Short Story Criticism

Guide to Gale Literary Criticism Series

For criticism on	Consult these Gale series
Authors now living or who died after December 31, 1999	*CONTEMPORARY LITERARY CRITICISM (CLC)*
Authors who died between 1900 and 1999	*TWENTIETH-CENTURY LITERARY CRITICISM (TCLC)*
Authors who died between 1800 and 1899	*NINETEENTH-CENTURY LITERATURE CRITICISM (NCLC)*
Authors who died between 1400 and 1799	*LITERATURE CRITICISM FROM 1400 TO 1800 (LC)* *SHAKESPEAREAN CRITICISM (SC)*
Authors who died before 1400	*CLASSICAL AND MEDIEVAL LITERATURE CRITICISM (CMLC)*
Authors of books for children and young adults	*CHILDREN'S LITERATURE REVIEW (CLR)*
Dramatists	*DRAMA CRITICISM (DC)*
Poets	*POETRY CRITICISM (PC)*
Short story writers	*SHORT STORY CRITICISM (SSC)*
Black writers of the past two hundred years	*BLACK LITERATURE CRITICISM (BLC)*
Hispanic writers of the late nineteenth and twentieth centuries	*HISPANIC LITERATURE CRITICISM (HLC)*
Native North American writers and orators of the eighteenth, nineteenth, and twentieth centuries	*NATIVE NORTH AMERICAN LITERATURE (NNAL)*
Major authors from the Renaissance to the present	*WORLD LITERATURE CRITICISM, 1500 TO THE PRESENT (WLC)*

ISSN 0895-9439

Volume 37

Short Story Criticism

Criticism of the
Works of Short Fiction Writers

Anja Barnard, Anna Sheets Nesbitt
Editors

GALE GROUP

Detroit
New York
San Francisco
London
Boston
Woodbridge, CT

STAFF

Janet Witalec, *Managing Editor, Literature Product*
Anja Barnard, Anna Sheets Nesbitt, *Editors*
Mark W. Scott, *Publisher, Literature Product*

Jenny Cromie, *Associate Editor*
Patti A. Tippett, Timothy J. White *Technical Training Specialists*
Kathleen Lopez Nolan, Lynn M. Spampinato, *Managing Editors*
Susan M. Trosky, *Content Director*

Maria L. Franklin, *Permissions Manager*
Edna Hedblad, Kimberly F. Smilay, *Permissions Specialists*
Erin Bealmear, Sandy Gore, Keryl Stanley, *Permissions Assistants*

Victoria B. Cariappa, *Research Manager*
Andrew Guy Malonis, Barbara McNeil, Gary J. Oudersluys, Maureen Richards, Cheryl L. Warnock, *Research Specialists*
Tamara C. Nott, Tracie A. Richardson, *Research Associates*
Scott Floyd, Timothy Lehnerer, and Ron Morelli, *Research Assistants*

Mary Beth Trimper, *Composition Manager*
Evi Seoud, *Assistant Production Director*
Carolyn Fischer, Gary Leach, *Composition Specialists*

Dorothy Maki, *Manufacturing Manager*
Stacy Melson, *Buyer*

Randy Bassett, *Image Database Supervisor*
Robert Duncan, *Imaging Specialist*
Mike Logusz, *Graphic Artist*
Pamela A. Reed, *Imaging Coordinator*

Library of Congress Catalog Card Number 88-641014
ISBN 0-7876-3083-7
ISSN 0895-9439
Printed in the United States of America

10 9 8 7 6 5 4 3 2 1

Contents

Preface

Short Story Criticism (*SSC*) presents significant criticism of the world's greatest short story writers and provides supplementary biographical and bibliographical materials to guide the interested reader to a greater understanding of the authors of short fiction. This series was developed in response to suggestions from librarians serving high school, college, and public library patrons, who had noted a considerable number of requests for critical material on short story writers. Although major short story writers are covered in such Gale series as *Contemporary Literary Criticism* (*CLC*), *Twentieth-Century Literary Criticism* (*TCLC*), *Nineteenth-Century Literature Criticism* (*NCLC*), and *Literature Criticism from 1400 to 1800* (*LC*), librarians perceived the need for a series devoted solely to writers of the short story genre.

Scope of the Series

SSC is designed to serve as an introduction to major short story writers of all eras and nationalities. Since these authors have inspired a great deal of relevant critical material, *SSC* is necessarily selective, and the editors have chosen the most important published criticism to aid readers and students in their research.

Approximately eight to ten authors are included in each volume, and each entry presents a historical survey of the critical response to that author's work. The length of an entry is intended to reflect the amount of critical attention the author has received from critics writing in English and from foreign critics in translation. Every attempt has been made to identify and include the most significant essays on each author's work. In order to provide these important critical pieces, the editors sometimes reprint essays that have appeared elsewhere in Gale's Literary Criticism Series. Such duplication, however, never exceeds twenty percent of an *SSC* volume.

Organization of the Book

An *SSC* entry consists of the following elements:

- The **Author Heading** cites the name under which the author most commonly wrote, followed by birth and death dates. Also located here are any name variations under which an author wrote, including transliterated forms for authors whose native languages use nonroman alphabets. If the author wrote consistently under a pseudonym, the pseudonym will be listed in the author heading and the author's actual name given in parenthesis on the first line of the biographical and critical introduction. Uncertain birth or death dates are indicated by question marks. Single-work entries are preceded by the title of the work and its date of publication.

- The **Introduction** contains background information that introduces the reader to the author and the critical debates surrounding his or her work.

- A **Portrait of the Author** is included when available.

- The list of **Principal Works** is ordered chronologically by date of first publication and lists the most important works by the author. The first section comprises short story collections, novellas, and novella collections. The second section gives information on other major works by the author. For foreign authors, the editors have provided original foreign-language publication information and have selected what are considered the best and most complete English-language editions of their works.

- Reprinted **Criticism** is arranged chronologically in each entry to provide a useful perspective on changes in critical evaluation over time. All short story, novella, and collection titles by the author featured in the entry are printed in boldface type. The critic's name and the date of composition or publication of the critical work are given at the beginning of each piece of criticism. Unsigned criticism is preceded by the title of the source in which it appeared. Footnotes are reprinted at the end of each essay or excerpt. In the case of excerpted criticism, only those footnotes that pertain to the excerpted texts are included.

- Critical essays are prefaced by brief **Annotations** explicating each piece.

- A complete **Bibliographical Citation** of the original essay or book precedes each piece of criticism.

- An annotated bibliography of **Further Reading** appears at the end of each entry and suggests resources for additional study. In some cases, significant essays for which the editors could not obtain reprint rights are included here. Boxed material following the further reading list provides references to other biographical and critical sources on the author in series published by Gale.

Cumulative Indexes

A **Cumulative Author Index** lists all of the authors that appear in a wide variety of reference sources published by the Gale Group, including *SSC*. A complete list of these sources is found facing the first page of the Author Index. The index also includes birth and death dates and cross references between pseudonyms and actual names.

A **Cumulative Nationality Index** lists all authors featured in *SSC* by nationality, followed by the number of the *SSC* volume in which their entry appears.

A **Cumulative Title Index** lists in alphabetical order all short story, novella, and collection titles contained in the *SSC* series. Titles of short story collections, separately published novellas, and novella collections are printed in italics, while titles of individual short stories are printed in roman type with quotation marks. Each title is followed by the author's last name and corresponding volume and page numbers where commentary on the work is located. English-language translations of original foreign-language titles are cross-referenced to the foreign titles so that all references to discussion of a work are combined in one listing.

Citing *Short Story Criticism*

When writing papers, students who quote directly from any volume in the Literature Criticism Series may use the following general format to footnote reprinted criticism. The first example pertains to material drawn from periodicals, the second to material reprinted from books.

Henry James, Jr., "Honoré de Balzac," *The Galaxy* 20 (December 1875), 814-36; reprinted in *Short Story Criticism*, vol. 5, ed. Thomas Votteler (Detroit: The Gale Group, 1990), 8-11.

Linda W. Wagner, "The Years of the Locust," *Ellen Glasgow: Beyond Convention* (University of Texas Press, 1982), 50-70; reprinted and excerpted in *Short Story Criticism*, vol. 34, ed. Anna Sheets Nesbitt (Farmington Hills, Mich.: The Gale Group, 2000), 80-82.

Suggestions are Welcome

Readers who wish to suggest new features, topics, or authors to appear in future volumes, or who have other suggestions or comments are cordially invited to call, write, or fax the Managing Editor:

Managing Editor, Literary Criticism Series
The Gale Group
27500 Drake Road
Farmington Hills, MI 48331-3535
1-800-347-4253 (GALE)
Fax: 248-699-8054

Acknowledgments

The editors wish to thank the copyright holders of the excerpted criticism included in this volume and the permissions managers of many book and magazine publishing companies for assisting us in securing reproduction rights. We are also grateful to the staffs of the Detroit Public Library, the Library of Congress, the University of Detroit Mercy Library, Wayne State University Purdy/Kresge Library Complex, and the University of Michigan Libraries for making their resources available to us. Following is a list of the copyright holders who have granted us permission to reproduce material in this volume of *SSC*. Every effort has been made to trace copyright, but if omissions have been made, please let us know.

COPYRIGHTED EXCERPTS IN *SSC*, VOLUME 37, WERE REPRODUCED FROM THE FOLLOWING PERIODICALS:

American Imago, v. 36, Summer, 1979. Copyright 1979 by the Association for Applied Psychoanalysis. Reproduced by permission.— *American Quarterly*, v. XV, Summer, 1963. © 1963. Reproduced by permission of The Johns Hopkins University Press.—*Ariel: A Review of International English Literature*, v. 25, January, 1994 for "'To Understand this World Differently': Reading and Subversion in Leslie Marmon Silko's Storyteller" by Linda J. Krumholz. Copyright © 1994 The Board of Governors, The University of Calgary. Reproduced by permission of the publisher and the author.—*The CEA Critic*, v, 55, Fall, 1992. Copyright © 1992 by the College English Association. Reproduced by permission.—*Chicago Tribune Books*, September 10, 1995 for "Moving Beyond Gothic: The Different Reality of María Luisa Bombal" by Penelope Mesic. © 1995 Tribune Media Services, Inc. All rights reserved. Reproduced by permission of the author.—*Deutsche Vierteljahrs Schrift*, July 2, 1981 for "Reading Representation in Franz Grillparzer's Der arme Spielmann" by James Porter. Reproduced by permission of the author.—*English Language Notes*, v. XXVI, March, 1989. © copyrighted 1989, Regents of the University of Colorado. Reproduced by permission.—*The Explicator*, v. 55, Fall, 1996. Copyright 1996 by Helen Dwight Reid Educational Foundation. Reproduced with permission of the Helen Dwight Reid Educational Foundation, published by Heldref Publications, 1319 18th Street, NW, Washington, DC 20036-1802.—*The German Quarterly*, v. XLV, November, 1972. Copyright © 1972 by the American Association of Teachers of German. Reproduced by permission.— *The Germanic Review*, v. 55, Summer, 1980. Copyright © 1980 Helen Dwight Reid Educational Foundation. Reproduced with permission of the Helen Dwight Reid Educational Foundation, published by Heldref Publications, 1319 18th Street, NW, Washington, DC 20036-1802./v. LIII, Spring, 1978 for "Proportion and Disproportion in Grillparzer's 'Der arme Spielmann'" by W.C. Reeve; v. LVI, Fall, 1981 for "'Der arme Spielmann' and the Role of Compromise in Grillparzer's Work" by Ian F. Roe. Copyright 1978, 1981 by Helen Dwight Reid Educational Foundation. Both reproduced by permission of the respective authors.—*Hispanofila*, v. 28, September, 1984; v. 112, September, 1994. Both reproduced by permission.—*Kentucky Romance Quarterly*, v. 26, 1979. Copyright © 1979 Helen Dwight Reid Educational Foundation. Reproduced with permission of the Helen Dwight Reid Educational Foundation, published by Heldref Publications, 1319 18th Street, NW, Washington, DC 20036-1802.—*Latin American Literary Review*, v. IV, Fall-Winter, 1976; v. X, Spring-Summer, 1982. © 1976, 1982 Latin American Literary Review. Both reproduced by permission.—*Modern Austrian Literature*, v. 3, Fall, 1970. © International Arthur Schnitzler Association 1970. Reproduced by permission.—*Modern Fiction Studies*, v. XI, Spring, 1965; v. XIV, Winter 1968-9; v. 20, Summer 1974; v. 31, Summer, 1985. © 1965, 1969, 1974, 1985 by Purdue Research Foundation, West Lafayette, IN 47907. All rights reserved. All reproduced by permission of The Johns Hopkins University Press.—*Modern Languages*, v. 70, December, 1989. Reproduced by permission.—*Mosaic: A Journal for the Interdisciplinary Study of Literature*, v. IX, Spring, 1976. © Mosaic 1976. Acknowledgment of previous publication is herewith made.—*Revista de Estudios Hispánicos*, v. XIV, January, 1980. Reproduced by permission.—*Seminar*, v. XII, November, 1976. © The Canadian Association of University Teachers of German 1976. Reproduced by permission of the publisher.—*Steinbeck Quarterly*, v. VII, Summer-Fall, 1974 for "The Original Manuscripts of Steinbeck's 'The Chrysanthemums,'" by Roy S. Simmonds; v. XXII, Winter-Spring, 1989 for "'The Chrysanthemums' Revisted" by C. Kenneth Pellow; v. XXI, Summer-Fall, 1993 for "Longing for the Lost Frontier: Steinbeck's Vision of Cultural Decline in 'The White Quail' and 'The Chrysanthemums,'" by Christopher S. Busch. All rights reserved. All reproduced by permission of the copyright owner and the respective authors.—*Studies in American Fiction*, v. 15, Autumn, 1987. Copyright © 1987 Northeastern University. Reproduced by permission.—*Studies in Short Fiction*, v. VII, Spring, 1970; v. IX, Winter, 1972. Copyright 1970, 1972 by Newberry College. Both reproduced by permission.—*Wascana Review*, v. 21, Spring, 1986. Reproduced by permission.

PHOTOGRAPHS APPEARING IN *SSC*, VOLUME 37, WERE RECEIVED FROM THE FOLLOWING SOURCES:

María Luisa Bombal
1910-1980

Chilean novella and short story writer.

INTRODUCTION

Hailed by José Donoso as "the first contemporary Chilean novelist" and Carlos Fuentes as "the mother of us all," María Luisa Bombal is credited for altering the form and substance of Chilean letters, which prior to 1935 was overtly realistic, masculine, and regional. Although she wrote only two novellas and a handful of stories, Bombal's avant-garde works have won consistent praise for their narrative experimentation, complex poetic imagery, and psychologically convincing characters. Even so, criticism of Bombal's oeuvre has been slight. This has been attributed to a number of causes, including her unwillingness to adopt the popular literary methods of her day, her modest output, and her preoccupation with themes centering around women during a time and in a place where such themes were not in vogue.

BIOGRAPHICAL INFORMATION

Born into a privileged family in Viña del Mar, Chile, Bombal moved to Paris at the age of twelve where she attended Nôtre Dame de L'Assomption and La Brùyere before graduating from La Sorbonne with a degree in French literature. In Paris her intellectual development coincided with the rise of the avant-garde movement, an exciting period in the arts marked by experimentation and innovation. Shortly after returning to Chile in 1931, Bombal moved to Buenos Aires where she soon became acquainted with such literary figures as Victoria Ocampo, Jorge Luis Borges, Federico García Lorca, and Pablo Neruda. The 1930s were productive years for Bombal; she published two novellas and wrote stories for Ocampo's journal *Sur* while lodging with Neruda and his wife. After shooting and seriously wounding her lover Eulogio Sánchez, Bombal moved to New York in 1941. There she married Count Raphael de Saint-Phalle and translated several of her works, including a significantly revised and expanded edition of *La última niebla*. The last years of her life were spent in Chile where she died after a brief illness.

MAJOR WORKS

In highly poetic works about women trapped within the constraints of a patriarchal society, Bombal fused realism with the supernatural, or fantastic, to express the displacement, isolation, frustration, and loneliness of her female protagonists. In *La última niebla,* for example, a woman trapped in a loveless marriage takes a lover one evening while lost in a deep mist. Because the story contains a first-person narrative and takes place in the immediate present, the lines between concrete reality and fantasy are blurred. As the story progresses, both the protagonist and the reader begin to doubt that the lover exists, revealing the complex and dismal state of the protagonist's mind. In *La amortajada* a dead woman reflects on past experiences and observes those who knew her from the confines of her coffin. Multiple narrators in this work—the dead woman, individuals surrounding her coffin, and an omniscient narrator who provides alternating panoramic and closeup views of the setting—offer varying perspectives of the woman's character, lending it shape and credibility. All of Bombal's works are replete with imagery, particularly nature imagery. According to Celeste Kostopulos-Cooperman, "the natural world becomes a type of magical looking glass through which these women protagonists perceive and depict their inner dramas."

CRITICAL RECEPTION

Despite early acknowledgment of Bombal's significance in Latin American literature, her fiction has incited little critical response until recently. Many scholars have focused on her craftsmanship or have sought to interpret the many images in her fiction. The majority, however, have been drawn to her depiction of the feminine experience. As Phyllis Rodríguez-Peralta has written: "The woman in her novels is caught in the confusion of her roles. She reflects present-day themes of futility and alienation and she appears as a marginal figure, an outcast like the contemporary authors' version of her. She is, therefore, far from the stereotyped woman of Latin American literature before this era, and she does not reflect the traditional Hispanic concepts of femininity. At the same time she herself offers little or no positive rebellion against her diminished humanity, and, instead, longs for the romantic role once assigned to her. She feels human estrangement, but she has nothing to substitute for the old ideals."

PRINCIPAL WORKS

Short Fiction

La última niebla [The House of Mist] (novella) 1935
La amortajada [The Shrouded Woman] (novella) 1938
New Islands and Other Stories (short stories) 1982

*Later editions of this work include the stories "El árbol" and "Las islas nuevas."

CRITICISM

M. Ian Adams (essay date 1975)

SOURCE: "María Luisa Bombal: Alienation and the Poetic Image," in *Three Authors of Alienation: Bombal,
Onetti, Carpentier,* University of Texas Press, 1975, pp.
15-35.

[*In the following essay, Adams comments on Bombal's use
of poetic imagery to express alienation in* La última niebla, *focusing in particular on the symbolic value of the
mist in the novella.*]

María Luisa Bombal's first novel, *La última niebla,* was
published in 1935 in Buenos Aires.[1] Her second novel, *La
amortajada,* appeared in 1938. In 1947 she published *The
House of Mist,* a novel in English based on *La última
niebla.* These three books and a few short stories are all
that she has written. In 1963 she was supposed to be working on another novel, *El Canciller,* which had originally
been written in English in 1953 and was called *The Foreign Minister.*

María Luisa Bombal was chosen for this study because
her treatment of alienation and loss of self seen in *La última niebla* represents two fundamental possibilities of the
theme. She shows alienation, as a human experience, arising from personal, internal forces. Cedomil Goić states:
"The world exposed in *La última niebla* has as its only
base the personal existence of a woman reflectively turned
upon her own destiny. This novel is distinguished by its
personal structure."[2] This evaluation is not completely accurate. Although the personal element is predominant,
there are social conditions, secondary in nature, that are
important in terms of alienation. These will be examined
later.

Bombal's literary treatment of the theme is its other fundamental possibility; the mode of presentation, development, and structure is poetic. Amado Alonso in his introduction to *La última niebla* emphasizes this: "The natural
and direct form of narration is due, if I am not mistaken,
to the sure knowledge of having a poetic concept to present
. . . "[3] Thus the nature and function of the imagery will
be central to an examination of alienation and loss of self.
It will be seen that concrete entities are used to symbolize
and give poetic value to the alienated state. In addition, literary or thematic devices serve to distance the reader from
the material, again creating a poetic experience of alienation.

Amado Alonso and Cedomil Goić both consider the date
of publication of *La última niebla,* 1935, to be important
because it marks a change in Chilean literature. Novelists
up to then had been writing under the influence of naturalism, but around 1935 literature in Chile began to reflect
surrealism and other contemporary movements of world
literature. Goić says: "When María Luisa Bombal begins
to write, she does so completely within the system of pref-
erences of the new sensibility. She belongs to a younger
generation than the surrealists; she moves with comfort
and surety of means within the new rules imposed on the
contemporary novel."[4]

Although the emotional states described in *La última niebla* are of great complexity and artfully constructed, the
overall emotional trajectory of the protagonist is quite
simple; starting from an unhappy marriage, the protagonist
moves away from the real world into herself, through a
process of increasing fantasy, and then is forced to retreat
from this created world to face the realities of aging and
emotional barrenness. Her interior movement is the focus
of the novel.

However, there are exterior social dimensions that, although they never come into the foreground, provide a
hidden influence that tends to push all Bombal's women
into themselves, giving them a feeling, frequently not expressed, of lack of control over their lives. The position of
women in the society described in her novels is the most
outstanding of these forces, in that it makes marriage the
central issue of their lives. On the emotional level, the
most important one within Bombal's works, this position
gives men the power of choice as opposed to women's
relative helplessness, turning men into an external alienating force. This is one of the meanings of the complaint in
La amortajada: "Why, why is the nature of woman such
that a man always has to be the center of her life?"[5]

Near the beginning of *La última niebla,* this social function of man—as the one with the power to choose and,
consequently, to make woman feel a lack of control over
her life—is emphasized. On their wedding night the husband asks:

> "Why did we marry?"
>
> "To marry," I answer.
>
> Daniel gives a small laugh.
>
> "Do you know that you've been lucky in marrying
> me?"
>
> "Yes, I know," I reply, overcome with weariness.
>
> "Would you have liked being a shriveled old maid,
> who sews for the poor of the hacienda?"
>
> I shrug my shoulders.
>
> "That's the fate awaiting your sisters . . . " (P. 42)

In direct opposition to the cultural background implied in
this dialogue is the other important male-female relationship of the book, that between the woman narrator and her
fantasized lover. It is characterized by a total lack of social
or cultural context. The central element is that the narrator
is desired as a woman, for herself and for her body. "Once
nude, I remain seated on the edge of the bed. He moves
away and contemplates me. Under his attentive glance I
throw my head backwards, and this gesture fills me with
intimate well-being. I hold my arms behind my neck,
crossing and uncrossing my legs, and each movement
brings me an intense and complete pleasure, as if, at last,
my arms, my legs, and my neck had a reason for being.
Even if this enjoyment were the only purpose of love, I
would consider myself well rewarded" (pp. 59-60).

Thus Bombal shows woman's position in society to be a
force that causes alienation. This opinion is reinforced by
another man-woman relation that is of less importance
than the two already mentioned but causes the narrator's
first emotional crisis. Her first encounter with passion in

reality occurs when she surprises Regina and her lover embracing. This is a relationship that breaks all social rules, of course, and the aspect of scandal is stressed toward the end of the novel by the tragic results of the union. But the protagonist is driven to desperation by the realization that the love she desires exists outside social boundaries.

The achievement of extramarital love in Bombal's world involves the destruction of self, either physically, in the case of Regina, or mentally through escape into fantasy, in the case of the narrator in *La última niebla.*

Because of the existence of a social dimension, manipulated by the author through contrast and implication, Margaret Campbell's definition of a general theme in Bombal's works is somewhat inaccurate. She states, "In general the theme seems to consist of two parts: unrequited love and an attempt to deal with the situation."[6] However, Campbell's article does not examine or recognize that aforementioned social background. A better and broader statement of the theme would be that it is woman and love. This allows for the existence of the different types of love that are present in Bombal's works. If unrequited love were taken to be the main theme, it would be impossible to understand a story like **"Islas nuevas,"** which is structured around the contrast between a sudden erotic passion and a shifting background of many kinds of love—the love of a man for his dead wife, of a mother for her son, and of father and son.

Another external aspect seen in *La última niebla* and most of the other works of Bombal is the contrast between town and country. It is probably most important in *La amortajada,* but it also plays a decisive role in *La última niebla.* This contrast is really one of a series of external elements used by the author to symbolize interior states, but in addition it has a structural function. Emotionally, the city represents lack of isolation and the presence of human contact (this is not true in *House of Mist*) and the country isolation and withdrawal. The protagonist creates her lover in the city. Returning to the country, she begins a long process of withdrawal and fantasy that leads to a state of total alienation. The abrupt return to reality and the acceptance of a barren life occurs in the city. Thus the major spatial movement of the novel involves elements that symbolize parallel emotional movement.

Amado Alonso considers the use of external elements to be a characteristic of Bombal's art, giving it its special poetic quality. "No descriptive note represents mere information or, even less, a documentation of the objective; instead each one is an element of interior life" (p. 20). He refers to the "structural role of the accessory," saying: "The evident and admirable unity of tone in this short novel arises because the author has used material according to poetic need and not according to literary convention: as elements of architecture, not as themes of an exercise . . . " (pp. 15-16).

An example of the structural role of the accessory is seen at the beginning of the novel when what at first glance seems to be an insignificant detail is really that which provides access to the most hidden parts of the narrator's character. When the narrator surprises Regina and her lover, "two shadows suddenly separate, one from another,

with such little skill that the half undone hair of Regina remains hanging from the buttons of the coat of a stranger. Surprised, I look at them" (p. 46). She has, as already mentioned, come face to face with the possibility of passion. But the element that leads her to desperation is the hair caught between two lovers. Its immediate function is, of course, to symbolize the love between the two, but it starts a process of self-examination that terminates with a full realization on the reader's part of the narrator's mental and emotional condition.

The protagonist's first thought is a comparison between herself and Regina: "I think of the too-tight braid that gracelessly crowns my head" (p. 47). The hair symbolizes different emotional lives. Both Goić and Amado Alonso point out the parallelism between Regina and the narrator. Alonso's description is "Regina, a passionate life lived and real; she, a passionate life dreamed and imagined" (p. 19). However, this parallel is still at the level of external character comparison. The next level of revelation in the novel, still based on the external element of hair, is a vision of the depths of the narrator's being. "In front of the mirror in my room, I undo my hair, also dark. There was a time when I wore it loose, almost touching my shoulders. Very straight, tightly drawn at my temples, it shined like glowing silk. My coiffure seemed to me, then, an unruly bonnet that, I'm sure, would have been pleasing to Regina's lover. Since then my husband has made me gather together my extravagant locks, because in everything I should force myself to imitate his first wife, his first wife, who, according to him, was a perfect woman" (p. 47).

She continues the comparison with Regina, showing how in the past they were equal, her hair as free as Regina's. The next step is the central reality of her emotional life. Her hair—and thus her life—is a form forced upon her by her husband to imitate his dead wife, an imitation she can never successfully carry out because the husband considers the first wife to have been perfect.

Bombal is telling the reader that the narrator has allowed herself to be destroyed, that she has allowed her body to become the imitation of another body, and that her function as a woman is not to be herself but to be another. The presentation of this state of total alienation from the self is arrived at through the use of a single external element—hair.

In the context of the book the hair incident, with all it reveals, is bracketed by two scenes that directly concern the body-self relation. The first is of great importance both structurally and emotionally. In it the major integrating element of the book, the mist, appears for the first time.

This first scene is the one in which the protagonist sees a child in its coffin. It is the first time she has seen a dead person. The physical contrast between a dead and a live body is emphasized; movement is opposed to imprisoned rigidity. After the initial external contrast, other reactions are successively more internal, as in the hair scene. First is a description of the dead girl's face as empty of all feeling. The visual impact of the body suggests a word—*silence*—to the narrator. "Silence, a great silence, a silence of years, of centuries, a dreadful silence that begins to grow in the room and in my head" (p. 44). The terror of the connotations of the word causes her to flee, but outside she finds more silence and a countryside covered with mist. The mist destroys physical reality. "I avoid silhouettes of trees so ecstatic, so vague, that I stretch out my hand to convince myself that they really exist" (p. 45).

She personifies the mist, and, because of its destruction of external reality, she feels that it is attacking her and her reality. "I exist, I exist—I shout—and I'm beautiful and happy! Yes. Happy! Happiness is nothing more than having a young, slim, and agile body" (p. 45).

Her reaction is unexpected and, at first glance, inexplicable. The terms she uses to affirm her existence are those of physical beauty and of happiness. The confusing part of her reaction is the further definition of happiness—having a young, slim, and agile body. It could be explained as the shallow idea of a young girl, but the emotions leading to it are not shallow. Only in the light of the following scene does this definition of happiness become more meaningful. By denying her own body, by allowing it to be turned into someone else's, the narrator has become alienated from herself, both physically and emotionally. Her frantic affirmation of existence is made in the face of a strong feeling of nonexistence. The linking of a body and happiness must be seen as an unfulfilled desire since she has in reality disassociated herself from her body. What she is really saying is that if she could feel vitally related to her body she would be happy.

R. D. Laing in *The Divided Self* describes this condition in the section on the unembodied self. He believes that the normal sense of being alive, of feeling real, is related to the way one feels one's body to be alive and real. However, many people become detached from their bodies through stress or illness. "The body is felt more as one object among other objects in the world than as the core of the individual's own being. Instead of being the core of his true self, the body is felt as the core of a false self, which a detached, disembodied, 'inner,' 'true' self looks on with tenderness, amusement, or hatred, as the case may be." [7]

The results of disembodiment, according to Laing, are that the unembodied self cannot participate directly in any aspect of life perceived through the body. The unembodied self becomes an onlooker and observes, controls, and criticizes the body's activities.

The scene following the narrator's encounter with Regina and her lover is important, because it specifically explores the body-self relation. Faced with Regina's intensity of life, and surrounded by two husbands and Regina's lover, the narrator cannot control her inner emotions. "It seems as though they had poured fire through my veins. I go into the garden, I flee" (p. 49). The reader does not know what these emotions are, nor does he have a very good idea of what caused the emotional outbreak. The narrator only describes Regina's "intensity of life, as though she were living an hour of interior violence" (p. 48). Her reaction is to seek solitude.

After the narrator flees, the reader becomes partially aware of her internal state through a series of physical images and their connotations, which convert to interior emotions. The first of these occurs when the narrator throws herself against a tree trunk. The physical sensations are not described, but their emotional impact is. "Oh, to throw my arms around an ardent body and tumble with it, entwined, suspended forever!" (p. 49). A tactile experience becomes a longing for the physical sensations of love. Once this desire for primary physical experience of love is expressed, the woman undresses to swim and explores her own body. "I didn't realize I was so white and so beautiful. The water lengthens my features, which assume unreal proportions. I never before dared to look at my breasts, now I look at them. Small and round, they seem to be diminutive flowers suspended above the water" (p. 49).

In one sense this is a moment of discovery. She wants love, but she wants to experience it through her own body, which she looks at for the first time and surrounds with physical sensations, both real and imaginary. However, something more complex is taking place, as the imagery of the scene reveals. Although the woman is searching for and encounters primary physical sensation, her vision connected with this experience is distorted. The imagery destroys the visual dimension of the physical world.

The description of her body in the water is an example of visual distortion; its outline lengthens to unreal proportions. Her breasts seem to detach themselves from her body to float on the water. To further destroy her form, the water plants entwine themselves about her body in a human caress.

Visual distortion is not limited to this scene. It is the dominant mode of vision in the book and is directly related to the central structural element of the work, the mist. The title of the novel indicates the importance that Bombal attached to the mist in relation to the entire work.

Amado Alonso discusses the function of mist, calling it a leitmotiv and saying, "But the constant poetic function of the mist is that of being the formal element in which the protagonist lives, engulfed" (p. 24). Cedomil Goić extends Alonso's concept: "Though one can conceive that the function of the mist is that of being the formal element of the dream, as does Amado Alonso, it really is much more than that and, as a point of narrative construction, definitely something else. We should not, in general, rely on the common conception of the dream atmosphere as something vague or nebulous. Dreams are sharp and clear. That which is shadowy is the border between dream and wakefulness." [8]

A detailed study of the use of mist in relation to its meaning in the crucial scenes of the novel will clarify its function as a literary element.

The first appearance of mist in the book has already been partially discussed. When the narrator flees from the child's funeral, she immerses herself in a mist-covered countryside. The exact wording of the description is important: " . . . a subtle mist has diluted the countryside, and the silence is even more immense" (p. 45). The mist distorts and destroys visual reality. It also becomes a barrier, isolating the protagonist from any emotional contact with external reality. "I avoid silhouettes of trees so ecstatic, so vague, that I stretch out my hand to convince myself that they really exist" (p. 45). The mist, personified, coincides with her unexpressed internal emotional turmoil: "And because it attacks me for the first time, I react violently against the assault of the mist" (p. 45).

It has already been shown that at this point the narrator is suffering a crisis of lack of identity, loss of self, and disembodiment. The mist in this scene is a complex symbol functioning on several levels, providing further insight into her condition. It is a visual quantitative measure of the narrator's isolation from external reality. It is also an emotional symbol of her internal confusion. Overall its function is to externalize her interior state of withdrawal, confusion, and fantasy and, through its connotations, to create an emotional identification between reader and character. It is important to realize that the narrator does not describe her emotional state, leaving it to be deduced by the reader from the use of an external symbol.

At the rational level there is an important opposition in this scene that recurs through the novel: the existence of the protagonist against the nonexistence represented by the mist. Throughout the first part of the book, the mist invades more and more territory and the protagonist is less and less in contact with herself. Before the crucial journey to the city, where she meets an imaginary lover, the mist, functioning symbolically, has destroyed almost everything. "The mist closes in, more each day, against the house. It has already made the pines disappear, whose branches used to beat on the balustrade of the terrace. Last night I dreamed that it was infiltrating, slowly, through the crevices in the doors and windows, into my room, blurring the color of the walls, the shape of the furniture, and entwining itself in my hair, sticking to my body, it consumed everything, everything . . ." (p. 53). What remains is the image of Regina's face, full of passion. Here mist is functioning as a clear symbol. The loss of body is central to the narrator's loss of self and complete alienation, and it is her body that the mist dissolves. The image of another body fulfilled by passion, that of Regina, withstands the assault of the mist. The mist is not the border between "dream and wakefulness." Instead it represents nonexistence destroying existence.

Also, in addition to its symbolic importance, the mist here has a structural function. By symbolically condensing the emotional condition of the protagonist to the point that only one element is able to resist the destruction of being, the book—and thus the narrator's life—must move in the direction of this element, toward a moment of passion.

Before this moment arrives, there is a brief section in which the narrator talks about her present and future life. She sees boredom and the lack of and impossibility of attaining love and desire. Facing her situation, she feels a desire for death. She says: "Of dying, yes, I feel capable. It is very possible to desire death because one loves life too much" (p. 56). For her, of course, the life she loves is not part of her existence; she hates the life she is leading.

This is the first time in the book that Bombal has described the situation of her central figure without using imagery as the method of description. This section seems to serve the function of firmly fixing the reader in a logical, rational relation to the situation of the protagonist so that this conviction of reality will carry over into the next scene, the encounter with a lover. Thus the reader and the protagonist are both convinced of the existence of the lover, and both coincide in their gradual discovery that he and the entire scene are fantasy.

In the love scene the imagery concerned with mist is reduced to its essential elements, with resonances, of course, of its earlier meaning. The physical setting is similar to others already seen; unable to sleep, suffering an emotional crisis, the narrator goes out at night, into the fog-covered city. The imagery refers to the scene in which she fled from the funeral and leaned against a tree, converting the physical sensation of the tree into a desire for physical love. Bombal, using the same images, relies upon the memory of emotions already created to set the scene. "Through the darkness and the mist I glimpse a small plaza. As if in the country I lean, exhausted, against a tree. My cheek searches for the humidity of its bark" (p. 56). What follows is a complete love scene that later is seen to be fantasy.

Mist as an image occurs only once during the scene, and the narrator makes a clear and concise statement about its meaning. This occurs when her lover takes her to his bedroom. "All the warmth of the house seems to have been concentrated here. The night and the mist can beat in vain against the windowpanes; they will not succeed in introducing a single atom of death into this room" (p. 58). She is, of course, referring not to physical death but, instead, to death in life, to nonexistence caused by lack of a body to experience love.

Because the love scene is put forth as the negation of the world symbolized by the mist, the form that love takes is of great importance to an understanding of the narrator's loss of self and the conditions that seem to allow her to temporarily (and mistakenly) experience herself. A careful study of the scene reveals its basic unreality.

The first unreal aspect is that no verbal communication takes place. The communication is at an emotional level and corresponds to the wishes of the narrator. The physical contact is described in terms of her gratification alone.

More important is the way the narrator refers to her body as a separate entity, expressing her feeling of disembodiment. "The beauty of my body yearns for, at last, its share of homage" (p. 59). Not only is she maintaining detachment from her body, as shown by her point of view, but she is also removed from her feelings. "I embrace him and with all my senses listen" (p. 60). The use of the present tense in the description adds to the feeling of detached observation.

The narrator's disembodiment and detachment are reinforced a few pages later when, becoming aware of the passing of time and of advancing age, she looks back upon her moment of love and says, "What difference does it make that my body withers, if it knew love!" (p. 64). This quotation shows how she remains separate even from the memory of the central event in her life, thinking of it as something that happened to her body and not to her intimate self.

At any rate, it is clear that the forces of disembodiment and loss of self that caused her desperation are present to a great degree in what she sees as a moment of fulfillment. This fact alone casts the reality of the scene in doubt, even without the other unrealistic details concerning the lover and the form of the encounter. The rest of the book is concerned with the gradual discovery by the protagonist of the fantasy of the situation.

As far as the relation of mist as an image to the scene is concerned, one more aspect should be mentioned. When the narrator leaves her lover, she describes the trees, again, as immobile, but the mist is not described. Its absence is important in that it underlines the mist's function as a symbol referring to the interior state of the protagonist. It and its threat of nonexistence are absent after a moment of ostensible fulfillment.

The experience, of course, changes the existence of the narrator, and the images connected with her interior life have to reflect this change. However, several problems arise from the direction and form her life takes after what she has described as an experience of love.

The general emotional movement of the rest of the novel is easy to delineate. The narrator moves farther into her fantasy world. At the same time she feels a growing need for definite proof of her lover's existence, a need that leads to the eventual destruction of the myth she had created. During this process the mist plays an important role in several crucial scenes.

The first problem in dealing with the narrator's emotional life concerns her extreme passivity after her moment of love. She makes no effort to contact her lover or to have any further experience. She says: "My love for 'him' is so great that it overcomes the pain of his absence. It is sufficient for me to know that he exists, that he feels and remembers in some corner of the world" (p. 66). There is no imagery to aid in the interpretation of this emotional state. The only help is the narrator's own words in the following paragraph: "My only desire is to be alone to dream freely. I always have so much to think about! Yesterday afternoon, for example, I left suspended a scene of jealousy between my lover and myself" (p. 66).

Her words reveal that her experience of love did not help her to establish contact with herself but, instead, allowed her to create a false self, building a world around this self. The only way to explain her passivity is to consider that the object of her desire is her fantasy world rather than real experience, which is forbidden her by the form of her external existence. Her response to her initial loss of self is to create a myth that allows her to increase her alienation by erecting a fantasy, false self. Sustaining this false self makes conflict with reality inevitable.

Bombal again employs mist as an image when the narrator seeks affirmation of the existence of her lover. She first looks for concrete evidence and finds it in her straw hat, which she believes she lost when she met her lover. This evidence is not emotionally satisfying, but her lover's appearance is.

The setting for the scene is interesting in itself. The narrator is bathing in the pond. The importance of the pond in revealing her state of separation from her body has already been shown. Thus her physical actions, on a symbolic plane, show continuing separation from her body. When the lover comes, he comes through the mist. "I was emerging from those luminous depths when I saw in the distance, through the mist, completely closed, a coach coming silently, as though it were an apparition" (p. 70). Her lover is in the coach. He stops, looks at her nude body, and goes on "as if the mist had devoured him" (p. 71). These two quotations couple mist with unreality and nonexistence. In the first the lover is in the mist and appears unreal. In the second the mist destroys even his ephemeral existence by seeming to swallow him. Thus the mist in this scene seems to be an external symbol related to the existence of the lover, and only by extrapolation does it relate to the interior condition of the narrator. The image that does serve as an indicator of her emotional state is the pond, referring to associations previously established in the first part of the book.

In addition, the importance of the narrator's body-self relation is emphasized in that when her lover does look at her, he looks at her nude body, reminding the reader of the love scene and the importance the protagonist attached to having her body admired.

The unreality of the lover is more pronounced in this scene, and there is an additional feature that provides a new dimension. The narrator cannot communicate with or contact her lover for the simplest of reasons: she does not know his name. This inability could be construed as an indicator of how far her loss of self and fragmentation have progressed. She is unable to communicate with a fantasy of her own creation.

Her immediate need for verification of her lover's existence is another indication of increasing difficulty, which she counters with attempts to believe that he is near. She also renews physical contact with her husband. She cannot accept the physical gratification resulting from this contact, because she feels guilt about betraying her lover. However, the physical pleasure allows her to realize more clearly his importance. "My lover is for me more than a love; he is my reason for being, my yesterday, my today, my tomorrow" (p. 88). This is a clear statement of her desire to maintain a fantasy world and a fantasy self in preference to a real world and an authentic self, and in retrospect it helps to explain her passivity in the real world.

Mist imagery is again a central element in the crucial scene in which reality finally overpowers her fantasy world. Two events that are the direct cause of the scene need to be examined beforehand because of their aid to understanding.

The first event is the renewed communication with her husband, which exposes her to direct physical gratification and, however unacceptable, renews her contact with her own body. Also, her husband is responsible for pushing her into direct action to verify the existence of the lower; he denies that she ever went out in the night and thus destroys the factual basis of her adventure.

The other critical event is Regina's attempted suicide. In terms of plot it allows the narrator to return to the place of her encounter. It also provides part of the closed structure of the book. The narrator's emotional trajectory starts when she is confronted by Regina and her lover and ends when she is faced with the results of Regina's affair.

The major function of the scene is to provide the narrator with an objective way of examining and evaluating her own life by comparing it with Regina's. "Behind Regina's gesture is an intense feeling, an entire life of passion. Only a memory maintains my life, a memory I keep alive day by day so that it doesn't disappear. A memory so vague and so distant that it seems to me almost a fiction" (p. 92). The perspective gained makes her realize the extent of her misfortune and unhappiness, something she has never done before. This is the first encounter she has had with her real self, that is, the self based in reality, and the result is a decision to abandon her passivity, to search for her lover or to prove his existence.

The mist has a minor role in the aforementioned scene as background to the emotional discovery that is the major element. When the protagonist comes into Regina's hospital room, she sees Regina in bed, turns away, and presses her head "against the windowpane blurred with fog" (p. 92). The physical situation is reminiscent of the love scene; the mist is outside and cannot enter the room. Whereas in the love scene it was ostensibly the life created by the intensity of passion that restrained the mist and its symbolic meaning of nonexistence, in the hospital the encounter is with truth. The only thing that can be said then, based on the elements presented within the scene, is that the opposition is between a moment of truth through self-discovery and the surrounding mist-covered world where truth is absent. Obviously, at this point the symbolic meaning of the mist is the total of all the meanings attached to it during the course of the novel.

The first few lines of the next crucial scene support this interpretation. The protagonist again goes out in the city at night in an active search for her lover and for the place where her encounter occurred. It must be emphasized that this is the first time she has actively tried to establish contact. She describes the night: "In the middle of the mist, which immaterializes everything" (p. 93). This immaterialization has been the basic symbolic function of the mist throughout the novel; it destroys reality. In this part of the scene it prohibits her from determining the physical reality of the surroundings in her search.

An additional and highly important quality of the mist is described. "The mist, with its smoky barrier, prohibits any direct vision of beings and of things, provoking a withdrawal into one's self" (p. 94). That the mist frequently is a symbolic poetic externalization of the narrator's interior emotional state has already been inferred from the previous scenes, but this clear statement by the protagonist indicates a much greater degree of self-knowledge and allows the reader to understand logically what before had to be inferred symbolically.

In addition, the narrator's definition of the action of the mist upon herself gives the entire scene symbolic meaning. She is wandering in the mist of her fantasy, within herself. The mist in this scene thus has become a symbol of the emotional vision of the protagonist, a vision about to be shattered against reality.

The protagonist finds a house she believes to be her lover's. But it is not; it is furnished in bad taste, and its master, blind, had died fifteen years before. Her dream of love can no longer stand.

When she realizes that all has been a fantasy, she talks about the destructive power of the mist in the same words she had used to describe its action upon her lover when he appeared while she was bathing in the pond. Also, her words show that she has abandoned her struggle to maintain the fantasy and instead has accepted the reality of her unhappiness. "Besides, why struggle? It was my destiny. The house, and my love, and my adventure, all have disappeared in the mist" (p. 98).

The mist as described here by the protagonist is an external destructive force. It is capable of destroying emotions and fantasies in addition to physical reality. However, behind the protagonist's description of the external function of the mist, there is another level of meaning. The narrator's words must be examined in the light of the perspective possessed by the reader with his knowledge of the emotional life of the protagonist and of the change that has just taken place in that life. At various places in the novel the mist, at its maximum level of emotional intensity, has been a symbol of the protagonist's emotional vision, physically representing her peculiar inability to distinguish between reality and fantasy. When she finally and unequivocally can identify reality and can establish contact with herself, she describes her fantasies as being destroyed by the same element that has previously destroyed reality. The tone of her statement puts the final action of the mist in the past, but at the same time it generalizes its action. Thus the mist acquires a universal quality as a mysterious force inimical to human happiness. At the same time it maintains its individual character as a form peculiar to a large part of the protagonist's life. The former meaning is well described by Cedomil Goić: "The specific function of the mist is to represent the ominous, the presence of the hostile forces of the world."[9]

In part, the final scenes represent the triumph of this hostile force. Although the protagonist has abandoned a false self she constructed through fantasy, the real self she encounters is that of a desperately unhappy woman, aging, with no possibility of future happiness. She further realizes, again through Regina's life, that it is not love she is lacking. What she has missed is direct, primary experience, be it love or pain, and by her own nature she has denied herself such experience. "And I feel, suddenly, that I hate Regina, that I envy her suffering, her tragic adventure, and even her possible death. I'm assailed by a furious desire to shake her violently, asking her what she has to complain about, she, who has had everything! Love, vertigo, and abandon" (p. 100). The protagonist's realization that she has wasted her own life leads her to attempt suicide. Her tragedy, the triumph of the hostile forces, is that the self and the life she accepts are without life and without hope. "But an implacable destiny has robbed me even of the right to search for death, it has been binding me, slowly, insensibly, to old age without fervor, without memories . . . without past" (p. 102).

The mist is the closing image. The narrator, after being stopped by her husband from throwing herself in front of a car, accepts the fact that what remains of her life is linked to his. "I follow him to carry out an infinity of insignificant tasks; to fulfill an infinity of pleasant frivolities; to cry by habit and to smile because of duty. I follow him to live properly, to die properly, some day.

"Around us the mist gives things a character of definitive immobility" (p. 102).

This acceptance is of course a complete change. The narrator is no longer totally alienated from her everyday life, and she has abandoned her false fantasy self. To a lesser degree than before, her being remains split between unfulfilled desires and the knowledge that in the life she has accepted these longings can never be gratified. The rest of her life will be lived in the unhappiness caused by this split.

In the final sentence the mist symbolically defines this frozen state of unhappiness. "Around us the mist gives things a character of definitive immobility." The universal meaning of the mist, dominant in the final scenes, is functioning here. It is a generalization and judgment applied to the rest of the narrator's life.

Although there is no direct textual evidence, other than the ambiguous parallel between the word *final* in the title (*última*) and the phrase "definitive immobility," it seems obvious that the meaning shown by the mist in the last sentence of the book is that referred to by the title.

This detailed study of the mist as it appears in different scenes has shown that it is an element used by Bombal for a variety of purposes and with many different meanings. It is used to describe both interior and exterior conditions with respect to the protagonist, and it ranges in meaning from a simple symbol of non-existence to a universal symbol of forces opposed to human happiness. The total and final effect of the use of a multifaceted element is the sense of mystery produced as the different meanings merge into a vague, diffuse, complex reaction to the element with each new appearance. The scene-by-scene analysis has stressed the separate meanings deduced from the context of the situation, but the response to the accumulation of meanings should not be ignored.

The same sense of mystery surrounds the character of the protagonist. Although it is possible to analyze the basis of her actions, no information is given about the conditions that caused them. Thus the reader sees the loss of self beginning with the acceptance, emotional and physical, of her role as replacement for her husband's first wife; yet her reasons for accepting this role are not presented. Again, although her passivity after her imagined encounter with a lover can be explained, her final passivity in the face of an immobile, unhappy life has no explanation within the novel. Thus the protagonist's character and the major literary element used throughout the book—the mist—coincide in that their meaning and nature are limited to the events presented in the book and do not extend beyond the actual narrative content.

However, one aspect of the image of the mist that is totally outside the book should be discussed: the quality and meaning of the type of vision associated with the image. Mist as a physical phenomenon has several visual characteristics. It destroys a sense of depth. Without a sense of depth, visual impressions become superficial. This superficiality is characteristic of schizoid vision. Joseph Gabel, in his work on alienation, describes several aspects of this type of vision: "Finally, the live space of melancholics is characterized by the loss of the dimension of living depth, and this, in apparently paradoxical fashion, is followed by the exaggeration of live distances, which change from human to superhuman."[10] Anton Ehrenzweig defines a similar

kind of vision: "Depersonalized vision tends to have a clearer peripheral field, but is also flatter, and in a sense unreal."[11] He further describes schizoid vision in art: "True schizophrenic art only offers the surface experience of fragmentation and death without being redeemed by low-level coherence" (p. 122).

The schizoid disembodiment of the protagonist has already been described, but her other schizoid traits have not. Her retreat into a world of fantasy corresponds to a description by R. D. Laing: "The unrealness of perception and the falsity of the purposes of the false-self system extend to feelings of deadness of the shred world as a whole, to the body, in fact, to all that is, and infiltrate even to the 'true' self. Everything becomes entirely unreal or 'phantasticized,' split, and dead, and no longer able to sustain what precarious sense of its own identity it started with."[12] This correspondence should not be surprising because the difference between alienation and schizophrenia is one of degree and not of kind. Erich Fromm considers the two conditions to be complementary and Erich Kahler treats them as different stages of the same process. R. D. Laing, seeming to utilize the same concepts as Kahler, makes the further distinction, followed here, between schizoid and schizophrenic: "The term schizoid refers to an individual the totality of whose experience is split in two main ways: in the first place, there is a rent in his relation with his world and, in the second, there is a disruption of his relation with himself."[13] The schizoid, however, is sane, whereas the schizophrenic is psychotic.

Nevertheless, the exact psychological classification and analysis of the protagonist in **La última niebla** are not important. Her character has been presented through implication, suggestion, and connotation, not through analysis. What is important is the additional use of mist to evoke a poetic qualitative and quantitative experience of an abnormal state of mind. This is the highest poetic level of the novel in that the reader emotionally and irrationally shares the protagonist's experience of life.

Notes

1. María Luisa Bombal was born in Viña del Mar, Chile, on the eighth of June, 1910. Upon the death of her father she, her two sisters, and her mother went to Paris, where she studied at Notre Dame de l'Assomption. She had studied before at the school of Franciscan nuns at Viña del Mar. She graduated from the Sorbonne with a degree in philosophy and letters. She also studied drama in the school of Charles Dullin, director of the Théâtre Atelier in Paris. When she returned to Chile in 1931 she was active in theater, participating in a company directed by Luis Pizarro Espoz.

   Bombal moved to Buenos Aires in 1933. In 1939 she made a short trip to the United States, where she made contact with William Faulkner, Sherwood Anderson, and Erskine Caldwell. After the trip she returned to Buenos Aires and resumed her job with the magazine *Sur*. A brief return to Chile in 1941 was followed by another trip to North America.

   She married in 1944 and has one daughter. She now resides in New York and has published versions of her novels in English. In 1961 she returned briefly to Santiago. In 1963 she was reported to be working on another novel.

All of the foregoing information was taken from the introduction to *El árbol* in *Antología del cuento chileno*, pp. 433-436.

2. Cedomil Goić, *La novela chilena: Los mitos degradados*, p. 149. My translation.

3. María Luisa Bombal, *La última niebla*, p. 14. My translation. All subsequent references will be to this edition with page numbers given in the text.

4. Goić, *Novela chilena*, p. 144.

5. María Luisa Bombal, *La amortajada*, p. 99. My translation.

6. Margaret V. Campbell, "The Vaporous World of María Luisa Bombal," *Hispania* 44, no. 3 (September 1961), p. 415.

7. R. D. Laing, *The Divided Self*, p. 69.

8. Goić, *Novela chilena*, p. 156.

9. Ibid.

10. Joseph Gabel, *La fausse conscience*, p. 152. My translation.

11. Anton Ehrenzweig, *The Hidden Order of Art*, p. 14.

12. Laing, *Divided Self*, p. 138.

13. Ibid., p. 17.

Mercedes Valdivieso (essay date 1976)

SOURCE: "Social Denunciation in the Language of "El Arbol" [The Tree] by María Luisa Bombal," in *Latin American Literary Review*, Vol. IV, No. 9, Fall-Winter, 1976, pp. 70-6.

[*In the following essay, which was translated from Spanish by Ellen Wilkerson, Valdivieso explores the symbolic value of the tree in Bombal's short story.*]

Among Chile's outstanding women writers, Maria Luisa Bombal is perhaps the most complex and permanent figure. Born in Viña del Mar, Chile, she studied at the Sorbonne, returned to Chile, and then settled in Buenos Aires. Her first stories, **"Las islas nuevas"** [**"The New Islands"**], and **"El arbol"** [**"The Tree"**], were published in the Argentine review, *Sur*. In 1935 the publishing house of that magazine brought out a volume of short stories titled *La ultima niebla*, [*The House of Mist*], and, in 1938, the novel, *La amortajada* [*The Shrouded Woman*]. Recently she has returned to her country, and now lives in Viña del Mar.

Her short stories and her novel remain always in a zone which seems about to slip into a dream world. Perhaps the realities of her time, in conflict with her sensibilities as artist and woman, accentuated the evasion of reality so apparent in her work.

In **"The Tree"** one sees clearly one of the conflicts generated within a bourgeois society which has assigned definite roles to its members from which they can free themselves only by outright rupture of accepted rules and acceptance of the ensuing punitive attitudes of the society. In this society, woman's role has had a mythical quality. Certain static concepts are routinely attributed to her. "Beauty," "Sorrow," "Romance," "Hatred"—grandiose ideas with which one supposes her to be naturally concerned. Society, with compromising intent, has made a myth of woman. Rather than a temporal and widely varying individual, she has become a fixed and eternal concept.

But in Brígida, the protagonist of **"The Tree,"** María Luisa Bombal gives us a woman not mythical, but historic; not static, but dialectic; flesh and suffering, the reflection of a social situation from which she tries to free herself with only a presentiment of the wholeness of being which is denied her.

The presentation of events is logical and not chronological. The principal character is Brígida, who, at the beginning of the story, appears seated in a concert hall. As she listens to the music, she recalls her past: the lonely childhood, the futile longing to be close to her father, the frustrations of her marriage, the same rejection repeated by her husband who thinks of her only as a toy, a "necklace of birds." Finally, she contemplates her present, alone, but free at last to make a life for herself. Through the music, almost imperceptibly, she hears the rustling of the leaves of the tree.

The other character is the triple figure of father-husband-tree, projections of a single image, of Brígida's unchanging search for a man, a protector who will keep her safe from a world which she does not understand.

The tree will come to signify for her that protection which she lacked from infancy to young womanhood. It is the body which intervenes between the brutal reality of the outside world and the refuge within. The tree replaces father and husband, both indifferent to her needs, and offers life and perenniality. But one day the tree is cut down, and Brígida has to accept death. With it she accepts life and understands that the tree-father-husband was protecting her, not from death, but from life. When the tree falls, it becomes imperative for Brígida to go out into the world.

Brígida's life has a clear sequence: childhood and adolescence passed within the limits of the family circle, which is dominated by the figure of the father who remains always at a distance. The image which the author projects of him is that of a man overwhelmed by the prospect of having six daughters to marry. He is a sorrowful figure who complains within the family trap which fate has laid for him.

> "I will give anyone this burden of an unhappy widower with daughters to bring up. Poor Carmen! How she would have suffered over Brígida. The child is retarded." Brígida was the youngest of six girls, all of different disposition. When the father came at last to his sixth daughter, he was so perplexed and exhausted by the five elder that he preferred to simplify the situation for himself by calling her retarded.[1]

Exhausted by the responsibility of five daughters, when he comes to Brígida, the father no longer concerns himself neither with her education nor her anxieties. In the end, the child is left to herself in the house, safe from the world.

"Poor Carmen!" The reference of Brígida's father is to the dead wife who bore no sons, but his compassion is, in fact, directed to himself and refers concretely to the world of business and money which is important to him. 'Poor father with no sons, who can expect neither success nor power through his progeny.'

From this childhood lacking any affective structure—the only person who interests her is her father—Brígida passes to youth and to marriage. She marries her father's best friend, a man who shares her father's interests, emotions and affinities. But the change does not produce the relationship that she had longed for. Her husband is as distant and inaccessible as her father was, and he tolerates her as her father tolerated her birth, her fantasies, and her sex.

The relationship with Luis prolongs in her a frustrated and inconclusive childhood. She resists the transition to maturity because she has not completed the self-defining process of growing up. He is a taciturn, absentminded man who is half amused at her nonsense and her idleness. He calls his wife "collar de pajaros" ["necklace of birds"], a name he gave her when, as a child, she would run to him for comfort. The very name is indicative: in Spanish, "collar" is necklace, but it can also mean a collar or chain, a restraining bond only slightly softened by plumage and song.

> Since she was very small, when all the rest abandoned her, she used to run to Luis. He would lift her up, and she would throw her arms around his neck with gurgles of laughter like the twittering of a bird, scattering kisses in profusion over his eyes and forehead and on his hair, even then turning grey. (Had he never been young?) "You are a necklace," Luis would tell her. "You are like a necklace of birds."
>
> It was why she had married him. Because at the side of that solemn, taciturn man, she felt no guilt in being just what she was: foolish, playful and idle.[2]

Between father and husband the continuity is maintained: the one has six daughters to bring up and marry; the other acquires a child-bride to care for and support. Neither of the two has ever given a thought to the possible maturity of Brígida. Both leave her completely to her own devices—so long as these remain inconsequential and cause no major problems.

There is no erotic passion between husband and wife, and Brígida accepts passively that serious and incomprehensible task of men.

Then the tree appears. After her every effort to communicate, first with her father and later with her husband, has failed, the tree becomes a part of Brígida's life.

In the concert hall, listening to Beethoven, Brígida thinks about the tree. "How it chattered, that huge old gum tree. Every bird in the neighborhood came to take refuge there."[3] The association is very clear. Her husband calls her "necklace of birds."

In the story, the character, Father-husband-tree, is a trinity, and the figures alternate, not competing, but complement-ing each other. The bedroom where she slept with Luis had an unbearable light, white and glaring. But in the dressing room, shaded and sheltered by the tree, every-thing was different, restful, "like a world submerged in an aquarium."[4] The uterine connotation of refuge, is evident. The protagonist, "retarded child" in her father's view, and later the child-bride of an aging husband, still is not able to attempt a break at the conscious, language level. At that time, instead of pushing toward life, she withdraws to a world on another level. If communication with man is im-possible, then Brígida sublimates the desire for that com-munication and relates to the tree, saving herself from an actual break from the social frame which surrounds her.

In the dressing room, her husband's indifference is forgot-ten. In the bedroom is Luis, in the other, the tree. Each loves her in his own way, but both demand of her the same submission. When Brígida, in the first outburst of in-dignation that she is able to express in words and gestures, thinks of leaving the house and her husband, it is the tree who calls her to order and restrains her.

Referring to the tree, the narrator, taking refuge in a third person which all but identifies itself with the protagonist, uses an erotic frame of reference which neither narrator nor protagonist would have dared to use referring to a man, even though he had been her husband. In the child-woman that is the character of Brígida, the limitations be-come much more evident. But eroticism is here too and manifests itself, albeit unconsciously.

Brígida, furious, was preparing to leave the house when the tree calls her to order:

> It was the tree, the gum tree waving in a great gust of wind, who was beating with his branches against the window panes, he who, from outside, summoned her to watch him twisting in the wind, transformed into an impetuous black flare under the burning sky of that summer night.[5]

The tree demanded of her, the tree desired her to watch him twisting in the wind. The adjectives in the following sentences, "impetuous," "burning" ascended in rising cre-scendo in the description of the rain-whipped tree to cul-minate in the climactic expression, "What delight."

And Brígida then would slip "between the sheets of the wide bed, very close to Luis."[6]

The transference from her husband to the tree has been ac-complished, repeating the former transference from father to husband. But Brígida still cannot free herself from her childhood, nor from the consequent dependence that it sig-nifies. The world that surrounds her is designed to prevent it: Father-Husband-Tree.

Up to this point in her life, Brígida's psychological devel-opment has been limited to the search for fulfillment of her childish yearnings. Now, the emotional break between husband and wife deepens, and her attachment to the tree supercedes her longing for her father. Her husband's indif-ference is no longer so painful. Brígida converses with the tree, it "chatters" to her, descending to her level of a bab-bling child. At last Brígida feels secure.

But one otherwise remarkable day produces a revelation. A thunderous crash announces the falling of the gum tree, and a bright light, white and terrifying, fills the dressing room. They have cut down the tree, and suddenly the world enters through the window. In her mirror, where once were green shadows and moving foliage, now are "nickel plated balconies and clothes lines and cages with canaries."[7]

Suddenly the brutal images of the street have come in, and over the fallen tree death has entered. Life comes with it to shatter the game of fantasies that Brígida has been playing. The last thing that Brígida will see in the moment of revelation will be, symbolically, a cage of canaries. The mirrors that used to reflect and re-reflect the foliage of the tree have suddenly begun to reflect life with all its uncertainties and transitoriness. It is not possible now to accept illusion. Luis appears as he is—an old man, and the father figure who used the branches of the gum tree to recall her to the order established by society has fallen with the tree into the middle of the street. The umbilical cord has been broken. Brígida leaves her husband's house.

In the story, the entire sequence is developed psychologically (the actual time sequence is the duration of a concert) and the reader is not surprised with any kind of suspense. From the very beginning, he is prepared to witness the process which will culminate in that black clad woman seated in the concert hall. But even knowing the outcome in advance, the narrator holds the reader's attention, bringing ever closer the voice which tells the story. The death of the tree (Brígida dressed in black) brings her world into that of the reader and the story is unified, given meaning, and is closed with the beginning of reality and with death. The story ends with the freedom of the protagonist.

Until the revelation of freedom, Brígida has looked at the world with alien eyes, without trying even remotely to assert herself or "to be"—to be, that is, something more than a "necklace of birds." But this non-existence that Brígida has confused with the essence of life breaks down with the blow which fells the tree. Brígida realizes then that she wants to live, and if her lack of education limits the things she can want, then she must want what she can, things that she has never had: "love . . . yes . . . love, and trips and fun and foolishness . . . and love . . ."[8]

To live, for our heroine, is first the rebellion of her body in the fullness of a sensuality that was scarcely manifested during her adolescence and the first years of her marriage:

> . . . and Mozart leads her. He leads her across a bridge suspended over crystal waters that flow on a bed of rosy sand. She is dressed in white with a lace parasol, intricate and fine as a spider's web over her shoulder.[9]

All during the development of the story, the masculine and feminine worlds confront each other with no trace of mutual understanding. It was the habitual, the established thing. Brígida's sisters went everywhere with their husbands, and this amazed her. But her sisters did not go, they were taken by their husbands. The dependence was diminished, thanks to masculine gallantry and to the complacent attitudes of a refined society, but it existed. Her sisters could have been taken nowhere, as happened in her case.

Her sisters, nevertheless, were taken everywhere by their husbands, but Luis—why hadn't she admitted it to herself?—was ashamed of her, of her ignorance, of her timidity, even of her eighteen years.[10]

But for Brígida, the social structure falls with the tree, since in the world in which she has lived, power is exercised on the man's part, and therefore, it is he who represents it. The brutal and immediate reality will have to relegate the myth that surrounds woman to a secondary position, replacing it with an urgent and historic task. The grandiose words dissolve in a useless heaven. Brígida has come down to earth.

> It is necessary to agree with Macherey when he emphasizes that a literary work transposes the conflicts of an ideology, and that, consequently, the study of that transposition itself will permit one to discern in what manner that complex ideology has conditioned a literary production.[11]

Concerning the liberation of Brígida, one knows only the concrete fact of her break with her husband, and as an extension of this, with the world he represents. Of her totality as a liberated being one has no more knowledge. It takes time to adjust one's mental processes after a leap across the abyss.

Notes

1. María Luisa Bombal, *La última niebla* [*The House of Mist*] (Nascimiento: Santiago, Chile, 1962) p. 106.

2. *Ibid.*, p. 109.

3. *Ibid.*, p. 112.

4. *Ibid.*, p. 112.

5. *Ibid.*, p. 117.

6. *Ibid.*, p. 117.

7. *Ibid.*, p. 124.

8. *Ibid.*, p. 125.

9. *Ibid.*, p. 107.

10. *Ibid.*, p. 113.

11. Michel Zéraffa, *The Novel and Society* (Buenos Aires: Amorrortu Editores, 1973) p. 80.

Claudia Waller Orlandi (essay date 1979)

SOURCE: "Mist, Light and the Libido: *La Ultima Niebla*," in *Kentucky Romance Quarterly,* Vol. 26, No. 2, 1979, pp. 231-42.

[*Here, Orlandi presents a psychological reading of Bombal's novella.*]

Novels of the early twentieth century such as *Alsino, El hermano asno,* and *Don Segundo Sombra,* through their poetic and lyrical texture, together with the spiritual and psychological identification of author and character, influenced the continent's subsequent development of modern fiction. Old themes and atmospheres prevailed under new perspectives with writers no longer treating the conflict between man and his world but rather their fusion. From about 1935 we may speak of the emergence of a new novel in which an anguished search for the meaning of human destiny finds expression in themes of existentialist suffering and mythical reality. Weighed down by the devastation of world war, the depression, the Spanish Civil War, the rise of Hitler, the threat of atomic powers, and the mechanization of a computerized world, man, disillusioned and alone, became more intellectually and morally concerned. With the passage of time, old values lost their meaning. As Professor Schwartz points out: "Many novelists saw the tragedy of the human condition and of the individual, analyzed what it meant to be human, and sought for constants and new options in an absurd world, using, in the process, the findings of twentieth century sciences, philosophy and psychology."[1]

Combining myth, magic realism, allegory, and existentialism with a new twentieth century aestheticism of interior monologues, dream sequences, flashbacks, and cinematographic techniques, the continent's contemporary fiction developed much in the way of psychological treatment and structure. Authors injected European concepts of Freud and Jung into the craftsmanship of their works and in so doing produced not only regional but also universal expressions of ethical and moral conflict.

Psychically, twentieth century man lives constantly on the edge of a volcano, "al filo del agua"; in the words of Jung, "there is, so far as we know, no way of protecting ourselves from a possible outburst that will destroy everybody within reach."[2] In light of this, Freud's theory of repression inevitably characterizes modern man's anguished emotional view of a disillusioning demise of universal brotherhood and ideals:

> Freudian Psychology is characterized by one central idea, the repression of incompatible wish tendencies. Man appears as a bundle of wishes which are only partially adaptable to the object. His neurotic difficulties are due to the fact that environmental influences, education, and objective conditions put a considerable check on the free expression of instinct.[3]

Seemingly based on this idea, contemporary Spanish American writers explored a reality of dreams and the subconscious, of suppressed fantasies and fears. In 1935 María Luisa Bombal (Chile, 1910-), one of Latin America's outstanding magic realists, wrote a short masterpiece, *La última niebla,* an important contribution to the development of modern fiction in Spanish America. She joins Jorge Luis Borges, and later novelists such as Juan José Arreola, Alejo Carpentier, Miguel Angel Asturias, and Juan Rulfo in solidifying the trend of "lo real maravilloso" in Spanish America. For critics like Amado Alonso and Cedomil Goic, *La última niebla* represents the start of a new Chilean mode. In the words of the former, "el arte de la Bombal queda extraña al [arte naturalista] de sus compatriotas . . . no tiene el menor residuo de naturalismo."[4]

The first-person narration in *La última niebla* takes place within the mind and soul of a passionate, fantasy-ridden young woman. A curtain of mist pervades the entire novelistic atmosphere, forming a psychological and artistic counterpoint for the protagonist's escape into a hallucinatory world of dreams. Within the mist, we are never certain what is real and what is invented reality. The story opens with the unnamed protagonist's marriage to Daniel, her cousin and former childhood playmate, who, from the beginning, compares her unfavorably to his deceased first wife, "una mujer perfecta." Desirous of an understanding her husband is unable to provide, the protagonist awakens one misty night, goes out into the street, and, meeting the unknown man of her dreams, finally discovers real love. From this point on her entire existence is given to a fervid emotional fidelity to and dreaming of her lover, whom she sees once more on a foggy day as he rides by in a carriage only to be immediately swallowed up again by the mist. After years of dream-like reality she finally realizes her lover is but a figment of her imagination. She attempts suicide, is unsuccessful, and eventually resigns herself to the boredom and emotional sterility of her life and marriage.

Within the protagonist's world of repressed emotion, mist and dreams (or sleep), two elements of chiaroscuro, provide the unity of tone throughout *La última niebla.* Amado Alonso speaks of the "niebla" motif in terms of an artistic vehicle, " . . . el elemento formal del ensueño en que vive zambullida la protagonista. La niebla, siempre cortina de humo que incita a ensimismarse. . . . "[5] Goic differs in the focus of his analysis, viewing the motif as symbolic of " . . . lo ominoso, la presencia de las potencias hostiles del mundo. Es una construcción imaginaria de sorprendente efectividad narrativa como elemento fundamental de la estructura cerrada de la obra."[6]

It is our opinion that mist in *La última niebla,* in addition to its obvious poetic dimension, performs a psychologically oriented function: that of establishing a barrier between the protagonist and her vision of reality. Indeed, towards the close of the novel she is to remark: "Bien sé ahora que los seres, las cosas, los días, no me son soportables sino vistos a través del estado de vida que me crea mi pasión" (p. 89). This barrier of repressed emotion is associated with a screen of mist: "La niebla, con su barrera de humo, prohibe toda visión directa de los seres y de las cosas, incita a aislarse dentro de sí mismo" (pp. 94-95).

In his study, "A Waking Screen Analaogous to the Dream Screen," Joseph Kepecs speaks of a patient with similar impressions, who often remarked he did not see reality clearly and that between him and the world was an "impalpable screen. "[7] Kepecs equates this "screen" of the waking state to the maternal breast symbolism of Lewin's Dream Screen. He explains:

> In a sense the interposition of the screen had kept him [the patient] 'asleep' as far as real contact with life was concerned, and the disturbers of his 'sleep' were the activities he was avoiding. However, in a more real and functional sense the screen was a barrier to his perception of reality rather than an expression of a wish to sleep.[8]

Kepecs concludes that "it is quite likely that many people are unable to perceive the real world clearly because between it and themselves they interpose a phantom of the maternal breast through which everything else is seen."[9] In its obstruction of reality, it seems evident that the mist motif in *La última niebla* effects the same function as Kepec's concept of a waking screen. Bertram D. Lewin, the originator of the Dream Screen theory,[10] states: "The dream screen can appear in the waking state too, as in the case reported by Kepecs (1952), but then it usually is not so much the flat screen of dreams as it is an opaque something of unspecifiable density, . . . The use of the term *dream screen* . . . is, of course, by analytic poetic license."[11]

The protagonist's initial encounter with "niebla" comes with her first contact with death. Viewing the body of Daniel's former wife, she says:

> Me acerco y miro, por primera vez, la cara de un muerto.
>
> . . .
>
> . . . afuera, una sutil neblina ha diluido el paisaje y el silencio es aún más inmenso.
>
> Desciendo la pequeña colina . . .
>
> Y porque me ataca por vez primera, reacciono violentamente contra el asalto de la niebla.
>
> ¡Yo existo, yo existo—digo en voz alta—y soy bella y feliz! (pp. 42-43)

Symbolically linked with overtones of death, the ominous power of the mist impels the protagonist to reaffirm her own existence. "Niebla," as a metaphor of destruction and death, recurs frequently throughout the novel: "la noche y la neblina pueden aletear en vano contra los vidrios de la ventana; no conseguirán infiltrar en este cuarto un solo atomo de muerte" (p. 57). Death is also conveyed in terms of a colorless, static realm of mist: " . . . lo neblina . . . lo inmaterializa todo" (p. 94). Finally, the "niebla" motif may combine with a devouring aspect of the Dream Screen (which Lewin tells us may also be equated to the dark insides of the maternal womb): "El carruaje . . . se perdió . . . como si lo hubiera tragado la niebla" (p. 70); "era mi destino. La casa, y mi amor, y mi aventura, todo se ha desvanecido en la niebla" (p. 98).

Impeding a direct communication with and perception of reality, within an aesthetic and functional framework of external description, a waking screen of mist pervades the entire atmosphere of *La última niebla*: "los cazadores parecen haber sido secuestrados por la bruma" (p. 49); "la niebla se estrecha, cada día más, contra la casa" (p. 51); "fue una noche de niebla" (p. 81); "la mañana es fría y brumosa" (p. 90).

The novel's concept of mist as a waking screen relates to a latent expression of a wish to sleep, to a desire to escape into a world of the subconscious, characteristic of uroboric incest. Freud defines sleep as an instinct to return to the intrauterine womb, signifying on a uroboric level a return to the Great Mother. Metaphors of sleep and dreams constitute a second major element of chiaroscuro in *La última niebla*, augmenting the imaginary, illusory reality of the novelistic cosmos. "Mi único anhelo es estar sola para poder soñar, soñar as mis anchas" (p. 65), says the protagonist. Gutheil tells us (italics his): "Some people have a strong *desire to sleep and to indulge in dreams*. People of this kind are in the main not sufficiently satisfied with their life and attempt to escape from the emptiness of their daily existence to a realm of pleasure as presented to them in their dreams."[12] Observe the following sleep imagery

from the novel: "Mi cansancio es tan grande que en lugar de contestar prefiero dejarme caer en un sillón" (p. 41); "me siento desfallecer y en vano sacudo la cabeza para disipar el sopor que se apodera de mí" (p. 47).[13]

The conceptual framework of sleep in the novel at times presents a variety of what Lewin terms a near blank dream class. He tells us that near blank dreams " . . . contain elements, visual and nonvisual, such as screens which indicate nonvisual sensations, or dreams that are not so much visions as states of mind difficult to describe and name, which are called 'elusive', 'vague', 'like a pure emotion.' . . . "[14] At the opening of the novel, the protagonist indicates a similar occurrence: " . . . desde hace mucho, flota en mí una turbia inquietud. Cierta noche, mientras dormía, vislumbré algo, algo que era tal vez su causa. Una vez despierta, traté en vano de recordarlo. Noche a noche he tratado también en vano de volver a encontrar el mismo sueño" (p. 44). Seemingly a catalyst for deeper emotions in the character, this type of elusive, vague dream is followed by a nocturnal dream some time later, in which artistic and psychological effects of "niebla" compose a more visual Dream Screen:

> Anoche soñé que, por entre las rendijas de las puertas y ventanas, se infiltraba la niebla lentamente en la casa, en mi cuarto, y esfumaba el color de las paredes, los contornos de los muebles, y se entrelazaba a mis cabellos, y se me adhería al cuerpo y lo deshacía todo, todo . . . Solo en medio del desastre, quedaba intacto el rostro de Regina, con su mirada de fuego y sus labios llenos de secretos (p. 52).

Lewin tells us that in some types of dreams "the screen equivalent is not distinct from the subject; . . . the whole dreamer may be immersed in the substance of the dream, or screen equivalent"[15] ("la niebla . . . se me adhería al cuerpo"). He goes on to say: "Dreams made up of . . . pure atmospheric and ghostly material may be as intense, energetically speaking, as many others, often more intense. They may be nightmares or recurrent anxiety dreams, or on the other hand libidinal to the point of orgasm."[16]

Various dreams in *La última niebla* bear evidence of a psychological, sexual symbolism which relates to the protagonist's desire and need for love. Freud tells us: " . . . there exists a psychological technique by which dreams may be interpreted, and . . . upon the application of this method every dream will show itself to be a senseful psychological structure which may be introduced into an assignable place in the psychic activity of the waking state."[17]

Freud treats the dream as a symptom of repressed desire (*ID*, 84) and proclaims that the content of the dream is . . . the fulfillment of a wish, that its motive is a wish (*ID*, 100). Psychologists have discovered that there are a certain number of dreams which have been dreamed in the same manner and which indicate the same significance in the case of every dreamer. As a representation of latent, suppressed thoughts there thus exist many symbols which almost regularly mean the same thing. Sexual symbols are among the most prevalent of these disguised manifestations present in dreams. Gutheil states: "Sex plays a remarkable part in our unconscious, for it is one of the instincts which cannot be indulged in to its fullest extent . . . it appears in our dreams in disguised and undisguised form . . . (*LD*, 52-53).

Although the most valid dream interpretations require a detailed analysis of a patient's emotional and personal history, dreams, within a hypnogogic framework of chiaroscuro, in *La última niebla* reflect a number of standard sexual symbols, the examination of which augments the significance of the work's artistic imagery and character development. A combination of breast, genital, and coitus symbols seem to recur not only in the protagonist's nightly dreams but also in her day-time reveries.

Her nocturnal dream which we previously discussed as an atmospheric type of Dream Screen, and which described the mist as slowly penetrating the house, destructively enveloping her, may also be viewed, in psychological terms, as a disguised expression of sexual desire and suppressed emotions. An integral part of the manifest dream content in this case centers around the appearance of Regina, the protagonist's sister-in-law: "Anoche soñé que, por entre las rendijas de las puertas y ventanas, se infiltraba [la niebla] lentamente en la casa, en mi cuarto, y esfumaba el color de las paredes, los contornos de los muebles, y se entrelazaba a mis cabellos y se adhería al cuerpo y lo deshacía todo, todo . . . Solo en medio del desastre quedaba intacto el rostro de Regina, con su mirada de fuego y sus labios llenos de secretos" (p. 52). Her relative's extramarital affair and secretive love life represents the romantic, emotional type of existence so ardently desired by the protagonist, and defines the motive of the latter's dream as a hidden, repressed wish to imitate Regina, whom she outwardly disdains. Freud tells us: "Relatives in the dream generally play the role of genitals" (*ID*, 248),[18] an interpretation which reinforces the appearance of Regina as a subconscious portrayal of sexuality and a wish-fulfilling symbol of passion on the part of the dreamer. Regina's "mirada de fuego" may be interpreted as an expression of the dreamer's impulse, symbolized by fire (*ID*, 51), while "labios" convey the idea of the female organ which is indicated by openings of the body such as mouth, eyes, etc. (*LD*, 56). "Lips filled with secrets" expands the dark mystery of the female genitals.

Penetrated by the mist, the doors, windows, house and room also imply symbols of the female sexual organ, the latter generally corresponding to little cases, boxes, caskets, closets, stoves, and the like (*ID*, 246). The "niebla" enters and destroys everything but the image of Regina, characterizing the symbolic presence of love as the only force able to overcome the ominous power of mist throughout *La última niebla.* Indeed, later, when the protagonist consummates her sexual desires in another dream, she is to remark at that moment: "La noche y la neblina pueden aletear en vano contra los vidrios de la ventana; no conseguirán infiltrar en este cuarto un solo átomo de muerte" (p. 57).

This reference constitutes part of the novel's longest dream sequence which covers some nine pages of narration. Appearing at the midpoint of novelistic development, it represents the emotional climax of the protagonist's existence. The dream's most salient psychological manifestations have been selected for purposes of analysis:

> . . . Me ahogo. . . . Salto del lecho, abro la ventana. Me inclino hacia afuera y es como si no cambiara de atmósfera.
>
> Una idea loca se apodera de mí. Sacudo a Daniel, que entreabre los ojos. (p. 53)

. . .

—Me ahogo. Necesito caminar. ¿Me dejas salir?

—Haz lo que quieras—murmura . . .

. . .

Me visto. Tomo al pasar el sombrero de paja con que salí de la hacienda. (p. 54)

. . .

Entre la oscuridad y la niebla vislumbro una pequeña plaza. Como en pleno campo, me apoyo extenuada contra un árbol. Mi mejilla busca la humedad de su corteza. Muy cerca oigo una fuente desgranar una sarta de pesadas gotas.

La luz blanca de un farol, luz que la bruma transforma en vaho, baña y empalidece mis manos, . . . Y he aquí, de pronto, veo otra sombra junto a la mía. (pp. 55-56)

Un hombre está frente a mí, . . .

Comprende que lo esperaba y que le voy a seguir como sea, donde sea. . . .

. . . Me guía hasta una calle estrecha y en pendiente. . . . Tras una verja, distingo un jardín abandonado. El desconocido desata con dificultad los nudos de una cadena enmohecida. . . . Dentro de la casa la oscuridad es completa, . . . Subo a tientas la larga escalera. . . . Quedo parada en el umbral de una pieza que, de pronto, se ilumina. (pp. 56-57)

. . .

. . . Él está nuevamente frente a mí, desnudo. . . . la luz de la lámpara, lo envuelve de pies a cabeza en una aureola de claridad. (p. 59)

. . .

. . . Su cuerpo me cubre como una grande ola hirviente, me acaricia, me quema, me penetra, me envuelve, me arrastra desfallecida. (p. 60)

. . .

Ya estoy fuera. Abro la verja. . . . Y he aquí que estoy extendida al lado de otro hombre dormido [su marido]. (p. 61)

Feelings of suffocation often indicate a suppression of emotion and desire. Within this context Gutheil tells us that "opening a window may symbolize 'giving an outlet to one's urges'" (*LD*, 56). Once again the presence of mist forms an atmospheric Dream Screen which envelops the protagonist. Expression of a need to walk conveys a wish for sexual intercourse (*LD*, 58), an idea which is reinforced by the protagonist's straw hat, the latter significant as a symbol of the male genital. Freud tells us: "Of articles of dress the woman's hat may frequently be definitely interpreted as the male genital" (*ID*, 247).

Approaching a small plaza, she rests her cheek against a tree, expressing a figurative contact of the male organ ("árbol" [*LD*, 54]) with the female breast or buttock ("mejilla"). Complementing the sexual interpretation of such imagery, the sound of falling water from a near-by fountain may be a symbolic parallelism for intercourse. Gutheil states: "In symbolic parallelism all secretions and excretions, . . . are equal to each other and may be substituted for each other. Of interchangeable value are: blood, urine, pus, water, semen, milk, tears, vomiting, etc." (*LD*,

57). He goes on to say that urinating, or flowing water, may mean "intercourse" (*LD*, 57).

The protagonist's vision of the lighted street lamp adds to an illusory atmosphere and, more importantly, figuratively coincides with the presence of an unknown male figure. Light constitutes an archetype of the masculine principle and in the form of a street lamp may be interpreted as a symbol of the phallus. Freud states: "All elongated objects, sticks, tree-trunks, and umbrellas (on account of the stretching-up which might be compared to an erection); all elongated and sharp weapons, knives, daggers, and pikes, are intended to represent the male member" (*ID*, 246). The presentation of the protagonist and the stranger as two "sombras" seems a subconscious projection of Regina and her lover, whom the protagonist had seen earlier: "Entro al salón . . . En la penumbra dos sombras se apartan bruscamente . . . la cabellera medio desatada de Regina queda prendida a los botones de la chaqueta de un desconocido" (p. 44). The description of both Regina's lover and the man in the protagonist's dream as "sombras" and "desconocidos," in addition to relating the two events mentally, also characterizes the concept of an affair in terms of a passionate and mysterious adventure.

As the protagonist follows the stranger, a number of sexual symbols become evident. The walking together up a narrow street, according to Gutheil, is a coitus symbol. To climb up something expresses "the effort and the increasing excitement" (*LD*, 58) of the sexual act. Continuing the theme of the latter image, the two figures come to an iron gate behind which is an abandoned garden, both standard symbols of the female genital. The stranger's act of unlocking the chain may be interpreted as a symbolic expression of entering the woman.

Inside the house they ascend a staircase, again symbolic of intercourse. Freud states: "Staircases, ladders, and flights of stairs, or climbing on these, either upwards or downwards, are symbolic representations of the sexual act" (*ID*, 246). The naked body of her lover is presented within the glow of a heavenly halo, and symbolically fuses sensuous effects of illumination with the archetype of divine masculinity. Prefaced by a series of disguised meanings, the theme of repressed sexual desire now passes from latent to manifest dream content in which sexual manifestations are directly expressed.

Sometime following the occurrence of this dream (which the protagonist considers to be a reality), as she is bathing in a pool her lover appears before in a daydream:

> Emergía de aquellas luminosas profundidades [del estanque donde me bañaba] cuando divisé a lo lejos, entre la niebla, venir silencioso como una aparición en carruaje todo cerrado.
>
> . . .
>
> El carruaje avanzó lentamente, hasta arrimarse a la orilla opuesta del estanque.
>
> . . .
>
> Tras la ventanilla estrecha del carruaje vi, entonces, asomarse e inclinarse, para mirarme, una cabeza de hombre.
>
> Reconocí inmediatamente los ojos claros de mi amante.

. . .

> El carruaje echó a andar nuevamente y sin darme tan siquiera tiempo para nadar hacia la orilla, se perdió de improviso en el bosque, como si lo hubiera tragado la niebla. (pp. 69-70)

Once again the protagonist's dream includes the presence of a waking screen of mist. The water symbolism of this narration is interesting. Gutheil says: "*Water* we usually consider (with Freud) as a symbol of birth. Yet we know now (Stekel) that it is also a symbol of life, a symbol of the psyche, of impulses (which sometimes can flood, break through the barriers) . . . " (*LD*, 60). The latter case of water as a symbol of life seems to apply here, for it is only when the protagonist senses contact with her lover that she feels truly alive. The appearance of the closed carriage with her lover inside may be interpreted as a symbolic representation of the phallus ("lover"[19]) penetrating the vagina ("carriage"). The ominous power of the mist manifests itself again as it swallows up the carriage.

The protagonist's last dream, although brief, continues the sexual symbolism of previous dreams:

> Salto del lecho, abro la ventana y el silencio es tan grande afuera como en nuestro cuarto cerrado. Me vuelvo a tender y entonces sueño.
>
> Hay una cabeza reclinada sobre mi pecho, una cabeza que minuto a minuto se va haciendo más pesada, más pesada, y que me oprime hasta sofocarme. Despierto. ?No será acaso un llamado? (p. 80)

Here the presence of a weight on the protagonist's chest fits exactly a coitus symbol described by Gutheil (italics mine): "A man may express the act of intercourse by the picture of fishing, plowing, bowling, riding, shooting, etc. Erection means 'rising,' 'flying,' etc. A woman may express the act by: earthquake, a *burden on her chest,* etc" (*LD*, 58).

As we have seen, the above dreams constitute a series of psychological manifestations which revolve around a number of recurrent sexual symbolisms. Freud speaks of dream sequences: "It happens very often that a second dream confirms and continues the interpretation assumed for the first. A whole series of dreams running for weeks or months rests on a common basis, and is therefore to be interpreted in connection" (*ID*, 415).

There remains one more sexually oriented symbol meriting closer analysis in *La última niebla*: the image of light. Illumination appears both within the character's dreams, as we have seen ("la luz blanca de un farol y el desconocido;" "la luz.. lo envuelve [al desconocido] . . . en una aureola de claridad"), and within her waking descriptions. As previously stated, light constitutes an archetype of the masculine sexual principle, which takes on a symbolic significance early in the novel when the protagonist sees Regina and the latter's lover:

> Parece que me hubieran vertido fuego dentro de las venas. Salgo al jardín, huyo. Me interno en la bruma y de pronto un rayo de sol se enciende a través, prestando una dorada claridad de gruta al bosque en que me encuentro; hurga la tierra, desprende de ella aromas profundadas y mojadas. (p. 47)

The image here of "fuego" may be taken as a symbol of the passionate emotions stirred in the protagonist after seeing Regina with her "amante." As she flees into the garden (symbolic of the female organ) a ray of light, symbolic of the phallus, penetrates the forest. The entire composite reflects a manifestation of the sexual act, which is thematically reinforced through use of sensuous descriptive counterpoint: "hurga la tierra, desprende de ella aromas profundas y mojadas."

The element of light as a metaphor of erotic pleasure appears in the following description of the bedroom in which the protagonist abandons herself to a series of purely physical, sexual encounters with her emotionally estranged husband: "herméticamente cerradas las claras sedas de las ventanas y sumido así en una semioscuridad resplandeciente, nuestro cuarto parecía una gran carpa rosada tendida al sol . . . " (p. 79).

Fire constitutes one of the novel's most recurrent symbols of passion: "Vivo como con una quemadura dentro del pecho" (p. 82); "ahora, mi cuerpo entero arde como una brasa" (p. 95). Becoming synonymous with the image of her lover, fire represents a symbol of love and life: " . . . todo a mi alrededor estaba saturado de mi sentimiento, todo me hacía tropezar contra un recuerdo: . . . el fuego en la chimenea, porque en él surgía para mí, cada noche, su imagen [la de su amante]" (p. 87). She tells us earlier in the novel: "me gusta sentarme junto al fuego y recogerme para buscar entre las brasas los ojos claros de mi amante. Bruscamente, despuntan como dos estrellas y yo permanezco entonces largo rato sumida en esa luz" (pp. 65-66). These images of light as symbols of love carry overtones of suspended time. In another place she is similarly to remark (italics mine): "Yo me he hundido en un mundo misterioso [el estanque] donde *el tiempo parece detenerse* bruscamente, donde *la luz pesa* como una sustancia fosforescente" (pp. 68-69).

With the final realization that her lover has been but a dream, light, for the protagonist, takes on a symbolization of crude, disillusioning reality: "Veo en seguida el amanecer infiltrar, lentamente, en el cuarto, una luz sucia y triste" (p. 85). At the close of the novel she seeks escape from the truth: "Aunque la luz no es cruda, entorno los ojos penosamente deslumbrada. ¿No esperaba acaso sumirse en la penumbra?" (pp. 96-97). This desire to lose oneself in darkness, symbolic of the unconscious, perpetuates a theme of uroboric incest. With the novel's closing line, the protagonist remains without light, in "la última niebla" and its ominous character of death: "Alrededor de nosotros, la niebla presta a las cosas un carácter de inmovilidad definitiva" (p. 103). With the disappearance of an illusory realm of dreams and love, the mist, no longer capable of creating phantom images, conveys a tone of definitive reality and hopelessness.

The symbolic, psychological implication of much of the imagery in **La última niebla** is interesting not only from the viewpoint of the novelistic characters but also for what may perhaps be an unconscious extension of Bombal, the author. As Erich Neumann states: "the work of art . . . the dream in all its meaningfulness, rises up from the depths of the psyche and yields its meaning to the discerning interpreter, though often enough it is not grasped spontaneously by the artist or dreamer himself."[20]

Notes

1. Kessel Schwartz, *A new History of Spanish American Fiction* (Coral Gables: University of Miami Press, 1972), II, 98.

2. Carl Gustav Jung, *Psychological Types,* trans. R. F. C Hull, Vol. VI of *Collected Works* (New York: Pantheon Books, 1957), p. 61.

3. Jung, *Psychology and Religion: West and East,* trans. R. F. C. Hull, Vol. XI of *Collected Works* (New York: Pantheon Books, 1958), p. 15.

4. Amado Alonso, "Nota preliminar," *La última niebla* by María Luisa Bombal, 5ta ed. (Buenos Aires: Editorial Andina, 1970), pp. 9, 11. Quotes from the novel are from this edition.

5. "Nota preliminar," p. 24.

6. Cedomil Goic, "*La última niebla*: Consideraciones en torno a la estructura de la novela contemporánea," Anales de la Universidad de Chile, 121 (1963), 76.

7. Joseph G. Kepecs, "A Waking Screen Analogous to the Dream Screen," *Psychoanalytic Quarterly,* 21 (1952), 158.

8. *Ibid.,* p. 169.

9. *Ibid.,* p. 171.

10. Lewin tells us: "The dream screen, as I define it, is the surface on to which a dream appears to be projected. It is the blank background, present in the dream though not necessarily seen, and the visually perceived action in ordinary manifest dream content takes place on it or before it. . . . The dream screen appears to represent the breast during sleep, but it is ordinarily obscured by the various derivatives of the preconscious and unconscious that locate themselves before it or upon it. These derivatives, according to Freud, are the intruders in sleep. . . . The dream screen is the representative of the wish to sleep. The visual contents represent its opponents, the wakers." Quote taken from Kepecs' article: "A Waking Screen Analogous to the Dream Screen," p. 167.

11. Bertram D. Lewin, "Reconsideration of the Dream Screen," *Psychoanalytic Quarterly,* 22 (1953), 189.

12. Emil Arthur Gutheil, *The Language of the Dream* (New York: The Macmillan Company, 1939), p. 190. This work hereafter cited in the text as *LD*.

13. Additional examples include: "paseos insólitos alrededor de mi lecho, provocan desgarrones en mi sueño" (p. 48); "Regina se ha quedado dormida sobre el diván" (p. 49); "tumbado en un diván, Daniel bosteza" (p. 65); "me vuelvo a tender y entonces sueño" (p. 88); "mientras pugno por rechazar el aturdimiento de un sueño bruscamente interrumpido . . . " (p. 89); "pero en aquello soñarémás tarde" (p. 89).

14. Lewin, "Reconsideration . . . ", p. 179.

15. *Ibid.,* p. 184.

16. *Ibid.,* p. 190.

17. Sigmund Freud, *The Interpretation of Dreams,* trans. A. A. Brill (London: George Allen and Unwin, Ltd., 1923), p. 1. Hereafter cited in the text as *ID*.

18. The name "Regina," meaning "queen," may also take on the significance of the mother. As Freud tells us: "Emperor and Empress (King and Queen) in most cases really represent the parents of the dreamer" (*ID*, 246).

19. Bertram D. Lewin, "The Body as Phallus," *Psychoanalytic Quarterly,* 2 (1933), 24-47.

20. Erich Neumann, *Art and the Creative Unconscious,* trans. Ralph Manheim (New York: Pantheon Books, 1959), p. 104.

Phyllis Rodríguez-Peralta (essay date 1980)

SOURCE: "Maria Luisa Bombal's Poetic Novels of Female Estrangement," in *Revista de Estudios Hispánicos,* Vol. XIV, No. 1, January, 1980, pp. 139-55.

[*In the essay below, Rodríguez-Peralta compares Bombal's two novellas, noting in particular their unique position in Hispanic literature.*]

Many women writers in Latin American literature have presented a feminine world overtly concerned with emotional responses which often carefully cover underlying repressive forces. In these works, man generates the impulses and reactions in the spatial corridors structured around him, whether or not his own space is focused at the center or at a distance. Baroque profusion enabled Sor Juana Inés de la Cruz to conceal her total personality. But Gertrudis Gómez de Avellaneda in the nineteenth century was openly dependent upon passionate relationships, and the twentieth century poetesses Mistral, Agustini, Storni, and Ibarbourou, although completely different in their responses, react to personal factors invariably designated as feminine concerns. (And only Juana de Ibarbourou clearly rejoices in her femininity.) In the line of developing female consciousness, the novels of María Luisa Bombal present the psyche of a young woman in the 1930's curiously poised between the attributes of the conventional, traditional woman of her era and the dissatisfactions of the contemporary woman. The structure and technique of these novels also position them in the antechambers of the New Narrative in Latin America.

Bombal's first novel, *La última niebla* (1935), flows from the personality of a nameless woman protagonist whose perception of reality comes from the dreaming states of her mind. Amado Alonso writes in his Prologue: "Todo lo que pasa en esta novela pasa dentro de la cabeza y el corazón de una mujer que sueña y ensueña."[1] This woman is married to a man whose love belongs to his first wife, his beloved bride who died three months after their marriage. The protagonist, therefore, is an outsider, even an intruder in a second marriage. Without tenderness or understanding, she sinks into great weariness until she is stirred by the blaze of emotion she witnesses between Reina, her husband's sister-in-law, and a lover. Hugging this borrowed warmth, she creates her own world: in the mist it is she who is found by a lover, and with him she experiences one night of rapture which enables her to dream and to imagine throughout the days and years that pass. She grows older, but it does not matter, for she can endure a long life of tedium cushioned by the memory of one beautiful adventure. She guards her precious hours alone so that she can dream and converse with her lover. Days of expectation drift by when she knows that he will come for her. And once, out of the fog that envelops the land, his carriage appears and he waves gravely to her before he is swallowed up in the mist. In time, when she and her husband resume their conjugal life, she begins to forget her lover's features, nor can she remember his voice, and this doubt of his existence brings the heaviness of mourning.

A telegram, with the news that Reina is dying after a suicide attempt, jolts her into actuality. They must go to the city. And there in the mist she sets out to find the house of her memory. But it has all been imagined. It is Reina who has experienced everything: love, emotion, abandonment. She takes a step toward throwing herself in front of a car, but her husband pushes her back. "Lo sigo para llevar a cabo una infinidad de pequeños menesteres, lo sigo para vivir correctamente, para morir correctamente, algún día. Alrededor nuestro, la niebla presta a las cosas un carácter de inmovilidad definitiva." (p. 85)

The unfulfilled and unfulfilling woman whose personality exists at the center of this novel can be reached only by surrender to the art forms chosen by the author. Thus, in her own way, Bombal has anticipated contemporary Latin American writers who consider narrative form as a creative entity in their work. Total subjectivity is achieved in *La última niebla*. A sense of a stream-of-consciousness comes about through the structural flow of the novel as a whole rather than in its stylistic segments (such as interior monologues which attempt to approximate the mind's switch from one thought to another). The spatial movement within the novel is consistently forward with only the barest indication of the passage of time. Hence without explanation, an immediate shift occurs from the emptiness of the wedding night to the protagonist's contemplation of a girl lying in her coffin, her face devoid of feeling. Silence, a great silence of years, of centuries, rises in that room given over to death, and, in panic, the protagonist rushes out into the mist which envelops her with a greater silence. She cannot even hear the leaves she is crushing in her flight because they are humid and decomposing. Losing a sense of reality, she feels that the mist is attacking her, and she cries out: "¡Yo existo, yo existo . . . y soy bella y feliz! Sí ¡Felíz! La felicidad no es más que tener un cuerpo joven y esbelto y ágil." (p. 38) The entire frenetic scene becomes a metaphor of the impression created by the young girl's dead body, indicative in itself of her own insensible marriage.

To accompany this structural flow, Bombal adds the stylistic technique of inserting external details which subsequently will be taken into the protagonist's mind and converted to emotions. Inadvertently seeing Reina's hair tangled in her lover's vest, she thinks of her own hair now kept within the rigid confines of a braid in imitation of the first wife. Later, before her mirror, she remembers when her hair was loose and flowing, then that it is losing its luster, then, with anguish, that there will be no one to appreciate her own beauty. More complex is a later scene where the original detail is prolonged into a series of poetic images. In their bedroom, lulled by the sound of rain, her husband offers her a cooling drink. The bedroom becomes submerged in the lilac twilight, and the mirrors, shining like compressed waters, make her think of the trickling of clear pools. She imagines dusty highways, cities chastised by the implacable sun, and then the rain falls again. A feeling of well-being comes over her. She seems to feel the water slipping sweetly over her feverish temples and over her breast replete with sobs.

In reverse procedure, while sitting in front of the fire and searching for her lover's eyes, she tries consciously to evoke his image by removing the ashes of her memory so that a spark can leap up. Suddenly a great wind comes which blows down three oaks. The wind, the trees, and the mother-in-law crossing herself in fear are all real, but it is this great wind which returns her lover to her.

M. Ian Adams[2] deals with Bombal's use of poetic imagery in expressing alienation, particularly imagery associated with the mist which shrouds both countryside and city scenes and fragments reality in the mind of the protagonist. As her withdrawal deepens, so does the mist, which prevents direct vision and induces an isolation within herself. It filters into the house, into her room, through her hair, effacing everything. (Only the face of Reina, beloved, adored, remains intact.) Erasing the corners and muting the sounds, the fog seems to choke her. But safe with her lover, the mist beats its wings in vain against the window panes and cannot infuse a single atom of death into their room. (Here the mist does not necessarily symbolize physical death, but the death of feeling, which is akin to death.) In the end, everything disappears in the mist—her lover's house, her love, and her adventure, to be taken up by the final imagery of "definitive immobility."[3]

Although the personality of the woman protagonist is psychologically convincing, Bombal avoids the probing analysis of a psychological novel and remains constant in her presentation of the woman through impressionistic techniques. Living within herself, she reflects her sensual perception of subtle fragrances and sifted sounds. Her death wish is projected through autumnal imagery: she feels nostalgia for abandoned parks and wants the autumn leaves left on the grass until the humidity turns them into silence. To parallel her own joylessness, there are no natural rhythms of nature, no joyful awakenings of a blossoming springtime. Unable to escape the monotony and boredom of her life, she escapes into her mind. A constant fatigue accompanies her in this flight, which at times also acts as her defense against an unwelcome reality. A sweet sadness brings a tired smile to her lips as she drifts in a dreamlike state, interspersed with an occasional resolve to dedicate herself to daily household tasks in order to bring peace of mind. The dirty, sad light of dawn filters into her room to interrupt the reality of her dreaming. As her depression increases, there is a peculiar loss of identity together with a loss of will, and she seems faceless as well as nameless.[4] Her self-perception is indistinct, like the mist.

In *La amortajada* (1938)[5] the death wish of the first novel has been accomplished. Encircled by silence, Ana María lies in death. But she sees and she feels, and an immense happiness invades her being because those who surround her can admire her beauty, pale and smooth-skinned again, without a sign of care or worry. As each mourner approaches to gaze on her for the last time, the dead woman's thoughts flow through those portions of her life which each has shared.

The first to come is Ricardo, the love of her early youth. His presence annuls the long years and takes her back to their childhood. Even as a child, she had felt the force of his attraction, and later, with overwhelming emotion, she had given herself to him. His desertion and her pregnancy and miscarriage had been bewildering. Her father comes to her gently, her father who used to ask if she remembered her mother. She knows he will suffer alone, barring any entrance to his grief. She notices her sister praying next to her, and she talks to her, mentally, of their differing concepts of God. Her sons look upon her quickly, those sons who did not want to recognize her right to remain young and yet were secretly pleased when friends praised their youthful mother. The cry of grief from her daughter surprises her, her daughter so proud of her twenty years, who smiled indulgently when her mother showed photographs to prove that she, also, had been charming and attractive at twenty.

Fernando's visit disconcerts her with memories of their self-destructive relationship. Confidant of her marital misery, she looked to him to deny her complaints of her husband's neglect; but envy and egotism always sealed his lips. She hated the desire that shone in his eyes, and yet that daily, unswerving homage flattered her. Indifferent to his feelings, she was sometimes rude and belittling, but "Oh, Fernando, para sentirme vivir, necesité desde entonces a mi lado ese constante sufrimiento tuyo." (p. 79)

At last the principal figure in her life arrives: Antonio, her husband, adored, hated, unreachable. Her thoughts return to their early married life, to his ardor and her lack of response, her desire to return to her father's house, his delay in coming for her, and his courteous indifference from then on. Even the birth of their first son did not bring back his love. She remembers her schemes to re-interest him, her reliance on her legitimate position, her ire at his infidelities. Irritation and rancor permeated her suffering, which over the years turned into a sustaining hatred. She contemples his bowed head. She is amazed that he is crying, and from her vantage point of death, she knows that now he will always feel a strange sensation of loneliness which will never allow him to enjoy anything completely. Her hatred evaporates. How can she hate a being destined for sadness and old age?

In neither loving nor hating him, she feels that the last knot of her life structure has been undone. Putting her cheek against the hollow shoulder of death, she floats out beyond herself. A current—someone, something—pushes her through tropical vegetation, under pale foliage, into the watery pulp of nature. She returns. They are putting her in her coffin, and they carry her through the house, down the steps, out through the forest and the swamp. It is infinitely sweet to be transported, with her hands folded on her breast, like something fragile and very beloved. They reach the cemetery and enter the chapel. Father Carlos's thoughts accompany the final blessing. And then begins her descent, slowly, slowly, avoiding strange beings, colliding with human skeletons whose knees are pulled up as though again in the womb of their mothers. She reaches the bed of an ancient sea and reposes there among the millenary snails. From her body she feels an infinity of roots sinking and spreading in the earth like a powerful cobweb through which the constant palpitation of the universe ascends to her: . . . "Había sufrido la muerte de los vivos.

Ahora anhelaba la inmersión total, la segunda muerte: la muerte de los muertos." (p. 143)[6]

Creativity of concept in **La amortajada** is matched by creativity of technique. While the residue from surrealist currents remains, the structure and style flow toward the techniques of the contemporary novel. With complete mastery, Bombal has blended the supernatural with reality. In commenting on the novel, Jorge Luis Borges[7] says that he had advised Bombal of the impossibility of writing such a work, among other reasons because the magical zone would invalidate the psychological, and vice versa. Yet when she presented him with the manuscript, he saw that the dilemma and the risks that he had predicted had been overcome to the extent that the reader was not even aware of their existence.

Although the dead woman's memories and thoughts remains at the center of the work, Bombal moves toward an interchange of narrative perspectives. This is particularly true in the segment between Ana María and Fernando. Each speaks mentally to the other, using "tú" directly, but without attempting to cross the barrier of death that separates them. Thus the reader enters the thoughts of each one concerning the other. At the same time within this segment sections appear in the third person which fluctuate between the dreaming state of Ana María and a traditional exterior narration:

> ¡Este hombre! ¡Por qué aún amortajada le impone su amor!
>
> Es raro que un amor humille, no consiga sino humillar.
>
> El amor de Fernando la humilló siempre. La hacía sentirse más pobre. No era la enfermedad que le manchaba la piel y le agriaba el carácter . . .
>
> Lo despreciaba porque no era feliz, porque no tenía suerte. (59)

In contrast, the segments with Ricardo and with her husband have only the perspective of her thoughts and her comments, a stylistic approach which underlines their failure of communication in life. The segment with her father is presented in the third person, while the closer relationship with her sister is evident by her soft mental conversation framed in "tú." When the casket is placed before Father Carlos, the narration comes from his memories of her, conveying the impression that her consciousness has left her body momentarily in order to exist within those memories.

Throughout the novel there is the constant marking of "I remember," or "She remembers," or directly to the person, "Do you remember?" An added dimension enters these memories when Ana María incorporates conversations once spoken to her by others. She does not always move in chronological order in her reminiscences. Thus when her husband appears in the long segment belonging to him, the reader has already met him through the mental conversations of Ana María and Fernando and the confidences which she has shared with the latter.

A "leitmotiv," "El día quema horas, minutos, segundos," indicates the passage of time (and is associated with the candles flickering around her as she lies in state). The passing hours are also shown by the slow disintegration of her body, which she herself notes. The consciousness beyond death which floats through the novel is centralized in the psyche of one woman; nevertheless, the evocation of this essence can be called a prelude to the collective consciousness present in Juan Rulfo's *Pedro Páramo* (1955).

Imagery formed from nature is part of the poetic texture of both Bombal's novels, even though the focus and the emphasis differ between **La última niebla** and **La amortajada.** The symbolic quality of the fog, together with other attributes of nature, is clearly evident in the first novel. At times in this novel creatures may relate symbolically to the woman (the hunter's trophy of the wild pigeon, still warm and bleeding, which Reina's lover tosses in her lap, takes the place of the woman victim). Or with symbolist-surrealist technique, a nature object can be carried from one scene to another (an unfeeling tree which the woman embraces in a gesture of longing appears later as her support which she is leaning against, weakly, when her imagined lover comes for her out of the mist). In *La última niebla*, Bombal often uses aspects of nature to accompany the mood she is projecting: a dismal rain dripping through the broken tiles of the old country house greets the bride on her sad wedding night, while on other occasions light rain brings consolation. Bombal's sensitivity enables her to escape an obvious use of nature in the sense of the romantics, although a rare brush stroke in this novel comes perilously close to romantic stylization.[8] The sensual richness of nature is an integral part of **La amortajada,** always present in the thoughts and memories of the dead woman, as well as in the perceptions and sensations she continues to possess. But the relationship between nature and the woman is lyric more than symbolic. And in the end, she merges into nature to become part of the oneness of the universe.

Poetic similes and metaphors, characteristic of Bombal's style, enhance the lyric quality of both novels. She speaks of a silence so absolute that it creates a desire "de removerlo como a un agua demasiado espesa." (*La amortajada,* p. 71) In this same novel Ana María's hands, crossed over her breast and clasping a crucifix, have acquired "la delicadeza frívola de dos palomas sosegadas." (p. 12) In *La última niebla* the rain withdraws slowly, "como una bandada de pájaros húmedos." (p. 65) The woman protagonist in this novel must move about as the only way to impose a certain rhythm on her dreams, widening them, making them describe a perfect curve. "Cuando estoy quieta, todos ellos se quiebran las alas sin poderlas abrir." (p. 57) [9]

As part of the poetic process in her novels, Bombal conveys an exquisite sensation of motion. This is always presented through the perception and sensitivity of the central character. For the nameless woman in **La última niebla,** the sound of barking constantly approaches and withdraws. A nocturne, scattering the grains of its notes, doubles and multiplies in the air. She listens. The frogs stop their song. Then, in the distance, from the heart of the night, she hears his steps. They press down the moss, they stir the dry leaves, they advance to the gate. And then there is silence. The keenest sensation of motion (paralleling the stillness of death) is achieved in **La amortajada** as Ana María is taken from her home to the cemetery. Lying in her casket, the dead woman sees the ceiling above her swinging back and forth as they turn through the rooms, the halls, the front door.[10] She feels the narrowness of the vestibule, the jolting of the steps, the sway of her coffin on its journey. From this perspective, she sees the undulating reflections of the tall trees, she hears the wind lifting the dry leaves that strike the casket, and as they pass into the forest, she breathes the acrid perfume of plants that envelopes her with another shroud.

The relationship of the real and the unreal in these novels has a peculiar opposition. In one, there is the unreality of a dead woman projecting the reality of remembered actions. In the other, the unreality of fantasized actions functions against reality. But the narrative world of both novels emanates from the mind of the respective protagonist. Therefore, beneath the poetic texture and the imaginative techniques lies the personality of a woman whose character reflects both personal and contemporary social factors.

The narcissism of the two women protagonists is their most salient characteristic.[11] Neither ever loses sight of the fundamental importance of her physical beauty. Almost the first thought that Ana María expresses in death is to rejoice that her dark hair looks lovely as it cascades around her in her coffin. The nameless woman of the first novel constantly thinks with horror of losing her beauty in old age and of having to hide a body that will no longer deserve love and desire. Concerned only with herself, each woman relates exclusively to her own personal world, and the dream-like flow of the narration makes it possible for each to become surfeited with herself without exterior considerations. The self-insight that each possesses is pitifully limited, particularly in the case of the unnamed woman. Wrapped up in herself, it is equally impossible for the latter to achieve any insight into the indistinct beings who surround her. In the second novel, and from the perspective of death, Ana María gains some knowledge of qualities in other persons which she had not perceived during her contacts with them in life. However, both women remain singularly superficial in their self-knowledge and in their dealings with others.

Ana María has many more facets to her nature than the dreaming protagonist of *La última niebla.* Nevertheless, both live in spiritual and mental estrangement, particularly from their husbands, and they suffer from loneliness and rejection. This isolation seems symptomatic of the area often reserved for women, even if their own inertia, lack of perception, and inability to communicate have helped to build the barriers that hedge them in. They use feminine defenses, both weak and strong, against this crippling aloneness. The first woman, increasingly neurotic and exhausted, occasionally goads herself from her dreaming retreat into spurts of domestic activity. Ana María also busies herself with daily household tasks, and she learns to take refuge in her family and to combat her anguish by surrounding herself with her children. Her concern for feminine details of domesticity is never far from the surface: even while the pall-bearers are carrying her through the house to her tomb, she is upset because they have put her blue rug in the hall, where it will soon fade.

The character of Ana María is more fully developed than that of the nameless woman, partially because she touches many more lives and partially because the shift of perspectives in the second novel allows the reader to view her occasionally through the eyes of others. Like the first woman, Ana María often feels fatigued; she finds it difficult to comb her hair, to take responsibilities, to smile; she cries frequently. But in an atmosphere of indifference, she adapts her own vehement love to what she considers to be the mediocre and limited love of others. She learns to restrain herself from throwing her arms around her husband or her children, feigning frivolity in order not to frighten away the little love coming toward her. Ana María also incorporates vengeful streaks into her character, particularly in her dominant role with the ever-attentive Fernando which she flaunts in front of a husband who merely tolerates her. Her ideas of revenge enable her to conjure up great plans which almost always end in petty acts.

Bombal's novels deal openly with a woman's sensuality and sexuality. In *La última niebla* the protagonist's repressed desires produce various sexually oriented scenes. Fleeing from the passion that she senses swirling around Reina and her lover, she runs from the house into a mist pierced with sun rays. Throwing herself against the insensitive bark of a tree, she feels a strange lassitude, and in the floating sunlight she removes her clothes and sinks into a pond. She had never dared look at herself like this: the waters lengthen her body into unreal proportions, the currents caress her, and her breasts, small and round, seem diminutive corollas suspended over the water.[12] The vivid sexual scene with her lover is presented from the viewpoint of a woman, heightened because it takes place with an imagined lover and therefore is comprised entirely of a woman's longings. With abandon she rejoices in his adoration of her physical beauty, and with all her senses she follows him into complete fulfillment. The sexual scenes in *La amortajada* are revealing of a woman's initial psychological problems with sex. In spite of Ricardo's great attraction, Ana María knows that he found her to be cold since she was unable to share his ecstasy and desired only his kisses. With her husband she tries to remain passive in order to discourage his constant desire, and she describes her unwilling pleasure as a union in the same shame. It is significant to note that the *detailed* sexual scenes, appearing only once in each novel, occur between an imagined lover in the first novel, and the husband in the second. The identities of the men, plus the poetic texture of the descriptions, keep the scenes from straying very far beyond the confines of contemporary convention in the 1930's. Other details, such as Ana María's reactions, also reflect the mores of that era.

A strong maternal instinct does not appear as a corollary to the sexuality of the two women. The childless protagonist of *La última niebla* never includes any aspect of motherhood in her dream fulfillments. Ana María, the mother of three grown children who seem distant and uninvolved, does not direct any memories to the days when they were babies and she their nurturing force. Even though she remembers happy family scenes as she is being carried from her home for the last time—and although the reader knows that Fred is her favorite—the relationship between parent and children is not structured as part of the center space. On the other hand, Ana María does turn her thoughts to her first pregnancy, which ended in miscarriage. These memories flow from the impressions of a pregnant woman, in combination with conventional descriptions of whims and cravings. Although she reflects on being "confinada en mi mundo físico" (p. 38), the memories encompass a sense of wonder, and they are free of complaints.

In Bombal's novels, where the woman exists at the center, the male characters are projected through a female consciousness. From this perspective, all men are seen as incomplete figures, distant and unreachable. In the opening scenes of *La última niebla,* the husband, momentarily focused from a short distance, is aggressively sarcastic and totally unfeeling toward his wife, with wounding words that seem designed to cover a suppressed rage. Never again is he focused in close proximity, and from a distance he lives withdrawn and disinterested, existing in a world incomprehensible to her. Even when they resume their physical relations after several years, he remains an estranged, indistinct figure. Her lover is totally nebulous. In their wordless love scene he is the dominant one, but the circumstances and the surroundings hazily waver and float around them. Years later, when her retreat from reality has deepened, he comes again, and the dreamlike quality attached to him is much more evident. She sees his carriage appearing out of the mist; the horses do not make the slightest sound as they pass over the dead leaves, and when they lower their heads to drink, they do not open a single circle in the polished surface of the water. In anguish she tries to call his name—unknown—but there is no answer. Focusing both the husband and the lover from a perspective of great distance not only keeps them distant from the reader but illustrates the distance between the male characters and the protagonist.[13] Incapable of going beyond herself, her lack of comprehension makes both men seem like hollow shells to the reader, as indeed they are to her.

The men in *La amortajada* are varied in their relationships to Ana María, including sons, father, admirer (all marginal figures); but the lover and the husband retain most of the attributes of their counterparts in the first novel. Ricardo's actions remain an enigma to Ana María. With veiled contempt, her husband treats her like a foolish creature who bores him. Their failure of communication was solidified early in their marriage when Antonio, still ardently enamored, was unable to understand her nostalgic desire to return to her father's house, and she, without space to become accustomed to the city and time to mature, was incapable of expressing her feelings. A stunted marriage of alienation and mutual discontent resulted.

While it is evident that neither woman establishes mature bonds with men, it is equally clear that their goals and aspirations revolve entirely around their relationships with the principal men in their lives. The first woman dreams of being given over completely to the will of a man who adores her. Ana María believed that she had this relationship with her youthful lover, and belatedly she seeks the same thing with her husband. With the perception that death has added, she ponders; "¿Por qué, por qué la naturaleza de la mujer ha de ser tal que tenga que ser siempre un hombre el eje de su vida? Los hombres, ellos, logran poner su pasión en otras cosas. Pero el destino de las mujeres es remover una pena de amor en una casa ordenada, ante una tapicería inconclusa." (pp. 103-4)[14]

The nameless woman who spins out the workings of her mind, or the dead woman who spins out her memories, came into view just before the New Narrative in Latin America, which dates from the Second World War. The "boom" writers are men. In general, their concept of woman varies from earth-mother, to goddess, to sex-object,

to willing dispenser of comfort and well-being, to destroyer-force; but regardless of her functions, she remains outside their principal concerns. In Bombal's novels, the woman's concept of herself embodies some but not all the roles assigned to her by these writers. She is not earth-mother, procreator, goddess, or destroyer. On the other hand, she is dependent, subservient, passive, and yielding. She obeys docilely, yet without any apparent wish to please or to serve. Certainly she does not conceive of herself as bringing comfort and healing, nor is she the "heart of the home" in either a maternal or a religious sense. Her dreams of fulfillment concern only her own gratification which comes from adoration by the male.

The imagery applied to males in the New Narrative is associated with hard, stony earth, cutting implements, cruel, shining knives. This is contrasted in Bombal's novels with the softer imagery of mist, light rain, wind—subtle images that float or drift, that are formless, shapeless, insubstantial, like water that molds itself to the vessel that holds it. The tenuous fiber of these novels reflects inner needs and unconsciously reveals the tensions of transitional currents.

In both technique and in content, Bombal has reached the crossroads of the old and the new. The woman in her novels is caught in the confusion of her roles. She reflects present-day themes of futility and alienation and she appears as a marginal figure, an outcast like the contemporary authors' version of her. She is, therefore, far from the stereotyped woman of Latin American literature before this era, and she does not reflect the traditional Hispanic concepts of femininity. At the same time she herself offers little or no positive rebellion against her diminished humanity, and, instead, longs for the romantic role once assigned to her. She feels her human estrangement, but she has nothing to substitute for the old ideals.

Notes

1. Prologue to the 1941 edition. (Santiago de Chile: Nascimento, p.11). All quotations from the novel will be taken from this edition.

   The original publication in 1935 (Buenos Aires: Sur) was a very limited edition.

2. *Three Authors of Alienation.* Austin: Univ. of Texas, 1975, Chap. 2. "María Luisa Bombal: Alienation and the Poetic Image," pp. 15-35.

3. Amado Alonso considers the constant poetic function of the mist to be the formal element of the dream state in which the protagonist lives. *Op. cit.* p. 21.

   Cedomil Goic extends the functions of the mist to include a suggestive quality indicative of uncertainty toward reality (of the nameless woman, but by extension, the metaphysical insecurity of mankind), and as an obsessive element representing the ominous and the presence of hostile forces threatening annihilation of personality. *La novela chilena.* Santiago de Chile: Universitaria, 1968. Cap. 7. *"La última niebla,"* pp. 144-162. (See pp. 156-160).

4. The protagonist, Reina's lover, and her own lover have no names.

5. (Buenos Aires: Sur). The novel received the Premio Municipal de Novela (Santiago) in 1942.

All quotations will be taken from a recent edition published in Buenos Aires: Andina, 1972.

6. Both novels seem oblivious to the presence of the reader, who must adjust himself to the protagonists' sights. Even so, there is a pause after the final scene of *La amortajada,* and then Bombal faces the reader and directs six lines to him beginning with "Lo juro," and ending with the words quoted in the text.

7. "*La amortajada,*" *Sur.* viii. No. 47 (agosto de 1938), pp. 80-81.

8. For example on page 38. After her flight into the mist, a cold gust of wind whips her forehead. "Sin ruido, tocándome casi, ha pasado sobre mí un pájaro de alas rojizas, de alas de color de ontoño."

9. Arturo Torres-Ríoseco dwells on the poetic form of Bombal's style, and, selecting illustrations with modernist shading, he writes that the author still uses old instruments but with hands that move them with new skill. *Ensayos sobre literatura latinoamericana.* Berkeley: Univ. of California, 1958. "El estilo en las novelas de María Luisa Bombal," pp. 179-190. (See p. 189.)

   Cedomil Goic, uninterested in this aspect and applying different methods of critical analysis to *La última niebla,* considers that this work contains many elements found in the contemporary novel. Among these: the narrator's renunciation of dominion over the narrative world; an impression of time that passes with velocity and simultaneously remains; a confusion of levels of reality; cyclic structure; parallelism and contrast; the complexity of a narrative process based on a personal relationship to the narrated world; the self-sufficiency of the narrative structure. *Op. cit.* pp. 145-156.

10. This journey was anticipated in *La última niebla* when the protagonist muses that Reina, lying face up on the stretcher, must have seen all the autumn stars swaying in the sky. (p. 83)

11. Rosario Castellanos shows little compassion for this kind of woman which she describes with thinly veiled scorn in her chapter "María Luisa Bombal y los arquetipos femeninos." (*Mujer que sabelatin.* México: Secretaría de Educación, pp. 144-149)

12. M. Ian Adams refers to the visual distortion in this scene, and in others, which he calls the dominant mode of vision, directly related to the central structural element of the novel which is the mist. *Op. cit.,* p. 23.

    Amado Alonso, referring to this same scene in his Prologue, stresses that the coherence of all the images and sensations is the expression of a poetic and organically intuitive vision. In his view, no descriptive note represents mere information but is an element of interior life, and the swiftly passing images leave their energy in the style without the strict requirements of visual perception. *Op. cit.,* p. 18.

13. Thus Bombal could be cited as an added example in the section. "Variations of Distance" in Wayne Booth's *The Rhetoric of Fiction.* Chicago: The Univ. of Chicago, 1961, pp. 155-159.

14. Bombal rewrote both novels in English. The English version of the first novel (*House of Mist.* New York: Farrar, Straus & Co., 1947) tears to shreds the original sensitive novel of a woman's subconscious. Dedicated to her husband "who helped me to write this book in English," Bombal takes a few strands from the Spanish work and extends them into a very inferior episodic novel more than four times the length of the original. Subtle imagery has disappeared, almost as though the author had not realized the significance. Instead, a comedy of errors results where the two-dimensional characters are constantly misinterpreting appearances, and even the dreamed amorous adventure is merely the result of the champagne which Helga drank (Helga being the name of the protagonist, now seen as a stock character in a theater piece). Even the change of title to "House of Mist" negates the floating essence of the Spanish title *La última niebla,* meaning the "last" or "final" mist. The loss of the original technique and structural flow removes the artistic and subjective quality from this novel in exactly the same manner as the loss of the tree in Bombal's famous story "El arbol" shatters Brígida's sense of protection and beauty.

    Bombal's translation of her second novel, *The Shrouded Woman* (New York: Farrar, Straus & Co., 1948), is also considerably extended beyond the original text. The new characters who approach the dead woman, such as her brother and Sofía, the foreign wife of her first love, are easily intermingled in Ana María's contemplations. But the sections which amplify the circumstances of this first love and the reasons for Ricardo's desertion are unnecessary; and the insertion of a long segment centered on her daughter-in-law and the effects of her beauty is detrimental to the unity of the novel, both structurally and stylistically. (The latter appeared originally as a short story entitled "Historia de María Griselda," published in *Sur,* No. 142, 1946, eight years after the publication of *La amortajada.*) In spite of these weaknesses, however, *The Shrouded Woman* keeps the essence of the original novel, especially in the exquisite English translation of the most poetic portions.

    It is significant that the character of the husband shifts in the English versions of both novels. In *House of Mist* he materializes into a somewhat tricky, unpleasant fellow rather than the enigmatic, distant figure that the protagonist of *La última niebla* was unable to reach. The discovery that for years the husband in *The Shrouded Woman* has been jealous of Ana María's memories of Ricardo puts him in a more sympathetic light.

Lorna V. Williams (essay date 1982)

SOURCE: "'The Shrouded Woman': Marriage and Its Constraints in the Fiction of María Luisa Bombal," in *Latin American Literary Review,* Vol. X, No. 20, Spring-Summer, 1982, pp. 21-30.

[*Below, Williams investigates the theme of confinement and its effects on the women protagonists of Bombal's* La última niebla, La amortajada, *and* "El árbol."]

Over the past decade, most Americans have come to assume that achievement in the public domain is a variable pursuit for both men and women. At the same time that American women were affirming their right to be self-oriented and not merely other-oriented, as they have been for centuries, the Chilean novelist, María Luisa Bombal (1910-1980), was acknowledging that there was an archetypal woman, whose natural sphere of interest was the life of the emotions. As she stated in a recent interview:

> I do not believe that the social rights now being granted to women officially can change their basic nature. I believe we are, and will continue to be, the eternal woman: the idealistic, sensitive, self-sacrificing woman, eager above all to love and be loved.[1]

It could be easily assumed that Bombal's is simply an outmoded voice that is not in tune with contemporary reality. However, several observers of the Latin American scene have commented on the absence of a feminist consciousness that would negate the validity of Bombal's assessment of the female condition in Spanish America.[2]

Various explanations have been given for the persistence in Spanish America of the view on women endorsed by María Luisa Bombal. The most recurrent is that which regards such views as the female equivalent of *machismo,* the widespread cult of virility.[3] Presumably, women who express a belief in their inherent passivity, and give priority to their relationship with others, have accepted the premise of inequality on which the dominant patriarchal values of their society are based. Nevertheless, there is an ambivalence at the center of María Luisa Bombal's perceptions of women. While in an interview she is willing to concede that women are inherently incapable of acting in their own interests, in her works of fiction she calls into question the very posture of the self-sacrificing woman that she has chosen to regard as an eternally feminine characteristic in the statement quoted above.

Like their male counterparts, all Bombal's female protagonists are members of the privileged classes of their society. However, unlike the male characters, the women are ill-equipped to play an active role in maintaining their class position. Either because of parental neglect of their education, as in the case of the protagonist of the story, **"The Tree,"** or because of their exposure to a curriculum that stresses piano lessons, needlework and religious history, as in the case of the protagonist of the novel, ***The Shrouded Woman,*** Bombal's female characters are intellectually unprepared to act to shape their social situation.

In addition to their educational deficiencies, prevailing social attitudes about appropriate feminine behavior impede their ability to live for themselves. Since the other members of their society generally believe that a single woman cannot choose to make a life of her own—a position articulated by the narrator's husband in the novel, ***House of Mist***—these women are all expected to achieve self-realization through marriage. However, in all three instances to be discussed in this essay, there is a discrepancy between the public expectation that marriage satisfy a woman's desire for fulfillment and the wife's experience of the limitations of marriage as a field for female development.

As if to indicate the primacy of social institutions in determining a woman's place in the world, all three works are founded on the premise that marriage is the primal event of a woman's life. The act of getting married is never described, nor is marriage presented as a goal toward which Bombal's female characters strive consciously, because in all three works, marriage is a state into which the protagonists have already entered prior to the opening paragraphs of the narrative. Since all three works end with the protagonist's re-evaluation of her relationship to her husband and/or family, development here is not an organic process, paralleling the evolution from childhood to maturity, because the significant changes in the protagonists' situation all take place within the context of marriage.

Even as the lives of Bombal's female protagonists are textually enclosed within the domain of marriage, so too they themselves are spatially confined within the domestic sphere. In a literal sense, ***The Shrouded Woman*** presents the most dramatic expression of the wife's confinement because Ana María's position in the coffin is the place from which the entire work is narrated. Once the story begins to unfold, it becomes clear that the dimensions of the coffin replicate those of Ana María's social environment throughout her life. Like Brígida of **"The Tree,"** Ana María goes from the confines of her father's house to the confines of her husband's town house, and, like the protagonist of ***House of Mist,*** when she is not encircled by the walls of the town house, she is isolated on her husband's country estate.

In a broader sense, the physical confinement of Bombal's female protagonists is the symbolic equivalent of their narrow social existence. The structures of confinement that recur in all three works represent the multiple barriers that thwart the women's full development as human beings. On the other hand, the conflict between the public definition of their destiny and their private notions of self-development leads to a desire to transcend the socially prescribed limits of their proper place. Thus, structures of escape are an essential element in all three works. However, the mechanisms of escape assume a particular form because the women are denied access to the means of creating an autonomous existence.

Since all three women interact only with members of their extended families, the other characters are of limited usefulness in enabling the protagonists to arrive at a meaningful alternative to the domestic role with which they are dissatisfied. For Ana María and Brígida, the lack of a suitable role model is even more acute because both were brought up in isolation by a widowed father, and their more conformist older sisters merely serve to reinforce the prevailing social values which both protagonists seek to repudiate.

While the other characters are simply extensions of the protagonists' domestic situation, and therefore serve as inadequate mediators in the protagonists' attempt to close the gap between aspiration and achievement, the circumscribed world in which they move provides them with little opportunity for evolving an alternative mode of existence. For the protagonist of ***House of Mist,*** both country and city constitute the same existential landscape because she only goes beyond the boundaries of her husband's hacienda when she accompanies her husband to visit his relatives in the city. For her, a change of locale means the substitution of one domestic sphere for another rather than an opportunity to broaden her knowledge of the workings of the larger society. Similarly, for Ana María and Brígida, location is immaterial as a field of experience. Both women, whether in town or country, are usually at home, awaiting the return of a lover and/or husband, and therefore they stand in marked contrast to the men who move about freely in pursuit of their socioeconomic interests.

Because the women are constrained in their outward movements, their inner development is of central importance in all three works. Given the fact that it is their dependent status as wives which causes them anxiety, for all three women, the quest for selfhood involves some form of separation from their husbands.

In *The Shrouded Woman,* Ana María initially attempts to resist her husband's domination by physically separating herself from him within a few months of marriage. However, her lack of resources for achieving true autonomy makes this a regressive movement since she can only return to her father's country estate. Nevertheless, the return home is crucial for her emotional growth because while she is away from Antonio, she comes to realize that her relationship with him has changed her significantly. Her recognition and acceptance of her sexual maturity enables her to express the desire to resume her relationship with her husband, and she subsequently returns to bear him three children. In this respect, Ana María's relationship with Antonio is qualitatively different from her premarital affair with Ricardo, which had resulted in pregnancy and miscarriage. Her emotional development is also reflected in her reactions to her unequal relationship with both men. Whereas she had been sexually passive with Ricardo, and had harbored self-destructive feelings when he eventually abandoned her, with Antonio, she becomes more assertive, albeit through traditional feminine gestures of seduction, in an attempt to make their marriage function on her own terms.

That her initiatives ultimately fail to produce the desired results stems from the fact that her assertiveness conflicts with Antonio's view of himself as the decisionmaker in the family. Consequently, Ana María must resort to a less threatening means of self-expression. Because physical separation has already proven to be unworkable, particularly in the light of Ana Maria's lack of the basic requirements for personal independence, she has no choice but to accommodate herself to being an unequal partner in the marriage. The following cry of protest represents her awakening to her secondary status when she is compelled to organize her life around Antonio's needs:

> Why, why must the nature of woman be such that a man always has to be the axis of her life?
>
> As for men, they manage to put their passion into other things. But the destiny of women is to displace the hurt of love onto a tidy house, before unfinished tapestries. (p. 84)[4]

Despite the biological interpretation of Ana María's situation, it is the social value that is ascribed to women which precludes the possibility of Ana María's becoming a self-determining individual. But if she is denied the opportunity to exist her herself in the realm of the real, she

achieves a margin of freedom in the psychological realm when she chooses Fernando as her confidant.

As a relationship based on her own need to relieve the frustrations of marriage and motherhood, Ana María's involvement with Fernando marks a new stage in her personal development. For the first time, it is Ana María's terms which establish the ground of the relationship. Her interaction with Fernando is also significant in that even though it is strictly platonic, it is her only relationship with a man that is based on his recognition of her as a complete person. Unlike Ricardo, for whom she was a purely sexual being, and unlike Antonio, who, through his love affairs, comes to separate her social existence as his wife from her sexual identity as a woman, Fernando acknowledges that the source of Ana María's appeal is as rooted in her aging body as in her intelligence.

In a society where divorce does not exist, the fact that Ana María is indissolubly linked to Antonio blocks the development of a relationship that might have enabled her to exist as a separate individual within the traditional sphere of marriage. Moreover, as Antonio's legitimate wife, the social respectability in which she is enshrined not only denies her the sexual freedom that Antonio enjoys, but, in the words of her lawyer, it also prevents her from acting to make her legitimate status coincide with her actual experience:

> "No, this shouldn't be done, Ana María. Remember that Antonio is the father of your children: remember that there are steps that a married woman cannot take without lowering herself." (p. 87)

Even though Ana María is denied freedom of movement in life, she achieves a measure of mobility in death when the coffin is lowered into the ground and she thereby enters the realm of nature. Thereupon, she begins to grow organically, as the vital forces that were trapped within her body become part of the cosmic order. Death thus enables her to escape the constraints of the coffin, and therefore of family ties, permitting her an expansive form of growth that was denied her in life.

The circumstances that restricted Ana María's social growth, and which only made it possible for her to develop physically, emotionally and psychologically, or to become coextensive with nature, also prevail in *House of Mist.* Like Ana María, the nameless protagonist of the novel becomes aware of the disparity between her expectations and the state of her marriage on her wedding night:

> The storm the night before had damaged the roofing of the old country house. When we got there, rain was dripping in all the rooms.
>
> "The roofs are not prepared for a winter like this," the servants said as they let us into the living room. And since they seemed to give me a strange look, Daniel explained quickly:
>
> "My cousin and I got married this morning."
>
> I was perplexed for two seconds.
>
> "However little importance he may have given to our unexpected marriage, Daniel should have informed his people," I thought, scandalized. (pp. 39-40)[5]

As young brides, both women experiences discomfort in the very domain that has always been considered woman's natural place. For the protagonist of *House of Mist,* initial discomfort is compounded when she discovers on her wedding night that her body is simply a familiar object to her husband:

> "Felipe and I have spied on all the girls in the family, and seen them dive in the river. I don't even need to undress you. I am even familiar with the scar from your appendectomy." (pp. 40-41)

The threat to her individuality, contained in Daniel's statements, is intensified by his subsequent efforts to transform her into a replica of his dead wife.

Two incidents arouse the protagonist into an awareness of her arrested development. The first, the sight of a dead girl in her coffin, leads the protagonist to recognize that, in a similar manner, her own vitality has been stifled because of her entrapment within her husband's conceptions of an ideal wife. And like Ana María, the protagonist initially attempts to resist engulfment by fleeing from the site where the threat to her identity is experienced most intensely. However, physical escape for her is even more short-lived than it was for Ana María because she merely escapes from her husband's house into the garden. Once she is in the open air, standing on the grounds of her husband's property, she becomes aware that she is not totally free from the danger of disembodiment. The mist which she perceives enveloping the landscape comes to stand as an objective equivalent of the immaterial presence—the memory of Daniel's dead wife—that threatens her constantly with non-being. Thus, she subsequently attempts to resist loss of self by affirming her biological existence:

> I am afraid. There is a kind of hidden danger in all that immobility and in the immobility of that dead girl stretched out upstairs.
>
> And because it is attacking me for the first time, I react violently against the mist's asault.
>
> "I exist, I exist," I say out loud, "and I am beautiful and happy! Yes. Happy! Happiness is simply having a young, slender and agile body." (p. 45).

By anchoring her identity to her material self, the protagonist seeks to overcome her husband's efforts to empty her of her physical distinctiveness.

Having taken a preliminary step toward recovering her individuality, the protagonist is enabled to take another step in that direction as a result of her second encounter. When she accidentally perceives Regina, Felipe's wife, passionately embracing her lover, she becomes aware not only of her own loss of identity because of having to assume the style and manners of Daniel's dead wife, but she also becomes conscious of the possibility of achieving self-realization outside the boundaries of marriage. That Regina is willing to assert the primacy of her own needs in defiance of social conventions inspires the protagonist to emulate Regina in giving priority to her own desires. And her discovery of her body as an object of beauty as well as a source of pleasure becomes an intentional act toward that end. But whereas Regina dares to go beyond acceptable social limits in her quest for personal fulfillment, the protagonist chooses to remain within those limits, and

therefore the direction of her project for self-development is necessarily inward.

Through the powers of her imagination, she invents a lover, who not only gazes at her appreciatively but he also desire her body for itself:

> I am aflame with the desire for his looks to discover me as soon as possible. The beauty of my body yearns, at last for its share of homage.
>
> Once nude, I remain seated on the edge of the bed. He moves away and contemplates me. Under his attentive look, I throw my head back and this gesture fills me with innermost well-being. I fold my arms behind my neck, I cross and uncross my legs, and each gesture gives me an intense and total pleasure, as if, at last, my arms and my neck and my legs had a reason for being. Even if this pleasure were the only purpose of love, I would feel amply rewarded! (pp. 59-60)

But even though the protagonist now dares to conceive of a totally satisfying existence on the other side of marriage, the projections of her imagination are still structured by her actual situation. While the frustrations of marriage to a domineering husband are transformed into a fantasy of sexual pleasure with a more endearing partner, even then, the protagonist does not experience her body as the core of her own existence since she first needs to have its individual parts validated by her lover's eye.

Consequently, the attempt to escape the limitations of her situation through fantasy proves to be unsatisfactory because the locus of her selfhood is mediated by Daniel's presence. When the protagonist can no longer sustain the idealized image of the lover because of her husband's increasing sexual interest in her, she resorts to suicide in a final attempt to escape the constraints of marriage. For, as the following passage indicates, sexual frustration is only one element which makes her existence as Daniel's wife intolerable:

> "Tomorrow we will go back to the country. Day after tomorrow I will go to hear mass in town with my mother-in-law. Then, at lunch, Daniel will tell us about the work on the hacienda. Immediately afterwards I will visit the greenhouse, the bird cage, the orchard. Before supper, I will take a nap near the fireplace or read the local newspaper. After eating I will have fun stirring up minor disasters in the fire when I thoughtlessly poke the coals. The silence around me will indicate very soon that we have exhausted all topics of conversation and Daniel will put the bars on the doors noisily. Then we will go to sleep. And day after tomorrow it will be the same, and a year from now, and ten years from now; it will be the same thing until old age deprives me of all right to love and desire, and until my body shrivels and my face is all wrinkled and I am ashamed to appear in public without makeup." (pp. 55-56)

When Daniel restrains her from hurling herself in the path of an oncoming car, the protagonist eventually accommodates herself to her situation, thereby admitting the impossibility of ever achieving self-realization:

> I follow him in order to perform an infinity of little tasks; to fulfill an infinity of pleasant frivolities; to cry out of habit and to smile out of duty. I follow him in order to live correctly, to die correctly, some day. (p. 102).

As if to underscore the protagonist's sense of being frozen in a situation of endless duration, the predominant time of narration throughout the novel is the historic present. References to the protagonist's wedding night, her tenth wedding anniversary, and her suicide attempt are all given in the present, as if they all constituted the same experiential moment. When the protagonist ultimately shows an awareness of the passing of time, it is to take note of the marks of the ravages of time on her own body and on that of her husband: which simply heightens her despair at seeing her body deteriorate without her having had a chance to develop fully.

The idea of marriage as a state of stagnation for the protagonist also underlies the story, **"The Tree."** For Brígida, like Bombal's other heroines, finds little meaingful activity within the domestic realm. Moreover, like the narrator of *House of Mist,* Brígida also faces the threat of disembodiment because of her husband's insistence on imposing al alien identity on her. Unlike the absent presence of Daniel's dead wife, however, the figurative language which Luis applies to Brígida—"You are like a necklace of birds" (p. 108);[6] "you have a frightened deer's eyes" (p. 110)— not only implies that she is basically flawed but it also relegates her to a lower order of social existence. At the same time, Luis's essentialist terms are similar in effect to Daniel's sarcastic remarks in that, at the outset, Brígida, like the narrator of *House of Mist,* internalizes her husband's perceptions of her. When Luis shows little interest in her, conveying through his recommendation, "eat and go to bed" (p. 112), that he perceives her as a creature with only elemental needs, Brígida assumes that it is her own deficiencies that are responsible for her frustrations as Luis's wife rather than the obvious difference in age and temperament between husband and wife.

Because it is her husband who defines her sphere of activity, Brígida, like Bombal's other heroines, must repress her own desires. But unlike Ana María and the narrator of *House of Mist,* who subsequently seek a satisfactory means of self-expression in the world of men—real or imagined—Brígida turns to the realm of nature as a avenue of personal freedom. If, on the one hand, her communication with the gum tree seems to indicate her continued acceptance of her husband's naturalistic definition of her, on the other hand, it marks the beginning of her emotional independence from Luis, a movement that will culminate in her decision to leave him.

Unlike Ana María, for whom coextension with nature provides an arena of development in death, for Brígida, the world of nature is a separate realm which enables her to make the transition from dependence to self-determination in life. When the tree is cut down, Brígida comes to realize that the tree, like Luis, who had embodied a similar promise of eternal satisfaction, does not exist in a timeless dimension, but is subject to social process and death. Once Brígida is forced to recognize the impingement of the social world upon the natural one, she becomes aware that she, too, exists in a social dimension, and therefore, like the tree, she must also come to terms with the world of change. Having recognized her own temporality, Brígida perceives that neither tree nor Luis can provide a stable core for her existence. Thereupon, she rejects the stasis of her earlier life and assumes the risk of restructuring her existence according to her own desires: "Lie! Her resigna-

tion and serenity were lies; she wanted love, yes, love, and trips and foolishness, and love, love . . . " (p. 125) Having expressed the desire to begin living in her own interest, Brígida consciously assumes her individuality as a social being by abandoning the naturalistic environment of her husband's house and making the trip to the concert hall.

Even though Brígida appears to be different from Ana María and the protagonist of *House of Mist* in that she moves beyond the confines of her own body as well as beyond the domestic realm, she is basically similar to Bombal's other heroines, despite her willingness to assume responsibility for shaping her own life. Both her inexperience and the gaps in her education make in unlikely for her to succeed in attaining her goal of autonomy. Moreover, the circular structure of the story suggests that progress for Brígida is impossible, bracketed as she is by the moment between the beginning and the end of the concert. Thus, while Brígida takes the step of going out into the world, there is no indication that her social position is qualitatively different than that of Bombal's other heroines.

The limited options available to the women in all three works cause marriage to be the only arena of social development available to them. Yet, the marital relationships portrayed by Bombal indicate that for the women, marriage is incompatible with self-realization. Wives either stagnate or lose themselves in marriage. Consequently, even Brígida's modest attempt to act in her own interest requires her to become separated from her husband. Because the path of social development is blocked for Bombal's female characters, death, dream or fantasy become the only authentic avenues to personal growth available to these "shrouded" women.

Notes

1. Marjorie Agosín, "Entrevista con María Luisa Bombal," *The American Hispanist,* 3 (November 1977), 6. My translation.

2. See, for example, Elsa M. Chaney, "Old and New Feminists in Latin America: The Case of Peru and Chile," *Journal of Marriage and the Family,* 35 (May 1973), 338-41; Marysa Navarro, "Research on Latin American Women," *Signs,* 5 (Autumn 1979), 113-14; Evelyn P. Stevens, "The Prospects for a Women's Liberation Movement in Latin America," *Journal of Marriage and the Family,* 35 (May 1973), 313-21.

3. See Jorge Gissi Bustos, "Mythology about Women, with Special Reference to Chile," in *Sex and Class in Latin American,* eds. June Nash and Helen Icken Safa (New York: Praeger Publishers, 1976), pp. 30-45; Salvador Reyes Nevares, "El machismo en México," *Mundo Nuevo,* 46 (April 1970), 17; Sebastián Romero-Buj, "Hispanoamérica y el machismo," Ibid., 31.

4. References are to my translation of *La amortajada* (Havana: Casa de las Américas, 1969), originally published in 1938. Bombal subsequently published a modified version of the Spanish novel in English, entitled *The Shrouded Woman.*

5. References are to my translation of the novel, *La última niebla* (Santiago, Chile: Editorial

Nascimento, 1962), originally published in 1935. This edition of the novel also includes the story, "The Tree" "El árbol", which I discuss later. In 1947, Bombal published an English version of *La última niebla*, entitled *The House of Mist*, which was an expansion rather than a translation of the Spanish work.

6. María Luisa Bombal, "El arbol," in *La última niebla*. All translation are by the author.

Thomas O. Bente (essay date 1984)

SOURCE: "María Luisa Bombal's Heroines: Poetic Neuroses and Artistic Symbolism," in *Hispanofila*, Vol. 28, No. 1, September, 1984, pp. 103-13.

[*In the following discussion of* La última niebla, La amortajada, *and* "El árbol," *Bente examines the "neurotic" demeanor of Bombal's woman protagonists. The critic concludes: "her literature of neuroses and frustration, illustrated through clearly defined women protagonists and executed through poetic and artistic symbolism, achieves the highest tradition of life and literature as a conveyance of the perplexities of the human condition."*]

Whether due to increasing appreciation of the short stories and novels of María Luisa Bombal as a precursor of the Spanish American New Narrative, or to contemporary interest in the status of women in Spanish American society, the last several years have seen a partial redress of the semi-obscurity of critical interest in Bombal's work. Indeed, a number of convincing studies have appeared and will appear, bearing testimony of awakened esteem for the artistic quality, if not the quantity, of the Chilean novelist's writing. Although the current critical interest in Bombal acknowledges in common her novelistic craftsmanship, a trend of thought and interpretation of the central women characters also seems to be emerging; it suggests that they are shallow, frivolous, and fatuous, characters incapable of self-realization and fulfillment—which they are, almost without exception—because they exist in a literary world that mirrors the male-dominated, bourgeois society of Chile, and one assumes Spanish America in general, in the 1930's. In quasi-Naturalistic terms, the neurotic behavior of Bombal's heroines is attributed to the *milieu* and *moment* of their existence.[1] While this study does not aspire to be a polemic against such interpretation, recognizing that there is some evidence for it, it does seek to question topical conclusions, to add a more central focus to the explanation and interpretation of the women characters, and to show how skillfully María Luisa Bombal has elaborated their frustrations, which result in neurotic behavior, through the artistic symbolism in each of her works. Three will be examined: *La última niebla, La amortajada,* and **"El árbol."**

La última niebla, published in 1935, is the surrealistic study of the woman protagonist's sexual frustration. Unlike Bombal's other two works which will be commented on here, *La última niebla* deals very little with the emotional level of the nameless central character, although, curiously, the work specifically mentions in the opening pages the emotional needs of Daniel, the protagonist's

cousin and new husband. Their marriage, executed precipitously without great consideration on either part, is characterized when Daniel asks her "¿Para qué nos casamos?," to which she replies, with a casualness that borders on contemptuous indifference, "Por casarnos."[2] Bombal rather explicitly explains why Daniel has remarried to ameliorate the loneliness in his life caused by the unexpected death of his first wife three months after they were married a year earlier. Neither partner is prepared to bring to the new marriage what the other needs and expects; rather callously, Daniel tells his new wife that he and Felipe, his brother, used to observe the girls in the family when they were children swimming in the river, and that "No necesito ni siquiera desnudarte. De ti, conozco hasta la cicatriz de tu operación de apendicitis."[3] For Daniel, physical familiarity has preceded their marriage; physical intimacy is of secondary importance or, indeed, totally out of the question for him at this point. Opposed to his sexual lack of interest, the protagonist manifests even greater callousness and indifference in the face of Daniel's emotional turmoil, doubtless caused by the memory of his adored first wife. As they enter the nuptial chamber, she realizes that Daniel is crying; rather than attempting any consolation, "Me aparto de él, tratando de persuadirme que la actitud más discreta está en fingir una absoluta ignorancia de su dolor. Pero en mi fuero interno, algo me dice que ésta es también la actitud más cómoda.

"Y entonces, más que el llanto de mi marido, me molesta la idea de mi propio egoísmo."[4] By her own admission, the heroine[5] characterizes herself as insensitive, complacent, apathetic, and unsolicitous. She has, unconsciously, paralleled her husband's temporary sexual impotence, caused by the trauma of reenacting the wedding night with his new wife, with her own emotional frigidity, a basic, integral part of her own personality. Bombal stresses the immature, undeveloped nature of her heroine by further telling the reader, vis-à-vis a third person narrator "la muchacha que yace en ese ataúd [i.e., the protagonist gains a distant perspective of herself] blanco, no hace dos días coloreaba tarjetas postales sentada bajo el emparrado."[6] Witless, insensitive, and capricious, she has whimsically contracted marriage without the slightest awareness of the demands her new role might make. The author repeatedly has emphasized the absence of warmth in the house, symbolic of the vacuum of compassion and sexual interest that prevails; least there be any doubt whether the marriage is consummated the first night, the heroine informs that "A la mañana siguiente, cuando me despierto, hay a mi lado un surco vacío, . . . "[7] imagery that is clearly a reference to the lack of fertilization of their wedding night.

The emotional and sexual sterility of their first night together is followed by the first plainly surrealistic scene, in which the heroine gains a perspective of herself as a dead person (see footnote 6); the house, characterized as a tomb, provokes a silence that increases in the protagonist's head to a point of implosion, and she flees to the outside. The first reference to the mist, a poetic image-metaphor that continues to form a substantial part of the work, occurs as she frenetically seeks escape from the house.[8] Reacting against the silence and the image of herself as moribund, she states " . . . hay como un peligro oculto.

"Y porque me ataca por vez primera, reacciono violentamente contra el asalto de la niebla.

"¡Yo existo, yo existo—digo en voz alta—y soy bella y feliz! Sí. ¡Feliz! La felicidad no es más que tener un cuerpo joven y esbelto y ágil."[9]

This paroxysm, which further reinforces the shallowness of the protagonist as she proclaims only her sensuality, assumes greater importance than it has been accorded critically; it is nothing less than the first and last time the heroine will challenge the substitute-for-reality quality of the fog. Recognizing that her sexual desires have not been and may not be satisfied, given her frivolity and inadaptable nature vis-a-vis her husband's needs and the precipitous nature of their marriage, she defies the onslaught of the surrogate reality only momentarily by defiantly and brazenly reaffirming her own beauty. This brief and fleeting perceptions occurs once throughout the entire work; hereafter, she either passively or unconsciously indulges in fantasy encounters to relieve the sexual nullity in her life.

Masterfully, Bombal introduces a scene charged with sensuality and suggestion immediately after the heroine has challenged the mist: the arrival of Felipe, Daniel's brother, with his wife Regina, and an unnamed male companion referred to simply as "un amigo." The protagonist, as far as the reader knows at this point, is the only outsider aware that the *amigo* and Regina are lovers. The latter, whose appearance and every action exude a voluptuous, provocative aura, functions as a counterpoint to Daniel's wife who, burning with envy and desire, again flees the house into the mist. She states, "Cierro los ojos y me abandono contra un árbol. ¡Oh, echar los brazos alrededor de un cuerpo ardiente y rodar con él, enlazada, por una pendiente sin fin . . . ,"[10] clearly an action of frustration with the tree as a symbol for the male, perhaps a phallic symbol,[11] as she then participates in her fantasy in a poetic, metaphorically described sexual encounter in the pond.

The occasion for the visit of Felipe, Regina, and her lover is a hunt, which takes place the following day. At dusk, amidst symbolic imagery of heat and light, the men return, whereupon Regina's lover drops and forcibly holds one of the dead birds, still warm and bleeding, in the protagonist's lap. The scene is grotesque; in addition to its obvious sexual innuendoes and overtones, it plainly points up the male sexual dominance and female susceptibility that characterize *La última niebla*. The novel does not, either in this scene or any other, illustrate male moral, psychological, intellectual or emotional dominance over the female, however, one or all of which would be necessary if the reader were to accept the interpretation of exclusive male culpability for the neurotic behavior the protagonist displays.

The dream-like sequence, the mysterious encounter with a nameless lover in which the heroine participates in one night of sublime love, is a celebrated scene frequently commented on in critical discussions of the novel. Although the episode occupies only a few pages, the memory of the fantasy lover who finally assuages her sexual desires continues to nurture her through years of what becomes a platonic marriage. Her body ages, but she is indifferent. As though suggesting a progressively worsening mental and physical state, she is aware that "Estoy ojerosa y a menudo, la casa, el parque, los bosques, empiezan a girar vertiginosamente ante mis ojos."[12] Year pass, again

she fantasizes a meeting with her nameless lover in which she catches only a glimpse of him at the pond, and her inability to distinguish reality from the illusory worsens. Only when she and Daniel return to the city, a trip occasioned by Regina's suicide attempt, does she begin to acknowledge the possibility that her experiences may have been imagined. As she views Regina in the hospital, she admits, "Y siento, de pronto, que odio a Regina, que envidio su dolor, su trágica aventura y hasta su posible muerte. Me acometen furiosos deseos de acercarme y sacudirla duramente, preguntándole de qué se queja, ¡ella, que lo ha tenido todo! Amor, vértigo y abandono."[13]

Almost immediately thereafter, she contemplates and almost attempts suicide. Realizing its futility when her husband prevents it, she is then repelled by the thought, not because she wants to live, but because "El suicidio de una mujer casi vieja, qué cosa repugnante e inútil."[14] The novella closes with the protagonist following her husband, now deprived of her amorous memories because she realizes their chimeral nature, and resigned to a life of " . . . una infinidad de pequeños menesteres . . . una infinidad de frivolidades amenas; para llorar por costumbre y sonreír por deber."[15]

Most analyses of the central character would agree that she is infantile, shallow, narcissistic, and pococurante. Insensitive to her husband's needs, without any basis for marriage except to satisfy her concupiscence, she descends throughout the work into a replacement existence of wish fulfillment through her fantasy until she at last acknowledges its irreality and again confronts, albeit passively, the futility of her life. At no point in the work does María Luisa Bombal suggest that the behavior of the heroine is prompted or conditioned either by the prevailing social milieu or by male primacy. While the sexual dominance of the men characters over the women characters is acknowledged, the latter are frivolous and neurotic by their very nature. Hernán Vidal, viewing the collective women protagonists in Bombal's works as victims of capitalist bourgeois lives and primal men, states: "Las figuras masculinas que predominan en la narrativa de la autora son las de hombres de negocios, latifundistas y abogados, representantes del orden establecido, avejentados, canosos, fláccidos y desvitalizados. Sus mujeres, incapaces de encontrar junto a ellos identidad de tales en la comunión del amor fértil, quedan prisioneras de la enajenación mental."[16] I suggest that the responsibility for the "mental alienation" implicit in this statement is misleading; at the very least, it is confusing cause with effect.

Curiously, a substantive case for medical and/or psychosomatic reasons behind the protagonist's conduct and symptoms might be made. From a psychological point of view, her behavior is clearly schizophrenic, nearly bordering on the hysterical. Indeed, early in the work the author suggests that her character may be suffering from a mental disorder which, as we see, becomes progressively more severe. For example, the protagonist, immediately after challenging the mist, confesses, "No obstante, desde hace mucho, flota en mí una turbia inquietud. Cierta noche, mientras dormía, vislumbré algo, algo que era tal vez su causa. Una vez despierta, traté en vano de recordarlo. Noche a noche he tratado, también en vano, de volver a encontrar el mismo sueño."[17] Whether one accepts that the protagonist is afflicted by an identifiable mental disorder or is simply vainly juvenile in her marital priorities and ensuing relationship with her husband, she alone is perpetrator and victim of her own nervous disorders. Their acuteness is abetted by her circumstances, but it is she who has engendered them.

Ana María, the central protagonist of *La amortajada,* published in 1938, is a significantly more complex literary character than the unnamed heroine of Bombal's earlier novel. Moving from the realistic scenario with surrealistic overtones of *La última niebla,* the author reverses the process and creates a surrealistic atmosphere with realistic overtones in *La amortajada*: the wake and eventual interment of the shrouded woman who, although deceased, retains her faculties of thought. Through the visits a series of friends and relatives make to view Ana María in her coffin, the reader becomes aware—through stream of consciousness, monologue, dialogue, and a narrator who fluctuates between being omniscient and restricted—of the multiple and frequently ambiguous relationships she has had.

Basically, Ana María is—was—a far less troubled and neurotic woman than the protagonist in *La última niebla.* She shares with the former, however, a coquettish and accelerated vanity that borders on self-adulation. The third person narrator informs us early in the work that Ana María is preoccupied, and satisfied, with the style and touch that has been given to her hair in preparation for the wake and burial: "Pero ella no ignora que la masa sombría de una cabellera desplegada presta a toda mujer extendida y durmiendo un ceño de misterio, un perturbador encanto.

"Y de golpe se siente sin una sola arruga, pálida y bella como nunca."[18]

Immediately thereafter, in the presence of her daughter and sons, we are told " . . . sus hijos ariscos al menor cumplido, aunque secretamente halagados cuando sus jóvenes camaradas fingían tomarla [Ana María] por una hermana mayor."[19] Very carefully, Bombal has introduced her character as an obsessively egotistical woman who, even in death, revels in the admiration of others: "Saboreando su pueril vanidad, largamente permanece rígida, sumisa a todas las miradas, como desnuda a fuerza de resistencia."[20] Arrogant, proud, and self-flattering, she awaits the arrival of the first significant man in her life, Ricardo, whose force is symbolically heralded by the clashing of horses' hoofs in the distance. His presence evokes a chain of memories that extends to their childhood; gradually, the reader perceives the growing sexual attraction that characterized their relationship. Once, after having been reprimanded by his father, Ricardo disappeared for a night. Returning the next day, Ana María, addressing herself to him, remembers, " . . . Me arrimé a ti. Todo tu cuerpo despedía calor, era una brasa.

"Guiada por un singular deseo acerqué a tu brazo la extremidad de mis dedos siempre helados. Tú dejaste súbitamente de beber, y asiendo mis dos manos, me obligaste a aplastarlas contra tu pecho. Tu carne quemaba."[21] Masterfully, Bombal has counterpointed the physical sensuality and excitement of Ricardo with the suggestion of Ana María's lack of passion in her "dedos siempre helados." Ana María's inability to participate fully and with abandon in love is further accentuated after they become lov-

ers. Again addressing Ricardo in stream of consciousness monologue, she says "Durante tres vacaciones fui tuya.

"Tú me hallabas fría porque nunca lograste que compartiera tu frenesí, porque me colmaba el olor a oscuro clavel silvestre de tu beso."[22] Immediately thereafter, in a dramatic change of tone, she asks, "Aquel brusco, aquel cobarde abandono tuyo, ¿respondió a una orden perentoria de tus padres o alguna rebeldía de tu impetuoso carácter? No sé."[23] The structuring of particles of information, Bombal's sequence of insight into Ana María's character and psyche, suggests that a passivity that borders on frigidity is basic to her personality. The reader is left with the impression that Ricardo may, indeed, have left her because of her sexual indifference. Later in the novel, when Antonio, her husband, enters to view her, the same problem of amorous disharmony is recalled. In narrative which includes both the omniscient narrator and Ana María's stream of consciousness, the memories of sexual dissonance are recalled very explicitly as her dysfunction as a partner is emphasized. It is significant to note also that more important than their sexual incompatability, intimacy with Antonio produced an emotional frigidity in Ana María; sexual culmination brought no tenderness nor did it reaffirm affection, rather "¡Pobre Antonio, qué extrañeza la suya ante el rechazo casi inmediato! Nunca, nunca supo hasta qué punto lo odiaba todas las noches en aquel momento [i.e., physical culmination]."[24] She realizes she had married to spite Ricardo; regardless of Antonio's solicitations and entreaties to make her content, her capricious, self-centered neuroses militate against their establishing a marriage with even a modicum of happiness. At her request, Antonio returns her to her father's home; indecisive, she now longs for her husband. The separation results in a loss of Antonio's previously unwavering love; never again is it reclaimed after they are reunited.[25] Their marriage becomes routine as she acknowledges his extra-marital liaisons with a certain resignation. In a frequently cited passage, Ana María, followed by the narrator, ponders "¿Por qué, por qué la naturaleza de la mujer ha de ser tal que tenga que ser siempre un hombre el eje de su vida?

"Los hombres, ellos, logran poner su pasión en otras cosas. Pero el destino de las mujeres es remover una pena de amor en una casa ordenada, ante una tapicería inconclusa."[26] While it would be naive to overlook the socialcultural commentary implicit in this rumination, one is obliged to associate it in the perspective of Ana María's circumstances—Antonio has not consigned her to such a role; rather she has precipitated it. Curiously, even in death, Ana María seems totally unaware of her own partial responsibility for the outcome of her marriage and the repercussions caused by her compulsive behavior. She has lived and died assuming that impunity is a corollary of femininity.

By far the most psychologically complex female-male relationship in *La amortajada,* however, is Ana María's association with Fernando. As a widower friend, he and Ana María formed a mutually self-depreciating bond which only Fernando would acknowledge as such. While it is apparent that Fernando was drawn to Ana María through genuine love, albeit a love that flourished and nurtured itself precisely because of her rejection and diffidence, his relationship to her, as she views it, adds yet another dimension of her cunning nature. As a confidant and potential means to cause jealousy in her husband, Fernando provided little more than an outlet for her vindictive, tortured personality. She loathes him, not only for what he is but because of her dependence on him. Without the slightest genuine affection or friendship, by her own admission she has reciprocated in the exchange of confidences solely because he served her in a capacity that at first was iniquitous and then became routine, "un mal necesario." In many ways, Fernando is the most carefully drawn of Bombal's male personages in the works discussed here. His character, which thrives on unfulfillment and nonsuccess, curiously parallels the predicament of Bombal's heroines. As the antithesis of Bombal's standard masculine figures, Fernando stands out as a singularly unfortunate and hapless type—a victim of himself, but without the wiles of the author's women characters.

Bombal's well-known short story, **"El árbol,"** was included in the 1935 publication of *La última niebla.* Chronologically, it stands, therefore, in tandem with her earlier work, yet by virtue of the departure it evidences in the presentation of its major female figure, Brígida, it stands alone. Of the three women protagonists discussed here, Brígida is the only one who manages to surmount circumstances to confront a future that is unknown.

As a woman, she is characterized as naive without being superficial, ungifted without being shallow. María Luisa Bombal carefully stresses the childhood, formative roots of Brígida's untutored and intellectually complacent personality, emphasizing the indifference and near rejection her father demonstrated toward her and the fact that she married Luis, a much older man, "Porque al lado de aquel hombre solemne y taciturno no se sentía culpable de ser tal cual era: tonta, juguetona y perezosa"[27] Contrary to the unnamed heroine of *La última niebla* and Ana María in *La amortajada,* Brígida is neither as psychotic as the former nor as artful and vindictive as the latter; she shares with them, however, the same sexual-emotional frustration of her marriage. In this case, one is inclined to attribute the sterility of their marriage to Luis; there is not the slightest evidence of tenderness or physical interest on his part. Seeking refuge from the heated frustration of her marriage in the freshness of the dressing chamber, poetically presented in cool and aquatic imagery, Brígida attempts to cope with a barren and joyless life. Finally, when the protective tree that shaded the dressing room is cut down, she confronts external reality for the first time and leaves her husband. In a paragraph that completely captures the frenzy of Brígida's emotional state when she decides to abandon her marriage, the omniscient narrator says, "¡Mentira! Eran mentiras su resignación y su serenidad; quería amor, sí, amor, y viajes y locura, y amor, amor. . . . "[28] In taking this step, Brígida is remarkably singular in comparison with Bombal's other women protagonists. She is also the only heroine whose frustration and unhappiness are clearly the fault and responsibility of other people—her father and her husband—and not of herself.

This study has not attempted to vindicate entirely the culpability of the male protagonists María Luisa Bombal created. Clearly, they are often less than exemplary fictional characters. Daniel in *La última niebla,* dispirited and mournful over the death of his first wife, indeed does contribute to the heroine's inability to achieve a self-identity which could lead to fulfillment both as a person and as a wife-lover. Ricardo in *La amortajada* is overwhelmingly physical; once dissatisfied, Ana María becomes little more than a spurned paramour, and Antonio in the same novel obviously does not retain the same love and indulgence toward his wife throughout their marriage. Brígida's father in **"El árbol"** has wrought untold damage on his daughter by casting her as simplistic, a mold she grows to accept for herself which leads directly to an Oedipal marriage with disastrous results. None of these characters is exonerated. At the same time, the social pressures on the women characters must be acknowledged; each, with the exception of Regina in *La última niebla,* who indulges in an affair, and Brígida in **"El árbol,"** who seeks and achieves separation from her impotent and cold husband, conforms to a cultural milieu that demand fidelity and matronly propriety from women, while at the same time disregarding amorous liaisons and external interests of men.

Nevertheless, as has been shown, both *La última niebla* and *La amortajada* present central women figures who, by their very nature, directly contribute to the frustrations, neuroses, and disillusionment in which they become engulfed. Only Brígida in **"El árbol"** stands apart. Criticism of Bombal's works that minimizes or refuses to acknowledge this, risks converting the author into an avant-garde voice for female equality, casting her in the vanguard of Spanish American writers who illustrate the disparity of the sexes in their writing, and viewing her works as tendentious social commentary, Bombal achieved much more; her literature of neuroses and frustration, illustrated through clearly defined women protagonists and executed through poetic and artistic symbolism, achieves the highest tradition of art as a reflection of life and literature as a conveyance of the perplexities of the human condition.

Notes

1. M. Ian Adams, in his perceptive study, "María Luisa Bombal: Alienation and the Poetic Image," states, for example,

   However, there are exterior social dimensions that, although they never come into the foreground, provide a hidden influence that tends to push all Bombal's women into themselves, giving them a feeling, frequently not expressed, of lack of control over their lives. The position of women in the society described in her novels is the most outstanding of these forces, in that it makes marriage the central issue of their lives. On the emotional level, the most important one within Bombal's works, this position gives men the power of choice as opposed to women's relative helplessness, turning men into an external alienating force. pp. 16-17.

   The essay appears in *Three Authors of Alienation* (Austin: Univ. of Texas Press, 1975), pp. 15-37.

   In a similar vein, Hernán Vidal in *María Luisa Bombal: La feminidad enajenada* (Barcelona: Colección Aubí, 1976) concludes,

   Excluida la posibilidad de una armoniosa integración en el orden masculino burgués, la mujer tiene sólo dos opciones: traicionar su feminidad para cooperar servil y anestesiadamente, o recluirse en sí misma sin complementar sus potencialidades irracionales con una activa participación en el mundo como ente social. Ambas opciones sólo pueden tener como resultado la suspensión del amor como fuerza de cohesión social, el predominio del resentimiento y el espíritu vengativo contra quienes obstaculizan el normal desarrollo del ser y, finalmente, el deterioro mental por la violencia que todo esto implica contra los instintos humanos. pp. 138-139.

2. *La última niebla,* 3.ª edición (Santiago de Chile: Nascimento, 1962), p. 42. All quotations from the novel are taken from this edition.

3. Ibid., p. 41.

4. Ibid., p. 43.

5. A good case could be made in favor of calling María Luisa Bombal's women protagonists "anti-heroines." The term "heroine" is used throughout this study as simply a synonym for "woman protagonist," to whom few, if any, of the attributes of the "traditional" heroine may be attached.

6. *La última niebla,* p. 44.

7. Ibid., p. 43.

8. M. Ian Adams' discussion of the symbolic function of the mist, in *Three Authors of Alienation,* will doubtless become the definitive statement. Briefly, he contends

At various places in the novel the mist, at its maximum level of emotional intensity, has been a symbol of the protagonist's emotional vision, physically representing her peculiar inability to distinguish between reality and fantasy. When she finally and unequivocally can identify reality and can establish contact with herself, she describes her fantasies as being destroyed by the same element that has previously reality. The tone of her statement puts the final action of the mist in the past, but at the same time it generalizes its action. Thus the mist acquires a universal quality as a mysterious force inimical to human happiness. At the same time it maintains its individual character as a form peculiar to a large part of the protagonist's life. The former meaning is well described by Cedomil Goić: "The specific function of the mist is to represent the ominous, the presence of the hostile forces of the world." p. 32.

9. *La última niebla,* p. 45.

10. Ibid., p. 49.

11. For a discussion of symbols and their values in María Luisa Bombal's works, see the "Introduction" by Ángeles Cardona de Gilbert to Vidal's study of the author.

12. *La última niebla,* p. 68.

13. Ibid., p. 100.

14. Ibid., p. 101.

15. Ibid., p. 102.

16. Hernán Vidal, p. 54.

17. *La última niebla,* p. 68.

18. *La amortajada,* 5.ª edición (Santiago de Chile: Editorial Orbe, 1969), pp. 8-9. All quotations from the novel are taken from this edition.

19. Ibid., p. 9.

20. Ibid., p. 10.

21. Ibid., p. 20.

22. Ibid., p. 25.

23. Loc. cit.

24. Ibid., p. 83.

25. This interpretation is notably different from Professor Phyllis Rodríguez-Peralta's reading. She writes,

The men in *La amortajada* are varied in their relationships to Ana María, including sons, father, admirer (all marginal figures); but the lover and the husband retain most of the attributes of their counterparts in the first novel [ie., *La última niebla*]. Ricardo's actions remain an enigma to Ana María. With veiled contempt, her husband treats her like a foolish creature who bores him. Their failure of communication was solidified early in their marriage when Antonio, still ardently enamored, was unable to understand her nostalgic desire to return to her father's house, and she, without space to become accustomed to the city and time to mature, was incapable of expressing her feelings. A stunted marriage of alienation and mutual discontent resulted.

Prof. Rodríguez-Peralta's study of Bombal's work, "María Luisa Bombal's Poetic Novels of Female Estrangement," was scheduled to appear in the January, 1980, issue of *Revista de estudios hispánicos.*

26. *La amortajada,* p. 99.

27. "El árbol," *La última niebla,* 3.ª edición (Santiago de Chile: Nascimento, 1962) p. 108.

28. Ibid., p. 125.

Celeste Kostopulos-Cooperman (essay date 1988)

SOURCE: "Antithetical Mirror Images and the Poetic Imagination in the Narrative of María Luisa Bombal," in *The Lyrical Vision of María Luisa Bombal,* Tamesis Books Limited, 1988, pp. 69-78.

[*In the following essay, the critic discusses recurring images in Bombal's novellas and stories that serve to portray the futile state of her women protagonists.*]

Imagination is a strong, restless faculty. When she shows us bright pictures, are we never to look at them, and try to reproduce them? And when she is eloquent, and speaks rapidly and urgently in our ear, are we not to write to her dictation?

Charlotte Brontë, in a letter to George Henry Lewes[1]

The desire to translate and to render artistically her inner fantasies and thoughts into the written word is not a novel experience for the literary woman. However, as Charlotte Brontë's questions clearly imply, fiction was not always considered a legitimate domain for the woman writer. Indeed both Sandra Gilbert and Susan Gubar brilliantly disclose in their panoramic study of the woman writer and the nineteenth-century literary imagination, how several generations of women were either prevented or strongly dissuaded from "attempting the pen".

Anomalous figures in the annals of a predominantly masculine engendered literary domain, women have until quite recently, been denied their place in literature.[2] However interesting it is to speculate and to discuss the probable causes and origins of this conspiracy of silence, it is even more essential to examine the distinctive manner in which the woman writer has not only designed her craft but has also confronted and transcended the conventional strictures that have been given her.

Although María Luisa Bombal initiated her literary career in the Buenos Aires of the thirties amidst a highly respected group of artists and intellectuals—among these, Jorge Luis Borges, Oliverio Girondo, Norah Lange, Pablo Neruda and Victoria Ocampo—and her first two novels, *La última niebla* (1935) and *La amortajada* (1938), appeared in the prestigious journal *Sur,* the recognition and interest that these works initially inspired, suddenly and mysteriously waned, plunging the poet-novelist into the silent abyss of literary anonymity that was to accompany and to plague her for a period of almost three decades. So few acknowledged the originality of her prose, that an incredulous Amado Alonso found himself compelled to ask:

> ¿Por qué la crítica local no habrá anunciado *La última niebla* como un libro importante? . . . Una novelista que en su primera obra nos da una construcción poética con tan artística realización y con tan sobrios y eficaces elementos de estilo bien merece ser saludada y presentada por la crítica con especial atención.[3]

Unwilling to subscribe to the literary dogmas that were still in vogue in her native Chile and responding to an inner voice that differed from conventional techniques of storytelling in its tonality, substance, and form, María Luisa Bombal was destined to become a marginal and somewhat problematic figure. Her preoccupation with feminine themes, her revitalization of traditional models of narration and her voluntary exile also undoubtedly contributed to her enigmatic disappearance from the literary mainstream.

María Luisa's narrative evokes a poetic vision of the self and its relationship to its world. Implicit within the dissonant mirror images that pervade her fiction, is the antithetical nature of this association. Since her heroines are the primary vehicles through which her lyrical point of view is conveyed, they subsequently become literary screens behind which the poet as concealed narrator creates and depicts her fictional microcosm. As experiencing protagonists they also expand the poetic dimension of Bombal's prose through the depersonalized and aesthetic images that they continuously generate.

By activating the imaginations of her alienated heroines, the artistic sensibility of our poet-novelist creates an expanding tapestry of vivid symbolic images that often represent idealized perceptions of their individual dramas. Through an aesthetic objectification of their inner selves, these women not only elude the anguish that haunts them in struggling for self-realization but they simultaneously endeavor to redefine and assert their own identities. Paradoxically, however, their creative attempts toward redefinition are entirely futile when viewed from a feminist perspective, for by frequently identifying themselves with essentially patriarchal images, Bombal's heroines cannot possibly achieve the full autonomy that they desire. As Gilbert and Gubar observe,

> Before the woman writer can journey through the looking glass toward literary autonomy . . . she must come to terms with images on the surface of the glass, with, that is, those mythic masks male artists have fastened over her human face both to lessen their dread of her "inconstancy" and—by identifying her with the "eternal types" they have themselves invented—to possess her more thoroughly. Specifically, . . . a woman writer must examine, assimilate, and transcend the extreme images of "angel" and "monster" which male authors have generated for her. Before we women can write, declared Virginia Woolf, we must "kill" the "angel in the house". In other words, women must kill the aesthetic ideal through which they themselves have been "killed" into art. And similarly, all women writers must kill the angel's necessary opposite and double, the "monster" in the house, whose Medusa face also kills female creativity.[4]

Ubiquitous images in the lyrical narrative of María Luisa Bombal, the angel and the monster emerge as antagonistic emblems of a divided self as it struggles to reconcile its own anxieties and impulses with the hostile and repressive social order in which it exists.[5] According to Ellen Moers " . . . nothing separates female experience from male experience more sharply, and more early in life, than the compulsion to visualize the self".[6] This can truly be said of all Bombalian heroines. In *La última niebla* Daniel's wife spends several hours immersed in a pond, gazing at her reflection and imaginatively recreating a timeless and aesthetic image of herself. Ana María likewise gazes at her image in the water. Yolanda is discerned, absorbed in the contemplation of her body. Brígida is often surrounded by by the mirrors which line her dressing-room walls, and María Griselda frequently bathes in the waters of the río Malleco.[7] Curiously, the perceptions that these women have of themselves, differ greatly from others' perceptions of them. In the particular cases of María Griselda and of the anonymous protagonist in Bombal's first novel, each is also haunted by an antithetical double who, like the Queen in the Grimm tale of *Little Snow White,* threatens to usurp and destroy her idealized form of existence.[8]

The docility and alienation of Bombal's angelic heroines are continuously juxtaposed against portraits of monstrous figures who are nothing more than antithetical mirror images of their own submission and despair. Significantly, however, the Medusas, Sirens and Amazons that populate María Luisa's mythical narrative originate in the imaginations of male characters who are both perplexed and disconcerted by their vain attempts to penetrate and to possess the illusive and enigmatic qualities of their female counterparts. According to Gilbert and Gubar:

. . . the female monster is a striking illustration of Simone de Beauvoir's thesis that woman has been made to represent all of man's ambivalent feelings about his own inability to control his own physical existence, his own birth and death. As the Other, woman comes to represent the contingency of life, life that is made to be destroyed. "It is the horror of his own carnal contingence", de Beauvoir notes, "which [man] projects upon [woman]". In addition, as Karen Horney and Dorothy Dinnerstein have shown, male dread of women, and specifically the infantile dread of maternal autonomy, has historically objectified itself in vilification of women, while male ambivalence about female "charms" underlies the traditional images of such terrible sorceress goddesses as the Sphinx, Medusa, Circe, Kali, Delilah, and Salome, all of whom possess duplicitous arts that allow them both to seduce and to steal male generative energy.[9]

Whether or not the appearance of these female monsters in Bombal's narrative represents a basic male dread of feminine creativity, mystery, and power is open to speculation. It is nevertheless interesting to examine how the lyrical point of view associates her heroines with the monster's angelic opposite, an identification that clearly accentuates the debilitating passivity that prevents these women from actively asserting their own needs.

The bird imagery that pervades her prose becomes the central vehicle through which María Luisa creates this antithetical figure.[10] It is also though these winged creatures of the air that our poet-novelist reveals the discordant and equivocal relationships that exist between her heroines and their male companions. Significantly, Regina's lover tosses a dead and still bleeding ring-dove into the lap of Daniel's terrified and speechless wife; Fernando kills a barn owl for Anita, Ana María's daughter; Juan Manuel and his comrades consume most of their days hunting and killing wild waterfowl, and Alberto madly pursues and kills his wife's frightened and defenseless doves. The antagonism implicit in these examples reflects a fundamental hostility between hunter and prey which pervades María Luisa's narrative from beginning to end.

> Simone de Beauvoir has commented that the human male's "transcendence" of nature is symbolized by his ability to hunt and kill, just as the human female's identification with nature, her role as a symbol of immanence, is expressed by her central involvement in that life-giving but involuntary birth process which perpetuates the species. Thus, superiority—or authority— "has been accorded in humanity not to the sex that brings forth but to that which kills".[11]

Paradoxical signs, birds are also metaphors for artistic inspiration. María Luisa, herself, once said, "Escribir es un aliento de la tierra, un aliento de Dios. Llega a uno como el viento, como un viento de Dios, que pasa . . . Escribir es *un ángel* que pasa"[12] [The emphasis is mine]. Like their angelic sisters birds have often been depicted as symbols of thought and of the imagination. For Bombal's heroines, however, their problematic association to the creative process is accentuated by their own distortion and confinement. As Ellen Moers observes in her analysis of the bird metaphor and its female association in literature by women, "Of all creatures, birds alone can fly all the way to heaven—yet they are caged. Birds alone can sing more beautifully than human voices—yet they are unheeded, or

silenced".[13] By comparing her dreams to birds with broken wings the anonymous heroine of *La última niebla* underscores the anguish of the female artist who must suppress her innermost feelings and stoically accept the solitude of her dark and silent world. Yolanda, the bird woman in **"Las islas nuevas"**, is similarly condemned to wander in the subterranean depths of her inner fantasies; Ana María is imprisoned within the shroud of her prior existence, and María Griselda painfully acknowledges the loneliness and despair of her alienated condition. Although Brígida is the only Bombalian heroine to eventually sever the yoke that has been maintaining her in captivity, her flight and subsequent freedom at the end of **"El árbol"** are ominously threatened by the stark and powerful images of the caged canaries that she sees as she boldly affirms her most intimate desires.

Through their poetic imaginations, María Luisa's female protagonists create worlds that are far less hostile than their patriarchal counterparts. Therefore, juxtaposed against the images of enclosure which permeate her narrative are also metaphors of escape that reflect a distinctively feminine need to liberate the self from the intolerable circumstances that have generated its despair. If we accept the premise that " . . . imagery of enclosure reflects the woman writer's own discomfort, her sense of powerlessness, her fear that she inhabits alien and incomprehensible places. Indeed [that] it reflects her growing suspicion that what the nineteenth century called 'woman's place' is itself irrational and strange",[14] then the imaginative flights of our Bombalian heroines into timeless regions of free and open spaces, seem to respond to a particularly female attempt to assert and to redefine the self in a realm that is antithetical to the dark, cold and sometimes stifling interiors that it is compelled to inhabit. It is precisely for this reason that Ana María loathes the immense and empty home of her husband's family and subsequently yearns to return to the countryside with its continuous signs of eternally pulsating life.

> La nueva casa; aquella casa incómoda y suntuosa donde habían muerto los padres de Antonio y donde él mismo había nacido; su nueva casa, recuerda haberla odiado desde el instante en que franqueó la puerta de entrada . . . Recuerda que erraba de cuarto en cuarto buscando en vano un rincón a su gusto. Se perdía en los corredores . . . No lograba orientarse, no lograba adaptarse . . . Y ella, acostumbrada al eterno susurrar de los trigos, de los bosques, al chasquido del río golpeando las piedras erguidas contra la corriente, había empezado a sentir miedo de ese silencio absoluto y total que solía despertarla durante las noches.[15]

All Bombalian heroines possess a poet's affinity to nature. The natural world is the aesthetic space within which they design and embrace new realities that reflect their uniquely feminine experience and vision. Significantly, it is also the central medium through which they attempt to mitigate the anxieties that emerge from their own seclusion and desolation. As the primary vehicle through which the poetic imagination experiences a series of symbolic encounters, the natural world becomes a type of magical looking glass through which these female protagonists perceive and depict their inner dramas.

María Luisa's narrative consists of a highly interiorized vision which originates within the subconscious realm of female experience. Although her heroines define and assert themselves through their relationships with their surrounding natural world, they are silent weavers of their own fate. Their language is a language of dreams and of fantasies, of ethereal journeys into symbolic territories in which self and world are combined through a lyrical and suggestive network of subjective associations. By retreating into the chimerical regions of their imaginations, these women not only create experiences that are continuously filtered by their point of view, but also rekindle their own faltering memories. "Her trip into the cavern of her own mind, despite (or perhaps because of) its falls in darkness, its stumblings, its anxious wanderings, begins the process of remembering . . . the female artist makes her journey into what Adrienne Rich has called 'the cratered night of female memory' to revitalize the darkness, to retrieve what has been lost, to generate, reconceive, and give birth."[16]

Concealed within the multiple layers of her heroines' consciousness, is the story of their own quest for self-realization, a story which essentially reflects their struggle " . . . to live their lives on their own terms, if only in the privacy of their own thoughts".[17] The silence within which they sustain their inner dramas not only reinforces the solitude of their alienated conditions, but also disguises rebellious impulses which they, alone, cannot bring to fruition. In the case of Brígida, it also paradoxically becomes a weapon through which Bombalian woman is able to assert tenaciously her autonomy from others.

> —?Qué te pasa? ?En qué piensas, Brígida? Por primera vez Luis había vuelto sobre sus pasos y se inclinaba sobre ella, inquieto, dejando pasar la hora de llegada a su despacho.
>
> —Tengo sueño . . . —había replicado Brígida puerilmente, mientras escondía la cara en las almohadas.
>
> Por primera vez él la había llamado desde el club a la hora del almuerzo. Pero ella había rehusado salir al teléfono, esgrimiendo rabiosamente el arma aquella que había encontrado sin pensarlo: el silencio.[18]

Duplicitous figures, María Luisa Bombal's heroines are continuously at odds with the surface realities that exist beyond their internal sphere of existence. The anguish that results from the irreconcilable conflict between their inner and outer worlds is either hidden behind a mask of feigned serenity and submission or displaced onto monstrous doubles that are nothing more than avatars of the heroine's own anger and despair.[19] Paradoxical beings, their individual dramas are interpreted by a poetic imagination which highlights the oppositional and antagonistic nature of their problematic conditions.

By portraying the plight of her heroines within a narrative framework of contrasting musical and pictorial motifs, María Luisa not only cultivated her dual vision as a poet and as a story-teller but also experimented with the artistic effects that could be created through the integration of lyrical elements into a primarily conventional narratorial genre. Like many other outstanding examples of lyrical fiction that were written in the early twentieth century, Bombal's creations are best characterized by their intensely inward projection of experience. According to Ralph Freedman,

> Few other forms allow the author or his 'persona' to penetrate so directly into the very act of knowledge

and to represent it in immediately accessible portraiture. The limitations of this approach are obvious enough: an underemphasis on character and an overemphasis on image, dream-like encounter, or allegory. The excitement instilled by the expectations of the lyrical process does not usually make up for it.[20]

Through her lyrical rendition of the inner lives of her protagonists, Bombal designs intimate and contemplative portraits of the despair, alienation, and solitude of the female artist as she struggles to articulate her own needs and aspirations. Since the movement of her narrative is interior in nature, most references to the outer world merely function as mirror images of the inner consciousness striving for personal autonomy. Experience is, therefore, fundamentally perceived as a mental quality, and the imagination becomes a medium that not only reflects but also creates realities that are often eclipsed by the visible world.[21]

As marginal figures, María Luisa's heroines are depicted in debilitating roles which conceal the creative and rebellious impulses that are often hidden within their individual psyches. Fragmented beings, they are denied the means that would physically release them from their traditional and submissive postures, and withdraw instead into an illusory world of dreams, fantasies and idealized realities.

Only through her imaginative and lyrical flights into these subconscious and interior realms is Bombalian woman able to transcend the anxieties that threaten to undermine her otherwise colorless existence. These angelic retreats into silence, however, are potentially more destructive than the despair that initially engendered them, for by outwardly perpetuating meek and powerless images of the self, they continue to reinforce a view of their sex that has historically denied women the authority to articulate their own stories. Although we as readers can penetrate their silent worlds, their voices are destined to drown in the metaphysical vacuum of their own mute and insular monologues.

Since María Griselda is an archetypal manifestation of the feminine ideal of acquiescent purity that has so frequently populated the pages of primarily male-authored texts, it is significant that María Luisa Bombal concludes her lyrical narrative with a portrait of this docile and selfless heroine. *The Story of María Griselda* that is narrated should more appropriately be identified as an anti-story, however, because it dramatizes the dire consequences that can befall a woman who becomes an aesthetic "object d'art", an object that can only inspire creativity but not engender it.

> Whether she becomes an *objet d'art* or a saint, however, it is the surrender of her self—of her personal comfort, her personal desires, or both—that is the beautiful angel-woman's key act. While it is precisely this sacrifice which dooms her both to death and to heaven. For to be selfless is not only to be noble, it is to be dead. A life that has no story . . . is really a life of death, a death-in-life. The ideal of "contemplative purity" evokes, finally, both heaven and the grave.[22]

María Griselda is like a cipher completely bereft of all generative power. "¡Un hijo! ¡Si pudiera tener un hijo! . . . Pero, ¡no parecía ya como que estuviese elegida y predestinada a una solitaria belleza que la naturaleza— quién sabe por qué—la vedaba hasta de prolongar!"[23] Her primordial connections associate her with life-giving forces, but she is denied the ability to experience them. As Bombal's paradigm of the female artist, Griselda is a victim of her own anatomy and gender. Trapped and frozen within the prison of her looking-glass self, she warily eludes the mirror madness that ultimately destroys Sylvia, and painfully endures her life with the resignation of an individual who is powerless to alter a destiny that has mercilessly been bestowed on her. Hidden behind the harmonious mask of infinite beauty that she projects is not only a woman who bemoans the alienation and solitude of her miserable existence, "¡Ah, la soledad, todas las soledades!",[24] but also an individual who fails to reconcile the contradictions that exist between who she really is and how others perceive her to be. A paradoxical figure, she cannot identify with the angelic image that she sees in the mirror, but is denied the opportunity to define herself in any other terms.

Although her heroines are deprived of the authority to change their life circumstances, it is through their rich and creative poetic imaginations that their point of view is articulated and revealed. It is also through María Luisa Bombal's sensitive and lyrical portraits of their problematic conditions that the depth and intensity of their inner dramas is ultimately apprehended and felt.

Notes

1. This quotation from Charlotte Brontë's personal correspondence, appears in Ellen Moers, *Literary Women—The Great Writers* (1963; rpt. New York: Oxford University Press, 1985), pp. 170-71.

2. I am here referring to the renewed interest in women's literature that arose from the women's movement of the sixties.

3. Amado Alonso, "Aparición de una novelista", prólogo de la segunda edición de *La última niebla* (1941; rpt. Buenos Aires: Editorial Andina, 1973), pp. 7; 34.

4. Sandra M. Gilbert and Susan Gubar, *The Madwoman in the Attic—The Woman Writer and the Nineteenth Century Literary Imagination* (New Haven: Yale University Press, 1979), p. 17.

5. See R. D. Laing, *The Divided Self—An Existential Study in Sanity and Madness* (1959; rpt. Harmondsworth: Penguin Books, 1965).

6. Moers, p. 107.

7. In several of these examples water metaphorically functions as a looking glass through which María Luisa's female protagonists examine and delineate images of themselves.

8. In *La última niebla,* Regina's presence continuously arouses the envy and the hatred of María Luisa's heroine. Her love affair and subsequent suicide attempt contrast painfully against the protagonist's turbulent and unfulfilled desires.

   Y siento, de pronto, que odio a Regina, que envidio su dolor, su trágica aventura y hasta su posible muerte. Me acometen furiosos deseos de acercarme y sacudirla duramente, preguntándole de qué se queja, ¡ella, que lo ha tenido todo! Amor, vértigo y

abandono. (1941; rpt. Buenos Aires: Editorial Andina, 1973), p. 101.

   Sylvia, on the other hand, obsessively contemplates her image in the mirror, struggling to find the key to her sister-in-law's extraordinary beauty and hoping, therefore, to possess and to control the source of Griselda's magical effects on others. "Por qué esa sensación de inferioridad en que la sumía siempre la presencia de María Griselda . . . ¿Por qué la intimidaba?" (*La historia de María Griselda* (1946; rpt. Valparaíso, Chile: Ediciones Universitarias de Valparaíso, 1977), pp. 53-54).

9. Gilbert and Gubar, p. 34. Dorothy Dinnerstein interprets male attitudes of dread toward women in the following manner,

   . . . man has magic feelings of awe and fear, sometimes disgust . . . toward all things that are mysterious, powerful, and not himself, and . . . women's fertile body is the quintessential incarnation of this realm of things. Alien, dangerous nature, conveniently concentrated near at hand in women's flesh, can be controlled through ritual segregation, confinement and avoidance; it can be subdued through conventionalized humiliation and punishment; it can be honored and placated through ceremonial gifts and adornments, through formalized gestures of respect and protectiveness. History and ethnography abundantly illustrate human use of this opportunity. (*The Mermaid and the Minotaur—Sexual Arrangements and Human Malaise* (New York: Harper Colophon Books, 1977), p. 125.)

10. As J. E. Cirlot observes, "Every winged being is symbolic of spiritualization. The bird, according to Jung, is a beneficent animal representing spirits or angels, supernatural aid, thoughts and flights of fancy". See his *A Dictionary of Symbols* translated from the Spanish by Jack Sage, (1962; rpt. New York: Philosophical Library, 1974), p. 26.

11. Gilbert and Gubar, p. 14. Also see Simone de Beauvoir, *The Second Sex* (New York: Knopf, 1953).

12. Agata Gligo, *María Luisa* (Santiago: Andrés Bello, 1984), p. 78. This quote originally appeared in María Luisa Bombal's "En Nueva York con Sherwood Anderson", *El Mercurio,* 5 de noviembre de 1939, Santiago.

13. Moers, p. 250.

14. Gilbert and Gubar, p. 84.

15. María Luisa Bombal, *La amortajada* (1938; rpt. Buenos Aires: Editorial Andina, 1978), pp. 89; 91.

16. Gilbert and Gubar, pp. 98-99.

17. Gilbert and Gubar, p. 74.

18. María Luisa Bombal, "El árbol", in *La última niebla* (Buenos Aires: Editorial Andina, 1973), pp. 117-18.

19. According to Gilbert and Gubar

   . . . By projecting their rebellious impulses not into their heroines but into mad or monstrous women (who are suitably punished in the course of the novel or the poem), female authors dramatize their own self-division, their desire both to accept the strictures of patriarchal society and to reject them. What this means, however, is that the madwoman in literature by women is not merely, as she might be in male literature, an antagonist or foil to the heroine. Rather, she is usually in some sense the *author's* double, an image of her own anxiety and rage. (p. 78)

It is interesting to observe that both Regina and Sylvia, antithetical reflections of their submissive counterparts, are suicidal victims of their own transgressive behavior.

20. Ralph Freedman, *The Lyrical Novel—Studies in Hermann Hesse, André Gide, and Virginia Woolf* (Princeton: Princeton University Press, 1963), p. 283.

21. See C. M. Bowra, *The Romantic Imagination* (Cambridge: Harvard University Press, 1949).

22. Gilbert and Gubar, p. 25.

23. María Luisa Bombal, *La historia de María Griselda,* pp. 67-68.

24. *La historia de María Griselda,* p. 68.

Catherine Boyle (essay date 1993)

SOURCE: "The Fragile Perfection of the Shrouded Rebellion (Re-reading Passivity in María Luisa Bombal)," in *Women Writers in Twentieth-Century Spain and Spanish America,* The Edwin Mellen Press, 1993, pp. 27-42.

[*In the following essay, Boyle discusses the significance of passivity in Bombal's women protagonists, especially in the novella* La amortajada.]

> Ella se había sentado en la cama, dispuesta a insultar. Pero en vano buscó las palabras hirientes que gritarle. No Sabía nada, nada. Ni siquiera insultar.
>
> —¿Qué te pasa? ¿En qué piensas, Brígida?
>
> Por primera vez Luis había vuelto sobre sus pasos y se inclinaba sobre ella, inquieto, dejando pasar la hora de llegada a su despacho.
>
> —Tengo sueño . . . —; había replicado Brígida puerilmente, mientras escondía la cara en las almohadas.
>
> Por primera vez él la había llamado desde el club a la hora del almuerzo. Pero ella había rehusado salir al teléfono, esgrimiendo rabiosamente el arma aquella que había encontrado sin pensarlo: el silencio.[1]
>
> ¡Mentira! Eran mentiras su resignación y su serenidad; quería amor, sí, amor, y viajes y locuras, y amor, amor . . .
>
> Pero, Brígida, ¿por qué te vas? ¿por qué te quedabas? había preguntado Luis.
>
> Ahora sabría contestarle:
>
> —¡"El árbol, Luis, el árbol! Han derribado el gomero."

A huff. It would seem that the protagonist of María Luisa Bombal's short story, **"El árbol"** (1939), spends its dura-

tion in a huff. Brígida is a young woman characterised by her languor, her silliness (only matched by her beauty) and her passivity, until she finally discovers the words that will explain her seemingly sudden abandonment of her husband, words that are meaningless to all but her. The rubber tree was her protection against the revelation of the truth of her marriage, without it she is forced to acknowledge that her marriage is worthless, she is forced to recognise the powerless place she occupies in her household, her world. The rubber tree gives her the means by which she is able to voice obtusely what she could not before. Because she did not choose her silence, it was imposed on her as a weapon, "without thinking", it was part of her total inability to articulate what she felt: she could not even find the words to insult. Her silence was pathetic, until words, coherent only in and from her experience, were forced out of her.

María Luisa Bombal's characters are outwardly silent creatures. It would be all too easy to say that their silence is a weapon, but it is not. It just is. It may become a weapon by default, it may be conceived of from outside as a weapon, a peculiarly easy, energy saving, infuriating, and manipulative weapon, but it is not. Silence is an imposition that they assume, and within which they nurture a multitude of lives, as in *La amortajada:*

> Te equivocas. Era engañosa mi indolencia. Si solamente hubieras tirado del hilo de mi lana, si hubieras, malla por malla, deshecho mi tejido . . . a cada una se enredaba un borrascoso pensamiento y un nombre que no olvidaré.[2]

La amortajada, the shrouded woman, was first published in 1938 in the famous journal *Sur* (Buenos Aires), whose editor was Victoria Ocampo. It was María Luisa Bombal's second novel, the first being *La última niebla* (Buenos Aires, 1935). In *La amortajada* a woman lies dead, first on her death bed and then in her coffin as she is taken to her grave, as relatives and friends come to pay their last respects. Through her half-shut eyes she can see the procession of people, watch them without their knowing:

> A la llama de los cirios, cuantos la velaban se inclinaron entonces, para observar la limpieza y la transparencia de aquella fanja de pupila que la muerte no había logrado empañar. Respetuosamente maravillados se inclinaban, sin saber que Ella los veía.
>
> Porque Ella veía, sentía. (9)

La amortajada is Ana María, wife of Antonio, mother of Anita, Fred and Alberto, ex-lover in her adolescence of her cousin, Ricardo, teaser of Fernando, her confidant, sister of Alicia. As these people come to mourn over her death bed, she watches them with an exhilarating freedom; their presence frees her memories, and through them she recalls the details of her life. As she observes them, she is sinking into the oblivion of death, but, every so often, someone, something, takes her, guides her again to a dubious surface of the living, tempting her with visions of life. In this process, she becomes another being, objectively observing her own wasting away, distantly aware of being laid out in all the paraphernalia of death, whose imagery, made most explicit in the candles that surround her, creeps into the reality of the day: "El día quema horas, minutos, segundos" (35). In the structure of the novel, Bombal uses different narrators. One is Ana María herself, in first person. The second is a third person narrator, a woman of whom María Luisa Bombal said:

> Es una mujer que contempla a otra mujer y siente compasión por lo que le ocurrió en la vida y sólo comprende en la muerte.[3]

Towards the end, in a section added much later on, yet another narrator appears, the dead woman's confessor. In 1968, at the age of 58 and after not having published anything in Spanish for over twenty years, María Luisa Bombal returned to her most famous novel one last time. In this new section she sought to resolve the religious tension in the novel, and add a passage in which the protagonist's confessor remembers her deeply personal relationship with established religion, guided primarily through her sensual reaction to the recounting of the lives of the saints and Biblical stories. By returning to *La amortajada* and adding this final section, María Luisa Bombal intensifies the peace of the end of the novel; without it Ana María is lowered in body but not in soul into the earth. María Luisa Bombal returned to this last part as a response to her own need to reconcile religion, living and death:

> Lo juro. No tentó a la amortajada el menor deseo de incorporarse. Sola, podría, al fin, descansar, morir.
>
> Había sufrido la muerte de los vivos. Ahora anhelaba la inmersión total, la segunda muerte: la muerte de los muertos. (107)

In interview the author talked of her feelings about death:

> No creo que existe. Soy religiosa. Creo en una vida en el más allá donde los seres que se han ido tienen influencia sobre los que permanecen en la tierra. . . . La muerte me aterra, me da una curiosidad inmensa. Creo que lo peor sería descubrir que detrás de la muerte no hay nada. Sería tan terrible como creer que todo termina con la muerte.[4]

The novel stayed with Bombal all her life, she helped with the translations into English and French, she was involved in the re-editions of the book, and in a project for a film script. She was constantly criticised for and questioned about her small literary output—her last published story was **"La historia de María Griselda"** (1946)—and about her decision to live outside Chile. Here, I want to tackle a question that, in the light of the novelist's own experience of life, the novel begs. How much of María Luisa Bombal is projected into the novel?

María Luisa Bombal was an extraordinary woman. Born and brought up in the Chilean resort of Viña del Mar, she had a privileged background, an education second to none, studying in Chile and in France, fluent in French and English, writing in both languages, with a real knowledge of Latin. She was attractive, romantic, lively, and given to exalted passions. This was painfully demonstrated in the case of her ill-fated love for Eulogio Sánchez, whom she finally attempted to murder, by shooting at point blank range from a doorway in Santiago. (She was let off when he did not press charges. She then went to New York, in 1941). She lived as a young woman in Buenos Aires, where she joined the vibrant artistic circles of the thirties—Jorge Luis Borges, Victoria Ocampo, Alfonsina Storni, Federico García Lorca, Pablo Neruda, with whom she fought over the kitchen table to write in the house where they both lodged. Pablo Neruda achieved fame, respect, literary prizes in his own country as well as abroad. Like Gabriela Mistral, Bombal's work sat on the edge of oblivion in Chile. But that is another issue. She married the Argentine artist Jorge Larco, but it was a short lived and problematic union; and she published in *Sur*. Everything after moving to New York was silence and dismay. In Chile her writing was new in conception, structure, theme, and in the sex of its author:

> No se ha escrito en Chile prosa semejante y, después de los poetas máximos, sólo buscando mucho en letras universales podría encontrársele paralelo.
>
> Mezcla singular, fenómeno digno de análisis el don gratuito, la poesía innata, la claridad, el orden y la lógica, unidos a no se sabe qué desdén que la fantasía visionaria siente por los datos concretos, aunque se afirme en ellos paso a paso.
>
> He aquí a la que inauguró con más derechos que nadie la nueva etapa de nuestra literatura posterior al criollismo, dejándola en pleno dominio estético, hallado y señoreado soberanamente, sin esfuerzo, sin propósito, porque sí.[5]

Yet, built into these declarations of praise are the seeds of her relegation to obscurity—that her writing was somehow intuitive, innate, that she broke literary traditions "porque sí". Not because she was setting out a new writing, or that she thought about the craft of writing. It was the terrain of others to defy consciously the *criollismo* of the previous generations. María Luisa did it because she felt like it, by intuition and osmosis—by dint of being a woman, and not being represented in these traditions in the first place? This attitude plagued her. It put the author into the limbo of the writer who is an attractive, intelligent, lively woman: an anomaly in the Santiago of the thirties. There is a famous quote, in which a writer said, "María Luisa tiene demasiada personalidad para ser mujer".[6] This was not a light observation, but a damning reproach, for it implied a lack of femininity, and succinctly sums up the dilemma that María Luisa Bombal suffered: how to reconcile her reality with her deep, deep desire for conformity to a social role she accepted, romanticised and longed to be able to perform adequately: that of lover, wife and mother. (She finally did marry a French count, Fal de St Phalle, in 1944, and lived in the United States until his death in 1973, after which she returned to Chile, where she died in 1980.)

How relevant is this? It is relevant in that María Luisa Bombal wrote a woman's experience, wrote, for the first time in Chile, works that grew from an experience "peculiar to the female",[7] and in that the knowledge, words and expression grew largely from her own experience, rooted in the unbearably ill defined place she occupied in her society, which she was not able through identification with other women or similar experiences, to define. It is this that she writes into her characters: the fact of being lost in this space. She does not write the attempt to move out of it, nor strategies for defiance, merely the being.

The writing of María Luisa Bombal is coherent in its use of a particular language, a particular syntax. She employs a rather restricted, but tightly connected network of images, made explicit, in the first instance, in the titles of her short stories and novels: *La última niebla*, **"El árbol"**,

"Trenzas", "Las islas negras". They are the physical expression of the inner worlds of the protagonists, worlds that find articulation only in this interior identification with natural elements, and seldom through verbal articulation, or action. It is a writing that, accepting notions of the mystery of womanhood, makes this the source of the work of the imagination, in finding the means to express the secrets of this mystery, known only to woman herself. Throughout all her work the same images and themes occur, occupying similar narrative functions: the narrators are led, passively, to places beyond their bounds, yet at the murky edges of their sensual imaginations; boring marriages trap innocent victims; silence becomes a refuge, but terrifying in its immensity, power and autonomous dynamics; time and its passage are threatening, and worlds are in an unstoppable process of decay, a decay finally made most explicit, and resolved in *La amortajada,* where decay becomes decomposition, and finally a union with the complexities of time. And almost every story has a shooting incident: attempted suicides, real suicides, the vengeful murder of a beautiful wife's doves in **"La historia de María Griselda".** Death as the final and only real solution is never far from this work—shooting is her favourite means. (Before her assault on her lover, María Luisa Bombal had actually shot herself, in the shoulder, in his presence).

On one level *La amortajada* describes a descent into the earth that will harbour the decomposing body, as little by little the protagonist sinks into a consciousness that is not that of the living, but that of the dead. The narrative structure provides the richness of image and experience that characterise the novel. Each narrative level opens a window into another world, onto another personal experience of the world that was Ana María's while alive, and that will leave its traces now that she is dead. Bombal assumes the role of the omniscient narrator, yet without imposing a firm vision of reality, as she once stated:

> el sentimiento de las realidades esenciales, encarnadas en símbolos y descifradas a través del arte son tanto o más verdaderas que las realidades cotidianas.[8]

She achieves control without control by evoking only blurred sketches of both the protagonist and of those who enter into silent dialogues with her:

> Reconsidera y nota que de su vida entera quédanle sólo en el recuerdo, como signos de identificación, la inflexión de una voz o el gesto de una mano que hila en el espacio la oscura voluntad del destino. (*La amortajada,* 74-75)

La amortajada becomes a vehicle for the narration, and for the thoughts, memories, sorrow and relief conveyed by each individual, each one sure that his or her words are protected and rendered silent by the unconsciousness of death. It is this narrative technique that imbues passivity with energy.

La amortajada is the writing of a moment: it is the writing of the dramatically charged moment before total loss of a wordly consciousness, when the world, in all its attractiveness, joy, ugliness, pain and smallness, is still alluring. Ana María is on a journey, and each person that visits her drags her back to a sensibility of a world that, in horrible irony, she is only now beginning to see clearly. If the

people that had populated her world bring her back to a former reality, then her own unease with the condition of death does the same, but in a much more oneiric way. At intervals a hand is held out to her, a voice urges her to follow, and transports her to different expanses of this huge, timeless instant between life and death:

> —"Vamos, vamos".
>
> —"¿Adónde?
>
> Alguien, algo, la toma de la mano, la obliga a alzarse.
>
> Como si entrara, de golpe, en un nudo de vientos encontrados,
>
> danza en un punto fijo, ligera, igual a un copo de nieve.
>
> —"Vamos".
>
> —"¿Adónde?"
>
> —"Más allá". (34)

In journeys that echo the night flights of the protagonist of *La última niebla,* and the transporting qualities of the music in **"El árbol",** where the imagination of the characters is set free by forces to which they cannot or will not put a name, a force beyond her control guides La amortajada, free, to and fro between different levels of consciousness, and as the mourners pass through her room, this independent force guides her inexorably to the deepest sleep, to which she begins to feel closer and closer:

> Fatigada, anhela, sin embargo, desprenderse de aquella partícula de conciencia que la mantiene atada a la vida, y dejarse llevar hacia atrás, hasta el profundo y muelle abismo que siente allá abajo. (43)

What is it that creates this continuing attachment to life, when she desires sleep and rest after her exhausting illness? The answer is that she is basking in the luxury of that moment, in the glorious freedom of her physical demise, in the final self-indulgent exorcism of her memory, which becomes the final indulgence of her senses, formerly so neatly packed and tied by her adherence to the rules of her role. As she listens to the rain, she "exhausts" the emotion it causes, to the last drop. Yet, it is a cruel, fatal thought, a horrible waste, to live an emotion to the full only in death. It is the ruthless freedom of her remembering. In her memories she can see the way her life was shaped, and it is now she says: "¡Ah Dios mío, Dios mío! ¿Es preciso morir para saber?".

In the final paragraphs of the book Ana María emerges briefly to the surface of life, where she still has the illusion that she can move, open the coffin, return, cold and straight, to the door of her home. But she does not:

> Pero, nacidas de su cuerpo, sentía una infinidad de raíces hundirse y esparcirse en la tierra como una pujante telaraña por la que subía temblando, hasta ella, la constante palpitación del universo. (106)

With this realisation of the roots that are spreading from her, of the universe that is pulsating beneath her, La amortajada finally establishes a new relationship with her death: she associates it with her life. This is one of the great narrative successes of the novel, linking life and death through threads of central vital images, her hair, the roots of the trees in the earth where she will be buried. Linking it also with her other writing:

> Porque la caballera de la mujer arranca desde lo más profundo y misterioso; desde allí donde nace y tiembla la primera burbuja; que es desde allí que se desenvuelve, lucha y crece entre muchas y enmarañadas fuerzas, hasta la superficie de lo vegetal, del aire y hasta las frentes privilegiadas que ella eligiera. ("Las trenzas", 73)

Through her confidant Fernando, who, by her death bed, enters into a silent and, at last, honest dialogue with the woman he had loved for so long and whose only response had been constant humiliation, the reader receives a different appreciation of Ana María's imaginative life, an expression of an experience of the world whose traces are seen to be implanted deep within:

> Te admiraba. Admiraba esa tranquila inteligencia tuya cuyas raíces
>
> estaban hundidas en lo oscuro de tu ser.
>
> —'¿Sabe lo que hace agradable e íntimo a este cuarto? El reflejo y
>
> la sombra del árbol arrimado a la ventana. Las casa no debieran ser
>
> nunca más altas que los árboles,' decías. (*La amortajada*, 50-51)

As in **"El árbol"**, the tree is sought out as a protector. Again, these images are at the heart of Bombal's writing; they are the physical elements that delimit the real experience of a world, extended into the expression of the imagination. Yet, recounted by Fernando, they have a grating edge of wonder that anything at all could be imagined inside a pretty little head. The reader becomes acquainted with layer upon layer of the protagonist's imagination, each layer, though hidden beneath the weight of subsequent years, reaping its own life. So, while the protagonists may be able, on one level, to mourn the losses in her life, in her death every memory, every experience has its own place, a place now awarded in a ruthless process of equalising. In this way, time loses any accepted meaning, it passes, it consumes life, but this does not mean that each moment past sinks inevitably into oblivion. No, life itself is a constant accumulation of time.

Time passes and mounts up hours, seconds, moments, yet somehow, María Luisa Bombal's characters are outside the experience of time. It is this that lends an exquisite tension to a novel whose identity must be essentially passive, and it is this that provides a central dilemma that may never be resolved.

Who is Ana María? She was a member of the land-owning Chilean elite, she was a woman whose childhood was spent in idyllic comfort, who fell in love with her cousin during her adolescence, who miscarried his child, and who harboured the remnants of this love whose end she never quite understood. She was the woman who married without love the man picked out for her, and she was the woman who never quite came to terms with the rules of the game according to which she was to live her life. In many ways, she was just another female product of her class. In life she had managed to exist behind a veil of conformity, outwardly accepting her role. She had passed on the values of her class; she had presumed dead, or as the perverted indulgence of suffering, all the passions and memories that are now, in her coffin, awakened. She is a woman who has to die to understand.

Can this construction of a stifling and typical female existence of a certain type be called a social statement? Is it a writing that suggests rebellion, that encourages and calls for rebellion, even a shrouded rebellion? Some critics have seen an implied revolt. And perhaps this is one of the dangers in an analysis of a novel like *La amortajada*: that we, now from the perspectives of the modern female, took for elements of rebellion against a role imposed, was that not what María. Luisa Bombal was suggesting when her protagonist can only find freedom of thought in death? At the roots of this problem is another unresolved tension, that of the identification of the author with her protagonist, into whom she wrote an imagination that sought its own escapes, its own expression, while the external self accepted the social codes into which she had been bred. At the time of writing these works, María Luisa Bombal longed to belong to that society, for it would be a society that would legitimise her existence, actually give her an existence as a person, as a wife, as a mother, and not as a child, an unthinking and irrelevant being, the state allotted to the unmarried woman, who has no social standing, no space where she can yield a certain power, no matter how small that may be. When *La amortajada* was written, women had not yet won the vote in Chile, that was not to happen until 1949. María Luisa Bombal explored the world of the woman complicit in her margination.

When she was in fact asked about the intentions of her work, if she had intended to denounce the role of women in society, she would reply:

> Yo tenía pasión por lo personal, lo interno, el corazón, el arte, la naturaleza. No, yo no perseguía nada . . .[9]

Yet, it is through this preoccupation with the internal and particular worlds of her protagonists that she finally poses questions that are central to a fundamental misunderstanding between the sexes.

All that the reader learns about Ana María's marriage is negative. It is an arranged marriage, through which she embarks on a route long mapped out for her and now personalised in her husband, Antonio, a good man that she has no legitimate reason, at first, not to love as a good husband. But she, through her marriage, enters a new world—they enter a possible new world. In their first months together Antonio shows her the pond made in the garden, a large, dark blue mirror in which she can comb her long hair, the essence of her vitality and sexuality. Yet all she can see is desolation, and when her husband, showing her how the images break and reform, throws a stone into the water, all she experiences is the violence of the gesture, the destruction of her image, the dis-arming of her self:

> Recuerda. Asiéndose de la balaustrada de hierro forjada, había cerrado los ojos, conmovida por un miedo pueril.—"El fin del mundo. Así ha de ser. Lo he visto". (67)

At this stage the language that is used speaks of the passivity of the woman, she allows her life to be lead by her husband, she sinks into a silence that awakes her at night. When her husband, looking to make his wife happy, asks her what she wants, her answer is desperate:

> Se había aferrado al brazo de su marido deseando hablar, explicar, y fue aquí donde su pánico, rebelde, saltó por sobre todo argumento:—"Quiero irme". (72)

Again there is no real articulation of the reasons for her unhappiness, there is no consideration of its roots or its solution. There is no consideration for another person, only the panicked whimper of an ego trapped, a whimper that could externally be interpreted as rebellion, but that is merely the only words she could find to seek a way out of a state of malaise. Once removed again from the novel, the reader can see another facet of this. It is a reaction against the role she is asked to play, and against the space she is asked to inhabit, and in which physically she cannot be at ease. Her "quiero irme" is her escape to the known and comfortable, a child's world she mistakenly thinks she can return to. Her unwitting rebellion maps out for her an endless married life of jealousy, love and sadness, and the loss of the sexual satisfaction that she had experienced with her husband, who has retreated into his own space, his own "selva negra". When she finally realises that she is no more than one of the passions in her husband's life, she begins to limit herself, she becomes smaller, meaner, she seeks protection in her own withering. It is here that María Luisa Bombal poses the dubious, but in the context relevant, question:

> Pasaron años. Años en que se retrajo y se fue volviendo día a día más limitada y mezquina. ¿Por qué, por qué la naturaleza de la mujer ha de ser tal que tenga que ser siempre un hombre el eje de su vida? Los hombres, ellos lograron poner su pasión en otras cosas. Pero el destino de las mujeres es remover una pena de amor en una casa ordenada, ante una tapicería inconclusa. (78)

Love becomes destructive in this circumstance, the lack of comprehension is almost total, and it is only now, in death, that she indulges in the luxury of attempting to understand how she controlled her love, how she learned the humiliation of giving too much love, learned to ration it, how, now, she understands that little by little she was complicit in the strangling of the most vital part of herself. And how she enjoyed her suffering for love because that was the passion through which she fed the strength to remain where she was.

María Luisa Bombal may not have written a novel that denounced woman's subordinate role in society, but from the depths of one woman's soul comes a chilling portrayal of a role defined by passivity, by an astounding lack of understanding, by the lack of another model of behaviour. It is only in death that Ana María begins to have some notion of the rules of the game by which her life had been governed. It is here that María Luisa Bombal excelled, for in the novel it is through the accumulation and manipulation of details that the identity of the protagonist and her surroundings are created. The most glorious example of this is when Antonio visits his dead wife and kneels by her bed. She finds him repugnant until:

> Repentinamente la hiere un detalle insólito. Muy pegada a la oreja advierte una arruga, una sola, muy fina,

tan fina como un hilo de telaraña, pero una arruga, una verdadera arruga, la primera. Dios mío, ¿aquello es posible? Antonio no es inviolable? (83)

It is glorious. She, who now feels herself new, young, beautiful and without wrinkles, is superior. Yet, in the way of María Luisa Bombal, this is not a consolation. The revelation of Antonio's vulnerability, of male weakness, of the human normality of the male, which she had not seen in life, does not come as a consolation. It comes as a surprise that he is not impervious to the passage of time, and she can no longer hate him the way she did, she can no longer feed her relationship on this hate. It is over, the life force between them is destroyed, and with it their present and their past. What would have happened in life if she had understood the weakness, the normality of her husband? How could she have sustained their relationship? Why does she have to discover the awful falsity of their marriage now, when all she wants is peace and reconciliation with the world she had formed around her, not this desire to live again through hate:

> No. No lo odia. Pero tampoco lo ama. Y he aquí que al dejar de amarlo y de odiarlo siente deshacerse el último nudo de su estructura vital. Nada le importa ya. Es como si no tuviera ya razón de ser ni ella ni su pasado. Un gran hastío la cerca, se siente tambalear hacia atrás. ¡Oh esta súbita rebeldía! Este deseo que la atormenta de incorporarse gimiendo: "¡Quiero vivir. Devuélvanme, devuélvanme mi odio!" (85)

All that is hers now is silence and the final descent. For, if she had known this before she could not have sustained the marriage, she hated any mirror of weakness. She despised Fernando for that reason, she denied his love because he wanted to unite their wounded souls, in a mutually manipulative relationship based on a perverse elongating of suffering.

In all of her works, María Luisa Bombal sets her protagonists against an unwelcome other. Most notably the protagonist of *La última niebla,* measured unfavourably against her husband's perfect first wife, enviously looks on as her sister-in-law indulges her sexual desires, which lead ultimately to an attempted suicide. But even that inspires on pity:

> Y siento, de pronto, que odio a Regina, que envidio su dolor, su trágica aventura y hasta su posible muerte. Me acometen furiosos deseos de acercarme y sacudirla duramente, preguntándole de qué se queja, ¡ella, que lo ha tenido todo! Amor, vértigo y abandono. (*La última niebla,* 53)

The protagonist's silence hides a most cruel projection of the ego. And it is in this way that Bombal most incisively subverts silence, for it is not merely a lyrical domain of trees, disappearing islands, misty towns. It is, much more than that, a place for an uninhibited assertion of the self, bound by no moral or social codes. In this place, the ego is an ego that can envy, hate, lust; in this place, the self—ignored as frivolous, childish and irrelevant in the social world the possessor inhabits—is reaffirmed. Sublimely. Immorally. The physical expressions that María Luisa Bombal creates are not those that relate to the external world, but that relate to this shameless, hidden self.

This self is shameless. From the literary world of geographic archeology that *criollismo* had become, emerged a writer who wrote exclusively and explicitly about female experience, in which female desire played an important role. Here was an author who described explicitly female orgasm, discovered, in the most female of ways, quite by accident: "¡El placer! ¡Con que era eso el placer! Ese estremecimiento, ese inmenso aletazo y ese recaer unidos en la misma vergüenza!" (66); an author who, in *La última niebla,* elaborated an intense sexual fantasy of ideal love, of all-consuming passionate love, narcissistic love, in which the protagonist's beauty is mirrored in the passion it inspires in her lover. Like the other protagonists, neither does this one clearly articulate the world into which she is drawn—for it is a forbidden world, a world that had not been acknowledged, that had not been given its words, its images, its expression. The Bombal protagonist is lead by the hand by someone, by a something that is, finally, sexual longing, that is the lust for the repetition of the once-experienced orgasm, that is the desire for freedom from a boring marriage, that is the search for another way of being beautiful beyond the male mind that tortures and manipulates beauty. In the protagonists these searches may be inarticulate, unknowing. But in the writing of Bombal, they are given exquisite expression. From the place of her abandonment in a literary world, María Luisa Bombal gave a voice to female desire and female loss. The ultimate expression of this is *La amortajada,* for it is a great artistic leap of the imagination, it is writing that seems to come from behind tightly closed eyes, a writer forcing her way into a deep inner space and squeezing out the means to express it. The fascination that death held for her was not only a fascination with its mystery, but with the mysteries of its literary expression; perhaps it is the fight against the dead woman in literature, woman as muse and inspiration, rather than as producer, creator. Total passivity, in this, the only stage of María Luisa Bombal's writing—for she wrote no more—becomes a goal, because it is the space for the release of the self. The dynamic of death is the dynamic of the space where an experience peculiar to the female meets the word.

Notes

1. See 'El árbol', in the collection of stories, *La última niebla. El árbol,* (Santiago: Editorial Andrés Bello, 1982) p.74. All further references will be to this edition.

2. See *La amortajada* (Santiago: Editorial Universitaria, 1981) p.65. All further references will be to this edition.

3. In Agata Gligo, *María Luisa (Sobre la vida de María Luisa Bombal)* (Santiago: Editorial Andrés Bello, 1985).

4. See Sara Vial, introduction to *La historia de María Griselda* (Santiago: Ediciones Universitarias de Valparaíso, 1977) pp.17-78.

5. See the introduction to *La amortajada* by the Chilean critic Alone in the edition quoted above.

6. See Agata Gligo, op. cit., p.56.

7. This is a reference to the poem by June Jordan, "A Case in Point".

8. See Agata Gligo, op. cit., pp. 20-21.

9. Ibid., p.77.

Gwendolyn Díaz (essay date 1994)

SOURCE: "Desire and Discourse in María Luisa Bombal's *New Islands,* " in *Hispanofila,* Vol. 112, No. 1, September, 1994, pp. 51-63.

[*In the following psychoanalytical study of Bombal's* New Islands and Other Stories, *Díaz addresses the theme of desire.*]

What does woman want? ask the psychoanalysts. Sigmund Freud posits what seems to be a logical answer as he develops his penis envy theory. Carl Jung's spiritual rapprochement to sexuality places woman's desire in the context of opposite and complementary male and female psychic tendencies or archetypes, as seen in the Yin and Yang of Taoist philosophy.[1] Jacques Lacan re-reads Freud in the light of Saussure and Derrida and offers alternative possibilities to the issue of woman's desire. For Lacan the penis becomes the phallus and the phallus in turn represents the signifier of desire, the power of authority and the structure of language.[2] The perspective of the writer offers new insight into this matter as seen in the narrative of María Luisa Bombal, who attempts to address this question from the stand point of a pre-Feminist Movement author who writes about woman's desire in a poetic, incisive and very serious way.

In *New Islands and Other Stories,* which appeared in 1982 and was published originally in Spanish in 1976 as *La última niebla,* Bombal's precision of expression, recurring imagery, structuring motifs and lyrical techniques create a fresh language and unique style of expression through which she explores the plight of women entrapped in traditionally confining situations. Although the book appears to be a collection of stories, it could also be considered an innovative novel with five chapters (stories) where the same female protagonist lives out a different yet similar life-plot. This elusive heroine is involved in a series of frustrating relationships with men in which desire for the other/Other (that which she does not know about) becomes more intense as the impossibility of reaching it becomes more evident.[3] As the locus of desire is in the female character, her desperate attempts to find satisfaction with male lovers appear to place Bombal's heroines as victims of a phallocentric Latin American ideology. However, these heroines seem to be searching for something beyond the male counterpart, their lack is not so much centered on the desire for the penis, nor for patriarchal power; it is a desire directed toward language itself, a new language to represent a female voice which is still silent, and perhaps ultimately, to create a discourse that reflects female experience.

Critics such as Lucía Guerra Cunningham have considered *The Final Mist,* the first novella in the collection, a puzzling love story of woman's lust and appetite for passion (48-9). However, if we read the text via Lacan's views on language and sexual identity the story offers a more significant message. It takes place in the consciousness of a nameless heroine, where we witness her recollection of her marriage to Daniel and the anguish she experiences in this unfulfilling relationship. She recounts his indifference towards her, his hostile attitude, and his condescending manner. Most humiliating of all is the fact he still yearns for his first wife, now dead, whom he considers the perfect woman. Why is his dead wife the perfect woman? Bombal subtly suggests the answer to this question; for Daniel, the perfect woman is the silent one. As the protagonist recalls viewing the coffin of the dead wife, she says: "She appears never to have been alive—her dead face bringing suddenly to mind the word *silence* [Bombal's emphasis]. Silence, a long silence invading the room, growing, filling my consciousness" (6). The mist, a recurrent motif, is also a symbol of silence and death which hangs over the landscape like an "immense veil" (7). The mist surrounds and encroaches; as fog it swallows and obliterates, threatening the protagonist's very being which she feels compelled to affirm: "I am alive, I exist!" (7) she cries out as the mist engulfs her figure. Also compared to a shroud, the mist is silence and death because it illustrates woman's lack of voice and language. Similarly, in Lacan's view, women's lack is related to the lack of a phallus, which represents the signifier or the word which organizes culture. He conceptualizes the phallus as the privileged signifier which structures society in its image. Consequently, the social structure is based on patriarchal values that derive from patriarchal discourse (*Ecrits* 284-87). Though at times the protagonist of **The Final Mist** may seem to affirm this idea of woman as lack, the character's silence represents a lack of appropriate discourse to describe her world view and it is seen critically as a reflection of a flawed social structure.

This position is reinforced in the episode in which the nameless protagonist observes the passionate interaction between Regina and her lover, whose gaze "follows her every step with desire" (Bombal 9). The protagonist envies all the passion and intensity of life that characterize Regina. Regina has a name; Regina plays the piano like "hundreds of notes spinning up and down like a flight of sparrows" (9), Regina has a lover whose gaze constitutes her as a significant subject, but mostly, Regina has a voice, the voice she creates by breaking the law of established order, by defying the social code and becoming an outcast, an adulteress. The episode between Regina and her lover awakens the heroine's hidden desire and at that moment she experiences her first fantasy or hallucination:

> I go into the garden, flee through the mist to a spot near the pond where a sunray pierces my path like a lance stuck in the earth, lending to the place the golden lightness of a grotto dank with the forest's deep aroma.
>
> A strange languishment overtakes me. I close my eyes, press myself against a tree. Oh, to throw my arms around a warm body and roll with it, bounding down an endless slope. In vain I shake my head to overcome this swoon-like lethargy.
>
> Then I remove my clothes, my undergarments, until my flesh glows with the same golden splendor afloat among the trees. And like this, naked and golden, I dive into the water . . . I sink to my ankles in thick velvety sand. Warm currents caress and penetrate me. Like silky arms, the aquatic plants embrace my body with their long tendrils. (9-10)

The sexual nature of these lines acquires significance in the light of Lacan's views on hallucination, which he believes not only makes present the objects of our need, but also sexualizes these objects (*The Four Fundamental* 155). In reading this passage, we must consider that desire is not merely desire for sexual rapport, but that it aims at a more profound want, it aims at knowledge of the other (that which we do not know). It attempts to find knowledge of who we are, of our unconscious being, in order to fill in the gap or the lack by which our conscious mind is characterized (Ragland-Sullivan, *Jacques Lacan* 292). Bombal's narrative allows this lack to surface in her use of certain key terms which become metaphors that are repeated throughout her works with multiple yet specific connotations. According to Lacanian theory, the metaphorical value of her terminology gives rise to a meaning which transcends the desire for sex and becomes desire for language. In this episode, the protagonist flees through the 'mist' which represents confusion, and arrives at a place near a 'pond' where a 'sunray' 'pierces' her path like a 'lance' stuck in the 'earth.' The 'pond,' the 'earth,' the 'forest' and the 'dank grotto' are images that Bombal uses to signify the female. The 'light' and the 'sun' are associated with the sexual virility of the male characters, as is the 'lance' which is 'stuck' in the earth. But light also represents knowledge and meaning as given by language, and the 'tree' against which she presses herself is not only the imaginary phallus, but also the Lacanian phallic signifier or *logos* (the word or speech which constitutes the controlling principle of culture). After removing undergarments, her flesh 'glows' with the 'same golden splendor' of the 'trees.' Her body acquires meaning as she is possessed; warm currents 'penetrate' her and aquatic plants embrace her with 'long tendrils,' leading us—for the moment—to conclude that here, man does indeed dominate the phallic signifier (i.e. language as a reflection of the patriarchal cultural order), and that she desires this man because she thinks he will bring to her the status and power possessed by him.

After we encounter her second hallucination, the heroine's desire for man as possessor of the signifier seems reinforced. The second hallucination takes place while she is lamenting the oppresive silence and sterile routine that have become her life and from which she wishes to escape. She escapes, indeed, into her fantasy where a sensuous young man guides her to a house ushering her into a room filled with brightness, while the fog and the darkness are without, waiting behind the window panes. His skin is "covered with fine chestnut hair to which the light clings, so that his body seems enveloped from head to toe in filaments of light" (Bombal 16). Once more, light becomes synonymous with meaning and voice. In the following sequence we find that her lover's body is described in terms of sound which she possesses as his body penetrates her:

> I *hear* the rise and fall of his *breathing,* the *pounding* of his heart—deep and powerful, *thudding* like a *gong, resounding* through his body as though each cell had somehow been transformed into a *sonorous echo.* Eager now, I tighten my embrace: wanting to enfold him, to feel the blood coursing in his veins. His strong muscles quiver under my fingers; *he sighs.* I hold in my arms a not a physical presence but another life—with all its fragility and mystery ebbing and flowing in my embrace. (17) (emphasis added)

As he possesses her she feels "faint with rapture, surprised to hear a sob rising from my throat, and for the first time I moan with pleasure . . . (18). Her 'sob' and her 'moan' come as a surprise because for the first time she realizes she too can possess a voice. It is not her lover that matters to her, she realizes, it is the fact that after 'knowing' him "the world seems now full of possibilities" (20). Here the text indicates that there is more to her desire than her lover's body.

Furthermore, during this same daydream the protagonist emphasizes the importance of her lover's gaze as a force that gives her power and significance:

> I burn with the need for him to see me naked, for my lovely body at last to receive the homage it deserves . . . Naked, I remain seated on the edge of the bed, he beside—having shifted forward to contemplate my body. Under his attentive gaze, I lean back, a gesture that fills me with infinite well-being. Locking my arms behind my head, I cross and uncross my legs, each gesture bringing me intense pleasure, as if at long last my arms, my neck, my legs had a reason to exist. (17)

In *The Four Fundamental Concepts of Psycho-Analysis,* Lacan argues that in dream the gaze shows us a closer picture of our being than we have when we are conscious. The gaze is characterized as well by a fading of the subject, a central lack or castration (74-77). In this daydream the woman portrays both her desire to be 'regarded' as a whole being (as opposed to a lacking one), and, also, her unconscious fear of physical and psychic fragmentation as exemplified by the reference to body parts. Here, she reconstructs her body through his gaze, where, her legs, arms and neck have a 'reason to exist.' If, as Lacan contends, the reality of a subject's desire is in hallucination and dream, the reality of this character's desire is to be constituted as, if not a whole being, a more complete one. She achieves this through the acquisition of an imaginary lover (as an agent of empowerment), who might regard her as a whole human being and not just a collection of body parts (155).

Woman's empowerment, however, is not wrought by coupling herself with a man who embodies power and authority. What is significant about Bombal's text is that she is presenting the possibility of a new language, molded and created by woman, a female based discourse that would reflect woman's "Weltanschauung." The task of creating a new language is one that happens at two levels: that of the protagonist and that of Bombal, the author. The heroine appears throughout the text as struggling to place her own perceptions into a world she does not understand. Her confusion is not due to ignorance, but to the fact that her view of the world does not coincide with the social reality she experiences. The confusion or the (mist)ifying aspect of the world she lives in is due to the clash between the phallocentric social structures she is subject to and her expectations of a reality quite different from the one that subjugates her like a suffocating fog. It is not the 'phallic' signifier that she desires, it is one that takes into account her world. In the following lines we see her efforts at constructing a new language:

> by walking I can *impress* a *rhythm* to my *dreams,* bring them into the open, make them describe a *perfect circle.* When I am *quiet* they plummet earthward in crazy spirals, like *birds with broken wings.* (Bombal 22) (emphasis added)

She wants to create a new 'rhythm,' a voice where her 'dreams' or unconscious come into her consciousness and describe a 'perfect circle' which would reflect a more complete view of a world now divided by sexual hierarchies. When she is 'quiet,' her dreams plummet like 'birds with broken wings'; that is, when she is silent or voiceless she is like a crippled animal. And where does she find inspiration for her creation? In the pond as womb where she sinks down:

> creating a gentle eddy on the surface while I glide ever lower in that mysterious world where time seems to stop, where light is solid as a phosphorescent substance, where my movements acquire a knowing and cat-like gracefulness as I carefully explore the dark windings in that cavern of silence. I find seashells, colorful crystals that, exposed to air, are transformed into nondescript black pebbles. I shift boulders from under which slippery creatures, roused from sleep, scuttle off into the gloom. (23)

As she explores the pond's 'cavern of silence' she finds hidden life forms, like hidden meanings, which populate a rich underworld that mirrors the life above. In so doing, she discovers the possibility of creating a voice for herself and a language that might express the hidden meaning of her world view. In this 'misterious world' she acquires 'knowing.' Within the womb-like cavern she finds life. However, this nameless heroine does not succeed in her quest. Her husband crushes her illusions of meaning when he shows her that her lover is merely a dream, her hallucinations were simply that. Interestingly, when he questions her about her supposed lover, he does not ask if he made love to her, he asks if he 'spoke' to her and requests that she describe his 'voice' (32). His concern is that she may have entered into dialogue, into the world of speech, since for him, the ideal woman is a dead or silent one. When the protagonist comes to the realization that her lover was merely a fantasy, she is "unable to distinguish anything through the fog" and she gives up her search. It is telling that upon coming to this realization she develops a physical symptom which attacks the site where voice is produced; she is stricken by an intense fever that "seized my throat like a burning claw" (43-44). Disillusioned by her aborted efforts she concludes that her destiny is to remain alone with a husband who does not love her, "Following him toward an infinity of insignificant tasks; toward a thousand trifling amusements; following him to live correctly—to cry from habit and smile out of duty; following him to die, one day, correctly" (47). To live 'correctly,' as the social constructs expect her to, is to be silent. As the novella ends, her fatal destiny becomes evident to her; she cries: "Around us the fog settles over everything like a shroud" (47).

The author's linguistic experimentation is clear throughout the collection. In *The Mist* she sets in motion a series of motifs that reappear in all the stories of the piece and function as structuring elements of each story, as well as of the book as a whole. This technique creates the effect of a novel, yet breaks with the traditional linear novel by placing a heroine whom we recognize as basically the same in similar though different positions with respect to men. In so doing she develops a new genre which borders somewhere between the story and the novel. Bombal also creates a new type of narrative structure through lyrical as well as musical techniques (metaphor, implied metaphor, simile, repetition, and other figures of speech, as well as rhythm and the precise use of the element of time in the composition of the piece).

In **"The Tree,"** her most frequently anthologized story, perhaps because it is somewhat less hermetic than the others, she focuses particularly on the motifs of music, the tree, the room/womb, light, darkness, the mirror and the mist. In this text the protagonist now has a name, Brigida. Though the narrative is framed within a concert hall where Brigida listens to the performance of three symphonies, the more significant space of the narrative is her consciousness. As the orchestra plays Mozart, Beethoven and Chopin, each composer's work triggers her memory of the past. Mozart reminds her of her childhood as the reader learns that her father had little time for her; he considered her pretty, but stupid and ignorant. She marries, Luis, much older than she, who calls her his little "necklace of sparrows" (Bombal 53) and compares her to a startled fawn. When she hears the Beethoven symphony, she recalls how her relationship with Luis deteriorates as he increasingly ignores her, leaving her abandoned at home. With Chopin's symphony, Brigida realizes that Luis never did love her. The tree, outside her dark boudoir where she often took refuge from her solitude, was cut down. Light entered her room and with it the realization that Luis, like her father, would never allow her to grow into a worthy individual.

In this story, Brigida tries to understand what it is about man's nature that makes him structure his life so differently from woman. She sees men as linear beings subject to habit, order and social custom: "Maybe life for men was based on a series of continuous customs. Rupturing this chain would probably produce disorder, chaos" (56-7). Within such a world, woman has value only in her relationship to her father or husband. She intuits this when she comments that Luis must have married her simply to "put the crowning touch on his old friendship with her father" (56). Luis sends her to her father's ranch for the summer to get her out of his way and she wants to insult him, yet she "could not find the hurting word. She knew nothing, nothing,—not even how to offend" (58).

Brigida takes refuge from this nullifying existence in her boudoir. It is warm, dark, fresh and gives her an overpowering sense of well-being. Outside this room's window is an immense rubber tree that shelters her from the outside world. This tree casts shadows that undulate on the walls of her room like cold moving water. Her mirrors refract its foilage creating the illusion of a green and infinite forest or of a world submerged in an aquarium (55-56). Here the room, as the pond in the previous story, is a symbol of woman's creative power. This dark, moist womb-like environment thrives with images of greenery and sea life and is a mirror-image of the real world in which the tree is no longer a protective element, but an obstacle. When the tree is cut down and her boudoir loses its cozy enchantment, her room is "invaded by a terrifying white light" (63). In this new light, she sees her existence for what it is, a loveless young woman enchained by an old, wrinked man incapable of love.

Once more we find the tree and light as symbols for the male. But here we see two readings of each symbol. In the real or outside world structured by phallic social interpretations of signifiers, the erect tree is viewed in its capacity to block light, it is an obstacle to knowledge in the guise a protection, as is the case in Luis' treatment of Brigida. Conversely, in her view the tree as she experiences it in her room/womb is an undulating shadow resembling moving water creating the illusion of an infinite forest. The rigid becomes undulating, the static becomes movement, the obstacle becomes an infinite possibility. Similarly, the light takes on dual values depending on whether it appears in her world or his. In her boudoir light is experienced as giving sumptuous color and movement, like the light of an aquarium which opens our eyes to the delicacies of a world submerged in water. On the outside, the light is a harsh, terrifying invader which entered the room as if it had ripped off the roof, entering crudely from every direction (55-56). Brigida's plight ends in a more positive manner than does that of the heroine of *The Final Mist* for she chooses to break away from the oppressive social structure that binds her. She leaves Luis to look for love, and in the context of Bombal's work, love represents woman's desire for self realization via a room/language of her own. Here, what woman wants is not just to be associated with or to employ the phallic signifier, she wants to create a new chain of signification. Bombal's stories attempt, in an incipient manner, to take on the task of creating a female centered discourse such as that envisioned by Julia Kristeva and Luce Irigaray. But while Kristeva seems to equate maternity to creativity privileging woman's reproductive function and Irigaray attempts to deconstruct phallocentrism and replace it with a discourse grounded in female sexuality, Bombal's work underscores the power play between the dominant discourse and the stifled one and emphasizes the difficulty of the struggle.[4]

Two short cryptic narratives link the first two stories with the final one. Though at first their inclusion may seem gratuitous, upon careful scrutiny we find that they are brief and clever fairy tales that encapsulate the modes of perception and expression that Bombal elucidates in her book. In **"Braids,"** which appears only in the English translation, she elaborates on the motif of woman's hair as a symbol of her power in her connection to the earth and reproduction. Two sisters of opposite nature live different life styles that end in the same tragedy. One renounces love, cuts her hair very short, dresses in a poncho and retires to the family's hacienda "determined to administer it with an iron hand" (71). She is nicknamed the Amazon for her strength and her apathy toward men. The other sister is beautiful and fragile and wears a single resplandescent red braid. "She would fall in love and love madly" when one day, after a ball, she falls faint on her carpet and the candelabra she was in the act of extinguishing catches fire. At this moment, many miles away, a fire begins to devastate the Amazon's forest. As the beautiful sister's body begins to lose life, her body takes on the semblance of death, expect for its red braid which still seems vivid and alive. Her hair finally dies as the forest is consumed. In the epilogue we are told that:

> the green clinging to plants that twine on the trees, the sweet algae clinging to the rocks, are but strands of hair: are the *word* [emphasis added], the coming and souring of nature . . . means of expression by which she gently instills her magic and wisdom into all living things. (74)

The narrator adds that the reason the women nowadays have lost their prophetic powers and no longer feel joy or possess magnetism is that they have reproduced their braids, that is, their feminine power to create the word.

The second tale, **"The Unknown,"** is the story of a pirate ship that sinks into the depths of the sea. The captain and his young mate encounter all sorts of bright sponges and shells and conches and sea life and creatures which belie an infinity of small and magic secrets. The sea and its creatures, just as the pond and the boudoir above, represent female knowledge and creativity as it springs from the unconscious. Beneath the sea: "A golden light radiates from gigantic sponges, yellow and resplendent as suns . . . and underneath certain deformed conch shells burrowed on the bottom there sits a little mermaid, weeping" (77). Under the sea (often a symbol of the unconscious) there is a different type of light and a message that is not readily understood. The conch shells, reminiscent of female biology, are occupied by a little mermaid who is weeping. The voice of the female, hidden in the depths of the unconscious, is a small, sad and stiffled voice. The pirates notice that the waves were whispering a message which they could not understand (78), and its their lack of understanding that leads them to their end for they do not realize that the moan beneath the sea was a "cry of affliction from someone desperate, burning with desire for something irrevocably lost" (82). Once more, Bombal's poetic view depicts the female as pregnant with meaning and message, but her messages are not understood by those who structure communication in a different way.

The final and most enigmatic tale is **"New Islands."** Appropriately the last story draws together many of the concerns expressed in the previous ones. The heroine is Yolanda, a strange elusive woman who walks like a bird and seems to come alive when she plays the scales on her piano. She lives in her country estate with her brother, who invites his friend Juan Manuel to go hunting and boating on their lake. This unusual lake produces the bizarre phenomenon of spurting-up new islands that emerge and disappear from one day to the next. Yolanda is bewildered by her brother and Juan Manuel who, seem to pursue silly hobbies and posture rather than act naturally.

> Men [exclaims Yolanda as she waches her brother] how absurd they were! Always in motion, forever willing to take an interest in everything. . . . If they go to a fireplace, they remain standing, ready to run to the other room—ready always to escape, to flee toward the futile. And they cough and smoke, speak loud as if they feared silence—indeed as if tranquility were a mortal enemy. (86)

Yolanda finds man's nature as alien as Juan Manuel views hers to be. He is intrigued by Yolanda, whose bewitching beauty resembles the grace of a sea gull in flight. One evening, as he returns from exploring the new islands teaming with sea creatures and aquatic vegetation, he gazes through the bathroom window, where Yolanda stands naked contemplating her left shoulder. What he sees next is that on her shoulder she is growing a wing, or the stump of a wing "a small atrophied member which she now strokes carefully" (106). Stunned and repelled, he flees from the estate and returns to Buenos Aires. He prefers to confort himself with the memory of his late sponse Elsa, another dead, hence silent and perfect wife, deciding to never again see the threatening Yolanda.

Again, as in *The Final Mist,* we see that for this character the perfect woman is the silent one. In turn, Yolanda is attracted to Juan Manuel who is "golden as though he were enveloped by a sunray" (94). The association between light and the command of the signifier is established once more. However, Yolanda resists Juan Manuel and runs away from him. Yolanda has also rejected the man she was in love with before she met Juan Manuel. She weeps because she feels she cannot explain to her lover why she cannot stay with him. The reason for her refusal to succumb to her love for these men is seen in the story's extended metaphor: Yolanda is growing a wing, that is, she is learning to be free of a male dominated social structure. The repeated motif of the musical notes played by Yolanda on the piano signify her attempt to voice her own language:

> Do, re, mi, fa, sol, la, ti, do . . . Do, re, mi, fa, sol, la, ti, do . . . Do, re, mi, fa . . . Do, re, mi, fa . . . Do, re, mi, fa . . . —the piano insists. And those notes repeated over and over beat against Juan Manuel's heart, striking where the see gull's wing has wounded him that morning. Without knowing why, he gets to his feet and starts walking toward that music chiming endlessly through the trees like summons. (94)

Her efforts to communicate her own way fail. Her notes fall on deaf ears as Juan Manuel refuses to listen to her view: "He fears losing his way in that wild world with its disorderly and poorly mapped pathways, strewn with an unsystematic confusion of clues" (112).

The mysterious new islands Juan Manuel discovers are teeming with sea life and strange vegetation: "islands afloat on the horizon, rising from a cloud of foam and wheeling birds . . . amid spirals of sea gulls" (93). But these islands are only a mirage. They existed only when he was with Yolanda. For as he returns to Buenos Aires to his son, and pulls out the jelly fish he found for the youngster in the islands, he sees that it has disappeared. Then, he thinks that perhaps he should call Yolanda so that everything would "seem less vague, less dreadful if I could hear her voice . . ." (109). To him, Yolanda's voice is like the disappearing islands, mysterious and incomprehensible.

This story can be understood only in the context of the previous ones, and as such, it interweaves the principle issues brought forth in the entire collection. In these narratives we find that birds and wings and flight and music are metaphors for a woman's attempt to voice her own language. When she shows signs of eloquence she takes flight like a bird or like notes in a scale; when she fails and falls into silence she is compared to a fallen bird with broken wings. Yolanda is associated as well with the new islands, full of steaming sea life, which, as shown above, represent female creativity. Unlike other women, she has dared to sprout her own wings. This has meaning within the poetics of Bombal's narrative, where wings, braids, sea life and plant life come to signify woman's effort to create a speech she hopes will allow her to take flight and achieve new heights. However, this achievement will not come without a cost. Women with wings or with long vine-like braids must live like Amazons; not without love or men, but within a new social structure where the meaning of the phallic signifier or male centered discourse is balanced by another signifier, perhaps the "small atrophied member" that Yolanda develops or the womb-like pond or room where the othe heroines find their voice.

It is significant to note that not one of the protagonists of these stories is a mother, yet the heroines are intimately involved with the process of creation. What they want to create is a language that reflects their subjectivity as a female individual not as a mother, for motherhood implies a relationship that in some ways alienates woman from herself. Jane Gallop reminds us that patriarchy is built upon the institution of motherhood, a motherhood where the woman is a complement of the child's subjectivity, a perfect selfless mirror of another subject's desire (324). It is at this juncture that psychoanalysis and feminism may part ways; one taking account of the child's wishes, the other focusing on the mother's desire (326). Bombal's powerless heroines suggest that what woman desires is a discourse of her own; not the surrogate authority she acquires via her association with the male as phallic signifier, as Lacan conceives, nor the traditional vicarious power she wields through her progeny, but the freedom to cultivate a discourse that would give her value and worth in and of herself. Gallop explains that:

> The question of language must be inserted as the wedge to break the hold of the figure of mother. *Ecriture Feminine* [a la Cixous and Irigaray] must not be arrested by the plenitude of the mother tongue, but must try to be always and also an 'other' tongue. The other tongue is hard to pronounce, but those of us who have learned critical interpretation from psychoanalysis and from feminism are learning how to read it. At its best, psychoanalytic feminist criticism is teaching us not how to speak the mother tongue, not only how to see the mother as other and not mirror, but how to read the other within the mother tongue. (329)

It is this 'other tongue' that Lacan refers to in "Homage to Marguerite Duras," where he noted that in her work "the practice of the letter converges with the workings of the unconscious" (Duras 124). It is precisely this merging of letter and unconscious that Bombal practices and that characterizes her view of a female voice.

Notes

1. For more on Jung's theories of archetypes and sexual difference see the sections on anima and animus in *The Archetypes.*

2. For a thorough analysis on the phallus see Lacan's "The Signification of the Phallus" in *Ecrits.*

3. According to Lacan the other/Other has various meanings. In this context we are refering to both the other (with small 'o') as the other persons, here the protagonist's lovers, and Other (with capital 'O') as the unconscious as it surfaces through language and speech. (For more on this see Lacan, *Ecrits* and Raglan-Sullivan, *Lacan*).

4. See *Speculum of the Other Woman* and *This Sex Which is Not One* for Irigaray's discussion of psychoanalysis' masculine bias and her perspective on creating a feminine discourse.

Works Cited

Bombal, María Luisa. *New Islands and Other Stories.* Trans. Richard and Luisa Cunningham. Ithaca: Cornell UP, 1982.

Duras, Marguerite. *Marguerite Duras.* San Francisco: City Lights Books, 1987.

Gallop, Jane. "Reading the Mother Tongue: Psychoanalytic Feminist Criticism." *Critical Inquiry* (Winter 1987): 314-29.

Guerra-Cunningham, Lucia. *La narrativa de Maria Luisa Bombal: una visión de la existencia femenina.* Madrid: Editorial Playor, 1980.

Jung, Carl G. *The Archetypes and the Collective Unconscious.* Trans. R.F.C. Hull. Vol. 9, part 1 of *Collected Works.* Princeton: Princeton UP, 1966.

Irigaray, Luce. *Speculum of the Other Woman.* Trans. Gillian C. Gill. Ithaca: Cornell UP, 1985.

Irigaray, Luce. *This Sex Which is Not One.* Trans. Catherine Poirier with Carolyne Burke. Ithaca: Cornell UP, 1985.

Lacan, Jacques. *Ecrits: A Selection.* Trans. Alan Sheridan, New York: Norton, 1977.

—. *The Four Fundamental Concepts of Psycho-Analysis.* Trans. Alan Sheridan. New York: Norton, 1974.

Ragland-Sullivan, Ellie. "Seeking the Third Term: Desire, the Phallus and the Materiality of Language. *Feminism and Psychoanalysis.* Ed. Richard Feldstein and Judith Roof, Cornell UP: Ithaca, 1989. 40-64.

—. *Jacques Lacan and the Philosophy of Psychoanalysis.* Urbana: U of Illinois P, 1987.

Penelope Mesic (review date 1995)

SOURCE: "Moving Beyond Gothic: The Different Reality of María Luisa Bombal," in *Tribune Books,* September 10, 1995, pp. 6-7.

[*In the following assessment of Bombal's English translations of* La última niebla *and* La amortajada *Mesic contends that, despite shortcomings, these works "both awake a feeling of genuine discovery, of minds and hearts not borrowed from European literature but indigenous to a New World of thought and feeling."*]

A frightened young bride dressed in black, who has heard the marriage ceremony hastily pronounced by a bored priest, is taken by her silent groom to his remote hacienda. The train stops at a station where the couple alone disembark. A carriage is waiting, and as it rocks them across a "dreary brown plain where great brambles stand motionless" the bride sees "the mist actually pushing forward to meet the carriage." "I'm so happy," she murmurs—surely in a effort to convince herself of it—but her new husband sits "unmoved, distant, indifferent." This, the opening scene of *House of Mist,* written in 1935 by Chilean novelist Maria Luisa Bombal, draws upon all the sure-fire devices of gothic romance: the timid heroine; the sullen, Byronic hero; the melancholy setting; and, above all, an air of gloom and mystery.

Yet Maria Luisa Bombal does not simply retrace the well-worn trail first blazed by Maria Radcliffe. She may begin with the elements of a familiar genre, but her objectives are different and reflect the values and legends, the landscape and habits of South America. It is as if someone living in Polynesia started with a French recipe, but in modifying the dish for local tastes, produced a flavor so distinctive that it becomes the basis for a genuine native cuisine. For Bombal—with her bold disregard for simple realism in favor of a heightened reality in which the external world reflects the internal truth of the characters' feeling, and with her deliberate mingling of fantasy, memory and event—is the precursor of the magical realism that is the flower of South American writing today. As the novelist Carlos Fuentes wrote, "Maria Luisa Bombal is the mother of us all."

House of Mist, long out of print and newly republished with the shorter novella *The Shrouded Woman,* was written while Bombal was staying in an apartment in Buenos Aires with the poet Pablo Neruda and his wife. Bombal's timid little heroine, Helga, who marries in black, may inhabit a traditional male-dominated and hierarchical society, where, as the illegitimate result of her parents' passionate love affair, she is something of an outcast. She may do needlepoint and worry about her virtue. But the story turns on something far more modern: Helga's search for the truth of her individual experience.

She has married Daniel, who thinks only of his first wife, a beautiful woman who drowned mysteriously in the *estancia*'s lake. Daniel's sister, sensing Helga's loneliness, introduces her to a handsome suitor, who accosts her at a costume ball. He leads her outdoors, across a dark garden to a crumbling gatehouse of magical charm, where they make love. With hallucinatory clarity she recalls the clock, its pendulum a brass arrow, that stands on the mantelpiece of their trysting place. And with a thrill of horror, she remembers propping her little fan, embroidered with seed pearls, against the clock, where it will serve as testimony to her betrayal.

But did this seduction really happen? Her maid swears that she led Helga, drunk on her first champagne, upstairs alone to bed. Her husband says he saw her asleep on a sofa distant from the ballroom. And the fan is nowhere to be found. But if it was a dream, why does Helga have such an accurate recollection of the cottage, which in fact exists?

In this psychological investigation, Bombal makes imagination, emotion and dream equal in importance to reality and creates a narrative linked by metaphor. The sign of Helga's unhappiness, of her disappointment in her loveless marriage, is the mist of the remote hacienda. But mist is also associated with her dreams, as if to imply that the root cause of her visions is sorrow.

"A giant impalpable snake seemed to be enfolding rings of smoke towards me. The mist! The mist now settled in the very core of my nature," Helga exclaims. And then she adds, "like the clock in the heart of Daniel's nature." For Daniel, still mourning his lost wife, has told her, "There's a clock everywhere in the world . . . and everything changes, everything moves away, disintegrates a little more. The irreversible reality of time is what memory and feeling conspire to undo."

The Shrouded Woman, a briefer novella included in the same volume, is the finer work. It recalls Faulkner's "As I Lay Dying" in being a narrative of the life of a wife and mother who speaks bitterly after her death about opportunities missed, and the selfishness that was mixed with her family's love and with her own. The appearance of relatives at her bedside yields both an account of her life and a portrait of an entire society. Her father sits stoically: "[He] will suffer in solitude, rebellious against any reference to his affliction . . . as if his grief were not within the reach of anyone." Her sister's presence causes Ana Maria to demand: "Where do you think I am? Rendering account to that terrifying God to whom you offer up day after day in your prayers the brutality of your husband?"

It is not only relationships but also the dead woman's surroundings that resonate with emotion. "The rain stops and [Ana Maria] hears clearly the rusty flat note that the wind is tearing out of the old windmill. And each wrench of the tin paddles seems to pluck a particular string in her shrouded breast. And for a long time, completely absorbed, she listens to that grave, sonorous note vibrating within herself, a note she never knew was there in her." This quiet passage contains a revolutionary implication that a woman has a self independent from her emotional life, and that her relation to the surrounding world is of equal importance to her relationship with a man.

And yet it is in describing her heroine's cousin and first lover, Ricardo, that Bombal is most eloquent. There are two moments of childhood contact between the characters, and both are as sharp and far from stereotype as can be imagined. One occurs when, playing hide-and-seek, Ana Maria finds her cruel older cousin defenseless, asleep in the hayloft. "You tossed about, sighing, and under the hay one of your bare feet touched mine. And I did not understand why the surrender in that gesture awakened such tenderness in me"

These works of fiction, particularly the over-long and discursive *House of Mist,* do have weaknesses. Bombal translated them herself, and her English, while correct, is occasionally stiff and faintly old-fashioned. Yet both awake a feeling of genuine discovery, of minds and hearts not borrowed from European literature but indigenous to a New World of thought and feeling.

FURTHER READING

Criticism

Scott, Nina M. "Verbal and Nonverbal Messages in María Luisa Bombal's 'El árbol'." *Modern Language Studies,* XVII, No. 3 (Summer 1987): 3-9.
> Linguistic study of Bombal's short story in which the critic examines "the contextual communication problems of the two principal characters and the formal aspect of narrative style."

Tolliver, Joyce. "'Otro modo de ver': The Gaze in *La última niebla.*" *Revista Canadiense de Estudios Hispánicos,* XVII, No. 1 (Fall 1992): 105-21.
> Explores the significance of the gaze as a form of empowerment in Bombal's novella *La última niebla.*

Additional coverage of Bombal's life and career is contained in the following source published by the Gale Group: *Hispanic Literature Criticism Supplement,* **Vol. 1.**

George Gissing
1857–1903

English short story writer, novelist, critic, and essayist.

INTRODUCTION

Gissing was a late nineteenth-century author whose short fiction exemplifies the changes that marked the transition from Victorian to modern literature. While his early works display a Dickensian concern for the plight of the poor and a belief in the effectiveness of social reform, later works manifest a distinctly modern sense of pessimism and moral uncertainty. Although Gissing's disillusionment is attributed to personal frustrations rather than to the failure of his Victorian ideology, critics note that his short stories and novels nevertheless express the evolving philosophical awareness of his entire literary generation.

BIOGRAPHICAL INFORMATION

Born in Wakefield, Yorkshire, Gissing was the eldest son of a drugstore proprietor. When the death of his father when Gissing was thirteen left the family destitute, concerned friends and neighbors established a fund that enabled Gissing and his two brothers to attend a boarding school at Alderly Edge, in the nearby county of Cheshire. Gissing proved to be a brilliant student and thus earned a full scholarship to Owens College. In his final year at the college, he met and fell in love with a sixteen-year-old alcoholic prostitute named Nell Harrison. To support and perhaps reform her, he began to steal from his classmates but was apprehended in May of 1876. He was immediately dismissed from Owens and was sent to America after serving a thirty-day jail sentence.

In America Gissing moved to Chicago and began to write short stories for the local newspapers. In late 1877 he returned to England, planning to earn his living as a writer. He wrote novels throughout the early 1880s, but his books sold poorly. However, with the publication of *New Grub Street* in 1891, his work began to garner critical and commercial attention. During the last phase of his career Gissing demonstrated his greatest versatility, producing short stories, novels, a travel memoir, criticism, and a fictionalized biography, *The Private Papers of Henry Ryecroft.* He died from a lung ailment in 1903.

MAJOR WORKS

Many of Gissing's stories are clearly autobiographical, and employ his recurring thematic concerns: his pessimism regarding human relationships; the repressive nature of familial expectations; class conflict; and the effects of industrialization, especially the loss of religious faith. In

his first published story, "Sins of the Fathers," which appeared in the *Chicago Tribune* in 1877, a middle-class student falls in love with an impoverished prostitute named Laura. As their relationship intensifies, the boy's father sends him to America, where he marries a woman of his own class. In a twist of fate, one night he attends a play in which Laura appears as a chorus girl. He meets with her only to find he still is attracted to her. Knowing that the relationship is doomed, Laura pulls him into the river and they die together. In a later story, "The House of Cobwebs," an aspiring writer named Goldthorpe moves into a run-down house owned by a man named Spicer. The two men form a peaceful and satisfying domestic partnership, but after Goldthorpe finishes his novel he falls ill; the doctor advises him to move to his mother's house and out of his "unhealthy" environment. After his recovery, he learns that Spicer has fallen ill and the house has been demolished, presumably a just punishment for a relationship that transgresses social conventions. Recently, there has been an effort to bring to light all of Gissing's short fiction, as evinced by the 1992 publication of *Lost in America,* a collection of several rare stories that originally appeared in American newspapers.

CRITICAL RECEPTION

Critics continue to debate Gissing's contribution to the short story genre. Although his early stories were derided as gloomy and drab, they were also noted for their lack of sentimentality and melodrama. Scholars agree that one of the most outstanding characteristics of Gissing's fiction is its intensely autobiographical nature, and many critics assert that his works can only be fully understood when considered in the context of his life. His insistence upon the importance of environmental factors in the development of his characters has led Gissing's name to be linked with that of Emile Zola. His stories were deemed mature and complex character studies, replete with deft insights into human perception and behavior. Most commentators agree that Gissing's short fiction has a clear place in English literary and social history, because it illuminates the economic and psychological currents of an era as well as the harsh social circumstances and realities of the day.

PRINCIPAL WORKS

Short Fiction

Human Odds and Ends (short stories and sketches) 1898
The House of Cobwebs, and Other Stories 1906
The Sins of the Fathers 1924
Brownie 1931
Stories and Sketches (short stories and sketches) 1938
George Gissing: Lost Stories from America 1992
The Day of Silence, and Other Stories 1993

Other Major Works

Workers in the Dawn (novel) 1880
The Unclassed (novel) 1884
Demos (novel) 1886
Isabel Clarendon (novel) 1886
Thyrza (novel) 1887
A Life's Morning (novel) 1888
The Nether World (novel) 1889
The Emancipated (novel) 1890
New Grub Street (novel) 1891
Born in Exile (novel) 1892
Denzil Quarrier (novel) 1892
The Odd Women (novel) 1893
In the Year of Jubilee (novel) 1894
Eve's Ransom (novel) 1895
The Paying Guest (novel) 1895
Sleeping Fires (novel) 1895
The Whirlpool (novel) 1897
Charles Dickens (criticism) 1898

The Town Traveller (novel) 1898
The Crown of Life (novel) 1899
By the Ionian Sea (travel essays) 1901
Our Friend the Charlatan (novel) 1901
The Private Papers of Henry Ryecroft (novel) 1903
Will Warburton (novel) 1905
London and the Life of Literature in Late Victorian England: The Diary of George Gissing, Novelist (diary) 1978

CRITICISM

The Academy (review date 1906)

SOURCE: A review of *The House of Cobwebs*, in *The Academy*, Vol. 70, No. 1776, May 19, 1906, p. 479.

[*In the following review, the critic offers a favorable assessment of* The House of Cobwebs.]

We are not of those whose pleasure in a man's work is necessarily increased by an intimate acquaintance with the circumstances of his life, yet it were idle to deny the power of that faculty (none the less irresistible for being frequently unconscious) which some writers have of exciting their readers' curiosity, and we well remember wondering, on taking up a book of George Gissing's for the first time, what manner of man this might be who could write with such bitter suavity, with such delicate irony, of a *milieu* which he appeared to know well and thoroughly to detest. The few hard, essential facts which invested Gissing's career with a not quite ordinary pathos are now well known to all who care enough to estimate an achievement standing in some sense apart; but the appearance of these fifteen short stories, aptly epitomising his personal attitude towards life as he found it, in conjunction with a strenuously condensed "chronological survey" of his work, justify a brief recapitulation. Educated at Lindow Grove School at Alderley and at Ownes College, Manchester, Gissing found himself at twenty, utterly poor and without a shred of influence, in London. Talented, delicate, and sensitive, of a shy geniality apt to freeze at an uncertain temperature into proud reserve, with a strong taste for the high romantic places of history, and a loathing for the sordid accompaniments of latter-day poverty, he seems to have had no assets but a fine comprehension of the significance of Dickens in English literature, a dogged industry, and the power begotten of dire necessity to pierce, with a pen naturally pointed for delicate introspection and æsthetic analysis, the tortured lives of the educated poor. In stress and poverty he produced his first book. *Workers in the Dawn*, in 1880. For three years he suffered under various yokes imposed by the necessity of earning a living wage. Then, most miserably lodged, he sat down to write, book after careful book, year after weary year. After six years one of these, *Demos*—not the best—brought him fifty pounds. He spent them in Italy, the land of his dreams from which "only death would have held me back." It proved more than a decade before he could sufficiently re-emancipate himself to wend South again. The interval was filled with those stories, one or more every year—*Born in Exile, The Odd Women, In the Year of Jubilee* are three of them—of which the governing idea, as Mr. Seccombe well summarises it, was to analyse as an artist the misery inherent in the sharp contrasts of modern life and to express it to the world. Equally suggestive is Mr. Seccombe's reflection that in forgetting that the "educated poor" are not all artists, Gissing underestimated those compensating "consolations of temperament, of habit, and of humdrum ideals which are common to the coarsest of mankind." He does not (he says) represent men as worse than they are; but he represents them as less brave. Gissing himself, at any rate, for all his dolorous note, was no coward, and he won through to an independence only too well deserved. Though he died young, he lived long enough worthily to glorify Dickens, to leave behind him that "gentle masterpiece of softened autobiography," *The Private Papers of Henry Ryecroft,* to throw his whole romantic soul into *Veranilda.* With all that Mr. Seccombe has to say of *Henry Ryecroft* we are in complete accord; but is not his praise of the *Dickens* and *Veranilda* excessive? That sentence, in the one case, about "a context in which every syllable is precious, reasonable, thrice distilled and sweet to the palate as Hybla honey"? That statement in the other that "Sir Walter himself could never in reason have dared to aspire to such a fortunate conjuncture of talent, grace, and historic accuracy"? It is, however, as a brief survey of the Gissing country designed to enable the reader to judge the author by eight or nine of his best books that this essay may most fairly be appreciated; and if, as we take it to be, it is intended for those who do not know Gissing well, it is either too long or too short. Those who have not read *New Grub Street* will scarcely care to learn that Reardon is "a greatly strengthened and improved rifacimento of Kingcote" (in *Isabel Clarendon,*) or that Amy Reardon is "a better observed Isabel," or that "Reardon was unlucky in marrying Amy." They will probably fight shy, too, of the foot-notes in their impatience to reach **The House of Cobwebs** and the rest. On the other hand, the reading of these often exquisite grey and mauve studies in semi-autobiography may leave a good many people eager to know more about their author than Mr. Seccombe has been able to compress within his fifty serried pages. He seems to write with a full knowledge of his country. Should he ever supplement his survey with a history, we would hope to find it a little less flamboyant.

Thomas Seccombe (essay date 1906)

SOURCE: An introduction to *The House of Cobwebs,* in *Gissing: The Critical Heritage,* edited by Pierre Coustillas and Colin Partridge, Routledge & Kegan Paul, 1972, pp. 509-17.

[*In the following excerpt, which was originally published as the introduction to the 1906 edition of* The House of Cobwebs, *Seccombe surveys the distinctive qualities of Gissing's fiction and places him in context with other nineteenth-century English authors.*]

In England during the sixties and seventies of last century the world of books was dominated by one Gargantuan type of fiction. The terms book and novel became almost synonymous in houses which were not Puritan, yet where

books and reading, in the era of few and unfree libraries, were strictly circumscribed. George Gissing was no exception to this rule. The English novel was at the summit of its reputation during his boyish days. As a lad of eight or nine he remembered the parts of *Our Mutual Friend* coming to the house, and could recall the smile of welcome with which they were infallibly received. In the dining-room at home was a handsomely framed picture which he regarded with an almost idolatrous veneration. It was an engraved portrait of Charles Dickens. Some of the best work of George Eliot, Reade, and Trollope was yet to make its appearance; Meredith and Hardy were still the treasured possession of the few; the reigning models during the period of Gissing's adolescence were probably Dickens and Trollope, and the numerous satellites of these great stars, prominent among them Wilkie Collins, William Black, and Besant and Rice.

Of the cluster of novelists who emerged from this school of ideas, the two who will attract most attention in the future were clouded and obscured for the greater period of their working lives. Unobserved, they received, and made their own preparations for utilising, the legacy of the mid-Victorian novel—moral thesis, plot, underplot, set characters, descriptive machinery, landscape colouring, copious phraseology, Herculean proportions, and the rest of the cumbrous and grandiose paraphernalia of *Chuzzlewit, Pendennis,* and *Middlemarch.* But they received the legacy in a totally different spirit. Mark Rutherford, after a very brief experiment, put all these elaborate properties and conventions reverently aside. Cleverer and more docile, George Gissing for the most part accepted them; he put his slender frame into the ponderous collar of the author of the *Mill on the Floss,* and nearly collapsed in wind and limb in the heart-breaking attempt to adjust himself to such an heroic type of harness.

The distinctive qualities of Gissing at the time of his setting forth were a scholarly style, rather fastidious and academic in its restraint, and the personal discontent, slightly morbid, of a self-conscious student who finds himself in the position of a sensitive woman in a crowd. His attitude through life was that of a man who, having set out on his career with the understanding that a second-class ticket is to be provided, allows himself to be unceremoniously hustled into the rough and tumble of a noisy third. Circumstances made him revolt against an anonymous start in life for a refined and educated man under such conditions. They also made him prolific. He shrank from the restraints and humiliations to which the poor and shabbily dressed private tutor is exposed—revealed to us with a persuasive terseness in the pages of *The Unclassed, New Grub Street, Ryecroft,* and the story of **'Topham's Chance.'** Writing fiction in a garret for a sum sufficient to keep body and soul together for the six months following payment was at any rate better than this. The result was a long series of highly finished novels, written in a style and from a point of view which will always render them dear to the studious and the book-centred. Upon the larger external rings of the book-reading multitude it is not probable that Gissing will ever succeed in impressing himself. There is an absence of transcendental quality about his work, a failure in humour, a remoteness from actual life, a deficiency in awe and mystery, a shortcoming in emotional power, finally, a lack of the dramatic faculty, not indeed indispensable to a novelist, but almost indispensable as an ingredient in great novels of this particular genre. In temperament and vitality he is palpably inferior to the masters (Dickens, Thackeray, Hugo, Balzac) whom he reverenced with such a cordial admiration and envy. A 'low vitality' may account for what has been referred to as the 'nervous exhaustion' of his style. It were useless to pretend that Gissing belongs of right to the 'first series' of English Men of Letters. But if debarred by his limitations from a resounding or popular success, he will remain exceptionally dear to the heart of the recluse, who thinks that the scholar does well to cherish a grievance against the vulgar world beyond the cloister; and dearer still, perhaps, to a certain number of enthusiasts who began reading George Gissing as a college night-course; who closed *Thyrza* and *Demos* as dawn was breaking through the elms in some Oxford quadrangle, and who have pursued his work patiently ever since in a somewhat toilsome and broken ascent, secure always of suave writing and conscientious workmanship, of an individual prose cadence and a genuine vein of Penseroso:—

> Thus, Night, oft see me in thy pale career . . . Where brooding Darkness spreads his jealous wings, And the night-raven sings.

Yet by the larger, or, at any rate, the intermediate public, it is a fact that Gissing has never been quite fairly estimated. He loses immensely if you estimate him either by a single book, as is commonly done, or by his work as a whole, in the perspective of which, owing to the lack of critical instruction, one or two books of rather inferior quality have obtruded themselves unduly.

[In later years] Gissing spent an increasing portion of his time abroad, and it was from St Honoré en Morvan, for instance, that he dated the preface of *Our Friend the Charlatan* in 1901. As with *Denzil Quarrier* (1892) and *The Town Traveller* (1898) this was one of the books which Gissing sometimes went the length of asking the admirers of his earlier romances 'not to read.' With its prefatory note, indeed, its cheap illustrations, and its rather mechanical intrigue, it seems as far removed from such a book as *A Life's Morning* as it is possible for a novel by the same author to be. It was in the South of France, in the neighbourhood of Biarritz, amid scenes such as that described in the thirty-seventh chapter of *Will Warburton,* or still further south, that he wrote the greater part of his last three books, the novel just mentioned, which is probably his best essay in the lighter ironical vein to which his later years inclined, *Veranilda,* a romance of the time of Theodoric the Goth, written in solemn fulfilment of a vow of his youth, and *The Private Papers of Henry Ryecroft,* which to my mind remains a legacy for Time to take account of as the faithful tribute of one of the truest artists of the generation he served.

In *Veranilda* (1904) are combined conscientious workmanship, a pure style of finest quality, and archaeology, for all I know to the contrary, worthy of Becker or Boni. Sir Walter himself could never in reason have dared to aspire to such a fortunate conjunction of talent, grace, and historic accuracy. He possessed only that profound knowledge of human nature, that moulding humour and quick sense of dialogue, that live, human, and local interest in matters antiquarian, that statesmanlike insight into the pith and marrow of the historic past, which makes one of

Scott's historical novels what it is—the envy of artists, the delight of young and old, the despair of formal historians. *Veranilda* is without a doubt a splendid piece of work; Gissing wrote it with every bit of the care that his old friend Biffen expended upon *Mr Bailey, Grocer.* He worked slowly, patiently, affectionately, scrupulously. Each sentence was as good as he could make it, harmonious to the ear, with words of precious meaning skilfully set; and he believed in it with the illusion so indispensable to an artist's well-being and continuance in good work. It represented for him what *Salammbô* did to Flaubert. But he could not allow himself six years to write a book as Flaubert did. *Salammbô,* after all, was a magnificent failure, and *Veranilda,*—well, it must be confessed, sadly but surely, that *Veranilda* was a failure too. Far otherwise was it with *Ryecroft,* which represents, as it were, the *summa* of Gissing's habitual meditation, aesthetic feeling and sombre emotional experience. Not that it is a pessimistic work,—quite the contrary, it represents the mellowing influences, the increase of faith in simple, unsophisticated English girlhood and womanhood, in domestic pursuits, in innocent children, in rural homeliness and honest Wessex landscape, which began to operate about 1896, and is seen so unmistakably in the closing scenes of *The Whirlpool.* Three chief strains are subtly interblended in the composition. First that of a nature book, full of air, foliage and landscape—that English landscape art of Linnell and De Wint and Foster for which he repeatedly expresses such a passionate tendre, refreshed by 'blasts from the channel, with raining scud and spume of mist breaking upon the hills' in which he seems to crystallise the very essence of a Western winter. Secondly, a paean half of praise and half of regret for the vanishing England, passing so rapidly even as he writes into 'a new England which tries so hard to be unlike the old.' A deeper and richer note of thankfulness, mixed as it must be with anxiety, for the good old ways of English life (as lamented by Mr Poorgrass and Mark Clark), old English simplicity, and old English fare—the fine prodigality of the English platter, has never been raised. God grant that the leaven may work! And thirdly there is a deeply brooding strain of saddening yet softened autobiographical reminiscence, over which is thrown a light veil of literary appreciation and topical comment. Here is a typical *cadenza,* rising to a swell at one point (suggestive for the moment of Raleigh's famous apostrophe), and the most gently falling, in a manner not wholly unworthy, I venture to think, of Webster and Sir Thomas Browne, of both of which authors there is internal evidence that Gissing made some study. . . .

Whatever the critics may determine as to the merit of the stories in the present volume, there can be no question as to the interest they derive from their connection with what had gone before. Thus **'Topham's Chance'** is manifestly the outcome of material pondered as early as 1884. **'The Lodger in Maze Pond'** develops in a most suggestive fashion certain problems discussed in 1894. Miss Rodney is a reincarnation of Rhoda Nunn and Constance Bride. **'Christopherson'** is a delicious expansion of a mood indicated in *Ryecroft* (Spring XII.), and **'A Capitalist'** indicates the growing interest in the business side of practical life, the dawn of which is seen in *The Town Traveller* and in the discussion of Dickens's potentialities as a capitalist. The very artichokes in **The House of Cobwebs** (which, like the kindly hand that raised them, alas! fell a victim to the first frost of the season) are suggestive of a charming passage detailing the retired author's experience as a gardener. What Dr Furnivall might call the 'backward reach' of every one of these stories will render their perusal delightful to those cultivated readers of Gissing, of whom there are by no means a few, to whom every fragment of his suave and delicate workmanship 'repressed yet full of power, vivid though sombre in colouring,' has a technical interest and charm. Nor will they search in vain for Gissing's incorrigible mannerisms, his haunting insistence upon the note of 'Dort wo du nicht bist ist das Glück,' his tricks of the brush in portraiture, his characteristic epithets, the *dusking* twilight, the *decently ignoble* penury, the *not ignoble* ambition, the *not wholly base* riot of the senses in early manhood. In my own opinion we have here in **'The Scrupulous Father,'** and to a less degree, perhaps, in the first and last of these stories, and in **'A Poor Gentleman'** and **'Christopherson,'** perfectly characteristic and quite admirable specimens of Gissing's own genre, and later, unstudied, but always finished prose style.

But a few words remain to be said, and these, in part at any rate, in recapitulation. In the old race, of which Dickens and Thackeray were representative, a successful determination to rise upon the broad back of popularity coincided with a growing conviction that the evil in the world was steadily diminishing. Like healthy schoolboys who have worked their way up to the sixth form, they imagined that the bullying of which they had had to complain was become pretty much a thing of the past. In Gissing the misery inherent in the sharp contrasts of modern life was a far more deeply ingrained conviction. He cared little for the remedial aspect of the question. His idea was to analyse this misery as an artist and to express it to the world.

One of the most impressive elements in the resulting novels is the witness they bear to prolonged and intense suffering, the suffering of a proud, reserved, and oversensitive mind brought into constant contact with the coarse and brutal facts of life. The creator of Mr Biffen suffers all the torture of the fastidious, the delicately honourable, the scrupulously high-minded in daily contact with persons of blunt feelings, low ideals, and base instincts. 'Human cattle, the herd that feed and breed, with them it was well; but the few born to a desire for ever unattainable, the gentle spirits who from their prisoning circumstance looked up and afar, how the heart ached to think of them!' The natural bent of Gissing's talent was towards poetry and classical antiquity. His mind had considerable natural affinity with that of Tennyson. He was passionately fond of old literature, of the study of metre and of historical reverie. The subtle curiosities of Anatole France are just of the kind that would have appealed irresistibly to him. His delight in psychological complexity and feats of style are not seldom reminiscent of Paul Bourget. His life would have gained immeasurably by a transference to less pinched and pitiful surroundings: but it is more than doubtful whether his work would have done so.

The compulsion of the twin monsters Bread and Cheese forced him to write novels the scene of which was laid in the one milieu he had thoroughly observed, that of either utterly hideous or shabby genteel squalor in London. He gradually obtained a rare mastery in the delineation of his unlovely *mise en scène*. He gradually created a small public who read eagerly everything that came from his pen, despite his economy of material (even of ideas), and de-

spite the repetition to which a natural tendency was increased by compulsory over-production. In all his best books we have evidence of the savage and ironical delight with which he depicted to the shadow of a hair the sordid and vulgar elements by which he had been so cruelly depressed. The aesthetic observer who wanted material for a picture of the blank desolation and ugliness of modern city life could find no better substratum than in the works of George Gissing. Many of his descriptions of typical London scenes in Lambeth Walk, Clerkenwell, or Judd Street, for instance, are the work of a detached, remorseless, photographic artist realising that ugly sordidness of daily life to which the ordinary observer becomes in the course of time as completely habituated as he does to the smoke-laden air. To a cognate sentiment of revolt I attribute that excessive deference to scholarship and refinement which leads him in so many novels to treat these desirable attributes as if they were ends and objects of life in themselves. It has also misled him but too often into depicting a world of suicides, ignoring or overlooking a secret hobby, or passion, or chimaera which is the one thing that renders existence endurable to so many of the waifs and strays of life. He takes existence sadly—too sadly, it may well be; but his drabs and greys provide an atmosphere that is almost inseparable to some of us from our gaunt London streets. In Farringdon Road, for example, I look up instinctively to the expressionless upper windows where Mr Luckworth Crewe spreads his baits for intending advertisers. A tram ride through Clerkenwell and its leagues of dreary, inhospitable brickwork will take you through the heart of a region where Clem Peckover, Pennyloaf Candy, and Totty Nancarrow are multiplied rather than varied since they were first depicted by George Gissing. As for the British Museum, it is peopled to this day by characters from *New Grub Street*.

There may be a perceptible lack of virility, a fluctuating vagueness of outline about the characterisation of 'some of his men. In his treatment of crowds, in his description of a mob, personified as some huge beast purring to itself in stupid contentment,' he can have few rivals. In tracing the influence of women over his heroes he evinces no common subtlety: it is here probably that he is at his best. The *odor di femmina,* to use a phrase of Don Giovanni's, is a marked characteristic of his books. Of the kisses—

> by hopeless fancy feigned
> On lips that are for others—

there are indeed many to be discovered hidden away between these pages. And the beautiful verse has a fine parallel in the prose of one of Gissing's later novels.

> Some girl, of delicate instinct, of purpose sweet and pure, wasting her unloved life in toil and want and indignity; some man, whose youth and courage strove against a mean environment, whose eyes grew haggard in the vain search for a companion promised in his dreams; they lived, these two, parted perchance only by the wall of neighbour houses, yet all huge London was between them, and their hands would never touch.

The dream of fair women which occupies the mood of Piers Otway in the opening passage of the same novel, was evidently no remotely conceived fancy. Its realisation, in ideal love, represents the author's *Crown of Life*. The wise man who said that Beautiful Woman was a heaven to the eye, a hell to the soul, and a purgatory to the purse of man, could hardly find a more copious field of illustration than in the fiction of George Gissing.

Gissing was a sedulous artist; some of his books, it is true, are very hurried productions, finished in haste for the market with no great amount either of inspiration or artistic confidence about them. But little slovenly work will be found bearing his name, for he was a thoroughly trained writer; a suave and seductive workmanship had become a second nature to him, and there was always a flavour of scholarly, subacid and quasi-ironical modernity about his style. There is little doubt that his quality as a stylist was better adapted to the studies of modern London life, on its seamier side, which he had observed at first hand, than to stories of the conventional dramatic structure which he too often felt himself bound to adopt. In these his failure to grapple with a big objective, or to rise to some prosperous situation, is often painfully marked. A master of explanation and description rather than of animated narrative or sparkling dialogue, he lacked the wit and humour, the brilliance and energy of a consummate style which might have enabled him to compete with the great scenic masters in fiction, or with craftsmen such as Hardy or Stevenson, or with incomparable wits and conversationalists such as Meredith. It is true, again, that his London-street novels lack certain artistic elements of beauty (though here and there occur glints of rainy or sunset townscape in a half-tone, consummately handled and eminently impressive); and his intense sincerity cannot wholly atone for this loss. Where, however, a quiet refinement and delicacy of style is needed as in those sane and suggestive, atmospheric, critical or introspective studies, such as *By the Ionian Sea,* the unrivalled presentment of *Charles Dickens,* and that gentle masterpiece of softened autobiography, *The Private Papers of Henry Ryecroft* (its resignation and autumnal calm, its finer note of wistfulness and wide human compassion, fully deserve comparison with the priceless work of Silvio Pellico) in which he indulged himself during the last and increasingly prosperous years of his life, then Gissing's style is discovered to be a charmed instrument. That he will *sup late,* our Gissing, we are quite content to believe. But that a place is reserved for him, of that at any rate we are reasonably confident. The three books just named, in conjunction with his short stories and his *New Grub Street* (not to mention *Thyrza* or *The Nether World*), will suffice to ensure him a devout and admiring group of followers for a very long time to come; they accentuate profoundly the feeling of vivid regret and almost personal loss which not a few of his more assiduous readers experienced upon the sad news of his premature death at St Jean-de-Luz on the 28th December 1903, at the early age of forty-six.

Frank Swinnerton (essay date 1923)

SOURCE: "Short Stories," in *George Gissing: A Critical Study,* Kennikat Press, 1923, pp. 125-36.

[In the following essay, Swinnerton offers a mixed assessment of Gissing's short fiction, but praises his adept characterization, particularly his female characters.]

The art of the short story, it has been sufficiently explained by critics who specialise in short stories, is very different from that of the novel. Mr. Max Beerbohm, in a reckless mood, once said that as the brick was to the house, so was the short story to the long one (and it is true that the novel makes in every way greater demands upon the imagination, the invention, and the staying powers of the author); but it is well known that Mr. Beerbohm is a law unto himself in these matters, and others, taking his words in a very literal sense, have thought differently. Gissing might have agreed with Mr. Beerbohm upon the most literal interpretation, for he wrote two little books which were either very long short stories or very short novels; and of his legitimate short stories (by "legitimate," I mean those which do not exceed eight or ten thousand words), quite a number are very small novels, while others again are the merest sketches. Some of these last, perhaps, do not quite justify themselves. They start, and they end; but otherwise have no positive qualities. Others, again, have a pleasant and enjoyable flavour, and justify themselves completely, since they have character and kindliness, and show the author's literary sense.

There are two volumes of Gissing's short stories—*Human Odds and Ends,* and that posthumous collection edited by Mr. Seccombe, *The House of Cobwebs.* The former contains twenty-nine "stories and sketches," the latter fifteen stories, mostly in the author's later key of gentleness and tolerance. Several of them cover ground already used by Gissing—or perhaps one should say that they are a second crop from the same ground—and they all have a quaint air of familiarity, very welcome to any reader acquainted with the author's longer works. They are by no means as good as some other short stories of their day; and their interest as a collection is a personal rather than a pressing one. But they are not negligible. In *Human Odds and Ends,* it seems to me that some of the sketches have no value—such a one as **"In No Man's Land,"** for example, is almost entirely without merit. It is about a man who knows of a string of houses without a landlord, in which people for years have lived rent-free. This man tries to take possession by peremptorily assuming control. He goes to the length of having the houses painted; but in the end he is forced to acknowledge defeat. Such an idea might possibly be made richly comic by a richly comic writer; but in Gissing's hands it produces but the ghost of a smile, as any damp joke might do in retelling. It becomes, in fact, pointless, since it is without character. Such another story as **"In Honour Bound"** is likewise difficult to explain. A philologist, finding himself ruined, confesses to his landlady that he has very little money; and she, on the point of buying a business, asks for some of it to assist in the purchase, and keeps him alive for months until he is again self-supporting. The philologist, intending "in honour bound" to ask if she cares to marry him, is then told of her marriage to another, and is warned by the woman's servant that the new husband would not like him about the house. The only real interest the story has is that it slightly foreshadows the idea of *Will Warburton,* where the hero, being ruined, hears from his landlady of a grocer's business which is for sale, and buys it. But **"In Honour Bound,"** even if it were true to an actual case, is not artistically probable; and Gissing's method does not give it verisimilitude. On the whole, therefore, it is not quite worthy of serious consideration.

Other stories in the same volume have far more value, even if it is slight. Such a story as **"An Inspiration,"** rather Dickensian and fairly sentimental, is interesting on two counts. First of all it imparts a faint warmth of pleasure to the reader, who is gratified at the spectacle of happiness for the downcast; secondly it relates to "Harvey Munden," an interlocutor several times employed by Gissing in both volumes of short stories. At first I supposed Harvey Munden to be intended for Gissing himself, but one of the stories in *The House of Cobwebs* is told in the first person, with Munden for a second figure, and in no case does he attain to any character at all. So his existence, or at least the recurrence of his name, is mysterious, and beyond explanation. **"Sing a Song of Sixpence," "The Day of Silence," "The Tout of Yarmouth Bridge"**—all have qualities of some description. **"The Justice and the Vagabond"** is another episode of interest, relating how a wife-ridden J.P. meets, in the course of his judicial work, a vagabond schoolfellow of his own. They take advantage of the absence of the J.P.'s wife to plan a dash to the far regions of the world; but the J.P. is overtaken by death before he can start. This is well told and good. For the rest, **Human Odds and Ends,** although modestly entitled, does not belie its name. It would have suggested poverty of invention had we not the far richer collection of *The House of Cobwebs* to restore our confidence.

II

Even in *The House of Cobwebs,* we become aware that Gissing had his own conception of the short story. Most of the stories in *The House of Cobwebs* are little narratives, depending hardly at all upon surprise or concentration, and consisting of a series of slight events which may be rounded off into a tale. They are, in short, undramatic. If, without pledging ourselves to any particular definition of what a short story should be, we notice the lack of drama in Gissing's two collections, we perceive a particular fact. That fact is, that the dramatic quality is implicit in most effective short stories—either in the sense of surprise, or unexpectedness, or conflict, or incident. When we find the incidents in Gissing's short stories humdrum, or mild, we recognise that we had expected to be stirred in some way, or to be given some precisely poignant moment, whether of suspense or sympathy. The lack of this emotional heightening in the whole of Gissing's work is notable; in his short stories it becomes, according to the dramatic test, a positive defect. It is a defect in the sense that the stories are not, regarded technically, short stories at all, but merely short as contrasted with long. There is, in essentials, no difference between **"A Song of Sixpence"** (in *Human Odds and Ends*), which is about a woman whose evil habits have been checked by disaster, or **"Humplebee"** (in *The House of Cobwebs*), and such a novel as *Eve's Ransom,* or *Denzil Quarrier.* The superficial difference is entirely one of area.

So it is with the volumes contributed to the "Autonym Library" and to Cassell's "Pocket Library"—*Sleeping Fires* and *The Paying Guest.* These stories are perhaps 30,000 words long, whereas many of Gissing's full-length novels contain 150,000 words; yet, except for the fact that they are written as separate tales, they might almost, as they stand, form contributory portions of longer books. This, strictly speaking, is not the art of the short story as it is generally understood. It is the art of the episode, an art which has hardly received acknowledgment as an art at all. So far, indeed, is that from being the case, that a book

like *The Nether World* may be rightfully condemned as episodic, which means that it does not progress unerringly from chapter to chapter, but is made up of segments or sections which show their joins and let the reader's interest lapse.

Yet if we take these short tales for what they are, we shall see how well they illustrate one aspect of Gissing's art—that of characterisation. He had a very keen sense of those slight personal eccentricities which, duly emphasised, may be made to suggest character in a book. His imagining of character, I should say, was not a strong point, because he never had the jolly visualising faculty of a Dickens, nor the detachment of a modern novelist. His bookish heroes were all inclined to run to one sensitive, retiring pattern, since his sympathy with other types of male was small. His women characters are very much stronger and better, possibly because a slight acquaintance with women, a good deal of intuition, and much self-communing may produce portraits of highly subtilised women transcending the acquaintance of ordinary men. That is to say, where portraits of men demand actual experience of men's ways, the woman of fiction is much more highly conventionalised, besides, of course, being much more interesting, experimentally, to a male novelist.

When Gissing drew character, he did it in firm outline; but he was not always equal to its expansion. His characters—particularly the men—gradually slide into sensitives, or they run between straight lines. Now the art Gissing possessed, of being able to shake up a character in a few words, was particularly useful to him in short stories of the kind we are now considering. A reader does not need to remember the characters in a short story: he wishes simply to retain an impression of the whole thing. So characterisation in short stories is required to be, for effect, sharp and typical; and Gissing's method, which, on a different plane, was the method of Dickens, was adapted to the short story. He would describe somebody as "a middle-aged man, bald, meagre, unimpressive, but wholly respectable in bearing and apparel"; or "A young woman of about eight-and-twenty, in tailor-made costume, with unadorned hat of brown felt, and irreproachable umbrella; a young woman who walked faster than any one in Wattleborough, yet never looked hurried . . . who held up her head . . . and frequently smiled at her own thoughts." The persons, once seen, are recognised sufficiently for the purposes of Gissing's short narrative. The reader has seen, or can delude himself into the belief that he has seen, just such people; and the short story has no room for subtleties of characterisation. Just so does Gissing hit off the people in his less notable novels: "A younger girl, this, of much slighter build; with a frisky gait a jaunty pose of the head; pretty, but thin-featured, and shallow-eyed; a long neck, no chin to speak of, a low forehead with the hair of washed-out flaxen fluffed all over it. Her dress was showy, and in a taste that set the teeth on edge. Fanny French, her name." In a long novel, such a method of characterising people loses its effect, because while it is desirable that the majority of the dramatis personæ should be easily referable to type by the reader, they should present themselves primarily as individuals. In the Gissing short story, on the other hand, the method is used with dexterity, and the stories, being easily read and admirably handled, are in every way enjoyable. They make no great demand upon the reader's emotion, but are intelligible and sufficiently absorbing. And they contain frequent portraits of Gissing's inveterate foes—landladies.

Gissing, whenever he writes about landladies, does so from first-hand knowledge. He writes of them always with feeling—in *Born in Exile*, in *Will Warburton*, in *Eve's Ransom*, in *The Nether World*—it would be possible to marshal such a collection of landladies as to reveal the species in hideous array. So in the short stories, particularly in **"The Prize Lodger"** (*Human Odds and Ends*) and in **"Miss Rodney's Leisure"** (*The House of Cobwebs*). Well does Gissing cry from his heart, in *In the Year of Jubilee*: "To occupy furnished lodgings, is to live in a house owned and ruled by servants; the least tolerable status known to civilisation." Mrs. Turpin, the minor heroine of **"Miss Rodney's Leisure,"** is seen with humour: presumably Miss Rodney treats her as Gissing would have wished all landladies to be treated by their tenants—in a spirit of chastening reproof.

"A Daughter of the Lodge" is a little pointless, as is **"A Poor Gentleman"**; and **"A Charming Family"** is, although clever, unpleasantly cynical. Otherwise, the contents of *The House of Cobwebs,* in addition to being cheerful, are well written and entertaining. To say that they do not challenge comparison with the best English short stories is in no sense to deny their merits. The lack of drama, the lack of any especial poignancy of motif, leaves them smooth and gracefully written tales.

III

The Paying Guest is a bright little story of the suburbs, rather similar in vein to *The Town Traveller*. A young couple, desirous of adding to their income, agree to receive as guest a girl who finds her own home unbearable. It seems that her mother has married a second time, and that her stepfather also has a daughter by his first marriage. The rival daughters quarrel particularly over a lover, who transfers his affections from one to the other. Accordingly, this rather flamboyant girl comes to stay with the suburbans, sets their circle in turmoil, and unexpectedly marries an old and determined suitor. This, however, does not happen until the house has been set on fire by reason of the suitor's ardour. The story is not very merry, and its humour runs to violent and grotesque action; but it is sustained, and does not fail to amuse.

In quite a different key is *Sleeping Fires,* which opens in Greece and deals with the meeting between a man and his illegitimate son (both ignorant of the relation), and their instant attachment. The son, however, dies before his identity is fully disclosed; and interest is then demanded for the father's resuscitated love-story. *Sleeping Fires* is slight; but it is characteristic Gissing, and has passages of good quality, which show how lightly Gissing could design and execute when he had a subject fit to his hand.

These two stories afford the author an opportunity for easy and pleasant writing, quite distinct from the labour which obviously belonged to the writing of their immediate chronological neighbours, *In the Year of Jubilee* and *The Whirlpool*. The year 1895, indeed, which saw the publication of *Eve's Ransom, The Paying Guest,* and *Sleeping Fires,* is one of happy tasks lightly performed; and while neither of the present stories is the equal or even the immediate infe-

rior of *Eve's Ransom,* it may perhaps be inferred from the author's success in such shorter works that he would have been more comfortable as well as more successful if the Victorian novel had died decently before he began to write. It is obvious from Reardon's painful struggles with the three-volume book that Gissing found irksome and laborious the excessive length required by the public. His own case is very little improved nowadays, when many commercial publishers stipulate beforehand that the stories they purchase shall consist of not fewer than 75,000 words; but it is clear that much of what went to the bulking of Gissing's long novels was strained and conscientious page-filling. How much better if the English reader did not count the number of words in the books he busy! If Gissing had written other simple narratives of the same kind as *Eve's Ransom* and these two short novels, his best work, by being purged and simplified, would have stood clear of the wreckage of the Victorian tradition by which it is now encumbered.

Conrad Aiken (essay date 1927)

SOURCE: A review of *A Victim of Circumstances*, in *The Dial,* Vol. LXXXIII, December, 1927, pp. 512-14.

[*In the following review, Aiken discusses Gissing's later works.*]

To this collection of short stories by George Gissing, "never before issued in book form," Mr Alfred Gissing contributes a preface, which is largely a discussion of "realism" in fiction; and in this preface Mr Gissing moves, a little naïvely, to the conclusion that the author of the *Private Papers of Henry Ryecroft* was something more, or better, than a mere realist, because his stories contained a "moral," or here and there pointed to a "higher truth." At this date, it seems a little odd to encounter a critic who is still worrying about the defence of the "ugly" in art, and who finds it necessary to discover a moral or social—if not aesthetic!—justification for such a portrait as that of Mrs Gamp. And it is odder still that Mr Alfred Gissing can proceed, as he does, with his pointing of Gissing's "moral," after quoting a passage from a letter in which Gissing wrote: "Human life has little interest for me, on the whole, save as material for artistic presentation. I can get savage over social iniquities, but, even then, my rage at once takes the direction of planning revenge in artistic work." This could hardly be clearer. If, in his early work (*Demos,* for example) Gissing was occasionally tendentious, in his maturity he was first and last an artist. His purpose, in his descriptions of lower middle-class life, was not moral at all, but aesthetic: his problem was a problem of presentation. His novels and stories were his reports of life as he knew it; he was, in his narrower field, as honest an observer as Trollope; and if he was of far smaller stature as an artist than Chekhov, less poetically gifted, he shared with that great man a tendency to minimize "plot" and to make of his stories mere evocations of life.

In this regard, Gissing was very much ahead of his time. When one reflects that it is now almost a quarter of a century since he died, one reads this posthumous collection of his short stories with astonishment: for with only one or two exceptions these stories are strikingly, in tone and manner, like the sort of thing which, in the hands of such a writer as Katherine Mansfield, critics hailed as revolutionary. In most of these tales the "story" amounts to little or nothing. If one compares them with the contemporary work of Hardy or Meredith or Henry James, one finds a difference as deep as that which severed Chekhov from Turgenev. Here is little or nothing of Hardy's habitual use of tragic or poetic background, his intermittent reference to the backdrop of the Infinite; here is none of Meredith's brilliant, and brilliantly conscious, counterpoint of comment, with its inevitable heightening of distance between the reader and the story; none of the exquisite preparation and elaboration of James. Much more than he admitted, or realized, Gissing *was* interested in "human life"; it is above all for his uncompromising fidelity to his vision that we can still read him with pleasure and profit. He seldom shapes or heads his narrative as these others did, attached less importance than they to dramatic climax. He is content with a bare presentation of a scene or situation.

To say that Gissing would have been liked by Chekhov is to say that he is a "modern"—he is decidedly more modern than Hardy or James. James, of course, would have disapproved of him, as he disapproved of Mr Arnold Bennett, on the ground that he offered his reader a mere slice of life, the *donnée* without the working out. Whatever we may feel about that, and however much this sort of modernity may ultimately make Gissing appear old-fashioned, we must unquestionably accept him as an artist of the Chekhov generation, and a good one. He is not great—he lacks force, depth, range, subtlety; he has almost nothing of Chekhov's poetic profundity, only a tithe of his exquisite sensibility; by comparison with him, Gissing seems prosy, bread-and-butterish. But he is good. He can almost always be counted upon to tell his story with a clear eye and a fine gravity of spirit. There is no rhetorical nonsense about him, he is capable of no literary pyrotechnics, his style is level and undistinguished; but within his limits he is an honest and just creator of people and pictures, exaggerating nothing, never forcing a mood, and often using understatement with the most delicate skill. What could be better than the ending of his charming story, **"The Fate of Humphrey Snell"**? Humphrey was a queer stick—lazy, dreaming, impractical, not very strong; he had a passion for countryside; and eventually found a happy solution of his difficulties by becoming an itinerant herb-collector. He tramped the country, slept where he found himself, enjoyed this simple existence hugely. And then one day he fell in love with a girl who was no better than she should be; applied for a job as steward to a Workman's Club; and asked the girl to marry him. And this is how Gissing ends his story: "Annie, whose handwriting was decipherable only by a lover's eyes, answered his news by return of post: 'Send me money to come i shall want all i have for my things i cant tell you how delited I feal but its that sudin it taks my breth away with heepes of love and—'. . . . There followed a row of crosses, which Humphrey found it easy to interpret. A cross is frequently set upon a grave; but he did not think of that."

That is all—and it is all we need. And Gissing is just as good in his story of the two Cockney families who go to Brighton for their Bank Holidays, or in the story of the matrimonial failures of Miss Jewell. These tales are, in their kind, perfect. The Budges, the Rippingvilles, Miss Jewell, and the two splendid Cockney girls, Lou and Liz,

are done from the life—they are as trenchantly recognizable as Mrs Laura Knight's etchings of Cockney folk on Hampstead Heath. And if the interior of an English middle-class boarding-house, with all its heavy smells and dreary sounds, its aspidistra plant and its scrubbed white step, has ever been better done, one doesn't know where to find it.

Q. D. Leavis (essay date 1938)

SOURCE: "Gissing and the English Novel," in *Scrutiny: A Quarterly Review,* Vol. VII, No. 1, June, 1938, pp. 73-81.

[*In the following review of* Stories and Sketches, *Leavis discusses the biographical background to Gissing's fiction.*]

These stories, which mistaken piety must have induced Mr. A. C. Gissing to publish, will unfortunately persuade no one to read George Gissing who is not already interested in him. They exhibit chiefly his weaknesses and give no indication of his virtues. This is nothing like as interesting a volume of stories as the better of his other two collections, **The House of Cobwebs,** which ought by now to have been put into one of the pocket libraries together with the interesting long 'Introductory Survey' Thomas Seccombe wrote for the 1906 edition. But if this new volume had persuaded reviewers to look up Gissing's novels, re-estimate his achievement, and demand for *New Grub Street* recognition as a classic, its publication would have been justified. There have been no such signs of a reviewer's conscience. It is odd that the Gissing vogue—subsequent to the Meredith vogue and much less widespread—has faded even out of literary history.

This is discouraging, but let us disinter Gissing nevertheless. He wrote twenty-two long novels but only one that posterity would want to read, two books of reminiscence (one the extremely popular *Private Papers of Henry Ryecroft*), two (now three) volumes of short stories, and the best existing critical introduction to Dickens, in twenty-six years of authorship (he died in 1903, aged only forty-six). He has already received adequate biographical and critical attention in *George Gissing: A Critical Study* by Frank Swinnerton, a capital piece of work which looks like remaining the last profitable word on Gissing as a man and a writer. [Nevertheless academic theses have since been excogitated on the same subject in English, German and American].

Gissing's life and temperament, with the problems that they raise, are the key to both his many failures and his single success as an artist. He made a false start in life, it is true (a blasted academic career, a spell in prison, a spell in America, an impossible marriage), but on the literary side his sending a copy of his first novel (*Workers of the Dawn,* 1880) to Frederick Harrison resulted much like Crabbe's application to Burke. Harrison recommended Gissing to Lord Morley, then editor of *The Pall Mall Gazette,* and engaged Gissing as classical tutor to his two elder sons, also helping him to get other pupils. He was thus, with the *entrée* to the *P.M.G.* and as many pupils as he could teach, provided for congenially enough—that is, congenially enough for any other man of letters. But his unfortunate idea of what was suitable for the possessor of literary genius interfered with Harrison's benevolent arrangements. He refused to write more than one sketch for the *P.M.G.* on the grounds that journalism was degrading work for an artist, and though Mr. Austin Harrison says that from 1882 onwards Gissing had a living income from teaching which he could increase at will, he continued to live, if not actually in cellars and garrets on one meal a day as before, at least in near poverty, because, says Mr. H. G. Wells, 'he grudged every moment taken by teaching from his literary purpose, and so taught as little as he could.' The interesting point here is not Gissing's romantic conception of what is due to genius, but that he continued to describe himself as the starving and unrecognized martyr of letters; he was for long neither well-to-do nor famous, but Mr. Austin Harrison characterizes his accounts of his 'continued struggles with abject poverty' as 'fiction of fiction.' Gissing apparently needed that fiction to support his self-esteem, his belief in his own genius, for actually he must have been well aware, like his wretched Edwin Reardon, that he had written mostly what was unworthy of his best abilities. He had to explain his failure by blaming material circumstances; and though his output was really enormous we find him in *Ryecroft,* in the year of his death, picturing himself as the writer obliged to earn his living uncongenially so that he could allow himself, ah but how rarely, the luxury of writing a novel at intervals of many years, and thus was his genius blighted. The facts, as we have seen, were otherwise.

It was not lack of time or means that hampered him, nor yet his unhappy temperament. The latter was perhaps his chief asset, since it produced an absolutely personal way of responding to life and his fellow-men, and when a measure of ultimate success came to (as they say) 'mellow' him the results on his work, as seen in *Ryecroft,* were deplorable. It is instructive to compare the benevolent portrait in *Ryecroft* of the writer N., the successful author and good mixer, with the earlier study of the same type, Jasper Milvain, in *New Grub Street* (when any nineteenth-century novelist names a character Jasper I think we may safely conclude that that character is intended to be the villain). Apart from his temperament all the other qualities he brought to his novels—his scholarship, his bookishness, his enlightened interest in all the leading topics of his day (religious reform, politics, education, emancipation of women, ethics, science, sociology . . . —bear witness to his being an exceptionally cultivated man and exceptionally alive in his age, yet apart from *New Grub Street* how those novels date, how unreadable they now are! [It is thus that I seem to hear the literary critic of *Scrutiny,* Vol. L, describing the novels of Mr. Aldous Huxley, whom Gissing in some respects resembles]. But there was no interaction between his subject-matter and his sensibility, so the exhibition of life he gives us seems arbitrarily blighted by a novelist always functioning below par as it were; Mr. Swinnerton, to account for his unpopularity, says 'he was condemned by novel-readers as a writer who whimpered at life.' But when he took as the subject of a novel his most vital interest—the problem of how to live as a man of letters, the literary world being what it is,[1] without sacrificing your integrity of purpose—he produced his one permanent contribution to the English novel. I think it can be shown to be a major contribution. The subject was both inside and outside him. The best way to suggest his achievement is to say that put beside the other best treatments of the same subject—Maugham's *Cakes and Ale* and the many fine short stories on aspects of the literary life by Henry James which should be read as a whole—Gissing's *New Grub Street* is quite different, equally serious and equally successful as a piece of art.

The Gissing temperament suitably colours the book, which, like *Cakes and Ale,* is consistently written in one tone, here an irony weighted with disgust. This strikes one as being the right outlook on the literary world ("such things were enough to make all literature appear a morbid excrescence upon human life,' the heroine reflects at one point), if less suited to life in general. However, life in general is here seen from the point of view of the slenderly talented Reardon who wants to support his family by his pen and yet at the same time write only novels and essays worthy of himself. We see him go under, weighed down by a wife who thinks social and material success the due of her beauty, by his lack of influential friends, most of all by his choosing to abide by the values of Dr. Johnson in an age where the policy of Alroy Kear had become requisite for success. We see his acquaintance Jasper Milvain deliberately choosing literature as a profitable field for his unliterary talents and ending up more successful than even he had dared expect, his marriage with Reardon's widow (become an heiress) symbolically ending the story. Delicacy and fineness, the strongly noble and the devotedly disinterested elements in human nature, are not ignored or denied, they are presented with complete success—this is a measure of Gissing's total success here—in the persons of Marian Yule, whom Milvain jilts and leaves to wretchedness, and Reardon's friend Biffen who is driven to remove himself from a world that has no use for his devoted labours. Such are shown doomed to misery and failure. The old-style man of letters, part hack and part stiff-necked enthusiast, is skilfully contrasted (Alfred Yule) with the new-style man of straw (Whelpdale) successful because pliant in his complete lack of any literary conscience. There are many masterly studies of the emotions and conduct peculiar to those who live by literature and journalism, and in spite of a certain stiffness of style from which Gissing was never for long free, the smallest touches are effective. The subject seems likely to remain of permanent interest and Gissing has raised crucial problems. The central problem, one ultimately of values, is put by Reardon to his wife thus:

> "'A year after I have published my last book, I shall be practically forgotten . . . And yet, of course it isn't only for the sake of reputation that one tries to do uncommon work. There's the shrinking from conscious insincerity of workmanship which most writers nowadays seem never to feel. "It's good enough for the market"; that satisfies them. And perhaps they are justified. I can't pretend that I rule my life by absolute ideals; I admit that everything is relative. There is no such thing as goodness or badness, in the absolute sense, of course. Perhaps I am absurdly inconsistent when—though knowing my work can't be first-rate—I strive to make it as good as possible. I don't say this in irony, Amy; I really meant it. It may very well be that I am just as foolish as the people I ridicule for moral and religious superstition. This habit of mine is superstitious. How well I can imagine the answer of some popular novelist if he heard me speak scornfully of his books. "My dear fellow," he might say, "do you suppose I am not aware that my books are rubbish? I know it just as well as you do. But my vocation is to live comfortably. I have

a luxurious house, a wife and children who are happy and grateful to me for their happiness. If you choose to live in a garret, and, what's worse, make your wife and children share it with you, that's your concern.'"

Whether Milvain could have existed at that or any time has, by way of objection, been doubted, but Seccombe, who was in a position to speak with authority, says 'Jasper Milvain is, to my thinking, a perfectly fair portrait of an ambitious publicist or journalist of the day—destined by determination, skill, energy and social ambition to become an editor of a successful journal or review, and to lead the life of central London.'

The original temper that the novel manifests is notable in every detail, *e.g.,*

> 'Alfred Yule had made a recognizable name among the critical writers of the day; seeing him in the title-lists of a periodical, most people knew what to expect, but not a few forebore the cutting open of the pages he occupied.'
>
> 'They had had three children; all were happily buried.'
>
> ' " . . . but I was never snobbish. I care very little about titles; what I look to is intellectual distinction."
>
> "Combined with financial success.'
>
> "Why, that is what distinction means."'
>
> 'Amy now looked her years to the full, but her type of beauty, as you know, was independent of youthfulness. You saw that at forty, at fifty, she would be one of the stateliest of dames. When she bent her head towards the person with whom she spoke, it was an act of queenly favour. Her words were uttered with just enough deliberation to give them the value of an opinion; she smiled with a delicious shade of irony; her glance intimated that nothing could be too subtle for her understanding."'

The last example is strikingly in the modern manner, and Gissing's best work, *New Grub Street* almost entirely, seems contemporary with us rather than with Meredith.

As a general thing, the same outlook characterizes Gissing's other novels, but elsewhere it seems merely depressed and therefore depressing. Poor Gissing was sliding down the hill which Dickens and his robust contemporaries had climbed in such high spirits. Seccombe explains it well: 'In the old race, of which Dickens and Thackeray were representative, a successful determination to rise upon the broad back of popularity coincided with a growing conviction that evil in the real world was steadily diminishing . . . In Gissing the misery inherent in the sharp contrasts of modern life was a far more deeply ingrained conviction. He cared little for the remedial aspect of the question. His idea was to analyse this misery as an artist and to express it to the world. One of the most impressive elements in the resulting novels is the witness they bear to prolonged and intense suffering, the suffering of a proud, reserved and oversensitive mind brought into constant contact with the coarse and brutal facts of life. The creator of Mr. Biffen suffers all the torture of the fastidious, the delicately honourable, the scrupulously high-minded in daily contact with persons of blunt feelings, low ideals and base instincts.' Outside *New Grub Street* however you too often feel that the provocation is inadequate to the suffer-

ing. Gissing's susceptibilities are not all equally respectable and in some cases he seems only a querulous old maid, too easily provoked on such subjects as bad cooking, slovenly lodgings, ungenteel personal habits and lack of secondary school education. But in *New Grub Street,* just as what is elsewhere merely bookishness becomes transfused into a passionate concern for the state of literature, so his other minor feelings have turned into positive values, and he produced the one important novel in his long list. It occurs less than half-way down, so its unique success is not a matter of maturity or technical development.

The difference between its technical efficiency and the incompetence of the rest is startling too. It might have been written by a Frenchman rather than an Englishman of those days, and Gissing's interest in and admiration for the nineteenth-century Russian and French novelists is significant. He was never able to make use of them as consistently as did Henry James or Conrad, but he was conscious that the English novel tradition he had inherited would not do and he was groping for help where it seemed to offer. [He later met Meredith and must have studied *The Egoist* with a certain degree of profit. Literary historians ought to inspect *Our Friend the Charlatan* (1901) which obviously was conceived and treated in the spirit of *The Egoist* though without ceasing to be Gissing's]. Gissing is an example of how disastrous it may be for a writer whose talent is not of the first order to be born into a bad tradition. A score and more of novels painfully sweated out of his system, the exceptional system of an exceptionally intelligent and well-educated and devoted writer, and only one that amounted to something. The absence of what now enables anyone in Bloomsbury to write a readable novel made Gissing's efforts mostly futile. Mr. Swinnerton justly talks of 'the wreckage of the Victorian tradition by which it [Gissing's best work] is now encumbered.' But in *New Grub Street* Gissing not only solved, if only temporarily, his own problems, he helped all later writers to solve theirs, and the recognition this novel at one time received from literary men is significant. It is probably an ancestor of the novel of our time.

It is an important link in the line of novels from Jane Austen's to the present which an adult can read at his utmost stretch—as attentively, that is, as good poetry demands to be read—instead of having to make allowances for its being only a novel or written for a certain public or a certain purpose. In the nineteenth century, to take the high lights, Jane Austen, *Wuthering Heights, Middlemarch, The Egoist, New Grub Street* connect the best eighteenth century tradition with the serious twentieth century tradition that Henry James, Conrad, Lawrence, Forster, Joyce and Mrs. Woolf have built up. There are inferior novels (*e.g., The Way of All Flesh*) in this tradition as well as good ones, and very minor successes (like Howard Sturgis's *Belchamber*) as well as major contributions, but they are all immediately recognizable as novels, distinct from what we may more usefully call fiction. It is time the history of the English novel was rewritten from the point of view of the twentieth century (it is always seen from the point of view of the mid-nineteenth), just as has been done for the history of English poetry. The student would undoubtedly be glad to be allowed to reorganize his approach and revise the list of novels he has to accept as worth attention; it would be a matter chiefly of leaving out but also of substitution, for the list consists only of conventional values. I don't know who will dare touch off the first charge to blow up those academic values. Mr. Forster once made an attempt on Scott and the response in the academic world was most interesting; the subsequent Scott centenary was a rally of the good men and true to batten down the hatches on Mr. Forster's wholesome efforts to have that reputation reconsidered. What is commonly accepted as the central tradition is most easily examined in the middling practitioner—such as Trollope or Charles Reade. *The Cloister and the Hearth* is a puerile example of what *Esmond* is a highly accomplished form of, but both are undeserving of serious attention and both are on the educational syllabus, at different ends; though I never knew anyone but the old-fashioned kind of schoolmaster who could bear the former, and the latter's ventriloquial waxworks in period costume (prick them and do they not bleed red paint) are a direct ancestor of Sir Hugh Walpole's own great trilogy which will in time, who can doubt, get on the list too. It is time also that we sorted out the novels which form or enrich the real tradition of the English novel from those which (like Trollope's and Wells's) are rather contributions to the literary history of their time and to be read as material for the sociologist, from those which (like Scott's and R.L.S.'s and George Moore's) perpetrate or perpetuate bogus traditions, from those which (like Charlotte Brontë's) are the ill-used vehicles for expressing a point of view or as in other novelists' hands (Aldous Huxley's), ideas; and from all the other kinds. As one step towards this desirable scheme I suggest that *New Grub Street* be made generally available by reissuing it in 'Everyman' or 'The World's Classics' editions. Sir Humphrey Milford has already ventured to make some surprising additions to the world's classic novels on his own responsibility (Constance Holmes for instance) and Messrs. Dent have similarly helped Galsworthy and Priestley to get on everyman's list of great novels, so they might do something for Gissing whose best novel will soon be due for a half-centenary.

Notes

1. It seems to have began to be as we know it in Gissing's time. Jasper Milvain differs from Alroy Kear (*Cakes and Ale*) only in being a simpler psychological study. Reviewing was much the same as now: 'The book met with rather severe treatment in critical columns; it could scarcely be ignored (the safest mode of attack when one's author has no expectant public) . . . ' '"The struggle for existence among books is nowadays as severe as among men. If a writer has friends connected with the press, it is the plain duty of those friends to do their utmost to help him. What matter if they exaggerate, or even lie? The simple, sober truth has no chance whatever of being listened to, and it's only by volume of shouting that the ear of the public is held."' Conditions governing material success were taking modern shape: '"Literature nowadays is a trade. Putting aside men of genius, who may succeed by mere cosmic force, your successful man of letters is your skilful tradesman . . . To have money is becoming of more and more importance in a literary career; principally because to have money is to have friends. Year by year, such influence grows of more account . . . Men won't succeed in literature that they may get into society, but will get into society that they may succeed in literature."'

Elsie B. Adams (essay date 1970)

SOURCE: "Gissing's Allegorical 'House of Cobwebs'," in *Studies in Short Fiction,* Vol. VII, No. 2, Spring, 1970, pp. 324-26.

[*In the following essay, Adams deems Gissing's short story "The House of Cobwebs" as an allegory depicting the fate of the artist in society.*]

Literary critics class George Gissing most frequently with the realistic-naturalistic writers of the late nineteenth century. However, as Wendell V. Harris has noted in "An Approach to Gissing's Short Stories," Gissing's stories lack "the omnipresent greyness and bitterness of tone" usually attributed to late nineteenth-century realistic fiction and contain instead warmth of tone, humorous touches, and subtle character portraiture.[1] These characteristics are especially notable in Gissing's short story **"The House of Cobwebs,"** which Mr. Harris finds typical of Gissing's best work. The story is, in fact, even further removed from the characteristics usually associated with realistic-naturalistic fiction in its being an allegory depicting the fate of the artist in middle-class society.

The plot of **"The House of Cobwebs"** is hardly eventful: a 23-year-old artist, Goldthorpe, decides to move to cheaper quarters until he has finished his first book; he discovers a dilapidated and decaying house, the "house of cobwebs," and rents a room from the owner, Mr. Spicer, who also lives there. A friendship develops and, as the weeks go by, Mr. Spicer gardens in the jungle-like, weed-filled yard, and Goldthorpe's novel progresses. But in the August heat Goldthorpe becomes ill and finishes his novel only with difficulty. Finally, very ill, he moves to his mother's house for recuperation, where the doctor tells him that he "must have been living in some very unhealthy place."[2] Goldthorpe returns to London when a publisher accepts the manuscript of his book, after numerous rejections. When he looks up his old friend at the house of cobwebs, he finds that the roof has fallen in and Mr. Spicer is in the hospital recovering from injuries. At the end of the story, Mr. Spicer is expressing pleasure at hearing of the acceptance of the book and resolving to continue to cultivate the garden of the now uninhabitable house. On the literal level, the story is primarily valuable, as Mr. Harris says, for its "description of Spicer's picturesque joy in having a garden of his own and in being allowed to shelter 'a literary man,' and in Goldthorpe's own experience in producing his first book."[3] But the primary meaning of the story resides, I think, on the allegorical-symbolical level.

The central symbol in the story, as the title suggests, is the house of cobwebs, and we can best understand the nature of the house by looking at the man who lives there, the epitome of middle-class virtue and aspiration, Mr. Spicer. He is an "unimposing person," a "respectable figure." He is middle-aged, dresses "like a decent clerk or shopkeeper," and has a "face of much simplicity and good-nature." He has "a soft, modest, deferential smile" and "a corresponding voice." His life history includes twenty-five years of employment in a midland town, where he rose from chemist's errand-boy to chemist's assistant. His lifelong ambition has been to own his own house, "not only a rented house, but one in which you could live and die, feeling that no one had a right to turn you out." When he inherited a London property from an uncle, he discovered, to his disappointment, that the property was in near ruins and due to revert soon to the ground-landlord. Nevertheless, he loves his house because, as he explains to Goldthorpe, "the sense of possession is very sweet. Property's property, even when it's leasehold and in ruins." In his "unimposing" appearance, in his unspectacular rise at the chemist's shop, in his desire to own a modest property and his delight in that ownership, Mr. Spicer would seem to be representative of ordinary middle-class character and ambition. And indeed his intellectual and aesthetic interests bear out this analysis of him. His chief pleasure is digging in his garden in an attempt to grow vegetables. We read that his "mental development had ceased more than twenty years ago, when, after extreme efforts, he had attained the qualification of chemist's assistant. Since then the world had stood still with him. Though a true lover of books, he knew nothing of any that had been published during his own lifetime." His library consists of "English classics or obscure writers of the early part of the nineteenth century"; his favorite poet is Cowper, "whose moral sentiments greatly soothed him"; he distrusts fiction and judges all literature "solely from the moral point of view." To counter-balance these essentially negative characteristics (at least they are negative to the young artist, "whose brain thrilled in response to modern ideas") are Mr. Spicer's kindness and his earnestness—what Gissing calls his "simple goodness." In the story, Mr. Spicer is neither satirized nor idealized: he is perhaps foolish in his reverence for the ruined property; his gardening produces vegetables which "for the most part. . . . lacked savour"; he is intellectually and aesthetically limited; but he is generous, earnest, and friendly, the sort of man Goldthorpe respects and likes.

However, close association with Mr. Spicer and his house almost destroys the artist, who, like Gissing himself, considers himself "the destined leader of a new school of fiction."[4] Goldthorpe first sees the house of cobwebs as he is walking through the London suburbs and his eyes turn to "a spot of desolation," a row of houses "once tenanted by middle-class folk, but now for some time unoccupied and unrepaired." He discovers that one of the houses is inhabited when he hears Mr. Spicer playing "Home, Sweet Home" on a concertina. Though Mr. Spicer loves it, his house is decaying, dirty, and ugly; it is called a "dead house." The brick is weathered, the windows and doors boarded up, the window panes broken, the paint faded and blistered, the garden strips in front filled with "a little wilderness of coarse grass, docks, nettles, and degenerate shrubs" and the gardens in back "threatened by a wild, rank growth of grasses and weeds, which had obliterated the beds, hidden the paths, and made of the whole garden plot a green jungle." The interior is dominated by cobwebs and a "peculiar odour": "The window was overspun with cobwebs, thick, hoary; each corner of the ceiling was cobweb-packed; long, dusty filaments depended along the walls"; "In the front passage, on the stairs, on the landing, every angle and every projection had its drapery of cobwebs. The stuffy, musty air smelt of cobwebs." In this house the artist is destined for destruction as surely as is the fly he hears one day "buzzing . . . entangled in one of these webs." However, because he is in need of money, Goldthorpe furnishes a room and moves into the house. He is "in the highest spirits, full of energy and hope," and confident that he will produce good work; "he was really

at home; the bed he slept on, the table he ate at and wrote upon, were his own possessions." In other words, the artist has now his own place in Mr. Spicer's world: he has relative comfort (at least freedom from pressing financial worries), companionship, and property.

Unfortunately, Goldthorpe cannot discuss his art with his friend, whose archaic literary tastes and moralistic attitude toward literature conflict with Goldthorpe's. Thus deprived of intellectual stimulation, Goldthorpe is overcome by "a treacherous languor"; his brain becomes "sluggish and the hand slow," and "Only with a great effort" can he finish his book. He eventually becomes despondent and feverish, learns "to dislike this strange abode," and realizes that "it would be impossible for him to dwell here much longer."

If my reading of the story is correct, Gissing is saying through the symbol of the cobweby and decaying house peopled by the kindly but inartistic bourgeois that the artist cannot survive in a middle-class world; it offers him security and companionship, but it stifles his brain and makes his work difficult, and finally incapacitates him. Significantly, when a publisher accepts Goldthorpe's avant-garde novel, the roof of the house of cobwebs collapses. This is probably an indication of the nature of Goldthorpe's "new school of fiction": like the hard-hitting, iconoclastic fiction of some late nineteenth-century realists, it causes to collapse the middle-class milieu out of which it grew. Though that collapse almost destroys Mr. Spicer, he remains attached to the old house, characteristically attributing the disaster to divine "chastisement for overweening desires" and resolving, Candide-like, to continue to cultivate his garden. On the other hand, Goldthorpe presumably has learned that he cannot survive in the house of cobwebs and that, though cultivation of the garden may produce a more or less contented life, it will produce no art, only savorless vegetables.

Notes

1. *Studies in Short Fiction,* II (Winter 1965), 138, 142.

2. In *The English Short Story in Transition, 1880-1920,* Helmut E. Gerber, ed. (New York, 1967), p. 235. All my references to "The House of Cobwebs" are to this edition, pp. 219-237, which makes the story readily available to students of late-Victorian and Edwardian literature.

3. Page 139.

4. Apropos of his social purpose as novelist, Gissing wrote to his brother (3 Nov. 1880), "Certainly I have struck out a path for myself in fiction." *Letters of George Gissing to Members of His Family,* Algernon and Ellen Gissing, eds. (Boston, 1927), p. 83. Throughout his career Gissing crusaded to emancipate the novelist from Mrs. Grundy.

Thomas C. Ware (essay date 1972)

SOURCE: "Jerusalem Artichokes in Gissing's Garden: A Postscript to the Allegorical Readings of 'House of Cobwebs'," in *Studies in Short Fiction,* Vol. IX, No. 1, Winter, 1972, pp. 86-9.

[*In the following essay, Ware expounds on the allegorical meaning of the Jerusalem artichokes in "The House of Cobwebs."*]

In her recent note in *Studies in Short Fiction,*[1] Miss Elsie B. Adams convincingly makes the point that in **"The House of Cobwebs"** George Gissing's principal theme is the difficulty (perhaps even the inability) of the artist's survival in the rank domesticity of the middle-class world. Such a world is symbolized in this work by the "cobweby and decaying house," inhabited—but only on lease-hold—by the kindly bourgeois Mr. Spicer, who offers an impoverished young writer a haven while he works on his novel. I would like to suggest that Mr. Gissing, who was not simply the flat realist nor the heavy-handed symbolist he appears to some readers, skillfully refined his theme in this story by the use of some details that Professor Adams either overlooked or deemed not important enough to analyze: the Jerusalem artichokes prized by the host, Spicer.

As readers of Gissing's story will note, Spicer is a fancier of eighteenth- and early nineteenth-century English literature; but he loved especially the moral sentiments of Cowper,[2] a soothing writer who romanticized a limited circle of domestic niceties. Cowper took pleasure, for instance, in tending his garden. Indeed, one long, popular section of his most famous poem, *The Task,* was subtitled "The Garden." It seems therefore that Gissing had Cowper and his virtues clearly in mind—rather than Candide—as he slyly characterized Spicer as a mild, retiring man of simple but enervating values, a man who loves to tend a disorderly garden of weeds and wild vegetables attached to the old house. Allegorically, Spicer is the antithesis of the young artist, Goldthorpe, "whose brain thrilled in response to modern ideas, and who regarded himself as the destined leader of a new school of fiction" (p. 230). And important for the discussion here, Spicer believes that his garden can produce a nourishment in the months ahead.

The Jerusalem artichokes are mentioned at several key places in the course of the narrative. While they are not central and unavoidable—as the "symbol" of the house is—nevertheless, as readers we are clearly led to inquire why the writer invested so much importance in them. Early in the story, for example, Goldthorpe recognizes them for what they are as he first sees them in the picturesque garden.

> "Why, there are potatoes growing there. And what are those things? Jerusalem artichokes? And look at that magnificent thistle; I never saw a finer thistle in my life! And poppies—and marigolds—and broad-beans—and isn't that lettuce?"
>
> Mr. Spicer was red with gratification. (p. 224)

The garden begins to yield food, but it is meager and savorless. The artichokes soon become, for these reasons, a great hope for the future. Through inquiries, Spicer has discovered that the edible portions of these plants are not ready to eat until the autumn—when, he announces, the "first frost is said to improve them. They're fine plants—very fine plants" (p. 231). Consequently, it would be deplorable for Goldthorpe, whose work at this point is steadily progressing, to quit the house before this tuber comes to maturity.

The plants flourish during the summer months, even as the two men grow increasingly friendly; but by contrast Goldthorpe's work goes slowly during the treacherous languor of the hot days. He thinks of other years at the seaside, where he believes he now ought to be. In a moment of luxuriating generosity, he promises to take Spicer there as his guest with the profits he already anticipates from the sale of his book. In short, he is almost lulled into domestic idleness, and with it, confusion about how to finish his project. Occasionally, he hears the sounds of a fly entrapped in one of the webs in his room—"It did not seem worthwhile to brush the new webs away" (p. 233). As Professor Adams indicated, this clear little symbolic pattern is foreboding evidence of the dangerous situation, where the artist begins to think of luxuries as necessities and material welfare as the principal by-product of his labors.

He does complete his novel, but its initial rejection drops him into an illness that seems at first catastrophic; in allegorical terms, however, it is a ritual of purification. The doctor's diagnosis confirms the obvious: that he has been living in an unhealthy place. And it is at this point ironic that a letter from Mr. Spicer expresses hope that his literary friend would soon be back "to taste the Jerusalem artichokes." (p. 235)

With perseverance, Goldthorpe finds a publisher, and as Professor Adams's summation points out, the collapse of the roof back at the old house, nearly destroying Spicer, symbolizes the impact of the avant-garde fiction on the entrenched but crumbling values of the late Victorian milieu.

More to the point here, Goldthorpe is denied by his fortunate illness the dubious joys of feasting on the artichokes, though he is assured by Spicer that they were worth the wait. The story closes with this dialogue.

> " . . . And how I grieve that you were not with me at the time of the artichokes—just at the moment when they were touched by the first frost!"
>
> "Ah! They were really good, Mr. Spicer?"
>
> "Sir, they seemed good to *me,* very good. Just at the moment of the first frost!" (p. 237)

The "first frost" clearly heralds the coming of bleak winter for Mr. Spicer and what he represents—and what he represents includes faith in the sustaining power of this curious wild vegetable, brought to our attention on at least three important occasions in the story.

Gissing's father, according to several biographical treatments, was an accomplished and enthusiastic botanist. Gissing himself was a precocious student, one we should expect to have more than a passing curiosity in his father's interests. One may easily find support for this assumption in the clear and specific references to botanical species in Gissing's published correspondence with H. G. Wells. For example, in one letter, (October 3, 1897) Gissing wrote Wells from Italy, noting that the wayside he had been traveling was "particularly English": " . . . very strange, amid grapes, olives and figs, to see hedges of bramble overgrown with traveler's joy, flowering dogwood, the hawkweeds, mints, and so on—"[3]

Doubtless Gissing knew a great deal about the history and the strange characteristics of the sunflower called the

Jerusalem artichoke (*Helianthus tuberosus*), a plant that had the reputation of spreading everywhere, so that no matter how carefully a gardener set it out, he must beware of its "choking" capabilities. If only for the immediate, recognizable implications of "ART-I-CHOKE," as this term would apply to Spicer's role and to the theme of this particular story, the species would draw our attention. Some aspects of the folk etymology suggest forcefully that there are ironic popular misunderstandings about the plant: "Jerusalem" from Italian *girasole*—i.e., "following the sun"; and "artichoke," derived from several Mediterranean languages suggesting "cabbage," but passing into English as roughly "choking the garden" (Latin *hortus,* for "garden"); hence "choking the heart." According to some versions of its history, this plant was introduced to Europe by Samuel de Champlain, who brought it back from Cape Cod. Evidently these "artichokes" were for a long time used extensively in eastern European countries as fodder for stock. But by Gissing's time, botanists had come to recognize that this tuber had little or no food value. Today, reference to any standard text on the subject will verify this conclusion.

In **"The House of Cobwebs,"** Mr. Spicer's insistence on the Jerusalem artichokes as promising a fine meal subtly elaborates the theme that the major symbol of the rotting old house only announces: that if the artist, Goldthorpe, continued to depend on the misguided energies and the imperfect understanding of his well-meaning host, Spicer, he would be in for somewhat less than nutritious offerings.

Notes

1. Elsie B. Adams, "Gissing's Allegorical 'House of Cobwebs,'" *Studies in Short Fiction,* 7 (Spring 1970), 324-326.

2. George Gissing, "The House of Cobwebs" in *The English Short Story in Transition 1880-1920,* ed. Helmut F. Gerber, (New York: Pegasus, 1967), p. 230. All subsequent references will be noted parenthetically in the text.

3. *George Gissing and H. G. Wells: Their Friendship and Correspondence,* edited with an Introduction by Royal A. Gettmann (Urbana: University of Illinois Press, 1961), p. 60.

Robert L. Selig (essay date 1983)

SOURCE: "Short Stories," in *George Gissing,* Twayne Publishers, 1983, pp. 112-23.

[*In the following essay, Selig outlines the themes and plots of Gissing's most accomplished short stories: "A Victim of Circumstances," "Comrades in Arms," "The Schoolmaster's Vision," and "The House of Cobwebs."*]

George Gissing's still-underrated short stories deserve to rank among the best of the late-Victorian era. He wrote some 110 in all, many very fine. Once he had mastered the art of brief narrative, it allowed him to break away from the wills, rival lovers, and theatrical climaxes that often clutter his novels. His finest short stories end, not with a melodramatic bang, but an ironic whimper. Yet even Giss-

ing's admirers tend to ignore his impressive short fiction, perhaps because it has become rather inaccessible.[1]

Gissing's work in the short-story form falls into three distinct periods. First came the 1877 journeyman pieces written in America and the few additional ones from 1878 to 1882 that he wrote back in England but could not sell. Because they follow such mid-Victorian fashions as Poe-like horror and Dickensian moral sentiment, these pieces have little resemblance to Gissing's mature work. Yet these amateurish tales have autobiographical interest. Their fictional themes of guilt seem closely related to Gissing's own crime and punishment in Manchester.

After these early pieces, Gissing produced only three more short stories in the 1880s: **"Phoebe"** (written 1883; pub. 1884; rpt. *SS,* 15-44), **"Letty Coe"** (written 1884; pub. 1891; rpt. *SS,* 47-68), **"Mutimer's Choice"** (written 1884; pub. 1970 in *EF,* 242-53). All three deal with a lower-class milieu like that of the early novels. In **"Phoebe"** an artificial-flower girl finds a much-needed sum of money only to have it stolen by another proletarian woman whom the good-natured heroine has befriended. In **"Letty Coe"** an accidental fire suffocates a costermonger's daughter, along with the donkey that he needs to earn his living. In **"Mutimer's Choice"** an injured workingman refuses to have his legs amputated, because he wishes to die and free his wife to marry the man whom she loves. Although these pieces display more skill than Gissing's earlier short fiction, they crowd too many calamities into too small a space for convincing emotional impact.

His most impressive proletarian short story came long after this period. **"Lou and Liz"** (1893; rpt. *VC,* 219-36) depicts the friendship of two working-girl roommates deserted by their men. Lou helps support both Liz and Liz's bastard child but considers herself superior until she learns that her own missing "husband" had committed bigamy with her. The subtle final scene of **"Lou and Liz"** shows how easily the resilient heroine gets over her chagrin at discovering herself unmarried. The whole piece reads like a correction of *Thyrza*'s idealizing softness.

By 1891 Gissing had perfected the art of short fiction. From then until his death, he wrote seventy-eight short stories, many of them remarkably fine. Their emphasis falls upon the lower middle class. A census of the fictional population of these mature pieces would include struggling writers and artists, traveling salesmen, shopkeepers, clerks, domestic servants, governesses, barmaids, and landlords. These pieces avoid the fault of the "exponent" male—that fantasy gentleman of leisure who inhabits Gissing's lesser novels. Above all, these stories emphasize an inextricable connection between social status and character.

Gissing's short fiction tends to center around one quintessential theme: the constrictive force of social class and narrow financial means upon aspiring men and women. Usually, the protagonists have shabby-genteel backgrounds and eke out livings in dreary or precarious work. The characters frequently clutch at an unwise marriage to escape from social frustration but find still more frustration as a husband or a wife than in unmarried loneliness. The plots hinge upon the characters' reactions to their straightened circumstances: trivial vexations, petty but stinging failures, ironically minor successes, and obscure struggles for a little self-esteem.

In these impressive yet understated pieces, Gissing shuns melodramatic twists. Instead his plot reversals remain fundamentally slight and subtle. An elderly governess saves just enough to buy a pathetically small retirement annuity (**"An Old Maid's Triumph"**—pub. 1895; rpt. *HOE,* 197-202). An overbearingly fastidious lodger marries his super-neat landlady and finds that she nags him incessantly (**"The Prize Lodger"**—written 1895; pub. 1896; rpt. *HOE,* 133-54). An impoverished book collector destroys his wife's health by cramming dusty books into their tiny living quarters, and only her near death persuades him to renounce his beloved scruffy collection (**"Christopherson"**—pub. 1902; rpt. *HC,* 47-67). An up-till-now sheltered middle-class woman takes work as a mere housemaid, proudly masters her lowly duties, but finds herself trapped in them for life (**"The Foolish Virgin"**—written 1895; pub. 1896; rpt. *VC,* 187-216). A rebellious young daughter of a gardener and a housemaid defies their aristocratic employers but later must beg humiliating forgiveness to save her parents' jobs (**"A Daughter of the Lodge"**—written 1900; pub. 1901; rpt. *HC,* 175-91). Taken as a whole, Gissing's mature short fiction portrays the ironic comedy of shabby-genteel frustrations. A detailed look at a few of his very finest pieces may help to suggest his achievement in this genre.

"A Victim of Circumstances"

Gissing's first truly excellent short story, **"A Victim of Circumstances"** (written 1891; pub. 1893; rpt. *VC,* 3-36), resembles Henry James's tales of artists and writers[2]. Within Gissing's other works, *New Grub Street*'s many vignettes of shabby-genteel authors provide the closest parallels to this splendid short piece. **"A Victim of Circumstances"** deals with a straightened artistic couple, Horace and Hilda Castledine. The talentless husband thinks himself a Victorian Michelangelo, yet the truly gifted wife regards her own work as scarcely worthwhile. When a famous landscape painter happens to visit the Castledines' house, he shows contempt for Horace's vast amateurish canvas but admires Hilda's watercolor landscapes. The mortified husband pretends that he himself painted his wife's pictures. Meanwhile, in order to support the family, she has sold a few to a local art collector but concealed that she has painted them. When she learns of her husband's lie, she allows him to take the credit for her art rather than expose him to public humiliation. She resolves to sign all her future landscapes as H. Castledine, so that Horace can continue to say that he has done them. Eventually she perceives her husband's lack of talent, as well as her own undeniable gift. Yet when he gives up painting for full-time teaching, she abandons her own landscapes in order not to shame him by her steady artistic achievement. After her ultimate death, Horace continues to boast of "his" early watercolors. He laments having lost his talent but insists that he would have painted many great pictures except for the burden of two children and a wife.

Within the story as a whole, the ironic contrast between Horace's grandiose daubings and Hilda's modest watercolors rests upon actual developments in nineteenth-century art. He attempts a form of academic history painting popular in the early Victorian period but already old-fashioned

by 1869—the time of the story's beginning (*VC,* 6). He labors, specifically, at a huge canvas called *The Landing of Joseph of Arimathaea in Britain*. He claims that the finished picture will rival Michelangelo, Raphael, and Leonardo da Vinci (*VC,* 5-6, 9-11, 21-22).[3] She, on the other hand, works at unpretentious landscapes. Modestly, she considers herself a mere amateur, although the visiting painter suspects that, with a few years' practice, her watercolors might someday approach those of David Cox (1783-1859) and Copley Fielding (1787-1855), fine English artists if not Michelangelos (*VC,* 11-13, 18).[4] If her husband has studied anatomy (*VC,* 8-9), Victorian prudishness has blocked an artist such as Hilda from working with the nude, so that her choice of genres has remained somewhat limited.[5] But, ironically, Hilda's landscapes have far greater relevance than her husband's garish work to late-Victorian trends in painting. Ultimately, though, she must renounce all creativity in order to protect his unjustified self-esteem.

Significantly, however, this wifely renunciation does not bring Hilda old-fashioned marital bliss but, rather, smoldering frustration, which she hides from her egocentric husband: "No one divined what lay beneath her tender smile, with its touch of sadness—least of all Horace himself. No one knew of the long sleepless nights when she wept silently over a glorious hope that had come only to vanish. She had her moments of rebellion, but subdued herself. . . . An artist no longer, however her artistic soul might revolt, the duties of wife and mother must suffice for all her energies, and supply all her happiness" (*VC,* 31-32). The passage hints that a wife's creative ambitions have as much legitimacy as those of her mate. Even the consoling hope that Hilda may derive compensatory "happiness" as a dutiful "wife and mother" melts away in the sardonic epilogue. Her renunciation, we learn, has failed to preserve the family's well-being: her boy dies prematurely, her girl marries unhappily, and her husband debases himself by concealing Hilda's sacrifice even sixteen years after her death (*VC,* 36). His self-pitying bleat—"You can't imagine how completely an artist is at the mercy of circumstances" (*VC,* 34)—applies, ironically, not to himself, but to the remarkable woman whose talents he and society had thwarted by the doctrine of masculine supremacy.

"Comrades in Arms"

The delightfully wry **"Comrades in Arms"** (written 1893; pub. 1894; rpt. *HOE,* 1-19) stands as Gissing's most sympathetic portrayal of a so-called unfeminine woman, although it also has some connection with **"The Poet's Portmanteau"** (written 1893, pub. 1895; rpt. *HOE,* 74-91) as an attack on feminine stereotypes. At Wilfrid Langley's usual lunchtime restaurant, this under-thirty novelist encounters Bertha Childerstone, his "comrade in arms"—an over-thirty newspaperwoman who has just reviewed his latest book very favorably. The unmaidenlike Miss Childerstone boasts of having earned enough from her scribbling to equip a younger sister with a trousseau and dowry and send her off to marry a "soft-hearted" man in Natal (*HOE,* 3-4). But Langley perceives that Miss Childerstone has made herself ill through her selfless journalistic drudgery. He hurries her home in a cab and writes her next article for her. He provides a doctor and nurse and also a generous loan. As Miss Childerstone slowly recovers, he suddenly perceives her subtle attractiveness.

But when he kisses this self-sufficient woman and then proposes marriage, she simply calls him "goosey" (*HOE*, 14). She promptly goes away without telling him where and refuses to see him again until they have "both recovered" (*HOE*, 17). As a sly suggestion that he also take a trip to cool down his sudden passion, she sends him "a large and handsome travelling-bag" (*HOE*, 18). He does travel abroad for a month, and then he and Miss Childerstone resume their old relationship as mere literary "comrades in arms."

The story emphasizes the spirited independence of its late-Victorian liberated heroine. Miss Childerstone takes pride not only in her professional career, but also in her role of substitute father for her conventional younger sister—specifically labeled "an old-fashioned girl, . . . an ideal housewife and mother" (*HOE*, 5). The emancipated woman journalist has resolved the basic tensions that Simone de Beauvoir found some fifty years later in twentieth-century career women. Unlike de Beauvoir's "independent" women, who accept the double burden of professional work and the feminine duty of maintaining a "scrupulously neat" home,[6] Miss Childerstone thrives in an untidy apartment strewn with books and newspapers. She herself connects her resistance to marriage with an unwillingness to dust and straighten like the usual domesticated female: " . . . I don't want to marry," she declares. "Look at this room, dirty and disorderly. This is all the home I care for" (*HOE*, 16, and see also 7 and 10). Unlike de Beauvoir's anxious professional women, Gissing's cheerful heroine feels no obligation to "do her own cooking" but goes to eat alone "at a restaurant as a man would in her place."[7] The story hinges, in fact, upon Miss Childerstone's unescorted encounter with the protagonist in a London restaurant. And unlike de Beauvoir's half-liberated women, Gissing's heroine feels no temptation to act girlishly and thus lure men by denying her superior "brain."[8] Indeed, Miss Childerstone teases and contradicts Langley with good-humored self-confidence. **"Comrades in Arms"** subverts the common belief that men must feel sexual repugnance for a genuinely masterful woman.

In an amusing passage toward the story's close, assembled party guests make fun of the absent heroine without knowing that the hero has become entranced with her:

> "Gone as war correspondent, I shouldn't wonder," said a young man; and the laughter of the company appreciated his joke.
>
> "Oh, she really is too mannish," remarked a young matron. "I suppose you study her as a curiosity, Mr. Langley?"
>
> "We're great chums," Wilfrid answered with a laugh.

The young man's ridicule of Miss Childerstone as probable war correspondent hints that she strikes him as an androgynous freak, a he-man in petticoats. And the young matron assumes that Langley can have only scientific interest in the apparently sexless heroine. But the hero's laughing description of himself and Miss Childerstone as merely "great chums" conceals the ironic truth: far from repelling him by so-called masculinity, she has had to fend him off, gently but firmly, to keep her contented independence.

"The Schoolmaster's Vision"

With its subtly ironic criticism of late-Victorian prudery, **"The Schoolmaster's Vision"** (written 1895; pub. 1896;

rpt. *VC*, 127-44) achieves greater objectivity than another notable Gissing piece about sexual frustration—**"A Lodger in Maze Pond"** (written 1893; pub. 1895; rpt. *HC*, 241-64). As a preparation for his "vision," the headmaster of a second-rate school for boys, forty-year-old Mr. Donne, feels sexually aroused by Mrs. Argent, the young widowed mother of his pupil Willie Argent.[9] Fifteen years previously, Donne had settled for this mediocre job in order to marry his fiancée and provide for her. But she soon revealed herself as a mindless homemaker—the boring embodiment of high-Victorian propriety. At occasional guilty moments, he had day-dreamed of supplementing his wife with a mistress, although Gissing avoids approval of Donne's adulterous thoughts by killing off Mrs. Donne long before the narrative starts. Previous to meeting Mrs. Argent, Donne thinks her selfish and neglectful because she has failed to visit her son. But when she finally does pay a visit, she whizzes in on a bicycle and captivates Donne by her emancipated manner, her spectacular good looks, and her daringly short skirts.[10] He conceals his lust, however, because of pedantic reserve but also because this wealthy young woman far outranks him socially. And before she rushes off on her bicycle, he has to confess that he does not even know how to ride one. The frustrated hero flees his campus and fails to return for the night. Instead, he takes a room at a small country inn and, alone in bed, experiences wildly erotic dreams.

Within his dream world, Donne miraculously rides a bicycle but cannot keep up with the cycling Mrs. Argent, who laughs at him scornfully. Then he sees her son weeping by the roadside, and, like the boy, the man begins to weep. Finally, his dream shifts to school, where Donne delivers a cynical harangue to a graduating student: beware of sexually dull and mindless wives. Upon awakening, the headmaster returns to his school and finds Mrs. Argent's son in actual tears. The boy has learned that his mother will remarry but will leave him in the care of an uncle. Donne comforts the boy with a falsely hearty speech about the character-building value of suffering. As the story ends, the hero seems as pompously donnish as ever.

Gissing makes his protagonist a schoolmaster because of the tendency of such academic authorities to indoctrinate the young in the sexual proprieties. Walter E. Houghton has noted how the most influential of all Victorian headmasters, Thomas Arnold of Rugby, felt obsessed by a need to eradicate schoolboy "sexual evil": "dirty jokes, masturbation, . . . sodomy."[11] Unlike Rugby's Doctor of Divinity, Donne is "not in orders," but "he could on occasion discourse with the true clerical impressiveness," and Mrs. Argent, in fact, mistakenly called him "Dr." (*VC*, 131, 132). If his long "magisterial gown" symbolizes propriety, Mrs. Argent's short bicycle skirt represents sexual freedom. As she speeds unchaperoned along the public road, her cycling suggests the sexual act itself—an act from which Donne stands excluded. And her hedonistic refusal to play the role of mother contrasts specifically with Mr. Donne's belief that duties to "wife and family" have crushed his free spirit (*VC*, 140). Within his extended nightmare, the bicycle represents not merely sexual love, but a sexual love without entangling domesticity—an unrestrained eroticism that the hero cannot achieve even in mere dreams. Mrs. Argent complains of his unsuccessful efforts to keep up with her cycling: "Oh, can't you do better than *that*? You really must be quick; I can't wait for you" (*VC*, 138-39).

Written five years before Sigmund Freud's *The Interpretation of Dreams* (1900), Gissing's fictional dream stands somewhere between Freud and mid-Victorian medicine. Instead of revealing suppressed unconscious thoughts, Mr. Donne's libidinous "vision" builds to a large extent upon his conscious waking fantasies. His acute shame while dreaming reminds one of the moralistic psychology of Dr. William Acton (1813-1875), a mid-Victorian specialist in sexual disorders: "The *character* is the same sleeping or waking. . . . If a man has allowed his thoughts during the day to rest upon libidinous subjects, he finds his mind at night full of lascivious dreams. . . ."[12] In Gissing's story, Donne experiences a wildly erotic dream because he has loosened his censorship of his waking sexual fantasies. Consequently, he feels shame merely at having allowed the dream to happen. By the story's end, however, he recovers his control and delivers a hypocritical lecture on the virtues of sexual repression. In essence, Gissing accepted the mid-Victorian belief that the waking release of sexual longing led directly to libidinous dreams. But in contrast to upholders of repression, Gissing approved of sexual release both in life and dreams.

"The House of Cobwebs"

"The House of Cobwebs" (1900; rpt. *HC*, 1-27) offers a genial correction of the Bohemian-artist myth—the moneyless genius who defies social conventions and expands his creative gifts with sex, alcohol, drugs, and defiant nonconformity. This short story reminds one of *New Grub Street*'s many fine vignettes of unglamorous literary struggles. The story's young hero, the aspiring writer Goldthorpe, decides to take inexpensive rooms until he can finish his first novel. On a stroll through a south-London suburb, he notices three apparently abandoned old houses but discovers their proprietor in the back playing "Home, Sweet Home" on a concertina. This man, a retired drugstore clerk named Spicer, reveals that he owns the houses only under a short-term lease, and he also confesses that he himself lives in one of the dilapidated rooms. Honored at his encounter with an actual living author, Spicer offers the hero another of the broken-down rooms at a merely nominal rent. Goldthorpe moves in among cobwebs and smashed window panes and becomes Spicer's friend. The good-natured proprietor spends his time in the unweeded garden, cultivating scraggly flowers, assorted vegetables, and especially Jerusalem artichokes. Goldthorpe's book progresses while the summer remains mild, yet by sweltering August he falls ill in his unsanitary home. He finishes the book anyway, but a publisher rejects it. Discouraged, moneyless, and now quite sick, he creeps away to recuperate with his mother in Derbyshire. By winter another publisher at last accepts the novel, and Goldthorpe returns to London to tell his ex-landlord. In the meantime, however, Spicer has narrowly escaped death from a falling chimney stack in his crumbling "house of cobwebs." Although no longer able to live there, he feels comforted that the hero wrote his successful book "under my roof, my own roof, sir!" (*HC*, 27).

This account of a writer's triumph over poverty contrasts strikingly with a famous glamorization of late-Victorian Bohemianism, George Moore's *Confessions of a Young Man* (1886). Gissing himself considered Moore's *Confessions* "interesting but disgusting."[13] The wealthy Moore describes his exotic adventures as a painter-writer in Paris and London, in Montmartre and Curzon Street, amid fellow geniuses and delightful women. He boasts of his amorality, of his joyous acquaintance with demimonde rogues. Gissing's writer, however, stoically survives in a pathetic suburban hovel. He lacks artistic friends or female seductresses, and he behaves with a dull but scrupulous decency. In contrast to a well-born writer like Moore, who could leave Bohemia whenever he chose, Gissing's hero struggles against an encompassing beggary.

Although Goldthorpe, like most Bohemians, suffers from poverty, he makes no attempt to disguise it as a glorious way of life. When Moore describes his Bohemian apartment, he emphasizes expensively unconventional emblems: a terra-cotta faun, Turkish couches, a Buddhist altar, statues of Shelley and Apollo, incense burners and candles.[14] Gissing instead stresses his impoverished hero's commitment to simple household pleasures: possessing his own humble bed and table, cooking and sharing meals with his landlord, strolling through the run-down neighborhood, and smoking inexpensive tobacco out in the unkempt garden (*HC*, 13-14). If Bohemians tend to scorn middle-class life, Goldthorpe clings to it stubbornly. The song that first draws his attention to his shabby future lodgings—"Home, Sweet Home"—idealizes the virtues of nineteenth-century domesticity. One familiar line from the song sums up the story's central irony: "Be it ever so humble, there's no place like home." Amid cobwebs, smashed windows, collapsing chimney stacks, and a literally poisonous atmosphere, this typical Gissing writer touchingly adheres to respectable middle-class proprieties.

The four short stories analyzed above can help to convey the high achievement of Gissing's extensive work in this genre. If his novels range from the excellent *New Grub Street* and *Born in Exile* to potboilers like *The Town Traveller* and *Sleeping Fires*, Gissing's mature short stories have an impressive consistency. His own characteristic version of the short narrative form suited his fundamental attitudes. Its inconclusive brevity seems particularly appropriate to his vision of human beings as fallible little creatures entangled in their petty social webs.

Notes

1. Over the years, Gissing's seven miscellaneous short-story collections have remained largely out of print. Some are hard to find even in good libraries. Soon, however, Professor Coustillas's planned collection of Gissing's complete short stories may rescue them from undeserved neglect. The total of 110 remains tentative. For the most recent discovery of Gissing stories, see "Unknown Gissing Stories from Chicago," pp. 1417-18. For an indispensable, although provisional, bibliography of Gissing's short stories, see Pierre Coustillas, "Gissing's Short Stories: A Bibliography," *English Literature in Transition* 7, no. 2 (1964): 59-72. Among the smattering of criticism on Gissing's short fiction, two essays deserve mention: J. M. Mitchell, "Notes on George Gissing's Short Stories," *Studies in English Literature* (Tokyo) 38 (March 1962): 195-205; W. V. Harris, "An Approach to Gissing's Short Stories," *Studies in Short Fiction* 2 (Winter 1965): 137-44. The finest short stories appear in George Gissing, *Human Odds and Ends: Stories and*

Sketches (London, 1898), hereafter referred to in the text as *HOE;* George Gissing, *The House of Cobwebs,* with an Introduction by Thomas Seccombe (London 1931; first pub. 1906), hereafter referred to in the text as *HC;* George Gissing, *A Victim of Circumstances and Other Stories,* with a Preface by Alfred C. Gissing (Boston, 1927), hereafter referred to in the text as *VC.* A later collection seems inferior to the previous three: George Gissing, *Stories and Sketches* (London, 1938); hereafter referred to in the text as *SS.* Two other collections contain Gissing's immature stories written in the United States in 1877: George Gissing, *Sins of the Fathers and Other Tales,* with an Introduction by Vincent Starrett (Chicago, 1924); George Gissing, *Brownie,* with six other stories attributed to him, with Introduction by George Everett Hastings, Vincent Starrett, and Thomas Ollive Mabbott (New York, 1931). Previously unpublished stories are printed from the extant manuscripts in George Gissing, *Essays & Fiction* (Baltimore, 1970), ed., with an introduction, by Pierre Coustillas; hereafter referred to in the text as *EF.*

2. For the argument that Gissing's fiction (particularly *New Grub Street*) influenced James's tales about authors, see Adeline R. Tintner, "Some Notes for a Study of the Gissing Phase in Henry James's Fiction," *GN* 16 (July, 1980): 1-15.

3. On the Victorian fondness for historical paintings, see William Gaunt, *The Restless Century: Painting in Britain 1800-1900* (London: Phaidon, 1972), p. 20, as well as the many plates of this genre scatered throughout the volume.

4. *Dictionary of National Biography* (1917 ed.; rpt. 1921-22 and 1937-38), S.V. "Cox, David" and "Fielding, Anthony Vandyke Copley." See Gaunt, pl. 57, for a reproduction of Cox's *A Windy Day* (1850).

5. On this point and on other problems faced by Victorian female painters, see Linda Nochlin, "Why Are There No Great Women Artists?" in *Woman in Sexist Society: Studies in Power and Power-lessness,* ed. Vivian Gornick and Barbara K. Moran (New York: Mentor, 1972), pp. 480-510.

6. Simone de Beauvoir, *The Second Sex,* tr. H. M. Parshley (New York, Alfred A. Knopf, 1957), p. 684.

7. Ibid.

8. Ibid., p. 685.

9. Somewhat unusually for Gissing, these are obvious type names. In colloquial English, *don* means a head, fellow, or tutor of a college. *Argent* (silver) suggests wealth.

10. On the connection between women's bicycling and their shortened skirts after 1889, see Ensor, *England 1870-1914,* p. 338.

11. Houghton, *Victorian Frame of Mind,* p. 357.

12. Quoted from William Acton, *The Function and Disorders of the Reproductive Organs* [(London?], 1857), by Steven Marcus, *The Other Victorians: A Study of Sexuality and Pornography in Mid-Nineteenth-Century England* (New York: Bantam, 1967), p. 24.

13. *Diary,* 25 April 1888, p. 27.

14. George Moore, *Confessions of a Young Man: Edited and Annotated by George Moore 1904 and Again in 1916* (New York: Capricorn Books, 1959), ch. vi, pp. 57-58.

Penelope A. Lefew (essay date 1989)

SOURCE: "Evidence of a Dickensian Gissing in 'Joseph Yates' Temptation'," in *English Language Notes,* Vol. XXVI, No. 3, March, 1989, pp. 82-7.

[*In the following essay, Lefew traces the influence of Charles Dickens on Gissing as demonstrated in "Joseph Yates' Temptation."*]

Seven years after the death of Charles Dickens, George Robert Gissing found himself penniless and starving in Chicago, Illinois, having left his native England following a brief imprisonment for stealing money to support his prostitute-lover, Marianne Helen ("Nell") Harrison. During his visit to the American midwest, Gissing wrote several short stories and sold them to various Chicago publications.[1] The process of discovering and identifying these obscure tales has received considerable attention. The stories themselves, however, are largely ignored.[2] To date, only two editions of these stories exist, and neither is comprehensive. *Sins of the Father* and *Brownie* preserve Gissing's early tales, but neither work offers any criticism or commentary on the stories except for brief references to influence, tradition, or style considered for the purpose of identification. The tales are presented as "potboilers of no real literary value."[3]

Though they are weakly plotted, melodramatic and predictable, the stories reveal important influences acting upon Gissing at age nineteen. Coustillas notes that the early stories "adumbrate themes which will recur in [Gissing's] maturer work and technical devices that he will later reject or keep."[4] One story which deserves particular attention for its theme and the influence at work in it is **"Joseph Yates' Temptation,"** first published in the *Evening Post,* 2 June 1877. As with several of Gissing's early works, **"Joseph Yates' Temptation"** reflects the potent and pervasive influence of Charles Dickens, undiluted by the later dominance of Schopenhauer, Zola, and Darwin. In fact, the story, which was unsigned, is attributed to Gissing largely because of the Dickensian plot, theme, and characterization.[5] Several scholars, including Vincent Starrett and Thomas Ollive Mabbott, have noted the Dickensian influence in **"Joseph Yates' Temptation,"** but none has identified the specific aspects of the tale which reveal this influence.[6]

Like the other Chicago tales, **"Joseph Yates' Temptation"** is a narrative about poverty and the constant lure of theft as a solution. Joseph Yates works for Mr. Peter Gale, a greedy, insensitive employer, co-owner of Gale and Company. Yates is in charge of receiving payments from customers, and one day the underpaid and overworked Yates forgets to deposit a one-hundred-pound check. He decides to keep the check overnight while contemplating the possibility of using the money to purchase Christmas gifts for his family. He takes a walk to deliberate about the crime and to escape the trusting, innocent eyes of his wife, Bessie. He meets a young boy, a pauper, selling evening papers on the street. Pity and curiosity lead Yates to the boy's home where he encounters the child's dying mother. She and the boy co-incidentally reveal themselves to be Peter Gale's long lost wife and son. Yates is humbled by their suffering and sense of pride, and shamed by his own self-pity. The next day, Yates confesses all to Gale and tells him of his wife and child. After leading Gale to his family, Yates returns home, certain he will be fired because of his admitted close call with crime. Gale, however, experiences a complete change of heart and character after his reunion with his wife and son. He raises Yates's salary and awards him a check for one hundred pounds.

Dickens' influence is evident in this tale, particularly in the obvious parallels with *A Christmas Carol.* The time, for instance, is Christmas Eve. Like Bob Cratchit, Yates finds himself feigning optimism in the face of a meager Christmas. And, like Ebenezer Scrooge, Peter Gale is somewhat less than inspired by the Christmas spirit and all of its trimmings. When Yates bravely requests an advance on his salary for the purpose of buying Christmas gifts, echoes of Scrooge's language resound clearly in Gale's reply:

> "I don't do those things, Yates, and you know it. I pay a man fairly when his work is done, and not a day before, and I never ask a man to pay me until my money is due. I know you want it for some stupid nonsense, but poor men like you had better save their money. This holiday business is bad for poor men like you."[7]

Gale's response is unmistakably similar to Scrooge's "poor excuse for picking a man's pocket" speech in answer to Cratchit's humble request for Christmas day off.[8]

The Scrooge-Gale, Cratchit-Yates analogies do not end with similarities associated with the holiday season. As Dickens transformed the character of Scrooge partly by revealing to him the errors of his past, so Gissing uses Gale's neglected past, represented by the impoverished condition of his wife and child, to create motivation for Gale's completely altered personality at the conclusion of the story. Gale raises Yates's salary, as Scrooge does Cratchit's, and, again like Scrooge, pleads for forgiveness from his clerk: "'Yates, I've been a hard master, I know, but you're a good man, and I couldn't spare you. I want you to stay and take charge at five-hundred pounds a year—will that do? . . . You brought me—oh, Yates, such a gift . . . I shall never forget—never, Heaven bless you, Yates—'" (71). Yates is rewarded after the transformation, however implausible, in Gale's character, just as Cratchit is made the beneficiary of Scrooge's moral rebirth. And Cratchit and Yates are not the only characters in the stories to enjoy improved living conditions as a result of their master's enlightened outlooks: Tiny Tim and Mrs. Gale, both on the verge of death, are saved through the income provided by their new-found philanthropists.

Though in their Christmas stories Dickens and Gissing view poverty less realistically than they do in other works, they nevertheless demonstrate a metonymical sensitivity for the struggles of the poor. Though humble, the homes of both Cratchit and Yates, for instance, represent warm, desirable places of refuge or, in Gissing's words, symbols of "beauty . . . beneath a humble roof."[9] There are always smiling faces and warm fires to greet tired, victimized men returning from the debased world of business. Realistic conditions of poverty (too little food, clothing, or coal) are eclipsed by the sense of charm and coziness that prevails in the modest living quarters of Cratchit and Yates. Gissing was later to abandon this Dickensian perspective on poverty in order "to bring home to people the ghastly condition (material, mental, moral) of our poorer classes."[10] But in 1877, the youthful Gissing could still write about the quaintness of poverty, though he undoubtedly saw nothing quaint about his own impoverished condition at the time.

In *A Christmas Carol,* one of the major reasons for Cratchit's satisfying home life is, of course, Mrs. Cratchit. A successful student of the art of living in poverty, she is the perfect poor man's wife. She knows how to make a small pudding feed any number of little Cratchits, and Dickens' initial description of her provides further evidence of her frugality: "Then up rose Mrs. Cratchit, Cratchit's wife, dressed out but poorly in a twice-turned gown, but brave in ribbons, which are cheap, and make a goodly show for sixpence" (81). Although Gissing would later question whether it was possible to make the best of the worst, at nineteen he had created a character who, like Mrs. Cratchit, suffered poverty well. Bessie Yates completes the picture of the humble, charming comfort of Joseph's metonymic home:

> Bessie Yates looked so bright and cheery in her crimson merino gown, with crimped ruffles at throat and wrists, and a few geranium leaves in her fair hair. And the room was cozy and inviting with the unsalable relics of former prosperity and Bessie's quick eye and fair fingers. His slippers were warming in the firelight, and his chintz-covered easy chair gave him welcome. (61)

Comfort, even in an indigent household, was possible through the efforts of a loving woman. Like her Dickensian counterpart, Bessie Yates understands the value of learning the art of living in poverty. She manages to provide gifts for every member of her family without spending money: "There are dresses for Nelly and Rose," she explains to her distraught husband, "made out of my blue poplin that you liked so well. No one would ever dream that it had been washed, and I made the old velvet do duty again" (63). Like Mrs. Cratchit, Bessie could find worth in a "twice-turned gown."

But Bessie Yates's significance goes beyond her economical use of materials. She also stands as a metonymic device for the moral of **"Joseph Yates' Temptation"**: poverty is not as low as dishonesty. She reminds Joseph that the condition of poverty is no excuse for theft, and she warns him that she will tolerate anything except disgrace. Gissing, familiar with Dickens' precedence in using literature to moralize and instruct, probably felt comfortable with the didactic tone of the tale. Certainly in his early work, Gissing was imposing a moral framework similar to the one he later attributed to Dickens: "From his duty as he conceived it, of teaching a moral lesson, Dickens never departs. . . . And his morality is of the simplest; . . . to follow the path of the just is to ensure a certain amount of prosperity, and reward unlimited in buoyancy of heart."[11] Following a Dickensian moral code, Gissing rewards Yates for adhering to "the path of the just" and avoiding temptation not only with "buoyancy of heart" but also with the very object of his temptation, the one-hundred-pound check, thus underscoring the themes of justice and honor at work in the tale. But it is Bessie Yates, with her insistence on the dignity of honest poverty, who represents the moral voice throughout the story.

The heavy moral tone and the two-dimensional treatment of the characters of Yates and Gale reveal Gissing's manner of addressing the theme of poverty in his early years as a writer. Halperin, referring to the later work of Gissing, observes that

> like Dickens, Gissing could sympathize with the plight of the poor without wishing to live among them; unlike Dickens, however, he did not fill his novels with people to whom he has attributed moral superiority because of the fact of their poverty.[12]

But what must be emphasized is that Halperin's observation does not apply to Gissing's early stories. Yates is inherently good because of his penniless circumstances, and he is therefore a better person than Gale, just as Cratchit is morally superior to Scrooge for the same reason. And Peter Gale is a negative character because of his wealth, another metonymic device, which, as Gissing implies, makes him corrupt. The same implication is made by Dickens in relation to Scrooge. In both Christmas tales, poverty is associated with nobility of character and goodness of heart; wealth is linked to greed and power over the weak.

Adopting the thematic and stylistic techniques of Charles Dickens was an integral part of Gissing's learning period in Chicago. Although he would eventually reject much of Dickens' philosophy and literary teachings, from his early years we possess some evidence of a time in Gissing's development when a dominant influence in his work was Charles Dickens.

Notes

1. According to Pierre Coustillas' "Gissing's Short Stories: A Bibliography" in *English Literature in Transition* 7 (1964):56-72, fourteen stories were initially attributed to Gissing. Coustillas revised this count to sixteen when he and Robert Sileg discovered two additional stories in 1980; see "Unknown Gissing Stories from Chicago," *Times Literary Supplement* 12 December 1980: 1417-18 and "Gissing in America: Two Tales Rescued from Oblivion," *The Gissing Newsletter* 16 (1980): 1-5. John Halperin reports in his Gissing biography, *Gissing: A Life in Books* (Oxford, 1982), that the most recent tally is seventeen. Both Halperin and Coustillas agree that there are probably more stories still hidden in Chicago publications.

2. For the most comprehensive study to date of Gissing's short stories, see Sister Mary Aurelia Parlati's dissertation, *A Critical, Sociological, and Technical Analysis of George Gissing's Short Stories and Sketches,* Fordham University, 1970. She

examines the Chicago stories briefly, noting obvious themes and influences.

3. George Gissing, *Brownie* (New York, 1931) and *Sins of the Father* (Chicago, 1924). Coustillas, "Bibliography" 60.

4. Coustillas, "Bibliography" 60.

5. Coustillas, "Bibliography" 65.

6. Thomas Ollive Mabbott and Vincent Starrett, Introductions, *Brownie,* by George Gissing.

7. Gissing, *Brownie* 59. Quotations from "Joseph Yates' Temptation" are taken from the *Brownie* collection; subsequent citations will be made parenthetically in the text.

8. Charles Dickens, *A Christmas Carol* (Philadelphia, 1977) 17.

9. George Gissing, *Charles Dickens: A Critical Study* (New York, 1898) 234.

10. Algernon and Ellen Gissing, eds. *Letters of George Gissing* (Boston, 1927) 83.

11. Gissing, *Charles Dickens* 101-102.

12. Halperin 5.

Robert L. Selig (essay date 1992)

SOURCE: "Gissing's Exile in America," in *George Gissing: Lost Stories from America,* edited by Robert L. Selig, Edwin Mellen Press, 1992, pp. 1-18.

[*In the following introduction, Selig investigates the circumstances surrounding the writing of Gissing's American stories, and asserts that "his large body of fiction accepted in America paved the way later for Gissing's success."*]

In 1876 an eighteen-year-old George Gissing, later to become a major English novelist, disgraced himself so utterly that friends shipped him off to America, far from the shame of his petty criminal acts. Without knowing the squalid details of this scandal, one cannot even start to understand his desperate courage during a hard year of exile. As a brilliant underaged scholarship boy at Manchester's Owens College, which lacked all student housing, he had remained throughout even his junior year in his old high-school dormitory, a train-ride away, where he often studied ascetically from 4:00a.m. to 10:00p.m. His asceticism ended disastrously in his senior college year when his family permitted him to move at last to a rooming house in the city, where he soon encountered a pretty blonde prostitute in a local bar—seventeen-year-old Marianne Helen (Nell) Harrison. Prostitutes swarmed in the bars around the Cobden House, the college's temporary home during Gissing's freshman year, and although the campus had moved by the time of his disgrace, he would have still known exactly where to find them. During these years a legend flourished of an Owens College porter enticed by a prostitute into an adjacent bar, "robbed," and "ejected" stark naked.[1] Without any conscious malice, Nell Harrison herself stripped Gissing of his money and also his moral defenses.

Unfortunately, she kept pleading for more and more money, which the poor young student could hardly provide from the annual £40 total of his two-year Shakespeare scholarship.[2] Seventeen-year-old Nell had already become alcoholic; had turned to prostitution in order to buy drinks; and if she gave it up, as her young lover urged, he would then have to support her drinking habit. His own quixotic schemes for Nell's reformation also cost money: a sewing machine to turn her into an instant seamstress and a healthy Spring escape from squalor to Southport by the sea, some forty miles away, where the once-perfect student began to cut his classes. Nell's continued prostitution and sexual promiscuity stung him into frantic action. Even after he had told a close college friend, John George Black, of falling in love with Nell, Black himself had sex with her, and his later confession appalled the infatuated Gissing. Neither the squalid and ridiculous shame of their both having caught gonorrhea from Nell nor the level-headed pleas of other close friends dissuaded young Gissing from his headlong self-destruction. No matter what it cost him, he would rescue poor Nell.[3]

Sometime after February 1876, Gissing began stealing money, books, and clothing from the Owens College cloakroom. Unlike the thieves in his American short stories or in his later novels, he gave in to the temptation far more than once. Over an extended period, he robbed fellow students at least five times.[4] Still, with mere odd change from petty thefts and the resale of secondhand books and clothing, he cannot have accumulated much for Nell. In the end, the college summoned police, and on May 31st, 1876, they planted marked coins in a cloakroom overcoat and caught Gissing in the act of stealing the pathetic sum of five shillings, twopence.[5]

Incredibly enough, Gissing had been expected for dinner on that very same night by the Principal of Owens, the classicist J. G. Greenwood, who, in shock and distress the next day in court, bailed out his prize scholar.[6] No wonder that, in Gissing's **"Too Dearly Bought"** (14 April 1877), the thief robs his benefactor. Yet in real life, Greenwood turned against Gissing as all the details came out at the June 6th trial: not one theft but many to support his relationship with a prostitute. After the court convicted and sentenced young Gissing to one month's imprisonment at hard labor, Greenwood, in the college's disciplinary council, denounced this pathetic first offender as having led "a life of immorality and dissipation." Consequently, the senate recommended and the council decreed his expulsion from Owens only a few days before he would have earned his Bachelor of Arts degree.[7] They had knocked him down when he was down already.

When Gissing emerged from jail, his friends agreed on a plan: ship the disgraced young man to the United States away from all the scandal and, not so incidentally, also away from Nell. Through money raised largely at the college itself as an afterthought of pity, they sent him off to Boston, where he did not know a soul, to work at self-reclamation, with only a few recommending letters.[8] Evidence exists that he himself had a different agenda than his friends. In an unpublished poem apparently addressed to Nell shortly before sailing, he calls her his beloved, embraces her, says that he always thinks of her, tries to soothe her misery over their forced separation, and promises their ultimate reunion.[9] Without this telltale lyrical farewell, we

could hardly understand his extraordinary behavior throughout his American year. Gissing hoped to make good in a very big way as the means to regaining Nell. Having concentrated on literature in college, he now aimed at success in the longest of all long shots—authorship. Yet surprisingly enough, in his twelve American months, he succeeded far better than one might have expected at becoming a writer and then keeping his word to Nell.

Sometime before October 5th, 1876, perhaps in late September, Gissing arrived in Boston—an important publishing center of the United States and a logical choice of cities for a would-be writer. Apparently through his letters of introduction, he met a major cultural figure from Boston's past, William Lloyd Garrison (1805-1879), the great abolitionist editor, then long past his prime. Through Garrison and his son Francis, Gissing tried to get a staff job on the *Atlantic Monthly,* but they had no need of his utter inexperience. Reverting to the interests of a literary scholar, he submitted an essay on Burns and Heine, but the *Atlantic* turned it down. Still thinking academically, he toyed with the idea of translating Heine's poems but feared that they would interest only English publishers. Two weeks later, though, the young man achieved his first small success as a writer: an unsigned art review in Boston's the *Commonwealth* about a painting, displayed locally, by one Tojetti of a scene from Tennyson's "Lancelot and Elaine" (1859), a blend of art criticism and literary comment.[10] At best such criticism paid very little, and Gissing now made the biggest decision of his entire life: to try prose fiction. He wrote and submitted to a local magazine "some" **"Sketches of Life in an English Manufacturing Town."**[11] But he found no takers for his first attempted tales. With only one acceptance during three months of writing—a piece of nonfiction—he had run through the funds collected for his exile. In spite of his wish to become a man of letters, he needed a steady job, and he needed it right away.

Sometime in December he found himself work in nearby Waltham, Massachusetts, as a temporary replacement in English, French, and German for a sick high school teacher at some eighty dollars a month. In Gissing's one letter home about it, he sounds temporarily relieved at having opted out from the lonely frustrations of a would-be man of letters. But of all possible jobs, teaching remained uncomfortably connected to his recent disgrace at college. His certificates recorded his brilliance in the First examinations for Bachelor of Arts—impressive enough for a high school position—but the British degree required three sets of exams, and, because of his expulsion, he had missed the last two. He may, indeed, have worried that the school would write to Owens to check his credentials and would learn about his shame. It must have alarmed the guilty young man when a *Waltham Free Press* reporter asked him "where I came from and where I had studied" and then falsely described him in the newspaper piece as "a graduate of Owens College." Then, too, Pierre Coustillas has uncovered another personal factor that may have upset Gissing at Waltham: an incipient romance with his student, eighteen-year-old Martha Barnes—a potential betrayal of Nell. Furthermore, he may have come to regard this stopgap teaching job as an unwise detour from his literary aims. In any event, on March 1st, 1877, without telling anyone, he cut his waiting classes, packed his things, and left for unknown parts with money saved from his teacher's salary.[12]

After Gissing abruptly fled his teaching position, he ceased sending letters home, so that his last seven months of American exile have remained pretty much in darkness, a darkness relieved somewhat by the present writer's recent investigations. We know that Gissing next showed up in Chicago. As so often, *New Grub Street*'s fictionalized but largely confirmed account provides important clues about his movements:

> " . . . At last I got into perilous straits. I went to New York, and thought of returning home, but the spirit of adventure was strong in me. ' I'll go West,' I said to myself. . . . And go I did, taking an emigrant ticket to Chicago."[13]

Gissing would, in fact, have had to travel south from Boston to New York—a trip of at least six hours and forty-three minutes—to embark for Chicago on an "emigrant" train: a low-priced, unheated train that took twice as long as an ordinary one. Perhaps for a time he also held back from continuing on westward and toyed with the idea of sailing home to Nell. The emigrant train would have taken two whole days to creep from New York to Chicago. He cannot have arrived there earlier than March 3rd, 1877, and depending on how long he lingered in New York City, may have reached Chicago as late as March 6th.[14]

Just as in Boston, Gissing in Chicago sought a journalistic staff job. He cannot have foreseen the difficulties in his newly chosen town. If the whole United States had endured a steep depression since the 1873 panic, Chicago had its own additional and very special woes. The depression had hit the city very hard while it still was rebuilding from the great fire of 1871. Its 400,000 inhabitants lived and worked among as yet burnt-out lots and clumps of darkened bricks, and the people faced severe unemployment.[15] No magazine of literature had survived these ruinous times, as a quick look at a current directory would have told the arriving Gissing. The closest counterpart of Boston's *Atlantic Monthly*, Chicago's *Lakeside Monthly*, had collapsed from losses in the '73 panic as well as from the great fire,[16] and its editor-proprietor, the physically broken Francis F. Browne, had to settle for running the literary pages of a mere weekly newspaper—one that printed Gissing's own stories a few months before Browne himself took over.[17]

Gissing had to look, accordingly, for staff work on a paper, and he chose the *Chicago Tribune*, the most prominent one in town. Yet even as he walked toward the *Tribune* offices, he cannot have realized that he lacked the safety net back-up of his only previous work—high-school teaching. A definitive history of the city reveals that "at times, especially in the depression years of the later 'seventies, all teachers got only scrip, and in 1877 and '78 their pay was suspended."[18]

All unawares, Gissing approached the crucial moment of his life and career. He stood outside a five-story reddish sandstone building at Madison and Dearborn—rebuilt in 1872 about a year after the fire—and nerved himself for a seemingly hopeless effort. Even with help from the Garrisons during his months in Boston, he had failed to find a staff job at the *Atlantic Monthly*. Now in Chicago, friendless, unknown, unqualified, and down to his last few cents, he entered a street-level corridor and walked across a tiled floor of black, red, yellow, khaki, and blue. The tall, big-shouldered Englishman had not slept a wink during the all-night train ride from which he had just arrived, with only a short stop in-between at a local rooming house. His longish, pale-brown beard must have looked quite seedy, somewhat like a beggar's. He saw that on this level he had a choice of one of two *Tribune* offices, for the others were general businesses. He could inquire in the room of the paper's business manager or of its cashier, both with plate glass doors. Most probably he picked the business manager's door, adorned, as it was, with the *Tribune*'s monogram. Aiming as high as possible, Gissing asked if he might see the *Tribune*'s editor and, to his pleasant surprise, found out that he could. He was told that he should take the elevator to Room 24, up on the fourth floor, or, as *New Grub Street* puts it, "an upper storey." In the vestibule on the Dearborn side, he discovered the single elevator, an open, caged contraption. As it slowly rose he had an aerial view of each passing floor and its well-lit hallway. When the elevator stopped, he stepped out toward the doorway of his improbable future.[19]

Inside, a short-haired and quite youthful man sat before a desk littered with hand-written sheets and print, as he smoked a cigar stuck between his overhanging moustache and trim brownish beard. He turned out to be, not the editor-in-chief, the nationally known Joseph Medill (1823-1899), but his youngest and only brother to survive the Civil War, Samuel Medill (1841-1883), the *Tribune*'s managing editor, now thirty-five years old. During almost twenty years as a newspaperman and three as managing editor, he had earned a local reputation for brusqueness, impatience, and chilling reserve—one that might have intimidated Gissing if he had heard about it. Instead, in blissful ignorance, he plunged right ahead. Quickly introducing himself, he asked for a staff position on the paper.[20]

Here we should quote *New Grub Street*'s version of what Gissing and Medill said to one another:

> "'Can you give me work of any kind on your paper?' 'Well, what experience have you had?' 'None whatever.' The editor smiled. 'I'm very much afraid you would be no use to us.'"[21]

The interview might have ended there if Gissing had not seemed so pathetic. Instead, the usually gruff Medill asked this wholly unqualified man what he thought he could do at the *Tribune*. In reply Gissing asked if the paper used short fiction. Medill answered yes but said that it had to be "good." Then Gissing offered to write a short story if Medill would at least "consider it," and he said that he would gladly.[22]

For all the many confirmations of facts behind *New Grub Street*'s passage, a small but important detail sticks out as a departure, for the sake of drama, from what really happened. "'Well,' I said, 'if I write a story of English life, will you consider it?' 'With pleasure.'" In *New Grub Street*, the character next meditates down by Lake Michigan; returns to his shabby rooming house; and, in less than two days, composes a story from scratch.[23] The novel's phrase, "a story of English life," closely resembles Gissing's own description of his tales written in Boston but never actually accepted: **"Sketches of Life in an English Manufacturing Town."[24]** Indeed, the very first story that Gissing did submit to the *Tribune* concludes its opening sentence with the identical phrase: " . . . such a scene is but too common after nightfall in the heart of a great *English manufacturing town.*"[25] Obviously enough, Gissing offered to write a short story for Samuel Medill with a version of **"The Sins of the Fathers"** already in hand. Then he hurried away to revise a manuscript already rejected in Boston. Throughout his later literary career, he recycled parsimoniously earlier failed attempts and even one of his own forgotten successes—**"The Artist's Child"** from Chicago (*Alliance,* 30 June 1877), wholly rewritten in London but still called **"The Artist's Child"** (*Tinsleys' Magazine,* January 1878).[26] In addition, his second letter home from Boston suggests that Gissing carried more than one story in his bag when he stepped off the train in Chicago: "I have just been writing some **'Sketches of Life in an English Manufacturing Town.'** I have sent them to one of our Magazines [sic], but have not heard yet whether they are accepted."[27] The plural indicates clearly two or more stories about a Manchester-like city. Only the first of his Chicago tales fits this description, but he might have easily shifted others away from the outlying city to the more familiar London in order to appeal to his American readers. At any rate, in spite of the impression left by the passage in *New Grub Street,* Gissing sought to write fiction for the *Tribune* not from a sudden happy inspiration but the same ambitious plan that he had pursued since landing in America: to become a man of letters.

After less than two days of rewriting, Gissing took his sketch to the *Tribune,* just a few blocks away from his Wabash Avenue rooming house. Not only did he avoid the mails, but he also insisted on handing his work directly to Samuel Medill. Again Gissing rode up in the slow, caged elevator and again approached Room 24. Again Medill greeted him with kindness, promised to read his story by the very next morning, and asked him to come back then for a decision. Over the next few hours and throughout the night, the excited Gissing must have found it hard to wait. He badly needed an aceptance. Even though he had found cheap lodgings at $4.50 a week for both room and meals, he had used up all but small change to pay in advance. Outside, the lake-front weather was turning harsh. The Thursday, March 8th, papers predicted rain or snow, and by Saturday, March 10th, the temperature would drop to 9 degrees Fahrenheit. Unless the *Tribune* wanted his story, he would remain stuck in freezing Chicago without any shelter or food.[28]

When Gissing returned to the *Tribune* next morning, rode up on the elevator again, and again entered room 24, he saw a smiling Samuel Medill. *New Grub Street* provides a version of his words: "'I think your story will do. I'll put it into the Saturday supplement, Call on Saturday morning and I'll remunerate you.'" Surprisingly, almost magically, Gissing was "saved."[29]

The editor's exact words seem particularly significant. He had said from the first that fiction for the *Tribune* had to be "good." "I think the story will do" sounds, however, like less than a thunderous endorsement. Even without other clues, we might guess that Medill accepted Gissing's story more out of kindness than critical admiration. Wholly unaware of the editor's identity and speaking out of mere intuition, George Everett Hastings in 1931 jokingly called Gissing's man at the *Tribune* his "fairy godmother."[30]

The details in *New Grub Street*'s passage make the actions of this tender-hearted editor seem virtually miraculous. The editor meets with the suppliant four distinct times: when he asks for a staff job and then offers to write fiction, when he turns in his first story, on the following day when the editor declares that it will do, and on Saturday when the author shows up for his money.[31] During four and a half Chicago months, Medill published at least four and perhaps five Gissing stories, so that the novel's description of tender loving care—four interviews for the first piece and three for each of the others—suggests thirteen, sixteen, or even more meetings in Room 24.[32] No wonder that Gissing, through his fictional mouthpiece, Whelpdale, expresses amazement at the editor's kindness:

> "I have never come across an English editor who treated me with anything like that consideration and general kindliness. How the man had time, in his position, to see me so often, and do things in such a human way, I can't understand. Imagine anyone trying the same at the office of a London newspaper! To begin with, one couldn't see the editor at all. I shall always think with profound gratitude of that man with the peaked brown beard and pleasant smile."[33]

Neither Whelpdale nor Gissing himself had the slightest clue of what made the managing editor tick or made him behave like a cross between an editorial social worker and a saint. In 1985 the present writer discovered both the editor's identity and the reason for his many kindnesses to Gissing. During Samuel Medill's lifetime, only family, staff, and a few close friends knew the gentle secret of this normally brusque editor. Two days after his death at only forty-one, a *Tribune* editorial—a personal "In Memoriam"—at last revealed Samuel Medill's hidden benevolence:

> There was one quality of his character that was but little known, and that was his generosity, and his generosity was little known because it was bestowed in a quiet, private manner, and upon those whom he knew could never make any requital to him. He had a very warm heart, and could not resist the appeals of distress, but it was only those who knew him the best that really knew the nature and extent of his bounty. It was of a kind not blown by trumpets nor paraded in public acknowledgment, but among his sincere mourners there will be many in the humble and squalid ranks of life. There never was a time when he did not have some ragged little protégé whom he was clothing, some hungry mouth which he was filling, or some hopeless one he was encouraging. It was more often that he had a retinue of them depending upon him for support, and though he was occasionally deceived and imposed on it never dampened his charitable nature or relaxed his interest in the unfortunates. The first impulse of his heart was to relieve some one of his burdens as its last impulse was to inflict any of his own burdens upon others. There will be many obscure ones down among the unfortunates, among the ragged newsboys, bootblacks, and gamins of the streets, who will unaffectedly mourn the absence of the one who was so kind to them.[34]

In spite of his gruff exterior, Samuel Medill had secretly run an extensive personal and private philanthropy over many years. After all, he had worked through the great Chicago fire, had watched his own *Tribune* burn to the ground, and had seen the harm done to the humble and the poor, who could not, like the *Tribune,* quickly rebuild before the big depression hit them.[35] He had given regular handouts to the ragged, the foodless, the homeless, and especially to the young, had followed their troubles, and had often intervened to help. Rumpled young Gissing had encountered "no difficulty" at all in seeing the managing editor precisely because Gissing looked like just another of Medill's neediest cases.[36] When Gissing arrived in Room 24, his helplessness and seediness probably served to recommend him. Even the amateurishness of his very first story may have appealed to the editor's compassion. To Gissing himself it looked as though Medill had singled him out for unique personal favors, but Gissing joined, in fact, a whole "retinue" of shabby little protégés. To a man like Medill who concealed his philanthropy, the case must have seemed irresistible: he could pay Gissing cash for his stories and hide all elements of charity even from the recipient himself.

The fee that Medill paid for each Gissing story may hide further charity. Gissing himself in his later correspondence and Whelpdale in *New Grub Street* both cite a payment of $18.00 apiece.[37] Yet Gissing's long-time friend Morley Roberts, an old journalistic hand who later got to know Chicago the hard way—"dead broke"—doubted that any of its papers at the time would have paid that well.[38] Nevertheless, an $18.00 fee had particular appropriateness for Medill's disguised gift. Gissing's Wabash Avenue room cost him $4.50 a week,[39] a sum that divides exactly four times into $18.00. Medill had provided Gissing with about one month's rent. The editor may well have found out from Gissing how much he paid for board and lodgings and then set the high fee to cover it right down to the last cent.

Gissing's later *Tribune* acceptances may also have fit Medill's philanthropic plan. If we reject as Gissing's the "Browne-Vargrave" three (2 April, 28 April, 14 July 1877) and also, possibly, the unsigned "R.I.P" (31 March 1877), we arrive at an average of a Gissing story each month in the *Tribune* down through May,[40] three months' rent in all. Medill may even have timed each acceptance to keep Gissing from want. By May, though, Samuel Medill may have learned that his protégé had already won an acceptance from New York's *Appletons' Journal,* a distinguished magazine that would pay even more than the *Tribune*'s $18.00—$45.00, in fact. As a result, Medill may have felt less need than before of supporting his literary ward.[41] In any case, at midsummer Medill published one more Gissing story, **"Brownie"** (29 July 1877), after the exile had already left Chicago.[42] We can speculate that Gissing may have approached Samuel Medill one last time with this one last story and asked for and obtained payment in advance for the New York City trip—a final goodwill gesture from the extraordinary man "with the peaked brown beard and pleasant smile."[43]

Gissing's friend at the *Tribune,* however, probably never learned of anonymous other tales that by late April the exile had started to publish in rival Chicago papers.[44] The first Gissing attribution reprinted in this book from the *Chicago Daily News* suggests that he turned there next. We can reconstruct what he would have found at this recently established paper, which had just broken into the black after more than a year of struggle. Though it stood only three blocks away from the *Tribune* itself, the *News*'s building looked inadequate and cramped—architecturally

miles away from the big, successful *Tribune.* Gissing's tactics with the *Tribune*'s managing editor and later with James M. Hill suggest that he went in person to the *News* instead of simply mailing his submission there. As he stood near the corner of Madison and Fifth Avenue (now called Wells), he would have seen an unusually narrow four-story brick building. Inside, on the ground level he would have learned from the business office that the paper's editors were crammed together up on the top floor—by necessity, because a Norwegian language daily and a separate printing firm took up the other space. If he had asked for the elevator, he would have been told that only stairs existed. As he climbed them, he must have contrasted this do-it-yourself way of getting there with the Tribune Building's elevator. At the top, he would have found a tiny editorial space, some twenty-one feet square, without any windows and only a shaft to let in daytime sun.[45] Instead of having a private office like Samuel Medill at the *Tribune,* the *News*'s chief editor shared a single room with those who worked under him—a room small even for his limited staff. The young exile would have seen him there among the shabby furniture—including four humble kitchen chairs—sitting at a homemade table: four legs stuck onto joined pinewood boxes. Gissing must have approached the editor-in-chief, Melville E. Stone, for one simple reason. This brash twenty-eight-year-old journalist played some half dozen roles on his paper: chief editor, editorial writer, newswriter, receiver of advertisements, and even one of those who folded printed sheets down in the basement and bundled them up for delivery to the newsboys. Gissing would have seen a dapper young Stone, who had recently grown a dark, thick mustache along his upper lip—perhaps to disguise his youthfulness. He had a slightly turned up nose; deep-set eyes; a high, full forehead; and short-cut dark hair, parted quite sharply. The would-be contributor cannot have dreamed that this boyish newspaperman would one day become a power in the journalistic world: from 1893 to 1918, the managing editor of the influential Associated Press.[46] In any case, young Stone and the youthful *Daily News* ultimately published six unsigned stories now attributed to Gissing.

If Gissing had checked the fiction in this paper before actually approaching it, he would have noticed in its adjacent columns that Stone was an arch-enemy of the *Chicago Tribune* and especially of its editor-in-chief, Samuel Medill's brother, Joseph. In one short span right before Gissing appeared in the *News,* Stone had mocked the *Tribune* again and again in print: on April 7th; 9th; 14th; and then, embarrassingly enough, also on the 24th, in the very same issue that published Gissing's first story for the *News.* Stone kept ridiculing the *Tribune*'s editor-in-chief as "Aunt Nancy," "Nancy Medill," "Aunty Medill," or "Sister Medill," probably because of his prudishness as Chicago's reform mayor from 1871 to 1873 in shutting down taverns on Sunday and enforcing local blue laws. Stone also ridiculed Samuel Medill himself as "sad-eyed Sam" and mocked his affection for a large pet dog. Stone's attacks on the Medills and their paper kept on after Gissing's first *News* story appeared and even on the same day as his second. Gissing could hardly have read his own stories in the *News* and not have noticed Stone's assaults against the *Tribune,* for the stories appeared on the identical pages as the editor's sarcastic comments.[47]

Almost certainly, Gissing remained ignorant of Stone's real grievances against the Medills. In Stone's own words, "the *Tribune* had attacked" the *News* "even before" its "first copy . . . was issued," although it would "be in no sense a competitor," as the *Tribune* was "a morning paper" and the *News* "an evening" one.[48] Furthermore, when Stone needed money in 1876 to support his shoestring paper, an angry Joseph Medill had blocked Henry Demerest Lloyd, the *Tribune*'s financial editor, from raising a loan from his father-in-law to keep the *News* afloat. Unfortunately for Stone, the rich father-in-law, Illinois's ex-lieutenant-governor William Bross, not only was the *Tribune*'s president and second largest shareholder but also had an office close to Joseph Medill's. Bross had called him in, and the two bearded patriarchs had forced young Lloyd to withdraw as the *News*' s potential backer.[49] Even if Gissing did not know of this recent attempt to starve out the *News,* he surely perceived Stone's deep dislike of the *Tribune.* Perhaps in order not to offend his helper—Samuel Medill—Gissing left all of his stories for the *Daily News* unsigned. Because his last *News* piece appeared at least twenty-four days after Gissing had left Chicago, we must wonder if he ever got paid for it. In any case, each actual *News* payment must have been far less than the benevolent Samuel Medill's eighteen dollars a story.

Gissing next turned from the embattled little *News* to a second established daily and then to a third, both a block or so from the *Tribune:* the *Chicago Evening Journal* (28 April and 19 May 1877) and the *Chicago Post* (2 June and 28 July 1877), at 161 and 88 Dearborn respectively. Perhaps still playing it safe in a town full of quarreling journalists, he published anonymously in these rival big papers.[50] We cannot reconstruct what happened at either, for they had no philanthropic managing editor like Samuel Medill and no one-man journalistic band like Melville E. Stone. Yet Gissing's next overture—to a little-known humorous paper, Chicago's *National Weekly*—springs to life in his own words from his *Commonplace Book:*[51]

> There has come into my mind an odd incident in my literary experience in America. I wrote some stories for a man who combined the keeping of a dry-goods store with the editing of a weekly paper—and had always, by the bye, to wait about in the shop and dun him for payment due. I told him one day that I had finished a long story for serial publication, and asked him if he would have it. One of his chief inquiries was "Do you tell the *ends* of all characters?" An odd requirement with him, as I saw, a *sine qua non.*[52]

Through detective work in Chicago directories, the present writer has identified this clothing-store man and part-time managing editor. His name was James M. Hill, but no picture of him has survived, so that he remains a shadowy person. In the year before he encountered George Gissing. Hill had worked as a full-time salesman at the Boston Square Dealing Clothing House, 141 Clark, on the corner of Madison. When Gissing stepped into this shop, Hill was then its manager and also the part-time manager and proprietor of the *National Weekly,* just down the street at 114 Madison. One can see him shuttling back and forth between his two businesses. But Gissing soon discovered that the best place to find him and make him pay up was among the suits and shirts and near the money till.[53]

If Gissing's misadventures at the *National Weekly* seem unmistakably comic, that weekly itself featured low-comic writing in German-American dialect. For the two previous years and then the subsequent one, the paper carried the undignified name of *Carl Pretzel's Weekly* or *Carl Pretzel's Illustrated Weekly,* from the mock-German pseudonym of Charles Henry Harris, its contributing editor-in-chief, who composed humorous verses in a German-American patois rather like that of the later popular comic strip, *The Katzenjammer Kids,* by Rudolph Dirks in Hearst's *New York Journal* of 1897 and after. Gissing gained acceptance at Chicago's would-be comic weekly with his own first attempt at comedy, **"A Terrible Mistake"** (5 May 1877), but he signed it unjocosely G. R. Gresham, from his full initials. He published at least two other stories there, but they have vanished, along with most issues of this ephemeral little paper. Apart from Hill's perpetual stalling on money owed, Gissing can hardly have squeezed very satisfactory payments from this tight-fisted managing editor.[54]

The last Chicago paper to which Gissing turned, the weekly *Alliance,* also stood only a block or two from the *Tribune,* with business and editorial offices at 52 and 97 Clark. Throughout 1877 the *Alliance*' s editorial board—mostly clergymen—kept on changing, so that we cannot reconstruct whom Gissing met there. We do know that his mere presence at this religious paper required an intellectual compromise on his part, for he was and always remained a staunch nonbeliever.[55] He nevertheless published three *Alliance* stories, under the pseudonym G. R. Gresham, on 12 May, 2 June, and 30 June 1877. In contrast to his humorous one for the comic *National Weekly,* Gissing made his tales for the religious paper solemn and even somewhat moralistic, as if slanting them towards pulpit tastes.

Finally, while still in Chicago, he mailed a story to a New York magazine, the nationally sold *Appletons' Journal.* Most likely, he learned about it from advertisements in the *Tribune* of April 16th and May 17th, 1877, listing the contents of each forthcoming issue, including short fiction—a possible market for his own. Again he used the pseudonym G. R. Gresham. *Appletons'* accepted his story, **"An English Coast-Picture,"** well before June 18th, 1877, probably as early as May, and published it in July.[56] Nearly half a year after a Boston magazine had turned down Gissing's first attempted fiction, he broke into the pages of a New York one that paid him forty-five dollars—two and a half times as much as even the charitable Samuel Medill.[57] The young writer must have felt that he had at last arrived.

The *Appletons'* acceptance told the exile to go East, young man. Sometime before July 22nd, Gissing left Chicago for New York. Almost certainly, he aimed to continue at *Appletons'* his tried and proven tactic of approaching editors in the flesh and not just through the mails. But *New Grub Street*'s account suggests a still more basic reason for returning to the Atlantic coast:

> "And I began to grow homesick, wanted to get back to England, The result was that I found myself one day in New York again, but without money enough to pay for a passage home. I tried to write one more story."[58]

In Gissing's case, "homesick" for England almost certainly included homesick for Nell. But *Appletons'* seems to have turned down his second attempt for them and left him in the lurch on the Eastern seaboard. By leaving Chicago, he had, in effect, risked a writer's free fall, for he had given up his safety-net, those comforting payments from Samuel Medill.

Instead of winning glory as a writer in New York, Gissing blundered into a comedy of errors, an absurd anticlimax to his Chicago adventures. Apparently because he still expected his stories to come out in Chicago, he studied the out-of-town papers in a New York City reading room. There the former scholar of the classics chanced to notice a Homeric-sounding name: the *Troy* (New York) *Times*. He saw to his amazement that on July 14th it had stolen his own first story from the *Chicago Tribune* (10 March 1877). Squandering most of his remaining money, he rode a steamboat up the Hudson toward the *Troy Times* offices, where its editor refused to pay for further Gissing stories when he could steal them just as well. Without enough cash for combined food and lodgings, Gissing rented a tiny room by the day and lived five whole days on handfuls of peanuts from vendors in the street, the cheapest meal in town. Yet his utter pathos saved him once again. Marooned in a place with only one paper, he went to a lawyer's office to plead for copying work, but a merciful old custodian sent him instead to a local traveling photographer who hired him "on the spot" as a helper.[59]

In the words of *New Grub Street,* this "good-natured young" photographer took Gissing on a "five or six" week tour through nearby towns and cities to solicit "orders for . . . reproducing . . . old portraits." In each place they split up and went from house to house, yet Gissing had no talent for foot-in-the-door salesmanship. He averaged only one order a week. Because the photographer paid him a commission without any salary, the inept young assistant would have remained in the streets and starved if his kindly employer had not taken care of Gissing's food and lodgings.[60]

As the first anniversary approached of his having lost Nell, he determined now to keep his old promise of an ultimate reunion with her. But in spite of having published some twenty short stories, he still lacked money for the boat trip home and could hardly earn it from his scattered few commissions. As a result, he had to borrow from a Boston friend, a loan for which Gissing left belongings as security. He sailed from Boston to Liverpool sometimes after September 1st, 1877, and landed on October 3rd. He may well have hurried directly to Nell to resume their old relationship, for a gap in his movements occurs in the record. By October's second week, without any funds and, in fact, owing money, this prodigal son went back to his family in Wakefield and a very cool reception. At some point before October 18th, he departed to continue his career as a writer, this time in London, England's literary hub. No later than that autumn, he brought Nell to live with him there.[61]

Together again at last, Gissing and Nell Harrison did not, indeed, live happily ever after. During their first two years, he tried again to reform her, but Nell still went on drinking. Near the second anniversary of their reunion, he married her in an Anglican church. He may have hoped that this formality would enhance her sense of worth. Yet as Mrs. George Gissing, she behaved even worse than before. She squandered household money on drink, hid gin bottles in their apartment, disappeared for days from home, col-

lapsed on the street dead drunk, and needed an invalid's home and then a paid companion. She seems at times even to have gone back to prostitution. Finally, she got herself arrested for disturbing the public peace. On about the sixth anniversary of their reunion, he at last separated from her for good. Gissing had delayed the breakup much longer than he should have. Most probably it seemed to drain all meaning from his old disgrace at college and his troubled year of exile—sacrifices now for no one and for absolutely nothing.[62]

By propelling him into fiction, exile had nevertheless transformed his life. His achievement of living abroad for almost five months by writing short stories sustained his spirit in England during early years of failure. His one small English success sprang directly from an old Chicago success: he completely rewrote the *Alliance*'s tale **"The Artist's Child"** (30 June 1877) and got it published with the very same title in *Tinsleys' Magazine* (London) (January 1878), his first work under his own full name. Yet after that, he met with nothing but frustration. By 24 July 1878, he had ceased trying to sell his first attempted novel after many discouraging rejections. Sixteen months later, when he finished another book—*Workers in the Dawn*—many publishers turned it down. But he kept up his morale by recalling the many tales that he had sold in the United States—proof, he felt sure, of his writer's vocation. In order to get *Workers* into print, he stooped at last to vanity publication, paid £125 for producing his novel, and got sixteen shillings back in royalties.[63] He finished his next full-length book some two years later, *Mrs. Grundy's Enemies.* Yet although the firm of Bentley paid cash down for it, they never brought it out. Bentley himself grew disturbed at the absence of an elevated moral tone, and, after long delays, he canceled publication.[64] Rejection of all of Gissing's fiction continued until at last a double success in 1884: *Temple Bar'*s publication of his story **"Phoebe"** (March 1884) and Chapman and Hall's publication of his novel *The Unclassed.* Until then he had endured six London years without getting any novels or stories into print for pay.

Even as less-than-first-rate apprentice work, his large body of fiction accepted in America paved the way later for Gissing's success. America taught him the uses of adversity and also of a strong will. His surviving later diaries record a bulldog tenacity at putting words on paper, thousands a day in spite of many sordid troubles and frequent disappointments.[65] In the twenty-six years after his disgrace and American exile, he published twenty-two novels, four books of nonfiction, and over a hundred short stories—many of these works very fine. Without his early initiation, across the Atlantic, into the rewards and also the hardships of creating prose fiction, he might never have persisted in ultimately winning a distinguished place among English men of letters. In America he had taken his first small steps towards becoming the Gissing whom we know today: the author of *New Grub Street* (1891) and also *Born in Exile* (1892), major English novels very much alive one hundred years after he wrote them.

Notes

1. For Gissing's peculiar arrangement at the Lindow Grove school dormitory and his last-year move to Manchester, see John Spiers and Pierre Coustillas,

The Rediscovery of George Gissing: A Reader's Guide (London: National Book League, 1971), 21; [Pierre Coustillas], "Editor's Note" to "George Gissing at College," by Francis Noel Lees, Gissing Newsletter 5 (April 1969): 11. For young Gissing's study habits, see letters of George Gissing to Arthur Bowes, 21 February and 24 May 1874, The Collected Letters of George Gissing, Vol. 1: 1863-1880, ed. Paul F. Mattheisen, Arthur C. Young, and Pierre Coustillas (Athens, Ohio: Ohio University Press, 1990), 27, 32. For Gissing's meeting with Nell Harrison in a pub, see John Halperin, Gissing: A Life in Books (Oxford: Oxford University Press, 1982), 17—an account derived from Pierre Coustillas's as-yet-unpublished biography of Gissing. For the prostitutes near Cobden house and for the porter's humiliation, see Edward Fiddes, Chapters in the History of Owens College and of Manchester University, 1851-1914 (Manchester: Manchester University Press, 1937), 26-27, 54.

2. Gissing's general three-year scholarship at Owens had already run out and, in any case, had offered just free tuition. His two other cash scholarships won in 1875 applied only to the University of London, where he planned to attend later. For Gissing's scholarly awards, see Pierre Coustillas, "George Gissing à Manchester," Etudes Anglaises 16 (July-Sept. 1963): 260-61. For details about the three-year scholarship, see Fiddes, 302-3.

3. Halperin, 16-18; "George Gissing à Manchester," 255-60.

4. The Owens College disciplinary council document speaks of "several cases of theft," meaning a minimum of four, and distinguishes these from the time when Gissing was caught. See "George Gissing à Manchester," 260.

5. Halperin, 11.

6. "George Gissing à Manchester," 260; Halperin, 11, 19.

7. "George Gissing à Manchester," 260-61.

8. Halperin, 20.

9. George Gissing, "A Farewell" (August 1876), Notebook of Ms. poems 1869-1882, Beinecke Rare Book and Manuscript Library of Yale University.

10. Letter of George Gissing to William Gissing, 5 October 1876, and to Algernon Gissing, 13 November 1876, Collected Letters 1:46-48, 51-53; [George Gissing], "Art Notes: 'Elaine'—Rosenthal and Tojetti," Commonwealth, 28 October 1876, p 3.

11. Letter of George Gissing to Algernon Gissing, 13 November 1876, Collected Letters 1:53.

12. On Gissing at Waltham High School, see letter of George Gissing to Algernon Gissing, 28 January 1877, Collected Letters 1:55-58, which cites an annual salary of $800; Halperin, 22. The Beinecke Rare Book and Manuscript Library of Yale University possesses Gissing's certificates from the First Examination for Bachelor of Arts. On the three-exam requirement, see Joseph Thompson, The Owens College: Its Foundation and Growth and Its Connection with Victoria University, Manchester

(Manchester: J. E. Cornish, 1886), 206-7. The news item on Gissing appeared in the Waltham Free Press, 5 January 1877, p. 5.

13. George Gissing, New Grub Street: A Novel (London: Smith, Elder, 1891), 3:105.

14. Gissing must have studied a railroad guide carefully. One from about this time shows that, although he could have gone directly from Boston to Chicago, no emigrant trains traveled this route and the so-called expresses had long stopovers, so that they would have taken almost two whole days—more or less the same as the cheaper trains from New York City. By contrast, an "express" from New York reached Chicago in twenty-two hours and fifty-five minutes—a significant saving in time. See W. F. Allen, ed., Travelers' Official Railway Guide for the United States and Canada: Containing Railway Time Schedules, Connections, and Distances (Philadelphia: National Rail Publication Co., January 1879), 23, 55, 59. For the time from Boston to New York, see Allen, 35. Gissing's first Chicago story appeared March 10th, and in New Grub Street's account, he approached the Tribune's editor the same day as arriving in Chicago, took less than two days to write his first story, saw the editor again on two successive days, and then had to wait till Saturday to see his piece in print. These details would place his latest possible Chicago arrival at four days before the 10th. See New Grub Street 3:106-9.

15. Bessie Louise Pierce, The Rise of a Modern City, 1871-1893, Vol. 3 of A History of Chicago (New York: Alfred A. Knopf, 1957), 196, 224; Charles H. Dennis, Victor Lawson: His Time and His Work (Chicago: University of Chicago Press, 1935), 2.

16. Pierce, 3:405.

17. Francis John Mosher, "Chicago's Saving Remnant: Francis Fisher Browne, William Morton Payne, and the Dial" (Ph.D. diss., University of Illinois, 1950), 21, 27-28.

18. Pierce, 3:324.

19. The details about the Tribune building come from an account of its opening—"The Tribune," Chicago Daily Tribune, 15 February 1873, p. 2—including photograph and diagrams. Gissing's movements through the building come from the fictionalized but well-confirmed account in New Grub Street, 3:107. The description of Gissing's appearance at nineteen—later he had a droopy mustache and no beard—comes from George A. Stearns, "George Gissing in America," Bookman (New York) (August 1926): 683-84. Samuel Medill's appearance is based on his photograph from Charles D. Mosher, "Mosher's Centennial Historical Album," vol. 7, "Containing Photographs, Autographs and Biographies of Chicago Editors" (1876)—a photograph in the possession of the Graphics Department of the Chicago Historical Society.

20. For the identification of Samuel Medill, see Robert L. Selig, "Gissing's Benefactor at the Chicago Tribune: An Identification from a Passage in New Grub Street," Etudes Anglaises 38 (1985): 434-41. For the state of Medill's desk and his cigar and for

Gissing's approach to him, see *New Grub Street* 3:110-11. For Medill's career, see "Obituary: Samuel J. Medill," *Chicago Tribune*, 21 February 1883, p. 4. For his stern reputation, see "In Memoriam," *Chicago Tribune*, 22 February 1883, p. 4. From the office listings of 36 numbered ones and apparently two unnumbered ones on the ground floor—the cashier's and the business manager's—we can assume an even distribution of them through floors 2 to 5. This would put the managing editor's office, Room 24, on the fourth floor. See "Tribune Building Directory," *Chicago Tribune*, 28 March 1877, p. 4.

21. *New Grub Street* 3:107.

22. Ibid. 3:107-8.

23. Ibid.3:108-9.

24. Letter of George Gissing to Algernon Gissing, 13 November 1876, *Collected Letters* 1:53.

25. George Gissing, "The Sins of the Fathers: A Story in Three Chapters," *Chicago Tribune*, 10 March 1877, p. 11; italics added for emphasis.

26. For Gissing's habitual reuse of earlier failed attempts, see the many examples in George Gissing, *London and the Life of Literature in Late Victorian England: The Diary of George Gissing, Novelist*, ed. Pierre Coustillas (Lewisburg, Pa: Bucknell University Press, 1978).

27. Letter of George Gissing to Algernon Gissing, 13 November 1876, *Collected Letters* 1:53.

28. For both the Wabash Avenue rooming house and the second encounter of Gissing and Medill, see *New Grub Street* 3:106, 108-9. The novel describes the rooming house as full of actors, so it clearly stood near the theater district, indicated by *The Lakeside Annual Directory of the City of Chicago: Embracing a Complete General and Business Directory* (Chicago: Donnelly, Lloyd and Company, 1876-77), 1114-1117, 1204, as mainly in and around Clark Street between Randolph and Monroe. The *Directory*'s listing of hotels and lodgings on pages 1203-4 suggests that $4.50 a week lay in the lowest range. Gissing could have stayed at the St. Charles Hotel on Clark just above Madison for only $3.50 a week but without food included. For day-by-day weather, see "The Weather," *Chicago Journal*, 8 March 1877, p. 1, "The Weather," *Chicago Journal*, 10 March 1877, p. 1.

29. *New Grub Street* 3:110-11.

30. George Everett Hastings, introductions: pt. 1 to Brownie *by George Gissing: Now Reprinted from the* Chicago Tribune *Together with Six Other Stories Attributed to Him*, with introductions by George Everett Hastings, Vincent Starrett, and Thomas Ollive Mabbott (New York: Columbia University Press, 1931), 8.

31. *New Grub Street* 3:107-9.

32. In 1987 I rejected George Everett Hastings's attribution to Gissing of the "Browne-Vargrave" trilogy, leaving him no more than five stories from the *Tribune*. See Robert L. Selig, "Unconvincing Gissing Attributions: 'The Death-Clock,' 'The Serpent-Charm,' 'Dead and Alive,'" *The Library: The Transactions of the Bibliographical Society*, 6th ser., 9 (June 1987): 169-72. For a disagreement with my arguments and for my reply, see Pierre Coustillas and Robert L. Selig, "Correspondence: Unconvincing Gissing Attributions," *The Library: The Transactions of the Bibliographical Society*, 6th ser., 9 (September 1987): 274-77. Obviously, though, Medill could have met with Gissing at other times besides acceptances, and the editor may even have turned down some pieces.

33. *New Grub Street* 3:109-10.

34. "In Memoriam," 4.

35. Ibid., 4.

36. *New Grub Street* 3:107.

37. Letter of George Gissing to Algernon Gissing, 7 February 1880, *Collected Letters* 1: 238; *New Grub Street* 3:109.

38. Morley Roberts, *The Private Life of Henry Maitland: A Record Dictated By J. H.*, rev. and ed. Morley Roberts (London: Everleigh Nash, 1912), 37-38.

39. *New Grub Street* 3:106.

40. Unlike the highly improbable "Browne-Vargrave" attributions, the "R.I.P." one seems quite possible. Its French setting is unusual for early Gissing (he had yet to visit France), but it may connect with the signed "Gretchen" *Chicago Tribune* (12 May 1877). Still, these stories differ sharply: "Gretchen" depicts an English art-student in Paris, but "R.I.P." has a wholly French cast.

41. See the advertised contents of the forthcoming July *Appletons'*, including G. R. Gresham [George Gissing], "An English Coast-Picture", in the *Chicago Tribune*, 18 June 1877, p. 7; the lead-time for planning a monthly issue and advertising its contents suggests an acceptance of Gissing's piece before June. For *Appletons'* payment, see letter of George Gissing to Algernon Gissing, 7 February 1880, *Collected Letters* 1:238.

42. George Gissing's American Notebook in the Beinecke Rare Book and Manuscript Library of Yale University gives the following month-by-month itinerary on its first two pages: Chicago, March-July 1877; New York, July 1877; Troy, N.Y., July 1877; North Adams, Mass., July 1877; Greenfield, Mass., July 1877. *New Grub Street* 3:110 describes the writer as staying in New York at least one day and in Troy at least five and also provides for two July stopovers in nearby towns, so that if we add to these a forced-march itinerary of one day's travel from Chicago to New York and one from New York to Troy, he cannot have left Chicago any later than July 21, 1877, and, most likely, he left earlier.

43. *New Grub Street* 3:110.

44. Whelpdale says specifically that "for some months I supported myself in Chicago, writing for that same paper, and for others." See *New Grub Street* 3:110.

45. For a description of the *News*'s building and its office, see Charles H. Dennis, *Victor Lawson: His*

Time and His Work (Chicago: University of Chicago Press, 1935), 8, 10. The *News* remained in this very small space as long as the *Skandinaven* and the Anderson and Lawson printing firm stayed in the building. They were there throughout 1877. See *The Lakeside Annual Directory of the City of Chicago: Embracing a Complete General and Business Directory,* compiled by Thomas Hutchinson (Chicago: Donnelly, Lloyd and Co., 1877-78), 1244 and 1269. Not until the 1878-79 *Directory* does the *Skandinaven* appear at new quarters, 89 Franklin, and do Anderson and Lawson drop out altogether from the list of printing firms. See *The Lakeside Annual Directory of the City of Chicago: Embracing a Complete General and Business Directory,* compiled by Thomas Hutchinson (Chicago: Donnelly, Lloyd and Co., 1878-79), 1304, 1330-32.

46. Dennis, 8, 10, 12. The description of young Stone is based on an 1872 photograph of him without a mustache in Associated Press, *"M.E.S." His Book: A Tribute and a Souvenir of the Twenty-Five Years, 1893-1918, of the Service of Melville E. Stone as General Manager of the Associated Press* (New York: Harper & Brothers, 1918), opposite 46. See also the 1876 sketch of Stone with a mustache in Melville E. Stone, *Fifty Years a Journalist* (Garden City, N.Y.: Doubleday, Page & Co., 1921), 62. For his career at the Associated Press, see the accounts of various associates in *"M.E.S."*

47. See the editorial attacks on the Medills in the *Chicago Daily News,* 7 April 1877, p. 2; 9 April 1877, p. 2; 14 April 1877, p. 4; 24 April 1877, p. 2; 28 April 1877, p. 4; 1 May 1877, p. 2; 2 May 1877, p. 2; 10 May 1877, p. 2; 14 May 1877, p. 2; 24 May 1877, p. 2; 29 May 1877, p. 2; 11 June 1877, p. 2; 18 June 1877, p. 2. For Joseph Medill as the city's mayor, see Stephen Longstreet, *Chicago: 1869-1919* (New York: David McKay, 1973), 223.

48. Stone, 56.

49. For Lloyd's confrontation at the *Tribune* and Bross's position and relationship to Joseph Medill, see Lloyd Wendt, *Chicago Tribune: The Rise of a Great American Newspaper* (Chicago: Rand McNally, 1979), 230, 246-47, 261-62, 296. For Bross's *Tribune* office, Room 28, see "Tribune Building Directory," *Chicago Tribune,* 14 January 1877, p. 4. For the appearance of Joseph Medill in 1876, see the photograph from Mosher in the Graphics Department of the Chicago Historical Society. For a photograph of William Bross circa 1876, see [George P. Upton and Elias Colbert], *Biographical Sketches of the Leading Men of Chicago* (Chicago: Wilson, Pierce & Co., 1876), opposite 125.

50. Ten days before Gissing first published anonymously in the *Journal,* it was attacked by a *Tribune* editorial. See Editorial, *Chicago Tribune,* 18 April 1877, p. 4. Two months before he first published anonymously in the *Post,* it was attacked editorially by the *Tribune.* See Editorial, *Chicago Tribune,* 2 April 1877, p. 4.

51. The respective addresses of the three papers come from the *Lakeside Directory* (1877-78), 1242-44.

52. George Gissing, *George Gissing's Commonplace Book: A Manuscript in the Berg Collection of the New York Public Library,* ed. Jacob Korg (New York: New York Public Library, 1962), 52.

53. For an account of this detective work, see Robert L. Selig, "The *National Weekly:* A Lost Source of Unknown Gissing Fiction," *Gissing Newsletter* 18 (January 1982): 2-9. Hill's career can be traced in the *Lakeside* directories of 1876-77 and 1877-78. The location of the shop at the "corner of Clark and Madison" appears in a front-page advertisement of it in the *Chicago Daily Tribune,* 8 March 1877, p. 1, which Gissing may well have seen, though he probably learned of the *National Weekly* from the *Lakeside Directory* itself.

54. For details about the paper, see "The *National Weekly:* A Lost Source of Unknown Gissing Fiction," 2-9. Only at the Chicago Historical Society do the following few issues survive: 7 August 1875, 5 February 1876, 6 July 1878, and 11 September 1880.

55. For the *Alliance*'s address, see the *Lakeside Directory* (1877-78), 351. For its changing editors and for evidence that the distinguished nonclergyman Francis Fisher Browne did not take over its literary section until after Gissing had left Chicago, see Mosher, 26-27. For a summary of Gissing's agnosticism both early and late, see Jacob Korg, *George Gissing: A Critical Biography* (Seattle: University of Washington Press, 1963), 14-15, 243-44.

56. Advertisement of "*Appletons' Journal* for May," *Chicago Tribune,* 16 April 1877, p. 7; Advertisement of "*Appletons' Journal* for June," *Chicago Tribune,* 17 May 1877, p. 7; Advertisement of "*Appletons' Journal* for July," *Chicago Tribune,* 18 June 1877, p. 7, announcing among its contents Gissing's forthcoming story.

57. Letter of George Gissing to Algernon Gissing, 13 November 1876 and 7 February 1880, *Collected Letters* 1:53 and 238.

58. *New Grub Street* 3:110.

59. These details of the Troy misadventures, along with the quotations, come from *New Grub Street* 3:104, 110-12, as confirmed by George Everett Hastings's discovery—in introductions: pt. 1 to *Brownie,* 10—of the pirated "The Sins of the Fathers" in the *Troy Times.*

60. *New Grub Street*'s account of Gissing's commercial tour is confirmed by the itinerary in his American Notebook: Troy, N.Y., July 1877; North Adams, Mass., July 1877; Greenfield, Mass., July 1877; Boston, Aug. 1877; Portland, Me., Aug. 1877; Boston, Sept. 1, 1877 *New Grub Street*'s estimate of a "five or six weeks" tour comes out just right if, as we have already indicated, he left Troy in late July. See *New Grub Street* 3:112-13.

61. For the loan, see *Collected Letters* 1:86. For the dates of Gissing's arrival in Liverpool, see American Notebook. For his arrival at Wakefield and his departure, see Halperin, 25. The October 18th date comes from the first extant letter to Gissing on his return home. See letter of William Gissing to George Gissing, 18 October 1877, *Collected Letters*

1:60-61. The later white lie of Algernon and Ellen Gissing that George was married by "the autumn of 1877" shows that by then he was already living with Nell. See the commentary in George Gissing, *Letters of George Gissing to Members of His Family,* collected and arranged by Algernon and Ellen Gissing (London: Constable, 1927), 22.

62. For a summary of these events, see Robert L. Selig, *George Gissing,* Twayne's English Authors Series, no. 346 (Boston: Twayne, 1983), 8-9. For further details, see Halperin, 26-31, 41-44, 50.

63. Letters of George Gissing to Algernon Gissing, 24 July 1878, 3 November 1879, 25 January 1880, 26 February 1880; letter of William Gissing to George Gissing, 21 February 1878, *Collected Letters* 1:98, 214-15, 235-36, 240-41, 238, 75. For the tiny royalty, see *Rediscovery,* 31-32.

64. The manuscript of "Mrs. Grundy's Enemies" has not survived. See Royal A. Gettmann, *A Victorian Publisher: A Study of the Bentley Papers* (Cambridge: Cambridge University Press, 1960), 215-22.

65. For Gissing's steady labor at writing, see almost any page of *London and the Life of Literature in Late Victorian England.*

Pierre Coustillas (essay date 1993)

SOURCE: An introduction to *The Day of Silence and Other Stories,* edited by Pierre Coustillas, J. M. Dent, 1993, pp. xiv-xx.

[*In the following essay, Coustillas provides a thematic analysis of the short fiction comprising* The Day of Silence and Other Stories.]

Despite the considerable interest in George Gissing's life and works in the last four decades—witness the steady flow of biographies and critical studies, of new editions and translations of his novels—his short stories have received very little attention from publishers and critics. Ten years ago Robert L. Selig deplored the situation, observing that in his opinion 'the author's short stories deserve to rank among the best of the late Victorian era'.[1] Whereas *The Odd Women,* his feminist novel, has been dramatized successfully and is available in three paperback editions, and *New Grub Street,* an acknowledged masterpiece, can be obtained from as many publishers, none of his four main collections of short stories is currently in print.

Not that admirers have been wanting. A.H. Bullen, Gissing's own publisher in the 1890s, was one of them. In his *Guide to the Best Fiction* (1913), Ernest A. Baker declared **Human Odds and Ends** and **The House of Cobwebs** to be 'very significant and representative fragments' which show 'how admirably Gissing could work on a small scale.'[2] Christopher Morley admired the latter collection so much that he claimed to read it 'again and again at midnight with unfailing delight.'[3] In the novelist's lifetime his stories found favour with editors as far away as New Zealand, and they have enjoyed an extraordinary vogue in Japan since the interwar years.

It was as a short-story writer that Gissing made his debut in literature, some three years before he turned to the novels on which his reputation mainly rests. The *Chicago Tribune* published his first story, **'The Sins of the Fathers'**, on 10 March 1877, and it was sheer material need that forced it and another twenty into existence. Young Gissing, after being expelled from Owens College, Manchester, had been packed off to America, where it was hoped that he would live down the disgrace that his quixotic attempt to redeem a young prostitute had brought upon him. The stories that appeared in the Chicago press, for the most part anonymously or pseudonymously, constitute the first group of the 115 or so which he wrote for newspapers and magazines until his death in 1903. Inevitably, as he was then nineteen, they are prentice work, more valuable as an index to their author's tormented state of mind than a promise of the indelible mark he was to leave on late Victorian fiction. None of these stories remains uncollected—they may be read in **The Sins of the Fathers** (1924), **Brownie** (1931) and **Lost Stories from America** (1992)—but some additional tales which are known to have been written in Chicago may still emerge from oblivion if a file of the paper containing them ever turns up.[4] Exile, robbery, imprisonment loom large among other gloomy themes in those early tales that testify to Gissing's vain struggle to forget and be forgiven his youthful folly. He now and again ventured into thematic areas unconnected with his own predicament, for example the eerie in **'Brownie'**, or indulged in the jocularity that we associate with him as a schoolboy. A fictionalized backdrop of the few months he spent on the fringe of the Middle West literary bohemia is supplied by the well-known chapter of *New Grub Street* in which Whelpdale gives a spirited account of his American adventures, but Gissing is not known to have ever looked back light-heartedly upon his first encounter with starvation, a lost soul wandering on foreign ground.

The second group of his short stories extends over the years 1878-84—from the time of his first, unpublished novel to the publication of *The Unclassed,* his second novel, admired by both George Meredith and Thomas Hardy. Only two of the nine stories in this group appeared in Gissing's lifetime, **'Phoebe'** and **'Letty Coe'**, which George Bentley somewhat reluctantly accepted for his popular magazine *Temple Bar,* feeling guilty after purchasing the rights of, but failing to publish, Gissing's naturalistic novel *Mrs Grundy's Enemies.* Try though he did to vary his subjects and force his naturally pessimistic self to take a more sanguine view of life, Gissing only met with rejections. Neither a gleefully farcical story like **'My First Rehearsal'** nor the brisk social comedy of **'My Clerical Rival'** was deemed acceptable. The tales of this second group were eventually collected in four volumes of varying length, **An Heiress on Condition** (1923), **Stories and Sketches** (1938), **Essays and Fiction** (1970) and **My First Rehearsal and My Clerical Rival** (1970).

Masochistically Gissing convinced himself in the early 1880s that he had no gift for short fiction, and for seven years—the seven years Bentley took to publish **'Letty Coe'**—he concentrated on novels, making his name known among the intelligentsia and those well-educated young men without money, not uncommon in his fiction, who read his books in the copies they borrowed from libraries. No one familiar with his fine series of working-class novels, culminating with *The Nether World* in 1889, was aware of his failure to dispose of equally characteristic but shorter stories. It was the accident of a visit to Glastonbury, the ancient Somerset country town celebrated for its tor and its Arthurian associations, that tempted him to try his hand again at short stories likely to win the approval of magazine editors. The acceptance of **'A Victim of Circumstances'** in 1892 proved decisive. He now realized that if he returned to London, after a couple of years in Devon, he could capitalize on his reputation as author of *New Grub Street* and *Born in Exile,* his two strongest books to date. An unexpected request for a story (which was to be **'Lou and Liz'**) 'like the Bank Holiday scene in *[The] Nether World*'[5] confirmed his feelings. It came from Clement King Shorter, who edited the *Illustrated London News,* the *English Illustrated Magazine* and the *Sketch,* and was bent on improving the cultural tastes of the new readers turned out by the board schools.

Gissing was prepared to meet the challenge if it entailed no lowering of his artistic standards. With the assistance of William Morris Colles, his literary agent, he embarked on a second career. From then on many of his short stories were commissioned by editors, chiefly C.K. Shorter and Jerome K. Jerome. The demand reached such a peak in 1895 that he thought he must learn to refuse (and occasionally did refuse) the least tempting offers for the simple reason that he might, in those days of small novels and ever shorter short stories, never be able to write any more full-length novels like his last two three-deckers, *The Odd Women* (1893) and *In the Year of Jubilee* (1894). Yet he readily admitted that this kind of work, to which he soon became accustomed, even though it required an altogether new technique, suited him well. Furthermore, shorter pieces were less incompatible with a disorderly domestic life than protracted novels. If the dedicated artist that he remained to the end mildly regretted having entered upon the commercial path, his 'Account of Books' attests that the sharp rise of his income in the mid-1890s is largely explained by the fees he received from editors. His short stories were read by a much wider audience than his novels. His work was printed in a variety of publications—popular newspapers and *avant-garde* quarterlies, as well as illustrated monthlies and stylish publications that were content to capture an audience of connoisseurs. The very last piece he completed, a few days before the outbreak of his fatal illness, and just when the ending of his historical novel *Veranilda* was at long last in sight, was a short story urgently requested by the *Daily Mail,* **'Topham's Chance'** . With a few exceptions, all those which make up the third and by far the most important group were distributed haphazardly among four volumes, three of them posthumous, which have delighted generations of book-collectors, **Human Odds and Ends** (1898), **The House of Cobwebs** (1906), *A Victim of Circumstances* (1927) and **Stories and Sketches** (1938).

Ranging chronologically from 1893 to 1903, the present selection first glances back to the days when Gissing made of working-class life his main study. Indeed the link between **'Lou and Liz'** and *The Nether World* was specified by the editor of the *English Illustrated Magazine,* although the gloomy atmosphere of the bank holiday merry-making in the novel has lifted. The narrator is amused rather than distressed by the rowdiness of the scenes in which Lou, Liz and the latest common-law wife of Bishop/Willox join

to unravel his precise status in the eye of the law. Respectability is a relative value, and the cawing rooks of Rosherville Gardens that witness this episode look wiser than the squabbling holiday-makers they watch. The story also links up with *In the Year of Jubilee* (1894), in which Gissing was to review official celebrations and popular rejoicings with the soberness of hindsight. Its natural complement is **'One Way of Happiness'**, whose setting he had studied at close quarters in the 1880s when he would occasionally seek rest from metropolitan turmoil in Eastbourne. Bank holiday crowds had long since robbed him of the political and social illusions he had entertained in his radical days. Thus his alter ego Osmond Waymark in *The Unclassed* admits that his former 'zeal on behalf of the suffering masses was nothing more nor less than disguised zeal on behalf of [his] own starved passions.'[6] By the next decade he had come to consider the people more serenely, however, as appears in **'The Day of Silence'**, an admirably conducted tragedy of lowly life; his compassion could still be as easily roused as his condemnation of human folly. Yet another facet of his response to the *mores* of the people is revealed in the only story reprinted [in ***The Day of Silence and Other Stories***] that is notable for its suspense, **'Fleet-Footed Hester'**, with its apparently happy ending. The discreet classical allusion to Atlanta in the title echoes the classical metaphors and similes in his proletarian novels.

The love interest which prevails in **'Lou and Liz'** and **'Fleet-Footed Hester'** has ramifications in a few of the other tales. Mr Whiston, the 'scrupulous father', may look startlingly different from John Rayner, Hester's future husband, but Gissing points with ironic subtlety to their one common characteristic—an undue concern for conventions which, in both stories, nearly has the better of emotional impulses. Class-consciousness, traced again in a different milieu, crops up obtrusively in **'An Inspiration'**, and is just as much of an obstacle to emotional fulfilment; it is also present in the only other story which concludes, rather wryly, with the prospect of a union, **'The Fate of Humphrey Snell.'** The poor herb-gatherer has a personality of a kind which rarely meets with approval, and we leave him precariously happy and under sufferance largely for reasons that smack of social prejudice. A misfit he was and he remains in a world where frustrations are in proportion to the consciousness of misery fostered by education—for as Gissing, with a note of self-pity, remarked in *New Grub Street:* 'To the relatively poor (who are so much worse off than the poor absolutely) education is in most cases a mocking cruelty.'[7]

Of the quandaries that stem from the conflict between poverty and aspirations, however unclearly formulated, a few touching examples are offered. Among the male characters elderly Mr Tymperley, the shabby-genteel prototype, is driven by his pathetic discretion to feign philanthropy only to be ultimately unmasked by dire necessity. Christopherson, the gentle, obsessive book-collector, is brought to choose between a chance of his wife's survival in a rural, bookless environment and the prospect of his own withering away through lack of cultural nourishment. As for Humplebee, a victim of good fortune and a temperamental relative of Humphrey Snell, he has been too sorely tried not to see himself smilingly as a born loser. But the female characters have greater resilience, for—with the exception of the antiphrastically named Miss Jewell—the narrator of **'A Daughter of the Lodge'** encourages us to view May Rockett as a profitably chastened young woman with a modest future, while Miss Rodney's triumphant nature sublimates all her difficulties into a capacity for creating 'a sort of order in [her] little corner of the world.' So that everything is not for the worst in the worst of all possible worlds. By the side of the bleak tragedy related in **'The Day of Silence'** and of the half dozen stories that end on a neutral note there are as many that allow of hope for the struggling underdogs that populate the scene. Foolishness and social oppression may well still be endemic in this late Victorian world—Gissing had a knack for spotting them—but generosity is not altogether absent from it. Above all, we are led to ponder the sanity of revolt—whether conscious and reasoned, or instinctive and bred by the humdrum working of the social organism. An urgent need for emancipation, a hankering after a larger life are perceptible throughout and, quite naturally, are felt more distinctly by women.

Yet Gissing's position was not that of a radical feminist. As Sandra Enzer has noted, 'he advocated neither militancy nor covert rebellion against traditional male supremacy.'[8] There is rich evidence in **'Their Pretty Ways'**, for instance, that he held trenchant opinions on a certain type of frivolous, spendthrift Victorian wife he had observed round his suburban home, but about the time he wrote this story, he had already convinced himself that hope lay in female emancipation through better education, even though this would entail a phase of sexual anarchy. He was sensitive to the effects of inadequate training on the individual, on family life and on society at large. The irrational or shallow women he introduced into his stories of the 1890s are by no means an extinct race in his two post-1900 novels of modern life, where he continued to pity the socially handicapped and emotionally starving spinster so aptly sketched in **'The Foolish Virgin.'** For the boredom that time causes to descend on married life he saw no better remedy than a sound, liberal education. In retrospect, his level-headed approach to the problems of married life is more valuable from both literary and historical standpoints than the shrill pessimistic vignettes of a trendy female writer like George Egerton or even the romantic class-ridden pictures of Hardy's *Group of Noble Dames*.

The thematic affinities between the short stories and the novels, especially *The Nether World, The Odd Women, In the Year of Jubilee* and *Our Friend the Charlatan*, are striking—alongside Gissing's refusal to sensationalize or sentimentalize. The ideal, he knows, is as unreachable as a shooting star. The young man who had composed **'An Ode to Truth'** at Owens College remained a truth-teller to the end of his life, as well as a demanding artist. He delighted in his craftsmanship. Irony, humour, pathos are the dominant notes; a commendable restraint can be noticed throughout. Nor is there any monotony in the studiously subdued narrative voice. Deliberately written in a minor key, with an artistic discipline only approached by his three 1895 novellas, *Eve's Ransom, Sleeping Fires* and *The Paying Guest*, his short stories are memorable for the perfect subserviency of plot to character. Above all, whether crepuscular like **'Christopherson'**, or matutinal like **'Fleet-Footed Hester'**, they have meaningful beginnings and quietly summarizing endings. No good short story can be effective without such assets.

Notes

1. Robert L. Selig, *George Gissing* (Boston: Twayne Publishers, 1983), p. 112.

2. London: George Routledge & Sons, 1913, p. 118.

3. *Modern Essays,* selected by Christopher Morley (New York: Brace and Company, 1921), p. 316.

4. Indeed, an entry in Gissing's *Commonplace Book,* edited by Jacob Korg (New York Public Library, 1962), shows that other early stories from his pen still have to be traced in the *National Weekly,* a grandiosely entitled but trashy paper, no number of which is known to have survived for 1877.

5. Diary entry for 30 March 1893, *London and the Life of Literature in Late Victorian England: The Diary of George Gissing, Novelist,* edited by Pierre Coustillas (Hassocks: Harvester Press, 1978), p. 300.

6. Edited by Jacob Korg (Hassocks: Harvester Press, 1976), p. 211.

7. Edited by Bernard Bergonzi (Harmondsworth: Penguin Books, 1968), p. 70.

8. Sandra Solotaroff Enzer, 'Maidens and Matrons: Gissing's Stories of Women', *Dissertation Abstracts International,* August 1978, p. 894-A.

FURTHER READING

Bibliographies

Collie, Michael. *George Gissing: A Bibliographical Study.* Winchester, England: St. Paul's Bibliographies, 1985, 167 p.

> Comprehensive information regarding the composition, sale, and publication of Gissing's works, including the locations of extant manuscripts.

Coustillas, Pierre. "Gissing's Short Stories: A Bibliography." *English Literature in Transition* 7, No. 2 (1964): 59-72.

> Provides a primary bibliography of Gissing's short fiction, including Japanese translations.

Biographies

Collie, Michael. *George Gissing: A Biography.* Folkestone, England: William Dawson and Sons, 1977, 189 p.

> Concentrates on the relationship between Gissing's life and his work.

Donnelly, Mabel Collins. *George Gissing: Grave Comedian.* Cambridge: Harvard University Press, 1954, 254 p.

> Critical biography.

Halperin, John. *Gissing: A Life in Books.* Oxford: Oxford University Press, 1982, 426 p.

> Comprehensive critical biography.

Korg, Jacob. *George Gissing: A Critical Biography.* Seattle: University of Washington Press, 1963, 311 p.

Chronicles Gissing's life and works, providing critical commentary on his novels.

Tindall, Gillian. *The Born Exile.* London: Temple Smith, 1974, 295 p.

Biographical and critical study.

Criticism

Coustillas, Pierre, ed. *Collected Articles on George Gissing.* London: Frank Cass, 1968, 186 p.

Collection of significant essays by prominent critics and Gissing scholars.

Coustillas, Pierre and Partridge, Colin, eds. *Gissing: the Critical Heritage.* London: Routledge and Kegan Paul, 1972, 564 p.

Reprints criticism of Gissing's work from 1880 through 1912.

Goode, John. *George Gissing: Ideology and Fiction.* London: Vision, 1978, 205 p.

Thorough analysis of Gissing's work.

Poole, Adrian. *Gissing in Context.* Totowa, N.J.: Rowman and Littlefield, 1975, 231 p.

Discusses Gissing's work in the context of late nineteenth- and early twentieth-century literature.

Additional coverage of Gissing's life and career is contained in the following sources published by the Gale Group: *Contemporary Authors,* **Vols. 105, 167;** *Dictionary of Literary Biography,* **Vols. 18, 135, 184; and** *Twentieth-Century Literary Criticism,* **Vols. 3, 24, 47.**

Franz Grillparzer
1791-1872

Austrian dramatist, novella writer, poet, and critic.

INTRODUCTION

Grillparzer was a well-known Austrian writer who wrote in an age of transition, between the classical romanticism of Johann Wolfgang von Goethe and Friedrich Schiller and the realism of the middle and late nineteenth century. Known primarily as a dramatist, Grillparzer's reputation as a short story writer is based on his novella, *Der arme Spielmann*. This story is considered a classic Austrian novella and has garnered much critical commentary throughout the ages.

BIOGRAPHICAL INFORMATION

Born on January 15, 1791, in Vienna, Austria, Grillparzer was raised in a wealthy and privileged family. His father was a lawyer; his mother possessed great musical talent. Like his father, Grillparzer studied law at the University of Vienna. Following his graduation in 1811 he worked as a private tutor for an aristocratic family. In 1814 he became an administrator at the Imperial Archives, and in 1832, he was appointed director. Grillparzer began to write for the stage, and on January 31, 1817, *Die Ahnfrau* was performed at the Theater an der Wien, launching his prestigious playwriting career. In 1826 he was arrested as a member of the Ludlamshöhle Club, a group of writers and artists suspected of propagating subversive ideas. The charges were dropped. On his retirement from the Imperial Archives in 1856, he was named Hofrat (privy councillor). Furthermore, he was appointed a member of the Upper House by Emperor Franz Joseph in 1861. Grillparzer died on January 21, 1872, at the age of eighty-one. He was so popular at his death that tens of thousands of people participated in his funeral procession.

MAJOR WORKS

Grillparzer wrote two novellas in his career: the little-known *Der Kloster bei Sendomir* and the renown *Der arme Spielmann,* which was written in 1848. As *Spielmann* opens, the narrator visits a street festival in a Viennese suburb and is intrigued by the horrible fiddling of a seventy-year-old street musician, Jacob. The two men meet, and a few days later Jacob relates his tragic background to the narrator. Raised in a respectable, middle-class home, Jacob was working as an unpaid copy clerk in a government office. One day he heard his neighbor, the grocer's daughter Barbara, sing a popular song, and at that moment, decided to devote his life to music. When Jacob visits Barbara to learn about music, a servant sees the two together and a scandal ensues. Jacob is expelled from his

father's house, and the tragedy is compounded when his father dies suddenly. He is befriended by Barbara as well as her father, who hopes for a share of Jacob's inheritance. When Jacob discovers that he has been swindled out of his inheritance by his father's clerk, Barbara's father discourages their deepening relationship. Eventually she marries a butcher. Jacob throws himself into music, becoming an itinerant street musician. After hearing Jacob's story, the narrator loses touch with him, only to find several months later that Jacob died of a fever. The narrator attempts to buy Jacob's violin from Barbara, but she refuses to part with the instrument. As he departs, the narrator sees her silently crying over the loss of her former lover.

CRITICAL RECEPTION

Der arme Spielmann is considered one of the best Austrian works of fiction in the nineteenth century. At the time of its publication, the novella was virtually ignored. In fact, serious critical examination of the work did not begin until 1925, when scholars began to explore the autobiographical aspects of the story. A recurring theme of commentary has been the perception that the narrator and Jacob should be considered as the two sides of Grillparzer: the pragmatic cynic and the idealistic artist. Jacob's problems with women and his inability to communicate his ideas seem to parallel Grillparzer's life. Several critics have attempted to place *Der arme Spielmann* within the literary and political context of the nineteenth century. Stylistic examinations of the novella focus on the role of the narrator and the effect of the frame story. In addition commentators have discussed the portrayal of Jacob and debated the role of music in the story.

PRINCIPAL WORKS

Short Fiction

Der arme Spielmann (novella) 1848

Other Major Works

Blanka von Kastilien (drama) 1809
Die Ahnfrau [The Ancestress] (drama) 1817
Sappho (drama) 1818
Das goldene Vliess [The Golden Fleece] (drama) 1821
König Ottokars Glück und Ende [King Ottocar: His Rise and Fall] (drama) 1825
Ein treuer Diener seines Herrn [A Faithful Servant of His Master] (drama) 1828
Des Meeres und der Liebe Wellen [Hero and Leander] (drama) 1831
Der Traum ein Leben [A Dream Is Life] (drama) 1834
Tristia ex ponto (poetry) 1835
Weh dem, der lügt! [Thou Shalt Not Lie] (drama) 1838
Die Jüdin von Toledo [The Jewess of Toledo] (drama) 1872
Ein Bruderzwist in Habsburg [Family Strife in Habsburg] (drama) 1872
Libussa [Libussa] (drama) 1874
Sämtliche Werke. 42 vols. (drama, novella, poetry, and criticism) 1909-48

CRITICISM

Ivar Ivask (essay date 1967)

SOURCE: An introduction to *The Poor Fiddler,* by Franz Grillparzer, translated by Alexander and Elizabeth Henderson, Frederick Ungar, 1967, pp. 5-25.

[*In the following essay, Ivask places* Der arme Spielmann *within the context of nineteenth-century fiction and assesses its impact on Austrian fiction.*]

". . . For it is by perfection of form that poetry enters life, external life. True emotion can convey only what lies within. But it is the task of all art to exemplify the inner life by the outer surface."[1]

The Poor Fiddler, the story of a failure, is told with genuine sympathy and yet objective detachment. It could well have had as its author one of the great Russian novelists of the last century—Gogol, Dostoevsky, or Turgenev. The first-person narrator characterizes himself as a dramatist and a passionate lover of his fellow men, especially the common people. He also stresses his strong anthropological bent and psychological curiosity. Indeed, he believes that "In truth, no one can understand the lives of the famous unless he has entered into the feelings of the humble. An invisible but continuous thread connects the brawling of drunken market porters with the strife of the sons of gods, and Juliet, Dido or Medea exist in embryo within every young servant girl. . . . " This rather astonishing credo of realism comes from a writer who was a contemporary of Goethe, writing at the height of idealism and romanticism in literature. The story was begun in 1831, completed some ten years later, but not published until 1847.

The author, Franz Grillparzer (1791-1872), was born and died in Vienna. His father was a lawyer; his mother possessed great musical talent. Grillparzer studied law at the University of Vienna and was later employed as a civil servant in various positions, finally as director of the State Archives (1832-56). After his mother's suicide in a fit of religious madness, he set out on an Italian journey. A poem, "Die Ruinen von Campo Vaccino" [The Ruins of Campo Vaccino], written on this journey, was received with hostility in court circles. In this poem, Grillparzer expressed sympathy with the fact that ancient Rome had had to yield to Christianity. Because of this, he was suspected of anticlerical sentiments by the ever-suspicious secret police of Metternich's reactionary regime. From that time on, he was beset by difficulties with the censors. In 1821, Grillparzer met Katharian Fröhlich, and a lifelong relationship outside marriage ensued. He traveled in Germany (1826 and 1847), France (1836), and visited Constantinople and Athens (1843). He knew personally many of his great contemporaries such as Goethe, Beethoven, Heine, and Hebbel. When his comedy *Weh dem, der lügt* [Woe to Him Who Lies], written in 1838, failed at its première, Grillparzer decided to publish no more plays. In 1856, he was retired with the rank of Court Councillor (*Hofrat*) and in 1861 was made a member of the *Herrenhaus* (House of Lords). Yet these honors came far too late to assuage Grillparzer's bitter awareness that he was not really at home in his own country: a very Austrian fate.

Grillparzer is considered by most critics to be the greatest Austrian dramatist. This claim is based on his verse plays, in which he tried to fuse elements of the Spanish and Austrian baroque and the Viennese popular theater with the classical drama of Goethe and Schiller. Grillparzer's deepest artistic sympathies were certainly with the colorful and passionate Spanish baroque dramatists, Calderón, Lope de Vega, and Tirso da Molina (many of whose plays he minutely annotated in his diaries); yet his critical mind was almost equally attracted by the rationalism of Enlightenment, which in Austria took the form of "Josephinism." Grillparzer's dramatic figures are often caught in the tragic dilemma of being compelled to act but hesitating to do so, because all action of necessity results in some guilt. His plays on Greek themes, such as *Sappho* (1819), or *Das goldene Vließ* [*The Golden Fleece*] (1822), are less successful than those that deal with Austrian and Slav history—for example, *Ein Bruderzwist in Habsburg* [*Family Strife in Hapsburg*] (1873), perhaps his greatest dramatic achievement. The love story of Hero and Leander has found a poetically sensitive presentation in the play *Des Meeres und der Liebe Wellen* [*The Waves of the Sea and of Love*] (1831); it reveals the dramatists's Austrian gift for creating psychologically believable, strong women characters. The English critic Ronald Peacock comments perceptively on Grillparzer's dramatic art: "In poetic power, in the creative use of language, he is inferior to the lyric poets of the great periods—Novalis, Hölderlin, George, Rilke; inferior even to a prose rhapsodist like Herder. *But in his sense of reality he is unique,* if we except the rather special case of Goethe. It may be that his Austrian nationality has something to do with it; for Austria, as the centre of power of the Holy Roman Empire and later the Austro-Hungarian, came nearer to political success than the modern German Reich has ever done."[2] This unique sense of reality stood Grillparzer in good stead when he wrote **The Poor Fiddler.**

Looking for parallels in German literature, we find a similar early rebellion against the canons of idealism and romanticism in Georg Büchner's story *Lenz* (written around 1835). "I demand of art," we read, "that it be life and the possibility that it might exist—nothing else matters; we then have no need to ask whether it is beautiful or ugly. The sense that what has been created has life stands above the other two precepts and is the only criterion in art. . . . Idealism is the most humiliating of insults to human nature. Let them try just once to immerse themselves in the life of the humble people and then reproduce this again in all its movements, its implications, in its subtle, scarcely discernible play of expression. . . . "[3]

Georg Büchner seemed to have the makings of a German Dostoevsky, but he died prematurely in 1837 at the age of twenty-four, and was duly discovered only much later by the naturalists and expressionists. So-called German "poetic realism," which dominated German literature from about Büchner's death until the final decades of the past century, had little of his bite and sheer creative energy, even less of his profound social concern. Büchner remained a lonely pioneer without establishing a German "great tradition" of the realistic novel that might be placed alongside the classics of the Russian, French, and English writers of the age. The German novel and novella of the later nineteenth century basically owed more to idealism and a lingering romanticism than to realism in the sense given it by the great European novelists.

Dostoevsky is supposed to have remarked once that "We all came out of Gogol's 'Overcoat.'" The same could be said in relation to the Austrian novelists after Grillparzer's truly seminal story **The Poor Fiddler.** More often than not the protagonists of Austrian stories have been variations on the theme first played by the poor fiddler on his cracked violin. A veritable procession of complex-ridden, indecisive anti-heroes, "superfluous men" (well-known to readers of the Russian novel), failures in practical life but pure of heart, people the Austrian novel and stage to this very

day. They are usually presented with warm understanding and a psychological insight such that even those works conceived well before Freud may strike one as being positively "Freudian." To name just a few random examples of this Austrian "great tradition": the misunderstood, miserly country parson in Adalbert Stifter's story, *Kalkstein* [*Limestone*], the first version of which was written in 1848, perhaps in competition with Grillparzer's story (which was hailed by Stifter as a masterpiece); Marie von Ebner-Eschenbach's *Dorf-und Schloßgeschichten* [*Village and Castle Stories*] (1883) contains a whole gallery of related types; Ferdinand von Saar's subtle analysis of the make-believe world of *Lieutenant Burda* (1889); Arthur Schnitzler's *Lieutenant Gustl* (1900) and his early, effective use of interior monologue to render the inner turmoil of an average fellow caught in an insoluble dilemma that involves his honor or dishonor, life or death; Robert Musil's first novel, *Die Verwirrungen des Zöglings Törless* (*Young Törless*) (1906), about the psychological and physiological confusions of adolescence; Rilke's hypersensitive poet, Malte, the subject of *Die Aufzeichnungen des Malte Laurids Brigge* (*The Notebooks of Malte Laurids Brigge*), in Paris, and Albert Ehrenstein's helpless *Tubutsch* in Vienna (both published in 1910); the host of frustrated and guilt-ridden bachelors in Kafka's stories and novels; Musil's paradoxical *Der Mann ohne Eigenschaften* (*The Man without Qualities*) (1931-33); the pathetic Lieutenant Trotta in Joseph Roth's novel, *Radetzkymarsch* (1932); Heimito von Doderer's widowed civil servant turned voyeur, Julius Zihal, in *Die erleuchteten Fenster* [*The Illuminated Windows*], and his Lieutenant Melzer whose separation from reality is gradually overcome in *Die Strudlhofstiege* [*The Strudlhof Stairs*], both published in 1951; and, in conclusion, Herbert Eisenreich's long story, *Der Urgroßvater* [*The Great-grandfather*] (1964), in which the rather ordinary protagonist becomes so pre-occupied with his origins that he loses touch with reality. More than a century of a fascinatingly and closely interrelated narrative tradition![4]

Obviously the Austrian Franz Grillparzer has been more fortunate than his German contemporary Georg Büchner. **The Poor Fiddler** did become the fountainhead of a rich prose tradition in which the "Insulted and Injured" (to use an apt formula by Dostoevsky), the surprising transformations of the poor fiddler, Jacob, have reappeared again and again. There are many reasons for this occurring in Austrian and not in German literature. The scope of this introduction permits to list only a few, and even these merely in passing. First of all, the Austrians are conservative *par excellence* and therefore great supporters of tradition (to the frequent grief of Austrian innovators and revolutionaries); secondly, Protestant idealism never had great appeal in Catholic Austria; and, thirdly, the baroque world view and style, oddly surviving well into the nineteenth century and beyond, immunized the Austrian writers against the lure of German romanticism. It could be formulated—boldly and paradoxically—that Austrian literature has been attracted time and time again to a kind of baroque realism, characterized by a constant tension between illusion and reality, being and doing. It is an existential tension that is to be borne, if not in faith, then at least with stoical equanimity, and it does *not* annihilate reality itself. After all, the Roman emperor and stoic philosopher Marcus Aurelius died in Vienna and it was on Austrian soil that he wrote the following remarks: "In the life of a man, his time is but a moment, his being an incessant flux, his senses a dim rushlight, his body a prey of worms, his soul an unquiet eddy, his fortune dark, and his fame doubtful. In short, all that is body is as coursing waters, all that is of the soul as dreams and vapors. . . . "[5] The emperor is still fondly remembered by the Viennese. Heimito von Doderer claimed only recently that it is "Marcus Aurelius Antoninus, with whose modern as well as profound notes Viennese literary history begins a few years before A.D. 180."[6] Indeed, the proverbial gaiety of the Viennese is not a diagnosis but a therapy for a fundamentally melancholy, self-analytical people at the crossroads of several nations (to refer to an enlightening formula by Hans Weigel). Austrian literature is by and large more deeply embedded in the country's landscape, filled with more affection for its capital and its society, evokes more lovingly a whole "way of life" than we are accustomed to in the literature of Germany. There is no doubt that Grillparzer is a truly representative son of his people.

Grillparzer was oversensitive, moody, hypochondriac, easily depressed, irritable, melancholy, self-tormenting; in short, an extremely complex man. (When traveling, he wanted nothing so much as to be home again; back in Vienna, however, he felt stifled and longed for freedom abroad.) His autobiography, abundant literary criticism, and dramatic works bear witness to this complexity. Yet nowhere does he present himself with as much clairvoyance and mature detachment as in his story about the poor fiddler. It seems truly to be an objective correlative of his own life and doubts, a self-contained work of art in no need of supporting biographical explanation to be fully appreciated and understood. Nevertheless, it constitutes an additional attraction for anyone acquainted with Grillparzer's biography to observe how the author's own taciturnity and his stiffly correct behavior (occasionally animated by plain human curiosity) are so well reflected in the outline portrait of the first-person narrator of the story. Although the fate of the poor fiddler occupies undisputedly the center of the stage, the story certainly gains in poignancy from the constant subtle counterpoint with the narrator's character and the framework that it adds to the story of the very much more unhappy and confused man—the fiddler.

But the attentive reader may be left wondering in the end whether Jacob has not lived more intensely and deeply amidst all his tribulations than the narrator ever has or will. Thus Grillparzer challenges through his art our very concept of what constitutes meaningful reality and healthy normalcy. We may ask further if Grillparzer is not only reflected in the courteous first-person narrator of the tale but, perhaps, in Jacob as well. Does not Jacob's highly questionable "art" mirror some of the Austrian dramatist's own self-lacerating doubts concerning the ultimate quality of his art when compared with the celebrated achievements of Goethe and Schiller? In Jacob, we find Grillparzer's own love of music, sense of measure, love of truth, enthusiasm, and penchant for pedantry, developed by the drudgery of office work that left only the evenings for creative activity. But then the effort of Jacob's life and art is consummated on an altogether different plane from that of the author, namely that of self-sacrifice and religious meaning. Jacob dies from the after-effects of having braved the cold waters of the Danube to save some children from the floods. The fact that the enlightened rationalist, Grillparzer, tries to mask his embarrassment at this religious turn of events in his own story—by making Jacob brave the flood-

waters yet another time, merely to salvage the tax books of a gardener—in no way devalues the tears that the woman, whom Jacob never was able to win, sheds for him. In the end, his cracked violin shares pride of place on her living-room wall with the crucifix. Grillparzer intimates here a solution for poor Jacob that was no longer open to himself. Thus Jacob, too, *is* and is *not* the author. The perplexing tension and mystery of great art remain intact.

It was around 1847-48 or a little later that Grillparzer replied to a question as to how he had found the real-life inspiration for his story:

> Quite by accident! For many years, I had been taking my meals at the restaurant "Zum Jägerhorn" in the Spiegelgasse. Often a poor fiddler came there to play. He attracted attention by the remarkable cleanliness of his shabby clothing, and his clumsy movements were touchingly comical. This old man always expressed gratitude for a gift with a short Latin phrase, which indicated an education and better days in the past. Suddenly he stopped coming and stayed away for a long time. Then the great flood of 1830 came. The Brigittenau, where a popular Saint's day is celebrated each year with a folk festival and much merrymaking, was striken hardest of all. I knew that the poor fiddler lived there, and as he did not come to play any more, I assumed that he had died as one of the many flood victims. I was asked to write a story for a pocket-almanac, and so I attempted one in which my poor good friend plays the main part.[7]

So simple and humble was the initial germ of our story. The final work was the result of more than ten years of writing and rewriting. In the story—now for the first time in an English translation that does it full justice—Grillparzer places against the background of a popular Viennese holiday the encounter between two men, one a somewhat sullen, sober dramatist, the other a naïve but serene beggar who makes a living with his fiddle. Both are very lonely and—in differing degrees—artists. Yet the one is at least sure of his social status and superior education, while the other reveals in his poverty flashes of better days, even a certain nobility in his demeanor. The narrator is fascinated by "people" in general, while the beggar is flattered by the gentleman's attention. What attracts the gentleman's curiosity in the first place, and thus triggers the action of the whole story, is that the seventy-year-old beggar plays the violin, following a score, and concludes the performance with a Latin phrase. The gentleman is struck by the incongruity of the caterwauling music and the surprising presence of a score, the very obvious distance between intent and realization. This discrepancy turns out to be the main theme of the story. It is repeated later in other symbolic gestures. The old man shares his room with some journeymen, but with chalk draws a line of demarcation to separate his cleaner living area from theirs; when he dares to return the kiss of the woman he loves, he does so through a glass door.

In the case of the poor fiddler, reality is so hostile and unattainable that he has no other escape than into the ideal. One of the most penetrating analyses of the story was written by J. P. Stern:

> The annihilating conclusion towards which this quiet, unadorned story takes us is no less than the intimation

of a deep and consistent distrust of the substantial world, which appears as a place radically incapable of yielding form and substance to the good will. The pure heart, in this vision, remains disembodied. The value of every thing in the world, of art even—its "objective value"—is as nothing to the purity and goodness and devotion that resides in the heart, mutely, unexpressed, perhaps inexpressible. The rift between being and doing, the severing of intention from realization, of spirit from matter—even the all but tangible "matter" of music—is complete.[8]

Reality has been everything but kind to Jacob in a life that seems to have consisted of nothing but a series of defeats or failures, depending on the vantage point of the judging reader. Born into a rich and influential family of a court councillor, with brothers who easily surpassed him in school by "jumping like chamois from peak to peak," Jacob would have been happy as a craftsman. "I would have liked nothing better than to become a turner or a compositor," he admits in awareness of his natural limitations. Yet such a solution would have been a disgrace for his family, and so the father inflicts upon his son one punishment after another, without the son in his meek obedience ever daring to challenge this cruel and unjust authority. Early in his life, Jacob loses his mother. When he learns of the death of his father, he faints from emotion, regretting that he did not have the opportunity to ask for his father's forgiveness. Devotion and submission could hardly be carried to more intolerable lengths. One is reminded of Kafka's stories *The Judgment* and *Metamorphosis,* with their nightmarish themes of inferiority complexes before paternal authority. (Heinz Politzer has explored the fascination and repulsion felt by the modern Austrian writer toward Grillparzer's story.)[9]

Jacob's job as a humble copyclerk is selected for him by his father. He is kept under constant surveillance, as if he were an irresponsible child. When Jacob finds sudden solace in a simple song that he hears from the neighboring grocer's daughter, Barbara, and visits her in order to get the score for the song, he is expelled from his parental home. But this song, nevertheless, marks a turning point in the life of Jacob, for he takes up the violin again, which he had forgotten since the days of his first instruction. Others may play Bach or Mozart, but no one plays *"den lieben Gott."* It is this that the poor fiddler strives for in his improvisations every evening, until he is reprimanded by his weary neighbors. And they are absolutely right by all normal standards, because the cacophony seems heavenly only to the musician's own ear and, Grillparzer seems to imply, perhaps to God.

Jacob's hopeless naïveté and clumsiness alienated him from his father and his brothers, later from the other clerks in the office where he is employed, and, finally, makes him lose the grocer's daughter to a butcher (which may remind some readers of the way Kafka's "hunger artist" is replaced by a strapping panther). After his father's death, Jacob is even swindled out of his meager inheritance. He dies from exerting his last strength to save a gardener's tax books and a bit of money. In short, Grillparzer has presented to us the tale of a total failure in practical life. A failure because his proud father could not accept that one of his sons would become a mere craftsman? Is Jacob crushed by an overwhelming father complex—somewhat like Georg Bendemann in Kafka's *The Judgment?* This

question certainly cannot and should not be answered unequivocally. Jacob's character is not merely the sum total of his environment. He has had, after all, the remarkable resilience of spirit to turn music into a religious escape, which has helped him to maintain a basic dignity, to achieve a stoic fortitude, and has given him the serenity, even a childlike gaiety, admired by the narrator. Art as a sublimation, a redemption from life's miseries—a familiar theme. Yet Grillparzer's story does not end there, for the "art" of Jacob is that of a deluded amateur, hence art proper cannot be called his salvation. If there is any salvation at all, it is strictly outside reality, a religious act of grace.

After the poor fiddler's tragic death, the narrator visits the butcher's family. He sees Jacob's fiddle on the wall "arranged symmetrically" opposite the crucifix. His idea is to buy the fiddle as a remembrance of the queer old fellow. Grillparzer could have added such a transaction as the last ironic twist to his story. Yet at this point, after the self-sacrifice of Jacob, hard practical reality is touched by the world of the spirit, and Barbara refuses to sell the violin, bursting into tears. What is she weeping about? Simply that the world is as it is, that Jacob deserved better treatment from her, or that his death was unnecessary? The story opens on a note of tumultuous gaiety among the holiday crowd; it ends with the tears of one woman, mutely witnessed by the narrator, "a passionate lover of his fellow men." The reader may ask whether the narrator was changed by the experience or was it merely another anecdote, another psychological "case" for him. And what is *the reader's* judgment and conclusion? Grillparzer's realism is a complex one, a baroque realism in which we still sense the tension between illusion and reality, heaven and hell. Although they are more subdued in the Austria of the nineteenth century, the metaphysical categories are still there, subtly implied by the Austrian writer in the narrative fabric of psychological realism. Grillparzer compares, at the beginning, the holiday crowd to a surging flood: " . . . And at last two rivers flow on triumphantly over and under each other—the Danube Canal follows its old river bed, the more swollen stream of people bursts forth from the narrows of the bridge in an all-submerging flood, to form a wide, turbulent lake." In the end it is the Danube, flooded in actuality, that claims the life of Jacob. It is against this background of billowing anonymous masses and raging forces of nature that Grillparzer has chosen to place the spiritual dignity of an individual fate, however ridiculous and insignificant it may appear in the eyes of the world, like a calm ship bound for other shores.

Notes

1. " . . . *Denn die vollendete Form ist es, wodurch die Poesie ins Leben tritt, ins* äußere *Leben. Die Wahrheit der Empfindung gibt nur das Innere; es ist aber Aufgabe aller Kunst, ein* Inneres *durch ein* Außeres *darzustellen."*—Franz Grillparzer, *Sämtliche Werke,* eds. Peter Frank and Karl Pörnbacher (Munich, 1964), 111, 286

2. Ronald Peacock, *The Poet in the Theatre* (New York, 1960), p. 62 [my ital.-I.I]. For the reception of Grillparzer's drama in the English-speaking world, see Arthur Burkhard, *Franz Grillparzer in England and America* (Vienna, 1961).

3. Georg Büchner, *Complete Plays and Prose,* trans. Carl Richard Mueller (New York, 1963), p. 151

4. The Austrian theater is no exception to this psychological curiosity: in his play, *Der Alpenkönig und der Menschenfeind* [The King of the Alps and the Misanthrope] (1828), Ferdinand Raimund created one of the first presentations of a split personality in world literature; Johann Nestroy entitled a play, *Der Zerrissene* (A Man Full of Nothing) (1844); Hugo von Hofmannsthal's most famous comedy is called *Der Schwierige* [The Difficult Man] (1921), about a man who is afraid to act and so terribly complicated that in the end the marriage proposal has to be made by the bride-to-be herself. These are but three examples; many more could be cited.

5. Marcus Aurelius, *Meditations,* trans. Maxwell Staniforth (Baltimore, 1964), p. 51.

6. Heimito von Doderer, "Einleitung," in Toni Schneider's *Österreich* (Zürich, 1958), p. 22.

7. Grillparzer, *Sämtliche Werke* (Munich, 1964), III, 1229

8. J. P. Stern, *Re-interpretations* (London, 1964), p. 74.

9. "Die Verwandlung des armen Spielmanns," in *Forum* (Vienna, October 1958), pp. 372-75

Otto K. Liedke (essay date 1970)

SOURCE: "Considerations on the Structure of Grillparzer's *Der arme Spielmann*," in *Modern Austrian Literature,* Vol. 3, No. 3, Fall, 1970, pp. 7-12.

[*In the following essay, Liedke compares the structure of* Der arme Spielmann *to a musical composition.*]

Grillparzer's ***Der arme Spielmann*** possesses the quality of all deeply poetic works to evoke responses of great variety, each one articulating the essence of the work through new insights into characters, incidents, images and language. Silz[1], examining social and psychological realism in ***Der arme Spielmann,*** points to the victory of the reality of ideas over the reality of things and people; Brinkmann[2], through an analysis of the narrative technique, sheds light on the discord between the ideal and the real at the core of Grillparzer's world; Politzer[3] discusses the theme of "Begegnung" and reveals transformations and humanizing effects brought about by the encounters in this novella. These studies may serve as examples for many others.[4] to illustrate the diverse possibilities that exist in the treatment of ***Der arme Spielmann.*** The study presented here proposes to approach the meaning of Grillparzer's novella through an examination of its structure. Such an investigation seems particularly justified since the similarity of this novella to a musical composition suggests that formal elements play an important part in indicating themes and ideas.

The structure of ***Der arme Spielmann*** resembles quite closely that of a sonata with its exposition, development and recapitulation or: statement of theme, variation of theme and summary restatement. In Grillparzer's novella, these divisions correspond to the opening frame ("Anfangsrahmen"), the main narrative and the concluding frame ("Schlußrahmen"). Just as the exposition of a sonata

commonly contains a tonic and a dominant, so also in the opening of ***Der arme Spielmann*** we can detect two related themes. We detect them visually in the movements of the narrator as he first goes with the stream of the people toward the Brigittenau and the "Volksfest" and then, just before reaching the fairgrounds, as he turns around and goes against the stream. These outward occurrences reflect, it would seem, an inner situation. As he slowly moves on toward the fairgrounds, the narrator desires only to give himself up to the joys of the festival, to join the masses and to get to know through them the source and origin of the loftier forms of life: " . . . wahrlich man kann die Berühmten nicht verstehen, wenn man die Obskuren nicht durchgefühlt hat. Von dem Wortwechsel weinerhitzter Karrenschieber spinnt sich ein unsichtbarer aber ununterbrochener Faden bis zum Zwist der Göttersöhne . . . " (p.227)[5]. To accomplish this purpose, the narrator patiently endures crowding and endless delays on the road toward his goal. However, chance—destiny—turns his attention into the opposite direction when he notices a beggar musician by the side of the road.

The common man, the porters, the servant girls and all the other "Kinder der Dienstbarkeit und Arbeit" no longer hold his attention; it is rather the strangeness, the uncommoness of the beggar musician that attracts the narrator now. The odd sight of the beggar playing from music placed on a music stand, marks him immediately as a person who does not really belong to the beggar type. The man's cleanliness together with the unmistakable signs of his poverty add to the strangeness of the appearance. When the musician then speaks the Latin words: "sunt certi denique fines," picks up his empty hat and leaves just when the prospects of getting some alms begin to improve, the character of the man stands out most clearly. Intrigued by such signs of the unusual, the narrator follows the beggar musician as he moves against the stream of the people. His only desire now is to penetrate the mystery surrounding this uncommon man. "Ich zitterte vor Begierde nach dem Zusammenhang." (p. 229) The original intention is forgotten and has turned into its opposite, and the external reversal of direction stands as a visible sign for the internal reversal.

In the dense crowd, the narrator loses sight of the *Spielmann.* When, by chance, he finds him again, the *Spielmann* is surrounded by a group of children who ask him to play a waltz. He does indeed play for them but the children do not thank him for it. Scornfully they leave him and run off to an organ grinder. In their opinion, the musician played nothing resembling a waltz, though he himself assures the narrator that it was one: "'Ich spielte einen Walzer', versetzte er, mit dem Geigenbogen den Ort des soeben gespielten Stückes auf seinem Notenpult bezeichnend . . . 'Aber die Kinder haben kein Ohr', sagte er, indem er wehmütig den Kopf schüttelte." (p. 230) This scene together with the preceding one makes it plain that the poor musician does not understand the world and the world, in turn, does not understand him.

In the development of the exposition or initial frame, three occurrences stand out at this point: the narrator's change of intention, the musician's leaving the holiday crowd without any reward for his art, and the children's rejection of the musician and his music. Against the background-image of movement and counter-movement, these occurrences offer a first indication of a structural design. Basically, it is a design made up of a pattern of opposites in the form of intention and reversal or failure of intention. Essential to the character of this structure is an ironic quality which stems from the sharp contrast between the elaborate manner in which the intention is expressed and the simple way in which the intention is given up through chance of circumstances or desire. If the structural theme appears here still somewhat vague, repetitions and variations of the same theme in the concluding frame can confirm it clearly and establish its validity. The striking parallels between the initial and concluding parts of the frame make it desirable to examine the final section of the novella before turning to a discussion of the main narrative.

In a musical composition, the main section varies, transforms, and even disguises the leading theme in order to accentuate and unfold fully its different aspects. Such treatment often creates a need for a reaffirmation and hence for a conclusion which will recapitulate the major themes, possibly through an intensified or reformulated statement of the theme. The concluding frame of *Der arme Spielmann* has decidedly the character of such a recapitulation.[6] It is, in fact, a reprise of the beginning: the narrator again sets out with a definite purpose in mind, but this time his intent is precisely the opposite. Originally he started out to find the common man and share his world. Now his aim is the unusual man, the poor musician, and he goes to visit him. Again, as in the beginning, the irony of fate intervenes and keeps him from carrying out his plan. He gets involved instead in a situation which in every respect is very much the opposite of what he had expected to find. Where he had hoped to meet again the bizarre and uncommon man, he now finds the common people and gets to know their cares and concerns. Jakob, the musician, is dead. During a flood that had ravaged the district where he lived, Jakob tried to help the people, went into the water to save some trivial possessions of his neighbor's and died soon after of the strain and exposure. The narrator arrives just in time for the funeral. Landlady, neighbors, school children, and even the woman Jakob loved years ago together with her husband and children join in the solemn procession; the narrator also takes part in the mourning.

Viewed in the light of the basic structure, these proceedings amount to a recapitulation of the original theme: a statement of intention followed by happenings that are an ironic reversal of that intention. However, this recapitulation not only restates the theme but even intensifies it. It does so through establishing an inverse relationship between the events of the opening and those of the concluding frame. Practically every detail of one part corresponds antithetically to a detail in the other. The mood of joy in the beginning has changed to sadness in the conclusion; the opening showed the narrator and the Spielmann struggling against the stream of people, at the end we see them as part of the people's doings; the chaos of the crowd on the way to the Brigittenau contrasts with the orderliness of the funeral procession; the people who had little regard for the poor musician now honor him, and the children no longer jeer him and his music but pay respect to him as they take their place in the procession. "Der Sarg ward erhoben, hinabgebracht und der Zug setzte sich in Bewegung. Voraus die Schuljugend mit Kreuz und Fahne, der Geistliche mit dem Kirchendiener. Unmittelbar nach dem Sarge die beiden Kinder des Fleischers und hinter ihnen das Ehepaar." (p.265)

These conversely arranged parallels between beginning and end confirm through their recurrence the pattern of opposites and reversal as basic to the structure of the theme. They confirm further the ironic character of the theme, since all intentions expressed in the first part (and later as well) find grotesque fulfillment in the second part. The narrator, for instance, joins the people as he had desired earlier, but he joins them in their sorrow not in their joy. Jakob had all his life hoped so sincerely to serve the people through "Veredlung des Geschmacks und Herzens" and now he had indeed served them but in a trivial rather than an edifying way. Only in death he receives the approval that was denied him throughout life. Fate's derisive laughter seems to echo through this fulfillment of human wishes—a fulfillment that in form and manner makes a mockery of the original hope. When Jakob endeavored to ennoble common taste and morals, he was looked upon as a fool, but in the end, when he did little more than to save a bit of petty cash and some unimportant account books, he was regarded with a love and respect he had never known in life. On a smaller scale, the narrator too went through a similar experience. He does participate in the life of the lowly as he had wished in the beginning, but this act of participation, as it finally takes place, has little resemblance to the original idea.

The theme identified in the first part and again in the conclusion can now be traced in several variations throughout the main narrative. Here, it becomes a pervasive force defining more and more character and idea of this novella. The beginning of the initial frame stressed the narrator's desire—a vain desire—to become part of the people. An experience containing the same elements of man's wish to belong and his failure to achieve this end occurred also in Jakob's life. He tried through all means of obedience and compliance to gain the approval of his family, but step by step he was forced into the lonely life of an outcast. First, after the failure in the examination, the family ignored him; Next he had to take his meals in a boarding house, and finally he had to move out of his father's house and into a furnished room. "Man hatte mir in einer entfernten Vorstadt ein Kämmerchen gemietet, und so war ich denn ganz aus der Nähe der Angehörigen verbannt." (p. 249) Here, just as in the beginning, we find physical occurrences reflecting inner experiences. Every change that moved Jakob physically farther away from the family represents also a greater degree of inner isolation. Not only human action but fate ultimately pronounced the separation as irrevocable when Jakob, too sick to attend his father's funeral, lost the chance to express his feeling of belonging in a last formal gesture. When the narrator eventually comes to see Jakob in the attic room, the isolation has reached an extreme. A chalk mark on the floor divides the room into two halves. The dividing line, to be sure, separates Jakob from chaos, but it also keeps him out of the world in which he has to live. Only death at last brings a reconciliation—an ironic one.

The aspect of the divided world makes the theme of wish and denial manifest. A variation of this appears in Jakob's relationship to Barbara. His bumbling attempts to win her favor and her companionship seem at first moderately successful but never attain any success greater than the kiss through the glass pane—the telling symbol of the ironic "almost", so much in keeping with the "almost"—motif of all central experiences in frame and narrative. For a short time, it looks as if Jakob's inheritance may have a good effect on his relationship to Barbara. The opposite occurs: it becomes the undoing of that relationship. True to the theme, Jakob's yearning for companionship ends in utter loneliness. Barbara's experience follows the same pattern. Her hope to live a life more decent than the one she knew with her father has a slight chance of realization for a while. This prospect dissolves into disappointment when Jakob naively loses almost all his father had left him. Barbara's words speak of this hope and disappointment: "Ich bin gekommen um Abschied zu nehmen. Ja, erschrecken Sie nur. Ist's doch Ihr Werk. Ich muß nun hinaus unter die groben Leute, wogegen ich mich solange gesträubt habe. Aber da ist kein Mittel . . . " (p. 260). We can recognize the theme of hope and disillusion again in the life of Jakob's father. All his planning and striving ended in failure marked by an irony that ultimately gave Jakob, the despised son, a place of respect among his fellow men, while the other sons, brilliant and promising at first, came to grief in disgrace and foolish venture.

These themes of hope and disillusion, of desire and non-fulfillment represent variations of the original theme of intention and reversal. Another important variation of this theme in disguised form can be seen in the repeated references to the idea of order and disorder. What relates this theme to the basic one is their common element of reversal as these examples can show. In the beginning of the novella, when the narrator describes the chaos of the people's exodus to the fairgrounds, he says: " . . . es ist in Wien ein stillschweigender Bund zwischen Wagen und Menschen, nicht zu überfahren selbst in vollem Lauf; und nicht überfahren zu werden, auch ohne Aufmerksamkeit." (p. 226) We are told here, jestingly, that the appearance of confusion and disorder is deceiving and that actually everything proceeds according to an inscrutable system. A little later, in the same jesting tone, the narrator remarks once more about the hidden forces of a mysterious condition: " . . . wie denn in dieser Welt jedes noch so hartnäckige Stehenbleiben doch nur ein unvermerktes Weiterrücken ist, . . . " (p. 226) A similar allusion to an order that underlies all phenomena occurs in the narrator's comment on the fine thread that connects the 'Karrenschieber' with the 'Göttersöhne' and the servant girls with the Julias, Didos and Medeas. References to the sense of order become serious, however, when Jakob describes the cause of his failure in school:

> " . . . Wenn ich mich recht erinnere, so wäre ich wohl imstande gewesen, allerlei zu lernen, wenn man mir nur Zeit und Ordnung gegönnt hätte. Meine Brüder sprangen wie Gemsen von Spitze zu Spitze in den Lehrgegenständen herum, ich konnte aber durchaus nichts hinter mir lassen und wenn mir ein einziges Wort fehlte, mußte ich wieder von vorne anfangen." (p. 238)

The same exacting sense of order prevails in Jakob's arrangement of his day: one part for practicing, one to earn his bread, and one to praise God. Jakob's remark about the chalk mark on the floor gives evidence of this tendency: "Die Unordnung ist verwiesen . . . " His dependence on written music rather than on the ear and his glowing discourse on the principles of harmony show what an important force this sense of order is in his life. Intention, hope, and desire fail to reach their goal in this story. In keeping with this structure, the sense of order too does not produce what one would normally expect. Adherence to order

should provide a means of entering and managing life, but here—at least from the observer's point of view—it produces the opposite: estrangement from life. The feeling for order actually turns into a paralyzing force when Jakob, as a pupil, reciting a memorized verse, forgot a word and then, despite prompting, could not continue, because the formal order of the verse was broken. His failure on this occasion led to the first separation between him and his family. His sense of order in the field of music, manifest in his close observance of the score and his dedication to the principles of harmony, leads to nothing but miserable scratching. Ultimately, it is the chalk mark that most vividly expresses the separation from the world brought about by Jakob's sense of order. Here, order is indeed established but it exists only in sterile isolation.

Life, the novella shows, turns man's intention into the opposite and eventually grants an ironic attainment of the goal; it raises man's hopes and shatters them and grants him in the end a mocking fulfillment; it endows man with a sense of order and perverts it into an inimical force. The persistent recurrence of these variations of the theme reveal Grillparzer's story as a deeply pessimistic one.[7] The pessimistic view does not relate so much to the life of the ordinary people, for the masses will reach their Brigittenau all right, the butcher will win his Barbara, and even the regular 'Bettelmusikanten' will get what they expect. The pessimism seems to relate much more to the unusual man.

Jakob, obviously, does not belong to the common crowd, his qualities give him distinction. He is a man without malice, living in ascetic simplicity; he is capable of love and loyalty and self-sacrifice, dedicated to the principles of order and reverent of God. Can we assume that Grillparzer wants to say that this kind of man must live estranged from the world without any sensible function? But such an assumption would only consider the virtues of the man and would overlook the fact that, according to the narrator and Jakob himself, the character of the Spielmann also includes some grave weaknesses—weaknesses that reduce what some have seen as "saintliness" and "other-worldliness" to perhaps incompetence and lack of good sense.[8] Despite his moral will, his gentleness and childlike ways, Jakob is a bungler. The story, however, emphasizes not so much the positive or negative in Jakob's character but rather the rift between internal worth and external ineffectiveness. This portrayal of life sees eccentricity and frustration as the only harvest of qualities that should lead to a life of human dignity and, no doubt, tragic dignity. When we find the grotesque where the tragic could be expected, we must ask for the view of man and his time from which such pessimism might stem.

In the opening frame, the narrator describes the people's fair as a pilgrimage and a devotion and in this context makes some enlightening observations about the union of man and fellow man that takes place here: "—als ein Liebhaber der Menschen, sage ich, besonders wenn sie in Massen für einige Zeit der einzelnen Zwecke vergessen und sich als Teile des Ganzen fühlen, in dem zuletzt das Göttliche liegt, ja, der Gott—als einem solchen ist mir jedes Volksfest ein eigentliches Seelenfest, eine Wallfahrt, eine Andacht." (p. 227) That union with the people, which the narrator here recognizes as a blessed state, Jakob failed to reach in every respect. His estrangement from life amounts then actually to an estrangement from the blessed state in which the divine, and, indeed, God exists. Jakob, reaching for a world of illusory order and perfection, must remain outside this union and must live in wretchedness—as the narrator sees it and as we see it. In essence, Jakob becomes the symbol of the wretchedness of an existence in which the realm of the ideal and that of the real live in total separation from each other.

To regard Jakob, however, simply as an individual out of touch with the demands of life would reduce his symbolic value severely. His sorrowful life reflects, after all, also upon the social and moral conventions of the time. The basic theme and its variations proclaim so persistently and pervasively the message of disillusion and ironic fulfillment that they cannot help but transcend individual importance. Jakob, whether taken as a "verunglückter Mensch"[9] or as the artist type points beyond himself to the fundamental agony that arises whenever man's hopes and ideals are denied a viable form of expression. The tragic isolation that results in such situations is a subject that occurs repeatedly in Grillparzer's works. He, evidently, saw this experience in a perspective broader than that defined by individual traits. Characters such as Sappho, Hero and certainly Rudolf II show how closely personal qualities are intertwined with social and moral forces in Grillparzer's portrayal of human destiny. Beyond that they reveal, just like *Der arme Spielmann,* the despair of a time when life conceived in the image of idealism loses its vitality, and life guided by the precepts of finite reality cannot gain full acceptance.

Notes

1. Walter Silz, *Realism and Reality* (Chapel Hill, 1954).

2. Richard Brinkmann, "Franz Grillparzer: 'Der arme Spielmann' in *Wirklichkeit und Illusion* Tübingen, 1957).

3. Heinz Politzer, *Franz Grillparzers "Der arme Spielmann"* (Stuttgart, 1967).

4. Some such studies are: Ernst Alker, "Franz Grillparzer, Ein Kampf um Leben und Kunst" in *Beiträge zur Deutschen Literaturwissenschaft* (ed. Ernst Elster) No. 36, 1930. Benno von Wiese, *Die Deutsche Novelle von Goethe bis Kafka,* (Düsseldorf, 1957). Walter Naumann, Grillparzer, *Das Dichterische Werk,* (Stuttgart, 1956). Johannes Klein, *Geschichte der Deutschen Novelle,* (Wiesbaden, 1954).

5. Page numbers refer to the Cotta edition by August Sauer, *Grillparzers Sämmtliche Werke,* (Stuttgart, 1892).

6. Ernst Alker, "Komposition und Stil von Grillparzers Novelle *Der arme Spielmann*" in *Neophilologus* 11, 1925. This study gives a factual account of structural relationships but does not go into the question of meaning.

7. Compare the conclusion of the Grillparzer study by Richard Brinkmann *op. cit.*

8. See Walter Silz *op. cit.*

9. See Johannes Klein *op. cit.*

John M. Ellis (essay date 1972)

SOURCE: "Grillparzer's 'Der arme Spielmann,'" in *The German Quarterly,* Vol. XLV, No. 4, November, 1972, pp. 662-83.

[*In the following essay, Ellis investigates the function of the narrator in* Der arme Spielmann.]

Grillparzer's story **Der arme Spielmann**[1] has long been regarded as one of his best works,[2] and its popularity even seems to be increasing; since 1964 no fewer than ten interpretations of the story have appeared, a remarkable number in such a short period.[3] Most interpretations have been concerned almost exclusively with the figure of the Spielmann, so that an evaluation of the story has seemed to be much the same thing as an evaluation of the Spielmann, and the question as to how we should understand the story has seemed to be identical with the question of how we should view the Spielmann.[4] Very often there has been a strong biographical slant in this criticism, so that the Spielmann has been identified in certain crucial respects as Grillparzer himself. "**Der arme Spielmann** ist Grillparzers offenstes Geständnis," said Alker in 1925,[5] a position adopted by many critics subsequently. The biographical identification, whether true or false, is of little use for criticism of the story; even granted that this were in some sense a confession, so are most works of literature in the same sense, and the critical question still remains to be considered: what kind of human experience is represented in the story, and how relevant is that experience to its readers? Even granted we knew what the Spielmann meant to Grillparzer, our analysis of the story as a work of literature must proceed from what he communicated in it; it is more relevant to take the Spielmann as a challenge for the reader than as a self-image by Grillparzer.

Since critical examinations of the story centered for the most part on the personality of the Spielmann himself, very little attention was given to its other important character, the narrator; indeed, he was rarely recognized as a character at all. This was an important omission, for almost a third of the text precedes the Spielmann's story, and this section is largely devoted to the narrator's talking about himself, his attitudes to the Spielmann, to the "Volksfest," and to other things. Klein's plot summary[6] avoids these expressions of his attitudes on the part of the narrator, while Bennett's account minimizes the existence of the story's long introduction.[7] This neglect of the function of so obtrusive a narrator is again partly to be traced to the biographical identification of narrator and Spielmann as two sides of Grillparzer;[8] once more, this identification is irrelevant to (and deflects attention from) the critical question of the nature and function of the juxtaposition of the two figures in the story.

Only a few recent critics (for example, Brinkmann, Swales and Politzer) have examined the position taken in **Der arme Spielmann** by the narrator, yet the value of their studies lies more in individual perceptions about specific parts of the text than in the emergence of any comprehensive view of the function of the narrator. Brinkmann's painstaking discussion of narration in the story is mainly concerned with the literary historical category of realism, and as a result treats narration as a technical rather than thematic element in the text.[9] Equating author and narrator,[10] he investigates only the question of the objectivity or subjectivity of the narrator's transmission of the story to the reader, not the function of the narrator's highly specific character in its system of values.

Swales and Politzer are the only critics so far to have taken the first step towards an investigation of the narrator's intrusion into his story by according him full status as a character in it, with his own reactions (not necessarily ours or the story's taken as a whole) to the Spielmann. Swales concludes that the narrator is ambivalent about the Spielmann, part of him wishing to identify with the old man while he also feels the need to defend against this identification as against a weakness.[11] But the Spielmann's own direct narrative already makes the reader ambivalent about him in just the same way, for there too we feel drawn to and exasperated by him; can the space and emphasis devoted by the text to the narrator's personality be considered justifiable if this contributes nothing that we do not already feel without him? A view which attributes so little function to so much text must remain unsatisfying. Politzer's account of the function of the narrator also has its problems; for when he abstracts the thematic point that the narrator, unlike the Spielmann, undergoes a "Verwandlung" through genuine "Begegnung" with another person at the end of the story in his encounter with Barbara, and thus that communication with another human being makes an impact on him,[12] we must surely agree with his reviewer[13] who points out that the text's ending contains no trace of all this. All the reader sees is the narrator's probing a sensitive spot in Barbara and looking without comment at the results, Barbara's tears, which he might easily have predicted. The function of the narrator must be derived not from non-existent material at the end of the story, but instead largely from the wealth of material in the first third of the text.

Though the Spielmann has often been said to be a problematic character, there are at least some important ways in which he is not. Much that is factual about him is not in any doubt; he tells his own story very openly, and there seems no reason to fear that he deliberately conceals anything from us. We do not feel that there are any secrets about him, or that we need further information and reports on more of his experiences; nothing new seems to be required to complete our picture of him. There seems also to be little difficulty in summing up and conceptualizing all that we know of his personality. I do not mean that there have not been misconceptions: when, for example, a critic asserts that the Spielmann's failures are compulsive, or another that he inhabits the ideal world of music, both seem to give insufficient weight to the fact that he is always shown to be genuinely simple-minded and incompetent;[14] this amply-demonstrated fact allows us neither to postulate a deep-seated efficiency behind it all, nor a world inside his head that can be thought of in terms of a communicable value like music. But these misconceptions are certainly very easy to clear up, and the available features of the text which show them to be misconceptions are extremely plentiful and obvious. Again, while one might take either a positive or negative view of the Spielmann, depending perhaps on one's taste,[15] there will be little disagreement as to the nature of the positive and negative sides of Jakob on which the whole judgment would be based; its ingredients are not obscure. His main characteristic is a lack of a certain kind of judgment and competence, a simple-mindedness visible both in his dealings with others, and in his abilities whether musical or otherwise. This makes him defenseless in his human contacts, and renders him of little practical value to anyone else, whether as musician or provider. But this defect has attendant advantages. Because he is without suspicion, he is also entirely without malice; because he cannot conceive of others being dishonest, he is himself entirely honest; and because he cannot recognize self-seekingness in others, he is entirely generous. Above all, because he is not in the least competitive, and because his ability to recognize the difference between good and bad playing is so limited, he is entirely without pose or pretensions; his most noticeable feature is his complete sincerity in his music and in his relations with others. As far as his happiness is concerned, he is almost without ability to produce or preserve situations which will make for his security and happiness, but is possessed of a remarkable ability to be happy with what he has. It is by no means certain, therefore, that he does not have a happier life than his more gifted father and brothers. To them, achievement meant so much that they could not be happy without it. Paradoxically, then, although Jakob seems to be exceptionally vulnerable in the world, he is in one sense invulnerable too; and in that sense his competitive family are very fragile indeed. His father is so vulnerable to a decline in his influence that a stroke, and death, result. One brother makes too ambitious a wager, and dies; the other chooses exile to escape the consequences of a dishonest attempt to harm a competitor. The Spielmann, on the other hand, survives them all, and appears to experience great happiness in his playing. The question remains of the real human value of happiness which depends on the reduction of one's horizons to this extent. But that, once more, is a problem for the reader; and its uncertainty is not caused by any uncertainty as to the facts of the Spielmann's existence. It is not necessary to quarrel, as critics in the past have done, over whether he is or is not a saint; we can simply say that it is natural that he should seem so to the "Gärtnerin" at the end (264) of the story, though we should usually reserve the use of such a word for one who displays the attractive features of the Spielmann *without* these features being produced by, and thus dependent on, his simple-mindedness.

So much for the characteristics of the Spielmann; but if as the central character he is perfectly comprehensible from his own story, then what can be the reason for the well-developed narrative framework? For it cannot change what we know of the Spielmann. I am, of course, assuming here that the Spielmann's story is indeed his own, in his own words. One critic, Brinkmann, does not share this assumption, believing that the Spielmann's story is colored by its being retold by the narrator. The narrator's emphasis and bias would have crept into the direct speech of the Spielmann after all, and on such a view we should (though Brinkmann does not draw this conclusion) need the narrative framework in order to evaluate the Spielmann, since it would be a key to the kind of bias which has been at work in the retelling of the old man's story. But there is no need for this conclusion. Brinkmann argues from such factors as the feat of memory required for the narrator to remember the Spielmann's story word for word after two years,[16] but overlooks the fact that this is one of those literary conventions without which fiction would be impossible. Direct speech in a work of fiction could never be given its full value if we did not accept the convention of the long memory of storytellers, just as theater is impossible without the acceptance of such conventions as the curtain, soliloquies, and so on. And so our question remains: given that the Spielmann presents himself fully enough, why the long preamble to his story? If with Jungbluth we want to call this device of two "Ich-Erzähler" a "raffinierter Trick," we have condemned it as an ingenious piece of irrelevance;[17] and if, with biographical critics, we say that Grillparzer here presents aspects of himself, we have still not considered their relevance to the Spielmann. Least of all can one agree with Stern that "the narrator's taciturnity about himself is one of its [the story's] minor triumphs," or that in the narrator's introduction there is established a laconic mode "with a sparseness, an economy of means rarely achieved elsewhere in German narrative prose."[18] These judgments seem most inappropriate to a text which is remarkable for precisely the reverse, a conspicuous presence of the narrator's personality, achieved by a particularly lengthy and digressive introduction to the story of the Spielmann.

If we are to take seriously this large part of the text as relevant to the whole, it would seem unavoidable to consider the contribution it makes in presenting the narrator as one of the two main characters of the story. He is not presented to us through the events of his life story as the Spielmann is, but nonetheless becomes a distinct character in his own right through the attitudes he strikes, the emphases of the descriptions he offers us, and on occasion through his direct comment on himself. From the very beginning of the story we must constantly evaluate what he says, and build up an impression of him. When, for example, he professes to a love for the common people, it is not enough to take this as a simple fact, to be accepted at face value and then passed over. The fact that the assertion is made so directly and explicitly is important, and we must consider both why the narrator raises the issue, and whether his actions are consistent with his claim.[19] Yet none of these questions is worth raising except in the context of the thematic structure of the whole story.

That there is something in these opening pages to which we instinctively react negatively seems clear; Alker, for example, found them a blemish on the story, badly and dilettantishly written.[20] Unlike many later critics, Alker allowed himself a direct response here, and yet his critical framework was inadequate to deal with it; what is unpleasant in these pages must be attributed not to the author's bad craftsmanship, but to the projection of an unpleasant character on the part of the narrator; and the particular kind of unpleasantness turns out to be very relevant to the Spielmann.[21]

The narrator begins his story by describing the July "Volksfest" in Vienna:

> In Wien ist der Sonntag nach dem Vollmonde im Monat Juli jedes Jahres samt dem darauffolgenden Tage ein eigentliches Volksfest, wenn je ein Fest diesen Namen verdient hat. Das Volk besucht es und gibt es selbst; und wenn Vornehmere dabei erscheinen, so können sie es nur in ihrer Eigenschaft als Glieder des Volks. Da ist keine Möglichkeit der Absonderung; wenigstens vor einigen Jahren noch war keine. (225)

Two pages later the narrator follows this with the assertion that "Ich versäume nicht leicht, diesem Feste beizu-

wohnen" (227). But this turns out not to be the case,[22] for he is very easily diverted from the festival by the sight of the Spielmann; and even when he loses the Spielmann he simply goes home instead of back to the festival. This is only one of the things said by the narrator which either immediately rings false, or turns out to be so in the light of later events. The rather self-conscious reference to the "Volk," with the immediately following introduction of class-awareness in the word "vornehm" distances the narrator from the people rather than shows his feeling for them; the choice of word in contrast to "Volk" is one suggesting superiority and refinement, and the resulting impression is of condescension to the inferior "Volk" by a man conscious of his own status as "Vornehmer," the pose of an aristocrat whose appreciation of a certain quaintness of the common people depends on his being quite safe from the realities of their life. These suspicions, derived from the tone of the first sentence, are confirmed in what comes later. There is a great deal of "Absonderung," no visible dropping of class barriers, and no levelling of human beings, in the description of what happens on the way to the festival:

> Schon mischen sich einzelne Equipagen der Vornehmeren in den oft unterbrochenen Zug. Die Wagen fliegen nicht mehr. Bis endlich fünf bis sechs Stunden vor Nacht die einzelnen Pferdeund Kutschen-Atome sich zu einer kompakten Reihe verdichten, die, sich selber hemmend und durch Zufahrende aus allen Quergassen gehemmt, das alte Sprichwort: Besser schlecht gefahren, als zu Fuße gegangen, offenbar zu Schanden macht. Begafft, bedauert, bespottet, sitzen die geputzten Damen in den scheinbar stille stehenden Kutschen. (226)

The narrator's description is concerned more than anything else with social levels. The "vornehme Damen" are as separate from the crowd as they could be, and description of the attitude to them of the people emphasizes that distance. The people behave as the "Vornehme" would expect them to, i.e. badly, thus allowing them a comfortable feeling of their own superiority.[23] The narrator goes on to reinforce this by a description of the "schreiende Weiber- und Kinderbevölkerung des Plebejer-Fuhrwerks" (226). There are here many pairs of words of opposite emotional force. "Plebejer" is as negative a word for the people as "Vornehme" was positive; the "Damen" of the latter correspond to the "Weiber" of the former, and while one group sits proudly and quietly on display, the other is "schreiend." The narrator himself in his language is producing that very "Absonderung" the lack of which he professes to find so valuable a feature of his favorite festival. The narrator may claim (225) that "Der Unterschied der Stände ist verschwunden," but it never disappears from his own consciousness or from the scene as he describes it. He separates himself from the people, remains always distant from them, and develops an interest in the Spielmann only after having heard him utter a piece of Latin: "Der Mann hatte also eine sorgfältigere Erziehung genossen, sich Kenntnisse eigen gemacht, und nun ein Bettelmusikant!" (229). The apparent move down the social scale is what attracts the narrator's attention, not the Spielmann's more evident (and more interesting) strangeness as a violinist. The phrase "sich Kenntnisse eigen gemacht" is an interesting key to the narrator's system of values too; education and knowledge is a possession of the privileged class, of which he too is a member. Throughout the story, the narrator is never really impressed by anything which represents the culture of the Viennese people as a whole. On the other hand, he is very impressed by the mention of Jakob's father, "Der Einflußreiche, der Mächtige" (238). And when Jakob gives the narrator his address, the latter responds to the information that it is "im ersten Stocke" with "'I der That,' rief ich 'im Stockwerke der Vornehmen?'" (232). By contrast, the narrator's references to the people are always pejorative; they are noisy and "genußlechzend" (228), and he is pleased to be away from them: "Die Stille des Ortes, im Abstich der lärmenden Volksmenge, that mir wohl" (233). As one who claims to be a lover of the people, the narrator is simply an impostor, and his lack of sincerity is well shown in the exaggerated tenor of his claim to be one:

> Als ein leidenschaftlicher Liebhaber der Menschen, vorzüglich des Volkes, so daß mir selbst als dramatischem Dichter der rückhaltlose Ausbruch eines überfüllten Schauspielhauses immer zehnmal interessanter, ja belehrender war, als das zusammengeklügelte Urteil eines an Leib und Seele verkrüppelten, von dem Blut ausgesogener Autoren spinnenartig aufgeschwollenen literarischen Matadors;—als ein Liebhaber der Menschen, sage ich, besonders wenn sie in Massen für einige Zeit der einzelnen Zwecke vergessen und sich als Teile des Ganzen fühlen, in dem denn doch zuletzt das Göttliche liegt, ja, der Gott—als einem solchen ist mir jedes Volksfest ein eigentliches Seelenfest, eine Wallfahrt, eine Andacht. (227)[24]

Both the tone of the passage, and its contradiction by all that the narrator says and does, inicate that this alleged love of the people is a pretentious aristocratic pose; only while safe from them, and feeling superior to them, can the narrator indulge it.

Yet this is only one example of the falseness of the narrator's claims about himself. Consider, for example, his claim to have an "anthropologischen Heißhunger" (229), or a "psychologische Neugierde" (265). Does the narrator show any real curiosity about or concern with other human beings, any desire to understand them? Again, his language is interesting. He refers to his meeting with the Spielmann not as something instructive, but as an "Abenteuer" (229). It is true that he is curious about Barbara and about the Spielmann, but it seems less the intellectual curiosity of the student of human nature than the kind of curiosity which we think of as prying into other people's affairs. He is always remote from both, and without any of that sympathy for them which would be necessary for him to begin to understand them. I am not here making the point that he is a neutral observer, since I believe that this is not the case;[25] on the contrary, the narrator shows a most unsympathetic attitude. When he leaves the Spielmann for the last time (262) while the old man is still playing his violin, the narrator's remarks are extremely cold: "Endlich hatte ich's satt, stand auf, legte ein paar Silberstücke auf den nebenstehenden Tisch und ging, während der Alte eifrig immer fortgeigte." There is no farewell, no expression of sympathy or concern, but instead only the very unsympathetic "hatte ich's satt," and the cold gesture of leaving some coins, as if to pay for his entertainment. Here, as elsewhere, the narrator never enters into the world of the Spielmann and his violin, instead recording his impatience with it. When going home after his first meeting (234) with the Spielmann, the narrator rather self-

righteously congratulates himself on his (as opposed to the Spielmann's) "Phantasieren" being something that disturbs no one. That the old man's playing is a disturbance is clear, but the narrator prefers to emphasize this side of the matter rather than that his violin playing is for the old man something very precious. There are a large number of such ungenerous, impatient responses to the Spielmann and his playing, which grate on the reader for their obsessive denigration of the Spielmann; they gradually become a gratuitous harping on what we already know. Even his report on Barbara—that she could never have been beautiful—concentrates on the ridiculous side of the Spielmann, and unnecessarily, since the old man had told us as much already (243). Likewise, the narrator's off-hand remark on Barbara's tune ("gemütlich, übrigens gar nicht ausgezeichnet" [241]) seems, however justified by the nature of the tune, to concentrate on the negative side—it is after all the tune's associations that make it distinctive for the Spielmann. Even against the background of his earlier behavior, his action at the end of the story is extraordinary. He visits Barbara, as he admits, out of curiosity, but ostensibly to attempt to buy Jakob's violin. Predictably, the request reduces Barbara to tears; and then the narrator goes away, having satisfied his curiosity. He has probed Barbara's response to a considerable provocation and wounded her in the process. This is wanton self-gratification; a pursuit of entertainment rather than of knowledge of humanity. The narrator is frequently careless and inconsiderate in his dealing with the Spielmann. His offer of money, to the end, is always as from benefactor to beggar, though the Spielmann had early in the story shown his sensitivity on this score (230 and 233); his pride demands that he accept money only as a fee for his performance. The narrator's attempt to elicit the old man's story is clumsy and demeaning; clumsy, in his baldly announcing that he is "nach Ihrer Geschichte lüstern" (237), and demeaning, in that his mentioning the Spielmann's display of Latin erudition allows the old man to see that it is his *fall* to the level of a beggar that interests the narrator. Such instances could be multiplied, and together they show that the narrator has no interest in or ability to enter into the world of other people. He refers to the people on occasion as a "Haufen," or a "Menschenwall" (229), and even the Spielmann is said, in a phrase whose overtones show his deeper attitudes to lesser categories of human being, to be "barhäuptig und kahlköpfig . . . nach Art dieser Leute" (228). His real interests lie in gratifying his idle curiosity, and in projecting a self-congratulatory image greatly at variance with reality.

The question must now arise: how is this personality relevant to the Spielmann? And the answer must surely lie in the fact that the narrator is shown to be the very opposite of the Spielmann. If the Spielmann's outstanding characteristic is his utter sincerity, that of the narrator is his complete lack of it, his incessant posturing and posing, his self-deception and pretense, even pretentiousness. The Spielmann is his opposite in every way, never worrying about social class, and being happy with any human being of whatever rank. He is concerned with other people, and respects them; he is saddened by their unhappiness, and always tries to be helpful, however inefficiently. The narrator, on the other hand, is always distant from everyone in the story, is insensitive to the Spielmann and his world, or to that of the common people around him, gratuitously hurts the feelings of the people he meets, and never shows a sign of regret at having done so. The Spielmann is so generous in his estimate of other people that he even thinks well of his father, in spite of the way his father has treated him. He is even sure that his father meant well, for after his death the Spielmann says that he hopes to find him again "wo wir nach unsern Absichten gerichtet werden und nicht nach unsern Werken" (250). On neither criterion would the Hofrat have done very well, but it is a touching thing that Jakob ascribes his own well-intentioned ineffi-ciency to his father, whose qualities were in fact the re-verse of his. The narrator, by contrast, is very ungenerous to the Spielmann and indeed to everyone else in the story. If at one point he calls the Spielmann his "Liebling," he quickly underscuts that compliment, for he speaks of the "Mißklängen meines und, ich fürchte beinahe, nur meines Lieblings" (235).[26] This underlines the fact that no one else can be expected to have any interest in the old man, which would in turn rob the old man of any *right* to the attention of the narrator too; this is, by implication, an odd quirk of the narrator, not a response to a deservedly interesting per-son.

It is evidently part of the story's strategy to have the old man introduced by one who is his opposite in certain fun-damental characteristics; thus a genuine but incompetent person is introduced by one who is capable but insincere. Yet the most interesting aspect of the contrast between the two lies in their attitudes to their art. The Spielmann's art is consistent with the rest of him: sincere, genuine, but so technically incompetent as to be of value only to himself alone. What of the narrator? He, we are told, is a dramatic poet, and we do not experience his dramatic work; how-ever, we do experience his qualities as a storyteller. Some distinct impressions emerge. Consider, for example, his description of the "Volksfest," and its metaphors:

> Und so fort und immer weiter, bis endlich der breite Hafen der Lust sich aufthut und Wald und Wiese, Musik und Tanz, Wein und Schmaus, Schattenspiel und Seiltänzer, Erleuchtung und Feuerwerk sich zu einem pays de cocagne, einem Eldorado, einem eigentlichen Schlaraffenlande vereinigen, das leider, oder glückli-cherweise, wie man es nimmt, nur einen und den nächst darauffolgenden Tag dauert, dann aber verschwindet, wie der Traum einer Sommernacht, und nur in der Erin-nerung zurückbleibt und allenfalls in der Hoffnung. (226)

The description of the festival hardly matches the image of it as a midsummer night's dream; nothing could be less appropriate. The festival is raucous, while the image is that of a delicate fantasy. Yet this is typical of the narra-tor's usually forced and pretentious imagery, which always seems to strive for an effect rather than to illuminate a situation. His earlier image of the stream of people is an-other example:

> Eine wogende Menge erfüllt die Straßen. Geräusch von Fußtritten, Gemurmel von Sprechenden, das hie und da ein lauter Ausruf durchzuckt. Der Unterschied der Stände ist verschwunden; Bürger und Soldat teilt die Bewegung. An den Thoren der Stadt wächst der Drang. Genommen, verloren und wiedergenommen, ist endlich der Ausgang erkämpft. Aber die Donaubrücke bietet neue Schwierigkeiten. Auch hier siegreich, ziehen endlich zwei Ströme, die alte Donau und die geschwoll-nere Woge des Volks, sich kreuzend quer unter und über einander, die Donau ihrem alten Flußbette nach, der Strom des Volks, der Eindämmung der Brücke

entnommen, ein weiter, tosender See, sich ergießend in alles deckender Überschwemmung. (225)

This time, the narrator has common speech to rely on: he is developing the metaphor inherited from ordinary speech, for in German as in English, we can quite normally speak of a stream of people. But he proceeds to develop this idea at length and in fact ad nauseum. He is obviously seeking after literary effect, but eventually mixes the metaphor di-sastrously. Over several pages the motif recurs: the crowd is "zuströmend" and "entgegenströmend" (229), it is a "weiter, tosender See," the fairground is a "Hafen der Lust," the festival itself constitutes dry land (226), while the German language allows the easy introduction of the embankment as a "Damm." The development appears, even on the surface, to be rather forced. But the absurdity of the sequence comes to light when it becomes apparent that the stream is heading for the harbor and land: for a stream reaches its destination when it gets to the sea, not to dry land! The narrator has developed his watery meta-phors in a grandiose way, but has confused the different perspectives of a stream running down to the sea, on the one hand, and a ship at sea looking for a harbor and land on the other; and so he has his stream reaching land, as fine an example of a mixed metaphor as one could wish for. The cry should not be "Land" but "Meer," and in that the moving stream of people reaches a larger, stationary concentration of people, this would not be inappropriate. What Grillparzer wants to show here is that the narrator is not interested in metaphorical illumination of what he is describing, but only in the creation of impressive lan-guage; the metaphor is not a genuine one which springs from the nature of his object, but a false one piled on to increase the appearance of a "literary" effect. This fact of his artistic performance illuminates his claim to being a student of humanity[27] from another direction. This too is part of the narrator's posture as a literary figure, and of his developing his image as a great writer. Another example of his consciously posing as the poet-dramatist is the much-quoted passage on the common people as literary material:

> Wie aus einem aufgerollten, ungeheuren, dem Rahmen des Buches entsprungenen Plutarch, lese ich aus den heitern und heimlich bekümmerten Gesichtern, dem lebhaften oder gedrückten Gange, dem wechselseitigen Benehmen der Familienglieder, den einzelnen, halb un-willkürlichen Äußerungen, mir die Biographien der un-berühmten Menschen zusammen, und wahrlich! man kann die Berühmten nicht verstehen, wenn man die Obskuren nicht durchgefühlt hat. Von dem Wortwech-sel weinerhitzter Karrenschieber spinnt sich ein unsicht-barer, aber ununterbrochener Faden bis zum Zwist der Göttersöhne, und in der jungen Magd, die, halb wider Willen, dem drängenden Liebhaber seitab vom Gewühl der Tanzenden folgt, liegen als Embryo die Julien, die Didos und die Medeen. (227)[28]

This is a gross and inflated piece of posturing again, no-ticeable both for the triteness beneath the self-importance and, as usual, for its irrelevance to what comes after it in the story. There is a pointed contrast between the grand, heroic figures it mentions, and the old unheroic Spiel-mann; and the verbs "durchfühlen" and "verstehen" are conspicuously inappropriate to the narrator, who makes no attempt to understand the world of the Spielmann's feel-ings. This is surely stereotype utterance for an author, and more stereotype author behavior can be found, for example, in his rather crude request for the Spielmann's story.

The old man's incredulity reinforces this impression, and in a sense constitutes a rejection of the resulting unnatural and self-conscious situation: "'Geschichte?' wiederholte er. 'Ich habe keine Geschichte . . . Das also nennen Sie meine Geschichte?'" (237). Grillparzer includes in the text equally self-conscious touches by the narrator when he seems to be taking notes in sentences without verbs; the impression created is that of image-projection on the part of that observant student of the world, the author, e.g., "Zank, Geschrei, wechselseitige Ehrenangriffe der Kutscher, mitunter ein Peitschenhieb" (226), or "Voraus die Schuljugend mit Kreuz und Fahne, der Geistliche mit dem Kirchendiener. Unmittelbar nach dem Sarge die beiden Kinder des Fleischers und hinter ihnen das Ehepaar" (265).

Just as his writing strives for effect, his criterion of artistic success is simply public acclaim, and hence his love of the people is, as he admits, greatest when they are applauding him; this is why he finds the "rückhaltlose Ausbruch eines überfüllten Schauspielhauses" more interesting and even instructive (though one might ask how it could possibly be so), than the judgments of his critics. Taken together with the evidence of his story-telling, this confession confirms that he is concerned with success but not integrity, and it also discredits his professed love of the people, for his concern with them seems now to be with their acclaiming him; and this will perhaps explain why it is that he shows no real interest in them for themselves, while claiming that he does. That we have here a truer profession of attitude is apparent, for the attack on the critics bursts in in an uncontrolled way, overriding the logic and grammatical shape of the sentence. Linguistically and in substance, it is an irrelevant intrusion. Grammatically it is out of place, as a clause having only a precarious link with the main clause by means of an adverbial phrase, and holding up the necessary arrival of the main verb; and as to the substance, it is just as much out of place to justify love of the people by referring to one's being applauded by them, or to express such a violent attack on the critics without any preamble or reported incident from which the attack would spring. In the absence of any reported incident we tend to draw our own conclusions as to the justifiability of the critics' strictures, taking into account the irrational tone of the outburst and the narrator's literary values as we have seen them; but the obsessive nature of the expression leaves no doubt that what the narrator says here is a genuine representation of his concerns, not another pose.

The contrast here with the Spielmann is striking. Rejection as an artist does not cause him to make such a vicious attack on his critics; he is without malice, resigned and forgiving. But this is in part due to another contrast between the two: the Spielmann plays according to his conscience, not to impress other people.[29] He is an incompetent, but not a compromiser. The two display very much the same contrast as artists that they show as men: the Spielmann technically incompetent, yet completely honest and sincere; the narrator technically slick and clever, conscious of literary effect, but without integrity, concerned with applause and a shallow kind of impact rather than with real artistic value. There are, to be sure, similarities between the two figures, and yet the main pattern is that of contrast; even these similarities function as common ground on which their differences may emerge in a more subtle way. An example of this is furnished by their both using religious terminology in the context of intensity of feeling. The Spielmann thinks of his music as something sacred:

> Als ich nun mit dem Bogen über die Saiten fuhr, Herr, da war es, als ob Gottes Finger mich angerührt hatte . . . Ich fiel auf die Knie und betete laut und konnte nicht begreifen, daß ich das holde Gotteswesen einmal gering geschätzt, ja gehaßt in meiner Kindheit, und küßte die Violine und drückte sie an mein Herz und spielte wieder und fort. (241)

As the Spielmann talks of music in these terms, the narrator reports an impression of intense conviction and involvement in what is said: "Ich kannte meinen Mann beinahe nicht mehr" (242). But the narrator has also spoken of his passions and needs in religious terms too; for him, it is the people who contain "das Göttliche" and the festival is therefore "ein eigentliches Seelenfest, eine Wallfahrt, eine Andacht" (227). Later, the narrator speaks of his need for something that will be spiritually uplifting early in the day:

> Die Morgenstunden haben für mich immer einen eigenen Wert gehabt. Es ist, als ob es mir Bedürfnis wäre, durch die Beschäftigung mit etwas Erhebendem, Bedeutendem in den ersten Stunden des Tages mir den Rest desselben gewissermaßen zu heiligen. Ich kann mich daher nur schwer entschließen, am frühen Morgen mein Zimmer zu verlassen . . . (234)

The Spielmann, too, preserves the morning for an activity that is "veredelnd":

> "Indem ich nun diese Stücke spiele," fuhr er fort, "bezeige ich meine Verehrung den nach Stand und Würden geachteten, längst nicht mehr lebenden Meistern und Verfassern, thue mir selbst genug und lebe der angenehmen Hoffnung, daß die mir mildest gereichte Gabe nicht ohne Entgelt bleibt, durch Veredlung des Geschmackes und Herzens der ohnehin von so vielen Seiten gestörten und irre geleiteten Zuhörerschaft. Da derlei aber, auf daß ich bei meiner Rede bleibe"—und dabei überzog ein selbstgefälliges Lächeln seine Züge—"da derlei aber eingeübt sein will, sind meine Morgenstunden ausschließend diesem Exercitium bestimmt." (232)

Yet the differences are obvious; the Spielmann acts on what he says, while the narrator does not. The narrator gives up his supposedly devotional presence at the "Volksfest," and also leaves his room in the morning to see the Spielmann. He seems to believe that the Spielmann's statements are as meaningless as his own; for though the old man has mentioned that his mornings are taken up exclusively with practicing, and that he would wish to be given advance warning of a visit in order to accommodate it into his round of daily tasks, the narrator ignores both points and exclaims: "So werde ich Sie einmal morgens überraschen" (232).

The most interesting of the contrastive parallels of the two characters lies in the narrator's early stream image and the flood through which the Spielmann dies. A precise and comprehensive account of this parallel is given by Walter Silz:

Despite this arithmetical discrepancy, the two frames give the impression of complete balance, and this impression is strengthened by a symmetrical correspondence of motifs, first and last. The public festival of the opening is balanced by the public calamity of the close, the flood of holiday folk at the beginning (a figure carried through at some length) by the flood of destructive waters at the end; a gateway in the park with the joyous living, a gateway in the flooded suburb with the bodies of the dead. Each flood casts its derelicts ashore: the wretched little company of 'Volksmusikanten' at the edge of the park road, and the corpses of the drowned awaiting the coroner.[30]

Papst has correctly observed that what was metaphor in the one case has become reality in the other;[31] but this is in a wider sense the contrast once more of the false and the genuine. The narrator's metaphor is a superficial piece of literary posturing, confused and inappropriate, while the flood and consequent deaths are harshly real.

The bearing of the narrator on the figure of the Spielmann is clearly a complex matter, involving many factors: among them his authorial pose, and the theme of descent in class. Also important here is his compulsive denigration of a man who is his opposite.[32] But the broader reason for the inclusion and juxtaposition of the two is that they represent the two sides of the main thematic contrast on which the story is based. This theme is that of integrity in relation to efficiency, and throughout, the narrator and Spielmann are systematically contrasted with each other in terms of it;[33] this is the meaning of the story which gives it a relevance transcending its possible biographical content.[34] The Spielmann, and perhaps even the narrator, may well represent the kind of extremes not met with in every day life; and yet the issue which is the basis of this contrasting pair is ever-present, and the need to balance the two sides of the contrast inescapable. It is easy to make the judgment that the Spielmann lacks competence in all that he does, and yet it is always possible for the honesty and trustingness which he preserves to become obliterated by the kind of technical expertness manifested by the narrator. The Spielmann's trusting nature has reached the point of sheer gullibility, yet the price of such gullibility may be excessive, bringing with it a permanently suspicious nature and a distance from all other human beings. All competence involves an act of emotional distance, and so a move away from the genuineness of the Spielmann's world, if continued too far, lands us in the narrator's world of insincerity and loss of contact with genuine feeling.

The ending of the story brings out the positive side of Jakob more strongly than had hithertoo been the case, since we are now shown not merely the narrator's reactions to Jakob, but those of Barbara and the "Gärtnerin." The tears of the former and the words of the latter show what an effect Jakob had had on them. More objective evidnce of his effect on the world is available: his name given to Barbara's child, his saving the lives of the children who had been threatened by the flood. Thus, the story closes by shifting the balance somewhat in his favor;[35]rightly, since if we have to err on one side or the other, sincerity or technique, gullibility or suspicion, we should all choose to lean to the Spielmann.[36]

Notes

1. References are to: *Grillparzers Sämtliche Werke in zwanzig Bänden,* ed. A. Sauer (Stuttgart, 1892), XIII, 225-266.

2. Cf., for example, Papst's judgment that the story "bears comparison with the best of his plays as one of his great masterpieces" (Grillparzer: *Der arme Spielmann and Prose Selections,* ed. E. E. Papst [London and Edinburgh, 1960], p. xviii).

3. These recent interpretations are the following: J. P. Stern, "Beyond the Common Indication: Grillparzer," in his *Reinterpretations* (London, 1964), pp. 42-77; J. de Cort, "Zwei arme Spielleute: Vergleich einer Novelle von F. Grillparzer und von Th. Storm," *RLV,* 30 (1964), 326-341; H. Politzer, "Die Verwandlung des armen Spielmanns. Ein Grillparzer-Motiv bei Franz Kafka," *JGG,* 4 (1965), 55-64; O. P. Straubinger, *"Der arme Spielmann,"* *GFF* (1966), 97-102; M. W. Swales, "The Narrative Perspective in Grillparzer's *Der arme Spielmann,"* *GL&L, N.S.,* 20 (1967), 107-118; H. Politzer, *Franz Grillparzer's "Der arme Spielmann"* (Stuttgart, 1967); A. Gutmann, "Grillparzers *Der arme Spielmann:* Erlebtes und Erdichtetes," *Journal of the International Arthur Schnitzler Research Association,* 6 (1967), 14-44; W. Paulsen, "Der gute Bürger Jakob. Zur Satire in Grillparzers *Armem Spielmann,"* *CollG* (1968), pp. 272-298; G. Jungbluth, "Franz Grillparzers Erzählung: *Der arme Spielmann.* Ein Beitrag zu ihrem Verstehen," *OL,* 24 (1969), 35-51; H. Krotkoff, "Über den Rahmen in Franz Grillparzers Novelle *Der arme Spielmann,"* *MLN,* 85 (1970), 345-366. Even before this a number of separate interpretations of the story had existed: E. Alker, "Komposition und Stil von Grillparzers Novelle *Der arme Spielmann,"* *Neophilologus,* 11 (1925), 15-27; B. Seuffert, "Grillparzers Spielmann," *Festschrift August Sauer zum 70. Geburtstag des Gelehrten am 12. Oktober 1925* (Stuttgart, 1925), pp. 291-311; W. Silz, "Grillparzer: *Der arme Spielmann,"* in his *Realism und Reality* (Chapel Hill, 1954), pp. 67-78; B. von Wiese, "Franz Grillparzer: *Der arme Spielmann,"* in his *Die deutsche Novelle von Goethe bis Kafka,* I, 134-53; R. Brinkmann, "Franz Grillparzer: *Der arme Spielmann.* Der Einbruch der Subjektivität," in his *Wirklichkeit und Illusion* (Tübingen, 1957), pp. 87-145; and the introduction to E. E. Papst's edition of the story (cited above). There are, of course, numerous treatments of the story in general works on Grillparzer and on the Novelle.

4. This is, for the most part, the emphasis of the interpretation of von Wiese, and on his p. 136 he gives a survey of previous critics who had a similar concern.

5. Alker, p. 17. Cf. also E. K. Bennett, *A History of the German Novelle,* p. 155: "It would seem rather that Grillparzer had at last arrived at the truth about himself." That the story had many roots in Grillparzer's life and experiences is by now so well documented and common ground to such a degree that it is surprising to see that many of the recent crop of interpretations consider the point to need further assertion; e.g., Straubinger (p. 98), noting the "widerstreitende Meinungen" concerning the story, suggests that biographical facts need to be taken into account; Gutmann's essay is entirely biographical; while Jungbluth recommends a return to a biographical approach such as that of Alewyn,

which he finds neglected: "Es ist eines der furchtbarsten und schonungslosesten Bekenntnisse der Weltliteratur" (R. Alewyn, "Grillparzer und die Restauration," *PEGS, N.S.,* 12 [1937], cited by Jungbluth, p. 38). Jungbluth also makes the assumption that in the narrator "man ohne Skrupel den Autor selbst erblicken darf" (p. 41).

6. J. Klein, *Geschichte der deutschen Novelle,* pp. 195-7. Klein himself calls his summary of the story a "Strukturskizze."

7. Bennett, pp. 152-158. Cf. especially his statement that Grillparzer's aim is to "present a complete picture of a given character . . ." (p. 158).

8. This is, in fact, now the most persistent cliché of *Spielmann* criticism, but is regularly "discovered" as if it were a new point. The first to make the point, according to Straubinger (p. 98) was WedelParlow, in his Grillparzer biography of 1932. But Seuffert (p. 295) made it in 1925. In the interpretations of the last twenty years, the point appears first in Silz, p. 74, and is repeated in von Wiese, p. 149; Brinkmann, p. 141; de Cort, pp. 340-1; Stern, p. 77; Swales, p. 115; and Jungbluth, p. 42. Papst warned against the dangers of this kind of interpretation in 1960, p. xxi.

9. Cf., for example, his conclusion on p. 131: "Was der Spielmann ist, was sein Wesen ist und wie er in der Welt steht, das erfährt man—formal—nicht durch entschiedene, zuordnende 'objektive' Aussagen, sondern nur aus den relativen Sichtweisen begrenzter 'empirischer' Subjekte, die *da* sind, nur insofern sie dem Erzähler wirklich begegnen."

10. Brinkmann makes this clear in saying: "Daß auch der Erzähler Grillparzer selbst ist, bedarf kaum der Erwähnung (so wenig selbstverständlich das auch *a priori* so sein müßte)" (p. 141).

11. Swales says that this is a narrator who "intellectually is determined to report from the perspective of the real world, but who emotionally assents to the ideal, if impossible world of the 'höchste Stufen der Kunst'" (p. 116).

12. Politzer, 1967, pp. 58-60.

13. F. Maxwell-Bresler's review of Politzer, 1967, in *MLR,* 64 (1969), 950-1. The point is actually not stated strongly enough; Maxwell-Bresler allows that this can only be "Vermutung," not categorical statement. But *some* evidence is needed for the former, too; even "Vermutung" has its limits.

14. Politzer, 1967, p. 40: "Es gibt, scheint Grillparzer sagen zu wollen, kein Versagen in der Wirklichkeit, das nicht in einem Seelenwinkel des Versagenden zu Hause wäre"; and Swales, pp. 115-116. Stern's (pp. 76-77) introduction of a Christian perspective also gives insufficient weight to the Spielmann's defective judgment. His attractiveness is a consequence of that defect, rather than a matter of faith.

15. Only in this sense do I agree with Papst that "either of two apparently conflicting assessments of the Spielmann seems to be equally tenable." These assessments are reactions to, not accounts of, the Spielmann.

16. Brinkmann, p. 126. Brinkmann's attempt to show stylistic features in the Spielmann's direct speech which are attributable to the narrator seems to me unconvincing.

17. Jungbluth (p. 43) does not draw this consequence of his view since he uses it as a bridge to a biographical excursion; the irrelevance can be explained ("findet daraus seine Erklärung") in biographical material. But this view of the process of artistic creation—haphazard inclusion of anything that happens to concern Grillparzer at a given moment—is not at all generous to Grillparzer's artistic talents.

18. Stern, pp. 63-64. It is not clear in any case why taciturnity should constitute a triumph; it is rather unusual for epic narrators to obtrude their presence.

19. Almost all critics accept the narrator's professions of love for the people and his claims to have an "anthropologischen Heißhunger" at face value, in spite of their obsessiveness: e.g. Straubinger, p. 100; von Wiese, pp. 137-38; H. Pongs, "Möglichkeiten des Tragischen in der Novelle," *Jahrbuch der Kleist-Gesellschaft,* 13-14 (1932), p. 79; Brinkmann, p. 88, and so on. Swales is the only critic who consistently evaluates rather than accepts the narrator's pronouncements concerning himself, though Politzer (1967, p. 13) questions the narrator's claim that he is "leidenschaftlich" about anything.

20. E. Alker, p. 18: "Doch die ersten drei Seiten können weder in stilistischer noch in kompositorischer Hinsicht als sehr glücklich gelten; sie machen einen jungdeutsch-dilettantischen Eindruck."

21. Politzer (p. 9) finds the narrator here pedantic. But while his style can be criticized, it must be criticized from the other end of the spectrum; it is a rather mannered, self-conscious and pretentious style.

22. Swales (p. 110) notes that his interest in the Spielmann seems "to be somewhat inconsistent with the narrator's avowed purpose in attending the Volksfest." Swales' interpretation of this discrepancy is mainly concerned with the relative importance for the narrator of Volksfest and Spielmann; I should think of it more as an indication of his insincere posturing.

23. It is unnecessary to introduce Grillparzer's possible fear of social revolution here, e.g. Brinkmann, p. 88 and Politzer, 1967, p. 10. The attitude of the narrator to the people is a motif in the story, only to be evaluated in relation to its other occurrences and to contrasting motifs. Only the complete results of this kind of analysis could be referred to Grillparzer's beliefs, or to anyone else's, not an isolated piece of text seen without the controlling factor of its position in the whole story.

24. It is strange to note how often this grotesque sentence has been taken at face value. Only Politzer appears to have responded to its style: "Dieser Satz ist nicht nur monströs; sein Gefüge straft auch seine Aussage Lügen" (1967, p. 12). My interpretation here, however, differs from that of Politzer; he believes that the narrator is interested in the people for their vitality, presumably because one with the

temperament of "ein hochnotpeinlich-scharfsichtiger Beobachter," feeling his deficiency, "sehnt sich nach der Begegnung mit einer Kraft . . . " (pp. 12-13). This seems to me not to do justice to the element of pretentious self-inflation by the narrator, the only real point of the style of the sentence.

25. Stern's view that the narrator is aloof, and "wishes merely to register" (p. 64) cannot be justified by the text. Many other critics have viewed the narrator's unsympathetic attitude as that of a distanced observer without an attitude; cf., e.g., Politzer: "Er ist die Linse, in der sich die Welt der Erscheinungen spiegelt" (1967, p. 13).

26. At this point occurs another of the narrator's unfulfilled protestations, and the discrepancy between what he says and what he does is again instructive. For having said that he will spare his reader any further description of the old man's playing ("dieses höllischen Konzertes") he in fact goes on to give a long description of it. Again, the discrepancy conveys his obsessive denigration of the Spielmann.

27. Swales (p. 111) is inclined to see this claim by the narrator as an attempt to excuse his interest in the Spielmann: "it is almost as if the narrator were ashamed of a moment of weakness for the Spielmann." But self-inflation seems to me a better explanation than the postulation of a conflict in the narrator's mind; for the narrator has no real personal sympathy for the Spielmann.

28. Swales alone among recent critics finds this passage suspect: " . . . do we not detect a certain strain, an element of self-deception in the language—does not our narrator perhaps 'protest too much'" (p. 110). But he draws no broader conclusions from this. It is remarkable how often it has been taken as a true confession by Grillparzer, and even a literary historical manifesto important for the time—as if by 1848 such a thing were necessary! Cf., for example, Politzer, p. 6; and von Wiese, p. 138: "Diese viel zitierte Stelle zeigt einen wichtigen geistesgeschichtlichen Wechsel in der Auffassung vom menschlichen Schicksal." Yet Seuffert already half a century ago found it an "etwas gezwungene Wendung," and the juxtapositions it contains a "gewaltsame Verknüpfung" (p. 292). Seuffert responded very accurately to the tone of these and other phrases early in the story, and it was only his lack of the theoretical distinction between author and narrator which prevented him from proceeding to a better understanding of the story. Having seen so much, he pronounces the "Dichter" to be Grillparzer himself (p. 296) and proceeds to explain away the interesting material he observes as due to Grillparzer's experiences and character; no more instructive example can be found of a critic whose intuitive response is very fine, but his theory so poor as to waste that advantage.

29. Politzer (pp. 15-16) notes the contrast in the reception given by the public to the art of the Spielmann and of the narrator, and part of their contrasting reactions to that reception, but without relating this systematically to the thematic structure of the story.

30. Silz, p. 69. This parallel has been proposed again by later critics, e.g. Swales, p. 109, and Politzer, 1967, p. 10. But it was already noted in 1925 by Seuffert (pp. 293-4) and, as Silz points out, by Alker (pp. 21-22).

31. Papst, pp. xxx-xxxi.

32. Unlike Swales, therefore, I do not find the kind of ambivalence which has as one of its sides a wish to identify with the Spielmann: "He can only—and this in spite of himself—offer a personal and instinctive belief, an emotional assent to the person and life of Jakob, the 'armer Spielmann'" (p. 116).

33. By contrast Stern says (p. 68) that "Jacob's devotion to his art (if we are to call it 'art' . . . emerges as the sole positive value intimated in the *Novelle*." But it is certainly not his art that wins him people who love or admire him.

34. Thus Jungbluth's conclusion is both irrelevant and erroneous: "Die Erzählung *Der arme Spielmann* ist nicht allein eine gnadenlose Abrechnung Grillparzers mit sich selbst, sie ist auch ein Zeugnis für extremen Selbstgenuß" (p. 51).

35. To be sure, these positive signs do not occur without something of their opposite; the contrast is maintained by Jakob's actual death coming as a result of his indiscriminately risking his life to rescue what is important (children) and what is unimportant (a small amount of money).

36. The interpretations of Paulsen and Krotkoff came to hand as this study was completed. Paulsen detects social satire in the story, but only through equating the narrator's attitudes and those of Grillparzer, e.g., referring to the opening of the story, his "Gerade dadurch, daß Grillparzer das Volk derart mythologisiert . . . " (p. 284), treats as authorial attitudes to society what should be viewed as part of the characterization of the narrator. Krotkoff's essay is concerned with the "Rahmen," but in an unproductive way: "In den autobiographischen Angaben des Erzählers hat mehr weltanschauliches Gedankengut Grillparzers in dichterischer Gestalt Eingang gefunden als man zuerst annehmen möchte" (p. 365). Thus she takes the narrator's remarks on the "Volk" as truths for the story's purposes.

W. E. Yates (essay date 1972)

SOURCE: "The Artist: Der arme Spielmann, " in *Grillparzer: A Critical Introduction,* Cambridge University Press, 1972, pp. 76-83.

[*In the following excerpt, Yates examines the portrayal of Jacob, the protagonist of* Der arme Spielmann, *and perceives the novella as a confessional work.*]

Der arme Spielmann, the last completed work that Grillparzer published in his lifetime, is the only other of his works in which the central character is actually an artist. It is also the only one of his works that is set in the Vienna of his own times. The city as a whole, indeed, is what the text begins with: Vienna in July. From there the focus narrows, first to the popular festival in Brigittenau (which lay by an arm of the Danube, to the north of the centre of the city), and then to the central figure, the mendicant fiddler who stands playing 'with a smiling, self-approving expression' (p. 40) as the crowds pass by. A few lines later this picture of his manner of playing is enlarged: '. . . he was belabouring an old much-cracked violin, beating time not only by raising and lowering his foot, but also by a corresponding movement of his whole bent body.' The picture the narrator presents—the fiddler bobbing in time with the music, so that his whole frame seems to gesture in lone accord with what he is playing—is a comic one; and it helps to set the mood for the whole portrait of Jakob, a portrait of 'so much artistic zeal with so much ineptitude' (41).

For the tone adopted by the narrator in the opening pages is a strongly ironic one—an irony which seems to set him as much apart from the background of festivities as Jakob himself. He ironizes as 'anthropological voracity' (41) his fascinated interest in the fiddler; but his self-irony does not mask the perceptiveness of his insight, and gradually the significance of his subject emerges. That the fiddler wends his way homewards in the opposite direction to the crowds as they arrive for the fair not only suggests an unexpected moral independence, but seems physically to exemplify, at the lowest possible level, the solitary nature of the artist's lot. Jakob leaves, the narrator tells us, 'as a man going home' (41); and this is meant not only in its physical sense, for Jakob is also returning to his spiritual home—what he is going to do is to devote himself to his music, in solitary improvisation. In his room, where the narrator visits him a few days later, the conscientious apartness of his lot is further symbolized by the chalk line which divides his meticulously ordered half of the room from the rank disorder of the other half (48).

The life-story Jakob has to tell is one not only of music but also of love, and the two threads are joined in the last view the narrator has of him, playing in rapt absorption the melody sung by Barbara, whom he loved and lost. But he is reluctant to tell his story: 'I have no story', he says (50). The reticence and discretion with which he talks of his past life distance us from the events and feelings in it; so too does the fact that his narrative is as it were filtered through the ironic viewpoint of the narrator, which the opening sequence has established. In the body of the story the narrator's voice unobtrusively but repeatedly interrupts, warding off too great an empathy on the part of the reader. By the interaction of the two voices we are allowed to see the absurdity as well as the tragedy in the story of the fiddler's love of Barbara and of his music; the laconic manner of both tellers prevents the story from descending either to the ridiculous or to the sentimental. The ultra-pathetic is told without sentimentality; irony and pathos are in perfect balance.

The pathos of Jakob's failure lies in the disparity between his intentions and his achievements. The earliest important example in his everyday life is his disgrace in a recitation exercise at school, which estranges his father from him (52): looking back at his father's death, he comments: 'I hope one day to see him again in that place where we are judged according to our intentions and not our deeds' (65). At work his slowness, a result of over-conscientiousness,

is taken as slackness (53) and his courtesy to Barbara is taken as philandering, so that he gains the reputation of being negligent and dissolute. His hesitancy in approaching the shop where Barbara lives appears so suspicious that he is apprehended as a thief by her father (61). His attempt to set himself up in business, based on an unpractical idea for a music-copying service, ends in his being cheated and brought to the edge of financial ruin. Equally, his performance as a musician falls short in practice: he enjoys a rich aesthetic life within his imagination, but cannot transform this inner beauty into sounds of beauty, whether in improvisation or in playing the classics. The disparity is suggested by the narrator, seeing him play from sheets of music, 'which doubtless recorded in perfect order what he rendered with such total lack of coherence' (41).

In love too Jakob's visions are cheated by reality. Though he tells his story unsentimentally, we learn from the narrator that both the sound of Barbara's song and the memory of her kiss can still bring tears to his eyes (54, 69): but while Barbara is sometimes kind to him, and understanding—she alone understands the good will of his intentions, his 'honest heart' (70)—the picture we are given of her is not a winsome one. She is mousy and pockmarked when young, and when she is old the narrator confirms that she looks as though she can never have been beautiful. Her reputation in the office where Jakob works is that she is coarse and that there is no good in her. Jakob himself observes her ill-temper. At home her behaviour is loud and vulgar. She is rude to customers; to Jakob she is cold at first, later she scolds him in the shop and mocks him in front of customers. The affection Jakob feels for her is inspired less by her unprepossessing real self than by the simple song she sings which captures his imagination. And even the song is, to the narrator's ear, 'not at all distinguished' (54). Jakob's hopes of happiness centre on illusions, on the constructions of his own imagination. Moreover the hesitancy with which he approaches Barbara at her home—first his dithering worry about displaying 'discourteous importunity' (60), then his trembling outside the shop—is evidence that he is too timid and unpractical ever to be able to grasp happiness in human relations. The most grotesque disparity between his intentions and his actual achievement in this sphere lies in the incident when at last he takes courage enough to kiss Barbara, but only through the glass pane of a closed door (69). He seems to fight shy of the sensual—even in old age his disapproval of the popular tunes played by most street musicians is based partly on the suspicion that they serve to revive 'the memory of the pleasures of dancing or other disorderly amusements' (44)—and it is characteristic that his attempt to return Barbara's impulsive kiss is made only when both his attempt and any further response on her part are physically impossible. And yet, despite the utter practical inadequacy of this reaction to her original kiss, the day remains for him a day of supreme happiness, the most blissful of his life (70).

The hardest day, by contrast, is the day of her farewell from him (75). It is the day on which for the first time she addresses him with the intimate *du;* but the feeling with which she parts from him is one of pity, '. . . And yet I'm sorry for you.' Bowing to practical necessity, she is at last doing what she says she has tried to resist having to do: she is marrying into 'the rough folk', where by character and upbringing she clearly belongs. Practical necessity has no place for so ineffectual a creature of the imagination as Jakob: Barbara has made this clear earlier in her plea, 'Give up your music-making and put your mind to practicalities!' (72).

Shy, unpractical, and ill-fitted to the world of his fellow-men, Jakob *cannot* do as Barbara demands; and having failed in the school of 'practicality', he devotes himself wholly to music. His first rediscovery of his violin, which he remembers as another of the happiest events in his life (53), took place when all his diligence in the office gained him a reputation for idleness; and so again now, having proved his incapability of achieving happiness in practical life, he devotes himself to his art as his sole consolation. He begins by studying the works of the classical masters. Even as an old beggar he practises and honours them still. But his playing is a means to an end, the recapturing of the divine ideal he glimpses within his imagination. Of other musicians he observes: "They play Wolfgang Amadeus Mozart and Sebastian Bach, but no-one plays the Good Lord himself" (55). Jakob—in his imagination— 'plays the Good Lord', and he speaks of his solitary improvisation as 'prayer' (44). When he first rediscovers the violin its sound seems to him like divine inspiration: 'And then, Sir, when I drew the bow across the strings, it was as though God's finger had touched me' (54); and the structure of fugue and counterpoint he regards as 'a whole heavenly edifice' (55). When he plays the effect is inebriating, it is as though the very air around him were 'pregnant with intoxication' (54); and this sense too seems a part of the divine inspiration: 'Speech is necessary to man, as food is; but drink too ought to be kept pure, for it comes from God' (55).

His devotion to music, then, is not a romantic sacrifice of the fruits of 'life', nor is it only a means of solace: it is a pure and whole devotion, and utterly serious. Even as an unregarded street fiddler he persistently upholds the dignity of his art. He refuses to pander to popular taste: he plays serious music and turns his back on the crowds at the *Kirtag*. He insists that he is not a mere beggar; and something of his artist's pride is brought out plastically in his insistence that money given him must not go straight into his hand but must be placed, like a well-earned tribute, in his hat (42f.). He regards the money he receives as an 'honorarium' (45).

The moral integrity and the idealism that inform the fiddler's life are finally made manifest in his death. We learn of this at the end of the *Novelle*, when we are back in the narrator's account that frames Jakob's own story. He has lost his life in the floods—not by drowning, but as a result of rescuing children and then plunging back into the waters to save his landlord's money, so that he has died of cold. His final action reveals the true motives and intentions of his life: he has given up his life in selfless service of humanity, despite the ingratitude and intolerant impatience he has met from humanity throughout his life. The humane reward, redressing the injustice of a lifetime, lies in Barbara's memory of him, her true affection and appreciation symbolized in her refusal to part with his violin, which—tearfully—she treasures and locks, defensively, in a drawer.

Her husband, one of the 'rough folk', would have been willing to sell it: Barbara's firm independence, her indif-ference to 'a few Gulden more or less', proves at the last that Jakob's life has not been totally without influence on the world around him. By the artistic standards of his own vocation, however, neither the practical achievement for which he dies nor Barbara's memory has redemptive value; for while the depth of his moral integrity, which is an essential factor in the quality of his *life*, most conspicuously informs his devotion to his music, nonetheless his performance as a musician is lamentably inadequate. From the very outset of his would-be professional career, his playing finds no appreciation, and though in Brigittenau he is competing with other beggars whose standard of musicianship (as the narrator makes very clear) is painfully low, they make more from their efforts than he does, and indeed play better. For 'what he played seemed to be an incoherent sequence of notes without tempo or melody' (41). When he obliges the children who demand waltzes from him, they cannot tell what he is playing. He blames the faulty discrimination of the children, saying that they 'have no ear for music'; and in an age which demands nothing but waltzes, public taste may well seem suspect to him. But the narrator, speaking as a dramatist, has already affirmed the value and validity of the judgment of the general public (39); and by any such objective criterion, the truth is that as a violinist Jakob is incompetent. His waltzes are unrecognizable because they are badly played—so badly that the narrator is dumbfounded to hear of his evenings of improvisation:

> Wir waren beide ganz still geworden. Er, aus Beschämung über das verratene Geheimnis seines Innern; ich, voll Erstaunen, den Mann von den höchsten Stufen der Kunst sprechen zu hören, der nicht imstande war, den leichtesten Walzer faßbar wiederzugeben. (43)[1]

The emphasis here is *not* placed on *faßbar*, to suggest—pathetically—a mere failure of communication or of comprehension; what he plays does not only *seem* a mere jumble. What is stressed, distancing us from the emotional implications of the fiddler's confession, is the narrator's astonishment, the incongruity in the situation. And indeed, as the narrator discovers at first hand, Jakob's improvisation is a 'hellish concert' (48); and his grotesque lack of natural musicianship is further brought out in the wonder with which he learns of Barbara's ability to sing the melody of her song by ear (59).

In the portrait of Jakob as an artist there is much of Grillparzer himself. The point is not that Grillparzer too loved music—he played the violin occasionally in boyhood (SB 97), and used later to improvise on the piano (*Gespr.* 58)— but that some of his deepest attitudes and experiences are ironically reflected in Jakob. Even the fiddler's reluctance to tell his story is akin to his own dislike in his mature years of exposing his inner self, which is attested in his diary (T 1656) and in verse (G 105); and if Jakob's reluctance rests psychologically on the failure of his efforts both in music and in love, this too corresponds to a side of Grillparzer, who once wrote towards the end of the 1840s, 'It makes me sad that everything I do in life is a failure&' (T 4026). His keen awareness of the disparity between ideas and achievements is attested in epigrams both early in his career (G 2) and—with rueful retrospection—in the 1860s (G 1688); and if it is interesting to see this awareness reflected in the delight with which at one stage he used to play an old stringless piano without any sense of missing the sound (SB 98f.), it is still more interesting that on one occasion in his youth, before he had written any of his tragedies, he related it specifically to dramatic writing—'I should like to be able to write a tragedy in *thoughts*. It would turn out a masterpiece!'(T 45)—and that it remained with him at the peak of his creative career: 'I always lived in my dreams and projects, but proceeded only with difficulty to executing them because I knew that I should never do it to my satisfaction' (SB 214). For Jakob's 'music-making'serves as a symbol for all art, including dramatic art; and if Jakob aspires to 'play the Good Lord', so Grillparzer once wrote proudly of himself as 'a poet of ultimate truths' ('ein Dichter der letzten Dinge': G 1310, ii). Jakob's sense of the intoxicating quality of music corresponds to his own conception of poetry, as opposed to prose: 'Prose is man's food, poetry is his drink, which does not nourish him but invigorates him'(T 3493 [1839]).

Hence the quick and persistent interest taken in Jakob by the dramatist narrator of *Der arme Spielmann*. For it is not only through Jakob's voice that this *Novelle* is a confessional work. Both the story-tellers—the intellectual artist and the imaginative artist—are fictional characters, but their roles correspond to a division that Grillparzer recognized in himself:

> In mir nämlich leben zwei völlig abgesonderte Wesen. Ein Dichter von der übergreifendsten, ja sich überstürzenden Phantasie und ein Verstandesmensch der kältesten und zähesten Art. (SB 135)[2]

The imaginative artist tells his story, and the ironic narrator adds his suggestive, occasionally even caustic, comments, implying a cumulative judgment on the artist's achievement, which he sees sympathetically but with realistic clarity.

Grillparzer recognized the paramount importance of emotion and the imagination in creative art; his intellect did not usurp the place of the imagination in his own dramatic writing, but was exercised in his wide reading, refining his taste and sharpening his critical sense. The late Fred O. Nolte, a distinguished American critic, has written that 'in the catholic, delicate appreciation of things poetic and artistic, Grillparzer is not impossibly the most patiently and sensitively cultivated mind in the whole range of European letters'. And all his patiently nurtured aesthetic sensibility was constantly directed critically at his own work: by the 1820s he was already a victim of 'the most merciless self-criticism' (SB 214). While he was also capable of assessing himself soberly as the first among the successors of Goethe and Schiller (SB 201), and while this is indeed not an immodest assessment, what he dwelt on most constantly in his works was not so much the positive achievement as the degree of failure; he could not compare his work with all his reading of Calderón and Lope, of Shakespeare, of Goethe, and of the ancients, without feeling his shortcomings. In short, this naggingly self-critical self, the 'intellectual' in him, judged his work by the highest standards there are, and found it wanting: and his fears of shotcomings are reflected—ironically yet affectionately caricatured—in the total artistic failure of the poor fiddler Jakob, who cannot reproduce his classical models, and to whom the art which is his sole solace and lasting ideal in life can never offer rewards to match the pinnacle of hap-

piness afforded by love—a happiness whose fleetingness is represented in Barbara's single kiss, but which is yet remembered as bringing the 'most blissful day' of his life.

Notes

1. 'We had both become quite silent: he, from embarrassment at this inmost sceret that he had betrayed; I, astonished at hearing a man speaking of the heights of art who was not able to give a recognizable rendering of the easiest waltz.'

2. 'There are in me two completely separate beings: a poet of the most overweening, even precipitate imagination, and an intellectual of the coldest and most unyielding kind.'

Robert M. Browning (essay date 1976)

SOURCE: "Language and the Fall from Grace in Grillparzer's *Spielmann*," in **Seminar: A Journal of Germanic Studies, Vol. XII, No. 4, November, 1976, pp. 215-35.**

[*In the following essay, Browning explores "a constitutive (but hitherto unnoted) theme of the novella—that of language or the word—and to offer some suggestions as to its possible meaning."*]

Grillparzer's most 'prosaic' work is also his most poetic. It is no doubt for this reason that it has found so many exegetes: with great poetry we are never done.[1] It is my primary purpose here to point out what seems to me to be a constitutive (but hitherto unnoted) theme of the novella—that of language or the word—and to offer some suggestions as to its possible meaning. In order to arrive at my main object I must unfortunately do what the novella also does, namely, adumbrate the themes introduced before the theme of language or the word itself assumes central importance, for it is this latter theme that shows the introductory themes in their true light, while they in turn give the theme of the word its real significance. *Der arme Spielmann* is structured on the principle of irony: what is first presented as of supreme importance is shown to be highly questionable and ethically hollow, while what at first appears insignificant and self-defeating turns out to be deeply meaningful and ethically salvational.

The opening frame, paragraphs 1-26,[2] introduces all the leading themes, with the exception of the one in which we are particularly interested, that of the word, though this theme may also be deduced. The overriding theme of the opening frame (as also of the closing one, but of that later) is the one and the many or the individual and the masses. It is first stated in terms of 'Volk' and 'Vornehme': the Brigittenkirchtag is a festival the lower classes 'give themselves'; the upper classes, 'die Vornehmen,' can participate in it only in their capacity as members of 'das Volk,' that is, only by temporarily assuming the character of the lower classes and merging with the commonalty, thus returning for the time being to the roots from which they sprang. The narrator, who only too obviously does not belong to 'das Volk' in the sense of being a member of the working classes, regards such a return in a very positive light—or at least he claims to: 'Ich versäume nicht leicht, diesem Feste beizuwohnen' (para. 6). St. Bridget's

Day is a feast of oneness: 'Der Unterschied der Stände ist verschwunden,' the narrator categorically informs us. The specific example adduced in the fourth paragraph, however, may hardly be said to bear this out—if anything, it indicates the opposite: 'Begafft, bedauert, bespottet sitzen die geputzten Damen' in their carriages stalled in the dense stream of the masses pressing towards the Brigittenau. The Holstein stallion seeks to take his way over the top of the plebian 'Korbwagen' filled with screaming women and children. The swift fiacre, immobilized in the traffic, 'berechnet ingrimmig' the lost time. These are images of divisiveness, not union.

Connected with the theme of (dionysiac) oneness is that of license and disorder. This is a 'saturnalische[s] Fest,' whose 'eigentliche Hierophanten' are 'die Kinder der Dienstbarkeit und der Arbeit.' The Roman Saturnalia were a time of celebration of freedom and equality, a memorialization of the Golden Age when man did not have to live by the sweat of his brow, but also a time of irresponsibility and license as the price of equality and oneness.[3] This theme is developed through images of a tremendous force escaping its proper confines: a mighty river overflowing its banks, a dense mass passing through a narrow opening—the city gate, the Danube bridge, the lane leading from the Augarten to the Brigittenau—until finally 'der breite Hafen der Lust' opens up to receive it. The Volksfest is seen as an escape from reality: a 'pays de cocagne,' an 'Eldorado,' a veritable 'Schlaraffenland,' which dissolves after two days and a night 'wie der Traum einer Sommernacht.' It is a regression or rebirth (we can easily construe the image of release through a narrow passage as a birth image) into a dreamy, womblike utopia of equality perhaps, of irresponsibility and license certainly. It is an 'Aufruhr der Freude' and exhibits 'Losgebundenheit der Lust.'

The crucial paragraph of the opening frame is the sixth, in which the narrator introduces himself in the first person singular. Here the theme of the one and the many appears in the variation of artist and audience. Emphatically a member of the upper classes, the narrator visits popular festivals in a double capacity: 'als leidenschaftlicher Verehrer des Volkes' and as a dramatist who finds here the opportunity to study character types. In a syntactically monstrous sentence, 95 words in length, the narrator enunciates the doctrine that the will of the people is the will of God and that submission to this will is equivalent to union with the divine. To him, as a dramatist, 'der rückhaltlose Ausbruch eines überfüllten Schauspielhauses' (a reprise of the image of overflowing) has always been 'zehnmal interessanter, ja belehrender . . . als das zusammengeklügelte Urteil eines an Leib und Seele verkrüppelten [!], von dem Blut ausgesogener Autoren spinnenartig aufgeschwollenen [!] literarischen Matadors . . .' For, 'als ein Liebhaber der Menschen,' he is convinced that there lies in the masses 'besonders wenn sie . . . für einige Zeit der einzelnen Zwecke vergessen und sich als ein Teil des Ganzen fühlen . . . denn doch das Göttliche . . . ja, der Gott.' For this reason every Volksfest must be for him 'ein eigentliches Seelenfest, eine Wallfahrt, eine Andacht.' This is certainly an astounding statement for a member of the upper classes, but its overheated rhetoric even more than its content is the thing that should give us pause. Here is a man who is trying to persuade *himself* of something; if we too are persuaded, it is because we have not been listening closely.

(Parenthetically it should be noted that the narrator does not state that the outburst in the theatre must be an outburst of *approval*, as some commentators assume.[4] Disapproval could be just as interesting and instructive. Approval or disapproval is not the point: in either case the many have spoken and the one must accept their judgment.)

The second half of paragraph 6 deals with the narrator's second reason for attending popular festivals: to study character types. It is obvious, however, that aloof observation is at odds with the attainment of dionysiac union with 'das Volk,' the narrator's passionately stated quasi-religious goal. Furthermore, the sentence pronounced with such a programmatic air: 'und wahrlich! man kann die Berühmten nicht verstehen, wenn man die Obscuren nicht durchgefühlt hat,'[5] shows that the narrator is not primarily interested in the 'obscure,' who are only a means to an end, but in the 'famous.' The final sentence bears this out: it is not the quarrels of drunken carters but the 'Zwist der Göttersöhne' that interests him; it is not the servant girl following her persistent lover away from the dance but the 'Julieen, die Didos und die Medeen' who are contained in her 'als Embryo' that he wants to fathom. The polarity between the famous and the obscure constitutes the third variation on the theme of the one and the many.

To summarize: the themes introduced thus far are: (1) the one and the many (shown forth in three variations: 'Volk' and 'Vornehme,' dramatist and audience, famous and obscure); (2) disorder und license as the price of voluptuous oneness; (3) union with the commonalty as union with the divine. Beneath, or concurrently with, these positively stated themes we become aware, almost subliminally, of certain inward contradictions, partly of a stylistic nature, partly in the form of images, partly as direct statements, that run counter to the doctrine of salvation through union with the masses, which is set forth with such evangelistic fervour. Our suspicions may be aroused that the narrator does not mean what he says or that he is not aware of what he is saying or that he does not know what he really means.[6]

The narrator (whom one should not naively equate with Grillparzer himself—he is a figure in a story *by* Grillparzer) is, we note, a dramatist. *His* way of achieving union with the 'das Volk' (the deduction is surely permissible) is through the power of the word. Though the masses themselves are inarticulate (we hear them murmuring, shouting, screaming, cursing, but never uttering a sentence), theirs is the final judgment on the verbal icon. Through his word the poet may either enter into oneness with the people or be excluded from it.

With the discovery of the Spielmann the themes stated in the first seven paragraphs begin to be inverted. The masses, described as 'lustgierig' (para. 7) and 'genußlechzend' (para. 8), stand in stark contrast to the Spielmann whose first words, a Horatian tag, speak of *limits* ('sunt certi denique fines') and whose decorous appearance contrasts so strikingly with the wild indecorum of the other mendicant musicians, this 'Gruppe aus dem sozial-pathologischen Tartarus' as Politzer (p. 14) calls it, posted along the narrow road to the Brigittenau. If the narrator, for all his protestations of quasi-religious yearning to merge with the 'Volk' and participate in the feast of oneness, now turns back just beyond the 'hölzernes Gittertor' that marks the boundary between the Augarten and the Brigittenau, between reality and dream, individuated separateness and oneness, it must be because there is something existentially more important to him than dionysiac union with the masses, namely, the fathoming of an individual who, even more emphatically than he himself, is *not* part of the masses.[7] The thematic inversions we now observe point the connection between narrator and Spielmann.

Paragraph 8 brings an inversion of the theme of the one and many or, more specifically, an inversion of the second variation of this theme as introduced in paragraph six, that of the relation of artist and audience. There the artist who bows before the voice of the people because in it lies 'finally' the divine, here the artist who blithely refuses to recognize their judgment. We need not rehearse the description of the Spielmann and his playing. Suffice it to say that once the narrator's attention has been riveted by the old fiddler in the threadbare overcoat his prose acquires a tone of complete conviction and authenticity. Despite the ironical overtones and a certain pretence of aloofness, the reader immediately senses that here is a subject with whom the narrator identifies, here at last is an 'Obscurer' whom he finds it worth his while to try to fathom. But can he, through him, learn to understand the 'Berühmten'? His 'ravenous anthropological appetite' is aroused by the *contrarieties* evinced by the Spielmann's appearance, behaviour, and station in life, in other words, by precisely those features which seem to contradict the doctrine of the oneness of mankind, for according to this doctrine the 'invisible but unbroken thread' spun between the obscure and the famous should run from the *other* mendicant musicians, not from the Spielmann. Everything about the Spielmann tends to cast doubt on the narrator's programmatic pronouncement concerning the connection between the high and the low. No wonder then that the narrator is "trembling with curiosity to discover the connection"(para. 9). The 'Volk' has now become merely an obstacle standing between him and his quarry and with the 'misadventure' that causes him to lose sight of the old fiddler he also loses all interest in the festival. Turning homeward, he hears in the distance the old man's fiddle and his pace quickens, he is filled with delight to find again the 'object of his curiosity.' It is a case of love at first sight.

A notable aspect of this passage is the irony of the narrator in describing the Spielmann, in whom he has such a burning interest, and which contrasts so emphatically with the quasi-religious fervency adopted in speaking of the masses, in whom, as his behaviour now proves beyond doubt, he has no true interest. This irony has a double function: it serves both to disguise the narrator's embarrassment at a sudden infatuation that contradicts his stated doctrine and it is an expression of Grillparzer's malicious delight in revealing the deeper nature of the narrator-artist, who is only half aware that he is concealing something not only from the world (i.e., the reader) but also from himself.[8]

When the narrator comes upon the Spielmann again, the latter is playing what he thinks is a waltz for a group of boys who in their turn are demanding that he play a waltz! Disgusted, they leave to gather around an organ-grinder. 'Die Kinder kennen eben keinen andern Tanz, als den Walzer,' says the narrator, trying to be kind. 'Ich spielte einen Walzer,'replies the old fiddler pointing to his sheet of music, 'Aber die Kinder haben kein Ohr.' Brinkmann (p. 111) puts the situation succinctly: 'Was die Welt von ihm [dem Spielmann] denkt, das scheint er von der Welt zu denken.' He is absolutely unmoved by his failure to reach the 'world' —it is not he who is at fault, it is the public, a complete rejection of the doctrine of the infallibity of the masses enunciated by the narrator. The 'question' the story sets itself to 'answer' is: who is right, the Spielmann or the world? As a figure, the Spielmann fascinates the narrator above all because he is a fellow artist, however unsuccessful. His interest in him is an interest in that which occupies him most: in the nature of the artist and of art and their relation to 'das Volk,' to the 'world.'

The next theme to be inverted after the narrator meets the Spielmann is that of license and disorder. The Spielmann is a person of pedantic order who considers it sinful 'andere durch Spiel und Gesang zu einem solchen widerlichen Vergehen anzureizen'; 'der Mensch [muß] in allen Dingen eine gewisse Ordnung festsetzen, sonst gerät er ins Wilde und Unaufhaltsame,' he declares (para. 15), and we must add: like the masses at their 'saturnalian' festivals, which are for the narrator 'ein Seelenfest, eine Wallfahrt, eine Andacht.' Through license and disorder the masses return to oneness, the Spielmann through order: 'Die drei ersten Stunden des Tages der Übung, die Mitte dem Broterwerb, und der Abend mir und dem lieben Gott, das heißt nicht unehrlich geteilt,' he explains, his eyes gleaming with tears (para. 18, end). 'Mir und dem lieben Gott'—the Spielmann also professes to find religious fulfilment in oneness, but not in union with 'das Volk.' It is not the first time he has betrayed emotion in speaking of how he spends his evenings: 'Abends halte ich mich zu Hause und'—his voice drops, he blushes and casts down his eyes—'da spiele ich dann aus der Einbildung, so für mich ohne Noten. Phantasieren, glaub' ich, heißt es in den Musikbüchern' (para. 16). Such improvising is for him prayer and 'gehört ins Kämmerlein' (para. 18), a reference of course to Matthew 6:6: 'Wenn du aber betest, so gehe in dein Kämmerlein und schließ die Tür zu und bete zu deinem Vater im Verborgenen; und dein Vater, der in das Verborgene sieht, wird dir's vergelten öffentlich.' It is now the narrator's turn to blush, though we do not hear that he does, for he is like the heathens (!) of whom the Lord speaks in the next verse, a man of many words: 'Und wenn ihr betet, sollt ihr nicht viel plappern wie die Heiden; denn sie meinen, sie werden erhört, wenn sie viel Worte machen.'[9] The Spielmann's rejection of the doctrine of the supremacy of the masses is the corollary of his attitude towards union with something higher. The narrator *must* believe that in the 'Volk' lies 'das Göttliche' as long as he accepts the commonalty as the arbiter of his art; the Spielmann *cannot*, for in the 'Volk' he sees chaos and license—in God alone lies order.

The *outward* manifestation of the order the Spielmann worships takes an amusingly pedantic or a naïvely touching form so far as his behaviour towards others is concerned: he expresses himself in a stiffly ceremonious fashion; he refuses to look upon himself as a mendicant but insists that any alms he may receive are an 'honorarium' for services rendered; he takes leave of the narrator by executing 'mit einer Abart von vornehmer Leichtigkeit einen ziemlich linkischen Kratzfuß' (para. 20). His private interpretation of his position in the world is so at odds with that of the world itself that he is bound to be an object of derision as long as we regard him merely as a phenomenon, an 'Original,' but a figure of deep poignancy as soon as we have heard his story.

The most striking manifestation of the rift between the Spielmann and the world is of course his music-making. The order the Spielmann cherishes within and which guides his private life manifests itself in his music as disorder, 'eine unzusammenhängende Folge von Tönen ohne Zeitmaß und Melodie' (para. 8) that only arouses the risibilities of the crowd and brings him no 'honorarium.' So far is he from attaining his goal of 'Veredlung des Geschmacks und Herzens . . . der Zuhörerschaft' (para. 18). Why this dissonance between inward and outward? Paragraphs 22-5 begin the revelation of the mystery.

On his solitary way home from the Kirchtag, after refreshing himself in a tavern, where he thankfully enjoys 'die Stille des Orts, im Abstich von der lärmenden Volksmenge' (para. 21)—a phrase which again reveals the speciousness of his fervant declarations about the divinity of the masses and his true inward kinship with the Spielmann—the narrator seeks out the old man's humble dwelling in a suburban street.[10] From the roadway he overhears him 'improvising,' that is, celebrating the divine order, at his garret window. To the neighbours, disturbed in their early slumbers, the Spielmann's concert not surprisingly sounds like 'Kratzen'; to the narrator it sounds like a series of long held tones separated by harmonic intervals: 'Hatte der Spieler sich vorher an dem Klange des einzelnen Tones geweidet, so war nun das gleichsam wollüstige Schmecken dieses harmonischen Verhältnisses noch ungleich fühlbarer.' But even for the narrator's trained ear the whole is little better than a hellish cacaphony. 'Und das nannte der alte Mann Phantasieren!' he exclaims, realizing, however, that 'es im Grunde allerdings ein Phantasieren war, für den Spielmann nämlich, nur nicht für den Hörer' (para. 22).

When he seeks out the old fiddler in the latter's room a few days later, having delayed his visit because for him—like the Spielmann!—the morning hours when the visit was to take place are sacred, he overhears him practising the masters and discovers the principle upon which the Spielmann's music-making is based. The passage, though often quoted by critics, has never to my knowledge been analysed for its analogical meaning. It is highly revealing (para. 25):

> Einige Zeit des Zuhörens ließ mich endlich den Faden durch dieses Labyrinth erkennen, gleichsam die Methode in der Tollheit. Der Alte genoß, indem er spielte. Seine Auffassung unterschied hierbei aber schlechthin nur zweierlei, den Wohlklang und den Übelklang, von denen der erstere ihn erfreute, ja entzückte, indes er dem letzteren, auch dem harmonisch begründeten, nach Möglichkeit aus dem Wege ging. Statt nun in einem Musikstücke nach Sinn und Rhythmus zu betonen, hob er heraus, verlängerte er die dem Gehör wohltuenden Noten und Intervalle, ja nahm keinen Abstand, sie willkürlich zu wiederholen, wobei sein Gesicht oft geradezu den Ausdruck der Verzückung annahm. Da er nun zugleich die Dissonanzen so kurz als möglich abtat, überdies die für ihn zu schweren Passagen, von denen er aus Gewissenhaftigkeit nicht eine Note fallen ließ, in einem gegen das Ganze viel zu langsamen Zeitmaß

vortrug, so kann man sich wohl leicht eine Idee von der Verwirrung machen, die daraus hervorging.

To grasp the force of this passage one must first of all obviate a misconception that is almost universal in the critical literature, namely, that the 'confusion' resulting from the Spielmann's performance is due to mere lack of skill.[11] True, he is no Paganini, but the resulting cacophony is not due to this: it is not because he is forced to play difficult runs at too slow a tempo. The basic reason is that he either skips or avoids as far as possible the *dissonances*, however harmonically necessary. At the same time he stresses and lengthens, even repeats contrary to all musical sense 'wohltuende Noten und Intervalle.' In the last analysis his playing of the 'revered masters' is not different from his improvising: harmony alone is permitted, dissonances disallowed. The Spielmann is transported by his own playing, the listener tortured and confused. The reason is of course that the work of art, insofar as it is a transfigured version of our *own* world, is not comprehensible without dissonances. The Spielmann's playing is a peculiar kind of theodicy: not a theodicy that accounts for the necessity of evil by showing that it is only an aspect of the good (this would be what Beethoven's music does), but a theodicy that leaves out evil altogether. It is evident that the Spielmann lives in a realm without dissonances and that it is this realm that is reflected in his music. We can call it the world before the Fall and the Spielmann the pre-lapsarian man. This is the reason why we, the fallen, cannot understand him, that is, cannot understand his music, which is his existential expression. That he is wholly without guile every interpreter points out,[12] but only unfallen man is completely guileless, because untouched by the Father of Guile.[13] That he cuts such a poignantly ridiculous figure in the fallen world only proves that he himself is not fallen: 'For the wisdom of the world is folly with God' and vice versa.[14]

Before the Spielmann begins to tell his story, the theme of disorder and license and its inversion is given unforgettable reinforcement in the 'Ding-symbol' of the chalk mark that divides Jacob's corner of the garret from that of the two journeymen: on the one side 'ein schmutziges, widerlich verstörtes Bett, von allen Zutaten der Unordentlichkeit umgeben,' on the other Jacob's couch, 'dürftig, aber reinlich und höchst sorgfältig gebettet und bedeckt' (para. 24). 'Die Unordnung ist verwiesen,' says the Spielmann, 'Nur die Tür ist gemeinschaftlich' (para. 25). The door into life is all that Jacob has in common with the 'Volk.' Once within (whether within his room or without), he lives utterly apart, sheltered by his own inner order which allows no dissonances.

When the narrator invites Jacob to tell his story (para. 26), we are not really surprised to learn that he is not aware that he has one. He lives timelessly: 'Ich habe keine Geschichte. Heute wie gestern, und morgen wie heute.' It is important to note—though seems not to have been noted!—that the narrator calls the Spielmann back into the realm of time by reminding him of the Latin *words* he uttered before picking up his music stand to leave the Volksfest. Mulling over the narrator's remark, the Spielmann begins to be recalled into time, the realm of 'einmal' and 'lange her': "Lateinisch," tönte er nach. "Lateinisch? das habe ich freilich auch einmal gelernt, oder vielmehr hätte es lernen sollen und können. Loqueris latine?" wandte er sich gegen mich, "aber ich könnte es nicht fortsetzen. Es ist gar zu lange her. Das also nennen Sie meine Geschichte?" And with this he settles down to tell 'wie es kam,' if not exactly to his auditor, at any rate to himself: 'Möchte ich mir's doch selbst einmal wieder erzählen.' The boundary between the Spielmann and the world, even a sympathetic representative of the world, is still preserved. The narrator is merely allowed to *overhear* the story Jacob tells primarily to himself.

Jacob's narrative occupies paragraphs 27-73. It is here that the theme of the word assumes central importance. Already in paragraph 27 it is stated with all clarity. Jacob, we learn, was not always content to talk to himself; there was a time when he made a valiant effort to communicate with the world in its own terms—but he could not learn its language. 'Wenn ich mich recht erinnere,' he recalls, looking back into the vistas of the past, 'so wäre ich wohl im Stande gewesen, allerlei zu erlernen, wenn man mir *Zeit und Ordnung* gegönnt hätte.' His two brothers 'sprangen wie Gemsen von Spitze zu Spitze in den Lehrgegenständen herum,' but he could never skip a thing, never leap: '*und wenn mir ein einziges Wort fehlte,* mußte ich von vorne anfangen' (para. 27, emphasis added). The order of the world in which his brothers are so thoroughly at home is not Jacob's order; it is an order he must laboriously learn, an order that in some inscrutable way is connected with *words*, and words are for him a source of excruciating difficulty. His lack of success makes him baulky and he takes refuge in his own order, an order without words: 'Abends im Zwielicht [ergriff ich] die Violine, um mich nach meiner Art ohne Noten zu vergnügen. . .' But the world, the other order, is adamant; if he is to live in it, he has to learn its language. The family confiscates his violin, claiming that his way of playing, that is, 'Phantasieren,' will ruin the instrument and that they cannot stand the torture. They tell him to wait for his violin lessons, but these lessons, also a kind of 'language' instruction, are for Jacob the true torture. Thus he comes to hate his violin.

The realm of *time*, which the Spielmann has now reentered in memory, Grillparzer is pointing out, is also the realm of the *word*. The equation of the word with time is good theology, not so much because of John 1:1-6 (where the Word equals Christ) as because of Genesis 1:3: 'And God said . . .' The *world*, which is the embodied word / Word, man interprets and thus controls through words, i.e., by 'saying' creation again, however imperfectly. Once, of course, before the Fall, he could 'say' it perfectly, for he was then one with the Word. If *now*, however, he were to 'say' it in that way, he would not be understood, but could talk only to God. We can no longer understand the *lingua adamica*, the *vox dei*. This, as I see it, is—in analogical terms—Jacob's case. He 'talks' to God through his music, but when he tries to communicate with his fallen fellows in the same medium, he meets only with blank incomprehension and derisive laughter.

The firmest support for this interpretation is found in paragraph 38, where the Spielmann so eloquently lectures his listener on the nature of music and makes his famous pronouncement about 'playing God': 'Sie spielen den Wolfgang Amadeus Mozart und den Sebastian Bach, aber den lieben Gott spielt Keiner.' No one, that is, except the Spielmann himself. *How* he 'plays God' we already know from paragraphs 22 and 25. God, in whom all opposites are in

concord, *coincidentia oppositorum*, is without discord like Jacob's music, which avoids the 'Übelklang' as far as possible and emphasizes (contrary to all earthly harmonic sense) the 'Wohlklang.' Nonetheless, he is quite aware of the role of the former: '. . .die Dissonanz [wird] herabgebeugt *als wissentliche Bosheit oder vermessener Stolz. . .*' (para. 28, emphasis added). The 'Übelklang' equals the evil that came into the world with the Fall. For us, who live in the world of Time/Word, music without discord is incomprehensible. Jacob says this himself, though he may not realize the implication. 'All but a few,' he reminds his auditor, impurify the 'breathing of the soul' that is music, by the addition of *words*, '"wie die Kinder Gottes sich verbanden mit den Töchtern der Erde; daß es hübsch angreife und eingreife in ein schwieliges Gemüt. Herr," schloß er endlich halb erschöpft, "die Rede ist dem Menschen notwendig wie Speise, man sollte aber auch den Trank rein erhalten, der da kommt von Gott."' 'Rede,' the word, is here equivalent to 'Übelklang,' dissonance, which the Spielmann, in his attempt to keep the divine drink pure, avoids.

Höllerer, as pointed out above (n. 11), does not make the mistake of attributing the incomprehensibility of the Spielmann's playing to mere lack of skill; rather he attributes it to his trying to give form to everything at once: '. . .er will Gott in seiner Kunst wirklich machen, alles auf einmal gestalten' (p. 260). If I understand him, Höllerer thinks the Spielmann is trying to give form to the divine as reflected in the world of appearances, the world of Time/Word, what he calls the 'Weltzusammenhang,' and this is the source of his failure: 'Wo er über das Menschliche hineingreift in den Weltzusammenhang, mordet er, so sieht es Grillparzer, die Kunst' (p. 260). Höllerer connects this 'playing the whole' with the narrator's words (for him, the narrator equals Grillparzer himself) in paragraph 6 about the divinity that resides in the masses as a 'whole': 'In der Kunst des. . .Spielmanns wird diese Idee, das Ganze, das Wesen schlechthin zu geben, zur Chimäre' (p. 261). My own conception, as I hope I have made clear, is almost the reverse of this: paragraph 25 shows that the Spielmann's playing *disregards* reality as we understand and experience it, thus becoming—in our eyes—anti-art. The Spielmann does not try to embody the world or the 'Weltzusammenhang' as we know it in his art; he plays God as reflected in his creation before the Fall.

The interpretation here offered is even more radically opposed to Politzer's (p. 46), who speaks of 'Jacob's Unfähigkeit, diesen Trunk [die Musik] rein zu erhalten, geschweige denn weiterzureichen. . .' This, in my view, is precisely the reverse of what the novella conveys: *because* Jacob keeps the drink pure, he cannot pass it on to others. Politzer (ibid.) also calls the story 'geradezu die Geschichte vom Sündenfall der Musik, ja der Kunst im Allgemeinen. . .' It is rather the 'story' of art *before* the Fall, and therefore of art incomprehensible to the fallen.

If Jacob is now able to control the spoken word with ease and naturalness and to tell his story with great plasticity, it is because, first, it *is* a story, i.e., a past event, and, second, because it is essentially the story of that period in his life when he was in intimate touch with the realm of Time/Word. We have seen how stiffly ceremonial and 'bookish' is his language when dealing with a situation in the *present*: it is almost as though he were speaking a foreign tongue and had to take special care to see that he made no slips. Now, however, he is able to say with colloquial ease (and unintentional deeper significance): 'Wir haben *Zeit*, und fast kommt mir die Lust zu *schwätzen* an' (para. 26). There is the same kind of change (*mutatis mutandis*) in the Spielmann's language between the frame and the story proper as there is in that of the narrator between his expatiations on the 'Volk' and his description of the Spielmann. In each case the change is due to the speaker's having found a subject close to his heart. The equivalent of Jacob's manner of telling his life story, we are soon to gather, is the way in which he renders the one piece of music he is capable of communicating to an audience: Barbara's song.

Jacob would gladly have escaped the martyrdom of the word by becoming an artisan: 'Ein Drechsler oder Schriftsetzer wäre ich gar zu gerne gewesen' (para. 28), but his father did not carry out his threat to remove him from school and apprentice him. It is worth considering why Jacob mentions these two trades. The reason, one can hardly doubt, is that both turners and typesetters follow intricate patterns from which they are not allowed to deviate. The typesetter deals with words, to be sure, but not creatively, only mechanically. He merely *copies* words, as the turner merely copies a pattern. Later, Jacob is 'recht an [seinem] Platze' (para. 31) as a copyist in the chancellery, and when he inherits his money the scoundrelly secretary easily fleeces him with a plan for establishing an 'Auskunfts-Kopier- und Übersetzungscomptoir' (para. 54). As a copyist Jacob can deal with the word without becoming existentially involved with it; his only 'social' relation to the world of words is purely formal, though it makes him touchingly happy to be granted even this: 'Ich hatte immer das Schreiben mit Lust getrieben, und noch jetzt weiß ich mir keine angenehmere Unterhaltung, [!] als mit guter Tinte auf gutem Papier Haar- und Schattenstriche aneinander zu fügen zu Worten *oder auch nur Buchstaben*' (para. 31, emphasis added). But alas if there is a word missing or a false mark of punctuation in the material to be copied! This can cause him 'bitter hours' of anxiety, for he is quite incapable of supplying a word or even a comma from the context. His purely formal relation to the fearsome world of the word could not be demonstrated more clearly.

The only sample of Jacob's penmanship that we are 'shown' is from the music he has copied. 'Musiknoten,' he says, 'sind nun gar überaus schön' (para. 31), but the narrator's impression of his skill as a music copyist is hardly favourable: 'Er zeigte dabei durchblätternd auf sein Musikbuch, in dem ich zu meinem Entsetzen mit sorgfältiger, aber widerlich steifer Schrift ungeheuer schwierige Kompositionen alter berühmter Meister . . . erblickte' (para. 18). 'Sorgfältig, aber widerlich steif' would also describe his use of language before he begins to tell the story of his life. He can only 'copy' the language of others; he cannot use it to express *himself*. His attitude towards the word as used by the rest of mankind is like ours might be towards ancient hieroglyphs—we could copy them no doubt, but we could not use them creatively.

Jacob's most traumatic experience with the word takes place at school during the public examination in Latin attended by his father when he forgets a word in a memorized passage from Horace's *Ars poetica*. We have already heard the Spielmann quote Horace: the first words we heard him utter were from the pen of that urbane master of language, and the narrator emphasized that he pronounced them 'mit der richtigsten Betonung, mit völliger Geläufigkeit' (para. 9). But there is a word that will not come to Jacob's tongue during the examination in spite of all dishonest prompting. This word is *cachinnum*, 'derisive laughter.' Politzer (pp. 21ff) has explicated this passage in detail. He does not, however, relate it to the theme of the word in general nor does he, as a matter of fact, seem to recognize any such theme *qua* theme. The *Ars poetica* is a work dealing above all with the doctrine of 'decorum,' i.e., the necessity of harmony of utterance with the subject treated: 'singula quaeque locum teneant sortita decentem' (v. 92: let each style keep its fitting place), that is, it treats exactly what seems (but only seems) so conspicuously lacking in Jacob, harmony between expression and that to be expressed.

The lines (also quoted by Politzer, p. 21) in which the fatal word occurs are 112-13: 'si dicentis erunt fortunis absona dicta, / Romani tollent equites peditesque *cachinnum*' ('If the speaker's words sound discordant with his fortunes, the Romans, in boxes and pit alike [knights and commoners], will raise a *loud guffaw*,' Fairclough's translation). It is obvious that one reason young Jacob subconsciously suppresses this word is that he feels himself to be the object (or fears to become the object) of just such a guffaw. (The word itself, one notes, is by its weighted position in the verse hard to forget.) Like the speaker referred to in Horace, his own character and his speech, 'his being and the expression of his being' in Politzer's words (p. 22), seem to gape apart when he is forced to express himself in the language of this world. Furthermore, the term *cachinnum* itself signifies something of which Jacob himself would be utterly incapable. There is nothing in his being that corresponds to it and thus it is for him an unword, an unsayable word. He can say it now of course, when it no longer makes any difference, and he could even say it the day after the examination, when it was already too late.[15]

This episode naturally also refers back to the opening frame (Politzer says nothing of this) and the crucial sixth paragraph with its enunciation of the doctrine of the necessity of the artist's submission to the voice of the crowd. It is not by accident, surely, that this is a *heathen* doctrine and that the Christian view is the exact opposite. We have already quoted 1 Corinthians 3:19: 'For the wisdom of the world is folly with God.' The world and its *cachinnum* are on the side of Horace, the Spielmann on the side of Paul.

His fiasco in the Latin examination leads to Jacob's 'silencing.' From this day onward his father refuses to speak to him, he is removed from school, made to take his meals alone in a restaurant, and treated altogether as a non-person. He has failed the test of the word and these are the awful consequences. He himself, to be sure, feels sorry for his father, whom he has so bitterly disappointed, rather than himself.

But Jacob's expulsion from the world of the word is more than compensated for by his re-entry into the wordless world of music: in his utter loneliness he hears Barbara's song. Not the words, as he himself stresses (para. 35), 'Wie ich denn überhaupt glaube, die Worte verderben die Musik.' It is the only piece of music he plays in a recognizable fashion. The narrator—and we can trust his judgment here—finds it 'gemütlich. übrigens gar nicht ausgezeichnet' (para. 35). But in playing it, Jacob is moved to tears. When one considers the matter, it is strange indeed that Jacob should be so moved by this very ordinary song: 'Es war so einfach, so rührend, und hatte den Nachdruck so auf der rechten Stelle,' he tries to explain (para. 35); then, describing how he had taken down his long unused violin and tried to play the melody, his words assume a positively mystical tone:

> Als ich nun mit dem Bogen über die Saiten fuhr, Herr, da war es, also ob Gottes Finger mich angerührt hätte. Der Ton drang in mein Inneres hinein und aus dem Innern wieder hinaus. Die Luft um mich war wie geschwängert mit Trunkenheit. Das Lied unten im Hofe und die Töne von meinen Fingern an mein Ohr, Mitbewohner meiner Einsamkeit. (Para. 36)

Politzer (p. 46) speaks of the effect of Barbara's song on Jacob in pietistic terms as an 'Erweckung.' One could also call it a return to the other order, the order without words that is/was/ever shall be. Jacob, exiled in the world of the word, has returned home.

The paradox is that song itself is also a 'word' and for Jacob even *the* word. It is the only word he can really understand and the only composition whose *content* he has ever concerned himself with. '. . . das jeweilige Was der Musik,' he states firmly, '*mit Ausnahme jenes Liedes*, [war] mir immer ziemlich gleichgültig und [ist es] auch geblieben bis zum heutigen Tag' (para. 38, emphasis added). Barbara's song is the only 'word' he can 'say,' because it is the only word to which he has ever had any but a purely formal relation. It is his single point of contact with the created world of the Word, the world of fallen man, which is why, when he 'says' it, it is also intelligible to fallen man: 'Er spielte, und zwar diesmal mit richtigem Ausdrucke, die Melodie . . . ' (para. 35). The song, in short, is for Jacob the connecting link between the 'two orders': 'Das Lied unten im Hofe *und* die Töne von meinen Fingern an mein Ohr, *Mitbewohner* meiner Einsamkeit.'

For Barbara of course the song is *only* words. When Jacob—after what difficulties and circumstantial preparations!—finally asks her for a copy of the music so that he may play the song properly, her incomprehension is total: '. . . die Abschrift? sagte sie. Das Lied ist gedruckt und wird an den Straßenecken verkauft. Das Lied? entgegnete ich. Das sind wohl nur die Worte.—Nun ja, die Worte, das Lied' (para. 43). Barbara lives wholly in the world of the fallen, which is the realm of the word; she is perfectly at home with 'das Volk.'[16] One need only recall the scene in the 'Grieslerladen' when Jacob, having been surprised by Barbara's father 'stealing' produce displayed on the sidewalk, is dragged into the shop where the butcher—her future husband—is talking to Barbara: 'Da lachte der . . . Fleischer laut auf und wendete sich zu gehen, nachdem er vorher dem Mädchen ein paar Worte leise zugeflüstert hatte, die sie gleichfalls lachend durch einen schallenden Schlag mit der flachen Hand auf seinen Rücken beantwortete' (para. 48). Barbara understands 'der Menschen Worte,' Jacob only 'die Stille des Aethers.'

In *Der arme Spielmann* it is not 'das Ewig-Weibliche' that draws us upward. It is Jacob who—for a time at

least—raises Barbara to purer spheres, as she herself recognizes when she comes to take leave of him: 'Ich muß nun hinaus unter die groben Leute, wogegen ich mich so lange gesträubt habe' (para. 66). And yet—is not Jacob more a woman than a man? Barbara at any rate seems to think so: 'Aber ändern müßten Sie sich!' she warns him during their conversation about a possible future together, 'Ich hasse die weibischen Männer' (para. 61, end). Masculine and feminine are curiously reversed in this story, Jacob representing the feminine pole and Barbara, whose 'mannish' traits have often been noted, the masculine.

It is not through his music, however, that Jacob raises Barbara. For her, as for everyone else, the Spielmann's playing is merely 'Kratzen.' 'Lassen Sie das Musizieren,' she instructs him, 'und denken Sie auf die Notwendigkeit!' (para. 62). They never speak of music when together, nor will Barbara sing for him (para. 57). If then Jacob raises Barbara to a higher plane, and we cannot doubt that he does, it is through the nobility of his being, and perhaps even through his very 'femininity,' which stands in polar balance to her 'mannishness.'

Barbara, on the other hand, as we have already indicated, connects the Spielmann with this world. She does this not only through her personality but also through her song, which is her existential expression and 'gar nicht ausgezeichnet.' Through words—'Nun ja, die Worte, das Lied'—Jacob is, for a while, embodied in the realm of time, the here and now—one could almost call it a creation. The way in which Barbara connects the Spielmann with this world, giving him a local habitation (and later a name), is shown most clearly in the passage (para. 57) where Jacob overhears her singing 'his' song as she works:

> Einmal aber, als ich unbemerkt zur Tür hereintrat, stand sie, auf den Zehenspitzen emporgerichtet, den Rücken mir zugekehrt, und mit den erhobenen Händen, wie man nach etwas sucht, auf einem der höheren Stellbretter herumtastend. Und dabei sang sie leise in sich hinein.—Er war das Lied, mein Lied!—Sie aber zwitscherte wie eine Grasmücke, die am Bache das Hälslein wäscht und das Köpfchen herumwirft und die Federn sträubt und wieder glättet mit dem Schnäblein. Mir war, als ginge ich auf grünen Wiesen.

So at home does this new Adam feel in the world that he even dares to try to embrace his Eve. The result, as we know, is tragicomic. Barbara hands him one of her notorious slaps, then kisses the hurt. He pursues her, she runs into the back room and leans against the door, he kisses her—through the pane. All the same, it is the 'Glückstag [seines] Lebens.'

The separation between the Spielmann and the world remains. This time, however, the chalk mark has been drawn by the world, not by the Spielmann, and Barbara later gives a clear indication that there is a possibility of its finally being erased. Having suggested that Jacob invest his money in a 'Putzladen' they can manage together, she says, 'Was sich etwa noch weiter ergäbe, davon wollen wir jetzt nicht reden' (para. 61, end). Whether the Spielmann would have been able to live in the world, however, whatever might have come to pass, is an open question. Barbara makes any future together dependent upon a radical change in Jacob's character: he must switch from the feminine to the masculine pole. Could he do that? Would he then still be Jacob?

The question never comes to a trial. Jacob's connection with the world is too tenuous for him to retain his foothold in it. He can live only in paradise with his Eve, not in the fallen world. His other-worldliness, which manifests itself as foolish saintliness, keeps him from even suspecting the world's wickedness and thus soon leads to his expulsion from it. The paradise myth is reversed: Jacob returns to the world of timelessness and worldlessness in which we first learned to know him. His sole connection between his world and ours is Barbara's song. It is the only composition he is later able to teach Barbara's son. It is the only 'word' he can 'say' and the summation of his 'story,' which is nothing more than an extended explication of the song. In playing it he only tells his story again, and even the narrator, who now knows its meaning, can bear to hear it repeated only so often. Jacob, however, tells it over and over again to himself. His tale ended, 'ergriff der Alte seine Geige und fing an das Lied zu spielen, und spielte fort und fort, ohne sich weiter um mich zu kümmern. Endlich hatte ich's satt, stand auf, legte ein paar Silberstücke auf den nebenstehenden Tisch und ging, während der Alte eifrig immer fortgeigte.'

The closing frame is essentially an ironic reversal of the opening one. At the beginning the masses, which are likened to a great natural force, overflow all within view; at the end it is they whom a great natural force overflows. At the beginning 'Aufruhr der Freude' and 'Losgebundenheit der Lust' (para. 2); at the end 'Von allen Seiten Weinen und Trauergeläute' (para. 76). At the beginning the narrator sets out to seek contact with the masses, at the end to find a particular individual, who, as we have come to see, lives in hermetic isolation from the masses. This theme itself is also reversed: in death the Spielmann finds identity with the masses, not because he seeks identity, however, but because, grotesquely and ironically, his other-worldliness prevents him from distinguishing between the necessary and the unnecessary, between saving lives and rescuing a few gulden. At the moment of death he returns wholly to that realm whose harmonies only he can hear: 'er . . . wendete Kopf und Ohr seitwärts, als ob er in der Entfernung etwas gar Schönes hörte, lächelte, sank zurück und war tot' (para. 76). He dies with the same ecstatic expression noted by the narrator when he surprised him at his morning practice, 'wobei sein Gesicht oft geradezu den Ausdruck der Verzückung annahm' (para. 25). What Jacob hears, we can never hear; what to us is cacophony is to him divine harmony; the two orders remain utterly distinct.[17] His union with the 'Volk' is a grotesque irony, his life, from the standpoint of the world, that of an outcast, he himself the object of derision, *cachinnum.*

An object of derision—or at best of sentimental pity—for all, that is, except Barbara and the narrator, the only ones who know his story. Whether we can say that Barbara 'loves' Jacob in the commonly accepted sense seems dubious. That she reveres him is beyond doubt. When the narrator pays his Sunday visit to the butcher's family in the hope of acquiring the old man's fiddle as a memento, he finds 'die Familie beisammen ohne Spur eines zurückgebliebenen besondern Eindrucks. *Doch* hing die Geige mit einer Art Symmetrie geordnet neben dem Spiegel einem Kruzifix gegenüber an der Wand' (para. 78, emphasis

added). Cross, mirror, fiddle—are we to interpret this constellation as an emblem of the world and the instruments of its overcoming? Here, in the final paragraphs, in contrast to the opening ones, it is fitting to apply Stern's term and speak of a 'laconic mode.' We are offered signs but no explication, as the story itself sinks into wordlessness. The final tableau shows us the butcher, who, 'ohne sich durch den Besuch stören zu lassen, mit lauter Stimme sein Tischgebet anhob, in das die Kinder gellend einstimmten,' while Barbara remains wordless, tears streaming down her face. The 'world' still has words, or at least formulas, but Barbara, who has been granted a glimpse of Jacob's realm and even been taken into it to a degree, has none. His life and its meaning remain finally unsayable, all that it meant symbolized in a precious relic to which, I think we must agree, Barbara has a better right than the narrator, his fellow artist. For Jacob touched the world, at least a tiny portion of it, by his being, not by his art.

Are we to read the story as a parable of the expressive dilemma of the artist? In my opinion, yes, although I would not maintain that reducing it to this formula significantly increases its depth and may even make it shallower. In *Libussa* Grillparzer treats the same theme in reverse and arrives at a similar conclusion: what is really worth saying cannot be said—the supernal order becomes disorder as soon as it is translated into the language of this world. When Libussa takes Primislaus as her interpreter of the divine order, this order becomes distorted beyond recognition and 'Vernunft' is degraded into 'Recht.' It is the same insight at which Rudolf has already arrived at the beginning of *Ein Bruderzwist* (v. 428f) when he tells Ferdinand: 'Dort oben wohnt die Ordnung, dort ihr Haus, / Hier unten eitle Willkür und Verwirrung.' The order of the stars, of which Rudolf is speaking, those lights that did not, like man, defect from the divine order, is also the order reflected in the Spielmann's life and music. The ridiculous and grotesque aspect arises of course from the fact that the Spielmann is unaware of the non-communication of his music, but assumes that his hearers are at any rate potentially open to a direct, non-dissonant revelation of the divine. But it is this same lack of awareness that makes us speak of his absolute good will and his saintliness, it is this that gives his story its deep poignancy.

Notes

1. I have consulted the following secondary literature which will be referred to in the text only by author and page: Bernhard Seuffert, 'Grillparzer's Spielmann,' *Festschrift August Sauer* (Stuttgart, 1925), pp. 291-311; Friedrich Gundolf, 'Franz Grillparzer,' *Jahrbuch des Freien Deutschen Hochstifts* (1931), pp. 9-93; Richard Alewyn, 'Grillparzer und die Restauration,' *Publs. of the Engl. Goethe Soc.,* NS 12 (1935-7), 1-18; Walter Silz, *Realism and Reality* (Chapel Hill, 1954), pp. 67-78; Walter Naumann, *Grillparzer: Das dichterische Werk* (Stuttgart, n.d. [1956]), pp. 20-32; Richard Brinkmann, *Wirklichkeit und Illusion* (Tübingen, 1957), pp. 87-145; Benno von Wiese, *Die deutsche Novelle von Goethe bis Kafka* (Düsseldorf, 1957), pp. 134-53; Walter Höllerer, *Zwischen Klassik und Moderne* (Stuttgart, 1958), pp. 240-94; J.P. Stern, *Re-interpretations: Seven Studies in Nineteenth-Century German Literature* (London, 1964), pp. 42-77; M.W. Swales, 'The narrative

perspective in Grillparzer's *Der Arme Spielmann,'
German Life & Letters,* 20 (1967), 107-16; Heinz
Politzer, *Franz Grillparzer's 'Der arme Spielmann'*
(Stuttgart, 1967); Günther Jungbluth, 'Franz
Grillparzers Erzählung: Der Arme Spielmann. Ein
Beitrag zu ihrem Verstehen,' *Orbis Litterarum,* 24
(1969), 35-51; Hertha Krotkoff, 'Über den Rahmen
in Franz Grillparzers Novelle *Der arme Spielmann,'
Mod. Lang. Notes,* 85 (1970), 345-66; Otto K.
Liedke, 'Considerations on the structure of
Grillparzer's *Der Arme Spielmann,' Journal of the
International Arthur Schnitzler Research
Association,* 3 (Fall 1970), 7-12; W.E. Yates,
Grillparzer: A Critical Introduction (Cambridge
University Press, 1972), pp. 76-83; John M. Ellis,
'Grillparzer's *Der Arme Spielmann,' German
Quarterly,* 45 (1972), 662-83. Of these, one can
single out only Jungbluth's contribution as almost
totally worthless.

2. As printed in the critical edition of Grillparzer's
works, ed. Reinhold Backmann (Wien, 1952), IV,
265-322, which is the edition followed here. In
Grillparzers sämtliche Werke, ed. Sauer, 5. Ausg. in
20 Bdn. (Stuttgart, n.d.), XIII, 223-66. the story is
printed in 77 paragraphs as opposed to 78 in
Backmann, paragraph 15 in Sauer corresponding to
15-16 in Backmann.

3. Krotkoff, pp. 347f, believes Grillparzer (whom she
equates with the narrator) 'versucht . . . den
christlich-religiösen Aspekt zu verwischen, indem er
das Fest mit dem Beiwort *saturnalisch*
charakterisiert.' Ideas associated with this word, she
adds, are: 'Heidentum, chaotische Umkehrung der
bestehenden Ordnung, lustbetonte Grundhaltung
. . .'

4. Ellis, p. 674, maintains that the narrator's 'criterion
of artistic success is simply public acclaim' and
implies that this is all he could be thinking of.
Politzer, p. 12, is of a similar opinion.

5. Cf. Krotkoff, p. 358: 'Auch läßt sich wohl
annehmen, daß [diesem] Satz . . .programmatischer
Charakter zukommt.'

6. I should hesitate to go as far as Ellis (p. 669) and
call the narrator 'simply an imposter,' though Ellis,
like Seuffert, Swales, and Politzer before him, is
undoubtedly right in adopting a suspicious attitude
toward what he terms the narrator's 'gross and
inflated posturing' (p. 674).

7. Liedke (p. 7) finds the design revealed in the
opening frame to be 'a pattern of opposites in the
form of intention and reversal or failure of
intention.' Cf. also von Wiese, p. 138, who points
out that as much as the frame speaks of the 'Volk'
and its divinity, the tale itself is concerned with the
Spielmann only, 'der aus diesem Rahmen der
allgemeinen losgebundenen Lust gerade herausfällt.'

8. Ellis (p. 669 and passim) apparently sees no irony
here. He denigrates the narrator as 'unsympathetic'
and 'prying.' But mere 'prying' can hardly be the
whole reason for his pursuit of an utter stranger;
some personal, 'existential' reason has to be
involved. Swales, p. 115, sees the situation much
more clearly. The narrator, he points out, is

connected with the Spielmann by his own isolation
from the crowd. 'It is because of this strange affinity
between them that the narrator is so fascinated by
the Spielmann; it is because he knows of this
embarrassing affinity that the narrator ironizes the
Spielmann,' thus laying bare 'his own uncertainty.'

9. One must agree with Ellis (p. 666) that J.P. Stern's
contention (p. 63) that 'here, in the narrator's point
of view, the laconic mode of the tale is established'
is 'most inappropriate to a text. . .remarkable for
precisely the reverse.'

10. Ms. Lorelei Beer of the University of Connecticut
(Storrs) has called my attention to the numerical
symbolism in the novella. I have no right to
anticipate her findings and will only titillate the
reader by referring to the fact that Jacob lives at 34
Gärtnerstrasse (3 + 4 = 7) and that the
Brigittenkirchtag takes place in the seventh month
of the year (July). There are several other
indications of the conscious employment of
symbolical numbers in the work.

11. Cf., e.g., Naumann, p. 31 (emphasis added): 'Im
Arme Spielmann ist das Fern-Halten des Lebens
dargestellt als *Nicht-Können*'; Jungbluth, p. 49:
'Trotz aller Übung bleibt [der Spielmann] ein. . .
Stümper'; Yates, p. 81: 'the truth is that as a
violinist Jakob is incompetent'; Silz, p. 79:
'ludicrous self-deception as to the quality of his
performance'; Stern, p. 70: 'utterly lacking in skill.'
Further examples could easily be adduced. Höllerer
seems to be the only exegete who clearly sees that
Jacob's ear-torturing music is not due to mere
inability (p. 259): 'Die mißgeschickte Kunst des
Spielmanns. . .wird nicht als ein Darunterbleiben
unter dem, was Kunst erfordert, abgetan, eher als
ein Zuviel-Wollen, ein Alles-zugleich-Wollen
geschildert.'

12. Stern, p. 72, regards Jacob (if I understand him) as a
symbol of 'the disembodied good will as the
absolute and only value.' If by 'disembodied' is
meant 'not translated into action the world can
understand,' then Stern is correct. But Jacob's good
will is surely not disembodied absolutely; on the
contrary, it is continually being embodied, both in
his 'art' and his actions; our incomprehension is a
sign of our own sinful, 'dissonant' state. By acting
according to the categorical imperative the good will
is 'embodied'; that is the only way we can
recognize it. That Jacob thus acts, one can scarcely
doubt; our consternation and amusement prove that
we do not and would not. Perhaps Stern means
something much like this when he speaks of 'the
substantial world. . .as a place radically incapable
of yielding form and substance to the good will' (p.
74).

13. Is it intentionally ironical that the Spielmann is
named after the patriarch noted for his guile and
deception?

14. The view we have been developing here, though
perhaps more radically stated, is by no means
without precursors in the critical literature.
Brinkmann (p. 114) speaks of the 'two orders' that
prevail in the story, that of the Spielmann and the
world, adding, 'Es ist an keiner Stelle deutlich, wer

nun eigentlich "ver-rückt," d. h. aus der rechten und richtigen Ordnung gerückt ist: der Spielmann order . . . die Welt,' Von Wiese, p. 145, while regarding the Spielmann's music as 'pure solipsism,' admits: 'Vielleicht wird sie noch von Gott gehört, so wie sie gemeint ist.' Krotkoff, p. 364, sees three 'worlds' in the tale: that of the people, still in the grip of a now decadent baroque piety, that of the narrator with his 'secularized religion of humanity,' and, finally, 'the pure filial relation to the divine' of Jacob. Naumann, p. 32, on the other hand, speaks of the Spielmann as being 'herausgelöst' '[aus] der Menge des Volkes' and claims (p. 22), 'Das Leben des armen Spielmanns. . .ist nichts als das reine Abbild des Wesens eines Menschen,' which would seem to mean that he sees Jacob as a representative of the 'Volk' in exemplary purity. If this is correct, Naumann's view is close to Alewyn's (p. 14): '*Der Arme Spielmann* ist die extreme Darstellung des totalen Privatmenschen, des idealen Untertans des Regimes Metternich.'

15. Politzer, p. 23, also interprets the forgetting of the word as a subconsciously purposive 'Fehlleistung' committed to gain a secretly desired end: to be removed from school and apprenticed to an artisan. I am sceptical of this explanation, though I cannot refute it. Jacob's contrition at having disappointed his father seems to me to speak against it.

16. Her name almost certainly indicates this connection, 'Barbara' equalling 'Barbar.'

17. One is strongly reminded of the legend of the death of another Jacob, Jacob Böhme, whose namesake 'our' Jacob may be, rather than the patriarch's. Cf. final words of the 'Erste Nachtwache' in *Nachtwachen. Von Bonaventura*: 'Den Sterbenden ist die Musik verschwistert, sie ist der erste süße Laut vom fernen Jenseits, und die Muse des Gesanges ist die mystische Schwester, die zum Himmel zeigt. So entschlummerte Jacob Böhme, indem er die ferne Musik vernahm, die niemand, außer dem Sterbenden, hörte.'

Martin Swales (essay date 1977)

SOURCE: "Grillparzer: *Der arme Spielmann*," in *The German Novelle*," Princeton University Press, 1977, pp. 114-32.

[*In the following essay, Swales discusses the importance of narrative perspective in* Der arme Spielmann, *in particular, the narrator's attitude toward the protagonist, Jacob.*]

Franz Grillparzer was born in Vienna on January 15, 1791. He studied law at the university, and from 1813 to 1856 he was employed as a civil servant, finally reaching the post of *Archivdirektor*. His was not a life rich in spectacular events; there were, admittedly, occasional visits abroad (to Italy, Germany, France, England, Greece), but on the whole, irresolution and timorousness prevailed (as in his agonized relationship to Katharina Fröhlich, the "eternal fiancée" whom he was never to marry). His career as an artist began with the considerable public success of *Die Ahnfrau* (*The Ancestress*) of 1817, but it was a triumph that was not to be repeated. The disastrous reception accorded to his comedy *Weh dem der lügt* (*Woe unto the Liar*) of 1838 so embittered Grillparzer that he never again attempted to have his plays performed publicly (although he continued to write for the stage). Both as man and artist Grillparzer was prey to nervous indecision and uncertainty; his relationship to his artistic calling was profoundly ambivalent, sometimes curiously arrogant, sometimes self-lacerating in its despair. Over and over again his art expresses his fear of passion, of intensity, of great and decisive activity, and upholds the values of a contained and tranquil life. Yet there is an intellectual toughness and honesty about Grillparzer that prevents him from becoming the philistine apologist for the values of "peace and quiet." In his story *Der arme Spielmann* (*The Poor Musician*) of 1848 he gives us the obliquely tender portrait of one man, the poor musician of the title, whose humility and serenity are both strength and weakness, both sublime and questionable.

In outline, at least, *Der arme Spielmann* is a character study, concerned with the life and death of Jakob, a poor street musician, whom the narrator happens to meet one year at a fair (*Volksfest*) in Vienna. Much of the work is taken up with Jakob's narration of his own life story, and at one point in that narration he describes the death of his father—and adds the following comment: "One day I hope to find him again where we will be judged by our intentions, and not by our works" (65).[1] In these words Jakob expresses the ambivalence that informs everything he tries to accomplish in this life. He is a man of infinite goodwill, of sublime intentions, who finds it impossible to translate his inner integrity into terms at all meaningful to the world in which he finds himself. It is precisely this split between the inward (*Innen*) and the outward (*Aussen*) that renders him incapable of performing even the most menial of clerical tasks and that ultimately destroys his relationship with Barbara. The high point of this relationship is a kiss, a kiss given through a pane of glass. For all the genuineness and intensity of his love for Barbara, Jakob can never put his love into practice—he can never convert his inner feelings into a workable human relationship.

Such is the picture that emerges of the *arme Spielmann*, "the poor musician," from his own narration. Although Jakob is without self-pity and his narration is utterly devoid of any attempts at self-justification, clearly one must ask oneself how valid this picture is. On his own admission, Jakob finds it difficult to communicate his inner feelings to the world outside, and hence we must have more evidence before we can accept his account of his life as in any sense valid. Here the narrator has a vital role to play. One notices immediately that the impression of Jakob that emerges from his own narration corresponds very closely to the narrator's assessment of the old man. Indeed, if one examines the narrator's opening description of the Spielmann, one sees that it is precisely because of the contradictions in his behavior—the poverty and the nobility, the commitment to music and the technical incompetence—that the narrator is so intrigued by him. When the narrator engages the Spielmann in conversation about his music, he is immediately struck by the contradiction between *Innen* and *Aussen*, between the Spielmann's ideals and their concrete expression in the music he actually plays. The narrator speaks of his "surprise at hearing the man speak of the very highest levels of art, who was at the same time incapable of giving a recognizable rendering of the simplest waltz" (43). Clearly, therefore, the narrator's estimation of the Spielmann's character is very much in accord with that of the old man himself. Moreover, certain aspects of the Spielmann's narration can be and are checked by the narrator. Particularly the relationship with Barbara is crucial. Does she in fact feel anything more than pity for Jakob? It would obviously be possible that Jakob, because of his feelings for Barbara, could offer a falsely colored picture of their relationship in order to compensate for his complete inadequacy in terms of their practical relationship. The structure of the story, the closing scene in which the narrator goes to see Barbara, means that the world of the Spielmann's narration is examined by the narrator, and hence we are enabled to test the validity of Jakob's account of himself. His death is at once sublime and foolish. Barbara's son *is* called Jakob; Barbara does weep for the dead Spielmann, and she cherishes his violin as an almost sacred relic of his existence on earth.

Hence, from what the narrator and the Spielmann tell us, and from the occasional glimpse they both give us of Barbara, we can build up a fairly consistent picture of the Spielmann's character. The contradiction between his inner intention and its outward expression, between "the goodwill and its profane realization"[2] lies at the very heart of his being. Yet is this all that needs to be said about the story? Does the work do no more than state the ambivalence of the Spielmann's situation? Are we given any evaluative perspective that tells us whether to judge according to intention (*Absichten*) or according to actual achievement (*Werken*)? The Spielmann can be seen either as a saintly figure whose practical failures are the measure of his commitment to an unattainable ideal or as a fool who erects a pretentious superstructure of impossible ideals to compensate for his inadequacy before the demands of everyday living. Do we, the readers, simply take our choice, or does the story help us at all in our evaluation of the Spielmann? If there is an answer, it can only lie in the narrative perspective, in the attitude of the narrator to his central character and, above all, in *our* evaluation of that narrator and his viewpoint.

When the narrator first meets the Spielmann we read: "I had, in order to observe the oddity undisturbed, withdrawn some distance on to the side of the embankment" (41). The implications of this are symptomatic of the narrator's whole attitude toward the Spielmann. Most commentators on the story have drawn attention to the narrator's laconic, ironical tone.[3] As J. P. Stern puts it, "As far as the narrator is concerned he merely reports but never identifies himself with the unheroic hero's point of view."[4] Could one not, however, go further than this and say that, far from identifying himself with Jakob, the narrator makes every effort to distance himself from him, while at the same time remaining strangely fascinated by him? His attitude is rather more complex than might appear at first sight. Indeed, one is tempted to say that there is something profoundly paradoxical in the narrator's overall relationship to the Spielmann, and the paradox is reflected in his remarks about himself and the *Volk*, the common people. The narrator describes himself as being a passionate lover of human beings (although we see remarkably little evidence of this love in the story he tells): "as a lover of human beings, I say, especially when they come together in masses, for a time forgetting their own wishes and becoming part of that wholeness in which ultimately the divine resides" (39).

Hence he is delighted by the fair, that one event in the year when individuals and social classes are absorbed into the sea of people all enjoying themselves. When one examines the narrator's description of the fair, however, one finds that he does not merge with the common people. Rather, he remains detached and aloof: an observer rather than a participant. Furthermore, he writes, as Richard Brinkmann puts it, "with a condescending, but clear, slightly intellectual distance."[5] Indeed, at times the irony seems to express not simply detachment but also criticism, an awareness of something violent and destructive at work in the spectacle before him: "the stream of the people, released from the containment of the bridge, a massive, roaring sea, pouring out and flooding everything" (37). It is perhaps significant that the only other time in the story when the narrator describes a crowd scene (the occasion of another deluge, the flooding of the Leopoldstadt) this, too, is something horrific. Its horrific quality resides unmistakably in the fact that it is a *mass* spectacle, with rows of bodies laid out for inspection by the authorities.[6]

The narrator's description of the crowd at the fair becomes intensified to grotesque proportions, as he narrows his field of vision from "the pleasure-hungry mass" to various beggar musicians who are attempting to entertain the passersby: "A lame, misshapen boy, he and his violin forming one inextricable tangle, who turned out endlessly unfolding waltzes with all the hectic violence of his twisted chest" (40). For all the horror of such performers, they are more at one with the crowd than is Jakob, the poor musician. This is made explicitly clear by the reactions of the crowd who simply laugh at the old man, giving him no money. Yet, suddenly the whole world of the fair fades and the narrator's attention is focused on Jakob:

> an old man, at least seventy, in a threadbare, but neat broadcloth coat, with a smiling, self-congratulating expression. He stood there, his bald head bared, having put, as these beggar musicians do, his hat on the ground before him as a collecting-box; and he was belaboring an old, very cracked violin, marking the beat not only by raising and lowering his foot, but also by the concerted movement of his whole bent body. But all this effort to bring unity into his performance was fruitless, for what he played seemed to be an incoherent sequence of notes, without shape or melody. Yet he was totally absorbed in his work; his lips twitched, his eyes never left the sheet music in front of him—yes, in all truth, sheet music! (40f.).

The contrast with the description of the other musicians is unmistakable. The whole tone of the language changes and the irony becomes more kindly: the mood is more relaxed, even good-humored, one of relief after the horrors that have preceded it. The quality of the language suggests that in the Spielmann the narrator finds an individual who attracts rather than repels him. Furthermore, it is significant that the narrator is attracted to the Spielmann not simply because he is unusual (the other musicians are unusual), but because his unusualness so manifestly divorces him from the whole quality and atmosphere of the fair. Suddenly the crowd is forgotten and only the Spielmann is of interest. This would seem to be somewhat inconsistent with the narrator's avowed purpose in attending the fair. Indeed, looking back on the narrator's praise of the fair, do we not detect a certain strain, an element of self-deception in the language—does not our narrator perhaps "protest too much"? "From the altercation of tipsy carters there runs an invisible, but uninterrupted thread up to the quarrel of the sons of gods, and in the young maid, who, half-unwillingly, follows her eager lover away from the mass of the dancers, are to be found, in embryo, the Juliets, Didos, and Medeas" (39). Is he really involved in the fair and all it stands for? If so, it is odd that he should be so easily deflected from his purpose by the meeting with someone who is, if nothing else, a complete outsider.

This is not, of course, to imply that our narrator immediately identifies himself with the Spielmann. The description of Jakob is ironic ("was belaboring"), with a touch of comic surprise ("yes, in all truth, sheet music!"). Yet, because of the tone of the passage and particularly in the light of what precedes it, one feels that the narrator is potentially more sympathetic to the Spielmann than he is to the general spectacle around him. Almost immediately, however, this gentle hint of some sort of involvement is negated by the rather pompous sentence: "The whole being of the old man was as though expressly designed to excite my anthropological hunger to the utmost" (41). It is almost as if the narrator were ashamed of a moment of weakness for the Spielmann—and immediately adopts an ironic and consciously withdrawn tone in order to distance himself from him.

The crowd now obscures the Spielmann and the narrator admits what has been implicit in his description of their meeting—that only the old man is of interest: "the lost adventure had taken away all my pleasure in the fair. I explored the *Augarten* in every direction, and finally decided to return home" (42). The fair, this inherently "divine" spectacle, is no longer worthy of the narrator's attention. Yet even this admission of the Spielmann's importance for the narrator is not without its distancing effect. Their meeting is described as an adventure, something out of the ordinary, but no more than that. Suddenly, however, the narrator hears the sound of the old man's violin: "I accelerated my pace and, lo and behold, the object of my curiosity stood playing for all he was worth before a circle of some boys who were impatiently demanding a waltz of him" (42). Once again, the language here is interesting. The narrator admits to a certain exultation and excitement at the prospect of seeing the Spielmann again. Yet lest we should mistake his feelings for sympathy and emotional involvement, he once again distances himself from the Spielmann by the way he describes the meeting—the self-conscious "lo and behold" (*"siehe da!"*), and the aloof "object of my curiosity" (*"Gegenstand meiner Neugier"*).

A conversation takes place between the two of them, a conversation the narrator decides to terminate as it is getting late. Almost instinctively he accompanies his words with the offer of further money. Yet here, too, any possible overtones of sympathetic involvement with the old man are neutralized by the narrator's stressing the diffidence and awkwardness of the old man's leave-taking: "And then, with a curious kind of aristocratic ease, he made a rather awkward bow and went off as fast as his old legs would carry him" (45). Even so, the Spielmann is uppermost in the narrator's mind as he pauses on his way home for a drink. The thought occurs to him that he is near the

Spielmann's house, and having made inquiries, he abandons his route home and turns off toward the *Gärtnergasse* where the old man lives. It is repeatedly stressed that the *Gärtnergasse* is not on the narrator's way home. We are told that, after leaving the inn garden, our narrator walked toward the town (46), whereas the *Gärtnergasse* "ran toward the open fields. I followed that direction" (46).

Furthermore, it is worth noting that, from the moment of his first meeting with the Spielmann, the narrator—in terms of his physical movements on that day—removes himself farther and farther from the crowd, from the flood of common humanity.[7] Once again, however, the narrator negates any suggestion of sympathy by the way he describes his thoughts as he enters the *Gärtnergasse*: "In which of these wretched huts could my oddity live? Typically, I had forgotten the number" (46). The insertion of the word "typically" (*"glücklich"*) here is intriguing. It implies that the narrator is irritated with himself for his forgetfulness, that he resents the thought that he might lose another opportunity of gaining insight into the Spielmann and his way of life. All this might seem to imply that there is an instinctive—almost spontaneous—involvement on the part of the narrator. Yet we are never allowed to forget that the present narrator is looking back on what he describes; he is reporting events that took place "two years ago" (39), and from the vantage point of his present narrative perspective he is able to play down his personal involvement at the time. Indeed, at times he is ironic at his own expense—as when he reports his journey home after finding the *Gärtnergasse*: "Only finding my way with difficulty in the unfamiliar streets, I embarked on my homeward journey, and I, too, improvised, but disturbing nobody, only in my head" (47). The irony here lightheartedly implies that an affinity existed between the Spielmann and the narrator of two years ago.

This curious half-identification occurs again when the narrator visits the Spielmann a few days later: "There has been almost an excess of reference to the ugly notes produced by my, and I almost fear that he is only my, favorite, that I will spare the reader the description of this hellish concert" (48). There is perhaps an implication here that the story of the narrator's encounters with the Spielmann is only of interest to the two people concerned—almost as if only the narrator could possibly be concerned with the doings of the strange old man. It is at this point that the Spielmann embarks on his narration. At first the narrator makes several comments, but only in order to fill in background detail (on the Spielmann's father) or to describe the Spielmann as he settles himself to tell his tale. Gradually, however, the narrator's interpolations become fewer and fewer until the old man is allowed to dominate the narrative completely. This whole scene is, then, remarkable for its lack of distancing commentary on the part of the narrator.[8]

Once the Spielmann's narration is ended, the narrator reasserts his usual laconic mode. Two sentences describe his leave-taking; no word is said about what the Spielmann has just told him. Several months are passed over in a few terse sentences—the narrator goes on a journey and only remembers the Spielmann when he hears of the terrible flooding in the Leopoldstadt. He decides to offer some help "to the address most of concern to me" (78). Once again, as with the description of that earlier flood—the people at the fair—the narrator offers a catalogue of horrors: "on all sides weeping, funeral bells, anxiously searching mothers and lost children" (78), before passing on to the specific case that interests him. The narrator arrives in time to witness Jakob's funeral. Without actually telling us as much, he clearly takes part in the funeral procession, or at least follows it at some suitable distance; from the concrete details of his description it is clear that he is present at the cemetery to witness the actual burial.

There then follows the closing scene—the meeting with Barbara—which brings together all the narrative features I have discussed, and which, in that reticent and understated way that is typical of the whole work, crystallizes the narrator's response to the Spielmann:

> A few days later—it was a Sunday—I went, impelled by my psychological curiosity, to the house of the butcher and took as my pretext that I wished to possess the old man's violin as a souvenir. I found the family together—with no particular impression left on them. Yet the violin hung on the wall, with a kind of symmetry, next to the mirror and opposite a crucifix. When I explained my intention and offered a relatively high price, the man seemed anything but disinclined to conclude a good deal. But the woman leaped up from her chair and said: "Whatever next! The violin belongs to our Jakob, and a few Gulden more or less do not make much difference to us!" She took the instrument from the wall, looked at it, turning it round in her hands, blew the dust off it and put it into a drawer, which she, as though fearing burglary, shut violently and locked. Her face was turned away from me so that I could not see what it might have expressed. As at this point the maid came in with the soup, and the butcher, without being embarrassed by the presence of the visitor, began to say grace in a loud voice—in which the children joined their shrill voices—I wished them a pleasant meal and went out of the door. My last glance fell on the woman. She had turned around and the tears were pouring down her face (8of.).

The paragraph opens with what is by now almost a familiar refrain: "impelled by my psychological curiosity." Surely, this sort of comment has by now become something repetitive and mechanical. Why does the narrator feel that he must explain his motives every time? Do we need to be constantly reminded that his curiosity is purely scientific? Indeed, could not the very obtrusiveness of such comments indicate to us that the narrator is trying to deceive himself—and us—about his true motives? Furthermore, for somebody who claims to have an insatiable scientific curiosity, the narrator is remarkably reticent about giving any psychological *interpretation* of the old man's life. Indeed, he does not allow himself one analytical statement about the Spielmann. In view of the repetitive references to "psychological curiosity" (*"psychologische Neugierde"*), one cannot help wondering whether he wants to see the old man only in order to prove to himself (and to us) that he is able—despite his fascination—to maintain a scrupulous detachment. This accounts for his obliqueness. He goes to see Barbara on the pretext that he wishes to buy the old man's violin. If this is only a pretext, we must ask ourselves what his real motives are. Psychological curiosity? But curiosity about what? After all, he has already seen Barbara on the day of the funeral; he has learned that she insists on paying the burial costs. He knows, therefore, that she does still feel something for the

old man, that she has not forgotten him. Yet, presumably, he wants to know more. We must assume that the extra information he wants can only be elicited by the direct approach of offering to buy the violin.

He finds the family "with no particular impression left on them. Yet the violin hung on the wall, with a kind of symmetry, next to the mirror and opposite a crucifix." Here one must note the conjunction "yet" (*"doch"*) by which the narrator fleetingly betrays his—almost embarrassed—intuition that he and a member of the family he is visiting have responded to the Spielmann in the same way. The other person is, of course, Barbara. That the narrator is embarrassed by his intuition is revealed in his attempt to understate the importance of the violin's position on the wall ("with *a kind of* symmetry"). The full significance of the violin is made abundantly clear by subsequent events. When the narrator offers money for the violin Barbara refuses violently. Her first, and instinctive, reaction is physical: she leaps to her feet. She then has to say something, to give reasons why it would be wrong to accept the narrator's financially favorable offer. She gives, in essence, two reasons for her refusal. First, "the violin belongs to our Jakob"—the violin belongs to their son Jakob and as parents they would be wrong to sell it. Second, "a few Gulden more or less do not make much difference to us"—they are not in need of the money. Of course, both these arguments could be perfectly valid reasons for her rejection of the narrator's offer. However, her subsequent actions suggest something very different: "She took the instrument from the wall, looked at it, turning it round in her hands, blew the dust off it and put it into a drawer, which she, as though fearing burglary, shut violently and locked." This sentence implies two things. In the first place, the fact that the violin has acquired dust on the wall suggests that her son has not played it, that it is not really *his* violin. Second, the violence with which she locks away the violin indicates that to her it is beyond price. Barbara's actions suggest the full importance the violin has for her, the importance of a sacred relic. Her actions intimate this—and yet, the statements she makes imply very different considerations on her part. They give mundane, practical reasons why the violin should not be sold. In other words, the truth of Barbara's feelings about the violin (and about the Spielmann) is something that she cannot say—perhaps because she does not fully understand it herself, perhaps because, even if she does know what she feels, she is convinced that nobody would comprehend the nature of her involvement with the old man, would understand why she so cherishes the last relic of his life on earth.

As a result of his pretext—his offer to buy the violin—the narrator finds out something important about Barbara. The funeral had told him that she grieved for the old man. What he needed to know was at what level she laments this loss. Pity? Nostalgic memory of her youth? With his offer to buy the violin, the narrator applies the crucial test to Barbara—and he discovers that she cares for the Spielmann in a way that she will not and cannot express. She asserts possession of the violin not simply against her family and the narrator, but ultimately against the real world, which in its unyielding material existence makes a mockery of her involvement with the "ideal" world of the Spielmann. The narrator knows—before he visits Barbara—that this is a possible response to the old man; hence he insists on seeing her again, on posing the crucial question. He senses this response, because at an unspoken—and unsayable—level of his being, this is his response to the Spielmann, a response that he masks as "psychological curiosity."

We now come to the narrator's last glimpse of Barbara. She has turned away and the narrator cannot see her face. The maid enters with the soup, the father and children begin to say grace, whereupon the narrator takes his leave: "I wished them a pleasant meal and went out of the door. My last glance fell on the woman. She had turned round and the tears were pouring down her face." Especially here the laconic, reticent style of the narrator implies infinitely more than it says. What the narrator does not mention (just as he never says that he follows the old man's funeral) is that, having turned to go, he pauses in the door and looks back at Barbara. Both the narrator and Barbara have turned around, and the final picture—almost a tableau—is one of a moment they have in common because of their feelings for the Spielmann. Yet it is a moment and no more. The narrator looks back at Barbara, but she, clearly, is utterly oblivious of him. There is no real communication between them at this point. Yet, the narrator and Barbara—for all the social differences that separate them—are analogous figures in terms of their response to the Spielmann. They have in common their embarrassment at having to *say* what the old man means to them. Yet the assent is there, and it is suggested by a very subtle parallel. If we turn to Barbara's last interview with the Spielmann, we find the conversation in which she most nearly *says* what she feels for Jakob. She resents his weakness, his utter impracticality. However, she also resents the alternative: "I must now go out among the coarse people—and I have resisted this so long" (77). This decision has to be taken; for Barbara (as for the narrator) objective social reality is binding. She repudiates the Spielmann and turns to go: "As she got to the door she turned round once again and said: 'The laundry is all in order. Take care that you do not lose any of it. Hard times will come.' And now she raised her hand, made a movement like the sign of the cross in the air and called: 'God be with you, Jakob!—For ever and ever, Amen!' she added more quietly and left" (77).

Her movements here are the same as the narrator's in the closing scene, and the reason for the crucial hesitation is made explicit by Barbara in the words she speaks to the old man. They are words of total assent; for the first and only time the *du* is used. Also, the words are not simply expressions of human tenderness—they have religious connotations. Barbara asks for God's blessing on the man whom she is rejecting. It is this response that binds Barbara to the memory of the dead Spielmann, it is this same response that binds the narrator to the old man. In spite of what unites them, however, there is no communication between Barbara and the narrator in the closing scene. This is surely because, by definition, there can be no community of those who have assented to the sheer saintliness of the old man. The violin may hang with a certain symmetry opposite the cross; but there can be no brotherhood of believers because the Spielmann's life—unlike Christ's passion—is not the story of a mediation between spirit and world. Rather, Jakob's life asserts the unbridgeable gulf between intention (*Absicht*) and work (*Werk*), between values and facts.

If one traces the religious references throughout the story one finds a significant pattern at work. The narrator praises the fair as a mass spectacle "in which ultimately the divine resides" (39). He tries to assert the presence of absolute values in the mass of common, ordinary humanity. However, he is deflected from the pursuit of this immanent divinity by his meeting with one man, a man whose efforts to make music are for him a link with the divine, who speaks of his art as a prayer, as "playing the dear Lord," a man for whom the Christian heaven is a world "where we are judged by our intentions and not by our works" (65). It is to that divinity, a divinity denied any substantial realization in the world that both Barbara and the narrator subscribe with part of their being. Both of them know that by this assent they threaten to isolate themselves from the real world, from any hope of human fulfillment deriving from practical achievement. Yet Barbara will not relinquish her hold on this world. She is an efficient wife and mother, she has practical good sense, she belongs to the world of the family, of impatient customers, of the simple, uncouth prayer spoken before a meal. Still, potentially the assent to the Spielmann is there. Similarly, the narrator, although manifestly different from the Spielmann in his intellectual sophistication and his social standing, displays an implicit affinity with the old man. When, for example, he first sees him at the fair, the narrator withdraws from the crowd "on to the side of the embankment" (41). At this moment both the narrator and the Spielmann stand apart from the crowd in total isolation. Both are oddities in the sense that they do not share in the merry-making of the crowd. It is because of this strange affinity between them that the narrator is so fascinated by the Spielmann, and it is because he knows of—and is embarrassed by—this affinity that the narrator adopts a stance of ironical distance from the Spielmann. Yet in so doing he lays bare his own uncertainty, he emphasizes the irony of his own precarious position.[9]

Many critics have interpreted this story in autobiographical terms. Quite clearly, Grillparzer is here examining with terrible and unflinching honesty his own agonizing self-doubts as a man and as an artist. Both Barbara and the narrator, however much they resent it or are embarrassed by it, subscribe with part of their nature to Jakob's world, to his ceaseless—and necessarily doomed—struggle to express the inner ideal in outward terms. Their resentment, their ambivalence is part of the honesty of the story. This is no facile affirmation of the idealist in a cold, materialist society. Barbara and the narrator know that to adopt Jakob's perspective fully is to negate the meaningfulness of life in the physical world, of family, of art created with material things. It is the specifically artistic aspect of the Spielmann's dilemma that is pertinent to the narrator's own situation. Unless he can believe that the "divine" does, potentially, reside in the mass, that "the unrestrained burst of applause from a fully packed theater" is "interesting, indeed instructive" (39), he condemns his art to a terrible isolation and to utter unrealization; he condemns himself to write for those few oddities who know that the "divine" has withdrawn into pure inwardness, who know that practical failure may be the measure of ideal intention. This involves so radical a devaluation of the real that the narrator must make himself repudiate it. He continues to repudiate it by his *present* act of narration, by insisting that his attitudes to the common people—and to the fair—have not changed despite the meeting of some two years previously with the Spielmann. It is, for example, significant that toward the beginning of his story he asserts his credo in the present tense: "I do not lightly miss this festival.. . . as a lover of human beings, I say, especially when they come together in masses, for a time forgetting their own wishes and becoming part of that wholeness in which ultimately the divine resides, indeed God himself—as such a person I find that every popular festival is actually a festival of the soul, a pilgrimage, an act of worship." (39). With this strident credo—affirmed as his present position—the narrator aligns himself with the real world of practical achievement. Accordingly, the perspective he adopts throughout his narration gives firm allegiance to externals, to the familiar universe of facts and events. That other interpretative possibility—of assent to the Spielmann—has to be implied, not stated, has to be intimated through irony, and not declared unambiguously. This is because any such explicit declaration to this effect would involve another credo—precisely that artistic and human credo that would render nugatory the attempt to write this story or any other story, for that matter.

The Spielmann, for all his reticence and self-depreciation, is both a radical and a disturbing figure. The confrontation with him—however much the narrator tries to play it down—is a shock, a shock to which he continues to subject himself in order to be able to withstand it. One is reminded here of Grillparzer's great contemporary, Baudelaire, and especially of the role of shock meetings in his work. Walter Benjamin argues that Baudelaire's decisive experience is that of the artist living within (but alienated from) the metropolis.[10] He distills the experience of the city—and its critique—from shock confrontations with the odd, the quirky, the freakish. The critique is channeled through an artistic concentration on the oddities that mass city life presents. Paradoxically, in the marginality of his human and social situation—and in the marginality of his thematic concern—the artist explores the central issue of the ruthlessly competitive, individualist society around him. This, too, behind all the oblique irony, is central to Grillparzer's vision in *Der arme Spielmann*.

It is a disturbing story, disturbing in the fact that it implies a deeply dangerous hermeneutic possibility: that we, its readers, may be tempted to relate to the Spielmann in the way that Barbara and the narrator, in spite of themselves, do. This central relationship of association and dissociation, of affinity and detachment, is perhaps put most succinctly, and with desperately appropriate ambiguity, by Franz Kafka in the *Briefe an Milena*. Kafka sends the story to Milena with the obliquely disparaging comment: "I am sending you *Der arme Spielmann* today, not because it has great meaning for me—it did once have it, years ago. I send it because he is so Viennese, so unmusical, so heartbreaking, because he looked down upon us in the *Volksgarten* (on us! You were walking beside me, Milena, just think, you walked beside me), because he is so bureaucratic, and because he loved a girl who had a good business sense."[11] Clearly, Milena's reaction to the story is a positive one, and Kafka replies to her with a more detailed commentary on his relationship to the work. Significantly, however, the more detailed commentary is no less ambiguous than his first statement. What Kafka does is to deepen the dialectic, to intensify both his acceptance and his rejection of the story. In so doing, he reenacts, as we do, the central dilemma of both Barbara and the narrator:

Everything you say about *Der arme Spielmann* is right. If I said that it did not mean anything to me, it was out of caution, because I did not know how you would get on with it, and then also because I am as ashamed of the story as if I had written it myself. And actually it does begin wrongly, has a number of things that are false, ludicrous, dilettante, grotesquely affected (especially when reading it aloud one notices it, I could show you the passages); and especially this kind of musical performance is surely a pitiably laughable invention, designed to make the girl so irritated as to throw everything, the whole shop, at the story, in a towering rage, in which the whole world, myself especially, would share, until the story, which deserves no better, would perish from within. Admittedly, there is no more beautiful fate for a story than to disappear—and in this way. The narrator, too, this comic psychologist, would fully agree with this, because he is probably the true poor musician who plays this story for us in the most unmusical way possible, thanked for his pains in an excessively abundant way by the tears from your eyes.[12]

Seldom has any novelle had such a devastatingly attuned reader.

Notes

1. References throughout are to Franz Grillparzer, *Sämtliche Werke*, vol. 13, ed. A. Sauer and R. Backmann, Vienna, 1930.

2. J. P. Stern, *Re-Interpretations*, p. 61.

3. See especially Heinz Politzer, *Franz Grillparzer's "Der arme Spielmann."* Politzer stresses (pp. 8f.) that the narrator's loftiness masks both diffidence and uncertainty.

4. *Re-Interpretations*, p. 67.

5. *Wirklichkeit und Illusion*, p. 96. John M. Ellis makes the same point, but his analysis suffers, in my view, from his undifferentiated deningration of the narrator figure. What he describes as "lack of sincerity" (p. 123), as "wanton self-gratification" (p. 125) is, in my view, symptomatic of a much more complex interpretative unease (*Narration in the German Novelle*).

6. On the implications of the narrator's distaste for the masses see especially Wolfgang Paulsen. "Der gute Bürger Jakob," and Hertha Krotkoff, "Über den Rahmen in Franz Grillparzers Novelle *Der arme Spielmann*."

7. I am grateful to my colleague Professor Ilse Graham for drawing my attention to this point.

8. On the importance—and the hermeneutic cohesion—of Jakob's account of his own life and on the significance of the narrator's withdrawal into silence see Roland Heine, "Ästhetische oder existentielle Integration?"

9. For a telling discussion of this affinity see Peter Schäublin, "Das Musizieren des armen Spielmannes."

10. In Walter Benjamin, *Schriften*, ed. T. W. Adorno, Frankfurt am Main, 1955. For an English version see Benjamin's *Illuminations*, pp. 157ff. See also Benjamin's *Charles Baudelaire: Ein Lyriker im*

Zeitalter des Hochkapitalismus, ed. R. Tiedemann, Frankfurt am Main, 1969.

11. Franz Kafka, *Briefe an Milena*, ed. W. Haas, Frankfurt am Main, 1966, p. 61.

12. Ibid., p. 77.

W. C. Reeve (essay date 1978)

SOURCE: "Proportion and Disproportion in Grillparzer's *Der arme Spielmann*," in *The Germanic Review*, Vol. LIII, No. 2, Spring, 1978, pp. 41-9.

[*In the following essay, Reeve examines the theatrical staging and spatial relationships in* Der arme Spielmann.]

In his psychologically oriented *Franz Grillparzer oder das abgründige Biedermeier*, Heinz Politzer noted with reference to the position of the violin and the cross in the final scene of *Der arme Spielmann*: "Der Abstand, der sich zwischen der Welt des Glaubens und dem Reich der Kunst aufgetan hat, wird im Raum offenbar. Die ganze Breite des Zimmers trennt die eine von dem anderen."[1] Not satisfied with Politzer's interpretation of "mit einer Art Symmetrie"[2] mentioned by the narrator in the same episode, James L. Hodge responded with an article entitled "Symmetry and Tension in *Der arme Spielmann*" in which he further explored the symbolic significance of what amounts to an example of skilful staging. "The mirror besides the violin, on the other hand, offers a ruthless reflection of the real. Together, the mirror and the violin express the total reality of Jakob's life—the dichotomy between human aspiration and human capability."[3] These two studies, in this one limited instance, cast light upon a principle of composition exploited by Grillparzer both in his dramas as well as in his famous narrative—a principle which, despite the recent wealth of critical material pertaining to *Der arme Spielmann*, has been either ignored or only alluded to briefly in passing.

As early as 1926, E. Alker underlined with mathematical exactitude and in chart form the structural symmetry inherent in the general composition of the Novelle: "Schon die beiden Rahmenstücke zeigen die streng parallele Komposition."[4] Since, in arriving at his scheme, Alker instinctively used the term "Szene" to describe each of the narrative's settings, he thus may be said to have been the first to point out the short story's predominantly dramatic character. Other critics such as Richard Brinkmann[5] or Walter Silz[6] have also dwelled upon the stage elements, but the real credit for outlining in some detail the nature of the dramatic in an epic form belongs to W. E. Yates who even goes as far as to classify Grillparzer's two creative prose works as "'Theatrical' Novellen."[7] Although he singles out the use of gestures rather than speech to express emotion, or the utilization of dialogue at climaxes "where speeches tend to be shorter and sharper, with an effect akin to stichomythia," Yates fails to grasp—except for one brief reference to "symbolic values . . . brought out by visual effects such as the use of Jakob's hat or the chalk-line down the centre of his room"[8]—the full import or implications of stage-setting and spatial relationships within *Der arme Spielmann*.

Grillparzer once wrote: "Das äct dramatische ist immer theatralisch, wenn auch nicht umgekehrt. Das Theater ist der Rahmen des Bildes, inner welchem die Gegenstände Anschaulichkeit und Verhältniß zu einander haben."[9] A drama must be seen in order to come to life.[10] The Viennese stage was firmly rooted in a long tradition dating back to the Baroque theatre which usually offered a feast for the eyes. One of the most obvious visual effects turned to account by the Baroque dramatist was the distinction between high and low, the former being associated with the realm of the gods, the Divine or the ideal, while the latter reflected the less than perfect domain of everyday earthly existence. If we turn to Grillparzer's plays, we can immediately ascertain how this same, most basic spatial contrast not only suggests a major psychological concern of the dramatist but also may even be said to summarize in concrete form a tragedy's main theme: Sappho casting herself from Mount Leucas into the sea; Medea and Hero in their respective towers with the loved one in the water below; Ottokar kneeling before Rudolf;[11] the land of deception (earth) versus the land of truth (heaven); "der Mann in dem braunen Mantel" standing above on the cliff, looking down upon Rustan; Rudolf II in his tower near the stars set opposite his illegitimate son Don Cäsar in the streets of Prague; King Alphons in a deserted throne room, gazing up at the symbol of the duty he owes to the state; or Libussa descending from the castle of her sisters to the fallible human realm. Grillparzer's complete command of the stage and its visual effects[12] served him equally well in the composition of the various scenes which make up his "'Theatrical' Novelle," *Der arme Spielmann*.

Before the reader catches his first glimpse of the fiddler, the narrator sets the stage with a detailed description of "das saturnalische Fest" (37), a Dionysiac folk celebration where "Der Unterschied der Stände" (37) has disappeared, where sociological distinctions such as upper and lower classes are rendered meaningless as all are caught up in the same flow of humanity, sharing a common fate. "Auch hier siegreich, ziehen endlich zwei Ströme, die alte Donau und die geschwollnere Woge des Volks sich kreuzend quer unter und über einander, die Donau ihrem alten Flußbette nach, der Strom des Volkes, der Eindämmung der Brücke entnommen, ein weiter, tosender See, sich ergiessend in Alles deckender Überschwemmung" (37). Grillparzer, who was fully aware of and put to good use the ancient, archetypal function of water as a symbol of the unconscious, employs the stream image to suggest a Dionysiac experience resulting from the surrender of the "principium individuationis" to an all-encompassing union with the whole. Although the higher flow of humanity presently remains above the inexorable flow of the river and indeed runs at right angle to its current, eventually the lower will rise to meet the upper with devastating effects for man.

Standing on the causeway, between the Augarten and the Brigittenau, Jakob opposes this general crowd movement. As an outcast he is immediately linked with the crippled musicians who, because of their handicaps, are excluded from the "pays de cocagne" (38). But the fiddler has no desire to enter, having consciously disassociated himself from the group. A paradise of indiscriminate, common human joys and pleasures holds no attraction for him so that, while his companions are ostracized because of a physical limitation beyond their conscious control, Jakob's exclusion is by free choice alone, for he remains to the very end totally unaware of the disastrous effect his music has upon others.

What really attracts the narrator, however, is the glaring sense of unbalance which characterizes this first confrontation and sets up the essential tension, proportion-disproportion, of the narrative. On the one hand, he observes the ordered world of the notes, the music stand, the immaculate although threadbare dress and the Latin phrase borrowed from Horace's satire I.1.106. The latter poem deals with the theme of greed and the unhappiness it leads to in keeping with the Horatian ideal of the middle path. The complete thought reads: "Est modus in rebus, sunt certi denique fines," which may be rendered in English as: "There is a proportion in things, and there are after all definite limits." In Jakob's first utterance, Grillparzer has very skilfully chosen a proverbial statement which aptly sums up his protagonist's attitude to the conscious world and which does not represent, as Politzer maintains, "die lateinische Fassung des wienerischen 'Ka Geld, ka Musi'."[13] On the other hand, the narrator cannot fail but hear the disordered world of his music which lacks normal spatial relationships: "was er spielte, schien eine unzusammenhängende Folge von Tönen ohne Zeitmass und Melodie" (41). This apparent dichotomy anticipates Jakob's unconscious dilemma. "Endlich hielt er ein, blickte, wie aus einer langen Abwesenheit zu sich gekommen, nach dem Firmament, das schon die Spuren des nahenden Abends zu zeigen anfing, darauf abwärts in seinen Hut, fand ihn leer . . ." (41). All the time he was engrossed in playing, he dwelled in a remote, ideal sphere, but now he returns to reality. The glance cast towards the sky, while having a practical cause, i.e., to verify the time of day, also indicates the upper realm (the Biblical term "Firmament" is consciously chosen) to which he aspires and thus prepares for the heavenly music he alone can hear in death. But almost immediately it is set in contrast with the downward motion towards the hat, the reminder of his practical needs and his social position. As a final confirmation of the dissonance inherent in the outward appearance of this old man, he leaves working his way "mühsam durch die dem Fest zuströmende Menge *in entgegengesetzter Richtung* . . ." (41) at the time when the real harvest begins for the beggar community.

In the next scene, the usual spatial relationship of an itinerant musician surrounded by children is established, but closer examination soon discloses the disproportional: The unrecognizable notes of the waltz and the cries of the dissatisfied children. The circle is soon broken and dissolved as the boys desert the fiddler in favour of the organgrinder. The young audience turns from a subjectively oriented system to a purely objective one of mechanical music produced with mathematical precision. As Herta Krotkoff has expressed it, "Die Wahl liegt zwischen übersteigerter Individualität bei Jakob und völliger Entseelung und Uniformiertheit beim Leierkastenmann. Die Wahl der Kinder fällt auf letzteren."[14]

"'Bitte! bitte!' rief der alte Mann, wobei er mit beiden Händen ängstlich abwehrende Bewegungen machte, 'in den Hut! in den Hut!'" (42-43). This emotional reaction, underlined by the four exclamation marks and by the dramatic gesture, to the narrator's attempt to hand his contribution directly to the *Spielmann* emphasizes the latter's love of and insistence upon order. The hat has become his link with the real world and its physical demands as well as a reminder of his semi-aristocratic past and the propriety it represented. His spatial relationship to the hat upon the ground corresponds to his desire to keep a certain protective distance between himself and the material world, specifically money, which ironically will eventually destroy him. The hat and its function thus anticipate the chalk-line drawn along the floor of the attic room. Once the money has received the consecration conferred by the hat, Jakob no longer fears to touch it since it has become part of his just payment for a service rendered. As the fiddler explains to the narrator in a logically determined fashion: "Erstens . . . zweitens . . . Drittens" (43) his reasons for retiring early, it becomes evident that, as Richard Brinkmann points out, "er begegnet der Welt durch das Medium einer selbstgesetzten Ordnung."[15] He seeks to live on the basis of a standard of order as dictated by the rational, conscious side of his personality. True to the principle: "der Mensch [muß sich] in allen Dingen eine gewisse Ordnung festsetzen, sonst gerät er ins Wilde und Unaufhaltsame" (43), he has strictly slotted his daily schedule according to a carefully worked out scheme, he refuses to become party to "Tanzfreuden oder sonst unordentlichen Ergötzlichkeiten" (44), and he even views his relationship to his public in terms of maintaining a balance. In short, on the surface "Maß" or proportion would seem to dictate his life. ""[Aber] der Abend gehört mir und meiner armen Kunst. Abends halte ich mich zu Hause, und'—dabei ward seine Rede immer leiser, Röte überzog sein Gesicht, sein Auge suchte den Boden—'da spiele ich denn aus der Einbildung, so für mich ohne Noten. Phantasieren, glaub' ich, heißt es in den Musikbüchern'" (43). Other than the reference to Jakob's state of mind as he stopped playing and gazed at the sky, this admission, not unlike a confession of love, is really the first indication of the disproportionate aspect of his inner world paralleling the music he produces in the outer world. The involuntary, emotional reaction of blushing and the fact that he rejects the ordering discipline of printed notes herald the movement from the rational-objective to the irrational-subjective.

At this point, it would seem advisable to investigate Grillparzer's attitude towards music, one which distinguishes him from the Romantics who sought to dispense with the boundaries separating the various art forms. "Wenn man den Grundunterschied der Musik und der Dichtkunst schlagend charakterisieren wollte, so müßte man darauf aufmerksam machen, wie die Wirkung der Musik vom Sinnenreiz, vom Nervenspiel beginnt und, nachdem das Gefühl angeregt worden, höchstens in letzter Instanz an das Geistige gelangt, indes die Dichtkunst zuerst den Begriff erweckt, nur durch ihn auf das Gefühl wirkt und als äußerste Stufe der Vollendung oder der Erniedrigung erst das Sinnliche teilnehmen läßt; der Weg beider ist daher gerade der umgekehrte. Die eine Vergeistigung des Körperlichen, die andere Verkörperung des Geistigen."[16] Following the examples of the philosopher he most admired, Kant, Grillparzer sees the effect of music as being predominantly physical and as appealing through the senses directly to human feeling. Man's rational faculties are therefore not necessary in the reception of music and indeed may without detriment be totally absent in its enjoyment. "Wenn eine Violinsaite gestrichen wird, so klingen die Saiten einer daneben liegenden unberührten Geige mit.

Wie, wenn ein ähnliches Nachleben unserer Nerven Ursache an der so großen Wirkung der Musik wäre? Bei mir wenigstens liegt gewiß so etwas zu Grunde, denn ich darf nur einen Ton hören, ohne noch Melodie zu unterscheiden, so gerät schon mein ganzes Wesen in eine zitternde Bewegung, deren ich nicht Herr werden kann" (*Zur Musik*, 121). As will be demonstrated, this is precisely the process in its simplest form in which Jakob indulges while improvising. Since for Grillparzer the result was an overwhelming physical experience over which he had no control, he learned to fear music and especially those composers such as Beethoven who flouted the classical conventions and whose compositions appeared to be on the verge of emotional anarchy or chaos. But perhaps Grillparzer's ambivalent attitude towards music has best been captured in his designation of "dunkle Gefühle" as "das eigentliche Gebiet der Musik. Hierin muß ihr die Poesie nachstehen. Wo Worte nicht mehr hinreichen, sprechen die Töne. Was Gestalten nicht auszudrücken vermögen, malt ein Laut. Die sprachlose Sehnsucht; das schweigende Verlangen; der Liebe Wünsche, die Wehmut, die einen Gegenstand sucht und zittert, ihn zu finden in sich selbst; der Glaube, der sich aufschwingt; das Gebet, das lallt und stammelt: alles was höher geht und tiefer als Worte gehen können, das gehört der Musik an" (*Zur Musik*, 128). Words, being logical constructs by which the mind operates and through which it seeks to impose a rational structure upon a world which is not necessarily rational, have reached the outermost limit of the expressible, and to cross that frontier into the realm of the irrational, one must have recourse to music.

Today, with the aid of psychology, one could easily interpret "dunkle Gefühle" as symbolic representations of the life urge. Indeed Grillparzer seems to have been very much aware of the sexual side of music, having once referred to the relationship between major and minor in terms of male-female (*Zur Musik*, 118) and to "die niedern Sinne, so süß sie auch sein mögen" (*Zur Musik*, 127) as not being a suitable basis for a free and beautiful art. It is also striking how closely his view of music approximates that of Nietzsche as expressed in *Die Geburt der Tragödie aus dem Geist der Musik*. Almost like an echo one reads: "die Musik selbst, in ihrer völligen Unumschränktheit, [braucht] das Bild und den Begriff nicht, sondern [erträgt] ihn nur neben sich . . . die *Sprache* [kann], als Organ und Symbol der Erscheinungen, nie und nirgends das tiefste Innere der Musik nach Außen kehren."[17] In lyrical music Nietzsche saw the glorification and the realization of the Greek god Dionysius, for in music the individual forgets and surrenders himself completely to a vision of universal union by which he becomes one with the all: "Unter dem Zauber des Dionysischen schließt sich nicht nur der Bund zwischen Mensch und Mensch wieder zusammen: auch die entfremdete, feindliche oder unterjochte Natur feiert wieder ihr Versöhnungsfest mit ihrem verlorenen Sohne, dem Menschen. . . . Singend und tanzend äußert sich der Mensch als Mitglied einer höheren Gemeinschaft."[18] In the words of Heinz Politzer, "Im übrigen fürchtete [Grillparzer], sich in der Welt der Töne zu verlieren. 1828 nannte er Paganini einen Selbstmörder."[19] Hence it may be assumed that as a therapeutic exercise Grillparzer has portrayed in the "Spielmann" what could conceivably have happened to him.

While the narrator listens below in the Gärtnergasse or later as he stands in the fiddler's room, he endeavours to discover the principle behind the performance. "Ein leiser, aber bestimmt gegriffener Ton schwoll bis zur *Heftigkeit*, senkte sich, verklang, um gleich darauf wieder bis zum lautesten Gellen empor zu steigen, und zwar immer derselbe Ton mit einer Art *genußreichem* Daraufberuhen wiederholt. Endlich kam ein Intervall. Es war die Quarte. Hatte der Spieler sich vorher an dem Klange des einzelnen Tones geweidet, so war nun das gleichsam *wollüstige Schmecken* dieses harmonischen Verhältnisses noch ungleich fühlbarer" (46-47). The sensually flavoured language which Grillparzer uses each time he describes the old man playing alone in his room points to music, or religion for that matter, as sublimations of the life instinct. Music has therefore become a means to express Jakob's frustrated vital urges,[20] an escape into a purely subjective world.[21] Because of a strict puritanical upbringing, he consciously aspires to the level of an Apollonian individual: "der Mensch [muß sich] in allen Dingen eine gewisse Ordnung festsetzen, sonst gerät er ins Wilde und Unaufhaltsame" (43), while unconsciously, in the Dionysiac experience of music, he can give free rein to the irrational side of his psyche. "Statt nun in einem Musikstücke nach Sinn und Rhythmus zu betonen, hob er heraus, verlängerte er die dem Gehör wohltuenden Noten und Intervalle, ja nahm keinen Anstand sie willkürlich zu wiederholen, wobei sein Gesicht oft geradezu den Ausdruck der Verzückung annahm" (48-49). An indulgence in excess, his playing rejects the accepted proportions and imposes its own according to a very basic pleasure principle: "Der Alte genoß, indem er spielte" (48). The result of this complete lack of discipline normally expected, indeed demanded in music, is "Verzückung," self-abandonment to an emotionalism having nothing to do with "Verstand" (Kant's designation adhered to by Grillparzer, *Zur Musik*, 127). Whereas the Apollonian creates an illusion of rationality which enables man to live despite the horror of the abyss, the Dionysiac, the basis of music, according to Nietzsche, brings man back to his primordial, irrational roots.

Bearing in mind the stress created by proportion versus disproportion in the mind of the reader (Jakob is totally unaware of this tension, which is reflected in the narrator, in this instance the reader's representative), we would have to reject as misleading Walter Silz' description of the old man as an example of "selflessness, which comes close to saintliness,"[22] for his enjoyment of music rests upon a purely selfish pleasure principle. It would be equally incorrect to refer to Jakob's life as "das Tragische der Innerlichkeit,"[23] for where there is no conscious conflict, there can be no tragedy. Also J. P. Stern's comment that "Grillparzer of course possessed none of Thomas Mann's up-to-date psychological skill and interest being concerned with effects rather than causes"[24] can be easily countered by reference to Politzer's study *Franz Grillparzer oder das abgründige Biedermeier* which demonstrates how "der frühe Seelenforscher Grillparzer,"[25] in addition to anticipating some of Mann's preoccupations (Politzer compares *Sappho* and *Tonio Kröger*), proves himself a match for the novelist, especially in his penetrating analysis of Otto von Meran.[26] And finally, something should be said about a persistent tendency in secondary literature to refer to Jakob's inner world as the realization of an unqualified ideal. For example, "Das Ideale und das Reale trennen sich, und das Ideale ist nur noch im Zurückziehen auf den esoterischen Bereich der Innerlichkeit zu bewahren."[27] If this is indeed the case, then we should have to alter radically our understanding of the ideal which since the time of Plato has stood for an intellectual realm free from the demands of the body with its, to use Grillparzer's phrase, "niedern Sinne, so süß sie auch sein mögen" (*Zur Musik*, 127). Surely, Grillparzer, by presenting his protagonist as sensually indulging in an orgy of sound, has seriously called this "Ideale der Innerlichkeit" into question by exposing "das Reale der Innerlichkeit."

If, however, we continue to accept with reservation the problematic distinction "ideal"-"real," then we must further come to terms with the setting and its symbolic value, because the location of Jakob's room renders a life of seclusion dedicated to art even more questionable. The street, the "Gärtnergasse" which "[lief] gegen das freie Feld hinaus" (46), is linked by its very name with down-to-earth needs and with people who earn their living from the soil. It is therefore significant that the first person the narrator encounters in the "Gärtnergasse" during his initial attempt to find Jakob's whereabouts is a man heavily laden with garden vegetables, incarnating the attitude of the everyday world down below in the street: "Kratzt der Alte einmal wieder . . . und stört die ordentlichen Leute in ihrer Nachtruhe" (46). Again, a spatial relationship sets up a discordant note between a very tangible, crude reality and aspirations towards a subjectively determined ideal.

The house Jakob lives in consists of a mere two stories and hence, from the very beginning, he is not that far removed from the ground level. As one might expect by now, the description of the attic room depends for its effect upon proportion-disproportion, order-disorder. The narrator observes "ein schmutziges, widerlich verstörtes Bette, von allen Zutaten der Unordentlichkeit umgeben," juxtaposed with "eine zweite Lagerstätte, dürftig, aber reinlich, und höchst sorgfältig gebettet und bedeckt" (48). A chalk-line which significantly the fiddler drew himself provides the border between these two contrasting realms. "Die Mitte des Zimmers von Wand zu Wand war am Boden mit einem dicken Kreidestriche bezeichnet, und man kann sich kaum einen grelleren Abstich von Schmutz und Reinlichkeit denken, als diesseits und jenseits der gezogenen Linie, dieses Aequators einer Welt im kleinen, herrschte" (48). The very use of the prepositions "diesseits" and "jenseits" is highly suggestive of the real and the ideal living in a state of forced co-existence, and one might wonder why Grillparzer introduced the "Handwerksgesellen" into the immediate proximity of the fiddler's world. The "Spielmann" lives solely for his music, an ideal vision of life which, although the reader may sympathize with it, has little to do with reality. The Biedermeier ethos was losing its faith in the absolute glorification of transcendental values, an article of faith proclaimed by both Classicism and Romanticism. Towards the middle of the nineteenth century, the real with its elementary demands was gradually winning the upper hand and would triumph briefly in Naturalism where the ideal would be denied completely as illusionary and incapable of filling an empty stomach. The workmen thus embody the unavoidable aspects of human existence which could no longer be ignored. This victory of the real over the ideal is intimated in Grillparzer's dramas as well, in Sappho's suicide, in the ascendency of the self-oriented spirit of Klesel over Rudolf II, in the defeat suffered by duty at the hands of sex in *Des Meeres und der Liebe Wellen* and *Die Jüdin von Toledo*, or in the transition from the matriarchial to the patriarchial state in *Libussa*.

As already noted, even the sacred domain of "deutsche Innerlichkeit" has been rendered suspect by its self-indulgent, disproportionate nature and its Dionysiac origin. In order to break the trance into which Jakob has retired, the narrator must finally resort to intentionally dropping his hat, the symbol of reality and social status. "Der alte Mann fuhr zusammen, seine Knie zitterten, kaum konnte er die zum Boden gesenkte Violine halten" (49). As the narrator's description indicates, the fiddler is violently forced out of a dream world, where individuality and self-control were dissolved, back into an awareness of self: "zu sich selbst kommend" (49). Having regained presence of mind, Jakob remarks in reference to the physical disorder of the other half of the room: "Die Unordnung ist verwiesen" (49), an ironic statement when one bears in mind the preceding expression of his "dunkle Gefühle" in music. The irony is compounded when he notes further: "[Die Unordnung] nimmt ihren Rückzug durch die Türe, wenn sie auch derzeit noch nicht ganz über die Schwelle ist" (49). Disorder has already invaded and made its presence felt both in the conscious (the attic room) and in the unconscious (music) realm. Even though he may try to deny the existence of the labourers by drawing his chalk-line, the fact still remains that he is the only one to honour this convention: "'Und respektieren diese Ihre Bezeichnung?'—'Sie nicht, aber ich'" (49) Even if man attempts to disavow life, the latter will not be denied and will triumphantly reassert itself and destroy man if necessary. "Nur die Türe ist gemeinschaftlich" (49). Both those who live the real and those who search for the ideal must enter by the same door of life. The two spheres cannot exist on a separate level and are both part of the same spatial plane. Whereas the workmen have no understanding of and hence show no respect for art, the fiddler must acknowledge the workers' existence even though he would prefer to ignore it altogether. Life states its claim, one that cannot be avoided. This desire to elude the ugly side of the real finds a parallel in Jakob's playing of the masters: because his conscientiousness will not permit him to dispense with the dissonances completely, he passes over them as quickly as possible while, in keeping with the principle of his improvisation, he dwells upon consonance.

Before Jakob relates his life story, another ritual must be performed as he takes the narrator's hat and places it upon the bed. As a gesture of politeness it points again to his aristocratic heritage, a social high point he once enjoyed and which will be confirmed by his autobiography. Furthermore, because of the hat's association with reality, it seems singularly appropriate that attention be drawn to it before he commences his tale. The surface qualities we have come to associate with the fiddler such as discipline, honesty, love of order etc., are evident in his narrative except for those passages which deal with music. "Wenn ich abends im Zwielicht die Violine ergriff, um mich nach meiner Art ohne Noten zu vergnügen, nahmen sie mir das Instrument und sagten, das verdirbt die Applikatur" (51). Even as a child, music represented the only brief release from the dictates of extreme discipline and order. His reintroduction to music many years later is skillfully staged, as usual with symbolic relationships in mind. Ostracized to "einem Hinterstübchen, das in den Nachbars-Hof hinausging" (53), that is to say, completely isolated without any vestige of social intercourse, he hears down below in the courtyard his song: "Es war so einfach, so rührend, und hatte den Nachdruck so auf der rechten Stelle, daß man die Worte gar nicht zu hören brauchte. Wie ich denn überhaupt glaube, die Worte verderben die Musik" (54). In Grillparzer's view, words constitute "Begriffe," rational concepts (and as such are part of the Apollonian tendency of the mind to systematize the world into a rational order), whereas music, dependent upon the senses and the nerves, appeals directly to man's feelings. The song, finding a strong resonance within Jakob's unconscious self, provides the means to express in a sublimated form the Dionysiac current long suppressed within. Interestingly enough, Nietzsche saw in the "Volkslied" "das perpetuum vestigium einer Vereinigung des Appollinischen und des Dionysischen" where "[die Melodie] ist auch das bei weitem wichtigere und nothwendigere [than the text] in der naiven Schätzung des Volkes."[28] Spatially, the song is associated with the courtyard and consequently with the people and the Dionysiac basis of life. The episode leads, of course, to the rediscovery of the violin. Reminiscent of the emotional upheaval Grillparzer underwent at the striking of a mere note: ". . . ich darf nur einen Ton hören, ohne noch Melodie zu unterscheiden, so gerät mein ganzes Wesen in eine zitternde Bewegung, deren ich nicht Herr werden kann" (*Zur Musik*, 121), Jakob's playing of a single note brings about a total abandon to emotional intoxication and its concomitant denial of "Maß." "Der Ton drang in mein Inneres hinein und aus dem Innern wieder heraus. Die Luft um mich war wie geschwängert mit Trunkenheit. Das Lied unten im Hofe und die Töne von meinen Fingern an mein Ohr . . . (54). Upper and lower are united in diction most suggestive of a sublimated sexual experience. As a further confirmation of the scene's erotic content, he "küßte die Violine und drückte sie an [sein] Herz und spielte wieder und fort" (55).[29]

"Das Lied im Hofe—es war eine Weibsperson, die sang—tönte derweile unausgesetzt" (55). It is of some importance to note that the song precedes the woman. Barbara is only desirable indirectly as the incarnation or medium through which the song is expressed; her incidental nature is reflected in the dashes. The fiddler's highly disciplined, prudish upbringing would never allow him to view a "Weibsperson" (both the word choice and the sentence structure suggest a conscious effort to place some distance between himself and the opposite sex) directly as a sexually desirable object, although Barbara is definitely connected spatially with the song and the lower courtyard. The "Lied" and music in general constitute a socially, consciously acceptable substitute, a symbolic representation of a repressed sexual drive, which perhaps nowhere becomes more transparent than in Jakob's description of harmony reaching a climax with "die Wunder der Bindung und Umkehrung, wodurch auch die Sekunde zur Gnade gelangt in den Schoß des Wohlklangs" (55). For Jakob, adding words to a song corresponds to "wie die Kinder Gottes sich verbanden mit den Töchtern der Erde" (55), a lowering of the divine origin of the music. But religion, like music, has its roots deeply embedded in the unconscious realm of the life instinct, and for one of the daughters of the earth, Barbara, who has a firm grasp on reality, the words are significantly more important than the music.

Barbara, solely as the bearer of the song, now becomes the object of Jakob's quest, one which is characterized frequently by excess. At their first confrontation, he describes the melody and in so doing renders a spatial image of his own life and indirectly of the fate of the ideal in the

"Vormärz." The melody "steigt gleich anfangs in die Höhe" (Jakob's search for the higher realm), "kehrt dann in sein Inwendiges zurück" (unable to find what he desires in the real world, he withdraws into himself) "und hört ganz leise auf" (—an intimation of his death) (59). As Barbara sings the song, "wobei sie das Haupt duckte, so schön, so lieblich" (59), she is physically transformed in the eyes of the fiddler into a concrete representation of the beauty she reproduces, and he grasps her hand to kiss it, an unheard-of, immoderate act in terms of his past life, but comparable to the passionate embrace of his violin. Because of Barbara's status as the mere material link with the immaterial and because of Jakob's psychological makeup, their relationship is based from the very beginning upon a misunderstanding of which neither is aware. By definition alone one cannot be conscious of the unconscious and hence I feel that Politzer goes too far when he maintains: "Was jedoch Barbara anlangt, so betrügt Jakob sie mit ihrem Lied, noch ehe er ihrer ansichtig geworden ist."[30] If it is a case of deception, it is not a conscious one.

After approximately three weeks, Jakob, in his desperation to have the notes of the song, resolves to visit the grocer's shop, and, in order to avoid suspicion, leaves his hat at home. Whereas the violin may be said to stand for the ideal aspirations of the protagonist, the hat leitmotif reflects the demands of the real world, and therefore it is also fitting that Jakob, in leaving the seclusion of his room to descend to the street in search of his ideal, leaves the hat behind. He is like a fish out of water. On a sociological level, it is indicative and prophetic of social degradation as noted by Barbara's father: "Ein Herr aus der Kanzlei? rief er, im Dunkeln, ohne Hut?" (62), and the fall is quick to assert itself. Jakob is obliged to leave home and Barbara is refused permission to enter the chancellery. Eventually, the fiddler's social decline is complete as he becomes a salesman in the store. This whole episode conducted on the ground level underlines his unsuccessful attempt to find some security, warmth and understanding in the day-to-day world of the shop, but events continue to prove that he remains singularly unfitted for this realm where "Von Musik oder Gesang . . . nie die Rede [war]" (68) and where profit, not politeness, counts.

One of the most memorable sequences in the Novelle is the series of events leading up to the kiss through the glass door. Coming upon the unsuspecting Barbara as she sings the song, Jakob is overcome by a self-induced vision triggered by the music: "Sie aber zwitscherte wie eine Grasmücke, die am Bache das Hälslein wäscht und das Köpfchen herumwirft und die Federn sträubt und wieder glättet mit dem Schnäblein" (68). Associating himself with the image, the fiddler becomes the hunter "auf grünen Wiesen" (68), stalking his prey. It would seem to me that sexual overtones are definitely present in this bird fantasy, although Politzer characterizes it as a "Vision, in der alles Erotische fehlt."[31] It is after all a bathing bird and one may recall that Leda, when she was raped by Zeus in the form of a swan, was bathing.[32] Also, to represent the loved one as a bird which the male hunter wishes to capture and put in a cage as his sole property is a well-known literary motif. In Jakob's mind the bird becomes synonymous with the music; the song, and for that matter the bird image in general as it appears in symbolic form in a dream sequence, are sublimations of the life instinct. Hence, he internalizes the whole experience so that "das Lied nicht mehr von außen, daß es aus mir herauszutönen schien, ein Gesang der Seelen" (68-69). When he seizes Barbara's waist, his imagination is merely taking possession of the song which is already part of him. The episode underlines his ability to disregard external reality, its proportions and its order at will and fulfils in Grillparzer's view the basic function of music: "die Musik [will] das Sinnliche vergeistigen" (*Zur Musik*, 115). The slap in the face only serves to intensify the pleasure: "Die Lichter tanzten mir vor den Augen.—Aber es waren Himmelslichter. Wie Sonne, Mond und Sterne; wie die Engelein, die Versteckens spielen und dazu singen. Ich hatte Erscheinungen, ich war verzückt" (69). This quasi-religious ecstasy is clearly a poetic representation of a sublimated erotic experience. In answer to Barbara's kiss offered both out of remorse and love, Jakob replies with a passionate kiss planted on the pane of glass which separates them. The staging is especially worthy of note: Barbara on one side of the door resisting "mit aller Macht" (69) and the fiddler on the other trying unsuccessfully to force it open. The image proves that Barbara is physically stronger, that Jakob will be unable to win the grocer's daughter at her level, that of the real world where the incident takes place, and that the fiddler is capable of passion which normally, however, has been obliged to find an outlet in the realm of subjective music. The kiss offered through the glass suggests his ineffectiveness in life and the resultant inappropriateness of their possible union. He must continue to deny his sexual drive any direct expression as if life were compelling him to lead an existence of self-denial, of half-measures. Since his childhood upbringing failed to develop or encourage the vitality necessary for survival, a mere pane of glass imposes an insurmountable obstacle. Again a hat, this time the grocer's (i.e., crass reality), which Jakob takes in his confusion by mistake, is utilized by Grillparzer as a concrete indication of a total loss of balance in his state of emotional upheaval on the ground floor.

The unsuitability of Jakob's presence in the lower realm is fully confirmed by the loss of his legacy through extreme naivety, his forced expulsion from the grocery store (paralleling his forced entry, on both occasions at the hands of Barbara's father) and his resigned, almost contented return to his upper room and its seclusion which is broken by Barbara's first and last visit. Here the up-down distinction is crucial to our interpretation. Having returned Jakob's belongings and offered her advice, Barbara descends the steps towards the street: "Wie ich aber die erste Stufe hinabstieg, sprach sie von *unten herauf*: 'Bleiben Sie!' und ging die Treppe vollends *hinab* und zum Tore hinaus" (57). The fact that she was able for a few brief minutes to climb up to Jakob's level intimates the drive within her towards a more refined, more ideal existence, but the distance that finally separates them, not unlike the glass pane, proves unbridgeable. Barbara's awareness of Jakob's inability to survive down below, where a life of suffering and deception would be inevitable, Grillparzer has succinctly captured in her command "Bleiben Sie!" Out of sheer financial necessity, she must go down "unter die groben Leute" and remain there (75), and it seems especially ironic if not tragic that she should be required to marry of all people a butcher. What could be more down-to-earth than a man who deals in animal flesh?

In the recounting of the flood which struck the Brigittenau with devastating effects, the narrator emphasizes the fid-

dler's relative security in his upper sphere. "Für des alten Mannes Leben schien nichts zu besorgen, wohnte er doch *hoch oben* am Dache, indes *unter* den Bewohnern der Erdgeschosse sich der Tod seine nur zu häufigen Opfer aussersehen hatte" (78). This same spatial distinction is also made by the "Gärtnerin": "Die ehrliche Seele saß da *oben* sicher in seiner Kammer" (79). If Jakob had adhered to Barbara's warning and had remained in the safety of his room, he would have been unharmed, but hearing the cries of drowning children, he descended and was destroyed. However, as Benno von Wiese has pointed out,[33] Grillparzer does not permit his protagonist the luxury of an heroic end. His return into the water, which then reached his chest, to save "Steuerbücher und die paar Gulden Papiergeld im Wandschrank" (79), not the rescue of the children, caused his death. Because money dictated Barbara's decision to go down "unter die groben Leute" and because it represented the sole reason why the fiddler ever left the safety of his room to earn a living by educating the people down below (with the exception of the final descent which was motivated by compassion), Jakob may be seen as a victim of the growing materialism of the times which Grillparzer deplored. However, his "Phantasie" (79) again came to his aid as he approached the final escape. "Denn er musizierte in einem fort, mit der Stimme nämlich, und schlug den Takt und gab Lektionen" (79). If we bear in mind the erotic undercurrent in Jakob's music as indicated by the narrator's description of his playing and by the fiddler's own explanation of the miracle of harmony, we come to realize that love and music are inextricably intertwined in a somewhat pathetic "Liebestod." "[Er] richtete sich plötzlich im Bette auf, wendete Kopf und Ohr seitwärts, als ob er in der Entfernung etwas gar Schönes hörte, lächelte, sank zurück und war tot" (79). There is created a strong suggestion in the spatial relationship implied in "Entfernung"—that which is just out of one's reach—of an ideal realm of celestial music. A smile upon his face, he sank back, submitting willingly to death, or in terms of his song he "hört[e] ganz leise auf" (59). The peace, calm, and confidence produced by his subjective illusion seems strangely out of proportion with the horror and concern of those who managed to survive the flood and who, in administering to the old man, "mehr dabei litten, als er selbst" (79).

To what conclusion then does an investigation of spatial relationships or proportion and disproportion in *Der arme Spielmann* lead? In a revealing analysis of the endings of Grillparzer's dramas, Herbert Seidler has observed: "Grillparzer gestaltet immer wieder den Widerspruch zwischen der Unvollkommenheit und Brüchigkeit der menschlich-geschichtlichen Welt und der göttlichen Seinsordnung in der Gesamtschöpfung. Diese göttliche Seinsordnung führt, weil sie die irdische überwölbt, doch zu einer letzten Geschlossenheit und Sinngebung. In dieser Auffassung wirkt noch die barock-christliche Weltan-schauung bei Grillparzer weiter. Zugleich aber erlebt und erkennt Grillparzer als Mensch des beginnenden positivistischen Zeitalters die langsam sich enthüllende Ungeborgenheit des modernen Menschen, dem jene überwölbende und sinnschließende göttliche Weltordnung fragwürdig wird und entschwindet."[34] Of course, the metaphysical superstructure can also be perceived in this "Novelle": the fiddler plays God, the "Gärtnerin," a simple woman from the people, is convinced that after Jakob's death he "musiziert jetzt mit den lieben Engeln" (79), and the description of Jakob's last moments as he responds to a celestial music and wills his removal to its source finds a parallel in Rudolf's departure in *Ein Bruderzwist in Habsburg*, a drama in which Rudolf adheres to the clear distinction between the two realms as described by Seidler. Is the issue merely left open, as M.W. Swales would have us believe? "It is because of the narrator's determination to state the intellectual problem [ideal versus real] and to have it as something open that the story itself is at all possible."[35] Grillparzer once wrote in his diary, "Die Novelle ist das Herabneigen der Poesie zur Prosa."[36] Art, the goddess whom Grillparzer worshipped and who to him was synonymous with the poetic drama, always enabled the dramatist to bridge the abyss by means of poetic apotheosis, perhaps best exemplified in Sappho's suicide. The Novelle, by Grillparzer's own definition more firmly anchored in the real, provided him with the opportunity to demonstrate reluctantly the ultimate triumph of life over the ideal.[37] Spatially, this unavoidable recognition is rendered in concrete, visible form by Jakob's position on the causeway, the location of his upper room with its chalk-line, which reality in the form of the workmen refuses to respect, and in the preponderant role of money in the lower realm, which Jakob, despite his subjective defence and escape mechanism, cannot ignore and which ultimately brings about his death. But above all, Grillparzer's amazingly accurate and perceptive analysis of "dunkle Gefühle" has both called the ideal into question and finally exposed it as a sublimation of a disproportionate sexual drive. "Apollo will die Einzelwesen gerade dadurch zur Ruhe bringen, daß er Grenzlinien zwischen ihnen zieht und daß er immer wieder an diese als an die heiligsten Weltgesetze mit seinen Forderungen der Selbsterkenntnis und des Maßes erinnert";[38] nevertheless, Dionysius, the god of life, demands and inevitably receives his due devotion. Through the medium of music, Jakob unconsciously joins the crowd at the beginning of the frame-narrative: "Menschen . . . wenn sie in Massen für einige Zeit der einzelnen Zwecke vergessen und sich als Teile des Ganzen fühlen, in dem denn doch zuletzt das Göttliche liegt" (39), an anticipation of Nietzsche's statement: "Unter dem Zauber des Dionysischen schließt sich nicht nur der Bund zwischen Mensch und Mensch wieder zusammen: auch die entfremdete, feindliche oder unterjochte Natur feiert wieder ihr Versöhnungsfest mit ihrem verlorenen Sohn, dem Menschen. . . . Singend und tanzend äußert sich der Mensch als Mitglied einer höheren Gemeinsamkeit."[39]

Notes

1. Heinz Politzer, *Franz Grillparzer oder das abgründige Biedermeier* (Wien, München, Zürich, 1972), p. 388.
2. Franz Grillparzer, *Der arme Spielmann, Sämtliche Werke*. Historisch-kritische Gesamtausgabe, ed. by August Sauer und Reinhold Backmann, 1. Abteilung, 13. Band (Vienna, 1909ff.), p. 81. All subsequent references to, and quotations from the text of *Der arme Spielmann* are taken from this edition. In quotations, italicized words or phrases are my own, unless otherwise indicated. I should like to express my gratitude to the Advisory Research Committee, Queen's University, for having enabled me to continue my research in Vienna in the summer of 1976.
3. James L. Hodge, "Symmetry and Tension in *Der arme Spielmann*," *The German Quarterly*, 47, no. 2 (1974), 263.
4. E. Alker, "Komposition und Stil von Grillparzers Novelle *Der arme Spielmann*," *Neophilologus*, 11 (1926), 19.
5. Richard Brinkmann, *Wirklichkeit und Illusion* (Tübingen, 1966), p. 92: "In der Tat, nur ein Dramatiker vom Format und der künstlerischen Erfahrung Grillparzers kann die Gestalten einer Erzählung in knappen Gesprächen so lebendig und leibhaft vor uns hinstellen."
6. Walter Silz, *Realism and Reality* (Chapel Hill: The University of North Carolina Press, 1965), p. 68. "Grillparzer's procedure is, moreover, essentially similar to that of the 'analytic' drama: he starts in just before the final catastrophe and, by progressively unrolling a past action while advancing a present one, he gives to his simple tale an uncommon depth and tension.
7. W.E. Yates, *Grillparzer. A Critical Introduction* (Cambridge: Cambridge University Press, 1972), p. 194.
8. Yates, p. 195.
9. Franz Grillparzer, *Sämtliche Werke*, 2. Abteilung, 10. Bd. Tagebücher und literarische Skizzenhefte, no. 3262.
10. Politzer, p. 287: "[Grillparzer] war, schließlich und endlich, zeit seines Lebens und trotz seiner Musikalität ein Augenmensch gewesen ein Dramatiker in jenem ursprünglichen Sinn des Griechischen, in dem das Theater das Geschaute schlechthin bedeutet."
11. Politzer, p. 174, explains the tragedy of Ottokar in terms of "ein überaus eindrucksvolles visuelles Symbol . . . das Knien Ottokars." Cf. also H. Seidler, "Prunkreden in Grillparzers Dramen *Studien zu Grillparzer und Stifter* (Wien, Köln, Graz, 1970), p. 113: "Ottokars Knien vor Rudolf, vom ganzen Lager am Schluß des dritten Aufzugs gesehen, entscheidet den weitern Handlungsverlauf."
12. Politzer, p. 205, has demonstrated convincingly how in *Ein treuer Diener seines Herrn* and *Die Ahnfrau* Grillparzer uses the staging to reflect the gradual penetration into the inner psyche of the protagonists. "Je tiefer der Blick des Dichters das Innere der Figuren durchdringt, desto dichter schließen sich die Kulissen um die Gestalten."
13. Politzer, p. 379.
14. Herta Krotkoff, "Über den Rahmen in Franz Grillparzers Novelle *Der arme Spielmann*," *Modern Language Notes*, 85 (1970), p. 361.
15. Brinkmann, p. 113.
16. Franz Grillparzer, *Sämtliche Werke*, 5. Ausgabe in 20 Bänden, ed. by August Sauer (Stuttgart, n.d.), Bd. 15, *Zur Musik*, p. 113. All Grillparzer's theoretical statements concerning music will be drawn from this edition.
17. Friedrich Nietzsche, *Werke*. Kritische Gesamtausgabe, ed. by Giorgio Colli and Mazzino Montinari (Berlin, New York, 1972), 3. Abteilung, Bd. 1, p. 47.
18. Nietzsche, pp. 25-26.

19. Politzer, p. 14.

20. Silz, p. 74. "No one can say—certainly Grillparzer himself could not have said—how much of the spiritual force that produced his poetic works was a compensation for this deep-seated sense of failure in his sexual life."

21. Brinkmann, pp. 113-114. "Und was ist die ganz willkürliche Weise seines Spiels, das 'höllische Konzert' seines Phantasierens, in dessen 'Tollheit' doch eine 'Methode' zu erkennen ist, was ist das anderes als ein Sichzurückziehen, ein Sicheinkapseln in ein selbstgebautes Refugium, in die höchstpersönliche Ordnung einer selbstkonstruierten Welt." See also Benno von Wiese, *Die deutsche Novelle von Goethe bis Kafka* (Düsseldorf, 1964), Bd. 1, p. 145: "Diese Musik ist vollendeter Solipsismus."

22. Silz, p. 75.

23. Hermann Pongs, *Das Bild in der Dichtung* (Marburg, 1963), 2. Bd., p. 222.

24. J.P. Stern, "Beyond the Common Indication," J.P.S., *Reinterpretations* (London, 1964), p. 71.

25. Politzer, p. 205.

26. Politzer, pp. 200-201. "Mit erstaunlicher Meisterschaft hat Grillparzer hier [Otto von Meran] die tendenziöse Doppelnatur einer psychosomatischen Krankheit gezeichnet: Leib und Seele verschränken sich im Übel; Innen und Außen verwirrt sich, so daß die Ursache zur Wirkung und das Symptom zum Erreger wird."

27. Brinkmann, p. 143.

28. Nietzsche, p. 44.

29. Politzer, p. 381. "All seine zurückgestaute Erotik bricht hier durch und vereinigt ihn mit seinem Instrument, wie er sich nie mit Barbara wird vereinigen können."

30. Politzer, p. 381.

31. Politzer, p. 378.

32. Grillparzer also used a bathing scene described by Eucharis to suggest Melitta's "Frühlingserwachen" in *Sappho.*

33. von Wiese, p. 147.

34. H. Seidler, "Die Schlüsse in den Dramen Franz Grillparzers," *Studien zu Grillparzer und Stifter* (Wien, Köln, Graz, 1970), p. 137.

35. M.W. Swales, "The Narrative Perspective in Grillparzer's *Der arme Spielmann,*" *German Life and Letters*, 20 (1966-1967), 116.

36. Franz Grillparzer, *Sämtliche Werke*, 2. Abteilung, 10. Bd., Tagebücher und literarische Skizzenhefte, no. 3281.

37. Walter Naumann, *Grillparzer. Das dichterische Werk* (Stuttgart, n.d.), p. 26. "Und doch ist das Leben, das was ist, das höchste Gericht. . . . Nicht weil Grillparzer objektiv von sich so klein denkt, im Verhältnis zu andern, sondern weil das Leben, das Mögliche, so viel größer ist, und er es nicht erfüllt, sieht er sich als den armen Spielmann."

38. Nietzsche, p. 66.

39. Nietzsche, pp. 25-26. Hence I cannot agree with Robert M. Browning's view: "Through license and disorder the masses return to oneness, the Spielmann through order." "Language and the Fall from Grace in Grillparzer's *Spielmann,*" *Seminar*, XII, No. 4, 1976, p. 221. Browning fails to take into account the "disorder and license" of Jakob's improvisations.

Peter B. Waldeck (essay date 1979)

SOURCE: "Franz Grillparzer: 'Der arme Spielmann' and *Die Jüdin von Toledo,*" in *The Split Self from Goethe to Broch,* Bucknell University Press, 1979, pp. 103-21.

[*In the following essay, Waldeck underscores the similar themes of* Der arme Spielmann *and Grillparzer's play* Die Jüdin von Toledo, *maintaining that the play "is the public, dramatic counterpart to the more private genre of the short story."*]

I

The split self has been widely acknowledged in Grillparzer's short story, **Der arme Spielmann.** The work has also been interpreted in unusual detail, particularly in the analyses of Richard Brinkmann and Heinz Politzer.[1] John M. Ellis has drawn together the numerous scattered critical references to the split self.[2] But Ellis believes that these lead into a fruitless biographism, and he prefers to dwell on the theme of "integrity in relation to efficiency" (p.134). This wariness of the biographical is justified only to the extent that the literature has not attempted to explore the identity of the narrator and the Spielmann, except to note that they both reflect aspects of Grillparzer. Günther Jungbluth, for example, has analyzed the correspondences between Grillparzer and the two main figures of the story. He concludes that it represents not only a "merciless judgment" of Grillparzer upon himself, but also—in connection with a diary comment—"a document of extreme self-pleasure."[3]

Of more immediate interest, at present, is the study of Eleonore Frey-Staiger: *Grillparzer: Gestalt und Gestaltung des Traums.*[4] She has treated the question of a *Spaltung* of Grillparzer in his work into the "play" and "spectator" (p.89), or inward and outward relationships to reality. She has followed this perspective into related issues, and her approach gains much from its broad application to Grillparzer's work as a whole. To be sure, she has little to say about **Der arme Spielmann,** where Jakob is a good example of the inward self (pp.115-16), and where the narrator can be understood in terms of an outward self (although she does not mention him). Beyond this, what the narrator and the Spielmann represent and the sense of their interaction have not been examined closely in the context of their function as part-selves. This will be our point of departure.

The relationship between the narrator and the Spielmann fits into the pattern we have designated as a norm for our theme. On the one hand is the Spielmann, with his childhood story of paternal oppression and his unrequited love for Barbara, a girl from the lower class. These two problems precisely match the characteristics of the oppressed earlier self. His counterpart is the narrator, intellectually and emotionally emancipated to the point where his polished exterior becomes suspect. Only an explicit inability to love cannot be directly confirmed in the text as an attribute of this personality. Since we learn almost nothing beyond what he reveals in his narration, his own part-self characteristics must remain largely masked; therefore, we cannot speak of a directly developed theme of his inability to love. Nevertheless, two telling details emerge in his narration: his condescending (or perhaps self-protective) distance from the Spielmann and the absence of any mention of his own social or family environment. We learn merely that when he is not engaged in the new hobby of following the Spielmann, his activities tend to vacillate between "thoughtless diversion" and "self-torturing melancholy."[5] Thus in following the Spielmann he betrays at least a lack of, and a need for, human involvement. Indeed, as the object of his curiosity implicitly suggests, he is the "beneficiary" ("der Beschenkte," p. 152) in their relationship.

While these facts in themselves are insufficient to establish the characteristics of the emancipated type, they gain definition against the broader backdrop of Christianity. Although this lightly but precisely developed theme is not immediate to the narrator's character, it is emphatic in its universality. The Christian symbolism begins with the narrator's attendance at the Brigittenau festival as "a pilgrimage, a religious devotion" (p.148). Later the Spielmann—goal of this pilgrimage—is described as feeling "his own wounds and those of others" (p.160), a combination pointing uniquely to Christ. At the end his violin, placed next to a mirror, is juxtaposed to a crucifix. If the violin represents the Spielmann and the crucifix Christ, then the mirror (in its proximity to the violin) can be seen to connect, through the content of its reflection, either Spielmann and Christ or Spielmann and the viewer; i.e., the narrator. If Christ represents above all the principle of love, then we find here a universal backdrop for the vague "freeing of pleasure" ("Losgebundenheit der Lust") associated with the narrator's "pilgrimage" (p.146). Through this Christian symbolism the festival thus expresses the narrator's need and search for—and hence presumably his relative lack of—love. The Christ symbolism is also directly tied to the split-self theme: "Teile des Ganzen, . . . in dem denn doch zuletzt das Göttliche liegt" (p.148).[6]

Each of these examples appears to serve a specific purpose: the Christ principle is established within the Spielmann; the search for Christ is revealed in the narrator; and the God-principle consists of the unity, if not necessarily of narrator and Spielmann, then at the very least of the social classes each represents. The Christ theme functions here not as a thick gratuitous layer of religious allegory to substitute for any lack of independent substance, but as an element carefully and minimally infused into the text. It is meant to suggest the universality of the Spielmann's condition, the narrator's possibly unconscious search for love, and the unity of the two. The evidence does not suggest a crude equation of the Spielmann and Christ.

Thus the constellation of the four basic characteristics of the split-self theme (oppression and love versus emancipation and inability to love) dominates the text. That Grillparzer also intended the narrator and the Spielmann specifically as parts of a single whole self is clear not only from his obvious relationship to them (as has been noted widely in the secondary literature), but explicitly from the text itself. At the beginning the narrator's description of the festival contains references that are less significant for their superficial function to describe a social phenomenon than for their applicability to the narrator and the Spielmann—the prime representatives here of the two social classes:

> In Wien ist der Sonntag nach dem Vollmonde im Monat Juli jedes Jahres samt dem darauf folgenden Tage ein eigentliches Volksfest, wenn je ein Fest diesen Namen verdient hat. Das Volk besucht es und gibt es selbst; und wenn Vornehmere dabei erscheinen, so können sie es nur in ihrer Eigenschaft als Glieder des Volks. Da ist keine Möglichkeit der Absonderung; . . . (P. 146)[7]

More emphatically, this event unites parts of a whole:

> . . . als ein Liebhaber der Menschen, sage ich, besonders wenn sie in Massen für einige Zeit der einzelnen Zwecke vergessen und sich als Teile des Ganzen fühlen, in dem denn doch zuletzt das Göttliche liegt— . . . (P. 148)[8]

The narrator continues, explicitly shifting the sense from the societal to the personal: ". . . als einem solchen ist mir jedes Volksfest ein eigentliches Seelenfest, eine Wallfahrt, eine Andacht" (p. 148).[9]

The psychological significance of this for the narrator is, to begin with, a "burst of joy, the freeing of pleasure" (p. 146); that is, if we may ascribe to the narrator the same basic motives he attributes to the visitors to the festival in general. All of this takes place in an atmosphere that a "new arrival" might find "dubious" ("bedenklich," p. 146). Leaving aside for the moment the question of where this problem may lead, we find in the Spielmann a corresponding yearning for unity, as expressed in his violin playing:

> . . . und so bearbeitete er eine alte vielzersprungene Violine, wobei er den Takt nicht nur durch Aufheben und Niedersetzen des Fußes, sondern zugleich durch übereinstimmende Bewegung des ganzen gebückten Körpers markierte. Aber all die Bemühung Einheit in seine Leistung zu bringen, war fruchtlos. (p. 149;[10]

"Unity" is not entirely the expected expression for the superficial sense of this passage. One would ordinarily expect something like "order," "accuracy," "intonation" or "proper rhythm." Unity here is better understood in connection with the unity that the narrator, as a counterpart to the Spielmann, seeks in the festival. If this is the case, then both narrator and Spielmann lack—and seek—unity.

This much would establish the story within the bounds of our narrowly defined split-self problem as a consciously manipulated theme. In contrast to most of his predecessors, however, Grillparzer seems to have benefited neither from the advice of a Herder nor from the confidences of a Goethe in gaining insight into this problem. Like Schiller, he may have perceived the theme in earlier works. If so—unlike Schiller—he gave no indication of having done so, either in the text or in his other writings. While he had used *Die Räuber* as a model for *Die Ahnfrau*, as Wolfgang Paulsen has demonstrated, it may be significant that he borrowed only one son figure (Karl, in Jaromir) and included no hint of a split self in this play. Similarly, while we know that he read *Götz von Berlichingen* in his youth, no other textual or biographical evidence points to Goethe as a source for his use of the split self.[11] In short, any of the works already discussed could have influenced him, but no concrete evidence appears to be forthcoming.

II

Having established substantial evidence of the split self here, we should consider some additional questions closely related to the theme. An important stylistic motif, often reiterated, points to the fairy tale, or perhaps the art fairy tale of the *Romantik*.[12] The superficial realism of the story is, above all, belied by the extreme relationship of the Spielmann to his father. With a violent gesture the latter rejects his son's attempt to kiss his hand and then condemns him prophetically: "Ce gueux" (p. 160). When the Spielmann is seen in Barbara's shop, he is presumably recognized as consorting with the lower classes, although realistically this cannot be all that much of a crime. Nevertheless, he is banished, Cinderella-like, to an isolated room, as though imprisoned. This scene points forward, to be sure, to Kafka, but also backward to the childlike exaggerations and stylisations of the fairy tale. Specific motifs suggest Eichendorff's "Aus dem Leben eines Taugenichts": the infinite guilelessness of the Spielmann, totally ignorant of society and oblivious to events he should be directing (the arrangements for his father's funeral and the disposition of the estate); the mysterious "secret warner" (p. 172); the simple satisfaction that, despite all adversity, he has "God's grace"; and the fairy-tale syntax:

> Ich fiel auf die Knie und betete laut und konnte nicht begreifen, daß ich das holde Gotteswesen einmal gering geschätzt, ja gehaßt in meiner Kindheit und küßte die Violine und drückte sie an mein Herz und spielte wieder und fort. (P. 162)[13]

Such tones bring Grillparzer's text close to a Jungian perspective on the fairy tale as manifesting archetypes of the unconscious. The simplemindedness and purity of the Spielmann suggest the Jungian analysis of the fairy-tale archetype of the disadvantaged child who is bullied by two siblings and a single parent of the same sex.[14] Frequently seen as simple or even mentally retarded, this figure represents the undeveloped unconscious—outwardly helpless but possessing great potential ("God's grace"). Thus the Spielmann appears as black sheep among three brothers and is oppressed by his father, with no mention of a mother. The two brothers are then replaced by the two "trade apprentices"—a suggestion that Grillparzer recognized or intuited the importance of maintaining this pattern.

Grillparzer may not in fact have had any inkling of such a level of significance. He may have used such fairy-tale material merely as a useful idiom to express the simplicity of the Spielmann and his harsh treatment at the hands of others. Still, this level—intentionally or not—perfectly corresponds to the Spielmann's role as the childhood part of the split self. The child is unsocialized and has not yet learned to repress completely those aspects of the psyche that form the unconscious. This pattern is also commensurate with his capacity for love and with the narrator as the juxtaposed adult, conscious ego, socialized to the point of pompous sophistication. The idea of a second self, repressed within or behind the public personality, may indeed constitute an inner meaning for what ostensibly refers to the universality of human characteristics: ". . . und wahrlich! man kann die Berühmten nicht verstehen, wenn man die Obskuren nicht durchgefühlt hat" (p. 148).[15]

Just as the Jungian unconscious is timeless and contains childhood experiences as though they were present, the Spielmann's relationship to reality is also characterized in numerous places as too slow, and it is mentioned that he has no watch (p. 158). This reinforces the idea that he represents a childhood stage of personality carried over into old age. Significantly, it also characterizes a major difficulty with his music:

> Da er nun zugleich die Dissonanzen so kurz als möglich abtat, überdies die für ihn zu schweren Passagen, von denen er aus Gewissenhaftigkeit nicht eine Note fallen ließ, in einem gegen das Ganze viel zu langsamen Zeitmaß vortrug, so kann man sich wohl leicht eine Idee von der Verwirrung machen, die daraus hervorging. (P. 157)[16]

In a significant recent contribution to the criticism of the story, Peter Schäublin has focused attention on the music of the Spielmann, where he discovers, among other things, both the distortion into atemporality and the lack of unity as principles central not only to the music, but to the work. He also relates these two principles to one another:

> Es genügt, sich zu vergegenwärtigen, daß mit der Sekunde als Urdissonanz [an interval the Spielmann avoids playing] die Zweiheit entsteht und daß mit der Zweiheit der Eintritt in die Zeit, in die Geschichte vollzogen wird.[17]

The narrator represents this normal temporal progression, as Schäublin sees it, and the Spielmann, in his music, expresses "Regression" (p. 45). All of this supports a specifically Jungian view of the Spielmann as the gifted, unconscious childhood personality juxtaposed to the libido-impoverished adult ego in the narrator. While one is reluctant to project twentieth-century concepts upon Grillparzer, it would be equally dangerous to deny him *a priori* all psychological insights, however vaguely understood, that achieved public status at a later date. Freud and Jung invented neither psychological phenomena nor psychological insight, and in fact supplemented their clinical observations with insights they had gathered from poets such as Grillparzer.

All of these levels—our typology of oppressed child versus emancipated adult, the Christ symbolism, and a Jungian Conscious versus Unconscious—are mutually consistent here and mutually reinforcing. None of these perspectives alone can do justice to the evidence. It is not clear, however, just how Grillparzer conceptualized all this material.

One specifically Grillparzerian dimension nevertheless does emerge from among these issues. We have not yet discussed the causes or origin of the suffering and broken existence of the Spielmann, apart from the paternal indifference and the religious symbolism. The fact of the split self is interpretatively crucial in an immediate formalistic context; so far, however, in the works already discussed it appears to serve also as a gateway to the largely hidden significance of the work as an expression of the poet's personality. This significance—whether Goethe's loss of childhood, Lenz's self-destructive reality, or Klinger's Oedipal theme—so far has served to provide a deeper, individual dimension beneath the common Jungian archetype we have hypothesized. It also provides the individual poets with a unitary theme and foundation for the duality of the split self. We should consider, too, whether Grillparzer also realized this underlying significance in the works under discussion.

Grillparzer in fact developed the concrete psychological character of the Spielmann's "problem" and of the narrator's distance from him—or at least he touched upon it:

"Ich hasse die weibischen Männer" (p. 177), Barbara informs Jakob. Kafka, at least, apparently drew the conclusion that the Spielmann's form of love is masochistic. We see this in "Die Verwandlung" which contains the borrowings of the kiss through the glass and the butcher's helper, as Heinz Politzer has noted,[18] and which Kafka also based on Leopold von Sacher-Masoch's *Venus im Pelz*. Thus the Spielmann enjoys the blow delivered by Barbara (p. 175). (To be sure, so also did Werther enjoy the box on the ear from Lotte.) Kafka apparently recognized in his "Fleischergeselle" that the butcher hints of an opposite sadism. This barely suggested theme accounts for the total paternal rejection that results when he is seen in Barbara's shop. Masochism also adds substance to the suggestion of yielding, against inhibition, to a forbidden desire (at the description of the festival, p. 147). Finally, this problem is commensurate with the chief themes associated with Christ: love, suffering, and rejection (by mankind). Grillparzer, not being Kafka, did not plumb the depths of this form of sexuality.

But both he and Kafka saw that the self-abnegation of masochism is only part of a larger problem of ego. Only suggestions of this are built explicitly into the text, such as Barbara's contemptuous, if unconscious, comparison of the Spielmann to a rotten pea: "Es ist ein Herr aus der Kanzlei, erwiderte sie, indem sie eine wurmstichige Erbse etwas weiter als die anderen von sich warf" (p. 169).[19]

While such explicit suggestions of a theme of threat to the ego are quite sparse, the general absurdity of the Spielmann's role in society implicitly inspires a powerful emotional reaction of vicarious ego-assertion in the reader— and all the more so in light of the failure of the narrator to step out from behind his self-protective distance and objectivity to do so. Kafka creates much the same atmosphere, only with greater intensity, in "Die Verwandlung" and in *Das Schloß*, where the absurdity of the social environment and the surveyor's low status encourage the reader inwardly to reject and transcend an intolerable and humiliating world.

III

If the themes of masochism and ego-assertion are so subtle and implicit that they raise serious doubts about the accuracy of this analysis—and indeed they cannot be said to be truly realized in **Der arme Spielmann**—confirmation of both themes can be found in *Die Jüdin von Toledo*. In significant respects this play is the public, dramatic counterpart to the more private genre of the short story. Based

loosely on Lope de Vega's *Las paces de los reyes y Judia de Toledo*, *Die Jüdin von Toledo* presents a medieval Spanish King Alfonso who, in the midst of a Moorish threat to his kingdom, succumbs to the attractions of the young Jewess Rahel. He indulges his infatuation temporarily, only to feel his royal dignity ebb and to experience rejection by his court. Finally, Rahel is murdered by members of the court and Alfonso returns to royal propriety. In the end, however, he abdicates in an attempt to resolve the conflict between social duty and deeper human emotions.

The relationship between the two works is close enough to contain a number of specific motifs common to both. King Alfonso describes himself explicitly, for example, as a "child grown into adulthood" ("großgewachsnes Kind"),[20] lending support to the suggestion that Grillparzer may have consciously conceived the function of the Spielmann in such terms. Similarly, our connection of the Spielmann's rejection by society with his Christ function is paralleled in Don Alfonso's view of contemporary Christianity:

> Wir [Christians] kreuzgen täglich zehenmal den Herrn/ durch unsre Sünden, unsre Missetaten,/ Und jene [Jews] habens einmal nur getan. (P.468)[21]

A split self also occurs in the play, if less prominently than in the story. As the central figure the king unites others in his personality:

> Denn wer mich einen König nennt, bezeichnet/ Als Höchsten unter vielen mich, und Menschen/ Sind so ein Teil von meinem eignen Selbst. (P.454)[22]

Other passages show that this is more than mere social metaphor. Specifically, Garceran represents the childhood, with its attendant lack of restraint and uninhibited nature—something the king never experienced. This aspect is a rather Jungian "energy" ("Kraft") juxtaposed to the "propriety" ("Sitte") of the surrogate father Manrique:

> *Manrique.* Die Kraft war mit der Sitte sonst vereint, / Doch wurden sie in jüngster Zeit sich feind. / Die Kraft blieb bei der Jugend, wo sie war, / Die Sitte floh zum altergrauen Haar. / Nehmt meinen Arm. Wie schwankend auch die Schritte: / Die Kraft entfloh, doch treulich hielt die Sitte. (P.496)[23]

In other words, both principles were harmoniously united with the person of the king, until the latter succumbed to the attractions of Rahel, appropriately aided by Garceran. It is the king, however, who makes decisions, rather than yielding control either to *Kraft* or to *Sitte*. This constellation anticipates the Freudian id (Garceran, if only in the one respect of *Kraft*), superego (Manrique), and ego (Alfonso). When Garceran yields to the authority of Manrique, however, the king is left deserted by his entire court. This pattern is strikingly reminiscent of Klinger's *Grisaldo*. Where the latter work proved a dead end for Klinger, one would like to have handed him Grillparzer's play with the explanation that this may be what he was trying to do. It is not known whether Grillparzer was familiar with Klinger's play; if so, we would have to suspect an influence.[24] Parallel to Klinger's Truffaldino and also resembling Barbara's father in **Der arme Spielmann,** the rascally Isak emerges as the king's representative in matters of state—a perversion in public to match the king's perversion in private.

The Klinger-like impoverishment of the king as ego, deserted by the harmony or balance of his representative attributes, appears to find concrete symbolization in the motif of the lame leg, either of man or horse, the animal whose healthy leg mythologically represents libido.[25] When the king is deserted by Garceran, his horse goes lame:

> Der Braune, sagst du, hinkt? Nun es ging scharf. / Doch hab ich seiner fürder nicht vonnöten. / Laß ihn am Zügel führen nach Toledo, / Dort stellt ihn Ruh als beste Heilung her. (P.496)[26]

Alfonso cries out for a horse as the symbol of what has been taken from him:

> Mein Pferd! Mein Pferd! / *Knappe.* Man hat die Pferde sämtlich weggebracht, / Mit sich geführt, vielleicht gejagt ins Freie. / Die Ställe sind geleert, so wie das Schloß. (P.504)[27]

The idea of drawing psychic energy from a biological level is expressed elsewhere in the play:

> Denn wie der Baum mit lichtentfernten Wurzeln / Die etwa trübe Nahrung saugt tief aus dem Boden, / So scheint der Stamm, der Weisheit wird gennant / Und der dem Himmel eignet mit den Ästen, / Kraft und Bestehn aus trübem Irdischen, / Dem Fehler nah Werwandten aufzusaugen. (P.456)[28]

A similar motif of the lame leg is seen in the two beggars—one an old men, one a child (suggesting the Spielmann's dual nature as childhood self and old man) and both lame—that accompany the narrator's first sight of the Spielmann (*op.cit.*, p. 149). But Grillparzer does not imply—as the mythological or Jungian symbolism requires and as already represented, for example, by Goethe's Mephisto—that the laming of the leg represents loss of libido. Despite the essentially positive reference to "Kraft . . . *aus trübem Irdischen,*" this energy is too threatening to (the bourgeois?) Grillparzer to appear as healthy. Thus the symbolism is inverted. The laming effect is apparently associated not with the inhibition but with the emergence of sexuality in the king's life.

At the beginning Rahel embraces his knee: *"Sie wirft sich vor dem Könige nieder, seinen rechten Fuß umklammernd."* (p.460)[29]

When finally free, Alfonso shows the effect:

> *Mit dem Fuß auftretend.* Hielt sie den Fuß mir doch so eng umklammert, / Daß er fast schmerzt.—Im Grunde wunderlich. (P.463)[30]

Elsewhere Grillparzer accounts for this apparent contradiction of the mythological significance by equating the right hand with matters of reason; i.e., of consciousness and ego, as opposed to feeling or heart, or to libido (if we can transpose this sense from the right hand to the right foot):

> *König.* Nicht beide Hände! / Die Rechte nur, obgleich dem Herzen ferner, / Gibt man zum Pfand von Bündnis und Vertrag. / Vielleicht um anzudeuten, nicht nur das Gefühl, / Das seinen Sitz im Herzen aufgeschlagen, / Auch der Verstand, des Menschen ganzes Wollen/ Muß Dauer geben dem, was man versprach. / Denn wechselnd wie die Zeit ist das Gefühl. / Was man erwogen bleibt in seiner Kraft. (P.498)[31]

The mention of Rahel's clinging specifically to Alfonso's *right* foot suggests that the same sense extends to the leg. Further, this passage underscores that the laming effect has more to do with will and ego than with a Jungian libido, despite the explicit mention of something like the latter concept, as noted above. It is worth observing that the right side of the body is governed by the left hemisphere of the brain, the seat of verbal consciousness and related social behavior, including moral precepts. Grillparzer appears intuitively—or perhaps only accidentally?—to have synthesized the libido symbolism of the leg with the laming of left-hemispheric functions. In the process, however, the specific idea of the emergence of a positive, healthy vitality, explicitly formulated elsewhere in the text, is sacrificed in this symbolism in favor of the inhibition of the conscious, moral personality. Grillparzer's complicated manipulation of this symbol is symptomatic of the conflict that the entire problem appears to have released in him as a dramatist.

The reason for the difficult and threatening quality of this material is the same one that was (barely) suggested in **Der arme Spielmann.** Thus the Biblical Jacob (cf. the Spielmann Jakob) is mentioned in the play as having *served* Rahel: "Von Jakob der um Rahel dienend freite—"(p. 467).[32] At the beginning the king is "captured" by Rahel (p.461). If these direct suggestions of masochism are muted, the theme of sadomasochism as a whole is not. Rahel's treatment of Alfonso's picture leaves no doubt as to *her* role in this relationship:

> Rück mir den Schemmel her, ich bin die Königin, / Und diesen König heft ich an den Stuhl. / Die Hexen, sagt man, die zur Liebe zwingen, / Sie bohren Nadeln, so, in Wachsgebilde, / Und jeder Stich dringt bis zum Herzen ein / Und hemmt und fördert wahrgeschaffnes Leben. . . . O, gäbe jeder dieser Stiche Blut, / Ich wollt es trinken mit den durstgen Lippen / Und mich erfreun am Unheil, das ich schuf. (P. 471)[33]

Later she sounds—ambiguously, to be sure—as though she were giving the king orders in matters relating to the court:

> O weh mir, weh! Bat ich euch denn nicht längst, / Zu scheiden, Herr, zurückzugehn an Hof / Und dort zu stören meiner Feinde Trachten. / Allein ihr bliebt. (pp. 487-88)[34]

But the king is no Spielmann. Like Klinger's king in *Grisaldo,* he is a seat of the ego and cannot simply succumb to the total destruction of his self-image necessary for the masochist to achieve union of self with his mistress. Rahel recognizes this:

> Ich habe nie geliebt. Doch könnt ich lieben, / Wenn ich in einer Brust den Wahnsinn träfe, / Der mich erfüllte, wär mein Herz berührt. (P. 484)[35]

Don Alfonso indulges only as long as he feels capable of reasserting himself:

> Doch weiß ich auch, daß eines Winkes nur, / Es eines Worts bedarf, um dieses Trauerspiel *(sic)* Zu lösen in sein eigentliches Nichts. (p. 483)[36]

He is only temporarily robbed of the outward layer of his royal self, symbolized by Rahel when she plays with his armor:

Empört sich der Geliebte und wird stolz, / Den Helm-
sturz nieder! *das I'isier herablassend* und er steht in
Nacht. / Doch wollt er etwa gar sich uns entziehn, /
Schickt nach dem Heer-Gerät uns zu verlassen, / Hinauf
mit dem Visier. (pp. 486-87)[37]

Thus *Die Jüdin von Toledo* is concerned not so much with
masochism as with the formidable, barricaded ego that is
driven to this extreme form of love as the only means to
reach the "Thou." This problem was treated implicitly in
Der arme Spielmann. Here it is the central concern of the
play, and it helps Grillparzer to counteract a distasteful
and threatening "Wahnsinn."[38] From the beginning the
king projects a sovereign willfulness of royal ego:

> *Manrique da alle schweigen.* Herr, du weißt, / Verboten
> ist der Eintritt diesem Volk / In Königs Garten, wenn
> der Hof zur Stelle. *König.* Nun, wenns verboten, so er-
> laub ichs denn. (P.461)[39]

When Rahel goes to work on his picture, she removes it
from its frame, symbolically releasing Alfonso as a human
being from his socially defined ego. As soon as he yields
to temptation, he finds himself intolerably threatened by
the need to hide from the court:

> Was fällt dir ein! / Soll ich verbergen mich vor meinen
> Dienern? / Und doch fürcht ich den Schmerz der Köni-
> gin. (P. 473)[40]

> Muß ich, noch gestern Vorbild aller Zucht, / Mich heute
> scheun vor jedes Dieners Blicken? (P.475)[41]

Alphonso's love must be adulterated by the protection afforded by an underlying "contempt" (p. 485), even "hatred" (p. 483). In the fourth act his self-assertion culminates in an attitude of moral omnipotence: "Ich spreche
mich von meinen Sünden los" (p. 499).[42] Equally dubious
is his subordination of nature to society: "Natürlich ist zuletzt nur was erlaubt" (p. 869).[43] This courtly stance is
contradicted by his more impressive summation to Esther:

> Ich sage dir, wir sind nur Schatten / Ich, du, und jene
> andern aus der Menge. / Denn bist du gut; du hast es
> so gelernt, / . . . Sie aber war die Wahrheit, ob verz-
> errt, / All, was sie tat, ging aus ihrem Selbst, / Urplötz-
> lich, unverhofft und ohne Beispiel. (P. 509)[44]

Thus the play vacillates. Alfonso's recognition of the validity of libido (Kraft aus dem Irdischen) and his indulgence of Rahel give way to a reassertion of ego. This, in
turn, is followed by the desire to punish Rahel's murderers
and by affirmation of her more intense reality. A dubious
one-sided assertion of "Sitte" then follows, finally countered by Esther's superior, humbling admonishment:

> Ich aber sage dir, du stolzer König: / Geh hin, geh hin
> in prunkendem Vergessen. / Du hältst dich frei von
> meiner Schwester Macht, / Weil abgestumpft der
> Stachel ihres Eindrucks. (P. 517)[45]

Unable, apparently, to reconcile the conflicting values of
social ego and sexual nature, Grillparzer seeks refuge in
Alfonso's withdrawal from both, giving up Rahel and ab-
dicating in favor of his son. This hardly is a solution to the
problem, for it leads only to a realization of man's weakness and to a general *nostra culpa*:

> *Esther.* Dann nehm rück den Fluch den ich gesprochen,
> / Dann seid ihr schuldig auch, und ich und sie. / Wir
> stehn gleich jenen in der Sünder Reihe, / Verzeihn wir
> denn, damit uns Gott verzeihe. (P. 518)[46]

It is significant that these final lines are spoken by Esther
and not by the king. One does not have the impression
that he is embarrassed and speechless. He has, after all,
saved his honor and dignity by yielding the throne. Rather,
we sense that these alternating positions have finally nulli-
fied his personality as a voice for the poet; that Grillparzer
must ultimately leave him aside and find a relatively un-
scathed person to express his final statement.

The larger sphere of these two (thematically, at least) mutually orbiting works thus affords a coherence only mar-
ginally and suggestively available in either one alone. The
theme of the split self, so clearly realized in **Der arme
Spielmann,** appears largely to lack the sort of explanation
supplied by the hobby-horse scene of *Die Räuber* or Goethe's autobiographical concerns in *Götz.* But the underlying
themes of ego and masochism, only subtly suggested, lead
outward and grow into certainties that are firmly anchored
and developed in *Die Jüdin von Toledo.* There, conversely,
the theme of the split self as such is easily overlooked. In
Grillparzer's work, the split self emerges as a concrete, if
disguised, outward manifestation of an inner, emotional
problem of self and sexuality that he apparently found
most difficult and dangerous to share with a Metternichian
society.

Notes

1. Richard Brinkmann, *Wirklichkeit und Illusion.
   Studien über Gehalt und Grenzen des Begriffs
   Realismus für die erzählende Dichtung des 19.
   Jahrhunderts* (Tübingen: Max Niemeyer, 1957),
   pp.87 - 145. Heinz Politzer, *Franz Grillparzer's
   "Der arme Spielmann"* (Dichtung und Erkenntnis,
   2: Stuttgart: Metzler, 1967).

2. John M. Ellis, *Narration in the German Novelle*
   (Angelica Germanica Series, 2. Cambridge:
   Cambridge University Press, 1974).

3. Günther Jungbluth, "Franz Grillparzer's Erzählung
   'Der arme Spielmann.' Ein Beitrag zu ihrem
   Verstehen," *Orbis Litterarum* 24(9) (1969): 35 - 51.

4. Eleonore Frey-Staiger, *Grillparzer: Gestalt und
   Gestaltung des Traums* (Zürcher Beiträge zur
   deutschen Literatur und Geistesgeschichte, 26:
   Zürich: Atlantis Verlag, 1966).

5. Franz Grillparzer, *Sämtliche Werke*, vol. 3; ed. Peter
   Frank and Karl Pörnbacher (Munich: Carl Hanser,
   1964), p.156. All quotations from Grillparzer's
   works are taken from this edition.

6. "Parts of the whole . . . in which in the final
   analysis the God-principle resides—. . ."

7. "In Vienna a folk festival—if ever a festival has
   deserved this name—is held on the Sunday after the
   full moon in the month of July of each year,
   together with the following day. The people attend
   and give it themselves; and if the higher classes
   appear, they do so only in their capacity as members
   of the people. There is no possibility of separation.
   . . ."

8. ". . . as one who loves people, I say, particularly when they forget as a group their individual concerns for a time and feel themselves as parts of a whole in which in the final analysis the God-principle resides—.. . ."

9. ". . . as such a person I find each folk festival a veritable soul-festival, a pilgrimage, a religious devotion."

10. ". . . and thus he belabored an old, cracked violin, whereby he marked the rhythm not only by tapping his foot, but simultaneously with a corresponding movement of his entire bent body. But all the efforts to bring unity into his work were fruitless."

11. Wolfgang Paulsen, *Die Ahnfrau. Zu Grillparzers früher Dramatik* (Tübingen: Max Niemeyer, 1962). Cf. also Joachim Müller, "Grillparzer und Goethe. Grillparzers Goetheverständnis und Goethe-Bild," *Chronik des Wiener Goethe-Vereins* 74 (1970); 30 - 57. For Grillparzer's reaction to *Götz*, p.32.

12. Zdenko Škreb has discussed the importance of the fairy tale for Grillparzer, as he was influenced by such institutions as the Viennese *Volksbühne* and such poets as Calderon and Lope de Vega ("Das Märchenspiel bei Grillparzer," *Jahrbuch der Grillparzer-Gesellschaft*, dritte Folge 7 [1967]: 37 - 55). Škreb also emphasizes Grillparzer's sensitivity to unconscious psychological material contained in fairy-tale sources and motifs—but unfortunately without discussing "Der arme Spielmann."

13. "I fell on my knees and prayed aloud and couldn't understand how, in my childhood. I once had thought so little of—yes, actually hated—the dear God, and kissed the violin and pressed it to my heart and played on and on."

14. Hedwig von Roques-von Beit, *Symbolik des Märchens. Versuch einer Deutung*, 2 vols. (Bern: Francke Verlag, 1960).

15. ". . . and indeed, one cannot understand famous men if one has not deeply comprehended the obscure."

16. "He did away with the dissonances as quickly as possible. In addition he played the passages too difficult for him much too slowly in comparison to the rest—and conscientiously insisted on playing every note. Thus one can get an idea of the resulting confusion."

17. "It is enough to remember that duality arises with the second as the basic dissonance [an interval the Spielmann avoids playing—P. W.] and that with duality the entrance is made into time, into history" (Peter Schäublin, "Das Musizieren des armen Spielmanns. Zu Grillparzers musikalischer Zeichensprache," *Sprachkunst 3* [1972]: 31 - 55).

18. Heinz Politzer, *Franz Kafka: der Künstler* (Frankfurt a/M: S. Fischer, 1965): 122 - 23.

19. "'It's a gentleman from the chancery,' she replied, flicking away a worm-eaten pea a bit farther than the others."

20. *Sämtliche Werke (op.cit.)*, vol.2 (1970), p.466.

21. "We [Christians] crucify the Lord / Ten times each day through sins, our misdeeds, / And they [Jews] did it but once."

22. "For he who calls me King, selects / Me from the crowd as highest, and they / Are thus a part of my own self."

23. "*Manrique.* Vitality was One with moral custom, / Yet now they have become antagonists. / Vitality remained with youth, as then / While moral custom fled to graying head. / Take my arm. However weak the stride, / Vitality has gone, but custom's true."

24. Fritz Martini has recently compared Klinger's *Simsone Grisaldo* with Grillparzer's *Ein treuer Diener seines Herrn* ("Die treuen Diener ihrer Herrn. Zu F.M. Klinger und F. Grillparzer," *Jahrbuch der Grillparzer Gesellschaft* 12 [1976]: 147-77). Although unable to establish concrete evidence of Klinger's influence on Grillparzer, Martini finds a significant similarity in the treatment of the theme of court intrigue. It is worth nothing here that Grillparzer also included a clear, if undeveloped, motif of the unity of Gertrude and Otto in *Ein treuer Diener*: "Ein Knabe wünscht ich mir zu sein—wie Otto. / Er wuchs heran, in ihm war ich ein Jüngling, / . . . Er ist mein Ich, er ist der Mann Gertrude, / Ich bitt euch, trennt mich nicht von meinem Selbst" (*Grillparzer Werke,* ed. Paul Stapf, 2 vols. (Berlin and Darmstadt: Der Tempel-Verlag, 1959), 1: 471-72).

25. Cf. the discussion of this concept in connection with Broch's use of the motif below, pp. 163-164.

26. "The brown one limps, you say? ' Twas run quite hard. / But now I have no further need for it. / To Toledo let the horse be led. / There give it rest as best of all the cures."

27. "My horse! My horse! *Page.* They took them all away, / Took them along, perhaps drove off to wander. / The stalls have been deserted, the castle too."

28. "For as the tree with darkly buried roots / Draws sustenance deep from the ground beneath, / So seems the trunk, with wisdom oft compared, / And with its branches suitable for heaven, / To suck vitality and lastingness / Not far from fault and error."

29. "*She throws herself down in front of the King, embracing his right foot.*"

30. "*Stepping about on his foot.* She held my foot so tightly / It almost hurts:—In truth it is quite strange."

31. "*King.* Not both hands! / The right alone, though farther from the heart, / One gives as pledge of unity agreed. / Perhaps to say, not feeling by itself, / Which in the heart its seat has well established, / But reason too, a person's total will / Must give a lastingness to pledge of faith. / For feeling vacillates like time itself. / What one has weighed stays in validity."

32. "Of Jacob who courted Rahel serving."

33. "Give me that stool, I am the Queen, / I pin this King to it. / The witches, they say, who force a man to love, / They plunge the needles, so, in waxen figures, / And every jab sinks deep into the heart / And holds and summons true-created life. . . . O if

each piercing thrust released his blood, / I'd drink it eagerly with thirsty lips, / Delight myself in harm that I inflicted."

34. "O woe is me! Did I not long since ask / My Lord, that you return at once to court? / To wreck the scheming of my enemies. / And yet you stayed."

35. "I have not ever loved. Yet I could love, / Were I to find in lover's heart the madness / Fulfilling me, then would my heart be touched."

36. "Yet I know well, a gesture merely, a word / Suffices well, this dream-play to dissolve / Into its proper nothingness."

37. "Should the lover revolt and proudly stand, / The visor down! *(lowering the visor)* and then he stands in night. / Yet if he wished to go from us away, / Sent off to find the army and to leave, / The visor up again."

38. Cf. Wolfgang Paulsen's discussion of the underlying emotional significance of the play for Grillparzer, and its reflection of his affair with Marie von Smolenitz ("Nachwort" to *Die Jüdin von Toledo* [Universalbibliothek no. 4394; Stuttgart: Reclam, 1968], especially pp.74-78).

39. "*Manrique, since all are silent.* Lord, you know / Forbidden is the entrance to this people / Into the royal park, when court is here. / *King.* Well, if forbidden, I permit it then."

40. "What are you thinking of? / Should I secret myself from my own servants? / And yet I fear the Queen's embarrassment."

41. "But yesterday a model of good breeding, / Must I retreat from every servant's glances?"

42. "I free myself from sins by me committed."

43. "Natural is only what's permitted."

44. "I say to you, we're only shadows / I and you and all the others there. / For if you're good; you've merely learned it so, / . . . But she was truth, perhaps herself distorted, / All that she did, went out from inner being. / At once, unique and unexpectedly."

45. "But I now say to you, you pompous King: / Go forth, go forth in proud forgetfulness. / You hold away the power of my sister / Because the sting of her effect is dulled."

46. "*Esther.* Then I take back the curse that I have spoken, / Then you are guilty too, and I—and she. / We stand like them in ranks of sinners jointly. / Let us forgive, that God forgive us too."

Ursula Mahlendorf (essay date 1979)

SOURCE: "Franz Grillparzer's *The Poor Fiddler:* The Terror of Rejection," in *American Imago,* Vol. 36, No. 2, Summer, 1979, pp. 118-46.

[In the following essay, Mahlendorf investigates autobiographical elements in Der arme Spielmann, *particularly the theme of rejection.]*

Grillparzer's story **The Poor Fiddler** (written from 1831–1842) portrays two artists, Jacob the fiddler, who is a total failure, and the narrator of the story, a dramatist in search of dramatic material, who lives and works in a manner entirely different from the fiddler. Narrator and fiddler are two different aspects of the author's own being. Both characters, though in different ways, are concerned with the problem of rejection. Through his two artist figures, Grillparzer compares and contrasts two different uses of art and two different media of art: in the case of the fiddler the medium of sound and in the case of the dramatist the medium of persons. The fiddler uses what he thinks of as his art as a defense against a rejecting world, a defense which works in well developed patterns and methods of pathological restriction and denial. Through the fiddler's developmental history, the reader finds out why he uses his violin to keep the world at bay. The dramatist, by comparison, is open and receptive to the world and to his material (in this case the old fiddler); he pursues it, he experiences it, and he lets it speak to him. However, the narrator does not accomplish what he sets out to do with his story—namely to show his entire creative process. Contrary to what he led us believe at the outset, the narrator does not shape the fiddler into a dramatic character nor his tale into a drama. He merely completes his report on external events and then falls silent. There is a break in the story between what the first half promises and what the second half fulfills.

The break in the story reflects Grillparzer's difficulty with his narrative, the first part of which he composed in 1831 while he completed the rest in 1842.[1] He began writing the novella when he experienced agonizing troubles with his playwriting. The novella is probably an attempt to resolve his own creative dilemma by objectifying it. The 1831 attempt seems to have been largely unsuccessful. Grillparzer had completed some ten plays during the preceding fifteen years (1816-1830). At the beginning of his career, he composed easily; after the first few plays, he encountered difficulties with writing. These difficulties were an ever increasing fear of the public's reaction to his work, paralyzing self-criticism, lack of concentration, and inability to feel empathy for his characters. During the next ten years, at the time when he was at work on the fiddler story, though repeatedly resuming dramatic work, he finished only one play, *Weh dem, der Lügt* (1837). He withdrew from theatrical production after the poor reception which this play got when it was performed in 1838. When he resumed the fiddler story in 1842, he wrote only for himself and with long intervening periods of artistic sterility. The completion of the story in 1842, while not resolving his creative dilemma, may have relieved his anxiety about it, so that during the ten years following he could finish, though not for production, the three plays of his maturity, *Libussa* (1843-45) and *Ein Bruderzwist in Habsburg* (1848), dramas of vast historical-philosophical scope and the less ambitious *Die Jüdin von Toledo* (1851). During the last twenty years of his life, he ceased writing altogether.

The fiddler's pathology would have less interest to the student of the *Künstlernovelle* and the creative process, aside from its value as a case history of schizophrenic withdrawal, oedipal problems, and sibling rivalry, if Grillparzer did not implicitly contrast the fiddler and his use of art with the artist as he appears in the work of the German Romantics, the wandering minstrel in the work of a Novalis, an Eichendorff, or an E. T. A. Hoffmann. The artist of the Romantics is childlike, devoted to art, unworldly, a seeker of the divine through beauty and love. An enthusiast for his ideals, he is estranged or even alienated from his contemporaries. The fiddler is all of this and with a vengeance! The narrator, on the other hand, has few of the characteristics of the Romantic artist of this convention. Yet he is, for Grillparzer, the genuine artist. The reasons for the fiddler's use of his art, the contrast he forms to the narrator, the possible causes for the narrator's failure with his dramatic task, the interrelationship of the two figures with each other, with their author, and with his difficulties in creating is the concern of my essay. A brief summary of the plot of the *Poor Fiddler* will furnish the background for further discussion.

THE PLOT

The story contains many Romantic elements (the outcast artist, his nightly violin playing, his unfulfilled love, *etc.*). In order to distort the Romantic ideal, Grillparzer projects these elements into a realistic lower class setting and reinforces the turn of events by his irony. Among artist novellas, **The Poor Fiddler** is so arresting because its protagonist, Jacob, possesses the singular devotion and enthusiasm for his art of the Romantic artist, the discipline in its exercise of the classic artist but so little 'talent' that he learns to play only a single simple and ordinary melody and for the rest produces screeches which cause him "sensuous enjoyment" (49)[2] but are a torment to everyone else's ears. The narrator, a dramatist and the story's other main character, finds him, the seventy year old beggar musician, at a popular festival and fair in a Viennese suburb. The narrator's curiosity is aroused by the discrepancy between the old man's devotion to his musical scores and the execrable shrieks produced by his instrument. The narrator follows him through the fair and finally accosts him to find out more about him. One third of the novella is occupied with the portrayal of the folk festival, the narrator and his relationship to his art and to the old fiddler.

A few days later at the fiddler's quarters, the old man tells the dramatist his story. He is the middle son of a former government clerk, he has had a good education but, overshadowed by more brilliant brothers and pushed too hard by an ambitious father, he never amounted to more than an unpaid copy clerk tolerated in a government office. Living abandoned in a backroom of his father's house, he heard one day a neighboring grocer's daughter, Barbara, sing a popular tune. The song moved him to such an extent that he discovered music and made violin playing the passion of his life. He visits the grocery shop to obtain the score for the song from Barbara. Because he is seen during the visit by a servant of his father's, he is expelled from home in disgrace. The father dies shortly thereafter and thus, unlike his Biblical namesake, Jacob never obtains his father's blessing. After his father's death, the grocer and his daughter befriend him, the grocer in hopes of getting a share of the fiddler's inheritance, the daughter in the knowledge that he needs care. The fiddler visits them every day, awkwardly helps in the store, and attaches himself to Barbara. When Jacob finds himself swindled out of his inheritance by a clerk of his father's, he loses their

friendship, and Barbara marries a butcher. Resigning himself to its loss and to that of Barbara, he takes up a career as a street musician. After a few years, Barbara having returned to town with her butcher husband, Jacob is once again befriended by her and gives violin lessons to her now teenage son.

The story told, the fiddler resumes his fiddling and the dramatist leaves his quarters in boredom. Some eight or nine months later, a flood devastates the suburbs. When the flood has receded, the dramatist visits the fiddler again to bring him help. He finds that the old man has died of a fever contracted during the flood. He comes just in time to observe Barbara and her family bury their friend. The dramatist's curiosity now fastens on Barbara and he visits her a few days later on the pretense of wanting to buy the old man's violin. Barbara refuses to sell it and, as the dramatist leaves her and her family, she turns to him a face bathed in tears.

While the dramatist describes himself as a successful artist who is used to the applause of a large public, the beggar violinist, by contrast, is jeered and rejected by his audiences. Yet both men are devoted to the exercise of their respective arts. Hence the question arises: What is the difference between them?[3] Let us first consider the fiddler. The mere plot of the tale poses a number of questions about him. What kind of a man is he? How old was he when he discovered music? Is his encounter with Barbara a love story? Why does he devote his life to art? Is he merely a man without a musical ear? Why does the butcher's wife weep so heartbrokenly over his death? What is the meaning of his death?

Unlike most of his critics who have found the fiddler a man "with inner richness," with "the happiness of a heart free of guilt," Grillparzer was aware of the pathology of his poor fiddler. Commenting on the difference between novel and novella during the time he was at work on the **Poor Fiddler,** he wrote in his diary: "The novel deals with psychology; the novella with psychopathology."[4] My analysis of the fiddler will stress the pathological aspects because they have been ignored in the past. Grillparzer's observation of the fiddler's psychopathology depends on his acquaintance with and "immediate observation" of an old fiddler, on his own family history, and on self-observation. Hence the developmental history and the characterization of a schizophrenic person with many autistic characteristics are much in advance of the psychological theory of his age.[5]

MECHANISMS OF DENIAL

When he is first asked by the narrator, about his story, the fiddler denies having one. He portrays himself as living outside of time, in a continuum in which "Today is the same as yesterday, and tomorrow as today. As for the day after tomorrow and beyond, who can tell" (51). His days are ordered in a mechanical, fixedly pedantic way. The first three hours of the day are devoted to "practice, the middle to earning a living, and the evening to myself and God" (43). The fiddler never deviates from this routine even when it might be advantageous to him, being anxious that he might slide "into undisciplined ways, into sheer anarchy" (4). His living space is as well ordered as are his temporal routines. He shares his room with two journeymen, but neatly divides off his part from theirs by a line of chalk which he never crosses. He keeps his part of the room in immaculate order. Spatial limitation, order, and time routines protect him from outer as well as inner stimuli and help him to ward off the social world. He defends his isolation and denial of reality by rationalizations. Thus, for instance, he does not speak up to his roommates when they disturb his sleep at night. He rationalizes that it is good to be awakened when one can go back to sleep again. His denial of reality appears most obvious in his violin playing. He is so "utterly absorbed in his task" (36) that the narrator has great difficulty in "recalling him to his whereabouts" (5). When he stops fiddling, he acts as if "recovering his wits after a long trance" (37). When interrupted in his playing, he is so startled that "his knees trembled, he could hardly keep hold of the violin" (50).

Lest the reader think (as many past readers in fact did) that the fiddler's absorption, his disinterest in monetary reward, his present ascetic and seemingly self-disciplined life-style are due to his devotion to art, Grillparzer provides in his past life history further background on his sensory deprivation and denial of reality. Before taking up his musical career at over forty, the fiddler spent almost thirty years as a copy clerk in similar mechanical routines with a similar deprivation of human contact. At his father's house (and for some time at a boardinghouse), he lived in a backroom, attended by none, spoken to by none, his meals being paid for and taken at a chop-house. During the day, he worked and copied, with great pains and little success, letters and documents that were incomprehensible to him. Required to return home half an hour after office hours, he spent the evening sitting idly in his dark room "because of my eyes which were weak even then" (58). His eyesight, however, like his intelligence, is selectively poor. For instance, he sees quite well when observing Barbara or when playing his scores; he understands Latin well and uses its phrases appropriately. Not being paid for his work, he has no money to buy cakes and fruit from the tradespeople as the other clerks do. He rationalizes this deprivation by saying that he does not regard food and drink "as a source of pleasure and enjoyment" (63). Thus from the time he can remember, he was deprived of sensory experience, be it by touch, sound, sight, or taste. Over the years, he learned to deprive himself by not seeing, hearing, touching, and tasting and by shutting out the external world.

The denial of the external world is accompanied by the denial and the repression of his inner world. He neither understands nor feels his deprived condition. As copy clerk and later as a fiddler, his temper is perfectly even. He sits alone in a dark room and is "neither sad nor happy" (58); scorned and laughed at by office mates and later by audiences at fairs and on streets, he keeps his "undisturbed cheerfulness" (37). Having learned to repress feeling, whether it be anger, hostility or grief, he substitutes cheerful, self-satisfied, and ornately phrased rationalizations for feelings. Thus, after telling of his father's obviously cruel, dictatorial and unjust treatment of him, he comments "my father was not a wicked man, only violent and ambitious" (55), "he meant well" (77).

The Function of the Fiddler's Pathological Art

From the beginning of the narrator's report, we know that the fiddler's music sounds dreadful. Yet he is not tone-deaf; in fact, he thrills to sound. Moreover, the narrator and the fiddler make sure that the reader knows of the utter seriousness with which Jacob approaches music. He not only practices passages from scores of Bach, Mozart, and other masters "fantastically difficult and thick with fast runs and double stoppings" (42), every day for three hours in the morning, but he also plays improvisations for his own pleasure every night. In addition, his street performance during the day consists of pieces whose score he has practiced. Despite the many daily practice hours over some twenty years, the fiddler's skill on the violin is minimal and the narrator draws our attention to "his clumsy fingers" (42). Yet there is more to the fiddler's poor performance than a lack of motor skill. Listening to the old man practicing passages, the narrator perceives the "method in his madness" (49). The narrator's understanding of this method is worth quoting in full:

> In his conception, there was only one distinction that mattered: consonance and dissonance. The former pleased, indeed delighted him, while the latter, even if harmonically justified, he avoided so far as possible. Therefore, instead of bringing out the sense and rhythm of a piece, he emphasized and prolonged the notes and intervals which struck mellifluously upon the ear, and did not hesitate to repeat them arbitrarily, his face often expressing utter ecstasy as he did so. As he skipped over the dissonances as quickly as possible and, too conscientiously to miss a single note, slowed down disproportionally in passages which were too difficult for him, it is easy to form an idea of the confusion which emerged from it all. (49-50)

The fiddler is as intolerant of disharmony in music as he is of "bad" feelings in his life. If at all possible, he represses both. He relishes harmony and uses repetition of harmonies to drown out the disharmonies of the score which he is too conscientious and obsessive to omit. Two tendencies therefore dominate his music as much as they do his life: on the one hand he represses disharmony (in feeling and sound) and, on the other, he obsessively adheres to established routine (time schedule or score or fixed environment).

He further emphasizes subjective musical routine by substituting his own invariant motions for the time values of the musical score. He attempts to keep time "not only by lifting and dropping his foot, but by a corresponding movement of his whole bowed body" (36). The motion, however, is not related to keeping time. Hence, his rhythm is reminiscent of autistic rhythmical rocking, his hand and finger motions in front of his face of autistic twiddling, the repetitiveness of each having the purpose to ward off stimuli from and contact with the external world. Even the fiddler himself is aware of this function of his playing because he says, "close to my ears the sounds I made with my fingers—they came to dwell with me in my loneliness" (59).

The fiddler has shut himself off from the external world. But that does not mean that he has developed an internal world of feeling and thought. He guards against sound becoming, let alone expressing, emotions, thoughts, symbols or ideas. In describing his reaction to music, he is aware only of sensation. When he struck the first sound on a violin, he felt "as if God's finger had touched me. The sound penetrated my inmost being and thence issued forth again"

(59). It is interesting that in this synaesthesia, he transforms hearing into touch. Moreover, as the sound touches him, he becomes the instrument. A similar merger of sensations and of object, sensation and perceiver occurs when he hears Barbara sing ("the song no longer seemed to come from outside but from right inside me," p. 83). The intensity of sensation causes a loss of self but it may also lead to an expansion of self which is equivalent to a loss of self ("the air around me was as if pregnant with ecstacy" 59). The fiddler experiences sound on an infantile, almost uterine level, a level so regressed that a self is not yet differentiated from the mother or the environment. It is probably not chance that at this point, the words "pregnant" ("geschwängert") and "ecstacy" ("Trunkenheit"), appear. We encounter here a regression to a primary process so basic that sensation is not yet clearly differentiated into hearing and touch. We further encounter the protoemotions pleasure and unpleasure as bound to sensation.[6] The fiddler plays with "voluptuous insistence," with "sensual enjoyment" (46). Since the fiddler has eliminated a distinct self while playing, a transformation of sensation and protoemotion into even simple emotions, images and primitive symbolizations has become impossible. Hence the primary process remains without mediation into expressive patterns. His reaction to sound is purely instinctual. By producing sounds, he satisfies the other instincts we see him deprived of—namely hunger and touch, that is the self-preserving and the social instincts. Thus the fiddler guards against the development of an inner world by the elimination of the self through sensation, and sensation in turn helps him to avoid a self and an inner world. It becomes clear now why he needs, for such an experience of regression through his violin playing, a safe, predictable, stimulus-free, routinized, autistically closed off environment. This environment makes possible the instinctual gratification. If we translate the fiddler's extreme case, his pathological use of art, into more general terms, we might say that Grillparzer shows that art enjoyed as pure sensation has a defensive function and is regressive and conservative.

The fiddler's attachment to sensation, however, is not satisfied by any sensation. He is selective and his selection is determined by his early history. He takes up music because of his encounter with Barbara who, as we shall see shortly, represents his mother. He takes up the violin because this was the instrument the rudiments of which he was taught as a child. He plays the scores of the famous old masters because they represent the upper class among whom he grew up and among whom, even as a beggar musician, he counts himself. How much early history determines the direction of his pleasure appears from his improvisations, which the narrator describes in some detail. His improvisations consist of very elementary scale relationships of the kind which the beginning violin student learns ("the single note . . . and interval . . . a fourth . . . the two notes now successively, now as a chord, haltingly linked . . . by the intervening scale. . . . the third . . . a fifth . . . always the same interval, the same notes" 46). Presumably improvisation is a measure of an artist's creativity. While a score imposes a high degree of secondary process functioning on the performing artist, improvisation because it permits the exploration of new, individual and personally felt musical relationships, presumably allows him to get in touch with his primary process. However, the primitive scale relationships which

the fiddler plays in improvising are not of the primary process but rather of the secondary process as it is taught to the beginner.[7]

The fiddler's improvising is directed to self-stimulation through sound just as is his playing of scores. The choice of the sound structure (score or scale) is irrelevant to the stimulation. Since stimulation has to follow some pattern, it follows the pattern of his earlier exposure to music. The fiddler uses the secondary process structures of score and of scale in the same way an autistic child uses a fantasized machine of which he imagines himself to have become a part. Scale and score for the fiddler are part of the protective environment in which his primary process takes place. Their individual sound components produce pleasurable stimulation. By producing the stimulation, the fiddler achieves a stable state of predictable pleasurable sensory input. This stable state blocks out external as well as internal reality.

The defensive system which dominates his music informs his entire life. The fiddler not only denies reality but, selectively and with skill, he makes it serve his purposes. Readers have found him an honest and simple man but they have rarely observed that these traits are supplemented by a considerable unconscious cunning. He sees and understands, forgets and remembers, just what serves his purposes. The fiddler not only defeats his father's ambitions for him but he also foils Barbara's plans for a common future. He remains unencumbered in the pursuit of his regressed existence.[8] Even though a beggar, he earns enough of an income to maintain himself. We can see his acuity of observation and aptness in social manipulation in his dealings with the narrator. He sizes up the dramatist stranger quite correctly and manages, by a combination of surmise and flattery ("a kind gentleman and a music lover" 40), by philosophical comment and learned allusion, by humility and ingratiating politeness ("My abode will be honored to receive such a distinguished visitor" 41), to receive a continuous supply of money. His self-satisfied rationalizations about his art serve a similar purpose. By maintaining that his listeners' "taste and feeling . . . is confused and misled" (43), that it is spoilt by "a few popular hits, . . . lewd song" (42) of the other street musicians, he negates their jeering and laughter and establishes himself, his values, and his way of life, as superior and hence inviolable.

Everything in the fiddler's life and music fits into a very tight and cunningly well-knit magic cycle of pathology. *The fiddler's art is not his fiddling but the artistry of his defenses against inner and outer reality.* How necessary and how airtight this defensive system has become appears from the fact that the fiddler does not relinquish it even in his mortal illness. He goes on fiddling and hearing sound even as he dies. In his regresse sterility and with his pathological artistry, the fiddler anticipates Kafka's hunger artist and negates the romantic portrait of the artist.

DEVELOPMENT AND OEDIPAL SITUATION

The fiddler must have had a profound need for defenses to have built them as tight as he has. In the fiddler's account of his childhood, Grillparzer provides the developmental reasons for the defensive structure. But since the story is told by the fiddler, the builder of artful defenses, we must attempt to penetrate the surface screen of his chronological account to find the real story. His is the account of singular parental and fraternal rejection, a rejection which appears behind the surface of distortion and rationalization of his story, a rejection against which the old fiddler must protect himself even as he tells his story, and a rejection from which the child fled into regressed withdrawal. Jacob is the middle son of an ambitious, very influential but low-ranking government official. He cannot satisfy, in competition with his brothers, any of his father's demands upon him. The enormity of the father's demands appears precisely in the discrepancy between the smallness of a task at which Jacob fails and the momentous consequences of the failure. For instance: young Jacob is removed from school because he cannot remember one word in a Latin poem during a public examination. But his punishment by removal from school is not enough. After this one failure, the father does not allow his son to enter a trade or an apprenticeship, or even to take a paid position as a clerk (it is his father who votes against his receiving a salary at the office). Moreover the father crushes any, even the most innocuous display of initiative by massive rejection, thus acting as if initiative were rebellion. Because of a visit at the grocery store, for instance, during which he is observed by a servant, Jacob is permanently evicted from his father's house.

Despite occasional resistance to and unconscious resentment of his father's severity (understandably Jacob feels the guilt of a murderer at his father's death from a stroke), Jacob internalizes his father's demands and obeys them to the end of his days. For instance, he makes restitution for omitting the single word of the Horace poem by never again omitting what is written, thus playing every note of his scores. Or, Jacob returns to his room before nightfall, because his father had once insisted upon it. He may give his own reason for doing so—his life needs order and he likes to improvise at night—but he remains obedient. From his story, we do not know when his ego was crushed so permanently that he can only live his father's commands; we only know that it was.

A child's ego cannot be so throughly annihilated by one parent acting alone. What about the role of the fiddler's mother? Jacob's mother is almost entirely omitted from his childhood story. He mentions her once in passing ("—my mother was long dead—," p. 58) when speaking of the meal arrangements at his father's house. Having repressed the memory of his own mother, Jacob projects her onto Barbara and relates to her as a pre-oedipal child does to his mother. This appears in his perception of her. Once when she hits out at him, she seems enormous to him and there is "something gigantic about" her hand (84). To appreciate the degree of regression in his "courtship" relationship to Barbara, let us look closely at the visit to the grocery shop which has such fatal consequences for him. Let us remember that Jacob at that time was in his forties and Barbara about twenty. His timidity is such that he dare not approach the grocery shop for several weeks; "whenever" he came "near the grocer's shop", he "was overcome by such violent trembling that willy-nilly," he "had to turn back" (69). When he finally desperately approaches the shop one evening, peeped through a crack in the door, trembling, saw Barbara in the company of "a rough, sturdy man" (70), he was "grabbed rudely from behind and dragged forward . . . inside" (71) to be punished. The

symbolism Grillparzar employs points to the preoedipal, even the oral period, to the context of the child's approaches to the forbidden mother, a prohibition he misunderstands (food and grocery shop, Barbara as a seller of cakes Jacob cannot buy, Jacob caught peeping, Jacob trembling at seeing, Jacob having the "painful sense of hiding something, of being in the wrong," p. 75, when visiting the grocery shop).

Jacob experiences his relationship to Barbara as an offense against his father, an offense for which Barbara's father is just about to punish him when Barbara rescues him. His own father, however, then punishes him by banishment from the family (p. 75). Jacob feels that in going to see Barbara, he has overstepped a serious paternal injunction, an injunction whose meaning he does not understand but one which he keeps to. And more than a breaking of the class barrier is at stake. He does not return to Barbara after his removal from his family even though he could hardly provoke further reprisals from his father. Figuratively, he keeps to his father's injunction to the end of his days and does not marry Barbara even when his father is dead. In his account, the fiddler strictly separates the story of his relationship to his father from that of his relationship to Barbara. If we superimpose the two relationships on each other, we understand Jacob's oedipal (or rather preoedipal) situation between father and mother. To sum up the oedipal conflict reflected in the fiddler's narration: the father interprets any action of his son as disobedience against him especially when this action has any reference to the mother. The child interprets the father's reaction to his actions as rejection and feels it so severely that it crushes him and forces him into regression and into withdrawal from human contact.

Barbara, the recipient of the mother-projection, acquiesces in her role in Jacob's life unwillingly, because she is, after all, a healthy child of the people (it is apt that she marries a butcher) and not his mother. She quickly realizes his inadequacy as a person; she objects to his "obsequiousness to customers" (82) which hide his incompetence in handling cash; she understands that he would "hardly be capable of looking after" his own affairs (87), and that he is a child whom she would need to shelter. When she offers to buy a milliner's shop with his father's inheritance and thus to provide for him, she is willing to settle for a mother's role in exchange for financial security and personal independence. Hence when Jacob loses his money, she leaves him. Being a realist, she sees that he is responsible for the loss of his inheritance ("It's your own fault" 96), that the loss reflects his unwillingness to stay with her, and that she cannot control him sufficiently to take care of him and herself. And she is not self-sacrificing enough to stay with him. Yet she never entirely loses her motherly affection for him, nor a sense of guilt for having forsaken him. The naming her own son Jacob hence is a propitiatory gesture. Moreover, she, on her return to town, gets in touch with Jacob and through the "violin lessons to their boy" (100) resumes her provident, motherly role towards him. When, after having taken care of the funeral, she refuses the narrator Jacob's violin, saying the "fiddle belongs to our Jacob" (108), her son and the fiddler have merged in her mind. Her fiercely protective gesture of the violin ("as though she were afraid of robbery" 108) is a compensation for having forsaken Jacob years earlier. Her surprising outburst of feeling, her stream of tears, is grief for a dead child, her tears are tears of regret and of old guilt.

What matters in all this to the fiddler is, however, that he is rejected by Barbara. Her rejection reflects and repeats maternal rejection. Maternal rejection complements the father's rejection. Hence the child retreats from any contract. His fear of his father (it is both fear of losing his father's protection and fear of castration, cf. his horror at "bloodshed and butchery as a calling," p. 56) first led him to fear any but the most infantile contact with his mother. Having internalized the father's injunctions too well, he cannot approach women in any other than infantile ways. Seeing Barbara (and all other women for that matter, cf. his approach to his landlady in asking for fruit, p. 50) as a mother, he cannot possibly marry her and thus "grow and multiply" as his name Jacob ironically promises. Therefore he remains at the pre-oedipal level of psychosocial development in his relationship to men and to women just as he remains at the level of his first violin lesson as an artist.

Grillparzer gives the name Jacob to the fiddler to draw attention to the importance of the parental blessing in the child's development. The biblical Jacob obtains, with his mother's help, the blessing of his father. The meaning of the paternal blessing appears to be that, by his blessing, the father encourages his son to grow. The son feels that, even if he transcends his father, he will neither lose his father's love nor be punished by him. Rather than a blessing, Grillparzer's Jacob receives a curse from his father, being called "ce gueux" (55) by him when he fails his examination. After having pronounced the curse, the father never again speaks to him and thus it becomes the prophecy which determines the course of his life. Yet Jacob waits for his blessing as long as his father is alive. This seems to be the meaning of his continued obedience to his father. Even thirty years after the father's death, he regrets that he did not attend him in his last illness because, as he says in his usually defensive manner, he could not obtain his pardon and "thank him for the indulgence" he supposedly received (p. 77—note that the German uses *Gnade*—grace for indulgence). In retrospect, therefore, Jacob almost succeeds in manufacturing a father's blessing for himself. But at the time of his father's death, he collapses "on the floor, unconscious" (77), realizing that he has lost his father's indulgence forever.

The mother figure compensates Jacob for the loss of the father's love, encouragement, and care. It is after all Barbara who gives Jacob the only gift of his life, her song, that is: his music and means of self-gratification. While the father's curse condemns him to poverty in literally everything, the mother's gift makes the poverty tolerable. In fact, once the fiddler has received the gift, there is no hope that he will relinquish the pleasure it offers him. Unwillingly and unknowingly, Barbara thus contributes to the stunting of his growth. Our interpretation is confirmed by the blessing Barbara gives Jacob as she leaves him: "Your linen is in order now. See that none of it disappears. You'll be having a hard time. She raised her hand, made the sign of the cross in the air, and cried: 'God be with you, Jacob!—For ever and ever, Amen'" (97). If we consider that a blessing is designed to further the child's productivity and fruitfulness, then Barbara's blessing discourages, admonishes him to keep to the parental order, and thus reen-

forces the father's injunction against growth and maturity. The mother thus becomes the collaborator in the father's oppression of the child. Kafka's letter to his father comes to mind.

THE NARRATOR'S CREATIVE PROCESS

The fiddler's story by itself would be interesting pathology, a fascinating account of what art is not and what stunts artistic development. In the counter story of the narrator, Grillparzer offers us insight into the artist's ability to delve into life, to derive substance from it, and to communicate this experience effectively. The narrator, unlike Jacob, does not live outside of time. He begins with a general evocation of the Viennese folk festival which forms the background of his meeting with the fiddler He feels the festival to be a flood of life. He explains that it is the matrix from which he, as an artist, derives his inspiration. Next, he turns to the near past and tells of his meeting the fiddler two years ago. Once he has firmly situated the reader in that time, he has the fiddler insert his story, in which time sequences are rather vague. In the somewhat too rapid concluding pages, treating of the flood of death which destroys the fiddler's life, the narrator returns to the near past of two years ago. By this ordering of time, the narrator shows himself to be in control of his material. Yet he is not obsessively controlling but rather open to the flow of life. He sees his task as an author to experience "the collective biographies of men unknown to fame" (33). He learns as a dramatist from the non-verbal communication of the common people, from their faces, from their gait, from their behavior toward each other, from their every "unpremeditated remark" (33). He feels empathy with the people because "no one can understand the lives of the famous unless he has entered into the feelings of the humble" (33). The people and the folk festival are for the dramatist what sound is for the fiddler, namely the "raw material" of his art. As the fiddler thrills to sound, the dramatist thrills to the people. There is, however, a world of difference between the fiddler and the dramatist in their respective relationships to their medium.

The most important difference between the two appears in the degree of each one's tolerance of and openness to disharmony, disorder and multiplicity. In the tumultuous flood of the festival, described at considerable length, the narrator, moved along by the crowd ("I had abandoned myself to the drifting throng" 34). In the identical situation, the old fiddler works "his way through the crowd coming to the fair, against the stream" (37); he cannot tolerate the drifting along in a stream of people. While being carried along by the crowd, however, the narrator scans the scene around him. The reader follows his glance as it gradually focuses on the old fiddler. By the wayside, he observes "a woman harpist, . . . an old cripple . . . a misshapen boy" (35-36) before his attention comes to rest on the old man. It is precisely the discrepancy between the old man's appearance and the sound of his music, a discrepancy that rapidly reveals a whole host of disharmonies, which catches the narrator's attention. The narrator, therefore, as he develops his narrative has us observe his creative process, his response to his medium, his selection of a particular part of the medium (the fiddler), and his criterion in this selection, namely the conflict in the fiddler, a conflict which he hopes to use as the basis for a play.

Once the dramatist has identified his subject and opened himself to its individual features in a lengthy paragraph which describes the fiddler in detail, he turns his attention to himself. In a short paragraph, he reports his feelings and thoughts and evaluates his impression of the fiddler. ("So the man had enjoyed a fairly good education, . . . now was a begging, itinerant musician! I was eager for an explanation" 37-38.) But because his medium is not static but has a will of his own, the dramatist, when his attention is centered on himself, loses the old fiddler as he moves away into the crowd. The narrator finds him again after a long search, quite significantly when he has almost given up searching. Moreover, he finds the fiddler in a place he has least expected him to be.

At the second encounter, the narrator moves in on his subject at once to hold it fast. He addresses the fiddler and expresses sympathy for him; he gives him money and openly states his curiosity, asking the fiddler for an explanation of the puzzling behaviour he has observed ("you go away just when . . . you could easily earn more" 39-40). The old man's explanation increases his curiosity so that he asks for permission to visit him to get to know him better. The narrator's interest in the fiddler is the interest of the artist for his subject matter. He is friendly because he needs the cooperation of his subject. He is direct ("I am curious to know your story" 51). He does not pretend that he wants more than material for his art.

On the evening of the day he has met him, the narrator checks on the old fiddler by returning home past his house. He goes by the house in the darkness, hears the scraping of the fiddler's "improvisations" and observes the neighbor's reaction to the disturbing "music." The nature of the improvisations and the reactions of the neighbors together with his previous impressions of the old man confirm the narrator in his hunch that he has found a valuable subject. Thus the narrator checks out his subject from many sides, in several different situations, and at several different times. The entire introduction of the novella is a dissertation on the dramatist's relationship to his material. This relationship contrasts sharply with the fiddler's relationship to sound. The dramatist is capable of giving himself over to impressions and to the flow of people. From this flow, the matrix of his creativity, he selects a character who seems promising. The narrator finds the promise, the attraction, in the character's conflicts, disharmonies, and discrepancies. Once he has found a promising subject, the dramatist examines it for further detail of flawing and promise just as a sculptor might tap a block of granite for its suitability for his special purpose, that is: whether the figure he has in mind fits the grain, the flawing, the contours, the strengths and weaknesses of a particular piece of stone. Unlike the fiddler, the narrator-dramatist uses his own emotional reactions to guide him in the further exploration of his theme and subject matter. He not only tolerates the conflict he feels in the fiddler's appearance and actions, but the discovery of every new conflict stimulates him to explore further.[9]

THE NARRATOR'S PROBLEM WITH DEATH AND REJECTION

When the narrator resumes his story after the fiddler's account, we seem to encounter a very different person, who reports in a markedly different style. The narrator of the introduction to the novella interacts with his environment and with the fiddler as he observes. He also registers his

own reactions, his feelings and thoughts. His attitude is reflective and analytical. His structure is complete, lengthy, subordinating. He displays his learning and his wit. He takes his time about furthering the plot. The narrator of the final pages completes the mere plot of the story in three pages. He restricts himself almost exclusively to a reportage of external detail. He does not display learning or wit. His interaction with the environment and with persons is sharply curtailed. For intance, when he approaches Barbara before the funeral, he does not get a chance to talk to her. When she answers his question the Sunday after, she turns away from him. Even more importantly, the narrator never expresses his feelings and thoughts about events. When he depicts the fiddler's funeral, he even moves from the perspective of the participant observer which he has maintained all through the story to the perspective of the all-knowing author. Thus, though walking behind the butcher's family in the funeral procession, he sees that the "husband was continually moving his lips as though in prayer" (106). The reader gets a feeling of distance from this perspective. As the narrative moves on, the sentences become very short and pithy. They report merely the external, visible details. "Thus the procession came to the cemetery. The grave was open. The children threw in the first handful of earth. Still standing, the husband did likewise. The wife knelt down and held her book close to her eyes. . . . The mourners separated and dispersed. The old fiddler was buried.

This style and manner of reporting is very effective. The reader no longer witnesses the events through the medium of the narrator's consciousness but is exposed to them directly. The narrator has lost his explanatory stance of the beginning of the story, he has been silenced, his mastery over the subject matter appears to have been shattered. The material appears to have taken on a life (or death) of its own. The nature of the flood, which leads to the fiddler's death, the curious perspective on the funeral procession, the cracked violin on the wall, the prayer of the butcher's family, Barbara's silent stream of tears, all these and many more symbols or symbolic events remain unaccounted for by him. We should remember that the dramatist earlier in the narrative promised to be on the lookout for dramatic characters (Juliets, Medeas, Didos, Achilles, and Agamemnons). The narrator succeeded in raising expectations in the reader, expectations of his mastery over a subject matter. At the end of the story, having been refused his request for the fiddler's violin and being turned out of Barbara's house by the solid front of the family against his advances, he is left with nothing. He has neither a human relationship (which finally even the fiddler did have) nor does he have the symbol of even a perverted art (the cracked violin which the butcher family keeps). Moreover, he has not yet used his poetic material to create a piece of dramatic literature (he has been on a journey instead).

The fiddler's story revolves around catastrophic rejection and defense against and avoidance of rejection. The narrator seems to be free of both. Yet, if we look at the story's ending, the situations of the two seem to be reversed. Able to overcome his regression during the flood (the proverbial emergency during which, temporarily, even the most regressed schizophrenic acts appropriately), the fiddler has saved children and his landlord's savings account (Grillparzer's irony is alive even here). As a consequence, the community accepts him and attends his funeral. Barbara and her family even grant him a kind of sanctification as they keep his violin on their wall "in symmetry with a crucifix" (108). The narrator, on the other hand, is rejected by Barbara and her family.

The fiddler's death, however, does not solve the problem of his rejection. After all, the fiddler is dead and cannot experience his acceptance. Moreover, he paid for the acceptance with his death. And personal death is feared because it is the ultimate rejection man can experience. Let us remember that the fiddler made himself dead psychically in order to survive a paternal and maternal rejection so severe that it would have killed him physically. If we take the flood as a consequence of which he dies to be the maternal element, it is maternal rejection which kills him in the end. The narrator may be rejected by the fiddler once he resumes his violin playing after telling his story. He may be rejected by Barbara and her family. But he, at least, remains alive. Though he does not succeed in his transformation of the fiddler into a dramatic character, (we might remember that the fiddler is part of the narrator's creative matrix) he, at least, survives his encounter with the maternal element.

All through the last pages of the story, something threatens the narrator. As he goes to see the fiddler after the flood, death lurks all about him The suburb is devastated. The building he enters by chance on his way contains, pressed against the window screens, the dead bodies of those who desperately struggled for their lives against the flood. As he approaches the fiddler's house, the narrator assures himself that the fiddler has not died in the flood but he is worried. When he finds him dead, he seems shocked. He acts as if he has not suspected the violence and anger of the maternal element.

Because Barbara (in his and our minds) has come to represent the maternal element, it is hardly surprising that she rejects his wish to talk to her. But what, after all, has he come to find out from her when he goes to see her the Sunday after the funeral? He says that his request to Barbara to be sold the violin is only a pretext (p. 106). A pretext for what? Earlier in the story, he needed no pretext to gratify his artistic curiosity. Has he come to find out why the maternal element is deadly? Or does he want Barbara to betray the dead fiddler by selling his violin? The story's symbolism and the dramatic characters mentioned earlier (Juliet, Dido, Medea) provide an answer to the narrator's unanswered question to and about Barbara. The reader understands her grief, her loyalty, and her remorse from her silence, her tears, and her refusal to sell the violin. Barbara represents the love of Juliet who laments dead Romeo, the loyalty of Dido who mourns faithless Aeneas, and the violent anger of Medea who weeps over the children she killed. In the figure of the woman and mother, love and deadly anger are inextricably mixed. For the narrator as much as for the fiddler, the encounter with woman is threatening. At the end of the story, the narrator does not indicate what he understands about Barbara and about women. His silence seems like flight. He has found a drama he cannot master.

Inasmuch as his heroes either founder in the midst of their creative task or are incapacitated by rejection or finally are killed by the maternal element, it is small wonder that the story did little to relieve Grillparzer of his writer's cramp.

And if to die a failure or to fail with his work was man's lot and if art did not help but rather endangered man, then why should he, Grillparzer, write plays!

Throughout his career as a dramatist, Grillparzer was exceedingly sensitive to criticism of his work. Like any successful author (and he was successful), he had his share of trouble with critics and with censorship (this was the Metternich area and even a conservative writer could be subject to the seasonal paranoia).[10] The inability to cope with adverse public reaction and criticism led him in 1838, after the unsuccessful performance of *Weh dem, der lügt*, to withdraw from the theater for good—that is: to reject the public, which had not altogether appreciated him. For a few more years, his rejection of the public may have given him enough strength to go on writing. Why was Grillparzer so keenly sensitive to criticism? For one thing, Grillparzer intimately identified with his plays; they were himself. To have a play of his performed meant to be exhibited in public. Indeed, Grillparzer, after attending and being mortified at the performance of his first drama (a disguised oedipal drama at that),[11] never again witnessed a performance of a play of his. A negative remark about his poetic products was thus a rejection of himself as a person.[12]

Grillparzer escaped from rejection of all kinds in ways very similar to the fiddler's. Especially during the 1830s, he experienced the same mindless states of regression and denial of reality as the fiddler. Hruschka reports that during these years, Grillparzer used "to play scales on the piano for two hours or more, saying that this rested his mind."[13] In his autobiography (1851) Grillparzer, in looking back on the early thirties, recognizes his own tendency to deal with personal difficulties by denial, by forgetting, and by distracting himself much as the fiddler does. He finds that this tendency harmed him permanently. Because of its insight, the passage is worth quoting in full:

> I am in great confusion about the sequence of events. The reason is that I have, until now, always tried to forget them. Perhaps somewhat hypochondriacally, I felt pressured and hemmed in by everything so that I knew no other help but to cut off the tormenting thoughts and to begin a new train of thought. As a matter of fact that harmed me much in other ways as well. Whatever in my character was stable originally (to express myself in a Kantian manner) was thereby made diffuse, and even my memory, which was excellent in my youth, became weak and unreliable through the continuous breaking off and distraction of thought. I would advise anyone who wants to achieve something, to think through his unpleasant thoughts until he has found a resolution. Nothing is more dangerous than distraction.[14]

By creating the figure of the fiddler, Grillparzer must have hoped to overcome his own sterility as well as his own fear of rejection. But even if he saw criticism of his work as personal rejection, this would not be reason enough for him to react with such an anxiety that it finally silenced him and made him act as if his very life were threatened. Whom did the critics represent? Two facts, one in the fiddler's story and one in Grillparzer's life, supplement each other and give an answer to this question.

In 1831, Grillparzer breaks off *The Poor Fiddler* in the middle of the fiddler's first visit to Barbara and her father. The break occurs when both together criticize his fiddling (the father by calling it scraping, the daughter by her scornful smile, p. 74). Grillparzer thus breaks off his narrative when Barbara and her father (who represents her more aggressive, outrightly rejecting self) reject the fiddler and his music, that is when his character experiences the same problem which plagued him, the author. We might then say that it is the mother's criticism, her rejection, which makes the author stop his writing though it does not make the fiddler stop his fiddling.

The kind of scorn the fiddler experiences with his musical efforts with Barbara, Grillparzer experienced from his mother during his piano lessons as a child. A keen lover of music, his mother was violently critical of his playing, screaming at him and snatching his hands off the keys at every wrong note. Thus piano lessons became a torture to him as violin lessons were a torture to the fiddler. Just as Barbara awakens the fiddler's love of music while rejecting his actual playing, so Grillparzer's mother instilled in him a love of music while violently rejecting his performance and causing him intolerable fear and anxiety. It is not surprising that despite his love of music, which found expression in his improvising on the piano, Grillparzer did not pursue a musical career. When he chose an artist's career, he chose literature, the art which, in his autobiography, he described as the province of his father. Grillparzer's choice of his artistic medium, literature, and the split in the story into narrator-dramatist (father-self) and fiddler-musician (mother-self) thus derives from his early experience with father and mother and each parent's preferred art form.

The depth of Gillparzer's fear of rejection can be estimated from his early relationship to his parents. Grillparzer testifies that he was loved by both. The brilliant first born Franz was his father's favorite. Like the fiddler's father, however, Grillparzer's father was an unsociable, cold, and ambitious man. A respected, busy, yet ultimately not very successful lawyer, the father was unable to demonstrate understanding and love to the child. Nevertheless, young Grillparzer was convinced of his unconditional love. This was not true of his mother. A profoundly disturbed, moody and dissatisfied woman, she preferred her eldest to the other children, but probably was not capable of giving much love. Moreover, what love she could give was conditional on what he could do for her.

The parents were very unhappy and often quarreled. They rejected all of their younger children in various degrees. Grillpazer thus knew vicariously from the treatment of his three brothers what rejection was. Moreover, with parents as rejecting and disturbed as his, he cannot have escaped their rejection entirely. Being the most loved child, he had most to lose and hence must have felt the threat of rejection most painfully. The psychic havoc these parents wrought can be appreciated from their children's lives. Grillparzer himself never married. His second brother was severely mentally ill. His third brother, in his younger days a promising musician, spent his life as a hypochondriacal, dissatisfied, bachelor minor official and in many respects resembled the fiddler. His youngest brother gifted and musical like his brothers, drowned himself at age seventeen. At the father's death, when Grillparzer was eigh-

teen, the mother expected him to take care of her and his brothers. He did so and was for her "son and husband," as he put it. There is no doubt that he was profoundly attached to her. She took care of household matters, but refrained from interfering in his "thoughts, feelings, work, and convictions."[15] After ten years of living with him, she committed suicide. Even during her lifetime, Grillparzer was remarkably silent about her. In his autobiography, he describes her death as due to a heart attack. None of the heroes in his plays have mothers. It seems that at least consciously, he avoided dealing with the son's relationship to his mother. The unconscious preoccupation with this theme, his fears about it, and its relationships to his creativity, dominates *The Poor Fiddler.*

The parental love which the child Grillparzer, unlike his brothers, received must have made the difference between his artistic genius and their failure. The father's and the mother's love and ambition for him must have inspired in the child the wish to excel. However, the need to perform in order to keep the mother's love, must have caused him terrifying anxiety, an anxiety which could easily lead to artistic paralysis. In any case, fear of his mother's rejection and of demands on him was greater than fear of his father's rejection. Hence, he chose an artistic career associated with his father's domain rather than with the music of his mother. Then, when he became exposed to the reaction to his plays of critics and the public, public criticism reactivated in his mind the early parental rejection, the mother's voice probably being louder than the father's. But since early parental rejection and criticism are deeply internalized, the awakening of their voices through public criticism became self-criticism and self-rejection. And self-rejection inspired by these parents could not have been an easy matter to deal with!

In writing *The Poor Fiddler* Grillparzer attempted a confrontation between his internalized mother-self, the fiddler, and his father-self, the narrator.[16] The narrator, who is the healthier part of Grillparzer's self, searches out the weaker, less developed part (the self Grillparzer would have become had he chosen the mother's art, music). The self with the greater ego-capacity (as represented by created mastery of reality, education, success, social standing) seeks the other in order to understand him, to make himself master over him, and to incorporate him or to cast him off. Yet, the mother-self is too regressed to allow assimilation through interaction or through conflict. Though the narrator perceives him as a conflicted subject, the fiddler does not lend himself to dramatic treatment. He is simply too autistic and too pathological. He is not a fit subject for drama. Hence after his first visit, the narrator leaves the fiddler to his fiddling and goes on his way. But the narrator cannot cast off the fiddler. At the end of the narrative and at the fiddler's death, there appears behind the fiddler's figure the flood, the maternal element, a Barbara grown to mythical proportions, and rejections unto death. And we realize then that the fiddler contained death all along. In his regressed and autistic state, the fiddler was death in life all along.

Thus, from an understanding of Grillparzer's biography, we derive insight into the narrator's dilemma. The narrator experiences material destructiveness through his encounter with the fiddler and withdraws in awe. From Grillparzer's biography and from our understanding of what this story meant to him, we can also appreciate Grillparzer's courage in writing the fiddler's and the narrator's story and in finishing the novella and further plays. Sooner or later, all creative activity put Grillparzer in touch with the deadly core which the narrator discovered in the fiddler and which Grillparzer felt in himself. And because Grillparzer had so little of a blessing from his father, it is not surprising that he finally fell silent as an author.

Notes

1. The manuscript of *The Poor Fiddler* shows how difficult its writing must have been for Grillparzer. The manuscript of the working copy of the first half of the story has many breaks, the author stopping often after only a few lines. The manuscriupt thus gives the impression of Grillparzer's working against resistance. Halfway through the fiddler's account, the manuscript breaks off. One reason for not completing the story at this time was the state of mind in which Grillparzer found himself as a result of the harsh criticism accorded the first performance of his play *Des Meers und der Liebe Wellen* in Spring, 1831. This increased his self criticism and hence his writing problems.

2. Franz Grillparzer, *The Poor Fiddler*, translated by Alexander and Elizabeth Henderson, Frederick Ungar Publishing Co., New York, 1967. All text references will be to this translation, the page reference following the quotation in parenthesis.

3. Heinz Politzer in *Franz Grillparzer's "Der arme Spielmann,"* J. B. Metzlersche Verlagsbuchhandlung, Stuttgart, 1967 and in *Franz Grillparzer oder das abgründige Biedermeier*, Verlag Fritz Molden, Wien, München, Zürich, 1972, and John M. Ellis in *Narration in the German Novelle: Theory and Interpretation*, Cambridge University Press, Cambridge, 1974, reflect two important critical attitudes to the narrator-fiddler problem. Politzer sees, as I do, the two figures as aspects of the author, and gives an excellent analysis of the fiddler's relationship to his father. He overlooks the severity of the pathology in the portrayal of the fiddler. Furthermore, he does not consider, as I do, the creative process and its failure to be the theme of the novella. Ellis pays more attention to the narrator than do most other critics of the novella. However, he considers the relationship between narrator and fiddler from an ethical perspective, a point of view which blinds him to the theme of creation. Ellis' account, however, contains the most recent bibliography on the novella and a valuable summing up of the most important recent critical literature in German and English.

4. Grillparzer, *Sämtliche Werke*, II: 4, p. 286. Author's translation. Grillparzer seems to mean that because the novella is a shorter piece of fiction than the novel, the author depends more on the extreme states of the psyche which produce a stronger and more suggestive effect on the reader.

5. None of the fiddler's individual characteristics are obviously pathological in themselves (such as hallucinations would be). It is their interplay and the severity of the regression which constitutes the pathology. As in the second stage of chronic schizophrenia, the fiddler's symptoms seem to have achieved an equilibrium while the more glaring symptoms have disappeared.

6. Cf. Silvano Arieti: *The Intrapsychic Self: Feeling, Cognition and Creativity in Health and Mental Illness*, Basic Books, Inc., Publishers, New York, London, 1967. Arieti's distinctions are particularly helpful, as they make clear on what level the fiddler experiences music, that is sound. When the fiddler says in reference to music that he finds other musicians lacking because "they play Wolfgang Amadeus Mozart and Johann Sebastian Bach, but no one plays God" (60), he associates sound itself, the protoemotion "pleasant sensation," with God. This protoemotion of pleasure in the sensation of sound has, for the fiddler, the force of an instinct, or rather it is clearly a substitution for an instinct.

7. Much has been made of the fiddler's remark that none but himself "plays God" (p. 60), that his interest is in playing as such, in the elements of music itself, "the whole heavenly edifice" (61). The elements the fiddler refers to are, however, rudimentary secondary process structures of scale and basic harmony. He could not tolerate the disharmony inherent in new combinations of sounds which are in fact characteristic of the primary process in music, cf. Anton Ehrenzweig: *The Psychoanalysis of Artistic Vision and Hearing: An Introduction to a Theory of Unconscious Perception*, The Julian Press, Inc., New York, 1953, particularly chapter 5. The reader might also think of the quality of Adrian Leverkühn's music and his creative exploration of, for instance, glissando effects, in Thomas Mann's *Doctor Faustus* (1948).

8. Politzer gives a detailed account of the fiddler's forgetting and of the skill with which his unconscious outwits his father as well as Barbara. Politzer in his two studies on the fiddler is concerned with sibling and father relationship. Like Grillparzer himself, Politzer omits the figure of the mother and her influence on the father-son-relationship; hence he stresses somewhat different aspects of the father-son problem.

9. A number of other contrasts between fiddler and narrator: While the fiddler's sacred hours for improvisation are at night, the narrator-dramatist's hours "of special value," presumably his hours for composition, are in the morning, like Grillparzer's own. The narrator is vastly more educated and sophisticated than the fiddler, he is wealthy and successful.

10. Grillparzer's problems with critics and censors were not all imagined. To mention the most outrageous case: in 1829, Francis I, after the performance of the perfectly loyal play *Ein treuer Diener seines Herrn* offered to buy the play so that it would never be performed again. Such treatment of his loyalty must have been a fearful threat to Grillparzer.

11. Politzer, *Franz Grillparzer oder das abgründige Biedermeier*, "Ödipus in Wien," p. 58-80.

12. This sensitivity is reflected in the following excerpt from his diary of 1928: "Unqualified applause surely would have raised me into the highest poet; the

continual squabbling and downgrading of the critics, however, leaves too much room for my hypochondria." *Sämtliche Werke*, Hanser edition, vol. IV, 443.

13. *Sämtliche Werke*, vol. 22, p. 64.

14. *Sämtliche Werke*, Hanser edition, vol. IV, pp. 163-164.

15. *Sämtliche Werke*, vol. XVI, 138.

16. On the father/mother-self as identifications, cf. Freud's *Group Psychology and the Analysis of the Ego*, VII, "Identification," *St. Ed.*, 18, p. 107, "identification is the earliest and original form of emotional tie . . .". In regression, "object-choice is turned back into identification—the ego assumes the characteristics of the object." The two characters, father-self and mother-self, both of which represent early internalizations, demonstrate nicely that the creative process of the author in forming his fictional characters, on the unconscious level, follows a parallel course and has a similar function as does symptom formation in pathology. For instance, the author experiences discomfort (anxiety, stress, cannot write). His psyche regresses to an earlier stage (oral-anal, cf. the oral symbolism which dominates the fiddler's account). The author then externalizes the early introjections as symptoms or characters. With respect to psychic origins, the fiddler's fiddling and Grillparzer's invention of his two characters do not differ. The purpose for which the author and the fiddler use their respective externalizations, makes one of the differences between pathology and art.

Ian F. Roe (essay date 1981)

SOURCE: "'Der arme Spielmann' and the Role of Compromise in Grillparzer's Work," in *The Germanic Review*, Vol. LVI, No. 4, Fall, 1981, pp. 134-39.

[In the following essay, Roe likens the character of Jacob with similar protagonists in Grillparzer's mature plays.]

Grillparzer's *Der arme Spielmann* has in recent years attracted considerable critical attention, and the debate concerning Jakob's negative or positive qualities shows no sign of ending. Nevertheless, as the titles of the two most recent full studies of Grillparzer's work indicate,[1] there is still a tendency to treat his one major prose-work in isolation from the dramas or, at best, to consider its relevance in an understanding of the author himself. Such biographical links are certainly of considerable interest: the echoes of the *Selbstbiographie* are only too obvious, whilst the ambivalent attitude of the narrator to the masses and their festival reflects Grillparzer's own equivocal approach to the emergence of nationalism and liberalism in the period which culminated in the upheavals of 1848. But in addition one may seek to demonstrate that in the picture of Jakob's isolation and artistic failure, despite all his acclaimed moral standards, there are clear links with similar characters in Grillparzer's mature plays.

As early as 1822 Grillparzer had suggested in his diary that there was a delicate balance between good and bad:

"die meisten Laster sind eigentlich nur der Exzeß guter Eigenschaften" (Tgb. 1202).[2] Grillparzer's early plays, however, are relatively unambiguous in their insistence on moral values—peace, purity, justice, limitation, moderation, humanity[3]—and *König Ottokars Glück und Ende*, with its specific comparison of Ottokar and Rudolf in moral terms, is the culmination of this early period. By comparison, *Ein treuer Diener seines Herrn* already reflects a more original treatment by Grillparzer of the problems inherent in ethical and moral standards. True morality must never be taken to extremes, as the King makes quite explicit:

> Doch Sitte hält ihr unverrückbar Maß
> Streng zwischen allzuwenig und zuviel.

(11.295-6)

Bancbanus's adherence to peace and justice is certainly excessive, if ultimately to be praised. From 1830 onwards such adherence is not to be praised; Grillparzer's plays repeatedly point to the dangers inherent in "zuviel des Guten," in an "Exzeß guter Eigenschaften." Increasingly one detects a tendency to put life higher than morality, to compromise, however reluctantly, for the benefit of activity and life as a whole. To take the most obvious example at this stage, Bishop Gregor comes to realize at the end of the comedy *Weh dem, der lügt!* that his demand for absolute truth was unnatural, inhuman even, that mistakes are human and a part of life. There is no question of rejecting morality; on the contrary, the plays reveal a constant stress on the need for the ethical standards that Grillparzer drew predominantly from German Classicism, and warn the audience of the dangers of ignoring such values. But equally the dramatic works contain numerous warnings on the quite different dangers of excessive morality in the world of reality and activity. It is these dangers that are fully evidenced also in *Der arme Spielmann*.

By the standards of the society in which he moves, Jakob does indeed lead "a life of failure at every step."[4] He fails at school, at work, in love, and in music. Again and again the other characters, or where necessary the narrator, point out this failure or the inadequate nature of his successes. His handwriting is "widerlich steif" (III, 153), Barbara's song "gar nicht ausgezeichnet" (162), his music "ein höllisches Konzert" (156), whilst of Barbara we are told: "es schien fast als ob sie nie schön gewesen sein könnte" (185). After saving the children from the floods, he dies of a chill because he returns to save ledgers and money. The happiest day of his life is a kiss through a glass door. He cannot pluck up courage to see Barbara, he is over-conscientious at school and at work, he is condemned as weak, effeminate, as a child who ignores important matters.

And yet one of the clearest indications of Jakob's isolation from others also gives a first pointer to the positive side of his character. The chalk line in his room divides "Schmutz" from "Reinlichkeit," chaos from order (156). Jakob himself insists, "die Unordnung ist verwiesen" (157), order was a theme of his first conversation with the narrator: "der Mensch (muß sich) in allen Dingen eine gewisse Ordnung festsetzen, sonst gerät er ins Wilde und Unaufhaltsame" (152). Similarly he believes he could have learnt at school, "wenn man mir nur Zeit und Ordnung gegönnt hätte" (159), if he had been given time to organize each item "im Zusammenhange mit dem übrigen" (160).

This search for order is a sign of Jakob's moral fibre. He disapproves of the activities of "Nachtschwärmer," which he considers "ein widerliches Vergehen" (152), he condemns the masses for their "genossene Tanzfreuden oder sonst unordentliche Ergötzlichkeiten" (153). His music must not encourage such dubious entertainment with "unartige Lieder," instead he hopes that the effect of his music will be "Veredlung des Geschmackes der ohnehin von so vielen Seiten gestörten und irregeleiteten Zuhörerschaft" (ibid.). Jakob is normally a man of modesty, self-critical, content with his lot, but he takes a certain pride in his appearance, upholds middle-class values of cleanliness, tidiness, order, as well as morality. Above all he has a pride in his music, he does not want to be thought of as a beggar, he insists on practising in order to put on a worthy performance.

The only song he can play, however, is Barbara's song. The reason why he cannot otherwise play a recognizable melody is fascinating, and becomes clear from two descriptions of his music, the first of which is introduced as the narrator visits Jakob:

> Der Alte genoß, indem er spielte. Seine Auffassung unterschied hierbei aber schlechthin nur zweierlei, den Wohlklang und den Übelklang, von denen der erstere ihn erfreute, ja entzückte, indes er dem letztern, auch dem harmonisch begründeten, nach Möglichkeit aus dem Wege ging.
>
> (156-7)

Jakob distinguishes between harmony and dissonance, between good and evil notes. He lengthens, repeats the good notes; the bad notes he skips over as quickly as possible. The reason for such a musical interpretation becomes clear in Jakob's own words later:

> Die ewige Wohltat und Gnade des Tons und Klangs, seine wundertätige Übereinstimmung mit dem durstigen, zerlechzenden Ohr, daß . . . der dritte Ton zusammenstimmt mit dem ersten und der fünfte desgleichen und die Nota sensibilis hinaufsteigt, wie eine erfüllte Hoffnung, die Dissonanz herabgebeugt wird als wissentliche Bosheit oder vermessener Stolz und die Wunder der Bindung und Umkehrung, wodurch auch die Sekunde zur Gnade gelangt in den Schoß des Wohlklangs.
>
> (163)

Harmony is seen by Jakob in moral, even religious terms as eternal grace and goodness, dissonance however is evil arrogance. So also he praises those aspects of music which suggest order and harmony (fugue, counterpoint, canon), the learning of which in his youth Grillparzer saw in terms of order (IV, 54). Jakob stresses the purity of music which must not be sullied by common words, and again he sees this in religious terms, "wie die Kinder Gottes sich verbanden mit den Töchtern der Erde." Music is a gift from God's finger, hence he desires to play music "überhaupt," absolute music, one might say; he even hopes to play God himself.

Sadly, Jakob has drawn his theories from listening to an expert; his own musical skill and insight are not equal to such considerations. The expert has told him how even the dissonant notes of a chord are taken up into a higher totality and harmony ("wodurch auch die Sekunde zur Gnade gelangt in den Schoß des Wohlklangs"), but it is clear that in practice Jakob cannot apply this knowledge to his playing as a whole. We discover that he has no ear for music, he is amazed by Barbara's natural ability to sing without notes. If this were not disastrous enough, he tries in addition to play the most complex passages of the old masters. Here of course there is a small autobiographical touch: Bach and Mozart, the musical masters of the eighteenth century, are Jakob's idols, as they were Grillparzer's, but Jakob's inability to play such pieces is presumably also an ironic indication of Grillparzer's fear that even, as it were, with notes he had failed to emulate the *literary* greats of the eighteenth century, Goethe and Schiller.

In the rather corrupt society in which he lives, Jakob's moral concerns encourage admiration. For J. P. Stern he is a man of integrity, of "disembodied good will," Walter Höllerer sees him in terms of a "schöne Seele," according to John Ellis we should all choose to lean in the Spielmann's direction, Heinz Schafroth writes of Jakob's "seelischer Aristokratismus," Walter Silz insists on his "rare saintly spirit," whilst in 1871 Gottfried Keller had spoken of the "Gewalt der absolut reinen Seele über die Welt."[5] More recently, Robert M. Browning has argued that "the Spielmann's playing is a peculiar kind of theodicy . . . a theodicy that leaves out evil altogether." Jakob, so Browning argues, lives utterly apart, in a world before the fall from grace, which consequently cannot be understood by others: "because Jakob keeps the drink pure, he cannot pass it on to others."[6] This interpretation, concentrating almost exclusively on Jakob's ideal, saintly qualities, seems somewhat extreme and one-sided, although admittedly less so than the recent assessment by W. C. Reeve that Jakob's enjoyment of his music "rests upon a purely selfish pleasure principle."[7] It is important to see Jakob's apparently religious approach to his music in more general ethical terms. Like Goethe, Grillparzer had no orthodox Christian belief. Alfred Anzenberger, in his study of Grillparzer's religious views, insists "also war Grillparzer kein Christ," and he justifiably concludes: "er war nicht atheistisch, sondern areligiös."[8] Numerous diary entries reveal Grillparzer's scepticism towards God,[9] although he insists that God be taken seriously rather than mutilated by Strauß, and the Hegelians. Grillparzer saw God as a personification of "das ewige Recht" (Tgb. 641), like Goethe he uses the idea of divinity as a symbol of a higher moral order ("daß das Gute und Wahre eine objektive Geltung erhält" [Tgb. 3313]), and one must agree with Andreas Oplatka that "Grillparzers Blick ist grundsätzlich auf das Diesseitige gerichtet," and with Ždenko Škreb: "Das Göttliche ist für Grillparzer die Bezeichnung für die höchste Ausprägung des Menschen."[10] Like Gregor in *Weh dem, der lügt!* and like the two Rudolfs, Jakob talks in religious terms which one may justifiably transfer to a wider ethical realm.

Jakob however is applying his concern for morality to the realm of art, to the actual process of playing music, not simply to types of music. At about the time that Grillparzer wrote his first draft of the story, we find two significant entries in his diary:

> Die sogenannte moralische Ansicht ist der größte Feind der wahren Kunst, da einer der Hauptvorzüge dieser

letztern gerade darin besteht, daß man durch ihr Medium auch jene Seiten der menschlichen Natur genießen kann, welche das Moralgesetz mit Recht aus dem wirklichen Leben entfernt hält.

(Tgb. 1775 [1830])

Die moralische Kraft gehört auch in den Kreis der Poesie, aber nicht mehr als jede andere Kraft, und nur insofern sie Kraft, Realität ist; als Negation, als Schranke liegt sie außer der Poesie.

(Tgb. 2064 [1832])

Certainly Jakob's attempt to treat art from an ethical standpoint is doomed to failure. His attempt to play only harmonious chords, only the good notes, results not in harmony, but in cacophony. He apparently cannot come to terms in practice with what has been explained to him in theory, namely that the totality of music is composed of harmony and dissonance, that discord can also be "harmonisch begründet." Schafroth argues that Jakob's artistic incompetence is irrelevant ("auf die geistige Haltung allein kommt es an"), but E. E. Papst rightly stresses Jakob's incompetence and the need for illogicality and dissonance in art.[11] Much more vital, however, is the wider context involved; his music is a sign of his dangerously solipsistic attitude to life in general. Jost Hermand describes Jakob as "lebensuntüchtig,"[12] and he is so because he fails to realize what Rudolf II does recognize in theory—"daß Satzungen der Menschen / Ein Maß des Törichten notwendig beigemischt" (*Bruderzwist*, 2336-7)—or what Zares insists on in *Esther*: "das Schlimme will auch sein Recht" (1.277). Jakob may indeed be an "absolut reine Seele" in Keller's words, but he has no "Gewalt über die Welt" as a result; on the contrary he can only exist in total isolation from everyday affairs: misunderstood, incompetent, unpractical. In ordinary life, not just in music, Jakob fails to see the unavoidability of dissonance. Perfection in one's work is impossible, life goes on too fast; people are not perfect, the inability to see this is dangerous in the extreme. Jakob's ideal concept of order and harmony cannot be applied to real life, his ordered life is artificial, a timeless, artistic realm of his own creation. One may, as Roland Heine suggests, see Jakob's life as an artistic whole rather than an existential totality,[13] and the depiction of Jakob's pure life and art does tally with Grillparzer's distinctions between poetry and prose and his fear that contemporary poetry was tending increasingly towards prose;[14] and yet Heine's distinction becomes insignificant once one remembers that Jakob cannot play. He is incompetent at all levels, he is competent only in an artistic world of his own creation that is cacophony to everyone else. One may indeed have a certain sympathy for Jakob, who upholds the cause of morality in the midst of sordid reality, and yet Jakob is a failure in all practical senses. The narrator, who has no obvious moral code, is a successful dramatist however. It is surely therefore significant that there is a shortage, even absence in the story of most of the ethical and moral concepts used by Grillparzer in his dramatic works; the narrator has no cause to stress them, whilst Jakob takes them to extremes, so that Grillparzer is not inclined to suggest that Jakob's attitudes are the right ones. Whilst there is undoubtedly justification for Martin Swales' assertion that the narrator "dare not answer the question whether Jakob is fool or saint,"[15] one may equally argue that Jakob's moral saintliness is also his foolishness in that it allows of no compromise with reality.

The artificiality and impracticality of Jakob's sense of order is noted by almost all recent critics, whether they judge his isolation in a positive or negative light. It would seem clear, however, that the picture of Jakob is symptomatic of Grillparzer's mature work as a whole. The fact that Jakob is incompetent in art as well as in life makes him an extreme case, but he is no more "lebensuntüchtig" than many of the characters in the plays: Bishop Gregor, Rudolf II, Libussa's sisters, the Queen in *Die Jüdin von Toledo* and Alphons also at the start of the play, the priest in *Des Meeres und der Liebe Wellen*. Within our present framework it will be possible to give only a brief analysis of the situation in these plays.

A study of the first drafts and variants of *Des Meeres und der Liebe Wellen* reveals that Grillparzer originally intended a greater emphasis on the laws, customs and order of the temple. Hero attacks Leander, or men in general, for having no concept "ob Recht nun oder Unrecht," but of merely following whatever is pleasing (HKA I/19, 195), and her condemnation of her mother is much stronger than in the final version:

Mit Recht bewahrt man heilige Gebräuche . . .
Wir kannten ja die bindend strengen Pflichten,
Als du hierher mich brachtest, halb noch Kind.

(I/19,277)

Even in Act IV one might have expected a greater insistence on the principles which the priest defends, and one cannot help thinking that this had been Grillparzer's intention. Originally Hero was to be seen as much more culpable, the stress was to be on her breaking of her vows and duties and on her being punished accordingly. The priest was seen very much as the agent of divine retribution, preserving the standards of right conduct, an instrument of fate that catches up with the lovers. In this role he was "herb und düster" (I/19,234), revealing "Verstandesschärfe und Kälte" (I/19,239).

In the play's final version, however, what is more important is that he is "keine moderne Humanität" (I/19,233). The priest can understand duty and responsibility, but not love and the human heart. His experience is bounded by the temple precincts. Marriage he sees as an institution which joins animals rather than human beings (364), whilst his denial of personal freedom of choice is a total rejection of the Classical insistence on "wollen" rather than "müssen." The priest is hence unable to judge people from a profound, humane viewpoint, but only in rigid moral terms. The priest's desire to see duty and responsibility in absolute terms is a dangerous one; such abstract concepts cannot cope with the complicated and exceptional aspects of life that confront them. Moral absolutes as defended by the priest destroy life instead of promoting it, as is true of Jakob's absolute moral approach to his art.

In his early work, and in his poems and diaries of the 1820s, Grillparzer had often longed for "Sammlung," for a state of complete concentration as a prerequisite for the achievement of aesthetic totality, as seen especially in the famous diary entry of 1826—"und doch ensteht nichts Großes . . . ohne Sammlung" (Tgb. 1413)—but also in early notes for *Des Meeres und der Liebe Wellen* (HKA I/19,206). In his later works there is an increasing awareness that such a state is inferior to the ordinary world of reality, however chaotic, discordant, or, in the words of Bishop Gregor, "buntverworren" this world may be. The realm of "Sammlung" is cast in its most ironic light in *Der arme Spielmann,* but its dangers are clearly seen in the portrait of the priest. He believes that only the priestly community can provide the key to full existence (11. 375-6), but in the final version the idea of "Sammlung" appears only once, and it is life and love that turn Hero and Leander into adults, whilst the priesthood is seen as the isolated and unnatural form of existence. After the completion of *Des Meeres und der Liebe Wellen*, Grillparzer makes little further use of the concept of "Sammlung," with the one admittedly important exception of the poem "An die Sammlung" (1833). The idea is however present in *Libussa.*

The realm of the sisters is also a haven of quiet aesthetic concentration, in which it is possible "all die bunten Kräfte / Im Mittelpunkt zu sammeln seines Wesens" (11.1146-7). Yet the sisters show the dangers of such a life; they are concerned with the spirit, with meditation, their search for totality causes them to avoid all limiting actions (11.218,440), they are above human considerations and need to remain untarnished by human affairs (11.128,439,469). Although Libussa leaves her sisters in order to enter the sphere of ordinary human activity, her first plans to found a matriarchal state that is based on instinctive humanity, on equality and complete trust in one's fellow men are still imbued with the idealism of her sister's realm. Only through marriage to Primislaus is a more realistic and practical assessment of political problems achieved which will ensure the continued existence of the state through the turmoils of the future. In marrying Primislaus she espouses the realistic social world and turns away from the sisters' isolated realm of spiritual concentration and also away from her first impractical idealism; her final prophecy, in which she seeks to return to the earlier state she has rightly left, is now beyond her powers and she dies.

For a similar situation we may turn to *Die Jüdin von Toledo*. Like Jakob, like the priest or Libussa's sisters, Alphons has had inadequate knowledge of the totality of life. He has had no time for "des Lebens Güter" (1.180), above all no time for women:

> Daß Weiber es auch gibt, erfuhr ich erst, Als man mein Weib mir in der Kirche traute.

> (11.182-3; cf. also 11.354-396)

As a result he is quite at a loss when he first meets Rahel, he has no defence against her, none of the immunization which the sowing of youthful wild oats would normally have provided (11.851-3, 863-4). But on a wider plane, his lack of experience is symptomatic of his earlier failure to live a normally balanced life, which includes the more instinctive, even the more sinful aspects. Manrique testifies to the King's being without fault, "fleckenols" (1.159), and Alphons himself agrees: "Mir selber ließ man nicht zu fehlen Zeit" (1.176). Yet Alphons is not proud of this, he realises the dangerous side of such a lack of faults:

> Bin ich nicht schlimm, so besser denn für euch. Obgle-ich der Mensch, der wirklich ohne Fehler, Auch ohne Vorzug wäre, fürcht ich fast. . . . Besiegter Fehl ist all

des Menschen Tugend, Und wo kein Kampf, da ist auch keine Macht.

> (11.162-75)

It has been Alphons' fate to grow up as a king, but not as a human being, and his great desire is to be a man among his people (11.94-7). Man, however, needs faults to be "ein Mensch," and it is precisely through his encounter with Rahel that Alphons becomes one. As a result he is able to distinguish between his role as King and "ich, Alfonso, ich der Mensch, der Mann/ In meinem Haus" (11.1519-20), between his regal life and his domestic circle, and he no longer wishes to lock himself away from the ordinary world (11.1395-1401). He now understands the difference subjectively, not simply as a result of "Bücherweisheit" (Tgb. 1330). Lola Montez, in the poem of that title, has a similar effect on Ludwig I of Bavaria:

> Drum kehrt euch nicht verachtend von dem Weib, In deren Arm ein König ward zum Mann.

> (I,311)

In the arms of his cold and frigid Queen, however, Alphons remains the child he was when he was first married to her. She is faultless to an extreme (1.184), but her excessive insistence on purity and morality is a sign of coldness and inhumanity which affects her husband adversely, as Alphons spells out to her:

> Das ist die Art der tugendhaften Weiber, Daß ewig sie mit ihrer Tugend zahlen. Bist du betrübt, so trösten sie mit Tugend, Und bist du froh gestimmt, ists wieder Tugend, Die dir zuletzt die Heiterkeit benimmt, Wohl gar die Sünde zeigt als einzge Rettung.

> (1499-1504)

Alphons had suggested the same at the start, as Eleonore and her ladies went off, leaving him with Rahel (335-6), and it is precisely what happens to Alphons. The Queen, in her exaggerated defence of purity and virtue, in her abhorrence of the sexual act, fails to satisfy Alphons' more sensual needs, or even his more modest desire for a happy home life; Rahel, on the other hand, is described as a ray of light and life illuminating the boredom of the court and its lifeless morality.[16] The Queen is of course "ohne Fehl," but Alphons would prefer her to have some fault which he might forgive (186), and it is for him a sign of her humanity when he detects a flaw in her, namely ordinary human jealousy:

> Wohl etwa Rachsucht gar? Nun, um so besser. Du fühlst dann, daß Verzeihen Menschenpflicht Und niemand sicher ist, auch nicht der Beste.

> (1415-7)

Forgiveness, one might say, is a human virtue practised in the recognition that one's partner is fallible, and as a result human.

In the course of the play the King acquires a full awareness of what at the beginning he can abstractly conceptualize, the need for a balanced view of life which eschews excesses and avoids meaningless absolutes. By the end of the play he has realized the need to apply both sides of his character, intellectual and sensual, to life as a whole. Man should put both "Gefühl" and "Verstand" into what he does and says (11.1366-8), previously he had had only the latter. Similarly, in a late essay "Zur Literaturgeschichte," Grillparzer ridicules any suggestion that one side of man's nature may take over the jurisdiction of the other: "der Trieb, die Neigung, das Instinktmäßige sind ebenso göttlich als die Vernunft" (III, 719). Even more vital in the present context are the ideas expressed in the poem "Lola Montez," written at the same time as work on *Die Jüdin von Toledo*:

> Denn harrtest du, bis aus Vernunft und Recht Entstünde, was das Recht und die Vernunft gebot, Schlimm wärs bestellt ums menschliche Geschlecht, Der Trieb erzeugt die Handlung, die uns not.

> (I,311)

Consequently, in pointing to Dona Clara, Alphons demands that man be inclined to virtue, that virtue be not merely "achtungswert" but also "liebenswürdig" (ll.1910-11), which is the Classical ideal of moral beauty and a further expression of the more balanced middle way that is sought.

Unfortunately, when Alphons returns to Toledo and his duties, having by now grown tired of Rahel, the Queen's inability to think in other than absolute moral terms, her inability to understand and forgive her husband, drive Alphons once again to compare Rahel's natural instincts with the unnatural life of the court that his wife represents. His defiance, his warning that he could go back to Rahel and his refusal to part with the portrait which he had until then forgotten are not signs of Rahel's continuing hold over him, but merely part of his insistence that he now understands his position as a human being, not just as King. Bruce Thompson is perfectly justified in underlining the superficial nature of the affair with Rahel, and in asking whether her death was really necessary; but his statement that "Rahel owes her death to a misunderstanding, indeed to a 'joke' on the King's part,"[17] is a view that needs some revision: Rahel owes her death to the gulf between King and Queen, to the Queen's continued insistence on excessive and absolute morality, which causes the King to reassert his newly found independence and manhood, even if the King is also to blame for losing control of himself and rising to the Queen's bait.

In *Weh dem, der lügt!* also, the isolated and artificial pursuit of absolute morality is replaced by the realization that true morals are learned and acquired in direct confrontation with the "buntverworrene Welt." Total truth is to be found only in heaven, real life is a confusing blend of truth and lies, good and evil. However, although the ending of the comedy seems to echo Goethe's famous dictum, "es irrt der Mensch, solang' er strebt," Grillparzer is not prepared to adopt the cavalier attitude to evil that is the hallmark of *Faust*; in a diary note of 1834, he specifically criticizes new ideas of "Gut und Böse eine Art Polaritätsgegensatz" (Tgb. 2169), and he attacked Goethe for the laxity of his moral standpoint in *Die Wahlverwandtschaften* (Tgb. 3538; III,55). *Ein Bruderzwist in Habsburg* clearly presents a more problematic picture than the other plays we have considered, yet even here excessive insistence on moral values, in this case the ideals of absolute right and perfect divine order,[18] lead to a dangerous inability and refusal to come to terms with reality. Like Bancbanus in *Ein treuer Diener seines Herrn*, Rudolf II is a man not cut out

for the world of politics, he is "blöd, langsam, verschlossen" (HKA I/21,107; he himself is conscious of his limitations, aware that he is "ein schwacher, unbegabter Mann" (ll.351,421) who is incapable of action (ll.446-7). Bancbanus, however, for all his "Borniertheit," is prepared to put his principles into practice and averts a greater tragedy as a result; by comparison, Rudolf refuses to act because his ideals cannot be realized and his inactivity produces a situation whereby men less morally equipped, less circumspect, less aware of the complexities of life, can arrogate the responsibility for action that is rightly his.

The notes for the play which appear to defend Rudolf were made during the 1820s, during a period of Grillparzer's life in which he clearly did see passivity and withdrawal as the only possible way to preserve the higher moral values of life. In this respect *Der Traum ein Leben* is very much a product of the period in which it was first planned, above all in its almost total rejection of ambition and its emphasis on peaceful withdrawal.[19] By comparison, Grillparzer's mature plays and **Der arme Spielmann** make a much more positive appeal for an understanding of mistakes and wrongs, and for the incorporation of them into a balanced view of life. The ideas of virtue, purity, truth, duty and order, which Grillparzer inherited from the Classical period, are not absolutes, and to treat them as such without an awareness of man's imperfections is to court danger and inhumanity, to banish man to a realm of artificial and potentially inhuman isolation. Grillparzer's more mature approach is expressed in the words of Zares in *Esther*:

> Niemand ist rein. Das Schlimme will auch sein Recht; Und wers nicht beimischt tropfenweis dem Guten, Den wirds gesamt aus Eimern überfluten.

> (11.277-9)

or in the words of advice to a friend reluctant to publish his work:

> Und doch soll er dran! Es ist einmal Pflicht des Menschen sich der Menschheit hinzugeben mit dem was er vermag. Im Grunde steht es auch den züchtigen Fräuleins nicht wohl zu heiraten und sich da allerhand sonst verabscheute körperliche Dinge gefallen zu lassen, aber der Mensch ist einmal nicht da um rein zu sein, sondern zu nützen, zu wirken.

Notes

The same link is referred to by Karl Eibl in a recent article ("Ordnung und Ideologie im Spätwerk Grillparzers. Am Beispiel des *argumentum emblematicum* und der *Jüdin von Toledo*," *Deutsche Vierteljahresschrift* 53 (1979): 84; unlike Eibl, however, I see no reason to distinguish between negative and positive aspects in the play and the poem respectively.

1. Ždenko Škreb, *Grillparzer. Eine Einführung in das dramatische Werk* (Kronberg/Taunus, 1976); Bruce Thompson, *A Sense of Irony. An Examination of the Tragedies of Franz Grillparzer* (Berne, 1976).

2. Reference is made to Franz Grillparzer, *Sämtliche Werke, ausgewählte Briefe, Gespräche, Berichte*, hrsg. von Peter Frank und Karl Pörnbacher (Darmstadt, 1969), or where necessary to the *historisch-kritische Gesamtausgabe* of Sauer and

Backmann (abbreviated HKA). Diary entries are abbreviated "Tgb."

3. The presence of such often-repeated ideals leads one to question Prof. McInnes' recent assertion that the early plays lack clear moral standards ("Psychological Insight and Moral Awareness in Grillparzer's *Das Goldene Vließ*," *Modern Language Review* 75 [1980]: 575-82).

4. J. P. Stern, "Beyond the Common Indication: Grillparzer," in J.P.S., *Re-interpretations* (London, 1964), p. 66.

5. J. P. Stern, *Re-interpretations*, p. 72; Walter Höllerer, *Zwischen Klassik und Moderne* (Stuttgart, 1958), p. 257; J. M. Ellis, "Grillparzer's *Der arme Spielmann*," *German Quarterly* 45 (1972): 678; Heinz F. Schafroth, *Die Entscheidung bei Grillparzer* (Berne, 1971), p. 67; Walter Silz, *Realism and Reality. Studies in the German Novelle of Poetic Realism* (Chapel Hill, 1954), p. 70; Gottfried Keller, conversation with Emil Kuh, 10/9/1871 (quoted in HKA I/22, 78).

6. Robert M. Browning, "Language and the Fall from Grace in Grillparzer's *Spielmann*," *Seminar* 12 (1976): 224, 227.

7. W. C. Reeve, "Proportion and Disproportion in Grillparzer's *Der arme Spielmann*," *The Germanic Review* 53 (1978): 44. According to Reeve, the more realistic form of the Novelle "provided him [Grillparzer] with the opportunity to demonstrate reluctantly the ultimate triumph of life over the ideal" (p. 48), which Reeve also sees intimated in the dramas (p. 45). For the reasons I have sought to demonstrate, one must take issue with the words "ideal" and "reluctantly."

8. Alfred Anzenberger, "Grillparzer und die Religion," (Diss., Vienna, 1948), pp. 39, 88.

9. See Tgb. 1680, 1681, 2803, 3288, 4073, etc.

10. Andreas Oplatka, *Aufbauform und Stilwandel in den Dramen Grillparzers* (Berne, 1970), p. 72; Ždenko Škreb, "Das Göttliche bei Grillparzer," *German Quarterly* 45 (1972): 627. For similar assessments, see also W. E. Yates, *Grillparzer. A Critical Introduction* (Cambridge, 1972), p. 202, and Schafroth, *Die Entscheidung bei Grillparzer*, pp. 55, 91.

11. Schafroth, *Die Entscheidung bei Grillparzer*, p. 110; Edmund Papst, "Grillparzers Theorie des psychologischen Realismus," *Grillparzer-Forum Forchtenstein*, (1973), pp. 15, 20.

12. Jost Hermand, *Die literarische Formenwelt des Biedermeiers* (Giessen, 1958), p. 112.

13. Roland Heine, "Ästhetische oder existentielle Integration? Ein hermeneutisches Problem des neunzehnten Jahrhunderts in Grillparzers Erzählung *Der arme Spielmann*," *Deutsche Vierteljahresschrift* 46 (1972): 650-83.

14. See Tgb. 1176, 2768, 3362, 3493.

15. M. W. Swales, "The Narrative Perspective in Grillparzer's *Der arme Spielmann*," *German Life and Letters* (New Series) 20: (1966-7): 116.

16. See ll.346-8, 511-2, 620-1, 726-7.

17. Bruce Thompson, "An Ironic Tragedy, Grillparzer's *Die Jüdin von Toledo*," *German Life and Letters* (New Series) 25 (1971-2): 215.

18. See ll.1169-78, 1215, 1470 ("Recht"); ll.427-9, 1266-7, 1467-8 ("Ordnung").

19. Even here, one detects signs of the play's later completion, and with some justification, Mark Ward has recently underlined the way that Zanga and the Dervish go off together at the end, which he sees as "this strange rehabilitation of the vital and active forces, for all their negative potential and consequences" (Mark G. Ward, "A Note on the Figures of Zanga and the Dervish in Grillparzer's *Der Traum ein Leben*," in *Essays on Grillparzer*, ed. Bruce Thompson and Mark Ward [Hull, 1978], p. 52). What is the merest hint in *Der Traum ein Leben* receives full treatment in the mature works. Grillparzer himself saw the play as a product of his earlier period and was annoyed to some extent by its success (report of Caroline Pichler [IV, 940]), complaining of the play's "Effektmacherei" (letter to Graf Redern, 4/11/1834).

James Porter (essay date 1981)

SOURCE: "Reading Representation in Franz Grillparzer's *Der arme Spielmann*," in *Deutsche Vierteljahrs Schrift für Literaturwissenschaft und Geistesgeschichte*, July 2, 1981, pp. 293-322.

[*In the following essay, Porter provides a literal, figurative, and formal reading of* Der arme Spielmann, *exploring how these readings give different perspectives on and insights into the novella. A corrected reprint of this essay appears in* Grillparzer's "Der arme Spielmann": New Directions in Criticism, *edited by Clifford Albrecht Bernd, Camden House, 1988, pp. 177–205.*]

> Es geht eben mit der Betrachtung von Kunstwerken wie mit der Beschauung von Naturgegenständen. Während der stumpfe Sinn des gewöhnlichen Hinschlenderers beim Anblick eines Baumes eben nichts bemerkt, als daß er grün ist, sieht das scharfe, wohl gar kunstgeübte Auge eine solche Welt von Abstufungen der Farbe und des Lichts, daß er stundenlang stehen und immer wieder den Baum betrachten kann, ja, wenn er Mahler ist und eine *Nachbildung* versuchen will, gerät er in Verzweiflung, auf der Palette jene Farbe zu finden, die der andere mit der allgemeinen Bezeichnung 'grün' so schnell abgefertigt hat.

> Franz Grillparzer, *Tagebücher*, ed. August Sauer,

> Nr. 3979

> Un kilo de vert n'est pas plus vert qu'un demi kilo.

In desperate need of interpretation, the line of Franz Grillparzer's **Der arme Spielmann** least remembered in the critical literature is also one which appears most to establish the blind fallibility of memory. For the statement recollected, itself containing a near self-contradiction, stands, on one reading at least, in flat contradiction to the events of the novella it claims to recall. The words are those of the Narrator, who concludes his introductory paragraph in this way:

> Da ist keine Möglichkeit der Absonderung; wenigstens vor einigen Jahren noch war keine.[1]

As anyone familiar with the story, or with the critical literature, will recognize, "Absonderung" in *Der arme Spielmann* is not the exception, the way the Narrator here seems to recall it, but the rule. It applies not only to the two major characters who first leap to mind, the Narrator and the Spielmann (". . . befand sich ein dichter Menschenwall zwischen mir und ihm." [p. 9]), but to every object of representation in the work. So all-pervading in the novella is "Absonderung," so deeply imprinted in the nature of representation itself, we can say this "rule of exceptions" colors and permeates the very textual fabric of *Der arme Spielmann*. What is more, it is the foundation of a philosophical posture that never attains full articulation in the work, but which, nonetheless, has rightly been identified with a dominant historical insight of Grillparzer's age.[2]

With this last observation we are a step closer to a neglected and potentially troubling consequence of one of the traditional interpretations of the novella: if "Absonderung" is the rule, it is the rule *based* on an exception, namely the subjective optic of the Narrator which distorts both his own and the reader's perception of the events. This line of interpretation stops short, however, of explaining us out of the paradox of a Narrator who states a false-hood while asserting its truth, when the conditions of truth and falsity are controlled exclusively by the Narrator himself. How, under these conditions, can we call the Narrator's statement false? How can we avoid making the identification, Narrator=text? The contradiction pointed out above demands an answer to these questions.[3]

One key lies in the near *self*-contradictory nature of the Narrator's statement. The Narrator asserts: (1) there is no possibility of "Absonderung"; (2) at least, a few years ago there was none; which implies that (3) there is or may well be, in fact, now the possibility of "Absonderung." The concession in (2) is thus a retraction, an admission of a weakness in the foregoing clause (1). The weakness can be pinpointed further: it is in the verb "is," the assertion of a (narrative) present, the making-present of an absence that underlies any mimetic enterprise (representation). The Narrator's equivocation, in other words, evokes in particular the self-contradiction of narrative fiction. This is one way the paradox dissolves into a thinkable form—a Narrator who "states a falsehood while asserting its truth" is the paradox of literary fiction, and rests on a two-edged convention: the convention of narrative fictitiousness (what is said in a text is not "really") and the convention of narrative fallibility (what is said in a text, even within the bounds of its own fiction, may not be "really"). We can thus deny outright that the Narrator controls the conditions of truth, "wie man denn nicht überall seine Augen haben kann" (p. 54; see footnote 3). Rather, it is the text and its conventions that condition truth and falsity, what we might call "literal" truth conditions.

Whether "Absonderung" numbers among the literal truth conditions of *Der arme Spielmann* or not, that is, whether

"Absonderung" is an objective circumstance in the novella and not simply a fabrication of the Narrator, will have to be determined by a "literal" reading of the text, in which statements by characters other than the Narrator are also given at least *prima facie* validity. And since the fact of "Absonderung" is already an accepted, "natural" reading of the text (since we intuitively allow the text to assert the truth of its own fiction), it will not require lengthy proofs, but only relevant elaboration.

On the other hand, a differing line of interpretation is also possible, one which sees in the above-given words of the Narrator a *faithful* representation of the state of affairs in the novella. This interpretation will initially require a still more deliberate literalism, and consequently a radically different *figural* reading not only of the quoted sentence, but of the entire text. The matter turns on how we interpret the "identity" of characters. For, while by the first reading, "Absonderung" (the necessity of exclusive identities for characters, where one character is identified as *distinct from* another) is not the exception but the rule, by the second reading, "Absonderung" is an impossibility ("da ist keine Möglichkeit der Absonderung"), and contact among characters (the equivalence and inclusiveness of their identities, where each character is virtually *identical with* another) is literally an exceptionless rule. Any differences construed or asserted by the Narrator are, on this reading, fantastic constructions of his imagination, transparent self-fictions: this does not mean that the "reality" behind these appearances belongs also to the Narrator's own invention, but merely that the reality is constituted by equivalences, and not by the differences attributed to it by the Narrator. The nature of *this* (figural) reality is determined entirely by the nature of literary language: not even the Narrator can escape the rule of his own fiction. This second, ruling out of exceptions is moreover the basis of a philosophical ideal and counterparts the historical insight into estrangement mentioned above—here expressed, it must be imagined, with all the earnestness of a wished-for ideal, but one that lies beyond the Narrator's means to secure it, beyond literal fact, but not beyond figural wishfulfilment.

But how, then, does this second (figural) reading correspond to the literal "facts" of the novella? By operating at a blind, counter-intuitive level in the text, against the text, challenging and obliterating the memory of expected differences, mimicking them, and the process of mimesis itself, with a literal reading of the *factorial* redundancy involved in re-presentation. Its source too is the original equivocation of the Narrator ("it is and is not"), the equivocal identity of fiction, that makes possible a radical assertion of identity ("this is that"), the total *satis-faction* of the mimetic ideal, total *self*-reference: in this way, the text asserts the fiction of its own truth.

Given these two, fundamentally opposed readings, I will try to show that they are necessarily conjoined by the text; that any choice made between them cannot help but be inadequate; that neither reading is *self*-sufficient or complete, since the independence of one is precisely the fallacy displaced and denied by the other. It is by locating such destabilizing incompatibilities that we gain access to the open structure of the text and its shifting, "empty" center, to the infinity of polyvalent meanings and intentions, structured about a difference, an ambivalence, and not a univocal truth. When choice is no longer in question, there is only the reflection of the *problem* of choice, which signifies the *impossibility* of choice ("da ist keine Möglichkeit der Absonderung") and of not choosing (since not to choose is not to read). The only exit from this double-bind is to make multiple re-readings, perpetual revisions, as we stand about the periphery of the text, at the turn of language, speaking in turns, in tropes, about a center that is itself a periphrasis.

What follows divides into three parts or readings, each part examining the novella in the light of a literary problem that occurs in *Der arme Spielmann* as a destabilizing factor in the text. The first two readings elaborate the two contradictory lines of interpretation drawn a moment ago, without attempting to smooth out the difference; no such reconciliation would be either desirable or necessary. Instead, we might look upon the first two readings as symptoms of a deeper problem, dealt with in the third reading, which poses the question: Can B be made in the image of A? (the problem of representation in a mimetic genre). The first two readings answer either affirmatively or negatively, but in such a way that the relevance of the originative question is cast into doubt: Yes, but the language of the text is so predominately self-referential (*recursive*) that we are hard-pressed to distinguish between original and copy; there are only multiple versions of the original ("da gibt es keine Möglichkeit der Absonderung"). No, because representation is conditioned by perspective, and so single commanding viewpoint is possible, nor could we, from our perspective, vouch for the accuracy of the representation even if there were; in any case, the *differential* structure of language closes this possibility: representation is a metalinguistic event ("Absonderung" affirmed).

This is, in sum, the way in which the argument of the paper is arranged. In a sense, the exposition of the readings is backward: the answers are considered before the question they pre-suppose (their pre-text) has been fully articulated. If so, this apparently non-aporetic method has been imposed by respect to the fundamentally paradoxical nature of a text which writes itself backwards, so to speak: a text which constantly generates more pretext, if only to make its self-explanation more available and more acceptable to the reader. I say "apparently" non-aporetic, because in fact textual presuppositions will be found called into question at every turn simply by virtue of the critical environment that harbors any text—selects, orders, and consequently represents the text, that is, while at the same time dissecting, disordering, and dis-representing the text; the critical environment is thus, *ipso facto* inimical to guised and inherently questionable textual pre-suppositions. And finally I draw attention to the organization of the paper to clarify a further potential misunderstanding. Because the readings themselves have been drawn from the same "filing cabinet of prefabricated representations"[4] we share as readers, it is essential to avoid an act of criticism that is itself a pre-defined reflex that never asks a question it thinks it does not already know the answer to. Such critical presuppositions are every bit as questionable as textual pre-texts. So, with this configuration in mind, we are ready to begin the first of the de-fined readings.

I. SIMILAR DIFFERENCES

"Similar Differences": the self-referentiality of a literary language. In as much as language is constitutive of literary characters, we might expect that characterizations exhibit the condition and structure of language, in other words, recursiveness and difference. What we find in *Der arme Spielmann,* however, is a figural representation of the mechanism of *self*-reference in narrative fiction. This representation is constructed in such a way that character identity, which is normally a differentiating identity, erodes before a literal reading of "identity," whereby characters loose their title to characterhood: they can be shown to be, in fact, identical. The claim to referentiality, to unique and extraneous reference, is thus called into question, shown inadequate, and compensated, in this uni-verse of the self, with an all-embracing self-referentiality: any singular reference in *Der arme Spielmann* looses its singularity to the plurality of applicable referents that weave into the tight fabric of the text, and that constitute its "innertextuality." The process that reveals such "similar differences" is not a total substitute for reference; it is, though, a particularly destructive force in the text, due to the stringent referential claims made by the Narrator on his language. For the inconsistencies that arise from the confusion of reference with self-reference rebound upon their source. The result is a *self-effacement* of language, achieved through the obliteration of meaningful differences by their sheer repetition. Self-affirmation, in *Der arme Spielmann,* entails self-negation: "Ich war wie vernichtet, . . . wieder zu mir selbst gebracht" (p. 32).

At stake in this dis-position of character is another aspect of literary language with special implications for the realist mode of literature: the speech-writing controversy. The text presents us with a dialogue, between a speaker-narrator (the Spielmann) and a writer-narrator (the Narrator), or more accurately, a discourse that is neither entirely committed to speech or to writing. For the speaker's narration is actually simulated writing. The placement of his recital and its dimensions alone insure its comparison with the foregoing narration; its continuity and general lack of intrusions by the Narrator add to the semblance. The writer's narration, on the other hand, is actually dis-simulated writing, as the realist convention dictates (and as the inclusions of "erlebte Rede," among other signs, indicates); not to mention the Narrator's efforts to submerge (or forge) himself in his own narrative, by citing his own words and finally by submitting to the narration of another character. The equivocation of the literal character is most penetrating: the character of the word is fully indeterminate; it (he) is neither spoken nor written, but is in fact that unstable combination of the audible and the mute—the read (the word as empty sign).[5]

(*i*) Both the Narrator and the Spielmann are lost in their own created fantasy worlds. It is this characteristic of self-absorption the Narrator singles out when he levels his criticism against the Spielmann (p. 15), without noting the self-reflection. The Narrator's obliviousness to the objects of his narration is simply the epistemological (or when the objects are persons, psychological) correlate of the oblivion that grounds fictional art, viz. the illusion of a Center. This claim is basic, and requires thorough elaboration. For now, though, we can illustrate the Narrator's blindness by his performance as narrator.

Originally aimed at establishing a rapport with the readership and replete with eager, confidential disclosures spliced with gnomic insertions, the narrative discourse grows increasingly self-centered ("Das ganze Wesen des alten Mannes war eigentlich wie gemacht, um meinen anthropologischen Heißhunger aufs äußerste zu reizen." [p. 8]), obsessively possessive ("mein Original" [p. 14]; "meines Lieblings" [p. 17]), and restrictive with regard to reader contact ("Wie soll ich *mir* das erklären?" [p. 10]). Ultimately, the Narrator will materialize himself before the reader's eyes as an element of his own narrative. Curiously, however, the centripetal movement "inward" runs contrary to the current that draws the Narrator from his lofty observation post into the text as a character, for the Narrator's disclosure of his many self-obsessions actually involves his *self-effacement* as a narrator-figure. After the early pages, the narration becomes noticeably less conspicuous, less self-designating, less disrupted by insertions and rhetorical figures which call attention to the narrative discourse or which retard or suspend it. The restrictions in the poetic function of the discourse are aimed at imposing a kind of economy on the narration so as to bring the reader all the more directly to the Spielmann's story.[6] But the dis-figuration of the narrative discourse also has the complementary effect of literalizing the narration. The narration, in other words, moves toward "transparent" mimesis, or rather, the narration is being *exchanged* for mimesis. The exchange, of course,[7] is never completed within the narrative, which is instead propelled by the centripetal movement to an appropriate culmination—a literal self-designation which is also a figure for the narrative proper: "und bald herrschte eine durch nichts unterbrochene Totenstille um *mich* her" (p. 15). Overruled by silence, by the impossibility of objective narration, the Narrator finds partial solace ("den Heimweg") in solipsism: "Ich trat, mühsam in den *mir* unbekannten Gassen *mich zurechtfindend*, den Heimweg an, wobei ich auch phantasierte, aber, *niemand* störend, für mich, im Kopfe" (p. 15).

That the Spielmann is absorbed by esoteric fantasies needs little discussion, except to point out that his oblivion ("Abwesenheit" [pp. 8, 17]) stems from, and culminates in, a performance no less impervious and alienating than that of the Narrator: ". . . und spielte fort und fort, ohne sich weiter um mich zu kümmern." (Cp. "Davon wird *niemand* etwas wissen bis auf wenige" [p. 25].)

(*ii*) Thus preoccupied with fantasies that are beyond the reach of their immediate environments, the Narrator and the Spielmann share a displacement that is both psychological and linguistic. The Narrator shows this in insisting on lifting ordinary details to the height of literary constellations ("bis zum Zwist der Göttersöhne" [p. 6]), sometimes through heavy borrowings in Fremdwörter and through allusions to the classics ("status quo," "Plutarch," "die Methode in der Tollheit"), but always in a tone that is tinged with disdainful irony. The pillars of the Narrator's allusions are not unshakeably grounded, though. In fact, it is just when the Narrator stands securely "bereits auf klassischem Boden" (p. 7), and when his discourse takes a singularly acrid twist toward condecension, that he encounters for the first time the Spielmann who can duplicate and thus put an end to, by jarring into perspective, his own literary pretensions: "Sunt certi denique fines" (p. 8). The Spielmann does not allow himself to be woven into a mythological framework as do the "Karrenschieber" and "die junge Magd" (p. 6). It is this same displacement in the Spielmann ("Exercitium" [p. 13]; "Ich will kein Bettler sein . . . Ich weiß wohl, daß die übrigen öffentlichen Musikleute sich damit begnügen . . ." [p. 12]) that lures the Narrator to seek out and confront his own likeness.

Consistent with this downward-looking perspective is a reverence for things of greater stature. The Narrator and the Spielmann stand in the shadow of "famous" persons, thus testifying to the definitive innertextuality of the text: ". . . und wahrlich! man kann die *Berühmten* nicht verstehen, wenn man die Obskuren nicht durchgefühlt hat" (p. 6); ". . . dann sah ich auch, daß *berühmte* Virtuosen, welche erreicht zu haben ich mir nicht schmeicheln konnte . . ." (p. 51).

(*iii*) If the elusiveness of their fantasies does not prevent the Narrator or the Spielmann from trying to realize them, it is less the passion of their desires than the *self*-ishness of their common need that determines what we might call the "economics" of their behavior. Both Narrator and Spielmann fall prey to possession-obsessions ("Ich zittere *vor Begierde* nach dem Zusammenhange" [p. 9]; "Da ich nun *vor Begierde*, das Lied zu haben . . ." [p. 30]). The motivation, given the two modes of their artistry, is identical. In the case of the Narrator, it is "um das Original ungestört zu betrachten" (p. 8), and ultimately to commit his quarry to writing. The Spielmann too is driven to obtain a written copy ("Abschrift") of the original "Lied," in order to reproduce it for himself ("nachzuspielen" [p. 29]). The difficulties of pure mimesis ("ich habe deshalb, teils weil mein Gedächtnis überhaupt nicht das beste ist . . . diese Hefte mir selbst ins *reine* geschrieben." [p. 12] prove to be major debilities for both the Narrator and the Spielmann: "Im Zweifel, ob ich mich genau ans Original halten oder aus *eigenem* beisetzen sollte, verging die Zeit angstvoll, und ich kam in den Ruf, nachlässig zu sein, indes ich mich im Dienst abquälte wie keiner" (p. 23). The words of the Spielmann speak for the Narrator as well; and the impurities (viz. the tortured, blackened script) of the Spielmann's "Hefte" (p. 12) implicate the Narrator's "Abschrift" by homology.[8]

(*iv*) Neither the Narrator nor the Spielmann is beyond exploiting a contact in order to obtain satisfaction for his needs: "Endlich hatte ich's *satt* . . ." (p. 52); ". . . ch gedachte aus dieser Bekanntschaft sogleich Nutzen für meinen Wunsch zu ziehen" (p. 27). Moreover, both are keenly aware of the positional advantages of others involved in some kind of economic exploitation, whether street-musicians (p. 7) or "die Gewerbsleute" (p. 26). It is significant, however, that the Narrator and the Spielmann are blind to exploitations of their own persons. The Spielmann's financial collapse (his total investment in a *"Kopieranstalt"*) is a case in point; his compliance with the Narrator's obsession is another. As for the Narrator, the loss he suffers in the exchange of narration for (apparent) mimesis, which in the long-run costs him not only the right to narration (this he yields to the Spielmann) but also the privilege of an authoritative point of view (this is put into question by the structure of the text he narrates), is an example of the extremest *self*-exploitation.

(*v*) Both Narrator and Spielmann are self-appointedly religious, or indicate religious tendencies, though each in his own manner ("besonders wenn sie in Massen für einige Zeit der einzelnen Zwecke vergessen und sich als Teile des Ganzen fühlen, in dem denn doch zuletzt das Göttliche liegt . . ." [p. 5]; "Das Gebet gehört ins Kämmerlein" [p. 11]). The Narrator's impulses are questionable, as his words ("*als ein Liebhaber der Menschen*, sage ich, *besonders* . . .") betray. But there are certain indications that we cannot take the Spielmann's religious sentiments at face value either.

For one, the Spielmann equates religious devotion with (nocturnal) music ("aber der Abend gehört mir und meiner armen Kunst" [p. 10]; "und der Abend mir und dem lieben Gott" [p. 13]), a narrow and rather questionable reduction, in light of certain other indications as well. The word he uses to describe this exchange with divinity is infelicitous: "Phantasieren" (p. 11). A further reduction: this "ganzes Himmelsgebäude" (p. 25), fantastic construction of his imagination ("Einbildung" p. 11), is not roomy enough for more than one mind. At the height of his euphoria, the Spielmann has left humanity behind in its traces ("Vielmehr stören sie dieses Ein- und Ausatmen der Seelen durch Hinzufügung allenfalls auch zu sprechender Worte . . ." [p. 25]). Sheltered and isolated, the Spielmann is like a lonely divinity ("den lieben Gott spielt").

That the Narrator seeks the divine presence in the fleeting outbursts of the masses (p. 5), which presence the Spielmann finds in private, nocturnal performances, is only an apparent difference. The obsessively self-centered aspect of the Spielmann's worship is too familiar to escape correlation with the Narrator's configurations: the Spielmann protects himself by converting felt pains into religious visions ("Ich stand wie von Donner getroffen. Die Lichter tanzten mir vor den Augen.—*Aber es waren Himmelslichter.*. . . Ich hatte Erscheinungen, ich war verzückt" [p. 42]). (That the Spielmann struggles "durch die dem Feste zuströmende Menge in entgegengesetzter Richtung" (p. 8) is a likewise misleading opposition: both Spielmann and "Volk" practice a different version of a religiosity left open to interpretation by its extremity alone. The Spielmann's ear is "durstig" and "zerlechzend" (p. 25), while the "Menge" is in its own euphoria "genußlechzend" (p. 7).)

(*vi*) Both the Narrator and the Spielmann readily take on the posture of narrator, or rather the Spielmann overtakes the Narrator's position: "'Möchte ich mir's doch selbst einmal wieder erzählen.' . . . und er nahm überhaupt die Lage eines mit Bequemlichkeit Erzählenden an" (p. 19). Their narrative techniques are closely similar: both display on the one hand a tentativeness rooted in the desire to be credible ("von mir aber sei fern zu betrügen" [p. 12]) which manifests itself in cautious qualifications, most often in concessive clauses subordinate to Truth, such as: "wenn ich mich recht erinnere" (p. 20); "wenigstens vor einigen Jahren noch war keine" (p. 1); compare the sentence, "Fast hätte ich gesagt: der einzige, was aber nicht wahr wäre, denn . . ." (p. 42). On the other hand, both Narrator and Spielmann exhibit an at times uncontrollable penchant for brash hyperbole and euphoric extravagance—fantasy, in other words. It is this curious admixture (or incompatibility) of reportage and lived event which is central to the novella as a theme, and which allows the Spielmann to say, without a sense of contradiction, "er verhielt sich aber *wirklich so und ging ins Riesenhafte*" (p. 42), just as the Narrator can rework events into subjective (mythic or figural) fabrications without suggesting he might have betrayed the "facts."

(*vii*) So close are their narrative techniques and standards of verity that their styles of narration are for all intents and purposes identical: the phrase "(bis) endlich" serves the Narrator as a way of controlling narrative rhythm, of clinching suspenseful expectations; "wie gesagt" (p. 13) is a rarer interjection used to organize material. The Spielmann employs freely both expressions as, for instance, in: "Endlich aber—wie gesagt— . . ." (p. 31). Another example of their *monologic* style: "Hart an dem Gleicher [Äquator, J.P.] hatte der alte Mann . . ." (p. 17); "hart vor dem Ladentische am Lichte sitzen . . ." (p. 32). Of course style is variable in its pecularities of expression: in similar situations, the Spielmann is more apt to say, "Ich nahm mir ein Herz" (pp. 28, 31), while the Narrator will say ". . . *ward* die *Ungeduld* meiner Herr" (p. 16); but deeper similarities reveal that the stylistic timing is the same ("endlich" occurs before each expression); the contexts are structurally homologous (this will be discussed below); and the impulse, impatience, is identical (earlier, the Spielmann has shown this: "ich *ward* fast *ungeduldig* von Zuhören" [p. 24]).[9]

So far, we have concentrated on shared superficial and deeper affinities between the two major figures of the novella. We have, in other words, begun a reading of the universe of the self.[10] This set of interrelations (similar differences) suggests what might be termed an "equivalent" effect, by which all members of the story (it is not restricted to the Narrator and Spielmann alone) are implicated in a single mesh, all equally involved in a reflexive mirroring. The mesh is of language, self-reflecting, self-referring. In the crowd, for instance, the Narrator spies two lovers, "und in der jungen Magd, die, halb wider Willen, dem drängenden *Liebhaber seitab* vom Gewühl der Tanzenden folgt, liegen als Embryo . . ." (p. 6). It is this same side-stepping that bonds the Narrator to the Spielmann ("Ich war, um das Original ungestört zu betrachten, in einiger *Entfernung* auf den *Seitenab*hang des Dammes getreten" [p. 8]), whose obliqueness persists up to the moment of his death: ". . . richtete er sich plötzlich im Bette auf, wendete Kopf und Ohr *seitwärts*, als ob er in der *Entfernung* etwas gar Schönes hörte . . ." (p. 54). Another instance of the equi-valent effect: Toward the end of the novella it is told that Barbara's son is named "Jakob" after the Spielmann (p. 52). He takes up the violin and even receives instruction from his namesake. But the child's progress is hampered by more pressing circumstances ("da ihn in der Woche der Vater beim Geschäft verwendet") and consequently he can only play on Sundays (music and religion, again; we meet the Spielmann on a Sunday). Moreover, "er hat *zwar* nur wenig Talent," though he has mastered to a certain degree "Barbara's Lied." Little Jakob is thus assimilated directly to the image of the Spielmann. (The "zwar" in the preceding citation reflects an inference drawn automatically from the facts of the analogy between the two Jakob's, and means "it could only be so"; the equi-valent effect is a compulsory, *over*determined relation.)

The equi-valent effect, consisting basically in a vertical projection, has in addition a horizontal extension that originates in reading the perspectival multiverse of the *other*. In this multiverse, which is also the universe of explicit self-criticism, differences generate a system of *cross*-reference that raises an evaluation problem for the reader: which point of view is correct? can we verify one by another? So, for instance, the question of Barbara's beauty is disputed among the Spielmann (p. 44), his "Kameraden" (p. 27), and the Narrator (p. 55).[11] By linking different points of view with identical referents (and with like but nuanced expressions), similar differences are distributed over a wide range of characters; the verbal echoes resonate through the whole of the text; and the resonances make it all the more difficult to assess characters either separately or in their ambiguous relations. Thus, the equivalent effect in its extension becomes the seed-plot of further difference, further discourse, that in turn becomes the subject of further assimilation. It is the differential, perspectival effect, however, that will take up our attention in the section to follow.

II. Points of view (metaphor and metonomy)

"Points of view (metaphor and metonomy)": the poetic structure within realist narrative. Literature originates in, or rather anticipates, an act of communication that the language perpetually strives to recover. For the origin-act is less of an utterance than a gesture or posture, the index of an unexpressed content, and the literal presentation of the gesture can at best take the form of a figural representation of the same. Thus, the reduplication of the shadow of literal meaning is nothing more than a persistent memory. In *Der arme Spielmann,* the duplicity of the shadow is attested to by the futile process of verification that is installed in the structure of the text (through opposed points of view and voices). Moreover, the conflict of reliabilities, which has its parallel in a necessary difference within the structure of literary language, namely between metaphor and metonomy, is symbolically represented in a dramatic confrontation between the Spielmann and the Narrator, or to put it baldly, between the representatives of poetry and prose, respectively. The foundations of the difference are imperiled by the reversals and exchanges of roles and desires, and the ensuing confusions. By the same token, the metaphorical foundation of (realist) representation is brought to light. While realistic prose has been correctly identified with the metonymic principle,[12] it is more correct to speak of a projection of the principle of *equivalence* onto the axis of combinative sequence,[13] or in the words of one critic,[14] the projection of a single moment of radical contradiction—the present—upon the temporal axis of a diachronic narrative."

The figural interplay of points of view in *Der arme Spielmann* creates, on the literal level, indecision between sentimentality and irony. If the origin of the literary moment is already written into its vehicle of expression, (and hence already [dis]figures the content of the expression), are we forever banned from the "real" meaning of the expression? We indeed are, to the extent that such a meaning is literally undecidable, and since the figural reading ironizes expression in the measure that an expressive content encourages a literal response.

"Endlich, wie denn in dieser Welt jedes noch so hartnäckige Stehenbleiben doch nur ein unvermerktes Weiterrücken ist, erscheint auch diesem status quo ein Hoffnungstrahl."[15]

The authority of the Narrator can be attested to only by examining the literary devices he has at his disposal and the way he deploys them, that is to say, disguises their strategic nature. Every position taken ("Stehenbleiben") masks a shift, a contradictory transposition or new edition, that creates in turn the illusion of space, of a difference, of dimensions and perspectives. In *Der arme Spielmann* two perspectives are particularly responsible for controlling the reader's approach to the recessive text, and these will be

the focus of our present discussion: the effectiveness of sentimentality and irony, taken as points of view. First we should determine how empathy and distance are given independent voice through the narrative discourse, and then we will consider their occurence at the more specific level of the sentence, where they coincide and interact. In this way, it will be possible to reconstruct the "sources" of these two, possibly incompatible, points of view.

To describe the emergence of an ironic point of view will involve tracing briefly the Narrator's gradual self-disclosure through the earliest paragraphs of the novella. Sweeping over the past through different time frames, returning to the present and finally retreating again into the past, the Narrator is concerning with establishing a fact (that of the "Volksfest") and an atmosphere in which to appreciate this fact (the "long expected" event). By this recursive technique, the Narrator is able to simulate the expectation, and thus lend it verisimilitude. Once the day of the festival is obtained ("erscheint endlich das saturnalische Fest") the Narrator continues in this strain of empathetic simulation, by incorporating the (literal) point of view of the masses within his own (figural) interpretation of the experience (the battling imagery—"siegreich," etc.—is too elaborate and too consistent to be common property; and yet, the ones battling their way to the "Lustort" are, at this moment at least, the impatient "Volk"). Thus the Narrator preserves his distance while constraining the fullest expression of his point of view for the purposes of "realistic" (simular) description.

While the object of narration is approaching a "Stillstand" ("Von Sekunde zu Sekunde wird der Abstand zwischen Wagen und Wagen kleiner. . . . Bis endlich fünf bis sechs Stunden vor Nacht die einzelnen Pferde- und Kutschen-Atome sich zu einer kompakten Reihe verdichten. . . ." [p. 4]), the movement of the narration itself by mimesis slows to an empirical conscientiousness: "Zank, Geschrei, . . ." (p. 4). It is no mere coincidence that at the point of greatest fusion for the celebrants, the narrative discourse revels in atomic detail. The narration is moving toward an independent focus, then culminates momentarily in a well-wrought ring composition comprising the whole of the paragraph beginning with the lines quoted at the head of this section. This richly-worked passage is the most poetical moment of the overture; its self-contained symmetry (we are in the synchrony of a metaphor) contradicts the movement of the proceding lines (which were an attempt at immersion in sequential time), while its sheathed ironies are an inevitably consequence of the presentation of that movement: it too contains the seeds of an independent, almost frivolous, point of view: ". . . zu einem pays de cocagne, einem Eldorado, einem eigentlichen Schlaraffenlande vereinigen, das leider, oder glücklicherweise, wie man es nimmt, nur einen und den nächst darauffolgenden Tag dauert, dann aber verschwindet . . ." (p. 5). The passage deserves closer inspection, even at the cost of a brief standstill.

In keeping with his previously established acumen it is fitting that the Narrator descry "ein *unvermerktes* Weiterrücken" when others fail to notice. (The line actually refers back to an earlier observation, ". . . sitzen die geputzten Damen in den *scheinbar* stillestehenden Kutschen" [p. 4]). Even more typical is his antipathy to the "Stillstand", and his acute orientation to the slightest break from the pause. "Stehenbleiben"—it is stasis, "the threat of an incompleted sequence,"[16] of equivalence, and the possibility for the Narrator of being himself observed, "begafft, bedauert, bespottet." The statement about *"hartnäckige* Stehenbleiben" does not agree with the present situation as closely as the thought which follows upon suggests: *"auch diesem* status quo." Nobody is being *obstinately* immobile at this point. The incongruence of the remark (its present inapplicability) is reflected back upon, and internalized by, the person of the Narrator. First of all, the rhetorical status of the figure is put into jeopardy: what is presented here as a gnomic insertion, an accepted wisdom, is actually a disguised personal outlook on the world. Second, the patency of a given narrative assumption exposes the redundancy of narration in general: the Narrator's words will have a *future* application, with regard to the Spielmann (whose stance toward the world might fairly be described as a "hartnäckige Stehenbleiben"), and so they create a proleptic contrast between two view-points (represented by two discourse patterns—see below) that are radically opposed.[17] Moreover, the temporality or the narrative sequence ("Weiterrücken") has been inter-rupted by the recurrence (transposition) of an event that has not yet even occured, thus indicating how the Narrator is confined to the status ("Stehenbleiben") of his own retelling, to a proleptic defense against constantly unstated objections. In the following lines the Narrator conceals his error by cloaking his viewpoint with that of the celebrants. In this tone, this half-convincing impersonation (simulation), or rather this simultaneous translation, the Narrator finishes the paragraph.

In between, a detectable and significant shift occurs in the Narrator's discourse, from the metonymic mode of description to the metaphoric. The former, based on the progress of a sequence, on the contiguity of details and their contextual intactness, has been identified as the underlying principle of prose, particularly of "realistic" prose.[18] It is also the mode native to the Narrator, as not only his style but also his motivations and attitudes attest. He is prompted by this characteristic to investigate the history of the Spielmann, to follow a trail of contiguous clues (the thread, "die Faden"), and to assemble them into a meaningful context ("Ich zitterte vor Begierde nach dem *Zusammenhange*" [p. 9]).

The set of metonymic operations that ultimately seeks out mediated Difference for the Narrator makes a sharp contrast with the way the Spielmann operates in the world. The latter figure may be said to embrace the metaphoric mode of language, the underlying mode of poetry.[19] Based on the principle of substitutibility, the metaphoric mode is actually opposed to temporal sequence and to the strictures of a context ("außer aller Zusammenhang" [p. 8]). The mode of metaphor naturally perceives Difference with In-difference. So the first response of the Spielmann to the Narrator's request that he tell his life-story is understandable in these linguistic terms: "Geschichte? . . . Ich habe keine Geschichte. Heute wie gestern, und morgen wie heute. Übermorgen freilich und weiter hinaus, wer kann das wissen?" (p. 19). That the Spielmann is baffled by a contextual orientation is evident in the school lesson scene (pp. 20-21): "Ich aber, der das Wort in meinem Innern und im Zusammenhang mit dem übrigen suchte, hörte ihn nicht." The metonymic/metaphoric distinction, elsewhere in the novella a latent but systematic difference, is here an observable fact made explicit by another similar difference. While the Spielmann's brothers are capable of progressing along a metonymic chain "wie Gemsen von Spitze zu Spitze in den Lehrgegenständen herum," the Spielmann never gets beyond his original station: ". . .ich konnte aber durchaus nichts hinter mir lassen, und wenn mir ein einziges Wort fehlte, mußte ich von vorne anfangen." Spielmann is in essence the victim of what Jakobson in "Two Aspects of Language and Two Types of Aphasic Disturbance" terms a "continuity disorder"[20] (" . . . ich begann stockisch zu werden."). His brothers do not necessarily suffer from the second type of disturbance, though their behavior is describable in terms of the metonymic principle the Narrator embodies, and whose behavior can truly be labelled a "similarity disorder." One criterion for the difference in aphasics is the marked variance of their linguistic performance where contextual structures play a role: "The less a word depends grammatically on the context, the stronger is its tenacity in the speech of aphasics with a contiguity disorder and the earlier it is dropped by patients with a similarity disorder."[21] Jakobson's generalization implies its converse, which suits our own case study, the school lesson scene: The more a word depends grammatically on the context (viz. "Cachinnum"), the weaker is its tenacity in the speech of aphasics with a contiguity disorder. The pathological or even psychological roots of the disturbance in the Spielmann (or Narrator) are of less interest to us than the linguistic patterns that underlie this "contexture-deficient" speech perception, and that translate into consistent patterns of discourse: "Wußte ich das eine, so hatte ich dafür das übrige vergessen." "Vergessen" is the key word here. Forgetfulness is the nemesis of anyone operating in the metonymic mode (which is also the mode of metalanguage and criticism), for whom details are not simply substitutible, and for whom a surplus of verbal denotations is tantamount to an amnestic condition;[22] on the other hand, indifference to sequence, denotative surplus, forgetfulness, is the principle of metaphor, and the regulative principle of the Spielmann's life.

But it is precisely forgetfulness the Narrator strives to approximate when he describes the scene of the festival[23] ("Alle Leiden sind *vergessen*"), by abandoning his prior careful application of the principle of difference and discrimination ("Aufmerksamkeit," p. 4) for the sake of the infinite ellipsis; the Narrator is, so to speak, "zum ersten Male seiner Natur ungetreu" (p. 4): "Die zu Wagen Gekommenen steigen aus und mischen sich unter die Fußgänger, Töne entfernter Tanzmusik schallen herüber. . . . *Und so fort und immer weiter . . .*" The narration strains to be impressionistic, to give as many predicates to any one substantive as it can (this is pure polysemy): "Wald und Wiese, Musik und Tanz, Wein und Schmaus, Schattenspiel und Seiltänzer, Erleuchtung und Feuerwerk (the coupling suggests equivalence) sich zu einem pays de cocagne, einem Eldorado, einem eigentlichen Schlaraffenlande *vereinigen* . . ."[24] This is the climax of the overture to the novella, which indicates that all along the Narrator has been resisting a tendency to lose himself in the metaphoric mode ("Der Unterschied der Stände ist verschwunden." [p. 1]) that acknowledges not difference but sameness. His ambivalence toward metaphoric description is evident even here, in the slight ironies that color his expression, and in the explicit prevarication, or is it simply in-difference?: "leider, oder *glücklich*erweise, wie man es nimmt."[25] Nonetheless, if the Narrator is not entirely committed to the logic of the rhetorical figure he has chosen, he is committed to closing the passage in a rhetorically satisfying way: the activity of the "Fest" finally subsides as an undifferentiated whole ("wie der Traum *einer* Sommernacht"), leaving a residual memory ("Erinnerung") and a lingering desire ("Hoffnung"). That these words reveal more than they should can be seen in the subsequent paragraph. There, the Narrator's praise for the totalizing powers of amnesia and the erasure of difference are clear: "besonders wenn sie in Massen für einige Zeit der einzelnen Zwecke *vergessen* und sich als Teile des *Ganzen* fühlen . . ."; but his inability to share in these collective experiences is even clearer from the sequel: "Wie aus einem aufgerollten, ungeheuren, dem Rahmen des Buches entsprungenen Plutarch lese ich aus . . . den *einzelnen* halb unwillkürlichen Äußerungen mir die Biographien . . . zusammen" (p. 5f.).[26] By comparison with this cultivated simile, the extended festival-description is a rare and nearly subversive indulgence in metaphoric language. Its ringform composition is built upon the two pairs words chiastically ordered:

Hoffnungsstrahl   Erinnerung
vergessen   Hoffnung

From the first sign of "Hoffnung," it was noted, the Narrator shifted into the metaphoric mode of description and into a certain oblivion. The final "Erinnerung," however, does not restore him to the properly narrative mode, nor is the accompanying "Hoffnung" the same at the end as it was at the beginning. These last form a circle, they bear *within* the metaphoric process ("Er *innerung*") and do not lead away from it. The original "hope" was teleological, a "Hoffnung*strahl*" opposed to "Stehenbleiben." The final "Hoffnung" is an imaginative reiteration of the experience that resists temporality; it is locked into its own "Stehenbleiben" ("zurückbleibt"). The Narrator must forcibly wrest himself from this "vicious" circle in order to restore himself to his self, the tenacious subject: "Ich *versäume nicht leicht* . . ."

As the narrative makes its final increment toward the confrontation with the "arme Spielmann" (whose name in the title is enough to create an expectation and to justify the delays), the Narrator's point of view grows still less empathetic and more emphatically his "own." The rupture in perspective requires a new mimetic strategy, and this in turn generates a rhetorical discontinuity in the Narrator's discourse: his distance is converted now into a tone vascillating between irony and sheer indifference; details are accordingly no longer exalted into, say, mythological figures, and if anything, their rudimentary, *dis*figured status is a glaring breach of the decorum demanded by their figural environment—the "klassische Boden" that recalls the earlier discussed "Stillestehen" (p. 7, cp. p. 5). "Eine Harfenspielerin mit widerlich starrenden Augen," for instance, does not conjure up a Homer. The Narrator's tone works against his images, and is capable of freezing over an object of otherwise warm compassion; the description of "ein alter invalider Stelzfuß, der . . . die Schmerzen seiner Verwundung dem allgemeinen Mitleid . . . empfindbar machen *wollte*" (p. 7) is a case in point. This is a critical moment for understanding the uses of sentimentality in this novella. How is it that we are aware of a participatory empathy (what is its source?) and simultaneously of an incompassionate, mocking voice? It is almost as if the sentimental message is conveyed *in spite of* the Narrator. It is important to determine whether these two voices, present

in *one* sentence, represent incompatible points of view, and if so, then we must identify their sources. There are other examples for comparison:

"Abends halte ich mich zu Hause, und"—dabei ward seine Rede immer leiser, Röte überzog sein Gesicht, sein Auge suchte den Boden—"da spiele ich denn aus der Einbildung . . ." Wir waren beide ganze stille geworden. Er, aus Beschämung, über das verratene Geheimnis seines Innern; ich, voll Erstaunen, den Mann von den höchsten Stufen der Kunst sprechen zu hören, der nicht imstande war, den leichtesten Walzer faßbar wiederzugeben. (p. 11)

The Spielmann has just confessed his most inner self and the Narrator is incredulous; it is not the emotional content that interests or affects the Narrator, but the incongruence between statement and context, a difference that cries out for elimination. Whether the Narrator can successfully account for all differences through a process of elimination has to be seen.

Other instances of an emotive quality show a kind of design to the representation of sentiment: it most often occurs through the barest of descriptions which involve the least intrusion of narrative commentary; and it always relies on the description of hands, of hands over a face, of tears over cheeks, in other words of (nearly) unvoiced gestures, simple signs, which in the context of overt narrative direction perform a kind of muting effect, a sudden and significant contrast. One classic example is found early in the text: "'Bitte! Bitte!' rief der alte Mann, wobei er mit beiden Händen ängstlich abwehrende Bewegungen machte, 'in den Hut! in den Hut!'" (p. 10). Compare: " . . . und dabei glänzten seine Augen wie feucht; er lächelte aber" (p. 13). "Dabei besah er mit auseinanderfallenden Händen seine ganze dürftige Gestalt" (p. 48). And so on. It is in moments when the Narrator reduces his commentary to a minimum, when he introduces his description with a perfunctory, formulaic "dabei" (as if to indicate, "this is the gesture that accompanied this word, that I have reproduced for you here in its unordained purity") that we are aware of an effect to which the Narrator himself is not entirely susceptible. For the sentiment (to be significant) requires a basis in objectivity that does not in turn require the sentiment.

In the Narrator's eyes, compassion is significant only in so far as it can be used to signify the ideal rapprochement of an object and its representation; and the maudlin connotations that are generated from this perspective are at least partially due to the nostalgic appeal and memory of the original. Removed from its presence and relieved from the need to re-present it, the Narrator allows the object to slip entirely from mind: in the solitude of space ("die Stille des Ortes" [p. 14]), the Narrator has no stake in the Spielmann ("mich verschiedenen Gedanken überlassend, an denen der alte Spielmann nicht den letzten Anteil hatte . . ."); following his second contact with the Spielmann, the Narrator proves again his transient susceptibility to the presence of images and his infidelity to those which are removed from his field of vision: "Die neuen Bilder hatten die alten verdrängt, und mein Spielmann war so ziemlich vergessen" (p. 52). By the same token, sentiment is a useful pretext ("zum Vorwande" [p. 56]) for approaching a desired object of representation, for fulfilling an empty obsession to possess it; this is certainly the Narrator's motivation at the end of the novella: "daß ich die Geige des Alten *als Andenken* zu besitzen wünschte," a doubly contorted pretext, since the Narrator is really after the confirmation of his representations as well as a final portrait (Barbara)—a crowning representation to represent all previous representations.

Sentimentality is a calculated effect and a special mode of representation.[27] If the sentimental affectations of the Narrator are taken "seriously," as genuinely representative of his point of view, then the affectation has been misleading; at the same time, sentimentality (in its emotive impact) is the reader's guide to a critical understanding of the work, and so must be taken "seriously," up to this point. Following the affectative trail to its ultimate source, the reader will find himself abandoned, and frustrated by what turns out to be a mere literary device. In this way the operations of the Narrator will be laid bare, and what originally serviced as a compositional technique will be converted into an alienating de-compositional element.

How, on the other hand, are we going to account for the generous narratorial allowances made to irony in *Der arme Spielmann* that seem to achieve this alienating effect of themselves? Irony too is a calculated mode of representation, generally signifying the distance between the word and the thing, though here it is a sign not for the categorical impossibility of representation but for the *mastery* of this impossibility through a discriminating awareness of the hazards involved. For the Narrator, irony is in fact a sign-post that points to the only possible *justification* of representation: the objective, *unaffected*, and purely distantiated perspective—this is the ideal position the Narrator actually strives to assume, whether in his ironical or sympathetic moments. The result is an illusory convergence of perspectives at a common vanishing point: when ultimately the differences between the two points of view (empathy and irony) become identical; when the emotive content of language becomes insignificant and indifferent; when, in other words, language performs its mimetic function to the point of effacing itself before the object, then the act of representation has exhausted its only viable grounds and sentenced itself to death. This self-immolation is timed by the Narrator so as to coincide with the last sentence of the novella. The question of his success or failure, which will hinge on the question of the authority of the Narrator, must remain open for discussion below.

This brings us back to the problems of point of view and verification, of similar differences and the structural ambivalences of the text itself. Sentimentality and irony employed as points of view serve to heighten the ambiguity of relations between characters, by charging and discharging the emotional atmosphere, by simulating the frustrations experienced by the characters which ultimately lead to their alienation, and incidentally an alienation that can only be overcome by affinities that transcend the structure: ". . . wobei ihm die Finger auf den Saiten zitterten und endlich einzelne *Tränen über die Backen liefen*" (p. 24); ". . . sie hatte sich umgewendet, und die *Tränen liefen* ihr stromweise *über die Backen*" (p. 56). Spielmann and Barbara are lovers who cannot make contact on their own, but only through the agency of a third party (like the Narrator), or through the mediation of a structured description that allows difference to become identical. Sentimentality is ambivalent in Barbara too, who in this respect *seems* to

have been assimilated to the Narrator's point of view. The similarity of their response to the Spielmann's monologues (it is minimal and judgmental) is evident from the line: "Dabei ließ sie mich aber immer allein sprechen und gab nur durch einzelne Worte ihre Billigung oder—was öfter der Fall war—ihre Mißbilligung zu erkennen" (p. 42).

Later Barbara tells Jakob point-blank, "Eigentlich verdienen Sie kein Mitleid" (p. 49) in words that belong and do not belong to her—words, that is, which testify to an innertextual lexicality. By their general currency among differing points of view, *"eigentlich"* and *"verdienen"* are made thematic (i.e. disputable) in the text; but since in *Der arme Spielmann* no single viewpoint taken by itself can stand independently of the text that creates it (the text cannot determine its own value), these normative terms come to signify the very categories they appeal to, and not the judgment they are being applied to. "Eigentlich" here is being used to make an (apparently) objective reference—to a judgment Barbara could assent to under other conditions, if she were not already affected by her contact with the Spielmann (or if she were not she)—an objective reference that is as equally beyond her scope as any objective representation by the Narrator.

The same words, however, appear at the outset of the Narrator's story where they ought to carry the weight of his authorial point of view: ". . . ein *eigentliches* Volksfest, wenn je ein Fest diesen Namen *verdient* hat" (p. 1). The apparent univocity of the statement when unmasked reveals an orchestra of contradictions: "eigentlich" here expresses the kind of enthusiasm that might come from the mouth of a proud compatriot or from a patronizing visitor. That the narrated sequel neither confirms nor denies the Narrator's local *origins* is itself a meaningful ambiguity, and one which he himself experiences; for the sequel gradually comes to suggest a third likelihood, that the Narrator is actually neither (neither proud compatriot nor patronizing visitor), or rather both (an expatriot within his own land, withdrawn and withholding his own source of identity even from himself). The process of naming and identifying is, as we have seen above, at the center of the value-laden process of representation.

The repeated occurence of these key, inter-subjective terms itself qualifies the status of so-called "objective" representation; their very redundancy already points to the *surplus-value* inherent in the mimetic enterprise. An example of one such qualification: the Spielmann, figure of the object-original, for instance, already repudiates the narrative assumptions when he turns down the offer by the Narrator of an *added* bonus of a money contribution ("und dabei fuhr ich in die Tasche, um das früher gereichte *gar zu kleine* Geldgeschenk allenfalls zu *verdoppeln*"): ". . . eines andern *Verdienstes* aber bin ich mir zur Zeit nicht bewußt" (p. 13). The exchange is further problematized by the fact that even the *original* "Geldgeschenk" was not part of "die *eigentliche* Ernte" forfeited by the Spielmann when he turned back home (p. 8). This entire sequence, in turn, is duplicated twice by the larger sequence of which it is a pre-figural moment: once in the narrative gesture of recuperation (of the Real, through representation) that ultimately must fail; and once again in the transposition from literal event to figural sign of the event that can never fail—for while a figure necessarily duplicates a literal meaning, it also *removes* itself from the value determinations of the process of representation, in as much as the figure, as a purely self-reflective sign (i.e. as reflective of a universe of discourse that is entirely self-referential) is pure surplus-value: in the example above, the failed exchange signifies *un*problematically the problematics of representation.[28]

The excess of wear on the terms we have been discussing ultimately results in the deflation of their meanings. Far from standing for determinate evaluations, they are often little more than gratuitous rhetorical figures easily susceptible to the ironies of trivialization (as in: "die *eigentlichen* Hierophanten dieses Weihfestes: die Kinder der *Dienstbarkeit* und der Arbeit" [p. 4]); or else they are the syllables of an exclusive language ("aber mit *mir* hat's *eigene* Wege" [p. 44]); or some conflation of the two ("Das ganze Wesen des alten Mannes war *eigentlich* wie gemacht, um *meinen* anthropologischen Heißhunger aufs äußerste zu reizen" [p. 8]). What is more, through their constant recurrence these terms become voided of all distinctive significance. In this world of the assimilative Self, dominated so by a tropological discourse, the literal Other does not have a language by which it can communicate (represent) its difference. The result is a confusion of viewpoints and sentiments such as we find in Barbara, whose words ("eigentlich verdienen Sie kein Mitleid") cannot even be taken at face-value, so wrongly does her representation of her emotion obscure her actual sentiments, which in the context of the story can be better shown than told: "Sie hatte sich umgewendet, und die Tränen liefen ihr stromweise über die Backen."

III. THE ORIGINS OF REPROACH, THE REPROACH OF ORIGINS

Now to return to the problem of representation itself where it is built most literally into the text, at a level of at least three removes from the unrepresented "reality": namely, the scene in which the Spielmann procures from Barbara a reproduction of "das Lied" that occassioned his musical conversion—the scene where the Spielmann proves himself to be the literal "Original" of the Narrator. In narrative terms, there are two layers of discourse embedded here for recuperation which can be schematized as follows:

Reader → (Narrator[1] → [Narrator[2] (Spielmann) → Barbara])

The Narrator seeks to reproduce a discourse which in part consists of the narration of a discourse. This, however, simply sets forth the structure of a more perplexing issue. The Narrator's attempt at representation is mirrored in the Spielmann's eagerness to reproduce "das Lied" ("nachzuspielen"). The Spielmann's attempts are met by only a qualified success ("Wären Sie etwa gar derselbe, rief sie aus, der so kratzt auf der Geige?") and the question of the Narrator's success is implicitly raised too. One obstacle to the Spielmann is the deficiency of his memory: ". . . das Kratzen rührt von daher, daß ich das Lied nicht in Noten habe, weshalb ich auch höflichst um die Abschrift gebeten haben wollte" (p. 29). How reliable are the Narrator's powers of recall?

Um die Abschrift? sagte sie. Das Lied ist gedruckt und wird an den Straßenecken verkauft. (p. 29)	"Geschichte?" wiederholte er. Ich habe keine Geschichte." (p. 19)

Barbara's startled response to the Spielmann's request parallels the Spielmann's response to the Narrator. Both the Spielmann and Barbara are innocent of the difference their interlocuter is pressing after:

Nun ja, die Worte, das Lied.	Heute wie morgen, und morgen wie heute . . .

"Schreibt man denn derlei auch auf?" asks Barbara, and the question might equally be put to the Narrator. The interrogators persist:

Und wie haben denn Sie's erlernt, werte Jungfer?	Wie es sich fügte - . . .

until recognition:

Ach, das wird wohl das sein!	Das also nennen sie meine Geschichte?

The sources ultimately volunteer their "originality," and they make preparations to assume the necessarily stylized posture:

. . . setzte den Korb wieder ab, stellte den Fuß auf den Schemel und sang . . .	Seine Gestalt verlängerte sich . . . (Er) schlug sitzend ein Bein über das andere und nahm überhaupt die Lage eines mit Bequemlichkeit Erzählenden an.

But the problems do not end here. If the Spielmann is convinced he has arrived at the ultimate original, then he is mistaken. Barbara too is implicated in the problem of (qualified) reproduction: "Ich hörte es singen, und da sang ich's *nach*." That the Spielmann is somewhat dissatisfied with the qualifications of his original is clear from his response. He goes on to praise her "natürlich Ingenium" and untutored "Talent," but reserves the word "Kunst" for himself: "Es ist aber doch nicht das Rechte, die *eigentliche* Kunst." "Eigentlich" recalls the difficulties (noted above) the Narrator falls into at the very outset of his effort ("ein *eigentliches* Volksfest"). The Spielmann cannot hide his despairing effort with the same ease ("Ich war nun neuerdings in Verzweiflung . . .") and Barbara comes closer to stating the problem than anyone else: "Aber welches Lied ist es denn *eigentlich*?" (The "es" might just as well have been omitted.) Not surprisingly, there is no one "original," but an unnumbered quantity of "originals" ("ich weiß so viele"). The Spielmann too seems to have discovered for himself more than one object of desire: "das Lied . . . so schön, so lieblich, daß sie noch zu Ende war, ich nach ihrer herabhängenden *Hand* fuhr." Thus are the string of desires and the string of "originals" proliferated into an unreachable infinity. The schema of imbedded discourse/desires stands in need of revision:

Reader → (Narrator[1] → [Narrator[2] (Spielmann) → Narrator[3] (Barbara) →?])

The string is graphically illustrated where the tales of the "Ohrfeige" are verified (p. 41). Barbara is busy in the store, standing on her toes, searching, *"den Rücken mir zugekehrt und mit den erhobenden Händen, wie man nach etwas sucht, auf einem der höheren Stellbretter herumtastend. Und dabei sang sie leise in sich hinein.—Es war das Lied, mein Lied!"* The Spielmann from behind is searching with his hands for her: " . . . *und faßte sie mit beiden Händen* . . . " With a small stretch of the imagination we can picture the Narrator standing behind the Spielmann with groping hands, and the reader behind him, etc. This scene follows a pattern of tensions familiar to the text: proximity leads to excitement (Spielmann: "Ich schlich näher und näher und war schon so *nahe,* daß . . . " [p. 41]; Narrator: " . . . ich war ganz *nahe* zu ihm getreten" [p. 10]); excitement leads to frustration. Barbara represents to both the Spielmann and the Narrator the ultimate "Original," the object most neglected by, and most ineluctable to, reproduction; the reproachful object that is ignorant of, and ignores, Art ("Von Musik und Gesang war nie die Rede" [p. 41]; "und [sie] kümmert sich wenig mehr um Musik" [p. 52]; the object that must submit to other laws and provisionally deny the lure and risk of approximation in order to endure indefinately in the face of harsh realities ("Aber da ist kein Mittel." [p. 49])—while for Art, the infinite duration of the moment, the expanse of the metaphor (the "Stillstand"), or the Center without periphery ("Mittel") is the core of experience.

Barbara's inaccessibility, however, implies still another kind of reproach, a reproach aimed at both the Spielmann and the Narrator for having condemned her to the inaccessible, for having wrapped her in the "mystique" that surrounds the object-original. This other reproach particularly escapes the notice of the Narrator, who presents the final scene in his conventional, narcissistic terms ("Ihr Gesicht war dabei von mir abgewandt, so daß ich nicht sehen konnte, was etwa darauf vorging." [p. 56]). The "last" glimpse she "affords" of herself, itself a pitiful commentary, is enjoyed as a perfecting conquest by the self-made hero of truth and detection. With all due conventionality, the Narrator makes his de-finitive statement with an appropriate gesture, by conceding the narrative entire to the object (since, according to the code of the mystique-(self-) worshippers, the last word—the silent word—must always return to the object):[29] "Sie hatte sich umgewendet, und die Tränen liefen ihr stromweise über die Backen." But the concession is only apparent: "stromweise" is a formal expenditure, a stylization or touch-up that lifts this object to the level of the other narrated objects: "[die] zwei Ströme, die alte Donau und die geschwollnere Woge des Volks" (p. 3). By *refusing* to concede to the object, the Narrator can protect its most precious "originality" from an exchange that would in turn fatally devaluate the "originality" of the narrative itself. The ultimate expense to the Narrator, the estimation of the Narrator's self*in*validation, is for the reader to measure against his or her re-collection of the original original.

This study began with an appeal to logic just as, in a most basic sense, do all readings of a text: to establish the reason of words ("der Ursprung des Namens" [p. 14]). Reenacting the urge of Adam harbored equally by the text, we encountered a difference, unbridgeable and irremediable, between the names and the things named. The discrepancy is fundamental, and owes less to the arbitrary nature of linguistic signs than to the respective referential orientations of the immediate naming-agents in the text (the Narrator and characters and the tacit informant occupying the space between conflicting points of view, the implicit authorial point of view). The evaluative problem that arises from these conflicting strains of logic is first reproduced in the text's own attempts to define the normative concepts of "Eigentlichkeit" and "verdienen." The text, however, cannot determine its own value, it cannot read itself. Ineffectual to name itself in this one respect (the individual voices mute one another, while the logic of the authorial "voice" is one of silent organization), the text anticipates without eclipsing the activity of reading by making this indeterminancy (this illegibility) descriptive of its own processes, by reading reading, with reading representing reading. Thus, the evaluative problem in turn becomes for the reader a problem of self-evaluation. And this, as I hope to have shown, is an activity without end.

Notes

1. Franz Grillparzer, *Der arme Spielmann, Erzählung,* mit einem Nachwort von Emil Kast (1977), p. 3. Henceforth in the notes, *"DAS."* All italics in the textual citations are mine, unless otherwise specified.

2. As the aim of this paper is to suggest an alternative, and at times close, reading of *DAS* in light of the general problem of realism, of mimesis and representation, I cannot hope to deal in any extensive way with the substantial body of literature on either the general or specific topics. For my theoretical insights I rely heavily on the classic work of the Russian Formalists (Shklovsky, Ehrlich, Jakobson) and on that of the more recent structuralists (Barthes especially) and post-structuralists. With regard to the Grillparzer text, I found the critical studies by Brinkmann, von Wiese, Politzer, and Heine quite helpful. It is only appropriate, then, that I acknowledge my debt in discussing each of these critical works briefly.

Richard Brinkmann's *Wirklichkeit und Illusion* ([3]1977) is the first analysis to identify the problem of realism in *DAS* as primarily a formal problem: what is "real" in a given work is not simply a (re)collection of identifiable artifacts; rather, the "real" is to be found in the formal organization of the work, in its structuration of experience, which is the visible projection of the assumptions and intentions the (implicit) author and/or narrator bring(s) to the work. So far, so good. In *DAS,* then, the Narrator has chosen a form of narration that commits him to authenticity, the "Ich-Erzählung." By making himself accountable for a second narration, that of the Spielmann, the Narrator puts himself in a (formal) bind: how can he preserve the authenticity of his own and the Spielmann's narratives without counterfeiting one or the other (pp. 123 and 129)? His options are two: either to comply with the limits of (and thereby preserve) his "Ich-Erzählung" and represent the Spielmann's narrative through indirect discourse, or to resort to (apparent) omniscience, and to qualified authenticity, by presenting the Spielmann's story in direct discourse. Is this a fair assessment? I think not, for two reasons. First, there is no reason to label the narrative tactic in the reported speechof the Spielmann "omniscient." By the conventions of realism, the Narrator is still working in his authentic first-person perspective: extraordinary retension of detail is in this kind of literature an uncontested given. Which brings me to my second point. Professor Brinkmann was right in challenging the authenticity of the narration where he did, at the juncture of the two narratives. But he failed to extend the challenge to other, equally crucial junctures: "Dagegen verstößt freilich nicht die gelegentliche Wiedergabe einer direkten Rede des Spielmanns" (p. 124). By this logic one could argue the briefer, earlier utterances of the Spielmann by their brevity alone would be the harder to retain; do they have any less of a claim to factitiousness than the later, reported monologue? "Nummer 34 im ersten Stocke" (*DAS*, p. 13). A few sparse hours after this remark is made, the Narrator has already forgotten where the Spielmann lives (*DAS*, p. 14)! Such signs encourage me to suspect that Grillparzer is toying quite deliberately with the "formal" problem of mimesis: by making salient the likely defects of mimesis due to the simple fallibility of memory, and by constructing an ambiguous two- (or even three- or more) way mirror of perspectives through which to observe and assess character, and through which we must learn to acknowledge the likely fallibility (or discrepancies) of perception. In short, Grillparzer both constructs and *deforms* the problem of realism: it is "problematized" by the structural organization of the text (in competing narratives, for instance), but it is replicated in each of the characters, but particularly in the person of the Spielmann, whose monologic representation is subject to the same pitfalls and doubts as the Narrator's. Moreover, the Spielmann is pathetic, and so the incongruities, the deformities, of his telling are all the more patent. "Der Spielmann sicht dabei mit einer Klarheit und Weite und mit objektiver Distanz, die dem Grundzug seines Wesens, der eigentümlich monomanischen Abgeschlossenheit widerspricht" (p. 132). As much can be said of the Narrator.

Benno von Wiese gives a clear and sensible account of *DAS* in his *Die Deutsche Novelle von Goethe bis Kafka: Interpretationen* (1964), I, 134ff. The essay, in my opinion, overcomes the limiting nature of the format: it is designed to be a brief thematic exegesis set in the context of a genre survey. Focusing on ambivalences in the Spielmann's character, von Wiese comes closer to the heart of the problem than more recent scholars who make the Spielmann into a saint. Among them: Peter Schäublin, "Das Musizieren des armen Spielmanns," *Sprachkunst* [1972], Heft 1/2, 32-55, see esp. p. 53; and Robert Browing, "Language and the Fall from Grace," *Seminar*, 12 (1976), 215-235. Notwithstanding, the study remains a character study, not does von Wiese take adequate pains to distinguish "Autor" from "Dichter" (i.e. Narrator from the biographic writer Grillparzer). The terms "(implicit) author," "narrator," "Grillparzer" will be used in this paper to make this necessary distinction.

Heinz Politzer's "Franz Grillparzers *Der arme Spielmann*" (1967) approaches the novella as though it were a piece of psychological realism. (The "intimacy" of this approach is assured in namecalling: Politzer's Spielmann is a "Jakob.") The theme of the story is successful "Begegnung" and alienation, and we have an example of each: the inner story of the Spielmann tends toward the tragic dysfunction of communication, while the outer narrative yields a promising comic solution: "Was Barbara mit Jakob nicht gelungen ist, gelingt ihr hier mit seinem Chronisten: er erlebt seine schöpferische Stunde, die Stunde der Begegnung, in der aus zweien eins wird, nämlich dieses Werk, dieser "Armer Spielmann" (p. 60). I cannot agree with this interpretation, though I find that Politzer is otherwise a close and sensitive reader. Politzer, however, comes closest to stating the "Similar Differences" thesis to be discussed below: "Daß zwischen diesen beiden Künstlergestalten . . . von vornherein tiefere Beziehungen gegeben sind, ohne daß der Erzähler dies bemerkte, gehört zu den vielen Ironien, die über ihrem Verhältnis walten" (p. 51). I would rather put it the other way around, that the "many ironics" are ordered under this most basic irony and "mishearing" which is easily translatable into the most persistant theme of the novella.

With the general hermeneutical perspective of Roland Heine's "Ästhetische oder existentielle Integration? Ein hermeneutisches Problem des 19. Jahrhunderts in Grillparzers Erzählung 'Der arme Spielmann' (*DVjs* [1972], 650-83) I find much to agree, and in particular with several of his close readings. I do not find his conclusions compelling though, nor do I think the Dilthey hermeneutic model on which they are based is applicable to our text. The Dilthey model forsees two possibilities for integrating a life and its meaning, and these are stated in Heine's title: a "Bedeutungszusammenhang" is either given *prior to* one's understanding ("existentielle Integration") or it is won *through* understanding ("ästhetische Integration") (cp. p. 667); in the case of the Spielman, I think it neither. The point Heine would make is the following: "Im Erzählzusammenhang von Jakobs Lebensgeschichte hat sich auch erst der Sinnzusammenhang seines Lebens ergeben" (p. 677). But nowhere does he specify in what respects the Spielmann has reached an *improved* understanding of his life, or how he is any more thoroughly integrated with his life-meaning after his telling than he was before it. The text certainly does not suggest that the act of narrating his past has altered the Spielmann's conception of the present ("Und damit ergriff der Alte seine Geige und fing an, das Lied zu spielen, und spielte fort und fort, ohne sich weiter um mich zu kümmern. Endlich hatte ich's satt . . ." [p. 52]), precisely because it has not altered his conception of the past. If anything, the Spielmann has in an almost retrogressive act renewed his bond with that part of the past that is for him immutable: "[Barbara] hat sich zwar sehr verändert in den vielen Jahren, ist stark geworden und kümmert sich wenig mehr um Musik, *aber es klingt noch immer so hübsch wie damals*" (p. 52). On the other hand, I do not think the text gives us any reason to suppose the original state of ignorance we must assume if we are to see in the Spielmann the coming to (self-/historical-) consciousness Heine sees in the "Entdeckung and Lösung" (p. 65) of "die erkenntnistheoretische Frage" posed in his title. Otherwise what are we to make of the words of the Spielmann: "Möchte ich mir's doch selbst einmal *wieder* erzählen" (p. 19)? or those of the Narrator: "[er] nahm überhaupt die Lage eines *mit Bequemlichkeit* Erzählenden an" (*ibid.*)? Even if the Spielmann ever achieved "aesthetic integration" it is unlikely that he achieves it here for the first time. It is more likely that the Spielmann comes, in the course of his life, to repeated partial understandings of his situation, just as he makes repeated attempts to reproduce Barbara's "Lied," but never achieving (total) integration, aesthetic or otherwise.

According to Heine, the Spielmann succeeds on a formal, hermeneutical level where he failed miserably existentially. I do not believe the two levels can be separated so easily as this, nor does the text encourage us to make this distinction. Heine himself notes the figural significance of the school-lesson scene: "Jakob muß erfahren, daß er in der Gesellschaft nicht am rechten Platze ist, daß er in sie ebensowenig hineinpaßt, wie ein unpassendes Wort in den Textzusammenhang" (p. 658). I would rephrase the formulation to: ". . . daß er in sie ebensowenig hineinpaßt, wie ein *passendes* Wort . . ." which could mean several things, but among them, that *Der arme Spielmann* heightens the fundamental ambiguity between a word and its context that stems from the general over-capacity of language. It is the words that *fit* the context (language in its ordinary, functional mode) that are susceptible to mis-readings (viz. to fictional narratives). The cohesiveness of *Der arme Spielmann* is due to its consistent figural representation of a literal problem such as this. Thus, the Spielmann's dyslexia serves as a metaphor for the general mis-reading of his life. The question remains, how is it possible for the Spielmann who fails so existentially (dyslexically) to succeed hermeneutically (to re-read his mis-reading), when the only difference between these two tests will be a new text? A closer look at the structure of *Der arme Spielmann* will show how the entire text is nothing if not a deliberate configuration of repeated instances of the same: in a world of duplicates everything fits, congruously: and so should (and do) the hermeneutical and existential events, viz. failures.

3. Although this line of interpretation does not *explicitly* acknowledge these conditions, I am suggesting that the paradox is an inescapable corollary to any over-definition of the Narrator's role in "objective" description. For instance: "Ebenso ist es etwa mit der Abschiedsszene zwischen Barbara und dem Spielmann. Auch sie ist überlegen und 'objektiv' gestaltet und in Worten dargeboten, die der Dichter dem Spielmann in den Mund legt, die aber doch nicht die seinen sind aus möglicher Erinnerung, sondern die aus des Dichters

'idealer' Vorstellungskraft kommen . . . Der Dichter ist es, der in Wahrheit hier spricht" (Brinkmann, *op. cit.*, pp. 134-135). One might object to these considerations on the grounds of interpretation alone; the Spielmann might well be capable of the same "clarity" of thought we look for and find in the Narrator, as I argue below. But another, more serious objection is a matter of theoretical interest. If we accept these conclusions, not only are we trammeling the conventions of realist narration that make great allowances for retention of detail by speaking subjects, we are also commited to the possibility that *everything* given by the Narrator is complete fantasy, that perhaps he is some kind of maniac who has concocted the whole story from ink for whatever motive (to conflate him with the author, in orher words). This seems to me both unnecessary and untenable. Below we will find an exact parallel for the Narrator's "fantasies" in the Spielmann; and seeing how the story is constructed in such a way that the narration of the Spielmann is "certified" by the appearance of Barbara, we should construe the narration of the Narrator in the same way—as ultimately certifi*able*, given the possibility. In pitting near-absurdities (the utterly fantastic narrator option) against conventions (that narrators are not generally *that* given to fantasy), Grillparzer is testing the bed-rock of fiction, not eliminating it. This kind of restraint is also a basic requirement of Professor Brinkmann's analysis: ". . . Grillparzer [steht] noch in der Tradition des 'objektiven' Dichters, obgleich nicht mehr so fest und fraglos, daß er auf realistische, das heißt hier: empirische Begründung und Legitimierung verzichten könnte" (p. 132).

4. R. Jakobson, "Two Aspects of Language and Two Types of Linguistic Disturbance," in *Selected Writings* (1962-1971), v. 2, p. 72.

5. "Ich habe von Natur keine Stimme" (p. 25).

6. In Jakobson's terms (see "Closing Statement: Linguistics and Poetics," in Sebeok (ed.), *Style in Language* [1960], pp. 353 ff.) the metalingual, (glossing), phatic (contact-prone) and poetic functions are reduced to different degrees, with the result that narrator-reader contact is radically modified. The speech-event functions are reduced to three dominants: emotive (expressive), conative (vocative and imperative), and referential (denotative). Consequently, the narrative discourse swings around emphatically to the Narrator's point of view. As the Narrator is less concerncd with coaxing the reader along, the reader must now consume the Narrator's imperatives. The reader is thus somewhat impersonalized ("so kann *man* sich wohl leicht eine Idee von der Verwirrung machen, die daraus hervorging." [p. 17]) and even hypostasized ("den Leser," [p. 17])—which, it seems, puts a great restriction on his earlier, hypothetical role as "listener" ("sage ich" [p. 5]). And it is the referent which is made the object of intensive investigation ("der Gegenstand meiner Neugier" [p. 9]).

7. "Of course," because a complete exchange would be impossible: the possibility for exchange is a

narrative fiction, a necessary ideal for forgetting that the narration is already mimesis.

8. The hardships of mimesis are endemic. Even the "übrigen öffentlichen Musikleute" suffer from it: "Daher spielen sie auch aus dem *Gedächtniss* und greifen *falsch* mitunter, ja häufig" (p. 12).

9. This phenomenon of "monologic" style is not restricted to Grillparzer. See, for instance, the article by Stephen M. Ross, "Voice in Narrative Texts: *As I Lay Dying*," *PMLA*, 94 (1979), 300-310. Faulkner's novel is narrated by several "voices" which not only "perceive the same phenomena, but . . . employ the same metaphors to describe them" (p. 304). Ross attributes this univocality of narration to an intimated ulterior consciousness which is "constituted by voice rather than revealed by it": "consciousness *is* the language used and shared by the narrators" (*ibid.*). Grillparzer is less concerned with consciousness than with the symbolic attitudes of his "notional" characters vis-à-vis the traditional "metaphysics" of meaning; representation is their language and constitutive consciousness.

10. The six-numbered similar differences are not by any means intended to be complete or exhaustive, but only indicative of the kind of reading the text allows.

11. Or the meaning of a word like "Ordnung" undergoes semantic torture: "Zweitens muß sich der Mensch in allen Dingen eine gewisse *Ordnung* festsetzen, sonst gerät er ins Wilde und Unaufhaltsame" (p. 11); "Kratzt der alte einmal wieder . . . und stort die *ordentlichen* Leuten in ihrer Nachtruhe" (p. 14); ". . . verdienen Sie kein Mitleid . . . wenn man so schwach ist, seine eigenen Sachen nicht in *Ordnung* halten zu können" (p. 49).

12. Jakobson, "Closing Statement," p. 275.

13. See Jakobson again, p. 375, and compare Barthes, *S/Z* (1970), p. 97: "Le récit n'engendre pas le récit par extension métonymique (sauf à passer par le relais du désir), mais par alternance paradigmatique: le récit est déterminé non par un désir de raconter mais par un désir d'échanger: c'est un *valant pour*, un représentant, une monnaie, un pesant d'or. Ce qui rend compte de cette *équivalence* centrale, ce n'est pas le 'plan' . . . c'est [l] a structure."

14. Paul De Man, *Blindness and Insight: Essays in the Rhetoric of Contemporary Criticism* (1971), p. 132.

15. *DAS*, p. 5.

16. Cf. Barthes, "Introduction à l'analyse structurale des récits," *Communications* 8 (1966).

17. This peculiar redundancy is never more transparent than when the Spielmann trys to achieve a rhetorical effect the facts of the situation will simply not tolerate: "Die Verkäuferin mochte mir, wie gesagt, das alles erzählt haben, aber ich hörte nicht und *stand regungslos*" (p. 50). Again, it is the "Stillstand" the obstruction to sequence, that creates a dangerous pause for metonymic, narrative discourse. Narration is thus a self-interrogating and self-implicating discourse ("einsame Übungen" [p. 11]) that must forge elaborate questions to re-member intentionally forgotten answers:

"*Erinnern Sie mich* auf einen Umstand, der schon früher meine Neugier rege machte!" (p. 10).

18. Jakobson, "Closing Statement," p. 375; "Two Aspects of Language and Two Types of Linguistic Disturbance" in *Selected Writings*, (1962-71), v. 2, p. 92.

19. *Ibid.*

20. *Ibid.*pp. 85-89.

21. *Ibid.*, p. 86.

22. See A. R. Luria's remarks on amnestic aphasia in "Theory of Aphasia," in *Roman Jakobson, Echoes of His Scholarship*, ed. D. Armstrong and C. H. van Schooneveld (1977), pp. 237-251: "Closer analysis shows, however, that underlying this symptom is not so much 'forgetting' of words and insufficiency of vocabulary but rather a SURPLUS of verbal denotations which may come to mind with equal probability and from which the patient cannot choose the one required."

23. Significantly, however, the Narrator can only attain this "Verbindungsweg" imaginatively; in the course of the story he never once sets foot on the other side of the bridge.

24. Barthes' account of the descriptive properties of language (*S/Z*, p. 120), which I re-discovered after having written this section, is uniquely appropriate: "Le blason consiste à prédiquer un sujet unique, la beauté, d'un certain nombre d'attributs anatomiques . . . L'adjectif devient sujet et le substantif prédicat . . . La phrase ne peut jamais constituter un *total*; les sens peuvent s'égrener, non s'additioner: le total, le somme sont pour le nagage des *terres promises* [italics mine], entrevues *au bout* de l'énumération, mais cette énumération accomplie, aucun trait ne pe la rassambler . . ." Barthes would no doubt regard the Narrator's indulgence in this "Schlaraffenlande" of metaphor as a fleeting realization or re-territorialization of the dream and desire of language.

25. The Narrator's inclination to willful blindness surfaces unmistakeably in a later passage where a second, significant "Stillstand" arrests momentarily the narrative sequence; and again, forgetfulness and in-difference are the essential ingredients of the experience: "Die Stille des Ortes, im Abstich der lärmenden Volksmenge, tat mir wohl, und mich verschiedenen Gedanken überlassend, *an denen der alte Spielmann nicht den letzten Anteil hatte* . . . Ich hatte die Hausnummer *glücklich vergessen*, auch war in der Dunkelheit an das Erkennen irgendeiner Bezeichnung kaum zu denken . . . Ich *stand stille*" (p. 14).

26. In a sense, these words are prophetic of the deconstruction of the Narrator's point of view to come ("aus dem Rahmen des Buches *entsprungen*").

27. Provocative and persuasive are Victor Shklovsky's thoughts on sentimentality in "A Parodying Novel: Sterne's *Tristram Shandy*," in *Russian Formalist Criticism*, ed. and trans. by Lee T.Lemon and Marion Reis (1965), p. 79ff.: "Sentimentality cannot be the content of art if for no other reason than that art does not have a separable content. The

representation of things from 'the sentimental point of view' is a special method of representation . . . In its essence art is outside emotion . . . 'Gore' in art is not gory, it rhymes with 'amor' . . ."

28. Respective discourses can be assigned different exchange values in like manner: metaphorical-discourse is satisfied by *qualitative* change ("die Nota sensibilis hinaufsteigt wie eine erfüllte Hoffnung" [p. 25]); metonymical-discourse requires *quantitative* change, total expropriation ("ein vorteilhaftes Geschäft" [p. 56]; original-discourse sets only one condition: *equivalence* of exchange ("So viel habe ich gehabt, so viel bring ich zurück." [p. 48]).

29. Barthes' brilliant reminder is apt here: "On en revient une fois de plus à la dure loi de la communication humaine: *l'originel* [italics mine] n'est lui-même que la plus plate des langues et c'est par excès de pauvreté, non de richesse, que nous parlons d'ineffable. Or c'est avec ce premier langage, ce nommé, ce trop-nommé, que la literature doit se debattre . . . On entend souvent dire que l'art a pour charge *d'exprimer l'inexprimable*: c'est le contraire qu'il faut dire (sans nulle intention de paradoxe): toute la tâche de l'art est *d'inexprimer l'exprimable*, d'enlever à la langue du monde, qui est la pauvre et puissante langue des passions, une parole *autre*, une parole *exacte*" (from the preface to *Essais Critiques*, [1964], p. 14).

Bruce Thompson (excerpt date 1981)

SOURCE: "Poetry and Prose," in *Franz Grillparzer,* Twayne Publishers, 1981, pp. 80-94.

[*In the following excerpt, Thompson contrasts Grillparzer's two works of short fiction,* Der arme Spielmann *and* Das Kloster bei Sendomir.]

In view of the fact that Grillparzer regarded poetry so much more highly than prose, it is more surprising that he should have written creatively in prose at all, than that he should have made only two contributions to the most popular genre of the nineteenth century in Germany, the shorter prose narrative. Grillparzer's two short stories, **Das Kloster bei Sendomir** and **Der arme Spielmann,** are dissimilar in content and atmosphere, and have also had markedly contrasting receptions. The former, published in 1827, has been generally regarded as a minor work and has received scant critical attention, but the latter, published in 1847, has been the subject of numerous critical studies, and has been acclaimed as one of the masterpieces in the history of the German *Novelle*. Both works are deeply rooted in Grillparzer's personal experience, treating respectively two of the dominant passions of his life, namely, love and devotion to his art. The autobiographical element is here even more than usually prominent, and it has been seen as the principal reason for Grillparzer's retreat in these two particular cases into the more protective form of prose narrative.[1]

With the sensational and improbable character of its subjectmatter, its atmosphere of tension and mystery, its lack of detailed characterization, and its violent, melodramatic conclusion, **Das Kloster bei Sendomir** [**The Monastery of Sendomir**] recalls aspects of Romantic horror literature, and Kleistian and Hoffmannesque qualities have been detected in it, both stylistic and atmospheric. Grillparzer had thus returned to the kind of material that had produced *Die Ahnfrau*, and to a genre that had really run its course. Yet it is a powerful story of dark passions and violence, treating the themes of adultery and murder, and presents a disturbing picture of an ill-fated marriage.

The story is narrated by a mysterious monk, who turns out to be the central character Starschensky, a Polish count who is lured into marrying a woman of voluptuous beauty called Elga, who accosts him at night on the streets of Warsaw. Though Elga is no prostitute in the technical sense, but the daughter of an impoverished nobleman, she ensnares Starschensky, who duly marries her and rescues her father from his precarious financial position. The couple settle down on Starschensky's estate and a daughter is born, but it is not long before their domestic harmony is disturbed. There are reports that a dark figure has been visiting the house at night, and Starschensky finds among Elga's possessions a portrait of her cousin Oginsky, which bears a strong resemblance to the child. The suspicious Starschensky returns to Warsaw, and inquiries reveal that Elga and Oginsky did indeed have a previous love affair. Later he reappears at home accompanied by a hooded figure whom he locks in a disused tower on the estate. In the final melodramatic scene Starschensky reveals to Elga that the figure is Oginsky himself, who has confessed to the paternity of the child. Oginsky flees, but Starschensky cuts Elga down with his sword and sets fire to the tower. Later he establishes a monastery near the site, becomes a monk, and does nightly penance for his monstrous crime.

Conceived as early as 1820, **Das Kloster** was based originally on Grillparzer's relationship with Charlotte, Oginsky's flight and Starschensky's violent revenge apparently representing Grillparzer's judgment on his own adultery with his cousin's wife. Yet the story was largely written in 1825, when Grillparzer had fallen under the spell of Marie and was already harboring suspicions about her character. Moreover, it is told from the viewpoint of the deceived Starschensky, rather than from that of the treacherous Oginsky, who remains a shadowy figure. Thus, as Douglas Yates has pointed out, the situation anticipates with uncanny accuracy Grillparzer's circumstances in 1826, when he felt himself betrayed by his friend Daffinger, who turned out to be the father of Marie's child.

Starschensky's story is narrated by himself, but in the third person so that he achieves a degree of objectivity about his own fate. His story is presented with sympathy, but also critically. Starschensky comes to Warsaw as an "innocent," having led a solitary existence and having had little contact with women, but this was due to his own love of independence and isolation. Thus he is particularly susceptible to Elga's charms, as she virtually seduces him into marrying her.[4] She takes the initiative in their physical relations, then tantalizes him by keeping him at a distance. When they are married, she indulges in a life of expensive pleasure-seeking. Yet Starschensky is still blissfully happy with her, blinded by passion, a victim both of his own naiveté and of this dangerously alluring creature. But though she is in some ways a forerunner of the coquettish Rahel of *Die Jüdin von Toledo*, no character in Grillparzer's work is reduced to such a level of cynical inhumanity as is Elga in the final nightmarish scene. This scene brings the work closest to some of Kleist's stories, when Starschensky threatens Elga with death, but indicates that he will spare her if she will kill the child. Elga at first protests, but soon she agrees in order to save her own life. But, before she can murder the child, Starschensky reveals that this was a trick, a test of her humanity, which she has failed, so he kills her nevertheless. In Elga the instinct for self-preservation has outweighed the instinct of maternal love; in Starschensky reason has become tainted with jealous passion, and the result is a cruelly difficult test of Elga's integrity, followed by brutal revenge. Perhaps a Kleistian Elga would have made an intuitive leap in the dark and perceived the meaning of Starschensky's test, but in Grillparzer's story there is no such salvation for the characters.

Just as Starschensky has been able to objectify his story through the medium of third-person narrative, so too has Grillparzer, through Starschensky, presented his own situation at an even greater distance. He has also exaggerated and distorted his experiences, translating his own pain, self-criticism, and, above all, his fears concerning both the nature of Marie and his own potential reaction, into a fictional situation. . . .

Grillparzer's second prose work, *Der arme Spielmann* [*The Poor Musician*], was begun in 1831, but not completed until about 1842. It is a more mature work than *Das Kloster*, but again a major problem concerns the relationship between author and subject, and the story has alarming implications for Grillparzer's misgiving concerning the value of his own art. The most immediately striking feature of the work is the framework which has been constructed round the central story of the musician. This takes up over a third of the work and is more elaborate than that used in his previous story. Like Starschensky, the musician gives his own account of himself, though here in the more usual form of first-person narrative. Yet Grillparzer again distances himself from his subject, in this case by interposing between reader and musician a narrator, a dramatist like himself, as though to discourage any assumption that the musician is simply a projection of Grillparzer's own self.

The narrator first notices the musician playing his violin to the crowds near the Augarten on the occasion of a popular festival, and the two have a brief conversation. Later that evening he listens to him from the street below as he plays in his room in the Leopoldstadt. But the musician's story is not told until the narrator actually visits him a few days later. Through the narrator's eagerness to get to know him Grillparzer convinces us that he is a case worth investigating. The impression received is that of an eccentric curiosity, for there is a striking element of incongruity in the musician's appearance and behavior. He stands alongside a group of beggar musicians, yet his dress and manner suggest a genteel and educated background, and he is serenely oblivious to his lowly surroundings. But his music is the most remarkable aspect of him. He is engrossed in his performance, which gives him obvious pleasure, and the sheet music on the stand before him suggests a more professional approach than that taken by the majority of

his kind. Indeed, he tells the narrator that he practices daily difficult compositions by the best composers. Yet what he produces is a disconnected sequence of sounds without melody or rhythm, a confusion unrecognizable as belonging to any particular piece of music and which is even painful to the ear.

Thus far the musician has remained a mystery to the narrator and it is only by having him tell his own story that he can get close to the truth about him.[2] As suggested by his appearance, the musician has indeed known better days, and his story constitutes a pathetic record of failure. Dull and painstakingly slow at his lessons, he becomes estranged from his father, who is an influential and ambitious man, and who obviously tries to forget his son's existence. He is given a menial copying job in the chancellery, and at home he leads a narrow and solitary life. When his father dies, he unexpectedly finds himself a rich man, but he imprudently entrusts his wealth to a rogue and is quickly ruined. This apparently empty and fruitless life is enriched by one engrossing experience, from which springs his passion for music. One evening he hears a girl in the courtyard below his room sing a song which entrances him, and which he finds he can play on the violin, an instrument he has not touched since childhood. The singer is a grocer's daughter, Barbara, and with timidity and embarrassment he seeks her acquaintance, initially to obtain the score of the song. She treats him with disdain, and when he visits her father's shop she ignores him. But, with the encouragement of her father, the visit is repeated, and gradually she begins to tolerate him. She even seems not to exclude the possibility of marriage when she advises him to take a shop, which she will help him run. Only when his financial ruin is discovered does she dismiss him, to marry a butcher whose proposal she had hitherto rejected. As for the musician, he is left to play his music and to give lessons to Barbara's children.

While the facts of the musician's story partly satisfy the narrator's curiosity, the story itself raises fundamental questions concerning our assessment of the man and his "music." He emerges from the story as a pathetic and occasionally absurd character, but though he is outwardly incompetent, there is no doubting either the honesty of his intentions or his moral integrity. In his office-job he works so slowly that he is thought to be lazy, yet this is because he is a perfectionist. His love for his father is such that instead of protesting against the harsh treatment that he suffers, he feels he should apologize for causing his father trouble. He allows himself to be cheated of his wealth, never imagining that not all possess the same honesty as himself. He has a decency that is occasionally misplaced or exaggerated, and that is literally too good for the world in which he lives. That his moral standards are not those of his fellowmen is suggested by the symbolic chalk line that he draws across the room to separate his own territory from that of the other lodgers. The order and cleanliness of his sector contrast with the disorder and dirt of theirs, but it is significant that whereas he observes the division, they do not. It is a one-sided and futile arrangement, from which he cannot profit in any practical sense, and there is a clear distinction between his interpretation of the situation and actuality. He is one of life's innocents lacking the practical fiber and judgment necessary for survival.

Eventually it is his lack of judgment that leads to his death, which occurs about a year after the musician's narration of his story, and which conveniently completes the framework and rounds off the work. It is set in February 1830, at the time of Vienna's great flood, and the Leopoldstadt is a major disaster area. Fearing for the musician's welfare, the narrator returns there to offer him assistance, only to discover that he has perished. He had behaved heroically, rescuing children from the flood, but it was not this that killed him. He died of a cold caught when he had gone back in foolhardy fashion to save his landlord's tax returns. Both actions were undertaken in the same spirit of selfless generosity, but in the exercise of his virtue he failed to discriminate between a matter of life and death and a triviality.[3]

The musician's inadequacies are most cruelly exposed in his relationship with Barbara. When they first become acquainted in the chancellery, where she sells refreshments, she asks for a piece of paper on which to place her cakes, a casual request, but he goes to ridiculous lengths to please her. Instead of simply taking a piece from the office, which he dare not do, he fetches a whole quire of paper from his home a few days later, a response which is well-meaning and which serves to further the acquaintanceship, but which at face value is absurdly inappropriate. From the reader's viewpoint the relationship seems a particularly humiliating one for the musician, for Barbara scolds him incessantly for his clumsiness and general ineptitude, showing us exactly what marriage to her would have been like for him. Yet the reader can detect in Barbara signs of genuine affection for him. When they part, she is emotionally distressed, and at the close of the work she is seen weeping over his memory. Clearly she senses something of value in his nature and character, yet at the same time she is exasperated that he is so weak, gullible, impractical, and effeminate. The musician is both saint and fool, a paradox which is reflected in the ambivalence of Barbara's feelings toward him.

It is possible that Grillparzer is offering through his presentation of the musician's unhappy fate a comment on the unscrupulous harshness of his own materialistic world, and we can despair that one so pure in soul becomes an outcast and beggar. The implication is that sterner qualities are required for survival in an unsympathetic world, qualities which the musician does not possess. Yet if he did possess them, he would lose something of his essential nobility. A similarly ironic combination of nobility of character and impracticality has been observed in the portraits of Bancbanus and Bishop Gregor, but in *Der arme Spielmann* greater emphasis is placed on the hero's inadequacies. He has been justly identified as one of the first true anti-heroes of nineteenth-century literature. One incident in particular, which stands at the center of the story, suggests that the blame for his failure rests more with his own character and personality than with society. This occurs at the climax of his relationship with Barbara when he attempts to embrace her for the only time. Her response is to strike him hard on the face, but then to kiss him lightly on the cheek. She then flees from him, and as she shuts the glass door in his face, he returns her kiss by pressing his lips passionately against the glass. The emotions that prompt Barbara's contradictory actions here are clearly identifiable. The blow represents a spontaneous reaction, her genuine anger at what she regards as an impertinence. Her kiss is only a fleeting gesture of remorse, in no sense an expression of love. Yet the musician is thrown into ec-stasies by the blow, and the memory of the kiss still brings tears to his eyes. His reaction is wholly inappropriate, for he invests in each of her actions a significance that is out of all proportion with reality. The gulf between reality and his own private view is symbolized by the glass which separates him and Barbara and in his ineffectual and grotesquely ridiculous attempt at a kiss. The incident both highlights his inadequacies as a man and suggests a profound division between himself and his fellow beings.

The musician's feelings for Barbara in themselves are also somewhat problematic. That this is no simple love story is suggested by the absence of any confession of love on his part. Nor is there any indication that he finds Barbara beautiful. Indeed, his colleagues find her pock-marked and generally unattractive, an opinion which he does not dispute. What does attract him is her song. It is the song that he finds beautiful, and it is his desire to possess the score of it that leads him to Barbara's home. It is when he finds her singing it that he attempts to embrace her; it is the song that he teaches to her elder child, that he plays after concluding his story, and that has retained its beauty for him over the years. The song thus possesses a unique significance for him and exercises over him a frightening demonic power. On the other hand, it affords him an ecstatic pleasure and is the only piece of music that he can play with any success. Indeed, he feels divinely inspired when he first plays it; it surpasses Bach and Mozart and provides access to God. When he dies, he smiles, as though he can hear something beautiful far away. It is thus arguable that his music has brought him close to "the divine source of truth and beauty,"[4] providing his life with spiritual and aesthetic riches which it would otherwise have lacked, and which transcend the ephemeral values of reality.

Yet if the musician's ears are attuned to some loftier ideal realm, he is unable to demonstrate this, for in that it fails to communicate anything of the feeling that has inspired the performer, his music is artistically worthless. The pleasure that he finds in his song is entirely private, for both to the narrator and to Barbara it sounds just like any ordinary popular song. Moreover, although he claims to have a serious artistic mission, he is totally unsuccessful in performance. Because he lacks the ability to communicate, to "perform" the ecstasy he feels, value cannot be ascribed to it in any absolute sense.[5] *Der arme Spielmann* underlines the fact that the power of the artist's vision is without value for others if it is not translated into intelligible art. As Grillparzer himself insisted, the basis of every art is craftsmanship, and any would-be artist who does not possess this quality is an incompetent, a *Stümper* (SB I, 14, 73). The musician's aesthetic experience may have significance for himself, but it is for his own pleasure alone. His devotion to his art and the evidence of the ecstasy that he derives from this are indicative of the capacity of art for the enrichment of life, but in that his art takes him into a private world which he cannot share with others, it is sterile. The gulf between the musician and reality, which exists in any case because of his shortcomings as a human being, is accentuated by the privacy of his art. Thus, although he has given his own subjective account of his story, we have still not got to the bottom of the mystery, for his deepest secret, the pleasure which he takes in his music, has remained impenetrable.

It is not without significance that **Der arme Spielmann** was completed at a time when Grillparzer's doubts as to the validity of his own art had reached a critical stage. The autobiographical element in this story is strong, and in an exaggerated and distorted fashion the portrait of the musician does reflect Grillparzer's relationship with his father, with Kathi Fröhlich, his own devotion to his art, and his tortured self-doubts both as man and artist.[6] If his earlier artist-figure Sappho also expressed Grillparzer's awareness of the gulf separating the artist from life, at least the value of her art was not questioned. But the value of the musician's art *is* questioned, and precisely because, in the true sense of the word, he is no artist. At most, he can represent Grillparzer's deepest fears as to the image that he himself might present to his unappreciative public. He is a distortion of the *unsuccessful* artist, and a warning of the dangers of an over-subjective, Romantic attitude to art. But he is also a forerunner of some of the sickly and decadent artist-figures of Thomas Mann, such as Detlev Spinell of *Tristan*, who enjoys the most exquisite, but uncommunicable private aesthetic experiences. In Grillparzer's musician's devotion to his song we may see an anticipation of the exclusive aestheticism and rarefied idealism that was to become such a cult at the turn of the century.

Notes

1. W. Paulsen, "Grillparzers Erzählkunst," *Germanic Review* 19 (1944): 59-68.

2. R. Brinkmann, *"Der arme Spielmann," Wirklichkeit und Illusion* (Tübingen, 1957), pp. 87-145, argues that despite Grillparzer's attempts to provide an objective, truthful depiction of the musician, he can only achieve a subjective account, whether from the narrator's or from the musician's own perspective.

3. A point made by Benno von Wiese, *"Der arme Spielmann," Die deutsche Novelle* (Düsseldorf, 1969), I, 147.

4. E. E. Papst, ed., *Der arme Spielmann* (London, 1960), p. xxvi.

5. J. P. Stern, *Re-interpretations* (London, 1964), writes: "What emerges as the sole positive value is . . . not the art which he has so faithfully 'practised' for a lifetime. . . . What emerges at the end . . . is the intention and the pure heart alone, the disembodied good will as the absolute and only value" (p. 72).

6. As argued by Papst, *Spielmann*, p. xx.

Roger F. Cook (essay date 1988)

SOURCE: "Relocating the Author: A New Perspective on the Narrator in *Der arme Spielmann*," in *Grillparzer's Der arme Spielmann: New Directions in Criticism*, edited by Clifford Albrecht Bernd, Camden House, 1988, pp. 322-36.

[In the following essay, Cook reassesses the function of the narrator in Der arme Spielmann, *arguing that it provides insight into the relationship between author and text.]*

Begun in 1831, but not completed until 1842 (published only in 1847), **Der arme Spielmann** was written during a period of transition for both German literature and the socio-political climate of the German-speaking regions. The development of a more volatile public consciousness, which had erupted in the violence of the 1830 July Revolution, added new significance to any literary work which dealt with contemporary social relationships. As the story of a social misfit, Grillparzer's novella reveals some problematical aspects of the emerging social order. Against the foil of the eccentric fiddler, the novella depicts the character of the Biedermeier period in which the larger populace had withdrawn from the public arena of strife back into the private realm of domestic simplicity. The view of the Viennese middle classes in **Der arme Spielmann,** however, does not reveal that idyllic quiet life of individual thrift which has typified the Biedermeier image in the eyes of subsequent generations. Instead, one finds among the lower middle classes a driving desire to attain the capital necessary for establishing a small trade and the willingness to swindle one's naive fellow man; one sees the exploitation of the petit bourgeois office worker; and in Jakob's father one has a figure representative of the upper bourgeoisie, who strives fanatically to instill in his sons the same rigorous classical education and disciplined work ethic which had brought him power inordinate with either his bureaucratic position or his class standing. Although primarily the burgher milieu is depicted in the novella, the atmosphere found there is far from the complacency associated with the larger public in the years 1830-1848. In fact, the only character who fits the Biedermeier topos is the outcast fiddler.

The focal point for most of the scholarship dealing with **Der arme Spielmann** has been the figure of the "poor fiddler." In a recent comprehensive discussion of the work's reception, Hinrich C. Seeba has shown that from 1847 through 1925 the interpretation of the novella was under the influence of the nostalgic memory of the Hapsburg Empire.[1] During this period the critic's attention remained fixed on the fiddler as an eccentric Biedermeier figure who embodies the bygone charm of preindustrial Austria. Under the influence of this course of reception, scholarly interpretation in the twentieth century has continued to ignore the novella's depiction of those social forces which alienate the fiddler from his fellow man. Since the end of World War II the novella has become the subject of numerous individual interpretations which, for the most part, concentrate on the psychological peculiarities of the artist. With the exception of Wolfgang Paulsen's essay "Der gute Bürger Jakob," which discusses Grillparzer's critical view of bourgeois society and his satirical mode of writing, these studies have neglected the critical picture of the social and political climate in which Jakob flounders.[2] This tendency has proliferated to the point that the call has gone out for a moratorium on such interpretations which fail to open up new perspectives on either the novella itself or on the historical standpoint of the literary scholar.[3]

The critics' concern with the fiddler's faith in an intact inner world of private sensibilities constitutes a form of identification—not with the fiddler, but rather with the narrator's point of view. Even where critics have focused on the particular standpoint from which the narrator presents Jakob's story, they have most often dwelled on the biographical points of reference and have seen **Der arme Spielmann** as either an expression of the writer's inner world or as an autobiographical character portrayal.[4] Literary criticism's general preoccupation with the author's role as a genial creator and the emphasis on the nature of the artist in *Der arme Spielmann* scholarship have engendered a particular bias in the analysis of the novella's narrative structure. With the aid of recent critical perspectives on the author as a function of literary discourse, it is possible to characterize this affinity between the narrator in *Der arme Spielmann* and the authors of the novella's interpretation and to provide a new context for understanding the fiddler's story.

In his disseminative essay which asks the question "What is an Author?" Michel Foucault claims that "in setting aside biographical and psychological references, one has already called back into question the absolute character and founding role of the subject."[5] *Der arme Spielmann* is a work particularly well-suited for this approach—because of the predominance of biographical and psychological interpretations in its reception history, but also because the figure of the narrator serves as an almost ideal model for the study of the author function which dominated literary discourse on the threshold between Romanticism and Realism in German literature. The narrator in Grillparzer's novella deems himself amply possessed of that creative force which has been attributed to the author of fiction since the eighteenth century: "We are accustomed . . . to saying that the author is the genial creator of a work in which he deposits, with infinite wealth and generosity, an inexhaustible world of significations."[6] It is my contention that in *Der arme Spielmann* Grillparzer exposes to critical analysis the idealist view of the author as a genial creative subject and illustrates expressly the regulatory influence it exerts on narrative. Moreover, in the narrator's sense of a mutually aggrandizing relationship with the larger public, to which his literary treatment of the fiddler contributes, one detects the specific ideological character of this author function in the time of apparent social harmony under the Metternich regime. In reassessing the narrator's role in *Der arme Spielmann,* I hope to offer here a contribution which, when seen in the context of the novella's reception in literary criticism, will offer insight into the forces of resistance that have sustained the author as a genial creator over two centuries. To arrive at this perspective, it is first necessary to establish the full scope of the narrator's role in the novella and the relationship between the two interlocking narrative strands which make up the story. With this focus it will be possible to see the narrator's self-acclaimed "anthropological voracity"[7] and "psychological curiosity" (186) not merely as biographical references to Grillparzer's character as a writer, but rather as signposts pointing to the problematical aspects in the relationship between the author and the fictional text.

Throughout the first hundred plus years of *Der arme Spielmann* reception the role of the narrator and the influence of his narrative perspective on Jakob's story were largely ignored. With Richard Brinkmann's 1957 realism study *Wirklichkeit und Illusion*, which addressed this question in *Der arme Spielmann* as well as other nineteenth-century prose works, a new perspective was opened to the role of the narrator.[8] Since Brinkmann's study appeared, other critics have addressed the role of the narrator in *Der arme Spielmann* and arrived at strikingly different conclusions. In the sixties Heinz Politzer[9] and M. W. Swales[10] imparted a much stronger importance to the narrator than in previous interpretations. Each of them draws conclusions about

the narrator which support their understanding of the story, but seem unjustified when one carefully considers the narrator's comments, actions, attitudes and, as these scholars have failed to do, the end product which he offers the reader. Politzer asserts that at the end of the story the narrator has undergone a transformation. He seems to imply that the change in the narrator redeems the fiddler's tragic existence: "Was Barbara mit Jakob nicht gelungen ist, gelingt ihr hier mit seinem Chronisten: er erlebt seine schöpferische Stunde, die Stunde der Begegnung, in der aus zweien eins wird, nämlich dieses Werk, dieser 'Arme Spielmann.'"[11] The redemption is in the aesthetic realm. The work of art produced from the fiddler's life as outsider and the narrator's encounter with him stand for Politzer as ample compensation for the suffering. Swales observes that the narrator's alleged involvement with the fiddler is negated by "pompous"[12] remarks and an ironic, distanced attitude toward him. He attributes this hypocritical stance to an ambivalence in the narrator. Swales detects in the narrator a genuine feeling of identification with the fiddler, but he explains that another part of him feels that this is a weak, sentimental tendency which he must overcome.[13] The following analysis of the narrator's role in the story will reveal problems in both these views of the narrator.[14]

When J. P. Stern says about the story, "the narrator's taciturnity about himself is one of its minor triumphs,"[15] he has missed one of the most salient features which define the narrator as a character. The narrator comments frequently and conspicuously on his attitude toward literary subjects and on his expectations regarding the fiddler. Repeatedly he refers to the fiddler as his "original" (150, 154) or "my fiddler" (183). Intrigued upon his first encounter with the fiddler, he describes to the reader his "anthropological voracity" with brimming conceit: "Ich zitterte vor Begierde nach dem Zusammenhang" (150). At the end of the story, after the fiddler's death, he states just as brazenly that in visiting Barbara's apartment he was driven by his "psychological curiosity" (186). His callous indifference toward the fiddler is displayed even more shamelessly in his inconsiderate treatment of him. When he finally visits him in his miserable hut (154), he scrutinizes him with a lingering stare without regard for the embarrassing predicament it creates. The fiddler, whose awareness and understanding the narrator underestimates throughout the story, is compelled to interrupt him: "'Sie sehen mich an,' sagte er, 'und haben dabei Ihre Gedanken?'" (158). His reply, "Daß ich nach Ihrer Geschichte lüstern bin" (158), is testimony to the narrator's total disregard for the fiddler as a human being with feelings and emotions. At the end of his visit the narrator's actions reveal again that the fiddler is for him simply a subject for a literary project: "Endlich hatte ich's satt, stand auf, legte ein paar Silberstücke auf den nebenstehenden Tisch und ging, während der Alte eifrig immer fortgeigte" (183). The narrator's comments about himself go beyond these references to the fiddler. They include self-evaluations that stand in contradiction to his treatment of the fiddler. In the opening description of the festival he refers to himself as "a passionate admirer of the people, particularly of the common people" (147-48). Yet he demonstrates a condescending attitude toward not only the fiddler, but toward the common people as a whole. In expressing his "love" for them, he maintains a patronizing attitude which brings out the differences in class and education;

this is evident in his references to them at the festival: "die eigentlichen Hierophanten dieses Weihfestes: die Kinder der Dienstbarkeit und der Arbeit" (146); "die schreiende Weiberund Kinderbevölkerung des Plebejer-Fuhrwerks" (147). When he decides to seek out the fiddler's living quarters in the Gärtnergasse, his snobbish attitude surfaces again: "Die Straße bestand aus zerstreuten einzelnen Häusern, die, zwischen großen Küchengärten gelegen, die Beschäftigung der Bewohner und den Ursprung des Namens Gärtnergasse augenfällig darlegten. In welcher dieser elenden Hütten wohl mein Original wohnen mochte?" (154). Why does the narrator describe these houses as "miserable huts"? Is it not because their inhabitants perform physical labor?

The exploitation of the fiddler as a literary subject continues even when the narrator goes looking for him a second time, allegedly out of concern for his welfare. After attaining his story, he had forgotten about him until the flood of the following spring recalls him to mind. The narrator attributes this to a trip which took him from Vienna in the months following his visit: "Bald darauf trat ich eine Reise an, von der ich erst mit einbrechendem Winter zurückkam. Die neuen Bilder hatten die alten verdrängt, und mein Spielmann war so ziemlich vergessen" (183). Although in this context the narrator is implying that he was worried about the old man, "my fiddler" is in actuality a metonymy for the literary work which he had intended to write based on Jakob's story. His casual attitude ("so ziemlich vergessen") also suggests that it is not the fiddler's sad and lonely existence which concerns the narrator, but rather the images which he won from his encounter with him and can work into a story. Nor is it sympathy which spurs him to go into Leopoldstadt after it has been ravaged by the flood. He wants to give the reader this impression, but his language betrays him: "Als aber die Wasser verlaufen und die Straßen gangbar geworden waren, beschloß ich, meinen Anteil an der in Gang gebrachten, zu unglaublichen Summen angewachsenen Kollekte persönlich an die mich zunächst angehende Adresse zu befördern" (184). The bureaucratic formulation [*Amtsdeutsch*] is a manifestation of the narrator's false pretenses in visiting the Gärtnergasse. It is also another example of his self-centered insensitivity, which in this case effects not only his dealings with other people, but his writing as well. Despite his claims that as a playwright he is in touch with the audience's expectations, he writes here in a style which has exactly the opposite effect from that which he desired—it reflects his inability to share the people's genuine sympathy for the flood victims.

Swales argues that the narrator's cold and distanced manner, both toward the people as a whole as well as toward Jakob, is due to his own uncertainties and self-doubts. He maintains that the narrator alternately is drawn to Jakob and then withdraws from him because he is "ashamed of a moment of weakness for the Spielmann."[16] For Swales, these contradictions are an intentional part of the narrator's strategy:

> . . . it is because he knows of this embarrassing affinity that the narrator ironizes his own precarious position. Only because of his self-awareness, only because he understands his own position and that of the fiddler is he able to adopt that ironic, intellectual position whereby he is able to write the story at all.[17]

The interpretation of the narrator's character hinges on this question of irony. The alternative to Swales's position is that the narrator was able to write the story because of his blind belief in the image of himself that he presents in the story. And indeed, several aspects of the story indicate that he possesses no ironic self-awareness of his weaknesses or of the fiddler's superior qualities. His comments about the common people contain, for example, no hint that the narrator is aware of his ingrained sense of class differences. Likewise, his pompous behavior is not counterbalanced by moments where his genuine concern for either the people or the fiddler shines through. And perhaps most convincingly, there is no indication that the narrator has been changed, or even moved, by the fiddler's story or death. The final product, the narrator's version of the fiddler's life story, is merely another literary triumph—in his own estimation—for the writer. In this sense, the flood provided the narrator the opportunity to give the story its final touches. The account of the flood and its tragic consequences forms a parallel to his own very contrived description of the "flood" of people at the folk festival.[18] What brought the narrator out to look up the fiddler was the aesthetic find, the stroke of luck which complemented his own literary genius and produced the well-rounded ending. As long as the aesthetic element had not presented itself, he was able to forget the fiddler and his insignificant existence.

The narrator's false representation of his own motives raises the question whether Jakob's first person narration of his life story should be taken as the narrator's fabrication or, if not, whether it has been altered by him. Brinkmann argues that the narrator's retelling of the fiddler's account will necessarily have imparted a certain tone to it, even if it is substantially the same.[19] I think that the question of this kind of alteration, although it might have a place in a thorough text analysis, does not play a role in a close reading of the text which belongs to the primary form of reception.[20] Despite the narrator's various contradictions and inconsistencies the fiddler's narration of his life story can be and is accepted by the reader as a word-for-word retelling. This can be argued by induction: if one questions the narrator's account of the fiddler's story, then one can just as well question the narrator's entire story and conclude that the fiddler is an invention of his literary imagination. But the overriding argument here is that of literary convention, the power of the quotation marks.[21] Direct speech in narrative fiction is accepted as the verbatim speech of the character, unless there is a clear, signaled undercutting of the particular passage or—as is often the case with twentieth-century authors such as Kafka—of the entire narrative point of view on which the story is based. This does not happen in *Der arme Spielmann.*

The question of the narrator's artistic liberty with the fiddler's story is played out on another plane. Jakob's narration of his life story stands in contrast to the literary framework which the narrator constructs for it. The novella revolves around the issue of narration—historical, biographical and fictional forms of telling stories and events and their interrelation. The fiddler raises this question at a pivotal point in the story. When the narrator so brazenly states his craving for Jakob's story, the latter is at first puzzled: "'Geschichte?' wiederholte er. 'Ich habe keine Geschichte'"(158). Learning what the narrator's interest in him is, he finally understands what he means by "Geschichte": "Das also nennen Sie meine Geschichte? Wie es kam?" (158). The fiddler's perplexity reveals how different the writer's perspective is from that of the insignificant "little" man who fascinates him. From his own point of view, his story consists of the suffering which loneliness and isolation from his fellow men have caused him: "Ich habe keine Geschichte. Heute wie gestern, und morgen wie heute. Übermorgen freilich und weiter hinaus, wer kann das wissen?" (158). The narrator, on the other hand, is interested in his "original" only as a subject for his next biography, the story of a most fascinating outsider that will captivate the readers. In his disbelief that anyone would be interested in his sad and inglorious fate, the fiddler reveals an intuitive understanding that history, narration, the telling of stories, does not concern itself with the pain and suffering of everyday life. He finally concedes that the conditions and course of events which led him to his present shameful state can form a story, even if common and uneventful in comparison to the grander events of which histories and stories usually consist. His straightforward narration of those events stands juxtaposed to the narrator's idea of the biography of a common person. It also is contrasted to the framework which the narrator deems necessary to make the fiddler's story worth telling.

The self-effacing naturalness with which he tells his story contrasts directly to the narrator's dramatically conceived sense of self-importance and his bombastic description of the folk festival:

> Er war während des Letzten zusehends ungezwungener geworden. Seine Gestalt verlängerte sich. Er nahm mir ohne zu große Umstände den Hut aus der Hand und legte ihn aufs Bette; schlug sitzend ein Bein über das andere und nahm überhaupt die Lage eines mit Bequemlichkeit Erzählenden an (158).

This posture as well as the ingenuous account of his life which follows are the essence of epic simplicity. Against this solid background, the narrator's penchant for heightened dramatic depiction presents itself to the scrutiny of the reader. What becomes the nucleus of the novella is not the interesting story of an unusual outsider, but rather the question of the literary fictionalization of real relationships, in this case, of a narrated life story.

Roland Heine examines the issue of narrated life experience in *Der arme Spielmann* in the context of the German hermeneutical tradition in the humanities [*Geisteswissenschaften*], specifically with reference to Dilthey.[22] He points to the two meanings of "Geschichte" to which the fiddler's words are alluding:

> Indem der Spielmann selbst den "Faden seiner Erzählung" fortspinnt, verwandelt er sein Leben im doppelten Sinn in 'Geschichte': (1) im *ästhetischen* Sinn in einen Erzählzusammenhang, (2) im *historischen* Sinn in einen Lebenszusammenhang. Das Leben als 'Geschichte' ist *story* und *history* zugleich, 'Geschichte' im ästhetischen und im historischen Sinn.[23]

When Heine claims, however, that the fiddler wins a historical perspective on his life, an overview that has failed him until he is encouraged to tell his life story to the narrator, he seems to imply that by doing so his life has gained some meaning that it did not previously have.[24] This new meaning is for the fiddler a gain only on the aesthetic plane. Heine maintains that with regard to the other characters his story exerts an influence on the historical level as well: "Die Bedeutung seiner Lebensgeschichte erschöpft sich also nicht in ihrer ästhetischen Sinnimmanenz, sondern wirkt noch über Jakobs Lebensende hinaus in der aktuellen Bedeutung, die der Verstorbene für die noch Lebenden hat."[25] He gives this explanation of the effect which Jakob's life has on Barbara: "Die 'Geschichte' des armen Spielmanns bleibt nicht bloß Fiktion, ein bloß ästhetischer Zusammenhang, denn Barbara verkörpert sie in persona."[26] The real effect which Heine envisions is the same one for which Politzer argued—a change in the narrator. Although he leaves open the question of whether or not the narrator understands the significance his narration of the fiddler's story gains ("da sich die Erzählperspektive auf den Leser hin öffnet"[27]), he implies that the last scene reflects a change in the narrator, in this case one made possible by the meaning which Jakob's "Geschichte" gains when he narrates it. On the other hand, Heine overlooks a more obvious and I think more consequential significance of the distinction between the aesthetic and historical sense of the fiddler's life story. The novella presents two contrasting modes of narrating his story—the fiddler's honestly and simply conveyed version of the events in his life and the narrator's pompous and pretentious framework in which it rests. In a very simplistic equation, the former represents the historical side of his story and the latter an exaggeratedly aestheticized version. The value of the hermeneutical perspective, which Heine established only to end with an unconvincing justification for the narrator's aesthetic product, is that it unravels the intricate relationship in the story between historical facticity (both narrated and unnarrated) and the aesthetic treatment of history. When the fiddler tells his story, it does not alter the hard reality of his life—"heute wie gestern, und morgen wie heute"; this explains his disinterest in his life story. The narrator's interest in the fiddler's story is a purely aesthetic one, centered on its value as literary subject matter. With the juxtaposition of the two accounts of the fiddler's life, his own and the narrator's, the novella brings into question the very idea of a significance which is immanently aesthetic ("ästhetische Sinnimmanenz").

Where I have suggested that a close reading of the text does not call for skepticism toward the narrator's second-hand account of the fiddler's story, it does demand a critical evaluation of the narrator's account of himself. At one point the narrator makes a comparison between his creative imagination and the fiddler's. On the evening of the festival he visits out of curiosity the street in which the fiddler lives. He listens to the old fiddler playing without notes, or "fantasizing," as he calls it. As the narrator returns home, he has his own fantasies: "Ich trat, mühsam in den mir unbekannten Gassen mich zurechtfindend, den Heimweg an, wobei ich auch phantasierte, aber niemand störend, für mich, im Kopfe" (155). He is referring here to his thoughts as he walks home, but another form of his "fantasizing," his writing, is at issue in the story. Immediately following this remark, he explains why he put off visiting him in the morning hours as the fiddler had requested:

> Die Morgenstunden haben für mich immer einen eigenen Wert gehabt. Es ist, als ob es mir Bedürfnis wäre, durch die Beschäftigung mit etwas Erhebendem, Bedeutendem in den ersten Stunden des Tages mir den Rest desselben gewissermaßen zu heiligen. Ich kann

mich daher nur schwer entschließen, am frühen Morgen mein Zimmer zu verlassen, und wenn ich ohne vollgültige Ursache mich einmal dazu nötige, so habe ich für den übrigen Tag nur die Wahl zwischen gedankenloser Zerstreuung oder selbstquälerischem Trübsinn (155-56).

What the narrator is referring to here as "something elevating, something meaningful" can be nothing else but his writing, his own fantasies about life. His "biographies of obscure people" (148), of which he had boasted, are glorifications of their lives which he can create only in the seclusion of his room, in the morning hours while his imagination is still unadulterated by the annoyances of reality. When the narrator states that his fantasizing does not disturb others, the reader must wonder if this applies as well to his writing and, in particular, to his account of the fiddler. It is, however, not merely a question of whether it is annoying; in the context of the hermeneutical interaction between history and story, and given his glorification of the fiddler's life and death, it becomes the question of the aesthetic veiling of real relationships.

The narrator does not think of his writing as fantasizing. He thinks of it in scientific (anthropological and psychological) terms. He feels that through objective observation and literary talent he can tell the story of a unified folk; he sees himself as a "Liebhaber der Menschen . . . besonders wenn sie in Massen für einige Zeit der einzelnen Zwecke vergessen und sich als Teile des Ganzen fühlen, in dem denn doch zuletzt das Göttliche liegt" (148). Although he views himself as a champion of the common people, his actions and comments in the story indicate that he can tolerate them only in moments which lift them above the realities of their everyday lives—at the festival, when they first empty out of the theater still caught up in the fictional world of the play, or in times of turmoil, such as the flood, when there is a strong feeling of solidarity and brotherhood. His interest in the people extends only to those moments when he can exult, as he does in describing the folk festival, "all suffering has been forgotten" (147). In the normal affairs of the world, when each person goes about his own individual interests, the narrator withdraws into his room to avoid the dissonances of reality. His interest goes only so far as the outside world, specifically that of the masses, offers material for his "occupation with something elevating, something meaningful." What qualifies as such material is the unusual and the dramatic, but not the real content of the common man's everyday life. What is "meaningful" for him is the aesthetic element which transforms the base level of history into something heroic and grandiose.

The narrator does not seem to impart this significance to the fiddler's story purposefully. Rather his fixation on the author as a creative subject leads per course to this appropriation of the fiddler's tragic story. The display of his—in his own opinion—considerable literary talents and his comments about the creative process offer the reader a critical perspective from which to evaluate how he portrays the fiddler. The narrator refers to himself as a "dramatic poet" who attaches more value to the response of the theater audience—described in his dramatic style as "der rückhaltlose Ausbruch eines überfüllten Schauspielhauses" (148)—than to the opinions of the critics: "das zusammengeklügelte Urteil eines an Leib und Seele

verkrüppelten, von dem Blut ausgesogener Autoren spinnenartig aufgeschwollenen literarischen Matadors" (148). This lavish invective attests to the harsh treatment he receives from the theater critics, just as it probably served to vent some of Grillparzer's frustrations as well, but it also lets the reader see the narrator in a critical light. His choice of the term "literary matador" is ironical in light of the dramatical flair with which he presents it. In fact, the opening description of the folk festival functions like the fanfare with which the matador is introduced into the arena. The narrator sees himself in the midst of the celebration like the matador surrounded by the cheering crowd: "Ich hatte mich mit dem Zug der Menge hingegeben und befand mich in der Mitte des Dammes, bereits auf klassischem Boden" (149). He also boasts of his skills as a writer much in the same way the matador demonstrates his virtuoso and elegance in the skills of the bullfight:

> Wie aus einem aufgerollten, ungeheuren, dem Rahmen des Buches entsprungenen Plutarch, lese ich aus den heitern und heimlich bekümmerten Gesichtern, dem lebhaften oder gedrückten Gange, dem wechselseitigen Benehmen der Familienglieder, den einzelnen halb unwillkürlichen Äußerungen, mir die Biographien der unberühmten Menschen zusammen (148).

His description of the festival is his bravura to display these skills. It builds in a crescendo of literary flair which is to dazzle the reader and to capture the excitement of the event. It ends in a dramatic outburst: "Und so fort und immer weiter, bis endlich der breite Hafen der Lust sich auftut und Wald und Wiese, Musik und Tanz, Wein und Schmaus, Schattenspiel und Seiltänzer, Erleuchtung und Feuerwerk sich zu einem pays de cocagne, einem Eldorado, einem eigentlichen Schlaraffenlande vereinigen" (147). One senses here the narrator basking in, if not the cheers of the spectators, then the anticipated admiration of the reader.

The temptation arises here to turn the analysis into a psychological study of the other artist figure, just as the scholarly reception of *Der arme Spielmann* has consisted mainly of biographically grounded studies into the psychology of the fiddler. The juxtaposition of the two artist figures and of their accounts of Jakob's life provides, however, a framework for a historical critique of the author function in literary discourse. In the eyes of the narrator the fiddler's account of his life, despite his curious eccentricity, could not stand alone without a twist to it which raises it into the realm of the meaningful. This is provided by the flood and the fiddler's "heroic" death. Grillparzer undermines, of course, this heroic element with the fact that the fiddler gave his last strength to save the tax records and a small amount of paper money belonging to his landlord. But this irony does not deter the narrator from finding the missing link in his story of the fiddler. By raising him to a mythical plane, by making him a hero of the common people, the narrator has concealed the deeper truths of his story. His private world of music and the "story" or "history" behind it, the "wie es kam," stands as a testimony to cracks in the social fabric of the nation. It points to the contradictions in the conception of the people and the nation as a homogeneous entity sharing common goals and purposes. The fiddler's life was a failure in part because his naive belief in man's benevolence allowed others to take advantage of him. Because of his selflessness, he was unable to manipulate people and situations to his own ends, and was thus exploited himself by all those with whom he came into contact—including Barbara and the narrator. The fiddler's narration of his life story reveals the tyranny which exists not only on a political level, but in the everyday relations between men of all walks of life. The narrator, who had shown that his interest in the masses was restricted to those occasions when the people felt a strong sense of unity, conceals this struggle of self-interests behind a picture of social harmony. The ultimate irony is that the fiddler, who suffered a lonely existence, alienated from his fellow men because he did not place his own private interests above everything else, is turned by the narrator into a symbol for the selflessness and common will of the people.

The fiddler's unwillingness—not his inability—to manipulate others for his own gain is carried over into the aesthetic realm. His music constitutes the extreme case of autonomous art: it eschews even those aesthetic conventions and practices which make art communicable. In this sense his peculiar music is an emblem of his existence as outsider. For in the realm of art the fiddler cannot circumvent the same kind of manipulation which left him an outcast from society. Having the need to express the loneliness he has experienced throughout his life, the fiddler naively turns to that realm which, ostensibly, serves this purpose. But as a direct expression of suffering, the Spielmann's music breaks the basic law of an idealist aesthetics—the pain and injustice in human existence is to be transformed by art into harmonious form. The dissonance of the fiddler's music stands in defiance of a dominant aesthetics which excludes the ingenuous representation of painful experience. As a form of expression which does not conform to the conventions and interests of the art world, his music is ridiculed and unable to establish its significance as an immanent critique of art's social function. Through its rejection, however, his music takes on another dimension of critique. It points to the particular hermeneutical bind of an idealist aesthetics: in its preoccupation with organic unity, art forms a self-referential closure of predetermined meaning.

The novella does not focus the reader's attention on the symbolic meaning of the fiddler's music, rather it highlights the significance which the fiddler and his music gain in the two-fold narration of his life story. In order to realize its potential for negative critique, the fiddler's music must be interpreted as such; it must have the right context of meaning transposed onto it. The narrator's pursuit of the fiddler's story offers the reader an opportunity to analyze, in process, the interpretative aspect of narration. The fiddler, who in performing his music acts genuinely as an autonomous creative subject, meets the first criterion for an artist in the narrator's conception. Yet his music consists of little more than painful cacophonies. It is this puzzling combination which intrigues and attracts the narrator. As he determinedly seeks to find out more about his fascinating subject, he becomes privy to what is seemingly the best context for understanding this strange music—it is the fiddler's own account of his life and how he came to be the "poor fiddler." However, the significance which his life and music win in the telling of his story is not acceptable to the narrator; for it undermines that glorified view of the creative subject which inspired his own life and work as writer. By turning the fiddler's death into a heroic act, the narrator revamps the context for interpreting this phenomenon and restores the positive view of the genial artist.

The manipulative power of fiction, the craft displayed by the narrator in his treatment of the fiddler, mirrors the manipulative social forces which rendered the naive and trusting Jakob a "poor fiddler." The novella exposes to critical analysis the creative function ascribed to the author in the dominant idealist aesthetic tradition. Foucault's description of this author function in "What is an Author?" recalls the narrator's estimation of himself:

> We are accustomed, as we have seen earlier, to saying that the author is the genial creator of a work in which he deposits, with infinite wealth and generosity, an inexhaustible world of significations. We are used to thinking that the author is so different from all other men, and so transcendent with regard to all languages that, as soon as he speaks, meaning begins to proliferate, to proliferate indefinitely.[28]

What the narrator, with his literary treatment of the fiddler, effects is not a proliferation of meaning. Rather he appropriates the fiddler's story for a self-serving glorification of the creative author. In doing so, he impedes that proliferation of meaning which Jakob's own account of how he came to be the "poor fiddler" could generate. By replacing the image of the hopelessly alienated individual, which presents difficulties for the idea of the genial creator, with the figure of the self-sacrificing hero, the narrator provides redemption for the traditional idea of the author. This is the narrator's manipulation, his aesthetic trick which elevates the fiddler's inability to function in a world where one must exploit or be exploited to a heroic virtue and thus secures his own status as a creative genius. The narrator functions in exactly the opposite fashion to that creative function which it is assumed the writer performs. Instead of endowing the fiddler's story with generative significations, the self-proclaimed biographer of the obscure little man appropriates it for his own literary eminence and robs it of its intrinsic potential to proliferate meaning. Thus, the narrator's story becomes an ideological product which conceals the significance of the fiddler's narrative for the Austrian social order. The novella, on the other hand, exposes the ideological disguising of the author function as a creative force which liberates.

Granting that **Der arme Spielmann** presents an early critique of the role of the author in literary discourse, it is not easy to discern how Grillparzer views the potential for change in the author function. Is he suggesting that within the basic functional role filled by the author the idealist view of the author could be replaced by a more sober understanding of the author's relationship to the text? Or is there in his novella even the anticipation of the recent critical challenge to the primacy of the author? Foucault maintains—while warning that calling for "a form of culture in which fiction would not be limited by the figure of the author . . . would be pure romanticism"[29]—that the author function will give way to a new, as yet undeterminable system of constraint. In **Der arme Spielmann** Grillparzer seems to suggest from a hermeneutical perspective that the author and his particular perspective cannot be eliminated. At the critical point of transition between Romanticism and Realism in German literature, his novella warns that there is no immediate realism, no purely objective description of events, conditions or causes—whether in fiction or in historical narrative—which is not interpretative and partial. The conclusion it suggests is not that the author function should become invisible; rather that it must belong explicitly to the literary "work" which presents itself to critical examination. Yet, in the course of its reception and interpretation critics and scholars have protected the privileged position of the author against the critical perspective which the novella opens up. What has been overlooked is both the example of and call for a literary narrative which displays the relationship between the text and its authors—not only the original "creative" author or the fictional authors of the text, but the authors of its reception and interpretation as well. That Grillparzer could only succeed in the first two instances is not a criterion for evaluating his novella, but rather a circumstance which reflects the author-function in the history of German literary criticism.

Notes

1. Hinrich C. Seeba, "Franz Grillparzer: *Der arme Spielmann* (1847)," *Romane und Erzählungen zwischen Romantik und Realismus: Neue Interpretationen,* ed. Paul Michael Lützeler (Stuttgart, 1983) 393-98.

2. Wolfgang Paulsen, "Der gute Bürger Jakob: Zur Satire in Grillparzer's *Armem Spielmann,*" *Colloquia Germanica* 2 (1968): 272-98. Paulsen mentions Benno von Wiese's claim that Grillparzer viewed the world around the fiddler "durchaus mit einem bösen Blick," Benno von Wiese, *Die deutsche Novelle von Goethe bis Kafka* 1 (Düsseldorf, 1956) 148. However, Paulsen points out that no one had actually examined this aspect of the novella: " . . . aber den 'bösen Blick' des Dichters hatte bisher doch noch niemand als solchen diagnostiziert" (283). See also Seeba 397-98, 401-6.

3. Paulsen suggested that such individual interpretations had run their useful course (272). After numerous new articles with similar approaches had appeared in the meantime, Seeba echoed Paulsen's concern, pointing to the lack of critical historical self-awareness in *Der arme Spielmann* scholarship: "Weil es wirklich so aussieht, wie Wolfgang Paulsen schon 1968 bemerkte, noch ehe weitere siebzehn Einzelinterpretationen und, zum 100. Todestag 1972, etliche Grillparzer-Monographien hinzukamen, 'als ob alles, was sich auf diese Weise erreichen ließe, inzwischen auch schon erreicht worden ist,' möchte man nach gründlicher Durchsicht des in 135 Jahren Erreichten künftigen Interpreten gewissermaßen ein Moratorium empfehlen. . . . [Es] sollte dieser Erzählung eine Schonfrist gegönnt werden, bis sich aus einer veränderten historischen Situation und entsprechend neuer Interessenlage grundsätzliche und übergreifende Fragestellungen ergeben, die auch diesen ausgewrungenen Text in einem wirklich neuen Licht erscheinen lassen, weil es—im Sinne eines lebendigen Forschungsfortschritts—das Verständnis seiner Interpreten und ihrer Leser bereichert, anstatt es im Relativismus sich im Kreise drehender Selbstbespiegelungen zu ermüden" (Seeba 401).

4. For interpretations in this direction, see von Wiese; Richard Alewyn, "Grillparzer und die Restauration," *Publications of the English Goethe Society* ns 12 (1935-37): 1-18; Walter Silz, *Realism and Reality*

(Chapel Hill, [4]1965) 67-68; Claudio Magris, *Der habsburgische Mythos in der österreichischen Literatur,* trans. Madeleine von Pasztory (Salzburg, 1969) 113-16; Günther Jungbluth, "Franz Grillparzers Erzählung: *Der arme Spielmann*: Ein Beitrag zu ihrem Verständnis," *Orbis Litterarum* 24 (1969): 35-51. For a more extensive account of this tendency in twentieth-century Grillparzer scholarship, see Seeba 412.

5. Michel Foucault, "What is an Author?" trans. Josue V. Harari, *Textual Strategies: Perspectives in Post-Structuralist Criticism,* ed. Josue V. Harari (Ithaca, 1979) 158.

6. Foucault 159.

7. Franz Grillparzer, *Sämtliche Werke,* eds. Peter Frank and Karl Pörnbacher, 3 (München, 1964) 150. Hereafter cited in the text; translations are my own.

8. Richard Brinkmann, *Wirklichkeit und Illusion* (Tübingen, [3]1977) 87-145.

9. Heinz Politzer, *Franz Grillparzers "Der arme Spielmann"* (Stuttgart, 1967).

10. M. W. Swales, "The Narrative Perspective in Grillparzer's *Der arme Spielmann,*" *German Life and Letters* ns 20 (1967): 107-16.

11. Politzer 60.

12. Swales 111.

13. Swales 110 11.

14. John M. Ellis also challenges the positions taken by Politzer and Swales as well as by Stern; John M. Ellis, "Grillparzer's *Der arme Spielmann,*" *German Quarterly* 45 (1972): 663-66.

15. J. P. Stern, "Beyond the Common Indication: Grillparzer," *Re-interpretations: Seven Studies in Nineteenth-Century German Literature* (New York, 1964) 63.

16. Swales 111.

17. Swales 115.

18. Ellis discusses in more detail the forced metaphor of the flood, which he concludes to be "a superficial piece of literary posturing, confused and inappropriate, while the flood and consequent deaths are harshly real" (677; see also 672-73).

19. Brinkmann 126.

20. The distinction made here is between an extensive analysis made by a literary scholar (secondary reading) and a close or competent reading of the text which is prior to the recognition or discussion of certain deep structures of literary discourse (primary reading). A primary reading, which can include an explicit interpretation of the text, may be complete and competent without engaging in certain valid questions raised in a secondary discussion of the text. Conversely, certain questions which are valid in the context of a secondary discussion based on the text may be invalid and misleading when applied to a primary reading. This is the case in Brinkmann's claim that the narrator's retelling of the fiddler's story will have influenced it. This question is an intrusion into the literary convention of direct speech which governs the reading of the text.

21. Ellis makes this point as well in response to Brinkmann. He argues that the narrator's memory of the fiddler's story and his retelling of it are to be accepted as "one of those literary conventions without which fiction would be impossible" (666).

22. Roland Heine, "Ästhetische oder existentielle Integration? Ein hermeneutisches Problem des 19. Jahrhunderts in Grillparzers Erzählung *Der arme Spielmann*," *Deutsche Vierteljahrsschrift* 45 (1972): 650-83.

23. Heine 654.

24. Heine 667.

25. Heine 681.

26. Heine 681.

27. Heine 682.

28. Foucault 159.

29. Foucault 159.

Roy C. Cowen (essay date 1988)

SOURCE: "The History of a Neglected Masterpiece: *Der arme Spielmann*," in *Grillparzer's* Der arme Spielmann: *New Directions in Criticism,* edited by Clifford Albrecht Bernd, Camden House, 1988, pp. 9-25.

[*In the following essay, Cowen places the critical reaction to* Der arme Spielmann *within a social, literary, and political context.*]

From the time of its first publication in *Iris: Deutscher Almanach für 1848* until today, the literary quality of Grillparzer's **Der arme Spielmann** has scarcely ever been directly questioned and has, in fact, been reaffirmed by some of the most established and influential literary figures from then to now.[1] Its initial appearance was, in this respect, quite auspicious, for in his review for Augsburg's *Allgemeine Zeitung* on 6 September 1847, Adalbert Stifter wrote: "Über scheinbar sehr ungefügige, ja fast widerstrebende Verhältnisse ist ein solcher Duft eines Seelenlebens ausgegossen, daß man allmählich hineingezogen wird, daß sich eine edle Rührung in unser Herz schleicht, und daß man am Schlusse die beruhigendste Auslösung und eine lohnende Erhebung empfindet."

Stifter's fame and reputation were beyond question, yet the introduction to the first reprint of the novella in volume 5 of Paul Heyse's *Deutscher Novellenschatz* (1871) concludes with the sentence: "Den Lesern der *Novelle* aber wollen wir durch keine weitere Zergliederung den Genuß dieser meisterhaften Charakterstudie beeinträchtigen."[2] And Heyse's previous statements also suggest a joy of discovery, both for his own audience and for the rest of the literary world. To what extent this is indeed the case can be gleaned from Gottfried Keller's comments in his letter of 10 September 1871, that is, the year of the publication of Heyse's anthology, to Emil Kuh, who has just sent him a copy of the original publication:

Die "Iris" habe ich seither auch erhalten und danke herzlichst für deren Zusendung; ich werde Ihnen das Buch nach Wien zurückschicken. Ich erinnerte mich plötzlich, daß ich den eleganten Band seinerzeit als Novität in den Händen gehabt aber nicht gelesen hatte. Mit großem Interesse hatte ich Ihre Bemerkungen über den "Spielmann" in Ihren Grillparzerartikeln gelesen und war begierig, die Erzählung kennen zu lernen. Das Buch befindet sich auf einer mir leicht zugänglichen Bibliothek hier, aber ich wußte nicht mehr, daß der kleine Schatz darin steckt, so daß ich die Erzählung doch erst aus Ihrer Sendung kennen lernte. Es liegt ein tiefer Sinn in der scheinbar leichten Arbeit, die Gewalt der absolut reinen Seele über die Welt.

Keller, however, is scarcely an exception, for we hear from Hieronymus Lorm in his article for the *Grillparzer-Jahrbuch* in 1894:

Eine größere Beachtung, eine weitere Verbreitung hat "Der arme Spielmann," so lange Grillparzer lebte, nicht gefunden, . . . Wäre für den deutschen Dichter ein gerechtes Schicksal vorhanden, so hätte die Novelle separat abgedruckt in Hunderttausenden von Exemplaren in die Welt geschickt werden können.[3]

This judgment, however, cannot help but evoke a smile among those who recall that Lorm, according to Reinhold Backmann[4] and his own admission in a letter on 3 August 1863 to Emil Kuh, rejected the **Spielmann** when it first appeared. In any case, we have a work of unquestioned quality that remained virtually unknown to a greater public from 1847 to 1871. The literary world's ignorance or neglect of Grillparzer's novella has frequently been attributed to the obscurity of the *Iris* as a publication. While there may well be some truth in such an assumption, we should not forget that Keller mentions having seen the original printing of the **Spielmann**; he simply did not read it. Moreover, Lorm makes the following comment in his article: "Auch das Taschenbuch 'Iris' zog unter seiner intelligenter Redaction die vornehmsten deutschen Literaturkräfte an sich, so daß es damals mit der Geltendmachung deutschen Geistes in Pest besser beschaffen war als in Wien."[5] This too seems to contradict the common notion that *Iris* was a poorly chosen organ for the publication, not in the least because it was, despite the turbulence of the Revolution of 1848 and other factors, reviewed. About such reviews, however, Lorm makes the following observation:

In Wien gab es für Belletristik und ihre Würdigung, mit Ausnahme vielleicht von Witthauers "Wiener Zeitschrift," nur verachtete und heute gänzlich verschollene Tagesblätter: "Theaterzeitung," "Sammler" etc. Sie brachten über den bezüglichen Jahrgang des genannten Taschenbuches nur hergebrachte Phrasen und behandelten die Novelle Grillparzers nicht anders als die kleinen lyrischen Verse "vaterländischer" Dichter; nicht die geringste Ahnung war ihnen aufgegangen, daß mit dem "armen Spielmann" die deutsch-österreichische Literatur plötzlich um ein Meisterstück bereichert worden war.[6]

In other words, the neglect of Grillparzer's novella can be attributed to the failings of its first reviewers. Since these reviewers limited themselves to "hergebrachte Phrasen" and thereby demonstrated their capitulation to the taste and trends of the times, any deeper understanding of the reception of the "neglected masterpiece" must be based on literary historical developments.

At the same time, however, we must take into consideration more than the period from 1848 to 1871. To be sure, in 1872 scholarship on Grillparzer and especially on *Der arme Spielmann* seemed to receive more than sufficient impetus. In one year after Heyse's reprint appeared also the first edition of the collected works, which contained the *Spielmann* as well as the last three unpublished dramas, and the important comparative work by Emil Kuh on Stifter and Grillparzer.[7] Yet, for all practical purposes, the critical confrontation with the *Spielmann* remained disappointingly rare, i.e., a second period of "neglect" began that cannot be ascribed to the work's lack of availability. Wolfgang Paulsen marks the effective limits of this "period" in the beginning of his essay on "Der gute Jakob":

> Da fällt zunächst auf, daß die kritische Auseinandersetzung mit dem "Armen Spielmann" erst um die Mitte der zwanziger Jahre unseres Jahrhunderts eingesetzt hat. Die für uns relevante Diskussion beginnt nämlich recht eigentlich mit Bernhard Seufferts Beitrag zur Sauerfestschrift im Jahre 1925, in dem die spezielle Problematik der Dichtung zum ersten Male umrissen wurde, ein Jahr später gefolgt von Ernst Alkers historisch insofern bedeutsamer Arbeit, als hier noch einmal versucht wurde, die positivistischen Methoden einer vergangenen Generation in den Dienst einer noch wenig zielsicheren Einzelinterpretation zu stellen.[8]

Admittedly, Paulsen adds in a footnote: "Alkers rein positivistische Textanalyse versetzt der Erzählung als Kunstwerk natürlich den Todesstoß." And, despite the appearance of the historical-critical edition by Backmann (1930) and two other studies, Paulsen sees the inception of a truly productive criticism in Walter Silz's "die psychologische Konfiguration der Dichtung erstmals genauer ins Auge fassenden Studie" (1954)[9] and Richard Brinkmann's monograph (1957),[10] in which he interprets this work "im wesentlichen von der Sprache und der Struktur her."[11]

One could, therefore, say that *Der arme Spielmann*—several essays and Hofmannsthal's inclusion of it in his anthology *Deutsche Erzähler* (1913) notwithstanding—suffered, if not from critical neglect, then from an inability to evoke criticism that did justice to its unique qualities. What obviously differentiates such a period from the first one of pure "neglect" is a shift in responsibility from the literary climate of the times to the critical method. For only with the post-war advent of *werkimmanente Kritik*, i.e. New Criticism, did Grillparzer's novella seem capable of coming into its own. In turn, any explanation of the "neglect" of this masterpiece must be twofold: 1) from 1848 to 1925 in terms of literary historical developments, and 2) from 1925 to 1954 in terms of critical approaches and assumptions.

I

Almost all literary historians, as little as they can otherwise agree on in respect to the nineteenth century, are unanimous in their use of 1848 as a turning-point in the social, political and literary history of Europe, especially Germany. It stands to reason that many scholars have, in turn, attributed the neglect of *Der arme Spielmann* to the turbulence of the Revolution of 1848 because its effects were so wide-reaching. As convincing as such non-literary events may be as explanations for major literary movements and developments, however, they seldom suffice in the case of an individual work, especially when we learn that the work was, despite the interruptions in the daily lives of the population, circulated widely enough for Heyse, Lorm, and Keller to find the original printing. Quite simply put: While the Revolution of 1848 may or may not have precluded the normal distribution of the *Iris* (even though the issue in question had already appeared in 1847), it most certainly did produce changes in the literary scene and thereby created the background against which Grillparzer could hardly expect an especially favorable reception of his novella.

Moreover, and lest we overestimate the importance of the one year 1848, we should note that in 1846 Grillparzer himself had, in fact, anticipated that *Der arme Spielmann* would not be a success. Reinhold Backmann cites from the author's letter in 1846 to Count Mailáth, the editor of *Iris*:

> Daß Ihnen die für die Iris bestimmte Erzählung gefallen hat, freut mich ungemein und ich wünsche nur, daß es mit dem Publikum derselbe Fall sey. Aber da von Deutsch-Einheit, deutscher Flotte und deutscher Weltmacht nichts darin vorkommt und der darin vorkommende Landsmann von jener Thatkraft gar nichts hat, die der Nazion auf einmal über Nacht angeflogen ist, so erwarte ich einen nur sehr geringen Beifall. Indeß da das Ding geschrieben ist, sey es gedruckt.[12]

And later, after he had been asked for another story for the *Iris* for 1849 (this issue never appeared), Grillparzer wrote the following:

> So sehr mich dieses Begehren erfreut, da es beweist, daß Sie mit der heurigen Leistung zufrieden sind, so muß ich nur bemerken, daß Erzählungen überhaupt nicht mein Fach sind und der alte Spielmann wirklich nur durch ein eigenes Erlebniß veranlaßt worden ist, ich auch bei meiner leider vorherrschenden Stimmung mich auf eine bestimmte Zusicherung nicht einlassen kann.[13]

Quite aside from the fact that the subsequent request for yet another novella substantiates the immediate recognition of the *Spielmann*'s artistic merits, we can glean two new points from these letters:

1. Whether Grillparzer correctly interprets the temper of the time before the Revolution or not, he already senses that his novella does not correspond to "modern" expectations, and he implies thereby that his work is the product of a by-gone literary era. This feeling toward all of his work is borne out by his letter of 16 June 1870 to Paul Heyse, for in it he still expresses his belief: "Von einer Ausgabe meiner sämtlichen Werke kann nur die Rede seyn nach meinem Tode, oder wenn Deutschland wieder poetisch geworden sein wird, welche zwey Zeitpunkte so ziemlich zusammenfallen dürften."

2. Grillparzer does not consider himself a narrator by nature, and, we may infer, he does not consider *Der arme Spielmann* as a personal or public refutation of this opinion.

While many of Grillparzer's remarks on his own work—including those cited above—must be weighed against his well-known psychological problems, we cannot ignore his own implied evaluation of *Der arme Spielmann* as outmoded in terms of social developments and of his individual talents. Obviously, his view of the situation explains why, despite his withdrawal from the public stage but continued interest in literature, he did not produce more prose narratives. His reluctance to do so seems especially noteworthy, as his decision comes at the on-set of an age that will be dominated by narrative prose, particularly the novella.

We cannot go into all of the indications on the coming dominance of the new genre that were available to Grillparzer, but the following recollection by Theodor Fontane in the twenty-first chapter of *Christian Friedrich Scherenberg und das literarische Berlin* reveals how obvious such indications must have been to everyone of the times:

> Über all dies hinaus aber begann eine große, tiefgreifende Geschmackswandlung in ganz Deutschland sich vorzubereiten, und mit dem Erscheinen von Freytags *"Soll und Haben"* [1855], welcher Roman so recht eigentlich den "Griff ins volle Menschenleben" für uns bedeutete, war der entscheidende Schritt getan. Man wollte Gegenwart, nicht Vergangenheit; Wirklichkeit, nicht Schein; Prosa, nicht Vers. Am wenigsten aber wollte man Rhetorik. Eine Zeit brach an, in der nach jahrzehntelanger lyrischer und lyrisch-epischer Überproduktion im ganzen genommen weing Verse geschrieben und noch weniger gekauft und gelesen wurden. Mit anderen Worten, es vollzog sich der große Umschwung, der dem *Realismus* zum Siege verhalf.

In turn, and despite or even because of all accolades that Grillparzer's **Spielmann** has earned as a "realistic" work and even as an anticipation of Naturalism (e.g. Gundolf),[14] we must compare it with the literary background of Realism as the dominant tendency during the period from 1848 to 1872, indeed, for long thereafter. Such a comparison can be justified not only as an exercise in literary history, but also as an explanation for the fact that Grillparzer, whose reputation in Germany was not that of a "Realist," had written a work that might well have been read—or at least "begun"—by many but never entered into discussions and was thereby for all literary historical purposes "neglected." Of course, it goes almost without saying that the results of such a comparison have virtually no relevance for the "realism"-question in a modern sense, for, as a contribution to the *Rezeptionsgeschichte* of the **Spielmann,** they must be based on the conception of "realism" that dominated the literary scene in Germany in the decades following 1848.

II

In terms of a complete picture of German literature for many years after the Revolution, one must consider the fact that many figures from Young Germany, e.g. Karl Gutzkow, continued to write popular novels and dramas; in fact, one such figure, Heinrich Laube, was later responsible for the rehabilitation of Grillparzer's dramas on the stage. But scarcely anyone familiar with *Die Ritter vom Geiste* (1850) and *Der Zauberer von Rom* (1858-61) would expect the author of these works to be receptive to **Der arme Spielmann,** and Laube's personal transformation after the abortive Revolution is only a part of the larger picture indicated by Friedrich Sengle when he writes:

> Es ist sogar möglich, daß die Biedermeiertradition eine Voraussetzung für die vielgetadelte idyllische Neigung des *deutschen* Realismus ist. *Aber es gibt im 19. Jahrhundert vor 1848 nirgends einen so deutlichen Klima-*

> *und Generationswechsel wie den, den der erste deutsche Revolutionsversuch bewirkte.*[15]

In 1848 an epoch came to a conclusion, but the unsuccessful revolution that ended it also gave birth to a new period. How important this new development was can be gleaned from Sengle's—albeit somewhat too forceful—statement, "daß die realistische Kritik der Biedermeierzeit der reinste 'Kahlschlag' und daher einwandfrei festzustellen ist."[16]

Following the lead of Sengle, many scholars have concentrated on the so-called "programmatic realism" (*programmatischer Realismus*) initiated by Julian Schmidt and Gustav Freytag in the pages of *Die Grenzboten* after they had assumed the editorship in 1848.[17] Whether 1848 also marks the inception of "Bürgerlicher Realismus," "Poetischer Realismus" or simply "Realismus" remains a moot point that goes beyond the present topic.[18] For, regardless of his direct or indirect influence on such later realists as Keller, Storm, Meyer, Raabe and Fontane, Julian Schmidt established himself in the years following the Revolution of 1848 as a literary pope by articulating a new generation's attitude toward the *Vormärz* and its demands for a "new" literature. Thus Schmidt writes in his article on the "Märzpoeten" in *Die Grenzboten* 9/1 (1850): "Aber wenn die Illusionen jener Tage aufgegeben sind, so ist ihre Geschichte nicht an uns verloren gegangen, und was wir in ihr gelernt haben, wird in der neuen Poesie zur Geltung kommen."[19]

Admittedly, *Die Grenzboten* did not review **Der arme Spielmann,** even though in 1852 it discussed Grillparzer together with Friedrich Halm and others under the collective title "Oestreichische Theaterdichter." Since the article concedes ignorance of *Melusine* and *Weh dem, der lügt!* by name, we can assume ignorance of the mere existence of **Der arme Spielmann.** Be that as it may, the following remarks on Grillparzer's *Sappho, Das goldene Vließ* and *Des Meeres und der Liebe Wellen* provide an indication of the reception Schmidt might have accorded **Der arme Spielmann**:

> Wenn wir die musterhafte Ausführung dieser drei Stücke erwägen, so werden wir zum höchsten Bedauern getrieben, daß ein so bedeutendes dramatisches Talent für uns verlorengegangen ist. Diese Probleme liegen zu weit seitab von dem, was den Pulsschlag unsrer Zeit bewegt. Nicht ungestraft entfernt sich der Dichter, namentlich der dramatische, von dem öffentlichen Leben seines Volks. So schön diese Gedichte im Einzelnen sind, sie machen doch nur den Eindruck von Schattenbildern, deren Wirkung mit dem Augenblick flüchtig vorübergeht.[20]

The review then calls the historical dramas *König Ottokars Glück und Ende* and *Ein treuer Diener seines Herrn* "viel schwächer." This journal speaks from the viewpoint of a new generation for which "ein so bedeutendes Talent . . . verlorengegangen ist." The main reason for Grillparzer's lack of modernity: He has removed himself "von dem öffentlichen Leben seines Volkes" and has left "nur den Eindruck von Schattenbildern." While such deficiencies are made to seem particularly telling for a "dramatic" writer, they are, as we shall see in Schmidt's other judgments, just as objectionable in narrative prose works.

Later in the review of Grillparzer's dramas we hear about *Ein treuer Diener seines Herrn*:

Der alte Bancbanus ist zu unter[t]hänig und zu altklug, als daß wir ihm unser Interesse schenken könnten, und die Reue, die später den Wahnsinn treibt, zu unklar und mystisch, als daß sie uns überzeugen und versöhnen könnte. Auch auf die Sprache hat die Sentimentalität dieser Anlage einen nachtheiligen Einfluß ausgeübt.[21]

More than one critic has compared Jakob to Bancbanus, and if such a comparison has any justification, then obviously Schmidt would have rejected the main character in **Der arme Spielmann** and probably the narrator's sentimentality as well.

Such suppositions are made even stronger when we learn which works Schmidt praised. For example, in 1850 he says in *Die Grenzboten*:

Ein erfreuliches Zeichen der Sehnsucht nach Realität, nach ursprünglichem, festem Leben war der Erfolg unsrer jungen idyllischen Poesie. Bei den Dorfgeschichten von Berthold Auerbach, Jeremias Gotthelf u.s.w. gewöhnte man sich wenigstens daran, mit Menschen umzugehen, die noch eine andere Beschäftigung hatten, als die Lectüre der Modejournale und die Fabrik von Sonetten an Blaustrümpfe; eine festere, concrete Bestimmtheit, als die vorübergehende Tendenz einer poetischen Doctrin.[22]

The author of these lines would scarcely have had the patience to read **Der arme Spielmann** and to think about why the main character plays his music the way he does. Moreover, the characters in Auerbach's and Gotthelf's works find their place in, and therefore reflect the value of, "real" life. Naturally, one could also point to the subject-matter of the *Dorfgeschichte* as one missing in Grillparzer's novella. As Werner Hahl correctly summarizes the situation, this genre, which is defined by its milieu, provided an important bridge between the literature of the *Vormärz* and the *Nachmärz*: "Der gemäßigte Auerbach war nicht nur der gefeierte Autor der vierziger, sondern die Brücke in die fünfziger Jahre, in den programmatischen Realismus."[23] But this genre soon came under fire from the new realists themselves, and in 1862 Freytag in his article for *Die Grenzboten* demands more than mere "Virtuosität in der Behandlung des Details" and relegates "das Absonderliche und Locale" to the function of "Farbe und Stimmung."[24] According to Freytag, the author of a "modern" *Dorfgeschichte* "muß verstehen, mühelos das allgemeine Menschliche, ewig Fesselnde in den Besonderheiten der Erscheinung darzustellen." Nonetheless, the commitment to, and success in, "real life" remains a mark of "realistic" prose narratives and their protagonists. Schmidt and Freytag would scarcely have found such qualities in Grillparzer's Jakob.

It is also questionable whether the programmatic realists would have accepted the narrator's commitment to life as they would like to see it portrayed. For, as a whole, **Der arme Spielmann** lacks the necessary bourgeois optimism. Many critics have attempted since then to interpret Grillparzer's description of the *Volksfest* in the first part of the novella as an indication of his association with the masses and "real life." But we must agree with Wolfgang Paulsen's statement that Grillparzer "mit dem Phänomen des 'arbeitenden Volkes' überhaupt nur fertig werden kann, indem er es mythologisiert."[25] While Paulsen attributes the first part of the novella and the mythological allusions in

the description of the *Volksfest* to the first period (1831) of the novella's genesis,[26] he continues the thought cited above with the judgment:

Der Realismus, auf den Grillparzers Erzählung ganz sicher schon hinstrebt, ist, wie sich an der Gestaltung gerade der Volksszenen ablesen läßt, noch eindeutig durch den Filter des klassischen Humanismus gegeben, wozu ihm wohl wirklich Goethes Gestaltung des "Römischen Karnevals" die Mittel zur Verfügung gestellt haben dürfte auch wenn er ihn nicht unbedingt gerade damals eben gelesen haben muß.[27]

To be sure, much has been written about Schmidt's and Freytag's implied demand for "Verklärung," and, as we shall see, even the later realists like Fontane made this demand of "realistic" prose.[28]

But the novel that seemed to fit best all of Schmidt's demands, including his more limited view of *Verklärung*, was Freytag's *Soll und Haben*, which, as we have heard from Fontane, set the trend for "realism" and, we must add, for the view of society for many years. This novel even carried as its motto Schmidt's own words: "Der Roman soll das deutsche Volk da suchen, wo es in seiner Tüchtigkeit zu finden ist, nämlich bei seiner Arbeit." From today's standpoint, we might not see Freytag's novel as especially "realistic," but we must take into consideration the point raised by Hartmut Steinecke in the following:

Sieht man Realismus jedoch nicht unter der Optik spekulativer "Wesensbestimmungen" von Literaturwissenschaftlern des 20. Jahrhunderts, sondern vom Verständnis der 1850er Jahre, so wird man die ältere Zuordnung sinnvoll finden. Realismus in diesem Sinne bedeutete zunächst formal: geschlossener Aufbau, klare Handlungsführung, Bemühung um Motivierung; sprachlichstilistisch: Verankerung des Romans in einer mittleren Sprachebene, Eindämmen der Rhetorik, des Pathos, der Reflexion; darstellerisch: detailgetreue Wiedergabe der "äußeren" Wirklichkeit, von Schauplätzen und Interieurs sowie von Personen, "wie sie im täglichen Leben stehen," mit einem an Dickens geschulten Humor; ethisch: "Optimismus" und "Gesundheit," positive Helden, die ihre Umwelt und ihr Schicksal fröhlich bejahen. . . . "Realismus" heißt hier also auch: Ablehnung der Gesellschaftskritik, Anerkennung des Vorhandenen, der bestehenden sozialen und politischen Verhältnisse.[29]

Obviously, such criteria can be applied not only to a novel but also to a shorter prose work. In turn, we recognize how little recognition these criteria allow for **Der arme Spielmann,** even if one ignores the social criticism implied by Grillparzer.

Naturally, some works were produced during the Fifties that both corresponded to the prevalent concept of "realism" and have at least a superficial similarity to **Der arme Spielmann.** These are especially the works that end on a note of resignation, particularly in a love-affair. These range from Otto Ludwig's *Zwischen Himmel und Erde* (1856) and Storm's *Immensee* (1850/51) to Keller's *Romeo und Julia auf dem Dorfe* (1856). In fact, Ludwig's tale was even strongly praised by Schmidt. But only Keller injects a question about the social order into his novella, and even here the protagonists' action at the end, by implication, affirms this order. Sali and Vrenchen refuse the offer of a life outside of society with the Black Fiddler, and after their suicide the narrator implies by his allusion to the newspaper comment that society should see the youngsters' action in its proper light. As many critics have pointed out, if Jakob does indeed sacrifice his life for a "social" value, it is for the superficial one of money, just as his brother before him drowned by carrying out—for honor's sake—a ridiculous bet.

III

As unreceptive as we might expect the "programmatic realists" to have been, we must remember that the zenith of realism was reached much later, indeed, not only after Schmidt and other critics of the Fifties had already said all that they had to say, but also after 1872, the year that had promised so much for a renewed interest in Grillparzer's *Spielmann*. During this period the major prose writers of the nineteenth century published their greatest and most enduring works, works on which we commonly base our definition of "Poetic Realism." It would contribute little to the present discussion to recapitulate all of the qualities of this movement, not in the least because Grillparzer's novella has much in common with the works of the Poetic Realists. In fact, like Droste-Hülshoff's *Die Judenbuche*, which Schmidt rejected, *Der arme Spielmann* is frequently counted among the works of Poetic Realism, almost as if these would have been possible in their present form and content without the intervening step of programmatic realism and the literary climate it created. Yet, given even the many similarities *Der arme Spielmann* has and Freytag's *Soll und Haben* does not have with the works of Keller, Storm, Meyer, Raabe and Fontane, there remains a crucial difference between Grillparzer's novella and those of the Poetic Realists, just as the latter writers are producing works popular in a society that is still reading Freytag's novel.

Before we move on to more basic distinctions, however, we should dismiss what seems to be a superficial similarity between Grillparzer's novella and the poetic realistic one: the emphasis on the "dramatic." On the one hand, much criticism has revolved around Grillparzer's talent as a dramatist and the relationship of this talent to his narrative style and presentation.[30] On the other hand, the interest of the poetic realists in the novella as an especially "dramatic" form is well-known. We need think only of Storm's dictum that the novella is a "Parallel-Dichtung des Dramas" (vid. his letter of 9 October 1879 to Erich Schmidt). Yet regardless of what we may consider today as "dramatic," Grillparzer's novella did not seem "dramatic" to the literary world of 1871. For we read in Paul Heyse's introduction to *Der arme Spielmann* in volume 5 of his *Deutscher Novellenschatz*:

> Die einzige Novelle, die der große Tragiker je gedichtet oder doch veröffentlicht hat, sind wir so glücklich, den Lesern unseres Novellenschatzes mittheilen zu dürfen. Und fürwahr, in mehr als einer Hinsicht hat diese Novelle Anspruch darauf, einzig in ihrer Art zu heißen. Wäre durch einen Zufall der Name des Verfassers verloren oder unbekannt geblieben, so würde man ihn gewiß unter den großen Dichtern, schwerlich unter den großen Dramatikern suchen. Denn Nichts von dem, was das Wesen und den Werth der dramatischen Kunst ausmacht, keine starkgegliederte Handlung, keine Spannungsmomente im theatralischen Sinne, kein rhetorisch erhöhter Ausdruck leidenschaftlicher Stimmung ist in

> diesen Blättern zu finden. . . . Wir können nun aber auch die psychologische Erklärung für jenen eigenthümlichen Zug seines Talentes geben: für die Neigung nämlich zu gebrochenen Farben, verhaltenen und verhüllten Stimmungen, zu dem räthselhaften oder doch nur der feineren Beobachtung zugänglichen Reiz des höchst individuellen, ganz persönlichen Seelenlebens, das sich gewöhnlich der dramatischen Form entzieht und der Novelle anheimfällt.[31]

Whatever we may think about Heyse's attempt to fit *Der arme Spielmann* into his scheme of the novella or about his distinctions between dramatic and narrative prerequisites, we must accept his description of the customarily accepted view of "dramatic" among *his* readers as that which was usually expected of any novella as—in Storm's words—"die Schwester des Dramas."[32] To what extent Heyse accurately describes the dramatic qualities of the novellas before 1871 may even be considered a moot point. In any case, his description of what Grillparzer lacks does correspond very well to what we find in the novellas by the Poetic Realists after 1871. And these are the very works with which *Der arme Spielmann* had to compete for public recognition.

Since Gerhart Hauptmann and the other Naturalists, we have of course come to accept an entirely different concept of "drama" on the stage, and consequently we might more readily accept *Der arme Spielmann* as dramatic. Yet more recent scholarship has concentrated on another quality of poetic realistic prose that both distinguishes it from that of other periods and is anchored in the principles of programmatic realism: *Humor*. While Wolfgang Preisendanz[33] and others can convincingly trace a line from the Romantics and Jean Paul through the works of Keller, Raabe and Fontane, there can be no doubt that "humor" was a specific quality demanded by Julian Schmidt, albeit a humor in the style of Dickens. Friedrich Sengle describes the orientation of the programmatic realists: "Freytag und Julian Schmidt bewunderten nach wie vor Scott wegen des untadeligen Aufbaus seiner Romane, Dickens aber, den Humoristen, priesen sie enthusiastisch. . . . Julian Schmidt erhob . . . Dickens, wodurch er noch musterhafter wurde, zum Deutschen: Dickens 'ist auch viel deutscher als unsre gesamte romantische Literatur von Tieck und Schlegel herunter bis auf Hebbel und Gutzkow'.[34] And in his review of *Soll und Haben* Theodor Fontane even calls it "eine *Verdeutschung* (im vollsten und edelsten Sinne) des neueren englischen Romans. . . . Dickens, Thackeray und Cooper sind unverkennbare Vorbilder gewesen." To what extent the element of "humor" plays a role in Schmidt's evaluation of all contemporary prose is nowhere more evident than in his review of Ludwig's *Heiterethei*, in which he writes:

> Mit einem Wort, die einzige poetische Form, durch welche dieser Realismus seine Berechtigung in der Kunst erwirbt, ist der Humor; der Dichter muß im Stande sein, die Unreife der Bildung, die er darstellt, unserer Anschauungsweise dadurch zugänglich zu machen, daß er den komischen Contrast hervorhebt, ohne dadurch den inneren Ernst seiner Erzählung abzuschwächen. . . . Von den deutschen Dichtern kannten wir bisher nur zwei, die ein eminentes Talent hatten, für dergleichen Zustände den richtigen Ton zu finden, Jean Paul und Jeremias Gotthelf. Wir freuen uns, daß wir nach der Heiterethei auch Otto Ludwig dazu rechnen können.[35]

Obviously, Grillparzer did not have the same models as Freytag or Ludwig. Yet it cannot be denied that there is a certain comic element in *Der arme Spielmann.*

Be that as it may, we must, however, question whether "humor" is simply a form of the "comic" and, in turn, whether Grillparzer's novella contains "humor," not merely in the sense that Julian Schmidt applies the concept to Jean Paul, Gotthelf, Freytag and Ludwig, but also in that which Fontane describes as the difference between Willibald Alexis and Walter Scott:

> Wie die *Stil*frage in einem nahen Zusammenhange mit jenen aufgezählten Unterschieden steht, so auch die Frage nach dem *Humor.* Der Humor hat das Darüberstehn, das heitersouveräne Spiel mit den Erscheinungen dieses Lebens, auf die er *herab*blickt, zur Voraussetzung. W. Alexis hatte den Kleinhumor, aber nicht den großen. Er wandelte in der Ebene, und was zufällig unter ihm lag, dafür hatte er eine humoristische Betrachtung; manches der Art ist ersten Ranges; Scott aber, in sein Tartanplaid gewickelt, ritt über die Grampians seiner Heimat, und die Schlösser und die Hütten, die Könige und die Kätner lagen gleichmäßig zu seinen Füßen, und nichts barg das Leben, zu dem er nicht, in spielenden Gestalten, eine heiter-superiore Stellung genommen hätte. Die Vorurteile steigerten nur noch den Effekt. Er war der Großhumorist, weil er persönlich groß und frei war. Wo W. Alexis eine ähnliche Position einzunehmen versucht, bleibt er, als Kind seiner Zeit und seines Landes, in der *Ironie* stecken. Er spöttelt, er persifliert; aber seine Seele bringt es zu keinem olympischen Lachen. Er war eben kein Olympier.[36]

Here we can see that "humor" goes far beyond the merely comic or amusing, in fact, that it really has little to do with the latter concepts.

What we are, in essence, dealing with is the question of narrative perspective or, as Wolfgang Preisendanz calls it, "angewandte Phantasie." Fontane says "looking down on the phenomena of life" is a prerequisite of humor. Certainly there has been no lack of critics who have pointed out the almost arrogant attitude of the narrator toward Jakob. Sengle, for example, writes:

> Zunächst muß noch, wegen der so beliebten biographistischen Identifikation des Dichters mit dem armen Spielmann, betont werden, daß Grillparzer die Existenz des Spielmanns wiederholt außerhalb der Erzählung erwähnt hat. . . . Dies erscheint mir deshalb wichtig, weil es absurd ist, den armen Spielmann mit Grillparzers Unzulänglichkeitsgefühlen in Verbindung zu bringen. Der Dichter hatte nicht ganz das erreicht, was er erstrebte, aber er sah sich niemals als Stümper. Die Distanz, mit der er erzählt, ist keine raffinierte Technik, sondern ergibt sich einfach aus der *liebevollen Herablassung des anerkannten Künstlers zum Nichtskönner.*[37]

On the other hand, John M. Ellis argues from an entirely different point of view, yet arrives at a judgment that emphasizes not "loving condescension" but an almost malicious attitude on the part of a narrator who lives in a "world of insincerity" and suffers from "loss of contact with genuine feeling."[38] For he finds:

> The bearing of the narrator on the figure of the Spielmann is clearly a complex matter, involving many factors: among them his authorial pose, and the theme of

descent in class. Also important here is his compulsive denigration of a man who is his opposite.[39]

Thus, whether one sees a sympathetic or an antagonistic narrator, the fact of his condescension remains a constant factor in interpreting the novella. While such a form of "Darüberstehn" obviously has nothing to do with the "comic," neither can it be interpreted as "humor" in a broader sense. For any form of arrogance or judgment over others is alien to the "Großhumor" that Fontane describes, indeed to the "heitersouveränes Spiel" he postulates for humor. On the one hand, the "liebevolle Herablassung" allows too much room for sentimentality, a feeling that keeps us from raising above the "Ebene" of the events and persons being portrayed. On the other hand, a "compulsive denigration" does not let the narrator transcend mere "Ironie." What Fontane means is a form of humor that is Olympian because it is tolerant, because it is neither too involved nor too prejudiced. It is, as Wolfgang Preisendanz following the lead of Hegel says, "objective humor."

Much has been said about the importance of an individual "tone," both by the Poetic Realists themselves and subsequent critics, and about the dominance of the *Rahmenerzählung* as the most fitting narrative form. Taken together, they indicate an emphasis on the human truth as opposed to a metaphysical one. Whether one sees in such novellas the influence of Ludwig Feuerbach, Rochau's *Realpolitik* or other writers and thinkers of the nineteenth century, it is self-evident that they could not, like the *Spielmann,* be interpreted as expressions of an *imitatio Christi* or a "Barockes Welttheater" (vid. von Wiese and Wittkowski).[40]

The truth of the poetic realistic *Rahmenerzählung* is a human truth that stems from one person, but a person who, because he sees events from his own viewpoint, evokes the readers' tolerance of every situation. In other words, we have in the *Rahmenerzählungen* of Storm, Keller, Meyer and Raabe a narrator who is clearly distinct from the author, and who manipulates or chooses the perspective, but is himself manipulated by the author. One can accept or reject the following assertion by Walter Naumann; in any case, it would not be made about a *Rahmenerzählung* of Poetic Realism:

> Der Rahmen der Erzählung **Der arme Spielmann** gibt ein Selbstbildnis des Dichters. Der Erzähler umreißt, ohne Umschweife, sich selbst als geistige Person, als Betrachtenden, der, durch menschliche Teilnahme bewegt, sich souverän dem Lebendigen zuwendet und es erkennt.[41]

Because the narrator in Poetic Realism is made so distinct from the author yet manipulated by him, we, as the readers, can consider this narrator as an objective but inadequate reporter who presents us with a "total" picture, albeit one seen only from his standpoint. We believe in the sincerity of this "witness," but we realize that he too is only human and that the "truth" he gives us is only the truth from his perspective. If other equally qualified persons had been there, they might have told a different story thereafter. This applies even in situations where, as in the case of Hans in Meyer's *Der Heilige* or the schoolmaster in Storm's *Der Schimmelreiter*, we seem to have a singularly qualified narrator. Because what may be mere appearance is, for such a narrator, the only reality, this reality may have been only the appearance of reality for others. No higher truth is offered than the strictly human one, but it must remain inadequate because we have heard only one of many possible witnesses.

Even from these few remarks, it is obvious that *Der arme Spielmann* requires a reaction that is no longer possible from an audience committed to the "inadequate" narrator of Poetic Realism. Stifter, as a member of the reading public before 1848, says "daß sich eine edle Rührung in unser Herz schleicht, und daß man am Schlusse die beruhigendste Auflösung und eine lohnende Erhebung empfindet." Grillparzer did not contradict this as his intention, nor could he have reasonably done so. When the tears roll down Barbara's cheek at the conclusion of Grillparzer's novella, the narrator is provided with a substantiation that the Poetic Realists seldom allow their narrators. Whether we like the narrator in *Der arme Spielmann* or not, and regardless of his own personal attitude toward Jakob, we believe in the accuracy of his portrayal of Jakob as the only one possible. He puts us—as Fontane says of Alexis—on the same "Ebene" as Barbara and the rest of Jakob's environment, even though everyone in this environment may not have "appreciated" Jakob as a person or *Spielmann.* Perhaps it is even against his (fictional) will that the narrator gives us a sympathetic and therefore a positive portrait of a social misfit, incompetent musician and ridiculously naive person; nonetheless—and unlike, for example, the events in the *Rahmenerzählung* in Meyer's *Der Heilige*—we know how we are expected to react emotionally. Because we are left with one valid impression of the central character, our own values—e.g. our belief that the intention should outweigh the result—determine only our attitude toward the narrator. Our curiosity about the musician and person Jakob has been satisfied, and we do not need another "witness." We could scarcely make such a statement about Hauke Haien in *Der Schimmelreiter*, Regine in *Das Sinngedicht* or *Stopfkuchen.*

IV

Today we benefit from many interpretations based on *werkimmanente Kritik.* They reveal how subtle Grillparzer's style and the structure of this novella are. Yet these interpretations provide their greatest benefits and, in fact, have their only real justification in making *Der arme Spielmann* accessible to a modern audience. In other words, they demonstrate why this or any other great work—regardless of its earlier reception—is relevant for today's reading public and therefore, by implication, "greater" than the many other works of that time. But in the case of "neglected masterpieces" one is too often tempted to assume that our critical faculties are more developed than those of earlier periods. Such an assumption—irrespective of our increase in critical breadth and methodology since 1848—could blind us to the accomplishments of writers and critics who "neglected" the works of a previous generation. Writers of today are producing literature with an eye on the criticism of today, but most of us who have a knowledge of literary history would probably wager that Grillparzer's *Der arme Spielmann* will still be read when most of the present-day literature has long ceased to find an audience. The same could be said of the works of many writers, not in the least those of the Poetic Realists, who, as products of a subsequent literary period, either ignored

or would not have fully understood Grillparzer's novella, yet themselves created timelessly "great" works.

Der arme Spielmann can indeed be praised as inherently "modern," and future criticism will undoubtedly bring even more insights into this aspect of the novella. But *textimmanente Kritik* does not necessarily concern itself with the "intention" of the author or the expectations of his and later audiences. In the same measure, it allows little insight into the relationship of a work to the literature that appeared between it and today. That is to say: *Der arme Spielmann* seems unquestionably more modern than most works of the *Vormärz,* but not because Grillparzer anticipated developments after 1848 or would have found approval among all Poetic Realists. After all, what Keller praises is not very different from what Stifter lauds in Jakob. But we would be hard-put to find a character in Keller's own works who could be described with Keller's words on Jakob. Keller expresses appreciation of Grillparzer's novella on the same level as the reader before 1848 would have done. Obviously, the programmatic realists like Schmidt would have found little to praise in a work that belonged to a period from which they wanted to divorce themselves. On the other hand, it might have found more tolerance among the less dogmatic Poetic Realists, but since only Fontane committed his literary views in any measure to print, we shall never really know for sure. In any case, they would not have praised it in terms of their own creations.

Notes

1. Interpretative summaries of the *Rezeptionsgeschichte* of *Der arme Spielmann* are presented by Wolfgang Paulsen, "Der gute Bürger Jakob: Zur Satire in Grillparzers *Armem Spielmann,*" *Colloquia Germania* 2 (1968): 272-98, and, more recently and in greater detail, by Hinrich C. Seeba, "Franz Grillparzer: *Der arme Spielmann* (1847)," *Romane und Erzählungen zwischen Romantik und Realismus: Neue Interpretationen,* ed. Paul Michael Lützeler (Stuttgart, 1983) 386-422. The following agrees with one of the main contentions of both authors, namely, that this work should be seen in the context of its time, not just as a great work of literature.

2. *Deutscher Novellenschatz,* eds. Paul Heyse and Hermann Kurz, 5 (München, 1871) 278.

3. Hieronymus Lorm, "Grillparzers *Der arme Spielmann,*" *Jahrbuch der Grillparzer-Gesellschaft* 4 (1894): 78.

4. Reinhold Backmann, "Grillparzer und Stifter in der Iris für 1848 (*Armer Spielmann* und *Prokopus*)," *Jahrbuch der Grillparzer-Gesellschaft* NF 2 (1942): 133-54.

5. Lorm 77.

6. Lorm 77.

7. Emil Kuh, *Franz Grillparzer und Adalbert Stifter: Zwei Dichter Österreichs* (Wien, 1872).

8. Paulsen 272.

9. Walter Silz, *Realism and Reality* (Chapel Hill, 1954).

10. Richard Brinkmann, *Wirklichkeit und Illusion* (Tübingen, 1957).

11. Paulsen 273.

12. Backmann 133.

13. Quotation from Backmann 135.

14. Friedrich Gundolf, "Franz Grillparzer," *Jahrbuch des Freien Deutschen Hochstifts* (1931): 9-93, claims: "Grillparzer läuft um ein Menschenalter den naturalistischen Elends- und Trübsinnsbildern des Flaubert, Zola, Maupassant, Tolstoi, Dostojewski, Hamsun, Hauptmann vor" (403).

15. Friedrich Sengle, *Biedermeierzeit* (Stuttgart, 1971-1980) 1:222.

16. Sengle 1: 222.

17. *Die Grenzboten* was, of course, not the only literary journal that called for a new realism. Helmuth Widhammer in his *Die Literaturtheorie des deutschen Realismus*, Sammlung Metzler 152 (Stuttgart, 1977) gives an extensive list that includes Hermann Marggraff's *Blätter für literarische Unterhaltung*, Robert Prutz's *Deutsches Museum*, and Rudolf Haym's *Preußische Jahrbücher.*

18. For discussions of the relationship of these concepts to each other see: Fritz Martini, *Deutsche Literatur im bürgerlichen Realismus 1848-1898* (Stuttgart, [4]1981); Clifford A. Bernd, *German Poetic Realism* (Boston, 1981); and Roy C. Cowen, *Der Poetische Realismus: Kommentar zu einer Epoche* (München, 1985).

19. Quotation from: *Realismus und Gründerzeit: Manifeste und Dokumente zur deutschen Literatur 1848-1880*, eds. Max Bucher et al. (Stuttgart, 1975) 2: 78.

20. *Die Grenzboten* (1852) 341.

21. *Die Grenzboten* 342.

22. Quotation according to *Realismus*—(note 19) 2: 81.

23. Werner Hahl, "Gesellschaftlicher Konservatismus und literarischer Realismus: Das Modell einer deutschen Sozialverfassung in den Dorfgeschichten," *Realismus*—(note 19) 1: 63.

24. Quotation from *Realismus*—(note 19) 2: 197.

25. Paulsen 282.

26. Paulsen 285.

27. Paulsen 282.

28. In his letter of 24 June 1881 to Emilie Fontane, Theodor Fontane writes about Turgenev: "Ich bewundere die scharfe Beobachtung und das hohe Maß phrasenloser, alle Kinkerlitzchen verschmähender Kunst; aber eigentlich langweilt es mich, weil es im Gegensatz zu den teils wirklich poetischen, teils wenigstens poetisch sein wollenden 'Jägergeschichten' so grenzenlos prosaisch, so ganz *unverklärt* die Dinge wiedergibt. Ohne diese Verklärung gibt es aber keine eigentliche Kunst, auch dann nicht, wenn der Bildner in seinem bildnerischen Geschick ein wirklicher Künstler ist. Wer *so* beanlagt ist, muß *Essays* über Rußland schreiben, aber nicht Novellen. Abhandlungen haben ihr Gesetz und die Dichtung auch."

29. Hartmut Steinecke, "*Soll und Haben* (1855): Weltbild und Wirkung eines deutschen Bestsellers," *Romane und Erzählungen des Bürgerlichen Realismus: Neue Interpretationen*, ed. Horst Denkler (Stuttgart, 1980) 143 f.

30. For example, Kurt Vancsa, "Grillparzers *Der arme Spielmann* und Stifters *Der arme Wohltäter*," *Festschrift für Eduard Castle zum 80. Geburtstag*, ed. Gesellschaft für Wiener Theaterforschung und Wiener Goethe-Verein (Wien, 1955) 105, still writes: "Gattungsgesetzlich . . . rangiert unzweifelhaft Stifters Novelle vor der Grillparzers. Grillparzer, eher in der Linie der Eigenwilligkeit Kleist'scher Epik, läßt sich völlig von seinen dramatischen Impulsen treiben, er verweilt nicht, beschreibt nicht, stellt nicht dar—, er spielt einfach den Part herunter, auch und gerade in der eingeschobenen 'Erzählung.' . . . Die Novelle Grillparzers ist das epische Konzept eines Librettos."

31. *Deutscher Novellenschatz* 278.

32. Theodor Storm, *Sämtliche Werke*, ed. Albert Köster (Leipzig, 1920) 8: 122.

33. Wolfgang Preisendanz, *Humor als dichterische Einbildungskraft: Studien zur Erzählkunst des poetischen Realismus* (München, [2]1976).

34. Sengle 1: 260.

35. Quoted from *Realismus*—(note 19) 2: 193.

36. Theodor Fontane, *Sämtliche Werke*, ed. Walter Keitel (München, 1962 ff.), Abt. III, 1: 161.

37. Sengle 3: 125.

38. John M. Ellis, "Grillparzer's *Der arme Spielmann*," *Germann Quarterly* 45 (1972): 677.

39. Ellis 677.

40. Benno von Wiese, *Die deutsche Novelle von Goethe bis Kafka* 1 (Düsseldorf, 1956) and Wolfgang Wittkowski, "Grenze als Stufe: Josephinischer Gradualismus und barockes Welttheater in Grillparzers Novelle *Der arme Spielmann*," *Aurora* 41 (1981): 135-60. To the extent that one accepts not merely a generally religious slant to Grillparzer's novella but rather a specifically Catholic one, one can opine that such programmatic realists as Julian Schmidt, coming as they did from a Prussian, Protestant tradition, would have had even more reason to reject it.

41. Walter Naumann, *Grillparzer: Das dichterische Werk* (Stuttgart, [2]1967) 31.

Ian F. Roe (excerpt date 1995)

SOURCE: "Prose and Poetry: *Der arme Spielmann*," in *Franz Grillparzer: A Century of Criticism*, Camden House, 1995, pp. 116-25.

[*In the following excerpt, Roe chronicles the critical reaction to* Der arme Spielmann.]

The exception to the overall history of neglect of Grillparzer's non-dramatic writing is **Der arme Spielmann (The Poor Musician)**, though the critical reception of Grillparzer's one major prose work has followed an uneven course. In 1988 Roy C. Cowen was still able to refer to it as a neglected masterpiece (Bernd 1988), and it has not been uncommon for it to be excluded from general studies of Grillparzer's work such as those by Reich (1894) or Skreb (1976), who choose to see him exclusively as a dramatist. E. K. Bennett, however, in his 1934 study of the German *Novelle*, claimed it as "without doubt the most perfect of all Grillparzer's works,"[1] and in the last few decades *Der arme Spielmann* has attracted such extensive interest in the Anglo-Saxon world that in 1983 Hinrich C. Seeba called for a moratorium on further criticism until there was anything new to say. This has had little impact on the eager battalions of scholars on either side of the Atlantic, as evidenced by the new contributions included in Bernd's 1988 collection of reprinted articles and by the essays that have continued to appear since.

In 1846 Grillparzer had forecast that the story's lack of any reference to German unity or Germany's military strength would limit its popularity, and despite Stifter's enthusiastic response when the story appeared the following year, *Der arme Spielmann* did not appeal to the advocates of social realism in the following decades and remained relatively unknown both before and after the author's death. Occasionally it even suffered the same fate as *Ein Bruderzwist in Habsburg*, being mistitled *Der alte Spielmann* (The *Old* Musician) not only in certain sections of the press but also in Wurzbach's book of 1871 (33). After Lorm's unsatisfactory attempt to reconstruct the author and the time in which the story is set from a reading of the work—the narrator's opening description, for example, gives us insight into the "metaphysical profundity of the Viennese character" (1894: 53)—serious exploration of the story did not begin until 1925. Bernhard Seuffert is predominantly concerned with the figure of Jakob and hence sees the narrator's introduction to Jakob's story as excessively lengthy, even irrelevant, as the festival makes no impression on the fiddler (1925: 293). Seuffert suggests that one could interpret the whole story along autobiographical lines, as Grillparzer no doubt wondered whether his own periods of optimism were as ill-founded as the musician's self-content. Alker also follows the autobiographical approach, seeing the musician as "Grillparzer's frank confession" (1926: 17), a presentation of all his problems in a nutshell, including his difficulties with women and his inability to express his ideas or to combine music and words so as to produce the great baroque *Gesamtkunstwerk*. Yet Allker also views the work as a modern novella that subordinates the depiction of events to psychology, not least in the author's self-denigration in the character of Jakob (24), and also provides a detailed investigation of the structure. This is considered symmetrical, with the narrator's framework enclosing a twofold inner story of music and Barbara; the symmetry is also found in Jakob's conception of music, which in turn is a statement of Grillparzer's aesthetic views. However, the two central themes and the length of the framework made Grillparzer conclude that the story did not satisfy the strict formal constraints of the German *Novelle*.

Critical interest increased in the 1950s with three writers (Brinkmann, Silz, and Wiese) examining the story in studies of the German novella or of nineteenth-century realism. Like Alker, Silz (1954) stresses the theme of psychological self-revelation, finding it in both the musician and the narrator. The latter is, in his opinion, Grillparzer's

outer social self, giving the views of neighbors and the public at large on the musician's elegiac tale of loneliness and inadequacy. Yet Jakob is the absolutely pure soul, with a selflessness bordering on saintliness, who upholds the virtues extolled by Rustan at the end of *Der Traum ein Leben*. Nevertheless, it is an ambivalent picture, both an ideal and a deterrent at the same time. According to Wiese, Jakob's music as the product of his loneliness is the ultimate expression of complete solipsism (1956: 145), and he questions the view of Silz and earlier critics that Jakob is a pure and innocent soul, seeing him instead as a pathological case, a distorted, even grotesque figure of incompetence and failure, despite hints of the indestructibility of the human and artistic soul.

The critical direction in Silz's essay is carried much further by Walter Naumann, for whom it is the narrator and the framework rather than Jakob that offers a self-portrait of Grillparzer the intellectual (1956: 21), the observer of life and humanity, though Jakob as the object of this interest also reveals many traits of the author. The festival described in the opening section indicates the judgment of the community on the fate of Jakob, the individual. Art can no longer be used as an excuse for failure in life, and Jakob is a failure in both. Brinkmann (1957) considers a further angle of the narrator's role: the extent to which he comments, interprets, and even distorts the story of the musician. Only toward the end is Jakob apparently allowed to speak for himself, but even then his words seem too educated and are clearly embellished by the narrator, who in any case could not possibly have remembered them so well after all the time that has elapsed. The narrator never approaches Jakob with kindness but only as an interesting specimen.

Brinkmann's implicit concern with the narrative perspective is pursued by Martin Swales (1967), who finds the narrator consciously distancing himself from the musician by the use of ironic and comic asides and deliberately playing down his personal involvement in Jakob's fate by his pompous references to anthropological curiosity. For Swales, the narrator "cannot and dare not answer the question whether Jakob is fool or saint" (116), and he takes issue with J. P. Stern's assessment, according to which the negative verdict of the world is reversed in the depiction of Jakob as the disembodied good will (1964: 72). The role of the narrator also features prominently in Heinz Politzer's short monograph that appeared in the same year as Swales's article. Politzer highlights the narrator's pedantry, his stylized baroque sentences that belie his professed interest in the crowds and their verdict on his work. As a dramatist he is the lens through which the world is reflected, but the lens breaks to reveal his own inner self (1967: 13). Jakob is a man of contradictions, at odds with his surroundings yet observing the boundaries that others overlook. The novella is full of failed encounters, and Jakob's music is itself a parable of men's estrangement from one another, their inability to communicate. The story consequently depicts the biblical Fall, but in this case of music or even of art as a whole (46), but Jakob remains attuned to the divine order of art that mere mortals cannot hear. A key theme of Politzer's monograph is echoed by Jungbluth (1969), who offers a psychological examination of Jakob as a reflection of Grillparzer's self-doubts as both man and artist.

The increasingly negative view of the narrator as expressed in the contributions of Brinkmann and Politzer took on the form of character-assassination in John M. Ellis's essay of 1972. For Ellis, the narrator is condescending in his attitude to the people and excessively conscious of being on a higher plane and of the need to escape from the noisy throng: "as one who claims to be a lover of the people, the narrator is simply an impostor" (669). His attitude to Jakob and to Barbara is equally cold and unsympathetic, and he goes out of his way to stress their negative aspects. With his posturing, his pretentiousness and self-deception, he is the complete opposite of Jakob, who is sincere, sensitive, helpful to all, and unaware of social divisions. The contrast also obtains in their respective approach to their arts: while Jakob's music is genuine and sincere, though technically incompetent, the narrator is concerned only with the creation of striking imagery and impressive language. For the narrator, success and acclaim are what count; he has no real interest in the people and makes no attempt to understand the musician's feelings. The main theme of the story is integrity and genuine feeling versus efficiency and competence, "honesty and trustingness" versus "technical expertness", and as a result "we should all choose to lean in the Spielmann's direction" (677-78). A more balanced view and a return to consideration of the story's increasingly neglected eponymous hero is to be found in W. E. Yates's monograph of the same year (1972): indeed, it is the narrator's role to prevent too great an empathy for Jakob on the part of the reader so that the story does not become ridiculous or sentimental. Yates declares that "the ultra-pathetic is told without sentimentality; irony and pathos are in perfect balance" (78). He stresses the moral integrity and idealism that inform the fiddler's life despite his lamentable inadequacy as a musician, which reflects Grillparzer's fears concerning his inability to reproduce his own literary classical models.

A political angle to the story had been briefly indicated by Alewyn in his 1937 essay on Grillparzer's political stance, which presents Jakob as an extreme representation of the totally private individual, the ideal subject of Metternich's regime. In 1954 Silz underlined that "the reality of Vienna, not romantic Alt-Wien" was to be found in the tale of Jakob, who clings to middle-class ideals and forms. This aspect is emphasized by Paulsen in his 1968 study of Jakob as "the good *Bürger*." Jakob adheres pedantically to bourgeois ideals but can no longer confirm their validity; his belief in order and cleanliness exaggerates externals at the expense of the essence of things (277). At first it may appear that the crowds and the festival are being mythologized as the repository of real values through the filter of classical humanism and the echoes of Goethe's description of the Roman carnival, but this is then equally revealed as a sham, and Grillparzer concentrates on the individual to the detriment of the whole. Like Alewyn (1937), Paulsen sees Jakob as the "totally private individual," unable to defend himself despite self-imposed limitations such as the chalk line in his room. The social theme is also pursued to a certain extent by Bruno Hannemann (1977), who views the narrator as an indication of the coldness of the *Vormärz* period, which had lost human warmth and with it an important source of poetic inspiration.

For Hannemann there is no doubt that Jakob is ethically superior to the narrator, a conclusion that was reached earlier in the decade by Schafroth (1971), who sees Jakob—

Grillparzer's second great self-portrait alongside Rudolf II—choosing a mission of improving people with his music. In this context it is irrelevant that he is technically a failure; only his attitude is what counts (110). Papst (1973), however, argues that Jakob's music reflects the author's dislike of genius without talent and is a sign of the contemporary malaise of the artist's inability to *present* his ideas, to achieve what for Grillparzer was the important artistic goal of *Darstellung*. Jakob's search for totally pure, religiously inspired music reveals the potential solipsism of his whole existence; it is the dissonances he omits that would facilitate its communication to the inhabitants of ordinary reality. In this way the story may also be seen as an indication of Grillparzer's rejection of abstract idealism in favor of a theory of psychological realism.

Roland Heine (1972) also views the story in a philosophical context, that of hermeneutics as defined by Dilthey. Jakob is indicative of the increasingly difficult search to make sense of life in the nineteenth century. His failure to find any connections or any order in life is indicated both by the chalk line in his room and by the glass door through which he kisses Barbara. Heine emphasizes the timeless aspects of Jakob's existence; he has no watch and no real understanding of time. However, his life is revealed as *Geschichte* in both the artistic and the historical senses of the German word, and it is in the aesthetic act of narration that his life acquires the missing coherence or *Zusammenhang* (677). In his life as in his music, however, this unity is artificially created by ignoring the discordant aspects. In his work also he destroys the necessary context and the links; he seeks to play God, and it is only in the divine realm that he can hope his intentions will be respected.

The increasing polarization of the critical view of Jakob, which often derived in part from very different understandings of the nature of his music, continued unabated throughout the 1970s and 1980s. For Robert Browning (1976), Jakob is sheltered from reality by his sense of order and even more by his music, which, in allowing only harmony and avoiding all dissonance, may be seen as "a peculiar kind of theodicy . . . a theodicy that leaves out evil altogether" (224). Jakob's art is not, as Politzer had argued, a parable of the biblical Fall, but in fact music before the Fall; because it is totally pure, it is incomprehensible to sinful ordinary mortals. Ordinary words are a mystery to Jakob—a mere comma causes him confusion—whereas Barbara as one of the fallen is entirely at home in that realm. "What is really worth saying," Browning concludes, "cannot be said" (234). W.C. Reeve (1978), however, sees Jakob's mystically emotional approach to music as an indication of egotistic tendencies. "His enjoyment of music rests upon a purely self-ish pleasure principle," according to Reeve (44), and shows clear signs of sublimated sensuality or even a repressed sexual drive. The erotic content of Jakob's devotion to his music is also pointed out in an essay of the same year by Lilian Hoverland, who highlights the contrast between Jakob's pure but solipsistic music and the realm of words and bodily sustenance represented by Barbara. Unlike Kafka's *Hungerkünstler*, with whom Hoverland detects certain similarities, Jakob's values are recognized at the end, as the narrator seeks access to the inner value of the fiddler. Hoverland consequently views Jakob as a martyr (75), as does Wolfgang Wittkowski (1981: 147), who gives an overly elaborate account of the vertical and horizontal demarcations

(*Grenzen*) in the work, which, he claims, reveal Grillparzer's adherence to the vertical hierarchy of baroque philosophy. In his survey of the Biedermeier period, Friedrich Sengle acknowledges that Jakob is completely inadequate in any real life situation yet insists there can be no question of Grillparzer's portrait of Jakob being satirical; this can be suggested only by young *Germanisten* with a lack of understanding of the Biedermeier (1980: 126).

Though he does not exactly argue for a satirical portrait, Roe (1981) nevertheless challenges the line of argument (that of Ellis, Browning, and Hoverland) according to which we should all lean in the Spielmann's direction. Roe takes up Browning's theme that Jakob's failure to play results from his attempt to play only the good and harmonious notes. This reflects his moralistic and religiously colored view of music's effect on others, but his attempt to avoid dissonance results only in cacophony. Far from being irrelevant, as Schafroth (1971) believes, or a sign of his superiority to uncomprehending lesser mortals, as in Browning's view (1976), Jakob's failure in music is seen to symbolize his equally impractical and idealistic attitude to ordinary life; here, despite frequent indications that the opposite is the case, he insists on seeing only the good in people (his father, the secretary who swindles him, even Barbara), and this results in a life of failure and isolation. Nevertheless, there is some sympathy for Jakob's moral stance in the midst of a sordid world, and the story is typical of Grillparzer's works as a whole, which highlight moral ideals such as purity and order but show the ineffectuality of absolute ideals and the consequent need for compromise. In his later monograph, Roe (1991) underlines the contradictions in Jakob that attract the narrator, who is, however, reluctant to admit his equally contradictory character and general similarity to Jakob—including the pomposity of language of which normally only the narrator is accused—and who therefore constantly denigrates Jakob and his surroundings. The contradictions remain to the end, not least in the ambivalent symbolism of violin and crucifix as mirror image or opposite. Ralf Nicolai also writes of the "tension between violin and crucifix" (1988: 82-83) and suggests that the violin may symbolize a chaotic or saturnalian element.

Returning once more to the motif of music, Gordon Birrell (Bernd 1988) argues that earlier critics, in common with the narrator of the story and other listeners, have completely failed to understand the nature of Jakob's music. Following up the theme of timelessness explored by Heine and others, Birrell sees Jakob's playing as far from prelapsarian purity but rather a precursor of modern atonal forms. Bruce Thompson also looks forward rather than backward, if in a more critical way, in linking Jakob's art with the "sickly and decadent artist figures of Thomas Mann" (1981: 94). The fascination with the nature of Jakob's music is further evidenced in a number of the new articles included in Bernd's 1988 collection and in the comments of Dagmar Lorenz, who somewhat unconvincingly presents Jakob's music as a deliberately antisocial act of revenge against his authoritarian upbringing (1986: 173-74).

In view of the interest in the aesthetic structures of the fiddler's music, it is strange that only occasional attention has been paid to the genre of ***Der arme Spielmann*** despite continual reference to the framework of the story (Krotkoff, 1970) and the narrative technique (Swales, 1967).[2] Paulsen

(1968) suggests that it is two intertwined tales rather than a "framework Novelle" in the form so often used in the nineteenth century. Kurt Franz (1980), however, while noting that Grillparzer himself rejected the designation *Novelle*, seeks to show what features it has in common with that genre: the apparent five-act structure and other similarities with the dramatic form, the symbolic content, and the all-important framework with its implications of order. In the story, Jakob's own sense of order prevents the influx of the wild and uncontrollable forces that Grillparzer detected in Kleist's stories.

More radical in their examination of the style of the story were a number of critics of the 1980s. James Porter (1981) first exposes the unreliability of the narrator that is revealed in the self-contradictory nature of his statement on the lack or existence of social divisions and consequently insists that it is "the text and its conventions" that condition truth and falsity (298). According to Porter, "the Narrator and the Spielmann share a displacement that is both psychological and linguistic" (303); the former increasingly departs from his avowed intention of establishing a rapport with the reader, and the latter will not allow himself to be woven into the narrator's mythological framework. After following up other similarities between the two main personae, Porter turns to the text's attempts to define what are believed to be normative concepts in it: *eigentlich* and *verdienen*. "The text, however, cannot determine its own value, it cannot read itself . . . the text anticipates without eclipsing the activity of reading by making this indeterminacy (this illegibility) descriptive of its own processes. Thus, the evaluative problem becomes for the reader a problem of self-evaluation. And this . . . is an activity without end" (322). More intelligibly, Ward (London 1987) also sees indications in the story of the contingent nature of truth and meaning, a move away from any established and preexistent system outside the text that is typical of nineteenth-century realism. This development is revealed in the use of images and metaphors without reference to external metaphysical boundaries. In an article of the previous year that compares Grillparzer's tale with Stifter's *Der arme Wohltäter* (the first version of *Kalkstein*), Ward had examined the narrator's failure to understand Jakob, his inability to find the appropriate *Zusammenhang* that he seeks, but this in turn reflects Jakob's position outside the prevailing system of social and musical norms. This emphasis on "connexion" is part of the text's "overt foregrounding . . . of the process of narration" (1986: 30), the open concern with its own attempt to establish Jakob's story or history (*Geschichte*); but Grillparzer differs from Stifter in seeing the "truth of tales" as only a relative truth.

The question of what Ward refers to as the "self-reflective capacity of narrative discourse" (18) is crucial to Roger Cook's analysis (Bernd 1988). For Cook, the narrator is not interested in the fiddler as a person but solely in exploiting his story as a literary subject; he has no awareness of his own weaknesses and his affinity to the musician. The contrast between the musician's self-effacing way of narrating his story and the narrator's bombastic self-importance indicates that the real nucleus of the novella is "not the interesting story of an unusual outsider, but rather the question of the literary fictionalization of real relationships" (330). The narrator is not concerned to proliferate meaning but seeks to appropriate the story for the self-

serving glorification of the creative author. Jakob's dissonant music is an emblem of his existence as an outsider,
"break[ing] the basic law of an idealist aesthetics" according to which, "in its preoccupation with organic unity, art
forms a self-referential closure of predetermined meaning"
(334-35).

If this is meant to indicate that there is no single or
straightforward "message" to the story, then most recent
critics would no doubt concur, even if it is the story itself
rather than the nature of Jakob's music that invites that
conclusion, and even if individual critics are still prepared
to go into battle convinced that the message they discover
is the right one. Even Hinrich Seeba, in his essay of 1983
with its much-quoted demand for an end to hostilities,
suggests that the historical context of the story has often
been neglected (and is presumably therefore worthy of further investigation), as the great Anglo-American interest in
the story, with its frequent emphasis on intrinsic criticism,
may have led critics such as Porter to completely dehis-
toricize it. Seeba argues (406) that Jakob dies trying to
reconcile private and public interests, helping to protect
material concerns that he himself has hitherto neglected,
not least in leaving the fair at the time he might start to
earn money. This potentially revolutionary social critical
center is defused, however, as the earlier laughter of the
masses gives way to an almost religious transfiguration
that has encouraged views of saintliness and martyrdom.
In contrast to critics such as Heine (1972), Seeba also underlines that Jakob is not in any way changed by telling
his story.

The publications connected with the bicentenary year have
found other neglected areas that postpone the day when
Seeba's call for a moratorium will be heeded. Boyd Mullan (*GLL* 1991) examines the story as a model for Storm's
Der stille Musikant. Werner M. Bauer (Innsbruck 1992)
suggests that it uses a number of motifs and techniques
from the "moral tales" of the Enlightenment, such as those
of Marmontel, which were popular in Austria and often
dramatized on the Viennese stage. Martin Sutton (Otago
1992) shifts the emphasis away from the continual contrast
of musician and narrator and argues that Barbara is the
one truly tragic figure in the story and that her struggle between the need for security and loyalty to Jakob suggests
similarities with Erny in *Ein treuer Diener seines Herrn*.
Most recently, Ingrid and Jürgen Hein have referred to the
parallel lives and thus the incompatibility of Jakob and
Barbara. In what might be considered an overzealous desire to demonstrate Grillparzer's modern credentials, they
also detect an anticipation of cinematic techniques in the
narrative: the use of flashbacks, cutting from one narrator
to another, showing close-ups of hands or other parts of
the body, and the interplay of sharp and soft focus (1993:
138).[3]

Notes

1. E. K. Bennett, *A History of the German Novelle*.
Cambridge: Cambridge University Press (1934):
156.

2. The same lack of reference to genre may be noted
in the most recent treatment of the story as this
book goes to press (Hein, 1993), even though the
article appears in a collection of essays on the
German *Novelle*.

3. Such claims have also been made for Grillparzer's
dramatic style by Morris (1957) and Kaiser (1980).

Sima Kappeler (essay date 1996)

SOURCE: "Exchange and Dispossession: Grillparzer's
'Der arme Spielmann'," in *First Encounters in French and
German Prose Fiction: 1830-1883,* Peter Lang, 1996, pp.
91-117.

[*In the following essay, Kappeler explores stylistic aspects
of* Der arme Spielmann, *in particular the effect of the
frame story on the novella.*]

> Le «sujet», c'est pour nous (depuis le Christianisme?)
> celui qui souffre: là où il y a une blessure, il y a un sujet: die
> Wunde! die Wunde! dit Parsifal, en devenant par là
> «lui-même»;
>
>   Roland Barthes[1]

Critical attention to Franz Grillparzer's narrative **Der arme
Spielmann** (1847)[2] has steadily increased in recent years.[3]
This interest in a text whose protagonist is presented as a
pathological failure can be viewed as attempts to pierce
the Spielmann's isolating layers and to reevaluate this verdict of failure.[4] One critic, annoyed at this avalanche of attention to the story, proposes others should leave the text
in peace.[5] Yet, this effort to block interference with the
governing interpretation of failure ironically parallels the
actions of the prohibiting father figures responsible for Jacob's isolation.[6]

Grillparzer's narrative in its use of a frame to embed the
encounter between the protagonists Jacob and Barbara resembles the structure of Balzac's "Sarrasine" and Stifter's
"Brigitta." The structure of a framed inner story inevitably
raises the question of the relationship between the outer
and the inner parts of the narrative. As in Balzac's narrative, the language and content of the frame are almost baroque in their abundant richness of detail and metaphor.
The interior story in contrast is more austere and structured, as if it had been stripped during the process of revision. This impression is supported by the fact that Grillparzer composed the first part in 1831 and completed the
story in 1842.[7] Significantly, the point that Grillparzer
stopped writing in 1831 was during the first encounter of
Jacob and Barbara in the presence of the girl's father; it
seems the threat of separation existed even on an extratex-
tual temporal plane.

The frame story, told by a first person narrator, examines
desire and satisfaction in its description of a popular festival where lower and upper classes mix. Here, once a year,
forces usually repressed are released. The narrator describes the festival as an instance of merging, where even
the noble appear as part of the people "und wenn Vorneh-
mere dabei erscheinen, so können sie es nur in ihrer Eigen-
schaft als Glieder des Volkes. Da ist keine Möglichkeit der
Absonderung" (357) [and any members of the upper
classes who put in an appearance can do so only as part of
the people. This is no occasion for being standoffish].[8] Yet
he presents himself as detached, functioning as a reader
who annually returns to reread the scene: "Wie aus einem
aufgerollten, ungeheuren, dem Rahmen des Buches ents-

prungenen Plutarch, lese ich aus den heitern und heimlich bekümmerten Gesichtern" (359) [As though from some vast Plutarch which has escaped from the bounds of the book and lies in an open scroll before me, I read the collective biographies of men unknown to fame. I read them in their faces, cheerful or worried by some secret] (32). Yet the festival has moments when it seems dangerous: a horse suddenly rears and frightens women and children; there are quarrels, shouts and lashes of the whip (*Zank, Geschrei, Peitschenhieb*). While violence is mostly subdued and denied in the interior story, in the frame it surfaces under the cover of pleasure and amusement. In one scene of supposedly harmless joy and pleasure, noble ladies are stuck in their carriages where they can be scrutinized with impunity: "Begafft, bedauert, bespottet, sitzen die geputzten Damen in den scheinbar stillestehenden Kutschen" (358) [The ladies in their finery sit in the seemingly motionless vehicles, stared at, pitied, made fun of] (31). This moment of constraint and full exposure to a critical glance can be interpreted as an instance of reading in which repressed forces in the crowd use the occasion to mock and sneer. This moment prepares for the encounter of the narrator as reader with the Spielmann as object of the gaze.

As in Stifter's "Brigitta," the narrator is introduced together with a simultaneous display of reading strategies. When encountered by the narrator, however, the Spielmann is not treated like a target for mockery, which is his usual fate. The encounter can be viewed as an instance of the narrator rereading and redefining a marginalized other. The earlier close-up of noble ladies can be seen as referring to the Spielmann's nobler past and his role as a target of mockery, but it also hints at the central scene between the Spielmann and Barbara. Like the female figures in the carriages who appear to be within reach but remain inaccessible, in one crucial scene Barbara is embraced by Jacob while separated from him by a glass door, an ambiguous symbol of inaccessibility that acts out the role of desire in the text.

The opening part of the frame story demonstrates the difficulty of making physical progress in festival streets so jammed with bodies. This concern for reaching one's destination appears in Stifter's and in Flaubert's texts. Here, the frame comments on the inner story, in that the crowd's impeded progress towards pleasure seems to mirror Jacob's stunted life.

The narrator implies he is willing to join the rowdy crowd because he is a "passionate lover of his fellow men," a declaration which both ties in and contrasts with the underplayed love plot of the interior story. He also portrays himself as a playwright who distinguishes himself from the critic, whom he characterizes in the following way:

> so daß mir selbst als dramatischer Dichter der rückhaltlose Ausbruch eines überfüllten Schauspielhauses immer zehnmal interessanter, ja belehrender war, als das zusammengeklügelte Urteil eines an Leib und Seele verkrüppelten, von dem Blut ausgesogener Autoren spinnenartig aufgeschwollenen literarischen Matadors. (358)
>
> [so that even as a dramatist I find the straightforward, if rowdy, response of the public in a packed theater ten times as interesting and indeed as instructive as the ex-

cogitated judgment of some literary matador, crippled in body and soul and bloated like a spider with the blood sucked from authors]. (32)[9]

This passage valorizes passion over reflection, juxtaposing an outburst of enthusiasm in a packed theater and the judgment of a literary critic. The use of a strange double image that superimposes a spider upon a matador, the former a natural and the latter a civilized killer, functions as a means to distance the narrator from the position of a critic. However, the narrator, like the critic, is engaged in reading the crowd and, like the spider/matador, he waits at the festival for prey to be drawn into his dramatic creation. The image of the spider/matador problematizes the relationship between the narrator/recipient and protagonist/reproducer of the story by establishing a link between loving and killing. We watch the "lover of his fellow men," as the narrator repeatedly calls himself, turn into a critic/predator when he appropriates Jacob's story.

The quest for a story foreshadows Jacob's description of his appropriation of Barbara's song, which leads Jacob to the advent of love and suffering in the interior story. From the narrator, the encounter with the other signifies above all the possible gift of a story. James Porter[10] emphasizes the figures' similarity: "Both narrator and Spielmann fall prey to possession-obsessions (Ich zitterte *vor Begierde* nach dem Zusammenhange[9]; Da ich nun *vor Begierde*, das Lied zu haben . . . [30]) [I was eager for the explanation] (38) [Desperate to possess the song] (67). Although I agree with the parallels being drawn, the Spielmann's "Begierde" reaches out beyond the song to Barbara, which I read as an attempt to surpass narcissistic structures. Both frame and inner story mirror each other in the quest for art, (the story, the song) which then leads to an encounter with the other.

When Jacob, the protagonist of the interior story, is seen by the narrator for the first time, he is outside the actual festival grounds. This positioning functions as an instance of fore-pleasure, significant with regard to the interior story's constant deferral of fulfillment: "Damit es nämlich der genußlechzenden Menge nicht an einem Vorgeschmack der zu erwartenden Seligkeit mangle" (359) [So that the pleasure-hungry crowd should not lack a foretaste of the delights to come] (34). While the Spielmann is positioned at an outpost, the narrator is characterized as one who can easily move to the center. Ursula Mahlendorf reads the narrator as a father figure whose possession of woman is implied: "In writing **The Poor Fiddler,** Grillparzer attempted a confrontation between his internalized mother-self, the fiddler, and his father-self, the narrator" (131). The opposition of the two figures' access to pleasure seems to support such a reading. While the Spielmann's location at the threshold of fulfillment seems justified by the ensuing relationship with Barbara, there are aspects of their relationship that undermine the finality of the position.

In his first encounter with the Spielmann, the narrator finds him among a group of deformed musicians. Their deformed and injured bodies hint at the repressed representation of the Spielmann as a wounded figure. While the pathetic musicians try to draw on-lookers into a position of identification "Ein alter invalider Stelzfuß, der . . . die Schmerzen seiner Verwundung dem allgemeinen Mitleid auf eine analoge Weise empfindbar machen wollte" (360) [an old cripple with a wooden leg, who labored . . . to bring home to the general sympathy by due means the aches and pains of his injury] (34), the Spielmann, so absorbed in his strangely warped performance, remains detached from the others. While the musicians reach out to the others, the Spielmann presents himself as narcissistically bent upon himself: "Mit lächelnder, sich selbst Beifall gebender Miene" (360) [with a smiling, self-congratulating expression] (36). The bodies of the deformed musicians are primarily oriented towards the other, but Jacob's body sways in time to his music-making, united with his violin. His body mimics harmony with the instrument, but the incongruous music lacks both timing and tune. This discrepancy between process and product turns the Spielmann into the pathetic figure announced by the narrative's title.

The narrator leaves the Spielmann undisturbed while he observes him from a distance. This distribution of two figures in space is suggestive of the first encounter between Jacob and Barbara, where Jacob is positioned at a distance when listening to the girl's singing. But the Spielmann in the frame is deliberately exposed to attract attention, while Barbara was singing to herself. Both the Spielmann and the narrator as observers use the other for their own purposes. The Spielmann is drawn to Barbara not as a baker and seller of cakes but as a singer and woman. The narrator is primarily interested in the Spielman as material for his own dramatic work. The narrator's detached interest in the other seems to mirror the blocking forces in the narrative represented by father figures. Both voyeuristic positions are further linked through metaphorical language which plays with the notion of hunger and arousal: "Das ganze Wesen des alten Mannes war eigentlich wie gemacht um meinen anthropologischen Heißhunger aufs äußerste zu reizen" (361) [The old man and everything about him were just made to excite my anthropological avidity to the utmost] (37). The applied "nutritive code," a term coined by Donaldson-Evans,[11] links Barbara, the seller of cakes, the Spielmann and the narrator; once again the image of the devouring spider is evoked. The "hunger" of the narrator assumes a more sexual tone in his desire for a coherent story that promises to explain the discrepant features of the Spielmann: "Ich zittere vor Begierde nach dem Zusammenhange" (361) [I tremble from desire for the explanation] (translation mine).

The question of the relation between desire and satisfaction, a central concern of the story, is seen in the narrator's curiosity about the musician and in the Spielmann's relation to his music. While music is usually shared, this musician is isolated and is applauded only by himself. As his performance lacks appropriate dynamics, rhythm and melody, what is pleasurable to him is unbearable to others. This unusual example of a musician who can give pleasure only to himself is opposed to the festival where pleasure is shared. However, what attracts the narrator is just this structure of disharmony which turns the musician into an outsider, a figure set against the general flow. While the festival posits an unproblematic access to satisfaction, the frame points to a possible collapse of fulfillment since the narrator does not accept the festival as a substitute after he loses sight of the musician: "Das verfehlte Abenteuer hatte mir die Lust an dem Volksfeste genommen" (361) [Cheated of my would-be-adventure, I had lost all pleasure in the fair] (38).

An avowed moment of desire is followed by the loss of its object. The Spielmann leaves the festival grounds and the narrator is unable to follow him. On his way home, the narrator hears the violinist; hardly lost, the Spielmann is found again. This renewed encounter is owed to the specific nature of Jacob's performance. As in the scene where Jacob first hears Barbara sing, sound precedes sight. This time the Spielmann is surrounded by a group of boys who ask for a waltz. Due to his inability to play a recognizable waltz, the Spielmann cannot make them dance; he, however, interprets this as unwillingness on their part. This scene reemphasizes the prevailing narcissistic structure and the Spielmann's inability to assess his effect on the other. This first mutual encounter between narrator and Spielmann demonstrates how the discrepancy between the intent and the actual performance of the musician leads to a proliferation of interpretation and misreading. The utter disjunction between intention and effect seems contagious.[12] While it looks as if the Spielmann is unwilling to play a waltz and that the boys do not want to dance, he is in fact unable to fulfil their request. The narrator tries to bridge this misunderstanding by rewarding the Spielmann for his performance with a silver coin; this initiates a sequence of exchange that is perpetuated throughout the story, as if such exchanges were the ultimate purpose of the encounters. Although the narrator observes the other's failure to meet the expectations of an audience, his gift to the Spielmann denies this fundamental discrepancy. In engaging in a sequence of exchange which valorizes the Spielmann's gift of the story, the narrator sets up a counter-model to the structure of disjunction.

In their first genuine encounter the musician is depicted as one who does not comprehend his effect on others. With the narrator, however, he takes on the role of one who assumes he has something to give: "'Sieht es doch beinahe aus', sagte der Alte lächelnd, 'als ob Sie, verehrter Herr der Beschenkte wären und ich, wenn es mir erlaubt ist zu sagen, der Wohltäter'" (362) ["It almost seems," said the old man with a smile, "as though you, my dear sir, were the one to receive a favor and I, if I may presume to say so, were the benefactor"] (41). The encounter focuses on the exchange of gifts and shows a reversal of donor and recipient by devaluing the material gift of money and privileging the satisfaction of curiosity in the form of a story. This reversal ties in with Naomi Ritter's assessment of the relation between all three main characters: "Both he [the narrator] and the 'barbaric' girl represent the world of commercial success that opposes Jacob; yet both have a weakness for him."[13]

The relationship between the narrator and the Spielmann appears to be satisfactory since the narrator, in singling out an object of desire from among the festival crowd, gets exactly what he wants, a story. The story he is told is a tale of discontinuity and deferred fulfillment which highlights the contrast between the narrator's far bolder pursuit of the Spielmann and Jacob's timid courtship of Barbara. This contrast suggests that contrary to the relation between frame and interior story in "Sarrasine," the frame story of **The Poor Fiddler** could be viewed as a counter-model to the inner tale.

After the narrator parts from the Spielmann in the street, he forgets Jacob's address. Again the Spielmann is lost and again his warped performance functions like a trace which enables the narrator to retrieve what was lost. The pleasure of repetition, acted out in these returns, is reflected in Jacob's improvisations: "und zwar immer derselbe Ton mit einer Art genußreichem Daraufberuhen wiederholt" (365) [It was always the same note, repeated with a sort of voluptuous insistence] (46). Music functions in the text as a symbol for the pleasure of repetition, but the Spielmann's music is a pleasure that cannot be shared and, therefore, emphasizes a distance between self and other that cannot be overcome. The repetition of single notes as well as of harmonic relationships sensually gratifies Jacob, implying that the production of music, usually directed towards others, is here directed towards the self in a narcissistic circle.

The narrator, who listens to both music and story, mirrors the position of the reader safely distanced from the text. However, by making examples of noble ladies who are scrutinized then marginalized through mockery and critics who are turned into monsters, the text itself points to the instability of the positions of observer and reader.

As the scene in Jacob's room continues and his story unfolds, what is spoken seems separate from what is transmitted to a recipient, since the Spielmann appears to be telling his story to himself rather than to the narrator: "Möchte ich mirs doch selbst einmal wieder erzählen" (368) [I wouldn't mind recalling it all, for my own sake] (52). This impression of a narcissistic structure is further supported by the fact that the narratee's reactions to the story seem to be ignored: "Der Alte schien mein Erstaunen nicht zu bemerken, sondern spann, sichtbar vergnügt, den Faden seiner Erzählung weiter" (368) [The old man did not seem to notice my surprise, but, visibly pleased, went on spinning his yarn] (53).

Mahlendorf pathologizes the Spielmann[14] and regards the narrator as a representation of "healthy" normality; indeed, the narrator presents himself as less obsessed and tormented; yet disorder lurks below a deceptive surface. The narrator's mornings are set to a strict timetable similar to the Spielmann's. The narrator devotes his morning hours to something significant, or else he feels beset by either "unthinking distraction or self-tormenting gloom." This instance undermines the assumption of a fundamental difference between the Spielmann's pathological structure and the narrator's "normality." This narrator, like the narrator in "Sarrasine," raises the question of how he is affected by the story.

In relating his life story, the Spielmann identifies himself as the son of a well-known, influential figure, *the Hofrat*. His rejection by his father and his father's sudden death transform this impressive origin into a negative beginning. While describing his relation with his father, Jacob examines the scene where he fails an exam before his father. The exam confirms the rift between father and son and consequently leads to the son's exclusion from any further schooling. After this humiliating scene Jacob protects himself from outward influences and creates an unbridgeable rift of compulsive perfectionism between self and other in memory of the rupture between father and son:

> Meine Brüder sprangen wie Gemsen von Spitze zu Spitze in den Lehrgegenständen herum, ich konnte aber durchaus nichts hinter mir lassen, und wenn mir ein

einziges Wort fehlte, mußte ich von vorne anfangen. So ward ich denn immer gedrängt. Das Neue sollte auf den Platz, den das Alte noch nicht verlassen hatte, und ich begann stockisch zu werden. (368)

> [My brothers leapt about like chamois from the summit of one subject to the next, but I could never skip anything at all, and if I missed a single word, I had to start again from the beginning. So I was always being pushed. New things were to take the place not yet vacated by old ones, and I became a refractory child]. (54)

What triggers the repetition compulsion is a missing word, a gap in his memory; that gap is a sign of absence. The gap can be read as characterizing the preparatory phase preceding the encounter with the other. While this gap is filled in Maupassant's text with anticipatory visions of the lover, it appears here as an unsettling sign that produces fear. As a copy clerk in a government office Jacob is caught in a painful predicament that reminds him of his failed exam. Whenever he comes upon illegible or missing words, he is torn between adhering to the original text and following his own ideas: "Im Zweifel, ob ich mich genau ans Original halten oder aus Eigenem beisetzen sollte, verging die Zeit angstvoll" (370) [Uncertain whether to stick precisely to the original or to add something on my own responsibility, I would timorously let the time pass] (57). In producing his unintelligible music, Jacob deviates from a musical score and calls it improvisation; but when confronted with language, any deviation pains him. This implies that the issue of the original and its reproduction is disregarded when its comes to music only to appear most painfully with regard to language. What appears to produce angst is absence: "Ein unrichtiges Unterscheidungszeichen, ein unleserliches oder ausgelassenes Wort im Konzepte, wenn es sich auch aus dem Sinne ergänzen ließ, machte mir bittere Stunden" (370) [One wrong punctuation mark, one illegible word or one missing from the draft, even if it could easily be guessed from the context, caused me hours of perplexity] (57). Jacob's fascination with the possibility of filling in the missing word seems to actualize the opposition between self and other. The absent other, represented as a draft to be copied, appears as that which cannot be deciphered.

Although Jacob continues to live in his father's house after his failure, his existence is an isolated one. This isolation is disturbed by an overheard song. He interrupts his story to the narrator in order to sing his melody. The reproduction of a song and the tears that accompany it create a trace of emotionality that points to a possible entrance into his protected self. His tears are reminiscent of Barbara's tears at their first separation and after Jacob's funeral, where they constitute the last statement of the entire text. The song, which continues to have a strong emotional impact, signifies, according to Mahlendorf (123), "the only gift of the Spielmann's life":

> Er spielte, und zwar diesmal mit richtigem Ausdrucke, die Melodie eines gemütlichen, übrigens gar nicht ausgezeichneten Liedes, wobei ihm die Finger auf den Saiten zitterten und endlich einzelne Tränen über die Backen liefen. (371)

> [He played, this time with correct expression, a tune which was pleasant enough, but by no means outstanding. His fingers were shaking on the strings, and soon a few tears trickled down his cheeks]. (59)

Jacob's tears are provoked by the memory of the only important female figure he mentions, apart from his mother who died young. This memory, elicits a bodily reaction and leads to the correct performance of a song. By singing, Barbara corrects Jacob's distorted relation to music which allows him to return to the instrument spoiled for him by lessons. What this instance further suggests is that the educational process cut off by a "bad" father figure is reinstated by the sudden appearance of a "good" mother figure. This related primal musical experience seems to reproduce the early mother-child dyad. When the Spielmann points out how he privileges music over words, he seems to situate himself at a preverbal stage that avoids language and its painful association with the law of the father:

> Wenn ich nun so saß, hörte ich auf dem Nachbarshofe ein Lied singen. Mehrere Lieder heißt das, worunter mir aber eines vorzüglich gefiel. Es war so einfach, so rührend und hatte den Nachdruck so auf der rechten Stelle, daß man die Worte gar nicht zu hören brauchte. Wie ich denn überhaupt glaube, die Worte verderben die Musik. (371)

> ["Sitting there, I would hear someone sing a song in the neighbor's yard-or rather several songs, but there was one which I liked especially, it was such a simple, such a moving song with just the right lilt, so that there was no need at all to hear the words. Besides, in my view, words only spoil music anyway"]. (58)

Like the first introduction of the anticipated other in *Une vie* who appears as the sound of steps in the park "elle entendit marcher dans la nuit" (13), here the introduction of the other is as a song separated from the singer "hörte ich ein Lied singen." This structure of separation presents the other as a trace separated both from itself and from the listener.

From a position of exclusion, deprivation and understimulation after his rift with his father, the protagonist moves to a state of ecstasy that recalls that scene of Sarrasine's first exposure to Italian theater and music. But while Sarrasine is immediately drawn to a visible, supposedly female figure, Jacob, oblivious of the presence of the female singer, imagines God as the agent of his awakening senses:

> Als ich nun mit dem Bogen über die Saiten fuhr, Herr, da war es, als ob Gottes Finger mich angerührt hätte. Der Ton drang in mein Inneres hinein und aus dem Innern wieder heraus. Die Luft um mich war wie geschwängert mit Trunkenheit. Das Lied unten im Hofe und die Töne von meinen Fingern an mein Ohr, Mitbewohner meiner Einsamkeit. Ich fiel auf die Knie und betete laut und konnte nicht begreifen, daß ich das holde Gotteswesen einmal gering geschätzt, ja gehaßt in meiner Kindheit, und küßte die Violine und drückte sie an mein Herz und spielte wieder und fort. (371)

> [[As I now swept over the strings with my bow, it was as if God's finger had touched me. The sound penetrated my inmost being and thence issued forth again. The air around me was as if pregnant with ecstasy. Down below in the yard the song, and close to my ear the sounds I made with my fingers—they came to dwell with me in my loneliness. I fell upon my knees and prayed aloud, and could not understand how I had ever, as a child, belittled and indeed hated this divine beauty, and I kissed the violin and pressed it to my heart and played again and again]. (59)

It is important to note how the pleasure of producing sound is linked with the pleasure of being touched, albeit figura-

tively. While Mahlendorf reads this instance of synaesthesia as "a regression to a primary process so basic that sensation is not yet clearly differentiated into hearing and touch" (118), it can also be read in connection with the appearance of a female figure as a displaced trace of the other. The ecstasy is experienced due to both the other's presence and absence and can be read as a sign of the problematic narcissistic structure which excludes the other. Similar to the passage in Balzac, the "woman's" song enters an interior space of the listener as if constituting his body as space.[15] Space is emphasized in the metaphor that evokes the pregnant female body: "Die Luft um mich war wie geschwängert mit Trunkenheit" (371) [The air around me was as if pregnant with ecstasy] (59).

In Balzac's "Sarrasine," the story also moves from the conflict between father and son to the ecstatic experience of music as a preparation for the first encounter. However, the Spielmann tries to suppress the actual female other with its implied threat of seduction and dependency: "Das Lied im Hofe—es war eine Weibsperson, die sang—tönte derweil unausgesetzt; mit dem Nachspielen ging es aber nicht so leicht" (371) ["The song in the yard—it was sung by a woman's voice—meanwhile went on ceaselessly; but I did not find it so easy to play"] (60). Jacob's difficulty in reproducing the song might be linked to his difficulty acknowledging the other as the source and origin of pleasure. In this context God "als ob Gottes Finger mich angerührt hätte" functions as a representation of the grandiose self, a manifestation of narcissistic disorder.

Jacob has been relegated to living in the rear quarters of his father's house when he first hears Barbara singing. Failure and punishment seem to be the prerequisites for Jacob's exposure to woman. It is only after his rejection by a hostile male order that he hears Barbara sing in the courtyard. She reaches Jacob's heart without any intention on her part; she is singing to herself, unaware of anybody listening to her. Jacob's attention is attracted by her voice and the motion of her body:

> Da ging eben die Sängerin über den Hof. Ich sah sie nur von rückwärts, und doch kam sie mir bekannt vor. Sie trug einen Korb mit, wie es schien, noch ungebackenen Kuchenstücken. Sie trat in ein Pförtchen in der Ecke des Hofes, da wohl ein Backofen inne sein mochte, denn immer fortsingend, hörte ich mit hölzernen Geräten scharren, wobei die Stimme einmal dumpfer und einmal heller klang wie eines, das sich bückt und in eine Höhlung hineinsingt, dann wieder erhebt und aufrecht dasteht. Nach einer Weile kam sie zurück, und nun merkte ich erst, warum sie mir bekannt vorkam. Ich kannte sie nämlich wirklich seit längerer Zeit. Und zwar aus der Kanzlei. (372)

> [Just then the singer crossed the yard. I saw only her back, and yet she looked familiar to me. She was carrying what seemed to be a basket of unbaked cakes. She went in through a little door at the corner of the yard, to where there was an oven, perhaps, for I could hear a scraping of wooden implements; she continued singing, but her voice sounded first duller and then clearer, as though its owner were bending down and singing into a cavity, and then standing up straight again. After a while she came back, and then I realized why she had seemed familiar to me. I had indeed known her for some time. From the office, as a matter of fact]. (61)

Jacob does not recognize the singing voice; he sees only her back yet he finds the figure familiar. The encounter with the other is presented as a gradual process of recovering what was once familiar but then forgotten. The other appears as fragmented, a voice and the back of a body; finally it is reassembled and recognized.[16] The immobilized male observer listening to a woman singing in the twilight evokes the early mother-infant relationship in which the maternal figure is constituted through her voice and her nuturing. The cake, the heat, and the cave-like opening are further reminders of the maternal realm. The maternal connotations of the first encounter are obvious, especially when unmasked as suggestive of an earlier forgotten encounter. This connection with the maternal must be repressed if a romantic plotline is to be pursued.

The female figure is presented as producing songs and cakes, hunger and love, the two great primary human instincts denied to Jacob. Jacob recognizes the young woman as part of a group of tradesfolk selling food in his office. Like the old musician who is selected by the narrator from a group of musicians at the fair, Barbara is selected by the officials for her tasty cakes. She is already chosen before Jacob notices her. Barbara is recognized as a public figure belonging to everybody. This configuration evokes that of Zambinella the singer. However, when Jacob observes her baking, he seems to discover Barbara's private self. His peek behind the scenes distinguishes him from his co-workers who only encounter Barbara's public self.

A more detailed portrayal of Barbara is presented through his colleagues' eyes, not Jacob's; it is as if he were not yet allowed to look at her. This strategy distances Jacob from his object of desire and implies his lack of easy access. Barbara's visual introduction differs from traditional descriptions of women; there is something undecided about the color of her hair and eyes. Her body is memorable, however, both for its figure and its strength; one day she slapped a man's face so hard that he still felt it a week later. The impression Barbara leaves is one that discourages access.

Barbara sells cakes at the office to satisfy oral needs. Since Jacob has little regard for his body, he cannot be one of her clients:

> Ich selbst gehörte nicht unter ihre Kunden. Teils fehlte mir's an Geld, teils habe ich Speise und Trank wohl immer—oft nur zu sehr—als ein Bedürfnis anerkennen müssen, Lust und Vergnügen darin zu suchen aber ist mir nie in den Sinn gekommen. Wir nahmen daher keine Notiz voneinander. (373)

> ["I myself was not one of her customers. First of all I had no money, and secondly food and drink was, no doubt, something I always had to accept as necessity, and sometimes only too much so, but which I never dreamed of regarding as a source of pleasure and enjoyment. So we took no notice of one another"]. (63)

Access to Barbara is through her role as a peddler. When Jacob does not buy, he is excluded from the exchange. "Lust und Vergnügen" are associated with the peddler and her cakes, but Jakob sees supplements to basic needs as unnecessary. Barbara and her tasty cakes along with the inevitable joking and flirting of the co-workers function as reminders of the link between need and desire.

The couple's encounter is arranged by Jacob's colleagues in order to tease him:

> Einmal nur, um mich zu necken, machten ihr meine Kameraden glauben, ich hätte nach ihren Eßwaren verlangt. Sie trat zu meinem Arbeitstisch und hielt mir ihren Korb hin. Ich kaufe nichts, liebe Jungfer, sagte ich.—Nun, warum bestellen Sie dann die Leute? rief sie zornig.—Ich entschuldigte mich, und sowie ich die Schelmerei gleich weg hatte, erklärte ich ihrs aufs beste. (373)

> ["Only once, to tcasc me, one of my colleagues led her to believe that I had asked for her cakes. She stepped up to my table and proffered her basket. 'I dont want to buy anything, thank you, miss,' I said. 'Well, in that case, why do you trouble people to come?' she exclaimed crossly. I apologized, and since I realized at once that it was a practical joke, I explained matters to her as best I could"]. (63)

Through his co-workers' interference, Jacob is presented as a desiring subject. A trick releases what has been repressed. Because of the co-workers' trick Jacob meets Barbara in spite of himself. Barbara's reaction is not to reject one who rejects her "Ich kaufe nichts," but to engage him in a structure of exchange.

Various figures, such as the mischievous colleagues, the hostile father, the reckless brothers, the rough butcher, and the treacherous secretary represent the aggressive forces behind sexual drives that in "Sarrasine" are seen as within the male protagonist. The ridiculed lover also appears in "Sarrasine"; but while Zambinella confesses to being an accomplice, Barbara is not implicated in the trick on Jacob.

Their relation is initiated from outside and revolves around the exchange of substitutes; Barbara offers Jacob cakes instead of the desired song. When he refuses her cakes, Barbara asks for paper, which, as property of the office, he cannot give. This structure opposes that of the frame story, where, at the fair, both music and food are offered. The inner story thus problematizes the availability of these symbols of pleasure and satisfaction.

The way that Barbara looks him over reveals a reversal of traditional gender roles at the initial moment of scrutiny: "Sie maß mich vom Kopf bis zu den Füßen, als ich näher kam, was meine Verlegenheit vermehrte" (374) [As I approached, she looked me up and down from top to toe, which did nothing to diminish my embarrassment] (65). For Jacob being scrutinized signifies measuring and judging which relates Barbara's assessment of Jacob to Jacob's disasterous exam and his relation to his father.

Later, Jacob again refuses her offer of cake in exchange for the paper he has brought her but admits he has a different request. Barbara braces herself and looks at him intensely as if she expected a sexual advance. In part Barbara's expectations are fulfilled as the theme of love does emerge displaced as a love of music: "Ich fiel rasch ein, daß ich ein Liebhaber der Tonkunst sei, obwohl erst seit kurzem, daß ich sie so schöne Lieder singen gehört, besonders eines" (374) [Hastily I blurted out that I was a lover of music, though only a recent one, and that I had heard her sing such lovely songs, one in particular] (65). Jacob's request for the song establishes Barbara as the origin of his love for music and makes clear her influence on and significance for Jacob.

Barbara admits having noticed Jacob, albeit negatively: "Wären Sie etwa gar derselbe, rief sie aus, der so kratzt auf der Geige?" (374) ["So you're the one," she exclaimed, "who scrapes away on the fiddle?"] (66). This moment of mutual recognition rewrites the initial script of mutual indifference: "Wir nahmen daher keine Notiz voneinander" (373) [So we took no notice of one another] (63). Their meeting follows a pattern of Jacob exposing his sensitivity and being wounded, followed by Barbara experiencing a moment of regret: "'Mir war es', setzte er seine Erzählung fort, 'Ganz heiß ins Gesicht gestiegen, und ich sah auch ihr an, daß das harte Wort sie gereute'" (374) ["The blood had rushed to my face," he said, picking up his tale again, "and I looked at her and saw that she was sorry for her harsh words"] (66). Since those who wounded Jacob in the past showed no regret, this sign of Barbara's sensitivity to Jacob's feelings might account for his attachment to her.

His relationship to Barbara at first is a means to an end, his appropriation of the song. Jacob desires to pass over the female figure and concentrate exclusively on the song, the actual site of desire. Jacob tries to separate the song and its performance as if the impact of the song were independent of its execution by that particular female voice. The attempt to split apart the inseparable, the female singer and the song, evokes the structure of the gap seen as a sign of Jacob's suffering as a copyist. Jacob's interest in the score rather than the performed song reads like a return to that scene where he suffers from the absence of a voice to guarantee the text.

The advent of the female figure shifts the emphasis to the neglected physical realm. Jacob hides his present for Barbara on his body, under his jacket. During their second encounter at the office Jacob becomes aware of his appearance and feels embarrassed by the young woman's gaze. Yet when Barbara sings the song for him, he is so moved that he tries to kiss her hand; this, despite their social differences so soon to be lost along with his inheritance.

Barbara's appearance complicates Jacob's life. After their second encounter at the office he cannot decide whether and when to get the promised score at her father's shop; either decision might be interpreted as impolite or forward or else as a sign of indifference, and Jacob wants above all to remain on neutral ground. He can no longer talk to the cake seller in the corridor since his colleagues are waiting for an opportunity to tease him again. The fact that he has opened himself up by turning towards Barbara makes him more vulnerable. His situation emphasizes how awareness and acknowledgment of desire are inevitably linked with the threat of wounding and frustration.

The advent of the young woman has various repercussions. Jacob has to hide his interest in Barbara from his father's servants. When Jacob nears the store owned by Barbara's father, he loses control of his body and trembles violently. Once these symptoms are overcome, he becomes again the secret observer as during the initial scene of watching Barbara in the courtyard. But he is caught by her father which emphasizes the supposedly forbidden nature of his enterprise. Barbara's father mistakes the silent observer for a thief, grabs Jacob and drags him into the store.

Inside the store, he sees Barbara in her "natural" environment, that is dependent on both her father and the butcher,

her future husband, who is present as well. Barbara is presented as already taken. Their unfolding relationship must fit into an already marked and restricted space.[17] Jacob competes as a suitor with Barbara's future husband from an oedipal position of exclusion and punishment. The entire scene shows Jacob as unwanted, wrongly identified, and confronted by a hostile father and a soon-to-be triumphant opponent.

In contrast to the maternal realm of the courtyard filled by Barbara's voice, this scene features a punishing father figure who creeps up from behind in order to punish a theft which never occurred. Barbara's father then curses him as did his own father for failing his exam. Yet this hostile set-up allows Jacob to admit that he has come about Barbara; the song turns into a pretext. When his confession is met by laughter, the oedipal character of this scene of complicity is reinforced.

Jacob's admission of interest in Barbara causes a collapse of his own identity; he is not a thief but he does not truly feel like the Hofrat's son so honored by Barbara's father: "Ich bin der Sohn des Hofrats, sagte ich, leise, als obs eine Lüge wäre" (377)[18] ["'I am the Hofrat's son,' I said, softly, as if it were a lie"] (73). His acknowledgment of the woman as an object of desire overlaps with a collapse of the self and encourages a reading of Jacob's quest for Barbara as a simultaneous quest for identity. A parallel can be drawn between Jacob and Maupassant's Jeanne who loses herself under the influence of the other. In both texts the appearance of the other reactivates the impact of the social order which redefines the social identity of the self.

The question of Jacob's status within his family is raised when one of his father's servants passes the shop and greets the grocer. In distress and confusion Jacob hurries off and forgets to take the music. The grocer runs after him, handing him the music as if offering his daughter. Hunter Lougheed views the first meeting of Jacob and Barbara's father as a "Verkaufsprozeß," [a deal] which emphasizes the woman's function as a commodity.[19] Jacob takes Barbara's father's identification of him as a thief more seriously than his acceptance of him as the Hofrat's son. Jacob relinquishes the song as the object of his desire; he then feels he has no right to court the woman, having been rejected and cursed by his father and hers. When one of his father's servants passes by, Jacob feels he is doing something secret and wrong. The fantasy and reality merge when the servant's report causes Jacob to be put out of his father's house. He seems caught in a male network that seeks to prevent his access to the woman. This network is composed of the rival butcher, the girl's father, his father, and his father's servant, an overwhelming host of adversaries. Jacob's desire for the woman must be intense if it is a force which has to be checked so thoroughly.

Jacob and Barbara are in fact punished like a couple since both are simultaneously expelled, Jacob from his father's house and Barbara from the office. The protagonists' mutual interest grows and is mirrored by an external, albeit negative, acknowledgment of their relationship. When Barbara loses her access to the government office, she also loses her relative independence from her father; while both protagonists strive in their relationship for emancipation, they actually lose it.

Soon after Jacob moves out, his father has a stroke but Jacob is not informed. Upon hearing of his father's death he becomes too ill to attend his funeral and consequently has no final encounter with his father. Once more Jacob is deliberately excluded and has no opportunity to ask forgiveness. The death of Jacob's father sets up an imaginary causal link between the son's desire for Barbara and the father's death as a consequence of Jacob's disobedience. Wolfgang Wittkowski sees a logical connection between imaginary evil acts and their actual consequences:

> Sein Tun verfolgt keine böse "Absicht" und fügt keinem Menschen Leiden zu. Im Gegenteil. Sein Tun nimmt aber hier deiktisch die Struktur eines Tuns aus böser Absicht an. Es wird als Geste symbolisch für ein Tun, "wie Kain, der Brudermörder" (65) es verübt— wie Jacob es sich selbst beim Tode seines Vaters zusprach und wie wir es—der Wirkung, nicht der Absicht nach—an ihm feststellten, als Barbara seinetwegen hinaus zu den groben Leuten mußte.[20]
>
> [His deeds have no bad intention and harm no one. But here his deeds deictically take on the structure of acts of bad intention and become a gesture which symbolizes a deed like that of Cain the murderer of his brother. Jacob himself views the death of his father this way and we can see his involvement in its effect not its intention when, because of him, Barbara has to join the rough folks].

Jacob's relation to Barbara and her father substitutes for the relationship between father and son that can no longer take place after the Hofrat's death. This process of substitution manifests itself when, during the course of one of his nightly guilt-ridden walks, Jacob sees Barbara and her father lit up like apparitions.[21] Although he wanted to avoid his father's house which horrifies him, he turns up in his old neighborhood at a decisive moment: a letter, presumably containing a marriage proposal from the butcher, is being considered. Jacob interrupts a scene that seems staged for him, but Barbara disappears and her father turns to him as yet another potential son-in-law. Later, in the street, Barbara's voice warns him not to trust anyone. That she appears only as a voice, an evocation of her song in the courtyard, somehow magnifies her; it is as if she were an ubiquitous maternal presence protecting him from ambiguous father figures. Barbara's apparent interest in him as well as in his inherited money begins to make him feel like a man and lessens the influence of his imagined sense of himself as an impostor "Ich bin der Sohn des Hofrats, sagte ich, leise, als ob's eine Lüge wäre" and a murderer "und nur des Abends irrte ich in den dunklen Straßen umher wie Kain, der Brudermörder" [Only in the evening I roamed about the darkened streets like Cain, the fraticide] (77). His assumption of the identity of a murderer reveals Jacob's unstable sense of self that causes him to associate success with a woman to a guilty feeling of responsibility for his brother's as well as his father's deaths.[22] Mahlendorf cautiously hints at the link between repressed aggression and guilt feelings but decides to view Jacob above all as the obedient son:

> Despite occasional resistance to and unconscious resentment of his father's severity (understandably Jacob feels the guilt of a murderer at his father's death from a stroke), Jacob internalizes his father's demands and obeys them to the end of his days. (121)

While Jacob can certainly be viewed as an obedient son, his persistent interest in Barbara and his opposition to the destructive forces of the flood suggest a counter-narrative.

Before the loss of his inheritance there is a brief and precarious moment of assertion when Jacob feels like a man. This feeling seems contingent on the diminution of his father's importance: "Die Sache war abgetan und ich fühlte mich erleichtert, erhoben, zum ersten Male in meinem Leben selbständig, ein Mann. Kaum, daß ich meines Vaters noch gedachte" (381) ["The matter was settled, and I felt relieved, exalted, for the first time in my life independent, a man at last] (81). The first occurrence of Jacob's assertion as a man, however, is shown as depending on his fading memory of his father rather than on his relation to the female other. Reassured, he seeks out his object of desire, but his identity as a rich heir is immediately undermined when he is greeted by Barbara's icy glance. He must start with her anew; nothing is consolidated, neither his sense of self nor its mirroring in the gaze of the other. Every renewed encounter necessitates a reconstruction of identity.

When Barbara describes Jacob in images that situate him among farm animals, his own sense of exclusion from humanity is accentuated: "Gott hatte mir zwei linke Hände erschaffen; mein Rock saß wie an einer Vogelscheuche; ich ging wie die Enten, mit einer Anmahnung an den Haushahn" (382) [She said I was clumsy; that my fingers were all thumbs; my jacket made me look like a scarecrow; that I walked like a duck trying to be cock of the roost] (82). Their initial relation as a member of a higher social class meeting a fairly unattractive working-class woman is reversed. Barbara's portrayal of Jacob reflects his difficulty assuming the male position already occupied by fathers and brothers who must first be eliminated for a male position for Jacob to become available. Barbara's characterization of Jacob seems to coincide with his own sense of self; she posits his innate clumsiness, questions his social identity with regard to his appearance, and undermines his sexual identity when viewing him as a female creature that wrongly assumes male behavior "ich ging wie die Enten, mit einer Anmahnung an den Haushahn." This view of Jacob ties in with his expulsion from the paternal house and loss of inheritance to constitute a history of symbolic acts of castration. Furthermore, these traits ascribed to Jacob help explain the discontinuity of his relationship to Barbara and Jacob's final manifestation as an appendix to a traditional family structure, when Jacob unexpectedly reappears as the music teacher of Barbara's son.

Strangely, it is after Barbara's assessment of Jacob that the relationship reaches its climax. Jacob enters the shop unnoticed and hears Barbara singing the song. As he gets closer to her, the song seems to join them, uniting their souls: "Ich schlich näher und näher und war schon so nahe, daß das Lied nicht mehr von außen, daß es aus mir herauszutönen schien, ein Gesang der Seelen" (382) [I crept up closer and closer until I was so near that the song no longer seemed to come from outside but from right inside me, a song of my own soul] (83). This moment of exaltation reverses inside and outside; both Barbara and her song seem to be Jacob's projection. At this imaginary point of fusion Jacob has the urge and the courage to hold Barbara around the waist; she slaps his face. But the violent encounter produces pleasure not pain and the slap is followed by a kiss on Jacob's cheek.

At this point the Spielmann interrupts his narration to the listening writer and touches his own cheek as if a trace of his physical encounter with Barbara could still be found. This pause suggests that part of his story is too painful and powerful to be reconstructed:

> "Was nun weiter geschah, weiß ich nicht", fuhr er fort. "Nur daß ich auf sie losstürzte und sie in die Wohnstube lief und die Glastüre zuhielt, während sie von der andern Seite nachdrängte. Wie sie nun zusammengekrümmt und mit aller Macht sich entgegenstemmend gleichsam an dem Türfenster klebte, nahm ich mir ein Herz, verehrtester Herr, und gab ihr ihren Kuß heftig zurück, durch das Glas. (383)

> ["What happened then, I don't know," he continued. "The only thing I remember is that I rushed at her and she fled into the living room and held the glass door closed, while I pushed at it from outside. Almost doubled up with the effort of holding fast, she had her face practically glued to the windowpane, and I, dear sir, I summoned up my courage and passionately returned her kiss, through the glass]. (85)

The violent potential of the physical act appears here displaced in the posture of defense Barbara assumes so that their bodies meet a glass surface instead of each other. This image sums up the entire relationship in its balance of both intimacy and separation. Jacob tries to overcome the glass barrier by a kiss but, of course, cannot reach the body of the other. Barbara's vehement defense of herself suggests her momentary recognition of Jacob as a man. The unique quality of the scene is, however, relativized by the fact that it evokes a former occurrence. The slap appears as a crucial characteristic in the portrait of Barbara given by Jacob's co-workers. The intimacy of the kissing scene is further tainted when it turns out that the two have been watched by Barbara's father, who gives the appearance of an approving procurer.[23]

Barbara, perhaps under some pressure from her father, suggests that Jacob buy the shop next-door so that she might set up a milliner's business. Otherwise she would have to accept the butcher's marriage proposal and move away. When Barbara reveals her vision of their common future, she seems like a queen to Jacob. While he idealizes her as a maternal figure whom he would follow anywhere, Barbara calls him a child.

But if he is a child then Barbara is here a mother offering a happy ending to the fairy tale she is telling. The fairytale attempt to create a "real" life for the couple is immediately shattered when Barbara learns that Jacob invested his money with his father's secretary, a confidence man. It fits the protagonist's unstable identity that he should be dispossessed. The narrative accelerates once Jacob has been betrayed by his father's former secretary, as if Jacob has now been fully defined by this betrayal and dispossession. Jacob's sudden loss of status transforms Barbara's eloquence into mute threatening gestures taken up by her father. The grocer immediately asserts himself as a patriarch. He throws out Jacob, now the wrong suitor, and contrasts him with the "real" man, the butcher: "Das, Herr, fuhr er fort, indem er auf den Brief zeigte, den Barbara vorher auf den Tisch geworfen hatte, das ist ein Mann!" (386) [Pointing to the letter which Barbara had thrown on the counter he continued: 'That, sir, that's a man!'] (92).

Jacob's loss means the grocer's ascendance and his first measure is to confine Barbara to her room. This echoes Jacob's father's prohibition of Barbara's access to the government office and emphasizes the link between patriarchy and territory. Jacob loses access to the store and Barbara's gaze; during his final appeal to her, she stares at the ground.

In a last attempt to recoup both his inheritance and his identity, Jacob looks for a trace of his name in the books of the commercial court: "Ich ließ in den Büchern nachschlagen, aber weder sein Name noch meiner kamen darin vor" (386) [I asked for a check in the books, but neither his name nor mine occurred in them] (93). The predicament of his missing name suggests a connection between identity, money and woman. The structure of absence links this scene to Jacob's inability to remember a certain word during his exam and to his suffering as a copy clerk when confronted with omitted words. Jacob's final heroic act of saving his landlord's money from the flood might, therefore, be viewed as an effort to reverse his traumatic erasure from the books and to reinscribe and reassert himself as real.

The Spielmann's narration returns to that painful scene of exposure and rejection and imagines a possible reversal of his misfortune. But he still comes to the sad conclusion that he would eventually have been rejected because of his appearance: "'aber sie hätte mich nicht gemocht.'— Dabei besah er mit auseinanderfallenden Händen seine ganze dürftige Gestalt" (387) ["But no, she probably did not care for me." He lifted his hands and let them drop, and looked down his whole shabby person] (94).

The bitter scene at the shop has a sequel. Barbara comes to say good-bye and to return Jacob's laundry. Jacob has just been imagining her and her father in their shop so her sudden unexpected appearance seems ghost-like to him, blending "reality" and imagination at a moment of imminent separation. Their last encounter as potential lovers is their first in Jacob's room, outside the palpable presence of father figures. This final meeting suggests the essence of their relationship:

> Darauf trat sie ein paar Schritte vom Schranke hinweg, und die Augen auf mich gerichtet, wobei sie mit dem Finger auf die offene Schublade zeigte, sagte sie: Fünf Hemden und drei Tücher. So viel habe ich gehabt, soviel bringe ich zurück. (387)

> [Then she stepped back a few paces from the cupboard, looked at me and pointed to the open drawer, and said: 'Five shirts and three neckcloths. That's what I had, that's what I bring back.']. (96)

The transfer of property connects this scene with the one in which Barbara enters Jacob's office as a peddler. Grillparzer's text examines their encounters in terms of the structure of exchange so that the transfer of goods raises the question of what else is traded in encounters. With the return of the laundry everything has been restored, yet Barbara's glance and her tears betray that there is more at stake. Barbara allows Jacob to hold her hand, then withdraws it and leaves, telling him not to follow her down the stairs. Later, Jacob visits the store and learns from the new owner that Barbara has already moved away to become the butcher's wife. To console himself, Jacob creates a vision of Barbara as secure and fulfilled:

Daß sie nun alles Kummers los war, Frau im eigenen Hause, und nicht nßotig hatte, wie wenn sie ihre Tage an einen Herd-und Heimatlosen geknüpft hätte, Kummer und Elend zu tragen, das legte sich wie ein lindernder Balsam auf meine Brust, und ich segnete sie und ihre Wege. (389)

[She was free of all worry now, mistress of her own house; free of the lot that would have been hers if she had tied herself to one like me, without hearth and home; she would be spared misery and grief. All this comforted my soul like a healing balm, and I blessed her and all her ways]. (99)

Although she is lost to him, Jacob envisions Barbara with many possessions, so that his loss has turned into her gain.

Years later after Barbara has returned to town, Jacob feels he cannot seek her out. Once again Barbara takes the initiative and calls him to her home under the pretext of having him give violin lessons to the son who bears Jacob's name; it is a common custom in Catholic countries for father and son to bear the same name. Her choice of name can be read as emphasizing the suppressed erotic nature of their relation rather than confirmation of Jacob's child-like identity. Through her son, their relation is renewed and their song reappears as a leitmotif taken on by the son to guarantee continuity and support the illusion of a natural family where the son inherits the song from the mother and his fiddling from the father.

It is Barbara's singing voice that evokes the past and mitigates the couple's unfulfilled relation: "Sie hat sich zwar sehr verändert in den vielen Jahren, ist stark geworden und kümmert sich wenig mehr um Musik, aber es klingt noch immer so hübsch wie damals" (389)[24] [She has changed a lot in all these years, she is fat now and has little thought of music, but nevertheless it sounds as pretty as ever"] (100). The thought of Barbara's singing moves Jacob to interrupt his story and begin playing their song on his violin. The song functions as a transitional link between past and present but also is a means to exclude the narrator.

The narrator, having heard the Spielmann's story, seems to forget all about him until the flood. At that point, he returns to the neighborhood and learns of Jacob's heroic death in the flood rescuing children as well as the landlord's money and tax-papers. While the Spielmann had been unable to attend his father's funeral, the narrator does participate in Jacob's as if to make up for the Spielmann's earlier omission. At the funeral the narrator sees the "real" figures of the Spielmann's story—the butcher, his wife, and their children. The following Sunday, the narrator seeks out Barbara to ask for Jacob's violin in return for a generous sum of money. Barbara's emphatic reaction emphasizes her need for closure which is contrary to the persistent narrator's indulgence in curiosity:

Die Geige gehört unserem Jakob, und auf ein paar Gulden mehr oder weniger kommt es uns nicht an!" Dabei nahm sie das Instrument von der Wand, besah es von allen Seiten, blies den Staub herab und legte es in die Schublade, die sie, wie einen Raub befürchtend, heftig zustieß und abschloß. (392)

["The fiddle belongs to our Jacob, and a few florins more or less won't make any difference to us." Whereupon she took the violin down from the wall, blew the dust off it, looked at it from all sides and placed it in a drawer which she vigorously closed and locked, as though she were afraid of robbery]. (108)

Barbara turns away as if to prevent an analysis of her expression, but this final expression of dismissal and closure is undermined when the text ends with a reading of Barbara's face: "Sie hatte sich umgewendet, und die Tränen liefen ihr stromweise über die Backen" (392) [She had turned round, and I saw that tears were streaming down her cheeks] (108). Barbara's feelings for Jacob are revealed in a way that suggests their need to be forever asserted. Barbara's tears, like those the old Spielmann shed when he remembers the song, affirm their relationship.

While Barbara's final gesture of locking the fiddle inside the drawer, like her departure from Jacob to marry the butcher, can be read as an attempt at closure, the narrative constantly returns to the question of desire and fulfillment. The assertive narrator symbolizes unproblematic gratification by his annual return to the popular festival and his successful appropriation of the Spielmann's story. However, both the narrator and the Spielmann seem to avoid the impact of the encounter with the other in their quest for the possession of a story or a song. As a Spielmann, Jacob professes his love for music, but his warped performance problematizes the meaning of such a love. Yet his performance of one song leads back to a blissful first encounter which asks to be repeated. The song points to the possibility of return, gratification and bliss found in the early mother-infant dyad. While the Spielmann remains forever positioned on the threshold of fulfillment by a network of hostile male figures, he seems able to return to that moment of hope through reproducing a song. The scene of the first encounter, when Jacob observes and listens to Barbara, constitutes an untainted moment. This moment is framed by a painful prehistory and a sequel of dispossession, rejection, and disconnection. However, the song's moment of hope and connectedness symbolically pierces the Spielmann's layers of isolation.

Notes

1. Roland Barthes, *Fragments d'un discours amoureux* (Paris: Editions du Seuil, 1977) 224. [The 'subject' is for us (since the Christian era?) he who suffers: where there is a wound, there is a subject: 'the wound, the wound, exclaims, Parsifal, and this is how he becomes 'himself''] (all translations without page reference are mine).

2. Franz Grillparzer, *Werke* (München: Carl Hanser Verlag, 1950),2: 357-392.

3. Clifford Albrecht Bernd, ed. *Grillparzer's Der arme Spielmann: New Directions in Criticism* (Columbia, SC: Camden House, 1988).

4. "By the standards of the society in which he moves, Jacob does indeed lead 'a life of failure at every step' He fails at school, at work, in life, and in music" in Jan F. Roe, "*Der arme Spielmann* and the Role of Compromise in Grillparzer's Work," *GR* 56.4 (1981): 134.

5. "Möchte man nach gründlicher Durchsicht des in 135 Jahren Erreichten künftigen Interpreten gewissermaßen ein Moratorium empfehlen" [After a thorough study of what has been achieved in 135 years, I want to recommend to future critics a

moratorium] in Hinrich C. Seeba, "'Ich habe keine Geschichte': Zur Enthistorisierung der Geschichte vom *Armen Spielmann*," Bernd (210).

6. Erhard Bahr, "Geld und Liebe im *Armen Spielmann*: Versuch einer sozioliterarischen Interpretation," Bernd (300).

7. Ursula Mahlendorf, "*The Poor Fiddler*: The Terror of Rejection," Bernd (112).

8. Franz Grillparzer, *The Poor Fiddler*, trans. Alexander and Elizabeth Henderson (New York: Frederick Ungar Publishing Co., 1967) 29.

9. For a better understanding of the underlying critique see Rolf Geissler, "Grillparzer und das Ende der Metaphysik," *Deutsche Vierteljahresschrift für Literaturwissenschaft und Geistesgeschichte* 67.1 (1993):125.

10. James J. Porter, "Reading Representation in *Der Arme Spielmann*," Bernd (187).

11. Mary Donaldson-Evans, A Woman's Revenge: The Chronology of Dispossession in Maupassaunt's Fiction (Lexington, KY: French Forum Publishers, 1986).

12. This structure surfaces as well in the narrator's reading of the critic, whose judgment instead of fitting the assessed object assumes a monstruous form: "das zusammengeklügelte Urteil eines an Leib und Seele verkrüppelten, von dem Blut ausgesogener Autoren spinnenartig aufgeschwollenen literarischen Matadors" (358). [the excogitated judgment of some literary matador, crippled in body and soul and bloated like a spider with the blood sucked from authors] (Henderson 32). The model of a contagious structure can also be traced in Balzac's "Sarrasine," where it takes the form of castration.

13. Naomi Ritter, "Poet and Carnival: Goethe, Grillparzer, Baudelaire," Bernd (349).

14. "None of the fiddler's individual characteristics are obviously pathological in themselves (such as hallucinations would be). It is their interplay and the severity of the regression which constitutes the pathology. As in the second stage of chronic schizophrenia, the fiddler's symptoms seem to have achieved an equilibrium while the more glaring symptoms have disappeared" 115 footnote.

15. "Quand la Zambinella chanta, ce fut un délire. L'artiste eut froid; puis, il sentit un foyer qui pétilla soudain dans les profondeurs de son être intime, de ce que nous nommons le coeur, faute de mot! (96) [When La Zambinella sang, the effect was delirium. The artist felt cold; then he felt a heat which suddenly began to prickle in the innermost depth of his being, in what we call the heart, for lack of any other word!] (Miller 238).

16. Woman as fragmented and reassembled appears as well in Flaubert's text. Reconnected to a prior scene Madame Arnoux is recognized as already known.

17. Dagmar C. G. Lorenz emphasizes the link between women in a misogynous world and the question of space: "In Grillparzers Diskurs befinden sich die weiblichen Charaktere ausnahmslos in Situationen der Unfreiheit—in einem misogynen Umfeld. Ihre Charaktere und Verhaltensweisen sind davon geprägt, wieviel oder wie wenig Spielraum ihnen zur Verfügung steht" [In Grillparzer's discourse women always find themselves in situations devoid of freedom-in a misogynous space. Their personalities and behavior are marked by how much or how little free play they are permitted] in "Frau und Weiblichkeit bei Grillparzer," *Der Widerspenstigen Zähmung: Studien zur bezwungenen Weiblichkeit in der Literatur vom Mittelalter bis zur Gegenwart*, eds. Sylvia Wallinger und Monika Jonas, (Innsbruck: Inst. für Germanistik: Univ. Innsbruck, 1986) 206.

18. The "as if" structure, which occurs repeatedly in the other texts, significantly appears here as well due to the impact of the encountered other.

19. Rosemarie Hunter-Lougheed, "Das Thema der Liebe im *Armen Spielmann*," Bernd (84).

20. Wolfgang Wittkowski, "Grenze als Stufe: Josephinischer Gradualismus und barockes Welttheater im *Armen Spielmann*," Bernd (170).

21. The other as apparition also appears in Flaubert's text where Madame Arnoux is first encountered in this way. The other as apparition emphasizes the elements of surprise, fantasy, and vision problematized by the figure's realistic cast.

22. For a discussion of Jacob's response to his father's death see Boyd Mullan, "Characterisation and Narrative Technique in Grillparzer's *Der Arme Spielmann* und Storm's *Ein Stiller Musikant*," *German Life and Letters* 44.3 (1991): 189.

23. Intimacy is also tainted when Marianina realizes that the ring scene has been watched by the narrator and the marquise.

24. We find a similar connection in "Sarrasine," where Marianina's singing plunges the old castrato into his own past as a singer.

FURTHER READING

Biography

Yates, Douglas. *Franz Grillparzer: A Critical Biography*. Oxford: Basil, Blackwell & Mott, 1946, 188 p.
    A biographical and critical study of Grillparzer's work.

Thompson, Bruce. *Franz Grillparzer*. Boston: Twayne Publishers, 1981, 165 p.
    Critical biography.

Criticism

Bennett, E. K. "The Novelle of Poetic Realism." *A History of the German Novelle*. London: Cambridge University Press, 1934, pp. 124-92.
    Contends that *Der arme Spielmann* "is certainly one of the most exquisite Novellen in German literature,

and without doubt the most perfect of all Grillparzer's works: that is to say, that less than any single drama it affords an opening for the criticism that the form and the content do not exactly coincide."

Bernd, Clifford Albrecht, ed. Grillparzer's *Der arme Spielmann: New Directions in Criticism.* Columbia, S.C.: Camden House, 1988, 361 p.

Collection of critical essay focusing on Grillparzer's novella.

Birrell, Gordon. "Time, Timelessness, and Music in Grillparzer's *Spielmann.*" *The German Quarterly<* 57, No. 4 (Fall 1984): 558-75.

Considers the role of music in the novella.

Hodge, James L. "Symmetry and Tension in 'Der arme Spielmann'." *The German Quarterly* XLVII, No. 2 (March 1974): 262-64.

Investigates the symbolism of Jacob's hanging violin.

Mullan, Boyd. "Characterisation and Narrative Technique in Grillparzer's *Der arme Spielmann* and Storm's "Ein Stiller Musikant."" *German Life and Letters* 44, No. 3 (April 1991): 187-97.

Finds similarities in theme and form between the two novellas.

Additional coverage of Grillparzer's life and career is contained in the following sources published by the Gale Group: *Dictionary of Literary Biography*, **Vol. 133 and** *Nineteenth Century Literature Criticism*, **Vol. 1.**

Gerhart Hauptmann
1862–1946

(Full name Gerhart Johann Robert Hauptmann) German dramatist, novelist, poet, short story writer, and autobiographer.

INTRODUCTION

Principally regarded for his plays of the late nineteenth century, Hauptmann is primarily recognized for initiating the naturalistic movement in German theater with his first drama, *Vor Sonnenaufgang* (1889; *Before Dawn*). Influenced by the work of Ibsen and Zola, Hauptmann become his country's most prominent exponent of dramatic techniques that sought to portray human existence with extreme verisimilitude, particularly focusing on the social problems of the lower classes. Hauptmann did not limit himself to drama, however, and produced a vast assortment of works in various genres throughout his long career. Likewise, his work ranges over a variety of styles from naturalism to romanticism to symbolic fantasy. Among his works of short fiction, Hauptmann composed a number of short stories and several novellas, including one that is widely considered his early prose masterpiece, *Bahnwärter Thiel* (1888; *Flagman Thiel*).

BIOGRAPHICAL INFORMATION

Hauptmann was born in Silesia in 1862. He received his early education in Breslau (now Wroclaw). After a varied academic career, during which he studied agriculture, sculpture, and history—and briefly attended the University of Jena and the Royal Academy of Dresden—he eventually settled in Berlin and married in 1885. An active member of the Berlin literary community, Hauptmann began his career writing novellas with *Fasching* (which first appeared in the periodical Siegfried in 1887 but was little noticed until its publication in book form in 1923) and *Bahnwärter Thiel*. Hauptmann produced his play *Vor Sonnenaufgang* in 1889, and the work was immediately successful. The previous year he had traveled to Zurich and there made the acquaintance of a man who would provide inspiration for his next-published novella *Der Apostel* (1890). During the 1890s Hauptmann focused on drama, writing his outstanding naturalistic plays. A visit to Greece in 1907 offered the source material for his travel narrative *Griechischer Frühling* (1908). Additionally, his encounter with the birthplace of Western classical mythology proved a rich source of inspiration for his later works. In 1912 Hauptmann received the Nobel Prize for Literature and undertook a series of public readings to commemorate the event. Between the wars he wrote the novella *Der Ketzer von Soana* (1918; *The Heretic of Soana*) and produced an epic poem, *Till Eulenspiegel* (1928). Though he was an active supporter of the Weimar democracy and a critic of

the Nazi regime, Hauptmann did not follow the example of many German artists who left the country during the Second World War. He consequently incurred much personal criticism for his wartime inactivity. The literary result of this period is *Die Atriden Tetralogie,* a reinterpretation of the classical myths surrounding the curse of Atreus. Having witnessed the bombing of Dresden and Nazi defeat by Soviet forces firsthand, Hauptmann died on 6 June 1946.

MAJOR WORKS

Overall Hauptmann's short fiction is principally focused on the lower classes or individuals who live in or retreat to the margins of society. Thematically bleak, these works offer a cultural critique of life in the modern world. Hauptmann's first novella, *Fasching,* was based upon a newspaper story detailing a couple's accidental drowning. Its title refers to the Shrovetide carnival from which the sail maker Kielblock, his wife, and child are returning. Crossing a frozen lake at night, the family falls through the ice and all three perish. *Der Apostel* features a nameless narrator, a preacher whose interior monologue reveals his mental instability. Afflicted by despair and spiritual delusions, the "apostle" endeavors to reenact the life of the Christ. *Der Ketzer von Soana* recounts the liaison of a young Italian priest with a country girl, which culminates in a departure from his congregation so that he may become a goatherd. A blend of naturalistic and symbolic strains, *Bahnwärter Thiel* follows the mental decline of a working-class railroad flagman, Thiel. Covertly worshipping his dead wife, Thiel has since entered into a new marriage with a sexually-dominating woman who abuses his child, Tobias. The violent death of Tobias by a locomotive precipitates Thiel's tragic collapse. In a fit of madness he kills his wife and their infant child. Hauptmann's final novella, *Mignon*, relates its narrator's obsession with a young, wandering orphan girl. His short story, "Das Märchen" (1941) reveals the influence of Goethe's 1795 work by the same name. The piece also evinces Hauptmann's interest in the mystical and supernatural late in his life.

CRITICAL RECEPTION

One of the most celebrated German-speaking literary figures of the late nineteenth century, Hauptmann earned his notoriety primarily through his works of drama. Still, considerable critical attention has been focused on his short prose, particularly since his death. While *Fasching* is generally considered the work of an apprentice, *Bahnwärter Thiel*, written the same year, has been hailed by critics as a masterful narrative. At the time of its first publication in 1918, *Der Ketzer von Soana* proved to be Hauptmann's most esteemed prose work, and though it is still highly regarded, most commentators reserve their highest praise for *Bahnwärter Thiel*, which has become a standard on reading lists for students of German literature. Several critics have evaluated the musical qualities of Hauptmann's prose in *Thiel*, numbering it among the finest achievements in the German Novelle genre. Others have analyzed the complex imagery and shifting narrative perspectives of the novella, qualities that place the work beyond the confines of purely naturalistic prose and contribute to the contemporary perception of *Bahnwärter Thiel* as a significant transitional work of modern German literature.

PRINCIPAL WORKS

Short Fiction

Fasching (novella) 1887

Bahnwärter Thiel [

Flagman Thiel] (novella) 1888

Der Apostel (novella) 1890

Der Ketzer von Soana[*The Heretic of Soana*] (novella) 1918

Mignon (novella) 1944

Lineman Thiel and Other Tales (novella and short stories) 1989

Other Major Works

Promethidenlos (poetry) 1885

Das bunte Buch (poetry) 1888

Vor Sonnenaufgang [*Before Dawn*] (drama) 1889

Das Friedenfest [*The Coming of Peace*] (drama) 1890

Einsame Menschen [*Lonely Lives*] (drama) 1891

Der Biberpelz [*The Beaver Coat*] (drama) 1893

Hanneles Himmelfahrt [*Hannele*] (drama) 1893

Die Weber [*The Weavers*] (drama) 1893

Florian Geyer [*Florian Geyer*] (drama) 1896

Die versunkene Glocke [*The Sunken Bell*] (drama) 1896

Führmann Henschel [*Drayman Henschel*](drama) 1898

Michael Kramer [*Michael Kramer*] (drama) 1900

Schluck und Jau [*Schluck and Jau*] (drama) 1900

Der rote Hahn [*The Conflagration*] (drama) 1901

Der arme Heinrich [*Henry of Auë*] (drama) 1902

Rose Bernd [*Rose Bernd*] (drama) 1903

Elga [*Elga*] (drama) 1905

Die Jungfrau vom Bischofsberg [*Maidens of the Mount*] (drama) 1907

Und Pippa tanzt! [*And Pippa Dances*] (drama) 1907

Griechischer Frühling (travel diary) 1908

Kaiser Karls Geisel [*Charlemagne's Hostage*] (drama) 1908

Griselda [*Griselda*] (drama) 1909

Der Narr in Christo Emanuel Quint [*The Fool in Christ, Emanuel Quint*] (novel) 1910

Die Ratten [*The Rats*] (drama) 1911

Atlantis [*Atlantis*] (novel) 1912

Gabriel Schillings Flucht [*Gabriel Schilling's Flight*] (drama) 1912

Festspiel in deutschen Reimen [*Commemoration Masque*] (drama) 1913

Lohengrin (novel) 1913

Der Bogen des Odysseus [*The Bow of Ulysses*] (drama) 1914

Parsival (novel) 1914

Winterballade [*Winter Ballad*] (drama) 1917

Indipohdi [*Indipohdi*] (drama) 1920

Der weisse Heiland [*The White Savior*] (drama) 1920

Anna (poetry) 1921

Peter Bauer (drama) 1921

Phantom [*Phantom*] (novel) 1923

Die blaue Blume (poetry) 1924

Die Insel der grossen Mutter [*The Island of the Great Mother*] (novel) 1925

Veland [*Veland*] (drama) 1925

Dorothea Angermann (drama) 1926

Till Eulenspiegel (poetry) 1928

Wanda (novel) 1928

Spuk: Die schwarze Maske (drama) 1929

Buch der Leidenschaft (novel) 1930

Vor Sonnenuntergang (drama) 1932

Die goldene Harfe (drama) 1933

Hamlet in Wittenberg (drama) 1935

Im Wirbel der Berinfung (novel) 1936

Ährenlese (poetry) 1939

Die Tochter der Kathedrale (drama) 1939

Ulrich von Lichtenstein (drama) 1939

*These four plays comprise *Die Atriden Tetralogie* published in 1949.

CRITICISM

Charles K. Trueblood (review date 1925)

SOURCE: "A Pagan Chorale," in *The Dial*, Vol. 79, October, 1925, pp. 339-41.

[*In the following review, Trueblood favorably assesses Hauptmann's novella* The Heretic of Soana.]

Hauptmann—the Ibsenist, the Zolaist, the psychologist-lover of man—is also a Nietzschean and a great lyric pagan. The two latter have joined minds, in *The Heretic of Soana,* to write in a great round hand what might seem to be a foot-note to Der Anti-Christ, or a tremendous hymn to Pan. It is both and neither. Hauptmann, by what may be rather provident use of a familiar narrative device, has made it simply the autobiography of the heretic's heart, and a *Novelle* of force and charm, which has been competently rendered by the translator.

One can hardly recollect the psychology of the Fall more ably studied in brief compass than in this tale of Francesco Vela, sometime priest, all but saint of Monte Generoso. It is a series of pictures of a man's heart, each melting imperceptibly into the other; and thus a development of that novel actualistic psychology which Hauptmann was studying in *Before Dawn, The Weavers,* and *Rose Bernd,* and for which he has been blamed as a weakener of dramatic technique. The kernel of the method lies less in the thoroughness with which it dredges up each detail—however trivial, however squalid, if only pertinent—than in the effort to reach *vraisemblance* by presenting the facts of a psychological situation as gradually as they would be presented by life itself. This method has been denounced as too snail-like for drama, though there seems to have been little question of its potency in *The Weavers.* In the present story it is velvety and inimitable. The intensification is accomplished with such skill that although Francesco Vela begins as a delicately cultivated young man, of the most genuine priestly promise, and ends as utmost anathema, each slope of his decline has a curious stealth, it so little increases the gradient of that above.

He comes upon his destiny in the noblest of business: the defeating hell of souls. It is characteristic of the stealing subtlety of the story that the young man is far gone upon the journey to a wild conclusion, before his undertaking ceases for him, to wear the fine smile of altruism, or justly to merit the blessings of holy church. Such were the arts of the then devil that, even when the young priest began to feel the sweet philtres of passion working in him, and vehemently prayed to be delivered from the fluent sorcery that set his blood-beats racing, and when he confessed the state of his feelings with literal exactness to his churchly superiors, he not only was freely absolved by these smiling, somnolent fathers, but received their command to proceed with what still seemed to them to be but the high and holy, though sorely beset, ransoming of souls. His prayers at first were for deliverance and purification, but not for long. There gradually slips into them a beseeching cry that the Holy Mother forgive, understand—approve. Once he thought of asking that his spiritual fathers send another priest, but the idea gained no ground. And imperceptibly we are made to know that had they really taken alarm from his later confessions and turned his mission over to another, the result upon his feelings would have but hurried the inevitable.

The pagan undersong which soon seizes and possesses the tale begins even before the telling. In the short prelude, before the actual story of Francesco has commenced, the author has interviews with the mountain heretic, Ludovico, and notices the expert care he takes in the procreation of his flocks, and his antique joy in the sturdiness and the fine, flashing, devilish eyes of his buck goats.

The tale has its first motion in Francesco's initial journey up the mountain to the stone hut of the wretched and iniquitous goatherds, the Scarabotas. Even before he has left the village, our attention is pointed to certain marble sarcophagi in the village square, into which a mountain stream pours, and where the village wives and girls carry their washing. These sarcophagi are but pointed out on his first journey. On the second we learn that their marble bas-reliefs display a procession of frantic maenads and contortive satyrs, and the tigers and chariot of Dionysus. Such hints would amount to nothing if the theme of passion did not promptly come to the surface to seize and be seized; to be elaborated in great eager lover phrases by the author's lyricism and his exquisite sense of beauty. We are soon impressed by the universal implications of the story; and the vast scene of it seems to become an echoing chamber for the thrill and resonance of the words. It is set among mountains, which we soon know he loves more than anything else in nature. It is set too, amid the leafy glory and ebullience of spring, which few are better able than he to render.

So, one by one, perhaps in spite of himself, he pulls out the stops upon an irresistible pagan diapason. The chords that are melted into this magnificence are without number, and are both heroic and exquisite. They range from the charm of immense landscape, of snowy peaks and battlements, and the majestic sky-circling of the fisher-hawks, to the vivid sleeping blue in the flowers of the mountain gentian. They vary from the dull thunder of the spring avalanches, and the sounding waterfalls, to the hum of bees about the shrines of the Virgin, the eloquence of birds, and the splendid soft singing of Agata, the mountain shepherd

Eve, for whom the priest of God forswore his vows, and was driven with stones from his parish, and became a shepherd Adam.

One wonders if so much lover's gold does not make the tale somewhat more pagan than the author intended. However, if the song of songs come up in the throat it will be sung. So perhaps the great lover in Hauptmann—who could not see his eternal pair go down to darkness and the end, after their mountain Eden—played into the hands of the Nietzschean in him. And the latter turned the frail priest, Francesco, into that determined heretic who, in the prelude to the tale, gave his name as Ludovico; who firmly cherished his hardy and lovely Eve; who was, into the bargain, a thorough-paced Zarathustran, genuinely caring nothing for the chattering curses of his fellows.

Walter Silz (essay date 1954)

SOURCE: "Hauptmann, Bahnwärter Thiel (1887)," in *Realism and Reality: Studies in the German Novelle of Poetic Realism,* University of North Carolina Press, 1954, pp. 137-52.

[*In the following essay, Silz describes* Bahnwärter Thiel *as poised between Poetic Realism and Naturalism.*]

With Gerhart Hauptmann's Novelle **Bahnwärter Thiel** we stand at the threshold of a new age in German literature, the period of "Naturalismus" that was to succeed "Poetischer Realismus." The little story was written and published in 1887, the year in which Berlin saw the performances of the visiting *Théâtre libre* that were to lead two years later to the establishment of the "Freie Bühne" and the debut of its chief talent, the young dramatist Hauptmann who quickly came to be regarded as the leader of the new literary revolt.

Bahnwärter Thiel, however, precedes that year of committal. It is a Janus-faced work, with traits both of the era which is coming to a close and of the era which is about to open. This makes it especially meaningful and appropriate as a termination for our present series of studies. In Hauptmann's life, too, it comes out of the middle of a critical period of transition, the Erkner years (1885-1888) which Hauptmann himself in his *Lebenserinnerungen* entitles "Lebenswende." It is Hauptmann's first narrative work, little regarde then or since because of the more sensational plays and longer stories that followed it; and yet it is a real masterpiece, and we can see in it already characteristic features of Hauptmann's style and of his *Weltanschauung.*

The young author of twenty-four, modestly conscious of being a beginner, entitled his tale a "novellistische Studie," not a Novelle outright. But it is a genuine Novelle nevertheless, fulfilling an unusual number of the familiar requirements of this "Gattung." It is brief (only thirty-seven pages in the standard edition) and limited in time, place, and action. It deals with only two, or at most three, adult persons. Strictly speaking, there is no evolution of character, as in the novel, but the revelation of a hitherto submerged side of character under the impact of crisis. There is a striking central event (the death of little Tobias), "eine

sich ereignete, unerhörte Begebenheit" in Goethe's terms, and we are shown its effect on an already matured or "fertig" hero. There is a distinct "Wendepunkt" in the middle of the story: Thiel's first vision of his dead wife, which is the first mental objectivation of the feeling of guilt and unfaithfulness that eventuates in murder. An "Idee" summarizing the action could readily be compressed into a brief and arresting statement. There are a number of impressive "Leitmotive," and one of these, Tobias's pathetic little brown cap, could qualify as a "Falke" in Heyse's sense. Certainly the story has the "scharfe Silhouette" stipulated by Heyse: its world, centered around a remote stretch of railroad-track and isolated by silent forest and solitude that encourage inward life, has a vivid and unique individuality. In this case, there is no "Rahmen" or frame; the author is "omniscient," but his presence is never suggested; there is complete objectivity of report.

The nature of the Novelle . . . favors dramatic procedures, and in *Bahnwärter Thiel* also one can pick out dramatic passages, such as the scene of the accident, where the author resorts to the lively present tense, some dialogue, and virtual "stage-directions."[1] In the weirdly "acted" brief scene on the tracks (41f.) we see only Thiel excitedly speaking and gesticulating, but are made vividly aware of the unseen "other one;" here, as in Kleist's *Bettelweib von Locarno,* one feels the hand of the dramatist. We are "present" at this scene, whereas Thiel's earlier vision came in a dream and was merely reported to us.

Yet, despite these occasional pseudo-dramatic interludes, the technique in **Bahnwärter Thiel** is decidedly epic. There is very little dialogue. Speech is often quoted, as in Kleist's Novellen, indirectly, in the subjunctive; the only direct speech of any considerable length is Lene's tirade against little Tobias (21f.). There is no "build-up" to scenes, but straightforward narrative procedure. Yet the story has a strongly propulsive action and intensification; it rises steadily, with "rest-periods" of description, to a climactic, explosive ending. The descriptive passages, for their part, are never allowed to become static or ends in themselves, but are integrated with the action, physical and above all psychological.

Throughout, Hauptmann maintains an even, epic tenor of factual report. His sentences are never very long, and are admirably clear and simple in structure. In climaxes of great emotional tension, like the account of the fatal accident, the sentences become even shorter, some consisting of three words, two words, even one word:

> Er ist es.
>
> Thiel spricht nicht. Sein Gesicht nimmt eine schmutzige Blässe an. Er lächelt wie abwesend; endlich beugt er sich; er fühlt die schlaffen, toten Gliedmassen schwer in seinen Armen; die rote Fahne wickelt sich darum.
>
> Er geht.
>
> Wohin?
>
> "Zum Bahnarzt, zum Bahnarzt," tönt es durcheinander.
>
> "Wir nehmen ihn gleich mit," ruft der Packmeister und macht in seinem Wagen aus Dienströcken und Büchern ein Lager zurecht. "Nun also?"
>
> Thiel macht keine Anstalten, den Verunglückten loszulassen. Man drängt in ihn. Vergebens. Der Packmeister

lässt eine Bahre aus dem Packwagen reichen und beordert einen Mann, dem Vater beizustehen.

Die Zeit ist kostbar. Die Pfeife des Zugführers trillert. Münzen regnen aus den Fenstern.

Lene gebärdet sich wie wahnsinnig (38).

An impressive device of style, but one that is not overused (as it may be said to have been, for example, in Bretano's Novelle), is that of the leitmotif. The great unbroken expanses of forest are thought of as a sea, and we hear of "ein schwarzgrünes, wellenwerfendes Meer" (20), "das schwarzgrüne Wipfelmeer" (26), or the forest surging "wie Meeresbrandung" in the tempest (28). The "Meldeglocke" that rings in the booth to announce the oncoming trains is heard repeatedly, and Thiel responds unfailingly; thus the motif contributes both to *milieu* and to characterization. The brown "Plüschmützchen" is emblematic of little Tobias and the mood of his one pathetic holiday; it becomes the fetish of the insane father, and the last, telling picture focuses our attention on this eloquent object.

Allied to the leitmotif is another device that might perhaps better be called correspondence or echoing, since it involves only two correspondent points and not a series. Thus we hear, early in the story, of a "Rehbock" that was run down by a train one winter night (15f.). Near the end of the story (44f.) a fine buck is shown leading his herd safely over the tracks that have just proved fatal to Tobias. Is an irony intended in the fact that Nature's creature heeds the danger-signal to which the child of Man did not respond?[2] Or are the two occurrences meant to show the same impersonal, now destructive now benevolent, operation of natural law that *Abdias* demonstrated? In any case, the "recall" has an artistic effect. The motif of "schwarzes Blut" on Tobias's lips (38) sets a pattern for Thiel's fell intent against Lene (41). In similar sinister fashion, the association "Eichhörnchen—der liebe Gott" (35), when it recurs, sets off a murderous reaction (43). On the way to the field, Thiel pushes the baby-carriage with an effort through the sand (33); on the sad return trip, it is Lene who does the same (45); the tragic events that the day has brought are thus tacitly signalized.

There is a striking use of sound-effects in the story; indeed, one would suspect it to be the work of a musically rather than sculpturally gifted writer. The account of the approach of the Breslau-Berlin express might be called a "Virtuosenstück" in this regard:

Durch die Geleise ging ein Vibrieren und Summen, ein rhythmisches Geklirr, ein dumpfes Getöse, das, lauter und lauter werdend, zuletzt den Hufschlägen eines heranbrausenden Reitergeschwaders nicht unähnlich war.

Ein Keuchen und Brausen schwoll stossweise fernher durch die Luft. Dann plötzlich zerriss die Stille. Ein rasendes Tosen und Toben erfüllte den Raum, die Geleise bogen sich, die Erde zitterte—ein starker Luftdruck—eine Wolke von Staub, Dampf und Qualm, und das schwarze, schnaubende Ungetüm war vorüber. So wie sie anwuchsen, starben nach und nach die Geräusche (26).

Or, again, the crescendo of the thunder, as it first awakens on the distant horizon and then draws nearer and increases, until its mighty voice fills the whole air and shakes the solid earth (29). There are passages of cacophony such as the braking and stopping of the work-train (44). On the other hand there are instances of verbal music that bear comparison with Storm's, especially in the alliteration on both vowels and consonants:

Die Kiefern bogen sich und rieben unheimlich knarrend und quietschend ihre Zweige aneinander. Einen Augenblick wurde der Mond sichtbar, wie er gleich einer blassgoldenen Schale zwischen den Wolken lag. In seinem Lichte sah man das Wühlen des Windes in den schwarzen Kronen der Kiefern. Die Blattgehänge der Birken am Bahndamm wehten und flatterten wie gespenstige Rossschweife. Darunter lagen die Linien der Geleise, welche, von Nässe glänzend, das blasse Mondlicht in einzelnen Flecken aufsogen (29).

One could call **Bahnwärter Thiel** the earliest Novelle of Naturalism, and adduce enough evidence from it to justify this classification. After these naturalistic elements had been extracted, however, there would be enough others left to make out a case for **Bahnwärter Thiel** as a work of Poetic Realism. The *milieu* of much of the story is typical of Naturalism. The picture of the "Arbeiterkolonie" on the Spree outside Berlin,[3] and the "close-up" of Thiel's own dwelling and his home life with its daily routine and its marital "scenes," all presented in factual, unvarnished detail, belongs to Naturalism, which preferred to emphasize the sordid and depressing aspects of lower-class life. Nothing of beauty or poetry is shown here, but a dull, unrelieved vulgarity. The hopelessness of Thiel's situation, the lack of "horizon" or mental resource, are characteristic of the atmosphere of Naturalism.

Furthermore, it may be thought indicative of the naturalistic trend in the story that, though the essential action is inward, it is set in a social matrix. We are constantly kept aware of a public, though this is, characteristically, anonymous and not even represented by typical individuals. There is a running commentary of public opinion, which is for the most part treated with light satire, as being based on very superficial evidence. "Wie die Leute meinten," Thiel's first wife was not at all suitable for him—because of the difference in their physiques (11). "Wie die Leute versicherten," Thiel was unaffected by her death—for were not his brass buttons as brightly polished, his red hair as sleeked, as ever (11)? "Die Leute," again on surface evidence, approve of his second choice: Lene is thought an ideal partner for him (12). Later, to be sure, the opinion of the neighborhood becomes more critical of her. "Die Leute" also censure Thiel for devoting so much time to the dirty brats (Rotznasen) of the settlement (19). Afte the accident to Tobias, Lene, whose callousness and hostility to the boy really caused his death, gets credit with the train passengers as "die arme, arme Mutter" (38), simply because of the way she "takes on," while the dazed and silent Thiel is comparatively unnoticed. At the end, the neighbors ("man") discover the frightful denouement, and its effect on them is reflected to us.

All the people in the story belong to the working class. We are not yet dealing with city "Proletariat," however; Thiel's neighbors are not factory workers, but fishermen and outdoor laborers. The author, to be sure, speaks of the collection of twenty houses (with a store in one room of one of them) as a "Dorf," but it is little better than a suburban slum, and we are conscious of the nearby metropolis, to which Thiel is finally transported. Nature itself is effete here, without the vigor of the true countryside; we see the river in the background, flowing sluggishly, black and glassy between scantily-leaved poplars (19). We get a glimpse of the village street, with the storekeeper's mangy dog lying in the middle of it and a crow flapping overhead with raucous cries (21). We see Thiel's little cottage, with its low cracked ceilings and narrow steep stairs. As we approach it, we are likely to hear the strident voice of Lene, the former "Kuhmagd," raised in vituperation. Coarse, burly, sensual, brutally passionate, domineering, and quarrelsome, she is a drastic contrast to Thiel's first wife, Minna, the quiet, frail, and spiritual.[4]

Lene climaxes a flood of vilification of her little stepson by spitting at the child (22). Her excitement in this scene brings out her voluptuous physical charms before her husband's spellbound eyes: we see "das Tier" in its full flush. We see her again spading the potato-patch, stopping only to nurse her child, with panting, sweat-dripping breast (34). Our last view is of her lying in her blood, her skull crushed, her face unrecognizable, butchered with the kitchen hatchet (47).

Of equally unsparing naturalism is the portrait of little Tobias, with his overgrown head and spindling limbs, his yellowish-red hair and chalky complexion and bloodless lips; in his bed, pestered with flies, or eating plaster out of cracks in the wall—a pitiable and at the same time repellent figure of an undernourished, abused, and almost cretinous child. Hauptmann does not spare us the details of the fatal accident: Tobias being tossed about between the wheels, the train grinding to a stop, the commotion and outcry, and finally a close-up picture of the horribly mangled and twisted little body on the stretcher.

This is "naturalistic" writing, no doubt of it. But Hauptmann was not only a Naturalist, and it may be questioned whether he was ever a very "consistent" one. "Konsequenter Naturalismus" calls for an undiscriminating and total "Wiedergabe" or reproduction of life, with no intrusion of the author's subjectivity and no factor of artistic selection. Naturalism of this "purity" is of course only theoretically possible. No real poet has ever been able to eliminate his artistic individuality from his work, and Naturalism itself could not dispense with selection; only it was resolved to select the sordid in human life, to the denial of every poetic element—and thus misrepresented the world quite as badly as did the most supernal idealists.

But there was a Poetic Realist left in Hauptmann. Indeed, one might say that in all periods of his life he betrays, like Goethe, a latent Romanticism. And one can prove both assertions by reference to *Bahnwärter Thiel.* The action in this story is chiefly an inner, psychological action, as it is in Ludwig's *Zwischen Himmel und Erde;* its "reality" is essentially that of the mind. It is significant that the most violent happening, the brutal murder of Lene and her infant, after being fully motivated psychologically, is not offered to our view as an act, but only in its results. The starkly sensual love between Thiel and Lene is strongly suggested, but not depicted, as outright Naturalism would have demanded. And the diction of all the persons in the story is kept above the low level of their actual speech.

The things of Nature, too, are not seen materially, but as they affect the mind. The forest is not a source of liveli-

hood or timber; it has no social or economic value at all, but a personal, poetic, religious one. When the din of Man and his machine has died away, Nature resumes its ancient solitary reign: "das alte heil'ge Schweigen schlug über dem Waldwinkel zusammen" (26)—this is the language of Romanticism.

And Man's machine itself, the train, is to some extent poeticized and given symbolical value. The railroads when they first appeared seemed to late-Romanticists like Justinus Kerner an abomination, ringing the knell of all poetry in life. Here, a half-century later, they have become productive of poetic "Stimmung" and wonder. Details of this railroad world are sharply seen and recorded, even to the number of bolts in a section of rail (36) or the items of equipment in the crossing-tender's shed. The phenomena of perspective, as they appear in the patterns of the right-of-way or in the oncoming and receding of a fast train; the "lag" in the sound that follows the white steam-puff of the whistle; the various noises of wheels and brakes and crunching gravel—all these are specific and exact.

And yet the account is shot through with imaginative comparisons: the floods of fog recoil from the embankment like a surf; the rails are strands in a vast iron net or, again, fiery snakes in the sunset red; the telegraph poles give forth mysterious chords, and the wires are like the web of some gigantic spider. The "panting" of a work-train locomotive slowing to a stop is like the heavy, agonized breathing of a sick giant. One can think, for contrast, of what a later realist would have made of "the tracks" as a scene of squalor and crime. But Hauptmann frames his stage with "Wald"—the very word, with all its connotations, cannot be fully rendered by an English one—and trains and tracks and telegraph poles are still things of much mystery and poetry, set in Nature.

The importance attached in this story to "Beruf" or calling is another trait characteristic of Poetic Realism. It appears in the very name of the hero; it is a part of his personality. More important than the external trappings of uniform and cartridge pouch and red flag are the qualities of character that fit Thiel for his work: his neatness, orderliness, and punctuality, symbolized by his old-fashioned but accurate watch and by the signal-bell to which he responds even under the most trying circumstances. Thiel does not yet typify the modern employee nor a class-conscious proletariat nor organized labor. He has still something of the loyal retainer of an earlier age. He belongs with Ludwig's forester Ulrich or slater Apollonius, men whose heart is in their work, and to whom "Beruf" has much of its old, full meaning of work to which one is called.

Thiel lives in two separate worlds. His actual "Wohnung" in the river "colony" is for sleeping and eating and the gratification of sex; but his spiritual home is the little booth on the lonely stretch of track, an island of inwardness and "Erhebung" set in a vast dark-green sea of forest. Nowhere else is Hauptmann's heritage from Romanticism so evident as in his use of the "Wald," even to the old magical word "Waldeinsamkeit" (24), which takes us straight back to Tieck and Eichendorff.

Throughout the story, the Nature-background is kept in view. There is a rich variety of "Naturstimmungen," and these moods of Nature are related to the states of mind of the persons, especially the hero. This linking of man with his natural out-of-doors setting is a persistence of Poetic Realism, quite different from the metropolitan *milieu* of which Naturalism became so fond. With its glorious sunrises and sunsets, Nature draws Thiel's soul out into infinite spaces; and then again with its winter storms it shuts him in to plumb the equally infinite depths of his soul and rise to mystic heights of ecstasy and vision. A stormy night with lightning and wind-tossed trees forms a background and parallel to his inner upheaval. A radiant morning that follows, with floods of sunlight and the sleepy dripping of dew from the leaves, helps to assuage his sense of guilt and impending tragedy. After the frightful accident, Nature itself seems paralyzed with horror: "Es ist still ringsum geworden, totenstill; schwarz und heiss ruhen die Geleise auf dem blendenden Kies. Der Mittag hat die Winde erstickt, und regungslos wie aus Stein steht der Forst" (39).

For the desolate scene of the work-train returning with Tobias's body a fit stage-setting is briefly indicated: "Ein kaltes Zwielicht lag über der Gegend" (43). As the stretcher with the unconscious Thiel is carried through the woods, the reddish moon pales to a funeral lamp, giving the faces of the little company a cadaverous cast, and its pallid light is swallowed up in the dark basins of the clearings (45). Sometimes a nature-scene is interpolated as "relief" after a scene of violence. Thus, after Thiel's second vision of Minna, which ends with the compulsive idea of a savage murder, we read: "Ein sanfter Abendhauch strich leis und nachhaltig über den Forst, und rosaflammiges Wolkengelock hing über dem westlichen Himmel" (41f.). Or, just before the catastrophe, there is a delicate picture of springtime Nature that might have come out of the late-Romantic world of Storm's *Immensee:* "Stücke blauen Himmels schienen auf den Boden des Haines herabgesunken, so wunderbar dicht standen kleine, blaue Blüten darauf. Farbigen Wimpeln gleich flatterten und gaukelten die Schmetterlinge lautlos zwischen dem leuchtenden Weiss der Stämme, indes durch die zart grünen Blätterwolken der Birkenkronen ein sanftes Rieseln ging" (35).

To the field of modern realism, on the other hand, belong the many small details of everyday living that characterize the hero in his outward appearance and demeanor, and the psychological finesse with which his inner life is exposed. Thiel is an orderly and dutiful man, slow, given to routine and set habits—for years the various things he carries in his pockets have been laid out on his dresser in a fixed order, and go back in that order (20). He has an animal-like patience and a childlike good-nature, a big and muscular frame, and coarse-cut features that nevertheless reflect "soul." He is a person of "mystische Neigungen," which are fostered by the isolation of his place of work and the uneventful monotony of his outward existence. With this religious-mystical bent is linked a sensitive, if inarticulate, feeling for Nature and a musical sense: listening raptly to the mysterious harmonies that issue from the telegraph poles, he can fancy himself in church, or in Heaven (35).

Outer events appear to make little impression on Thiel; he seems to possess infinite inner compensations: "Die Aussenwelt schien ihm wenig anhaben zu können: es war, als trüge er etwas in sich, wodurch er alles Böse, was sie ihm antat, reichlich mit Gutem aufgewogen erhielt" (13). His powers of expression are extremely limited; things that do

affect him, without outward sign, tend to "go down" and accumulate, and erupt later. He has something of the monumental simplicity and quietness of Brentano's Anna Margaret, and his slow, deep speech and "leiser, kühler Ton" (13) remind us of hers.

He reminds us also of another Common Man a half-century earlier, Büchner's Woyzeck, the most unheroic hero in the German drama up to his time. Both are simple, not to say simpleminded, faithful, "kinderlieb," inarticulate, concealing profound spiritual depths beneath a usually tranquil surface; easy-going, slow to suspicion and wrath, but finally capable of murderous violence against the women who have failed them. Lene also bears some resemblance to Woyzeck's Marie: a strapping, sensual woman, but one with a conscience and a capacity for acute contrition. Büchner, like Hauptmann, regards both these humble folk with deep compassion, though this feeling is not obtruded upon the narrative itself. It is interesting to recall that Hauptmann was one of the first "discoverers" of Büchner; just a few weeks after completing **Bahnwärter Thiel** he lectured on Büchner to the "Durch" literary club in Berlin, and he seems to have recognized Büchner as a literary forebear.[5]

Thiel exemplifies Faust's "zwei Seelen:" his consciousness is the battleground of man's spiritual and sensual natures, of sacred and profane love. He is a man placed in a sort of Grillparzerian triangle between two women of opposite types: one sickly, delicate, spiritual; the other robust, coarse, sensual. The two sides of his own nature correspond and respond to these two women: his pious, mystical, compassionate spirit to Minna; his brute strength and phlegma and primitive sensuality to Lene. Minna dies in childbirth, leaving a continuation of her being in Tobias— for Thiel's relation to both is spiritual: they call forth his pity, devotion, and tenderness divorced from sex in the ordinary sense.

Thiel's other nature comes to the fore in his second marriage. He justifies this, to be sure, as a step for Tobias's benefit; this is the only reason he gives the pastor, and it seems sanctioned by Minna's dying injunction (12); but one suspects a certain amount of rationalization in all this. At any rate, Thiel falls under Lene's physical spell, at times so completely that he is utterly unnerved and callously ignores Tobias's sufferings. Troubled in conscience by this apostasy, he then "compensates" by increased attention to Tobias (which intensifies Lene's jealous dislike of the child to the pitch of hatred) and by converting his lonely gate-tender's booth into a sort of chapel consecrated to the memory of Minna. He divides his time conscientiously between the living and the dead, thus fulfilling his obligations to both women and both sides of his nature. He keeps his worlds completely separate, withholding from Lene any knowledge of the number and location of his booth and keeping her, on one pretext or another, from ever accompanying him thither (14).

This arrangement functions successfully for a long while, and Thiel achieves a satisfactory equilibrium; only at certain times, when he "comes out of" an especially deep communion with the dead in his lonely devotions, does he feel disgust at his "other" life (15). The crisis, however, comes one evening when it dawns upon his slow-working brain that, because of necessary arrangements about a potato-patch, Lene will be invading his sanctuary in the woods and destroying the precarious balance of his mental and moral existence. At this instant, a thick black curtain of self-deception seems to be rent asunder, and he sees clearly what he has committed as it were in a two years' trance (28). Under the pressure of agonized repentance, he experiences a dream-vision in which his suppressed guilt-feelings take terrifying shape, dream and reality merging so convincingly that he all but stops a speeding train to keep the apparition of Minna from being run over.

The necessities of "real" life, represented by the potatoes which are such an indispensable staple for the poor, soon compel an adjustment, to be sure, and Thiel seems to accept the inevitable with a good grace, even going so far as to let Lene eat lunch with him in the sacred booth (36). But the psychological trauma, inflicted by this desecration of the past and vitiation of his conditions for normal existence, has of course not been overcome on a deeper level, and when Lene's carelessness causes the death of Tobias, the "other" world rises in a second and more compelling vision (41f.), and at its behest Thiel wreaks vengeance with a savageness in which there is a large amount of "displaced" consciousness of his own guilt and perfidy.

The psychological sequences which Hauptmann presents are extraordinarily lifelike and convincing. As a result of a surprise return home (he had forgotten his lunch), Thiel witnesses Lene's mistreatment of Tobias, previous signs of which he had "suppressed;" but, succumbing to Lene's physical and sexual power, he retreats in silent defeat. He loses himself in his duties at the tracks, in the contemplation of a magnificent sunset and the passing of a train. This defense of distraction wears thin, however—the more so as Nature's silent solemnity has stirred the deeper religious levels of his mind—and suddenly the name "Minna" comes up from below, as yet without conscious connection, to his lips. He succeeds in dropping it, while he absently sips his coffee and reads a scrap of newspaper he had picked up along the track. He begins to feel restless, thinks it is due to the heat in the booth, takes off his coat and vest, then decides to "do something" to get relief. He starts to spade up the garden patch, and the physical exertion proves soothing. But then apropos of this patch the thought arises that now Lene can no longer be prevented from coming out here, his carefully built up compensation will be lost and his guilt-feeling revived. Now he hates the patch he was so joyful over. Hastily, as though he had been committing a sacrilege, he pulls the spade out of the ground and puts it away. He is ready to fight some "invader" of his sanctuary; his muscles tense, he utters a defiant laugh; startled by this sound, he loses his train of thought, but finds it again—or it finds him, one might say, and holds him. Now in a flash he must recognize the reality of the domestic situation he has so long evaded, above all the plight of Tobias, that legacy from his earlier, better life; and he is wrung with pity, remorse, and a deep sense of shame over his long bondage (23-28).

In Thiel, Hauptmann has given a tragically impressive picture of a man seeking (in this case with no great mental resources) to reconcile two conflicting sides of his given nature, the needs of the spirit and the needs of the flesh. The balance which Thiel has for a space achieved, in his simple way, seems so insecure that one feels, had the fatal mishap to Tobias not occurred, some other crisis would surely have developed. The frightful "justice" which he wreaks on Lene and her child does not avail to redress Thiel's balance, for it is either the result or the contributory cause of the insanity which marks the final collapse of all effort.

It may not be too fanciful to think of Thiel as a sort of "gesteigerter Spielmann." Both are fundamentally good men, dutiful, kind, patient, trusting, utterly simple, relatively defenseless, yet distinguished by an uncommonly strong and deep inner life. Both defend this inner life, to some extent successfully, against the assaults of the outside world. But with a difference: Thiel has gone all the way along the road on which Jakob has been able to reach a stopping-place. The delusion which helps to shield Jakob from reality has reached a pathological extreme in Thiel; "Wahn" has become "Wahnsinn." One might say that Thiel's insanity constitutes the soul's retreat, in the face of unbearable torment, into its innermost fastness, from which there is no return, but also no expulsion. Thiel demonstrates in ultimate and desperate terms the superior reality of ideas over the "facts" of life which we observed in gentler form in the case of the poor fiddler.

The problem that has not become tragic for Jakob because of his very "Untüchtigkeit" and "Selbstbescheidung," but that becomes destructive for Thiel, is the problem of sex. The obsession with this problem, and its disillusioned, not to say cynical treatment in *Bahnwärter Thiel,* is a mark of Naturalism and not of Poetic Realism. The "Problematik" of sex and marriage dominates the story, and in the last analysis it is sex as affliction, as a source of guilt and destruction, as it was to be represented, a few years after this, in the plays of Frank Wedekind.

Bahnwärter Thiel could be described as a kind of bitter allegory of Man persecuted by Woman. Thiel is tyrannized and enslaved no less by the continuing spiritual influence of his first wife than by the sensuality of the second. The spirit of the first mercilessly condemns his physical sexuality and mercilessly exacts murderous atonement: "black blood" for black blood. The body of the second seems to Thiel the very incarnation of sexual vitality, overpowering, enervating, inspiring in man a mixture of lust, fear, and resentment at subjugation. Between these two opposite types of woman, Thiel is ground to pieces as between an upper and a nether millstone. He achieves no full happiness with either, but only an overwhelming sense of guilt that drives him to murder and madness.

But to the two women, who destroy Thiel, sex likewise brings destruction. Each is cut off early by anguish and death as a result of her sexual nature, and the offspring of each perishes violently. All these sufferers are viewed by the young author with that compassion which was to become so characteristic of his subsequent work that Hauptmann has been called "der Dichter des Mitleids."

Compassion is a saving grace left to an age that has lost hope and belief in an ultimate meaning in events. For Storm, too, death meant final annihilation. Yet man's end was heroic, and his work survived him, and perpetuated his name. Here, nothing survives. There is no "Ausblick," no vista of a better future, no uplift or ennobling effect of tragedy, but only dumb brute suffering that terminates in dull, savage destruction. Here is a pessimism that outdoes even Grillparzer's. For the poor fiddler achieved a triumph of the spirit. He rose at the end to heroism, even in the conventional sense of the word, and he was assumed into Heaven: "der musiziert jetzt mit den lieben Engeln, die auch nicht viel besser sein können, als er."[6] Thiel's course is not upward, but downward, and a not merely material but mental deterioration. Jakob becomes a hero and a benefactor, Thiel a murderer and an inmate of an asylum for the criminally insane.

Der Schimmelreiter, for all its scepticism, still looks back to the great age of Idealism, with its faith in salient individuals and indestructible spiritual values; Hauke Haien is a great man with a mission, a brother to Kohlhaas. ***Bahnwärter Thiel,*** on the other hand, despite its residual Romanticism, looks out upon a new age of materialism, mass humanity, and social "conditions;" its hero is a "kleiner Mann" of no prominence or formidableness, whose end brings a shudder of pathos rather than the sharp, tonic thrill of high tragedy.

Though ***Bahnwärter Thiel*** was actually written shortly before *Der Schimmelreiter,* it impresses us as a decidedly more modern work. For one thing, it deals with a contemporary situation, *Der Schimmelreiter* with one of the eighteenth century. Storm's theme comes out of the mists of folk tradition; Hauptmann's might have come out of the morning's newspaper. *Der Schimmelreiter* concludes an epoch, ***Bahnwärter Thiel*** opens an epoch. The one is the last work of a man of seventy-one, the other the first work of a man of twenty-four;[7] the one ends, the other begins, a long literary lifetime. Brentano's *Kasperl und Annerl* appeared in the year of Storm's birth, ***Bahnwärter Thiel*** just seventy years later; within that span, one may say, lies the achievement of Poetic Realism.

But that age was now ended. *Der Schimmelreiter* is its last great monument in the Novelle, and Storm the last great literary exponent of its middle-class ideals: "Er steht an der Grenze und ist der Letzte der grossen deutschen bürgerlichen Literatur."[8] With the death of Gottfried Keller in 1890 the greatest of the Poetic Realists expires. Storm had died two years earlier; Meyer lived on eight years longer, but his productive powers were blighted after 1891. With the passing of these three supreme masters of its most successful embodiment—the Novelle—the great period of Poetic Realism comes to a close.

In other spheres, too, the year 1890 was a demarcation. In that year the self-confident young Emperor William II forced the retirement of the veteran statesman Bismarck, and launched Germany on the course that was to end in the disaster of two world wars. New forces were coming to the fore on the world's stage: imperialism, economic internationalism, socialism, big business, and a mechanization of life such as the writers of Poetic Realism could have had no conception of. In literature, a new era was inaugurated when in 1889 the "Neue freie Bühne" in Berlin presented Hauptmann's *Vor Sonnenaufgang* and Sudermann's *Ehre.* The "Bürgertum," which had formed the social basis and the center of interest for Poetic Realism, was supplanted by the urban proletariat, whose misery writers sought to reproduce with photographic exactitude, in place of the artistic reflection of reality which was the ideal of Keller's generation. If the Poetic Realists seemed old-fashioned to the adherents of Naturalism, these in turn have become old-fashioned in the perspective of a half-century that has seen Neo-Romanticism, Impressionism, Neo-Classicism, Expressionism, Neue Sachlichkeit, Magischer Realismus, and other "waves of the future" recede into eddies of the past.

The achievement of Poetic Realism, for a time obscured by its successors, shone forth again with heightened lustre—not because there was any specific virtue in its poetic theory, but because of the excellence of many of its poetic productions. Great literature is made by poets, not by theorists (a poet is, etymologically, a "maker;" a theorist, a "viewer"). We divide the history of literature, for convenience, into periods and movements, and we treat it, for convenience, in such divisions, as has been done in the present book. But such procedures are only scaffolding, or fencing-off, to enable us to get close to what counts most: the individual artistic creation.

The supreme test of all poetry ("Dichtung" in the broad German sense) is its power to body forth new beings and their environing worlds, persons who *were* not before the inspired vision saw them and fixed them with the inexplicable magic of words, making them more real than the man who passes us in the street, for their reality is renewed, as the ordinary mortal's is not, each time those magical verbal symbols pass before the eyes of an imaginative reader or listener. If this creativity be the criterion of great literature, then the German Poetic Realists of the Novelle have added richly to its permanent store.

Notes

1. Gerhart Hauptmann, *Gesammelte Werke* in acht Bänden (Berlin: Fischer, 1921), V, 37-39. All subsequent references in the text are to pages of this volume.

2. Hauptmann uses irony elsewhere in the story, e.g., in the fact that Thiel, who has always been so scrupulous about lowering his gates (though hardly anyone ever passed over that remote crossing), must see his own child run over by a train; or that Lene, just before her death, is deeply changed for the better, yet the new woman, so to speak, is killed for the misdeeds of the old.

3. It is a "modern" feature of Hauptmann's story that he uses actual place-names of the vicinity of Berlin instead of the invented places of older fiction.

4. But Minna, too, is not idealized nor made especially attractive. Hauptmann gives the briefest, soberest "life" of her: she appears one Sunday with Thiel in church; another Sunday marries him, and shares his pew and hymn-book for two years, her delicate face a contrast to his; then one weekday the bell tolls for her, and the next Sunday Thiel is again alone in his pew (11).

5. Büchner's fragmentary narrative *Lenz* (1836) is a marvellous study in mental deterioration, far in advance of its times. Had it been completed, it would probably have been one of the great psychological Novellen of the century.

6. Grillparzer's *Sämtliche Werke,* Wien edition, Abt. I, vol. 13, p. 79.

7. *Promethidenlos* (1885) does not really count, as it was recalled after publication.

8. Georg von Lukács, *Die Seele und die Formen,* 165.

William H. McClain (essay date 1957)

SOURCE: "The Case of Hauptmann's Fallen Priest," in *German Quarterly,* Vol. 30, No. 3, May, 1957, pp. 167-83.

[*In the following essay, McClain considers Hauptmann's* Der Ketzer von Soana *as it displays a fallen priest's symbolic quest for meaning.*]

Few contemporary writers have expressed more eloquently than Gerhart Hauptmann the great spiritual quest of modern man for a meaning for his life and for values by which he can live creatively. Even Hauptmann's earliest heroes might be called souls in search in the sense that most of them experience a conflict between inner self and outer reality. Thiel, Loth, Crampton, Schilling, Kramer, Heinrich the bell-founder, Florian Geyer, Emanuel Quint, are all obsessed by an inward vision which they seek ardently to realize in face of an adverse reality. Unfortunately the striving of most of these characters ends in tragic failure. Personal failure, however, is far from being the most tragic aspect of their lives. At least equally tragic is the terrible isolation in which they carry on their struggle. All of these characters lack in varying degree the ability to communicate their innermost feelings, and from this inability springs their profoundest suffering. All stand thus alone in a world where true human understanding seems not to exist, and where man's natural human longing for genuine sympathy can never be satisfied. It is this basic situation of Hauptmann's early characters which makes them seem akin spiritually to the existentialist heroes of Hesse, Kafka, and Mann, for their great loneliness is also cosmic.

Only one of Hauptmann's earlier heroes seem to find the meaning and the workable set of values which his predecessors seek so vainly. This is the priest-hero of *Der Ketzer von Soana* who in the most decisive moment of his life courageously defies codes and conventions and renounces both church and priestly vows in order to build a new life with the woman of his choice. Most critics have unanimously praised this rhapsodical work in which Hauptmann seems to have vanquished for the first time the grim spectre of human inadequacy and failure which obsesses him and haunts his characters in the earlier works. The lyrical style and the poetical-mystic quality of the climactic passages of *Der Ketzer von Soana* do indeed give the tale profound affective power; and its deeply personal tone has caused many to feel it as an account of the spiritual *Durchbruch* of the author himself to a bold new affirmation of life and to a radical new conception of its meaning. Most critics have for this reason interpreted this challenging book as *Bekenntnisdichtung.* Even the author of one of the most recent works on Hauptmann speaks of it as "a single paean to the life-engendering forces of Nature and Eros."[1] To read *Der Ketzer von Soana* simply as a personal confession of faith, however, is to assign to it a far too limited meaning. Let us therefore try to look at the tale not only as a deeply personal work, which it undeniably is, but also as a stirring poetic articulation of human experience, in the hope that it may, when read from this broader point of view, take on a more universal meaning.

Since the meaning of *Der Ketzer von Soana* is revealed through the particular experience of the heretic himself, our principal problem is to find an adequate answer to a question which seems hitherto never to have been sufficiently considered: that of the symbolic meaning of Hauptmann's priest-hero.[2] We know that Hauptmann identified himself in a very personal way with this work and with its priest-hero. The setting, the tiny village of Rovio at the base of Monte Generoso, was a spot which held many pleasant memories; and the family names of both hero and heroine stem from reality.[3] The most touching indication of his fondness for the work, however, was his request during the troubled last days of his life that he be buried in the brown habit of a Franciscan monk which he had acquired in 1912 at the convent of Santa Marghareta in the vicinity of Rovio.[4] Legend had it for a while that Hauptmann had received this habit from the heretic of Soana himself, but according to Frau Hauptmann there is no truth to this intriguing legend.[5]

Spiritual roots of *Der Ketzer von Soana* are also discernible in numerous passages of *Griechischer Frühling* (1908), Hauptmann's account of his trip to Greece in 1907. This unusual travel book is an account not of visits to monuments and cities, but of Hauptmann's personal experience of the unchanging Greek countryside, which he discovered to be haunted still by all the gods and spirits of antiquity. The Greece which he evokes is not that of Winckelmann, but rather the pre-classical Greece of Nietzsche's *Geburt der Tragödie.* Riding over the Greek hills and meadows Hauptmann senses the living presence of the gods and spirits of old. At times he speaks of being overcome by a sort of dionysian ecstasy which enables him to transcend momentarily the limits of personality and individuality and to soar above the temporal and the ephemeral. In such moments he approximates mystical union with the primal forces of Being. In one characteristic passage he speaks of nature's opening her arms to receive his embrace, and when "with all the tenderness of Antaeus" he presses his face into the flowers covering the meadow he feels all the forces of earth rushing through his body, animating and revitalizing him.[6] The pan-erotic emotions which surge through Hauptmann during this and similar moments of mystical contact with the Greek countryside clearly anticipate those of his heretic-hero later, and they lead Hauptmann also to proclaim ecstatically that all true religion must be rooted in nature (147).

Der Ketzer von Soana is a *Rahmenerzählung* in which the author himself appears in the role of editor-publisher.[7] In the few pages of the frame (approximately twenty in all, out of a total of one hundred and sixty-five) Hauptmann, writing very soberly and objectively, presents the tale of the fallen priest as a hitherto unpublished manuscript, the authenticity of which he attempts to prove to his reader by having his narrator, the heretic, assert twice (22, 160) that it is based on actual fact. Indeed, he even describes the manuscript (23). The frame presents in brief outline, it will be remembered, the account of the friendship which developed between the heretic of Soana and the "editor-publisher" of his narrative. From the outset it is obvious that the heretic is a most unusual man. When we first see him he is tending a flock of goats. He is, however, no ordinary goatherd, for he is wearing spectacles, and his face, we are told, is that of an educated and cultured man. The first concrete visual image which we are made to associate with him is interestingly that of Donatello's John the Baptist, a comparison which at once conjures up a picture of the ascetic saint of the wilderness, the "forerunner" of Christ, who preached with such fiery intensity about the new way of life and salvation. Of the richness of his personality and the wide range of his erudition we learn only later. During this first encounter we are shown only an action: his calmly efficient, yet infinitely gentle treatment of the she-goat who has just given birth, a scene which may be cited at once as typical of the concentration and economy of the tale as a whole, since, as we see later, it is not only affective, but also quite functional from an artistic point of view in establishing the very important initial impression of the heretic-hero as a tender and compassionate man, and in sounding the note of the mystery of birth which will become one of the main leitmotifs of the work.

In the frame we also find the first exposition of the hero's unorthodox religious views. No longer does he stand with those who address their prayers to "einen Gehängten am Galgen" (19). To him a living buck or bull seems a far more fitting object. All peoples of antiquity have honored the bull, the ram, the buck, he declares, and he affirms the worship of these symbols of aggressive animal vitality: "Dazu sage ich: ja!—denn die zeugende Macht ist die höchste Macht, die zeugende Macht ist die schaffende Macht, Zeugen und Schaffen ist das Gleiche" (19). The Eros-cult which our heretic hero exalts is thus, as he says, "kein kühles Geplärr von Mönchen und Nonnen," but an active faith requiring of each of its adherents that he lead a creative life by exercising his procreative powers.

The *Erzählung des Berghirten* is the step by step account of the conversion of a young priest to this Eros-cult. It begins shortly after the hero, Francesco Vela, has received his first assignment to a mountain village parish on Lake Lugano. His most ardent wish has always been that he might be assigned after his ordination to a remote parish where he could dedicate himself completely to the service of God; and since coming to Soana he seems to have realized this wish, for already his intense piety has caused his parishioners to regard him as a saint. His natural introversion and his sheltered existence at home and later as a seminarian have prepared him for this complete withdrawal. Reality has, as it were, never touched him in any vital way hitherto. In this least likely of places, however, it suddenly intrudes itself in a most unexpected manner with the visit of Scarabota, a visit which is but the first of a series of strange new experiences which will completely transform Francesco's life.

Francesco's first ascent to the mountain dwelling of the Scarabotas occurs, it will be remembered, on a beautiful spring morning shortly before Easter. Hitherto the young priest, although named for St. Francis, has been insensitive to the beauty of nature. On this morning, however, new life seems to be stirring everywhere, and all creation seems to pulse with vital energy. In his own blood, too, the young man senses this "feine Gährung des Frühlings" (39), and he rationalizes his delight in this anomalous feeling by telling himself that it must be holy since it is so wonderful! In this sublime moment, as his senses are opened for the first time, he feels both "erhaben-gross" and "winzigklein" (39), and instinctively he expresses his awe by making the age-old sign of his faith, a sign which in this instance indicates both how profoundly he has been af-

fected and how deeply he mistrusts and fears his emotion. This as yet ineffable rapture becomes identifiable feeling a few moments later when the young priest, who has paused to ponder the strange experiences of the morning, is suddenly engulfed by another intense wave of emotion. This time, however his feeling is articulate, revealing itself as "eine klare und ganz grosse Empfindung von Dascin" (49), and as this great feeling of the fullness of Being courses through him for the first time he is significantly so overcome that he forgets momentarily both that he is a priest and that he has come on a priestly mission. He forgets even to make the sign of the cross.

This mystical pantheistic experience of Being with its attendant awakening of all of Francesco's senses prepares the young priest for two more fateful experiences on this same morning: his encounter with Scarabota's phallic symbol, and his first meeting with Agata. It is at once apparent to Francesco that Scarabota's wooden fetish is a talisman of the ancient Priapus-cult which his church has been seeking for centuries to eradicate in Italy. The highly ambivalent feelings which he manifests toward it accordingly strike us as quite strange. For he is both fascinated and repelled at the same time. He cannot repress an urge to touch the object and to examine it at close range. As he takes it into his hands, however, his fascination suddenly turns to anger, and in a moment of blind rage he throws the image into the fire. Both Francesco's initial fascination and his subsequent violent rejection of the provocative fetish betray the fact that it has troubled him deeply. It will trouble him from this moment on both in his dreams and during his waking hours, filling his nights with orgiastic visions and causing him to see phallic shapes everywhere in nature. Francesco is again troubled when Agata's shadow first falls over the threshold of the hut. As he sees the shadow "ein Schrecken unerklärlicher Art" (63) passes over him, and he crosses himself, as though he had received a premonition of impending danger. The young priest knows that this child must be "von Grund aus verderbt" (63); yet her grace and beauty, her calm self-assurance as she moves about the hut, and her seeming lack of any feelings of guilt soon allay his mistrust; and as he watches her "verstohlen durch die Brille" (64) he begins to doubt more and more whether a child of sin could ever become a creature of such magnificent composure. Her singing, which he hears a little later over the wild haranguing of her mother, confirms this impression of her essential purity; and as he listens once again a wave of emotion sweeps over him, associated this time with "einer Bangigkeit, wie er sie nie gefühlt hatte" (65). The smoke-filled, stall-like hut seems in this moment transformed, as if by magic, into the most charming of the crystal grottos of Dante's *Paradiso* (65-66), and the young priest is completely enraptured. Since ecstasy such as he now feels has always been a religious emotion for him hitherto, he can now feel only as holy the tremendous emotion which overwhelms him, and thus, though unconsciously, he rationalizes and justifies it.

Confused and perplexed after this experience, Francesco pauses before beginning his descent to collect his scattered thoughts and to regain his customary inner calm. Reading his breviary, however, does not help as he had thought it would, for even prayer cannot banish in this moment the very disquieting thought that he has somehow forgotten on this day to perform some vital part of his mission. As he sits thus meditating he falls into a reverie from which he is aroused by two incidents which, though in themselves inconsequential, assume in his by now overly stimulated brain an exaggerated significance. First the right lens of his spectacles cracks suddenly under the influence of the cold mountain air; and almost in the same moment he is assailed by two begging goats. From this predicament, which he accepts good-naturedly, he is rescued by Agata, who appears just in time to save his breviary which one of the goats has begun to devour, Francesco thanks the shepherdess for "rescuing" him, and as she returns his breviary jokingly remarks how strange it is after all that he is "trotz meines Hirtenamts" so helpless against her flock (70). Hauptmann's mention of the fact that Francesco looks upon these incidents with "erheblicher Uebertreibung" is sufficient to cause the reader also to focus attention on them; and it is important that he should, if he would appreciate fully the intricate and closely-knit structure of the tale. For here apparently trivial happenings bring out very important facts, in this instance the helplessness of the young priest in a real predicament (whose symbolic overtones are obvious), and his rescue from this situation by Agata. The reader who perceives this will notice later that this scene is not merely a humorous episode, but actually a prefiguration of very important later developments, and hence an integral part in the structure of the tale. The scene also illustrates Hauptmann's use of musical techniques in the composition of the tale. When Agata returns Francesco's breviary Hauptmann compares her, we remember, to a "young Eve." This is not only the first use of a metaphor which will recur and even become an integral part of the dominant imagery-complex of the tale later; it is also the first sounding of a musical motif, which we might call the "Adam-Eve-Paradise" theme, and which will recur again and again until it becomes at last a dominant theme in the purely symphonic passages of the climactic "Bergschlucht-Szene."

The young priest is first associated with Adam after his first "fall," his furtive embrace of the statue of the nude marchesina while locked in the studio of his deceased sculptor-uncle in Ligornetto (through this embrace he becomes, it will be remembered, a "fassungslos verwirrter und zerknirschter Sünder, dem nicht besser zumute war, als jenem Adam, der die Stimme des Herrn vernahm, nachdem er vom Apfel der Erkenntnis gekostet hatte" (82)). At this point Francesco's priestly moral code causes him still to look upon the tasting of the forbidden fruit as a sinful act, and hence to regard Adam as *fallen* man. Later, however, after he has himself tasted of the forbidden fruit, Adam will become for him the symbol of man-triumphant who dares to do that which he knows will make him like unto God. Again in this sequence we see exemplified the closely knit structure of **Der Ketzer von Soana,** for the fall which it describes occurs only after the way has been carefully prepared psychologically. After his first visit to the Scarabotas Francesco seeks relief from his anomalous desires, we recall, in confession. Ironically, however, the effect of disclosing these feelings is precisely the opposite of the desired one, for during confession these hitherto vague and undefined desires acquire an actual name and thus become articulate feelings. The inevitable next step is the overt act to which these newly formulated desires impel the young priest directly following his confession.

Weeks of self-flagellation follow this fall, but all suffering and anxiety are forgotten on the glorious May morning on which Francesco ascends Monte Generoso for the second time. Nature appears on this morning as the "Garden of Eden," and the young priest feels himself "surrounded by Paradise" (87). Leaving the village he greets a group of women who are gathered about the ancient stone sarcophagus which they habitually use for their laundry because of the clear mountain water which flows through it; and as he chats amicably with them suddenly he perceives a detail of the sarcophagus which had escaped him before: the ornamental frieze on its marble sides which represents a Bacchanalian procession. A few weeks earlier the exuberant sensuality of these figures would have shocked and incensed him; now, however, to his amazement he finds it not at all strange that the ancients should have decorated the coffins of their dead with figures reminiscent of the joys and pleasures of life. He finds it good too, that the vessel of death should continue to serve a useful function for the living. In this moment of insight Francesco realizes that the wonderful message of the continuity and indestructibility of life proclaimed by the figures on the sarcophagus is also an "Evangelium" (89) which is no less wonderful than the Christian gospel of the resurrection. This insight provides a key to the understanding of the wonders which rush in upon Francesco's consciousness during the ascent. Suddenly it is clear to him that the message proclaimed by the figures on the sarcophagus may be read in all nature, in every blade of grass, in every one of the sun's rays. With this realization all nature assumes "ein gleichsam sprechendes Leben" (89). The voices which speak, however, tell not of "dem Geschaffenen," but of "Schöpfung" (90). In the young priest's first moment of apocalyptic vision the world of nature thus reveals itself to his astonished eyes as a vitalistic world in which the driving force is the will to creative self-expression. "Wo gäbe es da irgend etwas in der Natur," he asks, "darin nicht ein drängender Wille sich betätigte?" (90-91).

The erotic overtones of the ecstasy which Francesco feels in this moment are revealed both in his sudden dejection at not seeing Agata with the others at the chapel, and in his unnatural exuberance while celebrating mass in her presence later. In this strange ritual, which becomes a bizarre combination of a Catholic mass and a bacchanalian revel (101-102), Francesco celebrates not only the mystery of the transubstantiation, but also the mysterious transformation which is taking place simultaneously in his own inner being. At the consecration he feels the love of the Saviour inundating him like a rain of divine fire and liberating all the love pent up in his heart, which now expresses itself as pan-erotic feeling: "Mit unendlicher Liebe weitete sich sein Herz in die ganze Schöpfung hinein und ward mit allen Geschöpfen im gleichen, entzückten Pulsschlag verbunden" (100). In this mystical moment he feels himself one of the elect, one whom God has chosen to exalt above the "wimmelnde Gezücht der Kirchen und ihrer Pfaffheit" (101); and as he stands before the altar with the elevated chalice he suddenly senses the surrounding presence of listening angels, saints, and apostles. Still more wonderful than these holy images, however, is the faint sound of clashing cymbals which resounds in this same moment outside as the accompaniment for the bacchanalian figures of the sarcophagus who, clearly visible through the chapel walls and dancing wildly "in verzückter Raserei," bear in triumphant procession the wooden fertility symbol of Luchino Scarabota.

The ambivalent emotions described symbolically here continue to trouble Francesco during the ensuing days. Even his prayers are affected, for though still fervent, they now often lack clarity and directness. At times he even wonders whether the feelings which he pours forth in them are of heavenly origin "oder aus anderen Quellen" (104). Two prayers, which occur only four pages apart in the narrative, reflect the rapidity with which the transformation begun during Francesco's second experience on the heights is accomplished in the troubled days which follow. The first is still humbly Christian in spirit: "Gib mir meine bisherige Enge und meine Sicherheit," the young priest implores, begging God to lead him back into the circumscribed existence in which he formerly found peace and comfort (104). The second, on the other hand, is militant in tone and culminates in the demand that God bless him by initiating him into the holy wonders of creation: "Lege mir nicht eine fertige Schöpfung in den Schoss, o Gott, sondern mache mich zum Mitschöpfer. Lass mich teilnehmen an deinem nie unterbrochenen Schöpfungswerk: denn nur dadurch, und durch nichts anderes, vermag ich auch deines Paradieses teilhaft zu werden" (108).

Even in demanding that he be made a "Mitschöpfer" Francesco wishes at this point still to participate as a *priest* in the work of creation. The dissolution of his priestly personality has, however, already progressed by now to a point where this has become almost impossible; and in the ensuing days this process continues uninterruptedly. Gradually the confines of the young priest's existence widen still further until he feels himself at last extended mystically into "das Allgemeine" (109). Nature becomes each day more vibrantly live before his enchanted gaze, and everywhere he sees gods being born in nature where before it had seemed dead (109). The ambivalent nature of these lofty feelings is revealed once again, however, in the "Höllenpein" which consumes the young priest when Agata fails to appear at his second mass for the Scarabotas. When he descends to the village after this mass he feels that he has been triply rejected, as a servant of God, as a dispenser of the sacrament, and, most important of course, as a man. In his imagination he pictures Agata in the embrace of some shepherd whose company she has preferred to attending mass; and he is far more relieved than he should be when he later unexpectedly encounters her astride her goat and leading her tiny bacchanalian procession. As he reprimands her he becomes aware for the first time that he is no longer master of his feelings in her presence, for he cannot conceal from himself that his exaggeratedly stern tone is but the outward expression of an inner elation which he hopes in this manner to conceal.

Francesco's next confession to the crude, ill-kempt priest of his native village is a depressing experience which, far from bringing solace, only alienates him further from the church. The last climactic step in the development of his illicit passion occurs, however, only when the villagers' cruel persecution of Agata forces him as the representative of mercy to identify himself with her. As he enters this last phase of his hopeless struggle against his love for Agata a host of images surging up from the depths of his memory reminds him at this fateful juncture of all that he has been and in this moment still is. But in the same instant another vision also rises up, effacing the first, the vision of a future "both sweet and terrible," but to which he knows that he is inevitably committed for the remainder of his earthly existence (134). In causing him to become responsible for Agata's safety, circumstances have given him, as he sees it, even "ein persönliches Anrecht auf sie" (140), and he sees no possibility of withdrawing from this commitment which coincides with what has been from the beginning his unconscious desire. Even the terrifying knowledge that he stands on the brink of mortal sin, even the apocalytic vision of the avenging angel with drawn sword are now powerless to hold him back. His conscious will, we have been told, is "gleichsam enttront" (134), and in its place another will now rules into whose power he is henceforth delivered "auf Gnade und Ungnade" (134), and which now leads him to follow his deepest desire. The word "Gnade," which arrests our attention here, occurs again a few pages later in an even more significant context when the young priest, after a last terrible moment with his conscience, sinks helplessly to his knees before Agata, uttering a sound which is "zugleich ein wildes, lebensbrünstiges Stöhnen und Röcheln um Gnade" (140). Here again we may admire the beautiful architecture of *Der Ketzer von Soana,* for, as we shall see, these two references are actually prefigurations whose full implications will become apparent only in the problematical last line of the tale with its otherwise incomprehensible reference to Agata's "gnadenlose Hände."

Up to this point the main course of the action of *Der Ketzer von Soana* might be described as a constant movement upward, since, as we remember, Francesco's most profound insights and his most formative experiences have come to him in the heights. The climactic final sequence, however, is laid in a deep ravine. The reasons are manifest. On the literal level Hauptmann is able to show in the descent of the lovers a willful withdrawal from the cruel world of bigotry and persecution into the protecting warmth of earth. On the symbolic level, however, he makes the scene serve a much deeper artistic purpose, that of suggesting a psychological process: Francesco's experience of the innermost depths of his own being. The young priest feels no regret at having sloughed off his old existence (which now seems like "Gewürm im Staub" (144), for before him, he knows, lies a wonderful new life in which he and his beloved will be like Adam and Eve in the first days of creation. The gates of Paradise seem to open once again to him and his beloved, and he enters with her. Within he feels complete security, even though he knows that his paradise is surrounded by a hostile world (144), for he is confident that no one can prevent his enjoyment of the transfiguring experience which now comes to him in the moment of love's fulfillment, that no one can deprive him of this momentary gift of "Gnade" (145). In this idyllic scene not only the action of the tale, but also the lyricism of its language reach their climax simultaneously. The main imagery-complexes, the plant and water images, combine now with the Adam-Eve-Paradise motif to produce a symphony of colors and sounds which doubly enhances the affective power of the sequence by adding a beautifully textured musical background and richly endowing the scene as a whole with symbolic overtones. All nature seems to become animate and to echo the lovers' abundant joy: the stars tremble with bliss; the clouds low like "schwelgerisch weidende Kühe"; exquisite purple fruits offer themselves as refreshment; and trees and flowers exhale a spicy fragrance. The water flowing endlessly about their tiny island bower suggests both their sense of satiety and abundance and, in a large metaphorical sense, the eternal streaming of all life in which both now participate creatively for the first time. The plant-images reflect their pulsating feelings and suggest their almost mystical sense of perfect integration in nature during this magic night. All of the wonders of this night are epitomized, however, in the highest wonder of all, in the Eve with whom Francesco-Adam, the "first created man" and "sole master of his Eden", shares his paradise, the Eve whom God has placed among all these wonders as "die Frucht der Früchte", die Würze der Würzen" (145). For to Francesco, who is overawed by the mysteries revealed to him this night, Agata, who has made this experience possible, seems the "Paradiesesfrucht", not from the "Baum der Erkenntnis des Guten und Bösen", but from the tree which makes one like unto God. The young priest desires no more transcendent experience than this night has brought: "Erstorben war . . . jeder Wunsch nach einer höheren, einer andren Glückseligkeit. Auf Erden nicht und im Himmel nicht gab es Wonnen, die mit der seinen vergleichbar waren." (154)

During this night of love an overpowering "Zauberei" transforms Francesco into a "vollständig willenlosen und, ohne Agata, vollständig leblosen Opfer des Eros" (159), and he is henceforth no longer "Herr seines Lebens". This reference to Eros recalls to the reader the heretic's profession of his own religious beliefs in the frame part of the tale (18) and thus identifies him at this critical moment with the hero of his narrative. In following the cult of Eros[8] the heretic has experienced, significantly, not a lessening, but a quickening of religious feeling; for if as a priest he has known moments of deep fervor, these have in no way equalled the experience of the first awakening to the joys of sensual love. The perpetual state of ecstasy in which he now seems to live springs, as he explains, from his awareness that through the expression of his own procreative powers he has at last become an integral part of the dynamic life-process as a "partner-creator" ("Mitschöpfer"). If he exalts the primeval generative forces of nature, however, this does not mean that he has become a mere sensualist in his new life. On the contrary, with the deepening of his emotional life has come seemingly a corresponding increase in intellectual power. Even outside the church he continues to live as a spiritual man dedicated to higher pursuits and devoting many hours to reading and meditation. Proof of the high level of his personal culture is the learning which he reveals in his conversations and the elevated tone of his narrative, which reflects a man both well-read and rich in human insights. In still another positive way Hauptmann has made it quite evident that his heretic-hero in divesting himself of his priest's garb has still not given up the best of his former life, for he has him first appear, we remember, as the good shepherd tending his flock.

The woman who shares the fallen priest's new life appears but once in a very brief sequence at the close. But the novel ends, and significantly I think, with a vision of her as she ascends into the heights. This final scene is described by the narrator who has just left his host and is on his way back to the village. Suddenly his musings over the strange things he has just heard are interrupted by the sound of a female voice singing. It is a voice of such beauty, he tells us, that all nature seems to hold its breath to listen. At last the singer herself comes into view carrying a clay vessel on her head "like a kanephoros of old"

and leading a little girl by the hand. Something almost awe-inspiring, even frightening about this proud, self-assured woman causes the narrator to feel "quite, quite small" in her presence. To those sweet, "almost scornfully curled lips" there could be no contradiction, he knows, nor would resistance be possible in face of the imperious demands of the woman's lithe and sensuous body. This superb female, who seems the incarnation of *natura naturans* (the narrator compares her here to the Syrian goddess, Atargartis) appears to have ascended from the depths of earth, and she is ascending still when she disappears at the close into the rays of the setting sun.

In harmony with the main course of the action of *Der Ketzer von Soana* this brief closing sequence is also a highly poetic vision of an ascent. As a final tableau it possesses great affective power and would certainly leave us with the loftiest of feelings, were it not for the rather disturbing last line which, if we consider its full implications, casts a troubling shadow not only over the radiance of the final scene, but over the work as a whole by pointing out forcibly at the very close of the novel that the hero's wonderful new life is actually a life of dependence to the same degree that it is a life of freedom. For if the narrative of the ex-priest is a glowing account of a courageous act of self-liberation from an existence in which he could not realize fully his potentialities as a human being, it is also undeniably the account of a lonely man who has built his life almost entirely around one individual into whose hands he has entrusted his entire personal happiness. And now, in the very last line, we are suddenly told that these hands are "gnadenlos"! The line reads: "Sie stieg aus der Tiefe der Welt empor und stieg an dem Staunenden vorbei—und sie steigt und steigt in die Ewigkeit, als die, in deren gnadenlose Hände Himmel und Hölle überantwortet sind." Curiously, only one critic, Paul Fechter, has devoted serious consideration to this line.[9] For him it expresses a "secret skepticism" which causes him to doubt whether the Eros-religion so enthusiastically proclaimed by the heretic hero could ever have supplied the final answer for Hauptmann himself. He goes so far, indeed, as to suggest in light of this line that we regard the Ketzer's profession of faith (and hence Hauptmann's, too, if we read the work as *Bekenntnisdichtung*) not as an actual expression of belief, but rather as an ardent desire to believe; and this reading leads him to conclude that the message of the work is essentially negative.

Fechter's sensitive explanation sheds most interesting light on this last line. Yet, if skepticism and even doubt are reflected in the adjective "gnadenlos," as he asserts, certainly optimism is expressed as well in the verb "steigen" which occurs four times in this one line, progressing from past to present tense, and literally forcing our gaze to travel ever higher as we watch Agata's figure ascending into the sunset. If one reads *Der Ketzer von Soana* as a confessional work one can scarcely escape Fechter's conclusion Even from our brief discussion above, however, it emerges, I believe, that the work is not merely an account of a variety of religious experience, but, much more important, the account of a great *human* experience in which an individual discovers a new meaning for his life. In one important sense, of course, the hero is still a seeker at the close, for he is still uncertain about his ultimate destiny. This uncertainty, however, seems almost inconsequential when compared to the glorious certainty that he is experiencing the fullness of Being. Formerly, as a priest, he was accustomed to seek transcendence only in the Beyond. Now he finds transcendence in the immanent and in the miracle of his own existence as a being in Becoming. His life is no longer an anticipation of something better in an indefinite beyond, but an active and creative existence in which he experiences perfect integration and full rapport with all Being. Inspiration akin to his former religious ardor fills him still in his new life, for he is now impassioned with the thought that he himself is a creative being before whom lie infinite possibilities for creative activity. Read with these considerations in mind the last line loses the negative meaning assigned to it by Fechter and acquires a positive significance more in harmony with the affirmative tone of the work as a whole. We see it then as the final summary statement of the fallen priest's new situation in the world as a man committed by his own decision to the "gnadenlose Hände" not only of Eros, but also of life; and if these hands offer no sustaining grace, they can nevertheless bear him upward, as the ascending figure of Agata reminds us at the close.

Der Ketzer von Soana allows us the unique experience of witnessing a spiritual dilemma in the life of a priest, a representative of a highest human calling, a dilemma in which an ordained spiritual guide and dispenser of religious truth is forced by a series of soul-shaking experiences to re-examine the premises upon which he has based not only his own life hitherto, but also his teachings of others. As we watch the hero struggling to resolve his dilemma, however, we become ever more aware of the fact that he is not only a priest facing a great crisis of conscience, but also a man actively engaged in working out his destiny as a human being; and with this realization the human significance of the work becomes even more strikingly apparent. For the man who emerges triumphant from this dilemma is not only the exponent of a new religion, as some have claimed; he is also a heroic human being who stands at the close as the symbol of humanity as a whole in all the great moments when man has had the courage to emancipate himself from ways of life which have threatened to stifle his creative powers. As the representative of the highest human calling he stands even as the arch-representative of humanity. It is difficult to imagine how Hauptmann could have endowed his work with greater affective power and with profounder human significance than by thus choosing as the setting for his great spiritual drama the soul of a priest; for by showing us this drama in the soul of one appointed to be a spiritual leader of men he keeps ever before us the great truth that even the highest human beings are men, and that they, too, because they are men and hence fallible, can reach the light only by the sweat of their own endeavor.

Notes

1. Hugh F. Garten, Gerhart Hauptmann, Cambridge, 1954, 42.

2. It should be mentioned here that Hauptmann seems at first to have been more interested in his heroine than in his hero, for the original version of the tale (begun as early as 1911) was entitled *Die syrische Göttin*. In the final version, however, the only reference to this earlier title is an allusion to Agata as "eine syrische Göttin" at the very close of the tale (164). This and all subsequent page references are to the Fischer ed. of *Der Ketzer von Soana*, Berlin, 1918.

3. The uncle of the young priest, Vincenzo Vela, was a well-known Italian sculptor from Ligornetto, near Soana, and a small museum there still houses some of his works. The name Scarabota belonged, as Hauptmann later revealed, to an Italian beauty whom he had met during a visit to Capri with his brother Carl.

4. C. F. W. Behl, *Zwiegespräche mit Gerhart Hauptmann,* Munich, 1948, 288. Also Gerhart Pohl, *Bin ich noch in meinem Haus? Die letzten Tage Gerhart Hauptmanns,* Berlin, 1953, 98.

5. C. F. W. Behl, *Gerhart Hauptmanns Leben: Chronik und Bild,* Berlin, 1942, 351.

6. Gerhart Hauptmann, *Griechischer Frühling,* Berlin, 1921, 46. All subsequent page references are to this edition.

7. As the "Herausgeber dieser Blätter," *op. cit.,* 15.

8. For Hauptmann, too, Eros was one of the sublime mysteries, and his works both prior to and following *Der Ketzer von Soana* reflect his repeated attempts to express this mystery in poetic form.

9. Paul Fechter, *Gerhart Hauptmann, Leben und Werke,* Dresden, 1922, 134.

John M. Ellis (essay date 1974)

SOURCE: "Hauptmann: Bahnwärter Thiel, " in *Narration in the German Novelle: Theory and Interpretation,* Cambridge University Press, 1974, pp. 169-87.

[*In the following essay, Ellis probes narrative technique and patterns of imagery in* Bahnwärter Thiel, *linking these to the work's theme of "rigid control and its loss."*]

With Hauptmann's *Bahnwärter Thiel*[1] we return to a narrative in which the story-teller neither figures as a character in the story nor presents himself as an identifiable man telling it, but remains as the unidentified epic narrator. His story is, in outline, a fairly simple one, but his descriptions of the settings in which it takes place are often outlandish. The forest, for example, has a strange appearance: ' Die Stämme der Kiefern streckten sich wie bleiches, verwestes Gebein zwischen die Wipfel hinein, die wie grauschwarze Moderschichten auf ihnen lasteten' (62). The moon appears as a ' riesige purpurglühende Kugel' (65), and the sun on a fine Sunday morning has a weird effect on the landscape: 'Die Sonne goß, im Aufgehen gleich einem ungeheuren, blutroten Edelstein funkelnd, wahre Lichtmaßen über den Forst . . .Von Wipfeln, Stämmen und Gräsern floß der Feuertau. Eine Sintflut von Licht schien über die Erde ausgegossen' (54). The description of the train is no less grotesque: 'Zwei rote, runde Lichter durchdrangen wie die Glotzaugen eines riesigen Ungetüms die Dunkelheit. Ein blutiger Schein ging von ihnen her, der die Regentropfen in seinem Bereich in Blutstropfen verwandelte. Es war, als fiele ein Blutregen vom Himmel' (53). In fact, the word 'description' fails to do justice to what can more accurately be thought of as the evocation of an apparition.

There is clearly a pattern, running through all of these examples, of an idiosyncratic and exaggerated language, and this kind of language is the most interesting and immediately arresting feature of the narration; to consider how it functions in *Bahnwärter Thiel* must surely be an important part of interpreting the story. But oddly enough, critics have often described the narrative as though its most central feature did not exist. Bennett we return to a narrative in which the story-teller neither figures as a character in the story nor presents himself as an identifiable man telling it, but remains as the unidentified epic narrator. His story is, in outline, a fairly simple one, but his descriptions of the settings in which it takes place are often outlandish. The forest, for example, has a strange appearance: ' Die Stämme der Kiefern streckten sich wie bleiches, verwestes Gebein zwischen die Wipfel hinein, die wie grauschwarze Moderschichten auf ihnen lasteten' (62). The moon appears as a riesige purpurglühende Kugel' (65), and the sun on a fine Sunday morning has a weird effect on the landscape: 'Die Sonne goß, im Aufgehen gleich einem ungeheuren, blutroten Edelstein funkelnd, wahre Lichtmaßen über den Forst . . .Von Wipfeln, Stämmen und Gräsern floß der Feuertau. Eine Sintflut von Licht schien über die Erde ausgegoßen' (54). The description of the train is no less grotesque: 'Zwei rote, runde Lichter durchdrangen wie die Glotzaugen eines riesigen Ungetüms die Dunkelheit. Ein blutiger Schein ging von ihnen her, der die Regentropfen in seinem Bereich in Blutstropfen verwandelte. Es war, als fiele ein Blutregen vom Himmel' (53). In fact, the word 'description' fails to do justice to what can more accurately be thought of as the evocation of an apparition. There is clearly a pattern, running through all of these examples, of an idiosyncratic and exaggerated language, and this kind of language is the most interesting and immediately arresting feature of the narration; to consider how it functions in *Bahnwärter Thiel* must surely be an important part of interpreting the story. But oddly enough, critics have often described the narrative as though its most central feature did not exist. Bennett[2] said that this work exhibited 'a detached transcription of reality . . . the transcription of reality is more meticulous, less artistically elaborated, than is usual with Saar'. This seems remote from Hauptmann's very unreal, and highly elaborate descriptions; yet its general direction is fairly typical. Martini, too, emphasises objective, realistic description:

> Wir müßen wiederholen: dem Realismus der Aufnahme entspricht die Haltung des Erzählers. Er bewahrt die Objektivität der Distanz, er steht dem geschilderten Gegenstande gegenüber, nimmt ihn beobachtend entgegen und verhält sich empfangend zu ihm. Realistisches Erzählen benötigt diesen Abstand des Erzählers . . .[3]

And so, too, does von Wiese: 'Die liebevolle Beschreibung des Kleinen und Dinglichen erinnert noch an die Prosa des Realismus.'[4] As for the stance of the story-teller, Martini believes that 'Hauptmann wählt den Standpunkt des Zuschauers.'[5]

There is little doubt that these views of the narration in *Bahnwärter Thiel* derive from the literary historian's awareness that the story stands between Realism and Naturalism, rather than from its text; for the text itself will not support the judgment that the narrator is an objective and distanced spectator who transcribes passively received impressions from the outside world, or who describes simply and realistically without any artistic elaboration. To be sure, there is little direct comment by the narrator on the sequence of events, but it would be misleading to note this fact without also noting that he colours his descriptions of those events in a highly idiosyncratic way.[6] Nor can the absence of direct comment be thought of as an absence of attitudes on the narrator's part;[7] on the contrary, his attitudes and evaluations are conveyed very strongly by his grotesque descriptions and by his choosing to dwell on and elaborate certain aspects of the events. Selection and emphasis can be just as expressive of attitude as direct comment.

If we conclude that the narrator of *Bahnwärter Thiel* is by no means 'objective', then the next step is to consider his distinctive characteristics and concerns in the story. We have already seen that he often produces strange, exaggerated and unreal descriptions in which, for example, colour is an obtrusive feature. But before considering the place of these passages in the thematic structure of the text, it is necessary to consider in more general terms the way in which the narrator tells his story. It is true that direct comment on and interpretation of the events and characters is not common, but it is not entirely absent; his attribution of 'brutale Leidenschaftlichkeit' to Lene (38), for example, is interpretation and expression of attitude rather than mere description. We are offered the interpretation *ex cathedra*, and thus accept it as fact, but it is no less a conclusion of the narrator for that. Yet for the most part his presence is indeed felt in less direct though scarcely less forceful ways. On the contrary: he exercises control over the narrative in a very blatant way, allowing it to become very obvious that he includes in or omits from his narrative whatever he thinks fit, without regard for the expectations of the reader; and his manner of telling the story can change abruptly, too. The reader is constantly reminded of his sovereign, almost dictatorial, control over the content and manner of the narrative. Some examples will illustrate this.

At a key point in the story, the narrator changes into the present tense from the preterite which he had used hitherto. But the change occurs in mid-paragraph: 'Thiel keuchte; er mußte sich festhalten, um nicht umzusinken wie ein gefällter Stier. Wahrhaftig, man winkt ihm— "Nein!"' (58). The present tense continues for two more pages, then is replaced by the past once more, again in mid-paragraph: 'Er meint sich zu erwecken; denn es wird ein Traum sein, wie der gestern, sagt er sich.—Vergebens.—Mehr taumelnd als laufend erreichte er sein Häuschen' (60). This might seem an arbitrary use of narratorial control, and yet while in one sense the entrance and exit of the present tense are equally unexpected, not occurring at natural breaks in the narrative, in another sense there is a logic to these transitions; both occur as Thiel is struggling to grasp what is happening to him. The change of tense functions as a switch to an unreal present scene, and we thus experience the whole episode of Tobias' accident in the present tense of what is before Thiel's eyes. Thiel's wondering whether it is all real signals an end to this unreal mode of experience, and a return to the more comfortable world of the story-teller's preterite, with its air of referring to credible past events. While the narrator's moving from one tense to another is definitely a ruthless and sudden shift, it is certainly functional—a point which must be borne in mind when the other examples of his apparently arbitrary procedure are examined. Take his relating the facts of Thiel's first and second marriages, for example; the sequence in which the information is given is again idiosyncratic. We see Thiel alone in church, then together with a wife, then alone again; and only after the last pseudo-fact are we told the important real fact, which would seem to overshadow the mere fact of his being alone in church by a long way: 'An einem der vorangegangen Wochentage hatte die Sterbeglocke geläutet; das war das Ganze' (37). But it is *not* 'das Ganze'; we still know only half the story. Only when Thiel wishes to marry again do we learn, as if by chance, what actually happened. The priest then asks Thiel why he wishes to remarry so quickly, and we are told that Thiel wants someone to look after his son. At last we find out, almost by a chance remark, that Minna died in childbirth, and the child lived (38). Now this withholding of information and subsequent introduction of it in a curiously accidental way is not indicative of a general tendency to be sparse in the provision of the detail of events; on the contrary, on the first page of the story, just as we are conspicuously not being told how Minna died, or of Thiel's child, we are instead told of his having been hit by objects thrown from the train, at a length which is disproportionate to the brevity of the account of the more important events. Again, a very arbitrary attitude to what deserves a further explanation, and what does not, seems to be shown.

Equally indicative of the narrator's blunt assertion of his prerogative is his brusque beginning of the second section of the story: 'An einem Junimorgen gegen sieben Uhr kam Thiel aus dem Dienst' (42). After the general and somewhat remote character of the narration up till now, this has an immediate effect, as if to announce through its determined and precise insistence on a definite time, place and occasion: now we are getting down to business! This closing in to definite events gives the impression that the narrator intends to select an important occasion from Thiel's daily life. All narration must be selective; but this narrator makes an issue of his selectivity, and draws our attention to it by his sudden switch from general comments about Thiel's household to this highly specific beginning.

Perspective can change in the same drastic way, as at the end of the story when the narrator stops seeing the whole story from the point of view of Thiel's presence. Throughout the story, for example, he gives us a view of only those actions of Lene which Thiel experiences, the others being hidden from us; now, instead of following Thiel to his murder of Lene and on the last journey through the forest, we switch to the perspective of outsiders: 'Nach Verlauf von einigen Stunden, als die Männer mit der Kindesleiche zurückkehrten, fanden sie die haustüre weit offen' (66). We then follow the men in their searching for Thiel and Lene, and so learn of what has happened through a radically different perspective to that chosen by the narrator hitherto.

Even in its style, the story shows the same decisive narratorial control in its alternating between terse, short sentences and long expansive ones; apparently, when the narrator wishes to expand he does, and otherwise the simplest and barest statement of a fact will suffice. The grotesque and unreal descriptions of natural objects fall into this same pattern; they are highly individual visions, in which the uniqueness of the way the narrator sees things is always uppermost.[8]

Taken together, all of this gives a strong impression of the narrator's being ever-present, dominating the narrative with obtrusive decisions and sudden changes in any of its aspects: how much information and of what kind, the balance of generality and detail, and the kind of perspective, style, or imagery. The narrator makes it very obvious that we experience everything through his mediation; though not obtrusively present in the classic manner of the explicitly moralising and interpreting narrator, he is in his own way just as evident, and a presence of which we cannot fail to be conscious. So much, then, for the extent of his presence; but what are the concerns shown in this presence, and how do they contribute to the meaning of the story? The best way into these questions is by means of his descriptions which link Thiel and the train, by showing Thiel in terms reminiscent of the train, and the train in terms reminiscent of Thiel. When describing either Thiel or the train the narrator often shows a sequence of events in which an initial calm is followed by the sudden onrush of a disturbance, which then gives way to a state of quiet once more. The first such description of the train is the fullest portrayal of the pattern. The feeling evoked by this sequence is important for the whole story, and I therefore cite it in full:

> Ein dunkler Punkt am Horizonte, da wo die Geleise sich trafen, vergrößerte sich. Von Sekunde zu Sekunde wachsend, schien er doch auf einer Stelle zu stehen. Plötzlich bekam er Bewegung und näherte sich. Durch die Geleise ging ein Vibrieren und Summen, ein rhythmisches Geklirr, ein dumpfes Getöse, das, lauter und lauter werdend, zuletzt den Hufschlägen eines heranbrausenden Reitergeschwaders nicht unähnlich war.
>
> Ein Keuchen und Brausen schwoll stoßweise ferner durch die Luft. Dann plötzlich zerriß die Stille. Ein rasendes Tosen und Toben erfüllte den Raum, die Geleise bogen sich, die Erde zitterte—ein starker Luftdruck—eine Wolke von Staub, Dampf und Qualm, und das schwarze, schnaubende Ungetüm war vorüber. So wie sie anwuchsen, starben nach und nach die Geräusche. Der Dunst verzog sich. Zum Punkte eingeschrumpft, schwand der Zug in der Ferne, und das alte heil'ge Schweigen schlug über dem Waldwinkel zusammen. (49-50)

The train begins as 'Punkt', and ends that way, but meantime has built up to a frightening climax of noise, vibration and smoke, to the point where it can not inappropriately be called a monster. Both before and after this frightening apparition there is silence. Now this climactic pattern is very characteristic of Thiel himself.[9] When, for example, he arrives home to find Lene illtreating Tobias, there is the following description of the rise and fall of Thiel's emotions:

> Der Wärter fühlte, wie sein Herz in schweren, unregelmäßigen Schlägen ging. Er begann leise zu zittern. Seine Blicke hingen wie abwesend am Boden fest, und die plumpe und harte Hand strich mehrmals ein Büschel naßer Haare zur Seite, das immer von neuem in die sommersproßige Stirne hineinfiel.
>
> Einen Augenblick drohte es ihn zu überwältigen. Es war ein Krampf, der die Muskeln schwellen machte und die Finger der Hand zur Faust zusammenzog. Es ließ nach, und dumpfe Mattigkeit blieb zurück. (46)

The same trembling begins the growing intensity, there is the same climax in a moment when something threatens to overwhelm him, and then the gradual disappearance of the tension. The same thing happens to him again a page later, as he looks at Tobias this time with a more explicit monster inside him which needs restraining: 'Einen Augenblick schien es, als müße er gewaltsam etwas Furchtbares zurückhalten, was in ihm aufstieg; dann legte sich über die gespannten Mienen plötzlich das alte Phlegma, von einem verstohlnen begehrlichen Aufblitzen der Augen seltsam belebt'. (47) This link between Thiel and the train is so well developed that the interpretation of the whole story depends on it. Its details radiate out into the rest of the text; the train becomes a complex symbol of Thiel himself, and even an interpretation of him. When Tobias is hit by the train, for example, Thiel 'reißt sich auf mit gewaltiger Anstrengung. Siene schlaffen Muskeln spannen sich . . .' (59). This is a subtle allusion to the earlier passage; the tensing of the muscles goes back to the previous occasion on which Thiel was nearly overwhelmed by something rising up within him, with its more explicit suggestion of danger, and so gently suggests the loss of control, the going berserk, which will result in his killing Lene and her child. Yet it also refers forward, for when the train starts off again it too 'stößt weiße, zischende Dämpfe aus ihren Zylindern und streckt ihre eiserne Sehnen' (60).

This anatomical and temperamental analogy between the two is extended into their being creatures of habit, governed by the strictest timetable. The train arrives on time, strictly according to the clock, but Thiel's life is no less ruled by time and order. Here is the point of the narrator's strangely incomplete and haphazard introduction of the events of Thiel's marriages. There is a logic to this haphazardness after all, for the whole of the first page of the story behaves as if Thiel were a mechanical thing that appeared at a certain place at a recurring time, just as his trains reach his part of the line at the same time each day. He is in church at exactly the same time, 'allsonntäglich' each week, like a train in a station. And just as Thiel's experience of the train is of things which he sees in the same place at the same time, irrespective of what has happened to them in the meantime, so we experience Thiel first of all in the same way; we wait for him to arrive week by week at the church, and only then learn what has happened since his last arrival there. The story's opening words refer to Thiel's appearance in church every Sunday as if reading from his timetable.[10] This is followed up by constant references to the rigidity of his behaviour; a 'peinlich gepflegte Uhr' (60) is among his few possessions, he is described as 'militärisch gescheitelt' (37) and as moving 'mit langsamem, fast militärisch steifem Schritt' (64), does things mechanically (48 and 58), and even his conversations with his little son are given much the same kind of appearance: ' "Was willst du werden?" fragte ihn der Vater und diese Frage war stereotyp wie die Antwort des Jungen: "Ein Bahnmeister"' (43). His leisure time is spent in a highly regular pattern, for 'Der ganze Ort hatte sich gewöhnt, ihm bei nur irgend erträglichem Wetter an dieser Stelle zu erblicken' (43), while his packing up his things to go off to his post is similarly automatic: 'Er brauchte dazu, wie zu allen seinen Verrichtungen, viel Zeit; jeder Handgriff war seit Jahren geregelt; in stets gleicher Reihenfolge wanderten die sorgsam auf der kleinen Nußbaumkommode ausgebreiteten Gegenstände: Messer, Notizbuch, Kamm, ein Pferdezahn, die alte eingekapselte Uhr, in die Taschen seiner Kleider' (44).

Taken together, this series of motifs linking Thiel and the train add up to an interpretation of him by the narrator. Both are regular of habit, and channelled, but also intrinsically very powerful; the train is a giant and a monster, while Thiel too, with his 'herkulische Gestalt' (37), is also a giant of a man. In both, a great natural force is channelled and put onto narrow rails, which make it predictable and harmless. Yet in spite of this domestication the primitive power seems always dangerous and about to erupt; the train as it passes by is a frightening apparition, while the threat of Thiel's being 'überwältigt' is just as ominous. With both, the danger is of their leaving the rails and bursting the inhibiting bonds which hold them in check.[11]

It is Thiel's allegiance to two very different women, representing different forces in his life, which is at the root of the imbalance in his mind, and makes his control at times seem precarious; but at those moments when his control is threatened, a restraining force seems to operate, and this restraining force finds its expression in another of the metaphors which link Thiel and the train. After Thiel's avoidance of a confrontation with Lene over her treatment of Tobias, he returns to his post in the wood. The scene there is then made the subject of one of the narrator's grotesque descriptions:

> Die schwarzen, parallellaufenden Geleise darauf glichen in ihrer Gesamtheit einer ungeheuren eisernen Netzmasche, deren schmale Strähne sich im äußersten Süden und Norden in einem Punkte des Horizontes zusammenzogen.

> Der Wind hatte sich erhoben und trieb leise Wellen den Waldrand hinunter und in die Ferne hinein. Aus den Telegraphenstangen, die die Strecke begleiteten, tönten summende Akkorde. Auf den Drähten, die sich wie das Gewebe einer Riesenspinne von Stange zu Stange frantrankten, klebten in dichten Reihen Scharen zwitschernder Vögel. (49)

The scene appears as a giant spider's web. But the key to this metaphor lies in its having been used to describe Thiel's feeling of helplessness with Lene shortly before: 'Eine Kraft schien von dem Weibe auszugehen, unbezwingbar, unentrinnbar, der Thiel sich nicht gewachsen fühlte. Leicht gleich einem feinen Spinngewebe und doch fest wie ein Netz von Eisen legte es sich um ihn, fesselnd, überwindend, erschlaffend. Er hätte in diesem Zustand überhaupt kein Wort an sie zu richten vermocht . . .' (47).[12] The railway and telegraph lines form a net, a spider's web, which surrounds the train, just as there is a net around Thiel which restrains him. The way in which repression and inhibition work here is unusual in its direction, for it is Lene's sexual power and Thiel's response to it that inhibits any direct expression of allegiance to Minna and to the other side of his personality. The eventual breakdown comes from his obsession with his dead wife, his visions of her and a sense of guilt at his betrayal of her and her child. Lene's unattractive qualities are, of course, dwelt upon and there is nothing positive in the narrator's tone as he reports that Thiel 'geriet durch die Macht roher Triebe in die Gewalt seiner zweiten Frau' (39). Yet these forces also inhibit his madness.

It is Thiel's physical dependence on Lene which shows most clearly that susceptibility to visual impressions which is a recurring theme in the story and the source of yet another motif linking Thiel with the train. As Lene undresses, Thiel watches her: 'Plötzlich fuhr sie herum, ohne selbst zu wissen, aus welchem Grunde, und blickte in das von Leidenschaften verzerrte, erdfarbene Gesicht ihres Mannes, der sie, halbaufgerichtet, die Hände auf der Bettkante, mit brennenden Augen anstarrte' (55). Earlier, it was his looking at Lene which had quietened his anger over her mistreating Tobias: 'Sekundenlang spielte sein Blick über den starken Gliedmaßen seines Weibes . . .' (47). But equally, it was his looking at Tobias that had threatened to produce an outburst: 'Seine Blicke streiften flüchtig das heulende Tobiaschen. Einen Augenblick schien es, als müße er gewaltsam etwas Furchtbares zurückhalten . . .' (47). In both these examples, a rather studied use of 'Blick' with a tactile verb gives an unusual aura and an extra importance to visual impressions; and the same kind of formulation is used when Thiel is about to enter the house, and wants to avoid the issue by not *looking* at anything: 'Seine Blicke hingen wie abwesend am Boden fest . . .' (46). When Thiel is said not to notice what is happening with Tobias and Lene, 'er schien keine Augen für sie zu haben' (42). It is after this introduction of the motif of Thiel's eyes and his 'Blicke' that the grotesque visual images in the text occur, and it is to this motif that these extraordinary descriptions must be related; but the description of the eyes themselves eventually becomes grotesque too. As he waits for news of his son 'seine gläsernen Pupillen bewegten sich unaufhörlich' (62), and Lene, after Thiel sees Tobias is dead, is afraid of 'ein unstetes Licht in seinen Augen' (64). As is usual with Thiel, any outstanding characteristic of his is matched by the train in dramatic fashion: 'Zwei rote, runde Lichter durchdrangen wie die Glotzaugen eines riesigen Ungetüms die Dunkelheit. Ein blutiger Schein ging vor ihnen her, der die Regentropfen in seinem Bereich in Blutstropfen verwandelte. Es war, als fiele ein Blutregen vom Himmel' (53). The monster engine has the same 'Glotzaugen' as Thiel has, the same staring and vacant eyes, which at one point (62) even give the impression of blindness. These 'eyes' produce the blood-red appearance of the rain, which is part of the riot of unnatural colour in the story, and of the series of highly unreal descriptions. The unreal visual images suggest in general not only something of Thiel's distorted vision, but also the extent to which he is attacked by and sensitive to visual impressions; this is the point of the impressionistic style[13] in the thematic structure of the story.

The variety and strangeness in its impression of colour are one of the story's most striking features. In the space of a paragraph of twenty-two lines (44-5) for example, we have 'die Wanduhr mit dem langen Pendel und dem gelbsüchtigen Zifferblatt', the pine forest 'dessen Nadelmaßen einem schwarzgrünen, wellenwerfenden Meere glichen', 'die rostbraunen Säulen des Hochwaldes', 'ein bläulicher, duchsichtiger, mit allerhand Düften geschwängerter Dunst', 'ein schwerer milchiger Himmel', and 'schwarze Wasserlachen'. These colours are almost all complex, and suggestive of a very strange light in which there can be black-green, transparent bluishness, and water that can look black. The unusual features of the colours—their unlikely compounding, colours unnatural for a particular object, and above all the obsession with blackness—all occur also in the first description of the train, where in a similarly short space there are a 'schwarzweiße Sperrstange', and 'der rötlichbraune kiesbestreute Bahndamm', 'die

schwarzen parallellaufenden Geleise', 'das schwarzgrüne Wipfelmeer', 'Ströme von Purpur', and 'Die Geleise begannen zu glühen, feurigen Schlangen gleich . . .' (48-9). This colouring finds its eventual climax in the sight of Tobias after the accident:

> Vor seinen Augen schwimmt es durcheinander, gelbe Punkte, Glühwürmchen gleich, unzählig. Er schrickt zurück—er steht. Aus dem Tanze der Glühwürmchen tritt es hervor, blaß, schlaff, blutrünstig. Eine Stirn, braun und blau geschlagen, blaue Lippen, über die schwarzes Blut tröpfelt. Er ist es. (59)

These visual impressions overload Thiel's brain and bring him to the point of madness; as he waits at his post after the little boy is taken away for medical treatment, he is obsessed with the colour of Tobias, and repeats over and over again 'braun und blau geschlagen' (62). Thiel's direct speech now contains the same kind of colours, which emphasises that the narrator's descriptions are to be taken as projections of his vision.

Consistent with the story's concern with grotesque and grim colour, and with the power of visual effects, is its series of images of light, and their seeming always to be destructive. The train spreads a light that looks like a rain of blood; the same unnatural redness was present in the 'Ströme von Purpur' of the sun during the first description of the scene at Thiel's post, and there too as the sun sets it leaves the trees 'in kaltem Verwesungslichte' (49). On the next morning the sun is blood-red: 'Die Sonne goß, im Aufgehen gleich einem ungeheuren blutroten Edelstein funkelnd, wahre Lichtmaßen über den Forst . . . Eine Sintflut von Licht schien über die Erde ausgegossen' (54). Flood, devastation and fullness of light occur together again in the last of the natural descriptions: 'Die Sonne goss ihre letzte Glut über den Forst, dann erlosch sie. Die Stämme der Kiefern streckten sich, wie bleiches, verwestes Gebein . . .' (62). This sequence of connected light imagery not only suggests the coming disaster, but also stresses the literally devastating character of visual impressions.

Much the same kind of pattern can be seen in other details of the story, among which the pattern of sounds is the most developed. The sound of the train is always given prominence: 'Ein Keuchen und Brausen schwoll stoßweise fernher durch die Luft. Dann plötzlich zerriß die Stille. Ein rasendes Tosen erfüllte den Raum . . .' (49). Contrasted with this noise is 'das alte heil'ge Schweigen', which returns as the train recedes into the distance. At the end, we have similar noises from the train, but a rather more personal image of it as Thiel hears: 'Das Keuchen einer Maschine, welches wie das stoßweise gequälte Atmen eines kranken Riesen klang . . .' (63). The last phrase suggests the breathing of the sick giant Thiel after Tobias' death: 'das schwere, aber gleichmäßige Atemholen' (66); but even without this more direct link, the verbal motif of 'keuchen' once more connects the two, for when Thiel witnesses the accident, his first response is: 'Thiel keuchte . . .' (58), just as he answers only with 'ein Röcheln' (59) when told there may be a chance for Tobias.

Apart from their more specific functions which I have already discussed, the light and sound imagery contribute to a much more general pattern of textual details which harp on the coming disaster and so help to create the effect of strain and impending breakdown of Thiel's world. A bird appears at the railway line early in the story: 'Ein Specht flog lachend über Thiels Kopf weg, ohne daß er eines Blickes gewürdigt wurde' (49). It reappears at the time of the disaster, but so does the final phrase of this sentence, in a different context; 'Das Hämmern eines Spechts durchdrang die Stille' (62), is followed shortly by 'Thiel würdigte sie [this time Lene] keines Blickes' (64). The signal bell is heard frequently throughout the early part of the story (48, 52, 58, 61), but eventually is transformed into a metaphor of the approach of madness, not the train: 'Aus dem nahen Birkenwäldchen kam Kindergeschrei. Es war das Signal zur Raserei' (63). Once more, the approach of the train and the approach of madness are juxtaposed. Even Thiel's madness has ironic pointers early on. First his wife is said to be 'rein närrisch' because of her joy over the new field (43), then Tobias is called 'närrischer Kerl' by Thiel himself in reply to Tobias' pointing to the squirrel and asking 'Vater ist das der liebe Gott' (57). Both wife and son having been lightly called 'närrisch', it is next Thiel's turn; but the third time is serious, and it is precisely the repetition of what Tobias had said at the sight of the squirrel that makes Thiel exclaim 'Aber mein Gott, das ist ja Wahnsinn' (63). The early mention of the accident involving a 'Rehbock' is another example: 'In einer Winternacht hatte der Schnellzug einen Rehbock überfahren' (41). This introduces the notion of the train's running over something living, and the figure of the 'Rehbock' returns to remind us of this: 'Ein Rudel Rehe setzte seitab auf den Bahndamm. Der Bock blieb stehen mitten zwischen den Geleisen' (64-5).[14] But the animal escapes, as if to emphasise that he is not the victim this time.

And so the impressionistic descriptions and the many forward-pointing details of the text build up a kind of pressure and create the sense of an overload of experiences and impressions in Thiel's mind. But perhaps 'overload' is not quite the right notion here to describe precisely what happens to Thiel, for the text provides its own idea: a slow fermentation. An apparently inconsequential detail of the story is its early account of how Thiel found and then later lost a bottle of wine near the railway-line:[15]

> An einem heissen Sommertage hatte Thiel bei seiner Streckenrevision eine verkorkte Weinflasche gefunden, die sich glühend heiß anfasste und deren Inhalt deshalb von ihm für sehr gut gehalten wurde, weil er nach Entfernung des Korkes einer Fontäne gleich herausquoll, also augenscheinlich gegoren war. Diese Flasche, von Thiel in den seichten Rand eines Waldsees gelegt, um abzukühlen, war von dort auf irgendwelche Weise abhanden gekommen, so daß er noch nach Jahren ihren Verlust bedauern mußte. (41)

Yet this passage has many echoes in the text. When, for example, Thiel overhears Tobias being illtreated by Lene, and then returns to his post, he is troubled: 'Thiel riss die Mütze vom Kopf. Der Regen tat ihm wohl und lief vermischt mit Tränen über sein Gesicht. Es gärte in seinem Hirn' (52). The fermentation is now in Thiel's brain and it too is cooled by water. As we might expect, Thiel's madness at the end of the story recalls this idea of fermentation: 'Alte, erfahrene Leute hatten kalte Umschläge angeraten, und Lene befolgte ihre Weisung mit Eifer und Umsicht. Sie legte Handtücher in eiskaltes Brunnenwasser

und erneuerte sie, sobald die brennende Stirn des Bewußtlosen sie durchhitzt hatte' (66). This, then, is the story's own way of seeing the effects of Thiel on the impressions which attack him. If one image of his going mad is the sudden interruption of calm and control by a monster which overwhelms him (the train image), the other, complementary image is that of slow ferment; the impressions received by his brain react together like the ingredients of a wine, until they build up so much pressure that the container erupts and overflows 'einer Fontäne gleich'. Within the framework of this notion of Thiel's development, some occasions seem to indicate sudden shifts, or distinct stages in the fermenting process. As Thiel begins to throttle the baby, for example, he suddenly comes to himself: 'Da fiel etwas in sein Hirn wie Tropfen heißen Siegellacks, und es hob sich wie eine Starre von seinem Geist' (63). This, and the shortly preceding 'Ein Lichtschein fiel in sein Hirn', both suggest sudden movements within Thiel's mind, its physical instability, but it is the verbal link with 'Sein Hirn gärte' that gives them their full meaning. A similar shift occurs immediately after the first train description: 'Und plötzlich zerriß etwas wie ein dichter, schwarzer Vorhang in zwei Stücke, und seine umnebelten Augen gewannen einen klaren Blick' (51). The process of 'gären' has moved on a stage. The other image of Thiel's madness is present here too, as the train's violence ('plötzlich zerriß die Stille') is suggested.

When we think of Thiel's final madness, it is easy to treat it as something caused by the experience of seeing his son's accident; but the text presents it as a process of mental ferment beginning much sooner. Very early in the story the slow reaction in Thiel's mind is hinted at in a slightly menacing way:

> Wohl wahr! Im Verlauf des Tages glaubte Lene mehrmals etwas Befremdliches an ihm wahrzunehmen; so im Kirchstuhl, als er, statt ins Buch zu schauen, sie selbst von der Seite betrachtete, und dann auch um die Mittagszeit, als er, ohne ein Wort zu sagen, das Kleine, welches Tobias wie gewöhnlich auf die Straße tragen sollte, aus dessen Arm nahm und ihr auf den Schoß setzte. Sonst aber hatte er nicht das geringste Auffällige an sich. (54)

This passage already suggests that something is evolving in Thiel's mind. And although he is said not to notice how Tobias is suffering at Lene's hands (42), his forgetting his lunch and consequently returning at an unusual time, suggests that at some level of his mind he is concerned about it; for it is the breakdown of his regular routine of packing his things that allows him to experience Tobias being illtreated, and the possible connection between this highly uncharacteristic behaviour and its result cannot be ignored. Thiel is otherwise never late and always meticulous in his preparations to go to work. The disturbance of his equilibrium is reflected in more deviations from his clockwork habits; he is late for work, then falls asleep and awakens believing that he has missed the signal-bell. Thiel's precarious balance between Lene and Minna is evidently in danger. The accident finally brings on his breakdown, but only finishes a process which began long before that,[16] by providing the final ingredient in the fermentation.

One last detail of the story remains to be considered, for it introduces another wine-bottle in the first paragraph:

> Im Verlaufe von zehn Jahren war er zweimal krank gewesen; das eine Mal infolge eines vom Tender einer

Maschine während des Vorbeifahrens herabgefallenen Stückes Kohle, welches ihn getroffen und mit zerschmettertem Bein in den Bahngraben geschleudert hatte; das andere Mal einer Weinflasche wegen, die aus dem vorüberrasenden Schnellzuge mitten auf seine Brust geflogen war. Außer diesen beiden Unglücksfällen hatte nichts vermocht, ihn, sobald er frei war, von der Kirche fernzuhalten. (37)

This might seem a lengthy digression, especially in view of its position in the text; but its relations with the rest of the text establish its importance. The two objects are contrasted, the one a rough piece of natural stone, the other a product of civilisation and culture. The first attacks Thiel by smashing his leg, the other hits him in the chest; here there are connotations of physical, as opposed to emotional attack. The contrast seems similar to that of the two wives: one rough, coarse and making a physical appeal to Thiel, the other more refined and the object of a 'eine mehr vergeistigte Liebe' (39). And yet, Minna's is the more dangerous attack on Thiel. It is she who is associated with the mental ferment of the wine-bottle, and a broken leg is less dangerous than a blow 'auf seine Brust'. In a curious way, it seems that she actually becomes synonymous with the wine-bottle; for Thiel's finding the bottle which becomes the source of the fermentation image, his hiding it in the wood, and his regretting years later his loss of it, is all suggestive of his lasting sorrow over Minna's death and his secret dedication of his woodland retreat to her. The literal story makes Tobias' death an accident but the symbolism of the story makes it seem otherwise. It is when Lene visits the place dedicated to Minna that Thiel's world breaks down. He can no longer keep the two forces in his mind in equilibrium by separating them. As we have seen, the train and Thiel are constantly juxtaposed, so that the train provides an interpretation of Thiel. But nowhere does the train seem more completely to be a symbolic expression of Thiel's mind than in this opening paragraph, for here the train throws out the emblems of the two different women, and it only destroys Tobias, on whom the harmonising of the two women in Thiel's mind depends, when that harmony is breaking down.

Bahnwärter Thiel is a more complex story than it would appear to be. It is only superficially the story of an accident told in vivid language. The impressionism of its descriptions is part of the bombardment of Thiel by experiences which he cannot digest and which must cause him more and more inner turmoil; the dominant symbols of the work, the wine-bottle and the train, bring out the slow process of fermenting of these impressions on the one hand, and the abruptness of the final eruption of violence on the other. Both images suggest a containment and inhibition of natural force. Thiel's outer calm and orderliness is a repression of the dangerous ferment of his mind, with its two opposing forces, which must be kept in strict control.[17] Meanwhile the narrator both creates this thematic network with his impressionistic and symbolic descriptions, and contributes to the theme of rigid control and its loss with his conspicuous domination of every aspect of his narrative.

Notes

1. References are to *Gerhart Hauptmann: Sämtliche Werke*, ed. Hans-Egon Hass (Frankfurt a. Main/Berlin, 1963), VI, 37-67. There are separate

essays by M. Ordon, ' Unconscious Contents in Bahnwärter Thiel', *Germanic Review*, XXVI (1951), 223-9; P. Requadt, ' Die Bilderwelt in Gerhart Hauptmanns *Bahnwärter Thiel*', in *Minotaurus. Dichtung unter den Hufen von Staat und Industrie*, ed. A. Döblin (Wiesbaden, 1953), pp. 102-11; W. Silz, ' Hauptmann: *Bahnwärter Thiel*', in *Realism and Reality*, pp. 137-52; B. von Weise, ' Gerhart Hauptmann: *Bahnwärter Thiel*', in *Die deutsche Novelle*, I, 268-83; F. Martini, ' Gerhart Hauptmann: *Bahnwärter Thiel*', in *Das Wagnis der Sprache*, (Stuttgart, 1954), pp. 56-98; W. Zimmermann, ' Gerhart Hauptmann: *Bahnwärter Thiel*', in *Deutsche Prosadichtungen unseres Jahrhunderts, Interpretationen für Lehrende und Lernende*, I (Düsseldorf, 1966), 69-87, first published as *Deutsche Prosadichtungen der Gegenwart*, I (Düsseldorf, 1956), 39-61.

2. Bennett, p. 238.

3. Martini, p. 74.

4. Von Wiese, p. 268.

5. Martini, p. 68. Once more, author and narrator are not distinguished.

6. E.g. von Wiese: 'Jede reflektierende Stellungnahme des Dichters ist vermieden' (p. 268), and Martini: 'Bewußt wird jede subjektive Identifikation mit dem Erzählten, jede direkte oder indirekte Selbstäußerung in ihm vermieden' (p. 65). At another point in his essay, von Wiese writes in a somewhat different vein: ' . . . es geht hier keineswegs um eine beliebige Wirklichkeitsnachahmung, der irgendwo anfängt und irgendwo aufhört, sondern um eine bestimmte Art künstlerischer Verwandlung, die sich zwar an die wirklichen Objekte hält, an die gegenständliche Umwelt oder an psychologisch erfassbare Seelenvorgänge, aber ihnen durch eine bestimmte Weise des Verknüpfens und Wiederholens eine durch das Sicht-und Meßbare weit hinausweisende Bedeutung verleiht' (p. 271). But it is still insufficient to see in this 'Verknüpfen und Wiederholen' the text's only deviation from or development of realism.

7. Silz (pp. 142-3) points to some of the theoretical inadequacies of the term 'Naturalism' which relate to this point.

8. These highly individual descriptions are on occasion thought of as stylistic defects; e.g., by Martini (p. 96), and by the array of early critics cited, apparently with sympathy, by S. D. Stirk in his introduction to the Blackwell edition of *Bahnwärter Thiel* and *Fasching* (Oxford, 1952), p. xxviii. This is a natural consequence of the assumption that the story is a 'realistic' or 'naturalistic' one; all that will not fit that assumption must be viewed as inconsistency and error.

9. Klein's (*Geschichte der deutschen Novelle*, p. 436) brief and undeveloped comment is certainly to the point here: 'Die Stille und die Stürme des Forstes, die unheimlichen Eindrücke, wenn ein Zug heranbraust—all das ist zugleich Ausdruck von Thiels Seele und Erlebnisweise. Stilles Grübeln und stürmische Erregung wogen ähnlich in ihm auf und ab.' Cf. also Martini: 'Die Antinomie dieser Mächte

ist das Symbol der Antimonie in Thiel selbst, in jenem Manne, aus dessen gelassener Ruhe und beseelter, stiller Innerlichkeit die wilde Gewalt vernichtend aufsteigen und ihn selbst zerstören wird' (p. 88). But a systematic development of this idea would necessitate his taking, for example, the later phrase 'spannten sich seine Muskeln' not as the poor attempt at theatrical effect which he believes it to be, but as part of the opposition of tension and relaxation which is to do with the sudden onrush of 'wilde Gewalt', in the train and Thiel. Requadt (pp. 105-6) also notes the connection of Thiel and the train, but thinks of this as showing Thiel's 'Verfallensein an das Maschinenwesen'.

10. The word 'allsontäglich' occurs twice in the first two pages; but the repetition cannot be considered a stylistic flaw in view of the importance here of the notion of similar actions repeated in a similar way. Cf. Requadt, p. 104.

11. Many critics, in talking of the forces unleashed here, are tempted to use rather generalised metaphysical and mythological language. For K. S. Guthke, the trains are 'Dämonen, Chiffren eines Unfasslichen', and in the outcome ' . . . bricht denn das Dämonische unaufhaltsam auf ihn [Thiel] herein' ('Gerhart Hauptmann', in *Einführung in die deutsche Literatur,* ed. J. Gearey and W. Schumann, New York, 1964, pp. 329-30). Von Wiese also invokes 'das Dämonische' (p. 280), and views the death of Tobias as the symbolic expression of 'das übermenschlich Chaotische' (p. 273). Martini speaks of 'überpersönliche Lebensmächte' (p. 73), finds in the descriptions of nature 'eine schaffend-zerstörerische Allmacht' (p. 83), and in those of the technological objects a 'nicht vom Menschen gelenkte und beherrschte, sondern aus sich selbst lebende Gewalt, als ein Elementares, welches das Elementare im Naturvorgang ablöst und überdonnert' (p. 86). My own view here is that notions such as 'das Dämonische' or 'das Elementare' are admittedly weighty but not very useful; they are too vague to say anything specific about this specific text, and they tend to inhibit further analysis by their grandiose air of finality. To talk of 'überpersonliche Mächte' in connection with Thiel, for example, does not help us to understand what he is or what happens to him, since the source of his personal catastrophe seems to be located elsewhere.

12. Von Wiese (p. 273) notes this parallel (following Ordon, p. 226, and Requadt, p. 105), and comments: 'Alles Unheimliche und Unbegreifliche verdichtet sich in dem Dingsymbol . . . ' But it is less helpful to call something a symbol than to say what it symbolises.

13. Stirk (p. xxv) also thinks the style of the story impressionistic.

14. Silz (p. 139) notes that 'the "recall" has an artistic effect', and he discusses possible meanings of it; von Wiese also notes the recall, but instead of interpreting it, sees 'Dämonie': 'Ist nicht alle Kreatur durch die Dämonie des Eisenbahnnetzes bedroht?' (p. 282).

15. Ordon (p. 229) does not interpret this motif in the light of its context in the story, but derives its significance directly from Jungian psychology: 'Mythology refers to it as the "waters of life" or the "rebirth" archetypal experience'. She concludes that the motif is not well worked out in the story, for otherwise it would mark 'rebirths' of Thiel's psyche.

16. Cf. Silz's accurate comment that ' . . . things that do affect him, without outward sign, tend to "go down" and accumulate, and erupt later' (p. 146).

17. Garten's view, shared in essence by many commentators, that Thiel is 'driven, by inexorable circumstances' (in 'Gerhart Hauptmann', *German Men of Letters,* ed. A. Natan, London, 1961, p. 240) is therefore not a useful view of his motivation.

James L. Hodge (essay date 1976)

SOURCE: "The Dramaturgy of Bahnwärter Thiel," in *Mosaic,* Vol. IX, No. 3, Spring, 1976, pp. 97-116.

[*In the following essay, Hodge interprets* Bahnwärter Thiel *as "a prose drama, patterned on classical Greek tragedy and influenced by a demonic, Dionysian concept of tragedy similar to that propounded by Nietzsche."*]

The symbolism ubiquitous in Hauptmann's novelle *Bahnwärter Thiel* (1888) has been interpreted from various perspectives. The trains and the weather have been interpreted by Professor Benno von Wiese[1] and by Professor Karl Guthke[2] as the expression of demonic forces. Professor Guthke specifically designates the demonic forces in *Bahnwärter Thiel* as "natural and technological." Some of the other symbols, such as the two stags and the two squirrels, have been interpreted by Marianne Ordon[3] as animal symbols for Thiel and Tobias.

Further interpretations of *Bahnwärter Thiel* should identify and explain the demonic power which underlies the technological and meteorological terror of trains and weather, and should encompass those other symbols which, Ordon suggests, should be the object of cooperative scholarly effort: the wine-bottles, the other animals, and so forth. One interpretation of *Bahnwärter Thiel* which comprehends all of the symbolism hitherto recognized in the story may be stated as a thesis: that *Bahnwärter Thiel* is a prose drama, patterned on classical Greek tragedy and influenced by a demonic, Dionysian concept of tragedy similar to that propounded by Nietzsche; that Hauptmann's story displays the full tragic rhythm (that is, tragic flaw, conflict, recognition, reversal, passion and resolution) and also the classical tragic conventions (chorus, prologue, complication, crisis, passion, denouement, exodus, and adherence to the unities); further, that this prose tragedy is founded, as was Greek tragedy, upon a "mythological" background, but that the mythology of *Bahnwärter Thiel* is a mixture of classical and modern motifs. The latter interpretation is, in a sense, an expansion and specification of Professor Guthke's analysis.

Because Hauptmann himself disclaimed Nietzsche as his "Vordermann," some justification of the above view may be in order. For example, Hauptmann had also referred to

Nietzsche as one of the shapers of the modern German theater.[4] Further, Professor Guthke describes a close affinity between Hauptmann's and Nietzsche's view of ancient Greece and of Greek drama:

> Man spürt: Im Gegensatz zur klassischen und frühromantischen Auffassung sieht Hauptmann mit Nietzsche die Daseinsform des griechischen Menschen nicht, genauer: nur in geringerm Grade als apollonisch massvoll, heiter and abgeklärt in der lebensbezwingenden Ordnungsstiftung, sondern vielmehr als dionysisch: als Hingabe an den elementaren Lebenstrieb, der ihn schon an Schopenhauers Philosophie gefesselt hatte, an den Rausch und die Ekstase, die hinabreissen in die Tiefen und in den Schmerz der Zerstörung, zugleich aber auch hinaufführen auf die Höhen des Genusses der "unsäglichen Wollust des Daseins," die Hauptmann auf griechischem Boden überkommt. Demeter, die Göttin der Erde . . .und Dionysos sind ihm entsprechend am stärksten gegenwärtig.[5]

A similar comparison is drawn in a discussion of *Indipohdi* in *Hauptmann und Shakespeare* by Felix A. Voigt and Walter A. Reichart: "Und wenn auch Hauptmann Nietzsche nicht als 'Vordermann' gelten lässt, so denkt man doch unwillkürlich an zwei Ideen dieses Philosophen: das ewig sich wiederholende Wunder des Lebenskreislaufes und den sich immer neu gestaltenden Willen zur Macht. . . ."[6]

Whether or not Hauptmann can be considered a disciple of Nietzsche, he does place a similar interpretation upon Greek life and drama. *Griechischer Frühling,*[7] especially that section which gives Hauptmann's impressions of Delphi—"shrine of Apollo and Dionysus" (p. 163)—is filled with reflections upon the nature and origin of drama. It is a lengthy homage to the people and the mythology whose influence he recognized even before he wrote *Bahnwärter Thiel* (pp. 15, 16). He speaks of myth and fantasy as the forces which created and encouraged Greek drama (p. 67), and several times ascribes the power of Greek drama to its function as a *Gottesdienst* (pp. 51-52, 79). He refers at least twice to the act of artistic creation as a "Dionysian act" (pp. 54, 72). He deplores the lack of such a creative force in his time (pp. 67-93) and also notes that Apollo and Dionysus still "people nature," for those who can perceive their influence (p. 77). In commenting on the worship of Demeter, he mentions the accompanying worship of Dionysus, implying the latter's influence upon the cult of Demeter, and further comparing the cult of Dionysus to the worship of Christ. The italics following are mine, emphasizing those words which bear most significance for this consideration:

> Man verehrte hier neben Demeter auch den Dionysos. Nimmt man hinzu, das der Mohn, als Sinnbild der Fruchtbarkeit, die heilige Blume der Demeter war, so bedeutet das, in zwiefacher Hinsicht, ekstatische *Schmerzens-* und *Glücksraserei.* Es bleibt ein seltsamer Umstand, dass *Brot, Wein* und *Blut,* dazu auch das Martyrium eines Gottes, sein Tod und seine Auferstehung noch heut den Inhalt eines *Mysteriums* bilden, das einen grossen Teil des Erdballs beherrscht.
>
> (p. 59)

The symbolism of *Bahnwärter Thiel* is drawn directly from this ancient creative force which Hauptmann experienced so personally twenty years after writing his Novelle. From the depth of emotion Hauptmann reveals in *Griechis-* *cher Frühling* in his discussions of Greek tragedy and its mythological and religious background, it may be surmised that the network of symbolism in *Bahnwärter Thiel* is partly a conscious and partly an inadvertent creation. Hauptmann's preoccupation with Greek drama, with Dionysus, and with the similarities between Dionysus and Christ had already provided him with material. Many passages of *Bahnwärter Thiel* could have been written in the heat of inspiration, incorporating automatically the demonic symbolism outlined below.

I

The mythology of *Bahnwärter Thiel* is not a commonly known story retold from the dramatist's own point of view, as is, for instance, the material of Sophocles' *Oedipus Rex.* Rather, it is a fund of common knowledge. The story was written just eighteen years after Nietzsche's *Geburt der Tragödie;* it was written during the period of Freud's first great influence, and it was written during the stress and turmoil of the Industrial Revolution. Hauptmann's predilection for social observation, for naturalistic description and for psychological characterization are encompassed here by a symbolism of contrasts. Persons and animals, natural and technical phenomena are a choric background for Thiel's thoughts and emotions. Violent sights and sounds are opposed to gentle creatures and mild weather. Night is opposed to day. In short, Dionysus is opposed to Apollo. The materials of this symbolic contrast are romanticized nature description, naturalistic social description, and pseudo- or pre-Freudian psychological description. These are the modern gods and demi-gods who lurk behind the scenes in the story, and who represent the latter-day incarnation of Pan, Dionysus, Apollo, *et al.*

The manifestations of this symbolism are perceived by Thiel, but they are not explained or analyzed for the reader. They are treated by the author just as the mythological material was treated by the Greek dramatist. The public is expected to recognize them—if not intellectually, then emotionally. It is their use, their placement in the story, and their frequent and seemingly unnecessary repetition which offer a clue to their deeper meaning.

At crucial moments in the story, certain creatures, objects and phenomena appear, and reflect the mood of the narration or of the main character. Night alternates with day in a significant pattern, storms occur during pivotal scenes, twilight separates one episode from another, trains rage by during violent emotional scenes, two stags are killed, two wine-bottles affect Thiel's life, a squirrel is called "der liebe Gott." These are the symbolic expressions of the mythology behind Hauptmann's tale. They give voice, in varying ways, to the greater conflict which underlies Thiel's conflict with Lene. They express for Thiel and the reader the dark, Dionysian force of life and death and, often only by contrast or implication, the opposed Apollonian world of reason, habit, and every-day reality. They are the choric media through which Nietzsche's dynamic division of tragedy has been adapted for application to psychological processes, and narrowed to fit the life of a railroad flagman.

This cosmic and psychological division is expressed through six discernible media: 1) the personalities of the three main characters; 2) the landscape or geography of the small area in which the story takes place; 3) the wine; 4) the weather and other natural phenomena; 5) the trains; 6) the various animals. These different media refer to the underlying mythology, to each other, and to events in the story.

The first medium of expression is the characters themselves. Thiel—a reserved and taciturn man—spends his working hours at night thinking of his first wife. He has made his shack a kind of memorial chapel in which he can commune with her memory, if not her spirit. He passes constantly from ecstatic thoughts and dreams of her to real-life confrontations with his second wife, whose aggressive forcefulness and sexual magnetism make him her subject. Tobias, who was born of the first marriage, is sacrificed systematically to the interests of his younger half-brother and to the bile of his stepmother. The only tender emotions displayed throughout the story are the feelings of Tobias and Thiel for one another. Thiel is paralyzed by Lene, and Tobias is victimized by her. The outstanding characteristics of the three personalities are Tobias' nearly constant misery, Lene's forceful and sensual brutality, and Thiel's terrible division between the real and the unreal, between agony and ecstasy, and between phlegm and passion.

Most of the "events" of the story are actually trains of thought in Thiel's mind, interspersed by actual occurrences. Such a psychological study would seem at first to have little to do with the stuff of Greek tragedy, but Hauptmann himself considered that thought, not action, was the true subject of the dramatist's art,[8] and that the task of modern drama was to present a "symbol of the soul."[9] In thought, he said, were all the elements of drama:

> Allem Denken liegt Anschauung zugrunde. Auch ist das Denken ein Ringen: also dramatisch. Jeder Philosophy, der das System seiner logischen Konstruktionen vor uns hinstellt, hat es aus Entscheidungen errichtet, die er in den Parteistreitigkeiten der Stimmen seines Innern getroffen hat: demnach halte ich das Drama für den Ausdruck ursprünglicher Denktätigkeit, auf hoher Entwicklungsstufe, freilich ohne dass jene Entscheidungen getroffen werden, auf die es dem Philosophen ankommt.
>
> Aus dieser Anschauungsart ergeben sich Reihen von Folgerungen, die das Gebiet des Dramas über das der herrschenden Dramaturgien nach allen Seiten hin unendlich erweitern, so dass nichts, was sich dem äusseren oder innern Sinn darbietet, von dieser Denkform, die zur Kunstform geworden ist, ausgeschlossen werden kann.[10]

As Hauptmann himself has noted, the period during which he wrote *Bahnwärter Thiel* was one in which he felt repulsed by the "barbarism" of the theater of his time. He had always felt himself drawn to the drama, had always felt the art of Shakespeare and Kleist to be his model. When he was "driven" to the Novelle and the novel as means of expression, this inclination was still strong within him, and thereafter reasserted itself emphatically.[11] It is difficult to believe that his inclination toward drama and his admiration for two masters of the psychological drama did not have some effect on the prose he wrote in this period. *Bahnwärter Thiel* is the dramatization of a man's thoughts. The symbolism which surrounds the three main characters elevates this psychological study to the level of a prose tragedy patterned on a Greek model, illuminated by Freud and interpreted according to Nietzsche.

The second medium for symbolism is the geography or landscape of *Bahnwärter Thiel.* As already mentioned, Thiel has created a sort of chapel in his shack by the railroad, and he passes daily from his misery at home to his happiness here. He also passes from a world of physical, sexual fulfillment to a world of spiritual and emotional fulfillment. His shack is located in an isolated waste (*Einöde*) and cut off from the town by a forest and a river.

The isolation of Thiel's place of work is a geographical reinforcement of his spiritual isolation from Lene, from Tobias, and in general from the everyday world. He communes with the spirit of his first wife and quite literally forgets everything else except the forcefully intrusive and demanding trains. Outside of the brief and frantic visitations of the trains, Thiel is alone in a world of his own. When he has night duty, he spends hours with a picture of Minna, a Bible and a song-book before him on the table. Sometimes he sings the whole night through. Or perhaps he "chants" for "[er] geriet hierbei in eine Ekstase, dic sich zu Gesichten steigerte, in denen er die Tote leibhaft vor sich sah" (p. 40).[12] When he thinks of Lene coming to his shack, he fears intrusion upon "sein Heiligstes" (p. 51).

The river Thiel crosses is the same river many others have crossed before him. They did not call it the Spree; they called it Styx or Lethe or some other name. It appears in many mythologies, and it functions as a barrier and a path to the "otherworld" of folk legend. To cross this river is to enter the realm of the dead, as Thiel enters the realm of Minna, his first wife. The dead were the first gods honored by men, and were still feared and honored as demi-gods within the framework of other, later religions. Thus the Spree is more than a stream to pass over on the way to work; it is the boundary between world and otherworld. As such, it always offers difficulties to those who wish to retrieve someone from the otherworld, e.g., the men who carry Thiel back home after Tobias' death: "Es kostete Mühe, ihn über die Spree zu bringen" (p. 65). That Thiel crosses the Spree at dawn and dusk is a reinforcement of this symbolism, as will be seen in the later consideration of the weather.

The forest through which Thiel passes is certainly a further separation of Thiel from reality, but it is also much more. Two elements of the description explain its symbolic purpose. The latter part of Thiel's walk to work leads through the edge of the forest, where older trees protect the seedlings planted there. Through nature, Hauptmann mirrors the relationship Thiel, like a parent of any species, should have with his offspring. Thiel passes daily through a reminder of his failure as a father.

The second element of the description is quite simple. This is a pine forest. Perhaps a pine forest is of no great botanical significance in Silesia, but it is of some symbolic significance to the interpretation of *Bahnwärter Thiel.* This forest, together with the wine-bottles, the weather and the trains to be mentioned below, defines the demonic forces which plague Thiel throughout the story. The *thyrsus* or staff carried by Dionysus and his followers was tipped by a pine-cone. The origin of certain Dionysian rites was connected with the hanging of village maidens from a pine tree.[13] This forest recalls the evergreen forests which Hauptmann himself peopled with bacchic worshippers in *Griechischer Frühling* (pp. 68-69). It represents the re-consecration of those trees and forests of Germany whose pagan sanctity was removed by centuries of Christian prejudice against devil worship—the forests of which he is reminded in *Griechischer Frühling* when he senses the presence of divinity in the Grecian landscape:

> Warum scheuen wir uns und erachten für trivial, unsere heimischen Gegenden, Berge, Flüsse, Täler zu besingen, ja ihre Namen nur zu erwähnen in Gebilden der Poesie? Weil alle diese Dinge, als Natur jahrtausendelang für teuflisch erklärt, nie wahrhaft wieder geheiligt worden sind. Hier, aber haben Götter und Halbgötter, mit jedem weissen Berggipfel, jedem Tal und Tälchen, jedem Baum und Bäumchen, jedem Fluss und Quell vermählt, alles geheiligt. Geheiligt war das, was über der Erde, auf ihr und in ihr ist. Und rings um sie her das Meer war geheiligt. Und so vollkommen war diese Heiligung, dass der Spätgeborene, um Jahrtausende Verspätete, dass der Barbar noch heut—und sogar in einem Bahncoupé—von ihr im tiefsten Wesen durchdrungen wird.

> (pp. 44-45)

The symbolism of the pine forest is continued and expanded by the third symbolistic medium: the wine-bottles. Not only did Dionysus invent wine; he spread its use throughout the world. The Greek drama—springing from Dionysian rites as later drama grew from Christian rituals—acknowledged its ancestry even by its use of make-up. On the stage of early Greek drama walked actors whose faces had been smeared with wine dregs.[14] As the Greek drama grew from one actor to two and at last to a decisive three, the primitive make-up Thespis had introduced was foregone, but the birth and development of drama were clearly due to, and influenced by, the cult of Dionysus, the god of wine.

Seen in this light, the two bottles of wine are extremely important in the symbology of *Bahnwärter Thiel*. The first bottle is mentioned at the very beginning of the story:

> Im Verlaufe von zehn Jahren war er zweimal krank gewesen; das eine Mal infolge eines vom Tender einer Maschine während des Vorbeifahrens herabgefallenen Stückes Kohle, welches ihn getroffen und mit zerschmettertem Bein in den Bahngraben geschleudert hatte; das andere Mal einer Weinflasche wegen, die aus dem vorüberrasenden Schnellzuge mitten auf seine Brust geflogen war.

> (p. 37)

The second bottle is one of the three things, outside of the above-mentioned accidents, which interrupted the regular course of Thiel's work. On a hot summer day, Thiel had found a corked wine-bottle whose contents felt glowing hot and, upon removal of the cork, "einer Fontäne gleich herausquoll, also augenscheinlich gegoren war" (p. 41).

What is the significance of one wine-bottle which brings a violent interruption to Thiel's routine of work and life, and of another which he finds, uncorks, hides away, and later cannot find? Do they represent the dark, emotional influence of Dionysus, " . . .the god who is destroyed, who disappears . . . and then is born again?"[15] Do they repre-

sent the "destructive demonic" force which Professor Guthke finds throughout *Bahnwärter Thiel*[16]—the same demonic force which Hauptmann has equated with Dionysus in *Griechischer Frühling* (p. 92)? Do they represent this same force bottled up in Thiel? Hauptmann has commented elsewhere on human psychology in remarkably similar terms: "Wer fühlt, fühlend denkt und erkennt, dem sind alle menschlichen Bekenntnisse und Erkenntnisse . . . gleich *verkorkten Flaschen* mit eingeschlossenen Notschreien. . . ."[17]

The force which causes an upset in Thiel's routine, which rises like a geyser from the uncorked bottle, is passion. The dark, Dionysian force of creation and destruction which underlies the world of reason and calm is mirrored in the upsetting accident and in the gushing, fermented liquid. The image is carried on after Thiel has dreamed of Minna in Part III of the story. In a long passage interspersed by images descriptive of intoxication or envelopment, Thiel's mental state is described idiomatically in the same terms as the contents of the wine-bottle: "Es gärte in seinem Hirn" (p. 51). Thiel's passions have reached a state of explosive fermentation. The dark and passionate life-force he had once recognized, felt, and lost, now wells up in him to sweep away all thought of reason and calm. Just as the first drinkers of wine neglected to add water, became intoxicated, and went temporarily insane, so Thiel is overcome by passions which have too long been undiluted by his gentler feelings.

Thiel's emotional sickness and its accompanying visions are merely the modern vestige of an ecstatic experience which was once vital, real, and even healthy to the early worshippers of Dionysus: "Eine grosse Summe halluzinatorischer Kräfte sehen wir heute als krankhaft an, und der gesunde Mensch hat sie zum Schweigen gebracht, wenn auch nicht ausgestossen. Und doch hat es Zeiten gegeben, wo der Mensch sie voll Ehrfurcht gelten und menschlich auswirken liess" (*Griechischer Frühling*, p. 31).

The fourth medium of expression is weather, and weather too has something to do with Dionysus. Robert Graves notes that the Hyades, who were entrusted with the care of the young god, were variously called the "passionate ones," the "roaring ones," and the "raging ones," and that their name itself means "the rain-makers."[18] Further, although Dionysus was originally the god of wine, "afterwards he became the god of vegetation and warm moisture."[19] William Fox notes also that the Bacchantes (whose relationship to Dionysus is well known) were the divinities of the winds and were conceived to be storms—wanton, wild and free." Their rites included the rending and eating of young animals.[20]

The characteristics of Dionysus and the deities connected with him, the above consideration of the wine-bottles, and the following consideration of the trains—especially of the monstrous spectacle they present and of the repetitive description of steam clouds issuing from their stacks—are signs along a trail blazed by Ordon. She states that a motif of *Bahnwärter Thiel* is: "God is a beast." The Bacchantes answer this description; the weather and the trains, as will be seen, also answer it. Ordon further notes the recurrence of gushing, warm liquid in descriptions of the wine-bottles, of the milk Lene pours for the baby, of the trains, and of the weather. She remarks that the recurrence of such a theme cannot be wholly accidental—although it may in part be inadvertent—and suggests that further interpretation on this point is needed. Hauptmann himself lends indirect support to these statements when, in *Griechischer Frühling,* he speaks of the "Gewitter der Tragödie" in the same passage which describes the diminution of the Dionysian force ("das Nachtgeborene") in the presence of daylight (pp. 46-47).

In several passages in *Bahnwärter Thiel,* Hauptmann has used the elements to complement and symbolize the Dionysian passions in the flagman. Rain, hail, mist and wind, together with various stages of darkness, predict and reflect. Thiel's inner storms of emotion. Stormy weather and darkness are constantly opposed to sunlight, calm, and the natural, quiet sounds of the forest. A quick review of the meteorological phenomena in *Bahnwärter Thiel* will demonstrate their relationship to Thiel's moods and to the events of the story, and will further emphasize their relationship to the Dionysian forces they symbolize.

The first mention of weather or time of day is in Part II, which begins by describing the fine June morning on which Thiel is coming home from work. After his arrival, Thiel takes Tobias down to the Spree where the children of the village gather to play and to be amused and taught by "Father Thiel." After lunch, Thiel lies down for a rest, and at 4:45 he leaves for work.

In the meantime, the day has changed markedly. A blue, transparent mist rises out of the earth and distorts Thiel's image of the landscape through which he passes. A heavy, milky sky hangs above, and black pools of water reflect "die trübe Natur noch trüber . . . " Thiel notes the "furchtbares Wetter." A moment later, "er fühlte dunkel, dass er etwas vergessen haben müsse." Thiel's mood is premonitory as he turns back to his house to retrieve his forgotten lunch. The landscape is rendered in shades of gray and black. a gloomy picture is reflected still more gloomily, and the weather promises to be "fearful." Darkness and dampness rise out of the earth to surround him and to predict the passion which will soon rise and be suppressed in him. Even the idiomatic use of "dunkel" in the phrase, "er fühlte dunkel," lends a note of glumness.

When Thiel arrives home, he overhears Lene scolding and beating Tobias. Lene's words are described in terminology which is both idiomatic and meteorological: "Unmittelbar darauf entlud sich ein neues Hagelwetter von Schimpfwörtern." When he witnesses the brutal treatment to which Tobias is subjected, Thiel suppresses an emotion which is described—in terms reminiscent of the weather in the previous passage—as "etwas Furchtbares." Thereupon he retrieves his lunch and returns to work. When he has arrived at his shack and has completed his preparations for the work ahead, the wind is rising and rushes humming through the telegraph wires. The sun casts a receding purple glow over the scene from under a huge cloud, and then begins slowly to withdraw the last light of day. At this point, Thiel sees the train coming. When the roaring machine has passed, Thiel wakes as from a dream and whispers, "Minna." Returning to the shack, he tries to dig a bit in the new plot of ground, but gives it up. In a few minutes he is gripped by his vision of Minna. The rising storm accompanies a rising outburst of emotion in Thiel. The meteorological and the psychological storms apparently suppressed so shortly before have only awaited the passing of sunlight and of reason, and now unleash their force on man and nature.

Thiel's vision of Minna is described by Professor von Wiese as the "novellistic middle point" of the novelle.[21] At last Thiel recognizes Tobias' misery, and he dreams of Minna fleeing painfully and fearfully along the rails. The weather again confirms Thiel's dark and raging emotions. Both his mental state and the aspect of nature have changed suddenly, violently and, to all appearances, simultaneously, from disquieted rest to uninhibited turmoil. The forest roars, the wind throws hail and rain against the shack. A reproduction of Lene's "Hagelwetter" and a barometer of Thiel's progressive emotional confusion is supplied: "Erst dumpf und verhalten grollend, wälzte er (der Donner) sich näher in kurzen, brandenden Erzwellen, bis er, zu Riesenstössen anwachsend, sich endlich, die ganze Atmosphäre überflutend, dröhnend, schütternd und brausend entlud." It is now pitch dark, the shack is shaking, nature has gone mad. Only the train is needed to complete the spectacle of raging, furious passion.

After this emotional seizure, Thiel regains his habitual composure by going on his rounds at dawn. The wind and rain have also grown quiet. As night and storm withdraw, Thiel recovers his self-control and his phlegmatic devotion to habit. At 6:00 A.M., he is relieved. One sentence, standing noticeably alone, reports: "Es war ein herrlicher Sonntagmorgen." The following passage describes a day that is indeed glorious, and Thiel returns home in a subdued mood.

There is no better or clearer interpretation of the above phenomena than a passage from *Griechischer Frühling.* In folkloric terms, Hauptmann speaks of the tragic figures of ancient drama and describes their resemblance to departed souls. In so doing, he defines indirectly Minna's nocturnal appearance, Thiel's double life, and the significant alternation of night and day, fair weather and foul in *Bahnwärter Thiel:*

> Es ist in ihnen etwas von den Qualen abgeschiedener Seelen enthalten, die durch die unwiderstehliche Macht einer Totenbeschwörung zu einer verhassten Existenz im Lichte gezwungen sind. Auf diese Weise wecken sie die Empfindung in uns, als stünden sie unter einem Fluch, der ihnen aber, solange sie noch als Menschen unter Menschen ihr Leben lebten, nicht anhaftete. Der schlichte Eindruck einer realen landschaftlichen Natur bei Tageslicht widerlegt jeden Fluch und zwingt der bis zum Zerreissen überspannten Seele den Segen natürlicher Masse auf.

> (p. 100)

The curse does indeed seem to have been laid temporarily. Sunday passes without incident, excepting Lene's announced intention to go out to the plot of ground the next morning, and excepting Thiel's hungry gaze as Lene disrobes for bed. The next day is clear of clouds. Lene plants, Tobias plays, Thiel works. And then the boy is killed. He is not killed during the night or during a raging storm, for this is the first and only invasion of Thiel's otherworld by any real person. Until now, Thiel has been in the company of no one but Minna and the brief, shadow-like figure of his relief man. When the world of sunlight and reason, habit and convention, comes to Thiel and to the scene of his recent, orgiastic emotional revelation, it comes as well to the altar of Dionysus.

After the accident, it is midday, and stifling hot. When Lene and the stranger have left with Tobias' body, Thiel finds that his throat is burning and that he cannot move. He sleeps, and is awakened by the signal for the local train. He envisions Tobias' broken body. A curt sentence reports: "Dann wurde es Nacht." And the narrative continues directly thereafter, making an unmistakable connection between Thiel's loss of consciousness and the fading of day: "Nach einer Weile erwachte er aus einer Ohnmacht." The day has been swept away by the events of the morning, and night is coming for Thiel in more than one sense.

When he wakes, he raves to his dead wife that he will kill Lene. The weather comments again on Thiel's mental state: "Die Sonne goss ihre letzte Glut über den Forst, dann erlosch sie. Die Stämme der Kiefern streckten sich wie bleiches, verwestes Gebein zwischen die Wipfel hinein, die wie grauschwarze Moderschichten auf ihnen lasteten." The last glow of the sun is seen briefly as it catches on a small cloud. Thiel's numbness is gone, his first unbelieving misery has passed, and he realizes fully that Tobias is dead. As the last, rose-colored cloud passes and cold, steel-blue sky remains, so Tobias passes and leaves his father empty and unforgiving. Everything is new and strange to Thiel. It becomes "keller-kalt." Thiel almost kills the baby before he realizes his madness. A solitary sentence starkly mirrors Thiel's mental state: "Ein kaltes Zwielicht lag über der Gegend." The previous twilight signaled the new day; this twilight is the harbinger of a night from which Thiel will not awake.

When the body is brought back, Thiel has sunk into a deep, terrible detachment: "Es wurde dunkler." When he faints, Thiel is carried home through the forest under the light of a moon which paints the faces of those in the forest a corpse-like shade. The last mention of natural phenomena occurs when Lene falls asleep. A cloud covers the moon and, presumably in the darkness, Thiel kills Lene and the baby. From the first to the last, the changing weather has reflected the basic conflict in Thiel's life. At the end, it predicts and reflects his permanent flight from reason and sanity.

The motif of the trains—the fifth medium of symbolic expression—is closely connected with those of the wine and the weather. Wine introduces and defines the demonic, Dionysian force present in the flagman, and does so in cooperation with the trains. The first wine-bottle, in fact, flies from a passing train and strikes Thiel on the chest, just as a piece of coal flew from a passing train and threw him injured into the ditch. The demonic force symbolized by the train and the symbolic meaning of the wine are allied early in the story by these events.

The imagery of the trains spouting clouds of steam recalls Dionysus' connection with warm moisture. It reminds us as well of the second wine-bottle and its explosive contents. The Silesian express is especially reminiscent of this. The train whistles—significantly, three times—and white rays of steam "quollen kerzengerade empor." This phenomenon is noted just before and just after Tobias' death. The train, which is the instrument of death, thus

emphasizes its relationship to the wine-bottles and to the god whose province comprehends wine, warm moisture and sacrificial death.

The weather, as shown above, reflects the demonic force which rises and subsides in Thiel. During the moments of greatest passion, or in scenes which predict these moments, the trains and the weather are combined to provide a massive, roaring, rushing spectacle. Even the coins thrown by sympathetic passengers provide a connection, for they are described as a "rain of coins"; the sparks which fly from the train are portentously described as a "rain of blood."

The first train appears shortly before Thiel's vision, and in conjunction with the first instance of bad weather, in Part IIIA—that is, in the first division of Part III. At the end of IIIA, which has been preparing gradually for the violent scene in Part IIIB, the train passes, and its description rivals that of the storm in its wildness of sights and sounds. A panting and roaring swells through the air, the quiet is ripped asunder, there is a frenzied raging, the earth trembles, a heavy wave of air passes, there is a cloud of dust, steam and smoke, and a snorting monster races by. Then, as it swelled, the sound dies away, just as Thiel's passion will swell and die away in IIIB, accompanied by the weather. Some of the words used in the description of the train are repeated twice or more in reference to the storm and to Thiel's emotions: e.g., "brausen" and "zerreissen."

The second train appears as Thiel struggles with the revelation that he has betrayed Minna and Tobias. Its sparks flame out like drops of preternatural light sinking into the earthly atmosphere. He stumbles outside to watch it roar by. The train lights shine like the eyes of a monster and the sparks seem to be a rain of blood from heaven. In his horror, he remembers the apparition of Minna on the tracks, and acts out the scene which is later to transpire with Tobias. He wants to stop the raging train, but he is too late.

Section IIIC begins with the Silesian express as it rolls over Tobias. Later, the panting machine appears again to return Thiel's dead son to him. Thiel collapses, " . . . in dem Augenblick, als der Zug sich in Bewegung setzen wollte." The last mention of the train records Thiel's first successful attempt to bring one of the monsters to a halt. The express has to stop because Thiel is sitting in the middle of the tracks—quite insane.

While the motif of the trains reflects the passions within Thiel, the signals for the trains partition the moods of the story. They always occur in threes; three, or a multiple thereof, is a "magic number" in most European folklores. The first signal introduces the ominous, rising wind of Part IIIA. The second shakes Thiel from his dream of Minna and brings him out to the reflecting horror of the train. The third introduces the express which kills Tobias. The fourth wakes Thiel from his mad attempt to kill the baby and leads into his imagined viewing of the doctor who examines Tobias. The fifth introduces the train which returns Tobias' body.

Even Lene has a connection with the trains. She too is a destructive force, and she too represents the passions by which Thiel is ruled. After the express has halted "anxiously," we are told that Lene is crying and anxious too. When she and the stranger carry Tobias away, they are described as "ein Zug." At several points in the story—for instance, when she is digging in the plot—Lene, like the train, is described as "eine Maschine."

The train motif alternately supports the imagery provided by descriptions of Lene, of the weather and of the wine. Its ultimate significance is based upon these comparisons, but is something more than their total. Whereas the wine-bottle and the pine forest announce the presence of Dionysus and the weather provides a manifestation of this presence, the trains are his earthly representative. While Lene is an agent of the destructive force, the trains are its instrument of death. As the rites of Dionysus required the sacrifice of a young boy,[22] so does the ritual passing of the train. Dionysus—the horned child crowned with serpents—takes his sacrifice on the railroad tracks which at one point are compared to serpents. Tobias, who has been sacrificed spiritually to his stepmother's malice because of his father's physical desire, is sacrificed bodily to the monstrous passion which is his father's unacknowledged god.

Tobias' death is a Bacchanalian rite and the "mysterious solemnity" which hovers over the passengers is the solemnity of those who have participated in a ritual mystery. They are the "schaudernde Menge" of which Hauptmann speaks in describing the Pythian rites.[23] The death of Lene and the baby are merely extensions of a ritual sacrifice which has been made to an allconsuming passion. After the murders, Thiel returns to the tracks—that is, to the sacrificial altar—where for the first time his passion is spent; and for the first time, he stops the express.

The repetitive symbolism of the trains and the wine—especially the descriptions involving blood, smoke and vapor—are reflected often in *Griechischer Frühling.* Similar terminology and imagery occur most noticeably in a long passage which begins by describing the Pythian rites and defining tragedy in terms of human sacrifice (italics are mine):

> Wenn zu Beginn der grossen *Opferhandlung, die das Schauspiel der Griechen ist,* das *schwarze Blut* des Bocks in die Opfergefässe schoss, so wurde dadurch das spätere höhere, wenn auch nur scheinbare Menschenopfer nur vorbereitet: das *Menschenopfer, das die blutige Wurzel der Tragödie ist.*

> (p. 79)

In the same passage (pp. 79-81), Hauptmann mentions the "bloody vapor" which rises from the stage to the blood-thirsty gods. He speaks of the springs which feed the souls of men, and especially that most important mystical source: "der springende Brunnen des Bluts." He speaks of the vapors of these springs as "pregnant with a fearful madness." He defines tragedy in the terms of Thiel's experience, as "Angst, Not, Gefahr, Pein, Qual, Marter . . .Tücke, Verbrechen, Niedertracht . . . Mord, Blutgier, Blutschande, Schlächterei—wobei die Blutschande nur gewaltsam in das Bereich des Grausens gesteigert ist." Finally, in terms parallel to the night-day opposition in *Bahnwärter Thiel,* he imagines to himself how the smoke, vapor and fumes of Dionysus' sacrificial altars roiled upward past the nearby cliffs and darkened the sun: e.g., Apollo himself.

The most interesting parallel to *Bahnwärter Thiel* occurs in one of Hauptmann's apparently casual descriptions of the Geek scenery and people in *Griechischer Frühling.* Hauptmann finds himself surrounded by "Parnassian shepherds and shepherd dogs." The blond heads of the men are unmistakably archaic in form. Their glance reveals a "Dionysian fire." Just as he believes that his Parnassian dream is dreamed out, his attention is arrested by something. Thereafter follows a description which is reminiscent, both in imagery and phraseology, of many scenes in *Bahnwärter Thiel.* It is specifically related to the train motif, to Tobias and to the animal symbols discussed below:

> . . . an der kleinen Haltestelle der Eisenbahn . . .finden wir ein gefesseltes schwarzes Lamm . . . Es trägt den Ausdruck hoffnungsloser Fügung im Angesicht . . . Schliesslich legt man das arme, unsäglich leidende, schwarze parnassische Lamm mit zusammengebundenen Füssen dicht an die Geleise, damit es leicht zu verladen ist. Ich sehe noch, wie es an seinen Fesseln reisst und verzweifelt emporzuspringen versucht, als die Maschine herandonnert und gewaltig an ihm vorüberdröhnt.

> (pp. 93-94)

With this dramatic flourish, Hauptmann ends his passage on Parnassus and his extended discussion of Apollo, Dionysus, and sacrificial tragedy.

The sixth medium for symbolism in *Bahnwärter Thiel* is the animals, and they are really supporting symbols. Some, like the woodpecker and the birds, perform the same predicting or reflecting function fulfilled by the weather. The crows in Part II accompany the premonitory weather. The birds of Part IIIA, which are ranged silently along the telephone wires, may predict the silent spectators of Part IIIC, who are silently ranged along the windows of the passenger cars. The woodpecker of Part IIIA flies "laughing" over Thiel's head, "ohne dass er eines Blickes gewürdigt wurde." As noted by Mrs. Ordon, the very same phrase is used later to describe Thiel's disregard of Lene when she cries hysterically after Tobias' death. The premonitory laugh is repeated just before Thiel's dream when a "short, challenging laugh" escapes his lips. As Grimm notes, the woodpecker in German mythology was a sacred bird, often associated with predicting the future.[24] In *Griechischer Frühling* Hauptmann speaks of birds as prophets (p. 61) and as incarnations of the gods (pp. 53-54).

The more meaningful animal symbols include the first crow and the poodle. Thiel passes a shabby poodle and a hooded crow in Part II on his way back to the house. The crow screeches, spreads its wings, and floats away on the wind. Seconds later Thiel arrives home to hear Lene screeching at Tobias, who merely "whimpers" in reply. The poodle and the crow predict the scene Thiel is about to witness at home. The very shabbiness of the poodle reflects Tobias' unhappy condition. Later, after Tobias' death, Thiel refers to Lene as "Stiefmutter, *Raben*mutter," thus reinforcing the symbol of the crow and again identifying Lene's predatory relationship to Tobias.

The poodle invites consideration of a related symbol: the "poodle-cap." This is not the only term Hauptmann could have used, as he reveals elsewhere in the story by using the name, "Plüschmützchen." If the crow is to be Lene and the poodle Tobias, then what is the poodle-cap? It is a living thing to Thiel when he sits on the tracks fondling it at the end of the story. It is the object of a tender regard which he might have shown to Tobias himself. Just as the shabby poodle has described Tobias' sorry condition, so the cap memorializes his sacrificial death on these very tracks.

Supporting the symbolism of the poodle are the two stags. The first, as noted by Ordon, is run over by the express and thus predicts Tobias' similar death. The incident is mentioned as one of the three "events" in several years of Thiel's routine existence. The others were the passing of the special, imperial train and the discovery of the corked wine-bottle. The second stag appears after Tobias' death. Upon hearing the train whistle, it leaps from the tracks and disappears into the forest with its family. Ordon suggests that this stage represents the proper, natural father protecting his family.

Thus the first stage predicts Tobias' immolation and the second—like the older trees of the pine forest—reproaches Thiel for his unfatherly behavior. To this we may add that the stag was a sacred animal in German mythology and was considered to be a "pathfinder" or one which "showed the way."[25] We may note also that the word "Bock" could have connotations of sacrifice for Hauptmann, for it is with the same word that he describes the ritual Greek sacrifice in *Griechischer Frühling* (p. 79).

We must come eventually to the squirrel who is "der liebe Gott." The animal is first seen by Tobias who stops picking flowers to ask suddenly, "Vater, ist das der liebe Gott?" Thiel replies, "Närrischer Kerl," and the narration continues. Later, after Thiel has said he would kill Lene, after the weather has turned cold and the sky steel blue, a single, late rose-colored cloud floats by. The cloud has already been suggested as a symbol for Tobias and for the last calm and tender emotions in Thiel's life. Immediately upon the passing of this cloud, Thiel notices a squirrel scurrying across the tracks. "Der liebe Gott springt über den Weg," he thinks. Thiel repeats his nonsense phrase several times, then realizes that he is raving. He fights to preserve his mental equilibrium, but he cannot. When he hears the baby cry, he goes temporarily mad: "Was wollte er tun? Was trieb ihn hierher? Ein wirbelnder Strom von Gefühlen und Gedanken verschlang diese Fragen." His passions have once again taken possession of him, and he does not know why. Suddenly he remembers. "'Der liebe Gott springt über den Weg,' jetzt wusste er, was das bedeuten wollte. 'Tobias'— sie hatte ihn gemordet."

Why should this phrase mean not only Tobias but Tobias' death? To Thiel the harmless squirrel may not symbolize God so much as Tobias' conception of God. In the boy's naïve world, God could perhaps be a lovable, small creature. Not in Thiel's world. When he sees the squirrel, Thiel must think of his harmless, helpless son. He must remember that Tobias too tried to "jump across the track," and was killed in the process. He must recall both Lene's guilt and his own. Driven by this poignant reminder of Tobias' immolation, he makes his first attempt on the baby's life. Sacrifice begets sacrifice.

The "mythology" behind *Bahnwärter Thiel,* then, is a combination of technological and natural symbols. Most of these symbols are portentous, sinister, demonic, Dionysian. Others, such as the poodle, the squirrel and the one stag, are representative of the innocent sacrifice to these demonic forces. Built upon this psychological, technological and natural "mythology" is a prose tragedy, which interprets its "myth" through the career of its protagonist.

II

Granted that the above may present a case for the "mythology" of *Bahnwärter Thiel,* what can be said for the story's technical similarities to a Greek drama? Let us consider first the three unities. Hauptmann has not restricted the time of action to twenty-four hours, as some Neo-Classicists might have insisted he do, but he has told the essential story of Thiel's life in little more than seventy-two hours. The convention of time is hardly disturbed by this slight expansion. The action itself begins when Thiel returns home from work on Saturday morning. The scene between Tobias and Lene and Thiel's dream take place on Saturday. Thiel returns home Sunday for an eventful day. Monday Tobias is killed; on Monday night, Thiel kills Lene and the baby. On Tuesday morning, Thiel is found sitting on the tracks.

Hauptmann adheres to the convention of place with classic formality. The "scenes" all take place in or around Thiel's home or near his shack at the railroad. Because of the compression of time, the small number of characters, and the concentration on Thiel's reactions to a situation which has finally and suddenly come to a climax, the convention of unity of action is also observed.

The number of actors and their roles are significant when *Bahnwärter Thiel* is regarded as a prose adaptation of Greek tragedy. There are just three "actors" in the story. When Sophocles created the third actor for the Greek stage, he gave Greek tragedy its final fullness of characterization and interplay of personalities. The *protagonist,* or primary speaker, took the longest part and spoke most of the lines. He was complemented by the *deuteragonist,* or second speaker, and by the *tritagonist,* or third speaker. The necessary tensions, conflicts and resolutions could be found within these three characters, with the minor characters and the chorus lending occasional background information and comment. Thus the tensions and even most of the information necessary to tragic drama in *Oedipus Rex* are contained in the characters of Oedipus, Tiresias and Jocasta. In *Bahnwärter Thiel* the flagman himself is the *protagonist* and "speaks" most of the lines through his varying trains of thought. The *deuteragonist* is Lene, who provides conflict and contrast; and the *tritagonist* is the unfortunate Tobias.

The perfect *protagonist* of Greek drama was of course a nobleman whose ruin was brought about by Fate and by his *hamartia,* or tragic fault. Thiel is by no means a nobleman, for he lives in an age when drama has taken the common man as its hero, as in *Die Weber.* On the other hand, Thiel is ruined by mysterious and god-like forces similar to the Fate implied in Greek tragedy, and he does exhibit a tragic flaw. Thiel's *hamartia* is the same fault which destroys Shakespeare's melancholy Dane. As we are told by Frank Lucas, "Hamlet's Tragic Error is his failure to act; and this is doubtless a moral flaw, such as it is usual to suppose that the *hamartia* must always be."[26]

Thiel, like Hamlet, does not act. His last chance to act is in Part II, when he comes upon Lene scolding Tobias. Lene could withstand nothing he might say or do at this vulnerable moment, but he suppresses his emotions and is silent. His silence allows Lene to turn the tables by scolding him for returning at this unusual time, and the issue of the story is decided. Thiel *will* not act. He will not act until too late when he thinks to save Minna from the train. He will not act to prevent Lene's carelessness, and he will not see Tobias until he has already been hit by the train. His life has been too routine, methodical and, in a strange way, comfortable, to allow him to act until he no longer has anything to lose. Just as Hamlet realizes the plot against his life and only then takes his revenge, so Thiel sees his son killed—and his life ruined—before he acts against Lene.

The *protagonist* has another, technical function to fulfill. He sings both solo and with the chorus. Thiel's thoughts are his solos, and the concert of weather, trains and other phenomena is manifestly a chorus accompaniment of certain of Thiel's "monologues." Thus Thiel fulfills the role of *protagonist* by speaking most of the lines, by yielding to his *hamartia,* and by singing both solo and with the chorus.

The chorus consists of nearly all the objects, animals and natural phenomena which appear in **Bahnwärter Thiel,** and consists further of the briefly seen, shadow-like, supporting characters, such as the conductor and the passengers. From the solemnity of the passengers to the raging tumult of the trains, from the laugh of the woodpecker to the eerie light of the moon, this chorus predicts, reflects, recalls, and comments upon events and emotions in Thiel's three day tragedy. Each of these symbols has some significance for Thiel and his tragic fate. The raging appearances of the trains, for instance, predict the nature of the tragedy, just as the phrase, "The pistols of my father" recurrently predicts the outcome of *Hedda Gabler,* and as the chorus ominously and recurrently mentions a "net" in *Agamemnon.*[27]

Of course a prose tragedy must evince more than a few of the proper conventions. There must also be a clearly discernible tragic rhythm. An outline of such a tragic rhythm and its conventions may be as follows:

1) *prologos* or prologue—background material supplied by a kind of narrator;

2) *parados*—the entrance of the chorus;

3) *epeisodia*—episodes or scenes.

The episodes are divided by:

4) *stasima*—the various utterances of the chorus when present on stage.

The last element is:

5) *exodos*—the final scene and often the last utterance of the chorus.

The *epeisodia* or scenes are further divisible into five steps which articulate the action surrounding the *protagonist.* These are:

1) complication—the events which entangle the character in a situation whose only resolution is his ruin or death;

2) crisis—the moment which may bring *anagnorisis* (recognition) or *peripateia* (a drastic turn of events) or both;

3) passion—the "Scene of Suffering" and/or "Death on Stage";

4) denouement—the inevitable unraveling of plot which completes the ruin of the *protagonist;*

5) *exodus*—the final judgment of the *protagonist* by himself or others.

The first dramatic division noted above—*prologos*—is purely expository and is not absolutely necessary to the form of the Greek tragedy. When present, it may help to inform the viewer of previous events which have led up to the concise tragedy he is about to witness. The play may then "begin in the middle" or even further along in the train of events. When the *protagonist*'s background and character have been sketched briefly in the *prologos,* the necessary action on stage may be reduced to a short complication, a crisis, a swift denouement, and a conclusion or *exodus.*

As this is true in *Oedipus Rex,* so it is true in **Bahnwärter Thiel.** Hauptmann has divided the story into three numbered parts; Part III is further separated, by spacing, into three sub-divisions, which I have called IIIA, IIIB, and IIIC. In a way, then, **Bahnwärter Thiel** is a five act tragedy, and Part I is clearly a *prologos.*

This first division tells of Thiel's routine life as a flagman, mentions the wine-bottles and the stag run over by the express, swiftly reviews his first marriage, describes the character of his first and of his second wife, and briefly describes Tobias' unfortunate situation in his father's home. The end of Part I takes note of Thiel's attitude toward the opinion of the town: "Thiel aber, welchen die Sache doch vor allem anging, schien keine Augen für sie zu haben und wollte auch die Winke nicht verstehen, welche ihm von wohlmeinenden Nachbarsleuten gegeben wurden." The townspeople have been mentioned before, but this is the first indication of Thiel's attitude toward them or relationship with them. As the heroes of Greek tragedy notoriously refuse to heed the advice and admonitions of the chorus, so Thiel ignores the well-meaning hints of his neighbors, and a relationship is established between the taciturn flagman and his environment. The logical end of *prologos* is *parados.*

The great bulk of the story must now be *epeisodia* of thought, dialogue or action interspersed by *stasima* (natural and technical phenomena, animals, and the like).

The first progression in the *epeisodia*—the complication—includes all of Part II and the first division of Part III. Thiel arrives home on Saturday, plays with the children, sleeps, starts out on the way to work, remembers his lunch, returns to witness the scene between Lene and Tobias, goes to work, notes the rising wind, hears the signal for the train, and watches the train pass. Thiel has seen evidence of Lene's maltreatment of Tobias, but has not yet reacted. The signal, the rising wind, and the train announce a new development, and Part IIIA ends.

Part IIIB begins with Thiel murmuring "Minna." Then, after a fruitless attempt to dig in the plot, he has his vision. Benno von Wiese calls this vision the novellistic center point of the novelle. Not only is this the novellistic center point, it is the exact center of the novelle. Parts I, II, IIIA and Part IIIB up to the vision occupy exactly thirteen pages. The vision is placed centrally because it is the crisis of the novelle.

The function of Thiel's central vision is clearly that of *anagnorisis,* or recognition. It is only now that Thiel awakes "aus einem zweijährigen totenähnlichen Schlaf" and perceives "die Leidensgeschichte seines Ältesten, welche die Eindrücke der letzten Stunden nur noch hatten besiegeln können." As Professor von Wiese notes of this scene: "Die Vision der wandernden ersten Frau mit dem blutigen Bündel wird zu dem entscheidenden Mittelpunkt, von dem aus das Geschehen erst seine volle Beleuchtung erhält."[28]

From the *anagnorisis* the episodes proceed to an apparent denouement. Thiel's recognition of the situation is complete. His actions, however, are the same. He cannot oppose Lene's desire to go to the plot on Monday and, as he thinks of what objections he could raise, he notices how happy Tobias has become at the prospect of this small excursion. His final decision seems to be made because he cannot bear to deny Tobias this outing. By assenting, Thiel prepares for Tobias' death, although his only motive is the boy's happiness. It is a complete reversal of fortune, which occurs, as Lucas says, "when a course of action intended to produce a result *x,* produces the reverse of *x,*"[29] that is, *peripateia.*

Tobias' death is preceded by an idyllic scene in which Thiel and his son walk the tracks, listen to the humming of the telegraph poles, and pick flowers. Later, even Lene is amused by Tobias' grimaces when the trains roar past. This all occurs in Part IIIB, which is roughly analogous to the fourth act of a play. Lewis Campbell describes such a relaxation of tension in Greek drama, and notes that the poet often inserts such a sequence in the fourth act, because he "has sufficient faith in the volume of sympathy which he has called forth to interpose a pause without fearing that emotion will subside."[30] In *Bahnwärter Thiel* the scene in question might be considered absolutely necessary, for the reader has just been assailed by a storm of emotions during Thiel's vision, and may well need a pause before the actual passion, or scene of suffering.

The pause ends when Thiel leaves Lene and Tobias to go on his rounds, and with the pause ends the fourth act, or Part IIIB. Part IIIC begins with another of the divisive train signals. Thiel then sees the train, sees the object bounced like a ball between the wheels, and learns that the object is, in fact, Tobias. Tobias' accident may, of course, be called a "death on stage," but the true scene of suffering begins a very short time later. This scene records Thiel's feelings after he is sure that it is Tobias who has been hit and before he passes into unconsciousness.

Hauptmann has marked the intensive scene of suffering in an interesting manner. For the first and only time in *Bah-*

nwärter Thiel, he changes from the past to the present tense. This change of tense begins abruptly after Thiel has dimly perceived Lene's cry. It begins with the statement: "Ein Mann kommt in Eile die Strecke herauf." This man announces the accident, Thiel runs to the scene, he sees Tobias, attempts to carry him away, the train leaves, Lene and the stranger carry Tobias away, and Thiel strikes his hand on his head in an effort to wake himself, "denn es wird ein Traum sein wie der gestern, sagt er sich." At this point, the story reverts again to the narrative past tense. The brief use of the present has set off more vividly than would otherwise be possible the presence of horror which Thiel perceives. All other thoughts—even his dream— were only premonitory. This is *real,* and his perceptions of the tragedy strike like one stimulus after another upon raw, open nerves. The present tense follows him in this state until he admits the truth to himself and collapses. Then the narrative resumes in the past tense to trace the grim denouement of Thiel's history.

The chorus makes a corollary comment directly after the scene of suffering. In the third sentence after the narrative returns to the past tense, we read that, "seine peinlich gepflegte Uhr fiel aus seiner Tasche, die Kapsel sprang, das Glas zerbrach" (pp. 60-61). The comfortable routine of Thiel's life and the protection it gave him have been destroyed. He will go on now only until he has fulfilled his vengeful purpose. When he is waked by the omnipresent signal bell, he goes out to the tracks: "Thiel konnte sich erheben und seinen Dienst tun." The chorus merges with the protagonist as the narrative reports:

> Am Ende sah er nur noch den zerschlagenen Jungen mit dem blutigen Munde. Dann wurde es Nacht.

> Nach einer Weile erwachte er aus einer Ohnmacht.

> (p. 61)

Thiel faints, wakes, inspects his watch: "Sie war trotz des Falles nicht stehengeblieben" (p. 61). Like Thiel the watch painfully continues to function until its last work is done.

Thiel counts the seconds and imagines the scene in the doctor's office. His fearful and vengeful thoughts are traced as he forms his resolve to kill Lene and the baby. Even the weapon he chooses to accomplish the murders is a parallel of the classical instrument. In his madness, he promises Minna that he will kill Lene "mit dem Beil—Küchenbeil, ja—schwarzes Blut!" (p. 62). As Hauptmann notes himself in *Griechischer Frühling,* the sacrificial instrument of the Greek rite was an axe (p. 80).

The last train signal announces the return of Tobias' body, and Thiel falls again into unconsciousness. The moon is the last comment of the chorus as the small group struggles homeward. The *exodus* or conclusion includes the discovery of the murders (which have been committed "offstage") and of Thiel's permanent flight into madness. Like Oedipus, Thiel has been crushed by his guilt, has disappeared into the wings, and has re-appeared as a living dead man. The curtain falls.

Notes

1. Benno von Wiese, *Die deutsche Novelle* (Düsseldorf, 1956), pp. 268-283.

2. Karl S. Guthke, *Gerhart Hauptmann* (Göttingen, 1961), pp. 54-57.

3. Marianne Ordon, "Unconscious Contents in 'Bahnwärter Thiel,'" *Germanic Review,* XXVI (October, 1951), 223-229.

4. Gerhart Hauptmann, *Die Kunst des Dramas,* ed. Martin Marhatzke (Berlin, 1963), p. 135.

5. Guthke, p. 110.

6. Felix A. Voigt and Walter A. Reichart, *Hauptmann und Shakespeare* (Goslar, 1947), p. 43.

7. Gerhart Hauptmann, *Sämtliche Werke,* ed. Hans-Egon Hass (Frankfurt, 1962), VII, 11-119. All subsequent citations from *Griechischer Frühling* will be from this edition.

8. See *Kunst,* pp. 175, 179, 186.

9. See *Kunst,* p. 207.

10. Gerhart Hauptmann, *Ausblicke* (Berlin, 1924), p. 13.

11. See *Kunst,* pp. 95-96.

12. All quotations from *Bahnwärter Thiel* are from: Gerhart Hauptmann, *Sämtliche Werke,* ed. Hans-Egon Hass (Frankfurt, 1962), VI, 37-67.

13. Robert Graves, *The Greek Myths* (Baltimore, 1955), I, p. 104.

14. Gilbert Norwood, *Greek Tragedy,* 2nd ed. (London, 1928), p. 68.

15. *Larousse Encyclopedia of Mythology,* ed. Felix Guirand, translated by Robert Aldington and Delano Ames (New York, 1959), p. 182.

16. Guthke, p. 54.

17. *Ausblicke,* p. 45.

18. Graves, p. 108.

19. *Larousse,* p. 178.

20. *The Mythology of All Races,* I, "Greek and Roman," ed. William S. Fox (Boston, 1916), p. 216.

21. Wiese, p. 276.

22. *Larousse,* p. 178.

23. *Griechischer Frühling,* p. 79.

24. Jakob Grimm, *Deutsche Mythologie* (Göttingen, 1854), pp. 1082-1085.

25. Grimm, p. 1093.

26. Frank L. Lucas, *Tragedy in Relation to Aristotle's "Poetica"* (London, 1930), p. 101.

27. See Lucas, pp. 64-65.

28. Wiese, p. 283.

29. Lucas, p. 92.

30. Lewis Campbell, *Tragic Drama* (New York and London, 1904), p. 93.

Larry D. Wells (essay date 1978)

SOURCE: "Words of Music: Gerhart Hauptmann's Composition *Bahnwärter Thiel,*" in *Wege der Worte: Festschrift für Wolfgang Fleischhauer,* edited by Donald C. Riechel, Böhlau Verlag, 1978, pp. 377-91.

[*In the following essay, Wells discusses musical imagery and the musicality of Hauptmann's prose in* Bahnwärter Thiel.]

"Mein Werk, aus Tönen ist es aufgebaut,
aus schnellen Lichtern und aus Funkenblitzen,
und mit dem Ohre wird es angeschaut."

(Gerhart Hauptmann, Der große Traum)[1]
"Die *Tonsprache* ist Anfang und Ende der Wortsprache . . . "

(Richard Wagner, Oper und Drama)[2]

Much of Gerhart Hauptmann's work is characterized by rich and at times flamboyant tonality and the synaesthetic blend of visual and acoustic imagery alluded to in *Der große Traum.* We may marvel at melodic masterpieces of the *Minnesänger* or the Romantics, but Hauptmann's works resound with no less tonality and effulgence. Certainly few Hauptmann readers could disagree with at least the first of Rolf Ibscher's observations "daß gerade das innige Verhältnis zur Welt des Klanges in weitestem Sinne, dieses *music in himself,* als schaffenspsychologische wesentliche Grundlage seiner Begabung, mithin als gewichtigste Komponente seines Schaffens, die eigene Note seiner Darstellungsmittel bestimmend, betrachtet werden muß, und daß diese immer schon latente musikalische Anlage als der Grund seines Wesens die zum Bildnerischen und Erdhaften drängende andere Seite seiner Natur vergeistigt."[3] Though most evident in those works originating after the mid 1890's and the start of the author's involvement with the musically gifted Margarete Marschalk,[4] this "music in himself" can be heard prior to this time. Already in his early dramas of Naturalism skillful use of dialect and verbal nuance bespeaks a finely tuned sense of tone and melody.[5] Some of his other dramas from this period were even written with music in mind. *Hannele* (1893) was a joint effort in collaboration with the composer Max Marschalk. Songs in *Die versunkene Glocke* (1896) became hits of the day, and the play inspired Respighi's opera *La Campana Sommersa.* How surprising then, that the early novella **Bahnwärter Thiel** (1888) should have escaped the ear of a scholar such as Ibscher, for it possesses both a pervasive musical interplay of word, tone, and motif and a structure "in tune" with trends in symphonic music of that era. It also invites comparison with musical innovations in the music of Richard Wagner.

For the most part critics have alluded only in passing, if at all, to the extensive acoustic imagery and musicality of this novella.[6] The one exception is Fritz Martini, whose exhaustive, almost word-for-word reading of the scene with Thiel standing in the evening sunset awaiting the train amounts to a *tour de force* for this type of literary analysis.[7] The flagman waits wordlessly beside his hut, while the train, an uncannily quivering speck at the convergence of two iron rails on the horizon, grows and grows, until, like a rapidly swelling monster, it explodes upon the forest tranquility in a cataclysm of fury, roaring, panting and snorting. This irruption of cacophony into the sylvan stillness symbolizes, in Martini's opinion, the elemental and anonymous forces of aggression ("elementare Gewalt des Dynamisch-Vitalen, des massenhaft und anonym Aggressiven") that beset and finally overwhelm Thiel.[8] Although Martini pinpoints Hauptmann's acoustic and visual artistry in a specific context, he does not consider the acoustic phenomena per se and as they relate to the musical composition of the work.

Much in the story suggests Hauptmann shared Wagner's somewhat metaphysical fascination with tone as the essence of language. Vowels and consonants continually strike the *Grundton*.[9] Repeatedly, assonance accentuates phrases, sentences, and entire passages. Even in the brief reference to Thiel's pocket watch falling to the floor: "seine peinlich gepflegte Uhr fiel aus seiner Tasche, die Kapsel sprang, das Glas zerbrach" (I, 253), assonating a's combined with harsh sch, sp, s, z and ch sounds produce a distinct, albeit somewhat dissonant musical measure that underlines acoustically, though not necessarily onomatopoetically, the symbolic import of the shattering timepiece.[10] Assonating chords dominate in more extensive examples too: "Zwei rote, runde Lichter durchdrangen wie die Glotzaugen eines riesigen Ungetüms die Dunkelheit. Ein blutiger Schein ging vor ihnen her, der die Regentropfen in seinem Bereich in Blutstropfen verwandelte. Es war, als fiele ein Blutregen vom Himmel" (I, 243f). Dark-sounding long and short o's and u's strike an ominous chord, with long u comprising the tonic, as it were, by virtue of its emphatic threefold recurrence in the word "Blut". Extending the musical analogy, the umlaut u in "Ungetüm" has the effect of an accidental, while assonating long and short i's and the diphthongs ie and ei furnish contrastive musical depth. Resonating m's, n's, and l's provide sustaining pedal for the chords of impending doom.

Alliteration also abounds in the story. The more than one hundred examples include practically every consonant or consonant cluster as well as the vowel a.[11] In addition to these, there are numerous instances where particular consonantal sounds predominate, though not necessarily alliteratively by strict definition: Ein fur*ch*tbares Wetter, da*ch*te Thiel, als er aus tiefem Na*ch*denken erwa*ch*te" (I, 233).[12] Invariably such consonantal sounds provide essential complement to the vocalic tonality of the language, but even when they do not—for at times Hauptmann gets carried away by his alliterative virtuosity—, they leave a distinctly acoustic stamp on his prose. Witness, for example the insistent, varied repetition of one consonant sound:

> "Auch die *Ge*leise be*g*annen zu *g*lühen, feuri*g*en Schlangen *g*leich" (I, 238),

or abrupt alliteration of one consonant upon another, with two consecutive letters of the alphabet no less:

> "Ein *R*udel *R*ehe *s*etzte *s*eitab" (I, 258).

Few sentences can surpass the following musical interplay of consonantal sounds:

> "*St*ücke *bl*auen *H*immels *sch*ienen auf den *B*oden des *H*aines *h*erabge*s*unken, *s*o wun*d*er*b*ar *d*icht *st*anden kleine, *bl*aue *Bl*üten *d*arauf" (I, 248f).

Musical in function are also the many word pairs, whether alliterative ("Tosen und Toben"), rhyming ("Brausen und Sausen"), or merely rhythmic ("Hagel und Regen"). For these Hauptmann uses a variety of grammatical forms: "knarrend und quietschend" (adverbial), "gurgelnde und

pfeifende Laute" (adjectival), "Ächzen und Stöhnen" (nominal), "zu husten und schreien" (predicative). He also employs the genitive construction ("Klappen der Sohlen," "Wühlen des Windes") and prepositional phrases without the article ("Gewühl von Tönen") for emphatic rhythmic effect. (The phrase "Bahre mit dem Bewußtlosen," for example, yields a less conspicuous rhythmic measure.) Not only do such word pairs add tonality and rhythm to Hauptmann's *Sprachmelodie*, they also function on the conceptual level by invariably describing and/or imitating sounds as well. They sound and denote simultaneously.

In combination, these various verbal approximations of sound and rhythm yield distinctly musical prose:

> "Als er noch damit beschäftigt war, diese [the gate] zu schließen, erklang die Signalglocke. Der Wind zerriß ihre Töne und warf sie nach allen Richtungen auseinander. Die Kiefern bogen sich und rieben unheimlich knarrend und quietschend ihre Zweige aneinander. Einen Augenblick wurde der Mond sichtbar, wie er gleich einer blaßgoldenen Schale zwischen den Wolken lag. In seinem Lichte sah man das Wühlen des Windes in den schwarzen Kronen der Kiefern. Die Blattgehänge der Birken am Bahndamm wehten und flatterten wie gespenstige Roßschweife. Darunter lagen die Linien der Geleise, welche, vor Nässe glänzend, das blasse Mondlicht in einzelnen Flecken aufsogen" (I, 242).

In addition to signaling an approaching train, the warning bell strikes the first note of the musical measures to follow. Numerous words allude to sounds in the nocturnal scene: "erklang," "zerriß," "rieben," "knarrend," "quietschend," "Wühlen," "wehten," "flatterten," "bogen." Yet the music itself derives from orchestration of tones. Repeating and alliterative b's, w's, and k's sound conspicuously, while s, sp, sch, and f sounds supply the acoustics of rustling canopies of leaves ("wie gespenstige Roßschweife"). One also hears persistent undertones of sonorous l's (particularly in the fourth and seventh sentences) m's, and n's. In the fourth sentence extended alternation of a and o vowels strikes an important chord for the passage, whereas lighter "notes" such as i, ie, and ei introduce contrastive richness and musical depth. Thus, vocalic and consonantal sounds complement each other in a rich display of *Tonsprache*. They also attest to deliberate musical composition on Hauptmann's part. For example, the contrasting of o and i vowels is "worked out" musically, since acoustic and syntactic separation of "Mond" (third sentence) and "Licht" (fourth sentence) finds resolution in the composite "Mondlicht" of the final sentence. Moreover, the same final sentence provides further opposition of contrasting light and dark sounding vowels ("Darunter lagen die Linien der Geleise") and harmonic variation of "blasse" and assonating a's in the first part of the sentence through "Nässe" with its ä accidental.

Word pairs influence both tone and rhythm. Like a modified refrain, "Kronen der Kiefern" echoes the rhythm of "Wühlen des Windes," only to repeat still again in the softened alliteration and rhythmical similarity of "Linien der Geleise." The musically attuned reader will perhaps hear in "Blattgehänge der Birken am Bahndamm" expanded repetition and variation of the same refrain, since the final two nouns of this sequence have a rhythm similar to that of the previous word pairs.

Here and in more than 140 other instances Hauptmann heightens the music of his prose with colors or contrastive light effects.[13] I am reminded of Brentano's tone-and-color poem "Abendständchen," for in this passage the blending of tones and colors results in synaesthesia and *Ton-farbe* in the most literal meaning of the term.[14] The a/o chord mentioned above is "colored" with golden hues implied by the very words containing the a and o notes: "Mond," "blaß-," "-golden," "Schale." These golden notes are then picked up again and musically varied through the a's, o's and ä's depicting the pale reflection of the moon in the wet rails: "vor Nässe glänzend, das blasse Mondlicht in einzelnen Flecken." Moreover, the contrastive interplay of light and dark tones accentuating the passage reflects, as it were, in the chiaroscuro of golden luminescence against the inky backdrop of night. Hauptmann has superimposed color and shadow upon the tones, thereby enhancing the acoustic and visual imagery of his prose through chromatic expression.

None of this musical prose necessarily imitates or reproduces specific sounds from the story. Rhythm and contrastive sounds in the phrase "knarrend und quietschend" may evoke acoustically the swaying and rubbing of spruces. Nevertheless, the primary effect is musical, for given no context, one would certainly not hear spruce trees in this phrase, nor rustling canopies of leaves in s, sp, sch, and f sounds. One would, of course, still hear sounds. The same holds true for program music, which, apart from rare exceptions, requires knowledge of the extramusical context put to music—usually stated in the title—for adequate understanding. Upon hearing a Wagnerian motif for the first time, the listener naturally suspects its function. To understand it, he must eventually associate the motif with happenings on stage. Hauptmann's prose demands no less. Only then can the willing ear hear certain phenomena and associate them with musical moments and, as we shall see, with major themes of the story.

We must bear in mind that literature and music, though sharing some features, are fundamentally different arts. Calvin S. Brown observes that music is "sound qua sound" without attached meaning external to the composition, whereas language, and by extension, almost any literary work, consists of sounds endowed with association and meaning.[15] In short, music *sounds:* language *denotes.* Music may, of course, also denote, but language rarely simply sounds. As the smallest conceptual compositional entity of language the word exists as a lexical item with meaning(s), though in contexts its meanings can change. Tones, on the other hand, possess no conceptual meaning of themselves, even though they may take on associative value in musical context. In **Bahnwärter Thiel** Hauptmann attempts to bridge the distinction between the two arts. By definition the novella is a work of words (*Wortkunstwerk*). Yet as we have seen, it is composed with tones, with pre-conceptual, phonological elements such as vowels, consonants, consonant clusters, and syllables, which together provide "word music"[16] and the unique instrumentation of the story.

Creating music in German prose is nothing new. One need but recall the virtuoso performances of Wackenroder, Hoffmann, and Heine.[17] New and surprising in a work foreshadowing Hauptmann's emergence as the foremost proponent of German Naturalism is the extent to which sound pervades a work without music as one of its explicit themes. In addition to tonal and rhythmic elements, there are more than two-hundred allusions to sounds in the story,

ranging from rustling leaves to snorting locomotives, from derisive laughter to outbursts of vilification and insanity. Like the diverse instruments of an orchestra, these sounds can be divided into four major groups. By far the smallest group (group I) consists of harmonious and gentle strains such as the wind in the trees, Thiel singing to Minna or teaching children the alphabet, and above all, the peaceful musical interlude with father and son prior to the accident:

> "Vor allem verwunderlich war ihm [Tobias] das *Klingen* der Telegraphenstangen . . . Oft blieb er, Tobiaschen an der Hand, stehen, um *den wunderbaren Lauten* zu lauschen, die aus dem Holze *wie sonore Choräle aus dem Innern einer Kirche* hervorströmten. Die Stange am Südende des Reviers hatte *einen besonders vollen und schönen Akkord.* Es war *ein Gewühl von Tönen* in ihrem Innern, die ohne Unterbrechung gleichsam in einem Atem *fortklangen,* und Tobias lief . . . um, wie er glaubte, durch eineÖffnung die Urheber *des lieblichen Getöns* zu entdecken. Der Wärter wurde weihevoll gestimmt, ähnlich wie in der Kirche . . . Er stellte sich vor, es sei *ein Chor seliger Geister,* in den sie Minna ja auch *ihre Stimme* mische . . . " (I, 248).[18]

Invariably such "chorales" are drowned out by the higher-volume "Brausen und Sausen" (I, 241) of the world around Thiel (group II) as, for example, when trains roar by the forest "Kapelle", intermittently interrupting Thiel's songs to his first wife: "Eine verblichene Photographie der Verstorbenen vor sich auf dem Tisch, Gesangbuch und Bibel aufgeschlagen, las und sang er abwechselnd die lange Nacht hindurch, nur von den in Zwischenräumen vorbeitobenden Bahnzügen unterbrochen . . . " (I, 227). Eventually the "Toben" of the train—one should note here the acoustic similarity with "Tobias"—and other barrages of sound engulf the flagman and the world dedicated to the memory of Minna.[19]

Most dominant throughout the story are the many distinct noises (group III) and unpleasing human sounds (group IV). Whistling, creaking, scraping, grating, rattling, hammering, shattering, howling, clanking, and a host of other predominantly dissonant noises (group III)[20] punctuate the forest tranquility, while, as an unceasing reminder of the flagman's monotonous routine, insistent signal bells sound the approach of trains.[21] There also seems to be no reprieve from groaning, moaning, whining, coughing, puffing, wheezing, choking, spitting, nose-blowing, scornful laughing, and the like, which mark the presence of humans in this dreary world.[22] Above all, there are frequent screams.[23] Continuous orchestration of these multifarious sounds, in particular the harsh noises and piercing screams, against a background of harmony and tranquility antedates the use of dissonance in symphonic works such as Bartok's *Allegro barbaro* (1911), Stravinsky's *The Rite of Spring* (1913), or Prokofiev's *Scythian Suite* (1916), although we find the scream already playing a role in the musical dramas of Wagner. Hauptmann most likely drew his musical inspiration from the general category of program music, of which at that time the symphonic poem was the most ambitious realization.[24] Richard Strauss's "tone poems" had not yet been composed, but ever since Berlioz' *Fantastic Symphony* (1830) composers like Liszt, Borodin, and Saint-Saëns, not to mention Wagner, had been using extramusical ideas as the basis of orchestral composition. Hauptmann's novella is the literary approximation of a symphonic poem on the theme of tranquility shattered, in which the calm and the harmonious group I sounds of the forest and the realm it represents on the personal level (Thiel's first wife, spiritual values) and the allegorical level (a romantic, pre-industrial state) are periodically invaded and finally engulfed by the sounds of the second wife and a technological age.[25]

Neither in symphonic poems nor in the novella are the sounds arranged arbitrarily. Here they are in phase with plot development, for the music of ***Bahnwärter Thiel*** is programmed to the themes of the work. Thus no matter how replete with tone and rhythm, each passage is part of the greater compositional and thematic structure, just as in musical composition. Leitmotifs and underlying themes ensure compositional unity:

> "In kurzer Zeit hatte er die Spree erreicht, setzte mit wenigen kräftigen Ruderschlägen über und stieg gleich darauf, am ganzen Körper schwitzend, die sanft ansteigende Dorfstraße hinauf. Der alte, schäbige Pudel des Krämers lag mitten auf der Straße. Auf dem geteerten Plankenzaune eines Kossätenhofes saß eine Nebelkrähe. Sie spreizte die Federn, schüttelte sich, nickte, *stieß* ein ohrenzerreißendes Krä-Krä *aus* und erhob sich mit pfeifendem Flügelschlag, um sich vom Winde in der Richtung des Forstes davontreiben zu lassen" (I, 233f).

The passage is word music, a rich interplay of vowels and consonants best exemplified by the sharp k sounds (thirteen times, including unvoiced g's in "stieg" and "lag") in combination with the seven plaintive ä's. Acoustically, these tones dominate the scene and anticipate the piercing "Krä-Krä" of the crow. But like the cawing itself, they function within a greater context by intensifying both a musical phase and a theme begun moments before with crows punctuating Thiel's muted walk through the forest on his way to work: "Krähenschwärme badeten . . .unaufhörlich ihre knarrenden Rufe *ausstoßend*" (I, 233). Yet in both instances the cawing crows are part of a developing sound sequence and a mild *mezzo-forte* compared to the force with which Lene's "kreischende Stimme" assaults the ear as Thiel approaches the house: "Ein Schwall heftig *herausgestoßener,* mißtönender Laute schlug an sein Ohr . . . " (I, 234). This flood of dissonance swells in wrath and volume, until it culminates in a *fortissimo* of anger and vilification: "Du erbärmlicher, niederträchtiger, hinterlistiger, hämischer, feiger, gemeiner Lümmel!" (I, 235). Thiel's unexpected return strikes Lene speechless as she struggles to regain composure. Not unlike the sudden musical break in symphonic poems, there is momentary silence, followed by a *pianissimo* of intense, half-muted anger. Hauptmann has not eliminated sound; he has reduced it by rendering Lene's renewed outburst toward Thiel in indirect discourse, where it is narrated, but does not sound directly: "und sie ermannte sich endlich so weit, ihren Mann heftig anzulassen: was es denn heißen solle . . . " (I, 235f). Wordlessly the flagman grabs his lunch sack und leaves. Plot and music pause on a note of smoldering passion and oppressive tension.

Essential to both musical build-up and thematic development in this section of the story is the use of leitmotif.[26] The italicized words ("ausstoßend," "stieß . . . aus," "herausgestoßener") suggest acoustic similarity between Lene and the crows. Association with the crows becomes unavoidable when the "stoß-" effect repeats a fourth time:

"Die Worte folgten einander in steigender Betonung, und die Stimme, welche sie *herausstieß,* schnappte zuweilen über vor Anstrengung" (I, 235). Repetition of the sound of the word itself fulfills a musical function. Through the sound it denotes, and in the contexts in which it occurs, the word also functions as a literary leitmotif, by enabling the "tuned-in" reader-listener to draw associations whenever the motif recurs. Thus he links Lene with the sound of the locomotive ("stoßweise"—I, 239), long before she is explicitly described as having the "Geschwindigkeit und Ausdauer einer Maschine" (I, 247). He hears in the "Riesenstößen" (I, 242) of thunder claps reverberating across the forest not only the echo of the train's intrusion into the forest hours before, but also Lene's imminent invasion of Thiel's "geheiligtes Land" (I, 226). Later, above the din of the fateful Silesian Express Lene's stream of abuse still echoes:

> "in unzählbaren, sich überhastenden *Stößen fauchte* der Dampf aus dem schwarzen Maschinenschlote" (I, 250); die Maschine *stößt* weiße, *zischende* Dämpfe *aus* (I, 252).[27]

There are other motifs. Not every ear will pick up subtle variations of "Ruderschlägen" in "Schläge" (I, 235), "Schlägen" (I, 237), "Hufschlägen" (I, 239), "Glockenschläge" (I, 253), and "Umschläge" (I, 260), all but the last of which not only sound the plaintive ä but denote sound as well. No one, however, can miss the tearing ("ohrenzerreißendes") quality of the crow's scream, nor the same shattering impact with which the train later destroys the forest tranquility: "Dann *plötzlich zerriß* die Stille" (I, 239). The same motif sounds again when the flagman finally realizes how Lene has tormented his son: "Und *plötzlich zerriß* etwas wie ein dichter, schwarzer Vorhang in zwei Stücke, und seine umnebelten Augen gewannen einen klaren Ausblick" (I, 241). It culminates with the accident and the penetrating scream, which links Lene and train together as very real manifestations of the forces that rip apart Tobias, the forest retreat, and the peaceful world dedicated to the past: "Ein Aufschrei *zerreißt* die Luft von der Unglücksstelle her . . . " (I, 251).

The theme of tranquility shattered provides the musical and thematic structure of the novella. The story follows a series of musical phases, each programmed to phases of thematic development and each following the same sequence of relative calm—build-up—*crescendo* climax—break or *decrescendo*—calm. In each phase interludes of *pianissimo* are shattered by *fortissimo* floods of sound (groups II, III, IV) in such a way as to accompany and echo the repeating and very real acoustic and physical intrusion of destructive forces (i.e., Lene, the train) into the peaceful remembrance of the past (Minna, the forest retreat, Tobias). Thus the composition conforms to the concept of the symphonic poem, for unlike the symphony with its inherently musical structure, it derives its structure from the text being put to music. Moreover, contrastive phases of interludes and crescendos were quite common in such "tone poems" around the time of Hauptmann's novella. Through contrast, thematic highpoints of the text could be readily accentuated. And of course, if the text contained plot development and was not purely descriptive, the music followed a similar development to a final climax. Since ***Bahnwärter Thiel*** is divided into three chapters, one might better speak of it as an abbreviated symphonic suite, that is, a symphonic poem in several movements.

Already in the first chapter, which sketches Thiel's past (Minna) and present (Lene) and the daily drudgery of his existence, bells, "Gekeif" (I,225), and the juxtaposition of Thiel's chants and the roaring trains anticipate motifs and themes to follow. The actual events of the story begin with Thiel's return from work one June morning (Chapter Two), reaching a first musical and thematic highpoint in the crescendo of vilification discussed above. Thiel's muted departure after the encounter with Lene concludes that phase and chapter. It also marks the prelude to the final chapter with its new series of crescendos. At first, only spasmodic coughing (I, 237) or sounds of Thiel at work in the hut interrupt the stillness. When the bell signals the approach of a train, there follows the rather loud train scene discussed at length by Martini (see above). The sudden silence ("das alte heil'ge Schweigen"—I, 239) that sets in after this intrusion of sound provides musical contrast within the crescendo-decrescendo sequence and a momentary interlude before the next crescendo. Again, only isolated sounds, such as Thiel's spade turning soil (potato patch and the Lene motif!) and his exclamations ("Minna"—I, 239ff), "Nein, nein, das geht ja nicht"—I, 240), interrupt the stillness and indicate the internal process taking place in Thiel. Thiel falls asleep and awakens hours later to the roar of a summer storm. This new explosion of sound in thunder claps repeats the previous crescendo in build-up and volume, for the retarding structure of the sentence can easily be heard as a description of an approaching locomotive: "Erst dumpf und verhalten grollend, wälzte er [the thunder] sich näher in kurzen, brandenden Erzwellen, bis er, zu Riesenstößen anwachsend, sich endlich, die ganze Atmosphäre überflutend, dröhnend, schütternd und brausend entlud" (I, 242). In the ensuing visual and acoustic interplay of night, wind, bells, train, golden hues, blood-like reds, and *Tonsprache* that follows, external occurrence and internal realization fuse in the ghastly apparition of the woman with the bloodied bundle (Thiel's guilt and premonition with respect to his neglected son) before the bloody glow of the lights of the on-coming locomotive (external reality). In this highly portentous moment, thematic development and musical expression coalesce in a moment of unsurpassed symbolic intensity and foreboding. Just as at the end of the other crescendo sequences, this phase also concludes on a note of relative silence with only Thiel's soles and wrench slapping distinct notes against the tracks as he checks them the next morning. There is a musical lull, a calm before the disaster.

The next crescendo, though not unexpected, nevertheless overwhelms by its suddenness, for it is preceded by a family idyl and musical interlude with Thiel and son walking the tracks a day later. Still, for all its peacefulness the scene is unsettling. The alert listener detects in the trains roaring by to Tobias' uncomprehending amazement musical repetition of the train motif and the theme of tranquility shattered. The accident, a staccato, second-for-second juxtaposition of frantic whistle bursts, screeching brakes, and Thiel's screams, rides a momentary wave of dissonance, followed by an immediate break of deathly silence. Figures dash to the rear of the train! A beckoning gesture! Silence! Then *the* scream, the primal utterance welling up from the depths of Lene's soul to split asunder the world of the flagman: "Ein Aufschrei zerreißt die Luft von der Unglücksstelle her, ein Geheul folgt, wie aus der Kehle eines Tieres kommend" (I,251)! The scream is climactic, for it not only marks the disaster to which all signs and motifs have been inevitably pointing, but also unites the central musical theme of shattered tranquility with Thiel's "torn" fate.

What follows is denouement, the outcome of the accident, but still part of the musical composition. Contrastive moments of silence and screams (Thiel's frenzied vows to avenge Tobias' death) accompany the flagman's descent into madness. With Thiel's collapse, stillness sets in, punctuated only by sudden raving outbursts, then by the wails of the villagers. Again quiet prevails, followed by screams of horror: "Mord, Mord! . . . Er hat seine Frau ermordet, er hat seine Frau ermordet! . . . Heiliger Himmel!" (I, 260f). To the end the "music" sounds, concluding on a final dissonant note of human outrage ("toben"—I, 261), as the insane flagman is forceably removed from the railroad tracks the next morning. Musically, this"toben" picks up one final time the dissonant refrain of the roaring trains and their destruction of the boy named "Tobias."

The screams, above all Lene's "Aufschrei" immediately after the catastrophe, strongly suggest Hauptmann's indebtedness to a particular composer. It was, after all, Wagner who established the scream as a vehicle of musical expression. In his Beethoven essay he cites the scream as the basis of verbal expression ("das Grundelement jeder menschlichen Kundgebung an das Gehör")[28] and thus a fundamental musical impulse. Although one may disagree with Wagner's musical metaphysics of the scream, one cannot ignore its conspicuous presence in his musical dramas. Hauptmann greatly admired Wagner. In *Marginalia* he confesses: "Ich bin als Jüngling in Wagners Bann gewesen, stand seiner Kunst lange fern und mußte ihrer fern stehen, um eigene Kräfte zu entwickeln" (XVII, 307). He may not have read the Beethoven essay, though I feel he must have. Indeed, he shared the composer's high regard of Beethoven, and in *Abenteuer meiner Jugend* he lauds the overpowering effect of the "Schrei" (XIV, 709) in the final chorale of Beethoven's *Ninth Symphony,* a work Wagner had specifically praised as that composer's greatest legacy to the development of "Vokalmusik," or what we would call the symphonic chorale. Moreover, Wagner is one of the composers whose works Hauptmann had by this time (1888) "kennengelernt" (XIV, 708) on frequent excursions to the opera and concert halls in Berlin. Thus there is at least the strong probability that Wagner's music did inspire the use of screams in *Bahnwärter Thiel.*

Summing up, we find Hauptmann does successfully integrate musical phenomena and musical structure with central themes, symbols, and occurrences of his "composition." It is also safe to assume that in this he was inspired by Wagner and by trends in symphonic composition of that era. Yet this novella should in no way be considered musical-literary exhibitionism on Hauptmann's part, for it issues from a deeply rooted scepticism regarding language as a means of communication. While not suffering the torments of "Sprachkrise" to the extent that Hofmannsthal did, he nevertheless laments throughout his works the inefficacy of words.[29] For this reason, his works, particularly the dramas, rely heavily upon meaningful gesture, sound effects, and silence as substitutes for speech. Some of his most dramatic moments are those of human muteness,[30] of the *stumme Gebärde,* such as when Thiel grabs his lunch and departs wordlessly, after Lene has mercilessly berated his son. Such gestures and moments of silence, like the screams, are part of the "music," with which Hauptmann attempts to transcend the limitations of words and thereby express the ineffable. The "railroaded" flagman's silence says more than words ever could.[31] So do the myriad noises all around him. Similarly, the tones, rhythms, and motifs of Hauptmann's music not only speak to us on an immediate and emotional level, they add a new dimension of communication, which infinitely expands the potential for thematic and symbolic association. This, of course, sounds very much like Wagner, and I would agree with Ibscher that much of Hauptmann's ouevre can be seen as a transposing of Wagnerian ideas on the *Gesamtkunstwerk* to the literary domain.[32] More importantly though, **Bahnwärter Thiel,** like much of Hauptmann's work, attests to the validity of his oft-quoted plaint: "Warum bin ich nicht Musiker geworden, der ich doch vor allem Musiker bin."[33]

Notes

1. *Das gesammelte Werk* (Berlin, 1942), XVI, 398. Subsequent quotations from this edition are indicated in the body of this paper by volume and page.

2. Gesammelte Schriften (Leipzig, 1914), XI, 199.

3. "Vom Geiste der Musik in Gerhart Hauptmanns Werk," DVjs., 27 (1953), 584. Ibscher cites "Klang" und "klangliche Schau" as "Urelemente" for Hauptmann. He explains Hauptmann's growing awareness of the "music in himself" and his "Wendung vom Optischen zum Akustischen," as a transition from the Apollonian to the Dionysian that explains the ever-increasing presence of irrational elements in his life and works.

4. For the past three-quarters of a century scholars have duly recorded Margarete's significance for Hauptmann's poetic development. Here again, Ibscher is informative, 599ff. For a somewhat more detailed discussion of Hauptmann's involvement with this woman, who in 1904 became his second wife, see Eberhard Hilscher, *Gerhart Hauptmann* (Berlin, 1969), pp. 191-216.

5. Ibscher, 588. For an opposing view see Paul Böckmann, "Der Naturalismus Gerhart Hauptmanns," in *Gestaltprobleme der Dichtung: Festschrift für Günther Müller,* ed. Richard Alewyn, Hans-Egon Hass, and Clemens Heselhaus (Bonn, 1975), pp. 239-258.

6. Marianne Ordon, "Unconscious Contents in *Bahnwärter Thiel," Germanic Review,* 26 (1951), 223-229, does not discuss acoustic phenomena. Paul Requadt, "Die Bilderwelt in Gerhart Hauptmanns Bahnwärter Thiel," in *Minotaurus,* ed. Alfred Döblin (Wiesbaden, 1953), pp. 102-111, provides a sensitive analysis of images in the story and their significance, but he does not treat acoustic images. Walter Silz remarks that sound effects would lead one to suspect the story to be the work of a musically gifted author, but he merely quotes two illustrative examples without commentary: *Realism and Reality* (Chapel Hill, 1954), pp. 137-152. Werner Zimmermann only touches on acoustic aspects, not mentioning them at all in connection with his structural chart of the story: *Deutsche Prosadichtungen der Gegenwart*: Teil I, 4th ed.

(Düsseldorf, 1962), pp. 39-61. In *Die deutsche Novelle* (Düsseldorf, 1962), pp. 268-283, Benno von Wiese cites the presence of many visual and acoustic images but is more or less content to quote or paraphrase them while recapitulating the story. Where he does offer genuine insights into Hauptmann's symbolism, they often echo those of Fritz Martini (see next note). John Ellis' insights, in *Narration in the German Novelle: Theory and Interpretation* (Cambridge, 1974), pp. 169-187, are original, in fact, too original: Ellis pays lip service to his professed concern with aspects of narration and then digresses into dubious insights of the square-peg, round-hole variety. His linking of the train to Thiel is overwhelmingly refuted by the events of the story, not to mention the conspicuous acoustic, symbolic, and thematic parallels between the iron monster and Lene. His assertion that the wine bottle, cast from a passing train and striking the flagman on the chest, is one of the two "dominant symbols of the story" (187) shows flagrant disregard for central symbols discussed by Martini and others. He does not dwell an acoustic phenomena. Irene Heerdegen, "Gerhart Hauptmanns Novelle Bahnwärter Thiel," *Weimarer Beiträge,* 4 (1958), 348-360, restricts herself to social implications of the story.

7. *Das Wagnis der Sprache,* 4th ed. (Stuttgart, 1961), pp. 56-98.

8. Martini, p. 86. Martini does not view these forces primarily as those of a technological age. Because of the mythical tone of Hauptmann's symbolism, he ascribes them to a greater, mythical presence: "Aber Natur wie technische Welt vereinigt, daß ihre empirische Wirklichkeit zugleich ins Visionäre überhöht und entschränkt wird, beide zur Erscheinung eines Übermenschlich-Elementaren, zum Symbol einer umfassenden, geradezu mythischen Vitalität werden" (p. 89). For Zimmermann these same forces are "es-hafte Mächte" (p. 48 ff), for von Wiese "das Irrationale" (p. 271), and "das übermenschlich Chaotische" (p. 273). I do not totally agree with these interpretations (see footnote 25).

9. In *Oper und Drama*Wagner comments extensively on the interrelationship of vowels and consonants as fundamental elements of musical expression. Of vowels, for instance, he writes: "Das Verständnis des Vokales begründet sich aber nicht auf seine oberflächliche Verwandtschaft mit einem gereimten anderen Wurzelvokale, sondern, *da alle Vokale unter sich urverwandt sind,* auf die *Aufdeckung dieser Urverwandtschaft* durch die volle Geltendmachung seines *Gefühlsinhaltes vermöge des musikalischen Tones.* Der Vokal ist selbst nichts anderes, als der *verdichtete Ton*": *Gesammelte Schriften,* XI, 245. The italics are Wagner's.

10. Strictly speaking, this brief passage is acoustic, though not necessarily musical in and of itself. But as should become clear as we progress, it is indeed conceived as a compositional element producing musical effect.

11. Random examples: "*Aufblitzen der Augen,*" "*bläulich blendend,*" "Ein . . . *d*urchsichtiger . . .

mit . . . *Düften geschwängerter Dunst*," "Die *F*erse des kleinen *Fußes*," "*goß* ihre letzte *Glut*," "Ein *H*immel *h*ing tief *h*erab," "*K*ronen der *K*iefern," "*l*agen die *L*inien der Ge*l*eise," "in den *M*ienen streckte der *M*ann seine Arme," "*p*ur*p*ur," "*Kn*arren und *Q*uietschen," "*R*udel *R*ehe," "Der *Sp*aten *sch*nitt knir-(*sch*)end," "*Thiel tas(t)e(t)e* ratlos," "*vor*sichtig schritt man *vor*wärts," "Das *W*etter und der *W*echsel," "von Zeit zu Zeit."

12. The italics here and in other such examples are mine.

13. An inventory of the colors in the story indicates that, as might be expected from the themes and images, reds, whites and blacks predominate with 24, 20, and 17 occurrences respectively. There are 14 allusions to blue, 13 to brown, a total of 13 to gold and yellow, 5 to grey, 3 to silver, and two to purple. In addition, there are numerous references to shades of light and dark.

14. "Tone color" or timbre is the "peculiar quality of a tone as sounded by a given instrument or voice." Willi Apel and Ralph T. Daniel, *The Harvard Brief Dictionary of Music* (New York, 1961), p. 305. In addition to the tone itself, of course, Hauptmann supplies color association. For an interesting discussion of some limitations of musical synaesthesia see Calvin S. Brown's chapter "Synaesthesia and the Confusion of the Arts" in *Tones into Words* (Athens, Ga., 1953), pp. 66-81. Brown cites the dubious practice of associating instrumental tones with certain colors as arbitrary and having no basis in a correlation between the two phenomena. Hauptmann's tones, however, are colored by the specific images to which they refer.

15. *Music and Literature: A Comparison of the Arts* (Athens, Ga., 1948), pp. 11 ff. Brown's book remains the most lucid treatment of the interrelationship between these two arts. Also informative is Horst Petri, *Literatur und Musik: Form- und Strukturparallelen* (Göttingen, 1964). For an historical, theoretical and bibliographical overview of this topic see Georg Reichert, "Literatur und Musik," in *Reallexikon der Literaturgeschichte*, II, 2nd ed., ed. Joseph Merker and Wolfgang Stammler (Berlin, 1965), 143-163, and introduction and appendix to Steven Paul Scher's *Verbal Music in German Literature* (New Haven and London, 1968), pp. 1-12, 155-166.

16. This term is used widely in criticism to denote literary imitation of sound and should be distinguished from "verbal music," which Steven Paul Scher applies to any literary work using a musical composition, whether real or fictitious, as its theme. Scher, pp. 8 ff.

17. Authors discussed by Scher.

18. The few other "chorales" are those of the forest: "tiefrauschend" (I, 233), "Der Wald draußen rauschte" (I, 241), "Geräusch der tropfenschüttelnden Bäume" (I, 244), "ein sanftes Rieseln" (I, 249).

19. References to such volumes of sound include: "Tosen und Toben" (I, 239), "Schneesturm . . .raste" (I, 227), "vorbeitobend[en]" (I, 227), "ein

Vibrieren und Summen" (I, 239), "dumpfes Getöse" (I, 239),"heranbrausend" (I, 239), "grollend" (I, 242), "in kurzen brandenden Erzwellen" (I, 242), "überflutend, dröhnend, schütternd und brausend" (I, 242), "vorübertoben" (I, 249), "heranbrausen" (I, 250).

20. Representative examples of these noises abound in the body of this paper. Particularly conspicuous are verbs such as "knarren," "klirren," "quietschen," and their corresponding substantives "Knarren," "Geklirr," "Klirren," and "Quietschen."

21. The bells comprise an acoustic motif in the story and are not limited to the railroad warning bell: "Sterbeglocke" (I, 223), "Türglocke des Krämers" (I, 230), "Glocke mit drei schrillen Schlägen" (I, 237), "die Signalglocke" (I, 242), "die Signalglocke" (I, 253), "drei Glockenschläge" (I, 253), "Signal zur Raserei" (I, 256), "Nachhall der Meldeglocke" (I, 257).

22. Most conspicuous are aspiratory sounds, such as "ausspeien," "husten," "keuchen," "schnauben," "fauchen," "röcheln," and references to tortured breathing.

23. In addition to the seven-fold occurrence of the verb "schreien," there are allusions to "kreischend[em] Gekeif" (I, 225), "knarrend[en] Rufe" (I, 233), "kreischenden Stimme" (I, 234), "Hagelwetter von Schimpfworten" (I, 234), "Aufschrei" (I, 251), "Geheul" (I, 251), "Kindergeschrei" (I, 256), "brach . . .in Klagen aus" (I, 259). Acoustically penetrating are the actual screams such as Lene's startled "Thiel!" (I, 246), Thiel's frantic "Halt!" (I, 250), or the "Mord! Mord!" (I, 260), of the villagers. We will return to the scream later.

24. The symphonic poem is a type of music in which an extramusical idea serves as the basis for the orchestral composition and developed from the efforts of composers to free their music from the formal restrictions of the symphony. *The Harvard Brief Dictionary of Music,* p. 290.

25. The overriding dissonance and metallic ring of many of the invading noises suggests the forces they express are more closely linked to technology than scholars have wanted to acknowledge. Martini and Zimmermann note that Hauptmann attempts to symbolically raise empirical reality to the level of myth. Hence the "es-hafte Mächte" (See footnote 8). For all the mythical overtones, I find these forces not to be "es-haft" at all, but rather explicit manifestations of the Industrial Age. The mythicizing of forces takes a back seat to the continual rendering of man and nature in images of technology. The forest reverberates not with the sounds of rustling leaves and chirping birds, but with "*Erz*wellen" (I, 242) ("Erz-" can mean bronze as well as arch-), humming wires, roaring trains, signal bells, and the "Hämmern" (I, 256) of a woodpecker. At different times the sky is milky grey ("Grau der Luft"—I, 233), "stahlblau" (I, 256), and "schmutziggrau" (I, 244). The setting sun pours molten streams of purple over the forest ("goß Ströme von Purpur"—I, 238), while trees bordering the tracks glow incandescently, like newly cast rails. The rails of the tracks are an "eiserne Netzmasche"

(I, 238), the wires a "Gewebe" (I, 238). Hauptmann uses the image of weight with metallic associations: Lene's physical power binds Thiel like a "Netz von Eisen" (I, 236). Later the forest is "wie aus Stein" (I, 253). Thiel feels held by an "eiserne Faust im Nacken" (I, 253), while his feet have become "bleischwer" (I, 253), and the tracks around him "wie die Speiche eines ungeheuren Rades, dessen Achse sein Kopf war" (I, 254).

26. Wagner made the leitmotif a popular musical device. But we should bear in mind that this device of characterization and repetition can be found in the literature of antiquity and is thus not necessarily musical in origin. Hauptmann attempts to fuse the musical and literary function of the leitmotif by letting his motifs simultaneously sound and denote.

27. The motif does not end here. It can be heard in Thiel's frenzied outbursts after the accident ("stieß er . . . hervor"—I, 255), in the sounds of Lene's child choking ("ausstieß"—I, 257), in the puffing of the locomotive ("wie das stoßweise gequälte Atmen eines kranken Riesen"—I, 257) bringing Tobias's body back, and, as a final grisly climax, in the sound of a neighbor bumping against the cradle of Lene's son with his throat slit ("einer stieß an die Wiege"—I, 261).

28. *Gesammelte Schriften*, VIII, 153.

29. Theodore Ziolkowski, "Gerhart Hauptmann and the Problem of Language," *Germanic Review*, 38 (1963), 295-306.

30. This insight comes from a relatively unknown gem of an essay: Oskar Seidlin, "The Shroud of Silence," in *Essays in German and Comparative Literature*, University of North Carolina Studies in Comparative Literature, No. 30 (Chapel Hill, 1961), pp. 228-236.

31. The pun is Oskar Seidlin's from a memorable classroom lecture at the Ohio State University a few years back.

32. Ibscher, p. 598.

33. Gerhart Hauptmann, *Ausblicke* (Berlin, 1924), pp. 26f.

Robin A. Clouser (essay date 1980)

SOURCE: "The Spiritual Malaise of a Modern Hercules, Hauptmann's Bahnwärter Thiel," in *Germanic Review*, Vol. 55, No. 3, Summer, 1980, pp. 98-108.

[In the following essay, Clouser examines the conflict between spiritual and physical natures in Bahnwärter Thiel, *equating Thiel with a failed Hercules.]*

Largely neglected until the middle of this century, *Bahnwärter Thiel* has recently begun to receive critical praise as a master *Novelle* and one of Gerhart Hauptmann's best prose pieces. Although it is an early work, *Bahnwärter Thiel* prefigures the major phases of Hauptmann's subsequent development—from poetic realism and naturalism, through mystic neo-romanticism and psychological realism, to modernizations of Hellenic myth. Thiel's story is both timeless and contemporary: the suffering of an oppressed human spirit at the dawn of the technical age. The soul of the protagonist, a meek signalman, is severely tried, first by the death of his adored wraith-wife Minna, then by his dominating and brutal second wife Lene. The emblematic wives and the tale's technological symbolism emphasize the opposite potentials of the human psyche.[1] Hauptmann's sympathetic delineation shows how a burly but gentle modern man comes to be spiritually subservient to physical forces. By subtle reference to Thiel's likeness to Hercules, Hauptmann ironically compares Thiel with a model of classical heroism. *Bahnwärter Thiel* is a myth of a modern strong man who fails to be a hero.

Scholars have long recognized that the conflict of the story is between man's spiritual and physical natures. Many consider the signalman's spiritual side weak and rather easily defeated by his physical appetites, low intelligence, and habit-prone ways.[2] Perhaps because the spirit seems to succumb so quietly in this tale, commentators have focused elsewhere—on imagery and symbolism, the unconscious psyche, animalism and the physical realm, and more recently on the narrator. Hence Hauptmann's subtle delineation of Thiel's spiritual life has been neglected and often misunderstood. Yet an awareness of Thiel's spirituality is fundamental to our understanding of the story, for upon it depends the degree of sympathy of Hauptmann and his reader with the signalman. Is Thiel's nature simply one of superficial piety and predominant bestiality? If so, the reader would feel pessimism concerning human nature and little sympathy for the *Bahnwärter*—for most readers do not think of themselves, whatever they think of some literary characters, as merely bestial beings. If, however, Thiel's spiritual life seems deep and real, and if his physical violence stems from an outrageous spiritual violation, then the reader may be moved to feel for Thiel a pity and fear that are similar to what he feels for classically flawed and spiritually suffering characters. When closely examined, the lines of causality in the tale suggest that it is the latter view which Hauptmann wishes the reader to see. We sympathize with Thiel because we fear that our own spiritual nature could be restricted or crushed altogether by superior and devious physical forces. If Thiel does possess a genuine spiritual nature, then he is not ignobly defeated like a naturalistic mad dog. He is, instead, a man gone mad in a belated defense of his beleaguered spirit. That he acts too late and excessively makes him in the end a pathetic and at least partially repugnant figure. In and of itself, however, the impulse to protest a spiritual violation is an heroic trait that we must admire, even though we are repelled by the means Thiel chooses. Thiel could have been a hero who successfully defended the soul—but he failed. In Thiel, Hauptmann represents every human being who lacks the firm will necessary to oppose brutish forces and whose spirit is consequently made subservient to the physical world.

Thiel's spirituality thus lies at the heart of Hauptmann's tale. The very first sentence tells a great deal about the flagman and his nature: "Allsonntäglich saß der Bahnwärter Thiel in der Kirche zu Neu-Zittau, ausgenommen die Tage, an denen er Dienst hatte oder krank war und zu Bette lag" (37).[3] Thiel is clearly dependable, even methodical, in his work and worship. Critics have consistently interpreted this opening line as a negative comment on Thiel's habit-prone ways.[4] But regularity of behavior is surely not the only trait suggested here; a strong positive inclination to the spiritual realm is intimated in Thiel's attendance at church whenever he can possibly be there. Although his work schedule only occasionally interferes with Thiel's care for his soul, the job exposes him to more serious dangers, as the next sentence reveals: "Im Verlaufe von zehn Jahren war er zweimal krank gewesen; das eine Mal infolge eines vom Tender einer Maschine während des Vorbeifahrens herabgefallenen Stückes Kohle, welches ihn getroffen und mit zerschmettertem Bein in den Bahngraben geschleudert hatte; das andere Mal einer Weinflasche wegen, die aus dem vorüberrasenden Schnellzuge mitten auf seine Brust geflogen war" (37). The dependence of this sentence on the first through the word "krank" implies that Thiel was not only hurt bodily, but also deprived spiritually by these sudden physical intrusions. Already we see the theme of the tale: the gradual succumbing of Thiel's vulnerable spirit to physical forces. Reinforcing the spiritual emphasis, the structure of the paragraph at once returns the reader to the central significance of the church to Thiel, for the final sentence repeats that nothing other than these two accidents had kept him from worship: "Außer diesen beiden Unglücksfällen hatte nichts vermocht, ihn, sobald er frei war, von der Kirche fernzuhalten" (37). The phrase "sobald er frei war" suggests that this is a free choice for spiritual commitment, not a mere act of habit. That Thiel is not lumpishly unreceptive in the sanctuary is indicated by the narrator's later comment, "Der Wärter wurde weihevoll gestimmt, ähnlich wie in der Kirche" (57). The central fact established by the first paragraph is the existence of an earnest soul that is about to be tried.

For fully eight of the ten years of Thiel's life given in the narrative, his spiritual and physical natures are in balance. The first page and a half of the *Novelle* show these eight mostly happy years: Thiel as a bachelor and then in his first marriage. At the start of paragraph two, we are told that for five years Thiel walked to church alone from Schön-Schornstein to Neu-Zittau, a statement that implies a lonely, steadfast devotion. As a single man, Thiel is a reliable, productive, God-fearing and law-abiding member of society. After his marriage to Minna, Thiel's spiritual and physical inclinations continue to be happily harmonized, for, despite her ethereality, Minna notably bears Thiel a son. Hauptmann's protagonist is established as having been initially a spiritually aware and well-adjusted man.

Although Thiel's life with Minna has the same duration in years as his later life with Lene, the former is ostensibly told in one brief paragraph. Perhaps because the narrator says relatively little about Minna directly, critics have tended to overlook or underestimate her significance to Thiel and to the tale.[5] Yet Minna is the single character who most completely symbolizes spirituality in this story. In life, she is always depicted in relation to the church, making her a perfect companion for the devout Thiel. The first time the reader sees her, she appears to be physically weak: "Eines schönen Tages war er dann in Begleitung eines schmächtigen und kränklich aussehenden Frauenzimmers erschienen. . . ." This sickliness suggests a relative incompatibility with the physical world. Next, there is a solemn wedding: "Und wiederum eines schönen Sonntagnachmittags reichte er dieser selben Person am Altare der Kirche feierlich die Hand zum Bunde fürs Leben" (37).

Then, in one sentence, we see their life together: "Zwei Jahre nun saß das junge, zarte Weib ihm zur Seite in der Kirchenbank; zwei Jahre blickte ihr hohlwangiges, feines Gesicht neben seinem vom Wetter gebräunten in das uralte Gesangbuch. . . ." Seen ever in sacred contexts, Minna's relationship with Thiel takes on a correspondingly spiritual quality. The repetition of the phrase "zwei Jahre" suggests to the reader that he or she should conceive of the couple's life together almost completely in terms of the sanctuary, as if their deeply felt and shared religiosity is both the basis of their relationship and the way they regard each other.

Then Thiel is suddenly pictured alone, and Minna's death, like her life, is reported indirectly and by means of omission: "und plötzlich saß der Bahnwärter wieder allein wie zuvor. An einem der vorangegangenen Wochentage hatte die Sterbeglocke geläutet; das war das Ganze" (37). The narrator accurately records here the fact of Minna's death. But, more profoundly, he hints that Minna was, in a manner of speech, "everything" to Thiel. The reader actually learns more about Minna and her effect upon the flagman after her death than during her life. The villagers falsely assess her loss as mattering little to Thiel: "An dem Wärter hatte man, wie die Leute versicherten, kaum eine Veränderung wahrgenommen. . . . Es war die allgemeine Ansicht, daß ihm der Tod seiner Frau nicht sehr nahegegangen sei . . . " (37).[6] But to the narrator's sharper eye, the flagman is in deepest mourning. He shows "den breiten, beharrten Nacken ein wenig gesenkt" and notes that Thiel worships "eifriger" than before (37). The "mehr vergeistigte Liebe" that Thiel and Minna had shared is now deeply missed (39). But judging from what we are told later, the narrator has withheld a great deal of information about Minna and Thiel: he has not yet even told us her name. This is the cryptic early portion of the narration which the reader understands only through hindsight. But the reader should not mistake emotionally freighted understatement for meaningless detail.

The two-year period with Minna has a profound impact on Thiel's conception of the spiritual world. Although her bodily presence begins and ends in the second paragraph, Minna's spirit may be said to endure beyond her physical death. Hereafter, the signalman's spiritual life is centered as much on mystical communion with Minna as on traditional religious worship. In a later revolt against his second wife, Thiel mentally declares his stretch of railroad "geheiligtes Land" (40), creates a chapel in his guard hut devoted to Minna, and places her picture beside his hymnal and Bible, thereby elevating his dead wife to the status of sainthood. Thiel's incorporation of Minna into his private worship services represents a fusion of the flagman's personal piety with the spiritualized intimacy he experienced with Minna. Although his daytime "geistiger Verkehr" is restricted to memories, by night Thiel is "recht innig mit der Verstorbenen verbunden" as he "las und sang . . . abwechselnd die lange Nacht hindurch . . . " (40). Only the passing trains—a reminder of the physical dangers of the first paragraph—interrupt Thiel's "Ekstase" as he envisions Minna "leibhaftig vor sich" (40). Thus it comes as no surprise when the narrator speaks of Thiel's "mystischen Neigungen" (40). During his oppressive second marriage, Thiel's mystic communications with Minna are his greatest spiritual resource and counterweight against Lene's physicality.

Minna's spiritual legacy to Thiel also takes physical form in the child Tobias. Only when Thiel is questioned by the skeptical pastor about his plan to remarry one year after Minna's death does the reader learn of the boy's existence. A second marriage, Thiel protests, is necessary because "Der Junge geht mir drauf . . . Mit der Toten kann ich nicht wirtschaften, Herr Prediger!" and because Tobias' present nurse has grossly neglected the boy (38). To protect his son's health, Thiel proposes to place him under the care of Lene—ironically, but unknown to Thiel, an even more abusive woman. Both father and son are daily endangered by the very means—job and nurse—that ought to assure their physical sustenance. Thiel perceives only part of the danger to his son, and his own hardly at all. Like his father, Tobias is threatened by physical forces against which he is defenseless. The abused Tobias, a spiritually precocious child who goes looking for God in nature, is an image of his father's own precarious spiritual-physical balance. Tobias' death will signal the onset of Thiel's madness.[7]

Like many fathers, Thiel invests his own special hopes and dreams in his son. Thiel keeps the "Sparkassenbuch des Tobias" under his pillow at night and in his pocket by day (44). When Tobias expresses an imitative desire to become "Bahnmeister," Thiel beams "von innerer Glückseligkeit." He devoutly hopes that "aus Tobias mit Gottes Hilfe etwas Außergewöhnliches werden sollte" (43). Like the arrows he carves for his son, Thiel's dreams for Tobias' future "verstiegen sich in der Tat in solche Höhen" (43). Indicative of their closeness are Thiel's carving of "Weidenpfeifchen" as well as other toys for the child and his singing and tapping time for Tobias' entertainment (44). Tobias is a tie to the spiritual world that later helps to tug Thiel's repressed conscience back to life from Lene's numbing influence.

In justifying his intent to remarry, Thiel also reveals for the first time a death-bed vow to Minna: " . . . und ferner, weil [Thiel] der Verstorbenen in die Hand gelobt, für die Wohlfahrt des Jungen zu jeder Zeit ausgiebig Sorge zu tragen . . . " (38). Thiel's concerted efforts to protect Tobias—even his contracting a second marriage—are thus undertaken not simply for the child's own sake, but, strangely, also for Minna's. In death as in life, Minna is the center of Thiel's universe. Her hand in his is a bond after death just as it had been a "Bunde fürs Leben."

Some scholars, however, share the pastor's skeptical reaction to Thiel's reasoning, believing that Thiel's motive for remarriage is not loyalty to Minna or Tobias but attraction to Lene's sexuality. The narrator, however, in contrast to the pastor, informs us that Lene's sensuality is not something Thiel is aware of: he contracts to marry a dominating, sensual, and quarrelsome bride "ohne es zu wissen" (38). Several distinctions can be made about this narrative statement and about Thiel's motives. On a conscious level, Thiel apparently wants only to remove Tobias from danger and to keep his pledge to Minna. Since we see that Thiel deeply loves his son and obviously still loves Minna, these are credible motives. Furthermore, even if we concede that on a subconscious level Thiel is probably motivated by a desire for a sexual outlet, this motive would by no means involve any prior, participative guilt on Thiel's part in the abuse and coercion to which Lene subsequently puts her sexual attractiveness. Her vicious misuse of her sexuality

for dominance is quite distinct from his innocent longing for sexual fulfillment. Thiel probably had had with Minna no experience of such sexual manipulation. This initial innocence does not, of course, excuse Thiel's subsequent passivity in allowing Lene to dominate him. Nor can he escape some responsibility for marrying without love, even if his motive is to provide for his son. But Thiel's motives for this second match—protection for Tobias and a subconscious need for sexual warmth—are ones we may defensibly call innocent. This reading accords with the narrator's insistence that Thiel "unknowingly" married a brutal, sensual woman.

When Lene enters the tale, the narrator does a strange thing. He interrupts his understated, objective manner to make a subtle but devastating revelation of his personal values. With one deft sentence, he divides his characters into the ensouled and the unsouled: "Auch war ihr Gesicht [Lenes] ganz so grob geschnitten wie das seine [Thiels], nur daß ihm im Gegensatz zu dem des Wärters die Seele abging" (38). Earlier, when the narrator compared Thiel's and Minna's faces, he mentioned only physical differences; we now infer retrospectively that Minna's face, like Thiel's, must have revealed this quality of "soul." Many scholars have noted that the narrator here begins the "psychological" dimension of the story, shifting to a more intimate tone hereafter, but no one has previously pointed out that the narrator also adds ethical and metaphysical dimensions to his tale with this sentence.[8] Up until now, the narrator's recital has been given without elucidation or any apparent narrative judgment; he has given the appearance of disinterested objectivity. But to see "soul" in one character and miss it in another is to hint that the former character possesses transcendent and more valuable traits and enjoys a greater degree of the narrator's sympathy than the latter character does. (The narrator has also with this one comment summarily removed his tale from the category of programmatic naturalism in which the soul is denied to exist.) Only by recognizing that the narrator has revealed his ethical bias—on the side of "Seele"—can the reader comprehend fully the implications of Thiel's life before and with Lene. The incalculable worth of spirit forms the basis of the narrator's viewpoint; he judges all characters and events from the touchstone of spiritual values. But scholars have recognized neither the narrator's partiality nor its implications, an oversight which has caused many a scholarly headache in explaining the narrative perspective in the tale.[9]

Although the narration changes in style at other points in the story, the narrator's sympathy with spirituality in general and with Thiel's spirit (though not with his deeds) does not change. Later shifts in technique occur at the beginning of section two, after the train accident, when Thiel's madness sets in, and in the last two sentences, where Thiel's fate is impassively recounted.[10] Taken as a whole, the narration is symmetric in style, beginning and ending with narrative distance and concentrating intimately upon the events just prior to and after Tobias' death. This pattern creates a kind of Doppler effect in the tale's pacing, pitch, and emotional intensity, reflecting the sound of the story's central *Dingsymbol,* the passing trains. But the narrator never abandons his focus on the state of Thiel's soul—never sympathizing with Lene's daily point of view, for example. And the most important stylistic shift of all remains the one that takes place when Lene enters Thiel's life. Like a traumatic shock, Lene's nature elicits a strong reaction in both the narrator and Thiel, sending each back to his spiritual values.

After the telling mention of "soul," the narrator then takes us into Thiel's inner world. We see his perceptions of his surroundings, their effects upon him, and how Thiel's previous balance between his spiritual and physical needs is gradually upset. Thus the reader is drawn closer to Thiel just as he is being alienated from Lene. We see how Thiel falls victim to a physical dominion much like that which threatens him on duty beside the passing trains. Like the roaring locomotives that momentarily blot out Thiel's mind and senses, the blustering, sensual Lene intermittently blots out his spiritual consciousness and values. As Thiel represses his awareness of the physical danger of standing close to an onrushing train, so he represses his sense of the danger of Lene's physical encroachment on his spiritual life, symbolized primarily by her abuse of Tobias. The bulk of the narration from this point on depicts Thiel's losing battle to stay spiritually alive. His insanity and sudden recourse to physical violence are his soul's death throes. The form his imbalance takes and precisely how he and Lene contribute to it are crucial, since these points are the bases from which we will later assess Thiel's guilt. But whatever his own guilt, there can be little doubt that the initiating cause of Thiel's spiritual malaise is Lene's physical intimidation and exploitation of his meekness, for before her entry into his life Thiel was spiritually at peace. In judging Thiel's character, we must also remember that this last, two-year-long struggle with Lene, though it forms the tragic principal portion of the tale, is but a short episode compared with his previous six quiet years as a bachelor and widower and his two years of intense happiness with Minna. The narrator would not have alluded so carefully to that calm, stable background had he not considered it significant to Thiel's story.

What do Lene's manipulative sensuality and lack of soul mean for someone like Thiel, who has thus far derived his life's order and meaning from spiritual values? Thiel's spirit withdraws, because his will is not strong enough to contest with Lene either his values or his right to a spiritual life. If Thiel had thought this was to be a marriage of convenience, the neighbors soon perceive that it is a disaster. They correctly conclude that Lene dominates the family; they pity Thiel (38), utter "Verwünschungen" about Lene's treatment of Tobias (42), and consider Lene a "Tier" who ought to be tamed "mit Schlägen" (39). But Thiel, to his credit, does not accept this easy solution. Instead, he struggles to control his impulses to use force against her (46-47, 51, 63) and invents a number of "außergewöhnlicher Hilfsmittel" (40) to shield his spirit. These aids include his sanctified railway hut, whose location he conceals from Lene. Because emotional scraps and physical violence are against his nature, Thiel's spiritual life goes, so to speak, underground.

Thiel and Lene relate as direct opposites. Thiel has at the beginning of his second marriage an air of uncorrupted innocence: "es war, als trüge er etwas in sich, wodurch er alles Böse, was sie ihm antat, reichlich mit Gutem aufgewogen erhielt" (39). The narrator thus explicitly associates Lene with evil ("Böse") and Thiel with goodness ("Gutem"). Referred to as "ein gutes Schaf' (38-39), Thiel is at first simply untroubled by Lene's irate antics and

long speeches. He is in certain ways the epitome of his religion's ideals: one who returns good for evil, who is meek, pure in heart, forgiving of others' faults, and a peacemaker. Thiel is called "kindgut" and "nachgiebig" (39), while Lene shows "eine harte, herrschsüchtige Gemütsart, Zanksucht und brutale Leidenschaftlichkeit" (38)—traits never even implicitly attributed to Thiel. Childlike Thiel seems to exist in an entirely different world than does his second wife: "Die Außenwelt schien ihm wenig anhaben zu können" (39).

The most striking physical difference between Lene and Thiel is their opposite relation to human speech. Thiel endures "die endlosen Predigten seiner Frau," remaining himself mostly "wortlos" (39). Hauptmann seems to have pitched their voices to incline us toward Thiel: " . . . und wenn er einmal antwortete, so stand das schleppende Zeitmaß sowie der leise, kühle Ton seiner Rede in seltsamstem Gegensatz zu dem kreischenden Gekeif seiner Frau" (39). The constantly noisy Lene sounds in marked contrast not only to the often speechless Thiel ("Er hätte wohl gern ein Wort dagegen gesagt, aber er wußte nicht, womit beginnen" [55]), but also to Minna, whom we never hear speak, and to Tobias, whose speech development is very slow. Even Lene's child is referred to as a "Schreihals" (41). In itself, Thiel's quiet forbearance seems admirable, especially in contrast to the irritating Lene. It is true that part of his calm demeanor is due to a certain mental slowness. But Thiel is not vacuous. He is described as "gedankenvoll" (43) and "sinnend" (57), often emerging "aus tiefem Nachdenken" (45) and thinking as he works:"Er tat es mechanisch, während sein Geist mit dem Eindruck der letzten Stunde beschäftigt war" (48). However attractive his mildness, Thiel's inability to articulate his thoughts or express his will against voluble Lene is nevertheless a fatal factor in their relationship and ultimately contributes to their tragedy. The extended aural contrast between Thiel and Lene warns the reader not to make the same mistake the villagers made, who judged at first only on visual appearance and so thought Lene and Thiel well matched because both have large, coarse "peasant" features. In spirit and temperament, Thiel is nearly as delicate as frail, silent Minna and no match for ear-splitting Lene.[11]

Meanwhile, at his work, Thiel shows his courage in a seemingly more dangerous duty. Thiel's job is a kind of secular calling to a physical guardianship, and his good works necessarily expose him to harm in obvious and insidious ways. He safeguards others from physical danger, becoming in one sense the equal of the train by bravely rising to meet its force rather than shrinking in a more natural retreat (49). In faithfully standing guard over these threatening machines, in daylight or darkness, good weather or storm, Thiel faces the hazard of death to protect his fellow men, thereby making him a kind of hero among men. But this is a specifically passive, rather than active, courage. Thiel merely meets and endures the passing of danger; he does not combat it. The signalman is in some ways the servant of the train, literally waiting upon and watching over its passing. His work entails a conditioned acceptance of the train's domination as it roars by and a momentary but brutal obliteration of his mind and senses.[12] The regularity of his exposure to this force tends to inure him to its danger. Ironically, Thiel's very ability to repress his fear of this danger is itself a weakness that contributes to his vulnerability to being dominated.

Thus, like other mortals and heroes, Thiel has flaws. His physical vulnerability—alongside the rails or at home with wily, seductive Lene—represents the mortal imperfection of every strong hero, just as Achilles was vulnerable at the heel and Siegfried upon his back, and just as most heroes are vulnerable to female beauty. Thiel's systematic, rather plodding quality is another flaw in his nature. But this is not, as some commentators seem to think, a flaw common only to a "lower" order of humanity; it has long been recognized by sociologists as a trait common to many human beings—literary critics included. The signalman's unusual lack of companions, relatives; or ancestors, the remoteness of his hut, and his preference for communion with the dead rather than with the living are circumstances common in stories of heroes, but they also reveal Thiel's existential aloneness and his isolation from advice and assistance. Powerful temperamental and physical forces are pitted against Thiel's spirit and his potential heroism.

Thiel has often been called "weak-willed" by scholars, and although there is justification for this accusation, finer distinctions can be made. The signalman clearly exercises his will early in the story when he productively manages his job and his free time. A year after Minna's death, Thiel forcefully defends his plans for remarriage against the pastor's objections. During the first year of his marriage to Lene, Thiel's will continues to exert itself. We hear of "Augenblicke, in denen er nicht mit sich spaßen ließ," and of his "Anstrich von Festigkeit, dem selbst ein so unzähmbares Gemüt wie das Lenens nicht entgegenzutreten wagte" (39). But this firmness gradually becomes a "gewisser leidender Widerstand." Although he had partially restrained Lene during the first year, an important change takes place in the second: "[Thiel] geriet durch die Macht roher Triebe in die Gewalt seiner zweiten Frau und wurde zuletzt in allem fast unbedingt von ihr abhängig" (39). The signalman has allowed his will to be almost totally subjugated to the physical desires that Lene has aroused and now manipulates. The pernicious result of this surrender appears on several occasions when Thiel chooses to ignore indirect evidence of Lene's abuse of Tobias. The inner workings of his subjugation are made clear when Thiel unexpectedly returns home to pick up a forgotten "Butterbrot." Accidentally confronting Lene in the very act of striking Tobias, Thiel is distracted by and elects to focus upon Lene's sexual charms (46-47). Thus he himself consents to have his will and spirit made prisoner to his sexual drives. But the narrator's qualifying word "almost" ("fast") indicates that Thiel's will yet retains some independence. His creation of secret spiritual hideaway and invention of private forms of worship testify to his greatly weakened but still surviving will. After a fearful midnight vision on his holy ground, Thiel belatedly tries to rouse his will to oppose Lene again and put a stop to Tobias' servitude at home: He brushes aside Lene's orders that Tobias attend her baby (54, 56). But Thiel's willpower is gradually sapped when pitted against Lene's, and thus Thiel must be called weak-willed in comparison with her. Still it is significant that even in contest with Lene's strong force, Thiel's independent will, deeds, and values do not entirely disappear.[13]

However serious Thiel's flaws, Lene's are more repulsive. She is characterized more truly by her physical bullying than by her coarse sensuality. The loose tripartite structure of the tale reflects the stages of Lene's progressive domi-

nance over her new family. By the end of part one, Thiel's submission to Lene's nagging has become an established pattern, and her abuse of Tobias begins; she presses the child into virtual slavery to her baby, and in Thiel's absence, Tobias is "unaufhörlich geplagt" (41). Early in part two, Lene extends her rule to include the right to strike her stepson, though still in private (42), and by the end of this section, when Thiel finds his son's facial bruise, he is too intimidated to rebuke Lene even for such a blasphemy against Minna's sacred trust. In part three, Lene invades Thiel's "holy ground." Thiel's story is thus inversely the tale of a female tyrant's progress.[14]

As the only person in the *Novelle* said to lack a "soulful" face, Lene is also the only one who regularly resembles a machine. Although several scholars mention in passing Lene's likeness to the trains, the nature of the resemblance has never been made explicit.[15] Like the "masculine" image she is associated with, Lene drives Thiel's spirit out of her space and unhouses his spiritual life. She allows only his physical needs to be filled in her house, thereby engendering a fatal schism in Thiel's personality. Like the locomotives, she shatters holy silences at home and in the forest (49). Both Lene and the trains sound "schrill," metallic, and cacophonous: "Der Ton einer [Lenes] kreischenden Stimme unterbrach die Stille so laut und schrill . . .Ein Schwall heftig herausgestoßner, mißtönender Laute schlug an sein Ohr . . . " (45); "Ein lautes Quietschen, Schnarren, Rasseln und Klirren durchdrang weithin die Abendstille, bis der Zug unter einem einzigen, schrillen, langgedehnten Ton stillstand" (64). Lene's scolding of Tobias intensifies like an advancing locomotive "im schnellsten Tempo" and "in steigender Betonung" (46). Muscular Lene digs up the potato patch "mit der Geschwindigkeit und Ausdauer einer Maschine" (56). Intermittently she suckles her baby "mit keuchender schweißtropfender Brust" (56); both the train from Breslau and the *Kiezug* are also characterized by the verb *keuchen* (49, 63).

Lene's hypnotic, paralyzing effect on Thiel, so like the trains' freezing influence on the signalman, is summed up in metallic, mechanical terms: "Eine Kraft schien von dem Weibe auszugehen, unbezwingbar, unentrinnbar, der Thiel sich nicht gewachsen fühlte. Leicht gleich einem feinen Spinngewebe und doch fest wie ein Netz von Eisen legte es sich um ihn, fesselnd, überwindend, erschlaffend" (47). Not only does this simile lay bare the physical and psychic intimidation behind Lene's power over Thiel, it also resembles the narrator's description of the iron rails: "Die schwarzen, parallellaufenden Geleise darauf glichen in ihrer Gesamtheit einer ungeheuren, eisernen Netzmasche, deren schmale Strähne sich im äußersten Süden und Norden in einem Punkte des Horizontes zusammenzogen" (49). Like the tracks that mark the path of the train, Lene's tyrannical course is indicated by the "Netz von Eisen" that she casts about her.[16]

Though oppressed in spirit, Thiel is intermittently aware of and conscience-stricken over the impropriety of his condition. Even after his initial resistance to Lene's dominance has faded, Thiel occasionally understands his relationship to her "im Lichte der Wahrheit" and feels "Ekel" and "Gewissensbisse" (40). One night he awakes as if "aus einem zweijährigen totenähnlichen Schlaf," sees "mit ungläubigem Kopfschütteln all das Haarsträubende," and watches with horror as "[d]ie Leidensgeschichte seines

Ältesten . . .trat deutlich vor seine Seele." He is seized with "Mitleid und Reue" and feels "eine tiefe Scham" about his failure to protect Tobias. Even his patience with Lene he perceives as "schmachvoll" (51). To his credit, Thiel focuses on his own sins rather than hers. Only a deeply sensitive and self-critical person would rouse himself to confront his past and present mistakes. The fact that Thiel still experiences these passing moments of clarity, spiritual acuteness, and shame is another indication that his spirit is not yet dead, nor his will altogether effaced.

On this confessional night, Thiel is overcome by "den selbstquälerischen Vorstellungen all seiner Unterlassungssünden" (51) and transfers his life's dilemma into the world of dream. A storm outside his hut becomes in his nightmare both an oncoming train and an uncanny analogue of Lene, whose physical and aural intimidation he recalls from a noisy encounter that afternoon. After he rouses himself to watch for the express train due, the storm's weird lighting perpetuates groggy Thiel's dream in a waking vision (51-53).[17] The dream-Minna's rags and haggard appearance embody the neglect Thiel has shown her through Tobias. She stumbles afraid and exhausted down the railroad tracks, fleeing from some unidentified pursuer; in her arms Thiel sees "etwas Schlaffes, Blutiges, Bleiches"—the brutalized Tobias. Minna's facial expressions reflect her foe's ferocity: "diese Blicke voll Herzensangst nach rückwärts gesandt. . . . O diese entsetzlichen Blicke!" Minna's unassisted attempt to prevent further injury to her bundle underscores Thiel's broken promise to care for her son. This betrayal results in Minna's disregard for Thiel in the dream-vision: "Sie war an Thiels Häuschen vorübergekommen, ohne sich darnach umzuschauen. . . . [Es] trat ihm klar vor die Seele: sie hatte sich von ihm losgesagt, ihn nicht beachtet. . . . Minna, the very image to Thiel of saintly spirituality, the grail and love-reward of his spiritual life, has abandoned as faithless the champion who promised to defend her.

Thiel's mind has presciently dramatized his life's crisis in a real setting of danger. By envisioning Minna and Tobias caught in the path of an actual approaching train, Thiel projects the climax of his conflict and foresees what literally will happen to Tobias on the following day. The symbol of the train has been especially intensified for this occasion, taking on the features of a carnivorous monster, an "Ungetüm" with bloody "Glotzaugen" (53). By making the train into a predator, Hauptmann symbolically frees the machine from its cage—the rails—and replaces the rational concept "train, servant of man" with a rampaging beast that will mutilate men.[18] This train-beast and Thiel's reaction to it in his vision are disguised phantoms of Lene and of his own guilty conscience. Thiel sees the monster-train as Minna's and Tobias' persecutor and himself as a shamefully passive, guilty bystander. But Lene is the true "soulless" beast who is hunting down Minna and Tobias. The real express train seems less dangerous to Thiel than Lene does, as his repression of her guilt indicates. For the train's arrival is announced by a bell, and it is still actually controlled in its direction by the tracks. Fierce Lene, however, attacks without warning and selects her victims unpredictably. Although the train usually passes away harmlessly, Lene encroaches more and more dangerously. Surely one of Thiel's greatest handicaps as a potential champion-hero is that the monster he is called upon to combat is female. The Greeks prepared their heroes for the psychic duress of duelling with malignant, destructive females. But what Christian knight was prepared to encounter Gorgon where he expected to find Minna?

Even before this weird night is over, Thiel is moved to act on the message of his vision. Feeling separated from his elder son "durch Jahre," the signalman is tempted to desert his post in order to go to Tobias. But after he does arrive home, he gradually seems to forget "die Bilder der Nacht" (54). The net effect of his nocturnal experience is an increased sense of distance from Lene, "etwas Befremdliches" in his manner toward her. He behaves especially strangely toward Lene in church, peering sideways at her instead of at the prayerbook (54). But Thiel's attempt to alter the course of things at home, handing the baby back to Lene and taking Tobias for a walk, is pathetically meager. It demonstrates how little Thiel has grasped of the serious ramifications of his domestic impasse.[19] Thiel is one of those people who seem to function only at two speeds: underreacting or overreacting.

To restore his world to balance, Thiel should have acted more firmly on his vision. Thiel's tragic flaw is his inability to put his spiritual values into action. Because he is unable to integrate his nighttime spiritual insights with Minna into his daytime life with Lene, unable even to express his spiritual values to Lene or do other than mutely mime them, as in his feeble attempt to free Tobias, the signalman's actions and emotions remain wholly disjunctive. The gift of forceful articulation might here have been his saving grace. Without it, Thiel's spiritual paralysis and schizophrenia of will—caused both by Lene's bullying and by his own temperamental meekness—will lead to insanity.[20] The unnaturally sundered and antagonized parts of Thiel's psyche—his spiritual and physical needs, his guilt and his obligations—must now either be rejoined or collide. His bloody vision foretells not only Tobias' fate but also the consequence of any failure to restore his own world to harmony: an impending mental breakdown and an eruption of retributive violence

Now Lene's advance is aimed more directly at Thiel himself: she plans to start a garden on his sacred stretch of railroad. Thiel "zuckte zusammen" when he hears she is coming to his post, feels "Mißbehagen" at her preparations the next morning, and walks in "Unruhe" with his family through the woods to work (55). Thiel senses deeply the danger of these developments but is too divided within himself to oppose Lene. Thus he allows the stage to be set for the reenactment of his disastrous dream.

Surprisingly, the highpoint of Thiel's relationship with Tobias comes during their walk that day along the tracks. In this scene, objects of modern technology take on, contrary to their previous ominousness in the tale, a spiritual aura. Thiel and Tobias hear "das Klingen der Telegraphenstangen . . . die aus dem Holze wie sonore Choräle aus dem Innern einer Kirche hervorströmten" (56). Though he has heard the sounds before, these secular tones now seem sanctified to Thiel by Tobias' companionship. For a few minutes with his son, Thiel feels as if his stretch of track were truly holy ground and is momentarily restored to happiness. The "Akkord" of the wires symbolized his long desired reunion with the boy and also the forgiveness of Minna, whose voice he believes he hears in a "Chor seliger Geister" (57). Nature and technology perform a heavenly pastorale for this imaginary family reunion. Little To-bias—revived and uplifted by his surroundings, his father's love, and his freedom from Lene—mirrors his father's spiritual experience when he thinks he sees God in a small brown squirrel: "Vater, ist das der liebe Gott?" (57). But the child's image of God, like his father's later grief-maddened recollection of it, pathetically reveals that to them God seems less powerful than Lene or the train. Their own feelings of helplessness and frustration are pro-jected in their image for the being who should be their source of spiritual comfort and aid. To the reader, the im-age suggests the effective absence of a Divine Providence that might intervene to prevent the coming tragedy.[21] Though God may continue to exist in the cosmos, His power to affect events has been radically reduced in the eyes of modern man.

The train's collision with Tobias is the turning point for Thiel's sanity and thus for the entire *Novelle*.[22] The image of Tobias bounced between the rails as if he were a rubber ball is the story's most naturalistic image, a fulfillment of his earlier nurse's dropping him as if "gekugelt" onto the floor (38). The accident marks at once the apex of Lene's abuse, here in the form of neglecting to watch over her stepson after Thiel has gone to stand guard, and also the complete destruction of Thiel's last tangible bond to Minna. Tobias' death therefore shatters the link that could have reunified Thiel's life and triggers his quick mental breakdown. The train's mangling of Tobias' body symbol-izes the psychic, physical, and emotional damage that Lene has done to the boy and to Thiel.

Thiel's insanity, Lene's surprising change of character, and the signalman's revenge constitute the final quarter of the tale. Thiel is transformed from a gentle father into a family-murderer. Only now does Hauptmann employ the vocabulary, syntax, and imagery that he used throughout the the text for Lene and the trains to describe the insane Thiel. Resemblance to the train indeed implies heartless brutality; but scholars have not pointed out that for Lene this is a way of life, while for Thiel it is a unique reaction in insanity and in "hot blood" to the loss of Tobias.[23] Only now does Thiel become the source of sharp, penetrating sounds: "'Ha-alt!' schrie der Wärter aus Leibeskräften" (58), and he cries out over his son's body "mit einer Stimme, als müsse der enge Raum davon zerbersten: 'Er muß, muß leben, ich sage dir, er muß, muß leben'" (61). Only now is Thiel associated with the verb *keuchen,* used earlier for Lene and the trains (58). Only now, when Thiel finally decides that Lene has murdered Tobias, does Haupt-mann describe him in words that recall the demonic train of the vision: "Ein roter Nebel umwölkte seine Sinne, zwei Kinderaugen durchdrangen ihn" (63). The presence in both passages of redness, eyes, and the past tense verb *durchdrangen* identifies Thiel with the killer train, and it is as if the train-monster has been reborn, this time to crush Lene and her child, as the Lene-train had borne down on Minna and Tobias. Thiel at last reacts to Lene's long op-pression of his spirit. Under the combined and unbearable stress of inner spiritual guilt, emotional outrage, and grief, Thiel physically and mentally explodes.

The problem of guilt in this tale is one critics have pre-ferred to avoid, perhaps because Thiel and Lene both seem to be so unaware of the consequences of their personalities and so unable to change until placed under extreme du-ress. At first it may seem that Hauptmann covertly sug-gests that if Lene has no soul and thus is not quite human, then perhaps Thiel is not quite guilty of murder in her case. Yet Lene changes dramatically after the accident. Feeling apparently for the first time some pangs of con-science, she fears her husband: "Thiel würdigte sie keines Blickes; sie aber erschrak beim Anblick ihres Mannes" (64). Crying and sobbing, Lene follows the men who later carry the unconscious Thiel home. With "Eifer und Um-sicht" she carries out her neighbors' medical advice and keeps close watch over his breathing. The narrator leaves no doubt of her change: "Sie war überhaupt eine andre ge-worden. Nirgend eine Spur des früheren Trotzes" (66). Lene's personality change shows that Hauptmann believes even an otherwise wholly sensual individual is capable, al-though here too late, of conscience and compassion. The reversal also makes her, in the reader's eyes, a more cred-ible and rounded character. In fact, Hauptmann inverts his characters' traits after the accident: Lene is transformed from an entirely negative, destructive personality into a tender, solicitous nurse, while Thiel changes by the same catalyst from meekness to violence. As Lene loses per-sonal force, the insane Thiel now dominates the forces he could not manage in his right mind: even asleep he is said to rule Lene, and later he successfully brings an express train to a halt. As Lene gains a degree of the reader's sym-pathy, Thiel elicits shock from the reader with his mad vengeance. The ill-matched pair's guilt and pathos rise and fall inversely, although the reader never sympathizes with Lene as much as with Thiel.

In combination Thiel and Lene create their own horrible fate. Both contribute to the tragedy and thus both are guilty. On the whole, however, Lene incurs the greater guilt, for the narrator depicts her as a heartless bully who habitually—and without the excuse of insanity—practices physical and mental brutality upon the defenseless, harm-less persons about her. She introduced violence to her gentle husband and eventually inspires it in him. Nor does Lene have for her violence any shred of spiritual justifica-tion or motive as the reader feels Thiel does. The initiating actor must be held more responsible than the long-restrained counter-actor.[24]

Nevertheless, the true villain of Hauptmann's tale is not Lene or Thiel but brute force—a trait he depicts in men, machines, and nature. The train is a man-made labor sav-ing miracle, but it also inherits its creator's capacity for brutality. The train is the *Dingsymbol* of brute force, but human beings cause themselves the greatest suffering. Hauptmann depicts Lene's and Thiel's brutality as stem-ming, respectively, from a lack of "soul" or spiritual incli-nation and from an inability to implement spiritual values. Only an active spiritual nature, Hauptmann implies, can safeguard man from being a brute in his relations with his fellow beings. Far from announcing man's lack of a soul, Hauptmann's *Novelle* emphasizes why man must struggle to keep his soul alive.

Another way of summarizing Thiel's simultaneous victim-ization and mad guilt is to compare him with the mythic hero Hercules. Although it may well be coincidental, Hauptmann seems to invite a comparison of the two men when at the outset he describes Thiel as having an "herkulisch[e] Gestalt" (37). Besides their imposing phy-siques, these men also share an emotional religiosity, self-slaughtered families, and an ambivalent reaction to women. Hercules and Thiel both live and judge by the heart, although the Greek hero, unlike lethargic Thiel, was always quick to act on his feelings. They have in common, too, a certain slow-wittedness in thinking an idea through. Both men are characterized by "greatness of soul."[25] W. H. Roscher, for example, attributes the demigod's heroic feats to his religious commitment: "Herakles aber, zu dessen religiösem Wesen die Überwindung böser feindlicher in Tiergestalten symbolisierter Dämonen gehört, bekämpft den Löwen. . . ."[26] It is Thiel's modern fate not to sense any divine assistance as he confronts his domestic "demon." Perhaps Thiel doubts that God should help a man with such a mundane foe. But Thiel is also the victim of a rational age in which God was not thought to show himself to help his devotees, as the Greeks believed Jupiter and his fellow gods could be relied upon to do.

Hauptmann may have recalled other details of the Hercules legends.[27] Xenophon's allegory of Hercules bears a curious resemblance to Hauptmann's depiction of the females in Thiel's life:

> Two women came toward [Hercules], both tall and uncommon in appearance: one, clad in white, majestic, and surrounded, as it were, with a halo of purity and holiness; the other, rounder and fuller in form, clothed in gauzy garments, mincing in gait and obviously inviting admiration.
>
> The latter ran quickly to Hercules and commenced to spread before his inexperienced judgment all the allurements which physical delights can offer. . . .
>
> "And by what name must I call thee, Lady?" asked Hercules. "My friends call me 'Happiness,'" was the reply; "but those who hate me call me 'Vice!'" . . .
>
> Then the other, whose name was "Virtue" . . . gave her description of a hero's duty, and the picture which she drew was so alluring to the soul of Hercules that he drove "Vice" from him and chose the long and narrow way, finding it true, as "Virtue" had promised. . . .[28]

Although Thiel does not meet simultaneously the two women in his life, they exist for him side by side, in spirit and flesh, for the greater part of the tale. But Thiel does not exercise Hercules' wisdom and will in his conduct toward the sensual woman. Although Hercules was later known for his sexual exploits, he never lost his self-command over a woman's attractiveness. Once Minna has been taken away, Thiel's weaker will allows Lene's sensuality to lead him into submission and to dissipate his spiritual strength.

The plot of Hauptmann's story reveals interesting parallels with Euripides' *Herakles,* wherein the Greek hero, in a fit of madness imposed on him by the jealous Hera, slays his wife and three sons.[29] In events early in the play, Herakles neglects his dependents, just as Thiel neglects Tobias. Thiel's and Herakles' insanities are described in similar length and details. The murders of both families take place in their own homes and are reported by a messenger. Herakles knows not that he is killing his own family, but Thiel seems conscious even in his madness that he is taking revenge upon Lene for Tobias. Both Herakles and Thiel think of God in their distress. The Greek hero blames Hera for his fate; Thiel "mußte an den lieben Gott denken, ohne zu wissen, warum" (63). Herakles blames a mali-

cious deity for his violent spiritual disorder. Thiel also looks to God in his spiritual derangement but finds no divine answer. The ancient hero had a divine scapegoat on whom to shift the guilt, but the modern Thiel has no one to blame but himself. If he blames God for His inaction, all the more must he blame his own. This is the modern man's burden: to rouse his own lonely strength as a spiritual, ethical being to combat brute force.

Both men contemplate suicide as a way of escaping the pain of their violence. Herakles wonders aloud (in the German version), "was stoß' ich nicht ein schwert in meinen busen / als richter und als rächer meiner kinder?" Thiel lies down on the tracks where Tobias was killed even though an express train is due. Theseus comes to talk Herakles out of suicide, persuading him to return to Athens and his expiatory twelve labors. Several employees of the railroad plead with Thiel to leave the tracks, but he is removed only by force, to be taken to an asylum from which he never emerges. Perhaps since Herakles' guilt was shared by Hera, he could shoulder a reduced and expiable burden of remorse. But Thiel is crushed by the unshared burden of his deeds and shame, for he has destroyed Lene, the only partner in his guilt. In both men, the inclination to suicide is an expression of their sense of guilt for lacking spiritual insight.

Even if Hauptmann did not intentionally juxtapose Thiel and Hercules, the contrast of their faiths, cultures, fates, and concepts of heroism is instructive. Thiel's differences from Hercules do not mean that he is not a tragic figure, for the modes of tragedy vary with the age. The two men represent extremes in the spectrum of tragic characters: the kindly demigod belongs to the high tragedy of dying but self-assured gods in the "Dionysiac" style of tragedy, while the mortal Thiel embodies tragic pathos in the low mimetic, "domestic" mode.[30] The typical *eiron* or humble hero of low mimetic tragedy is isolated, inarticulate, and self-deprecating, a predestined victim whose violent fate seems out of keeping with his mildness. He is an individual of vulnerable virtue who is dominated by a less scrupulous antagonist. He is not a socially elevated figure, yet he has experienced a great happiness that is now lost. The hero of domestic tragedy arouses not the admiring identification that an audience feels for King Oedipus or brave Hercules but rather an intense personal pity and terror, for the *eiron* appears—as the audience may often feel—powerless to control or influence his destiny. Like other low mimetic protagonists, Thiel seems "in a state of lower freedom than the audience." So when readers perceive that Thiel's realistic flaws are similar to their own, his chilling demise strikes home. Ultimately Thiel is a tragic figure—not just a just a pitiable one—because he consciously and spiritually suffers his fate and knows how he contributed to it.

Thiel's tragedy may have an even stronger impact on the reader than Hercules' death agony. For Hercules dies only to live happily and guilt-free in heaven, while Thiel experiences neither catharsis for his guilt nor remission from his grief and madness. The reader also is left with an unpurged feeling of helplessness and waste. But because of the narrator's spiritual values, Hauptmann's reader can hope for men in general if not for Thiel. If Thiel's tragic flaws were his failures to exert soul and will, then other men may find ways of bringing those faculties more effectively to bear on the forces of spiritual and physical oppression.

In Thiel, Hauptmann imagines how a contemporary Herculean man might fare. Thiel's most admirable traits are his compassion, his piety, and his gentleness toward others. His interest in the little children of the village—teaching them how to spell and play new games, listening to their lessons, and helping them to learn verses from the Bible and hymnal—earns him the title "Vater Thiel" and makes him a hero to the children (43). But it seems impossible for modern man to demonstrate heroism by feats of sheer physical strength. Thiel can never match the power of the locomotive, and sheer bludgeoning force is misapplied as a solution to his domestic problems. In the modern world, "herculean stature" and the old virtues of muscle no longer compose a hero. The well-spoken word can be as heroic as the powerful deed. The simple, tongue-tied, gentle, strong man is not properly equipped for the modern condition or for the burden that a withdrawn inactive God places on lonely human beings. The modern "herculean" man is destined to be a failed hero, a pathetic hulk huddled on the railroad tracks, insane and longing for death. Only strength of spiritual will, not physical prowess, could have made Thiel an admirable and successful modern Hercules.

Notes

1. For Hauptmann's stylistic development, see Walter A. Reichert, "Grundbegriffe im dramatischen Schaffen Gerhart Hauptmanns," *PMLA* 82 (1967): 142-51. The suffering of the human spirit is one of Hauptmann's main themes; see Thomas Mann, *Altes und Neues. Kleine Prosa aus fünf Jahrzehnten* (Frankfurt a. Main: Fischer, 1953), p. 450. Hugo F. Garten, "Formen des Eros im Werk Gerhart Hauptmanns," *Zeitschrift für deutsche Philologie* 90 (1971): 249, describes the man caught between two women as another of Hauptmann's favorite themes; and C. F. W. Behl, "Die Magie des Elementaren," *Gerhart Hauptmann Jahrbuch* 1 (1936): 51, discusses Hauptmann's interest in primitive psychic forces.

2. For formulations of the story's theme as a conflict between spirit and body, see F. B. Wahr, "The Art of Hauptmann's Shorter Stories," *GR* 24 (1949): 56; Marianne Ordon, "Unconscious Contents in 'Bahnwärter Thiel,'" *GR* 26 (1951): 225; Josef Kunz, "Geschichte der deutschen Novelle," *Deutsche Philologie im Aufriss,* ed. Wolfgang Stammler (Berlin: Schmidt, 1952), 2: 1830; Paul Requadt, "Die Bilderwelt in Gerhart Hauptmanns 'Bahnwärter Thiel,'" in *Minotaurus: Dichtung unter den Hufen von Staat und Industrie,* ed. A. Döblin (Wiesbaden: Steiner, 1953), p. 109; Werner Zimmermann, "Bahnwärter Thiel," in *Deutsche Prosadichtungen unseres Jahrhunderts: Interpretationen für Lehrende und Lernende* (Düsseldorf: Schwann, 1966), 1: 71; and Fritz Martini, "Bahnwärter Thiel," in *Das Wagnis der Sprache: Interpretationen deutscher Prosa von Nietzsche bis Benn,* 5th ed. (Stuttgart: Klett, 1964), p. 88. Many critics berate Thiel as a bestial sub-human with whose physical drives and mental

weaknesses they could not possibly have anything in common. Berthold Schultze, for example, speaks of Thiel's "zu derbe Natur," in "Die Eisenbahnstrecke in Gerhart Hauptmanns 'Bahnwärter Thiel,'" *Monatsschrift für höhere Schulen* 19 (1920): 299; Requadt claims that Thiel's "schwersinniges Wesen" sinks "in ein Zeitalter zurück, wo der Mensch in seiner Triebhaftigkeit dem Rationalen unzugänglich . . . war," p. 103; Martini believes Thiel exists in "dumpfer Primitivität," p. 91; John Ellis, *Narration in the German Novelle: Theory and Interpretation* (Cambridge: Cambridge Univ. Press, 1974), pp. 169-87, sees Thiel only in terms of his mechanical nature and his eventual madness and loss of self-control; and Manfred Schunicht calls Thiel's level of consciousness "pathologisch deformiert," in "Die zweite Realität. Zu den Erzählungen Gerhart Hauptmanns," in *Untersuchungen zur Literatur als Geschichte: Festschrift für Benno von Wiese,* ed. Vincent J. Günther et al, (Berlin: Schmidt, 1973), p. 442. For the most balanced appraisal of Thiel's strong and weak points, see Walter Silz, *Realism and Reality: Studies in the German Novelle of Poetic Realism* (Chapel Hill: Univ. of North Carolina Press, 1954), pp. 144-47, 149.

3. Gerhart Hauptmann, *Sämtliche Werke,* ed. Hans-Egon Hass (Frankfurt a. Main/Berlin: Propyläen, 1963), 6: 37. All subsequent references are to this edition; page numbers will be indicated parenthetically in the text.

4. Although most critics note that Thiel has a spiritual side, only one has recognized that the theme of spirituality is introduced in the first sentence. Requadt reads the first line in this way: "Die Einförmigkeit dieses Lebens ist schon im ersten Worte der Erzählung erkennbar . . . " p. 104; Ellis believes that the "story's opening words refer to Thiel's appearance in church every Sunday as if reading from his timetable," p. 177. Only Gottfried Mende notices the implications for Thiel's spirit: "Daß diese Seele sich nach oben sehnte, soll dadurch ausgedrückt werden, daß Thiel nie in der Kirche fehlte," in *Religiöse Betrachtungen über Werke Gerhart Hauptmanns* (Leipzig: Dieterich'sche Verlagsbuchhandlung, 1906), p. 19.

5. A surprising number of scholars speak negatively of Minna. Joseph Gregor describes her relationship to Thiel as "nicht viel mehr als Freundschaft," in *Gerhart Hauptmann: Das Werk und unsere Zeit* (Vienna: Diana, 1951), p. 79; Silz believes that the "spirit of the first [wife] mercilessly condemns [Thiel's] physical sexuality and mercilessly exacts murderous atonement," and concludes that Minna is one of the "two women, who destroy Thiel," pp. 149-50, 165; Benno von Wiese discusses "den Zugriff seiner [Thiels] ersten Frau," in *Die deutsche Novelle von Goethe bis Kafka* (Düsseldorf: Bagel, 1956), 1: 279; Zimmermann claims that Thiel's decline began with his marriage to Minna and argues that both wives are moved by "den gleichen Kräften des Triebhaft-Unbewußten," pp. 69, 85 (see also p. 77); and Ellis maintains that "Minna's is the more dangerous attack on Thiel," p. 186. In Minna's defense, Kunz notes her "Frömmigkeit," p. 1830; Silz regards Minna as "quiet, frail, and spiritual," p.

142; Gottfried Fischer perceives Thiel's "Innerestes" as "die Erinnerung an seine verstorbene Frau," in *Erzählformen in den Werken Gerhart Hauptmanns* (Bonn: Bouvier, 1957), p. 295; and Martini notices that Thiel looks to the departed Minna as to "der Rettenden," pp. 97-98.

6. Village and public opinions are throughout the tale randomly correct and incorrect. Each opinion must be evaluated in its context.

7. Wahr sees Tobias as "almost a symbol of [Thiel's] guilty conscience," p. 56. Silz believes the boy's cap "could qualify as a 'Falke' in Heyse's sense," p. 138.

8. Scholarly discussions of the narrator have not addressed the question of his values. Martini (p. 65) and Ellis (p. 171) maintain that the narrator evaluates as he tells the story, but they do not explain precisely what the narrator holds dear and what he deprecates. To date, commentators have focused instead upon the narrator's objectivity, omniscience, and techniques of narration. See Requadt, p. 103; Silz, pp. 138ff.; von Wiese, p. 268; Martini, pp. 65, 67, 72; and Ellis, pp. 171-74.

9. Like others before him, Ellis perceives shifts in the narrator's style, but does not unravel the ethical and emotional logic behind this particular shift. Instead, Ellis argues that the narrator is at times wrong, incomplete, or haphazard (pp. 172-73, 176). Ellis is correct in his insistence that the narrator in the early portion of the story does not tell everything he knows, but Ellis mistakes the techniques of selective narration and understatement for those of a mendacious or unreliable narrator.

10. Critics who note narrative changes in technique over the course of the story include Zimmermann, p. 72, and Ellis, pp. 172-74.

11. Silz (p. 146) and Zimmermann (p. 70) point out that Minna and Lene are diametric opposites. Not only their traits, but also their connotative names reinforce this opposition. "Minna" is the archaic word for poetic "love" and "remembrance," while "Lene" is a diminutive for both Helen(a) and Magdalena, mythical and Biblical women known for their physical and sensual qualities. For a general discussion of Hauptmann's "sensitivity to" names, see Warren R. Maurer, "Gerhart Hauptmann's Character Names," *GQ,* 52 (1979), 457-71; Maurer points out that Tobias' "Biblical namesake healed his father's blindness," p. 460.

12. Martini describes the effect of the passing trains on Thiel as "ein sprachloses Überwältigt-Werden," p. 87.

13. In *Die deutsche Novelle im 20. Jahrhundert* (Berlin: Schmidt, 1977), p. 25, Josef Kunz argues that Thiel, like other figures in Hauptmann's works, is without a will: "Eine solche Entscheidungsfreiheit in dem Werk Gerhart Hauptmanns zu suchen, wäre müßig. Der Mensch ist im Grunde willenlos in das Gegeneinander—noch nicht einmal in den Konflikt—von göttlichen und dämonischen Mächten, in das Gegeneinander von Gnade und Besessenheit hineingegeben." This seems to me an exaggerated charge, at least in Thiel's case. Hauptmann has

taken pains to portray the struggle of Thiel's will against Lene's, and surely to be weak-willed is not to be without a will altogether. If Thiel had no will and made no struggle, the tale would be deprived of its tension.

14. 14. For other explanations of the function of Hauptmann's threefold division of this tale, see Wahr, p. 56; Requadt, p. 103; von Wiese p. 273; Zimmermann, p. 79; Ellis, p. 173; and James L. Hodge, "The Dramaturgy of *Bahnwärter Thiel*," *Mosaic* 9 (1976): 114-15.

15. Scholars who mention Lene's similarity to the trains include Requadt, p. 106; Zimmermann, p. 77; Beverly Driver and Walter K. Francke, "The Symbolism of Deer and Squirrel in Hauptmann's 'Bahnwärter Thiel,'" *South Atlantic Bulletin* 37 (1972): 48; and Hodge, p. 108.

16. Scholars who interpret this simile in other ways include Requadt, p. 105; Ordon, p. 226; von Wiese, p. 273; Karl S. Guthke, *Gerhart Hauptmann: Weltbild im Werk* (Göttingen: Vandenhoeck und Ruprecht, 1961), pp. 54-55; Martini, p. 80; and Ellis, p. 179.

17. For commentary on the role of nature in this work, see Günter Taube, *Die Rolle der Natur in Gerhart Hauptmanns Gegenwartswerken* (Berlin: Ebering, 1936), pp. 20-21; Wahr, pp. 54, 56; Silz, pp. 142-45; von Wiese, pp. 276, 279-80, 283; and Requadt, p. 107.

18. For interpretations of Thiel's vision, see Kurt Sternberg, *Gerhart Hauptmann: Der Entwicklungsgang seiner Dichtung* (Berlin: Borngräber, 1910), p. 35; Gregor, p. 81; Silz, p. 147; von Wiese, p. 277; J. D. Stirk, "Introduction," *Gerhart Hauptmann: Bahnwärter Thiel and Fasching,* Blackwell's German Texts (Oxford: Blackwell, 1961), p. xxv; Guthke, p. 55; and Martini, pp. 66, 98. For the train as a symbol, see Requadt, p. 106; Silz, p. 143; Martini, p. 70; Driver and Francke, p. 48; and Ellis, pp. 176, 186-87. For a wide-ranging examination of the impact of technology, particularly trains, on the human imagination in the nineteenth century, see Leo Marx, *The Machine in the Garden: Technology and the Pastoral Ideal in America* (New York: Oxford Univ. Press, 1967).

19. Ellis traces Thiel's "process of mental ferment" to this passage (p. 185), but does not recognize that this is Thiel's attempt to put the lesson of his vision into practice.

20. Thiel's imbalance is thus the result of his and Lene's personalities and psychological make-up, not the result of an economic system; see Martini, p. 71. For a dissenting opinion on this point see Irene Heerdegen, "Gerhart Hauptmanns Novelle 'Bahnwärter Thiel,'" *Weimarer Beiträge* 4 (1958): 358. Heerdegen's conclusion that [Thiel's madness] represents "zumeist . . .eine Flucht aus dem unerträglich gewordenen gesellschaftlichen Verhältnissen des Kapitalismus" (p. 358), misses entirely, it seems to me, the pervasive personal tone of the story.

21. Interpreting the squirrel incident in quite different veins are Requadt, p. 111; Schultze, p. 301; Ordon,

pp. 226, 228; Driver and Francke, p. 50; Guthke, p. 56; and Hodge, p. 111.

22. Silz (p. 137) and Martini (p. 68) find other turning points. For a discussion of this story as a *Novelle*, see Silz, pp. 137-38.

23. See Requadt, p. 111; Ellis, pp. 174ff.; and Hodge, pp. 108-09. All three of these commentators neglect to notice that Thiel's resemblance to the train occurs only after the death of Tobias and is caused by it. In direct contrast, Lene has been depicted as the brutally mechanical equal of the train from the first time we saw her.

24. Assessments of guilt have differed. Silz believes that Thiel "callously ignores Tobias' sufferings," p. 147. Gregor blames Lene for the catastrophe: "Tobiaschen stirbt durch (unbewußt gewollte) Unachtsamkeit der Stiefmutter," pp. 81-82. Zimmermann defends Thiel's guiltlessness: "Thiel trifft keine Schuld an dieser Tat, er ist vielmehr selbst das Opfer," p. 86. Von Wiese (p. 270) and Martini (pp. 71-72) believe that Hauptmann makes no judgment of guilt whatsoever. Only Ordon suggests (p. 227) that Thiel did not want to save Tobias and thus may be directly culpable of his death.

25. Edith Hamilton, *Mythology* (New York: New American Library, 1942), pp. 160-61.

26. *Ausführliches Lexikon der griechischen und römischen Mythologie,* ed. W. H. Roscher (Leipzig: Teubner, 1916-24), 1:2:2195.

27. Hauptmann's extensive knowledge of Greek myth is documented by Felix A. Voigt in *Antike und antikes Lebensgefühl im Werke Gerhart Hauptmanns* (Breslau: Maruschke und Berendt, 1935), and in *Gerhart Hauptmann und die Antike* (Berlin: Schmidt, 1965); see especially Voigt's account of Hauptmann's education in the classics (*Lebensgefühl,* pp. 14ff.), and Voigt's comparison of Hauptmann and Euripides (*Lebensgefühl,* p. 69). See Hodge for a discussion of Thiel in relation to "Pan, Dionysus, Apollo, *et al*"—but not Hercules—pp. 100-11. Requadt takes the allusion to Hercules as a general heroic designation rather than a specific comparison, p. 106.

28. As rendered by Thomas Bulfinch, *Myths and Legends: The Golden Age,* ed. George H. Godfrey (Boston: Nickerson, n.d.), pp. 184-85.

29. See *Euripides Herakles,* trans. into German by Ulrich von Wilamowitz-Moellendorff (Berlin: Weidmann, 1879), an edition that young Hauptmann may himself have read.

30. For a wide-ranging discussion of the modes of tragedy, see Northrup Frye's *Anatomy of Criticism* (Princeton: Princeton Univ. Press, 1957), pp. 33-43. My analysis of the tragic aspects of *Bahnwärter Thiel* utilizes Frey's distinctions and terminology. Kunz's exclusion of this story from the genre of tragedy (*Novelle im 20. Jahrhundert,* p. 25) is based on his belief that Thiel does not possess freedom of will (see my discussion of this problem in note 13).

Warren R. Maurer (essay date 1982)

SOURCE: "Early Prose," in *Gerhart Hauptmann,* Twayne Publishers, 1982, pp. 13-24.

[*In the following essay, Maurer surveys Hauptmann's novellas* Fasching *and* Bahnwärter Thiel.]

FASCHING

In 1887, upon submitting **Fasching** for publication, Hauptmann requested that his first name be spelled Gerhar*t* (rather than Gerhar*d*), an orthography he retained for the rest of his life.[1] This minor change coincides with a much more significant change of aesthetic signature which was soon to lead to his most popular and enduring contribution: those many works that reflect an intimate amalgamation of personal experience, a vibrant sense of landscape, and warm portrayal of ordinary people confronted by forces and events too overwhelming to comprehend.

Due to the general disrepute of contemporary theater, combined with his attraction to Turgenev, Tolstoy, Zola, and Daudet,[2] Hauptmann turned to prose fiction and his first successful efforts in his new style were the novellas **Fasching** [Carnival] and **Bahnwärter Thiel** [Flagman Thiel]. While the former still bears traces of literary apprenticeship, the latter is an undisputed small masterpiece. Together they transcend Naturalism even before it reached its apogee and provide a more balanced insight into the future author than the more decidedly Naturalistic play *Vor Sonnenaufgang* which established his wider reputation in 1889.

Based on an actual event, the drowning of a shipbuilder named Zieb, his wife, and child, when they broke through the ice during a nocturnal crossing of the Flaken lake near Erkner on February 13, 1887, this story was long neglected, even after its rediscovery in 1922.[3] Using the event as a receptacle for his imagination and his emotions about the lake and the people around it, Hauptmann composed a somewhat contrived, melodramatic tale of hubris and death.

The plot is little more than an elaboration of the ironic title. After a dizzying round of celebrations, a man sets out for home, late at night, across a frozen lake. Skating on dangerous ice while pushing his wife and infant son before him on a hand sled, he loses his sense of direction when a dark cloud obscures the full moon and he is simultaneously deprived of the beacon of light from a lamp in his house upon which he had depended for orientation. Suddenly he finds himself plunged from a warmly animalistic enjoyment of life into the cold, dark waters of death in the one small portion of the large lake which had failed to freeze over completely. The next day all three bodies are fished from the lake and returned home, there to join in death the fourth member of the household, an old grandmother who, coincidentally, at about the same time, had died a natural death related to that of the others by the fateful lamp which had burned low because she could no longer attend to it.

Aside from the elemental depiction of the precariousness of human existence inherent in the central image of skating on thin ice, the story owes its effectiveness to the expressive characterization of its four principal characters, a demonization and estrangement of the natural surroundings, and a growing suspense maintained by an insistent foreshadowing of doom and an abundance of leitmotifs and effective visual and auditory imagery. The Zieb character, renamed Kielblock by Hauptmann in appropriate deference to his trade of sailmaker,[4] neglects his customers for the pleasures of carousing while, at the same time, speculating upon the death of his old mother whose strongbox full of savings—the result of a miserly lifetime—he hopes soon to acquire. His young wife Mariechen, instead of serving as a counterbalance to his excesses, is all too easily drawn into them herself. Her name, a diminutive form, suggests a lack of maturity which finds further expression in a favorite Hauptmann motif: child neglect and abuse. Far from considering him a blessing, the Kielblocks consider Gustavchen, their little son, a stroke of bad luck and a handicap to their preferred lifestyle. In Hauptmann's typology of characters Mariechen is also an early relative of those physically robust and erotically destructive women to whom he returned again and again.

Almost from the outset a mood of impending doom is evoked. It takes too many forms to be recounted in full here, but ranges from the very early description of Gustavchen's "death-like" sleep (6:16) to an incident in which Kielblock laughs off a fisherman's threat that he will have to fish him out of the lake in his net when he breaks through the ice (6:17); to his ridicule and parody of the cries of help of a boy who had almost drowned in the lake at the fateful spot in broad daylight (6:27)—cries later repeated almost verbatim in his own drowning (6:32). Especially evocative is Kielblock's behavior at a *Fasching* ball. Vaguely aware that a consciousness of death enhances the pleasure of living, he disguises himself as a corpse (whereas his wife, coquettishly attired in a red gardener's costume, represents life) and spends a few exuberant hours "teaching people the willies" (6:21).

As in *Bahnwärter Thiel.* albeit with less virtuosity, Hauptmann lavishes attention on the natural setting of his human drama. Nature goes its own way, hard and indifferent at best, malevolent and destructive at worst. The sun, a mere "piece of glowing metal" (6:24), and the moon a "silver knob" (6:28) observe with equal indifference the animal vitality and the death throes of the tiny human figures. As Kielblock struggles against drowning he is mocked by a flock of wild geese swimming effortlessly through the vast dome of stars and across the face of the full moon (6:32-33). More subjectively, the low "Tuba-call" of the cracking ice reminds him of standing upon "an enormous cage, in which hordes of bloodthirsty beasts are imprisoned, roaring from hunger and rage, and grinding their claws and teeth into the walls of their prison" (6:30). This is hardly the substance or language of "consistent Naturalism." Man is *a fated being,* an impression Hauptmann reinforces even in such subtle touches as the use of the same color (green) for the death-sled and the coveted strongbox. And, in spite of Naturalistic tendencies such as the accumulation of detail, the profuse use of dialogue (but sporadic and inconsistent use of dialect), and the *Sekundenstil* in which the moment of dying is recorded (6:33), the style is closer to magic realism—appropriate to the *aura magica* that the work exudes.

BAHNWÄRTER THIEL

Reminiscent of *Fasching* in style and certain motifs (e.g., child neglect) is *Bahnwärter Thiel,* written in 1887 and published the following year in the Naturalist periodical *Die Gesellschaft.* With this work Hauptmann "entered the world as a writer" (7:1044) and gave German Naturalism one of its most accomplished and enduring works. Praised extravagantly by its first readers,[5] it has enjoyed long popularity in German schools and in its motivation, psychological nuances, and form remains as fascinating today as on the day it appeared.

Again a product of life in Erkner, the character of Thiel seems to have been inspired by a railroad crossing guard who worked in that area.[6] The novella, of course, has more deeply personal roots as well. These undoubtedly include memories of railroad life acquired in Hauptmann's parents' railway restaurant; an early fascination with trains as an embodiment of the mixed blessings of technology (expressed also in the poems "Im Nachtzug" and "Der Wächter" ["In the Night Train" and "The Guard" (4:54-58)]; his attraction for Georg Büchner (7:1061); and an intense interest in psychology stimulated by Forel. For Hauptmann these elements began to coalesce after his "flight" to a new life in the "Waldeinsamkeit" ("forest solitude") of Erkner (7:1093): "I had never been so close to nature as then," he was to recall. "Through the mystery of birth [of a son] it was as though the earth too had opened itself up to me. The forests, lakes, meadows, and fields breathed within the same mystery" (7:1033).

Written in the early "hours before dawn,"[7] the novella relates the story of a large, seemingly phlegmatic and simpleminded crossing guard, Thiel, who is subjugated by two women: his first wife Minna, a delicate, ethereal creature who died in childbirth, leaving him to care for an equally vulnerable son Tobias; and an earthy, animalistic creature named Lene, whom he ostensibly marries to provide Tobias with a mother, whereas he actually does so for compulsive sexual reasons. Guilt-ridden by what he feels to be his betrayal of Minna, the stolid, punctilious anti-hero attempts to compartmentalize his life to accommodate two forms of love: accepting Lene's sexual domination during his off-duty hours at home but, simultaneously, transforming his little railway implement shack in the forest into a "chapel" where, with the help of quasi-religious relics of his dead wife, he achieves visionary states of communication with her. Thiel's attempts to keep the two areas of his life separated, however, are doomed to failure on account of little Tobias. Sickly, retarded, and undernourished though Tobias is, Thiel loves him as his link to Minna, thereby incurring the wrath of Lene who—veritable archetype of an evil stepmother—abuses the child at every opportunity and forces him to forgo the pleasures of childhood by burdening him with the responsibility of caring for her (and Thiel's) own infant son. Even though he accidentally witnesses a brutal beating of Tobias by Lene, Thiel's sexual bondage to her is so strong that he represses his rage and reverts to his usual torpor.

The crisis arrives in the aftermath of a mundane event. Given a small strip of land near his railroad shack for his private use, Thiel informs Lene of the fact without considering the consequences, i.e., the inevitable merging of the two realms he has so painstakingly kept apart. Having been told of the little field, Lene cannot be restrained from the urge to plant potatoes in it (a necessity, she claims, for the impoverished family) and one beautiful sunny morning finds the family heading for the fateful spot. At first the family's activity is a picture of idyllic harmony, impaired only by Lene's refusal to allow Tobias to accompany his father on his inspection round; she insists that he remain with her to care for his infant brother while she prepares the desolate little field for planting. As usual, her forcefulness prevails and suddenly tragedy strikes. Diverted by her work, Lene neglects to keep an eye on Tobias, as her husband had urged her to do, and the boy is brutally struck down by a raging locomotive. Efforts to save him by bringing him to the railway doctor prove futile. Thiel himself lapses into unconsciousness and then into a state of paranoia in which he promises revenge on Lene to his dead wife and catches himself in the act of strangling Lene's child. When the body of little Tobias is returned to the Thiel household a few hours later, Lene and her child are found dead; she with a shattered skull, the baby with a slashed throat. At first, Thiel, the murderer, cannot be located, but he is discovered the next day seated on the railway tracks at the scene of the accident, caressing the little brown cap of Tobias. An express train is made to halt while he is forcibly removed from the tracks. Taken to Berlin, he is eventually placed in an insane asylum.

Much of the original impact of this story must have resulted from its Naturalistic overtones. These include the depiction of a passive central character from a lower-class background in a specific milieu; problems of heredity (Tobias has his father's red hair but his mother's frailty and the mystical proclivities of both parents); emphasis on sexuality; the rather clinical description of mental derangement; a minutely detailed narrative style limited largely to a precise description of the few characters and their immediate environment; a preoccupation with the destructive forces of technology; the use of real place names, and the depiction of crass, almost sensational, reality (Lene's beating of Tobias, Thiel's attempted strangulation of the infant, and the discovery of the mutilated bodies.)[8] And yet, despite this impressive catalogue of attributes, even a first reading of the work reveals how inadequate the Naturalist label is. Compared to the "consistent" Naturalism of Holz and Schlaf, Hauptmann's novella is at once more traditional and more progressive, pointing to the past and to the future. An almost classical example of the novella genre as it flourished during the period of Poetic Realism, it also shares with that era a proclivity for describing in some detail the rudiments of a particular trade or occupation (here that of a railway flagman) without, however, placing it within the political context of a class-conscious proletariat.

Romantic elements also abound. Dreams become reality; natural surroundings are described subjectively so as to enhance the mystical experiences of the main character and to reflect his inner turmoil, while the language itself (e.g., in the use of the Romantic "code" word *Waldeinsamkeit* [6:47]) is, on occasion, almost indistinguishable from that of a Ludwig Tieck or Joseph von Eichendorff. Nor is this surprising in light of Hauptmann's lifelong latent Romanticism, detectable in even his most Naturalistic work. Indeed, it is largely these Romantic qualities that also tend to project the work into the future. Hauptmann's lack of faith in mere words as adequate vehicles of expression, his reliance on gesture, silence, symbolism, color imagery, the meaningful repetition of words and events, and an artistic control and fastidiousness second perhaps only to that of Thomas Mann, already point toward Neoromanticism.[9]

An important clue for locating *Thiel* more precisely in German literary history is provided by Hauptmann's admiration for Georg Büchner. Although Büchner had been almost a cult figure for him, and a few other Naturalists had instinctively recognized his relevance to their movement, his real discovery did not come until about 1911—just prior to the advent of Expressionism.[10] Although Büchner had died fifty years before *Thiel* was written, his work was still too progressive to be widely understood or appreciated. His drama *Woyzeck* and the novella *Lenz,* in particular, strike one as direct precursors of Hauptmann's work. Written in a similar style (a mixture of realism and symbolism), they represent two of the most sensitive analyses of mental aberration in German literature. The parallels between the hounded and abused soldier Woyzeck and Thiel are especially striking. As Silz has summed them up, "both are simple, not to say simple-minded, faithful, 'kinderlieb,' inarticulate, concealing profound spiritual depths beneath a usually tranquil surface; easy-going, slow to suspicion and wrath, but finally capable of murderous violence against the women who have failed them."[11] There are other similarities as well. Both men have a special relationship to nature and are subject to hallucinations; both are the victims of despotic, dehumanizing, materialistic "progress," both are obsessively attracted to women of robust sensuality, and, finally, both are spared the moral condemnation of their authors on the basis of a very similar outlook: that there are too many (and too obscure) determining forces acting upon human behavior to permit easy judgments.

In both *Woyzeck* and *Thiel* compassion for a poor, harassed individual from the lower classes far outweighs condemnation, and it is not surprising that both works have been the subject of Marxist-oriented criticism. Indeed, there are traces of a *j'accuse* tendency in *Thiel,* mostly in reference to little Tobias. For example, Hauptmann casually hints at his undernourishment in an episode in which the boy is described as using his finger to eat the lime from a hole in the wall (6:43). On the other hand, since Lene's own child is the picture of health, it would seem that this is more of a personal, family problem than a social one. More significant are some of the circumstances surrounding the accident. Inhumanely reduced to an object, "thrown to and fro like a rubber ball" (6:58) beneath the wheels of the train, Tobias's body is hurriedly wrapped up (in a red flag!) in the presence of the curious passengers: "Time is valuable. The whistle of the trainmaster trills. Coins rain from the windows. . . . 'The poor, poor, woman,' one hears in the compartments, 'the poor, poor mother'" (6:58). This confrontation of tragic loss with money, suffering with genteel banality, does seem to constitute a social statement—as does also the return of the boy's body in a gravel car (6:64). To try to impose the usual Marxist pattern upon the novella, however, to reduce Thiel's suffering to a catastrophe which "in the final analysis derives from the social problems of the hero," and to equate his religiosity with an "opiate of the people"[12] is, at best, an oversimplification. Even Irene Heerdegen, who broaches these views, seems aware of their limitation. On the one hand, she must regret that the work lacks a positive example for the proletariat and, on the other, admits that its basic orientation is more psychological than social.[13]

Psychological criticism of *Thiel* tends to fall into two categories: either features of the work itself are used to explore the psyche of the author, or the characters of the story are examined for psychological verisimilitude. An example of the former is Hauptmann's attraction to the theme of *mariage à trois*—typically a man between two women with contrasting natures and personalities. Whether or not one agrees with Jean Jofen that the third person in the triangle inevitably represents Marie Hauptmann, the author's mother (the name Minna is a diminutive form of her name), and therefore signifies oedipal complications, the theme is one that does occur again and again.[14] Similarly, the figure of Lene has been interpreted as a projection of Hauptmann's fear of sexually aggressive women during an era of pronounced feminine activism, and Tobias has been identified with the author's own childhood suffering.[15]

Less debatable is Hauptmann's skill in portraying the psychic life of his characters, especially of Thiel himself. Here we have a classic portrayal of repression avenged; of a man who bottles up both his sense of guilt and a growing rage beneath a pedantic orderliness. When, through the violent loss of his son, he is suddenly deprived of even the solace of hope for the future, it is more than he can endure. He loses his already tenuous hold on reality and his unconscious psyche wreaks vengeance on the world in a paroxysm of savagery that transcends mere revenge—reflecting instead a generous portion of self-loathing and "'displaced' consciousness of his own guilt and perfidy."[16]

Bahnwärter Thiel is, of course, more than a sociological case history or the study of an interesting psychopath. Hauptmann takes pains to universalize his hero's fate; to make of him an Everyman trapped between the spiritual and the temporal realms. That Hauptmann's artistic vision cannot be completely divorced from either the zeitgeist or his own outlook should, however, be obvious. In his loneliness Thiel embodies both the growing alienation which was the by-product of an increasingly materialistic late-nineteenth century culture and the desperate longing for spiritual solace which was its concomitant reaction. In addition, he reflects the author's own, somewhat eclectic, philosophical notions. For example, Hauptmann once compared tragedy "*cum grano salis,* with a breakthrough of subterranean forces" (7:101).

Whether or not these transcendental forces are benevolent or malicious, for Hauptmann, as for the ancient Greeks, they are a reality which reflects upon individual human destiny. Furthermore, like some Romantic thinkers he subscribes to the view that access to the transcendental realm is not only possible but that it is facilitated for certain individuals and under certain circumstances. In this regard, simple, primitive people living close to the soil are at an advantage, as the mysteries of existence, both divine and demonic, reveal themselves to them more directly than to their more highly civilized, excessively "rationalized" brethren. Especially in dreams, states of unconsciousness, and madness (frequently the result of great suffering) they acquire a foretaste of true being and, paradoxically, achieve their greatest clarity.[17]

Seen from this perspective, Thiel's life is "determined" not only in the scientific sense so dear to the Naturalist movement, but also in a metaphysical sense. His eventual madness, the result of profound suffering, represents the "breakthrough of subterranean forces," not merely an acute

case of psychological repression. As in the case of Büchner's *Woyzeck,* Thiel has been "struck a mortal blow, but in such a manner, that the genuine human values still shine brightly in destruction."[18] After the destructive paroxysm has run its course, he lapses into a new humaneness, expressed by his stroking of Tobias's cap. Indeed, even Lene, the "animal" (6:39), is humanized by the mystery of Thiel's suffering. Her sudden softening and reversal of character just before her death is more than the result of fear and remorse; and, although it would be presumptuous to equate it with the kind of "epiphany" Michael Kramer will later experience in the presence of his dead son, there is a tendency in that direction.

More important than content for imbuing the reader with the sense of irrational reality upon which the success of the work depends is the form in which it is presented. Paralleling the admixture of sharp Naturalistic detail and mystical obscurity in the plot is the intermingling of realistic and irrational elements in style and language. The dominant tone of the story, rather pedantically divided into three chapters (atypical for the novella), is that of an objective report interspersed with lyrical passages—the most effective of which depicts Thiel in his forest retreat in communion with his surroundings and Minna on the eve of the accident (6:48-51). Again, as in *Fasching,* the catastrophe itself is brought into relief in an excited, staccato *Sekundenstil* (6:58) but the subsequent events (with the minor exception of the discovery of the murders) are portrayed in cool, calm tones which tend to neutralize sentimentality. The narrator himself is anonymous but trustworthy. Occasionally he reveals a trace of irony, as when he describes Thiel's ambitions for Tobias who, as his father earnestly hopes, will someday achieve the exalted position of trainmaster (6:43), but Hauptmann avoids outright condescension. On the other hand, he allows the reader to experience the things Thiel experiences; to hear, see, and feel the things that affect him. Empathy with the hero is also facilitated for the educated reader by the lack of dialect, minimal dialogue (for a Naturalistic work), and by Hauptmann's tendency to ascribe to Thiel a sensitivity not normally associated with a character of his social class.

The growing sense of irrationality which precedes the catastrophe and makes it plausible is achieved in various ways; most effectively by a synthesis of two forces usually thought of as opposites: nature and technology. Hauptmann merges the two by describing each in terms of its apparent counterpart, and by imbuing both with the same mystical vitalism that also motivates the characters. Thus, a row of trees is "illuminated as though from within and glows like iron" (6:49); a locomotive stretches its "sinews" (6:60); the moon is described as a "signal lamp" (6:65); the singing telegraph lines become the threatening "web of a giant spider" (6:49); and Lene digs her field "with the speed and endurance of a machine" (6:56). Especially the locomotive, the most impressive representation of the raw power of technology available in 1887, is transformed into a demon of potential destruction. Appearing out of infinity like fate, a dark point on the horizon, suddenly growing into an enormous "black, snorting *Ungetüm*" (i.e., "violence personified" [6:50]), it disappears into unearthly stillness as suddenly and mysteriously as it came—paralleling in its inscrutable origins, sudden destructive force, and equally sudden lapse into deathly calm, Thiel's own fate.

In spite of its Naturalistic exterior a sense of fate pervades the atmosphere of the story. It is enhanced by some of the same techniques Hauptmann had experimented with in *Fasching.* The tragedy is foreshadowed almost from the beginning; ordinary events have symbolic value and their repetition fosters a feeling of inevitability; gesture, silence, and sound are manipulated for maximum effect, as is the virtuoso use of color.

We learn in the very first paragraph, for example, that during the past ten years only two events—both accidents caused by trains—have affected Thiel sufficiently to disrupt his routine and his religious worship. Once he suffered a broken leg when he was struck by a lump of coal falling from a tender, and another time he was struck on the chest by a wine bottle thrown out of an express train racing by him. A few pages later another wine bottle is mentioned, together with a further example of destruction. This time a roebuck has been killed by the Kaiser's special luxury train, and the event is immediately associated with a wine bottle Thiel had found. When he opened it some of the wine gushed forth and he placed it on the shallow edge of a lake only "to lose it somehow or other, so that even years later he still regretted its loss" (6:41).

Both the animal imagery and the symbolic "gushing" appear in meaningful context later. After the death of Tobias another roebuck standing on the fated tracks is spared at the last moment—as though the cravings of a monstrous deity for sacrifice had, for the time being, been satisfied. Likewise, in one of the most vivid scenes of the story— Lene has just been caught abusing Tobias, and Thiel feels an uncontrollable rage—a bottle of milk gushes over and Thiel is suddenly overcome by the sensuality of his wife's swelling breasts and powerful hips. Later Thiel's intuition of the impending accident is aroused by three vertical "milk-white" (6:58) jets of steam which presage the delayed sound of the futile emergency whistle-blasts.

The depiction and juxtaposition of these and similar events is neither coincidental nor gratuitous. They indicate a finely woven fabric of symbolic representation which recapitulates a central theme of the story: the mysterious interrelationship of death and Dionysian vitality.

A similar claim can be made for Hauptmann's use of colors. Sometimes the treatment is so subtle that one can only speculate on its intentionality. Thus, the neutral color brown, which occurs infrequently, links the deer on the tracks with a brown squirrel which Tobias confuses with God,[19] and with Tobias himself through the emblematic brown *Pudelmützchen* ("little poodle cap") which Thiel fondles in the asylum at the end of the story. Usually the color symbolism is more blatant, not to say melodramatic. Dominant by far are shades of red (representing blood, vitality, etc.) and those associated with death and decomposition (black, white, etc.). By careful manipulation of the choice of colors, the frequency of their occurrence and even their intensity (blood-red vs. rose, for example) Hauptmann is able to foreshadow events, enhance their emotional value, and contribute to the lyrical unity which has always been the hallmark of the very best *Novellen.*

Notes

1. Daiber, *G. H.,* p. 38.
2. Hilscher, *G. H.,* p. 97.
3. Cf. Hoefert, *G. H.,* p. 13.
4. For an interpretation of the name Kielblock see Ida H. Washington, "The Symbolism of Contrast in Gerhart Hauptmann's 'Fasching,'" *German Quarterly* 52 (1979): 248. For the autobiographical basis of the remaining names see Warren R. Maurer, "Gerhart Hauptmann's Character Names," *German Quarterly* 52 (1979):461-62.
5. See, for example, Michael Georg Conrad, *Von Emile Zola his Gerhart Hauptmann* (Leipzig: Friedrich, 1902), p. 78.
6. Cf. Behl and Voigt, *Chronik,* p. 24.
7. Zeller, *Leben,* p. 356.
8. Cf. also Hilscher, *G. H.,* pp. 99-100, and Walter Silz, *Realism and Reality* . . .(Chapel Hill: University of North Carolina, 1954), pp. 141, 165.
9. See Silz, *Realism,* pp. 137, 143-44; Roy C. Cowen, *Der Naturalismus* . . . (Munich, 1973), pp. 145-46; and Fritz Martini, *Das Wagnis der Sprache* . . . (Stuttgart, 1954), p. 77.
10. Maurer, *Naturalist Image,* pp. 226-28.
11. Silz, *Realism,* p. 146. Cf. Hilscher, *G. H.,* p. 98. For a detailed comparison of Büchner's *Lenz* and *Woyzeck* with *Thiel* see Heinz Fischer, *Georg Büchner: Untersuchungen und Marginalien* (Bonn: Bouvier, 1972), pp. 41-61.
12. Irene Heerdegen, "Gerhart Hauptmanns Novelle 'Bahnwärter Thiel,'" *Weimarer Beiträge* 3 (1958): 353, 359.
13. Ibid., 359-60.
14. Jean Jofen, *Das letzte Geheimnis* . . . (Berne, 1972), p. 51.
15. Ibid., p. 237, and Dieter Bänsch, "Naturalismus und Frauenbewegung," in *Naturalismus* . . . ed. Helmut Scheuer (Stuttgart/Berlin/Cologne/Mainz, 1974), pp. 142-43.
16. Silz, *Realism,* p. 148.
17. See Martini, *Wagnis,* pp. 66-69, 91; Benno von Wiese, "Gerhart Hauptmann," in *Deutsche Dichter der Moderne* . . . ed. Benno von Wiese (Berlin, 1965), p. 29; Karl S. Guthke, *Gerhart Hauptmann* . . . (Göttingen, 1961), p. 54.
18. Erwin T. Rosenthal, "Aspekte der dramatischen Struktur der beiden Tragödien Büchners," *German Quarterly* 38 (1965): 284.
19. Cf. Guthke, *G. H.,* p. 56.

Robin A. Clouser (essay date 1986)

SOURCE: "The Pilgrim of Consciousness: Hauptmann's Syncretistic Fairy Tale," in *Hauptmann Research. New Directions,* Peter Lang, 1986, pp. 303-22.

[*In the following essay, Clouser analyzes the syncretistic symbolism of Hauptmann's "Das Märchen," seeing that tale as one of a journey after death in the realm of another consciousness.*]

> Der Märchenerzähler gewöhnt die Leute an das Un-
> gewöhnliche, und daß dies geschehe, ist von großer
> Wichtigkeit, denn im Gewöhnlichen erstickt der Men-
> sch.
>
> Gerhart Hauptmann, **Einsichten und Ausblicke**([1])

When a writer undertakes to speak of unfamiliar things, he runs a great risk of not being comprehended. Such was the early fate of Gerhart Hauptmann's **"Das Märchen,"** written in 1941 at age 79 after his decision not to join other German authors in self-exile from National Socialism. Early commentators were disappointed in the work, partly because they felt it was embarrassingly inferior to Goethe's **"Märchen,"** upon which the tale is initially patterned. The main resemblance between the two works is their symbolic complexity, which, in the case of Goethe's tale, had already given critics more than a century of headaches. Goethe's fairy tale has the advantage of an obviously optimistic and tranformational ending. By comparison, Hauptmann's seemed to early readers opaque, goalless, and unrelievedly bleak.([2])

The opacity is due in part to the tale's thickly encrusted symbolism. It is not at all clear on a first reading what world view, mythology, or religious perspective provides the key to unlock these mysteries. Uwe Maßberg shows that Hauptmann drew on Christian alchemist-mystics, especially Paracelsus and Jakob Boehme, for concepts in his **"Märchen,"** he even gave his protagonist Paracelsus's first name, Theophrastus. Maßberg admits, however, that Christian mysticism does not lay bare the tale's secrets, and suggests that the inner motive of the work will not be found in the explication of external referents.([3]) The present essay attempts to locate the internal motive of Hauptmann's **"Märchen"** and to discover the reason for its extraordinarily wide-ranging syncretistic symbolism.

In 1957 Hans Mayer took the first step in getting beyond debilitating comparisons with Goethe's work when he remarked in passing that Hauptmann's fairy-tale "weit eher einen Vorgang der Selbstbefreiung darstellt als den einer Goethe-Imitation".([4]) Although Hauptmann does use Goethean and other symbologies, he makes clear early in the **"Märchen"** his belief that any depiction of the Other World ("jenseits des Stromes," 475) is idiosyncratic.

In the very first sentence, Hauptmann makes a subtle change as he invokes the setting of Goethe's **"Märchen".** "Das Märchen des wundervollen Weimaraners berichtet zunächst von einem übergetretenen Flusse—ich sage lieber Strome— . . . " (469). This slight but conspicuous substitution conjures up not just a physical river, or even the Styx, but the *Bewußtseinsstrom,* the "Strom des Erinnerns," as Hauptmann later calls it, that must have "banks" and "bulwarks" lest we be "deluged" (478). On the other side of this stream, the protagonist finds himself at first the only source of light, "eine Art Dämmerlicht," and the partial creator of his own surroundings: "er könne an der um ihn sich breitenden Schöpfung allenthalben mitwirken" (471). As the product of this pilgrim's unique consciousness, Hauptmann's Other World will naturally diverge from Goethe's, and Hauptmann prepares us to see his tale as the inner landscape of a single soul.

During his lifetime Hauptmann was fascinated by the idea that another realm of consciousness surrounded the living,
and that it was possible to perceive this alternative state. **"Das Märchen"** portrays a journey into the Other World of consciousness by one soul, not in life but in the realm of death. This theme structures the work and organizes its welter of mythological and religious allusions. In his travels through the Other World of the fairy tale, the pilgrim Theophrast represents all those mortals striving for answers not just to the mysteries of life, death, and afterlife, but to the mysteries of the self. "Selbstbefreiung," as Mayer calls it, becomes possible when one clearly comprehends the elements of the self.

Maßberg interprets Hauptmann's **"Das Märchen"** as a dream in which the pilgrim-protagonist-author journeys through a "Traumland". Although I agree with Maßberg that the non-sequitur logic of dreams is important to the story, this interpretation does not account for the tale's pervasive death and rebirth imagery. Maßberg's argument—that it must be a dream because the pilgrim enters the strange land "alive" and returns to the world at the end—assumes that Hauptmann wrote from a strictly Western, even Christian point of view, according to which a soul has but one life.([5]) Recent discoveries in the Hauptmann archives by Peter Sprengel and Philip Mellen, however, have shown that Hauptmann had extensive knowledge of comparative mythologies and eastern religions.([6]) In that context, the pilgrim's words—"[Es] ist mir nicht einmal klar, . . . ob ich sie [die Überfahrt] das erstemal oder schon zum tausendsten Male gemacht habe" (478)—make reincarnation rather than waking the more plausible reason for his return to life at the end of the tale.

Such a reading also makes sense in light of the density of death references in the work. The Charon imagery with which the tale opens; the ferryman's question whether the pilgrim is "traurig" (470) about making this crossing (one is not usually sad about having a dream); the pilgrim's discussion with a companion about how they died (477) and whether they knew each other "in der Körperlichkeit" (475); and the cryptic comment that some souls come alive, some dead into this "Mittelreich" (478)—all these clues combine to prepare the reader to experience Hauptmann's fairy-tale journey as a vision of consciousness not in a dream, but after death.

Hauptmann suggests that travelers to the *Mittelreich* create their own post-life existence according to what they believe. It is explained to the pilgrim that souls enter this "Delta" between the Tigris and Euphrates rivers in different states according to the direction from which they come. Those crossing from the west enter it dead, while those from the east enter alive: "Du bist vom Osten lebendig hereingekommen, der Tigris wird im Westen von Toten durchquert" (475). In this deceptively simple image Hauptmann depicts the belief of those to the west of the Tigris-Euphrates valley (Jews and Christians) that the soul is accorded but one life on earth and will not be reborn, while those to the east of the valley (Buddhists and Hindus) affirm the reincarnation of the soul in multiple lives, and thus enter the eerie realm "alive" and may return to earthly existence. But the image implies more. Hauptmann's pilgrim Theophrast was an historical Western personage; yet he enters the *Mittelreich* alive, which suggests that by altering beliefs one could change one's post-life reality.([7])

Not only the state of the soul, but the character of the *Mittelreich* itself is partly dependent on the individual consciousness. The land changes during the pilgrim's stay in it, depending on his mood. Sometimes Theophrast thinks it "eine liebliche Landschaft . . . man muß an den Garten Eden denken. . . . Vielleicht . . . bin ich im Paradiese" (471). At other times the realm is called "Hades" and reflects the pilgrim's "Schmerz und Sehnsucht" (482-83). By crossing to the *Mittelreich,* Theophrast had hoped to escape "das eiserne Zeitalter . . .Maschinen auf Geleisen . . . Brummen der Flugzeuge"; but the boatman warns him, "Das Alte lebt drüben in neuen Formen" (470). Another character later confirms the ferryman's view: "Es ist hier im Grunde dasselbe Ding wie am östlichen Flußufer. Die Dinge sehen genauso wie drüben aus, sind jedoch losgelöst von der Materie" (476). The pilgrim brings with him the problems of his own consciousness and of his earthly life into the personal"Mikrokosmos" (479) that he helps create.(⁸)

The power of consciousness to alter reality is but one of Hauptmann's theses in the **"Märchen."** The pilgrim can also try to change himself. A soul can retreat from its identity, or from certain aspects of its personality or consciousness. During most of the tale, Hauptmann's pilgrim does not know his own name or identity. The narrator informs us that he will call the pilgrim Theophrast (470), but the pilgrim himself does not know who he is: "Wer war nun eigentlich Theophrast? Nicht einmal er selber vermochte darauf zu antworten" (472). The pilgrim and a companion discuss "ein gewisser Arzt, namens Theophrastus" as if they were speaking of a third person (475). Only at the end of the work, after the pilgrim has undergone, as we shall see, a certain transformation, does he recognize that he was "once called Theophrastus" (485).

Into this psychic landscape Theophrastus projects a psychic population made from parts of himself. First he creates a lion merely by thinking of it ("Kaum hatte er nämlich an einen Löwen gedacht, so schritt der gelbbemähnte König der Tiere neben ihm," 471). Later he wishes for a person like himself to talk to: "gibt es hier herum keinen Mann meiner Art, mit dem ich ein wenig plaudern könnte?" (475); and his former famulus, Johannes Operin, appears. Like the lion, whose hunger is sated simply by watching the pilgrim eat (473), Operin is dependent on Theophrast: "es schien, als ob er von sich aus Lebenskraft nicht besäße und die des Pilgers notwendig habe" (476). Lion and famulus are thus projections of two aspects of the pilgrim's personality.

Other parts of Theophrast's nature appear, though in less obvious dependence. A snake manifests itself by touching the pilgrim's head and says she is an old friend. Later some saucy, arrogant will-o'-the-wisps claim to be related to him ("Bilde dir nur nicht ein, daß du selber kein Irrlicht bist: du bist und bleibst vom gleichen Geschlecht," 474). Each psychic character has both positive and negative sides, often illustrated by mythological or symbolic associations. The reader cannot take any single symbolic connection as definitive, but must weigh the character's total *Gestalt.*

The amnesia of the "nameless one, the poor one, the ignorant one, the barefoot one" ("der Namenlose, der Arme, der Unwissende, der Barfüßler," 475) could be interpreted simply as a sign that Hauptmann believes the soul operates subconsciously in the afterworld. But it also signifies,

as the pilgrim's change at the end implies, that he is questioning during this sojourn in death whether to continue his personality as it was previously constituted or to discard certain traits as he confronts himself in the identity-relaxing *Mittelreich.* As one part of his consciousness, Johannes Operin, says to the pilgrim: "Was indessen den Geist betrifft, so ist der deine mit meinem verschlungen und. . . . lange gemeinsam gewandert. Aus dieser Zweiheit ist manche Einheit hervorgegangen . . . [U]nsere Begegnungen sind ja doch irgendwie gesetzmäßig in Gegenwart und Vergangenheit—ob in Zukunft, das müßte sich erste noch herausstellen" (475-76). Hauptmann's pilgrim confronts himself internally and form that inner dissection and discovery derives a few hints for the improvement of human society. The characters in Goethe's "Märchen," on the other hand, confront a communal crisis, the rescue of a ruined culture, and only as a by-product resolve their personal weaknesses. Hauptmann's emphasis is on the reconstitution of the pilgrim's cacophonously divided soul.

The king of beasts, eternal companion of the pilgrim ("warst du nicht immer unsichtbar neben mir?" 472), represents his physical consciousness: awareness of hunger, movement, sickness or health, sensuality, mortality. Theophrast feels ambivalent about his physical self ("die Nachbarschaft eines Leuen war ihm zweideutig," 471). Sometimes the lion is described as "das Raubtier" (471), as "grimmig" (472), capable of "Wut" and of a "grausamen Tat" (474). At other times, it is called "zutunlich" (476) and "scheinbar demütig" (477). The pilgrim confesses, "er genießt deine Anhänglichkeit und Liebe" (472; cf. 471), and the lion often "schmiegte sich an ihn an" (479, 484; cf. 476). Theophrast muses: "Man müßte dich lieben, weil du so furchtbar gewaltig und dem Pilger dabei so nützlich bist . . .doch vielleicht: du willst ihn streicheln, und der Schlag deiner Pranke tötet ihn! So wären wir durch die Jahrzehnte gewandert, unzertrennlich, jedoch in Angstliebe" (472).

Theophrastus had long been very nearly at war with his physical self. In a previous life he undertook to change the lion's nature and make it less threatening. Famulus Operin explains:

> Um seiner Launen Herr zu werden, hat er Himmel und Erde nach Mitteln durchforscht. . . . Um dieses Tier zu zähmen, vor Krankheiten zu bewahren, in seinen Raubinstinkten unschädlich zu machen und ihm, das er doch auf Schritt und Tritt gefürchtet hat, ein wenig Leben zu vermitteln. . . . Er hat es chloroformiert und viviseziert. Aber es ist daran nicht gestorben. Und da es nicht umzubringen war, ist er darauf spazierengeritten (476-477).

Theophrast learned that his physical side is not in its essence alterable, and when in the end he couldn't kill it, he learned to accept it.

Later in the fairy tale, the pilgrim expresses a new appreciation of his physical consciousness, even though it makes him vulnerable to suffering: "ich habe es selbst erfahren, wie die grimmigsten Launen des Löwen mitunter ein weitaus höheres Dasein vermitteln als das trügerische Bewußtsein träger und fauler Sicherheit" (477). Too much physical security inhibits the development of higher sensibilities, a belief Theophrast shares with Goethe's Faust. Another character suggests that the lion keeps the intellectual pilgrim in touch with Everyman, with the average man's experience: "Was diesen sehr zu schätzenden kleinen Löwen anbelangt, so ist er ein Sohn des Aller-weltslöwen. Er spielt mit dem Menschen, wie dieser mit ihm. Und ohne das wäre das Dasein langweilig" (477). In the end, the Lion simply makes existence possible: "Ohne den Löwen geht es nicht" (478).

Thus the pilgrim comes to an accommodation with his physical self, having discovered that he can neither change nor do without it. He takes comfort in the thought that immaterial beings are deprived not only of the sufferings of physical existence but also of its joys. When the ferryman asks the pilgrim if he is sad to cross the river, he answers: "Ja und nein, . . . du weißt ja, daß selbst ein Gott, der das Leiden nicht kennt, auch auf das Glück verzichten muß" (470). Later it is said that another divinity became flesh to overcome that limitation: "Ans Kreuz genagelt hängt ein Gott, der sich selber aus unsäglichem Durst nach Leiden hat daran nageln lassen. Denn ihr müßt ja wissen, daß ohne Leid keine Freude ist" (477). Hauptmann's comment puts Christ's sacrifice in a different light: Was it done for mankind or for himself?

Although Theophrast recurringly fears that the lion is about to kill him—indeed, "der unvermeidliche Tatzenschlag dieser unberechenbar-tückischen Bestie" is what made an end of him in an earlier life (477)—nevertheless on this journey the fear proves groundless. The basically tame image of the lion in the *Mittelreich* ("Wo anders als dort könnte auch wohl ein so zahmer und menschenlieber Löwe zu finden sein," 471) may derive from the symbolic accommodation of man and beast at the close of Goethe's *Novelle*. Unlike Gottfried Benn, who earlier in the twentieth century ridiculed Goethe's complaisant lion, Hauptmann like Goethe accepts the physical side of man as basically benign. Not there do the most ugly of human vices originate, in the view of these two writers. As the pilgrim wends his way back to the river again, he takes the lion with him.

When the pilgrim's head is touched by the head of a huge snake hanging from a tree (471), that symbolic introduction alone will assure many readers that the snake represents the pilgrim's mental powers. Theophrastus and the snake need not speak to be heard by one another (472), but of the thousands of things she whispers, he retains only a few, like the fleeting germs of ideas that percolate up from the subconscious ("Der Pilger hörte sie zischeln und flüstern. Tausenderlei, wovon er nur wenig im Gedächtnis behalten konnte," 472). The snake's opalescent body sends off waves of flashing, sparkling light in every direction like waves of ideas, even when she is at rest (472-73). Appropriately, it is the snake, representing the intellect and imagination, who explains how a soul's beliefs affect its posthumous destiny and whether it enters the Delta alive or dead (475).

The snake recognizes that physical existence is prior to all other forms of consciousness ("Ohne den Löwen geht es nicht," 478), but claims to be the next closest influence on the soul of the pilgrim: "Aber auch ich bin, als er noch ein Kind war, bereits bei ihm gewesen" (478); "Ich kenne deinen Herrn . . . weit besser als du, guter Operin. Wir waren zeit seines Lebens die besten Freunde" (477). The snake, like the pilgrim, has reconciled herself to the lion's positive and negative impact ("Ohne Leid keine Freude," 477).

The decidedly un-biblical snake of Goethe's fairy tale was an eastern reptile who repeated the images of renewal and sacrifice associated with it in eastern symbologies. In contrast, Hauptmann's snake is initially identified as the Judeo-Christian serpent who misled Adam: "Bist du die Schlange des Paradieses, die Eva verführt und Adam ins Unglück gestoßen hat?" asks the pilgrim. "Du hast es erraten, sprach sie" (472). The snake admits to having seduced Adam and his sons for millennia ("Der Apfel . . . war weniger für sie [Eva] als für Adam bestimmt. Bald hab' ich denn mit ihm gebuhlt und seinen Söhnen, durch die Jahrtausende," 474). By making the archetypal temptation an intellectual seduction, Hauptmann lays the responsibility for sin not on Eve or the purely physical self (the lion), but on the corrupting intellect, man's ability to imagine all things and thus tempt himself.

Through his intellect and imagination, the pilgrim has come to resemble God himself. After the snake joined him in his childhood, Theophrast wanted to create his own worlds, "als ob die ihn umgehende wirkliche Welt des Alten vom Berge nicht vorhanden sei und er eine solche erst schaffen müßte" (478). To this end he blew "Seifenblasen, . . .unendlich regenbogenfarbige . . . wie kleine Welt-kugeln" (478). At first others laughed at his creations. "Nach und nach lernte er besser malen, und nun fand er, eigentlich erstaunlicherweise, Toren genug, die seine Wolk-enkuckucksheime schön fanden und sich in ihnen tatsächlich einnisteten" (479). Theophrast thus lured others to prefer his creations—novels? utopias? scientific or philosophical systems?—to God's. The snake specifically compares the pilgrim to Hauptmann's divine creator figure, the Old Man of the Mountain: "Wir haben indessen hier . . .in dem Pilger . . . eine Kreatur, die ihm [dem Alten vom Berg] nicht unähnlich ist" (478); she later calls him a "klein[es] Göttlein" (479). The inventive, satanic snake has helped Theophrast in all his God-like creations and experiments, filling gaps in God-given human wisdom with her perhaps too clever ingenuity: "Ihr unterschätzt den guten Bombast . . . den Gott selbst mit hoher menschlicher Weisheit erleuchtet hat . . . Und ich habe im übrigen nachgeholfen, wo dieser [Gott], wie oft, ein wenig knauserig gewesen ist" (477).

Thus through the exercise of his intellect and imagination Theophrast becomes a kind of god in his own right—at least in his own mind. But human participation in creation implies a partial responsibility for one's own destiny. Hauptmann's association of creativity with the satanic snake suggests that the Old Man of the Mountain is a jealous god who does not entirely approve of human creativity and punishes creative people for the sin of imitating his creation.([9])

The progeny of the snake from the men she seduces are the next characters in Theophrast's psychodrama *Die Irrlichter.* Already in crossing the river, Theophrast was accompanied by two unruly and charming will-o'-the-wisps (469), but he does not learn their connection to him and his intellect until they call the snake "Mütterchen," themselves her "Söhne" (473), and Theophrastus (perhaps euphemistically) their "Oheim" (474; cf. "meine Kinder,"

475). In Goethe's "Märchen," the *Irrlichter* offered other characters the opportunity to gain enlightenment or knowledge; Goethe's wisdom-seeking snake derived light from the will-o'-the-wisps' showers of gold. Hauptmann's "foolish fires" (Latin, *ignes fatui*) are similarly associated with a quest for knowledge: "Wir wissen, was gut und böse ist, wir haben vom Baum des Lebens gegessen," they say proudly; "wir haben . . .einen Tempel der höchsten Erkenntnis errichtet" (473). But Hauptmann mistrusts the reliability of human knowledge. In contrast to the will-o'-the-wisps' blithe certitude, Theophrast, the seeker par excellence, evinces modesty. He says he undertook this journey "um etwas Neues zu sehen, mehr noch zu erleben, was meine sogenannte Erkenntnis bereichern kann" (481)—thus expressing doubt about the possibility of absolute knowledge.

The danger of believing that humans can achieve supreme knowledge and unerringly distinguish good from evil is made clear by the swamp lights' chilling assertion that they have a program for doing away forever with human folly. Unlike the temple of wise government established at the close of Goethe's *"Märchen,"* the temple of Hauptmann's *Irrlichter* contains, they announce, "ein Krematorium. Von tausend Irrlichtern wird es bedient. Sie . . . brennen menschliche Torheit zu Asche: bald werden sie und wir beide sein wie Gott!" (473). The narrator immediately calls this assertion "Unsinn" (473). The lion, as if it felt personally attacked by their nonsense, strikes out at them, but succeeds only in doubling their number and making them more "arrogant" (473-74). The lion's act demonstrates both the foolishness of their program and of his attack; as the snake comments, "Ihnen nach dem Leben zu trachten heißt nichts weiter als sie vermehren" (474). To try to eliminate folly is only to commit another foolishness.

Instead of the black-and white morality of the *Irrlichter*, Hauptmann adopts in his fairy-tale the Taoist philosophy that life is a series of alternating, morally neutral opposites. The yin-yang pairs—female and male, dark and light, moon and sun, winter and summer, cold and warm—are complementary, not one-sidedly positive or negative. Hauptmann composes his own series of opposites: "Ohne Leid keine Freude, keine Gesundheit ohne Krankheit, ohne Gefahr keine Sicherheit" (477).([10]) Overhearing this, the *Irrlichter* chime in, "kein Licht ohne Irrlichter!" (478). Famulus Operin sneers at their pronouncement, yet it expresses the danger as well as reward in the human quest for knowledge. In one of the many uses of light and darkness imagery in the tale, Hauptmann has the Old Man of the Mountain momentarily extinguish all light, and with it all false lights: "Dies war er! . . . Wenn er das tut, erlöschen mit eins in der Welt alle Irrlichter. Doch schon glimmen sie wieder ein wening auf" (479). One cannot have the possibility of knowledge without the chance also for misinformation.

In his syncretistic combination of biblical and oriental wisdom, Hauptmann suggests that an ultimate truth does exist (in the form of the Old Man of the Mountain, who may be Brahma as well as Jehovah) within or behind life's yin-yang alternations, but that humans inevitably stray after false lights, especially when they arrogantly assume they can apprehend ultimate truth at their earthly level of consciousness. The very syncretism of Hauptmann's Other World makes it an admonitory revelation to those with narrowly limited cultural views who would seek, like the *Irrlichter,* to impose their "knowledge" of reality on others.

Over the course of his journey, Theophrast becomes resigned to limited knowledge and the undying foolishness of humanity. He recalls his own prior folly with Operin: "vergangene, gemeinsam verübte Torheiten in jener Welt" (480). Repeating the Edenic temptation, the *Irrlichter* offer the pilgrim another forbidden fruit of knowledge, this time "einen Apfel der Hesperiden"—golden apples that were sacred to Hera and Zeus in the Garden of the Gods and that provided Herakles entrance into Hades. But Theophrast refuses: "Er habe deren genug gegessen und im Augenblick keinen Appetit darauf" (485). Calling human folly "kein Leichnam, sondern ein unsterbliches Leben" (485), Theophrast refuses at the close of the tale to join the *Irrlichter* at their temple. He confesses to already having made the error of founding an earthly institution like the swamp lights' crematorium: "es gäbe dergleichen Zermalmungsmühlen auch auf dem Acker der Kartoffen . . .ja, er, einst Theophrastus geheißen, habe den Irrtum begangen, sich an ihrer Gründung hervorragend zu beteiligen" (485). The pilgrim "ließ . . .die Irrlichter stehen" as he turns to go back across the river (485). While no one can foreswear folly altogether, the pilgrim will at least have nothing to do with the will'o'-the-wisps' arrogant certitude and disastrous projects.

The fourth major psychic character, Johannes Operin, represents both the pilgrim's working self (Latin, *operari*, to work) and his scientific empirical skepticism. Of all the psychic cast, Famulus Operin is most closely tied to the pilgrim's prior historical identity as "Theophrastus Paracelsus Bombast von Hohenheim" (475), a Swiss physician, mystic, and alchemist (1493-1541) who supposedly made the first homunculus in his laboratory. Perhaps because the pilgrim has temporarily separated himself from that identity and the work he did, he shows great resistance to recognizing his former assistant (475). Operin is the only character to express uncertainty whether he and the pilgrim will continue to collaborate together in any future life (476).

Although he relies on Operin's informed guidance in the *Mittelreich* (475, 481), Theophrast also finds the famulus a burden ("Weiter sinnend, gestand er sich ein, daß Johann Operins Dasein seinen Zustand in einem belastenden Sinne veränderte. . . .Wenn ich, so dachte er, diese Belastung nur aushalte," 476). As one pinches oneself to keep from falling asleep with a boring companion, Theophrast jabs the yawning lion to keep it (himself) awake in Operin's presence (476). Later he halts the famulus's skeptical philosophizing by saying, "Ich bin eigentlich nicht hierher verschlagen worden, um lange Reden anzuhören und solche zu halten" (481). By comparison, the pilgrim seems to enjoy the snake's "langen Sermon" (477).

One reason for the pilgrim's distance from Operin may be their different reactions to divinity. When the Old Man of the Mountain sends darkness upon them, Operin's reaction is to sneer at the snake's explanation of the event, while the pilgrim is awed: "Theophrastus hatte die Hände gefaltet" (479). Later the companions come to a lovely lake that, in its shadows and sparklings, embodies the varying seasons of the year and moods of the pilgrim; as in Plato's cave, the viewer of the lake sees only reflections ("Spiegelungen") and shadows ("Umbraten"), not the original causes or "the painter" ("Der Maler an sich ist unsichtbar," (480).[11] Operin 'asserts that God is only one of the shadows, not the painter ("daß selbst der Alte vom Berge eine solche Umbrate ist") and scorns prayer to such a shadow as begging born of helplessness'(481). This cynicism evokes Theophrast's impatience with Operin's "lange Reden," and he voices in contrast his own wonder: "Und so wollen wir jetzt ein wenig aufmerken!—Kein Wunder, daß der Pilger diesen Entschluß faßte, denn der weite und wundersame See bot dafür von Augenblick zu Augenblick mehr Gelegenheit" (481). Operin is useful to the pilgrim as an excellent stater of facts and conditions, and as a factotum in carrying out experiments (e.g., upon the lion [476-477]). But the pilgrim's current reverence and Operin's empirical skepticism clash.

Both snake and famulus were accessory to Theophrast's earlier God-challenging writings and experiments, and contributed to his Faustian reputation. But the snake does not join Operin in doubting the power of the deity: "Ich bestreite die Macht des Alten vom Berge nicht. Ich würde mich sonst einer größeren Sünde als der mit dem Apfel . . . schuldig machen" (478). This is her response after Operin has applied his skeptical mockery not only to God but to Theophrast:"Mir scheint, der Alte vom Berge läßt seine Puppen tanzen, und du bist eine Puppe, so wie ich! bemerkte mit plötzlicher Schroffheit Operin" (478). The pilgrim admits he once wanted to shame the angel who turned mankind out of paradise and make the cherub think earth were heaven, paradise a hell (480). But Theophrast meekly and obediently accepts the sudden darkness as a sign that he should not try to call up old friends into his microcosm, but continue his introspective wanderings: "Soeben habe ich den Befehl erhalten, einige Meilen weiterzugehen" (479). If the pilgrim is the soul around which all the other forms of consciousness are draped, that soul is apparently now humble and reverent rather than skeptic—whatever it may have been in the past.

The final piece of psychic landscape that Theophrastus encounters is the wonderful lake, a marvel of syncretistic otherwordly symbolism and a barometer of the state of the soul. The snake calls it "das Nichts im Nichts" because it is "farblos, tonlos, geruchlos," etc.; but the pilgrim insists "daß es ein Allerhöchstes umschließt, was uns Menschen gegeben ist" (479). This description fits not only the ultimate locus of Being sought by Christian mystics, but also the Hindu and Buddhist Nirvana, that state of perfect satisfaction and union with creation in which the individual self is extinguished and freed from the cycle of reincarnation. For a time—hours or years, he isn't sure—the pilgrim floats in a Nirvana-like bliss upon the lake, where he and other fishermen "immer das Nichts aus dem Wasser herausfischten," under the impression that they are bringing up sun, moon, seagulls, azure, gold, stars, even the Milky Way in their nets—"höchstbefriedigt" (482-83).[12] At the same time, however, Hauptmann associates Hades imagery with the lake.[13] When Theophrast approaches it, he hears, like Aeneas, the fearful bark of a dog: "Man hörte plötzlich Hundegebell. Die mächtige Stimme, die tiefen Tons aus der Erde zu kommen schien, erregte dem Pilgrim ein leises Grausen" (481). This is Cerebus, the fierce three-headed dog who guards the Greek underworld.

The fishers pull their nets "aus dem schwarzen Meer des Hades" (183); yet as long as the men and their boats stay on the surface, the lake seems no hell but Nirvana. Only when the fishermen eerily submerge do they seem to have found the "Eingänge zum Hades"—of which, Hauptmann says, "ihrer sei Legion" (482), another mingling of classical and biblical allusions (Mark 5:9). Those who sink into the waters of hellish madnesses do not stay under forever, but later surreally reemerge (482), Hauptmann's Other World is as mutable as the soul's moods.

What makes Theophrast start to sink is sorrow over old friends and how quickly they vanished out of his life (483). No sooner do his thoughts turn in this direction than a glassy-eyed sleepy nodding comes over the fishery (483), a sign in the Aeneid of proximity to Hades. Instead of the shining cosmos, the pilgrim now sees old familiar faces in the reflecting lake. "Schmerz und Sehnsucht im Anblick der hier spukenden einst Gewesenen nahm bei ihm überhand"; he sees "die großen Zauberer; herrliche Musikanten des Alten vom Berge" (483). Whether these creative geniuses have been consigned to hell by a jealous God, or whether they are present only as reflections of the pilgrim's nostalgia is unclear. But like Aeneas and Odysseus, Theophrast finds the most wrenching part of the underworld the confrontation with old friends, in his case, his fellow creative "magicians." His soul no longer floats in Nirvana; he begins to sink slowly into the dark waters of hell.

But Theophrast is not yet destined to descend into Hades. At this point a group of rebirth images, also associated with Hades, comes onto play. As they first stood on the lakeshore, Operin had entertained the pilgrim with a tale from the Greek historian Pausanias about Persephone and Pindar the famed poet; typically, Operin had ridiculed the fable that Pindar wrote an ode to the neglected goddess of the underworld and had an old woman sing it at Delphi after his death (482).[14] Theophrast seizes upon the positive suggestions in the tale. Persephone spends half the year in the upper world and half with Hades, god of death, who stole her away to his kingdom in his chariot with the golden reins; hence she represents a cyclical rebirth motif in the Greek tradition, and Hades stands in this case for a death that holds sway over the soul only intermittently. Like Pindar, Theophrast decides to write about a deity of the underworld. "Wenn ich jemals aus diesem Bezirke wieder herauskomme . . .so werde ich darangehen, über diese goldenen Zügel des Todesgottes ein Werk zu schreiben. . . .dann würde es mir zugute kommen, daß ich kühnlich über den Fluß setzte und hier, wenn auch vorübergehend, heimisch gewesen bin" (482). For the first time the pilgrim anticipates his return to the living; writing a new book gives him a reason to want to live again, and also makes him feel "at home" with death and its cycles. He says that perhaps "ein goldenes Nichts besser als ein bleiernes Etwas ist" (482); in an "eisern[en] Zeitalter" (470) perhaps a golden fairy-tale about Hades and Nirvana is better than one more realistic novel about a leaden age.

The very nostalgia that made the pilgrim start to sink into the lake is another motive to be reborn. "Sollte ich je den Fluß nach rückwärts überqueren, . . . so werde ich feststellen, wem ich hier wiederbegegnet bin" (483), he says of his fellow fishermen. The Old Man of the Mountain had vetoed the pilgrim's impulse to call up old friends into his microcosm (479), so he must return to earthly life to satisfy his longing for friendship.

The snake becomes the final link in the pilgrim's chain of impulses toward rebirth. At the close of the tale, she sheds her western image of satanic tempter and takes on the eastern symbolism of Goethe's serpent. The sinking pilgrim suddenly spies "unzählige silberngeschuppte Schlangenhäute" upon the lakeshore and sees the snake, now called "a green, crowned viper," swimming to his aid (484). This is the only time the word "viper" (Latin, vivipara, to produce live young) is used in the tale, and the phrase symbolizes her new role: renewed intellectual innocence (new green skin) and the rescue of the pilgrim from his hell of sadness to set him back on the path to rebirth. Just as Goethe's snake encircled the Prince to preserve him until he could be revived by magic rites, the snake forms a circle with her buoyant body around the pilgrim's sinking boat. In both fairy tales, the snake is associated with magic words: Goethe's "Es ist an der Zeit" becomes Hauptmann's "Es ist höchste Zeit" (484), whispered by the snake to Theophrast as they return to shore. The intellect and its magic ability to articulate can redeem as well as corrupt. Like the lion, the snake accompanies the pilgrim back to the river to be reincarnated (484).

The pilgrim's snake-intellect is purified by shedding its skin. His raging lion-body finds, like Goethe's Faust, "den rechten Weg" as soons as it is reunited with the pilgrim on the lakeshore (484). But famulus Operin "wollte das Ufer des Sees nicht verlassen, ja, er verlor nach und nach seine Körperlichkeit" (484). The pilgrim leaves behind his skepticism, his commitment to scientific empiricism, at the lake of Hades-Nirvana. Perhaps Hauptmann had lost his faith in progress through science; he surely seemed disillusioned with the military ends to which mechanistic inventions were being put in that iron age.

But Theophrast does not abandon his creativity, the other major facet of his God-challenging Faustian persona. In his urge to be reborn to write again, Hauptmann's pilgrim affirms that "die großen Zauberer" transformed unsanctified flesh into something spiritual, god-like: "Diese seltsamen Nahrungsverschlinger nahmen zwar auch, ohne danach zu fragen, geschlachtete Tiere als Nahrung an, aber alles an ihnen setzte sich zuletzt in Geist, will heißen ins Göttliche um" (483-84). The pilgrim will write his book (or fairy tale) on Hades' golden reins, on the self-enlightenment that comes with self-distance in death, and on the humility that comes from the recognition of the limits of human knowledge.

Both Hauptmann and Goethe depict man's journey through the cosmos as cyclical in nature, but Hauptmann has far less hope that the cycle spirals upward. He knows "daß die Torheit kein Leichnam, sondern ein unsterbliches Leben ist" (485), and that *Irrlichter* are constantly being reborn. But the octogenarian Hauptmann looked into death and into his own soul in a horrific age and could still affirm his chosen profession as something worth living for, worth being reborn.

Notes

1. This comment on fairy tales comes from the "Kunst und Literatur" section in Hauptmann's *Einsichten und Ausblicke*. All quotations are from *Gerhart Hauptmann: Sämtliche Werke*, Centenar edition, ed. Hans-Egon Hass (Frankfurt on Main: Propyläen, 1963), VI, 1026. "Das Märchen" is found on pp. 469-485 of the same volume.

2. Typical of early criticism is Hermann Schreiber's comment that "Das Märchen" "vermittelt schon bei der ersten Lektüre den Eindruck geringer Selbständigkeit im Werke des Dichters," *Gerhart Hauptmann und das Irrationale* (Aichkirchen: Schönleitner, 1946), p.105. F.B. Wahr wrote that Hauptmann's "Märchen" "is reminiscent of Goethe's enigmatic effort of the same name and is likewise bafflingly allegorical and inconclusive in its attempt to suggest an interpretation of life," "The Art of Hauptmann's Shorter Stories," *Germanic Review* 24 (1949), 53. Recently Hans Daiber summarized early reaction: "Seine Verächter fanden den Vergleich und gar Wettbewerb mit Goethe lächerlich, Hauptmanns Verehrer fanden ihn peinlich, sie stellten ihn in Abrede, schon gar leugneten sie, daß Hauptmann diesen Vergleich begünstigte oder gar herausforderte," *Gerhart Hauptmann oder der letzte Klassiker* (Vienna: Molden, (1971), p.224. Hence, comparative commentary has been sparse. Hans Mayer captured the pieces' divergent tones: "Goethe beschließt seine Erzählung in einer Diesseitigkeit, in Bejahung der Außenwelt und ihre Realität, im Bild einer harmonisch gegliederten Gesellschaft, einer glücklichen Menschheit. Hauptmann verkündet ein Weltbild, worin sich erkenntnistheoretischer Idealismus mit kulturphilosophischem Pessimismus vereinigt. . . .Goethes 'Märchen' endete im Bild sozialer Harmonie, Hauptmanns gleichnamige Dichtung lebt aus dem Gefühl tiefster und bitterster Einsamkeit," ("Das 'Märchen': Goethe und Gerhart Hauptmann," in *Gestaltung Umgestaltung: Festschrift zum 75. Geburtstag von Hermann August Korff*, ed. Joachim Müller [Leipzig: Koehler and Amelang, 1957], p.105; rpt. in Mayer, *Von Lessing bis Thomas Mann: Wandlungen der bürgerlichen Literatur in Deutschland* [Pfullingen: Neske, 1959], pp.356-82). For further comparative comment, see Josef Gregor, *Gerhart Hauptmann: Das Werk und unsere Zeit* (Vienna: Diana, 1944), pp.611, 622-25; John Jacob Weisert, *The Dream in Gerhart Hauptmann* (Morningside Heights, New York: King's Crown Press, 1949), pp.83-85; and Daiber, pp.224, 276.

3. Uwe Maßberg, "Gerhart Hauptmanns Märchen in neuer Sicht," *Germanisch-Romanisch Monatsschrift* 52 (1971), 71: "Der Versuch, von den geistesgeschichtlichen Quellen her Licht in die Symbolik des Märchens zu bringen, muß naturgemäß wesentliche andere Aspekte des kleinen Werkes vernachlässigen. Dem Märchen als Dichtung könnte erst eine Interpretation gerecht werden, die die Funktion der einzelnen Motive innerhalb des sprachlichen Kunstwerks herausarbeiten würde."

4. Mayer, p.106.

5. Maßberg, pp.57-58. Other Hauptmann scholars who proceed from similar assumptions include Karl S. Guthke, "Die Zwischenreich-Vorstellung im Spätwerk Gerhart Hauptmanns, *Archiv für das*

Studium der neueren Sprachen 198 (1961), 253; Weisert, p.85; Schreiber, p.105.

6. Peter Sprengel, *Die Wirklichkeit der Mythen: Untersuchungen zum Werk Gerhart Hauptmanns aufgrund des handschriftlichen Nachlasses* (Berlin: Schmidt, 1982); and Philip Mellen, *Gerhart Hauptmann: Religious Syncretism and Eastern Religions.* (Bern: Lang, 1984).

7. Frederick Alvin Klemm sums up Hauptmann's conception of death: "Death provides an entrance into a new existence, the form of which varies according to the development and beliefs of the individual character. The poet does not attempt to answer the question of life after death in the light of a definite and consistent philosophy or religion. He rather reveals an approach from different standpoints together with a relativism which shifts the final responsibility onto the individual concerned," *The Death Problem in the Life and Works of Gerhart Hauptmann* (Philadelphia; n. p., 1939), p.96.

8. For interpretations of Hauptmann's Other World, see Guthke, pp.245-59; Felix A. Voigt, *Gerhart Hauptmann und die Antike* (Berlin Schmidt, 1965), p.134; Maßberg, p.58; and Manfred Schunicht, "Die 'zweite Realität': Zu den Erzählungen Gerhart Hauptmanns," in *Untersuchungen zur Literatur als Geschichte: Festschrift für Benno von Wiese* (Berlin: Schmidt, 1973), pp. 431-44.

9. Theophrastus resembles other artist figures in Hauptmann's works. See Karl S. Guthke, "Die Gestalt des Künstlers in Gerhart Hauptmanns Dramen," in *Neophilologus* 39 (1955), 23-40; rpt. in *Gerhart Hauptmann,* ed. Hans Joachim Schrimpf (Darmstadt: Wissenschaftliche Buchgesellschaft, 1976), 194-216. See also Voigt, p.49; and Mellen, pp.187-89, 237-38.

10. For Hauptmann's philosophical views on joy and suffering, see Mellen, pp.86-87, 111-14, 188-89; see pp.144-48 for Hauptmann's knowledge of Taoism.

11. Hauptmann's concept of *Umbraten* resembles Plato's metaphor of the cave; see Voigt, pp.133-34. Mellen, p.241, concludes in his discussion of *Der neue Christophorus* that "Umbraten denotes the somewhat deceptive images that are cast from the next world into ours . . . symbols of a higher reality"; see also Maßberg, p.67. Guthke (*Archiv*), p.255, and Mellen, pp.178, 186, 203, both link Hauptmann's use of the concept of *Umbraten* to Paracelsus. For additional commentary on Hauptmann's Other World in reference to Plato, see Guthke, *Archiv*, p.255, and Maßberg, p.58.

12. For Hauptmann's interest in philosophical concepts of nothingness, see Maßberg, p.65; and Mellen, pp.27, 57, 60. In a strange way the fishermen with their empty nets recall the disciples of Christ as they vainly attempted to draw fish from the Sea of Galilee. Christ instructed them to have faith, whereupon their nets were overburdened with a huge catch. To Hauptmann, belief creates reality, at least in the Other World.

13. For bodies of water associated with the underworld, see W.H. Roscher, *Ausführliches Lexikon der Griechischen und Römischen Mythologie* (Leipzig: Teubner, 1884-1937), VI, 42, 49.

14. Roscher explains that this hymn tells "vom Raube der Demetertochter, welche der Gott auf seinem mit vier schwarzen, unsterblichen Rossen bespannten, goldenen Wagen in die Tiefen seines Reiches gewaltsam entführte. . . . Es . . . bezieht sich auf die goldgeschmückten Zügel, mit denen Hades beim Raube sein Gespann lenkte," I/ii, 1784-85.

David G. Rock (essay date 1989)

SOURCE: "Interior Landscapes: Narrative Perspective in Hauptmann's *Bahnwärter Thiel,*" in *Modern Languages,* Vol. 70, No. 4, December, 1989, pp. 211-19.

[*In the following essay, Rock evaluates the narrative technique of* Bahnwärter Thiel, *viewing it as "Expressionistic" and "modern" in its abruptly shifting perspectives.*]

One aspect of the text **Bahnwärter Thiel** which has always presented problems for A-level candidates is the description of nature. Most candidates have used the old Blackwell edition ([1]), and they have not been entirely well served by the introduction, since the editor, S. D. Stirk, is misleading in his reading of certain aspects of the work, and this is most noticeable in his comments on some of the descriptive passages. For instance, on page xxv he notes: "Hauptmann gives a wonderful description of the setting sun. The moon rises, and for the last time the effects of light on the trees are described with the skill of a master-painter. The only word for this kaleidoscopic and flowing treatment of the line—its ever-changing aspects and moods—is *Impressionism*". Stirk is using the term Impressionism here clearly in the sense in which it is applied to the French painters of the 1860s and 1870s. Their work was characterised by a concern with the fleeting effects of light and a disregard for precise outlines, and by a general aura of delicate and mundane lightness of feeling. It will be shown in this article that the adjective *Impressionistic* is occasionally applicable to the style of **Bahnwärter Thiel,** but not in the sense in which Stirk uses it, when he clearly has in mind the delicate, pretty compositions of the French painters.

Stirk also uses the adjective "realistic" in his discussion of one of the descriptive passages, and critics of the descriptive passages, and critics in general have tended to fit **Bahnwärter Thiel** into a literary-historical category somewhere between Realism and Naturalism ([2]). Indeed, Stirk cites an array of critics who regard many of the descriptive passages as stylistic defects, and Stirk himself clearly endorses their views, quoting (p. xxviii), for instance, R. M. Meyer's comment that it is "märchenhafte Übertreibung" to assert that the two red lights on the train turned the raindrops into drops of blood! In *Realism and Reality.* Silz comments: "throughout Hauptmann maintained an even epic tenor of factual report" ([3]). Bennet argues that the work exhibits "a detached transcription of reality" ([4]). Martini stresses the realistic, objective depiction, the "Realismus der Aufnahme", and the narrator's stance as observer." Hauptmann wählt den Standpunkt des Zuschauers", whereby he constantly maintains his distance from his subject: "Der Erzähler hält sich in der Distanz, er steht dem von ihm erzähltem Schicksal gegenüber und berichtet es aus dem Abstand der scheinbar unbeteiligten

Objektivität. Bewußt wird jede subjektive Identifikation mit dem Erzählten . . . vermieden" (⁵).

The type of narrative voice which we have in ***Bahnwärter Thiel*** is the anonymous, unobtrusive third-person narrator, a conventional fictional intelligence. The story narrated to us is relatively straightforward in *outline,* and for the most part, the narrator relates the general situation and the events in a direct, almost matter-of-fact tone. Many aspects of the narration are consistent with the notion of Naturalistic "Zustandsschilderung" or "Detailmalerei", the objective analysis and detached depiction of the details of a situation in order to point to the "laws" which determine human behaviour, be they psychological or sociological—in this case the complicated factors which lead a man to murder his wife and child. Also consistent with the objectivity of the Naturalistic "stance" is the absence of any moral condemnation of the murderer by the narrator. For the Naturalists, the writer is objective analyst, not moral judge, because he portrays a world where men are ultimately not responsible for their actions since they are passive victims of circumstances over which they have no control. Categories like cause and effect replace those of guilt and expiation.

The story opens with a factual presentation of the general situation surrounding Thiel. The first statement is a matter-of-fact reference both to Thiel's piety and his mechanical regularity (⁶): "Allsonntäglich saß der Bahnwärter Thiel in der Kirche zu Neu-Zittau, ausgenommen die Tage, an denen er Dienst hatte oder krank war und zu Bette lag" (p.1). In this opening section, the information which we are given refers to a considerable expanse of time and is presented in the form of factual, indisputable details compressed into a relatively short space. We learn of his marriage to a rather delicate, sickly-looking woman, such a contrast to his own Herculean build, and her death after two years. However, the next statement introduces a note of uncertainty: "An dem Wärter hatte man, wie die Leute versicherten, kaum eine Veränderung wahrgenommen" (p.1). The narrative perspective has the effect here of restricting the reader's knowledge to what appearances seem to imply, what people who know Thiel think to be the case: "Es war die allgemeine Ansicht, daß ihm der Tod seiner Frau nicht sehr nahe gegangen sei" (p.2). With the benefit of hindsight, the reader later realises that these impressions are false. Moreover, the sequence in which the facts are given is misleading, since more important details are initially withheld and only revealed later—the fact that his first wife died in childbirth and that the child survived; that he has made a vow to his first wife to care for the child "zu *jeder* Zeit" (p. 2); that his second wife seems in physique "für den Wärter wie geschaffen" (p. 2), and yet lacks Thiel's spiritual side (of which no mention has been made up to now)—her gace lacks "im Gegensatz zu dem des Wärters die Seele" (p.2).

Thus, despite the detached, factual tone of this opening section, the reader's view of things is restricted at crucial points by the narrative perspective, the angle from which he is allowed to view things, and it would seem that the narrator, rather than being "objective" and detached, is highly selective in the way that he presents this sequence of facts, which seems intended to increase the readers's uncertainty. As a result of this technique, the reader actually "discovers" gradually that Thiel is a man with an in-ner life of depth and complexity which belies his outward appearance, a fact underlined by the first direct comment made by the narrator: 'Die Außenwelt schien ihm wenig anhaben zu können' (p. 3). It emerges, then, that the depth of Thiel's inner life is not appreciated by those around him, and the narrator uses his control over the sequence of what he narrates in order to enable the reader to actually *experience* this truth in the process of reading the story. The narrator then intervenes at crucial moments in his capacity as Naturalistic 'analytical psychologist' in order to *interpret* Thiel's inner life and attitudes. For instance, earlier on we are led to believe that Thiel has remarried for the sake of Tobias (the narrator actually inserts the direct conversation between the Pastor and Thiel on this subject on p. 2); but two pages later we read: 'Er, der mit seinem ersten Weibe durch eine mehr vergeistigte Liebe verbunden gewesen war, geriet durch die Macht roher Triebe in die Macht seiner zweiten Frau und wurde zuletzt in allem fast unbedingt von ihr abhängig' (p. 4). We are forced to reassess his motives, for now it would appear, in the light of the narrator's interpretation, that the real reason for his second marriage may be the irresistible sexual drive of a physically powerfully-built man.

Gradually, then, in this opening section, the reader is skilfully *confronted* with Thiel's problem on a general level: This is the case of a man split into two sides, the spiritual and the sensual, and the two opposite poles of his own nature are embodied in the two women who represent the two different but *equally dominant* forces in his life. The conflict between the two results in his feelings of guilt—the blatant sensuality of his second marriage is tantamount to sacrilege, a defilement of the memory of his first wife. Thiel is thus tyrannised by *both* the women in his life and can only appease his conscience by keeping the two sides clearly divided, so he transforms his lonely hut into 'geheiligtes Land', devoted to the memory of his first wife. This is underlined by the narrator in a clear statement: 'Dadurch, dass er die ihm zugebote stehende Zeit somit gewissenhaft zwischen die Lebende und die Tote zu teilen vermochte, beruhigte Thiel sein Gewissen in der Tat' (p.4). It should be noted that Thiel's problem is at first somewhat understated and is merely explained in terms of occasional pangs of conscience: 'Zuzeiten empfand er Gewissensbisse über diesen Umschwung der Dinge' (p. 4). A few lines on, however, we learn of the repulsion he feels for himself and the state of religious ecstasy he experiences in his lonely 'Wärterhäuschen' as he sees visions of his dead wife before him. Already we are given hints that his inner turmoil is so great that a complete imbalance of his mind threatens, but at this stage in the story the narrator seems to be at pains to play this down and interpret it in terms of environment ('Abgelegenheit') interacting with Thiel's 'mystischen Neigungen'. Moreover, the narrator subtly anticipates the crisis which dominates the last two sections of the story as early as the fourth page: 'Mit Hilfe von allerhand Vorwänden war es ihm in der Tat gelungen, seine Frau davon abzuhalten, ihn dahin zu begleiten'. In this indirect way, the narrator *prepares* the reader for the specific events which follow—the last detail which we are given in this section refers to Lene's ill-treatment of Tobias: 'Thiel aber, welchen die Sache vor allem anging, *schien* (my italics) keine Augen für sie zu haben und wollte auch die Winke nicht verstehen, welche ihm von wohlmeinenden Nachbarsleuten gegeben wurden' (p. 6).

The reader is already prepared to regard surface appearances with a degree of scepticism.

The narrative technique in this opening section thus draws the reader into direct involvement with the issues in the story on a general level, and the careful reader is already aware that this technique is realistic in the rather special sense of allowing the reader to actually experience the uncertainty of real life.

With the beginning of section 2, there is a sudden shift from these general comments about Thiel's life, and the narrator sharpens his focus onto a specific time and place: 'An einem Junimorgen gegen sieben Uhr kam Thiel aus dem Dienst' (p. 6). This is a clear indication by the narrator that from this point onward we will have a detailed sequence of specific events which form the main body of the story, and in contrast to the opening section, where a considerable expanse of time was compressed into a short space, a short period of time is presented in great detail. It is in this second section that the reader encounters the first of several descriptions of the natural setting. These descriptions stand out from the main body of the text because of their peculiarly expressive use of language and their weird unreal imagery, and also because not only the tone of the language but also the narrative perspective changes. Gone is the narrator reporting dispassionately and objectively ('Naturalistically').

The first description of nature precedes the first extraordinary episode in this narrower sequence of events—the break in the clockwork regularity of Thiel's everyday life, as he forgets his 'Butterbrot' and returns home at a time when Lene is not expecting him, and witnesses the beating of Tobias. The description of Thiel's daily journey through the forest to his hut appears at first to be 'objective' observation, and yet gradually a distinct mood of foreboding and oppressiveness is built up:

> "Er fand seinen Weg ohne aufzublicken, hier durch die rostbraunen Säulen des Hochwaldes, dort weiterhin durch dichtverschlungenes Jungholz, noch weiter über ausgedehnte Schonungen, die von einzelnen hohen und schlanken Kirfern überschattet wurden, welche man zum Schutze für den Nachwuchs aufbehalten hatte. Ein bläulicher, durchsichtiger, mit allerhand Düften geschwängerter Dunst stieg aus der Erde auf ließ die Formen der Bäume verwaschen erscheinen. Ein *schwerer*, milchiger Himmel hing *tief* herab über die Baumwipfel. *Krähenschwärme* badeten gleichsam im Grau der Luft, unaufhörlich ihre knarrenden Rufe ausstoßend. *Schwarze* Wasserlachen füllten die Ver*tief*ungen des Weges und spiegelten die *trübe* Natur noch *trüber wider*.
>
> Ein furchtbares Wetter, dachte Thiel, als er aus *tiefem Nachdenken* erwachte und aufschaute.
>
> Plötzlich jedoch bekamen seine Gedanken eine andere Richtung. Er fühlte *dunkel*, daß er etwas daheim vergessen haben müsse." (p. 9. My italics.)

In these latter two short paragraphs, the conventional omniscient narrator gives us a direct insight into Thiel's mind, pinpointing his thoughts and presentiments, but the description of the landscape which precedes this powerfully evokes Thiel's own subconscious state. What we have here is both an exterior natural landscape, but also an interior landscape, where Thiel's own mood of foreboding and

his inner, as yet unarticulated concern for Tobias (he feels deep down that something is wrong at home) is expressed in an indirect but powerful way: There is a direct correspondence here between the adjectives used to describe outer nature and Thiel's inner, mental activity ("schwer", "tief", "schwarz", "trüb", "dunkel"), and he goes home to hear Lene's "kreischenden Stimme" (p. 10), recalling the image of the ominous "krähenschwärme" and their "knarrenden" Rufe". (This association is actually repeated by Thiel later (p. 28) at the moment when his mind is going and he thinks that Lene has murdered Tobias: "Rabenmutter".) Then we read:

> "*Unschlüssig* blieb er einen Weile stehen, wandte sich dann aber plötzlich und eilte in der Richtung des Dorfes zurück.
>
> In kurzer Zeit hatte er die Spree erreicht, setzte mit wenigen kräftigen Ruderschlägen über und stieg gleich darauf, *am ganzen Körper schwitzend*, die sanft ansteigende Dorfstraße hinauf." (p. 9. My italics.)

In this indirect way, by suggesting Thiel's inner state, the narrator causes the reader to wonder whether it is not so much the forgetting of his sandwiches which troubles him but what he fears at home.

The second description of the natural setting comes after Thiel witnesses the beating of Tobias and when he has arrived at his work place. For the first time in the story strikingly bold imagery is used, here to describe the railway track and the telegraph wires. The passage is dominated by the two related similes of a montrous iron mesh and a giant spider's web:

> "Die schwarzen, parallellaufenden Geleise glichen in ihrer Gesamtheit einer ungeheureren, *eisernen Netzmasche*, deren schmale Strähnen sich im äußersten Süden und Norden in einem Punkte des Horizontes zusammenzogen.
>
> Der wind hatte sich erhoben und trieb leise Wellen den Waldrand hinunter und in die Ferne hinein. Aus den Telegraphenstangen, die die Strecke begleiteten, tönten summende Akkorde. Auf den Drähten, die sich wie das *Gewebe einer Riesenspinne* von Stange zu Stange fortrankten, klebten in dichten Reihen Scharen zwitschernder Vögel. Ein Specht flog lachend über Thiels Kopf weg, ohne daß er eines Blickes gewürdigt wurde." (p.13. My italics.)

The emphasis here is not on an "objective" description of nature—significantly Thiel does not take any notice of the *actual* woodpecker flying over his head: The predominance of unrealistic, fantastic yet clearly *visual* images suggests the distortion of Thiel's own vision of the world which is taking place during the course of the story. There is unmistakable "internal" evidence in the text which substantiates this view, because several of the grotesque metaphors used in the descriptions of nature are anticipated in some way beforehand. For instance, the two similies of the spider's web and the net of iron have already been anticipated in the previous scene with Lene. As he witnesses his second wife beating Tobias, Thiel feels helpless in the face of Lene's inescapable sexual power as he sees her half-naked breasts and her broad hips:

> "Eine Kraft schien von dem Weibe auszugehen, *unbezwingbar, unentrinnbar*, der Thiel sich nicht gewachsen fühlze.

Leicht gleich einem feinen *Spinngewebe* und doch fest wie ein *Netz von Eisen* legte es sich um ihn, fesselnd, überwindend, erschlaffend." (p.11. My italics.)

The description of the natural setting which follows shortly after this scene is thus dominated by the contours of Thiel's own inner life: His feeling of being helplessly ensnared in the web of his wife's sexual dominance is having a disturbing effect on his mind, distorting his vision of the world. The passage continues with the description of the train, which culminates in a terrifying metaphor: the train starts as "ein dunkler Punkt am Horizont" (p.14), and the sound of its wheels on the tracks builds up to a terrible apocalyptic climax resembling "den Hufschlägen eines heranbrausenden Reitergeschwaders". ([7]), and as the noise and smoke increase, the train actually *becomes* "das schwarze schnaubende Ungetüm". Again, the intensity which builds up in this passage is prefigured in the preceding incident as Thiel catches sight of his son's tears:

"Einen Augenblick schien es, als müsse er gewaltsam *etwas Furchtbares* zurückhalten, was *in ihm* aufstieg; dann legte sich über die gespannten Mienen plötzlich das alte Phlegma, von einem verstohlenen begehrlichen Aufblitzen der Augen seltsam belebt." (p.11.)

Just as this terrible thing inside him subsides and gives way to "das alte Phlegma", so too in the later description, as the train disappears, "das alte heil'ge Schweigen" returns to the forest. This scene then echoes in its powerful imagery the growing intensity of the uncontrollable feelings building up in Thiel himself, which threatens his mental equilibrium—significantly, as the train passes, Thiel is in a trance: "Minna", flüsterte der Wärter wie aus einem Traum erwacht" (p.14). Through the nightmarish image of the train, the narrator powerfully conveys to the reader the terrifying nature of Thiel's own inner experiences.

The narrator then informs us that Thiel is gradually overcome by a strange feeling of disquiet and that he suddenly realises that his second wife will now be coming out to visit the allotment on frequent occasions: The "holy" sanctuary dedicated to the memory of Minna is about to be desecrated by the profane, sensual Lene. The delicate balance which he has established by physically separating the two forces in his life (the spiritual and the sensual) is about to be shattered. The reader now senses that the story is approaching its climax, because the narrator makes it clear both directly and indirectly through his comments and through the descriptive passages, that a sense of all-consuming crisis inside Thiel himself is culminating, for he is now almost demented by feelings of guilt as he suddenly realises with horror that he has betrayed his dead wife and neglected his son for two whole years. The narrator now employs his omniscience to explain clearly how Thiel is losing control over his own mind:

"Es kam ihm vor, als habe er etwas Wertes zu verteidigen, als versuchte jemand, sein Heiligstes anzutasten, und unwillkürlich spannten sich seine Muskeln in gelindem Krampfe, während ein kurzes, herausforderndes Lachen seinen Lippen entfuhr. Vom Widerhall dieses Lachens erschreckt, blickte er auf und verlor dabei den Faden seiner Betrachtungen. Als er ihn wiedergefunden, wühlte er sich gleichsam in den alten Gegenstand.

Und plötzlich zerriß etwas ein dichter, schwarzer Vorhang in zwei Stücke, und seine umnebelten Augen

gewannen einen klaren Ausblick. Es war ihm auf einmal zumute, als erwache er aus einem zweijährigen totenähnlichen Schlaf." (p.15) ([8])

Overcome with fatigue as a result of his self-torment, he falls asleep:

"Ein Brausen und Sausen füllte sein Ohr, wie von unermeßlichen Wassermassen; es wurde dunkel um ihn, er *riß die Augen auf und erwachte*. Seine Glieder flogen, der Angstschweiß drang ihm aus allen Poren, sein Puls ging unregelmäßig, sein Gesicht war naß von Tränen." (p.16. My italics.)

The impact of this passage rests in the fact that although a storm would appear to be brewing outside, the reader is at first unable to determine from the given narrative perspective whether the sounds are real or merely the product of Thiel's tormented imagination—again Thiel's experience his own uncertainty, is expressed directly and effectively. He then staggers out into the storm, and the sound made by the trees is compared to "Meeresbrandung", a simile which has recurred several times, but now the link between the description of external nature and Thiel's perspective is established unambiguously: "Einen Augenblick kam er sich vor wie ein Ertrinkender" (p.16). The narrator again looks into Thiel's mind ("Es gärte in seinem Hirn", p.17), and indicates that Thiel now seems unable to separate dream and reality, for it now appears to him that the beating of Tobias was part of his dream (p.17, line 9 ff.); what he does recall clearly is the terrifying, guiltridden, prophetic image of his dead first wife walking along the railway track, carrying "etwas Schlaffes, Blutiges, Bleiches" (p.17). The reader is allowed to look directly into Thiel's troubled thoughts, but is then suddenly confronted with an apparition:

"Zwei rote, runde Lichter durchdrangen wie die Glotzaugen eines riesigen Ungetüms die Dunkelheit. Ein blutiger Schein ging vor ihnen her, der die Regentropfen in seinem Bereich in Blutstropfen verwandelte. Es war, als fiele ein Blutregen vom Himmel.

Thiel fühlte ein Grauen, und je näher der Zug kam, eine um so größere Angst. Traum und Wirklichkeit verschmolzen ihm in eins. Noch immer sah er das wandernde Weib auf den Schienen, und seine Hand irrte nach der Patronentasche, als habe er die Absicht, den rasenden Zug zum Stehen zu bringen. Zum Glück war es zu spät, denn schon flirrte es vor Thiels Augen von Lichtern, und der Zug raste vorüber." (p.18) ([9]).

This nightmarish description is typical of those effective moments in the story where the perspective shifts suddenly and dramatically, One moment we are looking into Thiel's thoughts, then without any warning we either see the outside world through the distorted mind of Thiel himself or the outside world actually takes on the contours of Thiel's inner world. Now dream and reality are no longer distinguishable for Thiel, as the raindrops are transformed in the lights of the train into the drops of blood which Thiel saw in his dream of Minna as she carried 'etwas Schlaffes, Blutiges'. The narrative technique actually allows the reader first to *experience* the terrible truth about Thiel, to which the narrator then points.

The fatal accident is preceded by a period of calm, as Thiel escorts Tobias around his 'Revier', but it is Thiel's

mental state which determines the mood of religious solemnity as he takes his son through this hallowed, consecrated domain (pp. 21-22), and as Thiel hears voices of
the dead in the telegraph wires and is moved to tears by
the thought that his first wife's voice is among them, we
realise that this is the calm before the storm. The portrayal
of the accident itself is remarkable in the way that the narrator, although inconspicuous, dominates every aspect of
the events. The incident itself is described with brutal
Naturalistic objectivity and from the standpoint of an outsider:

> 'Eine dunkle Masse war unter den Zug geraten und
> wurde zwischen den Rädern wie ein Gummiball hin
> und her geworfen. Noch einige Augenblicke, und man
> hörte das Knarren und Quietschen der Bremsen. Der
> Zug stand.' (p. 23)

But from this point on (p. 23 line 21 - p. 24 line 16), the
narrative technique is designed to convey to the reader the
shocked, stunned and confused reaction of Thiel, leading
only slowly and gradually to his realisation of the full horror of what has happened. The passage is remarkable for
its economy: For instance, the narrator's description of
Thiel is registered without comment, but there is sufficient
evidence for the reader to draw his own conclusion about
Thiel's state of mind—his sense of shock and horror are
clearly deducible from the description of his hair seeming
to stand on end and his turning pale. As D. Horrocks points
out:' Nor does the narrator explicitly state that the beginnings of Thiel's eventual derangement are detectable in his
reactions here, though it can obviously be inferred from
the strange movement of his eyes, the imbecilic expression
on his face and the incongruity of his absent-minded
smile.'([10]) Again, the dominant feature of the passage is
the technique of portraying the situation largely from the
perspective of Thiel himself, but the emphasis constantly
shifts to the reactions of Lene, the railway officials and
passengers, and then back to Thiel himself, producing an
impression of confusion. The details of Thiel's utterances,
movements and physical appearance are all reported to us,
whether directly by the narrator or from the perspective of
other figures. This is not the case, however, when it comes
to Thiel's thoughts. Nowhere in this key passage does the
narrator have recourse to conventional reported speech or
thought. Instead he allows us occasionally to enter into the
character's consciousness, to share his reactions, without
interposing himself as reporter. In two instances he does
so directly, presenting Thiel's thoughts immediately and in
exactly the form that they occur to him: 'Wer war das?!
Lene?! Es war nicht ihre Stimme, und doch . . . ' (p. 23)
and 'Er ist es.' (p. 24) Elsewhere the approach is the less
direct technique of *erlebte Rede,* 'free indirect speech', as
with the striking phrase 'Wahrhaftig, man winkt ihm',
where the reaction conveyed in the first word and the realisation that people are waving to him are Thiel's, not
comments from the narrator. The immediacy of the entire
passage is reinforced by the narrator's abrupt switch to the
dramatic present, which continues for two more pages. It
emphasises that Thiel is struggling to make sense of what
is going on, but it also forces the reader to experience the
dreadful episode in the present tense, as is going on before
Thiel's eyes:

> '—sein Ohr füllt das Geheul Lenens. Vor seinen Augen
> schwimmt es durcheinander, gelbe Punkte, Glühwürm-
> chen gleich, unzählig. Er schrickt zurück—er steht.

> Aus dem Tanze der Glühwürmchen tritt es hervor, blaß,
> schlaff, blutrünstig. Eine Stirn, braun und blau ge-
> schlagen, blaue Lippen, über die schwarzes Blut
> tröpfelt. Er ist es.' (p. 24)

These lines convey directly Thiel's gradual guilt-ridden realisation of the full horror of what has happened, with the
adjectives 'blaß, schlaff, blutrünstig' deliberately echoing
the 'etwas Schlaffes, Blutiges, Bleiches' which Thiel, in
his nightmarish vision of the previous Saturday night, had
seen Minna carrying along the tracks. By this point, of
course, we the readers are already well aware that the victim of the accident must be Tobias, but the narrative technique forces us to live through the experience of recognition with Thiel, and this adoption of Thiel's point of view
serves the purpose of enlisting the reader's sympathy for
the figure and his tragic loss.

The complex mixture of guilt and hatred in Thiel in the aftermath of the accident leads to his complete mental breakdown, and on the verge of madness, he follows an apparition down the track, muttering promises of revenge to his
dead wife. Thiel's actions are reported to use from the
standpoint of an outsider trying to interpret his gestures
and words:

> 'Während er, rückwärts schreitend, vor etwas zu we-
> ichen *schien* . . . '

> 'Er *schien,* als ob etwas an ihm vorüberwandle . . . '
> (p. 26)

> 'Er tastete in die Luft, *wie um* etwas festzuhalten . . . '
> (p. 27)

But as Thiel turns to walk back, the reader is given another description of nature:

> Die Sonne goß ihre letzte Glut über den Forst, dann er-
> losch sie, Die Stämme der Kiefern streckten sich wie
> bleiches, verwestes Gebein zwischen die Wipfel hinein,
> die wie grauschwarze Moderschichten auf ihnen
> lasteten. Das Hämmern eines Spechts durchdrang die
> Stille. Durch den kalten, stahlblauen Himmelsraum
> ging eine einziges, verspätetes Rosengewölk. Der
> Windhauch wurde kellerkalt, so daß es den Wärter
> fröstelte. Alles war *ihr* neu, alles *fremd.* (p. 27)

Again the perspective shifts abruptly, and we have a description of an eerie, alien natural landscape with powerful
images of death and decay which expresses Thiel's own
mental state—his torment over Tobias' probable death has
turned his world into a living death. The narrator then allows the reader to look again into Thiel's mind at the terrible moment when he suddenly becomes aware of his
own impending madness. In a moment of full consciousness, he realises that he is losing control of his own mind
and can no longer organise his thoughts: 'Er unterbrach
sich, ein Lichtschein fiel in sein Hirn: Aber mein Gott, das
ist ja Wahnsinn'.(p. 27)

After he has almost strangled the baby whose screams
were 'das Signal zur Raserei', Tobias' body is brought
back, and with this final confirmation of the death of his
son, Thiel collapses and loses all consciousness (p. 29,
line 37). Now that Thiel has clearly gone mad, we no
longer see things from his perspective. We are briefly allowed to see things from Lene's perspective (p. 30, line 35
- p. 31, line 15), for the purpose of encouraging us to

sympathise with her in her plight, but we witness the final events of the story from the standpoint of outsiders, as the bodies of Lene and the child are discovered by the men who bring back the body of Tobias. In marked contrast to many Naturalistic works with their emphasis on the detailed portrayal of gory details, the description of the bloody murder itself is avoided. The final two pages return to the tone of a factual report, and the reader is left with the image of the pathetic figure of Thiel holding his son's little brown hat in his hands in the madhouse.

The narrative perspective and in particular the descriptions of nature are thus crucial to any interpretation of the story, as we realise that Thiel's final madness is not something suddenly triggered off by his son's terrible death in the accident, but something which has been building up throughout the story, anticipated both in the descriptions and in the sudden, unannounced shifts to Thiel's perspective, which allow the reader to experience at first hand Thiel's gradual breakdown and the pressure building up through the moods and mental states which the descriptive passages evoke. By reference to them, we can chart out Thiel's own inner 'landscapes' and trace the development of his disorientation and final madness.

It is clearly misleading to simply label the work 'Naturalistic'. The empathy with which Thiel is portrayed goes far beyond the clinical observation of Naturalism. Moreover, the label 'Impressionistic' is also ultimately inadequate in so far as it only suggests the extent to which the descriptive passages reflect the ways in which the effects of light and sound affect a person's perception of reality. Indeed, with many of the passages where Thiel's inarticulated feelings are projected onto the natural world itself which is distorted by grotesque images and weird colours, the term 'Expressionistic' is arguably the most applicable, and Hauptmann can be seen to have anticipated, to a certain extent, the techniques of Expressionist painting, where subjective vision was expressed through distortion of colour and outline. Perhaps, however, the narrative technique is best simply termed 'modern', precisely because of the demands it makes on the reader, shifting its perspective abruptly, often unexpectedly, and yet precisely at those moments when the author's intentions demand it, leading the reader to empathise with the pathetic figure of Thiel himself.

Notes

1. A new Blackwell edition appeared in late 1988.

2. Two notable exceptions are John M. Ellis. *Narration in the German Novelle*, Cambridge, 1974. pp. 169-211, and Peter Sprengel, *Gerhart Hauptmann. Epoche - Werk - Wirkung*, Munich, 1984.

3. W. Silz, *Realism and Reality: Studies in the German Novelle of Poetic Realism*, Chapel Hill, 1954.

4. E. K. Bennet, *A History of the German Novelle*, Cambridge, 1961, p. 238.

5. F. Martini, *Das Wagnis der Sprache*, Stuttgart, 1954, p. 65.

6. The page numbers refer to the old Blackwell edition of the text, edited by S. D. Stirk, Oxford, 1961.

7. Martini sees this simile as a defect, cf. loc. cit., pp. 86-7: 'Was der Mensch um 1887 im Schauspiel des

kavalleristischen Manövers als die stärkste Ballung von übermächtiger und todbringender Gewalt noch konkret sehen und erleben konnte, ist heute zur nur militärgeschichtlichen Reminiszenz, damit mittelbar und abstrakt Ö geworden und längst durch größere Gewaltkonzentrationen im Technischen übertroffen. In dieser historischen Bindung des Bildes liegt eine Schwächung seiner Ausdruckskraft.' The apocalytic overtones of this image are surely consistent with Thiel's feelings of guilt—he suffers from what might almost be called a religious persecution mania.

8. This is close to the moment of anagnorisis in ancient tragedy, the moment of terrible recognition from which there is no escape.

9. Here the red lights are real enough—the lights of the train—and the effects they produce in the rain are just about plausible, but their personification as the googling eyes of a monster tells us more about Thiel's tormented mental state.

10. cf. David Horrocks' excellent and useful article. *How to tackle a commentary question in the German A-level literature paper (2)*, in *Treffpunkt*, Vol. 19 No. 1, March 1987, pp. 10-15.

Warren R. Maurer (essay date 1992)

SOURCE: "Symphony in Prose," in *Understanding Gerhart Hauptmann*, University of South Carolina Press, 1992, pp. 127-39.

[*In the following essay, Maurer explores the models and sources of* Bahnwärter Thiel, *discussing its relation to the German Novelle and analyzing its symbolism.*]

FLAGMAN THIEL

In Hauptmann's development as a dramatist, a distinct progression in the mastery of his craft is discernible from 1889 (*Before Sunrise*) to about 1911 (*The Rats*). In contrast to this pattern, **Bahnwärter Thiel** (1888) (**Flagman Thiel**) is a highly acclaimed masterpiece of prose fiction created at the beginning of his literary career and never quite equaled afterwards.[1] Written in Erkner during the early morning hours around the period of the birth of his second son and published in the Munich Naturalist periodical *Die Gesellschaft* (Society), this remarkable German novella marked Hauptmann's debut as an author of great potential. Although considerably milder than that occasioned by such dramas as *Before Sunrise, The Weavers,* or *Hannele*, this work also provoked its share of controversy. While some early readers welcomed in it primarily a Zolaesque Naturalism applied to the portrayal of distinctly German characters and circumstances, conservatives and Marxists alike decried its seemingly bleak and pessimistic depiction of the human condition.[2] Unconvincing Marxist interpretations to the contrary, the causes of the Thiel family tragedy derive more directly from universal human circumstances than from socioeconomic problems.[3] And while the novella has been widely read in German schools since around the end of the First World War as a classic example of Naturalism, it has also long been recognized by critics and scholars that such a rigid classification is much too narrow. ***Flagman Thiel*** features an early (but as we know from *Rose Bernd, The Rats,* and *Magnus Garbe,* recurrent) thematic complex of marriage, birth, and death, presented in a literary form skillfully amalgamated from naturalistic, symbolic, and mystical elements. In many respects it is paradigmatic for much of Hauptmann's future oeuvre; and, as a work with an established place in German literary history, it represents a transitional landmark reflecting past, contemporary, and future periods such as Poetic Realism, Naturalism, and Neoromanticism.

Because the story's salient characteristics are more powerfully atmospheric, lyrical, and musical than narrative (it has been convincingly described as a "symphonic poem"),[4] the plot of ***Flagman Thiel*** can be summarized in a few words. It examines the life, conflicts, and eventual destruction of a simple, almost child-like railroad-crossing guard and his family, whose situation is similar in many respects to the situation in *Drayman Henschel.* Like Henschel, Thiel is a widower who, ostensibly to provide a mother for Tobias, the son he has had with his deceased wife Minna, marries and becomes the guilt-ridden victim of a brutally sensual woman, Lene, who dominates him through the overwhelming power of her sexuality while simultaneously neglecting the child she had been expected to nurture. The climactic event is an accident in which the boy is struck and killed by a racing express train. Although neglectful of his safety, Lene can hardly be accused of consciously causing Tobias's death. Thiel, however, in an explosion of long-repressed and unarticulated rage, slaughters her and the child she has in the meantime borne him. The destructive paroxysm having run its course, Thiel lapses into a state of benign, lethargic insanity and is last seen in a charity hospital ward for the insane, guarding in his hands Tobias's little brown cap "with jealous care and tenderness" (6:67).

In spite of considerable effort expended on finding a real-life counterpart to the plot of ***Flagman Thiel*** (of the kind available for ***The Rats,*** for example), such searches have remained unproductive. When asked about a model for Thiel, Hauptmann was able to recall later only that he had spoken a great deal with a crossing guard in his little railroad shack located near the village of Fangschleuse.[5] The "humus" from which this particular narrative grew must, therefore, be sought elsewhere: in more general personal experiences of its author, in literary sources, and in the zeitgeist.

From the perspectives of personal experience two periods in Hauptmann's life seem especially promising here: the years immediately after 1877 and those following his move to Erkner with Marie in 1885. When Robert Hauptmann lost his hotel to creditors in 1877 and was reduced to the socially inferior status of running a mere railroad restaurant in Sorgau, the move was humiliating for the sensitive adolescent Gerhart, but it also steeped him in the railroad atmosphere that so thoroughly permeates ***Flagman Thiel.*** Difficult as it may be for someone in an age of hydrogen bombs and rockets to the moon to imagine, the steam engine was for young Hauptmann the embodiment of an awe-inspiring, quasi-diabolical technology. The noise and speed of "these iron colossi of locomotives" and their "inescapable, powerful rhythm" (7:724) stood in strong contrast to the idyllic natural surroundings of his boyhood.

That he was both fascinated and repelled by these monstrous intrusions into the landscape is clear from two early poems, **"Der Nachtzug"**(The Night Train) and **"Der Wärter"** (The Crossing Guard). The former plainly anticipates the admixture of romanticism, mysticism, and technology of ***Thiel,*** while the latter is more strongly oriented towards social criticism; it depicts the sufferings of a poor, deathly ill railway employee with a wife and child desperately in need of his support who collapses and dies beside the tracks.

While the Sorgau experience acquainted Hauptmann with the technology of the railroad (and with a variety of people employed in its demanding service), a second important aspect of the novella, the atmosphere and natural beauty of its setting, derives largely from the author's life in Erkner. "I had never been so close to nature as then," he was to recall later. "Through the mystery of birth [of a son] it was as though the earth too had opened itself up to me. The forests, lakes, meadows, and fields exhaled the same mystery. There was contained within it a somehow disconsolate magnificence, a grandeur through which one was placed before the gate (closed, to be sure) of ultimate comprehension" (7:1033).

In a search for literary models for ***Thiel*** it soon becomes obvious that, more than for any other of Hauptmann's works, Büchner is of central importance. Hauptmann confessed that "Georg Büchner's works, about which I had given a lecture before the *Durch* society [in 1887], had made an enormous impression on me. The incomparable monument that he had left behind after only twenty-three years of life, the novella *Lenz,* the *Woyzeck* fragment, had for me the significance of great discoveries" (7:1061). The importance of this Büchner "cult" (7:1061) has long been recognized and thoroughly explored in relation to ***Thiel.***[6] Attention has been focused on similarities between the two authors' weltanschauung, formal attributes of their prose, and characters. Both Büchner and Hauptmann are strongly fatalistic, and because the lives of their characters are determined by forces over which they have little or no control, their creators refuse to subject them to moral censure, preferring instead to reply to their failings and transgressions with compassion. Both authors are skillful at depicting stages of mental deterioration resulting in madness (see *Lenz*), and both employ a combination of realism and symbolism to achieve their desired results. Comparing Büchner's Franz Woyzeck with Hauptmann's Franz Thiel, Silz has pointed out that "both are simple, not to say simple-minded, faithful, 'kinderlieb,' inarticulate, concealing profound spiritual depths beneath a usually tranquil surface; easy-going, slow to suspicion and wrath, but finally capable of murderous violence against the women who have failed them."[7] Although neither of these antiheroes can escape completely the consequences of their low social status, it is their irrepressible and universal human qualities that shine forth in the end. Both are victims of a "progress" that has, outwardly at least, reduced them to a mechanical existence. For Woyzeck the dehumanizing force is embodied in the sadistic experiments of the medical doctor who sees in him only a human guinea pig; for Thiel it is a pedantic punctuality engendered by the demands of his railroad employment. Whereas Woyzeck has order imposed upon him by his superiors (and finds it difficult to subjugate his nature to their demands), Thiel seems to have adopted order as a defense mechanism. It is expressed not only in the mechanical precision with which he exercises his occupational obligations, in his regular church attendance, in the pedantic treatment of his few personal possessions, and in the monotonous rhythm of his daily existence, but, especially, in his effort to compartmentalize the central conflict of his life: his enthrallment by two women of totally opposite natures. Unable to resist the animalistic, physical blandishments of Lene (and feeling guilt for succumbing to them), he has established a shrine to his ethereal, spiritual, dead wife Minna in his lonely railroad shack, where he communes with her nightly. By keeping the physical and spiritual halves of his life scrupulously separated in this way, by imposing on them the same mechanical order he observes in his daily activities, he hopes to control them. However, as we know from Hauptmann's concept of the *Urdrama*, life is too chaotic to be managed so easily. A momentary lapse of caution, during which Thiel reveals that he has received a small strip of land near the tracks for his own use, becomes a fateful turning point when it leads to a merging of the two realms. Having once heard about it, Lene cannot be restrained from the urge to plant potatoes in the little plot—a necessity, she claims, for the poor family. As usual her forcefulness prevails, and tragedy is the result. Diverted by her work, she neglects to keep an eye on Tobias; he is killed, and Thiel's repressed emotions explode in fury.

Hauptmann has been aptly described as a "seismograph of his time."[8] Literarily this description seems especially apt for his early successes and can be illustrated by a closer look at the female characters depicted in *Flagman Thiel*. While Thiel is reasonably well-rounded and individualized, both Minna and Lene come close to representing melodramatic types who would have been at home in much of the popular literature of the day and who embody naturalistic stereotypes of women in general. At a time when women were struggling to achieve an enhancement of their status in society (equality with men remained a wistful dream), male writers and intellectuals found it both expedient and consoling to reduce them to two contradictory types: the idealized, pure—not to say immaculate—mother, and the sexually destructive whore, usually from the lower classes. Minna and Lene reflect these stereotypes. Minna (whose name associates readily with the medieval concept of *Minne*, a sublimated, spiritualized form of eros) is described as "a slender, sickly looking woman . . . who hadn't suited well Thiel's Herculean stature" (6:37) but who had been bound to him by "a more spiritualized love" (6:39). Outwardly Lene appears the more suitable spouse for Thiel. In strong contrast to her predecessor, "the former cowherd appeared as though made for the flagman. She was barely half a head shorter than he and surpassed him in fullness of limb. Also her face was carved quite as crudely as his, only that, in contrast to that of the flagman, it lacked soul" (6:38).

Although scornful of Strindberg's simplistic depictions of the battle of the sexes, Hauptmann, apparently unknowingly, shares a good deal of the Swede's misogyny. Not only is he partial to what he sees as an obsessive Strindbergian theme—the man trapped between and destroyed by two women[9] (compare *Henschel* and *Schilling*)—but he too seems to revel in the depiction of vulnerable males threatened by an all-powerful female sexuality. Surprised by Thiel as she is beating Tobias, Lene escapes her husband's wrath by paralyzing his ability to react: "Her full, half-naked breasts swelled from excitement and threatened to burst her bodice, and her gathered skirts made her broad hips appear even broader. An invincible, inescapable power, which Thiel felt unable to control, emanated from the woman" (6:47). Only the death of his son and the depths of suffering caused by it break the spell, and Thiel acts with devastating physical violence to escape and get revenge for the bondage he has been powerless to resist.

Perhaps because Lene's domination of Thiel is so blatant, Minna's role in his destruction tends to be overlooked. His love for his first wife is just as compulsive, irrational, and abnormal as his sensual enslavement by Lene. From a psychological perspective, Thiel (and some would claim his creator) fears both women. The good, spiritualized woman is banned to the realm of the dead; the evil, sensual one is beaten and butchered.[10] As Jofen has pointed out, the theme of *mariage à trois* tends to assume a special variation in Hauptmann's work, with the third person, a dead mother, continuing to dominate the unfortunate father from the grave.[11] (Compare not only *Thiel* and *Henschel* but also such later dramas as *Winterballade* [1917] [*Winter Ballad*] and *Veland* [1925]). Personally familiar to Hauptmann since the death of his cousin Georg and the death cult practiced on his behalf by his aunt in Lederose, such infatuation with the dead can exert a powerful influence on the daily lives of the living. By continuing to cede to Minna a controlling force over his inner life, Thiel, of course, exacerbates his anguish over Tobias.

It has been frequently noted that what separates Hauptmann's Thiel character from those of his Poetic Realist predecessors is a modern mood of isolation, an existential loneliness and sense of ultimate futility, and that his characteristic taciturnity and inarticulateness mirror a feeling of "external and inner abandonment."[12] This sense of abandonment is of a kind expressed by the famous "fairy tale" related by the character of the grandmother in Büchner's *Woyzeck*[13] and is manifested most poignantly in little Tobias, a sickly, abused child deprived of the warmth and emotional security of a loving, caring mother. As Klaus D. Post has convincingly shown, such a quintessential motherless state assumed for Hauptmann the force of a potent, recurring metaphor through which to express the inhumane coldness of modern existence.[14] Again it derives from a congruence of personal and zeitgeist elements. Although Hauptmann was strongly attached to his own mother, during his earliest formative years, as has been noted, her duties in helping run the hotel often deprived him of her coveted attention and left him to fend for himself or, worse still, in the dubious care of a brutal nursemaid. Even years later he vividly recalled a cosmic dream, reminiscent of the Büchner scene mentioned above, that epitomized his feelings of abandonment from that time: "There were dimensions of the most monstrous kind which were made graphic to me. I saw nothing less than the earth rolling along in space. I myself, however, was stuck to it, hopelessly, like a dizzying, minimal speck of life, doomed to death, in danger at every moment of plunging off into endless expanses" (7:489).

Leaving aside the autobiographical dimension, the Tobias character must have been of particular interest to Hauptmann's contemporaries. In no previous epoch had so much attention been focused on the study (social, political, pedagogical, or scientific) of childhood as during the Naturalist era. Given the appalling conditions in which children were often forced to work and live (see *The Weavers*), such attention was long overdue. The economic conditions which made it necessary for mothers to spend long hours each day away from home frequently resulted in their virtual abandonment of their offspring. A typical contemporary exposé provides a context within which readers of Hauptmann's novella could appreciate the emotional state of "motherless" children like Tobias. It reads in part, "A most horrible fact: Infants in their cradle, without care, day after day, without nursing, without motherly attention. Not a breath of love can warm them, no tender hand caress them, no mouth kiss them. No one to rock them to sleep, no one to sing songs to them, to laugh with them, to bathe them, to arrange their pillow, to enliven and refresh their little souls with games and dallying. The flat is empty and locked. No human being breathes in it, except the small, helpless mite of a child. The mother slaves in a factory. . . ."[15] Although Tobias's situation is somewhat different, the sense of motherless isolation it engenders is equally pervasive. His biological mother died when he was born, bequeathing him only her own delicate constitution and none of the benefits of genuine motherhood, and Lene actively abuses him both physically and psychologically—the latter in the time-honored manner of wicked stepmothers by letting him know how worthless he is.

More important than plot or characterization for an estimation of Hauptmann's narrative talent at this early stage of his career are some of the more formal aspects of his story. Although he was careful to label it a "study" (6:36)—thereby implying a more modest, tentative, and experimental approach—*Flagman Thiel* shares many of the attributes of the *Novelle* genre that flourished in Germany and Switzerland especially during the late nineteenth century. Silz includes among these its brevity; at least a relative limitation as to time and place; few adult characters; no real evaluation of character but, instead, the revelation of a hitherto submerged aspect of character under the stress of crisis; a striking central event (the death of Tobias); a turning point (Thiel's first vision of his dead wife); a straightforward plot easily summarized in a few sentences; a sharply profiled "silhouette"; and even, perhaps, Paul Heyse's notorious "falcon"—a physical object which plays a memorable role in the story (Tobias's little brown cap).[16]

Yet, in spite of such familiar traits, contemporaries must have been struck by Hauptmann's radical adaptation of the *Novelle* genre to a changed, modern zeitgeist. *Flagman Thiel* ends in chaos and disorder instead of the harmony more typical of Poetic Realism, and the shock of a brutal multiple murder (at a time when such crimes were still extremely rare) was not something readers of Gottfried Keller or Theodor Storm would have been prepared for. Indeed, it was such naturalistic elements that served most clearly to distance the work from more conventional literature of the day. These elements include the depiction of a passive central character from a lower-class background in a specific milieu; attention to details of heredity (Tobias has his father's red hair and his mother's frailty); an undisguised emphasis on sexuality; the rather clinical description of progressive mental derangement; a minutely detailed narrative style that, at times, comes close to Arno Holz's *Sekundenstil;* a preoccupation with technology; the use of

actual place names; and the depiction of ugly, crass reality (Lene's abuse of Tobias, Thiel's aborted strangulation of Lene's infant, and the final discovery of the mutilated bodies).

Nonetheless, such an impressive catalogue of naturalist traits notwithstanding, to simply consign Hauptmann's novella to the Naturalist movement is much too restrictive. Particularly in the character of Franz Thiel, for example, there is still a strong residue of Romantic ideology (for example, the belief that simple, down-to-earth, uneducated human beings have easier access to numinous levels of existence than their more sophisticated brethren). At the opposite extreme, there is considerable anticipation of future literary developments such as fin de siècle symbolism. The complex, virtuoso manipulation and control of every aspect of composition (symbols, leitmotifs, nature descriptions, and the like) is of such a higher order that it bears favorable comparison with Thomas Mann's *Death in Venice* (1912). (Like such rare masterpieces it must be absorbed whole through multiple readings, yields different secrets to individual readers of varied background, and will always retain elements of an ineffable, residual obscurity.)

Some sense of Hauptmann's "irrational realism"[17] can be conveyed by a closer inspection of a few symbols that provide for much of the compositional unity of the work. Superficially (and with the caveat that neatly separating them is contrary to the author's obvious intention) they can be categorized, for our purpose, as relating to technology and nature. Of the former, the railroad and its tracks, steam locomotive, telegraph wires, crossing-guard shack, and other accounterments figure most prominently.

Because of its omnipresence and the vitalistic terms in which it is depicted, it would not be too farfetched to consider the railroad as an important character in the story. It is a governing force of Thiel's external life as well as the locus of his inner existence. During ten years of servitude in its behalf, the reader learns in the first paragraph, he has suffered only two lapses of duty—both occasioned by the dangerous railroad itself: one as the result of a lump of coal that had fallen from the tender of a passing locomotive and "had struck him and flung him with a smashed leg into the ditch beside the track; the other time on account of a wine bottle which had flown out of an express train racing by, and had struck him in the middle of his chest" (6:37). At the end of the story, after the murders and the retreat into insanity, Thiel is found sitting between the rails at the precise spot where Tobias was killed. Briefly, for the first and only time, he is able to prevail over the train by forcing it to stop, but he is soon overpowered, bound hand and foot, and dispatched to the Charité hospital in Berlin. Throughout the novella the railroad is depicted in anthropomorphic terms as an all-powerful, demonic beast of destruction before which mere human beings are as helpless as before a natural cataclysm. "Panting" (6:63) or "stretching its sinews" (6:60), by night with "two red, round lights penetrating the darkness like the goggle-eyes of a gigantic monster" (6:53), it appears in daylight out of infinity, a dark point on the horizon, suddenly expanding into an enormous, black presence before disappearing into unearthly stillness as mysteriously as it arrived—paralleling Thiel's own fate in its inscrutable origin, sudden destructive force, and equally sudden lapse into deathly calm. It is almost as though this piece of cold technology were capable of mocking its human victims. After Tobias has been reduced to a lifeless object, "thrown to and fro between the wheels like a rubber ball," (6:58) a herd of deer watched over by a stag is seen standing on the tracks but gracefully escapes the oncoming locomotive.

Whereas the locomotive assumes vital, malicious overtones, Lene tends to be described in terms of a soulless machine. Depersonalized at one point with the inappropriate neuter definite article as *"das Mensch"* (6:38) (instead of *der Mensch* = human being), she beats Tobias "as though pieces of clothing were being dusted out" (6:46) and tills her little plot of land "with the speed and endurance of a machine" (6:56). Gradually and subtly Hauptmann establishes a parallel between Lene and the train so that when the catastrophe occurs they both seem culpable victimizers.

It is not only the train, however, but also the tracks which deserve attention. It may be stretching things to ascribe phallic significance to them as Jean Jofen does (she refers to the contention of Stekel, a disciple of Freud, that tracks—referred to at one point as resembling "firey snakes"—signify "path to woman"),[18] but it does seem clear that Hauptmann too has weighted them with symbolic value. Spatially, and as an irresistible "track of fate," they seem to run right through the middle of the narrative; and, running parallel to each other, like Thiel's attempt to keep the two halves of his life parallel but separate, they nevertheless converge in a "dark point" (6:49).

Thiel's mystical inclinations flourish especially in the railroad shack, which at night becomes a chapel for Minna. "A faded photograph of the dead woman before him on the table, open song book and Bible, he read and sang alternately throughout the long night, only interrupted at intervals by trains raging by, and, in so doing, fell into an ecstasy which intensified into visions in which he saw the departed bodily before him" (6:40). Reflections of his sexual bondage to Lene and of his guilt over his failure to protect Tobias from her abuse, these visions help push Thiel to the edge of insanity and make the subsequent catastrophe, if not inevitable, at least highly plausible.

Hauptmann's skill at saturating mundane, technological locales and artifacts with atmospheric significance is also shown by his recurring reference to the telegraph wires strung along the railroad embankment. The wind passing over them contributes to the subtle acoustical effects that complement so well the striking visual images of the narrative. Walking along the track with his son shortly before the accident, Thiel shares with him the pleasure of the mysterious music they produce.

> Holding little Tobias by the hand he often stopped to listen to the wonderful sounds that streamed forth out of the wood [of the telegraph poles] like sonorous chorales from the interior of a church. The pole at the south end of his section had an especially full and beautiful harmony. There was a turmoil of tones in its interior which continued to resound, without interruption as though from a single breath, and Tobias ran around the weathered wood in order, as he believed, to discover the originator of the lovely sound through an opening. The flagman fell into a solemn mood, as

though in church. Additionally, with time, he identified a voice which reminded him of his dead wife. He imagined it was a chorus of blessed spirits, into which she also mingled her voice, and this notion awakened a longing in him, a longing close to tears. (6:56-57)

This passage, which freely mixes technology, nature, religion, and psychology in a kind of magic realism, by no means exhausts the telegraph wire symbolism. While it successfully illustrates his dead wife's spiritual hold on Thiel, at a crucial point in the story the author is also able to expand the same imagery to include the threatening sexuality of Lene. Her strong identification with machines and technology, mentioned earlier, is further enhanced by association with the recurrent image of an iron net, based on both the iron rails of the railroad and the wires of the telegraph. "The black, parallel tracks . . .resemble . . . an enormous *iron mesh net* . . . and. . . . On the wires, which crept from pole to pole like the *web of a giant spider,* flocks of twittering birds were stuck in dense rows. A woodpecker flew away laughing over Thiel's head . . . " (emphasis added [6:49]). Two pages earlier Lene's feeling of dominance over Thiel had been suggested in similar terms. "Easily, like a fine *spider web,* and yet as tightly as a *web of iron,* it wrapped itself around him, binding, overpowering, and enervating him (emphasis added [6:47]). As original as such imagery may seem to us today, it too derives from that stock arsenal of symbols frequently invoked by contemporary authors and graphic artists at the turn of the century to epitomize lethal femininity—woman as black widow intent upon enticing, paralyzing, and devouring her mate.[19] Unlike the laughing bird, but very much like so many of Hauptmann's heroes and heroines still waiting in the wings, Thiel is unable to escape his own fateful "web of iron" without paying a heavy price—in this case his loss of sanity.

Among the most unnaturalistic aspects of *Flagman Thiel* are its nature descriptions and use of animal and color imagery. Although close to the author's own experiences— long walks in the forest solitude (*Waldeinsamkeit* [6:47]) of the pine woods near Erkner—nature is used to enhance the sense of a transparent reality behind which fateful, mysterious forces are constantly lurking. For Hauptmann "religious feeling has its deepest roots in nature,"[20] and in his novella nature descriptions are finely attuned to the requirements of plot, character, and atmosphere. As Martini has shown, the author, by his generous use of verbs of motion in describing nature, insures that it is rarely static.[21] In addition, he makes nature an integral part of his fictional cosmos by merging images appropriate to disparate aspects of Thiel's environment: tree trunks glow "like iron" (6:49); rain drops suffused by the red of a locomotive headlight are changed into "drops of blood" (6:53); the noise of a train is described in terms of a charging "cavalry squadron" (6:49); steel railroad tracks "suck up the pale moonlight" (6:52); and the moon itself becomes a "pale golden bowl" (6:52) or a "signal lamp" (6:65). Not surprisingly, Hauptmann also orchestrates nature freely to reflect Thiel's changing emotions and moods (fear, loneliness, calm, inner turmoil) or as a dramatic setting for enhancing the power of his visions. After Tobias's accident nature even seems to share his grief: "A gentle breath of evening air moved softly, steadily over the forest, and pink-flamed curls of clouds hovered over the western heavens" (6:62), and the moon shining on them "paints the faces of the men [carrying Tobias's body] in corpse-like tones" (6:65).

Animals also play a significant role in the artistic economy of **Flagman Thiel,** although those mentioned (including birds, squirrels, deer, and a poodle) do not belong to the "fang and claw" species so frequently identified with Naturalism. Instead, and appropriate for a hero who communes with the dead, they tend to be associated with a variety of superstitions, sometimes local ones. From time immemorial birds have been seen as messengers between the worlds of the living and the dead, and the crows and woodpecker mentioned in the story are considered to have special demonic attributes. (In Hauptmann's Silesia crows are messengers of death. According to local folklore their call is "Grab! Grab!" [grave]).[22] The squirrel Tobias encounters with his father just before the accident is likewise thought to possess oracular powers. Tobias's question on seeing it ("Father, is that . . . God?") has caused considerable puzzlement among interpreters; but, given the mystical tenor of Hauptmann's story, it is doubtful that much would be gained by a definitive, explicit explanation. (For what it is worth—or to add yet another element of ironic ambiguity—the superstitious of Silesia were accused of readiness to believe that the devil is a squirrel.)[23]

Color symbolism (often in synesthetic combination with sounds) adds another strong element of originality to **Flagman Thiel.** And while it would require a separate essay to do justice to this topic, it seems safe to say that no German writer before Hauptmann had so thoroughly saturated such a short prose work with such a profusion of meaningful colors, and that even the later Expressionists failed to surpass him in this regard. Not only do certain colors such as the polarity of black and white (the colors of the demonic locomotive and the pallor of death), red (sunsets, blood, vitality of life), and brown (Tobias's cap, a deer killed on the tracks, the squirrel mentioned above) suggest a metalanguage of symbolic gesture, but, as Krämer has pointed out, even the sequence in which colors are introduced appears to recapitulate the cycle of events depicted in the novella.[24]

"Everything that belongs only to the present dies along with the present."[25] This remark by Mikhail Bakhtin, Russia's greatest twentieth-century literary theorist and critic, would certainly have appealed to Hauptmann, who rejected fanatical, time-bound dogmatism in literature and politics alike. What he aspired to in his best work was permanence, and this could best be achieved by concentrating his talent on the depiction of eternally human qualities that can never lose their topicality and are a staple of great world literature (for example, the Bible; classical literature of Greece and Rome, and Grimms' *Fairy Tales*). As noted before, in recent years attempts have been made to link even Hauptmann's early work to models of such mythic stature. And, while the role of coincidence cannot be entirely discounted—erotic entanglements, child neglect, and murder are not unique in the annals of world literature— Clouser has shown a considerable number of detailed and interesting correspondences between Hauptmann's novella and the Hellenic myth of Hercules. These include but are by no means limited to physical traits (Thiel's "Herculean physique" [6:37]), "an emotional religiosity, self-slaughtered families, and an ambivalent reaction to women."[26]

Notes

1. See also, however, the short narrative *Carnival* (*Fasching,* 1887), 6:13-34, discussed in Warren R. Maurer, *Gerhart Hauptmann* (Boston: Twayne, 1982), pp. 13-15.

2. Cf. Klaus D. Post, *Gerhart Hauptmann, Bahnwärter Thiel: Text, Materialien, Kommentar* (Munich, Vienna: Hanser, 1979), pp. 47-50.

3. See, for example, Irene Heerdegen, "Gerhart Hauptmanns Novelle 'Bahnwärter Thiel,'" *Weimarer Beiträge* 3 (1958): esp. 353 and 359-60.

4. See Larry Wells, "Words of Music: Gerhart Hauptmann's Composition *Bahnwärter Thiel,* in *Wege der Worte: Festschrift für Wolfgang Fleischhauer* (Cologne, Vienna: Böhlau, 1978), p. 385.

5. See Eberhard Hilscher, *Gerhart Hauptmann. Leben und Werk* (Frankfurt/M.: Athenäum, 1988), p. 90.

6. For a summary discussion and secondary literature relating to this topic see Post, 100-108.

7. See Walter Silz, *Realism and Reality: Studies in the German Novelle of Poetic Realism* (Chapel Hill: University of North Carolina Press, 1954), p. 146.

8. See Ralph Fiedler, *Die späten Dramen Gerhart Hauptmanns: Versuch einer Deutung* (Munich: Bergstadt, 1954), p. 135.

9. Cf. Peter Sprengel, *Die Wirklichkeit der Mythen: Untersuchungen zum Werk Gerhart Hauptmanns* (Berlin: E. Schmidt, 1982), p. 182.

10. See Herbert Krämer, *Gerhart Hauptmann: Bahnwärter Thiel* (Munich: R. Oldenbourg, 1980), 18.

11. Jean Jofen, *Das letzte Geheimnis: Eine psychologische Studie über die Brüder Gerhart und Carl Hauptmann* (Bern: Francke, 1972), p. 51.

12. See Fritz Martini, *Das Wagnis der Sprache: Interpretationen deutscher Prosa von Nietzsche bis Benn* (Stuttgart: Klett, 1954), p. 63. Cf. also Post, 55.

13. See Georg Büchner, *Sämtliche Werke und Briefe,* ed. Werner R. Lehmann (Munich: Hanser, 1978) 1:427.

14. See Post, 55-64.

15. Quoted by Post, 138.

16. Cf. Silz, 137.

17. Martini, 60.

18. Jofen, 206.

19. For an especially drastic example of this attitude expressed in a work of art, see Alfred Kubin's 1902 drawing "The Spider" (*Die Spinne*) in Wieland Schmied, *Alfred Kubin* (New York: Ferdinand A. Praeger, 1969), plate 38.

20. Quoted by Martini, 60.

21. See Martini, 79.

22. See Krämer, 23.

23. See Krämer, 37 n. 75.

24. See Krämer, 33-35.

25. Quoted by Gary Saul Morson, "Bakhtin and the Present Moment," *The American Scholar* 60 (1991): 220.

26. Robin A. Clouser, "The Spiritual Malaise of a Modern Hercules, Hauptmann's *Bahnwärter Thiel*," *The Germanic Review* 50 (1980): 105.

FURTHER READING

Criticism

Baumgaertel, Gerhard. "Gerhart Hauptmann's Theme of Engagement Manqué in the Critical Treatment of His Early Characters." *Revue des langues vivantes / Tijdscrift voor Levende Talen*, No. 4 (Summer 1964): 307-35.
    Discussion of seekers of truth in Hauptmann's works, including his novella *Der Apostel*.

Carr, G. J. "Gerhart Hauptmann's Fasching: The Grandmother." *New German Studies* V, No. 1 (Spring 1977): 59-62.
    Analyzes the emblematic function of the grandmother in Hauptmann's novella *Fasching*.

Driver, Beverly and Walker K. Francke. "The Symbolism of Deer and Squirrel in Hauptmann's Bahnwärter Thiel." *South Atlantic Bulletin* XXXVII, No. 2 (May 1972): 47-51.
    Regards symbolism contrasting Thiel's metaphorical imprisonment and the freedom of animals in *Bahnwärter Thiel*.

Dussère, Carolyn Thomas. *The Image of the Primitive Giant in the Works of Gerhart Hauptmann*. Stuttgart: Akademischer Verlag Hans-Dieter Heinz, 1979, 182 p.
    Studies the giant figure as representative of irrational and vengeful forces in Hauptmann's works, such as *Bahnwärter Thiel* and *Der Ketzer von Soana*.

Hammer, A. E. "A Note on the Dénouement of Gerhart Hauptmann's Fasching." *New German Studies* IV, No. 2 (Summer 1976): 87-89.

Notes weaknesses and inconsistencies in the ending of *Fasching*.

Klemm, Frederick A. "A Return to Soana: Hauptmann's Diary and the Ketzer." In *Views and Reviews of Modern German Literature: Festschrift for Adolf D. Klarmann*, edited by Karl S. Weimer, pp. 61-69. Munich: Delp Verlag, 1974.
    Observes autobiographical elements in *Der Ketzer von Soana*.

McLean, Sammy. "Wife as Mother and Double: The Origin and Importance of Bipolar Personality and Erotic Ambivalence in the Work of Gerhart Hauptmann." In *Fearful Symmetry: Doubles and Doubling in Literature and Film*, edited by Eugene J. Crook, pp. 84-99. Tallahassee: University Presses of Florida, 1981.
    Considers psychological themes related to Thiel and his two wives in *Bahnwärter Thiel*.

Mellen, Philip. "Gerhart Hauptmann, Ingeborg Bachmann: Squirrels." *Germanic Notes and Reviews* 28, No. 1 (Spring 1997): 16-22.
    Sees the squirrel in *Bahnwärter Thiel* as a symbol of discord and miscommunication from German myth.

Turner, David. "Setting the Record Straight on Hauptmann's Fasching." *New German Studies* IV, No. 3 (Autumn 1976): 157-59.
    Examines inconsistencies in *Fasching* arising from the novella's status as both a work of literary naturalism and an old-fashioned morality tale.

Ulfers, Friedrich. "The Language of Reality and Symbol in Gerhart Hauptmann's Bahnwärter Thiel." *Teaching Language Through Literature* XVI, No. 2 (April 1977): 26-32.
    Studies overlapping naturalistic and symbolist elements in *Bahnwärter Thiel*.

Washington, Ida H. "The Symbolism of Contrast in Gerhart Hauptmann's Fasching." *German Quarterly* 52, No. 2 (March 1979): 248-52.
    Discusses Hauptmann's use of the symbolic oppositions of light/life and darkness/death in *Fasching*.

Additional coverage of Hauptmann's life and career is contained in the following sources published by the Gale Group: *Contemporary Authors*, Vols. 104, 153; *Dictionary of Literary Biography*, Vols. 66, 118; *DISCovering Authors: Dramatists Module;* and *Twentieth-Century Literary Criticism*, Vol. 4.

"The Legend of Sleepy Hollow"

Washington Irving

The following entry presents criticism of Irving's short story "The Legend of Sleepy Hollow" (1819). For additional information on Irving's complete short fiction, see *Short Story Criticism,* Volume 2.

INTRODUCTION

Considered the first professional man of letters in the United States and the first American author to win recognition abroad, Irving is noted for his contribution to the short story genre. In his most acclaimed achievement, *The Sketch Book of Geoffrey Crayon, Gent.* (1819–20), he created charming sketches, tales, and travel reminiscences. Widely read in its time, the book is remembered for the short stories "Rip Van Winkle" and "The Legend of Sleepy Hollow." In the latter of these tales—which details the run-in of a Connecticut schoolmaster, Ichabod Crane, with a headless horseman—Irving wove elements of myth, legend, folklore, and drama into a narrative that achieved almost immediate classic status. Critics generally agree that "The Legend of Sleepy Hollow" provided a model for the modern short story and introduced imagery and archetypes that enriched national literature. While Irving's other historical writings are valued for their graceful prose style and historical interest, critics generally agree that "The Legend of Sleepy Hollow" is—along with "Rip Van Winkle"—his most lasting artistic achievement.

PLOT AND MAJOR CHARACTERS

"The Legend of Sleepy Hollow" opens with a description of the Dutch New York community of Sleepy Hollow, located in a rural valley near the Hudson River. Irving introduces the tall, lanky schoolmaster Ichabod Crane as a figure of mild derision, a hard-nosed itinerant Yankee from Connecticut who takes himself too seriously and possesses an enormous appetite despite his slight build. Proud of his erudition, at least in comparison to the rustics he encounters in Sleepy Hollow, Crane is described as "an odd mixture of small shrewdness and simple credulity." He quickly discovers Katrina Van Tassel, the lovely daughter of a well-to-do Dutch farmer, Baltus Van Tassel, and resolves to win her heart. His principal rival, Brom Van Brunt, nicknamed Brom Bones, is a burly outdoorsman, strong and somewhat arrogant but with a well-developed sense of humor. Realizing that he cannot best Bones in feats of physical prowess, Crane sets out to woo Katrina by making regular visits to the Van Tassel farmhouse as a singing-master. Over time the competition between Crane and Bones intensifies.

At an autumn party at the Van Tassel home, Crane endeavors to impress Katrina with his singing and dancing. As he seems to gain the upper hand over Bones the conversation turns to local ghost tales—principally that of the Headless Horseman, an apparition of a decapitated Hessian soldier that haunts the area. Bones entertains the crowd by telling of his own adventure with the Horseman; later Crane recites extracts from the works of his favorite author, Cotton Mather. As the party winds down, Crane speaks with Katrina, but his advances are rebuked. Crestfallen, he departs on his horse. Shortly thereafter, while traveling through the darkness, Crane encounters the ghostly Hessian soldier who chases the schoolmaster until the frightened man is thrown from his steed. The following morning, the horse is found without its saddle or rider near the smashed remains of a pumpkin. Crane is never seen again in Sleepy Hollow, though a rumor spreads that he has become a lawyer and a judge in another town. The tale is retold of his harrowing confrontation with the Headless Horseman, which produces a spirited laugh from Brom Bones whenever the pumpkin is mentioned. Irving closes the tale with a postscript describing the original narrator of the story, "one tall, dry-looking old gentleman" who draws some conclusions from the extravagant yarn, but finally claims, "I don't believe one-half of it myself."

MAJOR THEMES

Thematic analyses of "The Legend of Sleepy Hollow" generally focus on the character of Ichabod Crane and the satirical implications of his rivalry with Brom Bones. Many critics maintain that Crane represents the outcast artist-intellectual in American society; although he has been considered, conversely, as a caricature of the acquisitive, scheming Yankee Puritan, a type that Irving lampooned regularly in his early satirical writings. Additionally, the work is seen as a regional contrast between Yankee Connecticut and Dutch New York, the latter personified in the figure of the backwoodsman Brom Bones. Other commentators have suggested that Crane represents a morally corrupt capitalist figure. Also, the tension between imagination and creativity versus materialism and productivity in nineteenth-century America is considered a significant theme in the story.

CRITICAL RECEPTION

Although much of Irving's fiction is today regarded as little more than petty and derivative, many critics agree that Irving did much to establish the American short story in 1819 with "The Legend of Sleepy Hollow." Commentators concur, moreover, that Irving set the artistic standard and model for subsequent generations of American short story writers with the tale. Among the technical innovations ascribed to "The Legend of Sleepy Hollow" include the integration of folklore, myth, and fable into narrative fiction; setting and landscape as a reflection of theme and mood; and the expression of the supernatural and use of Gothic elements.

PRINCIPAL WORKS

Short Fiction

The Sketchbook of Geoffrey Crayon, Gent. [as Geoffrey Crayon] 1819-20
Bracebridge Hall; or, the Humorists: A Medley [as Geoffrey Crayon] 1822
Tales of a Traveller [as Geoffrey Crayon] 1824
The Alhambra [as Geoffrey Crayon] 1832
The Crayon Miscellany [as Geoffrey Crayon 1835

Other Major Works

Salmagundi; or, The Whim-Whams and Opinions of Launcelot Langstaff, Esq., and Others [With William Irving and James Kirke Paulding] (satirical essays) 1807-08

A History of New York, from the Beginning of the World to the End of the Dutch Dynasty [as Diedrich Knickerbocker] (historical parody) 1809
A History of the Life and Voyages of Christopher Columbus (biography) 1828
A Chronicle of the Conquest of Granada (history) 1829
A Tour on the Prairies (travel sketches) 1835
The Works of Washington Irving. 15 Vols. [author's revised edition] (essays, short stories, sketches, history, and biography) 1848-51
Oliver Goldsmith (biography) 1849
The Life of George Washington (biography) 1855-59

CRITICISM

Daniel G. Hoffman (essay date 1961)

SOURCE: "Prefigurations: 'The Legend of Sleepy Hollow'," in *Form and Fable in American Fiction*, Oxford University Press, 1961, pp. 83-96.

[*In the following essay, Hoffman explains how "The Legend of Sleepy Hollow" dramatizes a conflict between two cultures—those of the Yankee city-dweller and the backwoodsman—that was to become a major theme in American literature.*]

ONE

The first important literary statement of the themes of native folk character and superstition was made, fittingly enough, in the first literary work by an American to win worldwide acclaim. When ***The Sketch Book of Geoffrey Crayon, Gent.*** appeared in London in 1819, its author became the first of a long series of expatriate Americans who found their native roots all the more poignant for viewing them from a distance.

Washngton Irving was fortunate, granted his special though restricted gifts, to be alive and in England at that moment in the history of literature. He sought out, and was taken up by, Sir Walter Scott, who was showing how the sentiment of nostalgia for the past could infuse fiction and become its informing principle. In his novels Scott projected that sense of historical continuity which formed a curious undercurrent of sensibility even before the Romantic movement began. Little though the Augustans attended the medieval or more recent past, there were important eighteenth-century successors to such early antiquarian works as Sir Thomas Browne's collection of *Vulgar Errors* (1648) and Samuel Pepys' collection of broadside ballads. Bishop Percy's *Reliques of Ancient English Poetry* (1765) and John Brand's *Observations on the Popular Antiquities of Great Britain* (1795) laid the groundwork for the two directions British folklore study has followed ever since. Scott took his prominent place in both with his ballad collection, *The Minstrelsy of the Scottish Border* (1802) and his comprehensive *Letters on Demonology and Witchcraft* (1830). Much more influential, however, than these formal studies in introducing a whole generation of readers—and authors—to such materials was his use of folklore in his own fiction. One of Scott's earliest and most popular disciples along this line was a young American *littérateur,* the London representative of P. E. Irving & Co., New York dealers in hardware.

Washington Irving was already something of an antiquary. His early *Knickerbocker's History of New York* reveals him to be enchanted with the very past he satirized. In *The Sketch Book* Irving used several themes to which he would again and again recur: the Gothic tale in the German manner of **'The Spectre Bridegroom,'** the antiquarian nostalgia of the four sketches on English Christmas customs, the character sketch of **'The Village Angler.'** The two selections destined for most enduring fame, however, were careful reconstructions of the scenes of Irving's own boyhood in the Dutch communities of the Hudson Valley. One of these retells a German folktale in this American setting, in which Rip Van Winkle sleeps away his twenty years after a heady game of bowls with the ghostly crew of the Half-Moon. In the other tale, **'The Legend of Sleepy Hollow,'** Irving brought into belles-lettres for the first time the comic mythology and folk beliefs of his native region. In Ichabod Crane and Brom Bones he dramatized that clash of regional characters—the Yankee versus the Backwoodsman—which would soon become a major theme in our literature, as well as a continuing motif in a century and a half of folktales, and in our national history.

It is surprising that the extent to which Irving drew upon native folklore has scarcely been acknowledged. The chief reason for this seems to be Henry A. Pochmann's convincing demonstration, in 1930, of the extent of Irving's indebtedness to his German contemporaries. Stanley T. Williams, in his definitive biography, gives us a further exploration of Irving's methods of composition.[1] When we see the extent to which Irving depended on other men's books, often translating without acknowledgment, we can understand why recent critics are reluctant to grant him credit for originality in interpreting American themes.

The foremost students of American humor have strangely overlooked **'The Legend of Sleepy Hollow.'** Walter Blair does call it 'a characteristic piece of American humor,' but his remark is relegated to a footnote. And Constance Rourke, writing with her usual felicity, remarks that 'in the Knickerbocker History and in Rip Van Winkle Irving created a comic mythology as though comic myth-making were a native habit, formed early . . . . But his Dutch people were of the past, joining only at a distance with current portrayals of native character.'[2] Why did Miss Rourke not mention **'Sleepy Hollow'**? I do not know; but I hope to show that in Ichabod and Brom Bones, Irving gave us portrayals of *current* native character projected backwards in time, rather than merely historical types unrooted in contemporary folklore.

There are of course good reasons why Brom and Ichabod have not been so recognized. For one thing, Irving's style is hardly what we expect in a folk document. For another, the Hudson Valley Dutch have long been thought an alien people by the Anglo-Saxons who conquered, surrounded, and outnumbered them. But the third and principal reason is Irving's own treatment of his Dutch materials. Almost everywhere *except* in **'The Legend of Sleepy Hollow'** he

deliberately altered the traditional characteristics of the Dutch for the purposes of his own fiction. As a consequence of Irving's popularity and of widespread ignorance of what the Dutch were really like, his caricatures were widely accepted as portraits of the Dutch-Americans. Paulding, writing *The Dutchman's Fireside* twenty-two years after the *Knickerbocker History,* imitated his friend in attributing chuckleheadedness and indolence to the brothers Vancour. In Cooper's *Satanstoe* (1845), however, we get a more realistic picture of the Dutch; his Guert Ten Eyck amply fulfills the historian Janvier's description: the Dutch 'were tough and they were sturdy, and they were as plucky as men could be.'[3] Only in **'The Legend of Sleepy Hollow'** did Irving give a Dutchman these attributes; everywhere else he made them fat, foolish, pompous, and pleasure-loving. Here his usual Dutchman does appear (Van Tassel), but only in the background. Brom Bones is his realistic Dutch frontiersman, who meets and bests a Yankee in the traditional conflict of our native folk humor. Why did Irving choose this theme, so different from his usual preoccupations?

When we admit his dependence upon books, we must look at the kinds of authors on whom he depended. Othmar and Musaeus were collectors and redactors of folktales and *märchen.* Irving knew personally a third folklorist, Dr. Karl Böttiger, 'who undoubtedly was able to give him expert advice on his folklore studies.'[4] Wherever Irving went he collected popular sayings and beliefs; he was prepossessed by a sense of the past, and recognized the power—and the usefulness to a creative artist—of popular antiquities. Brom and Ichabod had their beginnings in local characters he had known as a boy;[5] what made them take their singular form, however, was the direction in which Irving's imagination impelled them. And that direction was toward the fabulous. The fabulous was Irving's milieu.

In a reminiscence twenty years after *The Sketch Book,* Irving revealed that Diedrich Knickerbocker had learned the legend of Sleepy Hollow from an old Negro who gave him 'that invaluable kind of information, never to be acquired from books,' and from 'the precious revelations of the good dame at the spinning wheel.'[6] Of Musaeus' *Volksmärchen* he says nothing. But he may well indeed have heard such stories in the old Dutch chimney corners. H. W. Thompson recounts similar motifs in York State folklore: nightly visitations by a shrieking woman 'tied to the tail of a giant horse with fiery eyes'; and 'a curious phantom . . . uttering unearthly laughter, lights shining from her finger tips.' There were revenants aplenty in Catskills. Still another important part of Dutch folk culture was the lusty practical joking[7] which Cooper used in some of the most spirited pages in *Satanstoe.* Both aspects of Dutch folk life—the villagers' superstitions and their humor—are immortalized in **'The Legend of Sleepy Hollow.'**

Two

Irving sets his story in a folk society: 'It is in such little retired Dutch villages . . . that population, manners, and customs remain fixed; while the great torrent of migration and improvement, which is making such incessant changes in other parts of this restless country, sweeps by them unobserved.' And again: 'The neighborhood is rich in legendary lore . . . Local tales and superstitions thrive best in these sheltered long-settled retreats.' Into this community comes Ichabod Crane, 'a native of Connecticut, a State which supplied the Union with pioneers for the mind as well as for the forest.' Ichabod is Irving's Connecticut Yankee, the fictional ancestor of Mark Twain's Hartford mechanic. But his nearer descendants are Sam Slick, Jack Downing, Hosea Biglow. Before any of these was born in print Ichabod had already been a country teacher, a singing master, a sometime farmer; later he is to undergo still further metamorphoses which link him still more closely to these heroes of popular legend and literature. Like Ben Franklin, like Hawthorne's Holgrave, like the schoolmaster in *Snowbound* and Melville's marvelous Confidence Man, he was a jack of all trades. Metamorphosis is always magical, but now, in an egalitarian society, the magic is the power of self-reliance, not of Satan.

Ichabod's native shrewdness and perseverance are somewhat compromised by his credulity. 'No tale was too gross or monstrous for his capacious swallow.' Ichabod devoutly believed in all the remarkable prodigies retailed in Cotton Mather's *History of New England Witchcraft* (that is, the *Magnalia Christi Americani*). There he found spectral ships manned by ghostly women, heretics giving birth to monsters, revenants pursuing the innocent with invisible instruments of torture. But of all the ghostly tales in the valley, the one Ichabod Crane most liked to hear was that of the Headless Horseman.

Meanwhile, we remember, Ichabod falls in love with Katrina Van Tassel; more exactly, seeing her father's prosperous farm, he envisages 'every roasting pig running about with a pudding in his belly, and an apple in his mouth.' Considerations of this sort lead Ichabod into a most interesting reverie: he imagines 'the blooming Katrina, with a whole family of children, mounted on the top of a wagon loaded with household trumpery, with pots and kettles dangling beneath; and he beheld himself bestriding a pacing mare, with a colt at her heels, setting out for Kentucky, Tennessee, or Lord knows where.' Here we have Ichabod Boone—Connecticut's pioneer of the wilderness as well as of the mind. Traditionally the American frontiersman has resented the mercantile civilizer; in a thousand folktales the shaggy woodsman frightens the Yankee clear out of the district.

Ichabod's fatuous dream of pioneering prepares the way for his rival's entrance: 'a burly, roaring, roistering blade . . . Brom Van Brunt, the hero of the country round, which rang with his feats of strength and hardihood.' He had 'a mingled air of fun and arrogance,' and was 'always ready for either a fight or a frolic; but had more mischief than ill-will in his composition.' Famous for horsemanship, 'foremost at all races and cockfights' was Brom; 'and when any madcap prank, or rustic brawl, occurred in the vicinity, [the neighbors] always shook their heads, and warranted Brom Bones was at the bottom of it.'

Making allowances for Irving's smoothly flowing style, what we have here described is a Catskill Mike Fink, a Ring-Tailed Roarer from Kinderhook. While Irving was writing these lines in London, the real Mike Fink was somewhere west of Pittsburgh, shooting the heel off a nigger to make his foot fit the shoe, scalping Indians for the pure hell of it, roistering in towns along the Ohio. In Brom

Bones's good-natured mischief there is a tinge of Mike Fink's brutality, if not of his sadism. That other favorite frontiersman, Davy Crockett, had not by 1819 become a national figure; yet the type—the swaggering frontier braggart, the prodigious hunter and strong man, the daredevil, the mischief-maker—was already well established in oral tradition. Irving's depiction of Brom Bones certainly gave these characteristics new clarity as they are combined for the first time in a fictional portrait of the *genus* frontiersman.

Irving now pits his rival suitors against each other. Ichabod, the Yankee, 'had a happy mixture of pliability and perseverance in his nature.' Although he is caricatured unmercifully, he is not entirely unworthy of our grudging admiration; a thoroughly self-reliant citizen, he adapts his strategy to meet the case. 'To have taken the field openly against his rival would have been madness,' so Ichabod insinuates himself into Katrina's notice while masquerading as her singing-master. Here he outwits Big Brom in the contest, perennially fresh in American comic lore, between wit and strength. But Ichabod forces Brom Bones to draw upon his own resources—the rough fancy of the frontiersman—as well as upon brute strength. This proves a dangerous combination for the scholar.

At Van Tassel's quilting frolic, when the old Negro tunes the fiddle and rosins the bow, Ichabod finds his *métier*, fair grounds whereon he can excel Brom Bones. The ungainly form of the pedagogue achieves animation if not grace, for he is from Down East in Connecticut and is sufficiently sophisticated to know how to dance with a lady. Brom, the bumpkin, 'sorely smitten with love and jealousy, sat brooding by himself in one corner.'

The dancing over, talk now turns to the recently concluded Revolutionary War. Old soldiers' exploits become more heroic at each telling, as Irving skillfully moves us from the reality of the dance to mildly comic exaggerations of heroic truth, then to the supernatural itself. We are near Sleepy Hollow, and 'there was a contagion in the very air that blew from that haunted region.' The mythology of war blends with that of the otherworld, lending credence to the supernatural, as we learn that 'mourning cries and wailings [were] heard and seen about the great tree where the unfortunate Major André was taken'; and we hear of 'the woman in white, that haunted the dark glen at Raven Rock,' who 'was often heard to shriek on winter nights before a storm, having perished there in the snow.' But the presiding spirit at this haunted conference was the Headless Horseman, who tethers his horse in the graveyard, haunts the church, and chases travellers. Brom Bones has met him. Riding his horse, Daredevil, Brom challenged the ghost to race for a bowl of punch—'and should have won it too, for Daredevil beat the goblin horse all hollow, but, just as they came to the church-bridge, the Hessian bolted, and vanished in a flash of fire.'

Here is the bravado of the American hero, so confident of his own powers that he will risk everything for nothing, as Sam Patch did when he jumped Niagara just to prove that 'Some things can be done as well as others.' Such reckless daring makes the Faustus legend seem native in this land; Irving tried his hand at that in **'The Devil and Tom Walker'** a generation before Hawthorne gave the devil's compact more sombre treatment, a century before Stephen Vincent Benét outdid him in this comic mode.

But Ichabod reasserts the dominance of evil over American self-reliance: he quotes Mather on witches, and describes the ghosts he has seen himself. The homely Puritan cannot accept the bravado of the backwoods Natural Man; Ichabod and Brom inhabit different worlds although they live in the same village. When Ichabod bids Katrina good night, he is chagrined to find that his hopes for a prosperous match have somehow gone awry. Perhaps, having observed her rival swains' reactions to supernatural perils, she has decided not to be a Puritan's bride, however nimbly he may dance the quadrille. Ichabod steals away heavy at heart.

Now, in the best-known part of the story, comes Irving's debt to Musaeus. But the stylistic control of the atmosphere shows Irving's own talent at its best, while the conclusion of the story is of signal importance in the literary development of an American myth. The darkness deepens; all the tales of ghosts and witches crowd into Ichabod's brain. Now he crosses the stream where André was captured, a haunted brook. Ichabod is appalled to find he no longer rides alone. A silent horseman splashes beside him. Coming out of the valley, Ichabod gets a look at his companion and discovers, in terror, that he carries his head in his hands! Crane rushes toward the church-bridge, where the Hessian, pursuing Brom, had disappeared. Reaching the bridge, Ichabod turns 'to see if his pursuer should vanish, according to rule'—a fine pedantic touch!—but sees instead 'the goblin rising in his stirrups . . . hurling his head at him. Ichabod endeavored to dodge the horrible missile, but too late.' He falls from his horse, 'and the black steed, and the goblin rider, passed by like a whirlwind.'

Ichabod was never seen again in Sleepy Hollow. His landlord burns his copy of Mather's *Witchcraft* and determines to keep his own children from school, 'observing that he never knew of any good come of this same reading and writing.'

THREE

Here in this York State valley, Irving's Dutch braggart concocts the perfect backwoodsman's revenge on the Yankee.[8] This first statement of the theme is among the most memorable it has ever received in our literature; it is with us yet and ever has been, in Davy Crockett outwitting peddlers, in a thousand dime novels and popular magazines in which the yokel gets the best of the city slicker.[9]

The rustic hero may be naïve and honest, with only his common sense to help him make his way in the world; so he appears as Jack Downing, as Hosea Biglow, as Robin in Hawthorne's *My Kinsman, Major Molineux,* as Huckleberry Finn. Or he may be a swashbuckling braggart, half horse, half alligator, like all the ring-tailed roarers and Thorpe's Big Bear of Arkansas. No matter; in either form he represents the American élan, the pioneer, the Natural Man rebelling against the burden of guilt of the ages. It was he who cut the cords that bound him to the English throne, to all king-ridden Europe. Naked he stands in the wilderness, bereft of the past, confident that all human history begins—with *him.*

Who is his adversary? Perhaps an insufferable fop from the city to the East—traditions, culture, lineage, class distinctions always come from the East in American mythology: from New England, from Europe. Perhaps he is a shrewd, narrow-nosed Yankee peddler. No matter; in either form he stands for that ancient heritage of useless learning and inherited guilt against which the American, in each succeeding generation, must rebel.

Such are the roles in this ever-recurring fable of the American destiny. Washington Irving, whose birth coincided with that of the Republic, formulated a theme of its national literature with his dramatization of the Republic's dominant myth. Even Henry James is in his debt.

But what of Ichabod Crane? Did the pumpkin kill him? Of course not! Our folk heroes never die. Wearing the magic cloak of metamorphosis, they stave off death forever by simply changing their occupations. The ungainly pedagogue is no more—long live the New York City lawyer! For that is what Ichabod becomes after he makes his way from Sleepy Hollow. And onward and upward he goes: from the bar into politics, from his office to the press, thence to the bench. Far be it from Washington Irving to analyze or criticize the great American myth; where he finds a mythology of humor, he improves it on its own grounds. Responding instinctively to his fabulous materials, he makes Ichabod unforgettable in a stunning caricature. Brom, who is much more like life, is not so memorable, even though Americans always love a winner.

Yet Ichabod is not ultimately the loser in this legend. All he has lost is a farm girl's love and a measure of self-respect; the former was no real passion, the latter can be repaired. Ichabod Crane is a sorry symbol of learning, of culture, of sophistication, of a decayed religious faith, of an outworn order in the world. His very name suggests decrepitude: 'And she named him Ichabod, saying, The glory is departed from Israel' (I Sam. iv. 21). But Ichabod Crane is no Israelite; although an anachronism in all other respects, he is yet an American. And therefore he is immortal. Back to the city he goes, to find success.

Brom Bones stays in the village and gets the girl. He deserved her more than Ichabod did, for while the scholar danced and counted his stuffed pigs, Brom experienced two human emotions: jealousy and love.

Ichabod also knew two emotions, and two only. His were fear and ambition. He is not the loser, because he leads a full and prosperous life, experiencing to the brim the two emotions which give meaning to his existence: fear, in Sleepy Hollow, and ambition, in New York City. For it is the same ambition which led him to court Katrina Van Tassel that takes him later to the bar and the polls, to the editor's chair and the juror's bench. Ambition of this magnitude requires for its satisfaction a culture sufficiently complex to be capable of corruption. It cannot be gratified in the folk society of Sleepy Hollow Village, where the good people are as pure as the air.

Fear and ambition are Ichabod's, but not love. That is because Ichabod Crane is not wholly human. A sterile intellectual, his head aswim with worthless anachronisms, his heart set on material gain, Ichabod is gracelessly devoid of the natural human affections. He is the bumpkin's caricature of what life in the seat of a corrupt civilization can make of a man.

When one compares **'The Legend of Sleepy Hollow'** to the bulk of Irving's work it seems anomalous that he could have mustered the imaginative power to enrich us so greatly, for most of Irving's writing betrays a lack of creative energy, a paucity of invention. Irving, after all, was never able successfully to transcend the limited aims of a 'sketch,' and he continued to rework his old themes in new disguises,[10] telling a tale now set in old Dutch New York, now in Germany, now in England, now in Spain. *Bracebridge Hall, Tales of a Traveller,* most of *Wolfert's Roost* and **The Sketch Book** itself make tedious reading today. They show all too plainly Irving's faults: his dependence upon secondary sources, and the restricted range of emotional experience from which he was able to create fiction. But in the characters of Ichabod and Brom Bones, Irving found archetypal figures already half-created by the popular imagination. Among all of Irving's characters only Rip Van Winkle has as great a power to move us; and Rip, too, is what the highly developed but narrow gift of a storyteller whose milieu was the fabulous has made of a character from folklore. Although the original Peter Klaus was German, the themes of Rip Van Winkle are universal: the pathos of change, the barely-averted tragedy of loss of personal identity. And, as Louis LeFevre has pointed out,[11] Rip is indeed close to an aspect of the American national character—that yearning for escape from work and responsibility which is exemplified by a host of gadgets and the day-dream dramas of contemporary popular culture. Irving's Knickerbocker Dutchmen were, as Miss Rourke observed, remote caricatures resurrected from a distant past. But when Irving dramatized the homely comic figures he found in native American folk traditions, his Ichabod and Brom pass so readily into the reader's own imagination that they seem to be persons we have always known. **'The Legend of Sleepy Hollow'** sketches the conflict of cultures which the rest of our literature has adumbrated ever since. One could predict *that* from Irving's story; both Ichabod Crane and Brom Bones lived lustily ever after. They are rivals yet.

Notes

1. Irving's use of folk traditions of piracy is noted by W. H. Bonner, *Pirate Laureate: The Life & Legends of Captain Kidd* (New Brunswick, N. J., 1947), pp. 151-65; Leonard Beach discusses Irving's use of American themes and recognizes Ichabod as 'Irving's judgment of Puritanism': 'Washington Irving,' *University of Kansas City Review,* XIV (1948), 259-66. Pochmann notes 'Irving's German Sources in The Sketch Book,' *Studies in Philology,* XXVII (July 1930), 477-507; see also 'Irving's German Tour and Its Influence on His Tales,' *PMLA,* XLV (Dec. 1930), 1150-87. Pochmann shows, with parallel texts, that in 'Rip Van Winkle' Irving translated and expanded the story of Peter Klaus, a German goatherd who fell asleep for years, which he found in the *Volkssagen* of Othmar; and in 'The Legend of Sleepy Hollow,' he demonstrates Irving's indebtedness to the Rübezahl legends in *Volksmärchen der Deutschen,* by Musaeus. See also Williams, *The Life of Washington Irving* (New York, 1935), I, 177-86.

2. Blair, *Native American Humor,* p. 16, n. 3. Basing his judgment of Irving as a native humorist on the *Knickerbocker's History of New York,* Blair considers Irving as primarily 'a disciple of neoclassicism,' and concludes (p. 14) that 'he employed a technique which, admirable though it was, differed from that of typical American humor.' Rourke, *American Humor,* p. 77.

3. Thomas A. Janvier, *The Dutch Founding of New York* (New York, 1903), p. 4; Janvier takes issue with Irving's characterization of the Dutch on pp. 1-3, 9, 14, 46, 105, and 131-2.

4. Pochmann, 'Irving's German Tour,' *PMLA,* XLV, 1153-4.

5. Brom Bones was identified by Pierre M. Irving as a wag of Tarrytown who 'boasted of once having met the devil . . . and run a race with him for a bowl of milk' (*Life and Letters of Washington Irving,* London, 1892, I, 282). See Williams, *Life,* I, 429, n. 90, for a similar account; on p. 430, n. 91, he names Brom Van Allstyne of Kinderhook as the original of Irving's character. Ichabod Crane, Williams finds (p. 109), was modelled upon 'Jesse Merwin, the homespun wit' and village schoolmaster, as well as upon Fielding's Partridge and the schoolmaster in Goldsmith's *Deserted Village.*

6. 'Sleepy Hollow,' in *Biographies and Miscellanies,* ed. Pierre M. Irving (New York, 1866), pp. 514-16.

7. Thompson, *Body Boots & Britches* (Philadelphia, 1939), pp. 119-21; Carl Carmer, *The Hudson* (New York and Toronto, 1939), p. 35, lists some typical pranks.

8. The perfection of Irving's 'Legend' becomes even more apparent by comparison with 'Cobus Yerks,' Paulding's imitation of 'Sleepy Hollow.' Instead of Yankee vs. Backwoodsman, we find a stupid, superstitious Dutchman frightened by a ghostly dog, otherwise Tim Canty, a merry Englishman. Now the story is reduced to its supernatural motif only; the richness which Irving's 'Legend of Sleepy Hollow' holds for us, its reverberations on the themes of national and regional character, are entirely lacking in Paulding's caricature. *Tales of The Good Woman,* ed. W. I. Paulding (New York, 1867), pp. 285-99.

9. Mark Twain's first newspaper sketch was a version of this motif, called 'The Dandy Frightening the Squatter,' reprinted in *Tall Tales of the Southwest,* ed. F. J. Meine (New York, 1930), pp. 447-8; discussed by Bernard DeVoto in *Mark Twain's America* (Boston, 1932), pp. 90-91.

10. Much later Irving was to return to the frontier materials he used for Brom Bones in 'The Early Experiences of Ralph Ringwood,' a fictionalized biography of Governor Duval of Florida (*Wolfert's Roost,* New York, 1865. pp. 294-341). Some of the supernatural lore from 'The Legend of Sleepy Hollow' turns up here too, notably an apparition of a horse as a devil (pp. 298-9). Of his late frontier sketches Beach notes, 'Strange that Irving should have come so close to Longstreet's and Craddock's property! Strange too that he should not have known what to make of it' ('Washington Irving,' *University of Kansas City Review,* XIV, p. 266). Perhaps the

key to this puzzle is that Ralph Ringwood, a Kentuckian, meets only Westerners and hence there is no opportunity for Irving to give this sketch the dramatic power which the conflict of regional characters made possible in 'The Legend of Sleepy Hollow.' In view of the popularity, as well as the artistic success, of the earlier sketch, it is indeed surprising that Irving should have followed it with so poor an effort.

11. 'Paul Bunyan and Rip Van Winkle,' *Yale Review,* XXXVI (Autumn 1946), pp. 66-76.

Robert A. Bone (essay date 1963)

SOURCE: "Irving's Headless Hessian: Prosperity and the Inner Life," in *American Quarterly,* Vol. XV, No. 2, Pt. 1, Summer, 1963, pp. 167-75.

[*In the following essay, Bone considers the theme of materialism in "The Legend of Sleepy Hollow."*]

While the body of this essay is concerned with **"The Legend of Sleepy Hollow,"** I have tried to touch upon a central theme in our national letters: the relentless pressure of commodities on the American imagination. *Walden* is the classic statement of this theme. Thoreau went to the woods to escape the pressure of house and barn and mortgage; to free his soul from the tyranny of commodities. Since his aim was to confront essentials, his first requirement was to reduce the clutter of worldly goods which threatened to forestall the act of contemplation.

Nothing would seem more remote from contemporary sensibility than this ascetic strain. Yet consider the voluntary poverty of the Beat poet. Where Madison Avenue enjoins us to consume! consume!, the Beatnik demurs with a modern version of Thoreau's simplify! simplify! Deep in the American psyche, it would seem, lies a curious ambivalence toward the things of this world; a suspicion that material prosperity may be an impediment to the inner life.

It is not difficult, I think, to trace this conflict to its source in New England Puritanism. Seventeenth-century Americans were in many respects the heirs of the middle ages. Like their medieval ancestors, they regarded temporal affairs as a distraction from the serious business of salvation. Still in the grip of an otherworldly vision, the Puritan imagination experienced commodities as temptations of the world, the flesh and the devil.

Superimposed on this medieval base was the acquisitive drive of New England Puritanism. Maule's curse, after all, was not called forth by a morality of abstention. The main thrust of the Protestant Reformation was in a worldly direction, and in America the Protestant ethic was reinforced by the compelling needs of a frontier society. Faced with these cross-currents, the Puritan patriarchs devised a compromise formula which Perry Miller has described as "loving the world with weaned affections." In the spirit of the new age, one could love the world, if the primary commitment of the soul remained elsewhere.

Inevitably, as Puritan values were subverted by the growing prosperity of the colonies, this precarious equilibrium was upset. In the eighteenth century, the contemplative and acquisitive aspects of the Puritan temperament precipitated out. Autobiography, if not yet fiction, gave us two figures symbolic of the new division.

Here is a passage from the *Personal Narrative* of Jonathan Edwards:

> The whole book of Canticles used to be pleasant to me, and I used to be much in reading it, about that time; and found, from time to time, an inward sweetness, that would carry me away, in my contemplations. This I know not how to express otherwise, than by a calm, sweet abstraction of soul from all the concerns of this world; and sometimes a kind of vision, or fixed ideas and imaginations, of being alone in the mountains, or some solitary wilderness, far from all mankind, sweetly conversing with Christ, and wrapt and swallowed up in God.

The key word in this passage is *vision.* In Edwards, the imagination is an active faculty serving the soul in its communion with God.

Consider now a passage from the *Autobiography* of Benjamin Franklin, in which the author attempts to dissuade a young man from writing poems:

> He continued to write frequently, sending me large specimens of an epic poem, which he was then composing, and desiring my remarks and corrections. These I gave him from time to time, but endeavor'd rather to discourage his proceedings. One of Young's satires was then just publish'd. I copy'd and sent him a great part of it, which set in a strong light the folly of pursuing the muses with any hope of advancement by them.

Here the key word is *advancement.* In Franklin, the imagination is firmly subordinated to the acquisition of commodities.

By the early nineteenth century, the utilitarian ethic of Benjamin Franklin had emerged as the cultural norm. All value came to be defined in terms of use. By this measure, contemplation could scarcely be considered valuable, nor meditation, nor poetry, nor fiction. Increasingly the American writer found himself in an atmosphere of trade and commerce profoundly hostile to his art. In self-defense he turned to the Romantic movement, at the heart of which lay a spirited defense of the imagination.

During the Romantic period, the concept of imagination was itself transformed. Closely associated with devotional practices in the past, it now became more or less secularized. The contemplative principle was revived, as we have seen, in Thoreau, but devoid of specific theological content. Transcendentalism was perhaps the closest approximation to the spirit of Jonathan Edwards which a secular society would allow. As the role of the artist became increasingly differentiated from that of the clergyman or philosopher, the stage was set for a new phase in the history of the American imagination. *Henceforth the pressure of commodities would be experienced as a threat to the artistic process as such.*

It is Washington Irving's distinction first to have explored this theme. His interest in folklore, myth and legend provides him, in his best work, with a means of confronting the prosaic temper of his time. The folk tale, with its elements of fable and of fantasy, is an ideal medium, and it is here that Irving's creative powers reach fulfillment. **"The Legend of Sleepy Hollow"** is at once his finest achievement and his most enduring contribution to our literary history. For in the mythic encounter of Ichabod Crane and the Headless Horseman, the crisis of the modern imagination is first revealed.

The story begins with an epigraph from "The Castle of Indolence," by the Scottish poet James Thomson:

> A pleasing land of drowsy head it was,
> Of dreams that wave before the half-shut eye;
> And of gay castles in the clouds that pass,
> For ever flushing round a summer sky.

These lines serve primarily to establish the drowsy atmosphere of Sleepy Hollow, but are not without thematic relevance. "Dreams," "castles in the clouds," are suggestive of the imaginative faculty which is Irving's real concern. Moreover, the poem deals at length with the economic foundations of the arts; that is, with the question of patronage. This is one of the central issues which Irving means to raise.

Thomson is a spiritual cousin of Ben Franklin, and the poem amounts to a Calvinist homily on work. It is an allegorical attack on the slothful propensities of the leisure classes, and a sturdy defense of the Protestant ethic. Thomson is a poet, however, and he cannot suppress certain misgivings about the benefits of industry and progress. In particular, he deplores the loss of patronage which attends the passing of a cultured aristocracy. A jarring note thus intrudes upon his celebration of the Protestant virtues. In the old order, indolence brought social stagnation, but afforded a leisurely pursuit of art. The rise of the middle class portends great material prosperity, but leaves the fate of the poetic imagination in doubt.

This is precisely the mood of **"The Legend of Sleepy Hollow."** Dimly, uneasily, Irving sees the precarious position of the artist in bourgeois society. He is therefore of two minds as he contemplates the demise of Dutch colonial America. Fundamentally he approves of movement, activity and progress. Yet the story is saturated with nostalgia for the sheltered, protected, *embosomed* world of Sleepy Hollow, where dreams and reveries, ghosts and apparitions, still nourish the "visionary propensity."

Tarry Town emerges as a symbol of the colonial past, in which we tarry for a moment before moving on. The atmosphere is simple, uncomplicated, pastoral. It is established by such adjectives as quiet, listless, drowsy, dreamy, and such nouns as murmur, lull, repose, tranquillity. Captivated by the mood he has created, the narrator recalls his first exploit in squirrel hunting:

> I had wandered into [a walnut grove] at noon time, when all nature is peculiarly quiet, and was startled by the roar of my own gun as it broke the Sabbath stillness around, and was prolonged and reverberated by the angry echoes. [**"The Legend of Sleepy Hollow,"** p. 475. All quotations are from *The Works of Washington Irving,* Author's Revised Edition, Vol. II, **The Sketch Book** (New York, 1880).]

It was a shot heard round the world. The disruptive roar of the gun heralds the introduction of the Hessian trooper, "whose head had been carried away by a cannon-ball, in some nameless battle during the Revolutionary War." To the quiet repose of the opening pages, Irving counterposes the furious speed of the galloping Hessian. He is seen "hurrying along in the gloom of the night, as if on the wings of the wind." He embodies the sudden violence of the Revolution, which brought the pastoral phase of the national life to an end. A new spirit is abroad in the land, the mercenary spirit of a Hessian soldier.

At this point it may be well to review the basic features of the plot, so as to establish a solid foundation for a symbolic interpretation. In essence, we have a romantic triangle. Ichabod Crane and Brom Bones are rivals for the hand of Katrina Van Tassel, the daughter of a prosperous Dutch farmer. Ichabod is defeated under comic circumstances, and as a result, his values are profoundly altered. Humiliation and defeat transform his life, but what is the inner meaning of these events?

As the three principals are introduced, certain details of characterization point to Irving's theme. To begin with, Ichabod's New England origins are heavily underscored:

> He was a native of Connecticut, a state which supplies the Union with pioneers for the mind as well as for the forest, and sends forth yearly its legions of frontier woodsmen and country schoolmasters. (p. 478)

His favorite book is Cotton Mather's *History of New England Witchcraft.* Great stress is laid upon his appetite, which is at once natural and supernatural, encompassing both the gustatory and the marvellous. In this he reflects the dilemma of his Puritan ancestors: the contest in his soul might be said to turn upon the question of which appetite will come uppermost.

The ascetic circumstances of his existence are suggested by the shabbiness of his schoolhouse and the itinerant character of his life. As he moves from home to home among his pupils' families, he carries "all his worldly effects tied up in a cotton handkerchief." His poverty, however, is not without its compensations. Because of his itinerant habits, he is welcomed as a bearer of news and gossip. He is esteemed by his neighbors as a man of letters, "for he had read several books quite through." He instructs the young people in psalmody, and his tales of the supernatural are a popular feature of village entertainment. Ichabod embodies, in short, the primitive impulse of a frontier society toward culture.

Since culture is viewed with suspicion in frontier communities, Ichabod is thought, "by all who understand nothing of the labor of headwork, to have a wonderfully easy time of it." Highly vulnerable to criticism, he is forced to justify his existence on utilitarian grounds:

> That all this might not be too onerous on the purses of his rustic patrons, who are apt to consider the costs of schooling a grievous burden, and schoolmasters as mere drones, he had various ways of rendering himself both useful and agreeable. (p. 481)

There is something in the comic absurdity of Ichabod's situation which raises echoes of Cervantes. At one point, in fact, Ichabod rides forth "like a knight-errant in quest of adventures," astride a broken-down plough horse. In the light of these allusions, the character of Ichabod acquires a new dimension. Like Don Quixote, he is comic in appearance and behavior, but he must be taken seriously as a symbol of man's higher aspirations. Such a portrait requires a certain complexity of tone. For Ichabod is at once a comic and a tragic figure; he is, in Wallace Stevens' phrase, "A clown, perhaps, but an aspiring clown." In a portrait which is permeated with self-irony, Irving caricatures the position of the artist-intellectual in American life. Ichabod Crane is the first example in our literature of the comedian as the letter C.

Ichabod's antagonist is Brom Bones, "the hero of the country round." Brom's symbolic role is defined by a series of associations with the Headless Horseman. He is linked to the goblin rider by his skill in horsemanship and by the hurry-scurry of his midnight escapades. Like the Hessian, he scours the countryside with a squad of hard riders who dash about "like a troop of Don Cossacks." As the story reaches a climax, Brom becomes the literal incarnation of the Hessian trooper, for it is he, disguised as the Headless Horseman, who pursues Ichabod to his doom. Symbolically, Brom is the embodiment of the Hessian spirit, of mercenary values which threaten to engulf the imagination.

While Ichabod exists on the periphery of his culture, Brom occupies the very hub. Invisible spokes radiate from him to the entire male population of Sleepy Hollow. What is the "tough, wrong-headed, broad-skirted Dutch urchin who sulked and swelled and grew dogged and sullen beneath the birch" but a schoolboy version of Brom Bones? Brom's gang, whose behavior suggests the juvenile-delinquent phase of male development, harries the schoolmaster by smoking out his singing school and breaking into his schoolhouse after dark.

In Sleepy Hollow, hostility to learning is by no means confined to the young:

> Old Baltus Van Tassel was a perfect picture of a thriving, contented, liberal-hearted farmer. He seldom, it is true, sent either his eyes or his thoughts beyond the boundaries of his own farm. . . . (p. 486)

Toward the end of the story, Hans Van Ripper disposes of Ichabod's literary effects by a time-honored method. In his treatment of the scene, Irving betrays an animus ordinarily concealed beneath a gloss of genial humor:

> These magic books and the poetic scrawl were forthwith consigned to the flames by Hans Van Ripper; who from that time forward determined to send his children no more to school; observing, that he never knew any good come of this same reading and writing. (p. 517)

Katrina is a pivotal figure; she provides the measure of Ichabod's social worth. The bestowal of her favors amounts to a kind of community sanction, for if Ichabod's society takes him seriously it must supply him with a wife. It is of course Brom Bones that she chooses; she has been flirting with the schoolmaster only to arouse the jealousy and ardor of his rival.

Irving's sketch of Katrina blends humorously with his description of her father's farm. She is "plump as a par-

tridge; ripe and melting and rosy cheeked as one of her father's peaches." She wears "ornaments of pure yellow gold" whose colors call to mind the golden ears of Van Tassel corn, and "the yellow pumpkins . . . turning up their fair round bellies to the sun." As Ichabod surveys his future prospects, the metaphors proclaim his gustatory love:

> In his devouring mind's eye . . . the pigeons were snugly put to bed in a comfortable pie, and tucked in with a coverlet of crust; the geese were swimming in their own gravy; and the ducks pairing cosily in dishes, like snug married couples, with a decent competency of onion sauce. (p. 488)

Faced with such temptations, Ichabod is defeated from within. Consider the implications of his name. "Ichabod" is from the Hebrew; it means "inglorious," or literally, "without honor." Ichabod is a turncoat; in pursuit of material comfort, he betrays a spiritual tradition. Confronted with the opulence of the Van Tassels, he succumbs to the sins of covetousness and idolatry. His imaginative faculty is perverted, deflected from its proper object:

> . . . his busy fancy already realized his hopes, and presented to him the blooming Katrina, with a whole family of children, mounted on the top of a wagon loaded with household trumpery, with pots and kettles dangling beneath; and he beheld himself bestriding a pacing mare, with a colt at her heels, setting out for Kentucky, Tennessee, or the Lord knows where. (p. 489)

Here is the New England imagination turned mercenary, placed in the service of the westering impulse. Brom Bones has only to bury the body.

Ichabod's encounter with the Headless Horseman is the dramatic climax of the story. The stage is set so carefully, however, that a closer look at the backdrop is in order. Dominating the landscape is an enormous tulip tree known in the neighborhood as Major André's tree. André was a young British officer, appointed by his superiors to consummate with Benedict Arnold negotiations for the betrayal of West Point. Captured by American militiamen after a midnight interview with Arnold, he was executed as a spy. In effect, he was a scapegoat, hanged for Arnold's crime. As a result, he occupies an ambiguous position in American history. This ambiguity seems to be the point so far as Irving is concerned:

> The common people regarded [Major André's tree] with a mixture of respect and superstition, partly out of sympathy for the fate of its ill-starred namesake. . . . (pp. 510-11)

It is just this note of sympathy which Irving means to strike. Systematically he links "the unfortunate André" with "the unfortunate Ichabod," using the historical figure to control his tone. Let there be no mistake: Ichabod betrays the race of Cranes. The betrayal occurs at the quilting party, as he contemplates the possibility of becoming lord of the Van Tassel manor:

> Then, he thought, how soon he'd turn his back upon the old schoolhouse; snap his fingers in the face of Hans Van Ripper, and every other niggardly patron, and kick any itinerant pedagogue out of doors that should dare to call him comrade! (p. 503)

But Irving wishes to soften the effect of this betrayal by shifting the burden in large part from Ichabod to his society. The reader is to respond to Ichabod rather as an André than an Arnold: not entirely guiltless, but largely the victim of circumstance. Yet the veiled threat remains. Irving recalls, by his allusion to Arnold, a famous episode in which the nation's neglect and ingratitude was repaid by treason. Be niggardly with your patronage, he warns the Hans Van Rippers, and your artists will desert to the enemy camp.

At the very spot where Major André was captured, Ichabod is accosted by the Headless Horseman. The schoolmaster is an unskillful rider; he attempts an evasive maneuver, but to no avail. With a fizzle and a sputter, Gunpowder ignites from the spark of his rider's fear, and off they fly, with the apparition in hot pursuit. As they near the safety of the bridge, the goblin rider rises in his stirrups and hurls his head at Ichabod, tumbling him into the dust.

What is the meaning of this parable? Ichabod is overwhelmed by the new materialism, but at an awesome price to society. For in order to conquer, the Hessian must throw away his head. The next morning a shattered pumpkin is found in the vicinity of the bridge. The organ of intellect and imagination has become an edible. The forces of thought have yielded to the forces of digestion.

Defeated by the spirit of the age, Ichabod reconstructs his life along more worldly lines. As rumor has it,

> . . . he had changed his quarters to a distant part of the country; had kept school and studied law at the same time; had been admitted to the bar, turned politician, electioneered, written for the newspapers, and finally had been made a justice of the Ten Pound Court. (p. 518)

It is hardly necessary to recall the unfortunate Irving's legal career to sense the diminution of spirit which the author intends. "The Ten Pound Court" unmistakably conveys the pettiness and triviality of Ichabod's new occupation. The community suffers a loss, the nature of which is defined by Ichabod's curious estate. A book of psalm tunes, a broken pitch pipe, Cotton Mather's *History of Witchcraft,* a book of dreams and fortune-telling, and an abortive attempt at verse in honor of Katrina: these crude tokens of the imaginative life are left behind as the schoolmaster vanishes from Sleepy Hollow.

The postscript is an ironic defense of the literary imagination. The time is "the present," and it is clear that the descendants of Brom Bones are in the saddle. Folklore and legend, ghost stories and old wives' tales, have been superseded by an age of reason and common sense. Fiction itself has become suspect. Writing in a hostile climate, Irving supplies his fictional world with the trappings of historical research and objectivity. Hence the "Postscript, Found in the Handwriting of Mr. Knickerbocker."

This postscript recapitulates the theme; the dramatic situation alone has changed. The scene is "a Corporation meeting of the ancient city of Manhattoes, at which were present many of its sagest and most illustrious burghers." The role of Ichabod-Irving is played by a shabby narrator with a sadly humorous face, who is an entertaining storyteller, but is "strongly suspected of being poor." He has just told a tale called **"The Legend of Sleepy Hollow."** The role of Brom-Hessian is assumed by the sleepy aldermen who comprise his audience, and in particular by a literal-minded burgher who inquires as to the moral of the story, and what it goes to prove?

The narrator avoids a direct reply. The meaning of the story, Irving intimates, will not yield to purely logical methods. The art of fiction has nothing to do with "the ratiocination of the syllogism." The reader's imagination must supply the moral:

> The story-teller, who was just putting a glass of wine to his lips, as a refreshment after his toils, paused for a moment, looked at his inquirer with an air of infinite deference, and, lowering the glass slowly to the table, observed, that the story was intended most logically to prove:—
>
> That there is no situation in life but has its advantages and pleasures—provided we will but take a joke as we find it:
>
> That, therefore, he that runs races with goblin troopers is likely to have rough riding of it.
>
> Ergo, for a country schoolmaster to be refused the hand of a Dutch heiress, is a certain step to high preferment in the state. (pp. 520-21)

Martin Roth (essay date 1976)

SOURCE: "Post Mortem Effects," in *Comedy and America: The Lost World of Washington Irving,* Kennikat Press, 1976, pp. 155-69.

[*In the following excerpt, Roth examines the conflict between "the active and the imaginative life" in "The Legend of Sleepy Hollow."*]

"The Legend of Sleepy Hollow" is Irving's last attempt to preserve a festive America. Like *The History* and **"Rip Van Winkle,"** it is a tale of a Yankee invasion, but in it the Yankee is temporarily defeated, and his defeat is due primarily to the Yankee-American inability to assign any value to the world of dreams and imaginings. There is a hint of this theme toward the end of **"Rip Van Winkle":** the villagers who doubt the reality of Rip's tale and insist "that Rip had been out of his head, and that this was one point on which he always remained flighty" (*Washington Irving: Representative Selections,* 1934; Hereafter *RS,* 95) are the new Yankees who have conquered the sleepy community of Hudson, New York, and converted it into a secular logocracy. They can only identify imaginative vision as madness (which, in a positive sense, it is).

The identification of the American Cockaigne as the proper field for imaginative activity had been implicit in *The History* and **"Rip Van Winkle,"** but in this tale it is manifest:

> A drowsy, dreamy atmosphere seems to hang over the land and to pervade the very atmosphere . . . the place still continues under the sway of some witching power, that holds a spell over the minds of the good people, causing them to walk in a continual reverie. They are

given to all kinds of marvellous beliefs; are subject to trances and visions; and frequently see strange sights, and hear music and voices in the air (*RS,* 143).

Like almost all of the major American writers of the nineteenth century, Irving was concerned with the question of whether the creative imagination could take root in a country of such thin traditional soil; a country, moreover, which had been devoted by Adams and Jefferson to the practical arts alone. They had reasoned that the level of economic luxury necessary to foster a class of fine artists was incompatible with the nature of a democracy. But Irving did provide a formula for art in America. And while it may be difficult to take seriously the conception of an American culture growing out of Lubberland, the location of art (especially a comic art) within the context of creatural comfort, ceremony, festivity, and play does have validity.

On the other hand, Irving's aesthetic vocabulary—the passive and self-indulgent concept of the imagination suggested by words like *reverie* and *dream,* and the folk or fairy-tale vocabulary of spells, bewitching, and entrancement (which would be taken over by Hawthorne)—introduces yet again that note of ambivalence which is always found when Irving touches this subject.[1] In other essays in **The Sketch Book,** particularly "Westminster Abbey," Irving's doubts take the form of a fiction in which the imagination is unable to function at all. And in the later **"Stout Gentleman"** (the inner fusion of sense data and associations), it is not merely ineffectual, it is also morally reprehensible, resented by the stout gentleman, who, at the end of the tale, rebukes the artist by thumbing his ass at him without ever giving him a sight of his face:

> This was the only chance I would have of knowing him. I . . . scrambled to the window . . . and just caught a glimpse of the rear of a person getting in at the coach-door. The skirts of a brown coat parted behind gave me a full view of the broad disk of a pair of drab breeches. . . . and that was all I ever saw of the stout gentleman!

At any rate, Sleepy Hollow *is* a dreamer's paradise, and the narrator sees it as "a retreat, whither I might steal from the world and its distractions, and dream quietly away the remnant of a troubled life" (*RS,* 142-43).

The Yankee of *The History* and **"Rip Van Winkle"** had consisted of a body of generic traits associated with a name; in **"Sleepy Hollow,"** it is a single individual, Ichabod Crane, a "native from Connecticut." Crane has many of the qualities of Irving's earlier Yankees, and it will be useful to draw attention to these similarities, since criticism of the tale has raised questions about Irving's attitude toward Crane.

The first thing we are told of Ichabod is that he "sojourned, or, as he expressed it, 'tarried,' in Sleepy Hollow" (*RS,* 144), and the first thing that we are told of the earlier Yankee type is that he "is in a constant state of migration; *tarrying* occasionally here and there" (*A History of New York;* 1809; Hereafter *HNY,* 161). While Crane believes that he might one day possess Katrina Van Tassel's fortune, he dreams of investing the money "in immense tracts of wild land and shingle palaces in the wilderness":

> Nay, his busy fancy already realized his hopes, and presented to him the blooming Katrina, with a whole

family of children, mounted on the top of a wagon loaded with household trumpery, with pots and kettles dangling beneath; and he beheld himself bestriding a pacing mare, with a colt at her heels, setting out for Kentucky, Tennessee, or the Lord knows where (*RS,* 152).

This is precisely the life story of the earlier Yankee: "His whole family, household furniture and farming utensils are hoisted into a covered cart . . . which done he . . . trudges off to the woods. . . . A huge palace of pine boards immediately springs up in the midst of the wilderness . . . "

> . . . He soon grows tired of a spot, where there is no longer any room for improvement—sells his farm, air castle, petticoat windows and all, reloads his cart, shoulders his axe, puts himself at the head of his family, and wanders away in search of new lands—again to fell trees—again to clear corn-fields—again to build a shingle palace, and again to sell off, and wander (*HNY,* 163).[2]

In *The History* there is even a specific anticipation of Ichabod Crane in the "long sided Connecticut schoolmaster" who kidnapped and severely flogged Knickerbocker's grandfather when he was a boy (*HNY,* 263).

It has been argued by several critics that Sleepy Hollow dramatizes the conflict between the active and the imaginative life, and that Ichabod, despite the ridiculous figure he is made to cut, is a Quixotic projection of the artist—deliberately ridiculous as an emblem of the slightly comic position of the artist in America.[3] If, after fifteen years of trying, Irving finally managed to paint his enemy in rich colors, this can hardly be taken as evidence of an awakened sympathy for the type. For Ichabod Crane is definitely the enemy. Crane is not only a Yankee of Franklin's stamp, he also possesses many of the qualities of his earlier Puritan ancestors. Both attitudes involve a manipulation of nature, one for the purpose of accumulating material wealth and the other for the purpose of arousing piety through terror.

Irving's comic feud with schoolmasters and natives of Connecticut can be seen as early as *The Corrector,* and it was sustained throughout his subsequent works. The treatment of neither in **"Sleepy Hollow"** suggests any grounds for sympathy. Ichabod also corresponds to several other negative types in Irving's work. He is, for example, the sophisticated foreigner who debauches the tastes of the simple country girls (*RS,* 147), the homegrown equivalent of the French *émigré* in *Salmagundi.*

Ichabod Crane simply cannot be identified with the artistic imagination; there is too much sound evidence against this association. We are told "in fact" that Ichabod was "an odd mixture of small shrewdness and simple credulity" (*RS,* 148); these qualities are not imaginative, but they do relate directly to the Yankee-Puritan coupling referred to above.

Three times in the tale, Ichabod is seen engaged in "artistic" pursuits: he would amuse the maidens on Sunday by "reciting . . . all the epitaphs on the tombstones" (*RS,* 147), and a sheet of paper is found, "scribbled and blotted in several fruitless attempts to make a copy of verses in honor of the heiress of Van Tassel" (*RS*, 171). The third instance plays with the terms of creativity:

> As the enraptured Ichabod *fancied* all this, and as he rolled his great green eyes over the fat meadow-lands, the rich fields of wheat, of rye, of buckwheat and Indian corn, and the orchards burthened with ruddy fruit . . . his *imagination* expanded with the idea, how they might be readily turned into cash, and the money invested (*RS*, 151-52; italics mine).

Ichabod Crane is a petty capitalist and speculator.

Arguments linking Crane and the imagination generally hinge on his capacity for swallowing tales of the marvelous. Old Dutch wives tell him "marvellous tales of ghosts and goblins, and haunted fields, and haunted brooks, and haunted bridges, and haunted houses, and particularly of the headless horseman, or galloping Hessian of the Hollow."

> He would delight them equally by his anecdotes of witchcraft, and of the direful omens and portentous sights and sounds in the air, which prevailed in the earlier times of Connecticut; and would frighten them wofully with speculations upon comets and shooting stars; and with the alarming fact that the world did absolutely turn round (*RS*, 149).

Ichabod's voracious appetite for the supernatural is both "gross" and "monstrous." It is associated with his insatiable physical hunger which, as we shall see, is essentially sterile, an absorption which does not nourish.

There is a sense in which Crane does "create," however; he works at night, transforming nature into a place of terror:

> What fearful shapes and shadows beset his path. . . . How often was he appalled by some shrub covered with snow, which, like a sheeted spectre, beset his very path! . . . and if, by chance, a huge blockhead of a beetle came winging his blundering flight against him, the poor varlet was ready to give up the ghost, with the idea that he was struck with a witch's token (*RS*, 149, 148).

This is comparable to the world of Hawthorne's "Young Goodman Brown"; Crane is not imagining; he is projecting the terror of his isolation (the spiritual isolation of the mobile and manipulative Yankee) upon the neutral darkness of nature. By transforming nature into a place of terror he expresses his fear of the natural and his own body, just as the transformation of the abundance of the Van Tassel farm into the neutral sterility of money expresses a similar fear. And the images that are evoked by his "excited imagination" terrify him in turn: "His only resource on such occasions, either to drown thought, or drive away evil spirits, was to sing psalm tunes" (*RS*, 148). True creativity in **"Sleepy Hollow"** is represented by the Van Tassel farm and by Brom Bones.

Brom Bones, Ichabod's opponent, is Irving's final version of the traditional *buck* of *The Spectator*. He is a sympathetic character: "with all his overbearing roughness, there was a strong dash of waggish good-humor at bottom" (*RS*, 154). Although Ichabod Crane is not an artist, a case could be made for Bones—an artist, moreover, whose produc-

tions suggest Irving's own. After all, Brom Bones creates the legend of Sleepy Hollow out of the rumors of the community; its plot is the defeat of a Yankee, and its form is a hoax. Bones is a parodist—he "had a scoundrel dog whom he taught to whine in the most ludicrous manner, and introduced as a rival of Ichabod's . . . in psalmody"— and a burlesque artist—he "broke into the school-house at night . . . and turned everything topsy-turvy" (*RS*, 156).

Although the conflict at the center of **"The Legend of Sleepy Hollow"** is comparable to that of *The History*, Irving uses the symbolism of the earlier work in a contrapuntal way to express the conflict. It is Ichabod who is given the classical vision of Cockaigne—" . . . he pictured to himself every roasting pig running about with a pudding in his belly, and an apple in his mouth" (*RS*, 151)—but it is here contrasted unfavorably with the natural abundance of Sleepy Hollow and becomes simply a sign of Ichabod's avarice. Ichabod, like Pantagruel, is a huge gullet; not only does he eat enormous quantities of food, but he eats superstition as well, with a "capacious swallow" (*RS*, 148). He is a "huge feeder" (*RS*, 146), and Katrina Van Tassel is "plump as a partridge; ripe and melting and rosy cheeked as one of her father's peaches" (*RS*, 150). But although he eats voraciously, he remains as lean and skeletal as ever. The eating of Crane is likened to the devastations of a plague: he is compared to the grasshopper (*RS*, 158); and "to see him striding along the profile of a hill on a windy day, with his clothes bagging and fluttering about him, one might have mistaken him for the genius of famine descending upon the earth" (*RS*, 145).

Ichabod Crane is literally defeated and expelled from Paradise as a result of a prank played on him by Brom Bones. The essential cause of his defeat, however, is his fear of the powers of the imagination, his fear of art—common to both the Puritan and the Yankee. This is reinforced in the contrast between his aversion and Brom Bones's easy entrance into the very legend that sends Crane flying:

> [Brom Bones] made light of the galloping Hessian. . . . He affirmed that, on returning one night from the neighbouring village of Sing Sing, he had been overtaken by this midnight trooper; that he had offered to race with him for a bowl of punch, and should have won it too, for Daredevil beat the goblin horse all hollow (*RS*, 164-65).

The defeat of Ichabod Crane is the most glorious moment of Irving's career, artistically and, perhaps, psychologically as well; for it fuses into one image the various meanings that made up Irving's American period. Within the context of *The History*, Ichabod is defeated by his own conquest: the pumpkin was the Yankee emblem in that work, and it signaled the Yankee conquest of Fort Goed Hoop, where it "was hoisted on the end of a pole, as a standard—liberty caps not having as yet come into fashion" (*HNY*, 193).

Ichabod Crane is also defeated by his historical conquest. Irving has finally succeeded in undoing for a moment the American revolution by identifying the Dutch protagonist of his tale with the two historical enemies of Yankee America, the Hessians and the British in the person of Major André.[4] In the third place, the Yankee is defeated by that value to which he had devoted his existence, and that is mind to the exclusion of body. The Horseman throws his head at Ichabod as if to say that he does not much need it, that he is quite comfortable in his subsequent untroubled state. Finally, Ichabod is defeated by American art, Dutch art; for the legend is a creation of the Dutch community generally and Brom Bones particularly.

Ichabod Crane, however, is not defeated for long. The qualities that keep him thin in Sleepy Hollow allow him to grow and prosper in the outside world of American history, where his path is that of the *democratic toadeater* as defined in *The Corrector* and *Salmagundi*: after his dismissal by Katrina he had "studied law . . . been admitted to the bar, turned politician, electioneered, written for the newspapers, and finally . . . been made a justice of the Ten Pound Court" (*RS,* 172). The qualities represented by Ichabod Crane must overwhelm Sleepy Hollow as they did Hudson. This has already happened at the time the story is told: the tale is set "in a remote period of American history, that is to say some thirty years since . . ." (*RS,* 144). In the story itself, the abundance, which had been growing throughout Irving's early work, is an autumnal feast; it is a farewell banquet (*RS,* 158-59).

Like **"Rip Van Winkle,"** **"Sleepy Hollow"** is provided with a framework which seems to produce the tensions that we associate with the literary hoax. The tale is related at a meeting of the New York Corporation. And when doubts are raised as to the historical veracity of the tale, the story-teller ends the postscript by admitting, "Faith, sir . . . as to that matter, I don't believe one-half of it myself."

The story-teller is a "pleasant, shabby, gentlemanly old fellow, in pepper-and-salt clothes, with a sadly humorous face," and Knickerbocker strongly suspects him of being poor. His identity as a defeated Dutchman is conveyed by a device that Irving had used in **"Rip Van Winkle"**: the tale is approved and laughed at only by two or three deputy aldermen who are clearly Dutch, since they "had been asleep the greater part of the time."

The postscript is a reprise of the conflict between Dutch and Yankee, and this time overtly on the level of the imagination, since it is the value of the tale itself that is in contention. The story-teller's opponent is the artist's traditional foe, the Shandean man of gravity: a "tall, drylooking old gentleman, with beetling eyebrows . . . [and] a grave and rather severe face." I suspect that Irving meant us to entertain the possibility that he is Ichabod Crane. At any rate he demands to know "what was the moral of the story, and what it went to prove." In one sense, he is withholding both laughter and approval until he can be convinced that the tale is either socially useful or true. In a deeper sense he is asking what the world of Dutch abundance (and Irving's literary efforts) *mean* to an America of politics and business.

The major proportions of the postscript are the reverse of the tale. Here, the Yankee and his values are triumphant; the shabby Dutchman in that world can only recreate the past as an idle diversion and one whose meaning is not comprehended. And yet within the postscript the Yankee is defeated once again, for the Dutchman responds to his questioner with a triumphant leer and overwhelms him

with a weapon which has a comfortable place in the work of at least one writer of burlesque comedy—a nonsense syllogism.

How shall we finally read the final line—"Faith, sir . . . as to that matter, I don't believe one-half of it myself" (*RS,* 385)? It would be tempting to hear Irving defending his Dutch American vision as American imagining, made up in defiance of American fact *but still meaningful, still valuable.* It is more likely, however, that in this statement Irving is gently bidding farewell to his career as an American writer and a writer of burlesque comedy.

Notes

1. The tag to this tale associates American dreaming with the activity of the inhabitants of James Thomson's "Castle of Indolence."

2. By not having *The History* in mind, Hedges reads the passage from "Sleepy Hollow" as the expression of Crane's desire for a home of his own (*Washington Irving,* p. 142). On the contrary, it expresses the Yankee's "rambling propensity."

3. Hedges, *Washington Irving,* pp. 141-42. Because Robert A. Bone interprets Crane as a serious "symbol of man's higher aspirations"—"Irving's Headless Hessian," *American Quarterly,* XV (Summer, 1963), 167-75—he is forced to see Brom Bones, who frolics through the tale, as "the embodiment . . . of mercenary values which threaten to engulf the imagination."

4. The choice of the Hessian may have been an unfortunate one on Irving's part, if it reminds us of Paine's ravishers in *Common Sense,* although Franklin took a more sympathetic view toward these mercenaries. The choice of André strikes deeper chords of ambivalence. It must be significant that our first important Revolutionary drama, William Dunlap's *André,* should celebrate the death of a noble and virtuous, and innocent, British spy.

Albert J. von Frank (essay date 1987)

SOURCE: "The Man that Corrupted Sleepy Hollow," in *Studies in American Fiction, Vol. 15, No. 2, Autumn, 1987, pp. 129-43.*

[*In the following essay, Frank describes Ichabod Crane as a morally destructive force that enters Sleepy Hollow.*]

Washington Irving's reputation as a genial writer—as, indeed, America's *most* genial writer—has been firmly established for a century and a half, despite general agreement that his most enduring works are satires. *Knickerbocker's History* maintains its good humor largely by making its narrator appear foolish, but it is harder to say what keeps **"The Legend of Sleepy Hollow"** from seemingly overtly caustic, since in the portrait of Ichabod Crane Irving comes rather closer than in the *History* to adopting the controlling assumption of Augustan satire that the ridiculous and the evil are one. If Irving's genial reputation largely obscures the evil that Ichabod represents, it must also obscure the mythical structure of the story and, consequently, its formal relationship to such later works as "Young Goodman Brown," "The Man That Corrupted Hadleyburg," and a score of others. That Ichabod *is* evil needs all the more to be said since several modern readings of the story have made impressive moral claims on his behalf, or, alternatively, have transformed him into a pathetic hero, a figure more sinned against than sinning. One urges that he be taken "seriously as a symbol of man's higher aspirations," while another proclaims that "what he wants is simply a home, like anyone else."[1] Even those who regard Ichabod as a threat to the Dutch community differ significantly in assessing the nature and seriousness of the problem he presents.[2]

As Donald Ringe pointed out in 1967, the story is a work of regional satire, pitting Dutch New York against the restless spirit of New England; it is a story that "pleads in effect for the values of the settler and conserver over those of the speculator and improver."[3] Irving's satire, however, works most significantly not at the sociological or political level, but—as all permanently valuable satire does—at the level of the underlying moral issues. The success of the satirical method in **"The Legend of Sleepy Hollow"** lies in Irving's ability to see the familiar Yankee character as only superficially comic while at the same time discretely ventilating the deeper moral disease of which that comedy is the not quite independently conceived mask. The complexity of tone arising from such a polarized treatment may be traced more specifically to the two uses that Irving makes of the setting. The world of the New York Dutch is something more and other than an ethnic region realistically sketched; it is, indeed, a mythically conceived community, unfallen and changeless, a place of perfect ripeness. Irving establishes the setting in precisely this light and locates Ichabod's mock-heroic chivalry in the most incongruous of all possible contexts, while at the same time raising that portentous central issue of American literature, the moral spoliation of the New World garden. Inasmuch as both the serious and the comic themes converge on the setting, Irving has made the recovery of *its* meaning a precondition for any interpretation.

The setting is not a frontier. Although Daniel Hoffman has persuasively argued that the portrait of Brom Bones owes a great deal to the type of the "ring-tailed roarer,"[4] it is not a point with which one can do much more than Hoffman himself has done. Irving indicates that Sleepy Hollow is in most ways the precise reverse of a frontier. Not only has it long been a settled region (a rural one, to be sure), but it is also emphatically a European community with European values. Those forces which on the frontier operate to break down imported cultures—like the rest of the "incessant changes" that Irving abhors—are outside, beyond the "high hills," and simply do not function in "such little retired Dutch valleys, found here and there embosomed in the great state of New York," where "population, manners, and customs, remain fixed."[5] The true American frontier figures but once in the story and then only by way of the sharpest contrast with the Hudson Valley setting: knowing no more than Milton's Satan "to value right / The good before him," Ichabod proposes to exchange the "middle landscape" of the Van Tassel patrimony for a tract of wild land in "Kentucky, Tennessee, or the Lord knows where" (p. 280).

If the setting is not part of the frontier, it *is* a version of the American pastoral as Leo Marx has defined it,[6] though

ironically the distinction of Irving's version is that his innocent shepherds are all Europeans. They figure in this magic landscape as the stewards of their own abundant fruitfulness, which fertility takes on a sacramental character in the description of Baltus Van Tassel's farm, where architecture and institutions melt imperceptibly into the activity of farming, and that into a humanized version of the natural order, all under the benediction of an approving sun:

> Hard by the farm house was a vast barn, that might have served for a church; every window and crevice of which seemed bursting forth with the treasures of the farm; the flail was busily resounding within it from morning to night; swallows and martins skimmed twittering about the eaves, and rows of pigeons, some with one eye turned up, as if watching the weather, some with their heads under their wings, or buried in their bosoms, and others swelling, and cooing, and bowing about their dames, were enjoying the sunshine on the roof (p. 279).

This sequestered community is more than home to a company of Dutch farmers; in its sheltered resistance to change, its ungrudging fruitfulness, its feminine character, and, ultimately, its vulnerability, it is the fully elaborated symbol of home as a romantic moral concept.

Like other ideal settings, the larger Dutch community, Sleepy Hollow, and the Van Tassel farm are enclosed gardens, here concentrically framed, inviting, seductive, and as dangerous to itinerants as the island of the Sirens or the land of the Lotus-Eaters. The societies sheltered by these nested gardens are themselves closed and static (again, unlike the frontier), yet magically productive. Following pastoral convention, Irving describes the land in eminently hospitable feminine imagery, indicating in the first sentence that "in the bosom of one of those spacious coves which indent the eastern shore of the Hudson" lies the community named Tarry Town by the women of the region (p. 272). Two miles away is the smaller village of Sleepy Hollow, likened to a "mimic harbour, undisturbed by the passing current," where one might find even yet "the same families vegetating in its sheltered bosom" (p. 274). In the description of the Van Tassel farm these gender-specific topological features recur: it "was situated on the banks of the Hudson, in one of those green, sheltered, fertile nooks, in which the Dutch farmers are so fond of nestling" (p. 279). Each specific location is a repetition of the others; each involves the feminine principle, repose, and water, so the "small brook" that glides through Sleepy Hollow "with just murmur enough to lull one to repose" is made to well up on Van Tassel's quiet Xanadu as "a spring of the softest water" that bubbled along "among alders and dwarf willows" (p. 279).

Whatever significance may finally attach to the dandy-and-squatter form of Ichabod's conflict with Brom Bones, the moral satire surely depends on seeing Sleepy Hollow less as the frontier setting of a memorable joke than as Irving's romantic notion of any man's true home. The tone of the story is at all points favorable to the settled and home-loving Dutch; it supports their sense of tradition, their security, their relation to the land, their repose and plenitude, and, most of all, their imagination, while the interloper, Ichabod, is point for point the destructive antithesis of all these traits.[7]

Since the issue of the imagination has appeared to some to support a sympathetic view of Ichabod Crane, and since Irving himself indicates that Sleepy Hollow is an active abettor of the imagination, it is important to see how Irving discriminates between Ichabod and the Dutch on this point. "It is remarkable," writes Irving, "that the visionary propensity I have mentioned is not confined to the native inhabitants of the valley, but is unconsciously imbibed by every one who resides there for a time. However wide awake they may have been before they entered that sleepy region, they are sure, in a little time, to inhale the witching influence of the air, and begin to grow imaginative—to dream dreams, and see apparitions" (p. 273). As an Arcadian environment, Sleepy Hollow is necessarily a source of inspiration, and yet those who dream under its influence do so according to their personalities and capacities. The genuinely inspired acts of imagination all belong to the Dutch: to Brom Bones most conspicuously, the Pan by whom Ichabod is panicked, and a poet not of words, certainly, but of virtuous action; to Yost Van Houten, the inspired architect of the schoolhouse locking system, modelled on "the mystery of the eelpot," whereby, "though a thief might get in with perfect ease, he would find some embarrassment in getting out" (p. 274); or to Baltus Van Tassel, who monitors Ichabod's quixotic courtship of his daughter by recognizing and observing its appropriate symbol, that is, by "watching the achievements of a little wooden warrior, who, armed with a sword in each hand, was most valiantly fighting the wind on the pinnacle of the barn" (p. 282). Ichabod's imagination is a truly sorry thing in contrast, compounded, at worst, of Cotton Mather and simple credulity, and never, at its best, escaping the small shrewdness of his New England heritage. In his vision of the Van Tassel farm all its teeming life lies dead, served up as food for him alone, so that Irving's early description of Ichabod as "the genius of famine" (p. 274) comes finally to have a profounder point of reference than his gaunt and awkward appearance. He can easily imagine sacrificing all life to his own; the business of the story, however, is to force him to imagine his own death and ultimately to make that imagination feed and sustain the life of the community.

Nowhere is the difference between the Dutch imagination and Ichabod's more evident than in their respective superstitions. As the allusions to Cotton Mather suggest, Ichabod's superstitiousness is the vestige of a decadent Puritanism from which God and glory have departed equally. The schoolmaster is thus left with a system of infernal providences in which all of nature is supposed to have the power—even the purpose—of doing harm to Ichabod Crane.[8] Never wholly secure, he is especially skittish after dark when "every sound of nature . . . fluttered his excited imagination: the moan of the whip-poor-will from the hill side; the boding cry of the tree toad, that harbinger of storm; . . . or the sudden rustling in the thicket, of birds frightened from their roost" (p. 277). Ichabod is so radically disjoined from his environment that he and the natural world are fated enemies: nature frightens him, but, by the same token, he can and does frighten it. Put another way, the presence of death that he senses in nature, nature senses in him.

This development of the protagonist's character reveals an important aspect of Irving's method, because the frightening of the birds recalls the introduction of Ichabod as in appearance like a "scarecrow eloped from a cornfield" (p. 274) in a way that decisively alters its original comic application, just as the imagined devastation of the farm's teeming life recalled and deepened the earlier reference to Ichabod as the "genius of famine." The thematic aptness of Irving's humor becomes increasingly apparent as this kind of transformation is several times repeated: the comic details are simply funny when first seen undeveloped or apart from a larger social or moral context (which is to say, from Ichabod's perspective); but when Irving then replants them in a more coherent universe (when he provides them, in effect, some of the morally settled quality of the Dutch perspective), the regional comedy darkens into moral satire.

It is, of course, the basic coherence of the Dutch imagination that prevents their very pronounced superstitiousness from having anything monstrous about it. They are on the best of terms with their ghosts, who are, like themselves and unlike Ichabod, intimately attached to life and the local scene. The Dutch women tell of "haunted fields and haunted brooks, and haunted bridges and haunted houses" (p. 277); the men tell of "funeral trains, and mourning cries and wailings heard and seen about the great tree where the unfortunate Major Andrew as taken" or "of the woman in white, that haunted the dark glen at Raven Rock" (p. 289). These manifestations are, in the way of folk mythology, so localized, so much a part of familiar nature, that to apply the term "supernatural" to them seems almost inappropriate. They tell of unexpected life in the landscape, not of death or threats of death. The Dutch, moreover, tell these tales artistically, neither as first-hand accounts nor as "extracts" from books, as Ichabod does, but as still living legends. The sole exception is Brom Bones' account of his match with the Headless Horseman, a tale combining a youthful irreverence for the mythology of his elders with a point that not even the supernatural is to be dreaded. Generically, the Dutch tales are poles apart from Ichabod's monstrous and unfriendly indication to his female hosts of the "fact that the world did absolutely turn round, and that they were half the time topsy-turvy!" (p. 277).

These unsettled and unsettling traits in Ichabod are manifestly related to, and yet go deeper than, the New England character that on one level is the object of Irving's regional satire. Not content merely to display and ridicule the social behavior of the type, Irving probes the character of his Yankee to give the most basic kinds of moral explanations for the comic inappropriateness of his outward actions. The nature of these explanations is determined by the structure of the story, which involves the penetration of an outsider into the very heart of an earthly paradise. Seen in this light, Ichabod's unsettling traits seem less significantly those of an awkwardly displaced regional character or even of a sinful individual than, at last, those of sin itself. Indeed, the characterizing details of the story seem clustered around the seven deadly sins, even though it is not certain that Irving consciously meant it to appear so.

Ichabod's envy is indicated in one way by his "large green glassy eyes" which are mentioned first as a part of a ludicrous physical description and then again with the moral implications more fully in evidence (pp. 274, 279-80). His envy is indicated in another way, of course, in his whole attitude toward the domain of Van Tassel:

As the enraptured Ichabod . . . rolled his great green eyes over the fat meadow lands, the rich fields of wheat, of rye, of buckwheat, and Indian corn, and the orchard burthened with ruddy fruit, which surrounded the warm tenement of Van Tassel, his heart yearned after the damsel who was to inherit these domains, and his imagination expanded with the idea, how they might be readily turned into cash, and the money invested in immense tracts of wild land, and single palaces in the wilderness" (pp. 279-80).

This is not envy in the simple sense of wanting to own what others own but accords rather with the classic conception of the sin of envy in which, perversely, one seeks the annihilation of the object. The type of this sin is Satan's envy of the kingdom of God: he cannot hope to share in it, and so commits himself to its destruction. While it might be argued that merely *selling* the land would not destroy it, surely the point about these Dutch farms is that they never *have* been sold, never have had a "market value" or been held by strangers, and that what they represent would be forever lost if any of these conditions were to come to pass. Insidious as this threat is, however, it does not involve a passion that the Dutch, as the owners of the land, can directly be tainted with. In this sense, it is rather more disturbing that Ichabod has introduced envy in an altogether different way to people who seem never to have felt it before. While the schoolmaster escorts the village damsels about the churchyard on Sundays, "the more bashful country bumpkins hung sheepishly back, envying his superior elegance and address" (p. 276).

Ichabod's avarice is the concomitant of his envy and has already been suggested in the way his imagination is so casually dominated by the cash nexus. His plans for the Van Tassel-Crane estate show that he is interested not in the good life but in the immoderately wealthy life, which, for Ichabod, is the fiscal equivalent of never settling down. His "immense tracts" of frontier are for speculation, not for living on or farming, and reflect a characteristic desire that his wealth should come without labor.

Sloth ought to be a sin difficult to attain in this paradise, and yet Ichabod aspires even here. Aside from being a "flogger of urchins," he earns his bread not so much by the sweat of his brow as by assisting the Dutch "occasionally in the lighter labours of their farms" (p. 275). These labors comprise the sort of tasks then commonly assigned to women and children and include taking the horses to water and making hay. Even these he manages largely to avoid by becoming "wonderfully gentle and ingratiating" with the women: "He found favour in the eyes of the mothers, by petting the children, particularly the youngest, and like the lion bold, which whilome so magnanimously the lamb did hold, he would sit with a child on one knee, and rock a cradle with his foot, for whole hours together" (pp. 275-76). Ichabod's almost systematic avoidance of productive labor is depicted mainly through his alliance with female society and through his adoption of the least consequential of the activities traditionally associated with women. Thus, for example, he is a major source of gossip in the community and would also "pass long winter evenings with the old Dutch wives, as they sat spinning by the fire, . . . and listen to their marvellous tales" (p. 277). However, his masculinity is most directly challenged by his being a "man of letters" in a community of farmers,

where to work is perforce to have something to show for one's work. The women can appreciate his erudition, "for he had read several books quite through," though he was "thought, by all who understood nothing of the labour of headwork, to have a wonderfully easy life of it" (p. 276). It is a moral comment on Ichabod that a variety of his traits, including his problematic relationship to the world of work, divides a fundamentally coherent Dutch community along gender lines.

The subject of sloth appears to have been a complex and perhaps even a sensitive one for Irving, who, in the persona of Geoffrey Crayon, maintained a vested interest in the innocence of repose. The epigraph from Thomson's *Castle of Indolence,* a poem that successively celebrates the pleasures and indicts the decadence of indolence, contributes to the complexity of the issue by seeming to oblige the author to discriminate carefully in moral terms between the sloth he is condemning and the repose to which he is temperamentally and artistically committed. The distinction turns out, once again, to favor the Dutch, who never, throughout the course of the story, are shown at work. In the Van Tassel barn, "the flail was busily resounding . . . from morning to night," but workers neither work nor appear. The repose of the Dutch is simply prelapsarian, which means that they have, as the schoolteacher does not, something vital on which they *can* repose. Ichabod, who *is* shown working, who puts in his time at the schoolroom and performs his odd job, is nevertheless constantly preoccupied with schemes for rescinding the penalty of original sin in his own personal case, which is a large part of what Yankee ingenuity comes to in Irving's satire.

This fundamental difference parallels and at the same time further explains the qualitative distinction between the Dutch imagination and Ichabod's, the one effortless, natural, and supremely located, the other artificial, self-indulgent, and frenetic. From another point of view, Irving clearly had professional reasons for raising this issue, for if he was less personally concerned than Nathaniel Hawthorne with the public's perception of the value of the writer's vocation, he nevertheless knew that literature and scholarship in America were not always held in high esteem, that, indeed, they were often associated with idleness and self-indulgence.[9] By creating in Ichabod a slothful character at whom such charges might be levelled with perfect justice, he shows that they are most appropriately brought against the poseur, the man of self-deluding pretensions to literature, and not against the true writer (or artist) at all. And by creating in his Dutch characters an imagination rooted in innocent, even blessed repose, he affirms the value and explains the virtue of his own art.

If, in Eden, sloth is difficult, gluttony is simply ungrateful. It suggests a certain doubt as to the extent and continuance of divine providence, and, as Irving shows, leads to envy:

> [Ichabod] was a kind and thankful creature, whose heart dilated in proportion as his skin was filled with good cheer, and whose spirits rose with eating, as some men's do with drink. He could not help, too, rolling his large eyes round him as he ate, and chuckling with the possibility that he might one day be lord of all this scene of almost unimaginable splendour (p. 287).

Despite the narrator's gentlemanly imputation of thankfulness, the apparent fact is that Ichabod, having found heaven, aspires to *be,* not thank, its "lord." The appetite that prompts him is the sinister elaboration of the early, comic observation that "he was a huge feeder . . . though lank" (p. 275), while the transition from the physical fact to its spiritual implication has been prepared by Irving's intermediate use of the imagery of gluttony to describe Ichabod's mental processes. He is an intellectual gourmand: "His appetite for the marvellous, and his powers of digesting it, were equally extraordinary. . . . No tale was too gross or monstrous for his capacious swallow" (p. 277). After he is introduced to Katrina, it is, as the narrator says, "not to be wondered at, that so tempting a morsel soon found favour in his eyes" (p. 278), or that "his devouring mind's eye" could transform at a glance all the farm's life to food (p. 279). If Ichabod's imagination is thwarted and traversed by his sloth, it operates ineluctably in service to his belly. Even as he goes for his last interview with Katrina, he is "feeding his mind with many sweet thoughts and sugared suppositions" (p. 286).

There are three moments in the story that shed light on Ichabod's tendency to the sin of anger, and they appear to form, as in the case of his gluttony, a pattern of deepening seriousness. His willingness to flog his students, and particularly the stronger, more threatening children, is consistent with his personal insecurity and impatience with "inferiors." Beneath the artfully dispassionate surface of his behavior ("this he called 'doing his duty by their parents'" [p. 275]), the anger is, though visible, well submerged and controlled, so much so that Irving is content merely to hint at it and at the same time to warn his readers against concluding too quickly that Ichabod is "one of those cruel potentates of the school, who joy in the smart of their subjects" (p. 275). That Ichabod takes no "joy" in it is sufficiently easy to believe. The second moment occurs at the Van Tassel farm where Ichabod, flush with food, contemplates the possibility of being "lord of all this scene." Here the surface parts to reveal how he contends emotionally with the prospect of success: "Then, he thought, how soon he'd turn his back upon the old school house, snap his fingers in the face of Hans Van Ripper, and every other niggardly patron, and kick any itinerant pedagogue out of doors that should dare to call him comrade!" (p. 287). With perfect ironic aptness, his idea of success involves becoming the niggardly patron he despises, but the more important point is that his greatest wrath is reserved for his own alter ego. This mounting sense of anger when he ought to be most satisfied and placid is concisely indicated in the succession of verbs, which points ultimately to the self-hatred at the heart of the sin of anger. In the third and final moment, Ichabod's social controls, along with his great expectations, collapse at the end of the party in his private interview with Katrina. Here the surface parts in a different way: "Without looking to the right or left to notice the scene of rural wealth, on which he had so often gloated, he went straight to the stable, and with several hearty cuffs and kicks, roused his steed most uncourteously from the comfortable quarters in which he was soundly sleeping, dreaming of mountains of corn and oats, and whole valleys of timothy and clover" (p. 291). The horse, sharing Ichabod's physical traits and innermost dreams, is another alter ego, though now the kicking has become actual.

In the sentence describing this outburst of passion, much of the humor centers on the word "uncourteously," which signals the whole issue of the ill-starred lover's chivalric self-image. The narrator's sarcastic allusion is to the ruins of what had been, from the start, the preposterous vehicle of Ichabod's conscious pride: his assumption that he was a bit too good for a community of bumpkins. In point of pride, he is the opposite of Baltus Van Tassel, who is "satisfied with his wealth, but not proud of it" (p. 279). Unlike the man he seeks to supplant, he is eager to misapply the social leverage of his prospective good fortune by—class-consciously—kicking itinerant pedagogues out of doors.[10] But in perhaps the most telling revelation of all, Ichabod's pride appears at odds not with individuals but with sacred and communal values: "It was a matter of no little vanity to him to take his station in front of the church gallery, with a band of chosen singers; where, in his own mind, he completely carried away the palm from the parson" (p. 276). Appropriately, the profane Ichabod, the supercilious critic of the churchyard epitaphs, is avowedly the parson's self-anointed antagonist.

The treatment of lechery in **"The Legend of Sleepy Hollow"** is understandably circumspect, and yet it is very close to the effective center of the satire. The fact that Ichabod is a portrait of perverse and misdirected sexuality is arguably the author's final comment on his representative Yankee. Here Irving supplies two general contexts for Ichabod's behavior: one is the fertile feminine land that the schoolmaster threateningly lusts after, and the other is the prevailing sexuality of the Dutch, which is, for the most part, no sexuality at all. These are "general contexts" mainly in the sense that while they are rather inertly present all the while, they take on a heightened significance in conjunction with more particular details. For example, the first of these contexts is quickened when, on several occasions, Irving intimates that nothing is easier for Ichabod than to divert his sexual appetite into an appetite for food. After school he would sometimes follow students home "who happened to have pretty sisters, or good housewives for mothers, noted for the comforts of the cupboard" (p. 275). The change in the direction of this sentence, as the rest of the story goes to show, suggests a transformation rather than a competition of motives. By constantly pairing women and food in this metonymic way as objects of Ichabod's atention, Irving seems to imply that the gluttony is merely displaced lechery, and not, because food seems always to take precedence, that he is without lust.[11]

Irving's favorite phallic symbols—on which so much of his early bawdy humor centers—are guns, swords, and noses. In **"Rip Van Winkle"** there is the "clean well oiled fowling piece" that in twenty years of disuse became rusty and dysfunctional (p. 35); there is, too, among the men of Hendrick Hudson's crew playing at the masculine game of nine-pins, one whose face "seemed to consist entirely of nose, . . . surmounted by a white sugarloaf hat, set off with a little red cock's tail." This individual is singled out by the narrator from a group who carried "long knives in their belts" and of whom "most . . . had enormous breeches." The commander of this crew is further distinguished by having a "broad belt and hanger" (p. 34).[12] In **"The Legend of Sleepy Hollow"** the "long snipe nose . . . that . . . looked like a weathercock" belongs to Ichabod (p. 274), and Irving is even prepared to suggest, more directly than he ordinarily does, that this nose is a kind of reproductive organ: "There are peculiar quavers still to be heard in that church, and which may even be heard half a mile off, quite to the opposite side of the mill pond, of a still Sunday morning, which are said to be legitimately descended from the nose of Ichabod Crane" (p. 276). The final image in the story—that of a loitering ploughboy hearing these notes "among the tranquil solitudes of Sleepy Hollow" (p. 296)—seems in turn to allude to one of the very first images, that of the narrator breaking "the sabbath stillness around" by the startling "roar of [his] own gun" (p. 272), so that the story is framed by mutually defining instances of intrusion in which the virgin stillness of this enchanted feminine ground is symbolically violated by a foreign sexuality.

Another set of three images seems to work in much the same way, though it sheds a rather different light on the theme of Ichabod's lubricity. The transformation of the schoolhouse by the Dutch into an elaborate eelpot implicitly but quite directly casts Ichabod in the role of the eel. As though to underscore this impression, Irving shortly thereafter asserts, in one of the more surprising metaphors of the story, that Ichabod "had the dilating powers of an Anaconda" (p. 275). The effect of Irving's likening his protagonist to an eel becomes fully apparent only later, at the Van Tassels' harvest festival, where "the sons [appeared] in short square coats with rows of stupendous brass buttons, and their hair generally queued in the fashion of the times, especially if they could procure an eel skin for the purpose, it being esteemed throughout the country as a potent nourisher and strengthener of the hair" (p. 286). The schoolhouse, then, is explicitly an eel-trap constructed by a community that values eels as a source of male sexual potency. Apart from this connection, it is difficult to see why either detail should be in the story. Read, thus connected, in the general context of the prevailing Dutch sexuality—that is, in the division of the Dutch characters into menopausal and pre-pubescent groups—it becomes necessary to look upon Ichabod as, in a manner of speaking, the serpentine source of sex in paradise or as the necessarily extrinsic agent, procured by Yost Van Houten in the name of Dutch folk wisdom, to help Brom Bones over the portal of maturity. In this event, Katrina's coquettishness takes its place as a single element in a much larger ritual, one that manages to include the whole community.

The husband-to-be is near to the point of escaping the socially useless boy-culture of "Brom Bones and his gang," but so long as his "amorous toyings" continue to be "like the caresses and endearments of a bear" (p. 282) he will clearly never pass muster with the blooming Katrina. His rite of passage, as it turns out, involves more than the simple conquest of a rival. It involves him in the first socially useful act of his life, his first act as a member of the whole community. The expulsion of Ichabod simply *is* the defense of that whole community from moral taint and eventual destruction, while, considered in relation to the marriage that ensues—the marriage that, indeed, it makes possible—it is the rejection or expulsion of "Yankee sexuality," of the perverse and aggressive lust of one who "in form and spirit [was] like a supple jack—yielding, but tough; though he bent, he never broke; and though he bowed beneath the slightest pressure, yet, the moment it was away—jerk! he was as erect, and carried his head as high as ever" (p. 282). It is to break *this,* once and for all, that the "Headless Hessian" at long last carries *his* head

high, and, in the event, so frightens the hard-riding Ichabod as nearly to bring off the latter's castration "on the high ridge of his horse's back bone" (p. 294). Irving, though, is mercifully content with the symbolic castration of a blow to the "cranium," which is, appropriately yet problematically, the real seat of Crane's lechery.[13]

To read **"The Legend of Sleepy Hollow"** in this way is to see its formal relation to an important sub-genre of American fiction that Roy Male, in defining it, called "the Mysterious Stranger story."[14] This form is

> an inside narrative with an enclosed structure; its plot and characterization consist of the effect of a semi-supernatural and usually ambiguous stranger upon a crowd, a family, or an individual; its theme tends to center around faith and the contagiousness of good, or distrust and the contagiousness of evil and violence. . . . The trickster-god appears unexpectedly, usually in disguise, tests or transforms a mortal, and disappears.[15]

In Irving's Mysterious Stranger story all the elements are present, and yet, perhaps because he was more interested in the conflict than in its resolution and sequel, perhaps because he lacked the deeper ironic intelligence—certainly, in any event, because he made his devil too much the fool—Irving evades some central implications of the form, or, more particularly, has no use for the issue of "the contagiousness of evil and violence" that the structure of such a story raises. So far as the community is concerned, Ichabod is simply absorbed into the local mythology as the morally neutralized spectre that haunts the decaying schoolhouse. Death is absorbed into life. In a realm of such enchantment, there is no clear sign that Ichabod will have a lasting subversive effect on Sleepy Hollow or that anything serious will follow from the necessity that he himself created of expelling him by devious and forceful means. And if in the end there is no lurking worm of guilt, no paradise quite lost, yet it is to be remembered that Irving is attacking, not defending, the Puritan possibilities. Were he to insist that the expulsion of Ichabod is reflexively corrupting, it would be tantamount to giving the demonic mythology of New England precedence over the benign mythology of the Dutch. By refusing to give the devil his due, Irving in effect chooses to stress the preserving innocence which the recollection of home, safe from betrayal or violation, inveterately has in the memory.

Still, fictional forms have a force and a meaning of their own, built up of the uses to which they have previously been put by other writers. For this reason at least, Irving cannot quite escape the implication that Ichabod has forever changed Sleepy Hollow. Of the sorts of falls that such an agent as he might induce, consistent with Irving's fondness for his Dutch characters, there is the sort of pillow-soft, post-Miltonic fall of Brom, who, encountering evil without accepting it, passes from innocence to a knowledge of virtuous action and in the process gains his manhood. All that is shown of his life after marriage is that he would "look exceedingly knowing whenever the story of Ichabod was related," and that some were led to "suspect that he knew more about the matter than he chose to tell" (p. 296), a sort of deviousness which, harmless enough in appearance, is certainly no longer an Arcadian simplicity.

Another kind of fall is suggested by the whole retrospective, memorial tone of the narration, augmented, perhaps, by a knowledge of the historic fate of these Dutch communities. The story is set in the past, but the wistfully receding perspective in which it is presented is a function mainly of the layered narration, a device which, as Irving handles it, tells its own story of declining prosperity and increasing sophistication. The first narrator is "a pleasant, shabby, gentlemanly old fellow . . . with a sadly humourous face; and one whom I [Dietrich Knickerbocker, the second narrator] strongly suspected of being poor" (p. 297). He tells his story—orally—in the same spirit in which the supernatural tales are given at the Van Tassel party, neither as "literature" nor as veritable history, claiming in the end not to "believe one half of it myself" (p. 297). Knickerbocker, who writes it all down, has literary aspirations and a sense of wider audiences, though as the *History* indicates, he is ultimately defeated by poverty. He figures at last as a deadbeat fleeing from a hotel, a wandering solitary man survived only by his papers. With the emergence of Geoffrey Crayon as the executor of this literary estate, the tradition has passed from the Dutch altogether, and the fall seems complete.

Notes

1. Robert A. Bone, "Irving's Headless Hessian: Prosperity and the Inner Life," *AQ,* 15 (1963), 171, and William L. Hedges, *Washington Irving: An American Study* (Baltimore: Johns Hopkins Press, 1965), p. 142.

2. In *Form and Fable in American Fiction* (New York: Norton, 1973), Daniel Hoffman sees Ichabod as the comic Yankee who poses a threat to the Dutch, whose "magic is the power of self-reliance, not of Satan" (p. 88). Donald Ringe, in "New York and New England: Irving's Criticism of American Society," *AL,* 38 (1967), 455-67, presents perhaps the harshest view of Ichabod, but his brief treatment of the tale is mainly concerned with "the serious social implications" of Ichabod as a regional type. Martin Roth, in *Comedy and America: The Lost World of Washington Irving* (Port Washington: Kennikat Press, 1976), pp. 161-68, challenges the views of Bone and Hedges, though I believe he unduly diminishes the character of Ichabod by finding him little more than a "petty capitalist and speculator" (p. 164). Annette Kolodny, in *The Lay of the Land: Metaphor as Experience and History in American Life and Letters* (Chapel Hill: Univ. of North Carolina Press, 1975), pp. 68-70, sees Ichabod as the sexually aggressive male antagonist to the maternal pastoral. Specifically, he "threatens to intrude conscious thought and the feeble beginnings of art and learning" (p. 68).

3. Ringe, p. 463.

4. Hoffman, p. 89.

5. Washington Irving, *The Sketch Book of Geoffrey Crayon, Gent.,* ed. Haskell Springer (Boston: Twayne, 1978), p. 274. Hereafter page references to this edition will appear in the text.

6. In Leo Marx, *The Machine in the Garden: Technology and the Pastoral Ideal in America* (London: Oxford Univ. Press, 1964), passim. Because *The Sketch Book* predates the intrusion of technology, Marx does not discuss this tale;

however, its special relevance to the issues he raises is suggested by the epigraph to Chapter One, "Sleepy Hollow, 1844," an allusion, ready to hand, in the name of a wooded area in Concord, later a cemetery.

7. Ichabod Crane's mother was presumably another satirist: see I Samuel 4:21: "And she named the child Ichabod, saying, The glory is departed from Israel."

8. There is a strong analogy here to the character and situation of Simon Legree, another superstitious Yankee, another displaced flogger of the defenseless. In *Uncle Tom's Cabin,* ed. Kenneth S. Lynn (Cambridge: Harvard Univ. Press, 1962), p. 411, Stowe remarks that "no one is so thoroughly superstitious as the godless man. The Christian is composed by the belief of a wise, all-ruling Father, whose presence fills the void unknown with light and order; but to the man who has dethroned God, the spirit-land is, indeed, in the words of the Hebrew poet, 'a land of darkness and the shadow of death,' without any order, where the light is as darkness. Life and death to him are haunted grounds, filled with goblin forms of vague and shadowy dread."

9. A good and instructive example of this prejudice may be found in John L. Blake's *Geographical, Chronological, and Historical Atlas* (New York: Cooke and Co., 1826), p. 165: "There are none of those splendid establishments in America such as Oxford and Cambridge in which immense salaries maintain the professors of literature in monastic idleness. . . . The People of this country have not yet inclined to make much literary display—They have rather aimed at works of general utility."

10. Possibly Ichabod is smarting under the coincidence that the musician at the ball is yet another alter ego, "an old gray-headed negro, who had been the itinerant orchestra of the neighborhood for more than half a century" (p. 287).

11. Another instance would be Ichabod's entry at the Van Tassel party: "Fain would I pause to dwell upon the world of charms that burst upon the enraptured gaze of my hero, as he entered the state parlour of Van Tassel's mansion. Not of those of the bevy of buxom lasses, with their luxurious display of red and white: but the ample charms of a genuine Dutch country tea table, in the sumptuous time of autumn" (p. 287).

12. On this subject see William P. Dawson, "'Rip Van Winkle' as Bawdy Satire," *ESQ,* 27 (1981), 198-206.

13. Kolodny, in *The Lay of the Land,* p. 69, is surely correct in seeing a headless figure as the appropriate avatar of an anti-intellectual Sleepy Hollow, and equally correct in identifying Brom Bones' "removal and throwing away of the pumpkin-head" as a rejection of Ichabod's perverse blend of intellection and sexuality. She errs, I believe, in regarding the act as "a kind of symbolic castration" of Brom, whose marriage follows this victory, rather than of Ichabod, whose dark purposes are permanently thwarted in this moment of physical wounding.

14. "The Story of the Mysterious Stranger in American Fiction," *Criticism,* 3 (1961), 281-94. The examples that Male treats include Hawthorne's "Gray Champion," Melville's "Lightning-Rod Man" and *The Confidence-Man,* Harte's "Luck of Roaring Camp," Howells' *Traveller From Altruria,* Twain's *Mysterious Stranger* and "The Man That Corrupted Hadleyburg," as well as Porter's "Noon Wine" and Warren's "Blackberry Winter."

15. Male, p. 290.

Raymond Benoit (essay date 1996)

SOURCE: "Irving's 'The Legend of Sleepy Hollow'," in *The Explicator,* Vol. 55, No. 1, Fall, 1996, pp. 15-17.

[*In the following essay, Benoit explores Ichabod's loss of the imaginative bond between man and the world in "The Legend of Sleepy Hollow."*]

"There used to be gods in everything, and now they've gone . . . all the lonely summer night's become but fact" (19). These lines from Howard Nemerov's poem "The Companions" could have served as an epigraph for **"The Legend of Sleepy Hollow,"** for that legend is ultimately concerned with the loss of wonder and of a sense of life-as-mystery in the slow unraveling of imaginative attachment between man and things with the rise of human consciousness. Freud's words describe the process, for which Irving's fiction is in many respects an "objective correlative," that culminates when Ichabod, on his way home after Katrina's rejection has left him "with an air quite desolate and chopfallen" (290), reaches Major André's tree. Freud said: "Originally the ego includes everything, later it separates off an external world from itself. Our present ego-feeling is, therefore, only a shrunken residue to a much more inclusive—indeed, an all-embracing—feeling which corresponded to a more intimate bond between the ego and the world about it" (15). Until the evening at Van Tassel's, Ichabod's feeling is indeed an "all-embracing" experience, like the poet's experience described by Northrop Frye, "where the mind behind the subject and the world behind the objects are united, where nature and personality are one, as they formerly were in the sea-gods and sky-gods of ancient mythologies" (151)—and in the tree-gods of American mythology:

> What fearful shapes and shadows beset his path, amidst the dim and ghastly glare of a snowy night!—With what wistful look did he eye every trembling ray of light streaming across the waste fields from some distant window!—How often was he appalled by some shrub covered with snow, which like a sheeted specter beset his very path!—How often did he shrink with curdling awe at the sound of his own steps on the frosty crust beneath his feet; and dread to look over his shoulder, lest he should behold some uncouth being tramping close behind him!—and how often was he thrown into complete dismay by some rushing blast, howling among the trees, in the idea that it was the galloping Hessian on one of his nightly scourings. (Irving 278)

At Major André's tree, though, this imaginative and intimate bond slowly weakens and then breaks as Ichabod, "heavy hearted and crest fallen" (291), withdraws into himself in the distancing and analytic mood of subject to object, which develops as his thought becomes increasingly focused—"it was but a blast"; "a little nearer, he thought"; "but on looking more narrowly"; "it was but the rubbing":

> As Ichabod approached this fearful tree, he began to whistle; he thought his whistle was answered: it was but a blast sweeping sharply through the dry branches. As he approached a little nearer, he thought he saw something white, hanging in the midst of the tree: he paused and ceased whistling; but on looking more narrowly, perceived that it was a place where the tree had been scathed by lightning, and the white wood laid bare. Suddenly he heard a groan—his teeth chattered, and his knees smote against the saddle: it was but the rubbing of one huge bough upon another, as they were swayed about by the breeze. He passed the tree in safety, but new perils lay before him. (292)

The phrase, "it was but" functions like cock-crows to deny acquaintance with the larger one-life now in the process of splitting apart. For as Martin Buber wrote in *I and Thou,* "once the sentence 'I see the tree' has been pronounced in such a way that it no longer relates a relation between a human I and a tree You but the perception of the tree object by the human consciousness, it has erected the crucial barrier between subject and object; the basic work I-it, the word of separation, has been spoken" (74-75).

A new peril may lie ahead, but after the drama at Major André's tree, the ensuing confrontation with the headless horseman is anticlimactic; the crucial barrier has already been erected between Ichabod and Sleepy Hollow, the basic word of separation having been spoken by Ichabod himself.[1]

The postscript to the story is significantly an afterthought, an abstraction out of the whole, which ironically re-enacts the psychological drama of the short story epitomized in the episode at Major André's tree. The storyteller in the postscript, who has just concluded relating his "legend" at a corporation meeting in Manhattoes, diminishes his imaginative art into a shrunken syllogistic residue in response to a "dry-looking old gentleman" who demands to know "the moral of the story, and what it went to prove" (297). The storyteller mockingly obliges:

> "That there is no situation in life but has its advantages and pleasures, providing we will but take a joke as we find it:
>
> "That, therefore, he that runs races with goblin troopers, is likely to have rough riding of it:
>
> "Ergo, for a country schoolmaster to be refused the hand of a Dutch heiress, is a certain step to high preferment in the state." (297)

In contrast to the imaginative garden of the all-embracing narrative, these reductive words of reason are all that is left, and appropriately, as a "post-script," the real pieces of the broken pumpkin.

Notes

1. Cf. the biblical account in I Sam. 21-23: "She named the boy Ichabod, saying, 'The glory has gone from Israel,' thinking of her father-in-law and

husband and of the capture of the ark of God. She said, 'The glory has gone from Israel, because the ark of God has been captured.'"

Works Cited

Buber, Martin. *I and Thou.* Trans. Walter Kaufmann. New York: Scribner's, 1970.

Freud, Sigmund. *Civilization and Its Discontents.* Trans. James Strachey. New York: Norton, 1961.

Frye, Northrop. *A Study of English Romanticism.* New York: Random, 1968.

Irving, Washington. *The Sketch Book of Geoffrey Crayon, Gent.* Ed. Haskell Springer. Boston: Twayne, 1978.

Nemerov, Howard. *The Blue Swallows.* Chicago: U of Chicago P, 1967.

FURTHER READING

Criticism

May, Charles E. "Metaphoric Motivation in Short Fiction: 'In the Beginning Was the Story.'" In *Short Story Theory at a Crossroads,* edited by Susan Lohafer and Jo Ellyn Clarey, pp. 62-73. Baton Rouge: Louisiana State University Press, 1989.

> Examines "The Legend of Sleepy Hollow" as part of an assessment of the early development of the short story in American literature.

Piacentino, Ed. "'Sleepy Hollow' Comes South: Washington Irving's Influence on Old Southwestern Humor." *The Southern Literary Journal* XXX, No. 1 (Fall 1997): 27-42.

> Considers the impact of "The Legend of Sleepy Hollow" on subsequent works of nineteenth-century southern frontier humor.

Pryse, Marjorie. "Origins of American Literary Regionalism: Gender in Irving, Stowe, and Longstreet." In *Breaking Boundaries: New Perspectives on Women's Regional Writing,* edited by Sherrie A. Inness and Diana Royer, pp. 17-37. Iowa City: University of Iowa Press, 1997.

> Considers Irving's construction of the American storyteller and American literary hero as male in "The Legend of Sleepy Hollow" within a discussion of women regionalist writers.

Stone, Edward. "William Faulkner." In *A Certain Morbidness: A View of American Literature,* pp. 85-120. Carbondale: Southern Illinois University Press, 1969.

> Traces the influence of "The Legend of Sleepy Hollow" on William Faulkner's fiction, particularly *The Hamlet.*

Additional coverage of Irving's life and career is contained in the following sources published by the Gale Group: *Concise Dictionary of American Literary Biography, 1640–1865; Dictionary of Literary Biography,* Vols. 3, 11, 30, 59, 73, 74, 186; *DISCovering Authors; DISCovering Authors: British; DISCovering Authors: Canadian; DISCovering Authors: Most-Studied Authors Module; Nineteenth-Century Literature Criticism,* Vols. 2, 19; *Short Story Criticism,* Vol. 2; **and** *Yesterday's Authors of Books for Children,* **Vol. 2.**

Leslie Marmon Silko
1948–

American novelist, short story writer, poet and essayist.

INTRODUCTION

Silko is considered among the foremost authors to emerge from the Native American literary renaissance of the 1970s. In her writings she blends such literary forms as the novel, short story, and narrative poem with the oral traditions of her Laguna Pueblo heritage to communicate Native American conceptualizations of time, nature, and spirituality. Silko focuses on characters, often of mixed Laguna Pueblo and Anglo heritage, who occupy the fringes of both Native American and Western cultures. Through their struggles they must draw on the moral strength of their native community and its traditions in order to overcome the often repressive, alienating effects of Anglo-American society.

BIOGRAPHICAL INFORMATION

Of Laguna Pueblo, Plains Indian, Mexican, and Anglo-American descent, Silko was born in Albuquerque and raised on the Laguna Pueblo Reservation in northern New Mexico. Her family were storytellers among the Laguna; in fact, her relatives were among the Native Americans who taught early twentieth-century anthropologists, such as Franz Boas, traditional myths and stories. As a child Silko attended schools administered by the Bureau of Indian Affairs until she was able to commute to school off the reservation. She graduated with honors from the University of New Mexico in 1969 and briefly attended law school before deciding to pursue a writing career. By the early 1970s, Silko was garnering attention as a promising Native American author, known primarily for her short stories and poetry that explore the distinct oral tradition of the Laguna people. In 1969, while still an undergraduate, she published the short story "The Man To Send Rain Clouds" in the *New Mexico Quarterly.* This story served as the title piece for Kenneth Rosen's 1974 anthology in which he published six additional stories by Silko. The critical acclaim she earned from *Ceremony* (1977) solidified her position in the literary field and earned her numerous prestigious writing awards. Although she has taught at and has been associated with several universities, she now pursues writing full time from her home near Tuscon, Arizona.

MAJOR WORKS

Silko's first published collection, *Laguna Woman* (1974), consists of her narrative poetry based on the oral traditions and culture of her heritage. In *Ceremony,* her first novel, she interweaves free-verse poetry and narrative prose to

chronicle the story of Tayo, a World War II veteran of mixed white and Laguna Pueblo heritage who returns to the reservation shattered by his war experiences. He finds healing with the help of Bentonie, an elderly man who exists on the cusp of Laguna and white societies, and T'seh Montano, a medicine woman who embodies the feminine, life-giving aspects of the earth. In *Ceremony,* Silko introduces the unique elements that have characterized her fiction; a protagonist of mixed heritage, a conflict between Native and Anglo cultures; the destructive nature of the dominant white culture; and the restive powers of the traditional Native American life-style. Silko developed these themes in *Storyteller* (1981) and to a stronger extent in her second novel *Almanac of the Dead* (1991), a work about Native Americans who retain their native lands after whites, lacking the spiritual and moral force of the Native Americans, succumb to crime, perversion, drug addiction, and environmental degradation. In *Storyteller*—her volume of poetry, short stories, and recollections—Silko attempts to merge the oral tradition of storytelling with the literary form. She creates an unusual form of autobiography through which she describes her personal experiences and her family history by locating them within the larger Laguna society. Thus, she reflects the Pueblo belief that the individual is only significant in relation to their position within the whole. Silko demonstrates the dynamic nature of Laguna culture as she modernizes traditional myths such as "Yellow Woman." In stories such as "Storyteller," "Lullaby," and "Tony's Story," Silko's characters reside in a no man's land between cultures, destroyed by the tension between them. "Storyteller," the account of an Innuit girl who seeks revenge for her parents' death at the hands of whites, is one of Silko's best-known and most highly regarded short stories.

CRITICAL RECEPTION

Silko earned critical praise with the publication of her first short stories in the early 1970s. Reviewers noted their strong voice and coherent, tightly written structure. The publication of *Ceremony* cemented her reputation as one of the best contemporary Native American writers. Most scholars place her second only to N. Scott Momaday in terms of national influence and frequently compare *Ceremony* to Momaday's Pulitzer-Prize-winning novel *The House Made of Dawn.* Some reviewers noted that in *Ceremony* Silko does not maintain the same level of intensity and precision that characterizes her shorter works. However, critics are intrigued by Silko's efforts to replicate the oral tradition of Native American storytelling. Her subsequent work, *Storyteller,* earned Silko even greater national recognition. Kenneth Lincoln maintains that "Storyteller" "unfolds with an economy so lucid that nothing is lost." And N. Scott Momaday praises her sense of humor and her "sharp sense of the way in which the profound and the mundane often run together in our daily lives." Reviews were not uniformly favorable for her second novel *Almanac of the Dead.* While some critics praised her subject matter and her skill at handling such an extensive and controversial topic, other reviewers complained that Silko's tone is too dark, she portrays whites stereotypically, and that her plot is too complex and unwieldy. Despite mixed reviews of her other works, William M. Clements asserts that "it remains obvious that [Silko's] poetry and prose—both fiction and nonfiction—represent some of the most stimulating writing produced by a Native American in the late twentieth century."

PRINCIPAL WORKS

Short Fiction

Storyteller (poems and short stories) 1981

Other Major Works

Laguna Woman (poems) 1974
Ceremony (novel) 1977
Almanac of the Dead (novel) 1991
Sacred Water (nonfiction) 1993
Yellow Woman (nonfiction) 1993

CRITICISM

Arnold Krupat (essay date 1989)

SOURCE: "The Dialogic of Silko's *Storyteller,*" in *Narrative Chance: Postmodern Discourse on Native American Indian Literatures,* edited by Gerald Vizenor, University of New Mexico Press, 1989, pp. 55–68.

[*In the essay below, Krupat applies Mikhail Bakhtin's literary theories to Silko's* Storyteller *as he discusses the roles of authority and voice.*]

Autobiography as commonly understood in western European and Euro-American culture did not exist as a traditional type of literary expression among the aboriginal peoples of North America. Indeed, none of the conditions of production for autobiography—here I would isolate post-Napoleonic historicism, egocentric individualism and writing as foremost—was typical of Native American cultures.[1] To the extent that the life stories, personal histories, memoirs or recollections of Indians did finally come into textual form (traditional Indian literatures were not written but oral), it was as a result of contact with and pressure from Euro-Americans. Until the twentieth century the most common form of Native American autobiography was the Indian autobiography, a genre of American writing constituted by the principle of original, bicultural, composite composition, in which there is a distinct if not always clear division of labor between the subject of the autobiography (the Indian to whom the first-person pronoun ostensibly makes reference) and the Euro-American editor responsible for fixing the text in writing, yet whose presence the first-person pronoun ostensibly masks. Indian autobiography may thus be distinguished from autobiography by Indians, the life stories of those Christianized and/or "civilized" natives who, having internalized Western culture and scription, committed their lives to writing on their own without the mediation of the Euro-American. In autobiographies by Indians, although there is inevitably an element of biculturalism, there is not the element of compositeness that precisely marks Indian autobiographies.

The earliest examples of Native American autobiography are two by Indians dating from the decades surrounding the American Revolution. These did not attract much attention; indeed, the more extensive of the two by Hendrick Aupaumut was not even published until 1827 and then in a journal of rather limited circulation.[2] It was only six years later, however that the first Indian autobiography, J. B. Patterson's *Life of Black Hawk,* appeared. This book did gain widespread notice, coming as it did at a time of increased American interest in Indians (the book was occasioned by the last Indian war to be fought east of the Mississippi) and in the type of writing then only recently named autobiography (in 1809 by the poet Southey). Both of these interests are developed in this earliest type of Indian autobiography, which presents the acts of the world-historical chief or (of particular concern in the first half of the nineteenth century) the Indian hero. The historical orientation of Indian autobiography persisted in some form into the 1930s and 1940s after which none of the warriors was left alive to tell his tale. By that time there had already occurred a shift of interest on the part of Euro-

American editors from history to science. In the twentieth century professional anthropologists rather than amateur historians would most commonly edit Indian autobiographies.

In our time Indian autobiographies continue to be co-produced by historians and social scientists working with traditional native people, but their labors have very nearly been overshadowed by the autobiographical writing of a new generation of Indians, educated in Western literate forms yet by no means acculturated to the point of abandoning respect for the old ways. These autobiographies are not only contributions to historical and scientific record, but also works of art (particularly the autobiographies of N. Scott Momaday and Leslie Marmon Silko, whose claim to national attention came not from their relation to American religion, history or anthropology, but from their relation to American literature as previously established in their fiction and poetry).

The history of Native American autobiography could be charted thematically as a movement from history and science to art on a line parallel to the history of European and Euro-American autobiography.[3] To chart it thus would demonstrate that Native Americans have had to make a variety of accommodations to the dominant culture's forms, capitulating to them, assimilating them, sometimes dramatically transforming them, but never able to proceed independent of them. However, Native American autobiography differs materially from western European and Euro-American (though not strictly western American) autobiography through its existence in specifically individual and composite forms, or, both monologic and dialogic forms.[4]

To introduce the terms monologue and dialogue is to invoke an important recent development in literary theory: recent interest in the Russian theorist, Mikhail Bakhtin.

So much has been written on Bakhtin of late that any attempt to summarize his thought is bound to be incomplete.[5] In this country, at least, what is generally understood by reference to "Bakhtin," is very far from settled. To be sure "Freud" and "Marx" mean different things to different people as well; but there seems to be for Bakhtin, more than for these other major thinkers (and it is by no means generally agreed that comparison of Bakhtin to major thinkers is justified), a pronounced ambiguity. This openness may be functional, a practical illustration of what has been theoretically proposed. Perhaps it is not so much "openness," that Bakhtin's writing exhibits, but such inconsistency and ambiguity that it is difficult or pointless to specify the particulars of his thought. Hence, any attempt at an approximately neutral summary automatically becomes partial, a choice not between nuances but real differences. Nevertheless, the following briefly outlines what is at issue in Bakhtin and therefore at issue in any Bakhtinian reading of Native American autobiography.

Bakhtin calls human language "heteroglossic, polyvocal," the speech of each individual enabled and circumscribed not so much by language as a *system* as by the actual speech of other individuals. (In this he differs from Saussurian structural linguistics and its fascination with *langue*.) Speech is social and meaning is open and in flux, inevitably a dialogue among speakers, not the property or in the power of any single speaker. ". . . All there is to know about the world is not exhausted by a particular discourse about it . . ."[6] Bakhtin notes in a typical statement. Still some forms of written discourse and social practice seek to impose a single authoritative voice as the norm, thus subordinating or entirely suppressing other voices. It is the genre Bakhtin calls the "epic" that provides models of this monologic tendency in literature, while the totalitarianism of Stalinism under which Bakhtin lived provides the socio-political model of monologism. In opposition to the totalizing thrust of the epic, the novel testifies to its own (inevitable) incompleteness, its ongoing indebtedness to the discourse of others. The novel is the prime literary instance of dialogized speech.

Bakhtin seems to be committed to dialogue on empirical grounds, inasmuch as the term claims to name human communication correctly, pointing to the way speech and social life "really" are. But Bakhtin seems also to be committed to dialogue on moral and esthetic grounds; he approves of and is pleased by that which he finds bi-, hetero-, poly-, and so on. For him, truth and beauty are one, but what this equivalence is to mean ultimately in a dialogic theory of language and of social life remains to be determined.

Does Bakhtinian dialogic envision a strong form of pluralism in which all have legitimate voice: truth having its particular authority, beauty having its, and both having equal (cognitive) force over other voices, which, although worthy of being heard, can be judged decidably less forceful? Or does Bakhtinian dialogic envision a kind of postmodernist free play of voices with no normative means for deciding their relative worth or authority? We do not know whether Bakhtin's dislike of what he calls monologue permits some forms of relatively stable assertion, in particular truth and beauty. Such statements as "the last word is never said,"—and there are innumerable such statements in Bakhtin's writing—may intend a radically ironic, a schizophrenic refusal (in Jameson's very particular sense)[7] of any form, however relativized, of grounded meaning. Or they may insist only that no single language act has the capacity to encompass the entire range of humanly possible meaning, as no single mode of political organization can give full latitude to human potential.

In this latter regard the issue is particularly complicated because, while we do know from Bakhtin that the novel is supposed to provide the fullest literary illustration of relativized, dialogic discourse, we do not know whether the nearest thing he gives us to a socio-political equivalent of the novel, rabelaisian "carnival," represents an actual model for social organization or an escape from too rigid social organization. In either case, we do not know what Bakhtinian carnival might actually entail for current or future social formations. To examine Native American autobiography from a Bakhtinian perspective, then, is not only to consider it as a discursive type—a kind of literature, generically closer to the epic or the novel as Bakhtin understands these Western forms—but as a social model which allows for the projection of a particular image of human community.

Let me now offer a reading of Leslie Marmon Silko's *Storyteller* in relation to these issues.

Merely to consider *Storyteller* among Native American autobiographies might require some explanation, since the book is a collection of stories, poems and photographs as much as it is a narrative of its author's life. Of course a variety of claims have been made in the recent past for the fictionality of autobiographies in general, the autobiography being recognized as the West's most obviously dialogic genre in which a conversation between *historia* and *poesis,* documentation and creation, is always in progress. And some of these claims might easily be used to justify classifying *Storyteller* as an autobiography.

Indeed, to justify the book's classification as an autobiography in this way, would not be mistaken; it would, however, be to treat it exclusively from a Western perspective, failing to acknowledge that traditional Native American literary forms were not—and, in their contemporary manifestations usually are not—as concerned about keeping fiction and fact or poetry and prose distinct from one another. It is the distinction between truth and error rather than that between fact and fiction that seems more interesting to native expression; and indeed, this distinction was also central to Western thought prior to the seventeenth century. Thus the present "blurring of genres," in Clifford Geertz's phrase,[8] in both the social sciences and in the arts, is actually only a return to that time when the line between history and myth was not very clearly marked. But that is the way things have always been for Native American literatures.

From the Western point of view, Silko's book would seem to announce by its title, *Storyteller,* the familiar pattern of discovering who one is by discovering what one does, the pattern of identity in vocation. This is useful enough as a way to view Silko's text. In the West it has been a very long time since the vocational storyteller has had a clear and conventional social role. In Pueblo culture, however, to be known as a storyteller is to be known as one who participates, in a communally sanctioned manner, in sustaining the group; for a Native American writer to identify herself as a storyteller today is to express a desire to perform such a function. In the classic terms of Marcel Mauss, person, self and role are here joined.[9]

Silko dedicates her book "to the storytellers as far back as memory goes and to the telling which continues and through which they all live and we with them." Having called herself a storyteller, she thus places herself in a tradition of tellings, suggesting that her stories cannot strictly be her own nor will we find in them what one typically looks for in post-Rousseauan, Western autobiography or (as Bakhtin would add, in poetry) a uniquely personal voice. There is no single, distinctive or authoritative voice in Silko's book nor any striving for such a voice; to the contrary, Silko will take pains to indicate how even her own individual speech is the product of many voices. *Storyteller* is presented as a strongly polyphonic text in which the author defines herself—finds her voice, tells her life, illustrates the capacities of her vocation—in relation to the voices of other native and nonnative storytellers, tale tellers and book writers, and even to the voices of those who serve as the (by-no-means silent) audience for these stories.

It is Silko's biographical voice that commences the book, but not by speaking of her birth or the earliest recollec-

tions of childhood as Western autobiography usually dictates. Rather, she begins by establishing the relation of "hundreds of photographs taken since the 1890s around Laguna" that she finds in "a tall Hopi basket" to "the stories as [she] remembers them."[10] Visual stories, speaking pictures, here as in the familiar Western understanding will also provide a voice; and Silko's developing relation to every kind of story becomes the story of her life.

Dennis Tedlock has made the important point that Zuni stories are fashioned in such a way as to include in their telling not just the story itself but a critique of or commentary on those stories, and Silko's autobiographical story will also permit a critical dimension, voices that comment on stories and storytellers—storytellers like her Aunt Susie, who, when she told stories had "certain phrases, certain distinctive words/she used in her telling" (7). Both Aunt Susie and Aunt Alice "would tell me stories they had told me before but with changes in details or descriptions.. . . There were even stories about the different versions of stories and how they imagined these differing versions came to be" (227). Silko's own versions of stories she has heard from Simon Ortiz, the Acoma writer whom Silko acknowledges as the source of her prose tale, "Uncle Tony's Goat," and her verse tale, **"Skeleton Fixer,"** also introduce certain phrases and distinctive words that make them identifiably her own. Yet these and all the other stories are never presented as the final or definitive version; although they are intensely associated with their different tellers, they remain available for other tellings.[11] "What is realized in the novel," Bakhtin has written, "is the process of coming to know one's own language as it is perceived in someone else's language. . . " (365) and so, too, to know one's own language as bound up with "someone else's language." Any story Silko herself tells, then, is always bound up with someone else's language; it is always a version and the story as version stands in relation to the story as officially sanctioned myth, as the novel stands to the national epic. Silko's stories are always consistent with—to return to Bakhtin—attempts to liberate ". . . cultural-semantic and emotional intentions from the hegemony of a single and unitary language," consistent with a ". . . loss of feeling for language as myth, that is, as an absolute form of thought" (367).

Stories are transmitted by other storytellers, as Silko wrote early in her book:

> by word of mouth
> an entire history
> an entire vision of the world
> which depended upon memory
> and retelling by subsequent generations.
> . . . . .
> . . . the oral tradition depends upon each person
> listening and remembering a portion.. . .
>
> (6-7)

But the awareness of and respect for the oral tradition, here, is not a kind of sentimental privileging of the old ways. Indeed, this first reference to the importance of cultural transmission by oral means comes in a lovely memorial to Aunt Susie who, Silko writes:

> From the time that I can remember her
> . . . worked on her kitchen table

with her books and papers spread over the oil cloth.
She wrote beautiful long hand script
but her eyesight was not good
and so she wrote very slowly.

. . . . .

She had come to believer very much in books

It is Aunt Susie, the believer in books and in writing, who was of "the last generation here at Laguna, that passed an entire culture by word of mouth.. . . " Silko's own writing is compared to oral telling by a neighbor, who, finding her "Laguna Coyote" poem in a library book, remarks:

"We all enjoyed it so much,
but I was telling the children
the way my grandpa used to tell it
is longer."

To this critical voice, Silko responds:

"Yes, that's the trouble with writing. . .
You can't go on and on the way we do
when we tell stories around here.
People who aren't used to it get tired"

(110).

This awareness of the audience is entirely typical for a native storyteller who cannot go forward with a tale without the audience's response. As Silko writes:

The Laguna people
always begin their stories
with "humma-hah":
that means "long ago."
And the ones who are listening
say "aaaa-eh"

(38)

These are the stories, of course, of the oral tradition. Silko invokes the feel of "long ago" both in the verse format she frequently uses and in the prose pieces, although perhaps only those sections of the book set in verse attempt to evoke something of the actual feel of an oral telling.

It is interesting to note that there are two pieces in the book that echo the title, one in prose and the other set in loose verse. The first, **"Storyteller,"** is an intense and powerful short story which takes place in Alaska. The storyteller of the title is the protagonist's grandfather, a rather less benign figure than the old storytellers of Silko's biographical experience; nonetheless, the stories he tells are of the traditional, mythic type. The second, **"Storytelling,"** is a kind of mini-anthology of several short tales of women and their (quite historical, if fictional!) sexual adventures. The "humma-hah" (in effect) of the first section goes:

You should understand
the way it was
back then,
because it is the same
even now

(94).

[aaaa-eh]

The final section has its unnamed speaker conclude:

My husband
left
after he heard the story
and moved back in with his mother.
It was my fault and
I don't blame him either.
I could have told
the story
better than I did

(98).

In both these pieces (**"Storyteller"** and **"Storytelling"**) we find a very different sense of verbal art from that expressed in the West in something like Auden's lines (in the poem on the death of Yeats), where he writes that "poetry makes nothing happen.. . . " In deadly serious prose and in witty verse, Silko dramatizes her belief that stories—both the mythic-traditional tales passed down among the people and the day-to-day narrations of events—do make things happen. The two pieces refer to very different kinds of stories which, in their capacity to produce material effects, are nonetheless the same.

Among other identifiable voices in Silko's texts are her own epistolary voice in letters she has written to Lawson F. Inada and James A. Wright, the voices of Coyote and Buffalo, and those of traditional figures like Kochininako, Whirlwind Man, Arrowboy, Spider Woman and Yellow Woman—some of whom appear in modern day incarnations. In stories or letters or poems, in monologues or dialogues, the diction may vary—now more colloquial and/or regional, now more formal—or the tone—lyrical, humorous, meditative. Yet always, the effort is to make us hear the various languages that constitute Silko's world and so herself. If we agree with Bakhtin that, "The primary stylistic project of the novel as a genre is to create images of languages" (366), *Storyteller* is a clear instance of novelized discourse, Native American autobiography of the dialogic type. It remains to say what the implications of this particular dialogic discourse may be.

I have tried to read *Storyteller* as an example of Native American autobiography in the dialogic mode, that is, against the backdrop of Bakhtin's meditations on language and society. By way of conclusion, it seems useful to see what Silko's book has to say about these important subjects, or more accurately, what projections about language and society might be made from the book. To interrogate the text in this way is not to treat it foremost as ethnic or hyphenated literature (although it cannot be understood in ignorance of its informing context), but as a candidate for inclusion in the canon of American literature conceived of as a selection of the most important work from among national texts (*American* literature) and texts (for all the blurring of genres) of a certain kind (American *literature*).

Let me review the possibilities. In regard to its understanding of language and the nature of communication, on one hand a commitment to dialogism may be seen as a recognition of the necessity of an infinite semantic openness. Here the inescapable possibility of yet some further voice is crucial inasmuch as that voice may decisively alter or ambiguate any relatively stable meaning one might claim to understand. On the other hand, a commitment to dialogism may be seen as a type of radical pluralism, a more relativized openness, concerned with stating meanings provisionally in recognition of the legitimate claims of otherness and difference. In regard to its implied model of the social, a commitment to dialogism may be seen as envisioning, "a carnivalesque arena of diversity," as James Clifford has described it, "a utopian. . . space,"¹² where the utopian exists as a category of pure abstraction, an image out of time and oblivious to the conditions of historical possibility: diversity as limitless freeplay. Or a commitment to dialogism may envision—but here one encounters difficulties, for it is hard to name or describe the sort of democratic and egalitarian community that would be the political equivalent of a radical pluralism as distinct from an infinite openness. No doubt, traditional Native American models of communal organization need further study in this regard, although it is not at all clear how the present-day Pueblo or the nineteenth-century Plains camp circle might be incorporated into models of some harmonious world-community to come.

Let me, then, name the alternative to dialogism as carnival and polymorphous diversity, what Paul Rabinow has called *cosmopolitanism.* "Let us define cosmopolitanism," Rabinow writes, "as an ethos of macro-interdependencies, with an acute consciousness (often forced upon people) of the inescapabilities and particularities of places, characters, historical trajectories, and fates."¹³ The trick is to avoid "reify[ing] local identities or construct[ing] universal ones," a trick, as Rabinow notes, that requires a rather delicate balancing act, one that the West has had a difficult time managing. For all the seeming irony of proposing that the highly place-oriented and more or less homogenous cultures of indigenous Americans might best teach us how to be cosmopolitans, that is exactly what I mean to say. But here let me return to *Storyteller.*

Storyteller is open to a plurality of voices. What keeps it from entering the poststructuralist, postmodernist or schizophrenic heteroglossic domain is its commitment to the equivalent of a normative voice. For all the polyvocal openness of Silko's work, there is always the unabashed commitment to Pueblo ways as a reference point. This may be modified, updated, playfully construed: but its authority is always to be reckoned with. Whatever one understands from any speaker is to be understood in reference to that. Here we find dialogic as dialectic (not, it seems, the case in Bakhtin!), meaning as the interaction of any voiced value whatever and the centered voice of the Pueblo.¹⁴

If this account of *Storyteller's* semantics, or theory of meaning, is at all accurate, it would follow that its political unconscious is more easil conformable to Rabinow's cosmopolitanism than to a utopianized carnival. The social implications of *Storyteller's* dialogism might be a vision of an American cosmopolitanism to come that permits racial and cultural voices at home (in both "residual" and "emerging" forms¹⁵) to speak fully and that opens its ears to other voices abroad. This is an image, to be sure, not a political program; and to imagine the "polyvocal polity" in this way is also utopian, but perhaps only in the sense that it is not yet imminent.

Silko's book says nothing of this, offering neither a theory of communication nor of politics. To take it seriously,

however, is to see it as more than merely evocative, amusing, expressive or informative (to the mainstream reader curious about the exotic ways of marginalized communities). It is to see its art as a matter of values that are most certainly not only aesthetic.

Notes

1. For a fuller account see Arnold Krupat, *For Those Who Come After: A Study of Native American Autobiography* (Berkeley: University of California, 1985).

2. See Samson Occom, "A Short Narrative of My Life," *The Elders Wrote: An Anthology of Early Prose by North American Indians,* ed. Bernd Peyer (Berlin: Dietrich Reimer Verlag, 1982). Occom wrote in 1768; his manuscript reposed in the Dartmouth College Library until its publication by Peyer. Also see Hendrick Aupaumut, "Journal of a Mission to the Western Tribes of Indians," which was written in 1791 and published by B. H. Coates in 1827 in the *Pennsylvania Historical Society Memoirs,* II, part 1, 61–131.

3. This is William Spengemann's trajectory for Western autobiography which he sees as presenting "historical, philosophical, and poetic" forms, and a "movement of autobiography from the biographical to the fictive mode," in his *The Forms of Autobiography: Episodes in the History of a Literary Genre* (New Haven: Yale University Press, 1980) xiv.

4. An earlier and very different version of this paper was summarized as a presentation to the European Association on American Studies Convention (Budapest, Mar. 1986). It will appear in a publication of the selected proceedings of that Convention edited by Steve Ickringill, University of Ulster.

5. I hesitate to offer even a selected bibliography of recent work on Bakhtin, so voluminous are the possibilities. For what use it may be let me mention only two book-length studies. Katerina Clark and Michael Holquist's biography, *Mikhail Bakhtin* (Cambridge: Harvard University Press, 1984), is both indispensable and too-good-to-be-true in its shaping of Bakhtin's life and thought into a coherent, but largely anti-communist, whole. Tzvetan Todorov's *Mikhail Bakhtin: The Dialogical Principle,* trans. Wlad Godzich (Minneapolis: University of Minnesota Press, 1984) is a particularly subtle reading. Denis Donoghue's "Reading Bakhtin," *Raritan* 2 (Fall 1985): 107–19, offers a more sceptical account. The primary volumes in English of Bakhtin's work are *Rabelais and his World,* trans. Helene Iswolsky (Cambridge: MIT Press, 1968); *The Dialogic Imagination: Four Essays by M.M. Bakhtin,* ed. Michael Holquist, trans. Caryl Emerson and Michael Holquist (Austin: University of Texas Press, 1981); and *Problems of Dostoevsky's Poetics,* ed. and trans. Caryl Emerson (Minneapolis: University of Minnesota Press, 1984). The interested reader will find many special issues of journals devoted to Bakhtin, several with extensive bibliographies.

6. Mikhail Bakhtin, *The Dialogic Imagination: Four Essays by M. M. Bakhtin,* ed. Michael Holquist

(Austin: University of Texas Press, 1981) 45. All further quotations from Bakhtin are from this volume and page references will be documented in the text.

7. See Fredric Jameson, "Postmodernism, or The Cultural Logic of Late Capitalism," *New Left Review* 146 (1984): 53-82.

8. See Clifford Geertz, "Blurred Genres: The Refiguration of Social Thought," *Local Knowledge: Further Essays in Interpretive Anthropology* (New York: Basic Books, 1983), originally published 1980.

9. See Marcel Mauss, "A Category of the Human Mind: The Notion of Person; The Notion of Self." In M. Carrithers, S. Collins and S. Lukes, eds., *The Category of the Person: Anthropology, Philosophy, History* (Cambridge: Harvard University Press, 1985).

10. Leslie Marmon Silko, *Storyteller* (New York: Viking Press, 1981) 1. All further page references will be given in the text.

11. In fact there *are* other tellings because many of the stories in *Storyteller* have appeared elsewhere, some of them in several places. (Pieces of Silko's novel, *Ceremony*, also appear elsewhere.) What to make of this? On the one hand it may be that Silko is just trying to get as much mileage as she can out of what she's done, a practice not unknown to both fiction and essay writers, native and non-native. On the other hand, in the context of Native American storytelling, repetition of the "same" story on several different occasions is standard procedure, "originality" or noticeable innovation having no particular value. It should also be noted that the retellings of Silko's stories are not exact reprintings. For example, "The Man to Send Rain Clouds", as it appears in Kenneth Rosen's anthology of the same name (New York: Viking, 1974), and in *Storyteller*, have slight differences. In Rosen's anthology there are numbered sections of the story (one to four), while there are only space breaks in *Storyteller* (no numbers). In the first paragraph of the Rosen version, Levis are "light-blue" while in *Storyteller* they are "light blue"; "blue mountains were still deep in snow" (3) in Rosen while in *Storyteller* "blue mountains were still in snow" (182). If we turn to the story called **"Uncle Tony's Goat"**, in both books, we find differences in the endings. In Rosen the story ends this way:

. . . Tony finished the cup of coffee. "He's probably in Quemado by now."

I thought his voice sounded strong and happy when he said this, and I looked at him again, standing there by the door, ready to go milk the nanny goats. He smiled at me.

"There wasn't ever a goat like that one," he said, "but if that's the way he's going to act, O.K. then. That damn goat got pissed off too easy anyway" (99-100).

The ending in *Storyteller* goes:

. . . "He's probably in Quemado by now."

I looked at him again, standing there by the door, ready to go milk the nanny goats.

"There wasn't ever a goat like that one," he said, "but if that's the way he's going to act, O.K. then. That damn goat got pissed off too easy anyway."

He smiled at me and his voice was strong and happy when he said this (18).

The differences in the first example may not amount to much, while those in the second might suggest a slight change in emphasis; a systematic study of the differences in Silko's retellings (something I have not attempted to do) might tell us something about her development as a writer—or might not be all that substantial. My point here is that Silko's retellings in writing, whether she is aware of this or not (and it is always possible that different versions come into existence as a result of the demands of different editors rather than as a result of Silko's own determinations), tend to parallel what we know of the oral retellings of traditional narrators.

12. James Clifford, "On Ethnographic Authority," *Representations* 1 (Spring 1983): 137.

13. Paul Rabinow, "Representations are Social Facts: Modernity and Post-Modernity in Anthropology," *Writing Culture: The Poetics and Politics of Ethnography*, ed. James Clifford and George E. Marcus (Berkeley: University of California Press, 1986) 258.

14. This would not accord very well with what Silko said of herself in Rosen's 1974 volume, *Voices of the Rainbow* (New York: Viking Press, 1974) where she emphasized that " . . . the way we live is like Marmons. . . somewhere on the fringes . . . our origin is unlike any other. My poetry, my storytelling rise out of this source." As glossed by Alan Velie, from whom I take this quotation, this means like "mixed-blood[s] from a ruling family" (in *Four American Indian Literary Masters: N. Scott Momaday, James Welch, Leslie Marmon Silko, and Gerald Vizenor* (Norman: University of Oklahoma Press, 1982) 107). It goes rather better with what Silko put in her contributor's note to Rosen's 1975 *The Man to Send Rain Clouds*. She wrote, "I am of mixed-breed ancestry, but what I know is Laguna. This place I am from is everything I am as a writer and human being." (176)

15. These are values in relation to "dominant" values as defined by Raymond Williams in "Base and Superstructure in Marxist Cultural Theory," in his *Problems in Materialism and Culture* (London: Verso, 1980) 40ff.

Helen Jaskoski (essay date 1992)

SOURCE: "Words Like Bones," in *CEA Critic*, Vol. 55, No. 1, Fall, 1992, pp. 70-84.

[*In the following essay, Jaskoski maintains that by contextualizing stories between cultures, Silko transforms the Laguna tales in* Storyteller *into universal stories.*]

Out of her own body she pushed
silver thread, light, air
and carried it carefully on the dark, flying
where nothing moved.
Out of her body she extruded
shining wire, life, and wove the light
on the void.
From beyond time,
beyond oak trees and bright clear water flow,
she was given the work of weaving the strands
of her body, her pain, her vision
into creation, and the gift of having created,
to disappear.
After her,
the women and the men weave blankets into tales of
life,
memories of light and ladders,
infinity-eyes, and rain.
After her I sit on my laddered rain-bearing rug
and mend the tear with string.

—Paula Gunn Allen, "Grandmother"

The problem of contextualizing specifically tribal materials faces every Native American writer who presents such materials to a heterogeneous audience. The editors of *New Worlds of Literature,* an ambitious anthology of general literature, print Paula Gunn Allen's poem "Grandmother" with a brief introduction including the following comment by the author: "Language, like a woman, can bring into being what was not in being; it can, like food, transform one set of materials into another set of materials" (Beaty and Hunter 264). The only other annotation is two study questions, which bear examination:

1. What does "out of her own body she pushed / silver thread. . . extruded / shining wire, life, and wove the light / on the void" mean, in your own words?

2. "After" means "patterned on the model of" as well as next in time, and this seems to be the force of the word in the final verse paragraph. But what else in the relationship of speaker to grandmother is implied in the fact that the speaker is mending the rug that, apparently, the grandmother created? (265)

The first question appears to request a paraphrase of literal meaning: A female spider created the universe. The second question goes on to speak about "the rug that, apparently, the grandmother created," although the plain sense of the poem tells us that Grandmother (the spider) wove "the strands / of her body" (not a rug) "into creation" and that it is "the women and the men" who weave blankets "after her" (in both senses).

In Keresan (Laguna) tradition, with which Allen is familiar,[1] Ts'*its*'tc'ina k'o (identified in English translation as Thought-Woman or Thinking Woman), who is also the creator and great mother of Keresan peoples, is also known as Grandmother Spider. Thinking Woman/Grandmother Spider creates things by thinking of them and naming them (Boas 222, 276; Parsons 192; Silko, *Ceremony*). If the editors of *New Worlds of Literature* were familiar with this relevant bit of Keresan myth, which has been noted in discussions of the poem (Bannan; Jahner), one wonders why they suppressed the information. Or to put it another way, what does the student gain by attempting to make the paraphrase called for in study question 1 without knowing

that a Spider Creatrix is being talked about? Does such lack of contextualization invite students to make the same mistaken inferences as the writer of question 2? The difficulty for the student, or for any other reader, is unfamiliarity with the cultural lexicon of the poem. It is likely that the non-Laguna reader has not been introduced to the myths, heroes, stories, history, economy, lifeways, and geography that give meaning and substance to the poem. Mediating Allen's poem to a general audience demands more in the way of gloss than the editors of *New Worlds of Literature* provide.

The problem of contextualization is particularly acute with American Indian texts, which are inarguably "American" yet intractably different from "canonical" American literature. Contextualizing Native American materials has particular relevance for pedagogy: Besides giving access to the inherent richness of the works themselves, it can serve as a paradigm for the process of education.

Here, I will explore issues of contextualization as they are formulated in Leslie Marmon Silko's *Storyteller.* Silko, like Allen, draws on Laguna Pueblo heritage. *Storyteller,* her third book, is a mixed-media production: Composed of traditional tales retold, poems, bits of family history and written short fictions, it defies simple generic classification. *Storyteller* is a self-reflexive work that takes both form and theme from the traditional relationship between storyteller and audience. It challenges every reader to assume the role of storyteller's audience in co-creating text and context. For the non-native reader, the process may lead to a radical decentering, with a refocusing of signification from the putatively marginal Native American perspective. Indeed, the book calls into question whole categories of "center" and "margin," prodding the reader to rethink the means by which such positioning itself is accomplished (Babcock, "Tolerated").

I. STORYTELLER, AUTHOR, READER

Storyteller simultaneously addresses two different audiences, Laguna and non-Laguna. Cultural boundaries and integrity consistently figure in Silko's philosophy and practice. In **"An Old-Time Indian Attack,"** an important early essay, she criticizes writers such as Gary Snyder and Oliver LaFarge for improperly assuming a right to claim Indian materials as their own. For her Laguna audience, then, Silko's task is to validate her claim to the elder's role of teacher: She must establish her right to tell Laguna stories. In addressing a non-Laguna, non-Indian audience, the text invites the reader to participate in creating its meaning, yet it must do so without violating the integrity of cultural materials by complicity in an invalid appropriation. Mediation requires boundaries, but assimilation erases distinction and destroys otherness.

Silko's strategy for accomplishing these complicated interchanges is to reverse a (theoretical) historical development whereby oral story became transformed into written fiction and the function of the author displaced the performance of the storyteller. Michel Foucault's discussion of the concept of author offers a relevant paradigm for Silko's undertaking. While *Storyteller* conforms to the "author-functions" that Foucault says are the only real constituents of the author, it proposes to displace the absent author with the presence of the text *as* storyteller.

Reinventing the text as storyteller involves a radical reconstitution of audience as well as of author. Unlike writing, storytelling is a communal activity requiring the presence of both teller and audience. As Silko puts it, "Storytelling always includes the audience and the listeners, and, in fact, a great deal of the story is believed to be inside the listener, and the storyteller's role is to draw the story out of the listeners" ("Language and Literature" 57). *Storyteller* includes the advice of Hopi elder Helen Sekaquaptewa in *I'isau and the Birds:* "You must be very quiet and listen respectfully. Otherwise the storyteller might get upset and pout and not say another word all night" (254). A different translation of Helen's words affirms even more strongly the constitutive role of the audience in storytelling: "It is known that the storyteller is touchy. If you do not answer she may pout and not tell a story" (Wiget, "Telling the Tale" 299). In *Storyteller,* the author's text continually promises to revoke the frozen certitude of writing and devolve into the dynamic uncertainty of live performance. The reader, then, must assume the constitutive, creative task of the storyteller's audience.

One of *Storyteller*'s many paradigms for the storytelling performance is Silko's retelling of a tale given to her by her Aunt Susie: the story of Waithea, the little girl who ran away from her mother and whose clothes were transformed into butterflies. As Silko develops the text, she presents first a passage of reminiscence about Aunt Susie's background and education; the story proper follows. However, Silko takes care to embed the story of Waithea within a framing account of the storytelling situation and incorporates details of Aunt Susie's demeanor and expression as well as explanations of Laguna words:

> "Yashtoah" is the hardened crust on corn meal mush
> that curls up.
> The very name "yashtoah" means
> it's sort of curled-up, you know, dried,
> just as mush dries on top.
>
> (8)

The story embodies the complexities of audience participation noted earlier. The situation and Aunt Susie's intent are clearly didactic: Teaching of many kinds is going on as Aunt Susie instructs her audience in Pueblo language, geography, and history, thus contextualizing for the real little girl the marvelous experience of the legendary little girl. Silko's own role is complex. On the one hand, young Leslie's figurative presence in the story models the reader's role with respect to *Storyteller:* The reader takes the part of listener/learner, with the text as teller/teacher. On the other hand, Silko as author displaces Aunt Susie as transmitter—and teacher—of the text, while as author she is inevitably absent. The text as presence performs the storytelling function.

Using this story as a model, we may say that following the narrative and absorbing contextual information are activities this book requires of its readers. But this is not enough. The retelling of a traditional story that is printed near the end of *Storyteller* gives readers directions for more active participation in constructing the text. **"Skeleton Fixer,"** which Silko notes is "A Piece of a Bigger Story" (245), retells a version of the ubiquitous Bungling Host "collection."[2] In the opening of Silko's story, an unidentified

woman finds "[w]ords like bones / scattered all over the place" (242). Old Man Badger comes along and reconnects the bones, fitting back together even the ones that are not clearly recognizable, until—surprise!—"Old Coyote Woman jumped up / and took off running" (246). **"Skeleton Fixer"** recapitulates the process of fragmentation and reconstitution required of the reader of *Storyteller,* who must co-create the story by negotiating the apparently scattered, unrelated, and fragmentary texts and illustrations dispersed throughout the book. The synthesizing the reader undertakes will change with each rereading, just as each storytelling situation offers a new version of the "skeleton text."

Neither the process nor the metaphor is new. In the 1840s, Henry Rowe Schoolcraft—arguably the first non-Indian to pay attention to the native literatures of North America—defined the critical and scholarly work required of anyone seeking to understand (and not merely appropriate) the culture of the "Other":

> To seek among ruins, to decipher hieroglyphics, to unravel myths, to study ancient systems of worship and astronomy, and to investigate vocabularies and theories of language are the chief methods before us.. . . Who shall touch the scattered bones of aboriginal history with the spear of truth and cause the skeleton of their ancient society to arise and live? (Williams 303)

Schoolcraft's principles (if not his practice) counter the assumption of *New Worlds of Literature* that New-Critical readings attending exclusively to the internal dynamics of a text, unaided by cultural-contextual information, can revivify "the scattered bones" into anything even faintly resembling what they are supposed to represent.

II. AUTHENTICITY AND MEDIATION

Storyteller figures its diverse audiences and the processes of instruction and mediation it undertakes with respect to those audiences. In a brief vignette at the center of the book, Silko recalls stopping to chat with Nora, a neighbor in the village. Nora's children have brought home a library book with one of Leslie's poems in it: "We all enjoyed it so much," Nora says, "but . . . the way my grandpa used to tell it is longer" (110). Silko responds with a brief analysis of the distinction between writing and storytelling:

> "Yes, that's the trouble with writing," I said,
> "You can't go on and on the way we do
> when we tell stories around here.
> People who aren't used to it get tired."
>
> (110)

This passage brings the Laguna audience within the text, acknowledging the intertextuality of Silko's written and oral materials—even as it suggests for the reader both what is missing and what might be required in approaching the book. *Storyteller* does set out to recapture a sense of the recursive and elaborative "going on and on" of oral storytelling as it plays and replays themes of hunting, planting, rain-bringing, witchcraft, and, of course, storytelling itself (see Danielson, "The Storytellers"; Hirsch; Krupat).

Silko's address to her Laguna audience also involves functions of legitimation and authentication. Deep respect for elders as carriers of truth and tradition characterizes Laguna (and other Native American) values. Leslie Silko's Keresan audience might remark the audacity of a young woman who claims the important role of storyteller.[3] *Storyteller* can be read as a document authorizing Silko's appropriation of the storytelling role, and validating in particular her claim to the role of Laguna, American Indian storyteller. Silko's criticism of Snyder and LaFarge asserts in the strongest terms the background required of the authentic storyteller: "We are taught to remember who we are: our ancestors, our origins. We must know the place we came from because it has shaped us and continues to make us who we are" ("An Old-Time Indian Attack" 213). One function of the family history portions of *Storyteller* is to authenticate Silko's claim to the materials she includes in the book. The introduction of Aunt Susie, then, not only contextualizes the story of Waithea for the non-Indian reader and provides a paradigm for the storytelling experience but also documents the Laguna genealogy of the story and thereby authenticates the teller/author and her right to reproduce the text.

A non-Indian audience also appears in *Storyteller,* explicitly in the inclusion of passages addressed to Lawson Inada and James Wright. Portions of letters to these two writers elaborate the didactic, contextualizing functions of storytelling. Writing to Inada, Silko describes the relationship of storytelling to place, illustrating how and why "we must know the place we came from":

> I remember the stories they used to tell us about places that were meadows full of flowers or about canyons that had wide clear streams. I remember our amazement at these stories of lush grass and running water because the places they spoke of had all changed; the places they spoke of were dry and covered with tumbleweeds and all that was left of the streams were deep arroyos. But I understand now. I will remember this September like they remembered the meadows and streams; I will talk about the yellow beeweed solid on all the hills, and maybe my grandchildren will also be amazed and wonder what has become of the fields of wild asters and all the little toads that sang in the evening. Maybe after they listen to me talking about this rainy lush September they will walk over the sandrock at the old house at Dripping Springs trying to imagine the pools of rainwater and pollywogs of this year. (170)

Stories are important not (just) because they describe an ideal world or an imaginary one, but because they offer crucial information about the real, physical world. The stories Silko heard and the ones she will tell about Dripping Springs contain essential knowledge, hidden by drought from direct observation, about this "place where she comes from."

The letter to James Wright also instructs by example. Silko reflects on rooster stories in her family, on the complicated genealogy of family and story through which she has inherited a particular rooster anecdote, and on the connection between rooster stories of the past—like the one about what happened to Aunt Lillie and Grandpa Marmon's rooster—and her own rooster in the present (226-27). Like other brief, self-contained passages in *Storyteller,* the fragment recapitulates in miniature the exuberant abundance of the whole book (Silko and Wright 6-9, 22). The letters to Inada and Wright also have another mediating function.

Non-Indian readers learn that the text includes them. *Storyteller* addresses them (us) directly and holds out expectations for their (our) participation.

Implicit in the careful delineation of genealogy of story and storyteller is a related project of reclaiming Laguna (and other Native American) materials that have been appropriated by outsiders. Silko comments in *Storyteller* on ethnographers' collections of Laguna materials. Prefacing a redaction of a story told by her great-grandfather Marmon to Elsie Clews Parsons, she says,

> Boas, as it turns out
> was tone-deaf
> and the Laguna language is tonal
> so it is fortunate he allowed Ms. Parsons
> to do the actual collecting of the stories.

(254)

This epic critique of the ethnographic record takes the authenticating function from the outsider—ethnographer, linguist, anthropologist—and reclaims it for the subject's own storytelling voice. It also serves as implicit warning to the "tone-deaf" critic who, though well-intentioned, may engage in the colonizing activity of interpreting a work in ways inappropriate to its context.

III. LANGUAGE AND DIFFERENCE

The synthesizing that *Storyteller* requires of the reader also postulates a dynamic that requires maintaining difference. That is, the text mediates Indian culture to the non-Indian reader precisely by its delineation of boundaries between Indian and non-Indian. This maintaining of boundaries involves another project of reclamation and reinvention: the constitution of an Indian identity.

It is no secret that *Indian* is a construct of the non-Indian world. Gerald Vizenor writes of "the Indian" as an invention that European(ized) society uses to mask its failure to perceive the particular and the human (xxi). Hopi linguist Emory Sekaquaptewa offers the notion "Indian" as a mediating agent, a bridge to be left behind in the encounter with specific tribal reality.[4] Silko, on the other hand, proposes to reappropriate the designation from within. *Storyteller,* reinventing the stories and storytellers of Laguna culture and inventing the reader-listener for them, reclaims and reinvents the Indian as well. Like the reclaiming of Laguna texts long buried in anthropological volumes, Silko's invention of an Indian identity reasserts essential values that she distinguishes from and places over against the other, non-Indian world. In affirming "Indian" as a meaningful concept, *Storyteller* finds the locus of perceptible difference in language. In particular, the contes—the eight written short fictions in *Storyteller*—examine difference to postulate Indian identity.

These contes first of all focus on protagonists and settings from different Indian cultures: an Eskimo woman, an aged Navajo woman, the Apache Geronimo, a Laguna man visiting a Hopi village, a young soldier returning to an unspecified pueblo. All these diverse characters share a perception of their difference from a powerful, threatening world that speaks a different language. Ayah, the old Navajo woman at the center of **"Lullaby,"** reflects on the loss of her children. For many years, she had blamed her husband "because he had taught her to sign her name. Because it was like the old ones always told her about learning their language or any of their ways, it endangered you" (47). In **"Yellow Woman,"** the narrator, a young wife enjoying a romantic interlude with a seductive stranger, perceives that language difference is threatening to a white man the two lovers encounter: "The white man got angry when he heard Silva speak in a language he couldn't understand" (61). The woman's lover uses the tribal language to protect her by explaining how to escape the hostile rancher. In **"Tony's Story,"** Leon, a young veteran just returned to his pueblo, tries to protect the unnerved Tony from a bullying police officer with the excuse that "he doesn't understand English so good" (126; see Ruoff; Evers; Jaskoski, "From the Time"). What these three stories consistently dramatize is the importance of retaining one's tribal language—whatever it may be—as protection against a hostile and encroaching alien power.

Two contes, **"Storyteller"** and **"A Geronimo Story,"** explore in detail the significance of language boundaries. Placed toward the beginning and the end of *Storyteller,* they also suggest a linear thematic development that plays against the book's circular or weblike matrix (Danielson, "Grandmother"). **"Storyteller"** and **"A Geronimo Story"** recapitulate the major themes of *Storyteller*: relationship of story to teller and audience, displacement from the nominally marginal to the subjective point of view, decentering of the non-Indian reader across the boundaries of culture and background.

"Storyteller" traces the thoughts and memories of a Yupik Eskimo woman in a jail in the Arctic bush as she waits to be interrogated about the death of a "Gussuck" (non-Eskimo) storekeeper. The protagonist's attitude contradicts the polyvocality so abundant in the rest of *Storyteller.* Her single-minded adherence to the truth as she sees it is absolute and unyielding: Her story, and hers alone, has any relevance and meaning for her. It is this story, which we have followed through her central consciousness, that she begins to tell to her fellow villagers as **"Storyteller"** draws to an end.

A brooding fatalism hangs over this tragic tale of cruelty, misunderstanding, and revenge; its anonymous characters seem fated to act out some archaic, unfathomable myth. Nature itself seems about to disintegrate: "She told herself it wasn't a good sign for the sky to be indistinguishable from the river ice, frozen solid and white against the earth. The tundra rose up behind the river but all the boundaries between the river and hills and sky were lost in the density of the pale ice" (18–19). The protagonist's vision of nature reflects her perception of the Gussuck world as a hostile, colonizing force bent on dissolving the outlines of her own identity. Although she knows English, she refuses to speak it with the Eskimo jailer or the non-Eskimo attorney. These refusals reenact her previous insistence, at school, on her language as the sign and essence of her integrity: "The dormitory matron pulled down her underpants and whipped her with a leather belt because she refused to speak English" (19). Just as she sees the encroaching cold effacing all boundaries of place and identity in nature, she also realizes that the school's attempt to erase her language is meant to annihilate her as a Yupik woman by a process of assimilation.[5] The protagonist's

unyielding insistence on her truth as the only truth about these events corresponds with her equally rigid insistence on her own language; maintaining impermeable boundaries of language protects her sense of self in a world of imminent annihilation.

"A Geronimo Story," by contrast, choruses with many voices, many stories. The narrator, Andy, recounts a trip he took as a twelve-year-old boy when he rode with his uncle Siteye and other members of the Laguna Regulars under Captain Pratt; they were to assist Major Littlecock as he sought to encounter the legendary Apache chieftain Geronimo. **"A Geronimo Story"** is a deconstructionist parable in which the absence of Geronimo becomes the pretext for a deer hunt, and the subtext is the permeability as well as the toughness of cultural and linguistic boundaries. The story celebrates hunting, storytelling, and the common human ground of difference.

In **"A Geronimo Story,"** as in the contes discussed earlier, language protects identity and assists survival. However, this time it is a white man, Captain Pratt, who invokes the protective value of language—by refusing to translate. Speaking English, Major Littlecock makes a sexual slur against the Laguna men; Siteye responds in kind in Laguna; then, Captain Pratt deflects the potential hostility by lying: "I'm sorry, Major, but I don't speak the Laguna language very well" (221). This conte contrasts the uncompromising assertion of absolute truth that centers **"Storyteller"**: The hapless Littlecock must recognize and yet accept Pratt's obvious prevarication. Above all, **"A Geronimo Story"** insists that "language" is more than lexicon, orthography, or grammar. Although Littlecock lectures Pratt that "it is very useful to speak the Indian languages fluently" and although he himself has "mastered Crow and Arapaho, and. . . [is] fluent in Sioux dialects" (221), he cannot grasp the information about Geronimo's whereabouts that the Laguna scouts try to communicate to him, even though both Siteye and the captain "told him in good English" (220). (The sly sexual implications in the major's name also reflect the easy-going comedy of this tale, in contrast to the sadism and perversions that underlie the ominous, bitter world of **"Storyteller."**)

The Laguna men's commentary on the jokes they make at the expense of Major Littlecock and the white community serves as a gloss on the tragedy of **"Storyteller"** (and of **"Tony's Story"** and **"Yellow Woman"** as well): "Anybody can act violently—there is nothing to it; but not every person is able to destroy his enemy with words" (222). While the nameless protagonist of **"Storyteller"** believes she has destroyed her enemy, she remains within a cycle of violence and retribution, and *the* enemy remains. **"A Geronimo Story"** offers a different view: of boundaries that can be flexible, elastic, a permeable interfacing of differences. There is room for accommodation and compromise. Laguna men ride with U.S. troops, and Siteye admires Captain Pratt for—of all things—his devotion to afternoon tea: "I admire him for that. Not like a white man at all; he has plenty of time for some tea" (215). Captain Pratt is white (as are the storekeeper, priest, and construction workers in **"Storyteller"**), and paradoxically words do destroy him—*as* enemy—when he accepts the Laguna language's deep structure as well as its surface manifestations.

Language vanquishes other enemies as well. Geronimo, another putative enemy, is present only in the tracings he leaves—his abandoned campsites (if they are his) and the stories told about him. Pursued by soldiers and scouts, he retreats forever in an infinite regress of language and story. Poor Littlecock, left without enemies, can only fade away: "His face had a troubled, dissatisfied look; maybe he was wishing for the Sioux country. . . . If he hadn't killed them all, he could still be up there chasing Sioux" (223). This is the paradox of hunting and storytelling (and reading): Success is defeat, for the object is to search—not to find.

"A Geronimo Story" exemplifies the process of contextualization undertaken throughout *Storyteller*. Captain Pratt derives from Silko's great-grandfather, Robert G. Marmon, whose picture with his young wife—Silko's beloved Grandma A'mooh—opens the book. Marmon's image closes the text as well, in a photograph showing him surrounded by sons, son-in-law and two grandsons (the author's father and uncle). A third photograph, numbered 22, shows "The Laguna Regulars in 1928, 43 years after they rode in the Apache Wars" (224, 272). In it, Marmon stands to the far right of the dozen old soldiers standing under a great oak tree. Stories about Captain Pratt that Andy hears in **"A Geronimo Story"** echo details that Silko retells from family anecdotes about her great-grandfather: how he was called "Squaw Man" by his white neighbors (16), how he defended his young grandsons from the insults of an Albuquerque hotelier (17). Thus, *Storyteller* enacts for the reader the process that metamorphoses Robert G. Marmon into Captain Pratt, that invents Andy even as Andy and the scouts invent Geronimo, that reinvents the "history" of the "Apache Wars."

The contes of *Storyteller* decenter the non-Indian reader through language and point of view. Written in English, they are written against English. In every case, the reader is inducted by way of the central consciousness into the world of the Other, the putatively marginal. Kenneth Roemer points out that reconsidering supposedly marginal texts—his example being American Indian texts—can offer insight, available in no other way, into all literature. Silko's stories open for any reader the possibility of transformation that the author attributes to her great-grandfather Marmon: "I see in his eyes /he had come to understand this world /differently" (256). Here, we return to the transformative possibilities of language that Paula Gunn Allen asserts in her comment on Grandmother Spider.

IV. Transformation

The transformation into story of Geronimo and Marmon parallels the transformation of the old storyteller in **"The Storyteller's Escape,"** another of the narrative poems in *Storyteller*. The speaker of **"The Storyteller's Escape"** introduces an aged storyteller. This old woman "has been on every journey /and she knows all the escape stories" (247); she has become storyteller by "turning around /for the last look . . . so I could tell where these dear ones stopped" (248). Pursued by enemies and weakened by age, the old woman cannot go on. But then a child repeats the old storyteller's act: "A'moo'ooh, the child looked back" (250). Through the child's act of sympathetic imagination, the old woman returns: "This is the story she told, /the child who looked back, /the old teller's escape—the story she was thinking of" (253). The old storyteller makes her way home as part of the child's account, there to remain a living part of the community constituted by stories.[6]

"The Storyteller's Escape" in the last pages of *Storyteller* invites the reader back to Aunt Susie's story at the beginning of the book. In the earlier story, the child, Waithea, escapes from her mother; she undergoes transformation into a story even as her clothes metamorphoses into butterflies. In **"The Storyteller's Escape,"** the old storyteller is transformed into her story even as the "child who looked back" becomes the storyteller. The process of transformation and return through "looking back" parallels Leslie Silko's own relationship to Aunt Susie: Silko invents herself as storyteller and author in the process of "looking back" at Aunt Susie and her story and reinventing them for the readers of *Storyteller*.

Storyteller and the issue of contextualization have particular relevance to teaching and learning. Aunt Susie's instruction in Keresan vocabulary is but the overture to the compendium of lessons and models that Silko offers her readers. But contextualizing one's private experience and deepest thoughts in order to express, to communicate, to comprehend and be comprehended, is fundamental to the development of a public self that is the special project of education. Especially in the pluralistic society we live in, both locally and globally, the contextualizing of utterances—written and spoken, authored and received—to make sense of discourse across many ethnic, religious, language, and political boundaries has become critical to address. It is precisely in this way, I believe—by explicitly addressing the question of contextualization across these boundaries—that *Storyteller* reaches out from its local, family, and culture-specific grounding to engage its audience in recovering and repositioning the essential fictions by which we all live. "Storytelling brings us together," Silko says, "despite great distances between cultures, despite great distances in time" ("Language and Literature" 72).[7]

Notes

1. Keres is a linguistic category: Keresan languages and dialects are spoken at several of the New Mexico Indian pueblos, including Laguna, home of Leslie Silko and Paula Gunn Allen. Allen's maternal great-uncle, John M. Gunn, collected and translated Keresan history and literature at the beginning of this century (see Gunn, *Schat Chen*; Allen, *The Sacred Hoop* 282-83).

2. The classification "Bungling Host" comes from the Aarne-Thompson motif index. Among many printed versions of this tale are Tristram P. Coffin's "The Bungling Host" in *Indian Tales of North America* (145-46) and Sam Blowsnake's variations in *The Trickster* (Radin 41-49). T. C. S. Langen defines "version" and "collection" as a theoretical basis for understanding the relationship of individual instances of a given tale to a set of core elements.

3. Barbara Babcock ("At Home No Womens Are Storytellers") analyzes a dynamic of woman artist, traditional role, and change in convention with reference to the ceramics of Helen Cordero. Silko's appropriation of the storyteller role in the medium of print may be compared with Helen Cordero's stylistic and thematic innovations in figural pottery. Silko and Cordero (both members of Keresan pueblos) present their appropriation of material traditionally reserved for elders or males as affirmation rather than critique of tradition.

4. Sekaquaptewa writes,

   To the non-Indian, "Indian" may have some validity. But it does not derive from a particular Indian culture. It is something that has been concocted by the non-Indian.. . . It is a stereotype, and not an accurate reflection of our empirical reality.. . . In terms of bringing awareness of the Indian to the non-Indian, it serves well. Once the non-Indian becomes aware of the existence of Indians and the richness of their cultures, then he is ready to become interested in a specific tribe of Indians. If this is what is happening, then it is a good thing. (41)

   The conceptualization of "non-Indian" seems to require a notion of "Indian," notwithstanding tribally specific definitions of "self" and "not-self." I see Silko's construction of "Indian" emerging as response to the perception of "non-Indian." See Robert F. Berkhofer for analysis of the concept of "the Indian."

5. Kate Shanley Vangen discusses this story as an allegory of response to oppressive colonialism. Numerous autobiographies have documented the Dickensian character of U.S. and Canadian boarding schools for Native children; official policy was to destroy familial and tribal ties, thus extinguishing Indian identity. The autobiographies of Basil Johnston and Helen Sekaquaptewa (*Me and Mine*), for example, offer poignant accounts of this experience. Edgar S. Cahn documents the appalling state of Indian schools into the 1960s, and Roger Dunsmore recounts continuation of counterproductive policies into the 1980s.

6. The poem incorporates a frequent theme of autobiography and legend. Many versions are embedded in song, ceremony, or family history. Frances Densmore glosses the text of a Mandan song with such an account (Densmore 40-45; Jaskoski, "'My Heart Will Go Out'" 126-27); M argot Astrov reprints a Chiricahua Apache version (211-12); Chahadinelli Benally narrates the experience of his grandmother, who escaped from enslavement on a New Mexico ranch and walked by herself some hundred miles home, bearing a child on the way (Johnson 57-74). Silko has commented extensively on how she sees stories and storytelling constituting community; see especially "A Conversation with Leslie Marmon Silko" and "Language and Literature from a Pueblo Indian Perspective." In *Running on the Edge of the Rainbow,* Silko demonstrates storytelling in many modes.

7. Preparation of this paper was assisted by a grant from the California State University Fullerton Foundation.

Works Cited

Allen, Paula Gunn. "Grandmother." Beaty and Hunter, 264-65.

———. *The Sacred Hoop: Recovering the Feminine in American Indian Traditions.* Boston: Beacon, 1986.

Astrov, Margot. *The Winged Serpent.* 1946. Rpt. as *American Indian Prose and Poetry.* New York: Capricorn, 1962.

Babcock, Barbara. "At Home No Womens Are Storytellers: Potteries, Stories, and Politics in Cochiti Pueblo." *Journal of the Southwest* 30 (1988): 356-89.

———. "'A Tolerated Margin of Mess': The Trickster and His Tales Reconsidered." Wiget, *Critical Essays,* 153-84.

Bannan, Helen M. "Spider Woman's Web: Mothers and Daughters in Southwestern Native American Literatures." *The Lost Tradition: Mothers and Daughters in Literature.* Ed. Cathy N. Davidson and E. N. Broner. New York: Ungar, 1980, 268-79.

Beaty, Jerome, and J. Paul Hunter, eds. *New Worlds of Literature.* New York: Norton, 1989.

Berkhofer, Robert F., Jr. *The White Man's Indian: Images of the American Indian from Columbus to the Present.* New York: Random, 1978.

Boas, Franz. *Keresan Texts: Part I.* Vol. 8 of Publications of the American Ethnological Society. New York: American Ethnological Society, 1928.

Cahn, Edgar S., ed. *Our Brother's Keeper: The Indian in White America.* New York: New Community, 1970.

Coffin, Tristram P., ed. *Indian Tales of North America.* Philadelphia: American Folklore Society, 1961.

Danielson, Linda. "*Storyteller*: Grandmother Spider's Web." *Journal of the Southwest* 30 (1988): 325-55.

———. "The Storytellers in *Storyteller.*" *Studies in American Indian Literatures* 2d ser. 1.2 (1989): 21-31.

Densmore, Frances. *Mandan and Hidatsa Music.* BAE Bulletin 80. Washington, DC: Bureau of American Ethnology, 1923.

Dunsmore, Roger. "A Navajo High School and the Truth of Trees." *Studies in American Indian Literatures* 2d ser. 3.2 (1991): 36-40.

Evers, Lawrence J. "The Killing of a New Mexican State Trooper: Ways of Telling an Historical Event." Wiget, *Critical Essays,* 246-61.

Foucault, Michel. "What Is an Author?" *Textual Strategies: Perspectives in Post-Structuralist Criticism.* Ed. Josue V. Harari. Ithaca: Cornell UP, 1979, 141-60.

Gunn, John M. *Schat Chen: History, Traditions and Narratives of the Queres Indians of Laguna and Acoma.* 1917. New York: AMS, 1986.

Hirsch, Bernard A. "'The Telling Which Continues': Oral Tradition and the Written Word in Leslie Marmon Silko's *Storyteller.*" *American Indian Quarterly* 12.4 (1988): 1-26.

Jahner, Elaine. "A Laddered, Rain-Bearing Rug: Paula Gunn Allen's Poetry." *Women and Western American Literature.* Ed. Helen Winter Stauffer and Susan J. Rosowski. Troy NY: Whitston, 1982, 311-25.

Jaskoski, Helen. "From the Time Immemorial: Native American Traditions in Contemporary Short Fiction." *Since Flannery O'Connor: Essays on the Contemporary Short Story.* Ed. Loren Logsdon and Charles W. Mayer. Macomb: Western Illinois UP, 1987, 54-71.

———. "'My Heart Will Go Out': Healing Songs of Native American Women." *International Journal of Women's Studies* 4 (1981): 118-34.

Johnson, Broderick H., ed. *Navajo Stories of the Long Walk*. Tsaile, Navajo Nation, AZ: Navajo Community College P, 1973.

Johnston, Basil. *Indian School Days*. Norman: U. of Oklahoma P, 1989.

Krupat, Arnold. *The Voice in the Margin*. Berkeley: U of California P, 1989.

Langen, T. C. S. "Estoy-eh-muut and the Morphologists." *Studies in American Indian Literatures* 2d ser. 1.1 (1989): 1-12.

Parsons, Elsie Clews. *Pueblo Indian Religion*. 2 vols. Chicago: U of Chicago P, 1939.

Radin, Paul. *The Trickster*. 1956. New York: Schocken, 1978.

Roemer, Kenneth. "The Heuristic Powers of Indian Literatures: What Native Authorship Does to Mainstream Texts." *Studies in American Indian Literatures* 2d ser. 3.2 (1991): 8-21.

Ruoff, A. LaVonne Brown. "Ritual and Renewal: Keres Traditions in the Short Fiction of Leslie Silko." *MELUS* 5 (1978): 2-17.

Sekaquaptewa, Emory. "Hopi Indian Ceremonies." *Seeing with a Native Eye: Essays on Native American Religion*. Ed. Walter Holden Capps. New York: Harper, 1976, 35-43.

Sekaquaptewa, Helen. *I'isau and the Birds*. 1976. Words and Place Videocassette Ser. New York: Clearwater, 1982.

———. *Me and Mine: The Life Story of Helen Sekaquaptewa*. Ed. Louise Udall. Tucson: U of Arizona P, 1969.

Silko, Leslie Marmon. *Ceremony*. New York: Viking, 1977.

———. "A Conversation with Leslie Marmon Silko." *Suntracks* 3.1 (1976): 28-33.

———. "Language and Literature from a Pueblo Indian Perspective." *English Literature: Opening Up the Canon*. Selected papers from the English Institute, 1979. New Series 4. Ed. Leslie A. Fiedler and Houston A. Baker, Jr. Baltimore: Johns Hopkins UP, 1982, 54-72.

———. "An Old-Time Indian Attack Conducted in Two Parts." *The Remembered Earth: An Anthology of Contemporary Native American Literature*. Ed. Geary Hobson. Albuquerque: U of New Mexico P, 1979, 211-15.

———. *Running on the Edge of the Rainbow*. Words and Place Videocassette Ser. New York: Clearwater, 1982.

———. *Storyteller*. New York: Seaver, 1981.

———, and James Wright. *The Delicacy and Strength of Lace. Letters*. Ed. Anne Wright. Saint Paul: Graywolf, 1985.

Thompson, Stith. *Motif Index of Folk-Literature*. 6 vols. Bloomington: Indiana UP, 1955-58.

Vangen, Kate Shanley. "The Devil's Domain: Leslie Silko's 'Storyteller.'" *Coyote Was Here: Essays on Contemporary Native American Literary and Political Mobilization*. Ed. Bo Scholer. Aarhus, Denmark: SEKLOS, U of Aarhus, 1984, 116-23.

Vizenor, Gerald. *Earthdivers: Tribal Narratives on Mixed Descent*. Minneapolis: U of Minnesota P, 1981.

Wiget, Andrew, ed. *Critical Essays on Native American Literature*. Boston: Hall, 1985.

———. "Telling the Tale: A Performance Analysis of a Hopi Coyote Story." *Recovering the Word: Essays on Native American Literature*. Ed. Brian Swann and Arnold Krupat. Berkeley: U of California P, 1987, 297-336.

Williams, Mentor L., ed. *Schoolcraft's Indian Legends*. 1956. Westport: Greenwood, 1974.

Patricia Jones (essay date 1993)

SOURCE: "The Web of Meaning: Naming the Absent Mother, in *Storyteller*," in *"Yellow Woman": Leslie Marmon Silko,* edited by Melody Graulich, Rutgers University Press, 1993, pp. 213-32.

[*In the following essay, Jones analyzes Silko's use of the traditional Yellow Woman myth as a means of presenting the stories of the Laguna woman, her mother, and herself—merging myth and autobiography.*]

> They think
> I am stronger than I am.
> I would tell this like a story
> but where a story should begin
> I am left standing in the beat
> of my silences.
> There has to be someone to name you.
>
> —Wendy Rose, "Naming Power"

Storyteller by Leslie Silko begins with the image of "a tall Hopi basket . . . inside the basket are hundreds of photographs." The form and structure of the text reflect this image; it is a collage of stories, poems, myths, folktales, autobiographical notes, letters and pictures. And, like the photographs in the basket, the subjects are frequently the same—only the details change. Silko tells us that the photographs, many of which were taken by Grandpa Hank, "have always had special significance with the people of my family . . . [They] have a special relationship to the stories/ . . . because many of the stories can be traced in the photographs." The book itself is shaped like a picture album or a scrapbook, creating a certain intimacy and familiarity between text and reader. Silko seems to invite the reader to share with her a personal as well as a mythological, historical and fictional set of memories.

The book is, in fact, autobiographical in the sense that it places the emphasis on the shaping of the author's developing self through the influence of her family and friends, the myths and stories she was told, and the place where she was raised. In an interview with Per Seyersted, Leslie Silko says that she sees *Storyteller* "as a statement about storytelling and the relationship of the people, my family

and my background to the storytelling—a personal statement done in the style of the storytelling tradition, i.e., using stories themselves to explain the dimensions of the
process." By "naming" the people, places and stories that
were important to her, she defines herself through her relationship to the family, the community and the land. Storytelling for Silko is more than "just . . . sitting down and
telling a once-upon-a-time kind of story" (Barnes 86). It is
rather "a whole way of seeing yourself, the people around
you, your life, the place of your life in the bigger context,
not just in terms of nature and location but in terms of
what has gone on before, what has happened to other
people . . . a whole way of being" (Barnes 86). This is a
characteristic Native American point of view according to
Simon Ortiz, who regards storytelling as "a way of life
. . . a trail which I follow in order to be aware as much as
possible of what is around me and what part I am in that
life" (quoted in Lincoln 223). The reader, as he or she
turns the pages of this "album," is privileged to participate
in the journey.

We are introduced to Silko's family through the pictures
and the stories. We see and hear about her father, her sister, Aunt Susie, Grandpa Hank, Uncle Walter, Great Grandmother Anaya, Great Grandfather Marmon, Grandma
A'mooh, Aunt Bessie, Great Grandpa Stagner and his
brother Bill, Grandma Helen and even old Juana, who
raised Grandma Helen. Each photograph tells a story and
the story is "written" in the images present, the juxtaposition between photographs and text, and in the pictures
omitted. We "read" the pictures as we read the myths and
stories, looking for broader connections between them and
Silko's life as she presents it in the text. Terry Eagleton, in
Literary Theory: An Introduction, suggests that "the process of reading . . . is always a dynamic one, a complex
movement . . . unfolding through time" (77). The oral
storytelling tradition which forms the basic structure of
Silko's text involves the reader in such a dynamic process.
The reader, in effect, becomes participant in the text, connecting stories, finishing them, rewriting them, and constructing his or her own stories in the "gaps." These gaps
exist in every text according to Wolfgang Iser in "The
Reading Process" because

> no tale can ever be told in its entirety. . . . [It] is only
> through inevitable omissions that a story gains its dy-
> namism . . . [T]hus whenever the flow is interrupted
> . . . the opportunity is given to us to bring into play
> our own faculty for establishing connections—for fill-
> ing in the gaps left by the text itself.
>
> (55)

The gaps in Silko's *Storyteller,* however, form a greater
and more significant part of the story than those found in
traditional texts. Like many Native American and modern
texts, it is so fragmentary in form that "one's attention is
almost exclusively occupied with the search for connections between fragments" (Iser 55). As we are seduced
into the storytelling session, distinctions blur between the
teller and the told, and where one story ends, a new one
begins.

The most notable gaps and silences in *Storyteller* revolve
around the absence of Silko's mother. In a book that appears to be substantially autobiographical and largely about
the significance of female myths and forebearers, Silko's

mother is mentioned only once in the entire text and then
only in connection with Grandma A'mooh:

> It was a long time before
> I learned that my Grandma A'mooh's
> real name was Marie Anaya Marmon.
> I thought her name really was "A'mooh."
> I realize now it had happened when I was a baby
> and she cared for me while my mother worked.
>
> (33)

Stories about fictional, mythological and surrogate mothers, however, abound in the text. Not only does the book
begin with Aunt Susie who functioned as surrogate mother
to Silko, listening to her, answering her questions, and
passing "down an entire culture / by word of mouth / an
entire history / an entire vision of the world" (5-6), but it
is dominated by the myths and stories of Yellow Woman.
The Yellow Woman myths originate in traditional Cochiti
and Laguna Pueblo stories. There are many versions of the
story of Yellow Woman, but in each telling of the story
Yellow Woman is abducted or seduced by the sexually exciting, potentially dangerous ka'tsina spirit. When she is
drawn to him, her "physical sensations and desire . . .
blot out thoughts of home, family and responsibility"
(Ruoff 12). She leaves her husband and children to follow
him. Sometimes she returns to the family; other times she
does not. This union, however, almost always results in
positive benefits for the tribe. According to Paula Gunn
Allen in *Spider Woman's Granddaughters,* Yellow Woman
may be "a Spirit, a Mother, a blessed ear of corn, an archetype, a person, a daughter . . . an agent of change and
of obscure events, a wanton, an outcast, a girl who runs
off with Navajos, or Zunis, or even Mexicans" (211).
Whichever role she assumes, Yellow Woman functions as
a powerful image of freedom, sexuality, power and creativity. She is simultaneously the "good" mother who fulfills the traditional role of wife and nurturer and the "bad"
mother whose sexuality is a powerful force, capable of
both creation and destruction. As a daughter and as a
woman, Silko must come to terms with the female power
and sexuality she recognizes in her mother and in herself;
she must negotiate the dangerous territory between mother
and daughter, self and other, freedom and responsibility,
saint and wanton. To name her mother is to name herself;
to acknowledge her mother is to acknowledge her own divided self. Silko must, therefore, silence the literal mother
whose power, whose potential for wildness and wanton-
ness, frighten her. Only by putting her into a story, weaving both the mother's and daughter's stories into myths
and stories of Yellow Woman, can Silko find her own
voice, unite the dual aspects of her own psyche, and take
her rightful place in the line of strong women who preceded her.

Like Wendy Rose in "Naming Power," Silko "tells this
like a story" but where we expect her own personal story
to begin, with her own birth, with her own mother, we are
"left standing in the beat / of [her] silences." The mother
becomes simultaneously and paradoxically both absent
from the text, and through her palpable absence, the very
center of the text. This is a crucial "gap" in the text and
one which leads the reader to struggle for connections.
The mother is traditionally the central figure in a child's
life and perhaps even more significantly so in a female

child's life. It is generally through the mother that a daughter defines herself, her sexuality and her place in the world. As Susan Gubar suggests in "The Blank Page and Female Creativity," the gaps and silences in the text, the blank pages "contain all stories in no story, just as silence contains all potential sound and white contains all colors" (305). The absence of the mother implies her importance to Silko's sense of self. Furthermore, Silko's repeated retelling of stories of other mothers and wives, particularly in the form of the Yellow Woman stories, seems to reinforce this significance.

The centrality of the mother figure in Laguna life is discussed by Paula Gunn Allen in "Who is Your Mother? Red Roots of White Feminism." She writes that "at Laguna Pueblo in New Mexico, 'Who is your mother?' is an important question . . . [Y]our mother's identity is the key to your own identity" (209). Clearly Silko, who is of mixed Laguna, Hispanic and Anglo ancestry and who spent much of her childhood in and around the Laguna Pueblo, is aware of the importance of the mother figure on a mythical and metaphorical as well as literal level. The exclusion of the mother, then, from a text that focuses so strongly on the mythological aspects of motherhood, acquires increased significance. Certainly, as readers, we cannot overlook the silence; we must assume that this omission is both intentional and telling. Arnold Krupat suggests in "Post-Structuralism and Oral Tradition" that in reading Native American texts, we must "acknowledge that any meanings which appear to be present are never fully present" and conversely, "meaning (according to Terry Eagleton) . . . is a matter of what the sign is *not* as well as of what the sign seems to be" (128, italics added). The literal absence of the mother, therefore, invites us, as readers, to look for her in Silko's subtexts.

The mother, so conspicuously absent from Silko's personal memories, appears repeatedly in fictional and mythological forms. The opening story is one told by Aunt Susie about "the little girl who ran away" and drowned herself in the lake because her mother "didn't want [her] to have any *yashtoah*" (13). Yet after the child's death, the mother grieves and is "very sad" (14). In her grief, she scatters "the little clothing— / the little *manta* dresses and shawls / the moccasins and the *yashtoah*— / they all turned into butterflies— / all colors of butterflies / *And today they say that acoma has more beautiful butterflies—*" (15). The mother fails, at least in Western terms, to meet the child's needs and desires; yet, ultimately, good results for the community out of the individual tragedy. Aunt Susie's voice, relating the story, reflects this as she "spoke the words of the mother to her daughter / with great tenderness, with great feeling / as if Aunt Susie herself were the mother / . . . But when Aunt Susie came to the place / where the little girl's clothes turned into butterflies / then her voice would change and I could hear the excitement and wonder / and the story wasn't sad any longer" (15). Significantly, it is Aunt Susie, the surrogate mother, who tells this conflicted story of motherhood and establishes the sense of ambivalence and duality that is reflected in the many versions of the Yellow Woman stories that follow in the text.

Motherhood in Silko's stories has a duality that is based in history, tradition and myth and creates conflict for the Native American woman today; motherhood for the Lagunas is greater than a personal and familial state but has implications for the community and for the earth as well. This scope and the conflicts inherent in it are explored in the various tellings of the Yellow Woman stories. In their context Silko opens up the possibility for exploring the many dimensions of motherhood for herself and indirectly for the reader as well. The silences and the gaps in the text allow the reader the freedom to write and rewrite his or her own versions of Silko's stories just as Silko writes and rewrites them herself. The construction of Silko's text integrates the oral tradition into the reader's own experience. Just as Aunt Susie and Aunt Alice told Silko's stories "they had told . . . before but with changes in details," the text is open for our own storytelling. Silko remembers that

> The story was the important thing and little changes here and there were really part of the story. There were even stories about the different versions of stories and how they imagined these differing versions came to be. . . . I've heard tellers begin "The way I heard it was. . . ." and then proceed with another story purportedly a version of a story just told but the story they would tell was a wholly separate story, a new story with an integrity of its own, an offspring, a part of the continuing which storytelling must be.
>
> (227)

In the spirit of such a storytelling tradition, I will tell the stories "the way I heard it was . . . and then proceed with another story," my own version of the story just told and yet a "wholly separate story" as well.

In my first version of the story, I imagine that I am telling the story of Leslie Silko's childhood—the story of a little girl who grew up "around Laguna life without begin immersed in it . . . [living] somewhere on the fringes" (Smith, Allen 188). Silko knew that she was not full Laguna and that

> the white men who came to the Laguna Pueblo Reservation and married Laguna women were the beginning of the half-breed Laguna people like my family, the Marmon family. . . . I suppose at the core of my writing is the attempt to identify what it is to be a half-breed or mixed blooded person; what it is to grow up neither white nor fully traditional Indian.
>
> (Lincoln 233)

Like Yellow Woman, the women in Silko's family had been seduced into marriages that separated them from their culture, leaving Silko "somewhere on the fringes" of Laguna life. If, as Paula Gunn Allen suggests, two of the roles that Yellow Woman may take are that of an outcast and an agent of change, then the responsibility for the isolation and dissonance that Silko feels as a result of her mixed blood lies with the mother. By merging her mother's story and her own with the myth of Yellow Woman, Silko attempts to bring the disparate pieces together, to identify "what it is to be a half-breed." The process of the telling, revising and retelling of the old stories, the conversion of the traditional into the contemporary, binds Silko to her heritage, allowing her, like Yellow Woman, to return home with a new story to tell.

Since Laguna heritage is strongly matrilineal, the mother's story is particularly crucial in identifying the daughter and establishing her place in Laguna society. Women control the houses, the property, the lineage of the children, and many of the decisions about marriages (Fisher 23). The women in Silko's family provided strong role models for her. With her mother away at work, she was raised by "her grandmother Lillie, who had been a Model A mechanic, and her great-grandmother Marie or 'A'mooh,' a full blood from Paguate who . . . had gone to Indian School at Carlisle as soon as her many children were grown" (Seyersted 13). Aunt Susie attended Dickinson College and "when she returned to Laguna / she continued her studies / . . . even as she raised her family / and helped Uncle Walter run their small cattle ranch" (*Storyteller* 3). These women were not only remarkable in their accomplishments but in their ability to mesh the modern, westernized world of formal education and jobs with their traditional values and heritage. Grandma A'mooh "washed her hair in yucca roots and told the child about the old days" (Seyersted 13). Aunt Susie kept the oral tradition of storytelling alive and passed it down to Silko. Silko thinks of these women with affection and pride, saying "I grew up with women who were really strong, women with a good deal of power," but she adds a line which shows how difficult it is for her to reconcile this power with her mother's power, which she sees as negative: "And I think about that, and I try to think about my mother: is there something about the way she and I have gotten along, or how we related to each other? . . . If someone was going to thwart you or frighten you, it would tend to be a woman; you see it coming from your mother, sent by your mother" (Barnes 96-97). She can only "try" to think about her mother.

Silko's mother was a "mixed blood Plains Indian" and she kept Silko on the "customary cradle board until she was a year old" (Seyersted 13). Yet she also went out to work when Silko was a young child leaving Grandma A'mooh and her aunts to mother her. Thus, the mother is both present and absent in Silko's life; she weds the traditional Native American customs of mothering with the Western need to leave the home to work. Since much of Leslie Silko's sense of her place in the community is vested the identity of her mother and her mother's family, this dissonance sets up an inevitable conflict.

> Among the Keres, every individual has a place within the universe—and that place is defined by clan membership. In turn, clan membership is dependent on matrilineal descent. . . . [N]aming your own mother . . . enables people to place you precisely within the universal web of your life, in each of its dimensions: cultural, spiritual, personal, and historical.
>
> (Allen, "Who Is Your Mother?" 209)

Because of her mixed blood, Silko's position in the community was on the periphery. Her house was "situated below the village, close to the river . . . on the fringe of things" (Silko, "A Conversation," 29). She was included in clan activities, but not to the same extent as the full bloods; she helped out at ceremonial dances but did not dance herself (Seyersted 13). Silko seemed to belong nowhere and everywhere. Her place in the community is largely determined by her mother and, if her relationship with her mother is distanced or problematic, the consequences, according to Paula Gunn Allen, are the "same as being lost, isolated, abandoned, self-estranged, and alienated from your own life . . . Failure to know your mother, that is,

your position and its attendant traditions, history, and place in the scheme of things, is failure to remember your significance, your reality, your right relationship to earth and society" ("Who is Your Mother?" 209-210). The issues of motherhood in the literal, the figurative, and the metaphorical sense become central, therefore, to Silko's sense of self—her identity both as an individual and as a part of the whole.

Silko, then, must write about her mother in order to understand herself and her place in the community. Yet as Adrienne Rich points out in *Of Woman Born,* "the cathexis between mother and daughter—essential, distorted, misused—is the great unwritten story" (225). The daughter must both identify with and separate from the mother. It is difficult to see our own mothers in any way other than through their relationship to us, and if that relationship is conflicted, as it often is, we must look for our mother's stories and our own story in the stories of other women. It is both difficult and threatening to imagine our mothers with sexual and emotional needs similar to, yet separate from, our own. It is hard, in fact, to acknowledge those same feelings in ourselves. We, too, are daughters, and perhaps mothers, and in these roles, we bury the stories of our own sexuality as deeply as we do those of our mothers. Our sexuality makes us vulnerable and leaves us open to seduction. We are seduced by men, by words, by stories, by the experiences of others, and by our own needs and desires. The repeated storytelling of the Yellow Woman stories in *Storyteller* is an attempt on Silko's part to place her life in a larger context—to grapple with the sexuality and seduction of her mother, her grandmothers, herself and her people, to create a new story, a new myth, out of the old stories and the fabric of her life.

In *Storyteller,* the story of Yellow Woman is told at least six different times and each telling is both the same and different from the preceding telling. The effect of this succession of stories, merged with the content of each story, suggests that, like Silko, we all are caught in a web of storytelling in which the mythical stories that we have known since "time immemorial" inform the patterns that our lives take, the stories that we will live. Kenneth Lincoln in *Native American Renaissance* says that

> Words are believed to carry the power to make things happen, ritualized in song, sacred story, and prayer. This natural force is at once common as daily speech and people's names. The empowering primacy of language weds people with their native environment: an experience or object or person exists interpenetrant with all other creation, inseparable from its name. And names allow people to see themselves and the things around them, as words image the spirits in the world.
>
> (143)

The act of telling and of naming is an act of creation. Naming makes it so. In the Yellow Woman stories, Silko tries out a variety of stories and myths, telling each from a different stance. She tells traditional stories, mythological stories, modern versions, versions in which Yellow Woman goes home to her family and versions in which Yellow Woman is killed. Some stories are funny and others are sad; some stories are cynical and brittle, others are lyrical and touching. It is as though Silko tries on a new persona for each story, envisioning both herself and her mother as the Yellow Woman of the story, exploring the choices available to women and the compelling needs and desires that drive women to make those choices.

In **"Yellow Woman,"** it is the act of telling and naming that transverses the distance between myth and reality, between story and life, and merges the two into one. The stranger by the river calls the woman **"Yellow Woman,"** and she is seduced into the story, drawn inextricably into its pattern. She follows Silva: she "did not decide to go . . . [She] just went. Moonflowers blossom in the sand hills before dawn, just as . . . [she] followed him." Like the pattern in a spider web, the replication is inevitable. She wonders if

> Yellow Woman had known who she was—if she knew that she would become part of the stories. Maybe she'd had another name that her husband and relatives called her so that only the ka'tsina from the north and the storytellers would know her as Yellow Woman.

The story becomes her story. When Silko tells the story, it becomes her story as well; both Silko and Yellow Woman are "drawn inextricably into [the] . . . pattern" of the stories they create. Yellow Woman thinks that she "will see someone . . . and then I will be certain that he is only a man . . . and I will be sure that I am not Yellow Woman. Because she is from out of time past and I live now and I've been to school and there are highways and pickup trucks that Yellow Woman never saw." But all she can know is the moment. All she can feel is "the way he felt, warm, damp, his body beside me. This is the way it happens in the stories, I was thinking, with no thought beyond the moment." Perhaps we all live only in the moment and the moment is beyond our control, our stories written and determined by the stories that have gone before, that have already been told; we live out the stories unaware that we are recreating new versions of old stories and it is only in the telling that the patterns become real. In an interview in *Sun Tracks,* Silko suggests that "you know you belong if the stories incorporate you into them. There have to be stories . . . People tell . . . stories about you and your family . . . and they begin to create your identity. In a sense you are told who you are or you know who you are by the stories that are told about you" (29-30). Our very lives are an act of creation—making new versions of old stories for future storytellers.

Silva tells Yellow Woman that "someday they will talk about us and they will say, 'Those two lived long ago when things like that happened.'" And Yellow Woman knows that "if old Grandpa weren't dead he would tell them what happened—he would laugh and say 'Stolen by a ka'tsina, a mountain spirit. She'll come home—they usually do.'" In the end Yellow Woman decides to tell them "that some Navajo had kidnapped me, but I was sorry that old Grandpa wasn't alive to hear my story because it was the Yellow Woman stories he liked to tell best." In the telling, the story will become a new legend, a new myth, reinforcing the pattern that will inform the next story. As Elaine Jahner suggests, "transmission of the knowledge of 'stories,' . . . involves not only the sharing of knowledge but the sharing of how knowledge has been shaped through one's living with it" (41–42). It is through such stories that Silko is able to integrate past and present, to resolve the conflicts and to restore balance in her life.

In each telling of the Yellow Woman story, Yellow Woman abandons her family and goes off with the ka'tsina spirit, drawn to "his skin slippery against [hers]." Each time her actions are understandable, forgivable, inevitable. This story leads me back to the gaps, the silences, in the text about Silko's own mother. I imagine that this contemporary version of the myth is Silko rewriting her mother's story, justifying her mother's actions. In the story we are told that the "mother and grandmother will raise the baby like they raised me. Al will find someone else, and they will go on like before, except that there will be a story about the way I disappeared while I was walking along the river." Whether Silko actually felt abandoned by her mother physically, emotionally or spiritually is not relevant for, as Silko reminds the reader, "sometimes what we call 'memory' and what we call 'imagination' are not so easily distinguished." The telling of the story makes it real, turns pain into celebration.

Yet, in writing the Yellow Woman story, I imagine that Silko not only rewrites her mother's story, but writes her own story as well. This is a story conceived in both memory and imagination and its genesis is in both the myth and the modern world. In the *Sun Tracks* interview, Silko tells us that girls meet boyfriends and lovers at the river and that she used to

> wander around down there herself and try to imagine walking around the bend and just happening to stumble upon some beautiful man. Later on I realized that these kinds of things that I was doing when I was fifteen are exactly the kinds of things out of which stories like the Yellow Woman story [came]. I finally put the two together: the adolescent longings and the old stories, that plus the stories around Laguna at that time about people who did, in fact, just in recent times, use the river as a meeting place.
>
> (29)

Silko weaves together both her own stories and her mother's stories and in the process explores the power and dimensions of female sexuality. In the Yellow Woman stories, women are overcome time and again by their own overpowering passion. They are almost unhesitatingly willing to abandon one life for another. These women must negotiate between two worlds—the world of the family and that of self. The Native American version of this conflict, however, differs significantly from the Western version. In the Western tradition the mother who leaves her family is punished; in the Native American tradition she is celebrated. The Yellow Woman stories validate female sexuality, viewing the wildness and passion that leads to such improper, non-conformist behavior as an ultimately creative act. This sense of self as a sensual and sexual being may at certain times even work for the greater good of the community. Simon Ortiz suggests that "pueblo societies see the survival of the group as more important than the existence of the individual . . . [and] man as a minute part of an immense natural cycle" (Seyersted 17). The perpetuation of that cycle serves to "bring new blood into the pueblo [and] Yellow Woman becomes a symbol of renewal through liaisons with outside forces" (Ruoff 10). The sexual act, then, "channels the awesome power and energy of our human sexuality—the preserve of wilderness in human beings—into socially useful channels" (Smith, Allen 178). Accordingly, women who step outside the bonds of propriety often bring not disgrace but great good to the tribe. This pattern is reflected repeatedly in the various versions of the Yellow Woman stories.

In **"Cottonwood Part One: Story of Sun House,"** Yellow Woman leaves "precise stone rooms / that hold the heart silently" and "her home / her clan / and the people / (three small children / the youngest just weaned / her husband away cutting firewood)" (*Storyteller* 64). She is seduced by the "colors of the sun," in the form of a spirit who is the sun himself. She is inextricably drawn to him despite the fact that "the people may not understand." She does it "for the world / to continue / Out of love for this earth / cottonwood / sandstone / and sky." Because of her actions the sun comes again and again "out of the Sun House," and the earth will not freeze over and die.

This pattern is repeated in **"Cottonwood Part Two: Buffalo Story,"** in which Yellow Woman's actions result in bringing food to her people in a time of drought and starvation. Yellow Woman, who goes out searching for "water to carry back to her family," is seduced by "water . . . churning . . . [where] something very large had muddied the water." Frightened by her own sexuality, she turns "to hurry away / because she didn't want to find out," but it is too late. She is seduced by a spirit who is "very good to look at / . . . she had never seen anyone like him / It was Buffalo Man who was very beautiful," and when he says "Come with me," she follows. She is killed by her husband when he discovers she is unwilling to leave the Buffalo people whom she "loves." Yet, her death results in plentiful meat for her tribe. The community benefits from her actions:

> It was all because
> one time long ago
> our daughter, our sister Kochininako
> went away with them.
>
> (76)

Seduction stories follow one after the other and whether **"Yellow Woman"** (or her contemporary counterpart) is abducted by "that Mexican / at Seama feast," or "three Navajo men / headed north along / the Rio Puerco river / in a red '56 Ford" or is seduced "Outside the dance hall door / late Friday night / in the summertime," the result is always the same. When she is asked "Have you seen the way stars shine / up there in the sand hills?" she usually says "No. Will you show me?" The result of this acknowledgement and acting out of human sexuality generally climaxes in a positive outcome for the community or tribe in the form of the birth of magical children, the acquisition of food or water in time of need, or the gift of a new ceremony. Female sexuality is seen as a positive and creative force in the world, even outside the bonds of marriage.

I imagine that there is another story embedded in this story, however, and it is the story of the land. In **"Lullaby,"** Silko writes "The earth is your mother / she holds you / . . . There never was a time / when this / was not so" (51). The earth, as mother, is connected to the human, animal and spiritual world as mother/woman is to a lover. In an interview with Kim Barnes, Silko suggests that

> What's operating in those stories of Kochininako is this attraction, this passion, this connection between the human world and the animal and spirit worlds. Buffalo Man is a buffalo, and he can be in the form of a buffalo, but there is this link, and the link is sealed with sexual intimacy, which is emblematic of that joining of two worlds. . . . there's a real overpowering sexual attraction that's felt. The attraction is symbolized by or typified by the kind of sexual power that draws her to the buffalo man, but the power which draws her to Buffalo Man is actually the human, the link, the animal and human world, those two being drawn together. It's that power that's really operating, and the sexual nature of it is just a metaphor for that power.
>
> (95-96)

So Silko weaves a new story out of the old one—a story about power, sex, love and the earth. Intercourse occurs between mother earth and the spirit and animal world. And, like the other seductions in the Yellow Woman stories, this union results in good for the earth and the community. The mother, as sexual and sensual being as well as mother figure, is of central importance. For Silko to acknowledge and understand her own sexuality as well as her mother's, she must see it in the greater context of mother as earth as well as mother as individual. She must see sexuality as ultimately creative and productive; she must once again tell the story so that the mother's choice between self and child is not only an acceptable but a necessary act. Smith and Allen write:

> In such comings-together of persons and spirits, the land and the people engage in a ritual dialogue. . . . The ultimate purpose of such ritual abductions and seductions is to transfer knowledge from the spirit world to the human sphere. . . . the human woman makes little attempt either to resist or to tame the spirit-man who abducts her. Nor do men . . . attempt to control or dominate [the women]. . . . the human protagonists usually engage willingly in literal sexual intercourse with the spirits. . . . This act brings the land's power, spirit, and fecundity in touch with their own, and so ultimately yields benefit for their people.
>
> (178)

The mother who acknowledges her own sexuality and who acts on that acknowledgment offers men and women a paradigm for healthy and whole relationships with each other; a woman's role as wife, mother, earth is no longer viewed as constricting but as liberating.

This connection to the land must be particularly important to Silko. Today the Jackpile Mine is located in Laguna land, near Pagute. It is the largest open pit uranium mine in existence. The deepest uranium mine shaft is sunk into Mt. Taylor, the sacred Laguna mountain, which is the traditional home of the ka'tsina spirit. These mines have brought economic prosperity to Laguna but at the same time cancer is spreading at an alarming rate; the number of children born with birth defects at Laguna is growing significantly; the ecosystem is contaminated and drinking water has radiation levels two hundred times greater than those considered safe (Seyersted 12). If the mother is to survive, if the earth is to survive, Silko suggests that the relationship between the spiritual, the physical and the human must be one of passion, intercourse and love: We must sleep "with the river" and find "he is warmer than any man." We must listen to voices and stories that inform us:

Aging with the rock
of this ancient land
I give myself to the earth,
merge
my red feet on the mesa like rust, root
in this place with my mothers before me,
balance end by end like a rainbow
between the two points of my birth, dance
into shapes that search the sky for clouds
filled with fertile water.
Across asphalt canyons, bridging river
after river, a thirty year old woman
is waiting for her name.

Like this speaker from Wendy Rose's "Naming Power," through accepting and embracing our own passion and sexuality we can "give [ourselves] to the earth," connect with and come to understand "[our] mothers before [us]," and in so doing, achieve a "balance . . . like a rainbow."

The stories merge and converge. The absent mother at the center of the text is the figure around which all the other figures revolve. Each story is her story, Silko's story, and, in a sense, our story also. Just as the stories can be traced in the photographs in the Hopi basket, the stories are told through the blank pages, the silences, and the gaps in the text. When we look through Silko's album of pictures, the absence of a picture of her mother tells a story just as loudly as the presence of the pictures of others. Iser says in "The Reading Process" that

> although we rarely notice it, we are all the time engaged in constructing hypotheses about the meaning of the text. The reader makes implicit connections, fills in the gaps, draws inferences and tests our hunches. . . . [T]he text itself is really no more than a series of "cues" to the reader, invitations to construct a piece of language into meaning.
>
> (76)

The series of stories about Yellow Woman, like the pictures, each serve as a different pose, a different landscape, but the subject remains the same—the identity of woman as mother and wife and the tensions between those roles and her sexuality, creativity and productivity. In leafing through the album, telling the stories of the pictures, we see ourselves as well as others. Similarly, in reading the "gaps" in the text, we come to know a series of stories—some of them our own.

In Silko's **Storyteller,** we must listen to the silence as well as the words, and out of that silence construct our own stories to propel us into the future and connect us to the past. Leslie Silko is the storyteller and

> The storyteller keeps the stories
> all the escape stories
> she says "With these stories of ours
> we can escape almost anything
> with these stories we will survive."
> *"The Storyteller's Escape"*
>
> (247)

Works Cited

Allen, Paula Gunn. "Cochiti and Laguna Pueblo Traditional Yellow Woman Stories." *Spider Woman's Granddaughters: Traditional Tales and Contemporary Writing by Native American Women.* Edited by Paula Gunn Allen. New York: Fawcett Columbine, 1989, 210-218.

———. "Who is Your Mother?: Red Roots of White Feminism." *The Sacred Hoop: Recovering the Feminine in American Indians Traditions.* Boston: Beacon Press, 1986, 209-221.

Barnes, Kim. "A Leslie Marmon Silko Interview." *The Journal of Ethnic Studies* 134 (1986): 83-105.

Eagleton, Terry. *Literary Theory: An Introduction.* Minneapolis: University of Minnesota Press, 1983.

Fisher, Dexter. "Stories and Their Tellers—A Conversation with Leslie Marmon Silko." *The Third Woman: Minority Women Writers of the United States.* Edited by Dexter Fisher. Boston: Houghton Mifflin, 1980, 18-23.

Gubar, Susan. "The Blank Page and Female Creativity." *The New Feminist Criticism.* Edited by Elaine Showalter. New York: Pantheon Books, 1985, 292-313.

Iser, Wolfgang. "The Reading Process: A Phenomenological Approach." The Johns Hopkins University Press, 1980, 50-69.

Jahner, Elaine. "An Act of Attention: Event Structure in *Ceremony.*" *American Indian Quarterly* 5.1 (1979): 34-47.

Krupat, Arnold. "Post-Structuralism and Oral Tradition." *Recovering the Word: Essays on Native American Literature.* Edited by Brian Swann and Arnold Krupat. Berkeley: University of California Press, 1987, 113-128.

Lincoln, Kenneth. "Grandmother Storyteller: Leslie Silko." *Native American Renaissance.* Los Angeles: University of California Press, 1983, 222-250.

Rich, Adrienne. *Of Woman Born.* New York: W. W. Norton & Company, 1986.

Rose, Wendy. "Naming Power." *That's What She Said: Contemporary Poetry and Fiction by Native American Women.* Edited by Rayna Green. Bloomington: Indiana University Press, 1984, 218-220.

Ruoff, A. LaVonne. "Ritual and Renewal: Keres Traditions in the Short Fiction of Leslie Silko." *MELUS* 5.4 (1978): 2-17.

Seyersted, Per. *Leslie Marmon Silko.* Western Writers Series 45. Boise: State University, 1980.

Silko, Leslie. "A Conversation with Leslie Marmon Silko." *Sun Tracks* 3.1 (1977): 29-32.

———. *Storyteller.* New York: Seaver Books, 1981.

Smith, Patricia Clark and Paula Gunn Allen. "Earthly Relations, Carnal Knowledge: Southwestern American Indian Women Writers and Landscape." *The Desert is No Lady.* Edited by Vera Norwood and Janice Monk. New Haven: Yale University Press, 1987, 174-196.

Linda J. Krumholz (essay date 1994)

SOURCE: "'To Understand This World Differently': Reading and Subversion in Leslie Marmon Silko's *Storyteller,*" in *Ariel,* Vol. 25, No. 1, January, 1994, pp. 89-113.

[*In the essay below, Krumholz describes Silko's attempts to engage non-Native American readers in* Storyteller *in order to inform their understanding of Laguna culture.*]

Leslie Marmon Silko's *Storyteller* is a book of stories and a book about stories: it contains traditional Pueblo Indian stories, Silko's family stories, poems, conventional European style short stories, gossip stories, and photographs, all woven together to create a self-reflexive text that examines the cyclical role of stories in recounting and generating meaning for individuals, communities, and nations. *Storyteller* has been described as an uniquely Native American form of autobiography and as a simulation of the oral tradition in written form.[1] The book simulates the oral tradition both in the compilation of many stories that create their own interpretive context (functioning like an oral community) and in the lack of discrimination made between the many kinds of stories. By eliding distinctions between genres and between old and new stories, Silko creates a dynamic juxtaposition that duplicates the way in which meaning is created in the oral tradition through a constant interaction between the stories and the material circumstances of the community, between the old stories and the on-going creation of meaning. Her image for the oral tradition is a web: strong, flexible, resilient, ever-changing, interconnected, and in dynamic relationship with the rest of the world.

Silko's book functions in the "contact zone," a phrase coined by Mary Louise Pratt to describe "social spaces where cultures meet, clash, and grapple with each other, often in contexts of highly asymmetrical relations of power, such as colonialism, slavery, or their aftermaths as they are lived out in many parts of the world today" (444). Pratt describes a certain kind of text created by the colonized or conquered, by those made "other" by the dominating social group, as an "autoethnographic text," "a text in which people undertake to describe themselves in ways that engage with representations others have made of them" (445). Pratt argues that

> [autoethnographic texts] involve a selective collaboration with and appropriation of idioms of the metropolis or the conqueror. These are merged or infiltrated to varying degrees with indigenous idioms to create self-representations intended to intervene in metropolitan modes of understanding. Autoethnographic works are often addressed to both metropolitan audiences and the speaker's own community. Their reception is thus highly indeterminate.
>
> (445-46)

Silko's *Storyteller* is an autoethnographic text, a book that engages with the dominant representations of Native Americans in order to appropriate and transform those representations. The book contains many of the forms of expression and faces many of the perils that, according to Pratt, distinguish writing in the contact zone:

> Autoethnography, transculturation, critique, collaboration, bilingualism, mediation, parody, denunciation, imaginary dialogue, vernacular expression—these are some of the literate arts of the contact zone. Miscomprehension, incomprehension, dead letters, unread masterpieces, absolute heterogeneity of meaning—these are some of the perils of writing in the contract zone. (450)

Pratt emphasizes the perilous and indeterminate nature of the reception of texts in the contact zone. In this essay I focus on the role of the reader in Silko's book in an attempt to negotiate the charged terrain of the contact zone. I read *Storyteller* as a ritual of initiation for the reader into a Laguna Pueblo representation and understanding of the world, a reading that emphasizes the potential for the text to transform consciousness and social structures. Finally, I consider the position of literary criticism and my own work in this paper within this contact zone.

Silko explains in a talk entitled "Language and Literature from a Pueblo Indian Perspective" that "a great deal of the story is believed to be inside the listener, and the storyteller's role is to draw the story out of the listeners. This kind of shared experience grows out of a strong community base" (57). But how does the storyteller address both those inside the community base and those outside it as well? In describing *Storyteller* as an autoethnography and as an initiation for the reader, I will focus on the reader as outsider, the non-Laguna and non-Indian reader. What serves as an act of transformation for a non-Indian reader may serve as an affirmation for the Indian reader. But insofar as Silko engages with and challenges the dominant representations of Native Americans, she confronts the ideologies that all "Americans" are subject to in varying degrees—many Native Americans have also been educated in Euroamerican schools, for example. Silko begins *Storyteller* with stories that correlate with, and repudiate, the Euroamerican representation in which American Indians are tragic figures, scattered remnants of a dying culture. As the reader moves through the book, she or he gains greater familiarity with Native American stories and perspectives, until the final stories of the book use the humour and subversion of Coyote stories, stories of the quintessential Native American trickster, to show the vitality and humour of Indian culture, while also laughing at the dominant representations of power, of history, and of American Indians. Silko engages with the terms of the dominant culture and then moves them progressively into a Laguna context, shifting the reader's perspective from one interpretive position to another. Thus Silko creates "resistance literature"; she appropriates the terms of the colonizer in order to change forms of representation, to change readers, and to change the world.[2]

One of the central ways that Silko challenges dominant representations of Native Americans is by contesting the relegation of Native Americans to the past, and by breaking down the oral/written distinction that is used to support the past/present (them/us) dichotomy. Native American arts and storytelling were for a long time in the academic purview of anthropology, and European anthropologist Johannes Fabian argues that anthropological temporal categories served to construct the colonized "other" as part of the past, excluded from contemporaneity, in order to justify the colonial mission. He writes:

> Anthropology contributed above all to the intellectual justification of the colonial enterprise. It gave to politics and economics—both concerned with human Time—a firm belief in "natural," ie., evolutionary Time. It promoted a scheme in terms of which not only past cultures, but all living societies were irrevocably placed on a temporal slope, a stream of Time—some upstream, others downstream. Civilization, evolution, development, acculturation, modernization (and their cousins industrialization, urbanization) are all terms whose conceptual content derives from whatever ethical, or un-

ethical, intentions they may express. A discourse employing terms such as primitive, savage (but also tribal, traditional, Third World, or whatever euphemism is current) does not think, or observe, or critically study, the "primitive"; it thinks, observes, studies *in terms of* the primitive. *Primitive* being essentially a temporal concept, is a category, not an object, of Western thought. (17-18)

Clearly Fabian's analysis of Western temporal categories applies to the colonization of the United States, a colonization justified by a narrative in which Europeans discovered a New World that was empty except for a few nomadic savages who could only profit from contact with a more advanced society, primitives who needed to be brought from the past to the present (even if it killed them). There are also other contemporary manifestations of this evolutionary time concept, as in romantic ideas of Native Americans—new versions of the "noble savage"—that relegate them to some idyllic past to which other Americans wish they could return. Jimmie Durham, a Cherokee artist and writer, states that in "the United States, people phrase their questions about Indians in the past tense" (424).

The distinction between oral and written cultures has been used in anthropology to define the preliterate, prehistorical, and primitive (that is, static and dead) cultures in opposition to the literate, historical, and, by implication, contemporary (European) people. These reified divisions between oral and literate cultures have been criticized by contemporary Euroamerican anthropologists, such as Joel Sherzer and Anthony Woodbury, who argue that

> [some statements describing an oral/written distinction] do not come to terms with the nature of oral discourse, but tend rather to take written discourse as a model and then view oral discourse as less complicated, less advanced, and seemingly deficient in relation to the written texts of literate, technological societies. . . . there is no simple dichotomy between oral and written discourse, between nonliterate and literate societies. Rather there is considerable and quite interesting continuity between the oral and the written, showing diversity within each: There are oral genres in Native America that have such "written" properties as fixed text, "planning," and abstraction form context, and written genres in European-based societies have such "oral" properties as spontaneity and "repair," scansion into pause phrases, and context-dependent interpretability. (9-10)

In *Storyteller,* Silko challenges the distinctions between oral and written by constructing the written as a secondary and diminished version not simply of verbal presence but of the entire dynamic situation of place, people, and stories in the oral community.

Silko also works against the representations of traditional Native American stories as simplistic and static, without any contemporary applicability or pleasure, ideas perpetuated by anthropologists' stylistic choices in transcription and translation. Silko disdains the work of ethnologists Franz Boas and Elsie Clews Parsons, who "collected" stories of the Laguna Pueblo in their book *Keresan Texts* in order to preserve what they considered a dying culture ("A Conversation" 30). Dennis Tedlock, a Euroamerican anthropologist, has also criticized Boas's and Parsons's methods of transcription and translation as another way of rendering Native American people as primitive precursors. He writes:

> [When translating from oral to written] the direction of movement is opposite to that of translation as practiced between two written traditions: whereas the professional translator brings what was said in another language across into the saying of his own, the professional linguist takes his own language partway across to the other, artificially creating a new variety of broken English. Not only that, but as Dell Hymes has pointed out, those who wish to keep what was said in the other language at a great distance, whether giving it the status of an early link in their own evolutionary past or filling out the spaces in a literary bestiary, will even take this broken English as a sign of authenticity.[12]

Tedlock proposes that Native American oral narratives should be written on the page like dramatic poetry to emphasize oral and performative stylistics as they shape the meaning and aesthetics of oral narratives, thereby stressing the continuity of forms between the oral and the written. Silko uses some of the typographical devices that Tedlock suggests (not necessarily at his urging). She uses the ends of lines to indicate verbal pauses, she indents to indicate visually the structural importance of repetition, and she uses italics to indicate verbal asides to the audience. These textual indicators control the pacing and reception of the stories, increasing the accessibility and emphasizing the poetic and narrative effects for readers. Silko also blurs the distinction between oral Pueblo stories and written short stories as *Storyteller* progresses, in part by rendering them all in writing, but also by obscuring the formal differences on the page until in the final stories the forms of poetry, traditional stories, and European style short stories are virtually indistinguishable.

While blurring the distinctions between oral and written arts and asserting the contemporaneity of Native American verbal arts, Silko also carries Native American concepts of language into her written text. In Native American oral traditions, language is neither a lens offering a mimetic representation nor a problematic social structure—language has the power to create and transform reality. Numerous students of Native American culture have noted the efficacious power of the word. Kenneth Lincoln offers a description of "tribal poetics": "Ideally generative, words make things happen in Native America; language is the source of the world in itself" (20). Elsewhere, Brian Swann writes, "The Word, in fact, is a sacrament, a vital force, so that, for instance, a hunting song is not just a pleasant aesthetic experience, but possesses an active relationship with the hunting act" (xi). He elaborates: "A truly sacramental sense of language means that object and word are so fused that their creation, the 'event,' is itself creative, bringing into this time and place the enduring powers which truly effect that which the event claims, and such action cannot be undone" (xii). The term "sacramental," with its religious echoes, conveys a spiritual concept in which a symbol becomes what it symbolizes—there is no gap between signifier and signified. The spoken word is thus a powerful creative or destructive force.

The creative and transformative power of language connects linguistic acts to the transformative processes of ritual. Storytelling is a central element in Native American rituals, and Silko refers to the creative and destructive powers of language throughout *Storyteller.* Anthropological theories of ritual and liminality may be applicable to all acts of reading. But I wish to connect Silko's *Storyteller* to ritual in order to propose the transformative potential of this book in its particular position in the contact zone and to read the structure of the work as a tool in the transformative process.

Rituals are formal events in which symbolic representations, such as dance, song, story, and other activities are spiritually and communally endowed with the power to shape real relations in the world. The anthropologist Victor Turner divides the ritual process into three stages: rites of separation, rites of limen or margin, and rites of reaggregation or integration ("Are There Universals?" 8-18). Turner theorizes "marginality" or "liminality" as a space and time within ritual in which social classifications break down and social relations are transformed. The rites of separation and reaggregation frame and mediate between the social structure and the status-free experience of liminality. Within the limen, a time and space outside of categories is created, a place where dangers have free play within the limits set by the ritual. This is the arena of the "other" where the power of mystery supercedes the power of the social structure. Within the limen all participants, having temporarily put off their status, will see the world differently. Ritual thus creates a time and space in which the non-differentiation of *communitas* and the powers of otherness can break into, while being contained within, the preexisting power structures in the society (*Ritual Process* 128).[3]

Turner's three phases of ritual can also describe the process of reading, in which ritual processes of separation and reaggregation are compared to the (less formalized) actions of sitting alone with a book and then putting the book down. In this analogy, the act of reading correlates to the liminal phase of ritual. Liminality, according to Turner, is the central phase of ritual, a pedagogical phase in which neophytes about to be initiated are all of equal status outside of structures of social order while a ritual leader has absolute powers. Turner's description of the liminal phase as a time and space of possibility could well describe the ideal reading process:

> . . . the liminal phase [is] in the "subjunctive mood" of culture, the mood of maybe, might-be, as-if, hypothesis, fantasy, conjecture, desire . . . Liminality can perhaps be described as a fructile chaos, a fertile nothingness, a storehouse of possibilities, not by any means a random assemblage but a striving after new forms and structure, a gestation process, a festation of modes appropriate to and anticipating postliminal existence. ("Are There Universals?" 11-12)

The narrative is a liminal space, both within and outside daily life, a place and time in which a reader may take imaginative risks that may transform his or her perception of the world.

But the conjunction of reading and ritual also has a particular strategic value for Silko writing in the contact zone. Ritual is an indigenous idiom for many Native Americans, and it is a formal element in many contemporary Native American narratives. Paula Gunn Allen asserts that many contemporary novels by Indian authors "derive many of their structural and symbolic elements from certain rituals and the myths that are allied with those rituals" (79). This use of ritual can be read as autoethnography, a way of carrying Indian forms of representation into the European-derived form of the novel, which has the consequence of altering the novel. The convergence of ritual and written narrative brings into the novel—by implication, structure, or artistic effect—more of the physical, spiritual, and communal aspects of ritual that tend to be deemphasized in the individual, intellectual, and often secular experience of reading novels. Beyond this, the assertion of ritual properties in written narratives creates a potent model for change, similar perhaps to narratives aimed at religious conversion, in which the narrative seeks to provide a visionary experience. Silko gives *Storyteller* ritual properties: the sense of a community of voices, a spiritual vision, a visual, physical relationship to the text, and a structure that moves both progressively towards a vision and in a circle, suggesting cyclical and balanced relations rather than a sense of closure. But the complexity of *Storyteller* as a text correlates with the danger of the heterogeneity of meaning and the indeterminacy of reception that Pratt noted. As I trace some of the structures I find in the text, I hope my attention to reception can help me to avoid a homogenized reduction of the web of reading and meaning that Silko has constructed while making its powerful vision more accessible to the reader.

In order to describe the structural movements of *Storyteller* and the way it functions as a ritual of initiation for the reader, I designate six thematic divisions in the text. The first two sections are drawn from Bernard A. Hirsch's discussion of *Storyteller,* the four remaining sections correspond to those designated by Linda Danielson in her work on the book.[4] Hirsch designates the first section as the Survival section (1-53) and describes this section and *Storyteller* as a whole as "a self-renewing act of imagination/memory designed to keep storytellers as well as stories from so tragic a fate" as to be lost to memory (4). In this section, Silko establishes the familial and collective transmission of stories as vital cultural forces. The stories depict the determination of Native Americans to resist the forces that are dismantling Indian families, traditions, and interpretations. Most of the stories in this section are also tinged with a sense of loss and displacement caused by "European intrusion" (6) and the tensions between Native American and Euroamerican cultures. In the two short stories **"Storyteller"** and **"Lullaby,"** the characters reaffirm the power and continuity of the stories, but the situation of the storytellers is perilous. At the end of **"Storyteller,"** the Yupik protagonist is imprisoned literally by the Euroamerican authorities and figuratively by their interpretations of her story, for which they brand her as criminal or crazy.[5] In **"Lullaby"**, the old Navajo woman sings her songs of continuity as she sits outside with her husband, preparing to freeze to death after a lifetime of losing everything, including all of their children, to white social workers and doctors and white wars. In both **"Storyteller"** and **"Lullaby"** stories and songs provide consolation for Native American people beseiged by white culture and authority, but the survival of the people and the stories is threatened by Euroamerican legal and interpretive structures within which these stories are meaningless or unheard. This threatens not only Native Americans; the apocalyptic imagery of **"Storyteller"** suggests that the survival of the earth depends upon the perpetuation of these stories.

Some of the stories in the Survival section also tell of the matrilineage of storytelling, its power and its tensions.

Silko tells two traditional stories that her Aunt Susie told her as a young girl. Both stories—the story of the young girl who killed herself because her mother would not make her *yashtoah* (her favourite food) and the story of the two little girls who lost their mother in a flood and turned to stone—portray severed relationships between mothers and daughters, and may well have served as solace for Silko in her relationship with her mother.[6] Silko also shows her writing to be a continuation of a female lineage of storytellers, such as Aunt Susie, in her family photographs and reminiscences. When Silko recollects her Aunt Susie's stories she writes:

> I remember only a small part.
> But this is what I remember.
>
> (7)

In the balance of these two lines, Silko embodies both the loss of so much of the oral tradition, as well as the perpetuation of the oral tradition in her own memory and her own retellings. In the Survival section the reader is made to feel the depth of loss both of the stories and of the people who attempted to tell the stories and live by them. But Silko does not simply present the tragedy of the loss; she creates in her readers the need, the desire, and the ability to hear and understand those stories from a Native American interpretive perspective.

The second section (54-99), dubbed **"Yellow Woman"** by Hirsch, contains a number of stories about Yellow Woman, or "Kochininako" in Keres, a generic female character in Laguna Pueblo stories. Yellow Woman encompasses a great diversity of traits: in some stories she is loyal, beautiful, or powerful; in other stories she is selfish, thoughtless, or, worst of all, a witch.[7] Here, Silko focuses especially on the so-called abduction stories, in which Yellow Woman is taken from her husband and children by a powerful male figure—Whirlwind Man, Buffalo Man, or the Sun—but in Silko's stories the woman is drawn into the adulterous relationships as much by her own desire as by the man's. Hirsch argues that this focus on women's sexuality shows that "individual fulfillment can be equally important to a tribal community" as individual sacrifice (17), since in this section, and especially in the poem/story **"Cottonwood Parts One and Two,"** Silko's retelling of two traditional stories, Yellow Woman's desire and agency bring benefits to the people.

In the Yellow Woman section, Silko tells stories of women's roles developing within the dynamic exchange of old and new stories. In the short story **"Yellow Woman,"** for example, the first person narrator tries to figure out if, in her experience of abduction, she is Yellow Woman: "I was wondering if Yellow Woman had known who she was—if she knew that she would become part of the stories" (55). The narrator's relationship to the old stories is ambiguously resolved both in the title to Silko's story and in the last line of the story, when the narrator thinks "I was sorry that old Grandpa wasn't alive to hear my story because it was the Yellow Woman stories he liked to tell best" (62). The narrator's proximity with the old stories gives her experience a significance and a place in the life and stories of the people. As Silko writes in her poem **"Storytelling,"** a humorous juxtaposition of traditional and gossip stories, "You should understand / the way it was / back then, / because it is the same / even now" (94).

It is especially pertinent to consider the relations of old and new in the treatment of women's roles. Silko's description of her hunting experiences in this section, connected by a story she was told as a child about a great young girl hunter, point out some of the ways in which "traditional" roles for women mean something quite different for Native American and Euroamerican women. Rayna Green makes these differences explicit:

> The ironies multiply when, contrary to standard feminist calls for revolution and change, Indian women insist on taking their traditional places as healers, legal specialists, and tribal governors. Their call is for a return to Native American forms which, they insist, involve men and women in complementary, mutual roles. I underscore these differences because they may teach us more than analyses of Indian female "oppression." I am not suggesting that a return to tradition in all its forms is "correct" but that attention to the debate about the implications of such retraditionalization would mean healthier, culturally more appropriate scholarship on Indian women. (264)

Silko's focus on women's roles in this section of *Storyteller* compels the (white?) reader to reevaluate ideas of tradition, often considered by Euroamericans as something static, repressive, and unyielding. The way women construct and imagine their roles and their relation to tradition in Silko's stories parallels the give and take between old and new stories that gives the oral tradition its continuing vitality and relevance.

The next two sections, coming in the centre of the book, comprise a cycle from drought to rain. The Pueblo Indians, as well as the other Indians living in the arid southwest, focus many of their stories and rituals on the need for rain. Drought results from disruptions of harmony, from witchcraft, from bad thoughts or deeds, or from forgetting the old stories and the old ways. Rain results from an establishment of the right order and balance and sometimes from a ritual of healing to counter witchcraft.[8] In Pueblo and Navajo religions, witchcraft is a reversal of the right order and balance of things—it is a destructive rather than a creative use of power.

In the Drought section (100-57), Silko recasts the terms of power, so that white power, which is often represented as overpowering and absolute, is treated as a misunderstanding and a misuse of power—the sort of power to bring drought rather than rain. In two stories, the short story **"Tony's Story"** and the poem/story of the creation of white people by witches, the association between white power and witchery is explicit. In the creation story, in which a witch tells a story of white people that creates them as it is spoken, white people are described as people who objectify their surroundings and who bring death and destruction to people, animals, and land (with clearly historical allusions). The witch's evocation concludes with the white people's use of the rocks "in these hills": "They will lay the final pattern with these rocks / they will lay it across the world / and explode everything" (136).[9] In **"Tony's Story,"** Silko recounts a true story about a traditional Indian who killed a white state patrol officer. Since the story is told from Tony's (the Indian's) perspective, the reader is left to ponder both the delusions of Tony's vision and the logic of his assumption that the cop is a witch because his manifestation of power seems lifeless, arbitrary, and destructive.

The story of the Ck'o'yo magician connects white "power" to the illusions of "magic" by inference rather than by explicit reference. In the poem/story the magician disturbs the balanced relationships between the people and the land, the animals, and the spiritual powers, and thus he brings drought. The Ck'o'yo magician fools the people with tricks, "magic," that look like power but prove to be a false power. Like the power of technology, the Ck'o'yo magician can create magical and impressive visions while ignoring and even trampling on the cycles of worship, balance, and reciprocity required for fruitful relationships and necessary to bring the rain.

Following a group of photographs, the Rain section (158-186) begins with a rain chant, **"The Go-wa-peu-zi Song,"** written first in phonetic anglicized Laguna and then in English: "Of the clouds/ and rain clouds/ and growth of corn/ I sing" (158). This section continues from the previous one, but the emphasis has shifted from the disruptions that cause drought to the positive and creative forces the rain represents. The stories in the Rain section are lighter and more humorous, written in a light-hearted tone that celebrates the creativity, growth, and balanced relationships that bring the rain and that the rain signifies.

This section, halfway through the book, signals a shift into a Laguna Pueblo "language" and understanding. As Pratt has described it, autoethnography collaborates with and appropriates the representations the dominant group has of the dominated. In *Storyteller,* Silko uses the process of initiation to transform the reader and to shift the interpretive vantage point and the definition of terms from the Euroamerican to Native American. At this point in the book Silko moves toward affirmation and representation of Native American philosophical and spiritual beliefs from a more Native American centred world view. For example, both **"Tony's Story"** in the Drought section and **"The Man to Send Rain Clouds"** in the Rain section end with the promise of rain, but in the former story Tony's beliefs seem disturbing and out of touch with his surroundings, while in the latter story it is the Anglo priest whose beliefs seem disturbing and out of touch within the Laguna community. Although the perspective throughout the book is clearly Native American, the weight of Euroamerican representations lifts in this section, and the storyteller exhibits a greater confidence in the reader's ability to engage with Native American concepts and representations.

This shift in the emphasis of the collaborative enterprise is depicted most clearly in **"The Man to Send Rain Clouds."** In the story an old Laguna man is found dead by his relatives who prepare for his burial ritual and who ask him to send them rain clouds. It is believed that when the dead leave the fifth world (the world we are most familiar with) and travel to the other worlds below (which have no resemblance to Hades or Hell) they can carry an appeal to the rain clouds to bring rain to the fifth world. When the Anglo priest in the story is asked to bring his holy water to the burial ceremony, the Euroamerican character and belief system are put into the Native American context; the priest is the outsider who cannot comprehend the religious and cultural forms that surround him. The readers are put in the Laguna position, finding humour and pathos in his misunderstanding. In the end of the story, as the priest watches in bafflement as his holy water soaks into the sand, we see the sacred powers of the priest and the symbolism of his water get engulfed by the ceremony and beliefs of the Laguna and their (and our) understanding of the symbolism of the water.

The other stories in this section describe productive relationships and growth as part of the cyclical processes of the world. To illustrate the vastness of the natural and spiritual cycles, Silko depicts the dissolution of illusory boundaries of time and space. Four lyric poems in this section best exemplify this concept, especially **"Prayer to the Pacific"** in which the cycles of rain become a continual process that links the very origins of life and time to the present and the future, and every part of the globe to every other. Thus Silko presents a world of temporal and spatial coexistence, a world without boundaries, in which all things are interrelated.

The story **"The Man to Send Rain Clouds"** provides a link between the Rain section and the Spirits section (187-211), since the earth's cycles are connected with the processes of life and death and the presence of the spirits of the dead. The concept of temporal coexistence in the Rain section has direct bearing on concepts of ancestral presences, as Johannes Fabian observes:

> . . . all temporal relations, and therefore also contemporaneity, are embedded in culturally organized praxis. . . . To cite but two examples, relationships between the living and the dead, or relationships between the agent and object of magic operations, presuppose cultural conceptions of contemporaneity. To a large extent, Western rational disbelief in the presence of ancestors and the efficacy of magic rest on the rejection of ideas of temporal coexistence implied in these ideas and practices. (34)

The dissolution of temporal boundaries in the Rain section prepares the reader for an understanding of spiritual presences and our relationship to them.

In the Spirits section, Silko tells a number of stories about family members who have died, especially about her Grandpa Hank; the section is framed by photographs of her Grandpa Hank and her Grandma A'mooh. The Deer Dance becomes a model for the reciprocal relations between the living and the dead. Silko describes the Deer Dance which "is performed to honor and pay thanks to the deer spirits who've come home with the hunters that year. Only when this has been properly done will the spirits be able to return to the mountain and be reborn into more deer who will, remembering the reverence and appreciation of the people, once more come home with the hunters" (191). This cyclical relationship is also used in poems in the section to describe the pain and homage in love relations, in **"A Hunting Story," "Deer Dance / For Your Return,"** and **"Deer Song"**; and to describe the relations between the old stories and the new with a deeper spiritual dimension than in the Yellow Woman section. **"Where Mountain Lion Lay Down with Deer"** is a beautiful poetic evocation of the processes by which stories bring the spirits of the past back into existence. And in Silko's description of the anthropologists' explorations on the Enchanted Mesa, she describes a different kind of death that has threatened Indians, when pieces of the past are buried in museum basements, and the spirits and stories of the past are taken out of circulation.

In the last two stories of the section, which are two versions of a story, Silko describes spiritual transformations that affect the living. In one version a young boy taken by the bear people is brought back gradually to his humanity by a medicine man, but he will always be different after his connection to the bears. In the other version, **"Story from Bear Country,"** the reader, referred to as "you," is in the position of the young boy, and we are being lured back from the beauty of the bears' world by the narrator—the poem is the song by which the storyteller, in the role of the medicine man, calls the reader back. In these stories Silko conveys the power of stories to create spiritual transformations, thus offering stories that help to understand the reader's initiation and transformation in the ritual process of the book.

In the last section of the book, Silko tells stories of Coyote, the Native American trickster figure and ultimate survivor, to complete the shift to a Native American perspective and tradition. Coyote stories, common in the western and southwestern parts of North and Central America, differ among various people and regions, but the central feature of Coyote is his or her propensity for trickery, immorality, and deception. Exemplifying reprehensible, antisocial behaviours, Coyote is depicted as a lecher, a glutton, a thief, and a clown, whose uncontrolled appetites lead him to death again and again, though his death is never permanent. Jarold Ramsey describes Coyote's outlawry as a focus of social censure and of group humour that provides moral examples and psychological release, education and entertainment (xxxii). But Coyote's foolish errors, his appetite, and his laziness are not just amusing character flaws, they are characteristics that have shaped the world—thus he is also a very human character. William Bright argues that Coyote stories, while teaching morality through Coyote's negative examples, also depict the foolishness and the power of humanity (346).[10] In this last section of *Storyteller,* Silko introduces a character who represents human foibles and human creativity, as well as the power of Native American, and human, survival.

At this point, two structures can be seen in Silko's *Storyteller*; there is a progressive initiation into the Laguna Pueblo "language" and systems of belief and representation, and there is a mirror or circular structure. The Rain section responds to the Drought section, the Spirits section deepens the dynamics of change treated in the Yellow Woman section, and the Coyote stories reconsider the Survival section, and now the Indian perspective, traditions, and values pass judgment on the white world. The structure of the book can be envisioned as a butterfly: the two halves of the book provide two sides to a Native American perspective—on one side the sadness and struggle, on the other the humour and subversion—and both parts are necessary for a full understanding of power relations. At the same time, through the progressive movement of the book, Silko deflates the "dominant" vision of a "dominating" system of power.

The reader's experience of the text may be compared to the experience of Silko's great-grandfather Robert G. Marmon, a white man who married a Laguna woman and lived the rest of his life in Laguna. Near the end of *Storyteller* Silko looks at a photograph of Marmon as an old man, and she writes, "I see in his eyes / he had come to understand this world / differently" (256). Her observation, rendered in poetry to control the pace and emphasis, conveys the depth and importance of this difference in her great-grandfather's altered vision. Silko's book works to transform the reader's vision as a lifetime at Laguna did for her great-grandfather—to convey and reinforce the power and beauty of the Laguna vision.

This final section of my essay focusses on a story in the Coyote section, **"A Geronimo Story,"** that exemplifies the process of initiation that *Storyteller* as a whole enacts. In **"A Geronimo Story,"** the reader learns, along with the narrator's younger incarnation, how to "read" Laguna meanings through an understanding of the strategies of humour and subversion. The narrator, Andy, tells the story of a trip he made as a naive young man, when he accompanied the Laguna Regulars, led by his uncle Siteye and a white man, Captain Pratt, on an assignment to track and capture Geronimo. The United States Army, at war with Geronimo and the Apaches in the early 1880s, took advantage of inter-Indian hostilities and employed Laguna men to help them against their Apache enemies.

The narrative voice of the mature Andy follows the young Andy as he learns, through the subtlety of his uncle Siteye's humour and wisdom, about the ability of the trickster to turn white authority back on itself. The reader is put in the same position as the young Andy; the narrator provides the reader with the knowledge Andy already had when he went on the trip, but he does not explain the lessons he learns as the trip proceeds. To understand the story and how it affects Andy, the reader must, like Andy, learn to understand the humour of Siteye.

The story begins by establishing Andy's "horse sense"; he describes his uncle's larger Mexican horse and his own smaller Navajo horse as he ropes and saddles them for the trip. But Andy does not understand why the group heads for Pie Town when Siteye and Captain Pratt know Geronimo is not in that direction. Captain Pratt, a "squaw man" (as was Silko's great-grandfather Robert Marmon), has married a Laguna wife, adopted many of the Laguna ways, and is respected by the Laguna. Captain Pratt, in his respect for Siteye's opinions and for the Laguna people, is contrasted to other white men. Major Littlecock is the other kind of white man, whose authoritative stance, repeated errors of judgment, and racist underestimation of the Laguna are a source for the Laguna of amused contempt, a contempt also signified by his name.

The comradery, stories, and lessons of the trail end when the Laguna Regulars reach the white people's town, Pie Town, and encounter the white people's distrust and hostility, at which the full power of the Laguna sense of humour is released. The more fiercely and foolishly Major Littlecock acts out his authority and prejudice, the faster the jokes fly, until a joking session ends with Siteye's words and Andy's comprehension:

> Siteye cleared his throat. "I am only sorry that the Apaches aren't around here," he said. "I can't think of a better place to wipe out. If we see them tomorrow we'll tell them to come here first."
>
> We were all laughing now, and we felt good saying things like this. "Anybody can act violently—there is nothing to it; but not every person is able to destroy his

enemy with words." That's what Siteye always told me, and I respect him. (221-22)

The Laguna strategies of humour and collaboration become clearer to Andy by the end, when he puts them fully into the context of survival. First there is the following exchange with Siteye:

> Before I went to sleep I said to Siteye, "You've been hunting Geronimo for a long time, haven't you? And he always gets away."
>
> "Yes," Siteye said, staring up at the stars, "but I always like to think that it's us who get away." (222)

Siteye's sentence can be read two ways—to mean that it is "us" who escape from Geronimo, or that he *is* "us." Anything enigmatic in the statement is made clearer when, the following day, they prove to Littlecock that he was wrong about the Apaches' proximity. Andy thinks Littlecock was wishing he were still in Sioux country, which was more familiar to him. Silko writes, "Siteye felt the same. If he hadn't killed them all, he could still be up there chasing Sioux; he might have been pretty good at it" (223). The sarcasm and subtle humour of Silko's story suggest that the Laguna "collaboration" is both a strategy for survival and a deception of the white military authorities—a pretence of collaboration.

The journey becomes an initiation ritual for Andy, as he learns new places and the unspoken relations between Laguna and white men. Siteye teaches Andy tracking, explaining the process of memory based on an awareness of details and an ability to etch them into one's mind. The process of tracking Geronimo becomes a metaphor for Andy's initiation process, as he learns not only how to find him, but why they *do not* seek him. In Siteye's stories of the Apaches and the white soldiers, the soldiers' stupidity is a more prominent element than the murderousness of the Apaches; although there is no love lost between the Laguna and the Apache, the Laguna have even less respect for the white people with whom they ostensibly collaborate. The process of tracking and the idea of the hunt also become metaphors for the reader's initiation, as we trace through the subtlety of Silko's humour to figure out what Andy has figured out. Geronimo is, in a sense, the ultimate trickster figure of the story, the absent focus around whom the Laguna play with the whites and Silko plays with the reader. The hunt for Geronimo comes to mean much different things to the white authorities and to the Laguna. By the end of the story, Andy and the reader understand, without having heard it directly, that a successful hunt for Geronimo means *not* to find him, and that Siteye's final words in the story—"'You know,' he said, 'that was a long way to go for deer hunting'"—are a great joke on the white men.

Immediately following this story in *Storyteller* there is a photograph of "The Laguna Regulars in 1928, forty-three years after they rode in the Apache wars" (272). The photograph of a group of older men, some in jeans and workshirts, others in suits and ties, gives Silko's story historical authenticity, while also attesting to the survival of the Laguna Regulars. By bringing together the photograph with the story, Silko demonstrates how history can be rewritten as a Coyote story, which should subsequently enable the reader to reread history. In Silko's version, the power rela-

tion generally assumed is reversed. Her story suggests that the Laguna did not act in complicity with white people against other Indians, but instead that they had found better ways to survive white domination than direct retaliation.

In **"A Geronimo Story,"** Silko uses humour to establish a relationship with the reader and thus to insinuate the reader into another way of understanding Native American history and people; the humour becomes a means of reinterpreting history, power relations, and strategies for survival. Humour, the predominant feature of Coyote tales, is an essential ingredient in Silko's construction of a Native American perspective in the last section of *Storyteller*. In *Custer Died For Your Sins,* Vine Deloria, Jr. writes:

> One of the best ways to understand a people is to know what makes them laugh. . . . Irony and satire provide much keener insights into a group's collective psyche and values than do years of research.
>
> It has always been a great disappointment to Indian people that the humorous side of Indian life has not been mentioned by professed experts on Indian Affairs. Rather the image of the granite-faced grunting redskin has been perpetuated by American mythology.
>
> (146)

In humour, more than in other kinds of stories, the teller depends on common viewpoints and sensibilities. In the Coyote section, Silko uses humour as a final stage in an initiation process, showing Indian humour, resilience, and self-awareness along with her trust in the reader's ability to laugh with and at Coyote.

Throughout *Storyteller*, Silko reflects on the role of storytellers; in the final section, she connects the storyteller's art and her own role as storyteller to the strategies of Coyote. The storyteller is, like Coyote, a culture creator and transformer. But the analogy also connects to the subversive role of Coyote, in which Coyote's reversal of power relations and subversion of rules serve to expose the deceptions of white people or to represent Indians undermining white power. In an interview, Silko says:

> Certainly for me the most effective political statement I could make is in my art work. I believe in subversion rather than straight-out confrontation. I believe in the sands of time, so to speak. Especially in America, when you confront the so-called mainstream, it's very inefficient, and in every way destroys you and disarms you. I'm still a believer in subversion. I don't think we're numerous enough, whoever "we" are, to take them by storm. ("Interview" 147-48)

By the end of *Storyteller,* Silko appears to be a Coyote figure herself, as she subverts the dominant representations of history, power, and knowledge.

Finally, I want to raise a question: is it possible for white or non-Indian literary critics, or any critics in white academic institutions, to resist a reading practice that appropriates and diffuses Native American literature and its potentially subversive differences? As Fabian argues, objectification through distancing in time is not just a part of anthropology; it is part of Western epistemology. So although moving the study of Native American literature from the domain of anthropology to departments of English may be an improvement—a recognition that Native American art exists as art—the study still remains in the domain of the colonizer (and here I mean institutions more than individuals). Wendy Rose, a Hopi poet and anthropologist, refers to the current "literary-colonial canon" as another form of "cultural imperialism" (410). To revise Fabian's subtitle, how does literary criticism make its object, and is it possible to avoid objectification in our practice?

I have tried to suggest in this paper that one way to treat these stories may be to ask how they might change us as subjects, as readers—to rephrase Silko's description of the storyteller's role: what story does this book draw out of us? The concept of double consciousness could give those of us who are part of the white institutional structure a means of reconsidering our own subject positions, of viewing ourselves differently. The African American theorist W. E. B. Du Bois identifies "double consciousness" as both a gift of second sight and as an unwelcome psychological repercussion of racism; he describes "this sense of always looking at one's self through the eyes of others, of measuring one's soul by the tape of a world that looks on in amused contempt and pity" (17). Autoethnography is, in some sense, an act of double consciousness, a means of addressing the disparity between the two perceptions. The autoethnography, if it does capture the attention of the subjects in the "dominant" social position or institutions, can impose on those readers a "second sight" that reveals their own misunderstandings and misrepresentations of others and of themselves. In the process of initiating the reader in *Storyteller,* Silko puts the reader (and especially the Euroamerican reader) into this self-critical situation. The Native American perspective and interpretive context that Silko creates puts white readers in the position of feeling the humour *and* the discomfort of our historical roles and responsibilities. For the subject in the so-called "dominant" social position or institution to take on the responsibility of double consciousness may make possible a less authoritative and a more self-conscious approach to our own reading practice.

Perhaps it will also lead us to rethink our conception of the United States, replacing the vision of an inviolable, "indivisible" political, economic, and ideological entity with a vision of fragmented nation, a contact zone, in which colonized nations are demanding their land and their sovereignty, demanding that international laws and treaties be upheld. And maybe our ideas of contemporaneity as well as of the future will change. In this regard, I conclude with Silko's ideas about the future:

> The Pueblo people, of course, have seen intruders come and intruders go. The first they watched come were the Spaniards . . . But as the old stories say, if you wait long enough, they'll go. And sure enough, they went. Then another bunch came in. And old stories say, well, if you wait around long enough, not so much that they'll go, but at least their ways will go. One wonders now, when you see what's happening to technocratic-industrial culture, now that we've used up most of the sources of energy, you think perhaps the old people were right. ("Language and Literature" 67)

Perhaps we need to learn a Pueblo vision for the future, for the survival of all of us.

Notes

1. The self-consciousness of *Storyteller* and its roots in the oral tradition have invited critics before me to read it as more than a random collection of stories. Arnold Krupat describes *Storyteller* as an autobiography that manifests the biculturalism of all autobiographies by Native Americans. According to Krupat, Silko also reconceives autobiography: she rejects the authoritative individual voice common in Western autobiographies and replaces it with a polyphony that indicates the Native American conception of the individual's story as part of the collective stories of the people. Bernard A. Hirsch reads *Storyteller* as a simulation of the dynamic interaction of stories in the oral tradition. Hirsch suggests that by reading the stories in relationship to each other, the reader gets the sense of "the accretive process of teaching" inherent in the oral tradition. He proposes that Silko confronts the static nature of the written word and the absence of the dynamic context of storytelling by reproducing an episodic structure and a juxtaposition and compilation of stories. Linda L. Danielson describes *Storyteller* as a feminist work, a continuation of a Laguna matrilineal storytelling tradition, and as a work structured like a web in its circularity and intricate connections.

2. Barbara Harlow, in her study of postcolonial literatures, argues that the "dynamics of debate in which the cultural politics of resistance are engaged challenge both the monolithic historiographical practices of domination and the unidimensional responses of dogma to them. . . . the emphasis in the literature of resistance is on the political as the power to change the world" (30).

3. Turner uses the word "communitas" rather than community to indicate an attitude among people rather than mere proximity. Communitas is constituted by spontaneous, immediate, concrete relations rather than relations dictated by abstract structures (*Ritual Process* 128).

4. I got the first two categories and the very idea of thematic categories from Hirsch's article. Since by chance I read Hirsch's article before Danielson's, I owe his work a greater debt, but I was gratified to discover that Danielson's divisions of *Storyteller* correspond to my own, which suggests that these designations are not entirely arbitrary.

5. See Vangen's article on "Storyteller."

6. When, in an interview, Kim Barnes asked Silko about her ambivalent representation of mothers, Silko replied that in matrilineal and matriarchal society, the mother becomes the authority figure with which the child must reckon. She explains: "So the female, the mother, is a real powerful person, and she's much more the authority figure. It's a kind of reversal. Your dad is the one who's the soft-touch, and it's the mother's brother who reprimands you. . . . [You feel] more of an alliance with the father because he, in some ways, has less power in the household. . . . If someone was going to thwart you or frighten you, it would tend to be a woman; you see it coming from your mother, or sent by your mother" (97).

7. In the Pueblo Indian tradition, and in Native American traditions in general, witchcraft is not a specifically female practice as it tends to be in Christian traditions. I will treat witchcraft practices more thoroughly in my discussion of the Drought section of *Storyteller* below.

8. This is especially true of the Navajo, for whom witchcraft is more pervasive—see Silko's "Conversation," 32. The cycle from drought to rain that composes the centre of *Storyteller* is also the central ritual movement of *Ceremony*, which accounts for the fact that many of the stories in these two sections of *Storyteller* also appear in *Ceremony*.

9. Silko refers also to the uranium mines on the Pueblo reservations in her novel *Ceremony*.

10. See also Toelken and Wiget on Coyote.

Works Cited

Allen, Paula Gunn. *The Sacred Hoop: Recovering the Feminine in American Indian Traditions*. Boston: Beacon Press, 1986.

Bright, William. "The Natural History of Old Man Coyote." *Recovering the Word: Essays on Native American Literature*. Ed. Brian Swann and Arnold Krupat. Berkeley: U of California P, 1987, 339-87.

Danielson, Linda. "*Storyteller*: Grandmother Spider's Web." *Journal of the Southwest* 30.3 (1988): 325-55.

Deloria, Vine, Jr. *Custer Died For Your Sins: An Indian Manifesto* (1969). Norman: U of Oklahoma P, 1988.

Du Bois, W. E. B. *The Souls of Black Folk*. 1902. Greenwich, CN: Fawcett Publications, 1967.

Durham, Jimmie. "Cowboys and . . . Notes on Art, Literature, and American Indians in the American Mind." *The State of Native America: Genocide, Colonization, and Resistance*. Ed. M. Annette Jaimes. Boston: South End Press, 1992, 423-38.

Fabian, Johannes. *Time and the Other: How Anthropology Makes Its Object*. New York: Columbia UP, 1983.

Green, Rayna. "Native American Women." *Signs* 6 (1980): 248-67.

Harlow, Barbara. *Resistance Literature*. New York: Methuen, 1987.

Hirsch, Bernard A. "'The Telling Which Continues': Oral Tradition and the Written Word in Leslie Marmon Silko's *Storyteller*." *American Indian Quarterly* 12.1 (1988): 1-26.

Krupat, Arnold. "The Dialogic of Silko's *Storyteller*." *Narrative Chance: Postmodern Discourse on Native American Indian Literatures*. Ed. Gerald Vizenor. Albuquerque: U of New Mexico P, 1989, 55-68.

Lincoln, Kenneth. "Native American Literatures." *Smoothing the Ground: Essays on Native American Oral Literature*. Ed. Brian Swann. Berkeley: U of California P, 1983, 3-38.

Pratt, Mary Louise. "Art of the Contact Zone." *Profession 91*. New York: MLA, 1991. Rpt. in *Ways of Reading*. Ed.

David Bartholomae and Anthony Petrosky. New York: St. Martin's Press, 1993, 442-55.

Ramsey, Jarold, ed. *Coyote Was Going There: Indian Literature of the Oregon Country*. Seattle: U of Washington P, 1977.

Rose, Wendy. "The Great Pretenders: Further Reflections on Whiteshamanism." *The State of Native America: Genocide, Colonization, and Resistance*. Ed. M. Annette Jaimes. Boston: South End Press, 1992, 403-21.

Sherzer, Joel and Anthony C. Woodbury, eds. *Native American Discourse: Poetics and Rhetoric*. Cambridge: Cambridge UP, 1987.

Silko, Leslie Marmon. "A Conversation with Leslie Marmon Silko." *Sun Tracks: An American Indian Literary Magazine*. 3 (1976): 28-33.

———. Interview. *Winged Words: American Indian Writers Speak*. Ed. Laura Coltelli. Lincoln: Nebraska UP, 1990, 135-53.

———. Interview with Kim Barnes. *Journal of Ethnic Studies* 13.4 (1986): 83-105.

———. "Language and Literature from a Pueblo Indian Perspective." *English Literature; Opening Up the Canon*. Ed. Leslie A. Fiedler and Houston A. Baker, Jr. Baltimore: Johns Hopkins UP, 1981, 54-72.

———. *Storyteller*. New York: Little, Brown and Company, 1981.

Swann, Brian. Introduction. *Smoothing the Ground: Essays on Native American Oral Literature*. Ed. Brian Swann. Berkeley: U of California P, 1983, xi-xix.

Tedlock, Dennis. *The Spoken Word and the Act of Interpretation*. Philadelphia: U of Pennsylvania P, 1983.

Toelken, Barre. "Life and Death in the Navajo Coyote Tales." *Recovering the Word: Essays on Native American Literature*. Ed. Brian Swann and Arnold Krupat. Berkeley: U of California P, 1987, 388-401.

Turner, Victor W. "Are There Universals of Performance in Myth, Ritual and Drama?" *By Means of Performance: Intercultural Studies of Theatre and Ritual*. Ed. Richard Schechner and Willa Appel. Cambridge: Cambridge UP, 1989.

———. *The Ritual Process: Structure and Anti-Structure*. London: Routledge & Kegan Paul, 1969.

Vangen, Kathleen Shanley. "The Devil's Domain: Leslie Silko's 'Storyteller.'" *Coyote Was Here: Essays on Contemporary Native American Literary and Political Mobilization*. Ed. Bo Sholer. *The Dolphin* 9 (1984): 116-23.

Wiget, Andrew. "His Life in His Tail: The Native American Trickster and the Literature of Possibility." *Redefining American Literary History*. Ed. A. LaVonne Brown Ruoff and Jerry W. Ward, Jr. New York: MLA, 1990, 83-96.

Leslie Marmon Silko with Florence Boos (interview date 1997)

SOURCE: An interview with Leslie Marmon Silko, in *Speaking of the Short Story*, edited by Farhat Iftekharuddin, Mary Rohrberger, and Maurice Lee, University Press of Mississippi, 1997, pp. 237-47.

[In the following interview, Silko discusses her perceptions of herself as a writer, the role of oral tradition, women and men's roles in Laguna Society, and the nature of Native American political reform.]

Leslie Marmon Silko is noted for her haunting stories based on Laguna folktales, *Storyteller* (1981), and for the compassion and epic vision of her novels, *Ceremony* (1977) and *Almanac of the Dead* (1991). A MacArthur Foundation Fellow, Leslie Silko has also published *Laguna Woman* (1974), a book of poetry, *Sacred Water: Narratives and Pictures* (1993), and many individual stories and poems. However, Silko, a distinguished contemporary writer, is most well known for her compassionate novel, *Ceremony* (1977). It was the generous reception of this book that launched Silko headlong into fame, as well as giving her older stories new recognition. The most recent work of Silko's is *Sacred Water: Narratives and Pictures* (1993).

[Boos]: Do you consider yourself primarily a writer of stories or a novelist?

[Silko]: I've never tried to categorize what I do according to generic labels. I'm a writer, and I love language and story. I started out loving stories that were told to me. Growing up at Laguna Pueblo, one is immersed in storytelling, because the Laguna people did not use written language to keep track of history and philosophy and other aspects of their lives.

Imagine an entire culture that is passed down for thousands and thousands of years through the spoken word and narrative, so the whole of experience is put into narrative form—this is how the people know who they are as a people, and how individuals learn who they are. They hear stories about "the family," about grandma and grandpa and others.

When I started out at the University of New Mexico, I took a folklore class, and began to think about the differences between the story that's told and the literary short story. I started writing the "literary" short story, and tried to write it as closely as I could according to the "classical" rules which seemed to manifest themselves in my reading. I wanted to show that I could do it. But I've turned away from this since and haven't really written a short story in the usual sense since 1981. From 1981 to 1989 I worked on *Almanac of the Dead,* and so I don't think of myself as short story writer. Yet stories are at the basis of everything I do, even non-fiction, because a lot of non-fiction reminiscences or memories come to me in the form of narrative, since that's the way people at home organize all experience and information.

I found the rules of the "classical" short story confining. I think you can see why the post-modernist narrative and the contemporary short story went off in another direction. They're trying to escape the strictures of the formal story form.

I've now tasted the freedom one has with a novel, so I wonder if I'll turn back to more structured forms. I've written one short story, **"Personal Property"**, which I'm going to read tonight, and which purposely breaks some of the rules of the classical short story. Maybe I'm not done with making trouble with the short story form!

How are your poems related to your stories?

For me a poem is a very mysterious event . . . my poems came to me mysteriously. I started out to write a narrative, fiction or non-fiction, and something would happen so that the story would organize itself in the form of a narrative poem rather than a short story.

In fact, that happened with **"A Story from Bear Country,"** in *Storyteller.* I intended to make a note about a conversation I had had with Benjamin Barney, a Navajo friend, about the different ways our respective Navajo and Pueblo cultures viewed bears. I started a narrative of our conversation, but something shifted abruptly, and before I knew it, I was writing something that looked more like a poem. At the very end of that poem a voice comes in and says, "Whose voice is this? You may wonder, for after all you were here alone, but you have been listening to me for some time now." That voice is the seductive voice of the bears. Benjamin Barney and I had been discussing the notion that if humans venture too close to the bear people and their territory, the people are somehow seduced or enchanted. They're not mauled or killed, but they are seduced and taken away to live with the bears forever.

So I don't have control [over whether my tale becomes a tale or a poem]. I set out to narrate something—either something which actually happened or a story I was told—and after I begin the piece sorts itself into whether it will be a poem or a short story. I find a mixing of the two in **"The Sacred Water,"** a piece that I wrote a couple of years ago—a wanting to have the two together—so that there's really no distinct genre. This story also contained a bit of "non-fiction." I wanted to blend fiction and non-fiction together in one narrative voice.

So I am never far away from oral narrative, storytelling and narration, and the use of narrative to order experience. The people at home believe that there is one big story going on made up of many little stories, and the story goes on and on. The stories are alive and they outlive us, and storytellers are only caretakers of the story. Storytellers can be anonymous. Their names don't matter because the stories live on. I think that's what people mean when they say that there are no new stories under the sun. It's true—the old stories live on, but with new caretakers.

You present yourself as a narrative writer, but it struck me as I read **Storyteller** *that you also think visually. How do you decide where to put the words on the page?*

I'm a very aural person. On the other hand, my father was a photographer, and when I was a child, I would go in the darkroom, sit quietly on the stool, and watch as the images of the photographs would develop. As I've written in *Storyteller,* there was this old Hopi basket full of snapshots. One of us kids would pull a photograph and say, "Grandma, who's this," or "what's this?" A photograph would be tied to narration. And when I was a child walking in the countryside, I'd see a certain sandstone formation of a certain shape, or a certain mesa, and someone would say, "Look, see that hill over there? Well, let me tell you . . ."

Through the years I've done a lot of thinking about the similarities and differences between the "literary" story and the story that's told. I began to realize that landscape could not be separated from narration and storytelling. One of the features of the written or old-fashioned short story was the careful, detailed description of its setting. By contrast, in Laguna oral stories, tellers and audience shared the same assumptions, a collective knowledge of the terrain and landscape which didn't need to be retold. That's why something an anthropologist or folklorist has collected may seem sparser than a literary short story; sometimes the oral short story can seem "too sparse." I realized that all communities have shared knowledge, and that the "literary" short story resulted when all over Europe—and all over the world—human populations started to move. People didn't have this common shared ground anymore.

Storyteller seemed to evoke a whole context related to your deep kinship with your family. Even the shapes of the stories seemed to arise from your identification with those telling the stories.

Right. One of the reasons that *Storyteller* contains photographs was my desire to convey that kinship and the whole context or field on which these episodes of my writing occurred. The photographs include not only those of my family, but of the old folks in the village and places in the village. I started to think of translation [from Laguna]. I realized that if one just works with the word on the page or the word in the air, something's left out. That's why I insisted on having photographs in *Storyteller*. I wanted to give the reader a sense of place, because here place is a character. For example, in the title story, **"Storyteller,"** the main character is the weather and the free, frozen land itself. Or in the story I'm going to read tonight, **"Private Property,"** the community itself is a character—although places and communities are not ordinarily characters in the "classical" literary short story. I felt a need to add in these other [visual] components which before were supposed to be extraneous to the narrative, but which existed at Laguna Pueblo as visual cues—a mountain or a tree or a photograph.

When you advise your creative writing students, what suggestions do you give about choosing topics or about technique?

Usually I tell them just to think about a good story, not to think consciously about topic or theme. I tell them that their stories should contain something that they don't know, something mysterious. It's better not to know too much, but to have just the bare bones of an idea, and let the writing be a process of enlightenment for them.

I often say, "Well, you can tell me the idea for the story, so why can't you write it down?" There's a large difference between speaking and writing. But when I'm writing, it's as natural to me as if I were speaking, though the results are different. The most difficult element of writing to teach the student is that ease—writing as if you were talking to yourself or to the wall.

Students are traumatized by the writing process. I've noticed the traumatization begins right from the first grade. Usually kids withstand it till around the seventh or eighth grade, and then they experience a real terror of failure and scolding. People who can talk, who can tell you things, freeze when they sit down in front of a blank piece and a pencil. It shouldn't be difficult to make the transition from speaking to writing, and I blame the United States educational system for the fact that it is.

Though you speak of an oral narrative tradition, you also remark that you speak and write differently. What's different about the writing process for you, and why do you value that?

I was conscious that I wasn't as good a storyteller as the storytellers at home, for the people at home are so good at this. An oral performance is just that, so I needed to go off in a room by myself to evoke that same sense of wholeness and excitement and perfection that I seemed to hear all around me [during their performances].

Also, when I'm writing I'm alone. When I'm speaking to an audience, by contrast, I'm very sensitive to what people want from me or expect from me, whether the audience are becoming restless or whatever, and I'm anxious to please and to serve, putting the comfort of others ahead of my own. When I write I'm alone with the voices . . . with the people in my memory. Some of the voices that I'm alone with might even be those of people still living, so that I could go and talk to them outside that door, but when I'm alone in the room writing, a connection with the older voices occurs, which cannot happen for me when I'm storytelling.

Writing isn't just inscription of stories, then, but something that requires solitude as well?

Being alone allows me to hear those voices. I think it's aloneness to be able to hear Aunt Susie's voice, for example. If I were in a room with her I would only listen, not write or speak, but solitude enables me to hear [and transcribe] her very distinctive voice. I think it was meant to be distinctive so that I could never forget it.

I've thought a lot about this distinction between oral narration and writing. Storytelling was done in a group so that the audience and teller would respond to each other, and be grounded in the present. As I said, I'm not as good at that, but I learned that it's also dangerous to go into the room alone and hear the voices alone, because those are voices from spirit beings who have real presence . . . and bring dangers . . . There's a real danger of being seduced by them, of wanting to join them and remain with them. I'm forty-six, and things are becoming clearer to me, things that before I had only heard about and hadn't experienced, so I couldn't judge.

But now I'm beginning to understand. Old Aunt Susie used to say that when she and her siblings were children, her grandmother started storytelling by bidding the youngest child to go open the door "so that our esteemed ancestors may bring in their gifts for us." But when we tell the stories of those past folks telling stories, they are actually here again in the room. It's therefore dangerous for a storyteller to write in a room alone without others, because those old ancestors are really coming in.

In writing *Almanac of the Dead,* I was forced to listen . . . I was visited by so many ancestors . . . it was very hard. It changed me as a human being. I came to love solitude almost too much, and it was very frightening.

Don't you ever fear that the presences of the dead might view critically something you wrote?

No, I've never been afraid. I know the voices of the story-tellers, and I know that if you tell their truth and don't try to be self-serving, they aren't dangerous—in fact, they bring great protective power—*great protective power.*

How do you know what is true rather than self-serving?

I can tell. One method to avoid self-serving is to use a male protagonist, as in *Ceremony.* I wrote two stillborn versions of *Ceremony* now in the [Beinecke] Library at Yale—though I suspect that the rest of the university may had thought I was the Anti-Christ, so maybe they're not even catalogued! If anyone is interested, they can read the two stillborn drafts—each about sixty pages long—that lead up to *Ceremony.* "Stillborn" is of course such a grim term, but before I sold them to Yale University I looked at them again and saw that they're not really "stillborns" at all, but a necessary part of writing the novel. This gave me new confidence in the process of writing, and all young writers should understand that even those things that we throw in the trash can are necessary to get us to where we want to be. The first two stillborns had *female* protagonists.

Why would changing to a male protagonist have enabled you to transcend yourself?

When the characters were females, I identified too closely with them and wouldn't let them do things that I hadn't done or wouldn't do. It's not good to identify too closely with [one's own characters]. All this happened when I was very young; I started writing the "stillborn" versions of *Ceremony* when I was twenty-three.

Did you start to write short stories before you published poems? You published the poems of Laguna Woman quite early?

I wrote stories before I wrote poems, but the poems were easier to get out. That was because in writing stories I found myself too connected to the main character. Even though I wanted [her] to be a separate character, [she] wouldn't be. When on the third draft of *Ceremony,* I created Tayo, and I was so liberated by working with a male protagonist.

Also, in a matriarchy the young *man* symbolizes purity and virginity—and also the intellectual, the sterile, and the orderly. The female principle was the chaotic, the creative, the fertile, the powerful.

Ceremony struck me as a book about the bonds between men, very deep bonds. Why would it be liberating for you

to deal with male bonding and the recovery of a man's sense of himself?

When I was a little girl, I hung around adults. I was always the kid who wouldn't go off and play with the other kids, but liked to watch and eavesdrop on adults. I come from a culture in which men and women are not segregated, and so I had a great deal of opportunity to listen to the men talking. When I was really small, I listened to World War II and Korean War veterans. They had drinking problems and lacked regular jobs, but they had good souls and good spirits. Perhaps tragedy and anguish and trouble attracted me right away as a little girl, more than the easier parts of life.

Also, the Laguna people lived in a matriarchy, and in a matriarchy one is more afraid of what women may say and think about oneself. Children feel less powerful than their mothers, and men seemed more interesting to them because they too had less power and were more like themselves.

Needless to say, women are a lot happier in a matriarchy than in a patriarchal society. Also those elements that had given women their strength and continuity were not nearly as shaken by outside pressures as were those reserved for men. I think this was mainly because when outsiders came in, they didn't realize the women's power, and so they left them alone. They stopped more of the things that men did traditionally than those that women did. So you see the men were more broken apart by the invasion. The government imprisoned men for practicing the Pueblo religion. Then of course war came, and the Second World War and the Korean War were devastating for men.

The Pueblo world is the reverse of Anglo-American and mainstream culture, where the final word is the man's word. In the Pueblo world, women have the final word in practical matters. This is a simplification, but women own all the property, children belong to their mother's clan, and all the mundane business—quarrels, problems—are handled by women. The female deity is the main deity, and in the Kiva ceremonies, man dress as women. But formerly the matriarchy was more evenly balanced, for the men were responsible for the hunting and religious ceremonies.

On the other hand, I've heard the theory that because the Euro-American legal system was so patriarchal, it destroyed certain aspects of Indian life that favored or protected women (by enforcing nineteenth-century laws, for example, which gave a married woman's property to her husband). If so, imposition of foreign laws sometimes diminished women's authority.

Well, we're only seeing that starting with my generation. It's taken that long for western European misogyny to arrive in the Pueblo. It's true that the conquerors negotiated only with Pueblo men, ignoring the clan mothers, but in the long run, when they destroyed what they thought was important, they left behind the authority of women.

Yet it's true that women are sometimes disadvantaged. A lot of tribal councils were established which didn't give women the right to vote, even though tribal organization was matriarchal. But that's a superficial level of damage, when you think that if the Conquistadors had really understood how important women were, they might have tried to [undermine their power]. Patriarchal attitudes have touched the Pueblo people only in a superficial way.

Does your identification with Tayo perhaps suggest that an author should try to identify with someone of the opposite sex as a way of moving towards a full presentation of reality?

Totally. When I was growing up, for a long time I felt that I was "just me." That was easy to be in a matriarchal culture, where women have access to the wide world. Women are everywhere and men are everywhere women are. There isn't this awful segregation that you find even now in the Anglo-American world . . .

In university life!

Yes, in university life. In the Pueblo, women crack dirty jokes to men who aren't their husbands or close relatives. There's a lot of banter, and a real feeling of equality and strength within the community. There weren't places where a little girl was told, "Oh, you can't go there!," or things of which a little boy was told, "Oh, you shouldn't do that!" I wasn't told that because I was a little girl, I had to dress or act a certain way. So for along time, although I didn't think I was *really* a boy, I kind of . . .

. . . didn't learn not to identify with men.

Yes, I didn't learn not to identify with men. I had a horse and was kind of a tomboy, and I was glad of it. Although I was intensely attracted to men and males, I saw that as a part of being interested in them and watching their activities.

I finished writing *Ceremony* in 1977, when it was still not politically correct for a woman novelist to write from a man's point of view. Feminism in America was still so new that feminists wanted women to write of their own experiences, not those of men. Perhaps too, because my name is Leslie, which is kind of androgynous, they may not have realized that I was a woman author. For awhile I didn't hear anything from the feminists. I felt I was punished for using a male protagonist, but that was the only way I could write.

I'd like to ask you about some of your fellow contemporary women writers who have written novels about their own cultures—Michelle Cliff, Toni Morrison, and Maxine Hong Kingston among them. Are there contemporary women writers whose works you've read a great deal, or whose works you believe resemble yours in any way?

Of course Toni Morrison's work has been important to me, and that of Maxine Hong Kingston. Both women have encouraged me to believe that I'm on the right track, and that we share something—that it's not so lonely, for there are other women and other people thinking and writing about the same sorts of things.

It seemed to me that you portrayed discrimination profoundly from within, not preaching about it, but analyzing

its different layers and guises. Might I ask you to comment on contemporary Native American political issues and conflicts?

I'll tell you what's happening in terms of history. The largest city in the world is Mexico City, and officials don't really know its population. The uncounted ones are the *Indios*, the Indian people. A huge, huge change is on the horizon, indeed it's already underway—and there's nothing you can do.

A couple months ago at sundown, a freight train came up from Nogales through Tucson, covered, crawling with human beings. People were sitting on top, people were hanging on the side—and so the great return to Aztlan which the Chicano people talk about is coming to pass in a big way. The Zapatista uprising on January 1st, 1994, was one of the most important signalings of what is to come. After that small demonstrations were held all over Mexico and the United States and Canada, showing the solidarity of Native American people throughout the Americas. We sense that the rising on January 1st was a sign of this awakening.

The most important thing right now which people must watch out for is jingoism and hysteria about immigrants and immigration. [The U.S. government] is building an iron curtain, a steel wall—Rudolfo Ortiz calls it the Tortilla Curtain—but it's ugly. They're trying to seal off Mexico from the United States. But [those they are sealing off] are Indians, Native-Americans, American Indians, original possessors of this continent, and [those who hate them] want to create a hysteria here so that it will justify U. S. troops opening fire and shooting and killing. The future could be a horrendous blood bath and upheaval not seen since the Civil War.

Right now the border patrol stops [Indian] people. I've been stopped three or four times, and have had dogs put on me.

Oh!?

This happened to me on my way from Albuquerque to Tucson. Many people in the rest of the United States don't understand that the U.S. government is destroying the civil rights of *all* citizens living near the border. Something terrible is developing, and it's being sold to the American people, or shoved down their throats through this hysteria over immigrants and the fear that their jobs will be taken. But I see a frightening collision on the horizon! I'll tell you something—the powers that be, those greedy corrupt white men like Rostenkowski and all those criminals in the United States Congress—their time is running out very soon! The forces from the south have spiritual power and legitimacy that'll blast those thieves and murderers right out of Washington, D.C.

Are there particular Native-American groups that you see working effectively against government wrongs?

Ah, ah, this change that's coming will not have leaders. People will wake up and know in their hearts that it's beginning. It's already happening across the United States. The change isn't just limited to Native Americans. It can come to Anglo-Americans, Chicanos, African-Americans as well. Every day people wake up to the inhumanity and violence this government perpetrates on its own citizens, and on citizens all over the world. That's why the change will not be stopped, for it will be a change of consciousness, a change of heart.

We don't need leaders. They can't stop [this revolution.] They can shoot some, they can kill some—like they have already—but this is a change that rises out of the earth's very being—a Hurricane Andrew, a Hurricane Hugo, an earthquake of consciousness. This earth itself is rebelling against what's been done to it in the name of greed and capitalism. No, there are no groups which bring change. They aren't needed. This change that's coming is much deeper and much larger. Think of it as a natural force— human beings massed into a natural force like a hurricane or a tidal wave. It will happen when the people come from the south, and when the people here [in the North and Midwest] understand.

One morning people will just wake up, and we'll all be different. That's why the greedy powerful white men will not be able to stop what happens, because there will be nothing to grab onto. There are no Martin Luther Kings to shoot, so the F.B.I. can give up on that!

There's no one that can stop us, because [the return to Aztlan] will be a change inside of *you!* It will happen without your knowing it. And this won't happen because someone preached at you, threatened you with prison, put a gun to your head. No, you'll wake up [yourself]. It will come to you through dreams!

No Martin Luther King will have helped bring about change, but what about Leslie Marmon Silko? How do you see yourself contributing to this movement?

Just be telling people—"Look, this is happening!" As I tried to make clear in *Almanac of the Dead,* you don't have to do anything, for the great change is already happening. But you maybe might want to be aware of what was coming, and you might want to think about the future choices that you might have to make. Though as I said, in your yeart, you will already know.

Amen, and thank you.

FURTHER READING

Criticism

Barker, Adele Marie. "Crossings." In *Dialogues/Dialogi: Literary and Cultural Exchanges Between (Ex)Soviet and*

American Women, pp. 340-53. Durham, N.C.: Duke University Press, 1994.

Compares Silko's "Storyteller" and Anna Nerkagi's novel *Amiko.* Barker considers structure, narrative, language, and other literary devices through which the authors explore the boundaries of culture.

Barnes, Kim. "A Leslie Marmon Silko Interview." *The Journal of Ethnic Studies* 13, No. 4 (Winter 1986): 83-105.

Interview in which Silko discusses her purpose for writing *Storyteller.*

Danielson, Linda L. "*Storyteller:* Grandmother Spider's Web." *Journal of the Southwest* 30, No. 3 (Autumn 1988): 325-55.

Examines *Storyteller* from a feminist perspective, arguing that Silko reinterprets her culture outside the influence of European and male traditions.

Lappas, Catherine. "'The Way I Heard it Was . . .': Myth, Memory, and Autobiography in *Storyteller* and *The Woman Warrior.*" *CEA Critic* 57, No. 1 (Fall 1994): 57-67.

Explores the ways in which Silko and Maxine Hong Kingston blend myth and autobiography.

Nelson, Robert M. "He Said / She Said: Writing Oral Tradition in John Gunn's 'Ko-pot Ka-nat' and Leslie Silko's *Storyteller.*" *SAIL: Studies in American Indian Literatures* 5, No. 1 (Spring 1993): 31-50.

Compares John Gunn's novel *Schat-chen* to Silko's *Storyteller,* analyzing their different concepts of the role of the storyteller.

Stetsenko, Ekaterina. "Retelling the Legends." In *Dialogues/Dialogi: Literary and Cultural Exchanges Between (Ex)Soviet and American Women,* pp. 327-39. Durham, N.C.: Duke University Press, 1994.

Compares the use of oral tradition in Silko's "Storyteller" and Anna Nerkagi's *Amiko of the Nago Tribe,* contrasting the methods the authors use to depict Native and "civilized" cultures.

Vangen, Kate Shanley. "The Devil's Domain: Leslie Silko's 'Storyteller'." In *Coyote Was Here: Essays on Contemporary Native American Literary and Political Mobilization,* edited by Bo Schöler, pp. 116-23. Denmark: University of Aarhus, 1984.

Considers the tension between Silko's portrayal of the protagonist in "Storyteller" and traditional Western interpretations of women and sin.

Additional coverage of Silko's life and career is contained in the following sources published by the Gale Group: *Authors and Artists for Young Adults*, Vol. 14; *Contemporary Authors*, Vols. 115, 122; *Contemporary Authors New Revision Series*, Vol. 45; *Contemporary Literary Criticism*, Vols. 23, 74; *Dictionary of Literary Biography*, Vol. 143; *DISCovering Authors; DISCovering Authors: Canadian; DISCovering Authors: Modules*; **and** *Native North American Literature*.

"The Chrysanthemums"

John Steinbeck

The following entry presents criticism of Steinbeck's short story "The Chrysanthemums," first published in 1937. For an overview of Steinbeck's short fiction, see *Short Story Criticism*, Volume 11.

INTRODUCTION

One of Steinbeck's most accomplished short stories, "The Chrysanthemums" is about an intelligent, creative woman coerced into a stifling existence on her husband's ranch. The story appeared in *Harper's Magazine* in 1937; a revised version, which contained less sexual imagery, was published in the 1938 collection *The Long Valley*. Many critics believe the story reflected Steinbeck's own sense of frustration, rejection, and loneliness at the time the story was written. Some scholars also have speculated that the female protagonist of "The Chrysanthemums," Elisa Allen, was inspired by Steinbeck's first wife, Carol Henning.

PLOT AND MAJOR CHARACTERS

"The Chrysanthemums" opens at the Allen ranch, which is located in the foothills of the Salinas Valley. Elisa works in her garden, cutting down old chrysanthemum stalks, while her husband Henry discusses business with two men across the yard. After the men leave, Henry leans over the fence where Elisa is working and comments on her gardening talents. Elisa admits to her "gift," noting her mother also had "planters' hands." Henry then suggests that they dine out that evening. After Elisa agrees, Henry teasingly proposes that they go to the fights that night as well. Once Henry departs, a battered covered wagon driven by a tinker pulls up to the house. The tinker asks Elisa if she has any pots to mend. She declines several times, but once the tinker notices and compliments Elisa's chrysanthemums, her mood changes from slight irritation to exuberance. The tinker tells Elisa about a woman on his route who would like chrysanthemum seeds, and Elisa happily places several sprouts in a red pot for him. She then finds two saucepans for the tinker to repair before he leaves. Elisa rushes into the house, where she bathes, studies her naked body in the mirror, and dresses for the evening. As the couple leaves for dinner in their roadster, Elisa notices the chrysanthemum sprouts she had given the tinker lying in the road and asks her husband if they could have wine with dinner. A few minutes pass before she wonders aloud whether the boxers at the prize fights hurt each other very much and whether women ever attend. Henry asks Elisa if she would like to go to the fights, but she answers no, that "it will be enough if we can have wine." She then begins to cry, though unnoticed by Henry.

MAJOR THEMES

The primary theme in "The Chrysanthemums," one that appears throughout Steinbeck's canon, is Elisa's creative frustration. Some critics have viewed Elisa as a feminist figure, while others—arguing that Elisa both emasculates her husband and engages in an infidelity with the tinker—have argued that the story is an attack against feminism.

CRITICAL RECEPTION

"The Chrysanthemums" has garnered critical acclaim since publication. André Gide, who particularly admired the story, compared it to the best of Anton Chekhov. Other critics have detected the influence of D. H. Lawrence in "The Chrysanthemums." John Ditsky called the story "one of the finest American stories ever written." John H. Timmerman regarded the story as "one of Steinbeck's masterpieces," adding that "stylistically and thematically, 'The Chrysanthemums' is a superb piece of compelling craftsmanship." According to Mordecai Marcus "the story seems almost perfect in form and style. Its compelling rhythm underlines its suggestiveness, and nothing in the story is false or out of place." While some critics have praised Steinbeck's objectivity in the narrative, Kenneth Payson Kempton found the story "arbitrary, self-impelled, and fuzzy work . . . its effect annoyingly arty, muddy, and unreal." Most critics concede that it is Elisa Allen who makes "The Chrysanthemums" a memorable short story. Even so, R. S. Hughes argued that while the facets of "Elisa's personality are no doubt responsible for much of the story's appeal, ultimately Steinbeck's well-crafted plot and his skillful use of symbol make the story great."

PRINCIPAL WORKS

Short Fiction

Nothing So Monstrous 1936
Saint Katy the Virgin 1936
The Red Pony 1937; also published as *The Red Pony* [enlarged edition], 1945
The Long Valley 1938; also published as *Thirteen Great Stories from the Long Valley* [revised edition], 1943; and *Fourteen Great Stories from the Long Valley* [revised edition], 1947
How Edith McGuillicuddy Met R.L.S. 1943
The Crapshooter 1957

Other Major Works

Cup of Gold (novel) 1929
To a God Unknown (novel) 1933
Tortilla Flat (novel) 1935
In Dubious Battle (novel) 1936
Of Mice and Men (novel) 1937
Of Mice and Men: A Play in Three Acts (drama) 1937
The Grapes of Wrath (novel) 1939
The Moon Is Down (novel) 1942
The Moon Is Down: A Play in Two Parts (drama) 1942
Cannery Row (novel) 1945
The Pearl (novel) 1947
A Russian Journal (travel essays) 1948
Burning Bright (novel) 1950
East of Eden (novel) 1952
Sweet Thursday (novel) 1954
The Short Reign of Pippin IV: A Fabrication (novel) 1957
Once There Was a War (nonfiction) 1958
The Winter of Our Discontent (novel) 1961
Speech Accepting the Nobel Prize for Literature (speech) 1962
Travels with Charley: In Search of America (nonfiction) 1962
America and Americans (travel essay) 1966
Steinbeck: A Life in Letters (letters) 1975

Working Days: The Journals of "The Grapes of Wrath" (journal) 1989

CRITICISM

Joseph Warren Beach (essay date 1941)

SOURCE: "John Steinbeck: Journeyman Artist," in *American Fiction, 1920-1940*, The Macmillan Company, 1948, pp. 309-26.

[*In the following excerpt from an essay originally published in 1941, Beach compares "The Chrysanthemums" to the work of Anton Chekhov, calling the story's protagonist Elisa Allen "one of the most delicious characters ever transferred from life to the pages of a book."*]

There are many of Steinbeck's short stories that remind one of the Russian writer. [Chekhov]. There is the opening story of the volume entitled *The Long Valley* (1938). It is called **"Chrysanthemums."** It gives us the picture of a wholesome and attractive woman of thirty-five, wife of a rancher in that enchanting Salinas Valley where Steinbeck lived as a boy. This woman has what are called planter's hands, so that whatever she touches grows and flourishes. She is shown on a soft winter morning working in her garden, cutting down the old year's chrysanthemum stalks, while her husband stands by the tractor shed talking with two men in business suits. Nothing is said about the relationship of this married pair, but everything shows that it is one of confidence and mutual respect. He refers with simple pleasure to the size of her chrysanthemums. She applauds his success in selling his three-year-old steers at nearly his own price. And she welcomes his suggestion that, since it is Saturday afternoon, they go into town for dinner and then to a picture show. But she wouldn't care to go to the fights. The feminine note is sounded in the unaffected shrinking of the refined woman from the brutality of a sport which men enjoy. "Oh, no," she said breathlessly, "I wouldn't like fights." And he hastens to assure her he was just fooling; they'll go to a movie. It is not the author who tells us that he is making a sacrifice, and that he is glad to do so, for he likes his wife better thus than if she wanted to go to the fights. The beauty of this kind of storytelling is that the author does not waste words and insult his reader with that sort of explanation. He gets his effects with an elegant economy of words, and leaves some scope for the reader's imagination.

And now is introduced a third character, picturesque and individual, and a new balance of forces in human relations. The new character is an itinerant tinker who comes driving up in his queer covered wagon from the country road that runs along the bank of the river. He is a big stubble-bearded man, in a greasy black suit, graying but not old-looking, with dark eyes "full of the brooding that gets in the eyes of teamsters and of sailors." He is a shrewd, dynamic personality. And there ensues between him and Eliza Allen a combat of wits in which she shows herself a person of right feeling, one who doesn't let her charitable instincts run away with her, but who has at the same time a soft side where you can get round her. That is her love of flowers, and the pride she takes in her way with chrysanthemums. The author says nothing of this tug-of-war, nor of the shrewdness of the tinker, nor of the quality in Eliza Allen that makes her a victim. All these things he *shows* us in the brief dialogue—again with a richness of reference which makes us feel the whole quality of these two by no means commonplace lives. Among other things he makes us feel how, beneath her brisk and contented exterior, this woman harbors an unsatisfied longing for some way of life less settled than that of the rancher's wife, something typified by the shabby tinker camping nightly in his wagon underneath the stars.

Eliza Allen has nothing that needs mending, but the tinker does not want to leave without something to feed his hungry frame. He has the inspiration to take an interest in her chrysanthemums; he begs her for some of the shoots to take to a lady down the road who has asked him to bring her some. The upshot of it is that she finds some old pans for him to mend and he goes away with fifty cents in his pocket and a pot of chrysanthemum shoots. She watches him go down the road by the river, and is filled, as the author manages to make us know, with a kind of troubled joy at the thought of him on his vagabond trail.

And now she turns to the bustle of washing up and dressing for the trip to town. I wish I knew how the author manages here to convey the sense he does of the energy and well-being of this rancher's wife moved by thoughts unnamed and perhaps not brought above the level of consciousness. Her husband observes how "strong" she seems, but has no notion of the special occasion for it.

But Eliza Allen has a grief in store, and we have still the pleasure of seeing how mad and hurt she can be when she realizes that she has been outwitted by the man who means so much to her in the obscure places of her imagination. As she drives along to town with her husband she discovers a dark spot on the pavement where the tinker had thrown her chrysanthemums the moment he was out of sight of the ranch. The pot he kept. The thing remains a secret with her. She says nothing of it to her husband. We know it only by the tone she takes in asking him again about the fights. She asks him if the fighters do not hurt each other very much. "I've read how they break noses, and blood runs down their chests. I've read how the fighting gloves get heavy and soggy with blood." He is surprised and rather shocked that she should ever have thought of things like that; but he is willing to take her to the fights if she really wants it. "She relaxed limply in the seat. 'Oh, no. No. I don't want to go. I'm sure I don't.' Her face was turned away from him. 'It will be enough if we can have wine. It will be plenty.' She turned up her coat collar so that he could not see that she was crying weakly—like an old woman."

This is no tragic grief. But it does assure us that Eliza Allen is very much of a woman, and of the same flesh and blood with ourselves—that she shares with us our sensitive pride, our reluctance to let someone get the best of us, and more than that, our secret romantic longing for something more than "human nature's daily food." She is one of the most delicious characters ever transferred from life to the pages of a book. There is no doubt that she has a "soul." And she is much less simple than she seems.

Kenneth Payson Kempton (essay date 1953)

SOURCE: "Objectivity As Approach and As Method," in *Short Stories for Study*, Harvard University Press, 1953, pp. 115-52.

[*In the following excerpt, Kempton asserts that Steinbeck's "The Chrysanthemums" lacks objectivity.*]

No reader of "The Killers" will easily forget its opening sentence and paragraph: "The door of Henry's lunchroom opened and two men came in. They sat down at the counter." Behind this starkly matter-of-fact fluidity, one feels something impending; the objective writer gains a cumulative tension by omitting many details while confining his record to a stripped brief of action and speech. From first word to last, somebody is saying or doing something. In contrast, the first three paragraphs of **"The Chrysanthemums"** are static, are crowded with impressionistic detail—a description of the valley, the weather, the season, and the ranch: a vacant stage. They comprise a short essay on a scene not yet relevant to any story. The use of the word "tender" ("The air was cold and tender") misses the mark, for no one but the author could have admitted this personal sense impression. Now Maupassant, feeling his way through the beginning of "The Piece of String," used about three hundred words to describe a market day at Goderville; but it was a crowd of people and carts and animals his lens-diaphragm recorded, and briefly we glimpsed Hauchecorne in the mass, only to lose him again. The objective writer clings to persons, to humanity, in the mass or individually—to flesh and blood and spirit; he begins there, goes on there, ends there, the talk and behavior illuminating motives; he knows that to spend space on weather and scenery and season—unless these affect or are affected by persons—is to tax the reader's patience and give him time to question the impersonality of the method.

Once we see Elisa Allen, the rancher's wife (she has been waiting in the wings while her creator wrote the essay), the story overcomes its self-imposed inertia and begins to move. And it seems at first to move in a single direction. Here, at least, is a person, a woman in the prime of life, happy and busy in her flowerbeds. Interest picks up as we welcome her appearance and hope for a motive to follow; a strong motive in this strong, brisk woman, and some almost equally strong (or perhaps still stronger) yet understandable opposition. There may be, we feel, a story here after all.

We remember, though, that by the terms of objectivity the author will not have recourse to his own interpretation or to a character's thoughts for presenting and shifting or sustaining motives, he will do this only indirectly, by recording speech and behavioristic details that will create the motivating undertone and make drives and pressures, as well as the surface record, clear. So we must watch Elisa closely, stay alert, wait for small signs and portents, and be sure to catch each as it comes along.

Instead of catching, we are caught and misled. Elisa casts a frequent glance toward her husband and the two businessmen across the yard. Is this merely curiosity, is she fearful lest the two men somehow cheat Henry, or is she perhaps interested in one of those strangers? "Elisa started at the sound of her husband's voice," as he neared her, the men gone. (She feels guilt, then. The last inference was right.) At her husband's praise, "Elisa straightened her back and pulled on the gardening gloves again. . . . On her face there was a little smugness." (A sly one, she knows she can fool him.) But we learn later that this, if not a blind alley, is a crooked one. There is nothing between Elisa and either of those two men from town. The most we can say, after reading the entire story, is that perhaps Elisa, sexually frustrated, is interested in any man who comes along. But objective writing should not permit several possibilities held in abeyance; behavioristic detail should imply motive at the moment of reading. Hide-and-seek is easy for the author, hard on the reader.

Inferential alertness having failed us, it holds a weaker promise and we slack off somewhat. The author does too, using more and more behavioristic details that carry no certain undertone or those whose undertone he must all but state. In the first class: "Elisa looked up," "Elisa laughed," "her breast swelled passionately," "Elisa's voice grew husky," "Her upper lip raised a little, showing her teeth." (In context, this facial contortion may have been intended to indicate doubt, scorn, or disbelief.) "She sat unmoving for a long time," while Henry was changing his clothes. "Her eyes blinked rarely." (This I believe gets across; she is scheming something.) In the second class: "The irritation and resistance melted from Elisa's face," "Elisa's eyes grew alert and eager," "She stopped and seemed perplexed," "Elisa stiffened and her face grew tight"; then at Henry's repeated praise, "For a second she lost her rigidity," "She grew complete again." And finally, "She relaxed limply in the seat." No prize fights for Elisa. She weeps. The story ends.

Dimly through these behavioristic and almost expository tags one can perceive a broad motive (frustration) but only one that shifts before clear establishment and splits into five or six, none of which seems either comprehensible or dominant. Except for the tinker's treachery and her disillusionment in him, one can discover no opposition except of course what is provided by Elisa's mysteriously erratic nature. She is constantly defeating herself in one way or another, but why and over what issue only God and Mr. Steinbeck know. Everything is done *for* her, almost everything outside her goes right and gives her a chance to be happy; but, insisting on her neurosis when, as it were, rejected by the tinker, she refuses happiness. We know, at least, that she longs for something. But whether it is the freedom suggested by the nomadic life of the tinker, or children symbolized by her care of the young plants, or manliness as indicated by her delight in her strength and her masochistic scrubbing of her body in the bath, or a normal sex life hinted at by her tenseness when with her possibly impotent husband, or merely her lost youth as implied at the end—who can say? Ignorant of the desire that opposes her and creates frustration, we can't know what the story means. A conceivably premeditated idea—that Elisa wants something that she, therefore the author, therefore the reader can't identify—we must reject in deference to Mr. Steinbeck's known ability as a storyteller: such a meaning would make Elisa scarcely worth the reader's attention. The author has been commended as a symbolist. But surely, here, we are confronted with a mass of conflicting, disestablished symbols, and casually invited to take our choice. If we glance back at the title, often a key to comprehension in tough cases, **"The Chrysanthe-**

mums" is of little help. Elisa's behavior with and relation to her plants follows the pattern of all the other symbols of her unmotivated personality—mention without clarifying stress; and her varying emotions about the plants are all finally negated by her behavior toward the tinker, which is itself negated by what follows his departure. She is hurt by his act of throwing away her slips, yet at once seems to understand and forgive his keeping the pot. Again, we must discard as too far-fetched and fantastic the possibility that the source of Elisa's frustration lies in her compulsive behavior toward plants (nipping, cutting, rooting only to nip and cut again) carrying over into her behavior toward persons: with plants she is notably adjusted, uninhibited, not frustrated at all.

Thus, by any possible route we can take, we reach the same group of vague conjectures; and must reluctantly conclude that this is arbitrary, self-impelled, and fuzzy work, a disservice to the method under consideration, its effect annoyingly arty, muddy, and unreal.

Fortunately for beginning writers, a younger generation has done better with objectivity.

Mordecai Marcus (essay date 1965)

SOURCE: "The Lost Dream of Sex and Childbirth in 'The Chrysanthemums'," in *Modern Fiction Studies*, Vol. XI, No. 1, Spring, 1965, pp. 54-8.

[*In the essay below, Marcus explores the sexual symbolism of "The Chrysanthemums," concluding that Elisa Allen's frustration results from a longing for childbirth.*]

I will risk saying that John Steinbeck's **"The Chrysanthemums"** seems to me one of the world's great short stories, reassured by the fact that though it has received only scattered critical attention, Joseph Warren Beach called its protagonist, Elisa Allen, "one of the most delicious characters ever transferred from life to the pages of a book,"[1] and André Gide thought that the story resembles the best of Chekhov.[2] The story seems almost perfect in form and style. Its compelling rhythm underlines its suggestiveness, and nothing in the story is false or out of place. Criticism of the story, however, has only vaguely suggested the springs of its appeal.

On the simplest level **"The Chrysanthemums"** presents an attractive woman of thirty-five who wishes to escape from the limited domesticity of her ranch life to a world of wider experience. Joseph Fontenrose suggests that the weeping Elisa of the story's conclusion has learned to compose herself.[3] More accurately, F. W. Watt thinks that the conclusion shows "that the vitality she feels within herself will remain frustrated," and Watt earlier observes that Elisa's desires are "ambiguously sexual and spritual."[4] This ambiguity combined with Elisa's pervasive combination of femininity and masculinity, rather than the mere masculine rebellion against the passivity of her role as a woman suggested by Peter Lisca,[5] is central to the story.

Although the story's rich suggestiveness may call for a full analysis, I will concentrate on its sexual symbolism, especially as it suggests the elusiveness of various meanings. I will give Freud's theory of bisexuality[6] and Freudian views of sexual symbols only passing attention, for carried too far they lead away from the story's humanly felt experience to a forcing of ideas. I will not explore inherent bisexualty, penis-envy, or the idea that individuals desire to be self-created, though evidence of these ideas may be found in the story.

The story opens with a description of the surrounding Salinas Valley and Henry Allen's ranch, in December. Although harvest is over, the valley and the Allen ranch have been plowed and are waiting for a rain which is unlikely to come in time of fog. The plowed and waiting earth symbolize Elisa Allen's desire for fructification, for she has no child and her devotion to her chrysanthemum bed is at least partly an attempt to make flowers take the place of a child. Elisa's masculine dress; the strength of her hands; her exertions to plan, protect, and nurture her gigantic chrysanthemums; and her pride in their size and beauty suggest that circumstances have made her play both a feminine and a masculine role, though both roles merge at times, particularly in her protectiveness. The fog probably symbolizes her inability to see the nature of her dilemma. Denied a child, a wider world of experience, and that projection of oneself into the world of fresh and broad experiences which possessing a child fosters, she finds a substitute in her flowers, though she yearns for something more. The intensity of her pride in her ability to make things grow reinforces the likelihood that the flowers are a substitute for children.

At this point, however, her pride is much stronger than her sense of loss, and so when her husband proposes an evening in town as a celebration for his successful cattle sale, she can exclaim "Oh yes. That will be good." A similar exclamation towards the end of the story suggests that Elisa tends to accept conventional social pleasures as satisfying rituals because she feels that her most personal accomplishments and her husband's business acumen are authentically fulfilling. She has confused her strength and her husband's success with human completion. The second section of the story shows Elisa further convinced that her accomplishments are deeply fulfilling, but it moves her slowly to the realization that she does not possess much of what she wants.

The earlier suggestions that the chrysanthemums are her children expands in the second section to the feeling that the flowers are also a substitute for herself—just as a beloved child is. As the tinker first appears, there is nothing explicitly sexual about him. Despite his shabbiness, shallowness, and deceptivity, he clearly represents an independent and partially poetic life that Elisa yearns for, though this independence is painfully ambiguous. Elisa at first deals with the tinker as though she were a man—to reinforce her resistance against giving him work, to maintain a distant camaraderie with him, and because she feels—as he declares—that his mode of life is, if not impossible for a woman, certainly difficult. As her childlessness has made Elisa's strength both feminine and masculine, her social situation makes her desire for freedom both feminine and masculine. But interspersed with this ambivalence is her clearly feminine passion for flowers, reinforced by her reference to tending sprouts, by description of her shining eyes and pretty hair, and much more strongly by her asser-

tion of how her planting hands make her one with her plants, which situation suggests seeds, children, and sexual organs.

The tinker is puzzled and embarrassed by her talk, but he senses at least part of its meaning. Her passion for her plants leads him to comment on nights in the wagon, and when Elisa eagerly responds: "When the night is dark—the stars are sharp-pointed, and there's quiet. Why you rise up and up," the images suggest sexual excitement and fulfillment, both masculine and feminine, as well as spiritual aspiration. Her hesitant reaching towards the tinker's legs extends the sexual aura, which almost immediately melts into a maternal feeling as Elisa places the pot of chrysanthemums "gently in his arms." Her dreamy condition as he departs to what she calls "a bright direction" is movingly ambivalent. He is carrying off a symbol of the child she does not have—a substitute for it—and he moves towards the expanded world that such a child symbolizes.

As the story moves from its second to its final section, Elisa is exultant, for she feels the sexual and maternal triumph of having created her chrysanthemums and sent them out into the world. But she is clearly unconscious of the full meaning of her joy, for that joy leads to an ambivalent purification ritual and a continuing misunderstanding of the meaning of her strength. As she discards her clothing and scrubs herself with pumice, she is casting off the earth that—she ambivalently feels—makes her maternal, asserting a kind of masculine strength, and perhaps enjoying a quasi-sexual self-punishment; for this brief passage is intensely and subliminally suggestive. As she dresses, she tries to restore her femininity by thinking that her clothing and makeup emphasize her woman's role, but she is still confused about her sexual role, and her strange transformation is partly motivated by her entering a new social situation. She has tried to move from one kind of femininity to another, but neither is quite right. Both tend to be substitutions for biological femininity. In the garden her frustrated femininity has tended to become masculine. In the home she strains herself to assume social femininity.

Elisa's stance as her husband emerges dressed for the evening out—"Elisa stiffened and her face grew tight"—begins the most difficult sequence in the story. Her action suggests feelings of superiority over her husband, a sudden distaste for someone to whom she must play the woman, and on the deepest level the ambivalence of her desire to be seen as a woman. Her husband's painfully inadequate and puzzled "Why—why Elisa. You look so nice!" suggests that he has not perceived her adequately as a woman, has probably been blind to her needs as a woman. In a complex but brief dialogue, we see him perceive her strength as somehow masculine, to which observation she replies with violent ambivalence, asserting her strength but shocked at the implications that it is masculine. Surely Henry has little understanding of her needs or dilemma.

As Elisa sees her discarded chrysanthemums on the roadway, she reacts at first with an assertion of social norms: "It will be good, to-night, a good dinner," which shows that she is denying her real feelings and pretending that marriage, husbandry, and entertainment are part of a naturally fulfilling cycle. But as she turns from the quest for sensation in wine and in the spectacle of the violent prize fights, to pleasure in the thought of vindictive assault on men, we see that she is reacting to knowledge of her failure. Her feminine self, her capacity for fructification and childbearing, the very offspring and representative of her body, have been thoughtlessly tossed aside (just as they probably have been unrecognized by the man at her side), and the power in which she rejoiced is revealed to be a futile substitute for the power of being a woman which lay at the center of her aspirations.

Her sudden interest in the details of the boxing matches suggests many things. In proposing that she attend the fights she is again retreating from her failure as a woman, to an identification with men—the spectators at the fights. But her combination of horror and vindictiveness about the boxers shows a reassertion of her hurt femininity. She dreams of seeing men, who have failed her, punished, and she also wants to punish herself for her failure as a woman. As she abandons her interest in the fights and comforts herself with the thought that wine at dinner will be enough, she accepts her failure to be fully successful as a woman and again comforts herself with a mild symbol of extra-domestic excitement. At the end we see her as a woman, but only that ghost of a woman which nature and society have permitted her to be. She cries like an old woman because she has given in to passivity and potential desiccation, though tears like hers are shed by many a young girl.

It is unlikely that Steinbeck was generalizing about a masculine protest in woman, and unthinkable that he was suggesting that woman's role must be passive, but he has created an extraordinary portrait of a woman whose strength seems both masculine and feminine but who cannot center her power on what alone would help her to reach beyond a limited condition to an expansive happiness, though doubtfully any final one. Joseph Warren Beach's allusive suggestion that Elisa years for something more than "human nature's daily food" (p. 314) is perhaps unintentionally reminiscent of the Wordsworthian desire for the life of the child whose gates of the senses—or so we think—are open. In ways perhaps beyond our understanding, the desire for sexual mergence, the possession of children, and our repossession of the world through both of these conditions may underlie much of the power of this story.

Notes

1. *American Fiction, 1920–1940* (New York, 1941), p. 314.
2. *The Journals of André Gide*, trans. Justin O'Brien (New York, 1951), IV, 79.
3. *John Steinbeck, An Introduction and Interpretation* (New York, 1963), p. 63.
4. *John Steinbeck* (New York, 1962), pp. 42&-43.
5. *The Wide World of John Steinbeck* (New Brunswick, N. J., 1958), p. 95.
6. Freud confessed that he could not place his theory of bisexuality on a coherent biological or social basis. *New Introductory Lectures on Psycho-Analysis*, trans. W. J. H. Sprott (New York, 1933), pp. 155-158.

Elizabeth E. McMahan (essay date 1968–69)

SOURCE: "'The Chrysanthemums': Study of a Woman's Sexuality," in *Modern Fiction Studies*, Vol. XIV, No. 4, Winter, 1968–69, pp. 453-58.

[*In the following essay, McMahan identifies unfulfilled sexual desire as the source of Elisa Allen's frustration in "The Chrysanthemums."*]

Virtually every critic who has considered John Steinbeck's short story **"The Chrysanthemums"** has agreed that its basic theme is a woman's frustration, but none has yet adequately explained the emotional reasons underlying that frustration. In fact, Kenneth Kempton would consider such an explanation impossible. He professes his inability to find any consistent motivation for Eliza's behavior, and declares the work "annoyingly arty, muddy, and unreal."[1] But most critics who have examined **"The Chrysanthemums"** admire the story and find it meaningful. Warren French, after identifying the theme of the story as frustration, suggests that the central action concerns "the manipulation of people's dreams for selfish purposes"[2]—an interesting and valid idea but one which fails to incorporate the obvious sexual overtones of the story. Another critic who overlooks the sexuality is Joseph Warren Beach. He sees the conflict in the story as a contest of wits between Eliza and the pot mender; frustration results from damage to her pride when she is outwitted.[3] Ray B. West sees the story as "based on the assumed relationship between the fertile growth of plant life and physical violence and sexuality in human beings."[4] Peter Lisca explains Eliza's frustration as stemming from an unsuccessful "silent rebellion against the passive role required of her as a woman"[5]—an excellent idea but his treatment is too brief to account for all the elements of the story. F. W. Watt is on exactly the right track when he states that the story concerns Eliza's "struggle to express and fulfill desires which are ambiguously sexual and spiritual."[6] Unfortunately Watt, like Lisca, has not sufficient space in his book to give this story the thorough discussion that it deserves. The only such examination thus far is that of Mordecai Marcus.[7] But his interesting and persuasive argument that Eliza's frustration results essentially from a longing for childbirth is not entirely satisfactory. Marcus encounters difficulties with the story which I think disappear if we do not equate sexual fulfillment with a yearning for motherhood. Eliza's need is definitely sexual, but it does not necessarily have anything to do with a longing for children.

In order to understand Eliza's emotions, we first should look closely at the relationship between her and her husband. Beach, somewhat surprisingly, observes that "Nothing is said about the relationship of this married pair, but everything shows that it is one of confidence and mutual respect" (p. 311). Partially true, certainly, but confidence and mutual respect are not the only qualities that Eliza Allen desires in her marriage. The evidence points to an outwardly passive, comfortable relationship between the two which satisfies Henry completely but leaves Eliza indefinably restless with excessive energy which she sublimates into the "over-eager" cultivation of her chrysanthemums, and the care of her "hard-swept looking little house with hard-polished windows." Henry is a good provider, we can be sure; he has just received a good price for thirty head of cattle. He is also thoughtful; he invites his wife to go into town that evening to celebrate the sale. A good provider, a thoughtful husband. But what else? There is a distinct lack of rapport between these two, despite all that mutual respect. And the confidence which Beach observes is an assurance of each other's capability; it is not a warm mutual confidence of things shared.

We see this lack of rapport demonstrated early in the story as Henry makes a suggestion for their evening's entertainment:

> Henry put on his joking tone. "There's fights tonight. How'd you like to go to the fights?"
>
> "Oh, no," she said breathlessly. "No, I wouldn't like fights."
>
> "Just fooling, Eliza. We'll go to a movie."

The fact that husband and wife do not share an interest in sports is not remarkable, but the fact that Eliza responds seriously to Henry's "joking tone" suggests either that she lacks a sense of humor or that for some reason she is not amused by Henry's teasing. We discover later that she has a ready sense of humor when talking to someone other than Henry. Unmistakably, Henry has no gift with words. When he compliments his wife on her chrysanthemums, he praises their size not their beauty and does so in the most prosaic terms. When he wants to compliment his wife on her appearance, he stammers, as if in surprise—and Eliza is hardly elated by the banal adjective:

> "Why—why, Eliza. You look so nice!"
>
> "Nice? You think I look nice? What do you mean by *nice*?"
>
> Henry blundered on. "I don't know. I mean you look different, strong and happy."

Henry's word choice here is particularly unfortunate since his wife has just devoted her entire attention to heightening her femininity. She has put on her "newest underclothing and her nicest stockings and the dress which was the symbol of her prettiness." "Strong" is the way she least wants to appear. But Henry manages to make matters even worse. Bewildered by Eliza's sharp retort, he is inspired to his only attempt at figurative language in hopes of making himself clear: "'You look strong enough to break a calf over your knee, happy enough to eat it like a watermelon.'" It is hard to fancy the woman who would be pleased by Henry's agricultural comparison. Eliza is not amused.

We begin to sense the source of Eliza's discontent. She is a woman bored by her husband, bored by her isolated life on the farm. When the itinerant tinker arrives at Eliza's gate, we see that she is a woman who longs for what women's magazines vaguely call "romance." She wants, among other things, to be admired as a woman. The chrysanthemums that she cultivates so energetically produce great soft blossoms shaped like a woman's breasts. If one wishes to see the flowers as a symbol, they suggest the voluptuous softness of a sexually mature woman. There is no evidence to suggest that Eliza is a sex-starved female, that her husband is perhaps impotent, as Kempton suggests (pp. 122–123). Henry's placidity would seem to indicate the contrary. But neither is Eliza a sexually satisfied woman. Something is lacking in her relationship with Henry, and this something has a great deal to do with sex, but it is not as simple as a need for the sex act alone. This undefined longing becomes more clear as we examine her reaction to the tinker.

Unlike Henry, who has trouble finding the right words to please his wife, the tinker seems to know them intuitively. His greeting to Eliza is a mildly humorous remark about his cowardly mongrel dog: "'That's a bad dog in a fight when he gets started.'" Eliza gives no dead-pan response as she did to Henry's feeble joke. Instead, "Eliza laughed. 'I see he is. How soon does he generally get started?' The man caught up her laughter and echoed it heartly. 'Sometimes not for weeks and weeks,' he said." In contrast with Henry's uninspired comment on the size of her flowers, the tinker remembers that chrysanthemum blooms look "'like a quick puff of colored smoke.'" Eliza is obviously pleased. "'That's it. What a nice way to describe them,'" she says.

The man's physical appearance has little about it to warrant such a friendly response: "Eliza saw that he was a very big man. Although his hair and beard were greying, he did not look old."[8] His clothes are grease-stained and disheveled, his hands are cracked and dirty. But there is one physical characteristic which would make the man appealing to Eliza: "His eyes were dark, and they were full of the brooding that gets in the eyes of teamsters and sailors." Obviously he lacks the honest, dependable virtues of Henry, the virtues a woman should cherish in a husband. But the important thing he has that Henry lacks is an aura of freedom, unpredictability, perhaps adventure, maybe even poetry, which his gypsy life produces. It has got to be this element of the man that attracts Eliza to him. His first reference to his wandering, carefree existence produces an unconscious feminine response from her. The tinker says, "'I ain't in no hurry ma'am. I go from Seattle to San Diego and back every year. Takes all my time. About six months each way. I aim to follow nice weather.'" Eliza removes her unfeminine heavy leather gloves and "touched the under edge of her man's hat, searching for fugitive hairs. 'That sounds like a nice kind of a way to live,'" she said. But instead of continuing to talk about his roving existence, the tinker begins giving her his sales pitch about mending pots and sharpening knives and scissors. Eliza becomes suddenly distant: "Her eyes hardened with resistance." She is fast losing patience with him when, in an inspired move, he inquires about her chrysanthemums. She warms towards him again almost at once: "The irritation and resistance melted from Eliza's face." After the man shrewdly asks her if he can take some sprouts to a customer down the road, she becomes enthusiastic. "Her eyes shone. She tore off the battered hat and shook out her dark pretty hair"—a movement entirely feminine and essentially seductive. She immediately invites him into the yard.

Eliza is now clearly excited. She scoops up the soil into a flower pot, presses the tender shoots into the damp sand, and describes for him how the plants must be cared for. "She looked deep into his eyes, searchingly. Her mouth opened a little, and she seemed to be listening." She tells him about her "planting hands," which pluck buds instinctively and unerringly. But the reader is aware that such emotion could scarcely be generated solely by an enthusiasm for the care and clipping of chrysanthemums. Eliza, kneeling now before the man, "looking up at him," appears to be experiencing sexual excitement. "Her breasts swelled passionately." Not breast, but breasts. Not heaved, but swelled. The man is suspicious of her strange behavior, perhaps embarrassed: his "eyes narrowed. He looked away self-consciously." She has asked him if he understands her feelings, and he begins a response so in keeping with Eliza's mood that she quite forgets herself.

> "Maybe I know," he said. "Sometimes in the night in the wagon there—" Eliza's voice grew husky. She broke in on him. "I've never lived as you do, but I know what you mean. When the night is dark—why, the stars are sharp-pointed, and there's quiet. Why, you rise up and up! Every pointed star gets driven into your body. It's like that. Hot and sharp and—lovely."

The sexual implications of her last four sentences are unmistakable, yet the sexual impact lies just beneath the surface level of meaning in the phallic imagery. Eliza is, more than likely, unaware of the sexual nature of her outburst, but her next action, while probably still unconsciously motivated, is quite overt. "Kneeling there, her hand went out toward his legs in the greasy black trousers. Her hesitant fingers almost touched the cloth. Then her hand dropped to the ground. She crouched low like a fawning dog." The tinker's matter-of-fact comment jolts her at once back to her state of natural reserve: "'It's nice, just like you say. Only when you don't have no dinner it ain't.'" She is aware that he does not understand after all the feeling of erotic mysticism that she is trying to communicate. "She stood up then, very straight, and her face was ashamed. She held the flower pot out to him and placed it gently in his arms." To avoid further embarrassment, she goes at once to find some old saucepans for him to fix. After regaining her composure, she returns with the battered pots and chats with him as he works. She pays him for the repairs, and as he is leaving, calls out a reminder to keep the plants watered. She stands watching him go. "Her shoulders were straight, her head thrown back, her eyes half-closed, so that the scene came vaguely into them. Her lips moved silently, forming the words 'Good-bye—good-bye.' Then she whispered, 'That's a bright direction. There's a glowing there.' The sound of the whisper startled her. She shook herself free and looked about to see whether anyone had been listening. Only the dogs had heard."

After this the story returns to the portrayal of the relationship between Eliza and her husband, and in the final scenes her feelings toward Henry are clearly revealed. As the tinker's wagon moves out of sight, Eliza quickly returns to the house. The next scene portrays Eliza performing a purification ritual. She felt shame after her display of passion before the stranger. Now she cleanses herself before returning to her husband, the man to whom she should lawfully reach out in desire. "In the bathroom she tore off her soiled clothes and flung them into the corner. And then she scrubbed herself with a little block of pumice, legs and thighs, loins and chest and arms, until her skin was scratched and red." The abrasive action of the pumice suggests expiation for her imagined infidelity. Eliza then studies her naked body in a mirror: "She tightened her stomach and threw out her chest"—movements of a woman who wants to see her figure at its best, but also of a woman gathering resolution. The ceremonial preparation for her evening with Henry also has about it an element of resolve: "After a while she began to dress slowly. . . . She worked carefully on her hair, penciled her eyebrows and

rouged her lips." She is steeling herself for the coming evening. "She heard the gate bang shut and *set* herself for Henry's arrival" (Italics mine). Eliza, ready early, goes out onto the porch and sits "primly and stiffly down" to wait for her husband. "Henry came banging out of the door, shoving his tie inside his vest as he came. Eliza stiffened and her face grew tight." There follows the passage examined earlier in which Eliza bridles at each of Henry's inept attempts to compliment her. The scene culminates in his ill-chosen simile describing her in her carefully chosen finery as looking strong enough to break a calf over her knee. "For a second she lost her rigidity. 'Henry! Don't talk like that. You didn't know what you said.'" She seems to lose heart, to wonder if she can abide this insensitive man, but her resolution returns: "She grew complete again. 'I'm strong,' she boasted. 'I never knew before how strong.'"

In the final scene we see this strength tested to the breaking point, finally giving way and dissolving into despair. As the two are driving into town for their festive evening of dinner and a movie, "far ahead on the road Eliza saw a dark speck. She knew." The tinker has discarded her chrysanthemums, symbol of the femininity which she hopes will inspire the excitement she longs for. But he has kept the pot—an insult on any level of interpretation, to discard her treasure and keep its utilitarian container.

This symbolic rejection produces a need for female revenge in Eliza. The idea of attending a prize fight which was repugnant to her a few hours earlier has its appeal now. She asks Henry whether "the men hurt each other very much" and speculates on "how they break noses, and blood runs down their chests." But as her anger cools, she realizes the futility of vicarious vengeance. It can do little to salve her damaged ego or save her dying dream. Henry has promised her wine with dinner, and she tries to console herself with this small romantic touch. "'It will be enough if we can have wine. It will be plenty,'" she tells Henry. But she knows it will not really be enough. She knows that she will always have good, dull, dependable Henry, but how will she keep her mind from whispering, "There has got to be something more exciting, more beautiful in life than this"? No, wine will not be plenty. "She turned up her coat collar so he could not see that she was crying weakly—like an old woman"—like an old woman for whom all hope of romance is a thing of the past.

Notes

1. *Short Stories for Study* (Cambridge, Mass., 1953), p. 124.

2. *John Steinbeck* (New York, 1961), p. 83.

3. *American Fiction: 1920–1940* (New York, 1941), pp. 311–314. Beach was no doubt using the early version of the story which appeared in *Harper's* in October of 1937, which would account for his having missed the sexuality. The most explicitly sexual passage was added when the story was revised for publication in *The Long Valley* (New York, 1938). William R. Osborne pointed out the problem in "Texts of Steinbeck's 'The Chrysanthemums' " in *Modern Fiction Studies*, XII (Winter 1966–67), 479–484. He may be glad to know that Steinbeck has indicated that the text as published in *The Long Valley* should be considered

the correct version. All references to the story in this paper are, of course, to the revised version.

4. *The Short Story in America: 1900–1950* (Chicago, 1952), p. 48.

5. *The Wide World of John Steinbeck* (Brunswick, N.J., 1958), p. 95.

6. *John Steinbeck* (New York, 1962), p. 42.

7. "The Lost Dream of Sex and Childbirth in 'The Chrysanthemums,'" *Modern Fiction Studies*, XI (Spring 1965), 54–58.

8. Even though this line clearly states that "he did not look old," West refers to him as "the old man" (p. 48), and Lisca calls him "the old potmender" (p. 95).

Charles A. Sweet, Jr. (essay date 1974)

SOURCE: "Ms. Elisa and Steinbeck's 'The Chrysanthemums'," in *Modern Fiction Studies,* Vol. 20, No. 2, Summer, 1974, pp. 210–14

[*Here, Sweet asserts that "The Chrysanthemums" can be read as Steinbeck's response to feminism.*]

In a recent article on Steinbeck's **"The Chrysanthemums,"** Elizabeth McMahan began "Virtually every critic who has considered John Steinbeck's short story **'The Chrysanthemums'** has agreed that its basic theme is a woman's frustration, but none has yet adequately explained the emotional reasons underlying that frustration."[1] Indeed the conflict in the story derives from the relationship between Elisa Allen's sexuality and her interest in gardening, both elements that culminate with the visit from an itinerant fixer. In a lengthy interpretation Mordecai Marcus focuses on Elisa's desire for childbirth[2] as relating the elements while Elizabeth McMahan sees the motivation under the general desire for "what women's magazines vaguely call 'romance.'"[3] F. W. Watt is much too brief and ambiguous himself in deciding Elisa's is a "struggle to express and fulfil [*sic*] desires which are ambiguously sexual and spiritual."[4] Warren French simply notes that "Elisa Allen's passionate affection for the flowers . . . symbolize her feeling of closeness to a rhythm of nature."[5] Ray B. West, Jr. also sees this story in terms of an "affinity between human passion and the rich soil of the land."[6] Joseph Fontenrose only mentions that the tinker has "awakened dormant urges within her, so that she felt like breaking away from her secure domesticity and taking to the open road."[7] Kenneth Kempton almost gives up, complaining "one can perceive a broad motive [frustration]," and then finds that this motive deteriorates into "symbols of her unmotivated personality."[8]

There is motivation here but the majority of critics have so centered on the psychology of Elisa that they have neglected her relationship to the structure of the story and at least a semi-sociological approach that explains the relationship between the sexuality, the garden, and the fixer. In 1958 Peter Lisca dropped a hint (though he never elaborated) about the direction of future interpretation when he noted that "Elisa's silent rebellion against the passive role required of her as a woman (symbolized by her masculine manner of gardening) is triggered by the old pot-mender. . . ."[9] Yet, in 1965 Marcus probably summarized the critical reception by dismissing Lisca's observation as "It is unlikely that Steinbeck was generalizing about a masculine protest in woman. . . ."[10] Often contemporary situations shed new light on old problems, and so it seems that the best way of understanding Elisa Allen, her garden, and her sexuality can be accomplished by regarding her as an embryonic feminist, as Ms. Elisa Allen. In fact, **"The Chrysanthemums"** can then be read as Steinbeck's response to feminism.

In order to understand this idea fully, it is first necessary to note that Steinbeck has juxtaposed two parallel situations. Henry Allen is the successful owner of a ranch while Elisa Allen works her garden; that is, Elisa's garden functions as a microcosm of Henry's ranch. When the story opens, Elisa's attention and ours focuses on Henry Allen's conversation with two strangers. When Elisa inquires about the purpose of the meeting, Henry explains "They were from the Western Meat Company. I sold those thirty head of three-year-old steers. Got nearly my own price, too."[11] Thus, in the initial section of the story Henry Allen completes a successful business transaction.

The second section of the story likewise pivots around a business deal, Elisa's with the fixer. In fact, an understanding of Elisa is predicated upon seeing the relationship between the results of the two deals. First, however, the initial section has also provided an insight into Elisa's personality. Like her rancher-husband Elisa is always described as working. Furthermore, she is dressed in a masculine manner: in a "man's black hat," heavy gloves, and a big corduroy apron obscuring the dress which connotes her feminine identity. The Allen home has also been transformed into a masculine structure looking "hardswept" and "hard-polished." Elisa's lack of satisfaction with the female role is indicated also by her complacency in her ability and desire to extend these abilities into heretofore masculine areas. When Henry notes she has a "strong" crop on the way, Elisa likes the word for its masculine implications and Steinbeck adds, "In her tone and on her face there was a little smugness." When Henry jokes with her about working in his orchard, Elisa not only knows she is capable of doing it but also boasts about her "planters' hands." Henry undercuts her response by offering her a typical feminine evening—since she doesn't want to attend the fights—and reminds her he has been "Just fooling."

In the second section the business transaction begins with the arrival of the fixer who becomes for Elisa what the meat buyers were for Henry. Ms. Allen has learned from Henry how to conduct herself and so she begins by joking with the fixer, who like Elisa is dressed in masculine black. When the fixer asks for directions, Elisa not only gives them but makes a value judgment about his team and again jokes with him.

So far all of Elisa's actions have been conscious and calculated to operate in a masculine world, but after the fixer speaks, her actions becomes less conscious and more feminine. Unconsciously she removes the masculine work gloves and straightens her hair-do. Suddenly the fixer becomes more confident and tries some of his typical, sympathetic appeals to women. But Ms. Allen is ready for traditional approaches. So the fixer, realizing her self-assurance, alters his attack to the point of her expressed pride. But for Elisa her connection with flowers goes deeper than Henry's pride with his cattle.

While the cattle represent successful masculine strength, the chrysanthemums symbolize Elisa's masculine endeavors that are as illusory as the flowers—"like a quick puff of colored smoke." In the opening paragraph Steinbeck noted "the yellow-stubble fields seemed to be bathed in pale cold sunshine, but there was no sunshine in the valley now in December." Interestingly the fixer is also stubble-bearded and hence illusory in appearance. Furthermore, Steinbeck has Elisa place the chrysanthemums in a pot. In so doing Elisa runs "excitedly" and tears "off the battered hat and shook out her dark pretty hair." Emerging femininity then begins to thwart Elisa's attempt to operate in a masculine society and the main ingredient of Elisa's emotion is, as the pot foreshadows, her basic feminine sexuality. This embryonic sexuality colors and hinders her progress. In fact, as she kneels before the fixer reduced to a "fawning dog," her speech reveals the inherent weakness of her drive for equality in a masculine world. "I've never lived as you do, but I know what you mean. When the night is dark—why, the stars are sharp-pointed, and there's quiet. Why, you rise up and up! Every pointed star gets driven into your body. It's like that. Hot and sharp and—lovely."

Elisa is limited by her own feminine self which inextricably couples sexuality with equality. Therefore, Steinbeck seems to indicate that the sexuality inherent in woman prevents her from attaining equality. The fixer's response corroborates this notion. Confronted with a sexually excited woman, the fixer's mind is engaged, not his emotions; in fact, he is able to use Elisa's emotions against her. Initially he responds to her invitation very practically: "It's nice, just like you say. Only when you don't have no dinner, it ain't." Thus, his appeal is wrapped in sympathy, but unlike Elisa he is *not* involved with or completely unaware of the emotion. So when Elisa returns with materials to be repaired and her face "ashamed," she has become her own victim, not really that of the fixer who is now completely "professional." Caught up in the emotionality of her situation, Elisa's desires for equality are now bathed in failure; "It must be very nice," Elisa notes, "I wish women could do such things." After having watched the flaw in her scheme unveil itself, the fixer denies the possibility. Elisa ironically responds "How do you know?" Immediately afterwards she continues her delusion with "I could show you what a woman might do." But alas, she has already shown what a woman has done when activated by a male.

After the fixer's departure Elisa engages unconsciously in ritualistic purification. However, rather than cleansing herself of released emotion she is unawarely retreating further into pure femininity. Rebuffed in the masculine world she actually cleanses herself of the masculine situation by turning to the feminine world in which she best functions. Putting on her dress and her "newest underclothing" as well as making up her eyes and lips is a total withdrawal from equal competition and an unconscious admission that in her basic feminine nature is her power, not as a fawning supplicant but as an attractive, seductive female.

Upon returning Henry immediately notices her transformation which he so indicates by using the feminine adjective "nice" rather than the more masculine "strong." Although Elisa prefers "strong," for her the word's meaning has obviously shifted from "masculine equal" to "feminine overlord" and a false pride in her strength that Henry immediately undercuts. For when he describes her ability in a masculine manner as seeming "strong enough to break a calf over your knee," she momentarily looses her rigidity and composure. But if equality is impossible, dominance looms as better than suppression. So when Henry goes for the car, she waits until he not only brings it but also tires of waiting before she joins him.

Even before Elisa can discern the true shape of the dark speck, she knows what she has already unconsciously assimilated. In her business deal, which is the true test of her desired equality, she has been less successful than her husband. Where Henry had received almost his price for the cattle, Elisa has received nothing for her chrysanthemums. Instead she has paid the fixer fifty cents to perform a task she admittedly could do. She has failed to communicate with the fixer as he has taken her pot and thrown away the chrysanthemums; more importantly he has stripped her of her dignity and dreams of equality. And finally when he was faced with a fawning, sexually-aroused woman, he rejected her for that, too. Elisa can not even take refuge in her basic sexual femininity. And so she is even further reduced to the wife whose hard work is rewarded simply with a token Saturday night out. She accepts this lesser role by mentioning "It will be good tonight, a good dinner." Her desires for revenge are useless as she doesn't even want to go to the fights. And in the end her dreams of feminine equality are so shattered that her former state is impossible; she accepts her social role and turns the corner at thirty-five; now she is only "an old woman."

Mordecai Marcus, trying to negate the feminism in the story, has commented it is "unthinkable that he [Steinbeck] was suggesting that woman's role must be passive. . . ."[12] Yet, that is exactly what a close analysis of **"The Chrysanthemums"** reveals. Elisa Allen is no Myra Breckinridge wishing to be Myron but instead the representative of the feminist ideal of equality and its inevitable defeat. The point of the story is not, as previous critics have stressed, that Elisa possesses an unfulfilled sexual need, but rather that the feminist is still a woman and women are fundamentally emotional, as evidenced by tears or sexual arousal. Whereas a man can function unemotionally in the masculine business world and receive nearly his own price, a woman soon operates at less than a rational level and is victimized both by her basic nature and by others. There is nothing to suggest that Elisa's relationship with Henry is sexually inadequate. But Mailer and Miller aside, a woman has other dimensions than the sexual.

However, for Steinbeck a masculine-dominated society has so conditioned a female's basic emotional response that in such situations it is inevitably released. Thus, the fixer is only generically guilty. Moreover Elisa's frustration is compounded by being faced with an unfamiliar situation; a male has aroused her but does not want her—she has become a pure object. Though not to the degree of Hemingway, Steinbeck's world is a man's world, a world that frustrates even minor league women's liberationists.

Notes

1. "'The Chrysanthemums': Study of A Woman's Sexuality," *Modern Fiction Studies*, 14 (Winter 1968–1969), 453.

2. "The Last Dream of Sex and Childbirth in 'The Chrysanthemums,'" *Modern Fiction Studies*, 11 (Spring 1965), 54–8.

3. McMahan, p. 455.

4. *John Steinbeck* (New York: Grove Press, 1962), p. 43.

5. *John Steinbeck* (New York: Twayne Publishers, 1961), p. 83.

6. *The Short Story in America: 1900–1950* (Chicago: H. Regnery Co., 1952), p. 48.

7. *John Steinbeck* (New York: Barnes and Noble, 1963), p. 62.

8. *Short Stories For Study* (Cambridge: Harvard University Press, 1953), p. 124.

9. *The Wide World of John Steinbeck* (Brunswick, N.J.: Rutgers University Press, 1958), p. 95.

10. Marcus, p. 58.

11. All quotations come from *The Long Valley* (New York: Viking Press, 1958), the revised text Steinbeck designated as proper.

12. Marcus, p. 58.

Roy S. Simmonds (essay date 1974)

SOURCE: "The Original Manuscripts of Steinbeck's 'The Chrysanthemums'," in *Steinbeck Quarterly*, Vol. VII, Nos. 3–4, Summer-Fall, 1974, pp. 102–11.

[*In the following essay, Simmonds argues that Elisa Allen, contrary to popular opinion, is not a sympathetic figure.*]

In recent years what has almost amounted to a small critical industry has grown up around Steinbeck's short story, **"The Chrysanthemums."** It is obvious that this particular story has attracted a more than average share of expository attention due principally to the various interpretations which can be placed upon the behaviour of its central character, Elisa Allen, and upon the somewhat ambiguous relationship which seems to exist between Elisa and her husband, Henry. Surveys of these disparate interpretations have already been provided in Elizabeth E. McMahan's "'The Chrysanthemums': Study of a Woman's Sexuality"[1] and William V. Miller's more recent essay, "Sexual and Spiritual Ambiguity in "The Chrysanthemums',"[2] and it is not my intent here to go over such old ground again in detail.

This vexed question of interpretation has been complicated by the fact, as William R. Osborne established in his pioneer textual study,[3] that two published versions of the story exist: the version which Osborne designates "Text 1" which appeared in the October 1937 issue of *Harper's Magazine* and "Text 2" which was first published in the collection *The Long Valley* (Viking Press, 1938). Osborne

regretted that the author had not declared which of the two versions he himself preferred.

According to McMahan, however, Steinbeck "indicated that the text as published in **The Long Valley** should be considered the correct version."[4] We were thus given an authoritative opinion on the matter and this would seem, on the face of it, to have established a certain sequence of events. Indeed, both McMahan and Miller state that "Text 2" was the version Steinbeck *revised* for **The Long Valley,** in the process of which, according to McMahan, the "most explicitly sexual passage was added"[5] and, according to Miller, Steinbeck "stressed the sexual imagery"[6] of the story. Both these statements unfortunately contain a basic misconception of the true facts, as an examination of the original manuscript of **"The Chrysanthemums"** will reveal.

It is my purpose in this article to achieve two main objects: firstly, to suggest that the long-accepted view of Elisa as a wholly sympathetic character may possibly be open to question; secondly, to contend that a textual study of the original manuscript of the final version of the story makes it patently obvious that Steinbeck was obliged to tone down some of the sexual implications in the work to mollify the editors of *Harper's Magazine*.

The manuscript is in the Pascal Covici-John Steinbeck Collection at the Humanities Research Center, University of Texas at Austin, and forms part of the material in a notebook which contains, among other items, the manuscripts of the novel *Tortilla Flat* and of the short stories **"The Murder"** and **"A Leader of the People."** The manuscript of **"The Chrysanthemums,"** written in Steinbeck's small but extremely legible handwriting, occupies seven and a half sides of the 33cm. by 21.5cm. white blue-lined paper.

There is ample evidence to demonstrate that Steinbeck experienced some difficulty in getting the story off the ground. A few pages before the full manuscript version there is an earlier abortive version. For ease of reference I shall refer to the first, incomplete, version as "Manuscript A" and the second, complete, version as "Manuscript B." Steinbeck completed only the first paragraph of "Manuscript A" before he broke off and began setting down his random musings concerning both the story and the current circumstances of his life. He was apparently going through an unhappy period generally. It is possible to fix accurately the date on which he began working on the story for he mentions the date "Wednesday the 31st. January." The 31st. January fell on a Wednesday in the year 1934.

Steinbeck in these musings endeavours to reassure himself: "This is to be a good story. Two personalities meet [,] cross, flare, die and hate each other. Purple, if it were a little bit stronger, would be a good color for the story." The mention of the color purple relates to the color of the ink with which he was briefly experimenting. By the following day, he had abandoned the purple ink. "What is there about this story which makes it almost impossible for me to write it[?] There is a section of great ecstasy in it. It is a good story as I see it. I'm having a terrible time writing it. And I should get it done for I suspect I shall get a beastly reception for T.F. [*Tortilla Flat*] and much as I fight against it, I shall be upset by that reception." And later: "Now the story of the Chrysanthemums is to go on and may the [L]ord have mercy upon it. A story of great delicacy [,] one difficult to produce. I must do this one well or not at all. I'm getting the feel back." But he obviously was not. After two more pages, the second of which is impatiently scored through, the text breaks off again. "There's no sureness of touch in me today. I don't seem to be able to get to this story. I shouldn't be writing this story this way at all."

"Manuscript A" opens with a description of Elisa washing the noonday dishes at the kitchen sink. Her husband, Henry, is in the dining room and she knows he is waiting to tell her something. He is described as a "strange ceremonious man" who needs to arrange things exactly the way he wants before embarking on any announcement. Elisa plainly finds this attitude of his intensely irritating. She deliberately takes her time over the dishes. "She would wear down his patience and then start him wrong. It amused her to do this and it gave her a nice secret sense of power with which to combat the fact that she, Elisa, valedictorian of her class at the Salinas High School, winner of two State wide essay contests was the wife of a fairly successful farmer. She wiped the bottoms of the pans with the dishrag and put them away under the sink. She was not unhappy[,] only, [sic] the essay contests had placed her high, and sometimes this marriage with a farmer seemed to place her rather low."

When eventually she does go into the dining room she carries out her plan to "start him wrong" by immediately upbraiding Henry for not wiping the soles of his boots properly and, due to his carelessness, treading manure into the house. He protests against this false charge, but she presses the accusation and then further confuses him and ruins his little "ceremony" by asking him what is the "secret" he wishes to tell her. "How did you know?" he asks. "I wish you wouldn't do it. It makes me nervous to have anybody know what I'm thinking. It would make anybody nervous." He then informs her that he has completed an agreement with a seed company to plant twenty acres of sweet peas on his land. Elisa is delighted when she hears this and is a little ashamed of the way she has treated him. "Why the whole ranch will be perfumed. It will be beautiful. I'm terribly glad[,] Henry." There then follows a conversation more or less similar to the one in the published version when Henry proposes that they should celebrate by going into town for dinner and jokingly suggests that she might like to go to the fights. After he has left the house to attend to his afternoon's work, she daydreams about the fields of sweet peas in terms which contain explicit phallic imagery: "Twenty acres of sweet peas, solid squares of color and solid columns of scent, big towers of perfume if only you could see them."

In "Manuscript A," Henry's personality is more fully delineated than it is in "Manuscript B" and in the published version. He is presented in this earlier version as an unsympathetic and slightly ridiculous character. Elisa's reaction to him also makes her appear somewhat unsympathetic. There is very little subtlety inherent in the marital relationship Steinbeck here describes. Fortunately Steinbeck realized this comparatively early: "I had a story . . . and on a day I did not feel like writing, I sat down to write it. Two days of work passed before I realized that I was doing it all wrong. And now it must be done again.

Subconsciously I knew it was wrong from the beginning. But I blundered on, putting down words every one of which had an untrue ring. . . ."

A day or so later, he commenced the second—this time successful—attempt to write the story. On the next recto page of the notebook following that on which he recorded his admission of initial failure, the title **"The Chrysanthemums"** again appears, followed on that page and the ensuing six and a half pages by the first complete draft of the story. The opening sentence differs only very slightly in detail from the opening sentence of the published version: "The high grey flannel fog of winter close[d] off the Salinas valley from the sky and from the rest of the world." It is remarkable that Steinbeck could, after all the problems he had been encountering, produce in what appears to have been one flowing surge of creativity the short story which André Gide compared favorably with the best of Chekhov and which Mordecai Marcus unequivocally regards as "one of the world's great short stories."[7]

There are, naturally, considerable differences of detail by way of elaboration, deletion and refinement between "Manuscript B" and the published text. But the progression of the narrative line and the overall construction of the story are identical from one version to the other. A good example of the way in which Steinbeck carried out his revisions to the text is provided near the beginning of the story by comparing the introductory description of Elisa in the "Manuscript B" version with the description in the published version.

The description in "Manuscript B" reads:

> Elisa was thirty-five, but she looked older in her gardening costume, a man's hat pulled down on her head, clodhopper shoes and a big corduroy apron, littered with pockets, for snips, a little trowel, and seeds. Elisa wore leather gloves to protect her hands.

The published version is very much expanded:

> She was thirty-five. Her face was lean and strong and her eyes were as clear as water. Her figure looked blocked and heavy in her gardening costume, a man's hat pulled low down over her eyes, clodhopper shoes, a figured print dress almost completely covered by a big corduroy apron with four big pockets to hold the snips, the trowel and scratcher, the seeds and the knife she worked with. She wore heavy leather gloves to protect her hands while she worked.

This description of Elisa is in fact the passage which has undergone the most considerable elaboration from "Manuscript B" to published version. Steinbeck clearly wished to establish Elisa's physical appearance very carefully. It is surely not without significance that she evolves from the rather shadowy figure of the manuscript version into the almost masculine figure of the published version with her "lean and strong" face, her "blocked and heavy" figure and the "heavy leather gloves" she is wearing. Certainly, from the physical aspect she seems to exude precious little female sexuality. A little later, too, her face is described as "eager and mature and handsome," which again does not suggest a personality endowed with fragile feminine grace and beauty.

Indeed, as has already been mentioned, it is precisely this question of Elisa's sexuality and the ambiguity of the implied relationships in the story which have so fascinated scholars and commentators. D. H. Lawrence's influence on Steinbeck has often been noted,[8] and it is possible to regard Elisa and the tinker as representative Lawrentian characters: Elisa the sexually unfulfilled woman, the tinker the romantically virile man of nature who (only symbolically in this story however) seduces her.

Most scholars to date have postulated the theory that Elisa is a similarly frustrated woman, that her husband is unable to satisfy her sexual hunger. It has even been proposed that Henry is impotent. I would however suggest that there is a case for suspecting that Elisa is the one who is unable or unwilling to satisfy her partner sexually. All her sex drive seems to be directed towards the care and propagation of her flowers, the phallic symbols over which she exercises complete mastery. This feeling that Elisa has for her flowers is perhaps more forcibly expressed in the original wording of the "Manuscript B" text, which is reproduced below, rather than it is in the published text. The words in italics represent Steinbeck's above-the-line revisions and/or additions, and the words in parentheses represent deletions.

> *It's* [w]hen you're budding (your mind and your soul and your love) *everything* go[es] right down into your finger tips. You watch your fingers work (and) [word illegible] you can feel (the joy in them) *how it is.*

Elisa's carelessness in the matter of her everyday attire, her obvious reluctance to accept the fact of her femininity—exemplified by the manner in which she scrubs her body after the tinker has left (perhaps an over-reaction to his comment that his sort of existence was not "the right kind of life for a woman" as well as being the symbolic act of purification it is popularly accepted to represent) and by the belligerent manner in which she again over-reacts to her husband's surprised comment on how "nice" she looks dressed up for the trip to Salinas—indicates a personality who rejects the submissive female role, who even finds the act of love wholly distasteful and to be avoided whenever possible. "I'm strong," she boasts to Henry. "I never knew before how strong."

In the published version of the story we are given very little information about Henry. Not even the merest mention is made of his physical appearance. He remains a shadowy figure throughout the story and because of this indistinctness it is possible to regard him more sympathetically than the Henry of "Manuscript A." He is patently the weaker of the two personalities, as indeed he is unequivocally presented in "Manuscript A." In that first version, as we have seen, Elisa rejoices in her sense of dominance over her husband. Whilst I would agree that there could be considerable dangers in linking characterizations drawn in that first version with the protagonists as presented in "Manuscript B" and the published version, I would nevertheless submit that Eliza's behavior in "Manuscript A" goes some way towards explaining much of her behavior in the published version. The manner in which she mocks her husband when he compliments her upon her appearance and her perverse action in keeping him waiting while she puts on her coat, forcing him to idle the car motor, and then going out the moment he switches off

the motor have tended to be regarded as simply her reaction to the tinker's visit and a manifestation of the feeling of discontent he has engendered in her. To my mind, however, these actions are more indicative of what is probably the normal pattern of Elisa's and Henry's married life.

Elisa's need for this sense of dominance over the male is not confined solely to her feelings towards her husband. She experiences this need to assert her superiority over all men, contriving always to keep them at arm's length. Her flower garden is surrounded by a protective wire fence ostensibly to keep out animals, but the fence also serves to exclude her husband and the tinker. It is not until the tinker has verbally seduced her with his assumed interest in her chrysanthemums and is admitted to her side of the fence that Elisa finds her defenses in danger of collapsing to the extent that she almost allows herself to succumb to male dominance. Almost, but not quite. "Kneeling there, her hand went toward his legs in the greasy black trousers. Her hesitant fingers almost touched the cloth. Then her hand dropped to the ground. She crouched low like a fawning dog." When eventually she rises to her feet there is a look of shame on her face. Again, the general interpretation has been that her shame is the shame of a married woman briefly tempted by thoughts of possible clandestine sexual adventure. I would alternatively suggest that her shame is the shame of a woman who realizes that she has momentarily lowered her defenses and all but offered herself to the male dominance she so greatly despises. It is significant that for all the sexually-charged atmosphere that exists between Elisa and the tinker during the short time of his visit they never at any point make actual physical contact. She does not touch his trousered legs. She does admittedly hand him the flowerpot and the two saucepans and takes the saucepans back from him, but there would be no touching of hands in doing this. When she comes to pay him, she avoids physical contact by dropping the fifty cent piece into his hand.

Apart from the one little lapse, Elisa maintains, at least in her own mind, her dominance over the tinker. When the man first arrives, she deprecates (in semi-humorous fashion) the prowess of his dog and then of his mismatched team. Later she insists that she would be equal to living his rough open-air life with all that it entails and finally she challenges his own prowess, claiming that she could sharpen scissors and mend pots just as efficiently, if not better, than he.

An examination of the two original manuscript versions of the story thus provides further possible insights into Elisa's true nature and dispels some of the ambiguity that surrounds her. Additionally, such examination does to some extent resolve the confusion that has been generated by the two differing published texts. Even the most superficial examination of "Manuscript B" will show that the "most explicitly sexual passage" added, according to McMahan, when Steinbeck revised "Text 1" to produce "Text 2" for the Viking edition did in fact exist from the very beginning. The "Manuscript B" text reads:

> Elisa's voice (was) *grew* husky. *She broke in on him.* "I've never lived as you do but I know what you (want to say) *mean.* When the night is dark—(and) *why* the stars are sharp pointed and there's quiet. Why you (seem to) rise up and *up*[.] Every pointed star gets

driven into *you, into* your body. It's like that, hot and sharp and—all lovely." Kneeling there her hand went out toward his legs in the (dirty) *greasy* black trousers[,] *almost touched the cloth.* (Then h) Her hand dropped to the ground. She crouched low (and clamped her throat on the rising sobs *felt that*) *like a fawning dog.*

The inference is, of course, that the above passage was modified for consumption by the readers of *Harper's Magazine* and that Steinbeck simply restored the cuts (totalling four sentences) when the story was reprinted in **The Long Valley** the following year.

Similarly, the Viking text most closely follows the "Manuscript B" text in the passage describing Elisa's sighting of the discarded chrysanthemum shoots. Obviously, the perfect pithiness of the passage as originally written was gauged to be confusing to the magazine's readers and had to be made more expository. The "Manuscript B" text reads:

> When *far ahead on the road* Elisa saw a dark speck (far ahead on the road,)[.] (s)She knew. She tried not to look as they passed it but her eyes would not obey. She whispered to herself. ["]He might have thrown them off the road—that wouldn't have been much trouble, *not very much.* But he kept the pot—["]her throat tightened, ["]he had to keep the pot. *That's why he couldn't get them off the road.* ["]

And later:

> In a moment the thing was done. She did not look back.

In thus establishing firmly the correct sequence of the various texts some doubts must be cast on the validity of the additional expository material contained in "Text 1." It must be assumed that Steinbeck himself did write it, but reconsidered in the light of what the examination of the manuscripts reveals the description of Elisa's reactions in the *Harper's* text do not somehow ring true. "She felt ashamed of her strong planter's hands, that were no use, lying palms up in her lap." The Elisa who comes so clearly into vision, personality-wise in "Manuscript A" and by description in "Manuscript B" and the published versions, would never have been "ashamed" of her planter's hands. Her tears at the end of the story are the tears of a bitter, defeated woman. They stem not from the recognition that the tinker had tricked her into giving him work or from any hurt she might be suffering because he had discarded her precious chrysanthemums almost the moment he was out of sight of the farm. Rather her tears stem from her painful and reluctant acceptance of the fact that the tinker had, by that one action of throwing the flowers away, symbolically re-established the position of male dominance she imagined she had wrested from him, in exactly the same way as over the years she had deprived, emasculated, her husband. This interpretation surely provides a very different reading—though to my mind an equally valid one—from that based on Joseph Warren Beach's early assessment of Elisa as "one of the most delicious characters ever transferred from life to the pages of a book."[9]

Notes

1. Elizabeth E. McMahan, "'The Chrysanthemums': Study of a Woman's Sexuality," *Modern Fiction Studies*, 14 (Winter 1968–69), 453–8.

2. William V. Miller, "Sexual and Spiritual Ambiguity in 'The Chrysanthemums'." *Steinbeck Quarterly*, 5 (Summer-Fall 1972), 68–75.

3. William R. Osborne, "The Texts of Steinbeck's 'The Chrysanthemums'," *Modern Fiction Studies*, 12 (Winter 1966–67), 479–84.

4. McMahan, 454.

5. *Ibid.*

6. Miller, 73.

7. Mordecai Marcus, "The Lost Dream of Sex and Childbirth in 'The Chrysanthemums'," *Modern Fiction Studies* 11 (Spring 1965), 54–8.

8. See Richard F. Peterson's "The God in the Darkness: A Study of John Steinbeck and D. H. Lawrence" in *Steinbeck's Literary Dimension: A Guide to Comparative Studies*, ed. Tetsumaro Hayashi (Metuchen, N.J.: Scarecrow Press, 1973), pp. 67–82 and Reloy Garcia's *Steinbeck and D. H. Lawrence: Fictive Voices and the Ethical Imperative* (Steinbeck Monograph Series, No. 2, 1972).

9. Joseph Warren Beach, "John Steinbeck: Journeyman Artist," in *Steinbeck and His Critics*, ed. E. W. Tedlock, Jr. and C. V. Wicker (Albuquerque: University of New Mexico Press, 1957), p. 83.

> Quotations from the unpublished manuscripts of "The Chrysanthemums" are used by courtesy of the Humanities Research Center, University of Texas at Austin, Texas.

Stanley Renner (essay date 1985)

SOURCE: "The Real Woman Inside the Fence in 'The Chrysanthemums'," in *Modern Fiction Studies*, Vol. 31, No. 2, Summer, 1985, pp. 305–17.

[*In the following essay, Renner interprets "The Chrysanthemums" as "informed far less by feminist sympathies than by traditional 'masculist' complaints."*]

Steinbeck's classic short story **"The Chrysanthemums"** has long attracted admiration and respect from discriminating readers and eminent critics. But quite clearly the story's fame was enhanced during the last couple of decades as it was caught up in the eager discovery of works of literature dramatizing the female consciousness and was, in effect, included in the feminist canon.[1] Indeed, in the criticism of this period, **"The Chrysanthemums"** emerges as something of a feminist tract. The keynote was sounded in the late Fifties when Peter Lisca commented on "Elisa's silent rebellion against the passive role required of her as a woman" (95). As the woman's movement gathered momentum, critics enthusiastically followed the lead, and the standard reading developed: **"The Chrysanthemums"** is a story about a strong, capable woman kept from personal, social, and sexual fulfillment by the prevailing conception of a woman's role in a world dominated by men. Her husband, decent but dull, excludes her from the important business of the ranch. Content with the way things are in their marriage, he ignores her lack of fulfillment in keeping house and raising flowers. When an itinerant tinker happens by, Elisa's latent yearnings are awakened for the larger life that men enjoy of significant work, adventure, and sexual expression; and when she entrusts the tinker with cuttings from her chrysanthemums, she, in effect, reaches out to the wider world. But the tinker dumps her flowers in the public thoroughfare, thus rejecting her gesture toward a larger life, and she remains a pitiable victim of male domination and female disadvantage.[2]

I must make it clear at the outset that I have no objection to stories such as the one I have summarized. I simply want to question whether the story as it appears in the criticism is the one Steinbeck wrote. He himself implied that **"The Chrysanthemums"** might have a delayed and surprising impact on the reader (Steinbeck and Wallsten 91). The closer one looks at the story, the more one sees that the prevailing interpretation fails to square with its figurative design and structure, in which the female protagonist appears to be less a woman imprisoned by men than one who secures herself within a fortress of sexual reticence and self-withholding defensiveness. For one thing, Elisa Allen is a good deal more like the monstrously narcissistic Mary Teller of **"The White Quail,"** companion piece to **"The Chrysanthemums,"** than has yet been perceived. For another, the story's central image and its main and recurring action are a virtual obverse of the feminist view of a woman smothered by male domination. Finally, although, of course, biography need not inevitably determine a writer's perspective, Steinbeck's feelings about his marriage at the time the story was written were far from those of the implied author who would have written the essentially feminist version of the story.

As they are juxtaposed in *The Long Valley,* **"The Chrysanthemums"** and **"The White Quail"** are also often juxtaposed in discussions of Steinbeck's short fiction. Because of the presumption that the former is sympathetic to the female protagonist's plight and the latter is clearly not, Elisa Allen and Mary Teller are customarily discussed in terms of contrast.[3] In balance, I believe the story far more strongly supports the opposite conclusion: although there are minor differences between Elisa and Mary, physically and emotionally they are very much the same woman presented in different fictional contexts. **"The White Quail"** is something of a fable about a narcissistic female withholding herself from the grossness of physical intimacy in a marital relationship. To a significant extent **"The Chrysanthemums"** puts a quite similar female protagonist into a different kind of story, one more balanced and realistic.

Both Elisa and Mary, for example, are named after women famous for their virginity: Mary, of course, after the Madonna, whose virginity bespeaks her deeply spiritual calling, and Elisa for the Virgin Queen, whose virginity is associated with sexual reticence and fear. Both are married to men named Henry (Harry is a diminutive of Henry), meaning "ruler of a home or enclosure." The husband's name is ironic in both cases: Elisa and Mary are both associated with enclosures, but they control the enclosures, rejecting their husbands' attempts to enter. In physical terms both women are attractive. Mary is repeatedly described as pretty, while Elisa, perhaps because she is older, is described as "handsome" (10). Both, we are to understand, have a good deal of sex appeal. Mary makes her husband "kind of—hungry" (29); Elisa, with her "dark

pretty hair" (16), green thumb, and aura of glowing health and physical vitality, seems ripe for sensual enjoyment and sexual completion. Yet both women are childless. Both have their own room and presumably sleep apart from their husbands. Both women repulse the amorous advances of their husbands. Mary occasionally lets Harry kiss her, but when, night after night, he tries the door of her bedroom, he always finds it locked. Elisa, as we shall see, characteristically stiffens and turns cold at the approach of Henry, even as they prepare for a romantic evening in town.

Both Elisa and Mary are almost compulsive gardeners. Both grow flowers that, by universal agreement, symbolize themselves, their beauty, their femininity, and their sexuality. The gardens are carefully protected from natural intruders, Mary's by a cordon of fuchsias, Elisa's by a chicken-wire fence. In their gardens both women wear clothing that protects them from injury and contamination by the earth from which their flowers grow and from the insidious crawling predators that threaten their flowers. In **"The White Quail"** these predators have been recognized as suggestive of the sexual threat to Mary's fastidious sensibilities. In fact, both Mary and Elisa manifest an aversion to things such as "dirt, rust, disorder, and slimy things like the slugs" that represent the grosser implications of sexuality to their refined, carefully cultivated femininity symbolized by the flowers (Mitchell 308). Elisa's house is a virtual fortress—"hard swept" and "close-banked" all around with "red geraniums"—against the muddy earth and animal predators that threaten Elisa as flower (10). And in both cases the delicate, untouched flowers, associated with their femininity, stand as a sterile substitute for the children they do not have.

These extensive and detailed likenesses indicate not merely the close similarity between the two characterizations but a certain kind of similarity. In the paradoxical asexuality of these sexually appealing women we see the figure of woman rejecting her natural biological role in marriage. This is clearly true of Mary Teller, who has determinedly contrived to secure herself within a protective fortress of idealism, symbolized by the garden, which is pointedly identified as "herself" (28). In **"The White Quail"** Steinbeck attacks the idealization of love, woman, and marriage that has troubled Anglo-American culture since Victorian times.[4] As Mary withdraws from the sexual component of the marital relationship into her garden of the ideal, her husband, who in his conscious mind supports his wife's idealism, experiences a growing unconscious sexual frustration, which explodes in unintended violence in the story's striking climax. The figurative structure of **"The Chrysanthemums"** suggests that the problem in the Allens' marriage is an extension of the conflict in **"The White Quail,"** but with the emphasis on the consequences to the woman in such a sterile relationship instead of to the man.

The central image of **"The Chrysanthemums"** is that of a woman inside a fenced-in enclosure, cultivating flowers that symbolize her femininity. The central action of the story is that of men coming up to the fence and either inviting her to come out of the enclosure or endeavoring to be admitted inside the fence. The action unfolds in three movements. First, Elisa's husband, Henry, comes up to the fence to invite his wife out for an evening in town. She accepts his invitation, but he remains outside the fence, and she remains inside. Next, an itinerant handyman, an utter stranger, comes up to the fence and after some maneuvering is welcomed inside the enclosure. He carries off cuttings of her prized flowers, generally recognized as symbols of her vibrant, but somehow unfulfilled, sexuality. In the third movement, actually a continuation of the first, Elisa comes out of her garden and the couple get ready for the evening; but, curiously, she acts as though she is still inside her wire fence, and as the couple head for town it remains unclear, perhaps doubtful, whether her husband will be admitted inside her enclosure.

The focus of the action is the garden, a rich and complex symbol of Elisa's strong and healthy female potentiality. The flowers, as Elisabeth E. McMahan observes, suggest her ripe, glowing sex appeal: with "great soft blossoms shaped like a woman's breasts . . . they suggest the voluptuous softness of a sexually mature woman" (455). The descriptions of Elisa's skillful and productive gardening show that she is indeed a woman with capabilities far beyond those engaged by her flowers. Readers have been quick to note that at thirty-five she is still childless; thus, when the story states that the flowers "seemed too small and easy for her energy" (10), the rich sexual implications of the figurative context immediately call attention to the paradox of Elisa: here is a woman characterized as the epitome of sexual ripeness, a woman who seems to have been created in every way for reproduction—with the sex appeal to attract fertilization, the physical vitality to produce healthy offspring, and the strength, skill, and temperament to nurture living things through the growth cycle—but who, though she has been married presumably for several years, has no child. It is a major function of the figurative design of **"The Chrysanthemums"** to raise and answer the question "why?"

But the standard explanation, that Elisa's rich potential is being denied by the limiting conception of what a woman is and can do in a man's world, simply does not square with the figurative design of **"The Chrysanthemums."** The central figure of the story that emerges from the criticism is that of a woman imprisoned by men—the disadvantaged female fenced inside a garden of feminine triviality by a nexus of attitudes and circumstances by which men have asserted and maintained dominance over women. But in the actual story the central figure is that of a woman who has secured herself inside her own protective garden, fenced in against the unwelcome intrusion of men. Far from fencing Elisa inside the garden, the men in the story try to get her out from behind her fence or to open her fence to let them in.

In the story's terms there can be little doubt that the garden and fence are Elisa's own rather than imposed on her by her husband, men, or society. We first see her "working in her flower garden" behind a protective "wire fence" pointedly identified as "Elisa's wire fence" and "her wire fence" (9, 11, 13, 20). After the introduction, which establishes the natural setting to suggest a potential fertility not being fulfilled, the action begins. Elisa is in her garden, dressed in clothing that hides and protects her femininity, engaged in cultivating her flowers; Henry is across the yard selling the steers. The first movement of the action dramatizes Henry's approach to Elisa's fence and her response. Henry's approach is gentle, considerate—anything but that of the dominant male: "He had come near quietly, and he leaned over the wire fence" behind which Elisa and her flowers are protected from predators. In response Elisa "straightened her back and pulled on the gardening glove again" (11), behavior that seems natural enough but through repetition will come to suggest that she characteristically stiffens, puts on protective clothing, and erects defenses against her husband's approach.

What follows does not support the prevailing view of Elisa as relegated to the triviality of gardening and to "the passive role *required* of her as a woman" (my emphasis). Quite the contrary. In this scene she is extended two invitations to come out from behind her fence and join her husband in a more productive life: first to work in the orchard and "raise some apples" and then to go out with him for an evening in town. To grasp the full implications of the story's botanical symbolism, it is useful to remember Steinbeck's keen interest in biology, which began in the early Twenties.

Elisa's flowers are generally understood in the broad sense as evidence of her rich potential to take a more meaningful place in society and in a narrower sense as symbolic of her "very earthy sensuality" (Mitchell 305), her blooming but unrealized fertility, her "sublimation of powerful sexual desires" (Miller 70). In the light of Henry's invitation to raise apples, however, it is important to note that growing flowers is a fruitless occupation. In the life cycle of plants the flower stage is intermediate: a seed is planted and germinates, a plant grows and flowers, the flower is fertilized and develops into fruit containing the seeds of the next generation. If Elisa grows nothing but flowers, her life will remain sterile. But now it is vital to note *how* she grows flowers—asexually. The point of Steinbeck's elaborate descriptions of Elisa meticulously perpetuating her chrysanthemums by transplanting cuttings taken from the old stalks is that she methodically subverts the sexual method of reproduction in which the male stamen deposits pollen on the female pistil, fertilizing the flower and completing the reproductive cycle. Thus Elisa's garden will never bear fruit because her flowers will never be fertilized. Furthermore, her "over-eager" wielding of "powerful scissors," "cutting down the old year's chrysanthemum stalks" (10) standing erect, one may presume, to fulfill their reproductive purpose, is full of ominous sexual portent. William V. Miller has observed that "the flower stems can be regarded in the story's context as phallic," but he sees them as representing the masculine side of Elisa's ambiguous sexuality (70). It is far more faithful to the story's figurative logic to see her cutting down the phallic stems as an emasculation of the male principle. One must therefore question the view that the Allens' marriage "satisfies Henry completely" (McMahan 454) or that "there is no convincing evidence that their marriage fails in the sex act" (Miller 74).[5] Analyzing the curious infertility of a voluptuous female such as Elisa, McMahan finds no evidence of impotence in Henry (455). But as the natural image most closely associated with Elisa is the flower, so the natural image associated with Henry is the steer. It is an interesting measure of the urbanization of American life that even in the middle of Illinois very few of my students (and no critics of the story, to my knowledge) are aware that a steer is a castrated male cow. Very far from representing "successful masculine strength," then, as Charles A. Sweet, Jr., declares (212), the cattle in **"The Chrysanthemums"** suggest instead the extent to which Henry has been unmanned in his marriage to Elisa.[6]

Both Elisa and Henry are associated with images of sterility; small wonder their marriage remains infertile. But it does not appear in the terms of the story that, as Shigeharu Yano asserts, Elisa's "husband is the cause of her frustration" (56). It is she who has fenced herself inside her own garden. In keeping with traditional symbolism, both the woman herself and her sexual organs may be represented in the flower image. Thus Elisa is the sterile flower: avoiding completion of the reproductive cycle, she will produce no new life, only the perpetuation of her sterile beauty and pointless sex appeal. Thus, also, the flower of her sexual enclosure is fenced off, like the garden, against entry and fertilization by the male. Thus, finally, although Henry is not technically impotent, as we shall see, he has been rendered effectively sterile by Elisa's subversion of the natural sexual process.

Approached through the story's figurative design, Henry's invitation to Elisa to come out of her garden and to produce fruit should be understood as an appeal for her to join him in a procreative conjugal relationship. In perhaps the most thoughtless application of the feminist approach to the story, "Henry jokes with her about working in his orchard"—merely mocking her frustrated feminist "desires for equality" with men (Sweet 211, 212). But it is not until sixteen lines later in **The Long Valley,** that "Henry put on his joking tone." Although he keeps his feelings under control, except momentarily in the third movement, his veiled plea for a sexually productive marriage is in utter earnest. To judge the precise emotion informing Henry's invitation, it may be well to remember that Steinbeck himself wanted children and that his first marriage, which remained childless, was several years along when **"The Chrysanthemums"** was written.[7]

Henry's second invitation may now be seen as a logical continuation of the first: he asks his wife, in effect, for a date, thus initiating a time-honored ritual of courtship leading, especially for a married couple, toward culmination in sexual intimacy. Presumably, Saturday night in Salinas, dinner at the Cominos Hotel, and a movie afterwards are the best within reach of this ranch couple in the way of a romantic evening. But in this story replete with sexual imagery, both overt and oblique, the sexual implications of the invitation must be recognized. Henry is wooing his wife in the best tradition of the marriage manuals of the era: to enjoy a successful sexual relationship, because of the woman's more diffuse, more reticent, more emotional sexuality, the husband must continue to court his wife as a romantic lover. Although Elisa accepts Henry's invitation, she remains inside her fence; and her response to the erotic implications of his invitation is unpromising: "It's good," she says only, "to eat away from home" (12).

In the second movement of the action the tinker "pull[s] up to Elisa's wire fence" (13) and maneuvers to get inside. The explicit and oblique sexual imagery in this episode indicates pretty clearly that what is taking place is another implied sexual encounter between male and female, its successive stages marked by the tinker's progress through Elisa's fence. It is a classic confrontation between the hungry male and the reluctant female, who has no comple-

mentary hunger to satisfy. The tinker is the man with a sexual need, with brooding eyes like those "of teamsters and sailors" (13–14)—wandering men without women. Elisa is the woman who feels no sexual need, aloof and wary in her protective clothing behind her wire fence. What takes place, on the figurative level, is oblique sexual sparring as the tinker maneuvers to penetrate the enclosure of the female, discovers a weakness in her defenses, exploits it, and wins admittance inside Elisa's fence. First he rests his hands "on the wire fence"; then "He drew a big finger down the chicken wire" as if testing the fence. As he communicates his need to Elisa, "He leaned confidentially over the fence"; however, needing nothing from him, Elisa's "eyes hardened with resistance" (14). Getting nowhere, the tinker enjoys a flash of intuition. He has assumed in the female a physically oriented sexuality complementary to his own, symbolized by the pots—the containers—he is proposing to service; but Elisa's is an emotionally oriented sexuality, inner and spiritual, symbolized by the flowers that are contained in pots. When the tinker begins to court Elisa through her flowers instead of her pots, even making her a poem with delicate sexual implications about the flower she is protecting ("'Kind of a long-stemmed flower? Looks like a quick puff of colored smoke?'"), she immediately begins to dismantle her defenses, removing her protective clothing ("The gloves were forgotten now") and admitting the tinker "through the picket gate" and "into the yard" (15–16).

Although what happens may be only fantasized sexual surrender on Elisa's part, the imagery implies that, in the vernacular, she goes all the way. In explicit terms she voices her sexual arousal, describing the sensations of penetration somewhat ambivalently as "'Hot and sharp and—lovely'" (18), betrays her tumescence ("Her breast swelled passionately"[8]), and presents herself, as Marilyn L. Mitchell recognizes, "in the traditional female position for intercourse" (313). But the act is completed only in more oblique terms: the tinker does penetrate Elisa's enclosure as, simultaneously, in admitting him inside she opens her flower to him, shaking out "her dark pretty hair" (16). She does allow him in the end to service her pots, and when he leaves, he takes cuttings from her flowers, which, in vulgar terms of sexual conquest that might have crossed Steinbeck's mind, amounts to "getting a piece."

The last movement of the story, as Elisa and Henry bathe, dress, and set out for Salinas, reveals the outcome of Henry's courtship of his wife. Elisa's savage excoriation of her body as she bathes is usually understood as self-punishment for her fantasized unfaithfulness to Henry with the tinker.[9] But even more pertinently it dramatizes her sexual ambivalence—not the conflict between masculine and feminine impulses within her but between her glowing biological sexuality and her deep aversion to the earthy and animalistic realities of sexual life.[10] In the scene Steinbeck sets up an ironic counterpoint between a beauty magazine stereotype of the lovely woman bathing and dressing for a romantic evening and Elisa's ambivalent behavior. Instead of soaking langorously in her beauty bath, sensuously laving her delicate skin with fragrant feminine soap, she furiously attacks her body with harsh abrasive soap—Lava, perhaps. Dressing for the evening, she puts on clothing that emphasizes her sex appeal. She even puts on "her newest underclothing and her nicest stockings," an act of forethought that can only mean her awareness of the sexual implications of the evening, and pencils her eyebrows and rouges her lips like a courtesan. Yet when her husband comes to the house, instead of responding with the warm glow of romantic anticipation that these preparations imply, she "set herself for Henry's arrival" (20–21).

Although in body she is outside the fence, throughout this entire movement Elisa continues to erect barriers against her husband's courtship. As Henry hurries to get ready, she awaits him "primly and stiffly," her lack of romantic warmth underscored by the "frosted leaves," "high grey fog," "thin band of sunshine," and general Hardyesque neutral tones of "the grey afternoon" and the landscape in which "She sat unmoving" and unseeing. When Henry appears, she "stiffened and her face grew tight." Surprised and pleased by his wife's attractiveness, because she usually dresses to hide her sex appeal and thus to avoid activating his libido, Henry allows himself a surge of hopeful anticipation that his courtship is being successful and responds with a startled compliment to Elisa's unusual display of sexual attractiveness. But emotionally she is still inside her fence: she bristles with wiry defensiveness. Getting mixed signals from this cold stiff woman dressed to excite his sexual admiration, Henry naturally "looked bewildered. 'You're playing some kind of a game,' he said helplessly" (21). Having stifled his ardent response to her sex appeal, Elisa now reasserts her strong control over the relationship, which resumes its usual course, and Henry gets his emotion under control again: "when he brought his eyes back to her, they were his own again" (22).

This scene, showing Elisa turning away her husband's courtship, dramatizes what is wrong with the Allens' marriage and answers the story's central question: why is Elisa's life unfulfilled? Steinbeck concludes the scene with what may be a trifle too much ingenuity:

> Elisa went into the house. She heard him drive to the gate and idle down his motor, and then she took a long time to put on her hat. She pulled it here and pressed it there. When Henry turned the motor off she slipped into her coat and went out. (22)

Perhaps only now, concerned with conserving gasoline, are we struck by this curious and wasteful stalling. But it reveals how Elisa controls Henry's sexual interest in her: she keeps clear of him until his passion, awakened by her sex appeal, has cooled—until he idles down *his* motor and turns it off. Although he passes over the pointed sexual implications of the passage, Roy S. Simmonds observes that this behavior is likely "indicative of what is probably the normal pattern of Elisa's and Henry's married life" (108).

Now it becomes clear how the story works. It is about the Allens' marital relationship, and its main line of development dramatizes a husband's unsuccessful courtship of his sexually reticent wife. The central drama is interrupted by the episode of the tinker, which shows his success in getting through Elisa's fence, with all the sexual implications previously noted. This structure invites the hypothesis that the interaction between Elisa and the tinker is designed to illuminate the central drama of husband and wife and immediately raises the question: why does the husband fail while the utter stranger succeeds? The answer, I suggest, lies in the familiar observation that, unlike men, women

incline more toward romantic fantasies of sex than the act of love itself.[11] Clearly Elisa romanticizes the tinker. In the critical literature the tone of **"The Chrysanthemums"** is felt to be deeply sympathetic to her frustration, but there is a strong undercurrent of ironic impatience with Elisa's refusal of her sexual role that comes closest to the surface in the pointed contrast between the scruffy tinker, to whom she responds sexually, and clean-cut Henry, whom she turns away. In ironic mockery of Elisa's great and perverse capacity for romanticizing reality, Steinbeck makes everything about the tinker the utter antithesis of her fastidious tidiness, which symbolizes her delicate sexual sensibility. Unshaven, unwashed, his clothes "wrinkled and spotted with grease," he represents everything she furiously purges from her garden and scrubs out of her house. Yet she fantasizes sexual intercourse with him when he gratifies her hunger for romance because it is only a fantasy: he will presently climb back into his slovenly wagon and ride away into the romantic sunset. Henry, clean and reliable if a bit stodgy and clumsy, is reality pressing against Elisa's fence seeking an actual sexual relationship. But in rejecting reality, albeit unideal, as reality always is, for a patently falsified romantic fantasy, she defeats her own impulses toward a fuller life.

The consequences of Elisa's rejection of reality, and thus of life itself, are what we see in the coda, as the couple drive to town, back now in the rut of sexual inactivity that characterizes their marital life. Desiring only an ideal romantic love, Elisa has repulsed Henry's sexual overtures, but on the road to Salinas her hopes of being loved spiritually, poetically, *ideally*, are decisively crushed. She had responded ecstatically to the tinker's wooing of her inner selfhood, her soul, symbolized by the flowers that are the essence of her self. But he has only fed her a line, as the saying goes, in a calculated strategy to get through her defenses. The story dramatizes a familiar aspect of the battle of the sexes: women's resentment toward the direct genital nature of male sexuality. Henry's libido is activated by Elisa's sex appeal, so she hides her feminine charms from him, holding out for a more spiritual love. Nor is she deceived by his dinner invitation; she icily spurns the sexual implications of the evening. But then she discovers that the tinker, who had only pretended to admire her flowers—her inner spiritual being—had been interested only in her pot—her physical exterior: he kept the pot and discarded the flowers. Thus Elisa gives up on life. It is not what she dreamed of. There is no hope.[12]

I will not say that the story is utterly devoid of sympathy for Elisa's frustration, but it is critical of her refusal of life because it does not measure up to her ideal specifications. The brutal truth, in the story's biological terms, is that men *are* drawn to the external sex appeal of women, as Elisa's garden attracts earthy predators hungry to feed on her flowers. In view of the reality of sexual predation, the tinker does more than repulse Elisa's feminist desire for equality with men when he tells her that his life "ain't the right kind . . . for a woman." He speaks the truth: a woman *would* be threatened "with animals creeping under the wagon all night" (19). But the story laments Elisa's response to this problematical reality: in rejecting it she rejects the only way to fulfillment, because, in the story's terms, reality, however unideal it is, is all there is. Steinbeck would later observe that "Sex is a kind of war" (Steinbeck and Wallsten 509), thus clarifying after the fact the pugilistic metaphor of **"The Chrysanthemums."** Elisa's fenced-in enclosure is suggestive of the ring in which the fights Henry jokingly invites her to attend with him will take place. But because she cannot accept the kind of activity that goes on between male and female in the sexual arena, she refuses men, including her husband, admittance into the ring. Thus she stands alone, splendidly constituted physically for sexual life, but self-defeated emotionally, refusing the interaction that could bring, if not the ideal fulfillment she yearns for, at least the only fulfillment reality can provide.

For those who still want to see the tinker's sensitivity to Elisa's yearning as a positive foil for Henry's failure to provide the romance she craves, it is well to remember that he merely contrives to get inside her fence, brusquely making clear that there is no place for her in his wagon. Henry invites her to come out of her refuge of delicacy and to join him in a productive relationship. The tinker's poetic admiration of Elisa's flowers, her spiritual beauty, is pure calculation: he desires only to gain access to her pot. Henry's prosaic clumsiness is at least guileless and sincere, his overtures to Elisa considerate and straightforward. Indeed, he treats her more as an equal than, like the tinker, as a weaker vessel whose revulsion at the grossness of sexual reality and romantic yearning for a more poetically idealized love must be indulged before she can bring herself to respond in a sexual relationship. Let us at last be fair to Henry: he makes all the overtures toward a fuller relationship with Elisa, and she erects all the barriers. In preferring the tinker over Henry she foolishly chooses the negative over the positive manifestation of the same reality: to wit, that men tend to be interested more in a woman's body than in her soul, to desire a physical rather than spiritual love. The tinker is no more concerned about Elisa's emotional needs than Henry. But Elisa rejects Henry's honest invitation to meet him halfway, on equal terms, in a true procreative marriage, for the tinker's manipulative indulgence of her romantic delicacy. Ironically, it is the tinker who is the real chauvinist in the story: he treats Elisa as a weaker being, pampers and exploits her feminine weakness, and makes a sexual conquest. And thus Elisa invites her own exploitation, her subsequent disillusionment on the road to Salinas, and her ultimate defeat by life.

But may we not argue that the story is in the eye of the beholder—that to a feminist reader it may yet be read as a dramatization of woman's disability in a man's world and that the reading presented here merely reveals the masculine viewpoint of the writer? I am afraid not. Though, to be sure, in real life women have been and are fenced inside a garden of unproductive triviality in a world dominated by men, the story's evidence does not support the view that Elisa is a woman kept from fulfillment by male domination. Nor is there, in point of fact, any evidence that she is deliberately excluded from the important business of the ranch. The mere fact that we do not see her participating in the sale of the steers, together with our knowledge that women are and have been excluded from the conduct of the world, does not mean that, ipso facto, in this story the female protagonist is deliberately or even unintentionally prevented from participating in the financial affairs of the ranch. It must be said, I fear, that these assumptions have been imported into the story, where they are not supported by evidence, from the outside world,

where they are. The prevailing opinion on **"The Chrysanthemums"** thus stands as a cautionary lesson in the way criticism may be swept up and misdirected by the sympathies and enthusiasms of the moment.

Perhaps the criticism of **"The Chrysanthemums"** might have gotten off on sounder footing if its early critics had had access to Steinbeck's letters, published in 1975, which reveal his attitude toward his own marital relationship in the early Thirties when the story was written. To be sure, the letters reflect only his side of the story, and his impressions of the marriage are retrospective. And, of course, it does not inevitably follow that the marriage he presents in the story must necessarily be the one he was experiencing at the time he wrote it. Nevertheless, it is at least instructive that the relationship he looks back on in the early Forties, just after it broke up, is remarkably like the one presented in this discussion—in which the wife fences her husband out of a fulfilling sexual relationship—and not at all like the one implied in the prevailing criticism—in which the wife is fenced in by her husband's dominance and complacency. A brief summary must suffice of what becomes in the letters of the early Forties—and again in the late Forties after the breakup of Steinbeck's second marriage, ironically over much the same kind of conflict—a litany of frustration and bitterness at female sexual reticence. Clearly the problem in both cases involved sexual incompatibility. Although he had "tried for thirteen years," Steinbeck felt that he had "never been welcome" to his first wife; "maybe," he muses, "I'm good enough for someone else . . . who thinks in terms of giving as well as receiving" (Steinbeck and Wallsten 234, 240). With pointed reference to his first wife, he describes his new love interest as a woman who "likes being a woman and likes being in love," adding "This is a new experience for me" (242). As the underlying incompatibility of his second marriage approaches its climax, he writes of "natural spinsters" who "make much better mistresses than wives. They don't have to do it very often that way" (301). Steinbeck is not totally blind to the woman's plight in such a relationship: "It is an old story of female frustration," he observes, referring to his second wife: "She wants something I can't give her so she must go on looking." But the remark reveals more frustration at woman's unfulfillable idealism than sympathy for her disadvantage, for "maybe she will never find out that no one can give it to her" (319).

The clear import of Steinbeck's letters is that when he wrote **"The Chrysanthemums"** he was experiencing a frustrating marriage to a sexually reticent woman much like the relationship traced out in the foregoing analysis. The emotions that find a fictional outlet in the story are thus, presumably, those that he articulates openly years later when, now twice bitten, he comes to terms with the wreckage of his first two marriages. In what may be taken as one of his definitive observations on marriage (he claims it is "anything else" than "bitterness" [344]) he sums up the feelings that have evidently been developing through the years. And they are not feelings that would be likely to result in a story about women's disadvantage in a man's world:

> the breed of American women . . . they have the minds
> of whores and the vaginas of Presbyterians. They are
> trained by their mothers in a contempt for men. . . .

The American girl makes a servant of her husband and then finds him contemptible for being a servant. American married life is the doormat to the whore house. . . . The impulse of the American woman to geld her husband and castrate her sons is very strong. (343)

I suspect that this is the sentiment, in an early stage of development, that underlies the characterizations of Mary Teller and Elisa Allen, who shut their husbands out of a full sexual relationship in marriage. And in the weak, gelded husbands of these ironically strong women, Steinbeck appears to be dramatizing his own role in his first two marriages: "Well," he concludes, "I guess I wasn't a man or I wouldn't have put up with it" (343–344).

One feels some reluctance in depriving a writer of critical esteem, but it must be said that, at least for **"The Chrysanthemums"** and **"The White Quail,"** Steinbeck is undeserving of the feminist acclaim he has received over the last twenty-five years. Actually, the story is informed far less by feminist sympathies than by traditional "masculist" complaints: against the sexual unresponsiveness of the female, against an ambivalent female sexuality that both invites and repels male admiration, against the female's rejection of her biological role, against the sexual delicacy of the female, who, repelled by sexual reality, holds out for indulgence of her emotional and spiritual yearnings, and ultimately against female control over the sexual relationship itself.

Notes

1. It is included, for example, in the anthology *The Experience of American Woman*, where it is presented as the story of a woman "who has been relegated to performing activities which require only a fraction of her ability" and who comes to the painful awareness of "what a meager outlet she has for the energy and talent she possesses" (Solomon 13–14).

   Modern Fiction Studies, Volume 31, Number 2, Summer 1985. Copyright © by Purdue Research Foundation. All rights to reproduction in any form reserved.

2. Following is a representative sampling of the opinion I have summarized. Elisa is "a woman seeking a satisfactory identity" (Miller 72). The story is about the struggle of "strong women who must somehow express themselves meaningfully within the narrow possibilities open to women in a man's world." Elisa is "deliberately excluded" from the masculine "sphere of money, tobacco, and machines" (Mitchell 304, 311). She is "the representative of the feminist ideal of equality and its inevitable defeat" in "a masculine-dominated society" (Sweet 213, 214). "Her husband is the cause of her frustration" (Yano 56). She suffers from his "lack of understanding and affection" (McCarthy 27). Married to a dull, insensitive man, her need for romance makes her reach out to the tinker (McMahan 458). But "when Elisa threatened to encroach upon male territory, she was rebuffed and shepherded back to the refuge of her submissive and unproductive place" (Sullivan 217). A dissenting voice is that of Roy S. Simmonds, who suggests that "the long-accepted view of Elisa as a wholly

sympathetic character may possibly be open to question" (103).

3. Typical of this assumption is Yano's characterization of Mary Teller as "a woman who frustrates her husband" and of Elisa Allen as "a woman who is frustrated" (59). Similarly, Mitchell declares that although there are similarities in situation and setting, "Physically as well as emotionally . . . Elisa and Mary are almost complete opposites" (310).

4. See, for example, Rugoff, especially Chapter Three, "The Worship of Respectability" (35–45).

5. Sweet agrees that "there is nothing to suggest that Elisa's relationship with Henry is sexually inadequate" (213).

6. Simmonds agrees that "there is a case for suspecting that Elisa is the one who is unable or unwilling to satisfy her partner sexually" and that "over the years she had deprived, emasculated, her husband" (107, 111).

7. As Steinbeck, musing over the failure of his first marriage, sets out what he expects from his second, he writes "I want some babies" (Steinbeck and Wallsten 240).

8. I have found no support in any published version of the story for McMahan's quotation of this passage: "Her breasts swelled passionately" (457).

9. See, for example, McMahan (458) and Mitchell (313).

10. Simmonds notices in this scene Elisa's "obvious reluctance to accept the fact of her femininity" (108).

11. Simmonds describes Elisa as a woman "who even finds the act of love wholly distasteful and to be avoided whenever possible" (108).

12. Simmonds interprets Elisa's defeat as "her painful and reluctant acceptance of the fact that the tinker had, by that one action of throwing the flowers away, symbolically re-established the position of male dominance she imagined she had wrested from him" (110–111). I prefer to see it rather as a case of defeated romanticism.

Works Cited

Lisca, Peter. *The Wide World of John Steinbeck.* New Brunswick: Rutgers UP, 1958.

McCarthy, Paul. *John Steinbeck.* New York: Ungar, 1980.

McMahan, Elisabeth E. "'The Chrysanthemums': Study of a Woman's Sexuality." *Modern Fiction Studies* 14 (1968–69): 453–458.

Miller, William V. "Sexual and Spiritual Ambiguity in 'The Chrysanthemums.'" *Steinbeck Quarterly* 5 (1972): 68–75.

Mitchell, Marilyn L. "Steinbeck's Strong Women: Feminine Identity in the Short Stories." *Southwest Review* 61 (1976): 304–315.

Rugoff, Milton. *Prudery and Passion: A Study of Sexuality in Nineteenth-Century America.* New York: Putnam, 1971.

Simmonds, Roy S. "The Original Manuscripts of Steinbeck's 'The Chrysanthemums.'" *Steinbeck Quarterly* 7 (1974): 102–111.

Solomon, Barbara H., ed. *The Experience of American Woman*. New York: NAL, 1978.

Steinbeck, Elaine, and Robert Wallsten, eds. *John Steinbeck: A Life in Letters*. New York: Viking, 1975.

Steinbeck, John. *The Long Valley*. New York: Viking, 1958.

Sullivan, Ernest W. "The Cur in 'The Chrysanthemums.'" *Studies in Short Fiction* 16 (1979): 215–217.

Sweet, Charles A., Jr. "Ms. Elisa Allen and Steinbeck's 'The Chrysanthemums.'" *Modern Fiction Studies* 20 (1974): 210–214.

Yano, Shigeharu. "Psychological Interpretations of Steinbeck's Women in *The Long Valley*." *John Steinbeck: East and West*. Ed. Tetsumaro Hayashi, et al. Steinbeck Monograph Series 8. Muncie: Ball State UP, 1978, 54–60.

Louis Owens (essay date 1985)

SOURCE: "'The Chrysanthemums': Waiting for Rain," in *John Steinbeck's Re-vision of America*, The University of Georgia Press, 1985, pp. 108–13.

[*In the following essay, Owens correlates Elisa Allen's desire for rain with her need for personal fulfillment.*]

Of the first story in *The Long Valley*, **"The Chrysanthemums,"** Steinbeck wrote: "It is entirely different and is designed to strike without the reader's knowledge. I mean he reads it casually and after it is finished feels that something profound has happened to him although he does not know what nor how" (*Life in Letters*, p. 91). In light of the eagerness with which critics have rushed to praise this story, calling it "Steinbeck's most artistically successful story," and "one of the world's great short stories," it seems that most critics would agree that "something profound" happens in **"The Chrysanthemums."** And the great difficulty critics have encountered when trying to explain the "what" and "how" of this story suggests that Steinbeck's design has been very effective, has led, in fact, to what Roy Simmonds refers to as "a small critical industry" grown up around this story.

Like each of the stories in *The Long Valley* actually set in the valley, **"The Chrysanthemums"** is about the repression of powerful human impulses, the repression that would be necessary in any would-be Eden set in the fallen world of the valley. And like the subterranean current of the Salinas River that Steinbeck describes in *East of Eden*, these human urges throb just below the surface of everyday life and occasionally burst through to the surface in sudden floods. This theme of repression (which French labels "frustration") is introduced in the opening imagery of **"The Chrysanthemums"** when we are told that "the high grey-flannel fog of winter closed off the Salinas Valley from the sky and from all the rest of the world. On every side it sat like a lid on the mountains and made of the great valley a closed pot" (p. 9). In this fog-lidded valley,

it is "a time of quiet and of waiting" (p. 9). We enter here the lifeless winter of T. S. Eliot's *The Waste Land*, and the fertilizing rain is not likely to come soon, for, as we are told, "fog and rain do not go together" (p. 9). Like the plowed earth which waits "to receive the rain deeply when it should come," Elisa Allen cultivates her flower garden in a kind of suspended life, awaiting the fertilizing imagination of the tinker.

The difficulty posed by the "what" and "how" of this story is indicated in the fact that most Steinbeck criticism has tended to touch only briefly upon the story in passing. French is satisfied to call Elisa Allen "the victim of an unscrupulous confidence man," but he fails to shed any significant light on the story. More recent and comprehensive studies have been achieved in Mordecai Marcus's essay "The Lost Dream of Sex and Childbirth in 'The Chrysanthemums,'" Elizabeth McMahan's "'The Chrysanthemums': Study of a Woman's Sexuality," and William V. Miller's "Sexuality and Spiritual Ambiguity in 'The Chrysanthemums.'" As the titles suggest, each of these essays stresses the unmistakable significance in the story of Elisa's sexual frustration. The essays differ, however, about the importance of Elisa's frustrated maternal instinct. In a still more recent article, "The Original Manuscripts of Steinbeck's 'The Chrysanthemums,'" Roy Simmonds argues against the popular interpretation of Elisa's character, suggesting that "there is a case for suspecting that Elisa is the one who is unable or unwilling to satisfy her partner sexually."[2]

According to Marcus's reading of the story, Elisa's unfulfilled yearning for children gives birth to the tremendous current of frustration running through the story. Marcus argues that when the tinker coldly discards the flowers, "her feminine self, her capacity for fructification and childrearing, the very offspring and representative of her body, have been thoughtlessly tossed aside." McMahan, arguing correctly that no critic "has yet adequately explained the emotional reasons underlying [Elisa's] frustration," contends that "Elisa's need is definitely sexual, but it does not necessarily have anything to do with a longing for children"; instead, McMahan proposes that Elisa is discontented: "She is a woman bored by her husband, bored by her isolated life on the farm." Miller, in a more comprehensive and persuasive approach, locates Elisa's dream of fulfillment on three levels: "the conventional, the sexual, and the 'romantic.'"[3] Miller's reading would thus include the possibilities of sexual and maternal frustration (though Miller chooses to stress the former and to downplay the latter), while also accommodating McMahan's theory of "boredom." There is yet, however, a still more comprehensive basis for the tension and frustration which permeates this story, a basis involving once again the theme of commitment that runs in a steady current through Steinbeck's fiction.

It is obvious that these critics would all agree that "something profound has happened" in **"The Chrysanthemums,"** and just as obviously they would not agree precisely about what has happened or how it happened. To argue as McMahan and Miller do that Elisa's frustrated yearning for "fructification" does not play a very central role in this story is to ignore the full meaning and impact of the imagery of the story, imagery that introduces and reinforces the theme of procreation in the form of the ploughed land waiting for rain. Elisa, in middle age, is implicitly compared to the plowed furrows in winter, and to say that Elisa is simply bored with her life is to miss the force with which the opening paragraphs establish this parallel and the note of nearly hopeless expectancy dominating the story's atmosphere. At the same time, the theme of repression is very pronounced in the opening imagery and in Steinbeck's description of Elisa's "hard-swept looking little house" and her "over-eager, over-powerful" trimming of last year's flowers. Elisa's response to the tinker is violently sexual once he has made a connection between himself and the chrysanthemums, but only *after* he has made this vital link between himself and Elisa's "flower-children." The sexuality of Elisa's response to the tinker becomes unmistakable when she intones, "When the night is dark—why, the stars are sharp-pointed, and there's quiet. Why you rise up and up! Every pointed star gets driven into your body. It's like that. Hot and sharp and—lovely" (p. 18). Finally, Steinbeck has forced the sexual tension of the scene to such a pitch that Elisa becomes a parody of a bitch in heat: "She crouched low like a fawning dog" (p. 18).

While critics have been unanimous in recognizing the theme of repressed sexuality in this story, it is a mistake to attempt, as McMahan does, to limit the story's thematic significance to this alone. In Elisa the sexual and maternal impulses are blended into a single, frustrated urge, a longing for deep fulfillment. It is difficult not to see the "strong new crop" of flowers Elisa nurtures as surrogate children in her barren world. At the same time, the tinker's exotic life does symbolize a kind of escape for Elisa from the barrenness of the farm, an appeal to what Miller terms Elisa's "romantic" dream of fulfillment. All of these needs and urges come together, however, in the single powerful and unfulfilled yearning for the fertilizing potential inherent in deep human contact and commitment, the most significant symbols of which are sex, childbearing, and sacrifice. While the themes of sex and procreation are strong throughout the story, the theme of sacrifice is introduced in the story's conclusion.

After Elisa has seen the discarded flowers—evidence of the tinker's broken faith—she asks her husband, Henry, about the fights he has mentioned earlier. "I've read how they break noses," she says, "and blood runs down their chests. I've read how the fighting gloves get heavy and soggy with blood" (p. 23). Elisa's sudden interest in the fights which seemed to repulse her earlier has been seen as a rising desire for "vicarious vengeance" upon men, or simple "vindictiveness."[4] Such readings seriously undervalue the complexity of the story, however, and of Elisa's emotional response to what has taken place. Although Elisa does ask, "Do the men hurt each other much?" the emphasis here is not upon simple vengeance upon mankind or vicariously upon the tinker; nor does it necessarily indicate Elisa's need for a "sense of dominance over the male" as Roy Simmonds suggests.[5] Elisa's primary interest is in the blood. Coupled with her strong desire for wine at dinner, this imagery suggests another theme—that of commitment through sacrifice. Blood, as Mac knows well in *In Dubious Battle* and Joseph Wayne discovers in *To a God Unknown,* is the supreme symbol of commitment, and wine, of course, calls to mind the supreme Christian sacrifice. Elisa yearns here, in the wake of her abrupt awakening and disappointment, for a kind of futile sacrament—

reacting to the arousal and frustration of her deepest needs, Elisa is seeking symbols of commitment in a world of physical, spiritual, and emotional isolation and sterility. Like so many of Steinbeck's characters, she is acting out of a profound loneliness.

"The Chrysanthemums" is Steinbeck's finest story precisely because he does not tell us the "what" or "how" and because the powerful imagery of the story is woven brilliantly into a single fabric with theme and character. Elisa, on her isolated ranch in winter, waiting for the fructifying rain which is not likely to come, matched with a capable but not deeply sensitive husband, is cut off from fulfillment. In this story, the theme of human isolation and commitment central to *Of Mice and Men* is imbued with a strong current of repressed sexuality and maternity, and the result is the most emotionally forceful and subtly crafted of Steinbeck's stories.

Notes

1. Barbour, "Steinbeck as a Short Story Writer," p. 112; Mordecai Marcus, "The Lost Dream of Sex and Childbirth in 'The Chrysanthemums,'" *Modern Fiction Studies* 11 (Spring 1965): 54.

2. French, *John Steinbeck*, 1st ed., p. 83; Elizabeth E. McMahan, "'The Chrysanthemums': Study of a Woman's Sexuality," *Modern Fiction Studies* 14 (1968): 453–58; William V. Miller, "Sexual and Spiritual Ambiguity in 'The Chrysanthemums,'" in *A Study Guide to Steinbeck's "The Long Valley,"* ed. Hayashi; Roy S. Simmonds, "The Original Manuscripts of Steinbeck's 'The Chrysanthemums,'" *Steinbeck Quarterly* 7 (Summer-Fall 1974): 107.

3. Marcus, "Lost Dream," p. 57; McMahan, "'The Chrysanthemums,'" pp. 453–55; Miller, "Sexual and Spiritual Ambiguity," p. 72.

4. McMahan, "'The Chrysanthemums,'" p. 458; Marcus, "Lost Dream," p. 57.

5. Simmonds, "Original Manuscripts," p. 108.

John Ditsky (essay date 1986)

SOURCE: "A Kind of Play: Dramatic Elements in Steinbeck's 'The Chrysanthemums'," in *Wascana Review,* Vol. 21, No. 1, Spring, 1986, pp. 62–72.

[*Below, Ditsky praises the "Lawrentian values" and interpersonal drama that Steinbeck achieves in "The Chrysanthemums."*]

The longstanding critical assumption, routinely delivered and seldom questioned, that John Steinbeck represented an odd late flourishing of literary naturalism—rather than, as now seems increasingly clear, an innovative sort of romanticism—has had the predictable effect of retarding appreciation of his accomplishments. Among the latter are the ways in which Steinbeck's language emerges from his contexts: arises organically but not necessarily with "real-life" verisimilitude from situations which must therefore be seen as having demanded, and in a sense therefore also created, a discourse of a sometimes patent artificiality—of a rhetorical loftiness appropriate to the dramatic seriousness of the given subject matter, but unlikely as an instance of "observed" intercourse in English, American variety. For only from such a vantage point can we hope to make sense of many of the exchanges which animate such diverse works as *Cup of Gold, To a God Unknown, The Moon Is Down* and *Burning Bright*. Yet the sorts of usage I am referring to must necessarily give pause to the reader of even *In Dubious Battle, The Grapes of Wrath*, and *East of Eden*. Recently, however, Steinbeck criticism has increasingly begun to accept the writer on his own terms,[1] a process no more complicated than the reading closely of what heretofore has been often subjected to a routinely and callously applied imposition of extraneous critical assumptions. I think that the ways in which situation creates language—and action—can be seen in such a famously "naturalistic" piece as that famous short story which leads off Steinbeck's single lifetime collection of short fiction, *The Long Valley* (1938): **"The Chrysanthemums."**[2]

"The Chrysanthemums" occupies its keynote position in *The Long Valley* with good reason. Not only does it serve as a striking introduction to a number of Steinbeck's attainments and prepossessions, but it also achieves an astonishingly eloquent statement of Lawrentian values that is valuable in its own right. The story is usually perceived—quite rightly—as a study in psychological interconnection and revelation, and I have no wish to alter such assumptions. Rather, I would like to direct some further attention to the ways in which Steinbeck allows text to flow from context: that is, shows speech and gesture being spontaneously brought into being by means of the rigors, the labor, of interpersonal drama. It is, in short, the dramatist Steinbeck who concerns me here, though it is not one of his works created for the stage that I will use as my example.

In dramatic terms, **"The Chrysanthemums"** involves but three main characters: a ranch couple, Elisa and Henry Allen; and an unnamed tinker. It is December in the Salinas Valley. The Valley is shut off from the rest of the world by fog (p. 9), and the weather anticipates change: "It was a time of quiet and of waiting." The imminence of change is reflected in Nature herself, then: something is about to happen. Elisa Allen is already at work in her flower garden; she is a dramatic "giver," her present quantity clearly laid out by the narrator:

> . . . She was thirty-five. Her face was lean and strong and her eyes were as clear as water. Her figure looked blocked and heavy in her gardening costume, a man's black hat pulled low down over her eyes, clod-hopper shoes, a figured print dress almost completely covered by a big corduroy apron with four big pockets to hold the snips, the trowel and scratcher, the seeds and the knife she worked with. She wore heavy leather gloves to protect her hands while she worked. (p. 10)

Steinbeck's list of *dramatis personae* is thus fleshed out by being given the additional accoutrements of sexual misidentification: Elisa wears man's clothing, and carries tools meant to prod and poke. She is also at a stage that later would be taken for granted as constituting "mid-life crisis." Moreover, the constricted world that Elisa inhabits is further limited by being divided—as more notably, later on, the world of *The Wayward Bus* is divided—into male and female precincts, domains of activity into which the members of the opposite sex shall not intrude. Elisa's world, of course, is that of her garden; at work within it,

her femininity takes on a fullness it does not possess, apparently, inside her "hard-swept looking little house, with [its] hard-polished windows" (p. 10). She is mistress of her chrysanthemum milieu; indeed, "The chrysanthemum stems seemed too small and easy for her energy" (p. 10), and the flowers' insect enemies are no match for her "terrier fingers" (p. 11). As she looks towards where her husband is completing a deal to sell cattle to two other men—a deal he has not informed her of beforehand—"her face was eager and mature and handsome" in the enjoyment of indulgence in the creativity of helping beautiful things grow (pp. 10–11).

When her husband finally reports on his business transaction, Elisa is described as having "started" at the sound of his voice as he leaned "over the wire fence that protected her flower garden from cattle and dogs and chickens" and, presumably, husbands (p. 11). When he praises her prowess with growing things, we are told that "her eyes sharpened" at the notion that she might move over into the affairs of the ranch proper by raising apples as comparably big; she has "a gift with things," she confesses—something called "planter's hands" (p. 11). Her husband then suggests that they celebrate his successful transaction by going into Salinas for dinner and a movie; or, he jokes, they might attend "the fights." But she "breathlessly" admits that she "wouldn't like fights" (pp. 11–12). When her husband goes off to locate the cattle he has sold, she resumes her work with her flowers; the language here suggests a woman in total control of her surroundings: "square," "turned the soil over and over," "smoothed it and patted it firm," "ten parallel trenches," "pulled out the little crisp shoots, trimmed off the leaves of each one with her scissors and laid it on a small orderly pile" (p. 12).

Again, one must not perhaps make too much of these patently theatrical stage directions, but we are in fact being prepared for the sudden appearance of that oldest of dramatic devices—the Arrival of the Stranger. He comes on in the form of a "big stubble-bearded man" driving a wagon which advertises his prowess at fixing just about anything—anything metallic, that is (pp. 12–13). When the man's dog is faced down by the ranch shepherds, flirtation begins immediately between Elisa and the stranger; it takes the form of an admission that the latter's dog's aggressiveness may be not all that responsive to need. Easy in his masculinity, the stranger jokes about the dog's dubious ferocity; meanwhile, "The horse and the donkey [pulling the wagon] drooped like unwatered flowers" (p. 13). But here is a woman adept at making flowers thrive; and here is also a man with skills at fixing sharp tools. The banter falters, then continues: the man is off course; his animals, like his dog, are surprisingly vigorous "when they get started" (p. 14).

I should make note here of the alterations the stranger's arrival makes in the language of Steinbeck's narrative. When the husband reports his sale of cattle to his wife, her response is a tepid "Good." Indeed, she uses the same word four times in two lines, to react both to the cattle sale and to the prospect of dinner and the movies. "Good for you": it is his fine fortune and has little to do with her (p. 11). But the bland textures of Elisa's existence are disturbed by the arrival of the "curious vehicle, curiously drawn," and its driver (p. 12). The driver's eyes are "full of the brooding that gets in the eyes of teamsters and of sailors" (pp. 13-14); and if this perception is meant to be Elisa's as well, it marks her recognition of the appeal of the man's way of life—his ability to live by the simple "aim to follow nice weather" (p. 14). Her response is in the form of body language: she removes her gloves and hides them away with her scissors; and "She touched the under edge of her man's hat, searching for fugitive hairs" (p. 14). In short, she acknowledges his attractiveness by means of classic dramatic gestures.

The man's authority is equal to Elisa's within his own kingdom; "Fixed," his wagon proclaims, at the end of a listing of metallic objects which—no nonsense about it—he claims to be able to repair (p. 13). No matter that the lettering is "clumsy, crooked," or the words misspelled; Steinbeck's story is a drama that relies on subtext—the unspoken—throughout. Elisa and the stranger work through their temporary relationship through dialogue that has nothing to do, ostensibly, with the struggle for power that is going on. But when she is asked if she has anything needing repair or sharpening, "Her eyes hardened with resistance" (p. 14); she becomes a bit metallic herself in the process of making it clear that she is not so easily won as all that. In the process of telling the man—four times—that she has no work for him to do, she manages to make him play the role of dependent inferior: "His face fell to an exaggerated sadness. His voice took on a whining undertone" (p. 15). The man's demeanor becomes dog-like; like an actor, he uses expression and delivery to emphasize the import of his words: he is without a bit of work; he is off his usual road; he may not eat that day. Elisa is unmoved—is irritated, even.

Yet "irritation and resistance" melt from her face as soon as the man, resourceful, notices her chrysanthemums and asks about them (p. 15). Hers, she avers, are "bigger than anybody around here" can raise; and since she has been pouring her private emotional existence into the raising of chrysanthemums, her boasting has a nice kind of sexual irony about it. He responds to his cue with spontaneous poetry: the flowers look "like a quick puff of colored smoke" (p. 15). A brief confrontation over the flowers' smell is quickly resolved; the aroma is a "good bitter" one, "not nasty at all," and the man likes it. Fine, then; for hers, Elisa claims, have produced "ten-inch blooms this year." Ah, then, returns the fellow (the dialogue by now quite strongly resembles Pinter's), there is this "lady down the road a piece" who, though she does find difficult work for him to do, has no chrysanthemums in her otherwise splendid garden. Can Elisa help this unfortunate out?

She can; she will. Assuring the man that she can send along flowers for transplanting by the other woman— "Beautiful . . . Oh, beautiful" ones—she tears off her hat; she shakes out "her dark pretty hair"; and with her eyes shining, she admits the stranger into her yard. She strips off her protective gloves after running "excitedly" after a flower pot, and with her bare hands prepares a selection of her flowers for the man—who is described as standing over her as she kneels to work—to take (pp. 16–17). She indulges herself in the revelation of her private craft as she gives him instructions to transmit to the other woman; she looks "deep into his eyes, searchingly," as if trying to measure the degree of their mutual sympathy. As she does, "Her mouth opened a little, and she seemed to be listening" (p. 17). Mouth and eyes and ears are open to this

stranger as perhaps they have been to no one before as she explains her doctrine of "planting hands," the possessors of which can do nothing wrong. Her earnestness carries her away: "She was kneeling on the ground looking up at him. Her breast swelled passionately" (p.18).

Again, the psychological underpinnings of this story, so Lawrence-like, have been commented on before this; what I am attempting to do for perhaps the first time is draw attention to the ways in which Steinbeck's text moves along according to imperatives which can only be termed *dramatic*. In other words, can the standard definitions of literary naturalism adequately account for the rising action and intensity of "The Chrysanthemums," its quasi-musical climaxing? This is fairly far from *The Jungle*, from *Studs Lonigan*, this passage; it is closer surely to *Brief Encounter*. Now the man's eyes are said to narrow as he averts his gaze "self-consciously" and begins to make a comparison to his own life; "Sometimes in the night in the wagon there—"(p. 18), he starts. But she interrupts, carried away by her own unexpectedly-piqued emotional empathy:

> Elisa's voice grew husky. She broke in on him, "I've never lived as you do, but I know what you mean. When the night is dark—why, the stars are sharp-pointed, and there's quiet. Why, you rise up and up! Every pointed star gets driven into your body. It's like that. Hot and sharp and—lovely." (p. 18)

But Elisa's mystical attainment—her fusion of the psychosexual and the poetical—also has its natural and physical concomitant. The next paragraph says:

> Kneeling there, her hand went out toward his legs in the greasy black trousers. Her hesitant fingers almost touched the cloth. Then her hand dropped to the ground. She crouched low like a fawning dog. (p. 18).

She has opened herself to a stranger, and shown him a part of herself which presumably no one has seen before; and in the process, she has made herself as vulnerable to him as one of his subservient animals might be. Remarkably, for its time, the story also has Elisa adumbrating a world in which male and female experience might meld in an ecstasy of shared sensitivity—so unlike the one she has known on her husband's ranch.

But the stranger refuses this gambit. He reminds her that hunger is its own setter of standards; and so Elisa rises, "ashamed," and goes off to find the man some busy-work to do so that he can maintain his independence a bit longer. In the process, he reaffirms the radical dissimilarity of their two existences: when she speaks about a woman's being able to live such a life as his, he emphasizes its loneliness and frightfulness, wholly refusing to consider the implicit offer she is making. (Or is she?) Though they share body-language during this discussion—he concentratedly sucking his under-lip, she raising her upper lip and showing her teeth; both feral—he determinedly completes his routine repair work without deigning to consider her appeal for consideration of their shared romanticism (p. 19). Indeed, when he finishes his job and accepts his pay and turns to go, he has already almost forgotten the pretext of the chrysanthemums to be delivered to that other woman down the road (p. 20).

As the man and his animals depart, Elisa watches them off, silently mouthing "Good-bye" after him. "Then she whispered, 'That's a bright direction. There's a glowing there'"; and the sound of her whispering startles her, though only her dogs had heard (p. 20). This passage might seem extraordinary or simply inexplicable were it not for the consistent identification in Steinbeck's writing of "brightness" and "shining" with the quasi-divine power of absolute nature in the universe (as Blake's "Tyger" yields Steinbeck's title *Burning Bright*); and for that matter, the name "Elisa" and its variants are fairly commonly identified with idealized femininity in Steinbeck, from *Cup of Gold* onward. Elisa's next action is a sort of ritual purification followed by a donning of vestments: she tears off "her soiled clothes and flung them into the corner" of the bathroom. "And then she scrubbed herself with a little block of pumice, legs and thighs, loins and chest and arms, until her skin was scratched and red. When she had dried herself she stood in front of a mirror in her bedroom and looked at her body. She tightened her stomach and threw out her chest. She turned and looked over her shoulder at her back" (p. 20). Interestingly, Steinbeck's writing does not seek to titillate; the description of Elisa's *mikvah*, if I can call it that, is asexual, as though the operation were one which could be performed on any body as part of a ritual irrespective of gender. Yet Elisa's actions are also clearly narcissistic, her self-admiration clearly premised on a sense of having finally achieved, at her life's mid-point, some kind of summit of self-worth.

But now the naked Elisa begins to dress, again using makeup and costuming for theatrical effect—rather like Nora in Ibsen's *A Doll's House*, with the context of her presumably-imminent death giving abnormal beauty to what subsists of life. She begins with "her newest underclothing and her nicest stockings and the dress which was the symbol of her prettiness. She worked carefully on her hair, penciled her eyebrows and rouged her lips" (pp. 20–21). One dresses—or divests oneself of clothing—this attentively, this ceremonially, only with an implicit or explicit awareness of preparing for one of the ritual events of life (including, of course, one's death). It is interesting that Elisa retreats from the world of her mannish exercises in the garden, wearing men's attire, to what is described as "her bedroom" (p. 20); the two do not share a single sleeping-place. In this sort of dressing-room, then, Elisa prepares herself for a theatrical entry (or re-entry?) into life, an event in which she means to include her husband—who if he were but aware of the fact has been awarded this boon on the strength of a surrogate's efforts. Elisa neatly lays out her Henry's best clothes, so that he may do as she has finished doing, and then she goes out to the porch and sits "primly and stiffly" waiting for him, "unmoving," her eyes seldom blinking as they pursue the last of that bright glowing that she associates with the events of the afternoon, now disappearing beneath a "high grey fog" (p. 21).

When Henry finally appears, he is so taken aback at the appearance she has created for herself that he clumsily compliments her for looking "nice"—as though she seldom did. This reaction on his part comes in spite of the fact that her own self-assurance has made her "stiffen" at his approach, her face growing "tight" as she does (p. 21). Henry compounds his error by defining "niceness" as looking "different, strong and happy"—again as if these were unfamiliar aspects of Elisa's demeanour. Indeed, Henry is so flabbergasted at the change in his wife's image that he

unconsciously describes it as the theatricalization it actually is: "He looked bewildered. 'You're playing some kind of a game,' he said helplessly. 'It's a kind of a play. You look strong enough to break a calf over your knee, happy enough to eat it like a watermelon'" (pp. 21–22). Henry's flight of poetic utterance is a worshipful reaction to the irruption in his presence of the extraordinary in the ordinary, of the divine—the heroic, the Junoesque, if you will—into the human. At his tribute, her "rigidity" buckles briefly; she tells him that his venture into the domain of the ineffable was beyond his comprehension (instinctual?), and settles for the admission that "'I'm strong,' she boasted. 'I never knew before how strong'" (p. 22). She sends him for the car, deliberately fussing over the set of her hat until his turning off the engine signals an admission that a new sort of patience is now called for.

But Elisa's short happy life—the effects of her dramatic transfiguration, her irradiation—is destined for an abrupt conclusion. When she and Henry set off for dinner in Salinas, it is not all that long until she sees "a dark speck" on the road ahead. Steinbeck has told this story, as was his initial habit, largely from the outside of his characters, from close observation of their gestures and speech. In a sense, he violates that practice now, giving the reader in two words what would in the theatre be expressed through a reaction of the face and body: "She knew" (p. 22). It is as if Elisa had always possessed, deep down, the certainty that her self-assurance was built upon a deception. Now, she cannot even avoid following the discarded chrysanthemum shoots with her eyes as they pass, recognizing as she ponders the tinker's apparent cruelty the fact that he left the flowers along the road because he couldn't afford to throw away the bright red flower pot she had so carefully planted the flowers in—because it was the pot that had value in his world, and not—except as conversational pretexts—the flowers. She is able, however, to turn away from the sight of the tinker's wagon when their car overtakes it moments later (p. 22).

"In a moment it was over. The thing was done. She did not look back," Steinbeck tells us (p. 23). But her level of discourse, having fallen to the prospect of dinner, marks a change palpable enough for Henry to note it. "Now you've changed again" is his assessment; and the manner of his delivery is authorially noted as "complained": had Henry himself been buoyed by the brief brightening of Elisa? Now normality returns: he pats her knee; he makes small talk. Elisa has one last attempt at escape of the life-force within her. She makes what is apparently an unusual request, one that will make small ceremony out of the coming dinner out, itself a minor sacrament of sorts: ". . . could we have wine with dinner?" Henry agrees, and after a time of silence, she surprises her husband by an even more uncharacteristic question: do the boxers at prize fights "hurt each other very much?" (by which she means broken noses, she explains, with enough blood running down chests to get their gloves "heavy and soggy with blood" [p. 23]). Henry is startled, as are we; are these Elisa's Dionysiac propensities suddenly revealing themselves, or has her experience with the tinker taken an imaginative turn towards retribution, a perverse expression of the flowering of femininity he had seemed to foster? We are not told; but Elisa asks one more question: "Do any women ever go to the fights?" Some, yes, Henry answers, as if he cannot imagine his wife among them; not having been able to imagine her, a moment ago, as even having read about such things, he now offers to take her against his better judgment.

But Elisa's questioning has subsided, whether because of the unsuitability of her attending the fights or because of the torpor induced by the thought of attending them with a partner such as Henry. Withdrawing her face—on which tears have begun to show—she states that it will be enough to settle for "wine. It will be plenty." If the blood of Dionysiac sacrifice is not to be hers, she will settle for a conventional symbolism. Steinbeck alludes so obliquely to the Christian and the pagan at his ending that one is distracted, if at all, by the thought of how his final line—showing Elisa "crying weakly—like an old woman" (p. 23)—might have been ruined by claiming the strength of a metaphorical connection instead of making do with the subtlety of the simile. Elisa is, after all, only "like an old woman"; if she has nonetheless crossed a certain line in her life, it will take years, perhaps, for that fact to assert itself fully. Yet, as if she were one of the many animals mentioned throughout the story, she has made her sudden lunge towards a kind of life she may not have known she needed— only to have the constraints of her existence reassert themselves almost at once.

Whether or not **"The Chrysanthemums"** is what I would call it, one of the finest American short stories ever written, surely its craft is such as to reward reader attention and require critical inquiry. That craft, as I have suggested, is in great part a matter of introducing the materials of a naturalistic sort of fiction—the details of the occupations of tinker and gardener and the like—only to rise above them as a dramatist would: by raising the ante of artifice until the characters seem self-conscious of themselves as creative artists spontaneously creating a dialogue in a most poetic sort of drama, one in which the late flowers of a season of the human spirit can seem for a moment to be able to transcend their rootedness, to move farther down the road than just the town of Salinas. It is, finally, a craft by which seemingly ordinary individuals are made to see themselves as characters—persons moving in a world of "roles" and "symbols"—in search of an author who seems scarcely present at all. In the end, it is enough to make plausible a singular sort of epiphany: a bland sort of husband, likely one who has never been in a theatre in his life, being so astonished at the sight of his taken-for-granted wife suddenly appearing in "a kind of play" that he speaks, on the spot, his spontaneous rancher's ode.

Notes

1. I have tried to do as much in my 1984 Second International Steinbeck Congress (Salinas, CA; August) paper, "Steinbeck as Dramatist: A Preliminary Account," ed. Shigeharu Yano, Tetsumaro Hayashi, Richard F. Peterson, and Yasuo Hashiguchi (Tokyo: Gaku Shobo Press, 1986), pp. 13–23. But there are considerably more aspects of Steinbeck's works that need to be freed from the shackles of *a priori* critical constraints.

2. John Steinbeck, "The Chrysanthemums," in *The Long Valley* (New York: Viking, 1938), pp. 9–23.

C. Kenneth Pellow (essay date 1989)

SOURCE: "'The Chrysanthemums' Revisited," in *Steinbeck Quarterly*, Vol. XXII, Nos. 1–2, Winter-Spring, 1989, pp. 8–16.

[*In the following essay, Pellow calls into question the symbolic value of organic and mechanical elements in "The Chrysanthemums."*]

Scholars who have interpreted and analyzed John Steinbeck's short story **"The Chrysanthemums"** appear to have ignored several associations and parallels between animals and characters. These associations, and some contrasts between things organic and things mechanical, support an interpretation of the story that, while not altogether new, goes somewhat beyond previous critiques in seeing the story as radically feministic, an unusual venture for Steinbeck.

Roy S. Simmonds has stated most succinctly what has occurred to numerous other readers of Steinbeck—that "a small critical industry" has been produced by this story. Stanley Renner has summarized one reading, with the intent of debunking it. The female protagonist, in Renner's summary, is seen as prevented, by men in general and her husband in particular, from participating in important business. Then,

> When an itinerant tinker happens by, Elisa's latent yearnings are awakened for the larger life that men enjoy of significant work, adventure, and sexual expression; and when she entrusts the tinker with cuttings from her chrysanthemums, she, in effect, reaches out to the wider world. But the tinker dumps her flowers in the public thoroughfare, thus rejecting her gesture toward a larger life, and she remains a pitiable victim of male domination and female disadvantage.[1]

Renner's essay is the most recent lengthy study of this story and one that its author clearly intends to be corrective. It should be consulted as an opposing view to my own, as should that by Simmonds, which apparently inspired Renner's.[2] However, although Renner's argument includes some very clever readings of the story's symbolic import, there are several aspects of it that I find objectionable, primarily that it seems to ignore the story's ending. Our final glimpse of Elisa, relaxing "limply" while she tries to keep her husband from seeing her "crying weakly—like an old woman" hardly suggests that Steinbeck has meant to portray her unsympathetically, to treat her with "ironic mockery" (Renner, p. 313) in order to have the story be "critical of her refusal of life" (Renner, p. 314). Renner's concentrating his peroration, in the last page-and-a-half of his essay, on Steinbeck's life and letters seems to disregard his own sage observation, early, that "biography need not inevitably determine a writer's perspective" (Renner, p. 306). Similarly, he disregards his own summary of what has become a "standard reading" when he concludes his own reading with this claim: "Nor is there, in point of fact, any evidence that she is deliberately excluded from the important business of the ranch" (Renner, p. 315). The modifying adverb, of course, renders such "evidence" impossible to present. And finally, Renner employs a false disjunctive throughout his essay, as represented in this assertion, repeated at least once: "In the story's terms there can be little doubt that the garden and fence are Elisa's own *rather than* [emphasis mine] imposed on her by her husband, men, or society" (Renner, p. 309). The either/or is misleading; almost no reader can doubt that Elisa has shared in her own fencing-in and will probably continue to do so. That partly accounts for her tears at the end of the story.

The reader interested in this story's critical history should also see Louis Owens's book, *John Steinbeck's Re-Vision of America*,[3] where that history is briefly summarized with an emphasis different from Renner's. Owens also adds new dimensions to the story, based upon the symbolic function of weather therein, and at one point he comes near to the essence of my argument here, as I shall point out later.

As a starting point of my own contention about Elisa Allen's story, I refer to a 1966 article by William R. Osborne, apparently the first scholar/critic to notice that Steinbeck wrote two "versions" of this story.[4] Osborne's textual criticism demonstrates that the few portions of the original story added to or altered by Steinbeck for its 1938 publication in *The Long Valley*[5] tend to make even clearer Elisa's sexual and generic frustrations. One of the few lines, for instance, that Steinbeck added comes right after Elisa's passionate speech to the tinker, which seems to relate planting instincts to sexual awareness (a speech to be examined here, later). The line reads: "She crouched low like a fawning dog" (Osborne, p. 482; *LV*, p. 18).

Oddly, that line does not seem to have drawn much attention. Osborne does observe that the "dog simile" gives to Elisa's character "a carnality that is lacking" in the previous version of the story (Osborne, p. 482). And Owens has used the phrase to put this scene into the context of the story's sexual tension, noting that Elisa thus "becomes a parody of a bitch in heat" (Owens, p. 111). But no one has remarked upon the associations that the line provides: it links Elisa's response to the activities—more precisely, inactivities—of the tinker's mongrel dog, which Steinbeck had described earlier. When the tinker arrived at the Allen ranch, the dog rushed out from his place beneath the tinker's wagon and confronted the two ranch shepherds. He quickly decided, however, that discretion was preferable, and "feeling outnumbered, lowered his tail and retired under the wagon with raised hackles and bared teeth" (*LV*, p. 13). The tinker then observed that the dog was a tough fighter, "when he gets started" (*LV*, p. 13), and he and Elisa shared appreciation of the joke. Now Elisa, when she crouches "like a fawning dog," is also retiring from a potential fight, the struggle to free herself from a situation in which she feels trapped. (Likewise, the dog, in the story's last glimpse of him, "took his place between the back wheels" [*LV*, p. 20] as the tinker drove off.) Significantly, Elisa emulates that mongrel dog at least once more in the story. After she has indicated envy of the tinker's free-seeming, itinerant life, he claims that such is not "the right kind of life for a woman" (*LV*, p. 19). Before Elisa's challenging him on this point, "Her upper lip raised a little, showing her teeth." Elisa may be retiring from a struggle never really entered into, but she does so "with raised hackles and bared teeth."

When we have recognized that Elisa is associated with the mongrel dog, and that Steinbeck emphasized that association when he revised the story, we are led to realize that the association is part of a larger pattern in the story. All of the animals in it are oppressed, trapped, neglected, or overwhelmed by the mechanical and mechanistic world, much as is Elisa. Thus, steers exist only to be bought and sold, as on any ranch. The tinker's horse and burro, a "mismatched team" (*LV*, p. 22)—hardly the only such in the story—are shackled to the wagon where they droop "like unwatered flowers" (*LV*, p. 13), thus forming another association to Elisa, through her surrogate children, the chrysanthemums. When it is time to move on, and the dog has taken "his place" under the wagon, these two lean "into their collars" (*LV*, p. 20). In Henry Allen's metaphors, animals are treated unkindly: a calf is an item to be broken and eaten (*LV*, p. 22). The two ranch dogs, along with the "rangy mongrel," provide the only occasion of animal "dignity," but it is clearly a parody of dignity: "all three stopped, and with stiff and quivering tails, with taut, straight legs, with ambassadorial dignity, they slowly circled, sniffing daintily" (*LV*, p. 13). In the last animal image of the story, rabbits and cranes are driven into the brush and the riverbed, respectively, by the Allen roadster bouncing along the dirt road (*LV*, p. 22).

This last image puts the animal motif in this story into a yet broader context. Throughout **"The Chrysanthemums"** there runs a mechanical-and-organic contrast that also underscores Elisa's situation. She concentrates nearly all of her time and energy on raising flowers, while it becomes clear to her that it is in the mechanical world that one finds wealth, power, and, most important, self-determination. So, when Henry negotiates with the meat-packers who eventually buy his cattle, all three stand "by the tractor shed, each man with one foot on the side of the little Fordson" (*LV*, pp. 9–10). And near the end of the story, after Henry has been mildly chastised by Elisa for his "calf" metaphor and had been confronted by her boast of how "strong" she is, he "looked down toward the tractor shed, and when he brought his eyes back to her, they were his own again" (*LV*, p.22).

Part of Elisa's ultimate disenchantment with the tinker comes from much the same kind of opposition. This is not at first noticeable, at least to Elisa, for she and the tinker seem more alike than different. They are able, as noted earlier, to share a joke, and Elisa is taken by his ability to turn a poetic phrase, as in his likening of chrysanthemums to "a quick puff of colored smoke" (*LV*, p. 15). And both are transported when in the midst of what they love doing. Thus Elisa explains to the tinker about "planting hands." I will quote the entire speech, for, within the context of this story, it is a unique passage:

> Well, I can only tell you what it feels like. It's when you're picking off the buds you don't want. Everything goes right down into your fingertips. You watch your fingers work. They do it themselves. You can feel how it is. They pick and pick the buds. They never make a mistake. They're with the plant. Do you see? Your fingers and the plant. You can feel that, right up your arm. They know. They never make a mistake. You can feel it. When you're like that you can't do anything wrong. Do you see that? Can you understand that? (*LV* pp. 17–18)

Steinbeck here creates Elisa's breathlessness by deviating from the story's normal style. These eighteen sentences (only one is fragmentary) average less than six words each; none is longer than ten words. In a more typical paragraph of this story—the first, for instance—sentences run up to thirty words or more in length, and average twenty-three. Even in dialogue, syntax is not this terse; in Elisa's last speech before the one quoted above, sentences range up to twenty words in length, and average over ten. Immediately after this speech, it becomes even clearer that the breathlessness is sexual, for Elisa proceeds into the speech that ends: "Why you rise up and up! Every pointed star gets driven into your body. It's like that. Hot and sharp and—lovely" (*LV*, p. 18). As Elizabeth McMahan observes, "The sexual implications of her last four sentences are unmistakable" (McMahan, p. 457). Steinbeck enforced those implications when he revised the story, as he added the last three sentences.

As Elisa is transported when working with her flowers, so is the tinker when he performs his favorite work. When Elisa has decided that she does, after all, have some work he can do for her, "His manner changed. He became professional" (*LV*, p. 18). His gear set up, he goes to work at removing dents from her kettles: "His mouth grew sure and knowing. At a difficult part of the work he sucked his under-lip" (*LV*, p. 19). But there are differences, of course, between the kinds of work that they do. His is with things mechanical and profitably remunerative; hers is with things organic and financially, at least, profitless. It is all too typical of "woman's work." And that she is prohibited from participation in the other kind of work is emphasized by the tinker's observation that his profession "ain't the right kind of a life for a woman" (*LV*, p. 19). Elisa interprets this, probably accurately, as more prohibitive than protective. She says, as she pays him for his work: "You might be surprised to have a rival some time. I can sharpen scissors, too. And I can beat the dents out of little pots. I could show you what a woman might do" (*LV*, p. 19). The tinker represents more than sexual disillusionment to (and for) Elisa; he is also the enemy—the representative of the mechanical, self reliant fraternity that keeps her in her "place."

These animal/mechanical associations help to explain Elisa's disillusionment with the tinker. Partly, of course, she is disappointed at his lack of real sexuality. But there is more. Elisa, on this day in her life, senses more keenly than ever the contrast between herself and Henry. For him, living things, organic beings, are items to be sold, killed, broken, enslaved; to her, they are to be nurtured. And the tinker is just as much a disappointment to her as Henry is, for he also shuts her out of the mechanical, money-making, self-determining world.[6] It should not surprise us that the tinker keeps the manufactured, inanimate portion of Elisa's "gift" to him, while throwing away the part—the main part, indeed—that is natural and organic. Elisa appears to understand the separateness of his actions, when she sees her flowers lying in the road:

> She tried not to look as they passed. . . . But her eyes would not obey. She whispered to herself sadly, "He might have thrown them off the road. That wouldn't have been much trouble, not very much. But he kept the pot," she explained. "He had to keep the pot. That's why he couldn't get them off the road." (*LV*, p. 22)

Steinbeck added Elisa's explanation to herself in the story's revised version.

One more aspect of **"The Chrysanthemums"** remains to be explained here, the one that, perhaps, most needs explaining: that is, the story's final detail—Elisa's decision that she does not, after all, want to attend the prizefights. Mordecai Marcus's explanation is that as Elisa "abandons" her interest in the fights and comforts herself with the thought that wine at dinner will be enough, she accepts her failure to be fully successful as a woman and again comforts herself with a mild symbol of "extra-domestic excitement" (Marcus, p. 57). Marilyn Mitchell, on the other hand, contends that Elisa "acknowledges the fact that a man's freedom is denied her by agreeing with her husband that she would, after all, probably dislike the prizefights" (Mitchell, p. 33). My own understanding of this combines, but goes beyond, both views. First of all, it is clear that when Elisa felt attracted to the prizefights, she did so vengefully. When she speculated about what happens at them—"Well, I've read how the fighting gloves get heavy and soggy with blood" (*LV*, p. 23)—what she seemed to be anticipating, even hoping, was that the men in these fights would be more nearly cast in the role of animals (enslaved, oppressed, abused) than usual, as in the common analogy between prizefights and bullfights. But of course she drops her plan for vengeance, partly because she is a gentle, nurturing nonviolent person. Even those of us who most sympathize with her frustrations, who most resent the circumstances that bind her, would hardly wish for her to be otherwise. However, we might also notice, as Owens does, with a slightly different inference from mine (Owens, p. 112), the eucharistic symbolism of Elisa's consolatory choice—"wine will be enough" (*LV*, p. 23). She has, in a sense, opted for symbolic rather than real "sacrifice," for communion wine rather than the actual blood shed of prizefights. At the literal level, of course, Marcus's view is accurate: Elisa has decided that having wine with dinner will be romantic and adventurous "enough," that is, will be "enough" of a departure from the ordinary.[7]

Still, the day's accumulated effects weigh heavily upon Elisa, and she is well aware of their significance. In either version of the story, its final words portray Elisa "crying weakly—like an old woman" (*LV*, p. 23). Here McMahan's observation that Elisa weeps because "all hope of romance is a thing of the past" needs, I think, to be revised to "all hope for change is a thing of the past." To be young and female is to be still capable of altering one's status, once recognition of it has set in; but Elisa fears that she already grows old. It is worth noting that, although the question of her strength or weakness has come up before and the matter of her womanliness has been implicit throughout, this last line of the story is the first mention of the thirty-five-year-old Elisa's thinking herself "old." And "old" may be unchangeable. If she could continue to think of herself as young, she could, perhaps, confront men on their own terms, she could, perhaps, cease being just a rancher's wife, she could presumably be employed for renumeration. She could still, then, show the world—as she earlier threatened to show the tinker—"what a woman might do."

What Steinbeck has presented in this story, among other meanings, of course, is a feministic portrayal of a woman who is kept confined, restrained, and limited to a very small horticultural existence. That she has cooperated in her own confinement makes the portrayal no less convincing and no less dramatic. Steinbeck's symbolic intent becomes clear to us when we examine the organic/mechanical contrasts in the story, and he consistently reinforced that intent by the additions that he made to the story for its publication in **The Long Valley.** Particularly emphatic, in this respect, is his addition of Elisa's being "crouched" and "fawning" like the mongrel dog, as it anticipates the image of her "crying weakly" at the story's conclusion. Not only is such feminism an unusual theme for John Steinbeck, but it is not often found in any of America's best-known male novelists. Katha Pollitt has observed (in a review in *The Nation* of John Updike's *Witches of Eastwick*)[8] how "strange" it is that "the changes in sex roles vigorously under way" in our time have been "hardly mentioned in the novels of Bellow, Both, Mailer, Updike," *et al.,* and concludes that America's "celebrated writers just don't get the point, even when they try" (Pollitt, p. 775). She has named, I think, some of those males in whose works one might well have expected to find the sexual revolution chronicled—or at least recognized—but does not. How much more startling, then, to find traces of such recognition in Steinbeck's work—in 1938.

Notes

1. Stanley Renner, "The Real Woman Inside the Fence in 'The Chrrysanthemums,'" *Modern Fiction Studies*, 31 (Summer 1985), 305–17. The quotation appears on p. 306. Subsequent citation of this work will appear as "Renner," followed by a page number, all in parentheses in the body of my text. Renner cites most of the essays relevant to the "standard reading" that he has summarized. Of those, two in particular are influential upon my own reading: Elizabeth McMahan, "'The Chrysanthemums': Study of a Woman's Sexuality," *Modern Fiction Studies* 14 (Winter 1968–69), 453–58 (hereafter cited as "McMahan" plus a page number, in the text) and Marilyn L. Mitchell, "Steinbeck's Strong Women: Feminine Identity in the Short Stories," in *Steinbeck's Women: Essays in Criticism*, ed. Tetsumaro Hayashi (*Steinbeck Monograph Series*, No. 9) (Muncie, Indiana: Steinbeck Society, Ball State University, 1979). Subsequent citation of the latter will appear as "Mitchell," followed by a page number, all in parentheses in the body of my text. Another essay important to the history of this particular reading, but not cited by Renner, is Mordecai Marcus, "The Lost Dream of Sex and Childbirth," *Modern Fiction Studies* 11 (Spring 1965), 54–58. Subsequent citation of this work will appear as "Marcus," followed by a page number, all in parentheses in the body of my text. Only after having finished this essay did I become aware of the article by Ernest W. Sullivan, II, "The Cur in 'The Chrysanthemums,'" originally published in *Studies in Short Fiction*, 16 (Summer 1979), and reprinted in *The Heath Guide to Literature*, eds. D. Bergman and D. M. Epstein. (Lexington, Massachusetts: Heath, 1987), pp. 1387–89, where I discovered it. Sullivan begins with a point that is central to my argument—the association between dogs and Elisa Allen—but proceeds to conclusions substantially different from mine.

2. Roy S. Simmonds, "The Original Manuscripts of Steinbeck's 'The Chrysanthemums,'" *Steinbeck Quarterly*, 7 (Summer-Fall 1974), 102–11.

3. Louis Owens, *John Steinbeck's Re-Vision of America* (Athens: University of Georgia Press, 1985). See especially the section, "'The Chrysanthemums': Waiting for Rain," pp. 108–13.

4. William R. Osborne, "The Texts of Steinbeck's 'The Chrysanthemums,'" *Modern Fiction Studies*, 12 (Winter 1966–67), 479–84. Subsequent citation of this work will appear as "Osborne," followed by a page number, all in parentheses in the body of my text.

5. John Steinbeck, "The Chrysanthemums," *The Long Valley* (New York: Viking Press, 1938). Subsequent citation of this work will appear as *"LV,"* followed by a page number, all in parentheses in the body of my text.

6. Gerald Noonan, in a "brief footnote" to McMahan's article [*Modern Fiction Studies*, 15 (Winter 1969–70), 542], makes some observations of animal metaphors or "agricultural comparison" in this story, and comes to a conclusion somewhat near mine. The tinker, Noonan contends, is "businesslike," as is Henry. What Noonan does not observe, I think, is a crucial difference between the tinker's "agricultural comparison" ("I'm dry as a cow in there") and Henry's figure of the "calf": the tinker compares himself, figuratively, to the organic item. This more nearly explains, in my view, why Elisa is not offended by his figure of speech as she is by Henry's.

7. Owens sees the wine as being a communion symbol, as I do, but sees its importance as representing Elisa's "commitment through sacrifice" (p. 112)—commitment, that is, to human contact. I have written the first draft of this paper before reading Owens's essay on this story. I am now inclined to prefer his interpretation, but in the present context the difference is not crucial.

8. Katha Pollitt, "Bitches and Witches," *The Nation*, 238 (June 23, 1984) 773–75. Subsequent citation of this work will appear as "Pollitt," followed by a page number, all in parentheses in the body of my text.

R. S. Hughes (essay date 1989)

SOURCE: "The Chrysanthemums," in *John Steinbeck: A Study of the Short Fiction,* Twayne Publishers, 1989, pp. 21–7.

[*In the essay that follows, Hughes identifies elements responsible for the critical success of "The Chrysanthemums," specifically plot, characterization, symbolism, and overall objectivity.*]

Among Steinbeck's fifty or more pieces of short fiction, no story has been more highly praised than **"The Chrysanthemums."** Steinbeck began writing it on 31 January 1934,[1] and by the time he finished in February of that year, he sensed that he had created a subtly powerful work. In a letter to George Albee, Steinbeck says: "I shall be interested to know what you think of the story, **"The Chrysanthemums."** It is entirely different and is designed to strike without the reader's knowledge. I mean he reads it casually and after it is finished feels that something profound has happened to him although he does not know what nor how. It has had that effect on several people here."[2]

This subliminal quality sets the story apart. Critics have been responding favorably to **"The Chrysanthemums"** ever since Steinbeck composed it. Carol Henning Steinbeck, the author's first wife and perhaps most incisive critic of this period, said it was "the best of all [his] stories." Brian Barbour has praised it as Steinbeck's "most artistically successful story." Jackson J. Benson and Louis Owens consider the tale his "finest"; Roy S. Simmonds characterizes it as "one flowing surge of creativity." And Mordecai Marcus calls **"The Chrysanthemums"** "one of the world's great short stories."[3]

While its subtleties are difficult, if not impossible, to capture in retelling, **"The Chrysanthemums"** can be summarized as follows: One December afternoon on the Allen Ranch, a "greyflannel fog" seals the Salinas Valley like a "closed pot."[4] Elisa Allen, a vigorous woman of thirty-five, works in her fenced garden powerfully cutting down chrysanthemum stalks. Her husband, Henry, having just sold thirty head of cattle, appears and suggests they dine out that evening. When Henry returns to the fields, a rickety wagon drawn by a horse and burro wobbles toward the house. The big, bearded driver introduces himself to Elisa as a pot mender. Although Elisa three times declines his services, she warms to him when he expresses interest in her chrysanthemums. He tells her that a lady on his route wants some chrysanthemums, and Elisa excitedly prepares several sprouts in a red pot. As she talks with the tinker, Elisa becomes empassioned and reaches toward his leg, almost touching it. Then she scurries behind the house to find two old, dented saucepans, which he repairs for fifty cents. After the tinker departs, the exuberant Elisa bathes, exults in her naked body before a mirror, and dresses for dinner. When Henry returns and marvels at how strong she looks, Elisa confides that she never before knew how strong. As they leave for dinner in their car, Elisa spots the chrysanthemum sprouts she had given the tinker lying in the road. He has thrown them away and kept the red pot. She begins to cry, but hides her tears from Henry.

Since **"The Chrysanthemums"** is arguably Steinbeck's finest short story, Simmonds notes that a "small critical industry has grown up around [it]." Benson believes that many critics have addressed themselves to this enduring tale because, "like most outstanding stories, **The Chrysanthemums"** can be taken a number of different ways." Despite variant interpretations of the story, one theme critics keep coming back to is frustration, stemming from the protagonist's unfulfilled or thwarted desires. Critics have differed, however, on the specific source of Elisa Allen's frustration. Richard Astro, Robert M. Benton, and Elizabeth McMahan suggest a poor marriage as its source. Brian Barbour and William V. Miller blame a combination of ambiguous spiritual and sexual problems. Warren French argues that Elisa's behavior reflects sublimated "maternal instincts"; and, similarly, Mordecai Marcus says that she longs to bear children (a notion refuted by McMahan). Benson sees in her a woman trying to find a creative, significant role in a male-dominated society; Charles A. Sweet calls her the "embryonic feminist." And finally, John H. Timmerman finds in Elisa the artist's frustration with an unappreciative society. What all these readings have in common is that they suggest, in Owens's words, the "repression of powerful human impulses," which leads, as we have seen, to frustration.[5]

Central to almost any reading of the story is the protagonist, Elisa Allen, whom Joseph Warren Beach calls "one of the most delicious characters ever transferred from life to the pages of a book." Elisa is a Steinbeck "strong woman." According to Marilyn H. Mitchell (see her essay in part 3), such strong women have "a strength of will usually identified" with men, as well as an "ambiguous combination of traditionally masculine and feminine traits."[6] Elisa is in her prime—strong, talented, energetic, eager, and handsome. Yet she lives on an isolated ranch, is married to a well-meaning but unexciting cattleman, and has no creative outlets beyond the confines of her house and garden. And since Henry Allen, a traditional male, is the couple's sole breadwinner, Elisa's contribution to their material comfort and well-being is seemingly undervalued by herself, if not by her husband.

According to Benson, Steinbeck probably based the character of Elisa Allen on his own first wife, Carol Henning Steinbeck. Like Elisa, Carol was a woman of considerable talent and energy who wore "masculine clothes" and was "strong, large-boned" and "handsome rather than pretty." At the time **"The Chrysanthemums"** was composed, the Steinbeck's (like the Allen's) had no children. Although when she first met John Steinbeck, Carol was training for a career in advertising, after their marriage she took a series of temporary jobs as they moved from place to place. Benson says that **"The Chrysanthemums"** "indicates very strongly that Steinbeck was aware of and sympathetic to" forces frustrating his wife.[7] Basing his reading of the story on these biographical insights, Benson concludes: "Of the forces aligned against Elisa's freedom to be what she is capable of being, perhaps the most subtly destructive are, on the one hand, the basic understandings held by society of a woman's presumed limitations—a force that seems to permeate the atmosphere of the story—and, on the other hand, the misguided sympathy and kindness offered by the husband. It is the latter that is so terribly defeating—what is the feminine equivalent of 'emasculating'?"[8]

Evidence in the story suggests that Elisa, reflecting Carol Henning Steinbeck, is talented and energetic—as well as frustrated. She cuts her chrysanthemum stalks with excessive energy; "her work with the scissors [is] over-eager, over-powerful." The stalks seem "too small and easy for her energy" (10). She has "strong," "terrier fingers," which destroy pests "before they get started." Even her gardening clothes suggest power: "heavy leather gloves," "clodhopper shoes," "a man's black hat," and "a big corduroy apron with four big pockets" to hold gardening tools (10). Nearby behind the garden we see Elisa's "neat white farm house with red geraniums close-banked around it." The house looks "hard-swept" with "hard-polished windows, and a clean mud-mat on the front steps" (10). Everything about both the house and garden is orderly and immaculate—giving us clues as to how she spends her time.

We can also surmise that Elisa's marriage neither fills her time nor fulfills her desires. That she and Henry have less than complete rapport is evident from their first meeting in the story when Elisa "start[s]" at the sound of her husband's voice (11). And later, after she bathes and dresses for dinner, Elisa must "set herself" for his arrival; she [stiffens] and her face [grows] tight" (21). There is an unnatural or estranged quality to their relationship, so that at times they seem to be speaking different languages. When Henry puts on his "joking tone" and invites her to the fights in Salinas, for instance, Elisa takes him seriously, answering "breathlessly . . . 'No, I wouldn't like to go'" (12). For his part, Henry is "bewildered" by his wife's exuberance after her meeting with the tinker and then "complain[s]" when her spirits sink at the story's end (21, 23). He seems to have little understanding of her sensitive emotions.

While Steinbeck describes Elisa Allen with loving detail, he neglects to offer even a brief description of her husband. Henry Allen, a stereotypical rancher and husband, actually needs little introduction. A static, stock figure, he provides essential information about Elisa and acts as a measure of changes in her behavior. At the story's beginning, for example, he notes her unique talents as a gardener. "'You've got a gift with things,' Henry observed. 'Some of those yellow chrysanthemums you had this year were ten inches across'" (11). Henry also helps us to chart the rise and fall of her spirits. After Elisa's encounter with the tinker, Henry says to her. "You look strong enough to break a calf over your knee, happy enough to eat it like a watermelon" (21–22). But later when her spirits flag on discovering the pot mender's insincerity, Henry says, "Now you're changed again" (23). Thus, during these scenes and at other times in the story, Henry's words help to define the character of Elisa.

Henry Allen, whether from lack of interest or obtuseness, never enters the special world of his wife's garden. Yet, while Henry remains outside, restrained (like the ranch animals) by "the wire fence that protected [it] from cattle and dogs and chickens" (11), the itinerant pot mender breaches her special world after only a few minutes' conversation with Elisa. "'Come into the yard,'" she exclaims, and "the man came through the picket gate." (16). Compared to Henry Allen, the tinker is, indeed, an exciting and romantic figure. A casual traveler, who "ain't in any hurry," and aims "to follow nice weather" (14), what a contrast his life provides to the fenced-in existence of Elisa. Perhaps because of his fluid style of living, he brings out Elisa's sense of her own confinement and unfulfilled desires. Although the tinker is ragged and unclean in appearance, he taps Elisa's dormant passion. When she speaks with him her "breast swell[s] passionately" and her "voice [grows] husky" (18). At the height of her desire, the impassioned Elisa erotically describes the night ("Every pointed star gets driven into your body. It's like that. Hot and sharp and—lovely") and her "hand [goes] out toward his legs" and "her hesitant fingers almost touch the cloth" of his trousers (18). Thus, although her staid husband provides a measure for Elisa's change, it is the tinker who becomes the impetus of that change.

Elisa's most abrupt transformation occurs when she discovers that the tinker has tossed away her chrysanthemum sprouts. "Far ahead on the road Elisa saw a dark speck. She knew" (22). When she spots this "dark speck," Elisa's new sense of well-being is dashed and she begins to weep. The story's carefully foreshadowed surprise ending hinges on these few words. Earlier we are given clues about the

tinker's motives and his basic insincerity. After three failed attempts (using conventional persuasion) to sell Elisa his services, he finally notices her flowers. "What's them plants, ma'am?" he asks. Immediately, the "irritation and resistance melt[s] from Elisa's face" (15). By changing his tactics and feigning interest in her chrysanthemums, the manipulative fixer accomplishes his purposes—to make some money off a naive prospect. His insincerity is again underscored when Elisa reminds him before he leaves to keep the sand damp in the red pot. "Sand, ma'am . . . Sand?" he responds. "'Oh, sure. You mean around the chrysanthemums. Sure I will.' He clucked his tongue" (20).

These foreshadowings attest to Steinbeck's finely crafted plot in **"The Chrysanthemums."** According to Barbour, Steinbeck "succeeds in organizing this story in a way he does nowhere else."[9] The chrysanthemums themselves, the story's central symbol, provide the structural underpinning of the plot. Early in the story the chrysanthemum stalks resemble phalluses, and Elisa's "over-eager" (10) snipping of them suggests castration. Then in the "rooting" bed (12) Elisa's inserting the "little crisp shoots" into open, receptive furrows of earth suggests sexual coition. Sometime later the sprouts become Elisa's children, when she explains lovingly to the pot mender how to care for them ("I'll tell you what to do" [17]). And Elisa's full-grown chrysanthemums, which are yellow and giant (measuring "ten inches across" [11]) may represent the fruition of her talent and energy—the beautiful blooms of her desperation. Because Steinbeck did not try (as he did in "The White Quail") to peg this symbol to a single, static idea, **"The Chrysanthemums"** is rich in ambiguity.

The story is rich in other ways as well. Characteristic of Steinbeck's short fiction of the 1930s, **"The Chrysanthemums"** contains vivid seasonal imagery, as well as colorful images of flowers, plants, and animals. The tale opens in a December "grey-flannel fog" (9), suggesting not only the lack of sunshine in winter but also the coldness and sterility of this pallid season. Cleverly suggesting the oppressive closeness of winter, Steinbeck has the fog seal the valley "like a lid" on a "closed pot" (9). This "pot" image (like the house and garden imagery discussed above) underscores Elisa's circumscribed existence. Although fog seals the Salinas Valley in greyness, the "yellow stubble fields [seem] to be bathed in pale cold sunshine" and the "thick willow scrub . . . [flames] with sharp and positive yellow leaves" (9). These bright, sunny yellows (including Elisa's chrysanthemums) in the midst of winter suggest Elisa's hope, rekindled by the tinker, for a more fulfilling life. That the fixer represents such hope to Elisa is made clear when she whispers as she watches the tinker leave: "That's a bright direction. There's a glowing there." (20). Elisa's garden itself can also be thought of as a paradise or Eden, with Elisa as the innocent Eve who falls prey to the wiles of the deceptive tinker. The tinker dresses in (Satanic or reptilian?) black, his eyes are dark and "full of brooding" and his hands are calloused and cracked—in "every crack a black line" (13–14).

Animal imagery also abounds in the story. Ernest W. Sullivan argues that one "cannot help being struck by the repeated association of unpleasant canine characteristics with the otherwise attractive Elisa Allen."[10] For starters, Elisa has "terrier fingers" (11), as we have seen, and she crouches "low like a fawning dog" (18) before the tinker. Elisa also raises her upper lip, "showing her teeth" (19), as would an angry dog. The correspondences between the people and their dogs in the story elucidate the human characters' behavior. The two ranch shepherds and the tinker's mongrel, though Sullivan argues to the contrary, reflect their respective masters. The Allens, like their shepherds, are a distinct breed, and (despite Elisa's foiled rebellion) they live conventional, domesticated lives; the tinker and his mongrel, on the other hand, are homeless strays who wander about looking for their next meal.

One final feature of the story that deserves our attention is Steinbeck's point of view—third-person objective. This restricted point of view—in which the narrator reports events "objectively" without entering into the minds of the characters—is especially important in regard to the protagonist. Much of Elisa Allen's appeal stems from the ambiguity of her actions, and that ambiguity is maintained because we can only surmise what she is thinking and feeling. Mary Teller in **"The White Quail"** is less interesting than Elisa precisely because Steinbeck too explicitly tells us what Mary is thinking, while Elisa remains a mystery.

"The Chrysanthemums," to summarize, is probably Steinbeck's ultimate masterpiece in short fiction. In it he illustrates the frustrating limitations placed on women (and men) by sex-stereotyped roles and by traditional attitudes about "normal" female and male behavior. The sympathetically drawn Elisa Allen ranks as the most memorable female protagonist in Steinbeck's short fiction. The story's narrative, with its carefully foreshadowed surprise ending, is his most finely wrought. And the richly suggestive symbol, Elisa's chrysanthemums, allows the story to sustain widely diverse readings. Considering these strengths, it is no wonder that Mordecai Marcus calls **"The Chrysanthemums"** "one of the world's great short stories."

Notes

1. Roy S. Simmonds, "The Original Manuscripts of Steinbeck's 'The Chrysanthemums,'" *Steinbeck Quarterly* 7 (Summer-Fall 1974): 104.

2. Letter to George Albee, 25 February 1934, in *A Life in Letters*, 91.

3. Ibid.; Barbour, "Steinbeck as a Story Writer," 122; Benson, *True Adventures*, 276; Owens, *Steinbeck's Re-Vision*, 113; Simmonds, "Original Manuscripts," 104; Marcus, "The Lost Dream," 54.

4. *The Long Valley* (New York: Viking Press, 1938), 9. All subsequent references to this work appear in the text.

5. Simmonds, "Original Manuscripts," 102; Benson, *True Adventures*, 276; Richard Astro, *John Steinbeck and Edward F. Ricketts: The Shaping of a Novelist* (Minneapolis: University of Minnesota Press, 1973), 116; Benton, "Steinbeck's *The Long Valley*," in *A Study Guide to Steinbeck: A Handbook to His Major Works*, ed. Tetsumaro Hayashi (Metuchen, N.J.: Scarecrow Press, 1974), 71; Elizabeth E. McMahan, "'The Chrysanthemums': Study of a Woman's Sexuality," *Modern Fiction Studies* 14 (Winter 1968–69): 458; Barbour, "Steinbeck as a Story Writer," 122; William V. Miller, "Sexual and Spiritual Ambiguity in 'The Chrysanthemums,'" in

A Study Guide to Steinbeck's "The Long Valley," ed. Tetsumaro Hayashi (Ann Arbor, Mich.: Pierian Press, 1976), 1–10; Warren French, *John Steinbeck*, 2d rev. ed. (Boston: Twayne Publishers, 1975), 83; Marcus, "Lost Dream," 58; Charles A. Sweet, Jr., "Ms. Elisa Allen and Steinbeck's 'The Chrysanthemums,'" *Modern Fiction Studies* 20 (1974): 210–14; John H. Timmerman, *John Steinbeck's Fiction: The Aesthetics of the Road Taken* (Norman: University of Oklahoma Press, 1986), 67; Owens, *Steinbeck's Re-Vision*, 110–11.

6. Beach, *American Fiction*, 311–14; Marilyn H. Mitchell, "Steinbeck's Strong Women: Feminine Identity in the Short Stories," in *Steinbeck's Women: Essays in Criticism*, ed. Tetsumaro Hayashi, Steinbeck Monograph Series, no. 9 (Muncie, Ind.: John Steinbeck Society of America, Ball State University, 1979), 27, 33.

7. Benson, *True Adventures*, 145, 275–76.

8. Ibid., 276.

9. Barbour, "Steinbeck as a Story Writer," 122.

10. Ernest W. Sullivan II. "The Cur in 'The Chrysanthemums,'" *Studies in Short Fiction* 16 (1979): 215.

John H. Timmerman (essay date 1990)

SOURCE: "'The Chrysanthemums': Repression and Desire," in *The Dramatic Landscape of Steinbeck's Short Stories*, University of Oklahoma Press, 1990, pp. 169–77.

[*In the following essay, Timmerman contends that "The Chrysanthemums" is a classical example of Steinbeck's favored theme of artistic repression.*]

During his period of intense artistic activity during the first half of 1934, Steinbeck fought almost daily against an overwhelming sense of failure. There were days when the words flowed as if some divine muse guided them; there were others during which his ledger entries consisted of little more than despondent notes lamenting his lack of success. It is not surprising, in view of this symbiosis of exhilarating effort and exhausted despair, that one theme to surface regularly in the stories is society's failure to recognize the artistic gift and its consequent repression of the creative genius. Steinbeck explored that theme in three of his stories from *The Long Valley*: **"The Chrysanthemums," "The White Quail,"** and **"The Harness."**

"The Chrysanthemums" stimulated an unusual interest for Steinbeck. It was, as he noted in a ledger entry, the story of a woman that he could not get out of his mind. Perhaps this closeness to it led to the difficulties he endured in composing the story, for none other in *The Long Valley* seemed to give him quite so much trouble artistically. The labor was worth it, marking the story as one of Steinbeck's short masterpieces. Stylistically and thematically, **"The Chrysanthemums"** is a superb piece of compelling craftsmanship.

Perhaps the first reference to **"The Chrysanthemums"** occurs in an undated ledger held by the Steinbeck Research Center of San Jose State University. The notebook consists of only a few random notes, fragments of clippings, and some work of Carol Steinbeck. No unified work appears. One entry has work on a play that Steinbeck never finished called "The Wizard." He returned to it under the title "The Wizard of Maine" in 1944–45, completing about fifteen thousand words on thirty folio leaves.[1] In that notebook, however, one brief note appears in reference to **"The Chrysanthemums,"** probably jotted some time before he began composing the story in January 1934. The note is remarkable for its revelation of an author's discovery of his own story:

> My book, all empty. Maybe sometime you will be full. But not now. I am as empty as you are. I wish I could get the lady and the chrysanthemums chrysanthems [sic] out of my mind. If she goes much further and I haven't the least idea what she's about. I'm afraid she's going to get me and she isn't much of a story anyways. But she is interesting and if she did see them along the road—what the hell. She'd feel pretty terrible if she had built up a structure.

All other drafts of **"The Chrysanthemums"** appear in the *Tortilla Flat* notebook, held by the Harry Ransom Research Center of the University of Texas, Austin. The very early starts on the story give further indication of Steinbeck's process of artistic discovery. The first draft depicts Elisa in the kitchen:

> On a shelf over the kitchen sink, a little oblong mirror with fluted edges stood. In front of it lay four big hair pins, bent out of shape, shiny where the enamel was broken off at the U. Elisa, washing the noon day dishes, paused now and then to look in the mirror. Her face was now bloated now cadaverous as its reflection moved on the uneven glass. Her hands came out of the dish water and rested palms down on the spongy wooden sink board. Each finger drained soapy water. She leaned forward, peered in the mirror and then she picked up one of the hair pins, deftly captured a loose strand of light brown hair and pinned it in back of her ear. In the living room, her husband coughed to make his presence felt. Elisa regarded her fingers puckered and unhealthily white from the hot water and strong soap.

At this point, Steinbeck's ink ran out. He switched to purple ink and the switch itself, in a not unusual pattern in his ledgers, stimulated him to a reflection on his writing:

> This is to be a good story. Two personalities meet, cross, flare, die and hate each other. Purple, if it were a little bit stronger, would be a good color for the story. It is coming stronger and stronger. I have a definite feeling of change today, Wednesday the 31st of January. I feel that some change has taken place. Good or bad, I don't know. It will be interesting to see. I make the record for checking back. I think either tonight or tomorrow I will receive word of that change.

In the note Steinbeck dates the story-writing as Wednesday, January 31, thus placing the composition in 1934.

A day following, Steinbeck's mind was still absorbed with personal thoughts. He switched back to black ink, his preferred color, and determined to continue the story.

> Can the weather account for all of this gathering storm in my mind. What is there about the story which makes

it almost impossible for me to write it. There is a section of great ecstacy in it. It is a good story as I see it. I'm having a terrible time writing it. And I should get it done for I suspect I shall get a beastly reception for TF [*Tortilla Flat*] and much as I fight against it, I shall be upset by that reception.

Following some personal reflections, Steinbeck concludes the note:

> Now the story of the Chrysanthemums is to go on and may the Lord have mercy on it. A story of great delicacy, one difficult to produce. I must do this one well or not at all. I'm getting the feel back. Curious how my spirit was undermined a few days ago. Almost came crashing down too. I shouldn't like to start all over at the very beginning.

Evidently Steinbeck did not start all over. The next entry begins with a portrait of Henry Allen, following upon the earlier paragraph of Elisa washing dishes. Its importance lies in the insight it gives us to Henry's character:

> Henry was in the living room waiting for her, she knew. He wanted to tell her something. Strange ceremonious man he was. He couldn't come right out with it when he entered the house for lunch. No, he must keep silence, what he considered a poker face, he must arrange his scene, the living room, after she had finished washing the dishes—a little ceremony. Henry was always that way. And whatever his secret was, he thought it would be a surprise to Elisa. She would fool him as she had so often before. He thought she could read his mind. How many times had she not told him what he was thinking and amazed him.

Steinbeck suggests a potential conflict between Henry and Elisa; he being ritualistic and dependable, she intuitive and quick. The following paragraph accentuates the conflict, focusing now upon Elisa's native intelligence and Henry's rather dull, methodical pattern of living:

> Eliza [sic] took a towel from the rack and dried the dishes slowly. She would wear down his patience, and then start him wrong. It amused her to do this and it gave her a nice secret sense of power with which to combat the fact that she, Elisa, valedictorian of her class in Salinas High School, winner of two statewide essay contests, was the wife of a fairly successful farmer.
>
> . . . The essay contests had placed her very high, and sometimes this marriage with a farmer seemed to place her rather low.

Elisa goes into the sitting room to berate Henry for not wiping his feet, but then Henry shares his secret with her: "'Why the Ferry Seed People want me to put in sweet peas in that 20 acres out by the county road[,] ten of mixed and five of pink and five of blue. They say the land's perfect for sweet peas.'" Elisa thinks that the field of sweet peas, an idea later picked up in **"The Harnass,"** will be beautiful; Henry thinks only of the profit. To celebrate the decision, Henry invites her out: "'I thought we should have a little celebration tonight, go into town for dinner and then to a picture show.' He grinned. 'Or how would you like to go to the fights[?]' 'Oh no,' she said. 'I don't think I'd like fights.'" Elisa then decides to reset the chrysanthemums before going out.

But here Steinbeck broke off. In midsentence he switches from the narrative to his unease in writing it: "She heard Henry hammering metal in the tractor shed and she went to the back porch where she kept her gardening things— This was the day's work. There's no sureness of touch in me today. I don't seem to be able to get at this story. I should not be writing this story this way at all. It should be a hard finish story."

Several days passed before Steinbeck returned to the story, starting this time with the memorable opening lines retained in the published version, but focusing now upon Henry's labor in the field versus Elisa's work in the garden.

The versions from this point on have been ably analyzed by William Osborne in "The Texts of Steinbeck's 'The Chrysanthemums'" and Roy S. Simmonds's superb textual analysis in "The Original Manuscripts of Steinbeck's 'The Chrysanthemums,'"[2] the last particularly important for the sexual implications of the story arising from the scene where Elisa kneels before the Tinker. Simmonds observes, "A textual study of the original manuscript of the final version of the story makes it patently obvious that Steinbeck was obliged to tone down some of the sexual implications in the work to mollify the editors of *Harper's Magazine*."[3] The several starts on the story, however, also signify Steinbeck's efforts to relate his theme of repression to Elisa's femininity and native genius. Whether with Henry, who wishes she would use her gifts more profitably in service to the farm, or the Tinker, who frankly abuses her gifts, the pivotal center of the tale is the complex character of Elisa Allen.

Compulsively orderly and neat, Elisa has regimented her bursting creativity into rituals. While Steinbeck deleted the passage recounting her scholastic achievements, he retains her fierce eagerness in a more subtle imagery pattern allied with her gardening. She exudes energy. Her work with the scissors is rapacious, "over-eager, over-powerful." Her "terrier fingers" probe the flower stems with sureness and skill. Yet, for all her energy, her life is very much like the valley itself on this cloudy December day, "a closed pot."

In the story Elisa receives two contrary pulls from outside forces upon her energy. One emanates from the Tinker, who stands as her personal and physical opposite. Languid and disheveled, the Tinker poses a host of polarities to Elisa. While her body looks "blocked and heavy in her gardening costume," the Tinker slouches like a lean rail in a spindly fence. Her powerful force is frequently depicted in masculine terms—"handsome," "strong"—while the Tinker is effeminately deferential. Her energy is opposed by the Tinker's sad, melancholy disposition. Her eyes are "clear as water"; the Tinker's are "dark and full of brooding." She works with living things; he with inanimate objects. Her dog is a lively ranch shepherd; the Tinker's "a lean and rangy mongrel dog." She sports a yellow print dress; he a black suit worn to threads. Elisa's plants stand in soldierly rows of exuberant health; his horse and donkey "drooped like unwatered flowers."

The elaborate but artistically well-hidden list of juxtapositions function ironically, for this disheveled panhandler is also a master con man who manages to probe to the heart of Elisa's need in a way that her husband can never ap-

proach. He carries with him, beside the reek of long days on the road, the unqualified freedom to follow that road where he wills, his only aim "to follow nice weather." Freedom is the dream he brings.

Despite her keen awareness from the very start that the Tinker is a shyster, Elisa bows to the manipulation as she senses it opens on freedom. Her flowers have been her life, her children, her talent. Her gift is "planting hands," the chrysanthemums her offspring. When the Tinker acknowledges her gift, admitting its dangerous reality, Elisa reveals more of herself—physically and psychologically. She removes her hat and shakes out her long hair, removing layers of repressed desires from her soul. The unmasking comes to a climax, artistic as well as sexual, when she kneels before him to hand him one of her flowers. They are her progeny, her true and secret self. The sexual overtones of the passage are clear. Elisa exclaims, "'I've never lived as you do, but I know what you mean. When the night is dark—why, the stars are sharp-pointed, and there's quiet. Why, you rise up and up! Every pointed star gets driven into your body. It's like that. Hot and sharp and—lovely'" (p. 12).

And suddenly, like the dissipation of a sexual climax, it is over. The Tinker mends her pots, now once more just a slouch of a man rather than the revealer of her inmost heart. His retort cuts her to the quick: "It ain't the right kind of life for a woman." As she pays him, Elisa insists, "How do you know? How can you tell?" And he leaves, with the plant she knows full well is as doomed as her momentary dream. She whispers, "There's a bright direction. There's a glowing there." A bright direction opens, briefly, but it is a "gray afternoon" as she bathes to prepare for her evening out with Henry.

If the Tinker, almost inadvertently, opens a dream for Elisa and then quickly retreats, Henry is the second contrary tug upon Elisa's life. Having little sense of her gifts or her longing for full expression of them, Henry has also closed Elisa into a pot of routine expectations. From the start he is depicted as one who values the pragmatic more than the artistic, suggesting to Elisa that her gift could be put to better use in his orchard. When he tweaks her with the offhand compliment, "You look so nice!" he is hardly prepared for her response: "Nice? You think I look nice? What do you mean by 'nice'?" (p. 16). He will take her out for one more routine evening and return her to her routine at the ranch.

Steinbeck's creation of Elisa Allen is a remarkably insightful portrait with enduring relevance. She represents at once the repression of womanhood and of the artistic gift. Torn in one direction by the mechanisms of a slovenly Tinker who nonetheless opens a dream of recognition for her, and from the other by the routines of a pragmatic husband who fails to understand her, Elisa is left with little but her chrysanthemums. And the littleness of that is signified by her cherished progeny, this nurtured part of herself, that lies wilting by the roadside, tossed out by the Tinker so that he could keep the pot. It is no wonder that we are left with the portrait of her "crying weakly—like an old woman." It is all that others have permitted her to be.

It is possible, as Roy S. Simmonds has suggested, to consider Elisa as a headstrong woman blinded by her own femininity. In this view, the Tinker's abuses of her "symbolically re-established the position of male dominance she imagined she had wrested from him, in exactly the same way as over the years she had deprived, emasculated, her husband."[4] Read in this way, as Elisa's yearning for dominance, the garden signifies her surrogate kingdom, one in which she wields absolute authority in all matters of life and death. She is the sovereign queen. Simmonds argues,

> Elisa's need for this sense of dominance over the male is not confined solely to her feelings towards her husband. She experiences this need to assert her superiority over all men, contriving always to keep them at arm's length. Her flower garden is surrounded by a protective wire fence ostensibly to keep out animals, but the fence also serves to exclude her husband and the tinker. It is not until the tinker has verbally seduced her with his assumed interest in her chrysanthemums and is admitted to her side of the fence that Elisa finds her defenses in danger of collapsing to the extent that she almost allows herself to succumb to male dominance. Almost, but not quite. . . . Her shame is the shame of a woman who realizes that she has momentarily lowered her defenses and all but offered herself to the male dominance she so greatly despises.[5]

Support for such a revisionist view may be engineered from the fact that Elisa and Henry have no offspring and that Elisa has displaced both sexuality and femininity to her flowers. Some support may also be extrapolated from Steinbeck's personal relationship with Carol. The gardening costume Elisa wears, for example, is similar to one Carol wore frequently. She too could look "strong," "blocky," and "handsome." And more than once in his letters Steinbeck refers to the fact that Carol had great pride and that he sometimes could not feel close to her.

Such a reading of the story seems at odds with Steinbeck's strong rebellion against any repressive power in civilization's power bloc and his strong sensitivity toward any repressed individual. This is a theme that wends through the stories of *The Pastures of Heaven* and continues here in *The Long Valley*. Moreover, this revisionist view leaves begging this important question: What exactly would the "bright direction" that the Tinker opens for Elisa represent? Her "closed pot" of a valley does not seem, metaphorically, to be the action of her own mind, a kind of self-imposed willfulness. Rather, like the oppressive gray clouds on this December day, it is imposed upon her from without. Finally, with such a view, one wonders why Elisa would be weeping like an old woman at the conclusion. That final portrait is one of undeserved subjugation, not willful dominance.

"The Chrysanthemums" more likely should be understood as a unique and vital variation in Steinbeck's theme of social repression of the artistic gift. The personal disillusionment that Steinbeck felt at this point in his artistic career—the frequent rejections, the sense of a loss of self worth, the overwhelming loneliness—is also the guiding motif in shaping Elisa's character. The theme of the self-repressive female character more neatly fits Mary Teller of "The White Quail" than it does Elisa Allen, who typifies the individual whose gifts are ignored or repressed by the society about her.

Notes

1. In a description of the Harry Valentine Collection in *John Steinbeck: A Collection of Books and Manuscripts,* "The Wizard of Maine" is described as follows: "*The Wizard of Maine* is divided into six sections, and is the story of a traveling elixir salesman and magician who has set out from his home in Maine and travels across the country in hope of being discovered, so that he can perform his tricks on stage as a professional." The description states, "Composition date for the manuscript is unknown, but would seem to date from the 1940s based upon the style of the binder housing the paper." Jackson J. Benson dates the composition from the summer of 1944 (*True Adventures*, pp. 550–51).

2. See William R. Osborne, "The Texts of Steinbeck's 'The Chrysanthemums,'" *Modern Fiction Studies* 12 (Winter 1966–67): 479–84; and Roy S. Simmonds, "The Original Manuscripts of Steinbeck's 'The Chrysanthemums,'" *Steinbeck Quarterly* 7 (Summer-Fall 1974): 102–11.

3. Simmonds, "Original Manuscripts of 'The Chrysanthemums,'" p. 103.

4. Ibid., pp. 110–11.

5. Ibid., pp. 108–9. For other views on the sexuality and femininity of Elisa, see Mordecai Marcus, "The Lost Dream of Sex and Childbirth in 'The Chrysanthemums,'" *Modern Fiction Studies* 11 (Spring 1965): 54–58; Charles A. Sweet, Jr., "Ms. Elisa Allen and Steinbeck's 'The Chrysanthemums,'" *Modern Fiction Studies* 20 (June 1974): 210–14; and *Steinbeck's Women: Essays in criticism*, ed. Tetsumaro Hayashi.

Susan Shillinglaw (essay date 1991)

SOURCE: "'The Chrysanthemums': Steinbeck's Pygmalion" in *Steinbeck's Short Stories in "The Long Valley": Essays in Criticism,* edited by Tetsumaro Hayashi, Ball State University, 1991, pp. 1–9.

[In the essay below, Shillinglaw asserts that "The Chrysanthemums" was heavily influenced by the Pygmalion myth as utilized by Ovid and George Bernard Shaw.]

For John Steinbeck "life was not a struggle toward anything, but a constant process in it," writes Jackson J. Benson, and "that process for man . . . was largely a matter of learning. It was the major 'action' for both his life and work."[1] It is clearly the major "action" in his two most famous stories about women, "The Chrysanthemums" and "The White Quail." As Steinbeck records in his journals, the germ for each is that moment when a woman learns something profound about herself, a moment of insight either grasped or denied: Elisa seeing the chrysanthemums on the road; Mary in her garden, looking in the window. Before he composed "The Chrysanthemums" in 1934, Steinbeck wrote:

> I wish I could get the lady and the chrysanthemums out of my mind. If she goes much further, I'll have to write her and I haven't the least idea what she's about. I'm afraid she's going to get me and she isn't much of a story any way. But she is interesting and if she did see them along side the road—what the hell. She'd feel

pretty terrible if she had built up a structure. And if her structure were built on an inner joy, all the more.[2]

Clearly what intrigues Steinbeck is the instant when the structure, her envisioned life, topples completely. Such crises often appear in Steinbeck's work—although many of his characters certainly resist knowledge. But not Elisa. Hers is a story about change.

I would like to suggest a source for this tale about Elisa Allen's knowledge—the Pygmalion legend. For an author whose works frequently draw upon a mythic tradition, it is hardly surprising that this story of metamorphosis reveals his debts to both Ovid and George Bernard Shaw in delineating the stifling effects of both sexual repression and middle-class complacency.

In Ovid's version, the motive for transformation is sexual. Disgusted with the Propoctides, the whorish women he knows, the artist Pygmalion imagines an ideal woman, carves her in stone, and lovingly caresses her. And Venus, rewarding him for envisioning this ideal, grants Pygmalion the wish he dares not utter, the transformation of his statue into a woman. In Shaw's version of the legend, however, the sexual energy is diffused; Henry Higgins's sublime female is his mother, not the fair Eliza. Urging Eliza to stay with him at the end of the play, he offers her only a cozy triangle of her, Higgins, and Pickering, "three bachelors." He defines a complete life thus: "I care for life, for humanity, and you are a part of it that has come my way and been built into my house. What more can you or anyone ask?"[3] For him, Eliza Doolittle exists as an object, a useful piece of furniture. Triumphantly, he brags of the transformation she desires and he effects—not a sexual change but a social one, a change of class. Yet the metamorphosis does not free her. "Until the last scene of the play," notes one commentator, "Eliza is in a position of economic, as well as emotional and intellectual dependence on Higgins. She is a kept woman."[4] Pygmalion/Henry's dominance effects one metamorphosis, one that is, in effect, static, the creation of an articulate and finely dressed lady. But Lady Eliza must effect a second metamorphosis, specifically that from a kept woman to a free one. She must define life on her own terms. Thus, while making class the central issue, Shaw's play also studies the inadequacies of Pygmalion/ Henry's intellectual ideal. The creative mind in both the classical and the nineteenth-century versions envisions an ideal woman who must live in order to respond. In Ovid, life rewards the creator; in Shaw, life reveals the inadequacies of the creator.

Steinbeck fuses the different emphases found in Ovid and Shaw. He shows the sexual repressions a woman feels, not just in a broad social sense, but in the sense that class differences imply various degrees of empowerment and repression.[5] He has taken Ovid and Shaw and made their myths his own representation of men and women in a bourgeois world they uncritically accept as the only one imaginable, despite the possibilities for revolution held out, albeit deceptively, by the tinker. The open road is really a dead end for Elisa.

In the beginning of the story Steinbeck's Elisa, like Shaw's Eliza, is a kept woman. The opening paragraphs that describe the valley suggest her isolation, and, as Louis Owens notes, her "suspended life, awaiting the fertilizing imagi-

nation of the tinker."[6] But the figurative language also conveys a sense of mechanized, transformed nature, and this, too, helps characterize Elisa. Fog sits like a lid; the Salinas Valley is a closed pot; earth gleams like metal; willow shrubs "flame with sharp and positive leaves,"[7] as if etched. Nature, now held in check, has undergone a metamorphosis into something static and vaguely forbidding. And Elisa, the woman closest to nature, is similarly checked—fenced in when we first see her. In one of the best analyses of the story, Marilyn Mitchell argues that both Eliza and Mary Teller of **"The White Quail"** are "trapped between society's definition of the masculine and the feminine and are struggling against the limitations of the feminine."[8] More pointedly, it is the middle class—with all of the sexual, spiritual, and social inhibitions it enforces—that traps Elisa, as it does many throughout Steinbeck's work. She has been repressed by the very things which, while gardening, she achieves physical distance from—the tidy house behind her and the men conversing "down" to her. But no psychological escape follows. The syntax of the first sentence describing Elisa conveys her awareness of male prerogatives: "Elisa Allen, working in her flower garden, looked down across the yard and saw Henry, her husband, talking to two men in business suits" (*LV*, p. 4). The main clause addresses her awareness of the empowered male, but the phrase suggests her avocation. In the second page of the story that describes her gardening activities, there are four references to Elisa's glances toward this authoritative group, each of whom stands "with one foot on the side of the little Fordson" tractor. Steinbeck repeatedly shows that the bourgeois world restricts Elisa's self definition and creativity. When first described, she wears male clothing like a shield: "Her figure looked blocked and heavy in her gardening costume, a man's black hat pulled low down over her eyes, clodhopper shoes, a figured spring dress almost completely covered by a big corduroy apron with four big pockets. . . . She wore heavy leather gloves to protect her hands while she worked" (*LV*, p. 4). The male attire compromises Elisa's sexual identity, and this blurred identity causes much of her frustration. The softness that she later so poignantly reveals is, initially, concealed beneath the unwieldy clothing. Unconsciously, she "pulls on the gardening glove again" when Henry approaches, not only steeling herself against him, but revealing the impossibility at this point of identifying herself outside a male sphere. Furthermore, nothing in Elisa's world gives her pure pleasure. Even her creative outlet, gardening, is an adulterated delight: "The chrysanthemum stems seemed too small and easy for her energy" (*LV*, p. 10). When Henry first speaks to her, he taints their beauty by applying the language of commerce to the flowers, noting their size and wishing that she'd "work out in the orchard and raise some apples that big" (*LV*, p. 5). Henry speaks the language of power, particularly when compared to the tinker's later poetic rendering of a chrysanthemum as "a quick puff of colored smoke" (*LV*, p. 10). The paragraph that precedes the arrival of the tinker further reveals the psychological limitations of Elisa's gardening:

> With her trowel she turned the soil over and over, and smoothed it and patted it firm. Then she dug ten parallel trenches to receive the sets. Back at the chrysanthemum bed she pulled out the little crisp shoots, trimmed off the leaves of each one with her scissors and laid it on a small orderly pile. (*LV*, p. 6)

Her garden is as ordered and controlled as she is. The outlet she chooses is an inadequate substitute for the more fulfilling life that she, at this point, barely recognizes that she subconsciously craves.

For this earthy Elisa, like her Shavian predecessor, accepts the place that Henry/Pygmalion assigns her in his world, although chafing at its boundaries that limit physical, psychological, and sexual freedom. Throughout, it is the conversation between the two that best reflects the conventional nature of their partnership, the degree to which the metamorphosis that a husband effects is complete. Here, I would suggest that Steinbeck deliberately parodies the profession of Shaw's Henry Higgins, the grammarian. Although this Henry is a man of plain words, when Elisa is with him, his speech patterns hers. She speaks as plainly as he, often echoing his words. Coming toward her after completing his business deal, he first notes her "strong" crop, and she replies that "They'll be strong this coming year" (*LV*, p. 5). Henry then observes that she has a "gift with things" and Elisa agrees that she has "a gift with things, all right." When the conversation shifts from flowers, her responses become rote. To Henry's news and his proposal that they go to town, she repeatedly notes that his actions and suggestions are "good," a word to which she returns at the end of the story when she once again accepts her lot as the dutiful wife:

> She said loudly, to be heard above the motor, "It will be good, tonight, a good dinner." "Now you've changed again," Henry complained. He took one hand from the wheel and patted her knee. "I ought to take you in to dinner oftener. It would be good for both of us. We get so heavy out on the ranch." (*LV*, p. 17)

The blandness of "good" or "nice" reflects the sterility of their marriage. The word "heavy," earlier used to describe Elisa's male clothing, here suggests the oppression that she, in particular, feels on the ranch. And "strong," the other word that so frequently identifies Elisa or her activities, ironically underlines her powerlessness, in spite of her undoubted vitality. The few words that Henry knows, that Elisa echoes, and that the author uses to characterize both, identify not only the constrictions on their marriage, but more broadly the limitations of the bourgeois world.

In sharp contrast to this tight and tidy sphere, the tinker's entourage lacks order: "Up this road came a curious vehicle, curiously drawn" with squeaking wheels, a "crazy, loose-jointed wagon. . . . It was drawn by an old bay horse and a little grey-and-white burro," a mismatched team. "Words were painted on the canvas, in clumsy, crooked letters," some misspelled; paint drips beneath each letter (*LV*, p. 7). The wagon itself, compared to a prairie schooner, suggests a world far different from Elisa's—the myth of the West, of freedom, of enterprising souls, of self-sufficiency. Critics have suggested various reasons for her attraction to the tinker. In him, argues Marilyn L. Mitchell, she "finds a man whose strength seems to match hers" (Mitchell, p. 312). She responds, notes William V. Miller, to the romanticism of his "vagabond life"[9]; and to her "desire for the freedom of the male," Richard F. Peterson maintains.[10] Without discounting any of these suggestions, I would argue that she responds first not to his mode of life but to the man himself, a man from a class different from her own. Unlike her husband, he is a laborer, as the emphasis in Steinbeck's description of him makes vividly clear: his suit is "worn" and "spotted with grease," his hat battered; his eyes "were full of the brooding that gets in the eyes of teamsters and of sailors"; and his "calloused hands" are "cracked, and every crack was a black line" (*LV* p. 8). This big, disheveled itinerant works with his hands (an important focus throughout the story), as her bourgeois husband seemingly does not.

It is of less importance, I think, that this craftsman is false than that Elisa does not notice or care that he manipulates her. Both the tinker and Johnny Bear, observes Miller, embody "Steinbeck's ambiguous vision of the artist's morality," although "the tinker's manipulative art is conscious" (Miller, p. 71). This con artist immediately transforms Elisa, just as Steinbeck intended his own tale to have a startling impact on readers. This story, he wrote, "is designed to strike without the reader's knowledge. I mean he reads it casually and after it is finished feels that something profound has happened to him although he does not know what nor how."[11] Similarly, this rough-hewn Pygmalion causes something profound to occur; a dark Lawrentian man, as Peterson notes, he is the catalyst for Elisa's metamorphosis into a sexual, fulfilled woman.[12] With Henry she is cautious, stiff, and careful. With the tinker she expands immediately, laughing with him on his arrival. Then she stands up, takes off her gloves, and, when he mentions her flowers, she "melts," and her actions become eager and excited. Her language flows freely; gone are the staccato responses of her dialogue with Henry. Only when he uses the language of commerce, a speech all too familiar to her, does she resist him. But unlike Henry, he speaks both a commercial and a poetic language, and to the latter she responds, most particularly when he mentions her flowers. Elisa changes rapidly as she prepares her sprouts for the tinker to take, her gift to him of herself. Without discounting Mordecai Marcus's argument that the flowers represent her maternal urges, I would suggest that these "big," "strong" chrysanthemums more forcefully represent Elisa herself, just as the white quail represents Mary Teller.[13] So when the tinker seems to understand her soul—as Harry Teller cannot comprehend Mary's—Elisa imparts to him its meaning, the feeling expressed in her "planter's hands." Unlike her terse comments to Henry about these hands, Elisa's comments to the tinker are expansive. "I don't know how to tell you," she begins (*LV*, p. 11). Although Steinbeck again focuses on the potential inadequacy of language, in Elisa's longest, most impassioned speech, she finds words to express what Edward F. Ricketts called the experience of "breaking through," from contact with the earth to knowledge of the stars. It is an Emersonian moment of transcending the physical to the spiritual, what Steinbeck envisioned as "a section of great ecstasy" when he was still struggling to write the opening paragraphs.[14] And the climax, as most commentators have noted, is overtly sexual. To complete the metamorphosis from somebody's woman to her own, she must find both spiritual and physical fulfillment. From the tinker she needs only the briefest encouragement, for the moment is truly her own, and the change effected in her is complete, if, as all such heightened awareness must be, it is also transitory.

The rest of the story tells of Elisa's gradual withdrawal from this moment. In *The Long Valley* there are at least five stories about female sexuality, **"The Chrysanthe-**

mums," "The White Quail," "The Snake," "The Murder," "Johnny Bear," and possibly more, and each is patterned like a sexual encounter—expositions, a climax where the language is rather explicitly sexual, and the aftermath. After her own orgasmic moment, Elisa engages herself once again with her physical reality, first by reaching for another, the tinker, to share awareness: "her hesitant fingers almost touched the cloth. Then her hand dropped to the ground. She crouched low like a fawning dog" (*LV*, p. 12). When she reaches for his leg, she reaches out her "planter's hands" to connect with human life, and retreats. She is "like a fawning dog" because the spiritualized moment known only to humans is gone, and she must return to the physical world, to a man whose real concerns are not with her feelings but with a meal on the table and a pot to mend.[15] Her brave assertions about female capabilities—so similar to the speeches of Shaw's Eliza at the end of the play—and her dreamy farewell to the tinker once again identify precisely what her bourgeois existence lacks—ecstasy:

> "That's a bright direction. There's a glowing there."
> The sound of her whisper startled her. She shook herself free and looked about to see whether anyone had been listening. Only the dogs had heard. (*LV*, p. 14)

Once again, the dogs suggest her retreat to a world without visions, where she seeks physical compensations. The tinker's road is one she travels only in a car with her husband.

Unlike Shaw's flower girl, who is changed first to a lady, then to an independent woman, Steinbeck's Elisa, however "strong," cannot define herself in either sphere of male empowerment. A Shavian woman who has declared her independence is often unmarried, like Eliza, so can assert and act upon her sexual, economic, and social freedom. Elisa Allen, however, is trapped by the institution of marriage, the bulwark of middle class values. Whereas her predecessor exits triumphantly, Elisa shrinks in defeat. But she does not forgo her "strength" easily. After the tinker departs, she tries to transfer her heightened awareness into the physical pleasures that are hers also in her garden—vigorously scrubbing in the bath, carefully assessing her body, slowly dressing for dinner. But once again, the male presence begins to sap her strength, her sense of herself. She must "set herself for Henry's arrival," and, delaying his approach, sit "primly and stiffly down." Just as Elisa changes gradually back to her accustomed self, so, too, does the story return to the language and imagery of the first pages. As she awaits Henry, she "looked toward the river road where the willow-line was still yellow with frosted leaves so that under the high grey fog they seemed a thin band of sunshine. This was the only color in the grey afternoon. She sat unmoving for a long time. Her eyes blinked rarely" (*LV*, p. 15). Readjusting herself to her static world, Elisa is as unmoving as a statue—Henry/Pygmalion's creation once again. As a wife, she looks with clarity at the fog and the light that so poignantly suggest, as Miller argues, her feelings of entrapment and squelched hopes (Miller, pp. 69–70).

The end of the story reinforces her sense of failure. But readers are often unsettled and puzzled about Elisa's final retreat. Why does she ask about the fights? A glance at the original text may help answer that question. In an article

entitled "The Text of Steinbeck's 'The Chrysanthemums,'" William R. Osborne discusses the differences between the text Steinbeck first published in *Harper's Magazine* in 1937 and the one included in his collection of stories, ***The Long Valley***, in 1938.[16] One of the most substantive changes is in the paragraphs about Elisa's reaction to the "dark speck," her flowers thrown on the road. The original text ends with these sentences:

> She felt ashamed of her strong planter's hands that were no use, lying palms up in her lap. In a moment they had left behind them the man who had not known or needed to know what she said, the bargainer. She did not look back. (Osborne, p. 481)

Obviously more expository than the later version, this passage also returns the reader more insistently to her earlier transcendent moment with references to her hands, her explanation, and her shame. Through these verbal echoes, Steinbeck emphasizes the finality of her retreat from fulfillment. Furthermore, the reference to her hands gives us a clue, I believe, to the resolution of the story. Touch is Elisa's most acute sense, and she is attracted to the hands of a different class—to the tinker's calloused and skillful hands, to the "fighting gloves [that] get heavy and soggy with blood" (*LV*, p. 17). These males from a class lower than her own seem in contact with life, movement, freedom, and violence. As in Shaw's *Pygmalion*, Steinbeck contrasts the enervating effects of one class with the freedom and energy possible to the lower class. It thus seems wrong to argue that Elisa queries Henry about the fights because she wishes to punish men. Elisa does not hate men, but is fascinated by their power, the kind denied her. "Do any women ever go to the fights?" she asks her husband. "Some," but not many, and certainly not the wife Elisa who knows that she is once again inside her fence, or, at this point, inside Henry's car. Wine suffices because it must, and Elisa cries weakly—"like an old woman"—because she accepts her fate. She will never take the road again.

Steinbeck's treatment of the Pygmalion legend is thus much bleaker than either Ovid's or Shaw's, both of which, however different, end in self-assertion. As she exits, Elisa Allen cries not because she is yet weak or old, but because she is defeated by the bourgeois vision she must accept as her own. Ironically, the water that the land and the farmers so eagerly await at the beginning of the story arrives at last: tears of death, however, not of life.

Notes

1. Jackson J. Benson, *The True Adventures of John Steinbeck, Writer* (New York: Viking Press, 1984), pp. 250–51.

2. John Steinbeck, unpublished ledger book, Steinbeck Research Center, San Jose State University, p. 29.

3. George Bernard Shaw, *Pygmalion* (New York: Simon and Schuster, 1912), p. 95.

4. A. M. Gibbs, "The End of *Pygmalion*," *The Art and Mind of Shaw: Essays in Criticism* (New York: St. Martin's Press, 1983), p. 170.

5. Critics have been divided on precisely what oppresses and frustrates Elisa. Peter Lisca, among others, suggests that her role as a woman is the

source of her unhappiness. Mordecai Marcus disagrees, quoting F. W. Watt's observation that Elisa's desires are "ambiguously sexual and spiritual" and arguing that this "ambiguity combined with Elisa's pervasive combination of femininity and masculinity" is central to the story (p. 54). It does not seem to me that the two are mutually exclusive, and I wish to give the broadest possible definition for her unhappiness as a woman in a culture that frustrates many desires.

6. Louis D. Owens, *John Steinbeck's Re-Vision of America* (Athens: University of Georgia Press, 1985), p. 109.

7. John Steinbeck, "The Chrysanthemums," *The Long Valley* (New York: Viking Press, 1938), p. 3. Subsequent citations from this work will appear as *LV*.

8. Marilyn L. Mitchell, "Steinbeck's Strong Women: Feminine Identity in the Short Stories," *Southwest Review*, 61 (Summer 1976), 306.

9. William V. Miller, "Sexual and Spiritual Ambiguity in 'The Chrysanthemums,'" *Steinbeck Quarterly*, 5 (Summer-Fall 1972), 71.

10. Richard F. Peterson, "The God in the Darkness: A Study of John Steinbeck and D. H. Lawrence," *Steinbeck's Literary Dimension: A Guide to Comparative Studies*, ed. Tetsumaro Hayashi (Metuchen, New Jersey: Scarecrow Press, 1973), p. 69.

11. Elaine Steinbeck and Robert Wallsten, eds., *Steinbeck: A Life in Letters* (New York: Viking Press, 1975), p. 91.

12. Both Richard F. Peterson and Roy S. Simmonds note the similarities between Steinbeck and Lawrence; Simmonds observes that the tinker is a "romantically virile man of nature who (only symbolically in this story, however) seduces her." I would add emphasis to this point by noting that class differences here, as in Lawrence, contribute to the attraction. "The Original Manuscripts of Steinbeck's 'The Chrysanthemums,'" *Steinbeck Quarterly*, 7 (Summer-Fall 1974), 107.

13. Mordecai Marcus, "The Lost Dream of Sex and Childbirth in 'The Chrysanthemums,'" *Modern Fiction Studies*, 11 (Spring 1965), 54–58.

14. Simmonds, 104. It seems fairly certain that Steinbeck is referring to this section of the story; he envisioned both his scene and the one where Elisa sees the chrysanthemums on the road, as discussed above, before he wrote the story, showing how significant that moment of change or insight is to his conception of the tale.

15. In a recent article, C. Kenneth Pellow argues that Elisa is "like a fawning dog" because she retires, as do the tinker's dogs, "from a potential fight, the struggle to free herself from a situation in which she feels trapped" (p. 10). His interpretation of this moment is close to my own. "'The Chrysanthemums' Revisited," *Steinbeck Quarterly*, 22 (Winter-Spring 1989), 8–16.

16. William R. Osborne, "The Texts of Steinbeck's 'The Chrysanthemums,'" *Modern Fiction Studies*, 12 (Winter 1966–67), 470–84.

Christopher S. Busch (essay date 1993)

SOURCE: "Longing for the Lost Frontier: Steinbeck's Vision of Cultural Decline in 'The White Quail' and 'The Chrysanthemums'," in *Steinbeck Quarterly*, Vol. XXVI, Nos. 3–4, Summer-Fall, 1993, pp. 81–90.

[*In the following essay, Busch illuminates Steinbeck's preoccupation with an idealized frontier past in both "The Chrysanthemums" and "The White Quail."*]

In the course of his forty-year career, John Steinbeck consistently integrated elements of American frontier history, mythology, and symbolism into his fiction and nonfiction. Steinbeck's fascination with the frontier past germinated during his boyhood in Salinas, at that time a cowtown described by Jackson J. Benson as "a throwback to the frontier towns of a half-century before."[1] This vital interest in the frontier West remained with him throughout his life, impelling him in *America and Americans* to validate traditional mythic conceptions of the nation's Western heritage. He writes:

The dreams of a people either create folk literature or find their way into it; and folk literature, again, is always based on something that happened. Our most persistent folk tales—constantly retold in books, movies, and television shows—concern cowboys, gunslinging sheriffs and Indian fighters. These folk figures existed—perhaps not quite as they are recalled nor in the numbers indicated, but they did exist; and this dream also persists.[2]

While a number of critics have noted Steinbeck's focus on frontier themes, several seek to distance Steinbeck from the traditional Wild West mythology he embraces above, as well as from traditional visions of pioneers' agrarian and westering experiences on the frontier. In "'Directionality': The Compass in the Heart," for example, John Ditsky argues that *The Grapes of Wrath* shows "mere westering leads nowhere,"[3] and Chester E. Eisinger describes "the bankruptcy of Jefferson's ideal" in "Jeffersonian Agrarianism in *The Grapes of Wrath*" and claims that "we must seek another road to the independence and security and dignity we expect from democracy."[4] Warren French argues that *Grapes* represents "an attempt . . . to explode rather than perpetuate the myths and conventions upon which Western genre fiction [is] based."[5] And in his recent study, *John Steinbeck's Re-Vision of America* Louis Owens holds that

Steinbeck again and again in short story and novel held the dangers of the westering myth up to view. . . . Steinbeck saw no cornucopia of democracy in the retreating frontier, but rather a destructive and even fatal illusion barring Americans from the realization of any profound knowledge of the continent they had crossed.[6]

Though these views reflect a developing critical consensus regarding Steinbeck's vision of the frontier, Steinbeck's own words in *America and Americans*, and the words of a sympathetic farmer he presents in *Travels with Charley*, who laments, "This used to be a nation of giants. Where have they gone?"[7] haunt us and call us back to reconsider the nature of Steinbeck's deeply held vision of the frontier past.

Though French has distanced Steinbeck's work from the western genre, in fact Steinbeck's preoccupations closely parallel issues central to literary western stories and novels, particularly those that examine contemporary cultural degeneration. William Bloodworth discovers in the literary western "the sense of a vanished world in which action, gesture, and character had more significance than it does [*sic*] in the present."[8] Similarly, David Lavender, citing the works of Conrad Richter and Willa Cather, describes the frequent appearance of characters plagued by "a vitiation of energy" who experience "the universal tragedy of lost strength."[9] In "Steinbeck's 'The Leader of the People': A Crisis in Style," Phillip J. West describes Steinbeck's affiliation with this tradition, reflected in his depiction of the "diminished stature of society in the Salinas Valley . . . [which] is . . . hinted at in the epic devices that outlive epic greatness."[10] In fact, not only in *The Red Pony* but throughout his career, Steinbeck frequently exhibited concern that when compared to the frontier past, contemporary American life often lacks integrity and meaning, and that contemporary Americans increasingly resemble "a national kennel of animals with no purpose and no direction."[11] In delineating these deficits in culture and character, Steinbeck consistently represents the mythic frontier past and its prototypical figures—yeomen, cowboys, scouts, frontier fighters, hunters, wagonmasters, and westering pioneers—as an ideal or standard, while at the same time portraying modern characters who are, at best, diminished descendants of these idealized frontier types.

This comparative strategy appears, for example, in Steinbeck's characterization of such diverse figures as the hapless "hunter," Hubert Van Deventer, in *The Pastures of Heaven* (1932), the inept "scout," Pimples Carson, in *The Wayward Bus* (1947), and even the effete store clerk, Ethan Allen Hawley, in *The Winter of Our Discontent* (1961), who painfully recognizes the disparity between his own experience and that of his legendary ancestor.[12] Valuing the skill, self-reliance, and forthright vision of their cultural (and at times biological) forebears yet incapable of similar achievement themselves, such characters often live destructive lives that can only be described as diminished perversions of mythic frontier life. Steinbeck's effort to illuminate modern personal and cultural degeneration through reference to frontier types is also convincingly revealed in two stories from *The Long Valley* collection, **"The White Quail"** and **"The Chrysanthemums."**

In **"The White Quail,"** Steinbeck describes the protagonist, Mary Teller, as a diminished modern yeoman who attempts to create a perfect garden in the post-frontier West. Mary's husband, Harry, contributes to this project for a time, but ultimately recognizes its perverse nature and hunts down and kills the white quail, which, in Mary's mind, symbolizes the garden's perfection. Owens argues that "Mary's garden is an attempt to construct an unfallen Eden in a fallen world, a neurotic projection of Mary's self."[13] He concludes that the story ultimately reveals "the futility of holding to the Eden myth—even the danger of the illusion."[14] In describing Mary as yeoman and Harry as hunter, however, Steinbeck does not sharply undercut the myth of agrarianism as Owens suggests. Instead, by revealing the degenerate nature of the characters' personalities and actions, Steinbeck satirizes the narcissism and pathological self-delusion that cripple the modern American imagination and reflect the culture's degeneration.

As a frontier-based narrative, Steinbeck's story achieves much of its power through the dualistic quality of its setting and characters. Steinbeck purposely sets the story on a "frontier," or borderland possessing attributes of both a wilderness and a Crèvecoeurian "middle region" to emphasize the story's thematic connection with frontier history:

> Right at the edge of the garden, the hills started up, wild with cascara bushes and poison oak, with dry grass and live oak, very wild. If you didn't go around to the front of the house, you couldn't tell it was on the very edge of town.[15]

This setting functions as a modern suburban frontier, similar in appearance to the historical frontier, but diminished in size, a kind of mock frontier. The setting is both like the historical frontier and unlike it at the same time, just as the characters are both types and antitypes of mythic frontier figures.

In her effort to tame this frontier and transform it into a garden, Mary Teller appears to be a descendant of the homesteader, or yeoman, celebrated in the agrarian myth. Yet, in actuality, Mary is a diminished yeoman whose approach to nature inverts the yeoman's traditional approach to the land. Where the pioneer yeoman saw opportunity in the wilderness and approached it with expectancy, Mary sees danger in "the dark thickets of the hill": "'That's the enemy,' Mary said one time. 'That's the world that wants to get in, all rough and tangled and unkempt'" (pp. 26–27). Where the yeoman gained strength and virtue through contact with the soil, Mary protects herself from contact with nature by wearing a "sunbonnet" and "good sturdy gloves" (p. 25), and hires workers to carry out the actual labor.

Harry joins his wife on this suburban frontier as a diminished hunter, reminiscent of the Wild West hunter in the Leatherstocking tradition, yet curiously distinct from the type as well. Like the hunter, Harry appears near the story's end as a skilled marksman more at home in the wilderness of the hill beyond the garden than in the garden itself. But in his unconsidered acquiescence to Mary's neurotic wishes, his choice of an air gun as a weapon, and his pursuit of the harmless white quail as prey, Harry becomes a ridiculous figure, scarcely resembling the self-reliant frontier hunter whose "physical strength, adaptability to nature, resourcefulness and courage"[16] defined him as a heroic type.

As the story progresses, Steinbeck intensifies the distinction between the ideals of frontier yeoman and hunter and the modern setting and characters. Robert S. Hughes, Jr., argues that in both setting and plot, the story is "unusually static."[17] Implicit in the idea of frontier development is change and progress, but here stasis becomes the ideal: "'We won't ever change it, will we Harry?'" Mary begs. "'If a bush dies, we'll put another one just like it in the same place'" (p. 24). Whereas the yeoman harvested trees to build a shelter and food crops to feed a family, Mary's "harvest" consists of the sight of birds that "come to my garden for peace and for water" (p. 27), "bowls of flowers [which] were exquisite" (p. 25), and ultimately the white quail, "an essence boiled down to utter purity" (p. 33). And whereas the yeomen faced life-threatening challenges from Indians seeking to reclaim their land, droughts, floods, and fires, Mary and Harry must defend themselves against such dubious adversaries as snails and slugs:

> Mary held the flashlight while Harry did the actual killing. . . . He knew it must be a disgusting business to her, but the light never wavered. "Brave girl," he thought. "She has a sturdiness in back of that fragile beauty." (p. 26)

Near the story's end, the diminished Tellers face a final threat to their garden world in the form of a cat pursuing the quail. James C. Work argues that the white quail is a "life force,"[18] and Owens claims that the cat represents "the real world that Mary cannot keep forever from her garden."[19] Yet the Tellers' reaction to these two animals further emphasizes the protagonists' degeneration. As "an albino. No pigment in the feathers" (p. 35), the quail is indeed rare. But like the bowls of flowers and the garden itself, the quail is valued not for its genuine affinity with nature but rather for its distinctiveness, or isolation, from the "impurity" Mary imputes to the uncontrolled natural world. Similarly, though the cat is obviously a threat to the quail, it presents no real danger to the Tellers. What is significant in this minor conflict is that the Tellers elevate it to the stature of crisis, just as the snail hunt takes on exaggerated meaning earlier. The story's final episode thus becomes a testament to the Tellers' diminishment.

Harry's decision to kill the white quail, instead of the cat, at the end of the story may be seen, as Owens suggests, as an attack in frustration against "the heart of Mary's illusory garden." But Harry is not "an exile from the unreal Eden" as Owens claims.[20] Though they are at odds in their valuation of the white quail, the Tellers are much more alike in their misplaced values than they are different. As Steinbeck depicts them, they are both degenerate types: she a modern yeoman, he a modern hunter. They are Americans whose contracted imaginative vision interprets cats, slugs, and snails as adversaries to be destroyed, and whose unproductive suburban pleasure gardens provide meaningless challenges that ironically prove insurmountable. In their effort to create a "pure" landscape to mirror Mary's obsessive preconceptions and to give them both sensate pleasure, the Tellers lose perspective and forfeit any authentic relationship with the complex reality of nature and with each other. Their world is, as Owens argues, "an emotional wasteland without any certain hope for fructification, spiritual or physical."[21] Through this satire on modern western "settlement," Steinbeck exposes the suburban frontier and its "settlers," and questions what remains in American character of the physical capability and expansive vision of the West's pioneers.

In **"The Chrysanthemums,"** a second story in *The Long Valley* collection, Steinbeck again addresses the issue of cultural degeneration, this time in connection with the idea of westering. Work argues that "Elisa's life [on the foothill ranch] is dull, repetitive and vaguely frustrating," whereas "the itinerant tinker who pulls up to her fence one afternoon is a virile life-force who comes into her closed valley, arouses and confuses her emotions, and leaves."[22] Owens agrees with Work's assessment of Elisa's situation, claiming that "Elisa is seeking symbols of commitment in a world of physical, spiritual, and emotional isolation and sterility,"[23] a world revitalized in the story by "the fertiliz-

ing imagination of the tinker."[24] As Hughes persuasively argues, however, the tinker is a self-serving character who "lives for his own pleasure."[25] French identifies him as an "unscrupulous confidence man," and reads the story as an indictment against "the manipulation of people's dreams for selfish purposes."[26]

In contrast to the tinker's ambiguous character, Elisa can be seen as the truly vital life force in the story. Although her frustration with the limitations placed on her by her situation causes her to find the tinker's life attractive, Elisa's authentic connection to the earth validates her own life and serves as a strong contrast to the basic deception practiced by the tinker. The tinker, far from being a symbol of vitality, is rather a symbol of the degeneration of westering mythic energies, which were founded on acts of discovery and exploration. Although troubling in its apparent denigration of Elisa's situation, in actuality, the story celebrates her authentic connection to a realistic garden and reveals through the character of the tinker the absence of significant direction or purpose that debilitates modern American culture.

The story opens in late autumn, traditionally associated with the decline of the year and here symbolic of cultural decline as well.[27] In his portrayal of Elisa, Steinbeck creates an image of a person at home in nature, comfortable in a garden of her own making, and free of the neuroses that plague Mary Teller:

> Her face was eager and mature and handsome. . . . She brushed a cloud of hair out of her eyes with the back of her glove, and left a smudge of earth on her cheek in doing it. Behind her stood the neat white farm house with red geraniums close banked around it as high as the windows. (p. 4)

In tending her garden, Elisa has "a gift with things," Steinbeck writes, "planter's hands that knew" how to work in concert with nature's seasonal cycles (p. 5). Although critics often emphasize the sterility of Elisa's life, in fact, she operates, in contrast to both her husband and the tinker, as a vital force that maintains the yeoman's idealized connection with the land.

The tinker contrasts sharply with Elisa, functioning as a symbol of both personal and cultural degeneration. Steinbeck emphasizes the importance of this figure as a symbolic descendant of the westering pioneers by placing him at the reins of an anachronistic vehicle, "an old spring-wagon, with a round canvas top on it like the cover of a prairie schooner" (p. 7). Elisa and her husband own a roadster. The tinker enters the scene, then, as an important symbol of frontier westering that seems to emerge again on a post-frontier landscape. Yet degeneration, not vitality, distinguishes this modern westerer, who becomes an anti-type of the pioneers. His condition reflects both his own degenerate moral "vision," which neither values Elisa's patient nurturing of the land and gift of chrysanthemum sprouts nor exhibits any scruples about deceptively manipulating her emotions, and the decay of a central, once-grand westering tradition. Steinbeck highlights the disjunction between the tinker and the pioneers through his description of the wagon:

> Elisa . . . watched to see the crazy, loose-jointed wagon pass by. But it didn't pass. It turned into the

farm road in front of her house, crooked old wheels skirling and squeaking. . . . Words were painted on the canvas, in clumsy, crooked letters. "Pots, pans, knives, sisors, lawn mores, Fixed." Two rows of articles, and the triumphantly definitive "Fixed" below. The black paint had run down in little sharp points beneath each letter. (p. 7)

Reminiscent in shape only of the frontier settlers who pioneered the vast reaches of the continent and etched their destination and the epic stature of their adventure—"California or Bust"—on their canvases, the tinker and his rig, trade, and lack of direction all point symbolically to his degenerate state as a diminished descendant of the pioneers. In marked contrast to Elisa's vibrant flowers, the tinker's "horse and . . . donkey drooped like unwatered flowers" (p. 7), and unlike the westerers Grandfather celebrates in "The Leader of the People," the tinker has no destination, no purpose or goal in mind: "'I ain't in any hurry, ma'am. I go from Seattle to San Diego and back every year. Takes all my time. About six months each way. I aim to follow nice weather'" (p. 8). Roads and the places they lead figure prominently throughout Steinbeck's fiction. By contrasting the tinker's journey with the mythic westering trek in terms of both its directionality and relative significance of purpose, Steinbeck argues that not only this representative man but much of the culture is off its "general road," its historical road of destiny (p. 8). Unlike the pioneers, whose linear movement became a metaphor for both personal and cultural progress, this modern-day westerer simply travels in circles, not building a new culture but patching up the old, broken, worn-out one symbolized in the pots and pans he repairs.

The great irony of **"The Chrysanthemums"** is that a woman of tremendous vitality and connection with the natural world would be attracted to the aimless life of the tinker. Some critics argue that the narrowness of Elisa's life, symbolized by the fog-shrouded farm that resembles a "closed pot" in Steinbeck's opening description (p. 1), prompts her to idealize the tinker's carefree existence. Though Elisa's life clearly is not entirely satisfying, she seems nevertheless to misapprehend the truly bankrupt nature of the tinker's life. "'That's a bright direction. There's a glowing there,'" (p. 14) Elisa comments as the tinker departs, and through his gift of chrysanthemum sprouts she vicariously joins him on his circuitous route. But the trip into town undeceives her, for on the roadside she discovers her discarded chrysanthemums, symbol of her earth-based vitality, cast aside by the tinker, providing ample evidence, in Owens's words, of "the tinker's broken faith."[28]

Here Steinbeck clearly indicates that despite Elisa's dissatisfaction with human relationships in her life, her connection with the earth, a realistic yet beautiful garden, is authentic, just as her gift of chrysanthemums is authentic and vital. The life of the tinker, on the other hand, lacks physical, moral, and spiritual direction. By consciously manipulating Elisa's fascination with the pioneer spirit of freedom and adventure—in fact, by fraudulently posing as the modern embodiment of that spirit—simply to increase his trade, the tinker crushes Elisa's vital nature and destroys the momentary emotional and psychic pleasure she experiences by vicariously joining the tinker on his "adventurous" journey. Through his depiction of the tinker as a degener-

ate modern descendant of the westering pioneers, Steinbeck contrasts the aimlessness of modern American culture with the purpose and accomplishment of the westering heritage in American history. In his intrusion and despoilment of Elisa's imperfect but significantly productive and life-giving garden, the tinker becomes for Steinbeck a dark portrait of modern America's physical and transcendentally spiritual distance from its agrarian and westering past, a figure entirely lacking any respect for Elisa's wholesome connection with her land or a supra-material, visionary conception of personal or cultural advancement and progress.

Like *Travels with Charley, America and Americans*, and *The Wayward Bus*, among others, **"The White Quail"** and **"The Chrysanthemums"** reveal an important dimension of Steinbeck's fascinating, often paradoxical vision of America's frontier heritage. Whereas Ditsky, Owens, and French emphasize Steinbeck's self-distancing from traditional frontier mythology and history, here we see his appropriation of that legacy as a kind of ideal against which to measure contemporary American culture. Perhaps the greatest significance of these two stories, in addition to their thematic embrace of frontier ideals, is their date of publication; for although it may be argued that Steinbeck's celebration of the frontier past in *Travels with Charley* and *America and Americans* represents the nostalgic musings of an aging writer, these stories appeared, of course, as Steinbeck neared the pinnacle of his artistic powers in the thirties, indicating an early (and enduring) fascination with the mythic frontier West not yet fully appreciated.

Notes

1. Jackson J. Benson, *The True Adventures of John Steinbeck, Writer* (New York: Viking Press, 1984), 138, 134.

2. John Steinbeck, *America and Americans* (New York: Viking Press, 1966), 33–34.

3. John Ditsky, "'Directionality': The Compass in the Heart," *The Westering Experience in American Literature, Bicentennial Essays* (Bellingham, Washington: Bureau for Faculty Research, Western Washington University, 1977), 219.

4. Chester E. Eisinger, "Jeffersonian Agrarianism in *The Grapes of Wrath*," *A Casebook on "The Grapes of Wrath*," ed. Agnes McNeill Donohue (New York: Thomas Y. Crowell, 1968), 150.

5. Warren French, "Another Look at *The Grapes of Wrath*," *A Companion to "The Grapes of Wrath*," ed. Warren French (Clifton, New Jersey: Augustus M. Kelley Publishers, 1972), 222.

6. Louis Owens, *John Steinbeck's Re-Vision of America* (Athens: University of Georgia Press, 1985), 4.

7. John Steinbeck, *Travels with Charley in Search of America* (New York: Bantam Doubleday Dell, 1963), 168.

8. William Bloodworth, "Literary Extensions of the Formula Western," *Western American Literature* 14 (Winter 1980), 295.

9. David Lavender, "The Petrified West and the Writer," *American Scholar* 37 (Spring 1968), 301–302.

10. Philip J. West, "Steinbeck's 'The Leader of the People': A Crisis in Style," *Western American Literature* 5 (Summer 1970), 140.

11. Steinbeck, *America and Americans*, 139.

12. John Steinbeck, *The Pastures of Heaven* (New York: Viking Press, 1932); *The Wayward Bus* (New York: Viking Press, 1947); *The Winter of Our Discontent* (New York: Viking Press, 1961).

13. Owens, *Re-Vision*, 113.

14. *Ibid.* 114–115.

15. John Steinbeck, "The White Quail," in *The Long Valley* (1938) (New York: Viking Penguin, 1986), 21. Subsequent citations refer to this edition.

16. Delbert E. Wylder, "The Western Novel as Literature of the Last Frontier," *The Frontier Experience and the American Dream*, eds. David Mogen *et al.* (College Station, Texas: Texas A&M University Press, 1989), 121.

17. Robert S. Hughes, Jr., *Beyond the Red Pony: A Reader's Companion to Steinbeck's Complete Short Stories* (Metuchen, New Jersey: Scarecrow Press, 1987), 63.

18. James C. Work, "Coordinate Forces in 'The Leader of the People,'" *Western American Literature* 16 (Winter 1982), 280.

19. Owens, *Re-Vision*, 114.

20. *Ibid.*, 116.

21. *Ibid.*

22. Work, "Coordinate Forces," 280.

23. Owens, *Re-Vision*, 112.

24. *Ibid.*, 109.

25. Hughes, *Companion* 61.

26. Warren French, *John Steinbeck* (New York: Twayne Publishers, 1961), 83.

27. John Steinbeck, "The Chrysanthemums," in *The Long Valley* (1938), (New York: Viking Penguin, 1986), 3. Subsequent citations refer to this edition.

28. Owens, *Re-Vision*, 112.

FURTHER READING

Criticism

Gullason, Thomas A. "Revelation and Evolution: A Neglected Dimension of the Short Story." *Studies in Short Fiction* X, No. 4 (Fall 1973): 347–56.

Discusses how Elisa physically and emotionally "retreats and withdraws into herself" over the course of the story.

Mitchell, Marilyn L. "Steinbeck's Strong Women: Feminine Identity in the Short Stories." *Southwest Review* LXI, No. 3 (Summer 1976): 304–15.

Compares Mary Teller of "The White Quail" with Elisa Allen in "The Chrysanthemums," concluding that both women "have certain needs of the spirit, the abstract nature of which keeps happiness forever elusive."

Noonan, Gerald. "A Note on 'The Chrysanthemums'. " *Modern Fiction Studies* XII, No. 4 (Winter 1969–70): 542.

Footnote to Elizabeth McMahan's well-known article on the story, noting the use of agricultural language in the story.

Osborne, William R. "The Texts of Steinbeck's 'The Chrysanthemums'." *Modern Fiction Studies* XII, No. 4 (Winter 1966–67): 479–84.

Comments on the many differences between the two versions of Steinbeck's story, specifically changes Steinbeck made to Elisa and the overall sexual content

Sullivan, Ernest W., II. "The Cur in 'The Chrysanthemums'." *Studies in Short Fiction* XVI, No. 3 (Summer 1979): 215–17.

Examines dog imagery in the story.

Thomas, Leroy. "Steinbeck's 'The Chrysanthemums'." *The Explicator* XLV, No. 3 (Spring 1987): 50–1.

Brief discussion of the sexual symbolism that accompanies Elisa's encounter with the tinker in "The Chrysanthemums."

How to Use This Index

The main references

> **Calvino, Italo**
>   1923-1985 .... CLC **5, 8, 11, 22, 33, 39,**
>   **73; SSC 3**

list all author entries in the following Gale Literary Criticism series:

BLC = *Black Literature Criticism*
CLC = *Contemporary Literary Criticism*
CLR = *Children's Literature Review*
CMLC = *Classical and Medieval Literature Criticism*
DA = *DISCovering Authors*
DAB = *DISCovering Authors: British*
DAC = *DISCovering Authors: Canadian*
DAM = *DISCovering Authors: Modules*
       DRAM: *Dramatists Module;* *MST:* *Most-Studied Authors Module;*
       MULT: *Multicultural Authors Module;* *NOV:* *Novelists Module;*
       POET: *Poets Module;* *POP:* *Popular Fiction and Genre Authors Module*
DC = *Drama Criticism*
HLC = *Hispanic Literature Criticism*
LC = *Literature Criticism from 1400 to 1800*
NCLC = *Nineteenth-Century Literature Criticism*
NNAL = *Native North American Literature*
PC = *Poetry Criticism*
SSC = *Short Story Criticism*
TCLC = *Twentieth-Century Literary Criticism*
WLC = *World Literature Criticism, 1500 to the Present*

The cross-references

> See also CANR 23; CA 85-88;
> obituary CA116

list all author entries in the following Gale biographical and literary sources:

AAYA = *Authors & Artists for Young Adults*
AITN = *Authors in the News*
BEST = *Bestsellers*
BW = *Black Writers*
CA = *Contemporary Authors*
CAAS = *Contemporary Authors Autobiography Series*
CABS = *Contemporary Authors Bibliographical Series*
CANR = *Contemporary Authors New Revision Series*
CAP = *Contemporary Authors Permanent Series*
CDALB = *Concise Dictionary of American Literary Biography*
CDBLB = *Concise Dictionary of British Literary Biography*
DLB = *Dictionary of Literary Biography*
DLBD = *Dictionary of Literary Biography Documentary Series*
DLBY = *Dictionary of Literary Biography Yearbook*
HW = *Hispanic Writers*
JRDA = *Junior DISCovering Authors*
MAICYA = *Major Authors and Illustrators for Children and Young Adults*
MTCW = *Major 20th-Century Writers*
SAAS = *Something about the Author Autobiography Series*
SATA = *Something about the Author*
YABC = *Yesterday's Authors of Books for Children*

Literary Criticism Series
Cumulative Author Index

Anderson, Jon (Victor) 1940- . **CLC 9; DAM POET**
See CA 25-28R; CANR 20
Anderson, Lindsay (Gordon)
1923-1994 .... **CLC 20**
See CA 125; 128; 146; CANR 77
Anderson, Maxwell 1888-1959 .... **TCLC 2; DAM DRAM**
See CA 105; 152; DLB 7; MTCW 2
Anderson, Poul (William) 1926- .... **CLC 15**
See AAYA 5; CA 1-4R, 181; CAAE 181; CAAS 2; CANR 2, 15, 34, 64; CLR 58; DLB 8; INT CANR-15; MTCW 1, 2; SATA 90; SATA-Brief 39; SATA-Essay 106
Anderson, Robert (Woodruff)
1917- .... **CLC 23; DAM DRAM**
See AITN 1; CA 21-24R; CANR 32; DLB 7
Anderson, Sherwood 1876-1941 ..... **TCLC 1, 10, 24; DA; DAB; DAC; DAM MST, NOV; SSC 1; WLC**
See AAYA 30; CA 104; 121; CANR 61; CDALB 1917-1929; DA3; DLB 4, 9, 86; DLBD 1; MTCW 1, 2
Andier, Pierre
See Desnos, Robert
Andouard
See Giraudoux, (Hippolyte) Jean
Andrade, Carlos Drummond de ...... **CLC 18**
See Drummond de Andrade, Carlos
Andrade, Mario de 1893-1945 .... **TCLC 43**
Andreae, Johann V(alentin)
1586-1654 .... **LC 32**
See DLB 164
Andreas-Salome, Lou 1861-1937 ... **TCLC 56**
See CA 178; DLB 66
Andress, Lesley
See Sanders, Lawrence
Andrewes, Lancelot 1555-1626 .... **LC 5**
See DLB 151, 172
Andrews, Cicily Fairfield
See West, Rebecca
Andrews, Elton V.
See Pohl, Frederik
Andreyev, Leonid (Nikolaevich) 1871-1919 **TCLC 3**
See CA 104
Andric, Ivo 1892-1975 .... **CLC 8; SSC 36**
See CA 81-84; 57-60; CANR 43, 60; DLB 147; MTCW 1
Androvar
See Prado (Calvo), Pedro
Angelique, Pierre
See Bataille, Georges
Angell, Roger 1920- .... **CLC 26**
See CA 57-60; CANR 13, 44, 70; DLB 171, 185
Angelou, Maya 1928- .... **CLC 12, 35, 64, 77; BLC 1; DA; DAB; DAC; DAM MST, MULT, POET, POP; WLCS**
See AAYA 7, 20; BW 2, 3; CA 65-68; CANR 19, 42, 65; CDALBS; CLR 53; DA3; DLB 38; MTCW 1, 2; SATA 49
Anna Comnena 1083-1153 .... **CMLC 25**
Annensky, Innokenty (Fyodorovich)
1856-1909 .... **TCLC 14**
See CA 110; 155
Annunzio, Gabriele d'
See D'Annunzio, Gabriele
Anodos
See Coleridge, Mary E(lizabeth)
Anon, Charles Robert
See Pessoa, Fernando (Antonio Nogueira)
Anouilh, Jean (Marie Lucien Pierre)
1910-1987 .... **CLC 1, 3, 8, 13, 40, 50; DAM DRAM; DC 8**
See CA 17-20R; 123; CANR 32; MTCW 1, 2

Anthony, Florence
See Ai
Anthony, John
See Ciardi, John (Anthony)
Anthony, Peter
See Shaffer, Anthony (Joshua); Shaffer, Peter (Levin)
Anthony, Piers 1934- ..... **CLC 35; DAM POP**
See AAYA 11; CA 21-24R; CANR 28, 56, 73; DLB 8; MTCW 1, 2; SAAS 22; SATA 84
Anthony, Susan B(rownell)
1916-1991 .... **TCLC 84**
See CA 89-92; 134
Antoine, Marc
See Proust, (Valentin-Louis-George-Eugene-) Marcel
Antoninus, Brother
See Everson, William (Oliver)
Antonioni, Michelangelo 1912- .... **CLC 20**
See CA 73-76; CANR 45, 77
Antschel, Paul 1920-1970
See Celan, Paul
See CA 85-88; CANR 33, 61; MTCW 1
Anwar, Chairil 1922-1949 .... **TCLC 22**
See CA 121
Anzaldua, Gloria 1942-
See CA 175; DLB 122; HLCS 1
Apess, William 1798-1839(?) .... **NCLC 73; DAM MULT**
See DLB 175; NNAL
Apollinaire, Guillaume 1880-1918 .. **TCLC 3, 8, 51; DAM POET; PC 7**
See Kostrowitzki, Wilhelm Apollinaris de
See CA 152; MTCW 1
Appelfeld, Aharon 1932- .... **CLC 23, 47**
See CA 112; 133
Apple, Max (Isaac) 1941- .... **CLC 9, 33**
See CA 81-84; CANR 19, 54; DLB 130
Appleman, Philip (Dean) 1926- .... **CLC 51**
See CA 13-16R; CAAS 18; CANR 6, 29, 56
Appleton, Lawrence
See Lovecraft, H(oward) P(hillips)
Apteryx
See Eliot, T(homas) S(tearns)
Apuleius, (Lucius Madaurensis)
125(?)-175(?) .... **CMLC 1**
See DLB 211
Aquin, Hubert 1929-1977 .... **CLC 15**
See CA 105; DLB 53
Aquinas,Thomas 1224(?)-1274 ...... **CMLC 33**
See DLB 115
Aragon, Louis 1897-1982 .. **CLC 3, 22; DAM NOV, POET**
See CA 69-72; 108; CANR 28, 71; DLB 72; MTCW 1, 2
Arany, Janos 1817-1882 .... **NCLC 34**
Aranyos, Kakay
See Mikszath, Kalman
Arbuthnot, John 1667-1735 .... **LC 1**
See DLB 101
Archer, Herbert Winslow
See Mencken, H(enry) L(ouis)
Archer, Jeffrey (Howard) 1940- ...... **CLC 28; DAM POP**
See AAYA 16; BEST 89:3; CA 77-80; CANR 22, 52; DA3; INT CANR-22
Archer, Jules 1915- .... **CLC 12**
See CA 9-12R; CANR 6, 69; SAAS 5; SATA 4, 85
Archer, Lee
See Ellison, Harlan (Jay)
Arden, John 1930- .... **CLC 6, 13, 15; DAM DRAM**
See CA 13-16R; CAAS 4; CANR 31, 65, 67; DLB 13; MTCW 1

Arenas, Reinaldo 1943-1990 . **CLC 41; DAM MULT; HLC 1**
See CA 124; 128; 133; CANR 73; DLB 145; HW 1; MTCW 1
Arendt, Hannah 1906-1975 .... **CLC 66,98**
See CA 17-20R; 61-64; CANR 26, 60; MTCW 1, 2
Aretino, Pietro 1492-1556 .... **LC 12**
Arghezi, Tudor 1880-1967 .... **CLC 80**
See Theodorescu, Ion N.
See CA 167
Arguedas, Jose Maria 1911-1969 .... **CLC 10, 18; HLCS 1**
See CA 89-92; CANR 73; DLB 113; HW 1
Argueta, Manlio 1936- .... **CLC 31**
See CA 131; CANR 73; DLB 145; HW 1
Arias, Ron(ald Francis) 1941-
See CA 131; CANR 81; DAM MULT; DLB 82; HLC 1; HW 1, 2; MTCW 2
Ariosto, Ludovico 1474-1533 .... **LC 6**
Aristides
See Epstein, Joseph
Aristophanes 450B.C.-385B.C. .... **CMLC 4; DA; DAB; DAC; DAM DRAM, MST; DC 2; WLCS**
See DA3; DLB 176
Aristotle 384B.C.-322B.C. .... **CMLC 31; DA; DAB; DAC; DAM MST; WLCS**
See DA3; DLB 176
Arlt, Roberto (Godofredo Christophersen)
1900-1942 .... **TCLC 29; DAM MULT; HLC 1**
See CA 123; 131; CANR 67; HW 1, 2
Armah, Ayi Kwei 1939- . **CLC 5, 33; BLC 1; DAM MULT, POET**
See BW 1; CA 61-64; CANR 21, 64; DLB 117; MTCW 1
Armatrading, Joan 1950- .... **CLC 17**
See CA 114
Arnette, Robert
See Silverberg, Robert
Arnim, Achim von (Ludwig Joachim von Arnim) 1781-1831 ..... **NCLC 5; SSC 29**
See DLB 90
Arnim, Bettina von 1785-1859 .... **NCLC 38**
See DLB 90
Arnold, Matthew 1822-1888 ..... **NCLC 6, 29; DA; DAB; DAC; DAM MST, POET; PC 5; WLC**
See CDBLB 1832-1890; DLB 32, 57
Arnold, Thomas 1795-1842 .... **NCLC 18**
See DLB 55
Arnow, Harriette (Louisa) Simpson
1908-1986 .... **CLC 2, 7, 18**
See CA 9-12R; 118; CANR 14; DLB 6; MTCW 1, 2; SATA 42; SATA-Obit 47
Arouet, Francois-Marie
See Voltaire
Arp, Hans
See Arp, Jean
Arp, Jean 1887-1966 .... **CLC 5**
See CA 81-84; 25-28R; CANR 42, 77
Arrabal
See Arrabal, Fernando
Arrabal, Fernando 1932- ... **CLC 2, 9, 18, 58**
See CA 9-12R; CANR 15
Arreola, Juan Jose 1918-
See CA 113; 131; CANR 81; DAM MULT; DLB 113; HLC 1; HW 1, 2
Arrick, Fran .... **CLC 30**
See Gaberman, Judie Angell
Artaud, Antonin (Marie Joseph) 1896-1948 **TCLC 3, 36; DAM DRAM**
See CA 104; 149; DA3; MTCW 1
Arthur, Ruth M(abel) 1905-1979 ..... **CLC 12**
See CA 9-12R; 85-88; CANR 4; SATA 7, 26

Ballard, J(ames) G(raham) 1930- . CLC 3, 6,
14, 36; DAM NOV, POP; SSC 1
See AAYA 3; CA 5-8R; CANR 15, 39, 65;
DA3; DLB 14, 207; MTCW 1, 2; SATA
93

Balmont, Konstantin (Dmitriyevich)
1867-1943 .... TCLC 11
See CA 109; 155

Baltausis, Vincas
See Mikszath, Kalman

Balzac, Honore de 1799-1850 ... NCLC 5, 35,
53; DA; DAB; DAC; DAM MST, NOV;
SSC 5; WLC
See DA3; DLB 119

Bambara, Toni Cade 1939-1995 ...... CLC 19,
88; BLC 1; DA; DAC; DAM MST,
MULT; SSC 35; WLCS
See AAYA 5; BW 2, 3; CA 29-32R; 150;
CANR 24, 49, 81; CDALBS; DA3; DLB
38; MTCW 1, 2

Bamdad, A.
See Shamlu, Ahmad

Banat, D. R.
See Bradbury, Ray (Douglas)

Bancroft, Laura
See Baum, L(yman) Frank

Banim, John 1798-1842 .... NCLC 13
See DLB 116, 158, 159

Banim, Michael 1796-1874 .... NCLC 13
See DLB 158, 159

Banjo, The
See Paterson, A(ndrew) B(arton)

Banks, Iain
See Banks, Iain M(enzies)

Banks, Iain M(enzies) 1954- .... CLC 34
See CA 123; 128; CANR 61; DLB 194; INT
128

Banks, Lynne Reid .... CLC 23
See Reid Banks, Lynne
See AAYA 6

Banks, Russell 1940 .... CLC 37, 72
See CA 65-68; CAAS 15; CANR 19, 52,
73; DLB 130

Banville, John 1945- .... CLC 46, 118
See CA 117; 128; DLB 14; INT 128

Banville, Theodore (Faullain) de 1832-1891
NCLC 9

Baraka, Amiri 1934- . CLC 1, 2, 3, 5, 10, 14,
33, 115; BLC 1; DA; DAC; DAM MST,
MULT, POET, POP; DC 6; PC 4;
WLCS
See Jones, LeRoi
See BW 2, 3; CA 21-24R; CABS 3; CANR
27, 38, 61; CDALB 1941-1968; DA3;
DLB 5, 7, 16, 38; DLBD 8; MTCW 1, 2

Barbauld, Anna Laetitia
1743-1825 .... NCLC 50
See DLB 107, 109, 142, 158

Barbellion, W. N. P. .... TCLC 24
See Cummings, Bruce F(rederick)

Barbera, Jack (Vincent) 1945- .... CLC 44
See CA 110; CANR 45

Barbey d'Aurevilly, Jules Amedee 1808-1889
NCLC 1; SSC 17
See DLB 119

Barbour, John c. 1316-1395 .... CMLC 33
See DLB 146

Barbusse, Henri 1873-1935 .... TCLC 5
See CA 105; 154; DLB 65

Barclay, Bill
See Moorcock, Michael (John)

Barclay, William Ewert
See Moorcock, Michael (John)

Barea, Arturo 1897-1957 .... TCLC 14
See CA 111

Barfoot, Joan 1946- .... CLC 18
See CA 105

Barham, Richard Harris
1788-1845 .... NCLC 77
See DLB 159

Baring, Maurice 1874-1945 .... TCLC 8
See CA 105; 168; DLB 34

Baring-Gould, Sabine 1834-1924 ... TCLC 88
See DLB 156, 190

Barker, Clive 1952- .... CLC 52; DAM POP
See AAYA 10; BEST 90:3; CA 121; 129;
CANR 71; DA3; INT 129; MTCW 1, 2

Barker, George Granville
1913-1991 .... CLC 8, 48; DAM POET
See CA 9-12R; 135; CANR 7, 38; DLB 20;
MTCW 1

Barker, Harley Granville
See Granville-Barker, Harley
See DLB 10

Barker, Howard 1946- .... CLC 37
See CA 102; DLB 13

Barker, Jane 1652-1732 .... LC 42

Barker, Pat(ricia) 1943- .... CLC 32, 94
See CA 117; 122, CANR 50; INT 122

Barlach, Ernst (Heinrich)
1870-1938 .... TCLC 84
See CA 178; DLB 56, 118

Barlow, Joel 1754-1812 .... NCLC 23
See DLB 37

Barnard, Mary (Ethel) 1909- .... CLC 48
See CA 21-22; CAP 2

Barnes, Djuna 1892-1982 .... CLC 3, 4, 8, 11,
29; SSC 3
See CA 9-12R; 107; CANR 16, 55; DLB 4,
9, 45; MTCW 1, 2

Barnes, Julian (Patrick) 1946- .... CLC 42;
DAB
See CA 102; CANR 19, 54; DLB 194;
DLBY 93; MTCW 1

Barnes, Peter 1931- .... CLC 5, 56
See CA 65-68; CAAS 12; CANR 33, 34,
64; DLB 13; MTCW 1

Barnes, William 1801-1886 .... NCLC 75
See DLB 32

Baroja (y Nessi), Pio 1872-1956 ..... TCLC 8;
HLC 1
See CA 104

Baron, David
See Pinter, Harold

Baron Corvo
See Rolfe, Frederick (William Serafino Austin Lewis Mary)

Barondess, Sue K(aufman)
1926-1977 .... CLC 8
See Kaufman, Sue
See CA 1-4R; 69-72; CANR 1

Baron de Teive
See Pessoa, Fernando (Antonio Nogueira)

Baroness Von S.
See Zangwill, Israel

Barres, (Auguste-)Maurice
1862-1923 .... TCLC 47
See CA 164; DLB 123

Barreto, Afonso Henrique de Lima
See Lima Barreto, Afonso Henrique de

Barrett, (Roger) Syd 1946- .... CLC 35

Barrett, William (Christopher) 1913-1992
CLC 27
See CA 13-16R; 139; CANR 11, 67; INT
CANR-11

Barrie, J(ames) M(atthew)
1860-1937 .... TCLC 2; DAB; DAM
DRAM
See CA 104; 136; CANR 77; CDBLB 1890-
1914; CLR 16; DA3; DLB 10, 141, 156;
MAICYA; MTCW 1; SATA 100; YABC 1

Barrington, Michael
See Moorcock, Michael (John)

Barrol, Grady
See Bograd, Larry

Barry, Mike
See Malzberg, Barry N(athaniel)

Barry, Philip 1896-1949 .... TCLC 11
See CA 109; DLB 7

Bart, Andre Schwarz
See Schwarz-Bart, Andre

Barth, John (Simmons) 1930- ... CLC 1, 2, 3,
5, 7, 9, 10, 14, 27, 51, 89; DAM NOV;
SSC 10
See AITN 1, 2; CA 1-4R; CABS 1; CANR
5, 23, 49, 64; DLB 2; MTCW 1

Barthelme, Donald 1931-1989 ... CLC 1, 2, 3,
5, 6, 8, 13, 23, 46, 59, 115; DAM NOV;
SSC 2
See CA 21-24R; 129; CANR 20, 58; DA3;
DLB 2; DLBY 80, 89; MTCW 1, 2; SATA
7; SATA-Obit 62

Barthelme, Frederick 1943- ...... CLC 36, 117
See CA 114; 122; CANR 77; DLBY 85;
INT 122

Barthes, Roland (Gerard)
1915-1980 .... CLC 24, 83
See CA 130; 97-100; CANR 66; MTCW 1,
2

Barzun, Jacques (Martin) 1907- ...... CLC 51
See CA 61-64; CANR 22

Bashevis, Isaac
See Singer, Isaac Bashevis

Bashkirtseff, Marie 1859-1884 .... NCLC 27

Basho
See Matsuo Basho

Basil of Caesaria c. 330-379 .... CMLC 35

Bass, Kingsley B., Jr.
See Bullins, Ed

Bass, Rick 1950- .... CLC 79
See CA 126; CANR 53; DLB 212

Bassani, Giorgio 1916- .... CLC 9
See CA 65-68; CANR 33; DLB 128, 177;
MTCW 1

Bastos, Augusto (Antonio) Roa
See Roa Bastos, Augusto (Antonio)

Bataille, Georges 1897-1962 .... CLC 29
See CA 101; 89-92

Bates, H(erbert) E(rnest)
1905-1974 . CLC 46; DAB; DAM POP;
SSC 10
See CA 93-96; 45-48; CANR 34; DA3;
DLB 162, 191; MTCW 1, 2

Bauchart
See Camus, Albert

Baudelaire, Charles 1821-1867 . NCLC 6, 29,
55; DA; DAB; DAC; DAM MST,
POET; PC 1; SSC 18; WLC
See DA3

Baudrillard, Jean 1929- .... CLC 60

Baum, L(yman) Frank 1856-1919 ... TCLC 7
See CA 108; 133; CLR 15; DLB 22; JRDA;
MAICYA; MTCW 1, 2; SATA 18, 100

Baum, Louis F.
See Baum, L(yman) Frank

Baumbach, Jonathan 1933- .... CLC 6, 23
See CA 13-16R; CAAS 5; CANR 12, 66;
DLBY 80; INT CANR-12; MTCW 1

Bausch, Richard (Carl) 1945- .... CLC 51
See CA 101; CAAS 14; CANR 43, 61; DLB
130

Baxter, Charles (Morley) 1947- .... CLC 45,
78; DAM POP
See CA 57-60; CANR 40, 64; DLB 130;
MTCW 2

Baxter, George Owen
See Faust, Frederick (Schiller)

Baxter, James K(eir) 1926-1972 .... CLC 14
See CA 77-80

Baxter, John
See Hunt, E(verette) Howard, (Jr.)

Bayer, Sylvia
See Glassco, John

Baynton, Barbara 1857-1929 .... **TCLC 57**

Beagle, Peter S(oyer) 1939- .... **CLC 7,104**
  See CA 9-12R; CANR 4, 51, 73; DA3;
  DLBY 80; INT CANR-4; MTCW 1;
  SATA 60

Bean, Normal
  See Burroughs, Edgar Rice

Beard, Charles A(ustin)
  1874-1948 .... **TCLC 15**
  See CA 115; DLB 17; SATA 18

Beardsley, Aubrey 1872-1898 .... **NCLC 6**

Beattie, Ann 1947- ..... **CLC 8, 13, 18, 40, 63;**
  DAM NOV, POP; SSC 11
  See BEST 90:2; CA 81-84; CANR 53, 73;
  DA3; DLBY 82; MTCW 1, 2

Beattie, James 1735-1803 .... **NCLC 25**
  See DLB 109

Beauchamp, Kathleen Mansfield 1888-1923
  See Mansfield, Katherine
  See CA 104; 134; DA; DAC; DAM MST;
  DA3; MTCW 2

Beaumarchais, Pierre-Augustin Caronde
  1732-1799 .... **DC 4**
  See DAM DRAM

Beaumont, Francis 1584(?)-1616 .... **LC 33;**
  DC 6
  See CDBLB Before 1660; DLB 58, 121

Beauvoir, Simone (Lucie Ernestine Marie
  Bertrand) de 1908-1986 .... **CLC 1, 2, 4,**
  8, 14, 31, 44, 50, 71, 124; DA; DAB;
  DAC; DAM MST, NOV; SSC 35; WLC
  See CA 9-12R; 118; CANR 28, 61; DA3;
  DLB 72; DLBY 86; MTCW 1, 2

Becker, Carl (Lotus) 1873-1945 ..... **TCLC 63**
  See CA 157; DLB 17

Becker, Jurek 1937-1997 .... **CLC 7, 19**
  See CA 85-88; 157; CANR 60; DLB 75

Becker, Walter 1950- .... **CLC 26**

Beckett, Samuel (Barclay)
  1906-1989 .. **CLC 1, 2, 3, 4, 6, 9, 10, 11,**
  14, 18, 29, 57, 59, 83; DA; DAB; DAC;
  DAM DRAM, MST, NOV; SSC 16;
  WLC
  See CA 5-8R; 130; CANR 33, 61; CDBLB
  1945-1960; DA3; DLB 13, 15; DLBY 90;
  MTCW 1, 2

Beckford, William 1760-1844 .... **NCLC 16**
  See DLB 39

Beckman, Gunnel 1910- .... **CLC 26**
  See CA 33-36R; CANR 15; CLR 25; MAI-
  CYA; SAAS 9; SATA 6

Becque, Henri 1837-1899 .... **NCLC 3**
  See DLB 192

Becquer, Gustavo Adolfo 1836-1870
  See DAM MULT; HLCS 1

Beddoes, Thomas Lovell
  1803-1849 .... **NCLC 3**
  See DLB 96

Bede c. 673-735 .... **CMLC 20**
  See DLB 146

Bedford, Donald F.
  See Fearing, Kenneth (Flexner)

Beecher, Catharine Esther
  1800-1878 .... **NCLC 30**
  See DLB 1

Beecher, John 1904-1980 .... **CLC 6**
  See AITN 1; CA 5-8R; 105; CANR 8

Beer, Johann 1655-1700 .... **LC 5**
  See DLB 168

Beer, Patricia 1924- .... **CLC 58**
  See CA 61-64; CANR 13, 46; DLB 40

Beerbohm, Max
  See Beerbohm, (Henry) Max(imilian)

Beerbohm, (Henry) Max(imilian) 1872-1956
  TCLC 1, 24
  See CA 104; 154; CANR 79; DLB 34, 100

Beer-Hofmann, Richard
  1866-1945 .... **TCLC 60**
  See CA 160; DLB 81

Begiebing, Robert J(ohn) 1946- .... **CLC 70**
  See CA 122; CANR 40

Behan, Brendan 1923-1964 ...... **CLC 1, 8, 11,**
  15, 79; DAM DRAM
  See CA 73-76; CANR 33; CDBLB 1945-
  1960; DLB 13; MTCW 1, 2

Behn, Aphra 1640(?)-1689 .... **LC 1, 30, 42;**
  DA; DAB; DAC; DAM DRAM, MST,
  NOV, POET; DC 4; PC 13; WLC
  See DA3; DLB 39, 80, 131

Behrman, S(amuel) N(athaniel) 1893-1973
  CLC 40
  See CA 13-16; 45-48; CAP 1; DLB 7, 44

Belasco, David 1853-1931 .... **TCLC 3**
  See CA 104; 168; DLB 7

Belcheva, Elisaveta 1893- .... **CLC 10**
  See Bagryana, Elisaveta

Beldone, Phil "Cheech"
  See Ellison, Harlan (Jay)

Beleno
  See Azuela, Mariano

Belinski, VissarionGrigoryevich 1811-1848
  NCLC 5
  See DLB 198

Belitt, Ben 1911- .... **CLC 22**
  See CA 13-16R; CAAS 4; CANR 7, 77;
  DLB 5

Bell, Gertrude (MargaretLowthian)
  1868-1926 .... **TCLC 67**
  See CA 167; DLB 174

Bell, J. Freeman
  See Zangwill, Israel

Bell, James Madison 1826-1902 ... **TCLC 43;**
  BLC 1; DAM MULT
  See BW 1; CA 122; 124; DLB 50

Bell, Madison Smartt 1957- ...... **CLC 41, 102**
  See CA 111; CANR 28, 54, 73; MTCW 1

Bell, Marvin (Hartley) 1937- ...... **CLC 8, 31;**
  DAM POET
  See CA 21-24R; CAAS 14; CANR 59; DLB
  5; MTCW 1

Bell, W. L. D.
  See Mencken, H(enry) L(ouis)

Bellamy, Atwood C.
  See Mencken, H(enry) L(ouis)

Bellamy, Edward 1850-1898 .... **NCLC 4**
  See DLB 12

Belli, Gioconda 1949-
  See CA 152; HLCS 1

Bellin, Edward J.
  See Kuttner, Henry

Belloc, (Joseph) Hilaire (Pierre Sebastien
  Rene Swanton) 1870-1953 ...... **TCLC 7,**
  18; DAM POET; PC 24
  See CA 106; 152; DLB 19, 100, 141, 174;
  MTCW 1; YABC 1

Belloc, Joseph Peter Rene Hilaire
  See Belloc, (Joseph) Hilaire (Pierre Sebastien Rene Swanton)

Belloc, Joseph Pierre Hilaire
  See Belloc, (Joseph) Hilaire (Pierre Sebastien Rene Swanton)

Belloc, M. A.
  See Lowndes, Marie Adelaide (Belloc)

Bellow, Saul 1915- . **CLC 1, 2, 3, 6, 8, 10, 13,**
  15, 25, 33, 34, 63, 79; DA; DAB; DAC;
  DAM MST, NOV, POP; SSC 14; WLC
  See AITN 2; BEST 89:3; CA 5-8R; CABS
  1; CANR 29, 53; CDALB 1941-1968;
  DA3; DLB 2, 28; DLBD 3; DLBY 82;
  MTCW 1, 2

Belser, Reimond Karel Maria de 1929-
  See Ruyslinck, Ward
  See CA 152

Bely, Andrey .... **TCLC 7; PC 11**
  See Bugayev, Boris Nikolayevich
  See MTCW 1

Belyi, Andrei
  See Bugayev, Boris Nikolayevich

Benary, Margot
  See Benary-Isbert, Margot

Benary-Isbert,Margot 1889-1979 ..... **CLC 12**
  See CA 5-8R; 89-92; CANR 4, 72; CLR
  12; MAICYA; SATA 2; SATA-Obit 21

Benavente (y Martinez), Jacinto 1866-1954
  TCLC 3; DAM DRAM, MULT; HLCS
  1
  See CA 106; 131; CANR 81; HW 1, 2;
  MTCW 1, 2

Benchley, Peter (Bradford) 1940- . **CLC 4, 8;**
  DAM NOV, POP
  See AAYA 14; AITN 2; CA 17-20R; CANR
  12, 35, 66; MTCW 1, 2; SATA 3, 89

Benchley, Robert (Charles)
  1889-1945 .... **TCLC 1, 55**
  See CA 105; 153; DLB 11

Benda, Julien 1867-1956 .... **TCLC 60**
  See CA 120; 154

Benedict, Ruth (Fulton)
  1887-1948 .... **TCLC 60**
  See CA 158

Benedict, Saint c. 480-c. 547 .... **CMLC 29**

Benedikt, Michael 1935- .... **CLC 4, 14**
  See CA 13-16R; CANR 7; DLB 5

Benet, Juan 1927- .... **CLC 28**
  See CA 143

Benet, Stephen Vincent 1898-1943 . **TCLC 7;**
  DAM POET; SSC 10
  See CA 104; 152; DA3; DLB 4, 48, 102;
  DLBY 97; MTCW 1; YABC 1

Benet, William Rose 1886-1950 .... **TCLC 28;**
  DAM POET
  See CA 118; 152; DLB 45

Benford, Gregory (Albert) 1941- ..... **CLC 52**
  See CA 69-72, 175; CAAE 175; CAAS 27;
  CANR 12, 24, 49; DLBY 82

Bengtsson, Frans (Gunnar)
  1894-1954 .... **TCLC 48**
  See CA 170

Benjamin, David
  See Slavitt, David R(ytman)

Benjamin, Lois
  See Gould, Lois

Benjamin, Walter 1892-1940 .... **TCLC 39**
  See CA 164

Benn, Gottfried 1886-1956 .... **TCLC 3**
  See CA 106; 153; DLB 56

Bennett, Alan 1934- .... **CLC 45, 77; DAB;**
  DAM MST
  See CA 103; CANR 35, 55; MTCW 1, 2

Bennett, (Enoch) Arnold
  1867-1931 .... **TCLC 5, 20**
  See CA 106; 155; CDBLB 1890-1914; DLB
  10, 34, 98, 135; MTCW 2

Bennett, Elizabeth
  See Mitchell, Margaret (Munnerlyn)

Bennett, George Harold 1930-
  See Bennett, Hal
  See BW 1; CA 97-100

Bennett, Hal .... **CLC 5**
  See Bennett, George Harold
  See DLB 33

Bennett, Jay 1912- .... **CLC 35**
  See AAYA 10; CA 69-72; CANR 11, 42,
  79; JRDA; SAAS 4; SATA 41, 87; SATA-
  Brief 27

Bennett, Louise (Simone) 1919- ...... **CLC 28;**
  BLC 1; DAM MULT
  See BW 2, 3; CA 151; DLB 117

Benson, E(dward) F(rederic) 1867-1940
  TCLC 27
  See CA 114; 157; DLB 135, 153

Benson, Jackson J. 1930- .... **CLC 34**
  See CA 25-28R; DLB 111

Benson, Sally 1900-1972 .... **CLC 17**
  See CA 19-20; 37-40R; CAP 1; SATA 1,
  35; SATA-Obit 27

Benson, Stella 1892-1933 .... **TCLC 17**
See CA 117; 155; DLB 36, 162

Bentham, Jeremy 1748-1832 .... **NCLC 38**
See DLB 107, 158

Bentley, E(dmund) C(lerihew) 1875-1956
TCLC 12
See CA 108; DLB 70

Bentley, Eric (Russell) 1916- .... **CLC 24**
See CA 5-8R; CANR 6, 67; INT CANR-6

Beranger, Pierre Jean de
1780-1857 .... **NCLC 34**

Berdyaev, Nicolas
See Berdyaev, Nikolai (Aleksandrovich)

Berdyaev, Nikolai (Aleksandrovich)
1874-1948 .... **TCLC 67**
See CA 120; 157

Berdyayev, Nikolai (Aleksandrovich)
See Berdyaev, Nikolai (Aleksandrovich)

Berendt, John (Lawrence) 1939- ...... **CLC 86**
See CA 146; CANR 75; DA3; MTCW 1

Beresford, J(ohn) D(avys)
1873-1947 .... **TCLC 81**
See CA 112; 155; DLB 162, 178, 197

Bergelson, David 1884-1952 .... **TCLC 81**

Berger, Colonel
See Malraux, (Georges-)Andre

Berger, John (Peter) 1926- .... **CLC 2, 19**
See CA 81-84; CANR 51, 78; DLB 14, 207

Berger, Melvin H. 1927- .... **CLC 12**
See CA 5-8R; CANR 4; CLR 32; SAAS 2;
SATA 5, 88

Berger, Thomas (Louis) 1924- .. **CLC 3, 5, 8,**
11, 18, 38; DAM NOV
See CA 1-4R; CANR 5, 28, 51; DLB 2;
DLBY 80; INT CANR-28; MTCW 1, 2

Bergman, (Ernst) Ingmar 1918- ...... **CLC 16,**
72
See CA 81-84; CANR 33, 70; MTCW 2

Bergson, Henri(-Louis) 1859-1941 .. **TCLC 32**
See CA 164

Bergstein, Eleanor 1938- .... **CLC 4**
See CA 53-56; CANR 5

Berkoff, Steven 1937- .... **CLC 56**
See CA 104; CANR 72

Bermant, Chaim (Icyk) 1929- .... **CLC 40**
See CA 57-60; CANR 6, 31, 57

Bern, Victoria
See Fisher, M(ary) F(rances) K(ennedy)

Bernanos, (Paul Louis) Georges 1888-1948
TCLC 3
See CA 104; 130; DLB 72

Bernard, April 1956- .... **CLC 59**
See CA 131

Berne, Victoria
See Fisher, M(ary) F(rances) K(ennedy)

Bernhard, Thomas 1931-1989 ..... **CLC 3, 32,**
61
See CA 85-88; 127; CANR 32, 57; DLB
85, 124; MTCW 1

Bernhardt, Sarah (Henriette Rosine)
1844-1923 .... **TCLC 75**
See CA 157

Berriault, Gina 1926- .. **CLC 54, 109;SSC 30**
See CA 116; 129; CANR 66; DLB 130

Berrigan, Daniel 1921- .... **CLC 4**
See CA 33-36R; CAAS 1; CANR 11, 43,
78; DLB 5

Berrigan, Edmund Joseph Michael, Jr.
1934-1983
See Berrigan, Ted
See CA 61-64; 110; CANR 14

Berrigan, Ted .... **CLC 37**
See Berrigan, Edmund Joseph Michael, Jr.
See DLB 5, 169

Berry, Charles Edward Anderson 1931-
See Berry, Chuck
See CA 115

Berry, Chuck .... **CLC 17**
See Berry, Charles Edward Anderson

Berry, Jonas
See Ashbery, John (Lawrence)

Berry, Wendell (Erdman) 1934- ... **CLC 4, 6,**
8, 27, 46; DAM POET; PC 28
See AITN 1; CA 73-76; CANR 50, 73; DLB
5, 6; MTCW 1

Berryman, John 1914-1972 ... **CLC 1, 2, 3, 4,**
6, 8, 10, 13, 25, 62; DAM POET
See CA 13-16; 33-36R; CABS 2; CANR
35; CAP 1; CDALB 1941-1968; DLB 48;
MTCW 1, 2

Bertolucci, Bernardo 1940- .... **CLC 16**
See CA 106

Berton, Pierre (Francis Demarigny) 1920-
CLC 104
See CA 1-4R; CANR 2, 56; DLB 68; SATA
99

Bertrand, Aloysius 1807-1841 .... **NCLC 31**

Bertran de Born c. 1140-1215 .... **CMLC 5**

Besant, Annie(Wood) 1847-1933 ...... **TCLC 9**
See CA 105

Bessie, Alvah 1904-1985 .... **CLC 23**
See CA 5-8R; 116; CANR 2, 80; DLB 26

Bethlen, T. D.
See Silverberg, Robert

Beti, Mongo . **CLC 27; BLC 1; DAM MULT**
See Biyidi, Alexandre
See CANR 79

Betjeman, John 1906-1984 ...... **CLC 2, 6, 10,**
34, 43; DAB; DAM MST, POET
See CA 9-12R; 112; CANR 33, 56; CD-
BLB 1945-1960; DA3; DLB 20; DLBY
84; MTCW 1, 2

Bettelheim, Bruno 1903-1990 .... **CLC 79**
See CA 81-84; 131; CANR 23, 61; DA3;
MTCW 1, 2

Betti, Ugo 1892-1953 .... **TCLC 5**
See CA 104; 155

Betts, Doris (Waugh) 1932- ...... **CLC 3, 6, 28**
See CA 13-16R; CANR 9, 66, 77; DLBY
82; INT CANR-9

Bevan, Alistair
See Roberts, Keith (John Kingston)

Bey, Pilaff
See Douglas, (George) Norman

Bialik, Chaim Nachman
1873-1934 .... **TCLC 25**
See CA 170

Bickerstaff, Isaac
See Swift, Jonathan

Bidart, Frank 1939- .... **CLC 33**
See CA 140

Bienek, Horst 1930- .... **CLC 7, 11**
See CA 73-76; DLB 75

Bierce, Ambrose (Gwinett) 1842-1914(?)
TCLC 1, 7, 44; DA; DAC; DAM MST;
SSC 9; WLC
See CA 104; 139; CANR 78; CDALB 1865-
1917; DA3; DLB 11, 12, 23, 71, 74, 186

Biggers, Earl Derr 1884-1933 .... **TCLC 65**
See CA 108; 153

Billings, Josh
See Shaw, Henry Wheeler

Billington, (Lady) Rachel (Mary)
1942- .... **CLC 43**
See AITN 2; CA 33-36R; CANR 44

Binyon, T(imothy) J(ohn) 1936- .... **CLC 34**
See CA 111; CANR 28

Bioy Casares, Adolfo 1914-1999 ... **CLC 4, 8,**
13, 88; DAM MULT; HLC 1; SSC 17
See CA 29-32R; 177; CANR 19, 43, 66;
DLB 113; HW 1, 2; MTCW 1, 2

Bird, Cordwainer
See Ellison, Harlan (Jay)

Bird, Robert Montgomery
1806-1854 .... **NCLC 1**
See DLB 202

Birkerts, Sven 1951- .... **CLC 116**
See CA 128; 133; 176; CAAE 176; CAAS
29; INT 133

Birney, (Alfred) Earle 1904-1995 .. **CLC 1, 4,**
6, 11; DAC; DAM MST, POET
See CA 1-4R; CANR 5, 20; DLB 88;
MTCW 1

Biruni, al 973-1048(?) .... **CMLC 28**

Bishop, Elizabeth 1911-1979 ..... **CLC 1, 4, 9,**
13, 15, 32; DA; DAC; DAM MST,
POET; PC 3
See CA 5-8R; 89-92; CABS 2; CANR 26,
61; CDALB 1968-1988; DA3; DLB 5,
169; MTCW 1, 2; SATA-Obit 24

Bishop, John 1935- .... **CLC 10**
See CA 105

Bissett, Bill 1939- .... **CLC 18; PC 14**
See CA 69-72; CAAS 19; CANR 15; DLB
53; MTCW 1

Bissoondath, Neil (Devindra)
1955- .... **CLC 120; DAC**
See CA 136

Bitov, Andrei (Georgievich) 1937- ... **CLC 57**
See CA 142

Biyidi, Alexandre 1932-
See Beti, Mongo
See BW 1, 3; CA 114; 124; CANR 81;
DA3; MTCW 1, 2

Bjarme, Brynjolf
See Ibsen, Henrik (Johan)

Bjoernson, Bjoernstjerne (Martinus)
1832-1910 .... **TCLC 7, 37**
See CA 104

Black, Robert
See Holdstock, Robert P.

Blackburn, Paul 1926-1971 .... **CLC 9, 43**
See CA 81-84; 33-36R; CANR 34; DLB
16; DLBY 81

Black Elk 1863-1950 .... **TCLC 33;DAM**
MULT
See CA 144; MTCW 1; NNAL

Black Hobart
See Sanders, (James) Ed(ward)

Blacklin, Malcolm
See Chambers, Aidan

Blackmore, R(ichard) D(oddridge)
1825-1900 .... **TCLC 27**
See CA 120; DLB 18

Blackmur, R(ichard) P(almer) 1904-1965
CLC 2, 24
See CA 11-12; 25-28R; CANR 71; CAP 1;
DLB 63

Black Tarantula
See Acker, Kathy

Blackwood, Algernon (Henry) 1869-1951
TCLC 5
See CA 105; 150; DLB 153, 156, 178

Blackwood, Caroline 1931-1996 .... **CLC 6, 9,**
100
See CA 85-88; 151; CANR 32, 61, 65; DLB
14, 207; MTCW 1

Blade, Alexander
See Hamilton, Edmond; Silverberg, Robert

Blaga, Lucian 1895-1961 .... **CLC 75**
See CA 157

Blair, Eric (Arthur) 1903-1950
See Orwell, George
See CA 104; 132; DA; DAB; DAC; DAM
MST, NOV; DA3; MTCW 1, 2; SATA 29

Blair, Hugh 1718-1800 .... **NCLC 75**

Blais, Marie-Claire 1939- .... **CLC 2, 4, 6, 13,**
22; DAC; DAM MST
See CA 21-24R; CAAS 4; CANR 38, 75;
DLB 53; MTCW 1, 2

Carducci, Giosue (Alessandro Giuseppe)
1835-1907 .... **TCLC 32**
See CA 163

Carew, Thomas 1595(?)-1640 .... **LC 13**
See DLB 126

Carey, Ernestine Gilbreth 1908- ...... **CLC 17**
See CA 5-8R; CANR 71; SATA 2

Carey, Peter 1943- .... **CLC 40, 55, 96**
See CA 123; 127; CANR 53, 76; INT 127;
MTCW 1, 2; SATA 94

Carleton, William 1794-1869 .... **NCLC 3**
See DLB 159

Carlisle, Henry (Coffin) 1926- .... **CLC 33**
See CA 13-16R; CANR 15, 85

Carlsen, Chris
See Holdstock, Robert P.

Carlson, Ron(ald F.) 1947- .... **CLC 54**
See CA 105; CANR 27

Carlyle, Thomas 1795-1881 .. **NCLC 70; DA;
DAB; DAC; DAM MST**
See CDBLB 1789-1832; DLB 55; 144

Carman, (William) Bliss
1861-1929 .... **TCLC 7; DAC**
See CA 104; 152; DLB 92

Carnegie, Dale 1888-1955 .... **TCLC 53**

Carossa, Hans 1878-1956 .... **TCLC 48**
See CA 170; DLB 66

Carpenter, Don(ald Richard)
1931-1995 .... **CLC 41**
See CA 45-48; 149; CANR 1, 71

Carpenter, Edward 1844-1929 .... **TCLC 88**
See CA 163

Carpentier (y Valmont), Alejo 1904-1980
**CLC 8, 11, 38, 110; DAM MULT; HLC
1; SSC 35**
See CA 65-68; 97-100; CANR 11, 70; DLB
113; HW 1, 2

Carr, Caleb 1955(?)- .... **CLC 86**
See CA 147; CANR 73; DA3

Carr, Emily 1871-1945 .... **TCLC 32**
See CA 159; DLB 68

Carr, John Dickson 1906-1977 .... **CLC 3**
See Fairbairn, Roger
See CA 49-52; 69-72; CANR 3, 33, 60;
MTCW 1, 2

Carr, Philippa
See Hibbert, Eleanor Alice Burford

Carr, Virginia Spencer 1929- .... **CLC 34**
See CA 61-64; DLB 111

Carrere, Emmanuel 1957- .... **CLC 89**

Carrier, Roch 1937- .... **CLC 13, 78; DAC;
DAM MST**
See CA 130; CANR 61; DLB 53; SATA 105

Carroll, James P. 1943(?)- .... **CLC 38**
See CA 81-84; CANR 73; MTCW 1

Carroll, Jim 1951- .... **CLC 35**
See AAYA 17; CA 45-48; CANR 42

Carroll, Lewis .... **NCLC 2, 53; PC 18; WLC**
See Dodgson, Charles Lutwidge
See CDBLB 1832-1890; CLR 2, 18; DLB
18, 163, 178; DLBY 98; JRDA

Carroll, Paul Vincent 1900-1968 ...... **CLC 10**
See CA 9-12R; 25-28R; DLB 10

Carruth, Hayden 1921- ..... **CLC 4, 7, 10, 18,
84; PC 10**
See CA 9-12R; CANR 4, 38, 59; DLB 5,
165; INT CANR-4; MTCW 1, 2; SATA
47

Carson, Rachel Louise 1907-1964 ... **CLC 71;
DAM POP**
See CA 77-80; CANR 35; DA3; MTCW 1,
2; SATA 23

Carter, Angela (Olive) 1940-1992 ...... **CLC 5,
41, 76; SSC 13**
See CA 53-56; 136; CANR 12, 36, 61;
DA3; DLB 14, 207; MTCW 1, 2; SATA
66; SATA-Obit 70

Carter, Nick
See Smith, Martin Cruz

Carver, Raymond 1938-1988 ..... **CLC 22, 36,
53, 55; DAM NOV; SSC 8**
See CA 33-36R; 126; CANR 17, 34, 61;
DA3; DLB 130; DLBY 84, 88; MTCW 1,
2

Cary, Elizabeth, Lady Falkland 1585-1639
LC 30

Cary, (Arthur) Joyce (Lunel) 1888-1957
TCLC 1, 29
See CA 104; 164; CDBLB 1914-1945; DLB
15, 100; MTCW 2

Casanova de Seingalt, Giovanni Jacopo
1725-1798 .... **LC 13**

Casares, Adolfo Bioy
See Bioy Casares, Adolfo

Casely-Hayford, J(oseph) E(phraim)
1866-1930 ...... **TCLC 24; BLC 1; DAM
MULT**
See BW 2; CA 123; 152

Casey, John (Dudley) 1939- .... **CLC 59**
See BEST 90:2; CA 69-72; CANR 23

Casey, Michael 1947- .... **CLC 2**
See CA 65-68; DLB 5

Casey, Patrick
See Thurman, Wallace (Henry)

Casey, Warren(Peter) 1935-1988 ...... **CLC 12**
See CA 101; 127; INT 101

Casona, Alejandro .... **CLC 49**
See Alvarez, Alejandro Rodriguez

Cassavetes, John 1929-1989 .... **CLC 20**
See CA 85-88; 127; CANR 82

Cassian, Nina 1924- .... **PC 17**

Cassill, R(onald) V(erlin) 1919- ... **CLC 4, 23**
See CA 9-12R; CAAS 1; CANR 7, 45; DLB
6

Cassirer, Ernst 1874-1945 .... **TCLC 61**
See CA 157

Cassity, (Allen) Turner 1929- .... **CLC 6, 42**
See CA 17-20R; CAAS 8; CANR 11; DLB
105

Castaneda, Carlos (Cesar Aranha)
1931(?)-1998 .... **CLC 12, 119**
See CA 25-28R; CANR 32, 66; HW 1;
MTCW 1

Castedo, Elena 1937- .... **CLC 65**
See CA 132

Castedo-Ellerman, Elena
See Castedo, Elena

Castellanos, Rosario 1925-1974 .... **CLC 66;
DAM MULT; HLC 1**
See CA 131; 53-56; CANR 58; DLB 113;
HW 1; MTCW 1

Castelvetro, Lodovico 1505-1571 .... **LC 12**

Castiglione, Baldassare 1478-1529 ...... **LC 12**

Castle, Robert
See Hamilton, Edmond

Castro (Ruz), Fidel 1926(?)-
See CA 110; 129; CANR 81; DAM MULT;
HLC 1; HW 2

Castro, Guillen de 1569-1631 .... **LC 19**

Castro, Rosalia de 1837-1885 ... **NCLC 3, 78;
DAM MULT**

Cather, Willa
See Cather, Willa Sibert

Cather, Willa Sibert 1873-1947 ...... **TCLC 1,
11, 31; DA; DAB; DAC; DAM MST,
NOV; SSC 2; WLC**
See AAYA 24; CA 104; 128; CDALB 1865-
1917; DA3; DLB 9, 54, 78; DLBD 1;
MTCW 1, 2; SATA 30

Catherine, Saint 1347-1380 .... **CMLC 27**

Cato, Marcus Porcius 234B.C.-149B.C.
CMLC 21
See DLB 211

Catton, (Charles) Bruce 1899-1978 . **CLC 35**
See AITN 1; CA 5-8R; 81-84; CANR 7, 74;
DLB 17; SATA 2; SATA-Obit 24

Catullus c. 84B.C.-c. 54B.C. .... **CMLC 18**
See DLB 211

Cauldwell, Frank
See King, Francis (Henry)

Caunitz, William J. 1933-1996 .... **CLC 34**
See BEST 89:3; CA 125; 130; 152; CANR
73; INT 130

Causley, Charles (Stanley) 1917- .... **CLC 7**
See CA 9-12R; CANR 5, 35; CLR 30; DLB
27; MTCW 1; SATA 3, 66

Caute, (John) David 1936- ..... **CLC 29;DAM
NOV**
See CA 1-4R; CAAS 4; CANR 1, 33, 64;
DLB 14

Cavafy, C(onstantine) P(eter) 1863-1933
TCLC 2, 7; DAM POET
See Kavafis, Konstantinos Petrou
See CA 148; DA3; MTCW 1

Cavallo, Evelyn
See Spark, Muriel (Sarah)

Cavanna, Betty .... **CLC 12**
See Harrison, Elizabeth Cavanna
See JRDA; MAICYA; SAAS 4; SATA 1, 30

Cavendish, Margaret Lucas
1623-1673 .... **LC 30**
See DLB 131

Caxton, William 1421(?)-1491(?) .... **LC 17**
See DLB 170

Cayer, D. M.
See Duffy, Maureen

Cayrol, Jean 1911- .... **CLC 11**
See CA 89-92; DLB 83

Cela, Camilo Jose 1916- .... **CLC 4, 13, 59,
122; DAM MULT; HLC 1**
See BEST 90:2; CA 21-24R; CAAS 10;
CANR 21, 32, 76; DLBY 89; HW 1;
MTCW 1, 2

Celan, Paul .... **CLC 10, 19, 53, 82; PC 10**
See Antschel, Paul
See DLB 69

Celine, Louis-Ferdinand ... **CLC 1, 3, 4, 7, 9,
15, 47, 124**
See Destouches, Louis-Ferdinand
See DLB 72

Cellini, Benvenuto 1500-1571 .... **LC 7**

Cendrars, Blaise 1887-1961 ...... **CLC 18, 106**
See Sauser-Hall, Frederic

Cernuda (y Bidon), Luis
1902-1963 .... **CLC 54; DAM POET**
See CA 131; 89-92; DLB 134; HW 1

Cervantes, Lorna Dee 1954-
See CA 131; CANR 80; DLB 82; HLCS 1;
HW 1

Cervantes (Saavedra), Miguel de 1547-1616
**LC 6, 23; DA; DAB; DAC; DAM MST,
NOV; SSC 12; WLC**

Cesaire, Aime (Fernand) 1913- . **CLC 19, 32,
112; BLC 1; DAM MULT, POET; PC
25**
See BW 2, 3; CA 65-68; CANR 24, 43, 81;
DA3; MTCW 1, 2

Chabon, Michael 1963- .... **CLC 55**
See CA 139; CANR 57

Chabrol, Claude 1930- .... **CLC 16**
See CA 110

Challans, Mary 1905-1983
See Renault, Mary
See CA 81-84; 111; CANR 74; DA3;
MTCW 2; SATA 23; SATA-Obit 36

Challis, George
See Faust, Frederick (Schiller)

Chambers, Aidan 1934- .... **CLC 35**
See AAYA 27; CA 25-28R; CANR 12, 31,
58; JRDA; MAICYA; SAAS 12; SATA 1,
69, 108

Author Index

Author Index

Crabbe, George 1754-1832 .... **NCLC 26**
  See DLB 93
Craddock, Charles Egbert
  See Murfree, Mary Noailles
Craig, A. A.
  See Anderson, Poul (William)
Craik, Dinah Maria (Mulock) 1826-1887
  NCLC 38
  See DLB 35, 163; MAICYA; SATA 34
Cram, Ralph Adams 1863-1942 ..... **TCLC 45**
  See CA 160
Crane, (Harold) Hart 1899-1932 .... **TCLC 2,**
  5, 80; DA; DAB; DAC; DAM MST,
  POET; PC 3; WLC
  See CA 104; 127; CDALB 1917-1929;
  DA3; DLB 4, 48; MTCW 1, 2
Crane, R(onald) S(almon)
  1886-1967 .... **CLC 27**
  See CA 85-88; DLB 63
Crane, Stephen (Townley)
  1871-1900 .... **TCLC 11, 17, 32; DA;**
  DAB; DAC; DAM MST, NOV, POET;
  SSC 7; WLC
  See AAYA 21; CA 109; 140; CANR 84;
  CDALB 1865-1917; DA3; DLB 12, 54,
  78; YABC 2
Cranshaw, Stanley
  See Fisher, Dorothy (Frances) Canfield
Crase, Douglas 1944- .... **CLC 58**
  See CA 106
Crashaw, Richard 1612(?)-1649 .... **LC 24**
  See DLB 126
Craven, Margaret 1901-1980 .. **CLC 17;DAC**
  See CA 103
Crawford, F(rancis) Marion 1854-1909
  TCLC 10
  See CA 107; 168; DLB 71
Crawford, Isabella Valancy
  1850-1887 .... **NCLC 12**
  See DLB 92
Crayon, Geoffrey
  See Irving, Washington
Creasey, John 1908-1973 .... **CLC 11**
  See CA 5-8R; 41-44R; CANR 8, 59; DLB
  77; MTCW 1
Crebillon, Claude Prosper Jolyot de (fils)
  1707-1777 .... **LC 1, 28**
Credo
  See Creasey, John
Credo, Alvaro J. de
  See Prado (Calvo), Pedro
Creeley, Robert (White) 1926- .. **CLC 1, 2, 4,**
  8, 11, 15, 36, 78; DAM POET
  See CA 1-4R; CAAS 10; CANR 23, 43;
  DA3; DLB 5, 16, 169; DLBD 17; MTCW
  1, 2
Crews, Harry (Eugene) 1935- ..... **CLC 6, 23,**
  49
  See AITN 1; CA 25-28R; CANR 20, 57;
  DA3; DLB 6, 143, 185; MTCW 1, 2
Crichton, (John) Michael 1942- .... **CLC 2, 6,**
  54, 90; DAM NOV, POP
  See AAYA 10; AITN 2; CA 25-28R; CANR
  13, 40, 54, 76; DA3; DLBY 81; INT
  CANR-13; JRDA; MTCW 1, 2; SATA 9,
  88
Crispin, Edmund .... **CLC 22**
  See Montgomery, (Robert) Bruce
  See DLB 87
Cristofer, Michael 1945(?)- ... **CLC 28; DAM**
  DRAM
  See CA 110; 152; DLB 7
Croce, Benedetto 1866-1952 .... **TCLC 37**
  See CA 120; 155
Crockett, David 1786-1836 .... **NCLC 8**
  See DLB 3, 11
Crockett, Davy
  See Crockett, David

Crofts, Freeman Wills 1879-1957 .. **TCLC 55**
  See CA 115; DLB 77
Croker, John Wilson 1780-1857 .... **NCLC 10**
  See DLB 110
Crommelynck, Fernand 1885-1970 .. **CLC 75**
  See CA 89-92
Cromwell, Oliver 1599-1658 .... **LC 43**
Cronin, A(rchibald) J(oseph)
  1896-1981 .... **CLC 32**
  See CA 1-4R; 102; CANR 5; DLB 191;
  SATA 47; SATA-Obit 25
Cross, Amanda
  See Heilbrun, Carolyn G(old)
Crothers, Rachel 1878(?)-1958 .... **TCLC 19**
  See CA 113; DLB 7
Croves, Hal
  See Traven, B.
Crow Dog, Mary (Ellen) (?)- .... **CLC 93**
  See Brave Bird, Mary
  See CA 154
Crowfield, Christopher
  See Stowe, Harriet (Elizabeth) Beecher
Crowley, Aleister .... **TCLC 7**
  See Crowley, Edward Alexander
Crowley, Edward Alexander 1875-1947
  See Crowley, Aleister
  See CA 104
Crowley, John 1942- .... **CLC 57**
  See CA 61-64; CANR 43; DLBY 82; SATA
  65
Crud
  See Crumb, R(obert)
Crumarums
  See Crumb, R(obert)
Crumb, R(obert) 1943- .... **CLC 17**
  See CA 106
Crumbum
  See Crumb, R(obert)
Crumski
  See Crumb, R(obert)
Crum the Bum
  See Crumb, R(obert)
Crunk
  See Crumb, R(obert)
Crustt
  See Crumb, R(obert)
Cruz, Victor Hernandez 1949-
  See BW 2; CA 65-68; CAAS 17; CANR
  14, 32, 74; DAM MULT, POET; DLB 41;
  HLC 1; HW 1, 2; MTCW 1
Cryer, Gretchen (Kiger) 1935- .... **CLC 21**
  See CA 114; 123
Csath, Geza 1887-1919 .... **TCLC 13**
  See CA 111
Cudlip, David R(ockwell) 1933- .... **CLC 34**
  See CA 177
Cullen, Countee 1903-1946 .... **TCLC 4, 37;**
  BLC 1; DA; DAC; DAM MST, MULT,
  POET; PC 20; WLCS
  See BW 1; CA 108; 124; CDALB 1917-
  1929; DA3; DLB 4, 48, 51; MTCW 1, 2;
  SATA 18
Cum, R.
  See Crumb, R(obert)
Cummings, Bruce F(rederick) 1889-1919
  See Barbellion, W. N. P.
  See CA 123
Cummings, E(dward) E(stlin) 1894-1962
  CLC 1, 3, 8, 12, 15, 68; DA; DAB;
  DAC; DAM MST, POET; PC 5; WLC
  See CA 73-76; CANR 31; CDALB 1929-
  1941; DA3; DLB 4, 48; MTCW 1, 2
Cunha, Euclides (Rodrigues Pimenta) da
  1866-1909 .... **TCLC 24**
  See CA 123
Cunningham, E. V.
  See Fast, Howard (Melvin)

Cunningham, J(ames) V(incent) 1911-1985
  CLC 3, 31
  See CA 1-4R; 115; CANR 1, 72; DLB 5
Cunningham, Julia (Woolfolk)
  1916- .... **CLC 12**
  See CA 9-12R; CANR 4, 19, 36; JRDA;
  MAICYA; SAAS 2; SATA 1, 26
Cunningham, Michael 1952- .... **CLC 34**
  See CA 136
Cunninghame Graham, R(obert)B(ontine)
  1852-1936 .... **TCLC 19**
  See Graham, R(obert) B(ontine) Cunning-
  hame
  See CA 119; DLB 98
Currie, Ellen 19(?)- .... **CLC 44**
Curtin, Philip
  See Lowndes, Marie Adelaide (Belloc)
Curtis, Price
  See Ellison, Harlan (Jay)
Cutrate, Joe
  See Spiegelman, Art
Cynewulf c. 770-c. 840 .... **CMLC 23**
Czaczkes, Shmuel Yosef
  See Agnon, S(hmuel) Y(osef Halevi)
Dabrowska, Maria(Szumska)
  1889-1965 .... **CLC 15**
  See CA 106
Dabydeen, David 1955- .... **CLC 34**
  See BW 1; CA 125; CANR 56
Dacey, Philip 1939- .... **CLC 51**
  See CA 37-40R; CAAS 17; CANR 14, 32,
  64; DLB 105
Dagerman, Stig (Halvard)
  1923-1954 .... **TCLC 17**
  See CA 117; 155
Dahl, Roald 1916-1990 ...... **CLC 1, 6, 18, 79;**
  DAB; DAC; DAM MST, NOV, POP
  See AAYA 15; CA 1-4R; 133; CANR 6, 32,
  37, 62; CLR 1, 7, 41; DA3; DLB 139;
  JRDA; MAICYA; MTCW 1, 2; SATA 1,
  26, 73; SATA-Obit 65
Dahlberg, Edward 1900-1977 .. **CLC 1, 7, 14**
  See CA 9-12R; 69-72; CANR 31, 62; DLB
  48; MTCW 1
Daitch, Susan 1954- .... **CLC 103**
  See CA 161
Dale, Colin .... **TCLC 18**
  See Lawrence, T(homas) E(dward)
Dale, George E.
  See Asimov, Isaac
Dalton, Roque 1935-1975
  See HLCS 1; HW 2
Daly, Elizabeth 1878-1967 .... **CLC 52**
  See CA 23-24; 25-28R; CANR 60; CAP 2
Daly, Maureen 1921- .... **CLC 17**
  See AAYA 5; CANR 37, 83; JRDA; MAI-
  CYA; SAAS 1; SATA 2
Damas, Leon-Gontran 1912-1978 .... **CLC 84**
  See BW 1; CA 125; 73-76
Dana, Richard Henry Sr.
  1787-1879 .... **NCLC 53**
Daniel, Samuel 1562(?)-1619 .... **LC 24**
  See DLB 62
Daniels, Brett
  See Adler, Renata
Dannay, Frederic 1905-1982 .. **CLC 11;DAM**
  POP
  See Queen, Ellery
  See CA 1-4R; 107; CANR 1, 39; DLB 137;
  MTCW 1
D'Annunzio, Gabriele 1863-1938 ... **TCLC 6,**
  40
  See CA 104; 155
Danois, N. le
  See Gourmont, Remy (-Marie-Charles) de

Domini, Rey
See Lorde, Audre (Geraldine)
Dominique
See Proust, (Valentin-Louis-George-Eugene-) Marcel
Don, A
See Stephen, SirLeslie
Donaldson, Stephen R. 1947- .... **CLC 46; DAM POP**
See CA 89-92; CANR 13, 55; INT CANR-13
Donleavy, J(ames) P(atrick) 1926- .... **CLC 1, 4, 6, 10, 45**
See AITN 2; CA 9-12R; CANR 24, 49, 62, 80; DLB 6, 173; INT CANR-24; MTCW 1, 2
Donne, John 1572-1631 .... **LC 10, 24; DA; DAB; DAC; DAM MST, POET; PC 1; WLC**
See CDBLB Before 1660; DLB 121, 151
Donnell, David 1939(?)- .... **CLC 34**
Donoghue, P. S.
See Hunt, E(verette) Howard, (Jr.)
Donoso (Yanez), Jose 1924-1996 ... **CLC 4, 8, 11, 32, 99; DAM MULT; HLC 1; SSC 34**
See CA 81-84; 155; CANR 32, 73; DLB 113; HW 1, 2; MTCW 1, 2
Donovan, John 1928-1992 .... **CLC 35**
See AAYA 20; CA 97-100; 137; CLR 3; MAICYA; SATA 72; SATA-Brief 29
Don Roberto
See Cunninghame Graham, R(obert) B(ontine)
Doolittle, Hilda 1886-1961 . **CLC 3, 8, 14, 31, 34, 73; DA; DAC; DAM MST, POET; PC 5; WLC**
See H. D.
See CA 97-100; CANR 35; DLB 4, 45; MTCW 1, 2
Dorfman, Ariel 1942- ...... **CLC 48, 77; DAM MULT; HLC 1**
See CA 124; 130; CANR 67, 70; HW 1, 2; INT 130
Dorn, Edward (Merton) 1929- ... **CLC 10, 18**
See CA 93-96; CANR 42, 79; DLB 5; INT 93-96
Dorris, Michael (Anthony) 1945-1997 .... **CLC 109; DAM MULT, NOV**
See AAYA 20; BEST 90:1; CA 102; 157; CANR 19, 46, 75; CLR 58; DA3; DLB 175; MTCW 2; NNAL; SATA 75; SATA-Obit 94
Dorris, Michael A.
See Dorris, Michael (Anthony)
Dorsan, Luc
See Simenon, Georges (Jacques Christian)
Dorsange, Jean
See Simenon, Georges (Jacques Christian)
Dos Passos, John (Roderigo) 1896-1970 ... **CLC 1, 4, 8, 11, 15, 25, 34, 82; DA; DAB; DAC; DAM MST, NOV; WLC**
See CA 1-4R; 29-32R; CANR 3; CDALB 1929-1941; DA3; DLB 4, 9; DLBD 1, 15; DLBY 96; MTCW 1, 2
Dossage, Jean
See Simenon, Georges (Jacques Christian)
Dostoevsky, Fedor Mikhailovich 1821-1881 **NCLC 2, 7, 21, 33, 43; DA; DAB; DAC; DAM MST, NOV; SSC 2, 33; WLC**
See DA3
Doughty, Charles M(ontagu) 1843-1926 **TCLC 27**
See CA 115; 178; DLB 19, 57, 174
Douglas, Ellen .... **CLC 73**
See Haxton, Josephine Ayres; Williamson, Ellen Douglas

Douglas, Gavin 1475(?)-1522 .... **LC 20**
See DLB 132
Douglas, George
See Brown, George Douglas
Douglas, Keith (Castellain) 1920-1944 .... **TCLC 40**
See CA 160; DLB 27
Douglas, Leonard
See Bradbury, Ray (Douglas)
Douglas, Michael
See Crichton, (John) Michael
Douglas, (George) Norman 1868-1952 .... **TCLC 68**
See CA 119; 157; DLB 34, 195
Douglas, William
See Brown, George Douglas
Douglass, Frederick 1817(?)-1895 .. **NCLC 7, 55; BLC 1; DA; DAC; DAM MST, MULT; WLC**
See CDALB 1640-1865; DA3; DLB 1, 43, 50, 79; SATA 29
Dourado, (Waldomiro Freitas) Autran 1926- **CLC 23, 60**
See CA 25-28R; 179; CANR 34, 81; DLB 145; HW 2
Dourado, Waldomiro Autran 1926-
See Dourado, (Waldomiro Freitas) Autran
See CA 179
Dove, Rita (Frances) 1952- .... **CLC 50, 81; BLCS; DAM MULT, POET; PC 6**
See BW 2; CA 109; CAAS 19; CANR 27, 42, 68, 76; CDALBS; DA3; DLB 120; MTCW 1
Doveglion
See Villa, Jose Garcia
Dowell, Coleman 1925-1985 .... **CLC 60**
See CA 25-28R; 117; CANR 10; DLB 130
Dowson, Ernest (Christopher) 1867-1900 **TCLC 4**
See CA 105; 150; DLB 19, 135
Doyle, A. Conan
See Doyle, Arthur Conan
Doyle, Arthur Conan 1859-1930 .... **TCLC 7; DA; DAB; DAC; DAM MST, NOV; SSC 12; WLC**
See AAYA 14; CA 104; 122; CDBLB 1890-1914; DA3; DLB 18, 70, 156, 178; MTCW 1, 2; SATA 24
Doyle, Conan
See Doyle, Arthur Conan
Doyle, John
See Graves, Robert (von Ranke)
Doyle, Roddy 1958(?)- .... **CLC 81**
See AAYA 14; CA 143; CANR 73; DA3; DLB 194
Doyle, Sir A. Conan
See Doyle, Arthur Conan
Doyle, Sir Arthur Conan
See Doyle, Arthur Conan
Dr. A
See Asimov, Isaac; Silverstein, Alvin
Drabble, Margaret 1939- ...... **CLC 2, 3, 5, 8, 10, 22, 53; DAB; DAC; DAM MST, NOV, POP**
See CA 13-16R; CANR 18, 35, 63; CDBLB 1960 to Present; DA3; DLB 14, 155; MTCW 1, 2; SATA 48
Drapier, M. B.
See Swift, Jonathan
Drayham, James
See Mencken, H(enry) L(ouis)
Drayton, Michael 1563-1631 .... **LC 8;DAM POET**
See DLB 121
Dreadstone, Carl
See Campbell, (John) Ramsey

Dreiser, Theodore (Herman Albert) 1871-1945 .... **TCLC 10, 18, 35, 83; DA; DAC; DAM MST, NOV; SSC 30; WLC**
See CA 106; 132; CDALB 1865-1917; DA3; DLB 9, 12, 102, 137; DLBD 1; MTCW 1, 2
Drexler, Rosalyn 1926- .... **CLC 2, 6**
See CA 81-84; CANR 68
Dreyer, Carl Theodor 1889-1968 ...... **CLC 16**
See CA 116
Drieu la Rochelle, Pierre(-Eugene) 1893-1945 .... **TCLC 21**
See CA 117; DLB 72
Drinkwater, John 1882-1937 .... **TCLC 57**
See CA 109; 149; DLB 10, 19, 149
Drop Shot
See Cable, George Washington
Droste-Hulshoff, Annette Freiinvon 1797-1848 .... **NCLC 3**
See DLB 133
Drummond, Walter
See Silverberg, Robert
Drummond, William Henry 1854-1907 .... **TCLC 25**
See CA 160; DLB 92
Drummond de Andrade,Carlos 1902-1987 **CLC 18**
See Andrade, Carlos Drummond de
See CA 132; 123
Drury, Allen (Stuart) 1918-1998 .... **CLC 37**
See CA 57-60; 170; CANR 18, 52; INT CANR-18
Dryden, John 1631-1700 .... **LC 3, 21; DA; DAB; DAC; DAM DRAM, MST, POET; DC 3; PC 25;WLC**
See CDBLB 1660-1789; DLB 80, 101, 131
Duberman, Martin(Bauml) 1930- ...... **CLC 8**
See CA 1-4R; CANR 2, 63
Dubie, Norman (Evans) 1945- .... **CLC 36**
See CA 69-72; CANR 12; DLB 120
Du Bois, W(illiam) E(dward) B(urghardt) 1868-1963 ... **CLC 1, 2, 13, 64, 96; BLC 1; DA; DAC; DAM MST, MULT, NOV; WLC**
See BW 1, 3; CA 85-88; CANR 34, 82; CDALB 1865-1917; DA3; DLB 47, 50, 91, MTCW 1, 2; SATA 42
Dubus, Andre 1936-1999 ..... **CLC 13, 36, 97; SSC 15**
See CA 21-24R; 177; CANR 17; DLB 130; INT CANR-17
Duca Minimo
See D'Annunzio, Gabriele
Ducharme, Rejean 1941- .... **CLC 74**
See CA 165; DLB 60
Duclos, Charles Pinot 1704-1772 .... **LC 1**
Dudek, Louis 1918- .... **CLC 11, 19**
See CA 45-48; CAAS 14; CANR 1; DLB 88
Duerrenmatt, Friedrich 1921-1990 ... **CLC 1, 4, 8, 11, 15, 43, 102; DAM DRAM**
See CA 17-20R; CANR 33; DLB 69, 124; MTCW 1, 2
Duffy, Bruce 1953(?)- .... **CLC 50**
See CA 172
Duffy, Maureen 1933- .... **CLC 37**
See CA 25-28R; CANR 33, 68; DLB 14; MTCW 1
Dugan, Alan 1923- .... **CLC 2, 6**
See CA 81-84; DLB 5
du Gard, Roger Martin
See Martin du Gard, Roger
Duhamel, Georges 1884-1966 .... **CLC 8**
See CA 81-84; 25-28R; CANR 35; DLB 65; MTCW 1
Dujardin, Edouard (EmileLouis) 1861-1949 **TCLC 13**
See CA 109; DLB 123

Ekeloef, (Bengt) Gunnar
1907-1968 ... **CLC 27; DAM POET; PC
23**
See CA 123; 25-28R
Ekelof, (Bengt) Gunnar
See Ekeloef, (Bengt) Gunnar
Ekelund, Vilhelm 1880-1949 .... **TCLC 75**
Ekwensi, C. O. D.
See Ekwensi, Cyprian (Odiatu Duaka)
Ekwensi, Cyprian (Odiatu Duaka) 1921-
CLC 4; BLC 1; DAM MULT
See BW 2, 3; CA 29-32R; CANR 18, 42,
74; DLB 117; MTCW 1, 2; SATA 66
Elaine .... **TCLC 18**
See Leverson, Ada
El Crummo
See Crumb, R(obert)
Elder, Lonne III 1931-1996 .... **DC 8**
See BLC 1; BW 1, 3; CA 81-84; 152;
CANR 25; DAM MULT; DLB 7, 38, 44
Elia
See Lamb, Charles
Eliade, Mircea 1907-1986 .... **CLC 19**
See CA 65-68; 119; CANR 30, 62; MTCW
1
Eliot, A. D.
See Jewett, (Theodora) Sarah Orne
Eliot, Alice
See Jewett, (Theodora) Sarah Orne
Eliot, Dan
See Silverberg, Robert
Eliot, George 1819-1880 ...... **NCLC 4, 13, 23,
41, 49; DA; DAB; DAC; DAM MST,
NOV; PC 20; WLC**
See CDBLB 1832-1890; DA3; DLB 21, 35,
55
Eliot, John 1604-1690 .... **LC 5**
See DLB 24
Eliot, T(homas) S(tearns)
1888-1965 ...... **CLC 1, 2, 3, 6, 9, 10, 13,
15, 24, 34, 41, 55, 57, 113; DA; DAB;
DAC; DAM DRAM, MST, POET; PC
5; WLC**
See AAYA 28; CA 5-8R; 25-28R; CANR
41;CDALB 1929-1941; DA3; DLB 7, 10,
45, 63; DLBY 88; MTCW 1, 2
Elizabeth 1866-1941 .... **TCLC 41**
Elkin, Stanley L(awrence)
1930-1995 .. **CLC 4, 6, 9, 14, 27, 51, 91;
DAM NOV, POP; SSC 12**
See CA 9-12R; 148; CANR 8, 46; DLB 2,
28; DLBY 80; INT CANR-8; MTCW 1, 2
Elledge, Scott .... **CLC 34**
Elliot, Don
See Silverberg, Robert
Elliott, Don
See Silverberg, Robert
Elliott, George P(aul) 1918-1980 .... **CLC 2**
See CA 1-4R; 97-100; CANR 2
Elliott, Janice 1931- .... **CLC 47**
See CA 13-16R; CANR 8, 29, 84; DLB 14
Elliott, Sumner Locke 1917-1991 ..... **CLC 38**
See CA 5-8R; 134; CANR 2, 21
Elliott, William
See Bradbury, Ray (Douglas)
Ellis, A. E. .... **CLC 7**
Ellis, Alice Thomas .... **CLC 40**
See Haycraft, Anna
See DLB 194; MTCW 1
Ellis, Bret Easton 1964- ..... **CLC 39, 71, 117;
DAM POP**
See AAYA 2; CA 118; 123; CANR 51, 74;
DA3; INT 123; MTCW 1
Ellis, (Henry) Havelock
1859-1939 .... **TCLC 14**
See CA 109; 169; DLB 190
Ellis, Landon
See Ellison, Harlan (Jay)

Ellis, Trey 1962- .... **CLC 55**
See CA 146
Ellison, Harlan (Jay) 1934- ... **CLC 1, 13, 42;
DAM POP; SSC 14**
See AAYA 29; CA 5-8R; CANR 5, 46; DLB
8; INT CANR-5; MTCW 1, 2
Ellison, Ralph (Waldo) 1914-1994 .... **CLC 1,
3, 11, 54, 86, 114; BLC 1; DA; DAB;
DAC; DAM MST, MULT, NOV; SSC
26;WLC**
See AAYA 19; BW 1, 3; CA 9-12R; 145;
CANR 24, 53; CDALB 1941-1968; DA3;
DLB 2, 76; DLBY 94; MTCW 1, 2
Ellmann, Lucy (Elizabeth) 1956- ..... **CLC 61**
See CA 128
Ellmann, Richard (David)
1918-1987 .... **CLC 50**
See BEST 89:2; CA 1-4R; 122; CANR 2,
28, 61; DLB 103; DLBY 87; MTCW 1, 2
Elman, Richard (Martin)
1934-1997 .... **CLC 19**
See CA 17-20R; 163; CAAS 3; CANR 47
Elron
See Hubbard, L(afayette) Ron(ald)
Eluard, Paul .... **TCLC 7, 41**
See Grindel, Eugene
Elyot, Sir Thomas 1490(?)-1546 .... **LC 11**
Elytis, Odysseus 1911-1996 .... **CLC 15, 49,
100; DAM POET; PC 21**
See CA 102; 151; MTCW 1, 2
Emecheta, (Florence Onye) Buchi
1944- .... **CLC 14, 48; BLC 2; DAM
MULT**
See BW 2, 3; CA 81-84; CANR 27, 81;
DA3; DLB 117; MTCW 1, 2; SATA 66
Emerson, Mary Moody
1774-1863 .... **NCLC 66**
Emerson, Ralph Waldo 1803-1882 . **NCLC 1,
38; DA; DAB; DAC; DAM MST,
POET; PC 18; WLC**
See CDALB 1640-1865; DA3; DLB 1, 59,
73
Eminescu, Mihail 1850-1889 .... **NCLC 33**
Empson, William 1906-1984 ... **CLC 3, 8, 19,
33, 34**
See CA 17-20R; 112; CANR 31, 61; DLB
20; MTCW 1, 2
Enchi, Fumiko (Ueda) 1905-1986 ..... **CLC 31**
See CA 129; 121; DLB 182
Ende, Michael (Andreas Helmuth)
1929-1995 .... **CLC 31**
See CA 118; 124; 149; CANR 36; CLR 14;
DLB 75; MAICYA; SATA 61; SATA-
Brief 42; SATA-Obit 86
Endo, Shusaku 1923-1996 ..... **CLC 7, 14, 19,
54, 99; DAM NOV**
See CA 29-32R; 153; CANR 21, 54; DA3;
DLB 182; MTCW 1, 2
Engel, Marian 1933-1985 .... **CLC 36**
See CA 25-28R; CANR 12; DLB 53; INT
CANR-12
Engelhardt, Frederick
See Hubbard, L(afayette) Ron(ald)
Enright, D(ennis) J(oseph) 1920- .. **CLC 4, 8,
31**
See CA 1-4R; CANR 1, 42, 83; DLB 27;
SATA 25
Enzensberger, Hans Magnus
1929- .... **CLC 43; PC 28**
See CA 116; 119
Ephron, Nora 1941- .... **CLC 17, 31**
See AITN 2; CA 65-68; CANR 12, 39, 83
Epicurus 341B.C.-270B.C. .... **CMLC 21**
See DLB 176
Epsilon
See Betjeman, John
Epstein, Daniel Mark 1948- .... **CLC 7**
See CA 49-52; CANR 2, 53

Epstein, Jacob 1956- .... **CLC 19**
See CA 114
Epstein, Jean 1897-1953 .... **TCLC 92**
Epstein, Joseph 1937- .... **CLC 39**
See CA 112; 119; CANR 50, 65
Epstein, Leslie 1938- .... **CLC 27**
See CA 73-76; CAAS 12; CANR 23, 69
Equiano, Olaudah 1745(?)-1797 .... **LC 16;
BLC 2; DAM MULT**
See DLB 37, 50
ER .... **TCLC 33**
See CA 160; DLB 85
Erasmus, Desiderius 1469(?)-1536 ...... **LC 16**
Erdman, Paul E(mil) 1932- .... **CLC 25**
See AITN 1; CA 61-64; CANR 13, 43, 84
Erdrich, Louise 1954- .... **CLC 39, 54, 120;
DAM MULT, NOV, POP**
See AAYA 10; BEST 89:1; CA 114; CANR
41, 62; CDALBS; DA3; DLB 152, 175,
206; MTCW 1; NNAL; SATA 94
Erenburg, Ilya (Grigoryevich)
See Ehrenburg, Ilya (Grigoryevich)
Erickson, Stephen Michael 1950-
See Erickson, Steve
See CA 129
Erickson, Steve 1950- .... **CLC 64**
See Erickson, Stephen Michael
See CANR 60, 68
Ericson, Walter
See Fast, Howard (Melvin)
Eriksson, Buntel
See Bergman, (Ernst) Ingmar
Ernaux, Annie 1940- .... **CLC 88**
See CA 147
Erskine, John 1879-1951 .... **TCLC 84**
See CA 112; 159; DLB 9, 102
Eschenbach, Wolfram von
See Wolfram von Eschenbach
Eseki, Bruno
See Mphahlele, Ezekiel
Esenin, Sergei (Alexandrovich) 1895-1925
TCLC 4
See CA 104
Eshleman, Clayton 1935- .... **CLC 7**
See CA 33-36R; CAAS 6; DLB 5
Espriella, Don Manuel Alvarez
See Southey, Robert
Espriu, Salvador 1913-1985 .... **CLC 9**
See CA 154; 115; DLB 134
Espronceda, Jose de 1808-1842 ..... **NCLC 39**
Esquivel, Laura 1951(?)-
See AAYA 29; CA 143; CANR 68; DA3;
HLCS 1; MTCW 1
Esse, James
See Stephens, James
Esterbrook, Tom
See Hubbard, L(afayette) Ron(ald)
Estleman, Loren D. 1952- ..... **CLC 48; DAM
NOV, POP**
See AAYA 27; CA 85-88; CANR 27, 74;
DA3; INT CANR-27; MTCW 1, 2
Euclid 306B.C.-283B.C. .... **CMLC 25**
Eugenides, Jeffrey 1960(?)- .... **CLC 81**
See CA 144
Euripides c. 485B.C.-406B.C. .... **CMLC 23;
DA; DAB; DAC; DAM DRAM, MST;
DC 4; WLCS**
See DA3; DLB 176
Evan, Evin
See Faust, Frederick (Schiller)
Evans, Caradoc 1878-1945 .... **TCLC 85**
Evans, Evan
See Faust, Frederick (Schiller)
Evans, Marian
See Eliot, George
Evans, Mary Ann
See Eliot, George

Hamilton, Clive
See Lewis, C(live) S(taples)
Hamilton, Edmond 1904-1977 .... **CLC 1**
See CA 1-4R; CANR 3, 84; DLB 8
Hamilton, Eugene (Jacob) Lee
See Lee-Hamilton, Eugene (Jacob)
Hamilton, Franklin
See Silverberg, Robert
Hamilton, Gail
See Corcoran, Barbara
Hamilton, Mollie
See Kaye, M(ary) M(argaret)
Hamilton, (Anthony Walter) Patrick
1904-1962 .... **CLC 51**
See CA 176; 113; DLB 191
Hamilton, Virginia 1936- .... **CLC 26;DAM**
MULT
See AAYA 2, 21; BW 2, 3; CA 25-28R;
CANR 20, 37, 73; CLR 1, 11, 40; DLB
33, 52; INT CANR-20; JRDA; MAICYA;
MTCW 1, 2; SATA 4, 56, 79
Hammett, (Samuel) Dashiell
1894-1961 .... **CLC 3, 5, 10, 19, 47; SSC**
17
See AITN 1; CA 81-84; CANR 42; CDALB
1929-1941; DA3; DLBD 6; DLBY 96;
MTCW 1, 2
Hammon, Jupiter 1711(?)-1800(?) . **NCLC 5;**
BLC 2; DAM MULT, POET; PC 16
See DLB 31, 50
Hammond, Keith
See Kuttner, Henry
Hamner, Earl (Henry), Jr. 1923- ...... **CLC 12**
See AITN 2; CA 73-76; DLB 6
Hampton, Christopher (James)
1946- .... **CLC 4**
See CA 25-28R; DLB 13; MTCW 1
Hamsun, Knut .... **TCLC 2, 14, 49**
See Pedersen, Knut
Handke, Peter 1942- ... **CLC 5, 8, 10, 15, 38;**
DAM DRAM, NOV
See CA 77-80; CANR 33, 75; DLB 85, 124;
MTCW 1, 2
Handy, W(illiam) C(hristopher) 1873-1958
TCLC 97
See BW 3; CA 121, 167
Hanley, James 1901-1985 ..... **CLC 3, 5, 8, 13**
See CA 73-76; 117; CANR 36; DLB 191;
MTCW 1
Hannah, Barry 1942- .... **CLC 23, 38, 90**
See CA 108; 110; CANR 43, 68; DLB 6;
INT 110; MTCW 1
Hannon, Ezra
See Hunter, Evan
Hansberry, Lorraine (Vivian) 1930-1965
CLC 17, 62; BLC 2; DA; DAB; DAC;
DAM DRAM, MST, MULT;DC 2
See AAYA 25; BW 1, 3; CA 109; 25-28R;
CABS 3; CANR 58; CDALB 1941-1968;
DA3; DLB 7, 38; MTCW 1, 2
Hansen, Joseph 1923- .... **CLC 38**
See CA 29-32R; CAAS 17; CANR 16, 44,
66; INT CANR-16
Hansen, Martin A(lfred)
1909-1955 .... **TCLC 32**
See CA 167
Hanson, Kenneth O(stlin) 1922- .... **CLC 13**
See CA 53-56; CANR 7
Hardwick, Elizabeth (Bruce)
1916- .... **CLC 13; DAM NOV**
See CA 5-8R; CANR 3, 32, 70; DA3; DLB
6; MTCW 1, 2
Hardy, Thomas 1840-1928 .. **TCLC 4, 10, 18,**
32, 48, 53, 72; DA; DAB; DAC; DAM
MST, NOV, POET; PC 8; SSC 2;WLC
See CA 104; 123; CDBLB 1890-1914;
DA3; DLB 18, 19, 135; MTCW 1, 2

Hare, David 1947- .... **CLC 29, 58**
See CA 97-100; CANR 39; DLB 13;
MTCW 1
Harewood, John
See Van Druten, John (William)
Harford, Henry
See Hudson, W(illiam) H(enry)
Hargrave, Leonie
See Disch, Thomas M(ichael)
Harjo, Joy 1951- ...... **CLC 83; DAM MULT;**
PC 27
See CA 114; CANR 35, 67; DLB 120, 175;
MTCW 2; NNAL
Harlan, Louis R(udolph) 1922- .... **CLC 34**
See CA 21-24R; CANR 25, 55, 80
Harling, Robert 1951(?)- .... **CLC 53**
See CA 147
Harmon, William (Ruth) 1938- .... **CLC 38**
See CA 33-36R; CANR 14, 32, 35; SATA
65
Harper, F. E. W.
See Harper, Frances Ellen Watkins
Harper, Frances E. W.
See Harper, Frances Ellen Watkins
Harper, Frances E. Watkins
See Harper, Frances Ellen Watkins
Harper, Frances Ellen
See Harper, Frances Ellen Watkins
Harper, Frances Ellen Watkins 1825-1911
TCLC 14; BLC 2; DAM MULT, POET;
PC 21
See BW 1, 3; CA 111; 125; CANR 79; DLB
50
Harper, Michael S(teven) 1938- ... **CLC 7, 22**
See BW 1, CA 33-36R; CANR 24; DLB 41
Harper, Mrs. F. E. W.
See Harper, Frances Ellen Watkins
Harris, Christie (Lucy) Irwin
1907- .... **CLC 12**
See CA 5-8R; CANR 6, 83; CLR 47; DLB
88, JRDA; MAICYA; SAAS 10; SATA 6,
74
Harris, Frank 1856-1931 .... **TCLC 24**
See CA 109; 150; CANR 80; DLB 156, 197
Harris, George Washington
1814-1869 .... **NCLC 23**
See DLB 3, 11
Harris, Joel Chandler 1848-1908 ... **TCLC 2;**
SSC 19
See CA 104; 137; CANR 80; CLR 49; DLB
11, 23, 42, 78, 91; MAICYA; SATA 100;
YABC 1
Harris, John (Wyndham Parkes Lucas)
Beynon 1903-1969
See Wyndham, John
See CA 102; 89-92; CANR 84
Harris, MacDonald .... **CLC 9**
See Heiney, Donald (William)
Harris, Mark 1922- .... **CLC 19**
See CA 5-8R; CAAS 3; CANR 2, 55, 83;
DLB 2; DLBY 80
Harris, (Theodore) Wilson 1921- ..... **CLC 25**
See BW 2, 3; CA 65-68; CAAS 16; CANR
11, 27, 69; DLB 117; MTCW 1
Harrison, Elizabeth Cavanna 1909-
See Cavanna, Betty
See CA 9-12R; CANR 6, 27, 85
Harrison, Harry (Max) 1925- .... **CLC 42**
See CA 1-4R; CANR 5, 21, 84; DLB 8;
SATA 4
Harrison, James (Thomas) 1937- ...... **CLC 6,**
14, 33, 66; SSC 19
See CA 13-16R; CANR 8, 51, 79; DLBY
82; INT CANR-8
Harrison, Jim
See Harrison, James (Thomas)
Harrison, Kathryn 1961- .... **CLC 70**
See CA 144; CANR 68

Harrison, Tony 1937- .... **CLC 43**
See CA 65-68; CANR 44; DLB 40; MTCW
1
Harriss, Will(ard Irvin) 1922- .... **CLC 34**
See CA 111
Harson, Sley
See Ellison, Harlan (Jay)
Hart, Ellis
See Ellison, Harlan (Jay)
Hart, Josephine 1942(?)- .... **CLC 70;DAM**
POP
See CA 138; CANR 70
Hart, Moss 1904-1961 .... **CLC 66;DAM**
DRAM
See CA 109; 89-92; CANR 84; DLB 7
Harte, (Francis) Bret(t)
1836(?)-1902 ... **TCLC 1, 25; DA; DAC;**
DAM MST; SSC 8; WLC
See CA 104; 140; CANR 80; CDALB 1865-
1917; DA3; DLB 12, 64, 74, 79, 186;
SATA 26
Hartley, L(eslie) P(oles) 1895-1972 ... **CLC 2,**
22
See CA 45-48; 37-40R; CANR 33; DLB
15, 139; MTCW 1, 2
Hartman, Geoffrey H. 1929- .... **CLC 27**
See CA 117; 125; CANR 79; DLB 67
Hartmann, Eduard von
1842-1906 .... **TCLC 97**
Hartmann, Sadakichi 1867-1944 ... **TCLC 73**
See CA 157; DLB 54
Hartmann von Aue c.
1160-c.1205 .... **CMLC 15**
See DLB 138
Hartmann von Aue 1170-1210 ...... **CMLC 15**
Haruf, Kent 1943- .... **CLC 34**
See CA 149
Harwood, Ronald 1934- .... **CLC 32; DAM**
DRAM, MST
See CA 1-4R; CANR 4, 55; DLB 13
Hasegawa Tatsunosuke
See Futabatei, Shimei
Hasek, Jaroslav (Matej Frantisek)
1883-1923 .... **TCLC 4**
See CA 104; 129; MTCW 1, 2
Hass, Robert 1941- .... **CLC 18, 39, 99;PC 16**
See CA 111; CANR 30, 50, 71; DLB 105,
206; SATA 94
Hastings, Hudson
See Kuttner, Henry
Hastings, Selina .... **CLC 44**
Hathorne, John 1641-1717 .... **LC 38**
Hatteras, Amelia
See Mencken, H(enry) L(ouis)
Hatteras, Owen .... **TCLC 18**
See Mencken, H(enry) L(ouis); Nathan,
George Jean
Hauptmann, Gerhart (Johann Robert)
1862-1946 .... **TCLC 4; DAM DRAM;**
SSC 37
See CA 104; 153; DLB 66, 118
Havel, Vaclav 1936- ... **CLC 25, 58, 65; DAM**
DRAM; DC 6
See CA 104; CANR 36, 63; DA3; MTCW
1, 2
Haviaras, Stratis .... **CLC 33**
See Chaviaras, Strates
Hawes, Stephen 1475(?)-1523(?) .... **LC 17**
See DLB 132
Hawkes, John (Clendennin Burne, Jr.)
1925-1998 .. **CLC 1, 2, 3, 4, 7, 9, 14, 15,**
27, 49
See CA 1-4R; 167; CANR 2, 47, 64; DLB
2, 7; DLBY 80, 98; MTCW 1, 2
Hawking, S. W.
See Hawking, Stephen W(illiam)

Jones, Mick 1956(?)- .... CLC 30
Jones, Nettie (Pearl) 1941- .... CLC 34
　　See BW 2; CA 137; CAAS 20
Jones, Preston 1936-1979 .... CLC 10
　　See CA 73-76; 89-92; DLB 7
Jones, Robert F(rancis) 1934- .... CLC 7
　　See CA 49-52; CANR 2, 61
Jones, Rod 1953- .... CLC 50
　　See CA 128
Jones, Terence Graham Parry
　　1942- .... CLC 21
　　See Jones, Terry; Monty Python
　　See CA 112; 116; CANR 35; INT 116
Jones, Terry
　　See Jones, Terence Graham Parry
　　See SATA 67; SATA-Brief 51
Jones, Thom 1945(?)- .... CLC 81
　　See CA 157
Jong, Erica 1942- .... CLC 4, 6, 8, 18, 83;
　　DAM NOV, POP
　　See AITN 1; BEST 90:2; CA 73-76; CANR
　　26, 52, 75; DA3; DLB 2, 5, 28, 152; INT
　　CANR-26; MTCW 1, 2
Jonson, Ben(jamin) 1572(?)-1637 .. LC 6, 33;
　　DA; DAB; DAC; DAM DRAM, MST,
　　POET; DC 4; PC 17; WLC
　　See CDBLB Before 1660; DLB 62, 121
Jordan, June 1936- .... CLC 5, 11, 23, 114;
　　BLCS; DAM MULT, POET
　　See AAYA 2; BW 2, 3; CA 33-36R; CANR
　　25, 70; CLR 10; DLB 38; MAICYA;
　　MTCW 1; SATA 4
Jordan, Neil (Patrick) 1950- .... CLC 110
　　See CA 124; 130; CANR 54; INT 130
Jordan, Pat(rick M.) 1941- .... CLC 37
　　See CA 33-36R
Jorgensen, Ivar
　　See Ellison, Harlan (Jay)
Jorgenson, Ivar
　　See Silverberg, Robert
Josephus, Flavius c. 37-100 .... CMLC 13
Josipovici, Gabriel 1940- .... CLC 6, 43
　　See CA 37-40R; CAAS 8; CANR 47, 84;
　　DLB 14
Joubert, Joseph 1754-1824 .... NCLC 9
Jouve, Pierre Jean 1887-1976 .... CLC 47
　　See CA 65-68
Jovine, Francesco 1902-1950 .... TCLC 79
Joyce, James (Augustine Aloysius)
　　1882-1941 .. TCLC 3, 8, 16, 35, 52; DA;
　　DAB; DAC; DAM MST, NOV, POET;
　　PC 22; SSC 3, 26; WLC
　　See CA 104; 126; CDBLB 1914-1945;
　　DA3; DLB 10, 19, 36, 162; MTCW 1, 2
Jozsef, Attila 1905-1937 .... TCLC 22
　　See CA 116
Juana Ines de la Cruz 1651(?)-1695 .... LC 5;
　　HLCS 1; PC 24
Judd, Cyril
　　See Kornbluth, C(yril) M.; Pohl, Frederik
Juenger, Ernst 1895-1998 .... CLC 125
　　See CA 101; 167; CANR 21, 47; DLB 56
Julian of Norwich 1342(?)-1416(?) . LC 6, 52
　　See DLB 146
Junger, Ernst
　　See Juenger, Ernst
Junger, Sebastian 1962- .... CLC 109
　　See AAYA 28; CA 165
Juniper, Alex
　　See Hospital, Janette Turner
Junius
　　See Luxemburg, Rosa
Just, Ward (Swift) 1935- .... CLC 4, 27
　　See CA 25-28R; CANR 32; INT CANR-32
Justice, Donald (Rodney) 1925- .. CLC 6, 19,
　　102; DAM POET
　　See CA 5-8R; CANR 26, 54, 74; DLBY 83;
　　INT CANR-26; MTCW 2

Juvenal c. 60-c. 13 .... CMLC 8
　　See Juvenalis, Decimus Junius
　　See DLB 211
Juvenalis, Decimus Junius 55(?)-c. 127(?)
　　See Juvenal
Juvenis
　　See Bourne, Randolph S(illiman)
Kacew, Romain 1914-1980
　　See Gary, Romain
　　See CA 108; 102
Kadare, Ismail 1936- .... CLC 52
　　See CA 161
Kadohata, Cynthia .... CLC 59, 122
　　See CA 140
Kafka, Franz 1883-1924 . TCLC 2, 6, 13, 29,
　　47, 53; DA; DAB; DAC; DAM MST,
　　NOV; SSC 5, 29, 35; WLC
　　See AAYA 31; CA 105; 126; DA3; DLB
　　81; MTCW 1, 2
Kahanovitsch, Pinkhes
　　See Der Nister
Kahn, Roger 1927- .... CLC 30
　　See CA 25-28R; CANR 44, 69; DLB 171;
　　SATA 37
Kain, Saul
　　See Sassoon, Siegfried (Lorraine)
Kaiser, Georg 1878-1945 .... TCLC 9
　　See CA 106; DLB 124
Kaletski, Alexander 1946- .... CLC 39
　　See CA 118; 143
Kalidasa fl. c. 400- .... CMLC 9; PC 22
Kallman, Chester(Simon) 1921-1975 . CLC 2
　　See CA 45-48; 53-56; CANR 3
Kaminsky, Melvin 1926-
　　See Brooks, Mel
　　See CA 65-68; CANR 16
Kaminsky, Stuart M(elvin) 1934- ..... CLC 59
　　See CA 73-76; CANR 29, 53
Kandinsky, Wassily 1866-1944 .... TCLC 92
　　See CA 118; 155
Kane, Francis
　　See Robbins, Harold
Kane, Paul
　　See Simon, Paul (Frederick)
Kanin, Garson 1912-1999 .... CLC 22
　　See AITN 1; CA 5-8R; 177; CANR 7, 78;
　　DLB 7
Kaniuk, Yoram 1930- .... CLC 19
　　See CA 134
Kant, Immanuel 1724-1804 ..... NCLC 27, 67
　　See DLB 94
Kantor, MacKinlay 1904-1977 .... CLC 7
　　See CA 61-64; 73-76; CANR 60, 63; DLB
　　9, 102; MTCW 2
Kaplan, David Michael 1946- .... CLC 50
Kaplan, James 1951- .... CLC 59
　　See CA 135
Karageorge, Michael
　　See Anderson, Poul (William)
Karamzin, Nikolai Mikhailovich 1766-1826
　　NCLC 3
　　See DLB 150
Karapanou, Margarita 1946- .... CLC 13
　　See CA 101
Karinthy, Frigyes 1887-1938 .... TCLC 47
　　See CA 170
Karl, Frederick R(obert) 1927- .... CLC 34
　　See CA 5-8R; CANR 3, 44
Kastel, Warren
　　See Silverberg, Robert
Kataev, Evgeny Petrovich 1903-1942
　　See Petrov, Evgeny
　　See CA 120
Kataphusin
　　See Ruskin, John
Katz, Steve 1935- .... CLC 47
　　See CA 25-28R; CAAS 14, 64; CANR 12;
　　DLBY 83

Kauffman, Janet 1945- .... CLC 42
　　See CA 117; CANR 43, 84; DLBY 86
Kaufman, Bob(Garnell) 1925-1986 .. CLC 49
　　See BW 1; CA 41-44R; 118; CANR 22;
　　DLB 16, 41
Kaufman, George S. 1889-1961 ...... CLC 38;
　　DAM DRAM
　　See CA 108; 93-96; DLB 7; INT 108;
　　MTCW 2
Kaufman, Sue .... CLC 3, 8
　　See Barondess, Sue K(aufman)
Kavafis, Konstantinos Petrou 1863-1933
　　See Cavafy, C(onstantine) P(eter)
　　See CA 104
Kavan, Anna 1901-1968 .... CLC 5, 13, 82
　　See CA 5-8R; CANR 6, 57; MTCW 1
Kavanagh, Dan
　　See Barnes, Julian (Patrick)
Kavanagh, Julie 1952- .... CLC 119
　　See CA 163
Kavanagh, Patrick (Joseph)
　　1904-1967 .... CLC 22
　　See CA 123; 25-28R; DLB 15, 20; MTCW
　　1
Kawabata, Yasunari 1899-1972 ..... CLC 2, 5,
　　9, 18, 107; DAM MULT; SSC 17
　　See CA 93-96; 33-36R; DLB 180; MTCW
　　2
Kaye, M(ary) M(argaret) 1909- .... CLC 28
　　See CA 89-92; CANR 24, 60; MTCW 1, 2;
　　SATA 62
Kaye, Mollie
　　See Kaye, M(ary) M(argaret)
Kaye-Smith, Sheila 1887-1956 .... TCLC 20
　　See CA 118; DLB 36
Kaymor, Patrice Maguilene
　　See Senghor, Leopold Sedar
Kazan, Elia 1909- .... CLC 6, 16, 63
　　See CA 21-24R; CANR 32, 78
Kazantzakis, Nikos 1883(?)-1957 .... TCLC 2,
　　5, 33
　　See CA 105; 132; DA3; MTCW 1, 2
Kazin, Alfred 1915-1998 ..... CLC 34, 38, 119
　　See CA 1-4R; CAAS 7; CANR 1, 45, 79;
　　DLB 67
Keane, Mary Nesta (Skrine) 1904-1996
　　See Keane, Molly
　　See CA 108; 114; 151
Keane, Molly .... CLC 31
　　See Keane, Mary Nesta (Skrine)
　　See INT 114
Keates, Jonathan 1946(?)- .... CLC 34
　　See CA 163
Keaton, Buster 1895-1966 .... CLC 20
Keats, John 1795-1821 ...... NCLC 8, 73; DA;
　　DAB; DAC; DAM MST, POET; PC 1;
　　WLC
　　See CDBLB 1789-1832; DA3; DLB 96, 110
Keene, Donald 1922- .... CLC 34
　　See CA 1-4R; CANR 5
Keillor, Garrison .... CLC 40, 115
　　See Keillor, Gary (Edward)
　　See AAYA 2; BEST 89:3; DLBY 87; SATA
　　58
Keillor, Gary (Edward) 1942-
　　See Keillor, Garrison
　　See CA 111; 117; CANR 36, 59; DAM
　　POP; DA3; MTCW 1, 2
Keith, Michael
　　See Hubbard, L(afayette) Ron(ald)
Keller, Gottfried 1819-1890 .... NCLC 2; SSC
　　26
　　See DLB 129
Keller, Nora Okja .... CLC 109
Kellerman, Jonathan 1949- .... CLC 44;DAM
　　POP
　　See BEST 90:1; CA 106; CANR 29, 51;
　　DA3; INT CANR-29

Klein, A(braham) M(oses)
1909-1972 . **CLC 19; DAB; DAC; DAM MST**
See CA 101; 37-40R; DLB 68

Klein, Norma 1938-1989 .... **CLC 30**
See AAYA 2; CA 41-44R; CANR 15, 37; CLR 2, 19; INT CANR-15; JRDA; MAICYA; SAAS 1; SATA 7, 57

Klein, T(heodore) E(ibon) D(onald) 1947-
CLC 34
See CA 119; CANR 44, 75

Kleist, Heinrich von 1777-1811 ...... **NCLC 2, 37; DAM DRAM; SSC 22**
See DLB 90

Klima, Ivan 1931- .... **CLC 56;DAM NOV**
See CA 25-28R; CANR 17, 50

Klimentov, Andrei Platonovich 1899-1951
See Platonov, Andrei
See CA 108

Klinger, Friedrich Maximilianvon 1752-1831
NCLC 1
See DLB 94

Klingsor the Magician
See Hartmann, Sadakichi

Klopstock, Friedrich Gottlieb 1724-1803
NCLC 11
See DLB 97

Knapp, Caroline 1959- .... **CLC 99**
See CA 154

Knebel, Fletcher 1911-1993 .... **CLC 14**
See AITN 1; CA 1-4R; 140; CAAS 3; CANR 1, 36; SATA 36; SATA-Obit 75

Knickerbocker, Diedrich
See Irving, Washington

Knight, Etheridge 1931-1991 . **CLC 40; BLC 2; DAM POET; PC 14**
See BW 1, 3; CA 21-24R; 133; CANR 23, 82; DLB 41; MTCW 2

Knight, Sarah Kemble 1666 1727 .... **LC 7**
See DLB 24, 200

Knister, Raymond 1899-1932 .... **TCLC 56**
See DLB 68

Knowles, John 1926- . **CLC 1, 4, 10, 26; DA; DAC; DAM MST, NOV**
See AAYA 10; CA 17-20R; CANR 40, 74, 76; CDALB 1968-1988; DLB 6; MTCW 1, 2; SATA 8, 89

Knox, Calvin M.
See Silverberg, Robert

Knox, John c. 1505-1572 .... **LC 37**
See DLB 132

Knye, Cassandra
See Disch, Thomas M(ichael)

Koch, C(hristopher) J(ohn) 1932- .... **CLC 42**
See CA 127; CANR 84

Koch, Christopher
See Koch, C(hristopher) J(ohn)

Koch, Kenneth 1925- ..... **CLC 5, 8, 44;DAM POET**
See CA 1-4R; CANR 6, 36, 57; DLB 5; INT CANR-36; MTCW 2; SATA 65

Kochanowski, Jan 1530-1584 .... **LC 10**

Kock, Charles Paul de 1794-1871 . **NCLC 16**

Koda Shigeyuki 1867-1947
See Rohan, Koda
See CA 121

Koestler, Arthur 1905-1983 ... **CLC 1, 3, 6, 8, 15, 33**
See CA 1-4R; 109; CANR 1, 33; CDBLB 1945-1960; DLBY 83; MTCW 1, 2

Kogawa, Joy Nozomi 1935- .. **CLC 78; DAC; DAM MST, MULT**
See CA 101; CANR 19, 62; MTCW 2; SATA 99

Kohout, Pavel 1928- .... **CLC 13**
See CA 45-48; CANR 3

Koizumi, Yakumo
See Hearn, (Patricio) Lafcadio (Tessima Carlos)

Kolmar, Gertrud 1894-1943 .... **TCLC 40**
See CA 167

Komunyakaa, Yusef 1947- .... **CLC 86, 94; BLCS**
See CA 147; CANR 83; DLB 120

Konrad, George
See Konrad, Gyoergy

Konrad, Gyoergy 1933- .... **CLC 4, 10, 73**
See CA 85-88

Konwicki, Tadeusz 1926- .... **CLC 8, 28, 54, 117**
See CA 101; CAAS 9; CANR 39, 59; MTCW 1

Koontz, Dean R(ay) 1945- .... **CLC 78; DAM NOV, POP**
See AAYA 9, 31; BEST 89:3, 90:2; CA 108; CANR 19, 36, 52; DA3; MTCW 1; SATA 92

Kopernik, Mikolaj
See Copernicus, Nicolaus

Kopit, Arthur (Lee) 1937- .... **CLC 1, 18, 33; DAM DRAM**
See AITN 1; CA 81-84; CABS 3; DLB 7; MTCW 1

Kops, Bernard 1926- .... **CLC 4**
See CA 5-8R; CANR 84; DLB 13

Kornbluth, C(yril) M. 1923-1958 .... **TCLC 8**
See CA 105; 160; DLB 8

Korolenko, V. G.
See Korolenko, Vladimir Galaktionovich

Korolenko, Vladimir
See Korolenko, Vladimir Galaktionovich

Korolenko, Vladimir G.
See Korolenko, Vladimir Galaktionovich

Korolenko, Vladimir Galaktionovich
1853-1921 .... **TCLC 22**
See CA 121

Korzybski, Alfred (Habdank Skarbek)
1879-1950 .... **TCLC 61**
See CA 123; 160

Kosinski, Jerzy (Nikodem)
1933-1991 ... **CLC 1, 2, 3, 6, 10, 15, 53, 70; DAM NOV**
See CA 17-20R; 134; CANR 9, 46; DA3; DLB 2; DLBY 82; MTCW 1, 2

Kostelanetz, Richard(Cory) 1940- ... **CLC 28**
See CA 13-16R; CAAS 8; CANR 38, 77

Kostrowitzki, Wilhelm Apollinaris de
1880-1918
See Apollinaire, Guillaume
See CA 104

Kotlowitz, Robert 1924- .... **CLC 4**
See CA 33-36R; CANR 36

Kotzebue, August (Friedrich Ferdinand) von
1761-1819 .... **NCLC 25**
See DLB 94

Kotzwinkle, William 1938- ..... **CLC 5, 14, 35**
See CA 45-48; CANR 3, 44, 84; CLR 6; DLB 173; MAICYA; SATA 24, 70

Kowna, Stancy
See Szymborska, Wislawa

Kozol, Jonathan 1936- .... **CLC 17**
See CA 61-64; CANR 16, 45

Kozoll, Michael 1940(?)- .... **CLC 35**

Kramer, Kathryn 19(?)- .... **CLC 34**

Kramer, Larry 1935- .. **CLC 42; DAM POP; DC 8**
See CA 124; 126; CANR 60

Krasicki, Ignacy 1735-1801 .... **NCLC 8**

Krasinski, Zygmunt 1812-1859 .... **NCLC 4**

Kraus, Karl 1874-1936 .... **TCLC 5**
See CA 104; DLB 118

Kreve (Mickevicius),Vincas
1882-1954 .... **TCLC 27**
See CA 170

Kristeva, Julia 1941- .... **CLC 77**
See CA 154

Kristofferson, Kris 1936- .... **CLC 26**
See CA 104

Krizanc, John 1956- .... **CLC 57**

Krleza, Miroslav 1893-1981 .... **CLC 8,114**
See CA 97-100; 105; CANR 50; DLB 147

Kroetsch, Robert 1927- .... **CLC 5, 23, 57; DAC; DAM POET**
See CA 17-20R; CANR 8, 38; DLB 53; MTCW 1

Kroetz, Franz
See Kroetz, Franz Xaver

Kroetz, Franz Xaver 1946- .... **CLC 41**
See CA 130

Kroker, Arthur (W.) 1945- .... **CLC 77**
See CA 161

Kropotkin, Peter (Aleksieevich) 1842-1921
TCLC 36
See CA 119

Krotkov, Yuri 1917- .... **CLC 19**
See CA 102

Krumb
See Crumb, R(obert)

Krumgold, Joseph (Quincy)
1908-1980 .... **CLC 12**
See CA 9-12R; 101; CANR 7; MAICYA; SATA 1, 48; SATA-Obit 23

Krumwitz
See Crumb, R(obert)

Krutch, JosephWood 1893-1970 .... **CLC 24**
See CA 1-4R; 25-28R; CANR 4; DLB 63, 206

Krutzch, Gus
See Eliot, T(homas) S(tearns)

Krylov, Ivan Andreevich
1768(?)-1844 .... **NCLC 1**
See DLB 150

Kubin, Alfred (Leopold Isidor) 1877-1959
TCLC 23
See CA 112; 149; DLB 81

Kubrick, Stanley 1928-1999 .... **CLC 16**
See AAYA 30; CA 81-84; 177; CANR 33; DLB 26

Kumin, Maxine (Winokur) 1925- ..... **CLC 5, 13, 28; DAM POET; PC 15**
See AITN 2; CA 1-4R; CAAS 8; CANR 1, 21, 69; DA3; DLB 5; MTCW 1, 2; SATA 12

Kundera, Milan 1929- . **CLC 4, 9, 19, 32, 68, 115; DAM NOV; SSC 24**
See AAYA 2; CA 85-88; CANR 19, 52, 74; DA3; MTCW 1, 2

Kunene, Mazisi (Raymond) 1930- ... **CLC 85**
See BW 1, 3; CA 125; CANR 81; DLB 117

Kunitz, Stanley (Jasspon) 1905- .. **CLC 6, 11, 14; PC 19**
See CA 41-44R; CANR 26, 57; DA3; DLB 48; INT CANR-26; MTCW 1, 2

Kunze, Reiner 1933- .... **CLC 10**
See CA 93-96; DLB 75

Kuprin, Aleksandr Ivanovich 1870-1938
TCLC 5
See CA 104

Kureishi, Hanif 1954(?)- .... **CLC 64**
See CA 139; DLB 194

Kurosawa, Akira 1910-1998 .... **CLC 16, 119; DAM MULT**
See AAYA 11; CA 101; 170; CANR 46

Kushner, Tony 1957(?)- .... **CLC 81; DAM DRAM; DC 10**
See CA 144; CANR 74; DA3; MTCW 2

Kuttner, Henry 1915-1958 .... **TCLC 10**
See Vance, Jack
See CA 107; 157; DLB 8

Kuzma, Greg 1944- .... **CLC 7**
See CA 33-36R; CANR 70

Kuzmin, Mikhail 1872(?)-1936 .... **TCLC 40**
See CA 170

Matthiessen, Peter 1927- ... **CLC 5, 7, 11, 32, 64; DAM NOV**
See AAYA 6; BEST 90:4; CA 9-12R; CANR 21, 50, 73; DA3; DLB 6, 173; MTCW 1, 2; SATA 27

Maturin, Charles Robert 1780(?)-1824 .... **NCLC 6**
See DLB 178

Matute (Ausejo), Ana Maria 1925- .. **CLC 11**
See CA 89-92; MTCW 1

Maugham, W. S.
See Maugham, W(illiam) Somerset

Maugham, W(illiam) Somerset 1874-1965 **CLC 1, 11, 15, 67, 93; DA; DAB; DAC; DAM DRAM, MST, NOV; SSC 8; WLC**
See CA 5-8R; 25-28R; CANR 40; CDBLB 1914-1945; DA3; DLB 10, 36, 77, 100, 162, 195; MTCW 1, 2; SATA 54

Maugham, William Somerset
See Maugham, W(illiam) Somerset

Maupassant, (Henri Rene Albert) Guy de 1850-1893 .... **NCLC 1, 42; DA; DAB; DAC; DAM MST; SSC 1; WLC**
See DA3; DLB 123

Maupin, Armistead 1944- .... **CLC 95;DAM POP**
See CA 125; 130; CANR 58; DA3; INT 130; MTCW 2

Maurhut, Richard
See Traven, B.

Mauriac, Claude 1914-1996 .... **CLC 9**
See CA 89-92; 152; DLB 83

Mauriac, Francois (Charles) 1885-1970 .... **CLC 4, 9, 56; SSC 24**
See CA 25-28; CAP 2; DLB 65; MTCW 1, 2

Mavor, Osborne Henry 1888-1951
See Bridie, James
See CA 104

Maxwell, William (Keepers, Jr.) 1908- .... **CLC 19**
See CA 93-96; CANR 54; DLBY 80; INT 93-96

May, Elaine 1932- .... **CLC 16**
See CA 124; 142; DLB 44

Mayakovski, Vladimir (Vladimirovich) 1893-1930 .... **TCLC 4, 18**
See CA 104; 158; MTCW 2

Mayhew, Henry 1812-1887 .... **NCLC 31**
See DLB 18, 55, 190

Mayle, Peter 1939(?)- .... **CLC 89**
See CA 139; CANR 64

Maynard, Joyce 1953- .... **CLC 23**
See CA 111; 129; CANR 64

Mayne, William (James Carter) 1928- .... **CLC 12**
See AAYA 20; CA 9-12R; CANR 37, 80; CLR 25; JRDA; MAICYA; SAAS 11; SATA 6, 68

Mayo, Jim
See L'Amour, Louis (Dearborn)

Maysles, Albert 1926- .... **CLC 16**
See CA 29-32R

Maysles, David 1932- .... **CLC 16**

Mazer, Norma Fox 1931- .... **CLC 26**
See AAYA 5; CA 69-72; CANR 12, 32, 66; CLR 23; JRDA; MAICYA; SAAS 1; SATA 24, 67, 105

Mazzini, Guiseppe 1805-1872 .... **NCLC 34**

McAlmon, Robert (Menzies) 1895-1956 **TCLC 97**
See CA 107; 168; DLB 4, 45; DLBD 15

McAuley, James Phillip 1917-1976 .. **CLC 45**
See CA 97-100

McBain, Ed
See Hunter, Evan

McBrien, William Augustine 1930- .. **CLC 44**
See CA 107

McCaffrey, Anne (Inez) 1926- .... **CLC 17; DAM NOV, POP**
See AAYA 6; AITN 2; BEST 89:2; CA 25-28R; CANR 15, 35, 55; CLR 49; DA3; DLB 8; JRDA; MAICYA; MTCW 1, 2; SAAS 11; SATA 8, 70

McCall, Nathan 1955(?)- .... **CLC 86**
See BW 3; CA 146

McCann, Arthur
See Campbell, John W(ood, Jr.)

McCann, Edson
See Pohl, Frederik

McCarthy, Charles, Jr. 1933-
See McCarthy, Cormac
See CANR 42, 69; DAM POP; DA3; MTCW 2

McCarthy, Cormac 1933- ...... **CLC 4, 57, 59, 101**
See McCarthy, Charles, Jr.
See DLB 6, 143; MTCW 2

McCarthy, Mary (Therese) 1912-1989 .. **CLC 1, 3, 5, 14, 24, 39, 59; SSC 24**
See CA 5-8R; 129; CANR 16, 50, 64; DA3; DLB 2; DLBY 81; INT CANR-16; MTCW 1, 2

McCartney, (James) Paul 1942- . **CLC 12, 35**
See CA 146

McCauley, Stephen (D.) 1955- .... **CLC 50**
See CA 141

McClure, Michael (Thomas) 1932- ... **CLC 6, 10**
See CA 21-24R; CANR 17, 46, 77; DLB 16

McCorkle, Jill (Collins) 1958- .... **CLC 51**
See CA 121; DLBY 87

McCourt, Frank 1930- .... **CLC 109**
See CA 157

McCourt, James 1941- .... **CLC 5**
See CA 57-60

McCourt, Malachy 1932- .... **CLC 119**

McCoy, Horace (Stanley) 1897-1955 .... **TCLC 28**
See CA 108; 155; DLB 9

McCrae, John 1872-1918 .... **TCLC 12**
See CA 109; DLB 92

McCreigh, James
See Pohl, Frederik

McCullers, (Lula) Carson (Smith) 1917-1967 **CLC 1, 4, 10, 12, 48, 100; DA; DAB; DAC; DAM MST, NOV; SSC 9, 24;WLC**
See AAYA 21; CA 5-8R; 25-28R; CABS 1, 3; CANR 18; CDALB 1941-1968; DA3; DLB 2, 7, 173; MTCW 1, 2; SATA 27

McCulloch, John Tyler
See Burroughs, Edgar Rice

McCullough, Colleen 1938(?)- .... **CLC 27, 107; DAM NOV, POP**
See CA 81-84; CANR 17, 46, 67; DA3; MTCW 1, 2

McDermott, Alice 1953- .... **CLC 90**
See CA 109; CANR 40

McElroy, Joseph 1930- .... **CLC 5, 47**
See CA 17-20R

McEwan, Ian (Russell) 1948- .... **CLC 13, 66; DAM NOV**
See BEST 90:4; CA 61-64; CANR 14, 41, 69; DLB 14, 194; MTCW 1, 2

McFadden, David 1940- .... **CLC 48**
See CA 104; DLB 60; INT 104

McFarland, Dennis 1950- .... **CLC 65**
See CA 165

McGahern, John 1934- .... **CLC 5, 9, 48;SSC 17**
See CA 17-20R; CANR 29, 68; DLB 14; MTCW 1

McGinley, Patrick (Anthony) 1937- . **CLC 41**
See CA 120; 127; CANR 56; INT 127

McGinley, Phyllis 1905-1978 .... **CLC 14**
See CA 9-12R; 77-80; CANR 19; DLB 11, 48; SATA 2, 44; SATA-Obit 24

McGinniss, Joe 1942- .... **CLC 32**
See AITN 2; BEST 89:2; CA 25-28R; CANR 26, 70; DLB 185; INT CANR-26

McGivern, Maureen Daly
See Daly, Maureen

McGrath, Patrick 1950- .... **CLC 55**
See CA 136; CANR 65

McGrath, Thomas (Matthew) 1916-1990 **CLC 28, 59; DAM POET**
See CA 9-12R; 132; CANR 6, 33; MTCW 1; SATA 41; SATA-Obit 66

McGuane, Thomas (Francis III) 1939- .... **CLC 3, 7, 18, 45**
See AITN 2; CA 49-52; CANR 5, 24, 49; DLB 2, 212; DLBY 80; INT CANR-24; MTCW 1

McGuckian, Medbh 1950- .... **CLC 48; DAM POET; PC 27**
See CA 143; DLB 40

McHale, Tom 1942(?)-1982 .... **CLC 3, 5**
See AITN 1; CA 77-80; 106

McIlvanney, William 1936- .... **CLC 42**
See CA 25-28R; CANR 61; DLB 14, 207

McIlwraith, Maureen Mollie Hunter
See Hunter, Mollie
See SATA 2

McInerney, Jay 1955- ..... **CLC 34, 112;DAM POP**
See AAYA 18; CA 116; 123; CANR 45, 68; DA3; INT 123; MTCW 2

McIntyre, Vonda N(eel) 1948- .... **CLC 18**
See CA 81-84; CANR 17, 34, 69; MTCW 1

McKay, Claude .... **TCLC 7, 41; BLC 3; DAB;PC 2**
See McKay, Festus Claudius
See DLB 4, 45, 51, 117

McKay, Festus Claudius 1889-1948
See McKay, Claude
See BW 1, 3; CA 104; 124; CANR 73; DA; DAC; DAM MST, MULT, NOV, POET; MTCW 1, 2; WLC

McKuen, Rod 1933- .... **CLC 1, 3**
See AITN 1; CA 41-44R; CANR 40

McLoughlin, R. B.
See Mencken, H(enry) L(ouis)

McLuhan, (Herbert) Marshall 1911-1980 **CLC 37, 83**
See CA 9-12R; 102; CANR 12, 34, 61; DLB 88; INT CANR-12; MTCW 1, 2

McMillan, Terry (L.) 1951- .... **CLC 50, 61, 112; BLCS; DAM MULT, NOV, POP**
See AAYA 21; BW 2, 3; CA 140; CANR 60; DA3; MTCW 2

McMurtry, Larry (Jeff) 1936- .. **CLC 2, 3, 7, 11, 27, 44; DAM NOV, POP**
See AAYA 15; AITN 2; BEST 89:2; CA 5-8R; CANR 19, 43, 64; CDALB 1968-1988; DA3; DLB 2, 143; DLBY 80, 87; MTCW 1, 2

McNally, T. M. 1961- .... **CLC 82**

McNally, Terrence 1939- ... **CLC 4, 7, 41, 91; DAM DRAM**
See CA 45-48; CANR 2, 56; DA3; DLB 7; MTCW 2

McNamer, Deirdre 1950- .... **CLC 70**

McNeal, Tom .... **CLC 119**

McNeile, Herman Cyril 1888-1937
See Sapper
See DLB 77

McNickle, (William) D'Arcy 1904-1977 .... **CLC 89; DAM MULT**
See CA 9-12R; 85-88; CANR 5, 45; DLB 175, 212; NNAL; SATA-Obit 22

McPhee, John (Angus) 1931- .... **CLC 36**
See BEST 90:1; CA 65-68; CANR 20, 46, 64, 69; DLB 185; MTCW 1, 2

Morgenstern, Christian 1871-1914 .. **TCLC 8**
   See CA 105.
Morgenstern, S.
   See Goldman, William (W.)
Moricz, Zsigmond 1879-1942 .... **TCLC 33**
   See CA 165
Morike, Eduard (Friedrich) 1804-1875
   NCLC 10
   See DLB 133
Moritz, Karl Philipp 1756-1793 .... **LC 2**
   See DLB 94
Morland, Peter Henry
   See Faust, Frederick (Schiller)
Morley, Christopher (Darlington) 1890-1957
   TCLC 87
   See CA 112; DLB 9
Morren, Theophil
   See Hofmannsthal, Hugo von
Morris, Bill 1952- .... **CLC 76**
Morris, Julian
   See West, Morris L.(anglo)
Morris, Steveland Judkins 1950(?)-
   See Wonder, Stevie
   See CA 111
Morris, William 1834-1896 .... **NCLC 4**
   See CDBLB 1832-1890; DLB 18, 35, 57,
   156, 178, 184
Morris, Wright 1910-1998 .. **CLC 1, 3, 7, 18,**
   37
   See CA 9-12R; 167; CANR 21, 81; DLB 2,
   206; DLBY 81; MTCW 1, 2
Morrison, Arthur 1863-1945 .... **TCLC 72**
   See CA 120; 157; DLB 70, 135, 197
Morrison, Chloe Anthony Wofford
   See Morrison, Toni
Morrison, James Douglas 1943-1971
   See Morrison, Jim
   See CA 73-76; CANR 40
Morrison, Jim .... **CLC 17**
   See Morrison, James Douglas
Morrison, Toni 1931- . **CLC 4, 10, 22, 55, 81,**
   87; BLC 3; DA; DAB; DAC; DAM
   MST, MULT, NOV, POP
   See AAYA 1, 22; BW 2, 3; CA 29-32R;
   CANR 27, 42, 67; CDALB 1968-1988;
   DA3; DLB 6, 33, 143; DLBY 81; MTCW
   1, 2; SATA 57
Morrison, Van 1945- .... **CLC 21**
   See CA 116; 168
Morrissy, Mary 1958- .... **CLC 99**
Mortimer, John (Clifford) 1923- ..... **CLC 28,**
   43; DAM DRAM, POP
   See CA 13-16R; CANR 21, 69; CDBLB
   1960 to Present; DA3; DLB 13; INT
   CANR-21; MTCW 1, 2
Mortimer, Penelope(Ruth) 1918- .... **CLC 5**
   See CA 57-60; CANR 45
Morton, Anthony
   See Creasey, John
Mosca, Gaetano 1858-1941 .... **TCLC 75**
Mosher, Howard Frank 1943- .... **CLC 62**
   See CA 139; CANR 65
Mosley, Nicholas 1923- .... **CLC 43, 70**
   See CA 69-72; CANR 41, 60; DLB 14, 207
Mosley, Walter 1952- .... **CLC 97; BLCS;**
   DAM MULT, POP
   See AAYA 17; BW 2; CA 142; CANR 57;
   DA3; MTCW 2
Moss, Howard 1922-1987 ...... **CLC 7, 14, 45,**
   50; DAM POET
   See CA 1-4R; 123; CANR 1, 44; DLB 5
Mossgiel, Rab
   See Burns, Robert
Motion, Andrew (Peter) 1952- .... **CLC 47**
   See CA 146; DLB 40
Motley, Willard (Francis)
   1909-1965 .... **CLC 18**
   See BW 1; CA 117; 106; DLB 76, 143

Motoori, Norinaga 1730-1801 .... **NCLC 45**
Mott, Michael (Charles Alston)
   1930- .... **CLC 15, 34**
   See CA 5-8R; CAAS 7; CANR 7, 29
Mountain Wolf Woman 1884-1960 .. **CLC 92**
   See CA 144; NNAL
Moure, Erin 1955- .... **CLC 88**
   See CA 113; DLB 60
Mowat, Farley (McGill) 1921- .... **CLC 26;**
   DAC; DAM MST
   See AAYA 1; CA 1-4R; CANR 4, 24, 42,
   68; CLR 20; DLB 68; INT CANR-24;
   JRDA; MAICYA; MTCW 1, 2; SATA 3,
   55
Mowatt, Anna Cora 1819-1870 ..... **NCLC 74**
Moyers, Bill 1934- .... **CLC 74**
   See AITN 2; CA 61-64; CANR 31, 52
Mphahlele, Es'kia
   See Mphahlele, Ezekiel
   See DLB 125
Mphahlele, Ezekiel 1919- ... **CLC 25; BLC 3;**
   DAM MULT
   See Mphahlele, Es'kia
   See BW 2, 3; CA 81-84; CANR 26, 76;
   DA3; MTCW 2
Mqhayi, S(amuel) E(dward) K(runeLoliwe)
   1875-1945 .... **TCLC 25; BLC 3;DAM**
   MULT
   See CA 153
Mrozek, Slawomir 1930- .... **CLC 3, 13**
   See CA 13-16R; CAAS 10; CANR 29;
   MTCW 1
Mrs. Belloc-Lowndes
   See Lowndes, Marie Adelaide (Belloc)
Mtwa, Percy (?)- .... **CLC 47**
Mueller, Lisel 1924- .... **CLC 13, 51**
   See CA 93-96; DLB 105
Muir, Edwin 1887-1959 .... **TCLC 2, 87**
   See CA 104; DLB 20, 100, 191
Muir, John 1838-1914 .... **TCLC 28**
   See CA 165; DLB 186
Mujica Lainez, Manuel 1910-1984 ... **CLC 31**
   See Lainez, Manuel Mujica
   See CA 81-84; 112; CANR 32; HW 1
Mukherjee, Bharati 1940- .... **CLC 53, 115;**
   DAM NOV
   See BEST 89:2; CA 107; CANR 45, 72;
   DLB 60; MTCW 1, 2
Muldoon, Paul 1951- .... **CLC 32, 72;DAM**
   POET
   See CA 113; 129; CANR 52; DLB 40; INT
   129
Mulisch, Harry 1927- .... **CLC 42**
   See CA 9-12R; CANR 6, 26, 56
Mull, Martin 1943- .... **CLC 17**
   See CA 105
Muller, Wilhelm .... **NCLC 73**
Mulock, Dinah Maria
   See Craik, Dinah Maria (Mulock)
Munford, Robert 1737(?)-1783 .... **LC 5**
   See DLB 31
Mungo, Raymond 1946- .... **CLC 72**
   See CA 49-52; CANR 2
Munro, Alice 1931- .... **CLC 6, 10, 19, 50, 95;**
   DAC; DAM MST, NOV; SSC 3;
   WLCS
   See AITN 2; CA 33-36R; CANR 33, 53,
   75; DA3; DLB 53; MTCW 1, 2; SATA 29
Munro, H(ector) H(ugh) 1870-1916
   See Saki
   See CA 104; 130; CDBLB 1890-1914; DA;
   DAB; DAC; DAM MST, NOV; DA3;
   DLB 34, 162; MTCW 1, 2; WLC
Murdoch, (Jean) Iris 1919-1999 ... **CLC 1, 2,**
   3, 4, 6, 8, 11, 15, 22, 31, 51; DAB;
   DAC; DAM MST, NOV
   See CA 13-16R; 179; CANR 8, 43, 68; CD-
   BLB 1960 to Present; DA3; DLB 14, 194;
   INT CANR-8; MTCW 1, 2

Murfree, Mary Noailles 1850-1922 ... **SSC 22**
   See CA 122; 176; DLB 12, 74
Murnau, Friedrich Wilhelm
   See Plumpe, Friedrich Wilhelm
Murphy, Richard 1927- .... **CLC 41**
   See CA 29-32R; DLB 40
Murphy, Sylvia 1937- .... **CLC 34**
   See CA 121
Murphy, Thomas (Bernard) 1935- ... **CLC 51**
   See CA 101
Murray, Albert L. 1916- .... **CLC 73**
   See BW 2; CA 49-52; CANR 26, 52, 78;
   DLB 38
Murray, Judith Sargent
   1751-1820 .... **NCLC 63**
   See DLB 37, 200
Murray, Les(lie) A(llan) 1938- .... **CLC 40;**
   DAM POET
   See CA 21-24R; CANR 11, 27, 56
Murry, J. Middleton
   See Murry, John Middleton
Murry, John Middleton
   1889-1957 .... **TCLC 16**
   See CA 118; DLB 149
Musgrave, Susan 1951- .... **CLC 13, 54**
   See CA 69-72; CANR 45, 84
Musil, Robert (Edler von)
   1880-1942 ... **TCLC 12, 68; SSC 18**
   See CA 109; CANR 55, 84; DLB 81, 124;
   MTCW 2
Muske, Carol 1945- .... **CLC 90**
   See Muske-Dukes, Carol (Anne)
Muske-Dukes, Carol (Anne) 1945-
   See Muske, Carol
   See CA 65-68; CANR 32, 70
Musset, (Louis Charles) Alfredde 1810-1857
   NCLC 7
   See DLB 192
Mussolini, Benito (Amilcare Andrea)
   1883-1945 .... **TCLC 96**
   See CA 116
My Brother's Brother
   See Chekhov, Anton (Pavlovich)
Myers, L(eopold)H(amilton) 1881-1944
   TCLC 59
   See CA 157; DLB 15
Myers, Walter Dean 1937- ..... **CLC 35; BLC**
   3; DAM MULT, NOV
   See AAYA 4, 23; BW 2; CA 33-36R; CANR
   20, 42, 67; CLR 4, 16, 35; DLB 33; INT
   CANR-20; JRDA; MAICYA; MTCW 2;
   SAAS 2; SATA 41, 71, 109; SATA-Brief
   27
Myers, Walter M.
   See Myers, Walter Dean
Myles, Symon
   See Follett, Ken(neth Martin)
Nabokov, Vladimir (Vladimirovich)
   1899-1977 .... **CLC 1, 2, 3, 6, 8, 11, 15,**
   23, 44, 46, 64; DA; DAB; DAC; DAM
   MST, NOV; SSC 11; WLC
   See CA 5-8R; 69-72; CANR 20; CDALB
   1941-1968; DA3; DLB 2; DLBD 3;
   DLBY 80, 91; MTCW 1, 2
Nagai Kafu 1879-1959 .... **TCLC 51**
   See Nagai Sokichi
   See DLB 180
Nagai Sokichi 1879-1959
   See Nagai Kafu
   See CA 117
Nagy, Laszlo 1925-1978 .... **CLC 7**
   See CA 129; 112
Naidu, Sarojini 1879-1943 .... **TCLC 80**
Naipaul, Shiva(dhar Srinivasa) 1945-1985
   CLC 32, 39; DAM NOV
   See CA 110; 112; 116; CANR 33; DA3;
   DLB 157; DLBY 85; MTCW 1, 2
Naipaul, V(idiadhar) S(urajprasad) 1932-
   CLC 4, 7, 9, 13, 18, 37, 105; DAB;

411

Pirandello, Luigi 1867-1936 ...... TCLC 4, 29;
DA; DAB; DAC; DAM DRAM, MST;
DC 5; SSC 22; WLC
See CA 104; 153; DA3; MTCW 2

Pirsig, Robert M(aynard) 1928- ... CLC 4, 6,
73; DAM POP
See CA 53-56; CANR 42, 74; DA3; MTCW
1, 2; SATA 39

Pisarev, Dmitry Ivanovich
1840-1868 .... NCLC 25

Pix, Mary (Griffith) 1666-1709 .... LC 8
See DLB 80

Pixerecourt, (Rene Charles) Guilbert de
1773-1844 .... NCLC 39
See DLB 192

Plaatje, Sol(omon) T(shekisho) 1876-1932
TCLC 73; BLCS
See BW 2, 3; CA 141; CANR 79

Plaidy, Jean
See Hibbert, Eleanor Alice Burford

Planche, James Robinson
1796-1880 .... NCLC 42

Plant, Robert 1948- .... CLC 12

Plante, David (Robert) 1940- ...... CLC 7, 23,
38; DAM NOV
See CA 37-40R; CANR 12, 36, 58, 82;
DLBY 83; INT CANR-12; MTCW 1

Plath, Sylvia 1932-1963 ..... CLC 1, 2, 3, 5, 9,
11, 14, 17, 50, 51, 62, 111; DA; DAB;
DAC; DAM MST, POET; PC 1; WLC
See AAYA 13; CA 19-20; CANR 34; CAP
2; CDALB 1941-1968; DA3; DLB 5, 6,
152; MTCW 1, 2; SATA 96

Plato 428(?)B.C.-348(?)B.C. ... CMLC 8; DA;
DAB; DAC; DAM MST; WLCS
See DA3; DLB 176

Platonov, Andrei .... TCLC 14
See Klimentov, Andrei Platonovich

Platt, Kin 1911- .... CLC 26
See AAYA 11; CA 17-20R; CANR 11;
JRDA; SAAS 17; SATA 21, 86

Plautus c. 251B.C.-184B.C. ... CMLC 24; DC
6
See DLB 211

Plick et Plock
See Simenon, Georges (Jacques Christian)

Plimpton, George (Ames) 1927- .... CLC 36
See AITN 1; CA 21-24R; CANR 32, 70;
DLB 185; MTCW 1, 2; SATA 10

Pliny the Elder c. 23-79 .... CMLC 23
See DLB 211

Plomer, William Charles Franklin 1903-1973
CLC 4, 8
See CA 21-22; CANR 34; CAP 2; DLB 20,
162, 191; MTCW 1; SATA 24

Plowman, Piers
See Kavanagh, Patrick (Joseph)

Plum, J.
See Wodehouse, P(elham) G(renville)

Plumly, Stanley (Ross) 1939- .... CLC 33
See CA 108; 110; DLB 5, 193; INT 110

Plumpe, Friedrich Wilhelm
1888-1931 .... TCLC 53
See CA 112

Po Chu-i 772-846 .... CMLC 24

Poe, Edgar Allan 1809-1849 ..... NCLC 1, 16,
55, 78; DA; DAB; DAC; DAM MST,
POET; PC 1; SSC 34; WLC
See AAYA 14; CDALB 1640-1865; DA3;
DLB 3, 59, 73, 74; SATA 23

Poet of Titchfield Street, The
See Pound, Ezra (Weston Loomis)

Pohl, Frederik 1919- .... CLC 18;SSC 25
See AAYA 24; CA 61-64; CAAS 1; CANR
11, 37, 81; DLB 8; INT CANR-11;
MTCW 1, 2; SATA 24

Poirier, Louis 1910-
See Gracq, Julien
See CA 122; 126

Poitier, Sidney 1927- .... CLC 26
See BW 1; CA 117

Polanski, Roman 1933- .... CLC 16
See CA 77-80

Poliakoff, Stephen 1952- .... CLC 38
See CA 106; DLB 13

Police, The
See Copeland, Stewart (Armstrong); Sum-
mers, Andrew James; Sumner, Gordon
Matthew

Polidori, JohnWilliam 1795-1821 .. NCLC 51
See DLB 116

Pollitt, Katha 1949- .... CLC 28, 122
See CA 120; 122; CANR 66; MTCW 1, 2

Pollock, (Mary) Sharon 1936- .... CLC 50;
DAC; DAM DRAM, MST
See CA 141; DLB 60

Polo, Marco 1254-1324 .... CMLC 15

Polonsky, Abraham (Lincoln)
1910- .... CLC 92
See CA 104; DLB 26; INT 104

Polybius c. 200B.C.-c.118B.C. .... CMLC 17
See DLB 176

Pomerance, Bernard 1940- .... CLC 13;DAM
DRAM
See CA 101; CANR 49

Ponge, Francis (Jean Gaston Alfred)
1899-1988 .... CLC 6, 18; DAM POET
See CA 85-88; 126; CANR 40

Poniatowska, Elena 1933-
See CA 101; CANR 32, 66; DAM MULT;
DLB 113; HLC 2; HW 1, 2

Pontoppidan, Henrik 1857-1943 .... TCLC 29
See CA 170

Poole, Josephine .... CLC 17
See Helyar, Jane Penelope Josephine
See SAAS 2; SATA 5

Popa, Vasko 1922-1991 .... CLC 19
See CA 112; 148; DLB 181

Pope, Alexander 1688-1744 .... LC 3; DA;
DAB; DAC; DAM MST, POET; PC
26; WLC
See CDBLB 1660-1789; DA3; DLB 95, 101

Porter, Connie (Rose) 1959(?)- .... CLC 70
See BW 2, 3; CA 142; SATA 81

Porter, Gene(va Grace)Stratton 1863(?)-1924
TCLC 21
See CA 112

Porter, Katherine Anne 1890-1980 ... CLC 1,
3, 7, 10, 13, 15, 27, 101; DA; DAB;
DAC; DAM MST, NOV; SSC 4, 31
See AITN 2; CA 1-4R; 101; CANR 1, 65;
CDALBS; DA3; DLB 4, 9, 102; DLBD
12; DLBY 80; MTCW 1, 2; SATA 39;
SATA-Obit 23

Porter, Peter (Neville Frederick)
1929- .... CLC 5, 13, 33
See CA 85-88; DLB 40

Porter, William Sydney 1862-1910
See Henry, O.
See CA 104; 131; CDALB 1865-1917; DA;
DAB; DAC; DAM MST; DA3; DLB 12,
78, 79; MTCW 1, 2; YABC 2

Portillo (y Pacheco), Jose Lopez
See Lopez Portillo (y Pacheco), Jose

Portillo Trambley, Estela 1927-1998
See CANR 32; DAM MULT; DLB 209;
HLC 2; HW 1

Post, Melville Davisson
1869-1930 .... TCLC 39
See CA 110

Potok, Chaim 1929- ... CLC 2, 7, 14, 26, 112;
DAM NOV
See AAYA 15; AITN 1, 2; CA 17-20R;
CANR 19, 35, 64; DA3; DLB 28, 152;
INT CANR-19; MTCW 1, 2; SATA 33,
106

Potter, (Helen) Beatrix 1866-1943
See Webb, (Martha) Beatrice (Potter)
See MAICYA; MTCW 2

Potter, Dennis (Christopher George)
1935-1994 .... CLC 58, 86
See CA 107; 145; CANR 33, 61; MTCW 1

Pound, Ezra (Weston Loomis) 1885-1972
CLC 1, 2, 3, 4, 5, 7, 10, 13, 18, 34, 48,
50, 112; DA; DAB; DAC; DAM MST,
POET; PC 4; WLC
See CA 5-8R; 37-40R; CANR 40; CDALB
1917-1929; DA3; DLB 4, 45, 63; DLBD
15; MTCW 1, 2

Povod, Reinaldo 1959-1994 .... CLC 44
See CA 136; 146; CANR 83

Powell, Adam Clayton, Jr.
1908-1972 .... CLC 89; BLC 3; DAM
MULT
See BW 1, 3; CA 102; 33-36R

Powell, Anthony (Dymoke) 1905- . CLC 1, 3,
7, 9, 10, 31
See CA 1-4R; CANR 1, 32, 62; CDBLB
1945-1960; DLB 15; MTCW 1, 2

Powell, Dawn 1897-1965 .... CLC 66
See CA 5-8R; DLBY 97

Powell, Padgett 1952- .... CLC 34
See CA 126; CANR 63

Power, Susan 1961- .... CLC 91

Powers, J(ames) F(arl) 1917-1999 ..... CLC 1,
4, 8, 57; SSC 4
See CA 1-4R; 181; CANR 2, 61; DLB 130;
MTCW 1

Powers, John J(ames) 1945-
See Powers, John R.
See CA 69-72

Powers, John R. .... CLC 66
See Powers, John J(ames)

Powers, Richard (S.) 1957- .... CLC 93
See CA 148; CANR 80

Pownall, David 1938- .... CLC 10
See CA 89-92, 180; CAAS 18; CANR 49;
DLB 14

Powys, John Cowper 1872-1963 ... CLC 7, 9,
15, 46, 125
See CA 85-88; DLB 15; MTCW 1, 2

Powys, T(heodore) F(rancis) 1875-1953
TCLC 9
See CA 106; DLB 36, 162

Prado (Calvo),Pedro 1886-1952 ..... TCLC 75
See CA 131; HW 1

Prager, Emily 1952- .... CLC 56

Pratt, E(dwin) J(ohn)
1883(?)-1964 .... CLC 19; DAC; DAM
POET
See CA 141; 93-96; CANR 77; DLB 92

Premchand .... TCLC 21
See Srivastava, Dhanpat Rai

Preussler, Otfried 1923- .... CLC 17
See CA 77-80; SATA 24

Prevert, Jacques (Henri Marie) 1900-1977
CLC 15
See CA 77-80; 69-72; CANR 29, 61;
MTCW 1; SATA-Obit 30

Prevost, Abbe (Antoine Francois) 1697-1763
LC 1

Price, (Edward) Reynolds 1933- ... CLC 3, 6,
13, 43, 50, 63; DAM NOV; SSC 22
See CA 1-4R; CANR 1, 37, 57; DLB 2; INT
CANR-37

Price, Richard 1949- .... CLC 6, 12
See CA 49-52; CANR 3; DLBY 81

Prichard, Katharine Susannah 1883-1969
CLC 46
See CA 11-12; CANR 33; CAP 1; MTCW
1; SATA 66

Richardson, John 1796-1852 .... **NCLC 55; DAC**
See DLB 99

Richardson, Samuel 1689-1761 ...... **LC 1, 44; DA; DAB; DAC; DAM MST, NOV; WLC**
See CDBLB 1660-1789; DLB 39

Richler, Mordecai 1931- ...... **CLC 3, 5, 9, 13, 18, 46, 70; DAC; DAM MST, NOV**
See AITN 1; CA 65-68; CANR 31, 62; CLR 17; DLB 53; MAICYA; MTCW 1, 2; SATA 44, 98; SATA-Brief 27

Richter, Conrad (Michael) 1890-1968 .... **CLC 30**
See AAYA 21; CA 5-8R; 25-28R; CANR 23; DLB 9, 212; MTCW 1, 2; SATA 3

Ricostranza, Tom
See Ellis, Trey

Riddell, Charlotte 1832-1906 .... **TCLC 40**
See CA 165; DLB 156

Ridgway, Keith 1965- .... **CLC 119**
See CA 172

Riding, Laura .... **CLC 3, 7**
See Jackson, Laura (Riding)

Riefenstahl, Berta Helene Amalia 1902-
See Riefenstahl, Leni
See CA 108

Riefenstahl, Leni .... **CLC 16**
See Riefenstahl, Berta Helene Amalia

Riffe, Ernest
See Bergman, (Ernst) Ingmar

Riggs, (Rolla) Lynn 1899-1954 ..... **TCLC 56; DAM MULT**
See CA 144; DLB 175; NNAL

Riis, Jacob A(ugust) 1849-1914 ..... **TCLC 80**
See CA 113; 168; DLB 23

Riley, James Whitcomb 1849-1916 .... **TCLC 51; DAM POET**
See CA 118; 137; MAICYA; SATA 17

Riley, Tex
See Creasey, John

Rilke, Rainer Maria 1875-1926 .. **TCLC 1, 6, 19; DAM POET; PC 2**
See CA 104; 132; CANR 62; DA3; DLB 81; MTCW 1, 2

Rimbaud, (Jean Nicolas) Arthur 1854-1891 **NCLC 4, 35; DA; DAB; DAC; DAM MST, POET; PC 3; WLC**
See DA3

Rinehart, Mary Roberts 1876-1958 .... **TCLC 52**
See CA 108; 166

Ringmaster, The
See Mencken, H(enry) L(ouis)

Ringwood, Gwen(dolyn Margaret) Pharis 1910-1984 .... **CLC 48**
See CA 148; 112; DLB 88

Rio, Michel 19(?)- .... **CLC 43**

Ritsos, Giannes
See Ritsos, Yannis

Ritsos, Yannis 1909-1990 .... **CLC 6, 13, 31**
See CA 77-80; 133; CANR 39, 61; MTCW 1

Ritter, Erika 1948(?)- .... **CLC 52**

Rivera, Jose Eustasio 1889-1928 ... **TCLC 35**
See CA 162; HW 1, 2

Rivera, Tomas 1935-1984
See CA 49-52; CANR 32; DLB 82; HLCS 2; HW 1

Rivers, Conrad Kent 1933-1968 .... **CLC 1**
See BW 1; CA 85-88; DLB 41

Rivers, Elfrida
See Bradley, Marion Zimmer

Riverside, John
See Heinlein, Robert A(nson)

Rizal, Jose 1861-1896 .... **NCLC 27**

Roa Bastos, Augusto (Antonio) 1917- .... **CLC 45; DAM MULT; HLC 2**
See CA 131; DLB 113; HW 1

Robbe-Grillet, Alain 1922- .... **CLC 1, 2, 4, 6, 8, 10, 14, 43**
See CA 9-12R; CANR 33, 65; DLB 83; MTCW 1, 2

Robbins, Harold 1916-1997 ..... **CLC 5; DAM NOV**
See CA 73-76; 162; CANR 26, 54; DA3; MTCW 1, 2

Robbins, Thomas Eugene 1936-
See Robbins, Tom
See CA 81-84; CANR 29, 59; DAM NOV, POP; DA3; MTCW 1, 2

Robbins, Tom .... **CLC 9, 32, 64**
See Robbins, Thomas Eugene
See AAYA 32; BEST 90:3; DLBY 80; MTCW 2

Robbins, Trina 1938- .... **CLC 21**
See CA 128

Roberts, Charles G(eorge) D(ouglas) 1860-1943 .... **TCLC 8**
See CA 105; CLR 33; DLB 92; SATA 88; SATA-Brief 29

Roberts, Elizabeth Madox 1886-1941 .... **TCLC 68**
See CA 111; 166; DLB 9, 54, 102; SATA 33; SATA-Brief 27

Roberts, Kate 1891-1985 .... **CLC 15**
See CA 107; 116

Roberts, Keith (John Kingston) 1935- .... **CLC 14**
See CA 25-28R, CANR 46

Roberts, Kenneth (Lewis) 1885-1957 .... **TCLC 23**
See CA 109; DLB 9

Roberts, Michele (B.) 1949- .... **CLC 48**
See CA 115; CANR 58

Robertson, Ellis
See Ellison, Harlan (Jay); Silverberg, Robert

Robertson, Thomas William 1829-1871 **NCLC 35; DAM DRAM**

Robeson, Kenneth
See Dent, Lester

Robinson, Edwin Arlington 1869-1935 ... **TCLC 5; DA; DAC; DAM MST, POET; PC 1**
See CA 104; 133; CDALB 1865-1917; DLB 54; MTCW 1, 2

Robinson, Henry Crabb 1775-1867 .... **NCLC 15**
See DLB 107

Robinson, Jill 1936- .... **CLC 10**
See CA 102; INT 102

Robinson, Kim Stanley 1952- .... **CLC 34**
See AAYA 26; CA 126; SATA 109

Robinson, Lloyd
See Silverberg, Robert

Robinson, Marilynne 1944- .... **CLC 25**
See CA 116; CANR 80; DLB 206

Robinson, Smokey .... **CLC 21**
See Robinson, William, Jr.

Robinson, William, Jr. 1940-
See Robinson, Smokey
See CA 116

Robison, Mary 1949- .... **CLC 42, 98**
See CA 113; 116; DLB 130; INT 116

Rod, Edouard 1857-1910 .... **TCLC 52**

Roddenberry, Eugene Wesley 1921-1991
See Roddenberry, Gene
See CA 110; 135; CANR 37; SATA 45; SATA-Obit 69

Roddenberry, Gene .... **CLC 17**
See Roddenberry, Eugene Wesley
See AAYA 5; SATA-Obit 69

Rodgers, Mary 1931- .... **CLC 12**
See CA 49-52; CANR 8, 55; CLR 20; INT CANR-8; JRDA; MAICYA; SATA 8

Rodgers, W(illiam) R(obert) 1909-1969 .... **CLC 7**
See CA 85-88; DLB 20

Rodman, Eric
See Silverberg, Robert

Rodman, Howard 1920(?)-1985 .... **CLC 65**
See CA 118

Rodman, Maia
See Wojciechowska, Maia (Teresa)

Rodo, Jose Enrique 1872(?)-1917
See CA 178; HLCS 2; HW 2

Rodriguez, Claudio 1934- .... **CLC 10**
See DLB 134

Rodriguez, Richard 1944-
See CA 110; CANR 66; DAM MULT; DLB 82; HLC 2; HW 1, 2

Roelvaag, O(le) E(dvart) 1876-1931 .... **TCLC 17**
See CA 117; 171; DLB 9

Roethke, Theodore (Huebner) 1908-1963 **CLC 1, 3, 8, 11, 19, 46, 101; DAM POET; PC 15**
See CA 81-84; CABS 2; CDALB 1941-1968; DA3; DLB 5, 206; MTCW 1, 2

Rogers, Samuel 1763-1855 .... **NCLC 69**
See DLB 93

Rogers, Thomas Hunton 1927- .... **CLC 57**
See CA 89-92; INT 89-92

Rogers, Will(iam Penn Adair) 1879-1935 **TCLC 8, 71; DAM MULT**
See CA 105; 144; DA3; DLB 11; MTCW 2; NNAL

Rogin, Gilbert 1929- .... **CLC 18**
See CA 65-68; CANR 15

Rohan, Koda .... **TCLC 22**
See Koda Shigeyuki

Rohlfs, Anna Katharine Green
See Green, Anna Katharine

Rohmer, Eric .... **CLC 16**
See Scherer, Jean-Marie Maurice

Rohmer, Sax .... **TCLC 28**
See Ward, Arthur Henry Sarsfield
See DLB 70

Roiphe, Anne (Richardson) 1935- .. **CLC 3, 9**
See CA 89-92; CANR 45, 73; DLBY 80; INT 89-92

Rojas, Fernando de 1465-1541 .... **LC 23; HLCS 1**

Rojas, Gonzalo 1917-
See HLCS 2; HW 2

Rojas, Gonzalo 1917-
See CA 178; HLCS 2

Rolfe, Frederick (William Serafino Austin Lewis Mary) 1860-1913 .... **TCLC 12**
See CA 107; DLB 34, 156

Rolland, Romain 1866-1944 .... **TCLC 23**
See CA 118; DLB 65

Rolle, Richard c. 1300-c.1349 .... **CMLC 21**
See DLB 146

Rolvaag, O(le) E(dvart)
See Roelvaag, O(le) E(dvart)

Romain Arnaud, Saint
See Aragon, Louis

Romains, Jules 1885-1972 .... **CLC 7**
See CA 85-88; CANR 34; DLB 65; MTCW 1

Romero, Jose Ruben 1890-1952 .... **TCLC 14**
See CA 114; 131; HW 1

Ronsard, Pierre de 1524-1585 ..... **LC 54; PC 11**

Rooke, Leon 1934- ... **CLC 25, 34; DAM POP**
See CA 25-28R; CANR 23, 53

Roosevelt, Franklin Delano 1882-1945 .... **TCLC 93**
See CA 116; 173

Sevigne, Marie (de Rabutin-Chantal)
    Marquise de 1626-1696 .... **LC 11**
Sewall, Samuel 1652-1730 .... **LC 38**
    See DLB 24
Sexton, Anne (Harvey) 1928-1974 ..... **CLC 2,
    4, 6, 8, 10, 15, 53; DA; DAB; DAC;
    DAM MST, POET; PC 2; WLC**
    See CA 1-4R; 53-56; CABS 2; CANR 3,
    36; CDALB 1941-1968; DA3; DLB 5,
    169; MTCW 1, 2; SATA 10
Shaara, Jeff 1952- .... **CLC 119**
    See CA 163
Shaara, Michael (Joseph, Jr.)
    1929-1988 .... **CLC 15; DAM POP**
    See AITN 1; CA 102; 125; CANR 52, 85;
    DLBY 83
Shackleton, C. C.
    See Aldiss, Brian W(ilson)
Shacochis, Bob .... **CLC 39**
    See Shacochis, Robert G.
Shacochis, Robert G. 1951-
    See Shacochis, Bob
    See CA 119; 124; INT 124
Shaffer, Anthony (Joshua) 1926- ..... **CLC 19;
    DAM DRAM**
    See CA 110; 116; DLB 13
Shaffer, Peter (Levin) 1926- .. **CLC 5, 14, 18,
    37, 60; DAB; DAM DRAM, MST; DC
    7**
    See CA 25-28R; CANR 25, 47, 74; CD-
    BLB 1960 to Present; DA3; DLB 13;
    MTCW 1, 2
Shakey, Bernard
    See Young, Neil
Shalamov, Varlam (Tikhonovich)
    1907(?)-1982 .... **CLC 18**
    See CA 129; 105
Shamlu, Ahmad 1925- .... **CLC 10**
Shammas, Anton 1951- .... **CLC 55**
Shange, Ntozake 1948- ... **CLC 8, 25, 38, 74;
    BLC 3; DAM DRAM, MULT; DC 3**
    See AAYA 9; BW 2; CA 85-88; CABS 3;
    CANR 27, 48, 74; DA3; DLB 38; MTCW
    1, 2
Shanley, John Patrick 1950 .... **CLC 75**
    See CA 128; 133; CANR 83
Shapcott, Thomas W(illiam) 1935- .. **CLC 38**
    See CA 69-72; CANR 49, 83
Shapiro, Jane .... **CLC 76**
Shapiro, Karl (Jay) 1913- . **CLC 4, 8, 15, 53;
    PC 25**
    See CA 1-4R; CAAS 6; CANR 1, 36, 66;
    DLB 48; MTCW 1, 2
Sharp, William 1855-1905 .... **TCLC 39**
    See CA 160; DLB 156
Sharpe, Thomas Ridley 1928-
    See Sharpe, Tom
    See CA 114; 122; CANR 85; INT 122
Sharpe, Tom .... **CLC 36**
    See Sharpe, Thomas Ridley
    See DLB 14
Shaw, Bernard .... **TCLC 45**
    See Shaw, George Bernard
    See BW 1; MTCW 2
Shaw, G. Bernard
    See Shaw, George Bernard
Shaw, George Bernard 1856-1950 .. **TCLC 3,
    9, 21; DA; DAB; DAC; DAM DRAM,
    MST; WLC**
    See Shaw, Bernard
    See CA 104; 128; CDBLB 1914-1945;
    DA3; DLB 10, 57, 190; MTCW 1, 2
Shaw, Henry Wheeler 1818-1885 .. **NCLC 15**
    See DLB 11
Shaw, Irwin 1913-1984 .... **CLC 7, 23, 34;
    DAM DRAM, POP**
    See AITN 1; CA 13-16R; 112; CANR 21;
    CDALB 1941-1968; DLB 6, 102; DLBY
    84; MTCW 1, 21

Shaw, Robert 1927-1978 .... **CLC 5**
    See AITN 1; CA 1-4R; 81-84; CANR 4;
    DLB 13, 14
Shaw, T. E.
    See Lawrence, T(homas) E(dward)
Shawn, Wallace 1943- .... **CLC 41**
    See CA 112
Shea, Lisa 1953- .... **CLC 86**
    See CA 147
Sheed, Wilfrid (John Joseph) 1930- . **CLC 2,
    4, 10, 53**
    See CA 65-68; CANR 30, 66; DLB 6;
    MTCW 1, 2
Sheldon, Alice Hastings Bradley
    1915(?)-1987
    See Tiptree, James, Jr.
    See CA 108; 122; CANR 34; INT 108;
    MTCW 1
Sheldon, John
    See Bloch, Robert (Albert)
Shelley, Mary Wollstonecraft (Godwin)
    1797-1851 ..... **NCLC 14, 59; DA; DAB;
    DAC; DAM MST, NOV; WLC**
    See AAYA 20; CDBLB 1789-1832; DA3;
    DLB 110, 116, 159, 178; SATA 29
Shelley, Percy Bysshe 1792-1822 .. **NCLC 18;
    DA; DAB; DAC; DAM MST, POET;
    PC 14; WLC**
    See CDBLB 1789-1832; DA3; DLB 96,
    110, 158
Shepard, Jim 1956- .... **CLC 36**
    See CA 137; CANR 59; SATA 90
Shepard, Lucius 1947- .... **CLC 34**
    See CA 128; 141; CANR 81
Shepard, Sam 1943- .... **CLC 4, 6, 17, 34, 41,
    44; DAM DRAM; DC 5**
    See AAYA 1; CA 69-72; CABS 3; CANR
    22; DA3; DLB 7, 212; MTCW 1, 2
Shepherd, Michael
    See Ludlum, Robert
Sherburne, Zoa (Lillian Morin) 1912-1995
    CLC 30
    See AAYA 13; CA 1-4R; 176; CANR 3, 37;
    MAICYA; SAAS 18; SATA 3
Sheridan, Frances 1724-1766 .... **LC 7**
    See DLB 39, 84
Sheridan, Richard Brinsley
    1751-1816 .. **NCLC 5; DA; DAB; DAC;
    DAM DRAM, MST; DC 1; WLC**
    See CDBLB 1660-1789; DLB 89
Sherman, Jonathan Marc .... **CLC 55**
Sherman, Martin 1941(?)- .... **CLC 19**
    See CA 116; 123
Sherwin, Judith Johnson 1936-
    See Johnson, Judith (Emlyn)
    See CANR 85
Sherwood, Frances 1940- .... **CLC 81**
    See CA 146
Sherwood, Robert E(mmet)
    1896-1955 .... **TCLC 3; DAM DRAM**
    See CA 104; 153; DLB 7, 26
Shestov, Lev 1866-1938 .... **TCLC 56**
Shevchenko, Taras 1814-1861 .... **NCLC 54**
Shiel, M(atthew) P(hipps)
    1865-1947 .... **TCLC 8**
    See Holmes, Gordon
    See CA 106; 160; DLB 153; MTCW 2
Shields, Carol 1935- .... **CLC 91, 113;DAC**
    See CA 81-84; CANR 51, 74; DA3; MTCW
    2
Shields, David 1956- .... **CLC 97**
    See CA 124; CANR 48
Shiga, Naoya 1883-1971 ...... **CLC 33;SSC 23**
    See CA 101; 33-36R; DLB 180
Shikibu, Murasaki c. 978-c. 1014 ... **CMLC 1**
Shilts, Randy 1951-1994 .... **CLC 85**
    See AAYA 19; CA 115; 127; 144; CANR
    45; DA3; INT 127; MTCW 2

Shimazaki, Haruki 1872-1943
    See Shimazaki Toson
    See CA 105; 134; CANR 84
Shimazaki Toson 1872-1943 .... **TCLC 5**
    See Shimazaki, Haruki
    See DLB 180
Sholokhov, Mikhail (Aleksandrovich)
    1905-1984 .... **CLC 7, 15**
    See CA 101; 112; MTCW 1, 2; SATA-Obit
    36
Shone, Patric
    See Hanley, James
Shreve, Susan Richards 1939- .... **CLC 23**
    See CA 49-52; CAAS 5; CANR 5, 38, 69;
    MAICYA; SATA 46, 95; SATA-Brief 41
Shue, Larry 1946-1985 .... **CLC 52;DAM
    DRAM**
    See CA 145; 117
Shu-Jen, Chou 1881-1936
    See Lu Hsun
    See CA 104
Shulman, Alix Kates 1932- .... **CLC 2,10**
    See CA 29-32R; CANR 43; SATA 7
Shuster, Joe 1914- .... **CLC 21**
Shute, Nevil .... **CLC 30**
    See Norway, Nevil Shute
    See MTCW 2
Shuttle, Penelope (Diane) 1947- .... **CLC 7**
    See CA 93-96; CANR 39, 84; DLB 14, 40
Sidney, Mary 1561-1621 .... **LC 19, 39**
Sidney, Sir Philip 1554-1586 .... **LC 19, 39;
    DA; DAB; DAC; DAM MST, POET**
    See CDBLB Before 1660; DA3; DLB 167
Siegel, Jerome 1914-1996 .... **CLC 21**
    See CA 116; 169; 151
Siegel, Jerry
    See Siegel, Jerome
Sienkiewicz, Henryk (Adam Alexander Pius)
    1846-1916 .... **TCLC 3**
    See CA 104; 134; CANR 84
Sierra, Gregorio Martinez
    See Martinez Sierra, Gregorio
Sierra, Maria (de la O'LeJarraga) Martinez
    See Martinez Sierra, Maria (de la
    O'LeJarraga)
Sigal, Clancy 1926- .... **CLC 7**
    See CA 1-4R; CANR 85
Sigourney, Lydia Howard (Huntley)
    1791-1865 .... **NCLC 21**
    See DLB 1, 42, 73
Siguenza y Gongora, Carlos de 1645-1700
    LC 8; HLCS 2
Sigurjonsson,Johann 1880-1919 ..... **TCLC 27**
    See CA 170
Sikelianos, Angelos 1884-1951 .... **TCLC 39**
Silkin, Jon 1930- .... **CLC 2, 6, 43**
    See CA 5-8R; CAAS 5; DLB 27
Silko, Leslie (Marmon) 1948- .... **CLC 23, 74,
    114; DA; DAC; DAM MST, MULT,
    POP; SSC 37; WLCS**
    See AAYA 14; CA 115; 122; CANR 45, 65;
    DA3; DLB 143, 175; MTCW 2; NNAL
Sillanpaa, Frans Eemil 1888-1964 ... **CLC 19**
    See CA 129; 93-96; MTCW 1
Sillitoe, Alan 1928- ... **CLC 1, 3, 6, 10, 19, 57**
    See AITN 1; CA 9-12R; CAAS 2; CANR
    8, 26, 55; CDBLB 1960 to Present; DLB
    14, 139; MTCW 1, 2; SATA 61
Silone, Ignazio 1900-1978 .... **CLC 4**
    See CA 25-28; 81-84; CANR 34; CAP 2;
    MTCW 1
Silver, Joan Micklin 1935- .... **CLC 20**
    See CA 114; 121; INT 121
Silver, Nicholas
    See Faust, Frederick (Schiller)
Silverberg, Robert 1935- . **CLC 7;DAM POP**
    See AAYA 24; CA 1-4R; CAAS 3; CANR
    1, 20, 36, 85; CLR 59; DLB 8; INT

CANR-20; MAICYA; MTCW 1, 2; SATA
13, 91; SATA-Essay 104

Silverstein, Alvin 1933- .... **CLC 17**
See CA 49-52; CANR 2; CLR 25; JRDA;
MAICYA; SATA 8, 69

Silverstein, Virginia B(arbara Opshelor)
1937- .... **CLC 17**
See CA 49-52; CANR 2; CLR 25; JRDA;
MAICYA; SATA 8, 69

Sim, Georges
See Simenon, Georges (Jacques Christian)

Simak, Clifford D(onald) 1904-1988 . **CLC 1,
55**
See CA 1-4R; 125; CANR 1, 35; DLB 8;
MTCW 1; SATA-Obit 56

Simenon, Georges (Jacques Christian)
1903-1989 .... **CLC 1, 2, 3, 8, 18, 47;
DAM POP**
See CA 85-88; 129; CANR 35; DA3; DLB
72; DLBY 89; MTCW 1, 2

Simic, Charles 1938- ... **CLC 6, 9, 22, 49, 68;
DAM POET**
See CA 29-32R; CAAS 4; CANR 12, 33,
52, 61; DA3; DLB 105; MTCW 2

Simmel, Georg 1858-1918 .... **TCLC 64**
See CA 157

Simmons, Charles (Paul) 1924- .... **CLC 57**
See CA 89-92; INT 89-92

Simmons, Dan 1948- ...... **CLC 44;DAM POP**
See AAYA 16; CA 138; CANR 53, 81

Simmons, James (Stewart Alexander) 1933-
CLC 43
See CA 105; CAAS 21; DLB 40

Simms, William Gilmore
1806-1870 .... **NCLC 3**
See DLB 3, 30, 59, 73

Simon, Carly 1945- .... **CLC 26**
See CA 105

Simon, Claude 1913-1984 . **CLC 4, 9, 15, 39;
DAM NOV**
See CA 89-92; CANR 33; DLB 83; MTCW
1

Simon, (Marvin) Neil 1927- ... **CLC 6, 11, 31,
39, 70; DAM DRAM**
See AAYA 32; AITN 1; CA 21-24R; CANR
26, 54; DA3; DLB 7; MTCW 1, 2

Simon, Paul (Frederick) 1941(?)- ..... **CLC 17**
See CA 116; 153

Simonon, Paul 1956(?)- .... **CLC 30**

Simpson, Harriette
See Arnow, Harriette (Louisa) Simpson

Simpson, Louis (Aston Marantz)
1923- ...... **CLC 4, 7, 9, 32; DAM POET**
See CA 1-4R; CAAS 4; CANR 1, 61; DLB
5; MTCW 1, 2

Simpson, Mona (Elizabeth) 1957- .... **CLC 44**
See CA 122; 135; CANR 68

Simpson, N(orman) F(rederick)
1919- .... **CLC 29**
See CA 13-16R; DLB 13

Sinclair, Andrew (Annandale) 1935- . **CLC 2,
14**
See CA 9-12R; CAAS 5; CANR 14, 38;
DLB 14; MTCW 1

Sinclair, Emil
See Hesse, Hermann

Sinclair, Iain 1943- .... **CLC 76**
See CA 132; CANR 81

Sinclair, Iain MacGregor
See Sinclair, Iain

Sinclair, Irene
See Griffith, D(avid Lewelyn) W(ark)

Sinclair, Mary Amelia St. Clair 1865(?)-1946
See Sinclair, May
See CA 104

Sinclair, May 1863-1946 .... **TCLC 3, 11**
See Sinclair, Mary Amelia St. Clair
See CA 166; DLB 36, 135

Sinclair, Roy
See Griffith, D(avid Lewelyn) W(ark)

Sinclair, Upton (Beall) 1878-1968 ..... **CLC 1,
11, 15, 63; DA; DAB; DAC; DAM
MST, NOV; WLC**
See CA 5-8R; 25-28R; CANR 7; CDALB
1929-1941; DA3; DLB 9; INT CANR-7;
MTCW 1, 2; SATA 9

Singer, Isaac
See Singer, Isaac Bashevis

Singer, Isaac Bashevis 1904-1991 .. **CLC 1, 3,
6, 9, 11, 15, 23, 38, 69, 111; DA; DAB;
DAC; DAM MST, NOV; SSC 3; WLC**
See AAYA 32; AITN 1, 2; CA 1-4R; 134;
CANR 1, 39; CDALB 1941-1968; CLR
1; DA3; DLB 6, 28, 52; DLBY 91; JRDA;
MAICYA; MTCW 1, 2; SATA 3, 27;
SATA-Obit 68

Singer, Israel Joshua 1893-1944 .... **TCLC 33**
See CA 169

Singh, Khushwant 1915- .... **CLC 11**
See CA 9-12R; CAAS 9; CANR 6, 84

Singleton, Ann
See Benedict, Ruth (Fulton)

Sinjohn, John
See Galsworthy, John

Sinyavsky, Andrei (Donatevich) 1925-1997
CLC 8
See CA 85-88; 159

Sirin, V.
See Nabokov, Vladimir (Vladimirovich)

Sissman, L(ouis) E(dward)
1928-1976 .... **CLC 9, 18**
See CA 21-24R; 65-68; CANR 13; DLB 5

Sisson, C(harles) H(ubert) 1914- .... **CLC 8**
See CA 1-4R; CAAS 3; CANR 3, 48, 84;
DLB 27

Sitwell, Dame Edith 1887-1964 ..... **CLC 2, 9,
67; DAM POET; PC 3**
See CA 9-12R; CANR 35; CDBLB 1945-
1960; DLB 20; MTCW 1, 2

Siwaarmill, H. P.
See Sharp, William

Sjoewall, Maj 1935- .... **CLC 7**
See CA 65-68; CANR 73

Sjowall, Maj
See Sjoewall, Maj

Skelton, John 1463-1529 .... **PC 25**

Skelton, Robin 1925-1997 .... **CLC 13**
See AITN 2; CA 5-8R; 160; CAAS 5;
CANR 28; DLB 27, 53

Skolimowski, Jerzy 1938- .... **CLC 20**
See CA 128

Skram, Amalie(Bertha)
1847-1905 .... **TCLC 25**
See CA 165

Skvorecky, Josef (Vaclav) 1924- ...... **CLC 15,
39, 69; DAC; DAM NOV**
See CA 61-64; CAAS 1; CANR 10, 34, 63;
DA3; MTCW 1, 2

Slade, Bernard .... **CLC 11, 46**
See Newbound, Bernard Slade
See CAAS 9; DLB 53

Slaughter, Carolyn 1946- .... **CLC 56**
See CA 85-88; CANR 85

Slaughter, Frank G(ill) 1908- .... **CLC 29**
See AITN 2; CA 5-8R; CANR 5, 85; INT
CANR-5

Slavitt, David R(ytman) 1935- ..... **CLC 5, 14**
See CA 21-24R; CAAS 3; CANR 41, 83;
DLB 5, 6

Slesinger, Tess 1905-1945 .... **TCLC 10**
See CA 107; DLB 102

Slessor, Kenneth 1901-1971 .... **CLC 14**
See CA 102; 89-92

Slowacki, Juliusz 1809-1849 .... **NCLC 15**

Smart, Christopher 1722-1771 .. **LC 3; DAM
POET; PC 13**
See DLB 109

Smart, Elizabeth 1913-1986 .... **CLC 54**
See CA 81-84; 118; DLB 88

Smiley, Jane (Graves) 1949- ...... **CLC 53, 76;
DAM POP**
See CA 104; CANR 30, 50, 74; DA3; INT
CANR-30

Smith, A(rthur) J(ames) M(arshall)
1902-1980 .... **CLC 15; DAC**
See CA 1-4R; 102; CANR 4; DLB 88

Smith, Adam 1723-1790 .... **LC 36**
See DLB 104

Smith, Alexander 1829-1867 .... **NCLC 59**
See DLB 32, 55

Smith, Anna Deavere 1950- .... **CLC 86**
See CA 133

Smith, Betty (Wehner) 1896-1972 .... **CLC 19**
See CA 5-8R; 33-36R; DLBY 82; SATA 6

Smith, Charlotte(Turner)
1749-1806 .... **NCLC 23**
See DLB 39, 109

Smith, Clark Ashton 1893-1961 .... **CLC 43**
See CA 143; CANR 81; MTCW 2

Smith, Dave .... **CLC 22, 42**
See Smith, David (Jeddie)
See CAAS 7; DLB 5

Smith, David (Jeddie) 1942-
See Smith, Dave
See CA 49-52; CANR 1, 59; DAM POET

Smith, Florence Margaret 1902-1971
See Smith, Stevie
See CA 17-18; 29-32R; CANR 35; CAP 2;
DAM POET; MTCW 1, 2

Smith, Iain Crichton 1928-1998 .... **CLC 64**
See CA 21-24R; 171; DLB 40, 139

Smith, John 1580(?)-1631 .... **LC 9**
See DLB 24, 30

Smith, Johnston
See Crane, Stephen (Townley)

Smith, Joseph, Jr. 1805-1844 .... **NCLC 53**

Smith, Lee 1944- .... **CLC 25, 73**
See CA 114; 119; CANR 46; DLB 143;
DLBY 83; INT 119

Smith, Martin
See Smith, Martin Cruz

Smith, Martin Cruz 1942- .... **CLC 25; DAM
MULT, POP**
See BEST 89:4; CA 85-88; CANR 6, 23,
43, 65; INT CANR-23; MTCW 2; NNAL

Smith, Mary-Ann Tirone 1944- .... **CLC 39**
See CA 118; 136

Smith, Patti 1946- .... **CLC 12**
See CA 93-96; CANR 63

Smith, Pauline (Urmson)
1882-1959 .... **TCLC 25**

Smith, Rosamond
See Oates, Joyce Carol

Smith, Sheila Kaye
See Kaye-Smith, Sheila

Smith, Stevie .... **CLC 3, 8, 25, 44; PC 12**
See Smith, Florence Margaret
See DLB 20; MTCW 2

Smith, Wilbur (Addison) 1933- .... **CLC 33**
See CA 13-16R; CANR 7, 46, 66; MTCW
1, 2

Smith, William Jay 1918- .... **CLC 6**
See CA 5-8R; CANR 44; DLB 5; MAICYA;
SAAS 22; SATA 2, 68

Smith, Woodrow Wilson
See Kuttner, Henry

Smolenskin, Peretz 1842-1885 .... **NCLC 30**

Smollett, Tobias (George) 1721-1771 ... **LC 2,
46**
See CDBLB 1660-1789; DLB 39, 104

Snodgrass, W(illiam) D(e Witt)
1926- .... **CLC 2, 6, 10, 18, 68; DAM
POET**
See CA 1-4R; CANR 6, 36, 65, 85; DLB 5;
MTCW 1, 2

Stead, William Thomas
   1849-1912 .... **TCLC 48**
   See CA 167
Steele, Richard 1672-1729 .... **LC 18**
   See CDBLB 1660-1789; DLB 84, 101
Steele, Timothy (Reid) 1948- .... **CLC 45**
   See CA 93-96; CANR 16, 50; DLB 120
Steffens, (Joseph) Lincoln
   1866-1936 .... **TCLC 20**
   See CA 117
Stegner, Wallace (Earle) 1909-1993 .. **CLC 9,
   49, 81; DAM NOV; SSC 27**
   See AITN 1; BEST 90:3; CA 1-4R; 141;
   CAAS 9; CANR 1, 21, 46; DLB 9, 206;
   DLBY 93; MTCW 1, 2
Stein, Gertrude 1874-1946 .... **TCLC 1, 6, 28,
   48; DA; DAB; DAC; DAM MST, NOV,
   POET; PC 18; WLC**
   See CA 104; 132; CDALB 1917-1929;
   DA3; DLB 4, 54, 86; DLBD 15; MTCW
   1, 2
Steinbeck, John (Ernst) 1902-1968 ... **CLC 1,
   5, 9, 13, 21, 34, 45, 75, 124; DA; DAB;
   DAC; DAM DRAM, MST, NOV; SSC
   37;WLC**
   See AAYA 12; CA 1-4R; 25-28R; CANR 1,
   35; CDALB 1929-1941; DA3; DLB 7, 9,
   212; DLBD 2; MTCW 1, 2; SATA 9
Steinem, Gloria 1934- .... **CLC 63**
   See CA 53-56; CANR 28, 51; MTCW 1, 2
Steiner, George 1929- ... **CLC 24;DAM NOV**
   See CA 73-76; CANR 31, 67; DLB 67;
   MTCW 1, 2; SATA 62
Steiner, K. Leslie
   See Delany, Samuel R(ay, Jr.)
Steiner, Rudolf 1861-1925 .... **TCLC 13**
   See CA 107
Stendhal 1783-1842 .... **NCLC 23, 46; DA;
   DAB; DAC; DAM MST, NOV; SSC
   27; WLC**
   See DA3; DLB 119
Stephen, Adeline Virginia
   See Woolf, (Adeline) Virginia
Stephen, SirLeslie 1832-1904 .... **TCLC 23**
   See CA 123; DLB 57, 144, 190
Stephen, Sir Leslie
   See Stephen, SirLeslie
Stephen, Virginia
   See Woolf, (Adeline) Virginia
Stephens, James 1882(?)-1950 .... **TCLC 4**
   See CA 104; DLB 19, 153, 162
Stephens, Reed
   See Donaldson, Stephen R.
Steptoe, Lydia
   See Barnes, Djuna
Sterchi, Beat 1949- .... **CLC 65**
Sterling, Brett
   See Bradbury, Ray (Douglas); Hamilton,
   Edmond
Sterling, Bruce 1954- .... **CLC 72**
   See CA 119; CANR 44
Sterling, George 1869-1926 .... **TCLC 20**
   See CA 117; 165; DLB 54
Stern, Gerald 1925- .... **CLC 40, 100**
   See CA 81-84; CANR 28; DLB 105
Stern, Richard (Gustave) 1928- ... **CLC 4, 39**
   See CA 1-4R; CANR 1, 25, 52; DLBY 87;
   INT CANR-25
Sternberg, Josefvon 1894-1969 .... **CLC 20**
   See CA 81-84
Sterne, Laurence 1713-1768 .. **LC 2, 48; DA;
   DAB; DAC; DAM MST, NOV; WLC**
   See CDBLB 1660-1789; DLB 39
Sternheim, (William Adolf) Carl 1878-1942
   TCLC 8
   See CA 105; DLB 56, 118
Stevens, Mark 1951- .... **CLC 34**
   See CA 122

Stevens, Wallace 1879-1955 ...... **TCLC 3, 12,
   45; DA; DAB; DAC; DAM MST,
   POET; PC 6; WLC**
   See CA 104; 124; CDALB 1929-1941;
   DA3; DLB 54; MTCW 1, 2
Stevenson, Anne (Katharine) 1933- .. **CLC 7,
   33**
   See CA 17-20R; CAAS 9; CANR 9, 33;
   DLB 40; MTCW 1
Stevenson, Robert Louis (Balfour)
   1850-1894 . **NCLC 5, 14, 63; DA; DAB;
   DAC; DAM MST, NOV; SSC 11; WLC**
   See AAYA 24; CDBLB 1890-1914; CLR
   10, 11; DA3; DLB 18, 57, 141, 156, 174;
   DLBD 13; JRDA; MAICYA; SATA 100;
   YABC 2
Stewart, J(ohn) I(nnes) M(ackintosh)
   1906-1994 .... **CLC 7, 14, 32**
   See CA 85-88; 147; CAAS 3; CANR 47;
   MTCW 1, 2
Stewart, Mary (Florence Elinor)
   1916- .... **CLC 7, 35, 117; DAB**
   See AAYA 29; CA 1-4R; CANR 1, 59;
   SATA 12
Stewart, Mary Rainbow
   See Stewart, Mary (Florence Elinor)
Stifle, June
   See Campbell, Maria
Stifter, Adalbert 1805-1868 .. **NCLC 41; SSC
   28**
   See DLB 133
Still, James 1906- .... **CLC 49**
   See CA 65-68; CAAS 17; CANR 10, 26;
   DLB 9; SATA 29
Sting 1951-
   See Sumner, Gordon Matthew
   See CA 167
Stirling, Arthur
   See Sinclair, Upton (Beall)
Stitt, Milan 1941- .... **CLC 29**
   See CA 69-72
Stockton, Francis Richard 1834-1902
   See Stockton, Frank R.
   See CA 108; 137; MAICYA; SATA 44
Stockton, Frank R. .... **TCLC 47**
   See Stockton, Francis Richard
   See DLB 42, 74; DLBD 13; SATA-Brief 32
Stoddard, Charles
   See Kuttner, Henry
Stoker, Abraham 1847-1912
   See Stoker, Bram
   See CA 105; 150; DA; DAC; DAM MST,
   NOV; DA3; SATA 29
Stoker, Bram 1847-1912 .... **TCLC 8; DAB;
   WLC**
   See Stoker, Abraham
   See AAYA 23; CDBLB 1890-1914; DLB
   36, 70, 178
Stolz, Mary (Slattery) 1920- .... **CLC 12**
   See AAYA 8; AITN 1; CA 5-8R; CANR 13,
   41; JRDA; MAICYA; SAAS 3; SATA 10,
   71
Stone, Irving 1903-1989 .. **CLC 7;DAM POP**
   See AITN 1; CA 1-4R; 129; CAAS 3;
   CANR 1, 23; DA3; INT CANR-23;
   MTCW 1, 2; SATA 3; SATA-Obit 64
Stone, Oliver (William) 1946- .... **CLC 73**
   See AAYA 15; CA 110; CANR 55
Stone, Robert (Anthony) 1937- ... **CLC 5, 23,
   42**
   See CA 85-88; CANR 23, 66; DLB 152;
   INT CANR-23; MTCW 1
Stone, Zachary
   See Follett, Ken(neth Martin)

Stoppard, Tom 1937- ... **CLC 1, 3, 4, 5, 8, 15,
   29, 34, 63, 91; DA; DAB; DAC; DAM
   DRAM, MST; DC 6; WLC**
   See CA 81-84; CANR 39, 67; CDBLB 1960
   to Present; DA3; DLB 13; DLBY 85;
   MTCW 1, 2
Storey, David (Malcolm) 1933- . **CLC 2, 4, 5,
   8; DAM DRAM**
   See CA 81-84; CANR 36; DLB 13, 14, 207;
   MTCW 1
Storm, Hyemeyohsts 1935- .... **CLC 3;DAM
   MULT**
   See CA 81-84; CANR 45; NNAL
Storm, Theodor 1817-1888 .... **SSC 27**
Storm, (Hans) Theodor (Woldsen) 1817-1888
   NCLC 1; SSC 27
   See DLB 129
Storni, Alfonsina 1892-1938 . **TCLC 5; DAM
   MULT; HLC 2**
   See CA 104; 131; HW 1
Stoughton, William 1631-1701 .... **LC 38**
   See DLB 24
Stout, Rex(Todhunter) 1886-1975 ...... **CLC 3**
   See AITN 2; CA 61-64; CANR 71
Stow, (Julian) Randolph 1935- ... **CLC 23, 48**
   See CA 13-16R; CANR 33; MTCW 1
Stowe, Harriet (Elizabeth) Beecher
   1811-1896 .... **NCLC 3, 50; DA; DAB;
   DAC; DAM MST, NOV; WLC**
   See CDALB 1865-1917; DA3; DLB 1, 12,
   42, 74, 189; JRDA; MAICYA; YABC 1
Strachey, (Giles)Lytton 1880-1932 . **TCLC 12**
   See CA 110; 178; DLB 149; DLBD 10;
   MTCW 2
Strand, Mark 1934- .... **CLC 6, 18, 41, 71;
   DAM POET**
   See CA 21-24R; CANR 40, 65; DLB 5;
   SATA 41
Straub, Peter (Francis) 1943- . **CLC 28, 107;
   DAM POP**
   See BEST 89:1; CA 85-88; CANR 28, 65;
   DLBY 84; MTCW 1, 2
Strauss, Botho 1944- .... **CLC 22**
   See CA 157; DLB 124
Streatfeild, (Mary) Noel
   1895(?)-1986 .... **CLC 21**
   See CA 81-84; 120; CANR 31; CLR 17;
   DLB 160; MAICYA; SATA 20; SATA-
   Obit 48
Stribling, T(homas) S(igismund) 1881-1965
   CLC 23
   See CA 107; DLB 9
Strindberg, (Johan) August
   1849-1912 .... **TCLC 1, 8, 21, 47; DA;
   DAB; DAC; DAM DRAM, MST; WLC**
   See CA 104; 135; DA3; MTCW 2
Stringer, Arthur 1874-1950 .... **TCLC 37**
   See CA 161; DLB 92
Stringer, David
   See Roberts, Keith (John Kingston)
Stroheim, Erich von 1885-1957 ..... **TCLC 71**
Strugatskii, Arkadii (Natanovich) 1925-1991
   CLC 27
   See CA 106; 135
Strugatskii, Boris (Natanovich)
   1933- .... **CLC 27**
   See CA 106
Strummer, Joe 1953(?)- .... **CLC 30**
Strunk, William, Jr. 1869-1946 ...... **TCLC 92**
   See CA 118; 164
Stryk, Lucien 1924- .... **PC 27**
   See CA 13-16R; CANR 10, 28, 55
Stuart, Don A.
   See Campbell, John W(ood, Jr.)
Stuart, Ian
   See MacLean, Alistair (Stuart)

Stuart, Jesse (Hilton) 1906-1984 ... **CLC 1, 8, 11, 14, 34; SSC 31**
 See CA 5-8R; 112; CANR 31; DLB 9, 48, 102; DLBY 84; SATA 2; SATA-Obit 36
Sturgeon, Theodore (Hamilton) 1918-1985 **CLC 22, 39**
 See Queen, Ellery
 See CA 81-84; 116; CANR 32; DLB 8; DLBY 85; MTCW 1, 2
Sturges, Preston 1898-1959 .... **TCLC 48**
 See CA 114; 149; DLB 26
Styron, William 1925- .... **CLC 1, 3, 5, 11, 15, 60; DAM NOV, POP; SSC 25**
 See BEST 90:4; CA 5-8R; CANR 6, 33, 74; CDALB 1968-1988; DA3; DLB 2, 143; DLBY 80; INT CANR-6; MTCW 1, 2
Su, Chien 1884-1918
 See Su Man-shu
 See CA 123
Suarez Lynch, B.
 See Bioy Casares, Adolfo; Borges, Jorge Luis
Suassuna, Ariano Vilar 1927-
 See CA 178; HLCS 1; HW 2
Suckow, Ruth 1892-1960 .... **SSC 18**
 See CA 113; DLB 9, 102
Sudermann, Hermann 1857-1928 .. **TCLC 15**
 See CA 107; DLB 118
Sue, Eugene 1804-1857 .... **NCLC 1**
 See DLB 119
Sueskind, Patrick 1949- .... **CLC 44**
 See Suskind, Patrick
Sukenick, Ronald 1932- .... **CLC 3, 4, 6, 48**
 See CA 25-28R; CAAS 8; CANR 32; DLB 173; DLBY 81
Suknaski, Andrew 1942- .... **CLC 19**
 See CA 101; DLB 53
Sullivan, Vernon
 See Vian, Boris
Sully Prudhomme 1839-1907 .... **TCLC 31**
Su Man-shu .... **TCLC 24**
 See Su, Chien
Summerforest, Ivy B.
 See Kirkup, James
Summers, Andrew James 1942- .... **CLC 26**
Summers, Andy
 See Summers, Andrew James
Summers, Hollis (Spurgeon,Jr.) 1916- .... **CLC 10**
 See CA 5-8R; CANR 3; DLB 6
Summers, (Alphonsus Joseph-Mary Augustus) Montague 1880-1948 .... **TCLC 16**
 See CA 118; 163
Sumner, Gordon Matthew .... **CLC 26**
 See Sting
Surtees, Robert Smith 1803-1864 .. **NCLC 14**
 See DLB 21
Susann, Jacqueline 1921-1974 .... **CLC 3**
 See AITN 1; CA 65-68; 53-56; MTCW 1, 2
Su Shih 1036-1101 .... **CMLC 15**
Suskind, Patrick
 See Sueskind, Patrick
 See CA 145
Sutcliff, Rosemary 1920-1992 .... **CLC 26; DAB; DAC; DAM MST, POP**
 See AAYA 10; CA 5-8R; 139; CANR 37; CLR 1, 37; JRDA; MAICYA; SATA 6, 44, 78; SATA-Obit 73
Sutro, Alfred 1863-1933 .... **TCLC 6**
 See CA 105; DLB 10
Sutton, Henry
 See Slavitt, David R(ytman)
Svevo, Italo 1861-1928 .. **TCLC 2, 35;SSC 25**
 See Schmitz, Aron Hector
Swados, Elizabeth (A.) 1951- .... **CLC 12**
 See CA 97-100; CANR 49; INT 97-100

Swados, Harvey 1920-1972 .... **CLC 5**
 See CA 5-8R; 37-40R; CANR 6; DLB 2
Swan, Gladys 1934- .... **CLC 69**
 See CA 101; CANR 17, 39
Swarthout, Glendon (Fred) 1918-1992 .... **CLC 35**
 See CA 1-4R; 139; CANR 1, 47; SATA 26
Sweet, Sarah C.
 See Jewett, (Theodora) Sarah Orne
Swenson, May 1919-1989 ...... **CLC 4, 14, 61, 106; DA; DAB; DAC; DAM MST, POET; PC 14**
 See CA 5-8R; 130; CANR 36, 61; DLB 5; MTCW 1, 2; SATA 15
Swift, Augustus
 See Lovecraft, H(oward) P(hillips)
Swift, Graham (Colin) 1949- ...... **CLC 41, 88**
 See CA 117; 122; CANR 46, 71; DLB 194; MTCW 2
Swift, Jonathan 1667-1745 ..... **LC 1, 42; DA; DAB; DAC; DAM MST, NOV, POET; PC 9; WLC**
 See CDBLB 1660-1789; CLR 53; DA3; DLB 39, 95, 101; SATA 19
Swinburne, Algernon Charles 1837-1909 **TCLC 8, 36; DA; DAB; DAC; DAM MST, POET; PC 24; WLC**
 See CA 105; 140; CDBLB 1832-1890; DA3; DLB 35, 57
Swinfen, Ann .... **CLC 34**
Swinnerton, Frank Arthur 1884-1982 .... **CLC 31**
 See CA 108; DLB 34
Swithen, John
 See King, Stephen (Edwin)
Sylvia
 See Ashton-Warner, Sylvia (Constance)
Symmes, Robert Edward
 See Duncan, Robert (Edward)
Symonds, John Addington 1840-1893 .... **NCLC 34**
 See DLB 57, 144
Symons, Arthur 1865-1945 .... **TCLC 11**
 See CA 107; DLB 19, 57, 149
Symons, Julian (Gustave) 1912-1994 .... **CLC 2, 14, 32**
 See CA 49-52; 147; CAAS 3; CANR 3, 33, 59; DLB 87, 155; DLBY 92; MTCW 1
Synge, (Edmund) J(ohn) M(illington) 1871-1909 . **TCLC 6, 37; DAM DRAM; DC 2**
 See CA 104; 141; CDBLB 1890-1914; DLB 10, 19
Syruc, J.
 See Milosz, Czeslaw
Szirtes, George 1948- .... **CLC 46**
 See CA 109; CANR 27, 61
Szymborska, Wislawa 1923- .... **CLC 99**
 See CA 154; DA3; DLBY 96; MTCW 2
T. O., Nik
 See Annensky, Innokenty (Fyodorovich)
Tabori, George 1914- .... **CLC 19**
 See CA 49-52; CANR 4, 69
Tagore, Rabindranath 1861-1941 ... **TCLC 3, 53; DAM DRAM, POET; PC 8**
 See CA 104; 120; DA3; MTCW 1, 2
Taine, Hippolyte Adolphe 1828-1893 .... **NCLC 15**
Talese, Gay 1932- .... **CLC 37**
 See AITN 1; CA 1-4R; CANR 9, 58; DLB 185; INT CANR-9; MTCW 1, 2
Tallent, Elizabeth (Ann) 1954- .... **CLC 45**
 See CA 117; CANR 72; DLB 130
Tally, Ted 1952- .... **CLC 42**
 See CA 120; 124; INT 124

Talvik, Heiti 1904-1947 .... **TCLC 87**
Tamayo y Baus, Manuel 1829-1898 .... **NCLC 1**
Tammsaare, A(nton) H(ansen) 1878-1940 **TCLC 27**
 See CA 164
Tam'si, Tchicaya U
 See Tchicaya, Gerald Felix
Tan, Amy (Ruth) 1952- . **CLC 59, 120; DAM MULT, NOV, POP**
 See AAYA 9; BEST 89:3; CA 136; CANR 54; CDALBS; DA3; DLB 173; MTCW 2; SATA 75
Tandem, Felix
 See Spitteler, Carl (Friedrich Georg)
Tanizaki, Jun'ichiro 1886-1965 ... **CLC 8, 14, 28; SSC 21**
 See CA 93-96; 25-28R; DLB 180; MTCW 2
Tanner, William
 See Amis, Kingsley (William)
Tao Lao
 See Storni, Alfonsina
Tarantino, Quentin(Jerome) 1963- . **CLC 125**
 See CA 171
Tarassoff, Lev
 See Troyat, Henri
Tarbell, Ida M(inerva) 1857-1944 . **TCLC 40**
 See CA 122; 181; DLB 47
Tarkington, (Newton) Booth 1869-1946 **TCLC 9**
 See CA 110; 143; DLB 9, 102; MTCW 2; SATA 17
Tarkovsky, Andrei (Arsenyevich) 1932-1986 **CLC 75**
 See CA 127
Tartt, Donna 1964(?)- .... **CLC 76**
 See CA 142
Tasso, Torquato 1544-1595 .... **LC 5**
Tate, (John Orley) Allen 1899-1979 .. **CLC 2, 4, 6, 9, 11, 14, 24**
 See CA 5-8R; 85-88; CANR 32; DLB 4, 45, 63; DLBD 17; MTCW 1, 2
Tate, Ellalice
 See Hibbert, Eleanor Alice Burford
Tate, James (Vincent) 1943- ..... **CLC 2, 6, 25**
 See CA 21-24R; CANR 29, 57; DLB 5, 169
Tavel, Ronald 1940- .... **CLC 6**
 See CA 21-24R; CANR 33
Taylor, C(ecil) P(hilip) 1929-1981 .... **CLC 27**
 See CA 25-28R; 105; CANR 47
Taylor, Edward 1642(?)-1729 ..... **LC 11; DA; DAB; DAC; DAM MST, POET**
 See DLB 24
Taylor, Eleanor Ross 1920- .... **CLC 5**
 See CA 81-84; CANR 70
Taylor, Elizabeth 1912-1975 ..... **CLC 2, 4, 29**
 See CA 13-16R; CANR 9, 70; DLB 139; MTCW 1, 2; SATA 13
Taylor, Frederick Winslow 1856-1915 .... **TCLC 76**
Taylor, Henry (Splawn) 1942- .... **CLC 44**
 See CA 33-36R; CAAS 7; CANR 31; DLB 5
Taylor, Kamala (Purnaiya) 1924-
 See Markandaya, Kamala
 See CA 77-80
Taylor, Mildred D. .... **CLC 21**
 See AAYA 10; BW 1; CA 85-88; CANR 25; CLR 9, 59; DLB 52; JRDA; MAICYA; SAAS 5; SATA 15, 70
Taylor, Peter (Hillsman) 1917-1994 .. **CLC 1, 4, 18, 37, 44, 50, 71; SSC 10**
 See CA 13-16R; 147; CANR 9, 50; DLBY 81, 94; INT CANR-9; MTCW 1, 2
Taylor, Robert Lewis 1912-1998 .... **CLC 14**
 See CA 1-4R; 170; CANR 3, 64; SATA 10

Warner, Sylvia (Constance) Ashton
See Ashton-Warner, Sylvia (Constance)
Warner, Sylvia Townsend
1893-1978 .... **CLC 7, 19; SSC 23**
See CA 61-64; 77-80; CANR 16, 60; DLB
34, 139; MTCW 1, 2
Warren, Mercy Otis 1728-1814 ..... **NCLC 13**
See DLB 31, 200
Warren, Robert Penn 1905-1989 .. **CLC 1, 4,
6, 8, 10, 13, 18, 39, 53, 59; DA; DAB;
DAC; DAM MST, NOV, POET; SSC
4;WLC**
See AITN 1; CA 13-16R; 129; CANR 10,
47;CDALB 1968-1988; DA3; DLB 2, 48,
152; DLBY 80, 89; INT CANR-10;
MTCW 1, 2; SATA 46; SATA-Obit 63
Warshofsky, Isaac
See Singer, Isaac Bashevis
Warton, Thomas 1728-1790 ...... **LC 15;DAM
POET**
See DLB 104, 109
Waruk, Kona
See Harris, (Theodore) Wilson
Warung, Price 1855-1911 .... **TCLC 45**
Warwick, Jarvis
See Garner, Hugh
Washington, Alex
See Harris, Mark
Washington, Booker T(aliaferro) 1856-1915
TCLC 10; BLC 3; DAM MULT
See BW 1; CA 114; 125; DA3; SATA 28
Washington, George 1732-1799 .... **LC 25**
See DLB 31
Wassermann, (Karl)Jakob
1873-1934 .... **TCLC 6**
See CA 104; 163; DLB 66
Wasserstein, Wendy 1950- .. **CLC 32, 59, 90;
DAM DRAM; DC 4**
See CA 121; 129; CABS 3; CANR 53, 75;
DA3; INT 129; MTCW 2; SATA 94
Waterhouse, Keith(Spencer) 1929- .. **CLC 47**
See CA 5-8R; CANR 38, 67; DLB 13, 15;
MTCW 1, 2
Waters, Frank(Joseph) 1902-1995 ... **CLC 88**
See CA 5-8R; 149; CAAS 13; CANR 3, 18,
63; DLB 212; DLBY 86
Waters, Roger 1944- .... **CLC 35**
Watkins, Frances Ellen
See Harper, Frances Ellen Watkins
Watkins, Gerrold
See Malzberg, Barry N(athaniel)
Watkins, Gloria 1955(?)-
See hooks, bell
See BW 2; CA 143; MTCW 2
Watkins, Paul 1964- .... **CLC 55**
See CA 132; CANR 62
Watkins, Vernon Phillips
1906-1967 .... **CLC 43**
See CA 9-10; 25-28R; CAP 1; DLB 20
Watson, Irving S.
See Mencken, H(enry) L(ouis)
Watson, John H.
See Farmer, Philip Jose
Watson, Richard F.
See Silverberg, Robert
Waugh, Auberon (Alexander) 1939- .. **CLC 7**
See CA 45-48; CANR 6, 22; DLB 14, 194
Waugh, Evelyn (Arthur St. John) 1903-1966
**CLC 1, 3, 8, 13, 19, 27, 44, 107; DA;
DAB; DAC; DAM MST, NOV, POP;
WLC**
See CA 85-88; 25-28R; CANR 22; CDBLB
1914-1945; DA3; DLB 15, 162, 195;
MTCW 1, 2
Waugh, Harriet 1944- .... **CLC 6**
See CA 85-88; CANR 22
Ways, C. R.
See Blount, Roy (Alton), Jr.

Waystaff, Simon
See Swift, Jonathan
Webb, (Martha) Beatrice (Potter) 1858-1943
TCLC 22
See Potter, (Helen) Beatrix
See CA 117; DLB 190
Webb, Charles (Richard) 1939- .... **CLC 7**
See CA 25-28R
Webb, James H(enry), Jr. 1946- ...... **CLC 22**
See CA 81-84
Webb, Mary (Gladys Meredith) 1881-1927
TCLC 24
See CA 123; DLB 34
Webb, Mrs. Sidney
See Webb, (Martha) Beatrice (Potter)
Webb, Phyllis 1927- .... **CLC 18**
See CA 104; CANR 23; DLB 53
Webb, Sidney (James) 1859-1947 .. **TCLC 22**
See CA 117; 163; DLB 190
Webber, Andrew Lloyd .... **CLC 21**
See Lloyd Webber, Andrew
Weber, Lenora Mattingly
1895-1971 .... **CLC 12**
See CA 19-20; 29-32R; CAP 1; SATA 2;
SATA-Obit 26
Weber, Max 1864-1920 .... **TCLC 69**
See CA 109
Webster, John 1579(?)-1634(?) ... **LC 33; DA;
DAB; DAC; DAM DRAM, MST; DC
2; WLC**
See CDBLB Before 1660; DLB 58
Webster, Noah 1758-1843 .... **NCLC 30**
See DLB 1, 37, 42, 43, 73
Wedekind, (Benjamin) Frank(lin) 1864-1918
TCLC 7; DAM DRAM
See CA 104; 153; DLB 118
Weidman, Jerome 1913-1998 .... **CLC 7**
See AITN 2; CA 1-4R; 171; CANR 1; DLB
28
Weil, Simone (Adolphine)
1909-1943 .... **TCLC 23**
See CA 117; 159; MTCW 2
Weininger, Otto 1880-1903 .... **TCLC 84**
Weinstein, Nathan
See West, Nathanael
Weinstein, Nathan von Wallenstein
See West, Nathanael
Weir, Peter (Lindsay) 1944- .... **CLC 20**
See CA 113; 123
Weiss, Peter (Ulrich) 1916-1982 .. **CLC 3, 15,
51; DAM DRAM**
See CA 45-48; 106; CANR 3; DLB 69, 124
Weiss, Theodore (Russell) 1916- ... **CLC 3, 8,
14**
See CA 9-12R; CAAS 2; CANR 46; DLB 5
Welch, (Maurice) Denton
1915-1948 .... **TCLC 22**
See CA 121; 148
Welch, James 1940- ..... **CLC 6, 14, 52; DAM
MULT, POP**
See CA 85-88; CANR 42, 66; DLB 175;
NNAL
Weldon, Fay 1931- . **CLC 6, 9, 11, 19, 36, 59,
122; DAM POP**
See CA 21-24R; CANR 16, 46, 63; CD-
BLB 1960 to Present; DLB 14, 194; INT
CANR-16; MTCW 1, 2
Wellek, Rene 1903-1995 .... **CLC 28**
See CA 5-8R; 150; CAAS 7; CANR 8; DLB
63; INT CANR-8
Weller, Michael 1942- .... **CLC 10, 53**
See CA 85-88
Weller, Paul 1958- .... **CLC 26**
Wellershoff, Dieter 1925- .... **CLC 46**
See CA 89-92; CANR 16, 37
Welles, (George) Orson 1915-1985 .. **CLC 20,
80**
See CA 93-96; 117

Wellman, John McDowell 1945-
See Wellman, Mac
See CA 166
Wellman, Mac 1945- .... **CLC 65**
See Wellman, John McDowell; Wellman,
John McDowell
Wellman, ManlyWade 1903-1986 ..... **CLC 49**
See CA 1-4R; 118; CANR 6, 16, 44; SATA
6; SATA-Obit 47
Wells, Carolyn 1869(?)-1942 .... **TCLC 35**
See CA 113; DLB 11
Wells, H(erbert) G(eorge)
1866-1946 . **TCLC 6, 12, 19; DA; DAB;
DAC; DAM MST, NOV; SSC 6; WLC**
See AAYA 18; CA 110; 121; CDBLB 1914-
1945; DA3; DLB 34, 70, 156, 178;
MTCW 1, 2; SATA 20
Wells, Rosemary 1943- .... **CLC 12**
See AAYA 13; CA 85-88; CANR 48; CLR
16; MAICYA; SAAS 1; SATA 18, 69
Welty, Eudora 1909- ...... **CLC 1, 2, 5, 14, 22,
33, 105; DA; DAB; DAC; DAM MST,
NOV; SSC 1, 27; WLC**
See CA 9-12R; CABS 1; CANR 32, 65;
CDALB 1941-1968; DA3; DLB 2, 102,
143; DLBD 12; DLBY 87; MTCW 1, 2
Wen I-to 1899-1946 .... **TCLC 28**
Wentworth, Robert
See Hamilton, Edmond
Werfel, Franz (Viktor) 1890-1945 ... **TCLC 8**
See CA 104; 161; DLB 81, 124
Wergeland, Henrik Arnold
1808-1845 .... **NCLC 5**
Wersba, Barbara 1932- .... **CLC 30**
See AAYA 2, 30; CA 29-32R; CANR 16,
38; CLR 3; DLB 52; JRDA; MAICYA;
SAAS 2; SATA 1, 58; SATA-Essay 103
Wertmueller, Lina 1928- .... **CLC 16**
See CA 97-100; CANR 39, 78
Wescott, Glenway 1901-1987 ... **CLC 13;SSC
35**
See CA 13-16R; 121; CANR 23, 70; DLB
4, 9, 102
Wesker, Arnold 1932- ... **CLC 3, 5, 42; DAB;
DAM DRAM**
See CA 1-4R; CAAS 7; CANR 1, 33; CD-
BLB 1960 to Present; DLB 13; MTCW 1
Wesley, Richard (Errol) 1945- .... **CLC 7**
See BW 1; CA 57-60; CANR 27; DLB 38
Wessel, Johan Herman 1742-1785 .... **LC 7**
West, Anthony (Panther)
1914-1987 .... **CLC 50**
See CA 45-48; 124; CANR 3, 19; DLB 15
West, C. P.
See Wodehouse, P(elham) G(renville)
West, (Mary) Jessamyn 1902-1984 ... **CLC 7,
17**
See CA 9-12R; 112; CANR 27; DLB 6;
DLBY 84; MTCW 1, 2; SATA-Obit 37
West, Morris L(anglo) 1916- .... **CLC 6, 33**
See CA 5-8R; CANR 24, 49, 64; MTCW 1,
2
West, Nathanael 1903-1940 .... **TCLC 1, 14,
44; SSC 16**
See CA 104; 125; CDALB 1929-1941;
DA3; DLB 4, 9, 28; MTCW 1, 2
West, Owen
See Koontz, Dean R(ay)
West, Paul 1930- .... **CLC 7, 14, 96**
See CA 13-16R; CAAS 7; CANR 22, 53,
76; DLB 14; INT CANR-22; MTCW 2
West, Rebecca 1892-1983 ... **CLC 7, 9, 31, 50**
See CA 5-8R; 109; CANR 19; DLB 36;
DLBY 83; MTCW 1, 2
Westall, Robert (Atkinson)
1929-1993 .... **CLC 17**
See AAYA 12; CA 69-72; 141; CANR 18,
68; CLR 13; JRDA; MAICYA; SAAS 2;
SATA 23, 69; SATA-Obit 75

SSC Cumulative Nationality Index

ALGERIAN

Camus, Albert **9**

AMERICAN

Adams, Alice (Boyd) **24**
Aiken, Conrad (Potter) **9**
Alcott, Louisa May **27**
Algren, Nelson **33**
Anderson, Sherwood **1**
Auchincloss, Louis (Stanton) **22**
Baldwin, James (Arthur) **10, 33**
Bambara, Toni Cade **35**
Barnes, Djuna **3**
Barth, John (Simmons) **10**
Barthelme, Donald **2**
Beattie, Ann **11**
Bellow, Saul **14**
Benet, Stephen Vincent **10**
Berriault, Gina **30**
Bierce, Ambrose (Gwinett) **9**
Bowles, Paul (Frederick) **3**
Boyle, Kay **5**
Boyle, T(homas) Coraghessan **16**
Bradbury, Ray (Douglas) **29**
Cable, George Washington **4**
Caldwell, Erskine (Preston) **19**
Calisher, Hortense **15**
Capote, Truman **2**
Carver, Raymond **8**
Cather, Willa Sibert **2**
Chandler, Raymond (Thornton) **23**
Cheever, John **1**
Chesnutt, Charles W(addell) **7**
Chopin, Kate **8**
Cisneros, Sandra **32**
Coover, Robert (Lowell) **15**
Cowan, Peter (Walkinshaw) **28**
Crane, Stephen (Townley) **7**
Davenport, Guy (Mattison Jr.) **16**
Dixon, Stephen **16**
Dreiser, Theodore (Herman Albert) **30**
Dubus, Andre **15**
Dunbar, Paul Laurence **8**
Elkin, Stanley L(awrence) **12**
Ellison, Harlan (Jay) **14**
Ellison, Ralph (Waldo) **26**
Farrell, James T(homas) **28**
Faulkner, William (Cuthbert) **1, 35**
Fisher, Rudolph **25**
Fitzgerald, F(rancis) Scott (Key) **6, 31**
Freeman, Mary E(leanor) Wilkins **1**
Gardner, John (Champlin) Jr. **7**
Garland, (Hannibal) Hamlin **18**
Garrett, George (Palmer) **30**
Gass, William H(oward) **12**
Gilchrist, Ellen **14**
Gilman, Charlotte (Anna) Perkins (Stetson) **13**
Glasgow, Ellen (Anderson Gholson) **34**
Gordon, Caroline **15**
Grau, Shirley Ann **15**
Hammett, (Samuel) Dashiell **17**

Harris, Joel Chandler **19**
Harrison, James (Thomas) **19**
Harte, (Francis) Bret(t) **8**
Hawthorne, Nathaniel **3, 29**
Hemingway, Ernest (Miller) **1, 25, 36**
Henderson, Zenna (Chlarson) **29**
Henry, O. **5**
Howells, William Dean **36**
Hughes, (James) Langston **6**
Hurston, Zora Neale **4**
Irving, Washington **2, 37**
Jackson, Shirley **9**
James, Henry **8, 32**
Jewett, (Theodora) Sarah Orne **6**
King, Stephen (Edwin) **17**
Lardner, Ring(gold) W(ilmer) **32**
Le Guin, Ursula K(roeber) **12**
Ligotti, Thomas (Robert) **16**
Lish, Gordon (Jay) **18**
London, Jack **4**
Lovecraft, H(oward) P(hillips) **3**
Maclean, Norman (Fitzroy) **13**
Malamud, Bernard **15**
Marshall, Paule **3**
Mason, Bobbie Ann **4**
McCarthy, Mary (Therese) **24**
McCullers, (Lula) Carson (Smith) **9, 24**
Melville, Herman **1, 17**
Michaels, Leonard **16**
Murfree, Mary Noailles **22**
Nabokov, Vladimir (Vladimirovich) **11**
Nin, Anais **10**
Norris, Frank **28**
Oates, Joyce Carol **6**
O'Connor, (Mary) Flannery **1, 23**
O'Hara, John (Henry) **15**
Olsen, Tillie **11**
Ozick, Cynthia **15**
Page, Thomas Nelson **23**
Paley, Grace **8**
Parker, Dorothy (Rothschild) **2**
Perelman, S(idney) J(oseph) **32**
Phillips, Jayne Anne **16**
Poe, Edgar Allan **1, 22, 35**
Pohl, Frederik **25**
Porter, Katherine Anne **4, 31**
Powers, J(ames) F(arl) **4**
Price, (Edward) Reynolds **22**
Pynchon, Thomas (Ruggles Jr.) **14**
Roth, Philip (Milton) **26**
Salinger, J(erome) D(avid) **2, 28**
Saroyan, William **21**
Selby, Hubert Jr. **20**
Silko, Leslie (Marmon) **37**
Singer, Isaac Bashevis **3**
Stafford, Jean **26**
Stegner, Wallace (Earle) **27**
Steinbeck, John (Ernst) **11, 37**
Stuart, Jesse (Hilton) **31**
Styron, William **25**
Suckow, Ruth **18**
Taylor, Peter (Hillsman) **10**
Thomas, Audrey (Callahan) **20**

Thurber, James (Grover) **1**
Toomer, Jean **1**
Twain, Mark **6, 26**
Updike, John (Hoyer) **13, 27**
Vinge, Joan (Carol) D(ennison) **24**
Vonnegut, Kurt Jr. **8**
Walker, Alice (Malsenior) **5**
Warren, Robert Penn **4**
Welty, Eudora **1, 27**
Wescott, Glenway **35**
West, Nathanael **16**
Wharton, Edith (Newbold Jones) **6**
Williams, William Carlos **31**
Wodehouse, P(elham) G(renville) **2**
Wolfe, Thomas (Clayton) **33**
Wright, Richard (Nathaniel) **2**

ARGENTINIAN

Bioy Casares, Adolfo **17**
Borges, Jorge Luis **4**
Cortazar, Julio **7**
Valenzuela, Luisa **14**

AUSTRALIAN

Jolley, (Monica) Elizabeth **19**
Lawson, Henry (Archibald Hertzberg) **18**

AUSTRIAN

Grillparzer, Franz **37**
Kafka, Franz **5, 29, 35**
Musil, Robert (Edler von) **18**
Schnitzler, Arthur **15**
Stifter, Adalbert **28**

BRAZILIAN

Lispector, Clarice **34**
Machado de Assis, Joaquim Maria **24**

CANADIAN

Atwood, Margaret (Eleanor) **2**
Bellow, Saul **14**
Gallant, Mavis **5**
Laurence, (Jean) Margaret (Wemyss) **7**
Munro, Alice **3**
Ross, (James) Sinclair **24**
Thomas, Audrey (Callahan) **20**

CHILEAN

Bombal, Maria Luisa **37**
Donoso (Yanez), Jose **34**

CHINESE

Chang, Eileen **28**
Lu Hsun **20**
P'u Sung-ling **31**

COLOMBIAN

Garcia Marquez, Gabriel (Jose) **8**

SSC Cumulative Title Index

Title Index

Title Index

Title Index

Title Index

Title Index

Title Index

Title Index

Title Index

Title Index

Title Index

Title Index

Title Index

Title Index

ISBN 0-7876-3083-7

90000